This book is due for return not later than the last date stamped below, unless recalled sooner.

# Statistical Power Analysis
# for the Behavioral Sciences

## Second Edition

# Statistical Power Analysis for the Behavioral Sciences

## Second Edition

# Jacob Cohen

*Department of Psychology*
*New York University*
*New York, New York*

**LEA** LAWRENCE ERLBAUM ASSOCIATES, PUBLISHERS
1988　Hillsdale, New Jersey　　　　　　　　　　Hove and London

Lawrence Erlbaum Associates, Inc., Publishers
365 Broadway
Hillsdale, New Jersey 07642

First edition published 1969.
Revised edition published 1977.

**Library of Congress Cataloging in Publication Data**

Cohen, Jacob, 1923–
    Statistical power analysis for the behavioral sciences / Jacob
Cohen. — 2nd ed.
        p.   cm.
    Bibliography: p.
    Includes index.
    ISBN 0-8058-0283-5
    1. Social sciences — Statistical methods.  2. Probabilities.
I. Title.
HA29.C66   1988                          88-12110
300′.1′5195 — dc19                          CIP

PRINTED IN THE UNITED STATES OF AMERICA

10

*to Marcia and Aviva*

# Contents

# Chapter 10.  **Set Correlation and Multivariate Methods**

# Chapter 11.  **Some Issues in Power Analysis**

# Chapter 12.  **Computational Procedures**

# Preface to the Second Edition

In the quarter century that has passed since I first addressed power analysis (Cohen, 1962), and particularly during the decade that has elapsed since the revised edition of this book (1977), the escalation of the literature on power analysis has been difficult to keep up with.

In 1962, I published a survey of the articles in a volume of the *Journal of Abnormal and Social Psychology* from the perspective of their power to detect operationally defined small, medium, and large effect sizes [a meta-analysis before the term was coined (Bangert-Drowns, 1986)]. I found rather poor power, for example, a mean of .48 at the two-tailed .05 level for medium effect sizes.

Since the publication of the first edition (1969), there have been two or three dozen power surveys of either particular journals or topical areas, using its tables and (more or less) the same method. In addition to the half-dozen cited in the Preface to the Revised Edition in 1977, which were in the fields of counseling psychology, applied psychology, education, speech and hearing, and mass communication, there are numerous power surveys in many fields, for example: in educational research, in general education (Jones & Brewer, 1972), science education (Pennick & Brewer, 1972; Wooley & Dawson, 1983), English education (Daly & Hexamer, 1983), physical education (Christensen & Christensen, 1977), counselor education (Haase, 1974), social work education (Orme & Tolman, 1986) medical education (Wooley, 1983a), and educational measurement (Brewer & Owen, 1973). Power surveys have been done in social work and social intervention research (Crane, 1976; Judd & Kenny, 1981; Orme & Combs-Orme, 1986), in occupational therapy (Ottenbacher, 1982), abnormal psychology

(Sedlmeier & Gigerenzer, in press), personnel selection (Katzell & Dyer, 1977), and market research (Sawyer & Ball, 1981). A fairly large number have been accomplished in medicine: in clinical trials (Freiman, Chalmers, Smith, & Kuebler, 1977; Reed & Slaichert, 1981), public health (Wooley, 1983b), gerontology (Levenson, 1980), psychiatry (Rothpearl, Mohs, & Davis, 1981), and Australian medicine (Hall, 1982). Even further afield, a power survey was done in the field of geography (Bones, 1972). In addition to these published surveys, there have come to my attention about a dozen unpublished dissertations, research reports, and papers given at professional meetings surveying power in psychology, sociology, and criminology.

A corollary to the long neglect of power analysis is a relatively low awareness of the magnitude of phenomena in the behavioral sciences (Cohen, 1965). The emphasis on testing null hypotheses for statistical significance (R. A. Fisher's legacy) focused attention on the statistical significance of a result and away from the size of the effect being pursued (see Oakes, 1986; Gigerenzer, 1987; Chapter 11). A direct consequence of the recent attention to power, the last few years have witnessed a series of surveys of effect sizes: in social psychology (Cooper & Findlay, 1982), counseling psychology (Haase, Waechter, & Solomon, 1982), consumer behavior (Peterson, Albaum, & Beltramini, 1985), and market research (Sawyer & Ball, 1981).

The recent emergence of meta-analysis (Glass, McGaw, & Smith, 1981; Hedges & Olkin, 1985; Hunter, Schmidt, & Jackson, 1982; Kraemer, 1983) has been influenced by power analysis in the adoption of its effect size measures (Bangert-Drowns, 1986), and in turn, has had a most salutary influence on research progress and power analysis by revealing the level, variability, and correlates of the effect sizes operating in the areas to which it is applied.

The literature in power-analytic methodology has burgeoned during this period; pertinent references are given throughout this edition. Among the many topics here are applied power analysis for: nonstandard conditions (e.g., non-normality, heterogeneous variance, range restriction), nonparametric methods, various multiple comparison procedures, alternative methods of combining probabilities, and alternative stabilizing data transformations. There have been several articles offering simplified one-table methods of approximate power analysis including my own (1970) (which provided the basis for a chapter-length treatment in the Welkowitz, Ewen, & Cohen, 1982, introductory statistics text), Friedman (1982), and Kraemer (1985). The latter is particularly noteworthy in that it breaks new ground methodologically and is oriented toward teaching power analysis.

In marked contrast to the scene a decade or two ago, the current editions of the popular graduate level statistics textbooks oriented to the social and biological sciences provide at least some room for power analysis, and include working methods for the most common tests.

On the post-graduate front, as the word about power analysis has

spread, many "what is it" and "how to do it" articles have appeared in journals of widely diversified content, ranging from clinical pathology (Arkin,
1981) through applied psychology (Fagley, 1985) to biological community
ecology (Toft & Shea, 1983).

Microcomputer programs for power analysis are provided by Anderson
(1981), Dallal (1987), and Haase (1986). A program that both performs and
teaches power analysis using Monte Carlo simulation is about to be published (Borenstein, M. & Cohen, J., 1988).

It would seem that power analysis has arrived.

Yet recently, two independent investigations have come to my attention
that give me pause. Rossi, Rossi, and Cottril (in press), using the methods of
my power survey of the articles in the 1960 volume of the *Journal of Abnormal and Social Psychology* (Cohen, 1962), performed power surveys of 142
articles in the 1982 volumes of the direct descendents of that journal, the
*Journal of Personality and Social Psychology* and the *Journal of Abnormal
Psychology*. When allowance is made for the slightly different (on the average) operational definitions of small, medium, and large effect sizes of the
1962 paper, there is hardly any change in power; for example, the mean
power at the two-tailed .05 level for medium effect sizes of the 1982 articles
was slightly above 50%, hardly different from the 48% in 1960.

Generally, the power surveys done since 1960 have found power not
much better than I had. Some fields do show better power, but they are those
in which subjects are easily come by, so the sample sizes used are larger than
those in abnormal, personality, and social psychology: in educational research (Pennick & Brewer, 1972; Brewer & Owen, 1973), mass communication (Chase & Baran, 1976), applied psychology (Chase & Chase, 1975), and
marketing research (Sawyer & Ball, 1981). However, there is no comparison
of power over time in these areas.

Sedlmeier and Gigerenzer (in press) also studied the change in power since
my 1962 results, using 54 articles in the 1984 volume of the *Journal of
Abnormal Psychology*. They, too, found that the average power had not
changed over the past 24–year period. In fact, when the power of the tests
using experimentwise significance criteria (not encountered in my 1962 survey) were included, the median power for medium effects at the .05 level was
.37. Even more dismaying is the fact that in seven articles, at least one of the
null hypotheses was the research hypotheses, and the nonsignificance of the
result was taken as confirmatory; the median power of these tests to detect
a medium effect at the two-tailed .05 level was .25! In only two of the articles
surveyed was power mentioned, and in none were there any power calculations. Sedlmeier and Gigerenzer's conclusion that my 1962 paper (and the
extensive literature detailed above) "had no effect on actual practice" is
consistent with the available evidence.

Yet, I find some solace from the following considerations: First, this may
be a phenomenon on the abnormal-social-personality area and may not gen-

eralize to all behavioral-social-biological research areas. Second, to my certain knowledge, many journal editors and regular referees are quite knowledgable about power and make editorial decisions in accordance with this knowledge. Third, I am told that some major funding entities require power analyses in grant applications. (I've even heard an unlikely story to the effect that in one of them there is a copy of this book in every office!) Finally, the research surveyed by Rossi et al. (in press) and Sedlmeier and Gigerenzer (in press), although published in the early 1980's, was mostly initiated in the late 1970's. The first edition of this book was not distributed until 1970. In the light of the fact that it took over three decades for Student's t test to come into general use by behavioral scientists, it is quite possible that there simply has not been enough time.

Taking all this into account, however, it is clear that power analysis has not had the impact on behavioral research that I (and other right-thinking methodologists) had expected. But we are convinced that it is just a matter of time.

This edition has the same approach and organization as its predecessors, but has some major changes from the Revised Edition.

1. A chapter has been added for power analysis in set correlation and multivariate methods (Chapter 10). Set correlation is a realization of the multivariate general linear model, and incorporates the standard multivariate methods (e.g., the multivariate analysis of variance and covariance) as special cases. While the standard methods are explicitly treated, the generality of set correlation offers a unifying framework and some new data-analytic possibilities (Cohen, 1982; Cohen & Cohen, 1983; Appendix 4).

2. A new chapter (Chapter 11) considers some general topics in power analysis in more integrated form than is possible in the earlier "working" chapters: effect size, psychometric reliability, and the efficacy of "qualifying" (differencing and partialling) dependent variables.

3. The two sets of working tables used for power and sample size determination in multiple regression and correlation analysis (Chapter 9) have been greatly expanded and provide more accurate values for a denser argument. These tables, derived from the noncentral **F** distribution, are also used for power and sample size determination in set correlation and multivariate methods (Chapter 10).

References have been updated and greatly expanded in keeping with the burgeoning increase in the literature of power analysis, and the errors in the previous edition, mostly caught by vigilant readers (to whom I offer my gratitude), corrected. I am surprised that I had to discover for myself the most egregious error of all: this edition does not presume, as did its predecessors, that all researchers are male.

As in the previous editions, I acknowledge the never ending learning process afforded me by my students and consultees, and the continuing and unpayable debt of gratitude to my wife Patricia, who read, debated, and corrected all the new material despire a heavy workload of her own.

In their classic paper"Belief in the Law of Small Numbers," Tversky and Kahneman (1971) demonstrated how flawed are the statistical intuitions not only of psychologists in general, but even of mathematical psychologists. Most psychologists of whatever stripe believe that samples, even small samples, mirror the characteristics of their parent populations. In effect, they operate on the unstated premise that the law of large numbers holds for small numbers as well. They also believe that if a result is significant in one study, even if only barely so, it will most likely be significant in a replication, even if it has only half the sample size of the original. Tversky and Kahneman detail the various biases that flow from this "belief in the law of small numbers," and note that even if these biases cannot be easily unlearned, "the obvious precaution is computation. The believer in the law of small numbers has incorrect intuitions about significance level, power, and confidence intervals. Significance levels are usually computed and reported, but power and confidence limits are not. Perhaps they should be" (p. 110).

But as we have seen, too many of our colleagues have not responded to Tversky and Kahneman's admonition. It is almost as if they would rather follow W. H. Auden's proscription:

> Thou shalt not sit
> With statisticians nor commit
> A social science.

They do so at their peril.

September, 1987                                        South Wellfleet, Massachusetts
                                                                        Jacob Cohen

# Preface to the Revised Edition

The structure, style, and level of this edition remain as in the original, but three important changes in content have been made:

1. Since the publication of the original edition, multiple regression/correlation analysis has been expanded into a very general and hence versatile system for data analysis, an approach which is uniquely suited to the needs of the behavioral sciences (Cohen and Cohen, 1975). A new chapter is devoted to an exposition of the major features of this data-analytic system and a detailed treatment of power analysis and sample size determination (Chapter 9).

2. The effect size index used for chi-square tests on frequencies and proportions (Chapter 7) has been changed from $e$ to $w(=\sqrt{e})$. This change was made in order to provide a more useful range of values and to make the operational definitions of " small," " medium," and " large " effect sizes for tests of contingency tables and goodness of fit consistent with those for other statistical tests (particularly those of Chapters 5 and 6). The formulas have been changed accordingly and the 84 look-up tables for power and sample size have been recomputed.

3. The original treatment of power analysis and sample size determination for the factorial design analysis of variance (Chapter 8) was approximate and faulty, yielding unacceptably large overestimation of power for main effects and underestimation for interactions. The treatment in this edition is materially changed and includes a redefinition of effect size for interactions.

The new method gives quite accurate results. Further insight into the analysis of variance is afforded when illustrative problems solved by the methods of this chapter are addressed and solved again by the multiple regression/correlation methods of the new Chapter 9.

Thus, this edition is substantially changed in the areas for which the original edition was most frequently consulted. In addition, here and there, some new material has been added (e.g., Section 1.5.5, "Proving" the Null Hypothesis) and some minor changes have been made for updating and correction.

In the seven years since the original edition was published, it has received considerable use as a supplementary textbook in intermediate level courses in applied statistics. It was most gratifying to note that, however slowly, it has begun to influence research planning and the content of textbooks in applied statistics. Several authors have used the book to perform power-analytic surveys of the research literature in different fields of behavioral science, among them Brewer (1972) in education (but see Cohen, 1973), Katzer and Sodt (1973) and Chase and Tucker (1975) in communication, Kroll and Chase (1975) in speech pathology, Chase and Baran (1976) in mass communication, and Chase and Chase (1976) in applied psychology; others are in preparation. Apart from their inherent value as methodological surveys, they have served to disseminate the ideas of power analysis to different audiences with salutary effects on them as both producers and consumers of research. It is still rare, however, to find power analysis in research planning presented in the introductory methods section of research reports (Cohen, 1973).

As in the original edition, I must first acknowledge my students and consultees, from whom I have learned so much, and then my favorite colleague, Patricia Cohen, a constant source of intellectual excitement and much more. I am grateful to Patra Lindstrom for the exemplary fashion in which she performed the exacting chore of typing the new tables and manuscript.

New York

June 1976

Jacob Cohen

# Preface to the Original Edition

During my first dozen years of teaching and consulting on applied statistics with behavioral scientists, I became increasingly impressed with the importance of statistical power analysis, an importance which was increased an order of magnitude by its neglect in our textbooks and curricula. The case for its importance is easily made: What behavioral scientist would view with equanimity the question of the probability that his investigation would lead to statistically significant results, i.e., its power? And it was clear to me that most behavioral scientists not only could not answer this and related questions, but were even unaware that such questions were answerable. Casual observation suggested this deficit in training, and a review of a volume of the *Journal of Abnormal and Social Psychology* (JASP) (Cohen, 1962), supported by a small grant from the National Institute of Mental Health (M-5174A), demonstrated the neglect of power issues and suggested its seriousness.

The reason for this neglect in the applied statistics textbooks became quickly apparent when I began the JASP review. The necessary materials for power analysis were quite inaccessible, in two senses: they were scattered over the periodical and hardcover literature, and, more important, their use assumed a degree of mathematical sophistication well beyond that of most behavioral scientists.

For the purpose of the review, I prepared some sketchy power look-up tables, which proved to be very easily used by the students in my courses at New York University and by my research consultees. This generated the idea for this book. A five-year NIMH grant provided the support for the program of research, system building, computation, and writing of which the present volume is the chief product.

The primary audience for which this book is intended is the behavioral or biosocial scientist who uses statistical inference. The terms "behavioral" and "biosocial" science have no sharply defined reference, but are here intended in the widest sense and to include the academic sciences of psychology, sociology, branches of biology, political science and anthropology, economics, and also various "applied" research fields: clinical psychology and psychiatry, industrial psychology, education, social and welfare work, and market, political polling, and advertising research. The illustrative problems, which make up a large portion of this book, have been drawn from behavioral or biosocial science, so defined.

Since statistical inference is a logical-mathematical discipline whose applications are not restricted to behavioral science, this book will also be useful in other fields of application, e.g., agronomy and industrial engineering.

The amount of statistical background assumed in the reader is quite modest: one or two semesters of applied statistics. Indeed, all that I really assume is that the reader knows how to proceed to perform a test of statistical significance. Thus, the level of treatment is quite elementary, a fact which has occasioned some criticism from my colleagues. I have learned repeatedly, however, that the *typical* behavioral scientist approaches applied statistics with considerable uncertainty (if not actual nervousness), and requires a verbal-intuitive exposition, rich in redundancy and with many concrete illustrations. This I have sought to supply. Another feature of the present treatment which should prove welcome to the reader is the minimization of required computation. The extensiveness of the tables is a direct consequence of the fact that most uses will require no computation at all, the necessary answers being obtained directly by looking up the appropriate table.

The sophisticated applied statistician will find the exposition unnecessarily prolix and the examples repetitious. He will, however, find the tables useful. He may also find interesting the systematic treatment of population effect size, and particularly the proposed conventions or operational definitions of "small," "medium," and "large" effect sizes defined across all the statistical tests. Whatever originality this work contains falls primarily in this area.

This book is designed primarily as a handbook. When so used, the reader is advised to read Chapter 1 and then the chapter which treats the specific statistical test in which he is interested. I also suggest that he read all the relevant illustrative examples, since they are frequently used to carry along the general exposition.

The book may also be used as a supplementary textbook in intermediate level courses in applied statistics in behavioral/biosocial science. I have been using it in this way. With relatively little guidance, students at this level quickly learn both the concepts and the use of the tables. I assign the first chapter early in the semester and the others in tandem with their regular textbook's treatment of the various statistical tests. Thus, each statistical test or research design is presented in close conjunction with power-analytic considerations. This has proved most salutary, particularly in the attention which must then be given to anticipated population effect sizes.

Pride of place, in acknowledgment, must go to my students and consultees, from whom I have learned much. I am most grateful to the memory of the late Gordon Ierardi, without whose encouragement this work would not have been undertaken. Patricia Waly and Jack Huber read and constructively criticized portions of the manuscript. I owe an unpayable debt of gratitude to Joseph L. Fleiss for a thorough technical critique. Since I did not follow all his advice, the remaining errors can safely be assumed to be mine. I cannot sufficiently thank Catherine Henderson, who typed much of the text and all the tables, and Martha Plimpton, who typed the rest.

As already noted, the program which culminated in this book was supported by the National Institute of Mental Health of the Public Health Service under grant number MH-06137, which is duly acknowledged. I am also most indebted to Abacus Associates, a subsidiary of American Bioculture, Inc., for a most generous programming and computing grant which I could draw upon freely.

NEW YORK
JUNE 1969

JACOB COHEN

# The Concepts of Power Analysis

The power of a statistical test is the probability that it will yield statistically significant results. Since statistical significance is so earnestly sought and devoutly wished for by behavioral scientists, one would think that the *a priori* probability of its accomplishment would be routinely determined and well understood. Quite surprisingly, this is not the case. Instead, if we take as evidence the research literature, we find evidence that statistical power is frequenty not understood and, in reports of research where it is clearly relevant, the issue is not addressed.

The purpose of this book is to provide a self-contained comprehensive treatment of statistical power analysis from an "applied" viewpoint. The purpose of this chapter is to present the basic conceptual framework of statistical hypothesis testing, giving emphasis to power, followed by the framework within which this book is organized.

## 1.1 GENERAL INTRODUCTION

When the behavioral scientist has occasion to don the mantle of the applied statistician, the probability is high that it will be for the purpose of testing one or more null hypotheses, i.e., "the hypothesis that the phenomenon to be demonstrated is in fact absent [Fisher, 1949, p. 13]." Not that he hopes to "prove" this hypothesis. On the contrary, he typically hopes to "reject" this hypothesis and thus "prove" that the phenomenon in question is in fact present.

Let us acknowledge at the outset the necessarily probabilistic character of statistical inference, and dispense with the mocking quotation marks

**1**

about words like *reject* and *prove*. This may be done by requiring that an investigator set certain appropriate probability standards for research results which provide a basis for rejection of the null hypothesis and hence for the proof of the existence of the phenomenon under test. Results from a random sample drawn from a population will only approximate the characteristics of the population. Therefore, even if the null hypothesis is, in fact, true, a given sample result is not expected to mirror this fact exactly. Before sample data are gathered, therefore, the investigator selects some prudently small value **a** (say .01 or .05), so that he *may* eventually be able to say about his sample data, *"If the null hypothesis is true,* the probability of the obtained sample result is no more than **a**," i.e. a statistically significant result. *If* he can make this statement, since **a** is small, he said to have rejected the null hypothesis "with an **a** significance criterion" or "at the **a** significance level." If, on the other hand, he finds the probability to be greater than **a**, he cannot make the above statement and he has failed to reject the null hypothesis, or, equivalently finds it "tenable," or "accepts" it, all at the **a** significance level. Note that **a** is set in advance.

We have thus isolated one element of this form of statistical inference, the standard of proof that the phenomenon exists, or, equivalently, the standard of disproof of the null hypothesis that states that the phenomenon does not exist.

Another component of the significance criterion concerns the exact definition of the nature of the phenomenon's existence. This depends on the details of how the phenomenon is manifested and statistically tested, e.g., the directionality/nondirectionality ("one tailed"/"two tailed") of the statement of the alternative to the null hypothesis.[1] When, for example, the investigator is working in a context of comparing some parameter (e.g., mean, proportion, correlation coefficient) for two populations A and B, he can define the existence of the phenomenon in two different ways:

1. The phenomenon is taken to exist if the parameters of A and B differ. No direction of the difference, such as A larger than B, is specified, so that departures in either direction from the null hypothesis constitute evidence against it. Because either tail of the sampling distribution of differences may contribute to **a**, this is usually called a two-tailed or two-sided test.

2. The phenomenon is taken to exist only if the parameters of A and B differ in a direction specified in advance, e.g., A larger than B. In this

---

[1] Some statistical tests, particularly those involving comparisons of more than two populations, are naturally nondirectional. In what immediately follows, we consider those tests which contrast two populations, wherein the experimenter ordinarily explicitly chooses between a directional and nondirectional statement of his alternate hypothesis. See below, Chapters 7 and 8.

circumstance, departures from the null hypothesis only in the direction specified constitute evidence against it. Because only one tail of the sampling distribution of differences may contribute to **a**, this is usually called a one-tailed or one-sided test.

It is convenient to conceive of the significance criterion as embodying both the probability of falsely rejecting the null hypothesis, **a**, and the "sidedness" of the definition of the existence of the phenomenon (when relevant). Thus, the significance criterion on a two-tailed test of the null hypothesis at the .05 significance level, which will be symbolized as $a_2 = .05$, says two things: (a) that the phenomenon whose existence is at issue is understood to be manifested by any difference between the two populations' parameter values, and (b) that the standard of proof is a sample result that would occur less than 5% of the time if the null hypothesis is true. Similarly, a prior specification defining the phenomenon under study as that for which the parameter value for A is larger than that of B (i.e., one-tailed) and the probability of falsely rejecting the null is set at .10 would be symbolized as a significance criterion of $a_1 = .10$. The combination of the probability and the sidedness of the test into a single entity, the significance criterion, is convenient because this combination defines in advance the "critical region," i.e., the range of values of the outcome which leads to rejection of the null hypothesis and, perforce, the range of values which leads to its nonrejection. Thus, when an investigator plans a statistical test at some given significance criterion, say $a_1 = .10$, he has effected a specific division of all the possible results of his study into those which will lead him to conclude that the phenomenon exists (with risk **a** no greater than .10 and a one-sided definition of the phenomenon) and those which will not make possible that conclusion.[2]

The above review of the logic of classical statistical inference reduces to a null hypothesis and a significance criterion which defines the circumstances which will lead to its rejection or nonrejection. Observe that the significance criterion embodies the risk of mistakenly rejecting a null hypothesis. The entire discussion above is conditional on the truth of the null hypothesis.

But what if, indeed, the phenomenon *does* exist and the null hypothesis is *false*? This is the usual expectation of the investigator, who has stated the null hypothesis for tactical purposes so that he may reject it and conclude that the phenomenon exists. But, of course, the fact that the phenomenon exists in the population far from guarantees a statistically significant result,

---

[2] The author has elsewhere expressed serious reservations about the use of directional tests in psychological research in all but relatively limited circumstances (Cohen, 1965). The bases for these reservations would extend to other regions of behavioral science. These tests are however of undoubted statistical validity and in common use, so he has made full provision for them in this work.

i.e., one which warrants the conclusion that it exists, for this conclusion depends upon meeting the agreed-upon standard of proof (i.e., significance criterion). It is at this point that the concept of statistical power must be considered.

*The power of a statistical test of a null hypothesis is the probability that it will lead to the rejection of the null hypothesis,* i.e., the probability that it will result in the conclusion that the phenomenon exists. Given the characteristics of a specific statistical test of the null hypothesis and the state of affairs in the population, the power of the test can be determined. It clearly represents a vital piece of information about a statistical test applied to research data (cf. Cohen, 1962). For example, the discovery, during the planning phase of an investigation, that the power of the eventual statistical test is low should lead to a revision in the plans. As another example, consider a completed experiment which led to nonrejection of the null hypothesis. An analysis which finds that the power was low should lead one to regard the negative results as ambiguous, since failure to reject the null hypothesis cannot have much substantive meaning when, even though the phenomenon exists (to some given degree), the *a priori* probability of rejecting the null hypothesis was low. A detailed consideration of the use of power analysis in planning investigations and assessing completed investigations is reserved for later sections.

The power of a statistical test depends upon three parameters: the significance criterion, the reliability of the sample results, and the "effect size," that is, the *degree* to which the phenomenon exists.

## 1.2   SIGNIFICANCE CRITERION

The role of this parameter in testing null hypotheses has already been given some consideration. As noted above, the significance criterion represents the standard of proof that the phenomenon exists, or the risk of mistakenly rejecting the null hypothesis. As used here, it directly implies the "critical region of rejection" of the null hypothesis, since it embodies both the probability of a class of results given that the null hypothesis is true (**a**), as well as the definition of the phenomenon's existence with regard to directionality. For power to be defined, its value must be set in advance.

The significance level, **a**, has been variously called the error of the first kind, the Type I error, and the alpha error. Since it is the rate of rejecting a true null hypothesis, it is taken as a relatively small value. It follows then that the smaller the value, the more rigorous the standard of null hypothesis rejection or, equivalently, of proof of the phenomenon's existence. Assume that a phenomenon exists in the population to some given degree. Other things equal, the more stringent the standard for proof, i.e., the lower the value of **a**, the poorer the chances are that the sample will provide results which meet this standard, i.e., the lower the power. Concretely, if an investigator is prepared to run only a 1 % risk of false rejection of the null hypothesis, the probability of his data meeting this standard is lower than would be the case were he prepared to use the less stringent standard of a 10 % risk of false rejection.

The practice of taking **a** very small ("the smaller the better") then results in power values being relatively small. However, the complement of the power (1 − power), here symbolized as **b**, is also error, called Type II or beta error, since it represents the "error" rate of failing to reject a false null hypothesis. Thus it is seen that statistical inference can be viewed as weighing, in a manner relevant to the substantive issues of an investigation, these two kinds of errors. An investigator can set the risk of false null hypothesis rejection at a vanishingly small level, say **a** = .001, but in so doing, he may reduce the power of his test to .10 (hence beta error probability, **b**, is 1 − .10 = .90). Two comments may be made here:

1. The general neglect of issues of statistical power in behavioral science may well result, in such instances, in the investigator's failing to realize that the **a** = .001 value leads in his situation to power = .10, **b** = .90 (Cohen, 1962). Presumably, although not necessarily, such a realization would lead to a revision of experimental plans, including possibly an upward revision of the **a** level to increase power.

2. If the investigator proceeds as originally planned, he implies a conception of the relative seriousness of Type I to Type II error (risk of false null rejection to risk of false null acceptance) of **b/a** = .90/.001 = 900 to 1, i.e., he implicitly believes that mistakenly rejecting the null hypothesis under the assumed conditions is 900 times more serious than mistakenly accepting it. In another situation, with **a** = .05, power = .80, and hence **b** = 1 − .80 = .20, the relative seriousness of Type I to Type II error is **b/a** = .20/.05 = 4 to 1; thus mistaken rejection of the null hypothesis is considered four times as serious as mistaken acceptance.

The directionality of the significance criterion (left unspecified in the above examples) also bears on the power of a statistical test. When the null hypothesis can be rejected in *either* direction so that the critical significance region is in *both* tails of the sampling distribution of the test statistic (e.g., a **t** ratio), the resulting test will have less power than a test at the same **a** level which is directional, *provided that* the sample result is in the direction predicted. Since directional tests cannot, by definition, lead to rejecting the null hypothesis in the direction *opposite* to that predicted, these tests have no power to detect such effects. When the experimental results are in the predicted direction, all other things equal, a test at level $a_1$ will have power equal for all practical purposes to a test at $2a_2$.

Concretely, if an experiment is performed to detect a difference between the means of populations A and B, say $\mathbf{m_A}$ and $\mathbf{m_B}$, in *either* direction at the $\mathbf{a_2} = .05$ significance criterion, under given conditions, the test will have a certain power. If, instead, an anticipation of $\mathbf{m_A}$ greater than $\mathbf{m_B}$ leads to a test at $\mathbf{a_1} = .05$, this test will have power approximately equal to a two-tailed test with $\mathbf{a_2} = .10$, hence greater power than the test at $\mathbf{a_2} = .05$, provided that in fact $\mathbf{m_A}$ is greater than $\mathbf{m_B}$. If $\mathbf{m_B}$ is greater than $\mathbf{m_A}$, the test at $\mathbf{a_1} = .05$ has *no* power, since that conclusion is inadmissible. The temptation to perform directional tests because of their greater power at the same $\mathbf{a}$ level should be tempered by the realization that they preclude finding results opposite to those anticipated. There are occasional circumstances where the nature of the decision is such that the investigator does not need to know about effects in the opposite direction. For example, he will take a certain course of action if $\mathbf{m_A}$ is greater than $\mathbf{m_B}$ and not otherwise. If otherwise, he does not need to distinguish between their equality and $\mathbf{m_B}$ greater than $\mathbf{m_A}$. In such infrequent instances, one-tailed tests are appropriate (Cohen, 1965, pp. 106–111).

In the tables in this book, provision is made for tests at the .01, .05, and .10 significance levels. Where a statistical test may ordinarily be performed either nondirectionally or directionally, both $\mathbf{a_2}$ and $\mathbf{a_1}$ tables are provided. Since power for $\mathbf{a_1} = .05$ is virtually identical with power for $\mathbf{a_2} = .10$, a single power table suffices. Similarly, tables for $\mathbf{a_1} = .01$ provide values for $\mathbf{a_2} = .02$, and tables for $\mathbf{a_1} = .10$ values for $\mathbf{a_2} = .20$; also, tables for $\mathbf{a_2} = .01$ provide values for $\mathbf{a_1} = .005$, tables at $\mathbf{a_2} = .05$ provide values for $\mathbf{a_1} = .025$.

### 1.3   RELIABILITY OF SAMPLE RESULTS AND SAMPLE SIZE

The reliability (or precision) of a sample value is the closeness with which it can be expected to approximate the relevant population value. It is necessarily an estimated value in practice, since the population value is generally unknown. Depending upon the statistic in question, and the specific statistical model on which the test is based, reliability may or may not be directly dependent upon the unit of measurement, the population value, and the shape of the population distribution. However, it is *always* dependent upon the size of the sample.

For example, one conventional means for assessing the reliability of a statistic is the standard error (SE) of the statistic. If we consider the arithmetic mean of a variable $\mathbf{X}$ ($\overline{\mathbf{X}}$), its reliability may be estimated by the standard error of the mean,

$$\mathrm{SE}_{\overline{\mathbf{X}}} = \sqrt{\frac{\mathbf{s^2}}{\mathbf{n}}},$$

where $\mathbf{s^2}$ is the usual unbiased estimate (from the random sample) of the population variance of **X**, and **n** is the number of independent units in (i.e., the size of) the sample.

Concretely, if a sample of **n** = 49 cases yields a variance estimate for IQ of 196, then the standard error of the mean is given by

$$SE_{\overline{x}} = \sqrt{\frac{s^2}{n}} = \sqrt{\frac{196}{49}} = 2.$$

Thus, sample means based on 49 cases can be expected to have variability as measured by their own standard deviation of 2 IQ units. Clearly the greater the degree to which means of different samples vary among themselves, the less any of them can be relied upon, i.e., the less the reliability of the mean of the sample in hand. Note that in this instance reliability depends upon the unit of measurement (IQ) and sample size, but not on the value of the population mean or (to any material degree) on the shape of the IQ distribution.

On the other hand, consider the sampling reliability of a product moment coefficient of correlation, **r**. Its standard error is

$$SE_r = \frac{1 - r_p^{\,2}}{\sqrt{n - 1}},$$

where

$r_p$ = the population value of **r**, and

**n** = the number of paired observations in the sample.

Note that the reliability of the sample **r** depends upon the magnitude of the (generally unknown) population $r_p$ value and **n**, but not on the units in which the correlated variables are measured.

Not all statistical tests involve the explicit definition of a standard error of a sample value, but all do involve the more general conception of sample reliability. Moreover, and most important, whatever else sample reliability may be dependent upon, it *always* depends upon the size of the sample.

The nature of the dependence of reliability upon **n** is obvious from the illustrative formulas, and, indeed, intuitively. The larger the sample size, other things being equal, the smaller the error and the greater the reliability or precision of the results. The further relationship with power is also intuitively evident: the greater the precision of the sample results, other things being equal, the greater the probability of detecting a nonnull state of affairs, i.e., the more clearly the phenomenon under test can manifest itself against the background of (experimentally irrelevant) variability. Thus, we can directly formulate the relationship between sample size and power. As is intuitively obvious, increases in sample size increase statistical power, the probability of detecting the phenomenon under test.

Focusing on sample size as an invariant factor in power should not make the researcher lose sight of the fact that other research elements potentially under his control also affect power. Random measurement error, be it due to psychometric unreliability, observational carelessness, dirty testtubes, or any other source, because it increases the variability of the observations beyond their necessary "true" variability, also reduces the precision of sample results and thus reduces power. In general, *anything* which reduces the variability of observations by the exclusion of sources of variability which are irrelevant to the assessment of the phenomenon under study will serve to increase power. Experimental design is an area of inquiry wholly devoted to the removal of irrelevant sources of variability for the increase of precision and therefore for the increase of the statistical power of tests of null hypotheses (cf. Cox, 1958).

In this book, provision is made for the accomplishment of power analyses for the statistical tests associated with the most frequently utilized experimental designs and their accompanying null hypotheses. Issues such as the effects of a given level of random measurement error on power are not explicitly provided for. Sample size, the invariant feature of sample precision, is, however, a factor in all the power tables. It is used in both of the major kinds of analysis tables herein provided; in the power tables, sample size is one of the elements used to determine the power of the test, and in the sample size tables, it is the dependent variable of the function of the desired level of power (in both instances under given conditions of significance criterion and population effect size).

## 1.4   THE EFFECT SIZE

To this point, the phenomenon in the population under statistical test was considered as either absent (null hypothesis true) or present (null hypothesis false). The absence of the phenomenon implies some specific value for a population parameter. For example, in a study to determine whether there is a sex difference in incidence of paranoid schizophrenia, the investigator may draw a sample of patients bearing that diagnosis from the relevant population and determine the proportion of males. The null hypothesis being tested is that the population proportion of males is .50, a specific value.[3,4] Equivalently, we might say that the size of the "effect" of sex on the presence of

---

[3] The assumption is made here that .50 is the proportion of males in the population of interest.

[4] For the sake of simplicity, the null hypothesis is treated in this section for the nondirectional form of the significance criterion. For example, a directional (one-tailed) test here that the male proportion is greater than .50 implies a null hypothesis that it is equal to *or less than* .50. The reader may supply his own necessary qualifications of the null hypothesis for the directional case in each illustration.

the diagnosis is zero. In another study concerned with the IQs of children born in multiple births, the null hypothesis might be that the multiple birth population in question has a mean IQ of 100 (i.e., the general population mean), again a specific value, or that the size of effect of being part of a multiple birth on IQ is zero. As yet another example of a one-sample test, in a study of the construct validity of a neurophysiological measure of intro-version–extroversion, its product moment r with an accepted questionnaire measure for a sample of college students is determined. The null hypothesis here is that the population r is zero, or that the effect size of either on the other is zero.

In circumstances where two populations are being compared, the null hypothesis usually takes the form "the difference in the value of the rele-vant parameters is zero," a specific value. Thus, in a consumer survey research to determine whether preference for a particular brand A over its chief competitor B is related to the income level of the consumer, the null hypothesis might be: The difference in median family income of brand A and brand B users is zero, or, equivalently, that the size of the effect of income on brand preference is zero. Or, in a personnel selection study to determine which of two screening tests, A or B, is a better predictor of performance ratings (C), the null hypothesis might take the form: The difference between population product moment r's of A with C and B with C is zero.

Statistical tests involving more than two samples test null hypotheses that imply the constancy of a parameter over the populations involved. The literal statement of the null hypothesis depends upon the specific test involved. For example, the F test of the analysis of variance for $k \geq 2$ means has as its null hypothesis the proposition that the variance of a set of population means is zero, a condition that can only obtain when they are equal. Simi-larly, a test of whether a set of $k \geq 2$ population proportions are equal can be performed by means of the chi-square statistic. The null hypothesis here is that the variance of the population proportions equals zero (an exact value), a condition which can only obtain when they are all equal. In both of these instances we can think of the null hypothesis as the circumstance in which differences in the independent variable, the k populations, have no effect (have an effect size of zero) on the means or proportions of the dependent variable.

Thus, we see that the absence of the phenomenon under study is expressed by a null hypothesis which specifies an exact value for a population para-meter, one which is appropriate to the way the phenomenon under study is manifested. Without intending any necessary implication of causality, it is convenient to use the phrase "effect size" to mean "the *degree* to which the phenomenon is present in the population," or "the degree to which the

null hypothesis is false." Whatever the manner of representation of a phenomenon in a particular research in the present treatment, the null hypothesis
always means that the effect size is zero.

By the above route, it can now readily be made clear that when the null
hypothesis is false, it is false to some specific degree, i.e., *the effect size* (ES)
*is some specific nonzero value in the population.* The larger this value, the
greater the *degree* to which the phenomenon under study is manifested.
Thus, in terms of the previous illustrations:

1.  If the percentage of males in the population of psychiatric patients
bearing a diagnosis of paranoid schizophrenia is 52%, and the effect is
measured as a departure from the hypothesized 50%, the ES is 2%; if it is
60%, the ES is 10%, a larger ES.

2.  If children of multiple births have a population mean IQ of 96, the
ES is 4 IQ units (or $-4$, depending on directionality of significance criterion);
if it is 92, the ES is 8 (or $-8$) IQ units, i.e., a larger ES.

3.  If the population product moment $r$ between neurophysiological and
questionnaire measures of introversion–extroversion is .30, the ES is .30; if
the $r$ is .60, so is the ES, a larger value and a larger departure from the null
hypothesis, which here is $r = 0$.

4.  If the population of consumers preferring brand A has a median
annual income \$700 higher than that of brand B, the ES is \$700. If the
population median difference and hence the ES is \$1000, the effect of income
on brand preference would be larger.

Thus, whether measured in one unit or another, whether expressed as a
difference between two population parameters or the departure of a population parameter from a constant or in any other suitable way, the ES can
itself be treated as a parameter which takes the value zero when the null
hypothesis is true and *some other specific nonzero value* when the null hypothesis is false, and in this way the ES serves as an index of degree of departure
from the null hypothesis.

The reasons that the above discussion has proceeded in such redundant
detail are twofold. On the one hand, ES is in practice a most important
determinant of power or required sample size or both, and on the other hand,
it is the least familiar of the concepts surrounding statistical inference among
practicing behavior scientists. The reason for the latter, in turn, can be found
in the difference in null hypothesis testing between the procedures of Fisher
(1949) and those of Neyman and Pearson (1928, 1933).

The Fisherian formulation posits the null hypothesis as described above,
i.e., the ES is zero, to which the "alternative" hypothesis is that the ES is
*not* zero, i.e., *any* nonzero value. Without further specification, although
null hypotheses may be tested and thereupon either rejected or not rejected,

no basis for statistical power analysis exists. By contrast, the Neyman-Pearson formulation posits an *exact* alternative for the ES, i.e., the *exact* size of the effect the experiment is designed to detect. With an exact alternative hypothesis or specific nonzero ES to be detected, given the other elements in statistical inference, statistical power analysis may proceed.

Thus, in the previous illustrations, the statements about possible population ES values (e.g., "if the population product moment **r** between neurophysiological and questionnaire measures of introversion–extroversion is .30, the ES is .30") are statements of alternative hypotheses.

The relationship between ES and power should also be intuitively evident. The larger the ES posited, other things (significance criterion, sample size) being equal, the greater the power of the test. Similarly, the relationship between ES and necessary sample size: the larger the ES posited, other things (significance criterion, desired power) being equal, the smaller the sample size necessary to detect it.

To this point, the ES has been considered quite abstractly as a parameter which can take on varying values (including zero in the null case). In any given statistical test, it must be indexed or measured in some defined unit appropriate to the data, test, and statistical model employed. In the previous illustrations, ES was variously expressed as a departure in percent from 50, a departure in IQ units from 100, a product moment **r**, a difference between two medians in dollars, etc. It is clearly desirable to reduce this diversity of units as far as possible, consistent with present usage by behavioural scientists. From one point of view, a universal ES index, applicable to all the various research issues and statistical models used in their appraisal, would be the ideal. Apart from some formidable mathematical-statistical problems in the way, even if such an ideal could be achieved, the result would express ES in terms so unfamiliar to the researcher in behavioral science as to be self-defeating.

However, some generalization is obviously necessary. One cannot prepare a set of power tables for each new measurement unit with which one works. That is, the researcher who plans a test for a difference in mean IQs must use the same power tables as another who plans a test for a difference in mean weights, just as they will use the same tables of **t** when the research is performed. **t** is a "pure" (dimensionless) number, one free of raw unit, as are also, for example, correlation coefficients or proportions of variance. Thus, as will be seen in Chapter 2, the ES index for differences between population means is standardized by division by the common within-population standard deviation ($\sigma$), i.e., the ES here is not the difference between mean "raw" scores, but the difference between mean "**z**" standard scores (Hays, 1981), or the mean difference expressed in within-population $\sigma$ units. In the **F** test for $k \geq 2$ population means, the ES also uses such standardized means;

in testing "main effects" in the analysis of variance the ES is *their* standard deviation, $\sigma_m$, the standard deviation of standardized means (Chapter 8).

Each test for which power tables are provided thus has a metric-free ES index appropriate to it. A higher order of generalization is frequently possible. Specifically, several ES indices can be translated into the proportion of variance (PV) accounted for in the dependent variable. Where this is possible, it is discussed in the introductory material for the test. Also, each ES index chosen usually relates to yet other commonly used indices and these are also described in the same place.

The behavior scientist who comes to statistical power analysis may find himself grappling with the problem of what ES to posit as an alternate to the null hypothesis, or, more simply, how to answer the questions "How large an effect do I expect exists in the population?" He may initially find it difficult to answer the question even in general terms, i.e., "small" or "large," let alone in terms of the specific ES index demanded. Being forced to think in more exact terms than demanded by the Fisherian alternative (ES is any nonzero value) is likely to prove salutary. He can call upon theory for some help in answering the question and on his critical assessment of prior research in the area for further help. When these are supplemented with the understanding of the ES index provided in the introductory material to the relevant chapter, he can decide upon the ES value to adopt as an alternative to the null.

When the above has not provided sufficient guidance, the reader has an additional recourse. For each statistical test's ES index, the author proposes, *as a convention*, ES values to serve as operational definitions of the qualitative adjectives "small," "medium," and "large." This is an operation fraught with many dangers: The definitions are arbitrary, such qualitative concepts as "large" are sometimes understood as absolute, sometimes as relative; and thus they run a risk of being misunderstood.

In justification, several arguments may be offered. It must first be said that all conventions are arbitrary. One can only demand of them that they not be unreasonable. Also, all conventions may be misused and their conventional status thus abused. For example, the .05 significance criterion, although unofficial, has come to serve as a convention for a (minimum) basis for rejecting the null hypothesis in most areas of behavioral and biological science. Unfortunately, its status as only a convention is frequently ignored; there are many published instances where a researcher, in an effort at rectitude, fails to report that a much desired null rejection would be possible at the .06 level but instead treats the problem no differently than he would have had it been at the .50 level! Still, it is convenient that "significance" without further specification can be taken to mean "significance at no more than the .05 level."

Although arbitrary, the proposed conventions will be found to be reasonable by reasonable people. An effort was made in selecting these operational criteria to use levels of ES which accord with a subjective average of effect sizes such as are encountered in behavioral science. "Small" effect sizes must not be so small that seeking them amidst the inevitable operation of measurement and experimental bias and lack of fidelity is a bootless task, yet not so large as to make them fairly perceptible to the naked observational eye. Many effects sought in personality, social, and clinical-psychological research are likely to be small effects as here defined, both because of the attenutation in validity of the measures employed and the subtlety of the issues frequently involved. In contrast, large effects must not be defined as so large that their quest by statistical methods is wholly a labor of supererogation, or to use Tukey's delightful term "statistical sanctification." That is, the difference in size between apples and pineapples is of an order which hardly requires an approach via statistical analysis. On the other side, it cannot be defined so as to encroach on a reasonable range of values called medium. Large effects are frequently at issue in such fields as sociology, economics, and experimental and physiological psychology, fields characterized by the study of potent variables or the presence of good experimental control or both.

Since effects are appraised against a background of random variation, the control of various sources of variation through the use of improved research designs serves to increase effect sizes as they are defined here. A simple example of this is a study of sex difference in some defined ability. Assume that a difference of 4 score points exists between male and female population means, where each population has a standard deviation of 16. A research plan which randomly samples the two populations (simple randomized design or comparison between two independent means) is operating with an ES of $4/16 = .25$. Another research plan might proceed by comparing means of males and their sisters (comparison of two dependent means). Now, these populations can also be assumed to have a mean difference of 4 score points, but because of the removal of the variation between families afforded by this design (or equivalently when allowance is made for the brother–sister correlation in the ability), the *effective* standard deviation will be reduced to the fraction $\sqrt{1-r}$ of 16, say to 12 (when $r$ between siblings $= .44$), and the actual ES operating in the situation is $4/12 = .33$, a larger value than for the simple randomized design. Thus, *operative* effect sizes may be increased not only by improvement in measurement and experimental technique, but also by improved experimental designs.

Each of the Chapters 2–10 will present in some detail the ES index appropriate to the test to which the chapter is devoted. Each will be translated into alternative forms, the operational definitions of "small," "medium," and "large" will be presented, and examples drawn from various fields will illustrate the test. This should serve to clarify the ES index involved and make the methods and tables useful in research planning and appraisal. Finally, in Chapter 11, Section 11.1 is devoted to a general consideration of ES in the behavioral sciences.

## 1.5   TYPES OF POWER ANALYSIS

Four parameters of statistical inference have been described: power, significance criterion (**a**), sample size (**n**), and effect size (ES). They are so related that any one of them is a function of the other three, which means that when any three of them are fixed, the fourth is completely determined. This relationship makes formally possible four types of power analysis; in each, one of these parameters is determined as a function of the other three (Cohen, 1965, pp. 97–101).

1.5.1   POWER AS A FUNCTION OF **a**, ES, AND **n**. The preceding material has been largely oriented toward the type of analysis in which, given the specification of **a**, ES, and **n**, power is determined. For example, an investigator plans a test of the significance of a product moment **r** at $a_2 = .05$ using **n** = 30 cases. The ES he wishes to detect is a population **r** of .40. Given these specifications, he finds (by the methods of Section 3.3 in Chapter 3) that power equals .61. He may then decide to change his specifications to increase power.

Such analyses are usefully performed as part of research planning. They can also be performed on completed studies to determine the power which a given statistical test had, as in the power survey of the studies in a volume of the *Journal of Abnormal and Social Psychology* (Cohen, 1962). In each of Chapters 2–10, the power tables (numberd B.3.A., where B is the chapter number and A indexes the significance criterion) are designed for this type of analysis. The sections designated B.3 discuss and illustrate the use of these tables.

1.5.2   **n** AS A FUNCTION OF ES, **a**, AND POWER. When an investigator anticipates a certain ES, sets a significance criterion **a**, and then specifies the amount of power he desires, the **n** which is necessary to meet these specifications can be determined. This (second) type of power analysis must be at the core of any rational basis for deciding on the sample size to be used in an investigation (Cohen, 1965, pp. 97–99). For example, an investigator wishes to have power equal to .80 to detect a population **r** of .40 (the ES) at $a_2 = .05$. By the methods described in Section 3.4 in Chapter 3, he finds that he must have **n** = 46 cases to meet these specifications. (A discussion of the basis for specifying desired power and the use of power = .80 as a convention will be found in Section 2.4 of Chapter 2.)

This major type of power analysis is discussed and illustrated in the Sections B.4 (where B indexes the chapter numbers 2–8). Each of these sections contain sample size tables (numbered B.4.A) from which, given **a**, the ES, and desired power, the **n** is determined. A slightly different approach to **n** determination is employed in Chapters 9 and 10.

1.5.3   ES AS A FUNCTION OF **a**, **n**, AND POWER. A third type of power analysis is of less general utility than the first two, but may nevertheless be quite useful in special circumstances (Cohen, 1970). Here, one finds the ES which one can expect to detect for given **a**, **n**, and with specified power. For example, an investigator may pose the question, "For a significance test of a product moment **r** at $a_2 = .05$ with a sample of **n** = 30, what must the population **r** (the ES) be if power is to be .80, i.e., what is the *detectable* ES for these specifications?" The answer, obtainable by backward interpolation (in Table 3.3.5) is that the population **r** must be approximately .48. Were his **n** equal to 46, the detectable ES would be **r** = .40.

This form of power analysis may be conventionalized for use in comparisons of research results as in literature surveys (Cohen, 1965, p. 100). One can define, as a convention, a comparative detectable effect size (CDES) as that ES detectable at $a_2 = .05$ with power = .50 for the **n** used in the statistical test. So defined, the CDES is an inverse measure of the sensitivity of the test, expressed in the appropriate ES unit.

This type of power analysis is not discussed in detail in the ensuing chapters. However, when readers have become familiar with the use of the tables, they will find that it can be accomplished for all of the statistical tests discussed by backward interpolation in the power tables, or when it proves more convenient, in the sample size tables.

1.5.4   **a** AS A FUNCTION OF **n**, POWER, AND ES. The last type of power analysis answers the question, "What significance level must I use to detect a given ES with specified probability (power) for a fixed given **n**?" Consider an investigator whose anticipated ES is a population **r** of .30, who wishes power to be .75, and who as an **n** of 50, which she cannot increase. These specifications determine the significance criterion he must use, which can be found (by rough interpolation between subtables in Table 3.4.1) to be about $a_1 = .08$, or $a_2 = .15$).

This type of analysis is very uncommon, at least partly because of the strength of the significance criterion convention, which makes investigators loath to consider "large" values of **a**. We have seen that this frequently means tolerating (usually without knowing it) large values of **b**, i.e., low power. When power issues are brought into consideration, some circumstances may dictate unconventionally large **a** criteria (Cohen, 1965, p. 99ff).

This type of power analysis is not, as such, further discussed in Chapters 2–10, although it is indirectly considered in some of the examples. When the reader has become familiar with the tables, it can be accomplished for all the statistical tests discussed in this book by interpolation between subtables of the sample size tables (B.4.A), or when more convenient, between power tables (B.3.A), within the range provided for **a**, i.e., **a**$_2$: .01–.20, and **a**$_1$: .005–.10.

In summary, four types of power analysis have been described. This book is designed primarily to facilitate two of these, the solutions for power and for sample size. It is also possible, but with less ease, to accomplish the other two, solution for ES and for **a**, by means of backward interpolation in the tables.

1.5.5 "PROVING" THE NULL HYPOTHESIS. Research reports in the literature are frequently flawed by conclusions that state or imply that the null hypothesis is true. For example, following the finding that the difference between two sample means is not statistically significant, instead of properly concluding from this failure to reject the null hypothesis that the data do not warrant the conclusion that the population means differ, the writer concludes, at least implicitly, that there is *no* difference. The latter conclusion is always strictly invalid, and is functionally invalid as well unless power is high. The high frequency of occurrence of this invalid interpretation can be laid squarely at the doorstep of the general neglect of attention to statistical power in the training of behavioral scientists.

What is really intended by the invalid affirmation of a null hypothesis is not that the population ES is literally zero, but rather that it is negligible, or trivial. This proposition may be validly asserted under certain circumstances. Consider the following: for a given hypothesis test, one defines a numerical value **i** (for *iota*) for the ES, where **i** is so small that it is appropriate in the context to consider it negligible (trivial, inconsequential). Power $(1 - $**b**$)$ is then set at a high value, so that **b** is relatively small. When, additionally, **a** is specified, **n** can be found. Now, if the research is performed with this **n** and it results in nonsignificance, it is proper to conclude that the population ES is no more than **i**, i.e., that it is negligible; this conclusion can be offered as significant at the **b** level specified. In much research, "no" effect (difference, correlation) functionally means one that is negligible; "proof" by statistical induction is probabilistic. Thus, in using the same logic as that with which we reject the null hypothesis with risk equal to **a**, the null hypothesis can be accepted in preference to that which holds that ES = **i** with risk equal to **b**. Since **i** is negligible, the conclusion that the population ES is not as large as **i** is equivalent to concluding that there is "no" (nontrivial) effect. This comes fairly close and is functionally equivalent to affirming the null hypothesis with a controlled error rate (**b**), which, as noted above, is what is actually intended when null hypotheses are incorrectly affirmed (Cohen, 1965, pp. 100–101; Cohen, 1970). (See Illustrative Examples 2.9, 3.5, 6.8, and 9.24.) (Also, see Fowler, 1985.)

This statistically valid basis for extracting positive conclusions from "negative findings" may not be of much practical help to most investigators. If, for example, one considers a population $r = .10$ as negligigle (hence, $i$), and plans a test of the null hypothesis (at $a_2 = .05$) for power $= .95$ ($b = .05$) to detect $i$, one discovers that the $n$ required is 1294; for power $= .90$ ($b = .10$), the required $n = 1047$; and for power $= .80$ ($b = .20$), $n = 783$ (Table 3.4.1). For the much more liberal specification of $r = .20$ as $i$, the test (at $a_2 = .05$) for power $= .95$ ($b = .05$) requires $n = 319$; for power $= .90$ ($b = .10$) requires $n = 259$, and even for power $= .80$ ($b = .20$), the required $n = 194$ (Table 3.4.1). Thus, relatively large sample sizes are necessary to establish the negligibility of an ES. But if nothing else, this procedure at least makes explicit what it takes to say or imply from a failure to reject the null hypothesis that there is no (nontrivial) correlation or difference between A and B.

## 1.6   SIGNIFICANCE TESTING

Although the major thrust of this work is power analysis, a simple relationship between power and significance made it relatively simple in the computation of the power tables to provide an aid to significance testing which users of this handbook may find convenient. Generally, we can define the effect size *in the sample* (ES$_s$) using sample statistics in the same way as we define it for the population, and a statistically significant ES$_s$ is one which exceeds an appropriate criterion value. For most of the power tables, these criterion values for significance of the sample ES (for the given $a$ significance criterion and $n$) are provided in the second column of the power tables under the symbol for the ES for that test with subscript c (for criterion), e.g., $d_c$ for the $t$ test on means.

## 1.7   PLAN OF CHAPTERS 2–10

Each of the succeeding chapters presents a different statistical test. They are similarly organized, as follows:

*Section 1*. The test is introduced and its uses described.

*Section 2*. The ES index is described and discussed in detail.

*Section 3*. The characteristics of the power tables and the method of their use are described and illustrated with examples.

*Section 4*. The characteristics of the sample size tables and the method of their use are described and illustrated with examples.

*Section 5*. In Chapters 2–6 and 8, the use of the power tables for significance tests is described and illustrated with examples.

# CHAPTER 2

# The t Test for Means

## 2.1 INTRODUCTION AND USE

The arithmetic mean is by far the most frequently used measure of location by behavioral scientists, and hypotheses about means the most frequently tested. The tables have been designed to render very simple the procedure for power analysis in the case where two samples, each of **n** cases, have been randomly and independently drawn from normal populations, and the investigator wishes to test the null hypothesis that their respective population means are equal, $H_0: m_A - m_B = 0$ (Hays, 1973, p. 408f; Edwards, 1972, p. 86), referred to below as Case 0. The test is the **t** test for independent means. The tables can also be used to analyze power for (a) the **t** test on means of two independent samples when $n_A \neq n_B$ (Case 1), (b) an approximate **t** test on the means of independent samples when $\sigma_A \neq \sigma_B$ (Case 2), (c) a one-sample **t** test of the null hypothesis that a population mean equals some specified value, $H_0: m = c$ (Case 3) (Hays, 1981, p. 279), and (d) the **t** test on the means of dependent samples, i.e., paired values (Case 4) (Hays, 1981, pp. 296–298; Edwards, 1972, p. 247f). These latter four applications will be discussed below, following consideration of the (Case 0) **t** test for independent means drawn from equally varying populations and based on equal size samples. Finally, the tables can also be used for significance testing, as detailed in Section 2.5.

In the formal development of the **t** distribution for the difference between two independent means, the assumption is made that the populations sampled are normally distributed and that they are of homogeneous (i.e., equal) variance. Moderate departures from these assumptions, however, have generally negligible effects on the validity of both Type I and Type II error calculations. This is particularly true for nondirectional tests and as sample sizes increase above 20 or 30 cases. The only noteworthy exception to the above is under the condition of substantially unequal variances together with substantially unequal sample sizes (whether small or large). Summaries of the evidence in regard to the "robustness" of the **t** (and **F**) test is provided by Scheffé (1959, Chapter 10), and in less technical terms, by Cohen (1965, pp. 114–116). See also Boneau (1960, 1962).

## 2.2 THE EFFECT SIZE INDEX: **d**

As noted above (Section 1.4), we need a "pure" number, one free of our original measurement unit, with which to index what can be alternately called the degree of departure from the null hypothesis of the alternate hypothesis, or the ES (effect size) we wish to detect. This is accomplished by standardizing the raw effect size as expressed in the measurement unit of the dependent variable by dividing it by the (common) standard deviation of the measures in their respective populations, the latter also in the original measurement unit. For the two independent samples case, this is simply

$$(2.2.1) \qquad \mathbf{d} = \frac{\mathbf{m}_A - \mathbf{m}_B}{\sigma}$$

for the directional (one-tailed) case, and

$$(2.2.2) \qquad \mathbf{d} = \frac{|\mathbf{m}_A - \mathbf{m}_B|}{\sigma}$$

for the nondirectional (two-tailed) case,

where    $\mathbf{d}$ = ES index for **t** tests of means in standard unit,

$\mathbf{m}_A, \mathbf{m}_B$ = population means expressed in raw (original measurement) unit, and

$\sigma$ = the standard deviation of either population (since they are assumed equal).

The use of **d** is not only a necessity demanded by the practical requirements of table making, but proves salutary in those areas of the behavioral sciences where raw units are used which are quite arbitrary or lack meaning outside the investigation in which they are used, or both. Consider, for example, the question whether religious groups A and B differ in their favorableness toward the United Nations. The latter may well be indexed by an *ad hoc* attitude scale which yields a score expressed in points, such that the more points the more favorable the attitude. The absolute size of a point is a consequence of arbitrariness in the decisions made by the investigator, and/or in the scale construction method, and/or in the writing or selection of the items. If the A population has a mean of 280 and the B population a mean of 270, the question "How large is the effect?" can only be answered with "ten points," a generally unsatisfactory answer in the absence of a basis for answering the necessarily following question, "Well, how large is a point?"

**d** provides an answer to such questions by expressing score distances in units of variability. If, in the above situation, the common within-population standard deviation is $\sigma = 100$ scale points,

$$\mathbf{d} = \frac{\mathbf{m_A} - \mathbf{m_B}}{\sigma} = \frac{280 - 270}{100} = \frac{10}{100} = .1,$$

i.e., the means differ by a tenth of a standard deviation. Since both numerator and denominator are expressed in scale units, these "cancel out," and **d** is a pure number (here a ratio), freed of dependence upon any specific unit of measurement.

On the other hand, consider the circumstance when $\sigma = 5$ rather than 100. Now,

$$\mathbf{d} = \frac{10}{5} = 2.0,$$

i.e., the means differ by two standard deviations. This is obviously a much larger difference than is **d** = .1.

But *how* large are each of these differences, and how *much* larger is the second than the first? There are various ways the values of **d** may be understood.

2.2.1 **d** AS PERCENT NONOVERLAP: THE **U** MEASURES. If we maintain the assumption that the populations being compared are normal and with equal variability, and conceive them further as equally numerous, it is possible to define measures of nonoverlap (**U**) associated with **d** which are intuitively compelling and meaningful. As examples:

1. When **d** = 0, and therefore either population distribution is perfectly superimposed on the other, there is 100% overlap or 0% nonoverlap, hence $\mathbf{U_1} = 0$. In such a circumstance, the highest 50% of population B exceeds the lowest 50% of population A. We designate as $\mathbf{U_2}$ (50% in this example), a second percentage measure of nonoverlap, the percentage in the B population that exceeds the same percentage in the A population. Finally, as third measure of nonoverlap, $\mathbf{U_3}$, we take the percentage of the A population which the upper half of the cases of the B population exceeds. When **d** = 0, $\mathbf{U_3} = 50.0\%$.

2. When **d** = .1 as in the above example, the distribution of the population with the larger mean, B, is almost superimposed on A, but with some slight excess, i.e., some nonoverlap. $\mathbf{U_1}$ here equals 7.7%, that is, 7.7% of the area covered by both populations combined is not overlapped. For $\mathbf{U_2}$,

the value is 52.0%, i.e., the highest 52.0% of the B population exceeds the lowest 52.0% of the A population. For $U_3$, the value is 54.0%, i.e., the upper 50% of population B exceeds 54.0% of the values in the A population.

3. When we posited the smaller $\sigma$ ($= 5$), we found **d** $= 2.0$. $U_1$ then equals 81.1%, the amount of combined area not shared by the two population distributions. In this case, the highest 84.1% of the B population exceeds the lowest 84.1% of the A population, thus $U_2 = 84.1\%$. Finally, the upper half of the B population exceeds 97.7% of the A population, so that $U_3 = 97.7\%$.

Table 2.2.1

Equivalents of d

| d | $U_1$ | $U_2$ | $U_3$ | r | $r^2$ |
|---|---|---|---|---|---|
| 0 | 0.0% | 50.0% | 50.0% | .000 | .000 |
| .1 | 7.7 | 52.0 | 54.0 | .050 | .002 |
| .2 | 14.7 | 54.0 | 57.9 | .100 | .010 |
| .3 | 21.3 | 56.0 | 61.8 | .148 | .022 |
| .4 | 27.4 | 57.9 | 65.5 | .196 | .038 |
| .5 | 33.0 | 59.9 | 69.1 | .243 | .059 |
| .6 | 38.2 | 61.8 | 72.6 | .287 | .083 |
| .7 | 43.0 | 63.7 | 75.8 | .330 | .109 |
| .8 | 47.4 | 65.5 | 78.8 | .371 | .138 |
| .9 | 51.6 | 67.4 | 81.6 | .410 | .168 |
| 1.0 | 55.4 | 69.1 | 84.1 | .447 | .200 |
| 1.1 | 58.9 | 70.9 | 86.4 | .482 | .232 |
| 1.2 | 62.2 | 72.6 | 88.5 | .514 | .265 |
| 1.3 | 65.3 | 74.2 | 90.3 | .545 | .297 |
| 1.4 | 68.1 | 75.8 | 91.9 | .573 | .329 |
| 1.5 | 70.7 | 77.3 | 93.3 | .600 | .360 |
| 1.6 | 73.1 | 78.8 | 94.5 | .625 | .390 |
| 1.7 | 75.4 | 80.2 | 95.5 | .648 | .419 |
| 1.8 | 77.4 | 81.6 | 96.4 | .669 | .448 |
| 1.9 | 79.4 | 82.9 | 97.1 | .689 | .474 |
| 2.0 | 81.1 | 84.1 | 97.7 | .707 | .500 |
| 2.2 | 84.3 | 86.4 | 98.6 | .740 | .548 |
| 2.4 | 87.0 | 88.5 | 99.2 | .768 | .590 |
| 2.6 | 89.3 | 90.3 | 99.5 | .793 | .628 |
| 2.8 | 91.2 | 91.9 | 99.7 | .814 | .662 |
| 3.0 | 92.8 | 93.3 | 99.9 | .832 | .692 |
| 3.2 | 94.2 | 94.5 | 99.9 | .848 | .719 |
| 3.4 | 95.3 | 95.5 | * | .862 | .743 |
| 3.6 | 96.3 | 96.4 | * | .874 | .764 |
| 3.8 | 97.0 | 97.1 | * | .885 | .783 |
| 4.0 | 97.7 | 97.7 | * | .894 | .800 |

* Greater than 99.95

The reader is free to use whichever of these **U** measures he finds most meaningful to him in the context of his application. They are simply related to **d** and each other through the cumulative normal distribution. If **d** is taken as a deviate in the unit normal curve and **P** as the percentage of the area (population of cases) falling below a given normal deviate, then

(2.2.3)                         $$U_3 = P_d,$$

(2.2.4)                         $$U_2 = P_{d/2}$$

(2.2.5)                         $$U_1 = \frac{2P_{d/2} - 1}{P_{d/2}} = \frac{2U_2 - 1}{U_2}.$$

Table 2.2.1 presents $U_1$, $U_2$, and $U_3$ for values of $d = .1$ (.1) 2.0 (.2) 4.0. Its use will be illustrated after we have considered two other bases for the understanding of **d**.

2.2.2   **d** IN TERMS OF CORRELATION AND PROPORTION OF VARIANCE. Membership in the A or in the B population may be considered to be a simple dichotomy or a two point scale. Scoring it, for example, 0 for membership in A and 1 for membership in B (the values assigned are immaterial), one can express the relationship between population membership and any other variable as a Pearson product-moment correlation coefficient (**r**). Each member in the two populations may be characterized by a pair of variables, the "score" on population membership (**X**) and the value of the other variable (**Y**), and the **r** between **X** and **Y** can then be found by any of the usual computing formulas for **r** (Hays, 1973, p. 631f; Cohen & Cohen, 1975, pp. 32–35), or more readily as the point biserial **r** (Cohen & Cohen, 1975, p. 35ff). Investigators may prefer to think of effect sizes for mean differences in terms of **r**'s, rather than **d**'s, and they are related by

(2.2.6)                         $$r = \frac{d}{\sqrt{d^2 + 4}}.$$

Formula (2.2.6) is appropriately used when the A and B populations are such that they can be conceived as equally numerous. This will usually be the case when A and B represent some experimental manipulation (e.g., the presence or absence of a stimulus, or two different sets of instructions), or some abstract property (e.g., high versus low anxiety level, or native versus foreign speaker), as well as when the dichotomy represents real and equally numerous populations, as is the case (at least approximately) with males and females. The case of equally numerous populations is the usual one. This is the case assumed for the values of **r** given in Table 2.2.1.

When, however, the populations are concrete and unequal collections of cases, the inequality should figure in the assessment of the degree of relationship (e.g., finally diagnosed schizophrenics versus others on a diagnostic psychological test). The more general formula for **r** should then be used:

$$(2.2.7) \qquad \mathbf{r} = \frac{\mathbf{d}}{\sqrt{\mathbf{d}^2 + (1/\mathbf{pq})}},$$

where **p** = proportion of A's in combined A and B populations, and
    **q** = 1 − **p** (i.e., proportion of B's).

[The reader will note that when **p** = **q** = .5, formula (2.2.7) reduces to formula (2.2.6).]

Once a difference between population means of A and B can be expressed as **r**, it can also and usually most usefully be expressed as **r**², the proportion of the total variance (PV) of **Y** in the combined A and B populations associated with or accounted for by population membership (**X** = 0 or .1).

Table 2.2.1 present values of both **r** and **r**² equivalent to **d** for the case where equally numerous populations are assumed. If the means of two equally numerous populations on a variable **Y** differ by **d** = 1.0, then population membership relates to **Y** with **r** = .447, and **r**² = .200 of the combined population variance in **Y** is associated with A versus B membership (**X**).

2.2.3 "SMALL," "MEDIUM," AND "LARGE" **d** VALUES. When working with a variable **Y** which has been well studied, the selection of an effect size expressed in **d** offers no particular difficulty. On the one hand, estimates of the within-population $\sigma$ are readily at hand and the number of raw points difference between A and B population means to be detected (or to serve as an alternate hypothesis to the null) arise naturally out of the content of the inquiry. Thus, a psychologist studying the effects of treatment in phenylpyruvic mental deficiency will likely have an estimate of the $\sigma$ of IQ in such a population (e.g., $\sigma$ = 12.5) and be able to posit an interest in detecting a mean difference between treated and untreated cases of, say, 10 IQ points. Thus, he goes directly to **d** = 10/12.5 = .8. Similarly, an anthropologist studying social class differences in height in a preliterate culture would have an estimated $\sigma$ of height, for example, 2.5 in., and would posit the mean difference he was seeking to detect between two social class populations, say 2 in. He, too, could then find his difference expressed as **d** = 2/2.5, which (also) equals .8.

But consider now the frequently arising circumstance where the variable **Y** is a new measure for which previously collected data or experience are sparse or even nonexistent. Take, for example, an especially constructed test of learning ability appropriate for use with phenylpyruvic mental deficients. The investigator may well be satisfied with the relevance of the test to his purpose, yet may have no idea of either what the $\sigma$ is or how many points of difference on **Y** between means of treated and untreated populations he can expect. Thus, he has neither the numerator $(\mathbf{m}_A - \mathbf{m}_B)$ nor the denominator $(\sigma)$ needed to compute **d**.

It is precisely at this point in the apparent dilemma that the utility of the **d** concept comes to the fore. It is not necessary to compute **d** from a posited difference between means and an estimated standard deviation; one can posit **d** *directly*. Thus, if the investigator thinks that the effect of his treatment method on learning ability in phenylpyruvia is small, he might posit a **d** value such as .2 or .3. If he anticipates it to be large, he might posit **d** as .8 or 1.0. If he expects it to be medium (or simply seeks to straddle the fence on the issue), he might select some such value as **d** = .5.

The terms "small," "medium," and "large" are relative, not only to each other, but to the area of behavioral science or even more particularly to the specific content and research method being employed in any given investigation (see Sections 1.4 and 11.1). In the face of this relativity, there is a certain risk inherent in offering conventional operational definitions for these terms for use in power analysis in as diverse a field of inquiry as behavioral science. This risk is nevertheless accepted in the belief that more is to be gained than lost by supplying a common conventional frame of reference which is recommended for use only when no better basis for estimating the ES index is available.

SMALL EFFECT SIZE: **d** = .2. In new areas of research inquiry, effect sizes are likely to be small (when they are not zero!). This is because the phenomena under study are typically not under good experimental or measurement control or both. When phenomena are studied which cannot be brought into the laboratory, the influence of uncontrollable extraneous variables ("noise") makes the size of the effect small relative to these (makes the "signal" difficult to detect).

The implication of **d** = .2 as the operational definition of a small difference between means can be seen in Table 2.2.1. When **d** = .2, normally distributed populations of equal size and variability have only 14.7% of their combined area which is not overlapped ($\mathbf{U}_1$). If B is the population with the larger mean and A the other, the highest 54% of the B population exceeds the lowest 54% of the A population ($\mathbf{U}_2$). Our third measure of nonoverlap ($\mathbf{U}_3$) indicates that 57.9% of the A population is exceeded by the mean (or equivalently the upper half) of the B population.

From the point of view of correlation and maintaining the idea of equally numerous populations, **d** = .2 means that the (point biserial) **r** between population membership (A vs. B) and the dependent variable **Y** is .100, and $\mathbf{r}^2$ is accordingly .010. The latter can be interpreted as meaning that population membership accounts for 1% of the variance of **Y** in the combined A and B populations.

The above sounds indeed small (but see Section 11.2). Yet it is the order of magnitude of the difference in mean IQ between twins and nontwins, the latter being the larger (Husén, 1959). It is also approximately the size of the difference in mean height between 15- and 16-year-old girls (i.e., .5 in. where the $\sigma$ is about 2.1). Other examples of small effect sizes are adult sex differences on the Information and Picture Completion Subtests of the Wechsler Adult Intelligence Scale, favoring men, while a difference favoring women on the Digit Symbol Test which is twice as large (Wechsler, 1958, p. 147).

MEDIUM EFFECT SIZE: **d** = .5. A medium effect size is conceived as one large enough to be visible to the naked eye. That is, in the course of normal experience, one would become aware of an average difference in IQ between clerical and semiskilled workers or between members of professional and managerial occupational groups (Super, 1949, p. 98).

In terms of measures of nonoverlap (Table 2.2.1), a **d** = .5 indicates that 33.0% ( $= \mathbf{U}_1$ ) of the combined area covered by two normal equal-sized equally varying populations is not overlapped; that (where $\mathbf{m}_B > \mathbf{m}_A$) 59.9% ( $= \mathbf{U}_2$ ) of the B population exceeds 59.9% of the A population; finally, that the upper half of the B population exceeds 69.1% ( $= \mathbf{U}_3$ ) of the A population.

In terms of correlation, **d** = .5 means a point biserial **r** between population membership (A vs. B) and a dependent variable **Y** of .243. Thus, .059 ( $= \mathbf{r}^2$ ) of the **Y** variance is "accounted for" by population membership.

Expressed in the above terms, the reader may feel that the effect size designated medium is too small. That is, an amount not quite equal to 6% of variance may well not seem large enough to be called medium. But **d** = .5 is the magnitude of the difference in height between 14- and 18-year-old girls (about 1 in. where $\sigma = 2$). As noted above, it represents the difference in mean IQ between clerical and semiskilled workers and between professionals and managers (about 8 points where $\sigma = 15$). It is also the difference in means on the World War II General Classification Test for enlisted men who had been teachers versus those who had been general clerks (Harrell and Harrell, 1945, pp. 231–232). Depending on his frame of reference, the reader may consider such differences either small or large. We are thus reminded of the arbitrariness of this assignment of quantitative operational definitions to qualitative adjectives. See Section 11.2.

LARGE EFFECT SIZE: **d** = .8. When our two populations are so separated as to make **d** = .8, almost half ($\mathbf{U}_1 = 47.4\%$) of their areas are not overlapped. $\mathbf{U}_2 = 65.5\%$, i.e., the highest 65.5% of the B population exceeds the lowest 65.5% of the A population. As a third measure, the mean or upper half of the B population exceeds the lower 78.8% ( $= \mathbf{U}_3$ ) of the A population.

The point biserial **r** here equals .371, and **r**$^2$ thus equals .138.

Behavioral scientists who work with correlation coefficients (such as, for example, educational psychologists) do not ordinarily consider an **r** of .371 as large. Nor, in that frame of reference, does the writer. Note however that it is the .8 separation between means which is being designated as large, not the implied point biserial **r**. Such a separation, for example, is represented by the mean IQ difference estimated between holders of the Ph.D. degree and typical college freshmen, or between college graduates and persons with only a 50–50 chance of passing in an academic high school curriculum (Cronbach, 1960, p. 174). These seem like grossly perceptible and therefore large differences, as does the mean difference in height between 13- and 18-year-old girls, which is of the same size (**d** = .8).

## 2.3   POWER TABLES

The power tables are used when, in addition to the significance criterion and ES, the sample size is also specified; the tables then yield power values. Their major use will then be *post hoc*, i.e., to find the power of a test after the experiment has been performed. They can, of course, also be used in experimental planning by varying **n** (or ES or **a** or all these) to see the consequences to power of such alternatives.

2.3.1   CASE 0: $\sigma_A = \sigma_B$, $n_A = n_B$. The power tables are designed to yield power values for the **t** test for the difference between the means of two independent samples of equal size drawn from normal populations having equal variances (Case 0). They are described for such use below, and in a later section for other conditions (Cases 1–4). Tables list values for **a**, **d**, and **n**:

*1. Significance Criterion, **a**.* There are tables for the following values of **a**: $a_1 = .01$, $a_1 = .05$, $a_1 = .10$; $a_2 = .01$, $a_2 = .05$, $a_2 = .10$, where the subscripts refer to one- and two-tailed tests. Since power at $a_1$ is to an adequate approximation equal to power at $a_2 = 2a_1$ for power greater than (say) .10, one can also use the tables for power at $a_2 = .02$ (from the table for $a_1 = .01$), $a_2 = .20$ (from $a_1 = .10$), $a_1 = .005$ (from $a_2 = .01$), and $a_1 = .025$ (from $a_2 = .05$).

*2. Effect Size, ES.* It will be recalled that in formula (2.2.1) the index **d** was defined for one-tailed tests as

$$d = \frac{m_B - m_A}{\sigma},$$

where the alternate hypothesis specifies that $m_B > m_A$, and $\sigma$ is the common within-population standard deviation (i.e., $\sigma_A = \sigma_B = \sigma$).

Table 2.3.1

Power of t test of $m_1 = m_2$ at $a_1 = .01$

| n | $d_c$ | .10 | .20 | .30 | .40 | .50 | .60 | .70 | .80 | 1.00 | 1.20 | 1.40 |
|---|---|---|---|---|---|---|---|---|---|---|---|---|
| 8 | 1.31 | 02 | 03 | 04 | 05 | 08 | 12 | 14 | 19 | 30 | 43 | 57 |
| 9 | 1.22 | 02 | 03 | 04 | 06 | 09 | 13 | 16 | 22 | 35 | 49 | 63 |
| 10 | 1.14 | 02 | 03 | 04 | 07 | 10 | 14 | 18 | 25 | 40 | 55 | 70 |
| 11 | 1.08 | 02 | 03 | 05 | 07 | 11 | 15 | 21 | 28 | 45 | 61 | 76 |
| 12 | 1.02 | 02 | 03 | 05 | 08 | 12 | 17 | 23 | 31 | 49 | 66 | 81 |
| 13 | .98 | 02 | 03 | 05 | 08 | 13 | 19 | 26 | 34 | 53 | 71 | 85 |
| 14 | .94 | 02 | 03 | 06 | 09 | 14 | 20 | 28 | 38 | 57 | 75 | 88 |
| 15 | .90 | 02 | 04 | 06 | 10 | 15 | 22 | 31 | 41 | 61 | 79 | 90 |
| 16 | .87 | 02 | 04 | 06 | 10 | 16 | 24 | 34 | 44 | 64 | 82 | 92 |
| 17 | .84 | 02 | 04 | 07 | 11 | 18 | 26 | 36 | 47 | 68 | 85 | 94 |
| 18 | .81 | 02 | 04 | 07 | 12 | 19 | 27 | 38 | 49 | 71 | 87 | 95 |
| 19 | .79 | 02 | 04 | 07 | 13 | 20 | 29 | 40 | 51 | 74 | 89 | 96 |
| 20 | .77 | 02 | 04 | 08 | 13 | 21 | 30 | 42 | 54 | 76 | 91 | 97 |
| 21 | .75 | 02 | 05 | 08 | 14 | 22 | 32 | 44 | 56 | 79 | 93 | 98 |
| 22 | .73 | 02 | 05 | 08 | 15 | 23 | 34 | 46 | 59 | 81 | 94 | 98 |
| 23 | .71 | 02 | 05 | 09 | 15 | 24 | 36 | 48 | 61 | 83 | 95 | 99 |
| 24 | .70 | 02 | 05 | 09 | 16 | 25 | 37 | 50 | 64 | 85 | 95 | 99 |
| 25 | .68 | 02 | 05 | 10 | 17 | 27 | 39 | 53 | 66 | 87 | 96 | 99 |
| 26 | .67 | 02 | 05 | 10 | 17 | 28 | 41 | 55 | 68 | 89 | 97 | 99 |
| 27 | .65 | 02 | 05 | 10 | 18 | 29 | 42 | 57 | 70 | 90 | 97 | * |
| 28 | .64 | 02 | 05 | 11 | 19 | 30 | 44 | 59 | 72 | 91 | 98 | |
| 29 | .63 | 02 | 06 | 11 | 19 | 31 | 46 | 60 | 74 | 92 | 98 | |
| 30 | .62 | 03 | 06 | 11 | 20 | 32 | 48 | 62 | 75 | 93 | 99 | |
| 31 | .61 | 03 | 06 | 12 | 21 | 34 | 50 | 64 | 77 | 94 | 99 | |
| 32 | .60 | 03 | 06 | 12 | 22 | 35 | 51 | 66 | 79 | 94 | 99 | |
| 33 | .59 | 03 | 06 | 13 | 22 | 36 | 52 | 67 | 80 | 95 | 99 | |
| 34 | .58 | 03 | 06 | 13 | 23 | 37 | 53 | 69 | 81 | 95 | 99 | |
| 35 | .57 | 03 | 07 | 13 | 24 | 38 | 55 | 70 | 83 | 96 | * | |
| 36 | .56 | 03 | 07 | 14 | 25 | 40 | 56 | 72 | 84 | 96 | | |
| 37 | .55 | 03 | 07 | 14 | 26 | 41 | 58 | 73 | 85 | 97 | | |
| 38 | .55 | 03 | 07 | 15 | 26 | 42 | 60 | 75 | 86 | 97 | | |
| 39 | .54 | 03 | 07 | 15 | 27 | 43 | 61 | 76 | 87 | 98 | | |
| 40 | .53 | 03 | 07 | 15 | 28 | 45 | 62 | 78 | 88 | 98 | | |
| 42 | .52 | 03 | 08 | 16 | 30 | 47 | 64 | 80 | 90 | 98 | | |
| 44 | .51 | 03 | 08 | 17 | 31 | 49 | 67 | 82 | 91 | 99 | | |
| 46 | .49 | 03 | 08 | 18 | 33 | 51 | 69 | 83 | 93 | 99 | | |
| 48 | .48 | 03 | 08 | 19 | 34 | 53 | 71 | 85 | 94 | 99 | | |

Table 2.3.1 *(continued)*

| n | $d_c$ | .10 | .20 | .30 | .40 | .50 | .60 | .70 | .80 | 1.00 | 1.20 | 1.40 |
|---|---|---|---|---|---|---|---|---|---|---|---|---|
| 50 | .47 | 03 | 09 | 20 | 36 | 55 | 73 | 87 | 95 | 99 | * | * |
| 52 | .46 | 03 | 09 | 21 | 37 | 57 | 75 | 88 | 95 | * | | |
| 54 | .45 | 04 | 10 | 21 | 39 | 59 | 77 | 90 | 96 | | | |
| 56 | .45 | 05 | 10 | 22 | 40 | 61 | 79 | 91 | 97 | | | |
| 58 | .44 | 05 | 10 | 23 | 41 | 62 | 81 | 92 | 97 | | | |
| 60 | .43 | 05 | 11 | 24 | 43 | 64 | 82 | 93 | 98 | | | |
| 64 | .42 | 05 | 11 | 26 | 46 | 68 | 85 | 94 | 98 | | | |
| 68 | .40 | 05 | 12 | 27 | 49 | 71 | 87 | 96 | 99 | | | |
| 72 | .39 | 05 | 12 | 29 | 52 | 74 | 89 | 97 | 99 | | | |
| 76 | .38 | 05 | 13 | 31 | 55 | 76 | 91 | 97 | 99 | | | |
| 80 | .37 | 05 | 14 | 33 | 57 | 78 | 92 | 98 | * | | | |
| 84 | .36 | 06 | 15 | 34 | 60 | 81 | 94 | 99 | | | | |
| 88 | .35 | 06 | 16 | 36 | 62 | 83 | 95 | 99 | | | | |
| 92 | .35 | 06 | 16 | 38 | 64 | 85 | 96 | 99 | | | | |
| 96 | .34 | 06 | 17 | 39 | 66 | 86 | 96 | 99 | | | | |
| 100 | .33 | 06 | 18 | 41 | 69 | 88 | 97 | * | | | | |
| 120 | .30 | 07 | 21 | 49 | 77 | 93 | 99 | | | | | |
| 140 | .28 | 07 | 25 | 57 | 84 | 96 | * | | | | | |
| 160 | .26 | 07 | 29 | 63 | 89 | 98 | | | | | | |
| 180 | .25 | 08 | 33 | 69 | 93 | 99 | | | | | | |
| 200 | .23 | 09 | 37 | 75 | 95 | * | | | | | | |
| 250 | .21 | 11 | 46 | 84 | 98 | | | | | | | |
| 300 | .19 | 13 | 55 | 91 | 99 | | | | | | | |
| 350 | .18 | 16 | 61 | 95 | * | | | | | | | |
| 400 | .16 | 18 | 69 | 97 | | | | | | | | |
| 450 | .16 | 20 | 75 | 98 | | | | | | | | |
| 500 | .15 | 22 | 80 | 99 | | | | | | | | |
| 600 | .13 | 27 | 87 | * | | | | | | | | |
| 700 | .12 | 32 | 92 | | | | | | | | | |
| 800 | .12 | 37 | 95 | | | | | | | | | |
| 900 | .11 | 42 | 97 | | | | | | | | | |
| 1000 | .10 | 46 | 98 | | | | | | | | | |

* Power values below this point are greater than .995.

Table 2.3.2

Power of t test of $m_1 = m_2$ at $a_1 = .05$

| n | $d_c$ | .10 | .20 | .30 | .40 | .50 | .60 | .70 | .80 | 1.00 | 1.20 | 1.40 |
|---|---|---|---|---|---|---|---|---|---|---|---|---|
| 8 | .88 | 07 | 10 | 13 | 19 | 25 | 31 | 38 | 46 | 61 | 74 | 85 |
| 9 | .82 | 07 | 11 | 15 | 20 | 27 | 34 | 41 | 50 | 66 | 79 | 88 |
| 10 | .78 | 08 | 11 | 16 | 22 | 29 | 36 | 45 | 53 | 70 | 83 | 91 |
| 11 | .74 | 08 | 12 | 17 | 23 | 31 | 39 | 48 | 57 | 74 | 86 | 94 |
| 12 | .70 | 08 | 12 | 18 | 25 | 33 | 41 | 51 | 60 | 77 | 89 | 96 |
| 13 | .67 | 08 | 13 | 18 | 26 | 34 | 44 | 54 | 63 | 80 | 91 | 97 |
| 14 | .64 | 08 | 13 | 19 | 27 | 36 | 46 | 57 | 66 | 83 | 93 | 98 |
| 15 | .62 | 08 | 13 | 20 | 28 | 38 | 48 | 59 | 69 | 85 | 94 | 98 |
| 16 | .60 | 09 | 14 | 21 | 30 | 40 | 51 | 62 | 72 | 87 | 95 | 99 |
| 17 | .58 | 09 | 14 | 22 | 31 | 42 | 53 | 64 | 74 | 89 | 96 | 99 |
| 18 | .56 | 09 | 15 | 22 | 32 | 43 | 55 | 66 | 76 | 90 | 97 | 99 |
| 19 | .55 | 09 | 15 | 23 | 33 | 45 | 57 | 68 | 78 | 92 | 98 | * |
| 20 | .53 | 09 | 15 | 24 | 34 | 46 | 59 | 70 | 80 | 93 | 98 | |
| 21 | .52 | 09 | 16 | 25 | 36 | 48 | 60 | 72 | 82 | 94 | 99 | |
| 22 | .51 | 09 | 16 | 26 | 37 | 50 | 62 | 74 | 83 | 95 | 99 | |
| 23 | .50 | 10 | 16 | 26 | 38 | 51 | 64 | 76 | 85 | 96 | 99 | |
| 24 | .48 | 10 | 17 | 27 | 39 | 53 | 66 | 77 | 86 | 96 | 99 | |
| 25 | .47 | 10 | 17 | 28 | 40 | 54 | 67 | 79 | 88 | 97 | 99 | |
| 26 | .46 | 10 | 18 | 28 | 41 | 55 | 69 | 80 | 89 | 97 | * | |
| 27 | .46 | 10 | 18 | 29 | 42 | 57 | 70 | 82 | 90 | 98 | | |
| 28 | .45 | 10 | 18 | 30 | 43 | 58 | 72 | 83 | 90 | 98 | | |
| 29 | .44 | 10 | 19 | 30 | 44 | 59 | 73 | 84 | 91 | 98 | | |
| 30 | .43 | 10 | 19 | 31 | 46 | 61 | 74 | 85 | 92 | 99 | | |
| 31 | .42 | 10 | 19 | 32 | 47 | 62 | 76 | 86 | 93 | 99 | | |
| 32 | .42 | 11 | 20 | 33 | 48 | 63 | 77 | 87 | 93 | 99 | | |
| 33 | .41 | 11 | 20 | 33 | 49 | 64 | 78 | 88 | 94 | 99 | | |
| 34 | .40 | 11 | 20 | 34 | 50 | 66 | 79 | 89 | 95 | 99 | | |
| 35 | .40 | 11 | 21 | 34 | 50 | 67 | 80 | 89 | 95 | 99 | | |
| 36 | .39 | 11 | 21 | 35 | 51 | 68 | 81 | 90 | 96 | 99 | | |
| 37 | .39 | 11 | 21 | 36 | 52 | 69 | 82 | 91 | 96 | * | | |
| 38 | .38 | 11 | 22 | 36 | 53 | 70 | 83 | 91 | 96 | | | |
| 39 | .38 | 11 | 22 | 37 | 54 | 71 | 84 | 92 | 97 | | | |
| 40 | .37 | 11 | 22 | 38 | 55 | 72 | 84 | 93 | 97 | | | |
| 42 | .36 | 12 | 23 | 39 | 57 | 74 | 86 | 94 | 98 | | | |
| 44 | .35 | 12 | 24 | 40 | 59 | 75 | 87 | 95 | 98 | | | |
| 46 | .35 | 12 | 24 | 41 | 60 | 77 | 89 | 95 | 99 | | | |
| 48 | .34 | 12 | 25 | 43 | 62 | 79 | 90 | 96 | 99 | | | |

Table 2.3.2 *(continued)*

| n | $d_c$ | d | | | | | | | | | | |
|---|---|---|---|---|---|---|---|---|---|---|---|---|
| | | .10 | .20 | .30 | .40 | .50 | .60 | .70 | .80 | 1.00 | 1.20 | 1.40 |
| 50 | .33 | 12 | 26 | 44 | 63 | 80 | 91 | 97 | 99 | * | * | * |
| 52 | .33 | 13 | 26 | 45 | 65 | 81 | 92 | 97 | 99 | | | |
| 54 | .32 | 13 | 27 | 46 | 66 | 83 | 93 | 98 | 99 | | | |
| 56 | .31 | 13 | 28 | 47 | 68 | 84 | 93 | 98 | 99 | | | |
| 58 | .31 | 13 | 28 | 49 | 69 | 85 | 94 | 98 | * | | | |
| 60 | .30 | 13 | 29 | 50 | 70 | 86 | 95 | 98 | | | | |
| 64 | .29 | 14 | 30 | 52 | 73 | 88 | 96 | 99 | | | | |
| 68 | .28 | 14 | 31 | 54 | 75 | 90 | 97 | 99 | | | | |
| 72 | .28 | 15 | 33 | 56 | 77 | 91 | 97 | 99 | | | | |
| 76 | .27 | 15 | 34 | 58 | 79 | 92 | 98 | * | | | | |
| 80 | .26 | 15 | 35 | 60 | 81 | 93 | 98 | | | | | |
| 84 | .26 | 16 | 36 | 61 | 82 | 94 | 99 | | | | | |
| 88 | .25 | 16 | 37 | 63 | 84 | 95 | 99 | | | | | |
| 92 | .24 | 17 | 38 | 65 | 85 | 96 | 99 | | | | | |
| 96 | .24 | 17 | 40 | 66 | 87 | 96 | 99 | | | | | |
| 100 | .23 | 17 | 41 | 68 | 88 | 97 | * | | | | | |
| 120 | .21 | 19 | 46 | 75 | 93 | 99 | | | | | | |
| 140 | .20 | 21 | 51 | 80 | 95 | 99 | | | | | | |
| 160 | .18 | 23 | 56 | 85 | 97 | * | | | | | | |
| 180 | .17 | 24 | 60 | 88 | 98 | | | | | | | |
| 200 | .16 | 26 | 64 | 91 | 99 | | | | | | | |
| 250 | .15 | 30 | 72 | 96 | * | | | | | | | |
| 300 | .13 | 34 | 79 | 98 | | | | | | | | |
| 350 | .12 | 37 | 84 | 99 | | | | | | | | |
| 400 | .12 | 41 | 88 | * | | | | | | | | |
| 450 | .11 | 44 | 91 | | | | | | | | | |
| 500 | .10 | 47 | 93 | | | | | | | | | |
| 600 | .10 | 53 | 97 | | | | | | | | | |
| 700 | .09 | 59 | 98 | | | | | | | | | |
| 800 | .08 | 64 | 99 | | | | | | | | | |
| 900 | .08 | 68 | * | | | | | | | | | |
| 1000 | .07 | 72 | | | | | | | | | | |

* Power values below this point are greater than .995.

Table 2.3.3

Power of t test of $m_1 = m_2$ at $a_1 = .10$

| n | $d_c$ | .10 | .20 | .30 | .40 | .50 | .60 | .70 | .80 | 1.00 | 1.20 | 1.40 |
|---|---|---|---|---|---|---|---|---|---|---|---|---|
| | | | | | | | **d** | | | | | |
| 8 | .67 | 13 | 18 | 24 | 30 | 37 | 44 | 53 | 60 | 74 | 85 | 92 |
| 9 | .63 | 14 | 19 | 25 | 32 | 39 | 47 | 56 | 64 | 78 | 88 | 94 |
| 10 | .59 | 14 | 19 | 26 | 34 | 42 | 50 | 59 | 67 | 81 | 91 | 96 |
| 11 | .57 | 14 | 20 | 27 | 35 | 44 | 53 | 62 | 70 | 84 | 93 | 97 |
| 12 | .54 | 15 | 21 | 28 | 37 | 46 | 56 | 65 | 73 | 87 | 94 | 98 |
| 13 | .52 | 15 | 21 | 29 | 38 | 48 | 58 | 68 | 76 | 89 | 96 | 99 |
| 14 | .50 | 15 | 22 | 30 | 40 | 50 | 61 | 70 | 79 | 90 | 97 | 99 |
| 15 | .48 | 15 | 23 | 31 | 42 | 52 | 63 | 72 | 81 | 92 | 97 | 99 |
| 16 | .46 | 16 | 23 | 32 | 43 | 54 | 65 | 75 | 83 | 93 | 98 | * |
| 17 | .45 | 16 | 24 | 33 | 44 | 56 | 67 | 76 | 84 | 94 | 98 | |
| 18 | .44 | 16 | 24 | 34 | 46 | 58 | 69 | 78 | 86 | 95 | 99 | |
| 19 | .42 | 16 | 25 | 35 | 47 | 59 | 70 | 80 | 87 | 96 | 99 | |
| 20 | .41 | 16 | 25 | 36 | 48 | 61 | 72 | 82 | 89 | 97 | 99 | |
| 21 | .40 | 17 | 26 | 37 | 50 | 62 | 74 | 83 | 90 | 97 | 99 | |
| 22 | .39 | 17 | 26 | 38 | 51 | 64 | 75 | 84 | 91 | 98 | * | |
| 23 | .38 | 17 | 27 | 39 | 52 | 65 | 77 | 86 | 92 | 98 | | |
| 24 | .38 | 17 | 27 | 40 | 53 | 67 | 78 | 87 | 93 | 98 | | |
| 25 | .37 | 17 | 28 | 41 | 55 | 68 | 79 | 88 | 94 | 99 | | |
| 26 | .36 | 18 | 28 | 41 | 56 | 69 | 80 | 89 | 94 | 99 | | |
| 27 | .35 | 18 | 29 | 42 | 57 | 70 | 82 | 90 | 95 | 99 | | |
| 28 | .35 | 18 | 29 | 43 | 58 | 72 | 83 | 91 | 95 | 99 | | |
| 29 | .34 | 18 | 30 | 44 | 59 | 73 | 84 | 91 | 96 | 99 | | |
| 30 | .33 | 18 | 30 | 45 | 60 | 74 | 85 | 92 | 96 | 99 | | |
| 31 | .33 | 19 | 31 | 45 | 61 | 75 | 86 | 93 | 97 | * | | |
| 32 | .32 | 19 | 31 | 46 | 62 | 76 | 86 | 93 | 97 | | | |
| 33 | .32 | 19 | 32 | 47 | 63 | 77 | 87 | 94 | 97 | | | |
| 34 | .31 | 19 | 32 | 48 | 64 | 78 | 88 | 94 | 98 | | | |
| 35 | .31 | 19 | 33 | 48 | 65 | 79 | 89 | 95 | 98 | | | |
| 36 | .30 | 19 | 33 | 49 | 66 | 80 | 89 | 95 | 98 | | | |
| 37 | .30 | 20 | 33 | 50 | 66 | 80 | 90 | 96 | 98 | | | |
| 38 | .30 | 20 | 34 | 51 | 67 | 81 | 91 | 96 | 99 | | | |
| 39 | .29 | 20 | 34 | 51 | 68 | 82 | 91 | 96 | 99 | | | |
| 40 | .29 | 20 | 35 | 52 | 69 | 83 | 92 | 97 | 99 | | | |
| 42 | .28 | 20 | 35 | 53 | 70 | 84 | 93 | 97 | 99 | | | |
| 44 | .28 | 21 | 36 | 55 | 72 | 85 | 94 | 98 | 99 | | | |
| 46 | .27 | 21 | 37 | 56 | 73 | 86 | 94 | 98 | 99 | | | |
| 48 | .26 | 21 | 38 | 57 | 75 | 88 | 95 | 98 | * | | | |

Table 2.3.3 (continued)

| n | $d_c$ | .10 | .20 | .30 | .40 | .50 | .60 | .70 | .80 | 1.00 | 1.20 | 1.40 |
|---|---|---|---|---|---|---|---|---|---|---|---|---|
| 50 | .26 | 22 | 39 | 58 | 76 | 89 | 96 | 99 | * | * | * | * |
| 52 | .25 | 22 | 39 | 59 | 77 | 90 | 96 | 99 | | | | |
| 54 | .25 | 22 | 40 | 61 | 78 | 90 | 97 | 99 | | | | |
| 56 | .24 | 22 | 41 | 62 | 80 | 91 | 97 | 99 | | | | |
| 58 | .24 | 23 | 42 | 63 | 81 | 92 | 97 | 99 | | | | |
| 60 | .24 | 23 | 42 | 64 | 82 | 93 | 98 | 99 | | | | |
| 64 | .23 | 24 | 44 | 66 | 83 | 94 | 98 | * | | | | |
| 68 | .22 | 24 | 45 | 68 | 85 | 95 | 99 | | | | | |
| 72 | .21 | 25 | 47 | 70 | 87 | 96 | 99 | | | | | |
| 76 | .21 | 25 | 48 | 71 | 88 | 96 | 99 | | | | | |
| 80 | .20 | 26 | 49 | 73 | 89 | 97 | 99 | | | | | |
| 84 | .20 | 26 | 51 | 74 | 90 | 97 | * | | | | | |
| 88 | .19 | 27 | 52 | 76 | 91 | 98 | | | | | | |
| 92 | .19 | 27 | 53 | 77 | 92 | 98 | | | | | | |
| 96 | .19 | 28 | 54 | 79 | 93 | 99 | | | | | | |
| 100 | .18 | 29 | 55 | 80 | 94 | 99 | | | | | | |
| 120 | .17 | 31 | 60 | 85 | 96 | * | | | | | | |
| 140 | .15 | 33 | 65 | 89 | 98 | | | | | | | |
| 160 | .14 | 35 | 69 | 92 | 99 | | | | | | | |
| 180 | .14 | 37 | 73 | 94 | 99 | | | | | | | |
| 200 | .13 | 39 | 76 | 96 | * | | | | | | | |
| 250 | .11 | 44 | 83 | 98 | | | | | | | | |
| 300 | .10 | 48 | 88 | 99 | | | | | | | | |
| 350 | .10 | 52 | 91 | * | | | | | | | | |
| 400 | .09 | 55 | 94 | | | | | | | | | |
| 450 | .09 | 59 | 96 | | | | | | | | | |
| 500 | .08 | 62 | 97 | | | | | | | | | |
| 600 | .07 | 67 | 99 | | | | | | | | | |
| 700 | .07 | 72 | 99 | | | | | | | | | |
| 800 | .06 | 76 | * | | | | | | | | | |
| 900 | .06 | 80 | | | | | | | | | | |
| 1000 | .06 | 83 | | | | | | | | | | |

* Power values below this point are greater than .995.

Table 2.3.4

Power of t test of $m_1 = m_2$ at $a_2 = .01$

| n | $d_c$ | .10 | .20 | .30 | .40 | .50 | .60 | .70 | .80 | 1.00 | 1.20 | 1.40 |
|---|---|---|---|---|---|---|---|---|---|---|---|---|
| 8 | 1.49 | 01 | 02 | 02 | 03 | 05 | 07 | 09 | 12 | 21 | 33 | 46 |
| 9 | 1.38 | 01 | 02 | 02 | 04 | 05 | 08 | 11 | 15 | 25 | 39 | 54 |
| 10 | 1.28 | 01 | 02 | 03 | 04 | 06 | 09 | 12 | 17 | 29 | 45 | 61 |
| 11 | 1.21 | 01 | 02 | 03 | 04 | 07 | 10 | 14 | 20 | 33 | 50 | 67 |
| 12 | 1.15 | 01 | 02 | 03 | 05 | 07 | 11 | 16 | 22 | 38 | 55 | 72 |
| 13 | 1.10 | 01 | 02 | 03 | 05 | 08 | 12 | 18 | 25 | 42 | 61 | 77 |
| 14 | 1.05 | 01 | 02 | 03 | 06 | 09 | 14 | 20 | 27 | 46 | 65 | 81 |
| 15 | 1.01 | 01 | 02 | 04 | 06 | 10 | 15 | 22 | 30 | 50 | 70 | 85 |
| 16 | .97 | 01 | 02 | 04 | 07 | 11 | 16 | 24 | 33 | 54 | 73 | 88 |
| 17 | .94 | 01 | 02 | 04 | 07 | 12 | 18 | 26 | 35 | 57 | 77 | 90 |
| 18 | .91 | 01 | 02 | 04 | 08 | 12 | 19 | 28 | 38 | 61 | 80 | 92 |
| 19 | .88 | 01 | 02 | 05 | 08 | 13 | 21 | 30 | 41 | 64 | 83 | 94 |
| 20 | .86 | 01 | 02 | 05 | 09 | 14 | 22 | 32 | 44 | 67 | 85 | 95 |
| 21 | .83 | 01 | 03 | 05 | 09 | 15 | 24 | 34 | 46 | 70 | 87 | 96 |
| 22 | .81 | 01 | 03 | 05 | 10 | 16 | 25 | 36 | 49 | 73 | 89 | 97 |
| 23 | .79 | 01 | 03 | 06 | 10 | 17 | 27 | 38 | 51 | 75 | 91 | 98 |
| 24 | .78 | 01 | 03 | 06 | 11 | 18 | 28 | 40 | 54 | 78 | 92 | 98 |
| 25 | .76 | 01 | 03 | 06 | 11 | 19 | 30 | 42 | 56 | 80 | 93 | 99 |
| 26 | .74 | 01 | 03 | 06 | 12 | 20 | 31 | 44 | 58 | 82 | 95 | 99 |
| 27 | .73 | 01 | 03 | 07 | 12 | 21 | 33 | 46 | 60 | 84 | 95 | 99 |
| 28 | .71 | 02 | 03 | 07 | 13 | 22 | 34 | 48 | 63 | 85 | 96 | 99 |
| 29 | .70 | 02 | 03 | 07 | 14 | 23 | 36 | 50 | 65 | 87 | 97 | * |
| 30 | .69 | 02 | 03 | 07 | 14 | 24 | 37 | 52 | 66 | 88 | 97 | |
| 31 | .68 | 02 | 04 | 08 | 15 | 25 | 39 | 54 | 68 | 89 | 98 | |
| 32 | .66 | 02 | 04 | 08 | 15 | 26 | 40 | 56 | 70 | 91 | 98 | |
| 33 | .65 | 02 | 04 | 08 | 16 | 27 | 42 | 57 | 72 | 92 | 98 | |
| 34 | .64 | 02 | 04 | 08 | 17 | 28 | 43 | 59 | 74 | 92 | 99 | |
| 35 | .63 | 02 | 04 | 09 | 17 | 30 | 45 | 61 | 75 | 93 | 99 | |
| 36 | .62 | 02 | 04 | 09 | 18 | 31 | 46 | 62 | 77 | 94 | 99 | |
| 37 | .62 | 02 | 04 | 09 | 18 | 32 | 48 | 64 | 78 | 95 | 99 | |
| 38 | .61 | 02 | 04 | 10 | 19 | 33 | 49 | 66 | 80 | 95 | 99 | |
| 39 | .60 | 02 | 04 | 10 | 20 | 34 | 50 | 67 | 81 | 96 | * | |
| 40 | .59 | 02 | 04 | 10 | 20 | 35 | 52 | 68 | 82 | 96 | | |
| 42 | .58 | 02 | 05 | 11 | 22 | 37 | 55 | 71 | 84 | 97 | | |
| 44 | .56 | 02 | 05 | 12 | 23 | 39 | 57 | 74 | 86 | 98 | | |
| 46 | .55 | 02 | 05 | 12 | 24 | 41 | 60 | 76 | 88 | 98 | | |
| 48 | .54 | 02 | 05 | 13 | 26 | 43 | 62 | 78 | 90 | 99 | | |

Table 2.3.4 *(continued)*

| | | | | | | d | | | | | | |
|---|---|---|---|---|---|---|---|---|---|---|---|---|
| n | $d_c$ | .10 | .20 | .30 | .40 | .50 | .60 | .70 | .80 | 1.00 | 1.20 | 1.40 |
| 50 | .53 | 02 | 06 | 14 | 27 | 45 | 64 | 81 | 91 | 99 | * | * |
| 52 | .51 | 02 | 06 | 14 | 28 | 47 | 67 | 82 | 92 | 99 | | |
| 54 | .50 | 02 | 06 | 15 | 30 | 49 | 69 | 84 | 93 | 99 | | |
| 56 | .50 | 02 | 06 | 16 | 31 | 51 | 71 | 86 | 94 | * | | |
| 58 | .49 | 02 | 06 | 16 | 32 | 53 | 73 | 87 | 95 | | | |
| 60 | .48 | 02 | 07 | 17 | 34 | 55 | 75 | 88 | 96 | | | |
| 64 | .46 | 02 | 07 | 18 | 36 | 58 | 78 | 91 | 97 | | | |
| 68 | .45 | 02 | 08 | 20 | 39 | 62 | 81 | 93 | 98 | | | |
| 72 | .44 | 02 | 08 | 21 | 42 | 65 | 84 | 94 | 98 | | | |
| 76 | .42 | 03 | 09 | 23 | 44 | 68 | 86 | 95 | 99 | | | |
| 80 | .41 | 03 | 09 | 24 | 47 | 71 | 88 | 96 | 99 | | | |
| 84 | .40 | 03 | 10 | 26 | 50 | 74 | 90 | 97 | 99 | | | |
| 88 | .39 | 03 | 10 | 27 | 52 | 76 | 91 | 98 | * | | | |
| 92 | .38 | 03 | 11 | 29 | 54 | 78 | 93 | 98 | | | | |
| 96 | .38 | 03 | 11 | 30 | 57 | 80 | 94 | 99 | | | | |
| 100 | .37 | 03 | 12 | 32 | 59 | 82 | 95 | 99 | | | | |
| 120 | .34 | 04 | 15 | 39 | 69 | 90 | 98 | * | | | | |
| 140 | .31 | 04 | 18 | 47 | 77 | 94 | 99 | | | | | |
| 160 | .29 | 05 | 21 | 54 | 84 | 97 | * | | | | | |
| 180 | .27 | 05 | 25 | 60 | 88 | 98 | | | | | | |
| 200 | .26 | 06 | 29 | 66 | 92 | 99 | | | | | | |
| 250 | .23 | 07 | 36 | 78 | 97 | * | | | | | | |
| 300 | .21 | 09 | 45 | 86 | 99 | | | | | | | |
| 350 | .20 | 10 | 53 | 92 | * | | | | | | | |
| 400 | .18 | 12 | 60 | 95 | | | | | | | | |
| 450 | .17 | 14 | 66 | 97 | | | | | | | | |
| 500 | .16 | 16 | 72 | 98 | | | | | | | | |
| 600 | .15 | 20 | 81 | * | | | | | | | | |
| 700 | .14 | 24 | 88 | | | | | | | | | |
| 800 | .13 | 28 | 92 | | | | | | | | | |
| 900 | .12 | 33 | 95 | | | | | | | | | |
| 1000 | .12 | 37 | 97 | | | | | | | | | |

* Power values below this point are greater than .995.

**Table 2.3.5**

Power of t test of $m_1 = m_2$ at a. = .05

Non-Directional

| n | $d_c$ | .10 | .20 | .30 | .40 | .50 | .60 | .70 | .80 | 1.00 | 1.20 | 1.40 |
|---|---|---|---|---|---|---|---|---|---|---|---|---|
| 8 | 1.07 | 05 | 07 | 09 | 11 | 15 | 20 | 25 | 31 | 46 | 60 | 73 |
| 9 | 1.00 | 05 | 07 | 09 | 12 | 16 | 22 | 28 | 35 | 51 | 65 | 79 |
| 10 | .94 | 06 | 07 | 10 | 13 | 18 | 24 | 31 | 39 | 56 | 71 | 84 |
| 11 | .89 | 06 | 07 | 10 | 14 | 20 | 26 | 34 | 43 | 61 | 76 | 87 |
| 12 | .85 | 06 | 08 | 11 | 15 | 21 | 28 | 37 | 46 | 65 | 80 | 90 |
| 13 | .81 | 06 | 08 | 11 | 16 | 23 | 31 | 40 | 50 | 69 | 83 | 93 |
| 14 | .78 | 06 | 08 | 12 | 17 | 25 | 33 | 43 | 53 | 72 | 86 | 94 |
| 15 | .75 | 06 | 08 | 12 | 18 | 26 | 35 | 45 | 56 | 75 | 88 | 96 |
| 16 | .72 | 06 | 08 | 13 | 19 | 28 | 37 | 48 | 59 | 78 | 90 | 97 |
| 17 | .70 | 06 | 09 | 13 | 20 | 29 | 39 | 51 | 62 | 80 | 92 | 98 |
| 18 | .68 | 06 | 09 | 14 | 21 | 31 | 41 | 53 | 64 | 83 | 94 | 98 |
| 19 | .66 | 06 | 09 | 15 | 22 | 32 | 43 | 55 | 67 | 85 | 95 | 99 |
| 20 | .64 | 06 | 09 | 15 | 23 | 33 | 45 | 58 | 69 | 87 | 96 | 99 |
| 21 | .62 | 06 | 10 | 16 | 24 | 35 | 47 | 60 | 71 | 88 | 97 | 99 |
| 22 | .61 | 06 | 10 | 16 | 25 | 36 | 49 | 62 | 73 | 90 | 97 | 99 |
| 23 | .59 | 06 | 10 | 17 | 26 | 38 | 51 | 64 | 75 | 91 | 98 | * |
| 24 | .58 | 06 | 10 | 17 | 27 | 39 | 53 | 66 | 77 | 92 | 98 | |
| 25 | .57 | 06 | 11 | 18 | 28 | 41 | 55 | 68 | 79 | 93 | 99 | |
| 26 | .56 | 06 | 11 | 19 | 29 | 42 | 56 | 69 | 80 | 94 | 99 | |
| 27 | .55 | 06 | 11 | 19 | 30 | 43 | 58 | 71 | 82 | 95 | 99 | |
| 28 | .54 | 07 | 11 | 20 | 31 | 45 | 59 | 73 | 83 | 96 | 99 | |
| 29 | .53 | 07 | 12 | 20 | 32 | 46 | 61 | 74 | 85 | 96 | 99 | |
| 30 | .52 | 07 | 12 | 21 | 33 | 47 | 63 | 76 | 86 | 97 | * | |
| 31 | .51 | 07 | 12 | 21 | 34 | 49 | 64 | 77 | 87 | 97 | | |
| 32 | .50 | 07 | 12 | 22 | 35 | 50 | 65 | 78 | 88 | 98 | | |
| 33 | .49 | 07 | 13 | 22 | 36 | 51 | 67 | 80 | 89 | 98 | | |
| 34 | .48 | 07 | 13 | 23 | 37 | 53 | 68 | 81 | 90 | 98 | | |
| 35 | .48 | 07 | 13 | 23 | 38 | 54 | 70 | 82 | 91 | 98 | | |
| 36 | .47 | 07 | 13 | 24 | 39 | 55 | 71 | 83 | 92 | 99 | | |
| 37 | .46 | 07 | 14 | 25 | 39 | 56 | 72 | 84 | 92 | 99 | | |
| 38 | .46 | 07 | 14 | 25 | 40 | 57 | 73 | 85 | 93 | 99 | | |
| 39 | .45 | 07 | 14 | 26 | 41 | 58 | 74 | 86 | 94 | 99 | | |
| 40 | .45 | 07 | 14 | 26 | 42 | 60 | 75 | 87 | 94 | 99 | | |
| 42 | .43 | 07 | 15 | 27 | 44 | 62 | 77 | 89 | 95 | 99 | | |
| 44 | .42 | 07 | 15 | 28 | 46 | 64 | 79 | 90 | 96 | * | | |
| 46 | .41 | 08 | 16 | 30 | 48 | 66 | 81 | 91 | 97 | | | |
| 48 | .41 | 08 | 16 | 31 | 49 | 68 | 83 | 92 | 97 | | | |

Table 2.3.5 (continued)

| n | $d_c$ | .10 | .20 | .30 | .40 | .50 | .60 | .70 | .80 | 1.00 | 1.20 | 1.40 |
|---|---|---|---|---|---|---|---|---|---|---|---|---|
| 50 | .40 | 08 | 17 | 32 | 50 | 70 | 84 | 93 | 98 | * | * | * |
| 52 | .39 | 08 | 17 | 34 | 51 | 71 | 86 | 94 | 98 | | | |
| 54 | .38 | 08 | 18 | 34 | 53 | 73 | 87 | 95 | 98 | | | |
| 56 | .37 | 08 | 18 | 35 | 55 | 74 | 88 | 96 | 99 | | | |
| 58 | .37 | 08 | 19 | 36 | 57 | 76 | 89 | 96 | 99 | | | |
| 60 | .36 | 08 | 19 | 37 | 58 | 77 | 90 | 97 | 99 | | | |
| 64 | .35 | 09 | 20 | 39 | 61 | 80 | 92 | 98 | 99 | | | |
| 68 | .34 | 09 | 21 | 41 | 64 | 82 | 93 | 98 | * | | | |
| 72 | .33 | 09 | 22 | 43 | 66 | 85 | 94 | 99 | | | | |
| 76 | .32 | 09 | 23 | 45 | 69 | 86 | 95 | 99 | | | | |
| 80 | .31 | 10 | 24 | 47 | 71 | 88 | 96 | 99 | | | | |
| 84 | .30 | 10 | 25 | 49 | 73 | 90 | 97 | 99 | | | | |
| 88 | .30 | 10 | 26 | 51 | 75 | 91 | 98 | * | | | | |
| 92 | .29 | 10 | 27 | 52 | 77 | 92 | 98 | | | | | |
| 96 | .29 | 11 | 28 | 54 | 79 | 93 | 99 | | | | | |
| 100 | .28 | 11 | 29 | 56 | 80 | 94 | 99 | | | | | |
| 120 | .26 | 12 | 34 | 64 | 87 | 97 | * | | | | | |
| 140 | .24 | 13 | 38 | 71 | 92 | 99 | | | | | | |
| 160 | .22 | 14 | 43 | 76 | 95 | 99 | | | | | | |
| 180 | .21 | 16 | 47 | 81 | 97 | * | | | | | | |
| 200 | .20 | 17 | 51 | 85 | 98 | | | | | | | |
| 250 | .18 | 20 | 61 | 92 | 99 | | | | | | | |
| 300 | .16 | 23 | 69 | 96 | * | | | | | | | |
| 350 | .15 | 26 | 75 | 98 | | | | | | | | |
| 400 | .14 | 29 | 81 | 99 | | | | | | | | |
| 450 | .13 | 32 | 85 | 99 | | | | | | | | |
| 500 | .12 | 35 | 88 | * | | | | | | | | |
| 600 | .11 | 41 | 93 | | | | | | | | | |
| 700 | .10 | 46 | 96 | | | | | | | | | |
| 800 | .10 | 52 | 98 | | | | | | | | | |
| 900 | .09 | 56 | 99 | | | | | | | | | |
| 1000 | .09 | 61 | 99 | | | | | | | | | |

* Power values below this point are greater than .995.

Table 2.3.6

Power of t test of $m_1 = m_2$ at $a_2 = .10$

| n | $d_c$ | .10 | .20 | .30 | .40 | .50 | .60 | .70 | .80 | 1.00 | 1.20 | 1.40 |
|---|---|---|---|---|---|---|---|---|---|---|---|---|
| | | | | | | | | | | **d** | | |
| 8 | .88 | 11 | 12 | 15 | 20 | 25 | 31 | 38 | 46 | 61 | 74 | 85 |
| 9 | .82 | 11 | 13 | 16 | 21 | 27 | 34 | 42 | 50 | 66 | 79 | 89 |
| 10 | .78 | 11 | 13 | 17 | 22 | 29 | 37 | 45 | 53 | 70 | 83 | 92 |
| 11 | .74 | 11 | 13 | 18 | 24 | 31 | 39 | 48 | 57 | 74 | 86 | 94 |
| 12 | .70 | 11 | 14 | 19 | 25 | 33 | 42 | 51 | 60 | 77 | 89 | 96 |
| 13 | .67 | 11 | 14 | 19 | 26 | 34 | 44 | 54 | 63 | 80 | 91 | 97 |
| 14 | .64 | 11 | 14 | 20 | 27 | 36 | 46 | 57 | 66 | 83 | 93 | 98 |
| 15 | .62 | 11 | 15 | 21 | 29 | 38 | 49 | 59 | 69 | 85 | 94 | 98 |
| 16 | .60 | 11 | 15 | 21 | 30 | 40 | 51 | 62 | 72 | 87 | 95 | 99 |
| 17 | .58 | 11 | 15 | 22 | 31 | 42 | 53 | 64 | 74 | 89 | 96 | 99 |
| 18 | .56 | 11 | 16 | 23 | 32 | 43 | 55 | 66 | 76 | 90 | 97 | 99 |
| 19 | .55 | 11 | 16 | 24 | 33 | 45 | 57 | 68 | 78 | 92 | 98 | * |
| 20 | .53 | 12 | 16 | 24 | 35 | 47 | 59 | 70 | 80 | 93 | 98 | |
| 21 | .52 | 12 | 17 | 25 | 36 | 48 | 61 | 72 | 82 | 94 | 99 | |
| 22 | .51 | 12 | 17 | 26 | 37 | 50 | 62 | 74 | 83 | 95 | 99 | |
| 23 | .50 | 12 | 17 | 26 | 38 | 51 | 64 | 76 | 85 | 96 | 99 | |
| 24 | .48 | 12 | 18 | 27 | 39 | 53 | 66 | 77 | 86 | 96 | 99 | |
| 25 | .47 | 12 | 18 | 28 | 40 | 54 | 67 | 79 | 88 | 97 | 99 | |
| 26 | .46 | 12 | 18 | 29 | 41 | 55 | 69 | 80 | 89 | 97 | * | |
| 27 | .46 | 12 | 19 | 29 | 42 | 57 | 70 | 82 | 90 | 98 | | |
| 28 | .45 | 12 | 19 | 30 | 44 | 58 | 72 | 83 | 90 | 98 | | |
| 29 | .44 | 12 | 19 | 31 | 45 | 59 | 73 | 84 | 91 | 98 | | |
| 30 | .43 | 12 | 20 | 31 | 46 | 61 | 74 | 85 | 92 | 99 | | |
| 31 | .42 | 13 | 20 | 32 | 47 | 62 | 76 | 86 | 93 | 99 | | |
| 32 | .42 | 13 | 20 | 33 | 48 | 63 | 77 | 87 | 93 | 99 | | |
| 33 | .41 | 13 | 21 | 33 | 49 | 64 | 78 | 88 | 94 | 99 | | |
| 34 | .40 | 13 | 21 | 34 | 50 | 66 | 79 | 89 | 95 | 99 | | |
| 35 | .40 | 13 | 21 | 35 | 51 | 67 | 80 | 89 | 95 | 99 | | |
| 36 | .39 | 13 | 22 | 35 | 52 | 68 | 81 | 90 | 96 | 99 | | |
| 37 | .39 | 13 | 22 | 36 | 52 | 69 | 82 | 91 | 96 | * | | |
| 38 | .38 | 13 | 22 | 37 | 53 | 70 | 83 | 91 | 96 | | | |
| 39 | .38 | 13 | 23 | 37 | 54 | 71 | 84 | 92 | 97 | | | |
| 40 | .37 | 13 | 23 | 38 | 55 | 72 | 84 | 93 | 97 | | | |
| 42 | .36 | 13 | 24 | 39 | 57 | 74 | 86 | 94 | 98 | | | |
| 44 | .35 | 14 | 24 | 40 | 58 | 75 | 87 | 95 | 98 | | | |
| 46 | .35 | 14 | 25 | 41 | 60 | 77 | 89 | 95 | 99 | | | |
| 48 | .34 | 14 | 25 | 43 | 62 | 79 | 90 | 96 | 99 | | | |

Table 2.3.6 *(continued)*

| n | $d_c$ | .10 | .20 | .30 | .40 | .50 | .60 | .70 | .80 | 1.00 | 1.20 | 1.40 |
|---|---|---|---|---|---|---|---|---|---|---|---|---|
| | | | | | | d | | | | | | |
| 50 | .33 | 14 | 26 | 44 | 63 | 80 | 91 | 97 | 99 | * | * | * |
| 52 | .33 | 14 | 27 | 45 | 65 | 81 | 92 | 97 | 99 | | | |
| 54 | .32 | 14 | 27 | 46 | 66 | 83 | 93 | 98 | 99 | | | |
| 56 | .31 | 15 | 28 | 47 | 68 | 84 | 93 | 98 | 99 | | | |
| 58 | .31 | 15 | 29 | 49 | 69 | 85 | 94 | 98 | * | | | |
| 60 | .30 | 15 | 29 | 50 | 70 | 86 | 95 | 98 | | | | |
| 64 | .29 | 15 | 30 | 52 | 73 | 88 | 96 | 99 | | | | |
| 68 | .28 | 16 | 32 | 54 | 75 | 90 | 97 | 99 | | | | |
| 72 | .28 | 16 | 33 | 56 | 77 | 91 | 97 | 99 | | | | |
| 76 | .27 | 16 | 34 | 58 | 79 | 92 | 98 | * | | | | |
| 80 | .26 | 17 | 35 | 60 | 81 | 93 | 98 | | | | | |
| 84 | .26 | 17 | 36 | 61 | 82 | 94 | 98 | | | | | |
| 88 | .25 | 17 | 37 | 63 | 84 | 95 | 99 | | | | | |
| 92 | .24 | 18 | 39 | 65 | 85 | 96 | 99 | | | | | |
| 96 | .24 | 18 | 40 | 66 | 87 | 96 | 99 | | | | | |
| 100 | .23 | 18 | 41 | 68 | 88 | 97 | 99 | | | | | |
| 120 | .21 | 20 | 46 | 75 | 93 | 99 | * | | | | | |
| 140 | .20 | 22 | 51 | 80 | 95 | 99 | | | | | | |
| 160 | .18 | 23 | 56 | 85 | 97 | * | | | | | | |
| 180 | .17 | 25 | 60 | 88 | 98 | | | | | | | |
| 200 | .16 | 26 | 64 | 91 | 99 | | | | | | | |
| 250 | .15 | 30 | 72 | 96 | * | | | | | | | |
| 300 | .13 | 34 | 79 | 98 | | | | | | | | |
| 350 | .12 | 37 | 84 | 99 | | | | | | | | |
| 400 | .12 | 41 | 88 | * | | | | | | | | |
| 450 | .11 | 44 | 91 | | | | | | | | | |
| 500 | .10 | 47 | 93 | | | | | | | | | |
| 600 | .10 | 53 | 97 | | | | | | | | | |
| 700 | .09 | 59 | 98 | | | | | | | | | |
| 800 | .08 | 64 | 99 | | | | | | | | | |
| 900 | .08 | 68 | * | | | | | | | | | |
| 1000 | .07 | 72 | | | | | | | | | | |

* Power values below this point are greater than .995.

For two-tailed tests [formula (2.2.2)],

$$d = \frac{|m_A - m_B|}{\sigma},$$

where the alternate hypothesis specifies only that $m_A \neq m_B$.

Provision is made for $d = .10 (.10) .80 (.20) 1.40$. Conventional definitions of ES have been offered above, as follows:

small: $d = .20$,
medium: $d = .50$,
large: $d = .80$.

*3. Sample Size*, **n**. This is the size of *each* of the two samples being compared. Provision is made for $n = 8 (1) 40 (2) 60 (4) 100 (20) 200 (50) 500 (100) 1000$.

The values in the body of the table are the power of the test times 100, i.e., the percentage of tests carried out under the given conditions which will result in the rejection of the null hypothesis. The values are rounded to the *nearest* unit, and they are generally accurate to within $\pm 1$ as tabled (i.e., to within .01).

**Illustrative Examples**

**2.1**  An experimental psychologist designs a study to appraise the effect of opportunity to explore a maze without reward on subsequent maze learning in rats. Random samples of 30 cases each are drawn from the available supply and assigned to an experimental (E) group which is given an exploratory period and a control (C) group, which is not. Following this, the 60 rats are tested and the number of trials needed to reach a criterion of two successive errorless runs is determined. The (nondirectional) null hypothesis is $|m_E - m_C| = 0$. She anticipates that the ES would be such that the highest 60% of one population would exceed the lowest 60% of the other, i.e., $U_2 \cong 60\%$ (Section 2.2). Referring to Table 2.2.1, she finds that $U_2 = 59.9\%$ is equivalent to our conventional definition of a medium effect: $d = .50$. That is, the alternative hypothesis is that the population means differ by half a within-population standard deviation. The significance criterion is $a_2 = .05$. What is the power of the test? Summarizing the specifications,

$$a_2 = .05, \quad d = .50, \quad n_E = n_C = n = 30.$$

In Table 2.3.5 (for $a_2 = .05$), for column $d = .50$ and row $n = 30$, power equals .47. Thus, for the given sample sizes and using the $a_2 = .05$ significance criterion, the investigator does not quite have a fifty–fifty chance of detecting $d = .50$.

The choice of $d$ need not have proceeded by asserting the expectation that the ES was "medium" and using the conventional $d = .5$ value. Experience with the subjects and the maze in question or reference to the literature may have provided the experimenter with an estimate of the within-population standard deviation of trials scores, $\sigma$ (say 2.8), and theory or intuition may have suggested a specific value for the experimental effect, $|m_C - m_E|$ ($= 2$ trials, let us say). She would then use the explicit formula (2.2.2),

$$d = \frac{|m_1 - m_2|}{\sigma} = \frac{2}{2.8} = .71.$$

In this case, in Table 2.3.5 with $n = 30$ as before but now with $d = .70$, power is found to be .76 (or by linear interpolation for $d = .71$, power $= .77$).

It can also be argued that, given a theory, the psychologist would probably predict the direction of the difference, say $m_C > m_E$ (i.e., the animals profit from their exploratory experience) and that therefore a directional test should be used. In this case, Table 2.3.2 for $a_1 = .05$ would be used, with the results

for "medium" $d = .50$: $\qquad$ $n = 30$, $\qquad$ power $= .61$,
for explicit $d$ (from (2.2.1)) $= .71$: $\qquad$ $n = 30$, $\qquad$ power $= .86$.

As described above (Chapter 1, Section 1.2), power is greater for directional tests than nondirectional tests, other things equal, provided that the experimental results are in the anticipated direction. Experimenters are in an embarassing position when they obtain large experimental effects in the unanticipated direction (Cohen, 1965, pp. 106–111).

This example was chosen, in part, to point out that the frequently selected sample size of 30 does not provide adequate power at the conventional $a_2 = .05$ against a medium ES, which is frequently as large as can reasonably be expected. Only when a large ($d = .80$) ES can be anticipated, for $n = 30$ at $a_2 = .05$, is power as high as most investigators would wish, in this instance .86 (from Table 2.3.5). When a small ($d = .20$) ES is anticipated, for $n = 30$, $a_2 = .05$, power is only .12 (Table 2.3.5)—probably not worth the effort involved in performing the experiment.

**2.2** A psychiatric investigator, in pursuing certain endocrinological factors implicated in schizophrenia, performs an experiment in which urine samples of 500 schizophrenics and 500 comparable normals are analyzed for a certain relevant metabolic product which is approximately normally distributed with homogeneous variability. Since the implicated endocrinological factor is only indirectly related to the metabolic product in the urine and perhaps for other reasons, he anticipates only a small ES, specifically that $d = .20$. He selects the conservative significance criterion of $a_2 = .01$. What is the power of his **t** test? Summarizing the specifications:

$$a_2 = .01, \qquad d = .20, \qquad n_S = n_N = 500.$$

In Table 2.3.4 (for $a_2 = .01$), for column $d = .20$, row $n = 500$, power $= .72$.

Were he to be satisfied with the less stringent $a_2 = .05$ significance criterion, he would find (from Table 2.3.5) power equal to .88. Note that rather large samples are required to detect small effects (at least as we have conventionally defined them). Ordinarily, the investigator seeking to detect a small effect will hardly be able to afford the luxury of a stringent significance criterion such as $a = .01$. He may well want to consider increasing his Type I (**a**) error risk to perhaps .10 in order to keep the magnitude of his Type II (**b**) error risk from becoming so large as to make the experiment uninformative in the likely event of a nonsignificant difference. Naturally, the increase in **a** is made before, not after, the data are collected.

2.3.2   CASE 1: $n_A \neq n_B$, $\sigma_A = \sigma_B$. The power tables will yield useful approximate values when, from the two normal equally varying populations, samples of different sizes are drawn. In such cases, compute the harmonic mean of $n_A$ and $n_B$,

(2.3.1)                             $$n' = \frac{2n_A\,n_B}{n_A + n_B}$$

and in the **n** column of the table, find $n'$.

Power values found under these conditions will be underestimates.[1] However, within the values for **n** available in the table when $n_A/n_B$ is between .5 and 2.0, the true value will generally be within .01 of the tabled value. Further, once $n'$ is large (say greater than 25), even far greater discrepancies between $n_A$ and $n_B$ will result in trivially small underestimates.[2]

The fact that $n_A$ is not equal to $n_B$ will *not* effect the validity of the interpretation of **d** in terms of the **U** and **r** measures of Section 2.2, provided we continue to conceive of the *populations* as equally numerous, although the *samples* are of unequal **n**.

---

[1] This is because the table is treating the **t** test for **n** as based on $df = 2n' - 2$, when there are actually $df = n_A + n_B - 2$, a larger value.

[2] This is because of the speed with which the **t** distribution with $df > 50$ approaches that with $df = \infty$, i.e., the normal distribution.

**Illustrative Example**

**2.3** In a psychological service center, cases are assigned by an essentially random process to different psychotherapeutic techniques, a "standard" technique (A) and one featuring some innovation (B). After a period of time, 90 cases have been treated by Method A and 60 cases by Method B. The investigators wish to determine whether the new method (B) is better than the old (A), using final staff conference consensus ratings of improvement as the criterion. They posits an ES such that, with the B population higher, about 40% ($=U_1$) of the area covered by both population distributions would not overlap (see Chapter 2, Section 2.2). From Table 2.2.1, he finds that $U_1 = 38.2\%$ is equivalent to $d = .6$. The statement of the problem implies a directional test, since presumably they are indifferent to the possibility that B is worse than A. (Recall that the null hypothesis here is $m_A \leq m_B$, thus that B worse than A is indistinguishable from B = A.) Accordingly, they use a one-tailed test, with, say the $a_1 = .05$ significance criterion. Thus, the specifications are

$$a_1 = .05, \qquad d = .6\ (U_1 = 38.2\%), \qquad n_A = 90 \neq 60 = n_B$$

With unequal $n$, he finds [from (2.3.1)]

$$n' = \frac{2n_A\, n_B}{n_A + n_B} = \frac{2(90)\,(60)}{90 + 60} = \frac{10800}{150} = 72.$$

(Note that $n'$, the harmonic mean, is smaller than the arithmetic mean, which is $(90 + 60)/2 = 75$.)

In Table 2.3.2 (for $a_1 = .05$), column $d = .6$, row $n = 72$, he finds power equal to .97 (a trivially small underestimate).

Note that had they performed a *non*directional test which would have permitted the conclusion that B was worse than A, power (Table 2.3.5 for $a_2 = .05$) would have been .94. Power is less, but at this level not much less; they might consider the possibility of reaching the conclusion that B is worse than A worth the small loss of power.

2.3.3.  CASE 2: $\sigma_A \neq \sigma_B$, $n_A = n_B$. For normal populations of unequal variance, the formula for $t$ does not follow the tabled values for $t$, that is, this condition constitutes a "failure of the assumptions" (or more properly conditions) under which $t$ is generated. However, there is ample evidence for the robustness of the $t$ test despite moderate failure of this assumption provided that sample sizes are about equal (Scheffé, 1959; Cohen, 1965). Approximations to the true power values which are adequate for most purposes are available by using the tables in the ordinary way.

It should be kept in mind that when $\sigma_A \neq \sigma_B$, the definition of $d$ will be slightly modified. Since there is no longer a common within-population $\sigma$, **d** is defined as above (formulas (2.2.1) and (2.2.2)), but instead of $\sigma$ in the denominator, the formula requires the root mean square of $\sigma_A$ and $\sigma_B$, that is, the square root of the mean of the two variances:

$$(2.3.2) \qquad\qquad \sigma' = \sqrt{\frac{\sigma_A{}^2 + \sigma_B{}^2}{2}}.$$

The unequal variability need not affect the conception of **d** developed in Section 2.2. Given that there is a difference between $\sigma_A$ and $\sigma_B$, we merely are using a kind of average within-population standard deviation to standardize the difference between means. It is not the arithmetic mean of $\sigma_A$ and $\sigma_B$, but, as noted, the root mean square. (However, unless $\sigma_A$ and $\sigma_B$ differ markedly, $\sigma'$ will not differ greatly from the arithmetic mean of $\sigma_A$ and $\sigma_B$.)

In interpreting **d** for this case, the **U** (percent nonoverlap) measures can no longer be generally defined and the Table 2.2.1 **U** columns will not obtain. However, interpreting **d** in terms of **r** and $\mathbf{r}^2$ proceeds completely unaffected by $\sigma_A \neq \sigma_B$, and the conventional definitions of small, medium, and large **d** can also continue to be used.

Note that if $\sigma_A \neq \sigma_B$ and it is also the case that $\mathbf{n}_A \neq \mathbf{n}_B$, the nominal values for **t** and power at a given significance criterion, **a**, may differ greatly from the true values (Scheffé, 1959; Cohen, 1965, p. 115). Under these conditions ($\sigma_A \neq \sigma_B$ and $\mathbf{n}_A \neq \mathbf{n}_B$, simultaneously), the values in Tables 2.3 may be greatly in error.

### Illustrative Example

**2.4**   A labor economist plans a sample survey of men and women workers in a given occupation to determine whether their mean weekly wages differ. He proceeds to do a **t** test,[3] using random samples of 100 cases in each group and a nondirectional significance criterion of $\mathbf{a}_2 = .01$. He deems it quite possible that the wage variability differs between the two populations, i.e., $\sigma_A \neq \sigma_B$. He may arrive at the ES = **d** he is interested in detecting in any of the following ways:

*1. Explicit* **d**. He may plan for allowing that the difference between means, $|\mathbf{m}_A - \mathbf{m}_B|$, is \$2.00 a week, and that the "average" variability of the two populations is \$4.00. Note that this value is not the standard deviation of either the population of men workers or that of women workers,

---

[3] Departure from normality of the population distributions should not materially affect the validity of the **t** test and power estimate for samples of this size.

but the root mean square of their respective population standard deviations, $\sigma'$ (formula (2.3.2)). He then finds **d** by formula (2.2.2), at \$2.00/\$4.00 = .5.

*2. Direct Use of* **d**. From the experience with the **d** concept, he may directly posit **d** = .5, or arrive at that value as a convention. Although the unit he is using is $\sigma'$ and not $\sigma$, this need not substantially alter his conception of **d**.

*3. Correlation and Proportion of Variance.* If he finds it conceptually convenient to work in correlational terms, he may conceive of the ES he seeks to detect as a degree of (point biserial) correlation between sex and weekly wage as $r \cong .25$, or as the amount of wage variance associated with sex as $r^2 \cong .06$. In Table 2.2.1, he finds that $r = .243$ and $r^2 = .059$ are equivalent to **d** = .5. The fact that $\sigma_A \neq \sigma_B$ does not at all affect the validity of the correlational interpretation of a mean difference. Note, however, that under these conditions the **U** measures no longer apply.

Thus, by any of the above routes, we have the specifications:

$$\mathbf{a}_2 = .01, \qquad \mathbf{d} = .5, \qquad \mathbf{n}_A = \mathbf{n}_B = 100.$$

In Table 2.3.4, for column **d** = .5, row **n** = 100, he finds power equal to .82. If he is prepared to work with the less stringent $\mathbf{a}_2 = .05$, he would find from Table 2.3.5 power equal to .94. On the other hand, if he is prepared to restrict his test to detecting a wage difference favoring men workers and not the opposite, he would use the $\mathbf{a}_1 = .01$ level and from Table 2.3.1 find power = .88.

2.3.4 CASE 3: ONE SAMPLE OF **n** OBSERVATIONS. Up to this point we have considered the most frequent application of the **t** test, i.e., to cases involving the difference between two sample means where we test the hypothesis that two population means are equal or, equivalently, that their difference is zero. The **t** test can also be used with a single sample of observations to test the hypothesis that the population mean equals some specified value, $\mathbf{H}_0 : \mathbf{m} = \mathbf{c}$. The value specified is relevant to some theory under consideration. As an example, consider an anthropological field study of a preliterate group in which a random sample of **n** children is tested by means of a "culture-fair" intelligence test which yields an IQ whose mean, as standardized in Western culture, is 100. The null hypothesis then is that the population mean for the preliterate children is 100. As another example, consider an attitude scale so constructed that a neutral position is represented by a value of 6 (as in Thurstone equal-appearing interval scaling). For a single sample of **n** subjects, one can test the null hypothesis that the population from whence they are drawn is, on the average, neutral, i.e., $\mathbf{H}_0 : \mathbf{m} = 6$. Rejection with a sample mean greater than 6 yields the conclusion that the population is on the average "favorable" toward the social object, and with less than 6 that the population is on the average "unfavorable."

For the one-sample case (Case 3), we define

$$(2.3.3) \qquad\qquad d_3' = \frac{m - c}{\sigma}$$

as the ES index. Conceptually there has been no change: $d_3'$ is the difference between the (alternate) population mean ($m$) and the mean specified by the null hypothesis ($c$), standardized by the population standard deviation ($\sigma$). Since $c$ is conceived as the mean of a normal population whose standard deviation is also $\sigma$, i.e., the population specified by the null hypothesis, the interpretation of $d_3'$ proceeds exactly as described in Section 2.2 with regard to Table 2.2.1 and the operational definition of small, medium, and large effects.

However, the tables cannot be used as for the Case 0 two-sample test for two reasons:

1.   In the statistical test for Case 0, there are two sample means, each of $n$ cases, each contributing sampling error to the observed sample difference between means, while in the one-sample test, there is only one sample mean based on $n$ cases, the value $c$ being a hypothetical population parameter and thus without sampling error.

2.   The power tables were computed on the basis that $n$ is the size of each of two samples and that therefore the **t** test would be based on $2(n - 1)$ degrees of freedom. In the one-sample case, **t** is perforce based on only $n - 1$ degrees of freedom.

Thus, if one simply used the power tables directly for $d_3'$ and $n$ for the one-sample case, one would be presuming (*a*) twice as much sampling error with consequently less power and (*b*) twice the number of degrees of freedom with consequently more power than the values on which the tables' preparation was predicated. These are not, however, equal influences; unless the sample size is small (say less than 25 or 30), the effect of the underestimation of the degrees of freedom is negligible. On the other hand, the doubling of the sampling error would have a substantial effect for all values of **n**. However, the latter is readily compensated for. For the one-sample case, use the power tables with **n** and

$$(2.3.4) \qquad\qquad d = d_3'\sqrt{2}.$$

Multiplying $d_3'$ by $\sqrt{2}$ (approximately 1.4) compensates for the tables' assumption of double the error variance. The other problem resulting from the use of **n** is that the tabled value for power presumes that the degrees of freedom are $2(n - 1)$, when actually there are only $n - 1$ degrees of freedom. However, since $t$ approximates the limiting normal distribution fairly well even when its degrees of freedom are as few as 25 or 30, power values based on double the actual degrees of freedom will not be materially overestimated except in very small samples.

Seeking values for $d = d_3'\sqrt{2}$ raises the troublesome problem of numbers intermediate between the ones tabled. However, linear interpolation between power values will, except in rare instances, provide approximate power values which will differ from the true ones by no more than one or two units.

The value of $d_3'$ (*not* $d$) may be arrived at (or interpreted) through the equivalences with the $U$ and $r$ statistics (Section 2.2 and Table 2.2.1). It requires the further conceptualization that $c$ [the "null" value of the population mean, formula (2.3.3)] is the mean of a normal population whose $\sigma$ and size are equal to that of the population being sampled.

In summary, for Case 3, one defines $d_3'$ as above and interprets it exactly as described in Section 2.2, but values for power are sought in the power tables by means of $d = d_3'\sqrt{2}$. The resulting value is, except for very small samples, a very slight overestimate.

**Illustrative Example**

**2.5** It can be taken as known because of extensive record keeping over a long period, that under standard conditions a given strain of laboratory rats has a mean weight gain of 70 grams from birth to 90 days. To test the implications of a developmental theory, an experiment is performed in which a sample of 60 animals is reared from birth in total darkness. The investigator is interested in whether, under these experimental conditions, the mean weight gain of a population of animals departs from the standard population mean of 70 in either direction, even slightly. Thus, the null hypothesis he tests is $H_0: m = c = 70$. The investigator accepts $d_3' = .20$ [formula (2.3.3)] as a conventional operational definition of a slight departure. He uses the relatively lenient significance criterion of $a_2 = .10$.

In order to allow for the fact that we have only one sample mean contributing to error, rather than the two which the construction of the tables presumes, the tables must be considered not for $d_3'$, but using formula (2.3.4), for $d = d_3'\sqrt{2} = .20 \ (1.4) = .28$. Thus, the specifications for estimating power are

$$a_2 = .10, \qquad d = .28, \qquad n = 60.$$

In Table 2.3.6. (for $a_2 = .10$), for row $b = 60$, he finds power in columns $d = .20$ and $d = .30$ to be .29 and .50, respectively. Linear interpolation

between these values yields approximate power at $d = .28$ of $.8(.50 - .29)$
$+ .29 = .46$.

2.3.5   CASE 4: ONE SAMPLE OF **n** DIFFERENCES BETWEEN PAIRED OBSER-
VATIONS. Although the general one-sample case as described in Case 3
above does not occur with much frequency in behavioral science applications,
a special form of it appears quite often. Data are frequently gathered in
**X**, **Y** pairs which are matched in some relevant way so that there are **n** pairs
of **X**, **Y** observations. The **t** test of the $m_X - m_Y$ difference proceeds with the
paired differences, $X - Y = Z$. Since $m_X - m_Y = m_{(X-Y)} = m_Z$, the null
hypothesis that $m_X - m_Y = 0$, or equivalently that $m_X = m_Y$, is identical
to the null hypothesis that $m_Z = 0$. This in turn means that the one-sample
formula for $d_3'$ (2.3.3) has $c = 0$ and becomes

$$(2.3.5) \qquad\qquad\qquad d_Z' = \frac{m_Z}{\sigma_Z}.$$

The **Z** subscript is used to emphasize the fact that our raw score unit
is no longer **X** or **Y**, but **Z**. If the investigator is content to work with $\sigma_Z$
as the standardizing unit, he can proceed to do so as described for Case 3,
using $d_Z'$, and looking in the power tables for $d = d_Z'\sqrt{2}$ [formula (2.3.4) for
**Z**].

Note, however, that the **t** test predicated here is the one described in
textbooks as being for matched, dependent, or *correlated* means. If one were
to compute the product moment **r** between the **X** and **Y** values for each pair
in the population, the result would in general be a nonzero value. Indeed,
since matching is an experimental design technique used to remove irrelevant
sources of variance (see above, section 1.3), in practice such an **r** will be positive and material, say at least greater than $+ .30$. In contrast, with independent samples such as have been described in previous sections of this chapter,
the random pairing of **X** and **Y** values implied would perforce yield a population **r** of zero.

Now, the $\sigma_Z$ of the denominator in formula (2.3.4), and hence the unit in
which the ES index $d_Z'$ for the difference in matched pairs is expressed, is
given by

$$(2.3.6) \qquad\qquad \sigma_Z = \sigma_{X-Y} = \sqrt{\sigma_X{}^2 + \sigma_Y{}^2 - 2\,r\sigma_X\sigma_Y}.$$

Note that as **r** (the population between **X** and **Y** as paired) increases,
$\sigma_Z$ decreases. In the case of matched pairs here being considered, on the
assumption of equal variance, i.e., $\sigma_X{}^2 = \sigma_Y{}^2 = \sigma^2$,

$$(2.3.7) \qquad\qquad \sigma_Z = \sigma_{X-Y} = \sqrt{2\sigma^2 - 2r\sigma^2} = \sigma\sqrt{2(1-r)}\,.$$

Thus, the relative size of the standardizing unit for the $d_Z'$ of Case 4 (dependent) to the **d** of Case 0 (independent) is $\sigma\sqrt{2(1-r)}/\sigma = \sqrt{2(1-r)}$. In other words, a given difference between population means for matched (dependent) samples is standardized by a value which is $\sqrt{2(1-r)}$ as large as would be the case were they independent. Alternatively (and equivalently), the $d_z'$ value used as an ES index for means from matched samples, when expressed in the *same* terms as for independent samples, namely $\sigma$, the common within-population standard deviation, is $1/\sqrt{2(1-r)}$ larger than the **d** value for the same raw score difference in independent samples.

Although one can treat the matched pairs in Case 3 form, the standardizing unit, $\sigma_z$, will vary in size inversely with the size of r, as shown in formula (2.3.7.). When no estimate of **r** can be made, one has no choice but simply to apply the Case 3 procedure to the one sample of paired differences **Z**, keeping in mind that the $d_z'$ unit is $\sigma_z$. With an estimate of **r** available, a preferable procedure is to use as the ES index

$$(2.3.8) \qquad d_4' = \frac{m_X - m_Y}{\sigma},$$

Note that this is identically the same index as the **d** of formulas (2.2.1) and (2.2.2), the difference between means standardized by the within-population $\sigma$. As was the case for $d_3'$, all the interpretive material (e.g., **U**, **r**, $r^2$) of Section 2.2 holds. However, for correct power values, the value located in the power tables is *not* $d_4'$, but rather

$$(2.3.9) \qquad d = \frac{d_4'}{\sqrt{1-r}}$$

As in Case 3, this procedure leads to an overestimate of power which is trivial for all but small samples, since the tables assume $2(n-1)$ degrees of freedom where only $n-1$ are actually available.

The advantages of matching can now be made readily apparent. Consider an investigation which is to concern itself with the question of a sex difference in some aptitude variable. Assume that elementary school boys and girls each have population $\sigma = 16$, and one wishes to detect a difference in raw population means of 8 points, using samples of $n = 40$ subjects. Assume the test is to be performed at the two-tailed .05 level ($a_2 = .05$). The relevant power table is 2.3.5.

*Case 0.* Since the plan is to work with independent samples of 40 boys and 40 girls, we use $n = 40$ and

$$d = \frac{|m_A - m_B|}{\sigma} = \frac{8}{16} = .5$$

to find power $= .60$.

*Case 4.* Instead of independent samples of boys and girls, the investigator plans to draw 40 brother–sister pairs to detect the 8 point difference. There is the same ES, namely,

$$\mathbf{d_4}' = \frac{|\mathbf{m_x} - \mathbf{m_y}|}{\sigma} = \frac{8}{16} = .5.$$

However, he estimates the **r** between brothers and sisters on this aptitude variable as .6 and in Table 2.3.5 for **n** = 40 and

$$\mathbf{d} = \frac{\mathbf{d_4}'}{\sqrt{1 - \mathbf{r}}} = \frac{.5}{\sqrt{1 - .60}} = \frac{.5}{.6325} = .79,$$

he finds power $\cong .93$. Thus, given the same 8 point or .5 standardized difference between means to detect, the use of the matched pairs design with an estimated matching **r** of .60 has resulted in power of .93 instead of only .60.

Note that if **r** were .40 instead of .60, he would look for the value

$$\mathbf{d} = \frac{.5}{\sqrt{1 - .40}} = \frac{.5}{.7746} = .65,$$

and find power $\cong .81$ (by linear interpolation), a lesser increase because the matching **r** is smaller. See Section 11.4 for a general treatment of the relative power of difference and regressed difference scores.

**Illustrative Examples**

**2.6**  An educational researcher has developed two different programed tests for teaching elementary algebra. From a high school grade, he selects 50 pairs of pupils so that the two members of each pair have IQs within 3 points of each other. He randomly assigns the members of each pair to the A and B programs, and following instruction, tests all subjects on a common algebra achievement test. He wishes to detect a difference [formula (2.3.8)]

$$\mathbf{d_4}' = \frac{\mathbf{m_A} - \mathbf{m_B}}{\sigma} = .4,$$

a small to medium value, using the $\mathbf{a_2} = .05$ significance criterion. It would not be correct to look for the value in the power table $\mathbf{d_4}' = .40$, because this value does not take into account the advantageous effect of matching. The appropriate ES for this situation is [formula (2.3.9)]:

$$\mathbf{d} = \frac{\mathbf{d_4}'}{\sqrt{1 - \mathbf{r}}} = \frac{.4}{\sqrt{1 - \mathbf{r}}} .$$

**r** is the population correlation between IQ-matched pairs in algebra achievement. It is also the population **r** between IQ and algebra achievement.[4] From past educational research, or from the sample data (if this power analysis is being performed *post hoc*), he can estimate the population **r** as .55. Thus,

$$\mathbf{d} = \frac{.4}{\sqrt{1 - .55}} = \frac{.4}{.6708} = .60.$$

If he were lacking a basis for estimating **r**, the investigator would have reached the same result if he had postulated that the ES he was seeking to detect in terms of paired differences in the achievement test, $A - B = Z$ units, was [from formula (2.3.5)] $\mathbf{d_z}' = .42$, so that, in Case 3 fashion, he would use the power tables for $\mathbf{d} = .42\sqrt{2} \cong .60$ [formula (2.3.4)].

Thus, in either instance, summarizing his specifications:

$$\mathbf{a_2} = .05, \qquad \mathbf{d} = .60, \qquad \mathbf{n} = 50.$$

From Table 2.3.5, column $\mathbf{d} = .60$, row $\mathbf{n} = 50$, he finds power $= .84$.

Note that had the same problem been undertaken with *independent* random samples of 50 cases with the same ES, namely $\mathbf{d} = .40$, power would be only .50 (Table 2.3.5). The effect of matching with an **r** of .55 makes the effective **d** equal to .60 with a resultant large increase in power (from .50 to .84).

**2.7** Many behavioral science researchers use the "own-control" principle, i.e., each subject is observed under two conditions, **X** and **Y**, and the experimental issue is the existence of a difference between $\mathbf{m_X}$ and $\mathbf{m_Y}$. Thus, **X**, **Y** constitute the paired observations and the significance test is a straightforward instance of Case 4. Sometimes **Y** and **X** represent "before" and "after" some intervening experimental manipulation whose effect on a dependent variable is to be scrutinized. (In their failure to control for other concomitants of time, such studies may be misleading.)

Consider a study to appraise the efficacy of prescribing a program of diet and exercises to a group of overweight male students. The researcher gets from each subject his "before" weight **X**, prescribes the program, and checks the "after" weight **Y** 60 days later. The study employs a sample of 80 subjects. The researcher wishes to know the power of a test at $\mathbf{a_1} = .01$ to detect a mean loss $(\mathbf{Z} = \mathbf{X} - \mathbf{Y})$ of 4 lb where the estimate of the population $\sigma = 12$ lb. Thus [from formula (2.3.8)], $\mathbf{d_4}' = 4/12 = .33$. He may estimate

---

[4] Strictly speaking, this is true only if matching on IQ had been perfect. The postulated matching (within 3 points) approaches closely enough to make the equation of the two **r**'s substantially accurate.

that under these circumstances the population **r** of before with after weight would be in the vicinity of .80. Thus, his effective **d** [from formula (2.3.9)] is

$$\mathbf{d} = \frac{.33}{\sqrt{1 - .80}} = \frac{.33}{.4472} = .74.$$

Alternatively, he might have avoided the need to estimate **r** and reasoned that, considering the distribution of weight loss Z, he wanted to detect a mean loss of about .5 of the standard deviation of weight *losses*, i.e. [formula (2.3.5)]

$$\mathbf{d_z}' = \frac{\mathbf{m_z}}{\sigma_\mathbf{z}} = .5.$$

To find the effective **d**, $.5\sqrt{2} = .71$, or, in this instance, about the same value (.74) found from the approach via formula (2.3.9).

Summarizing the specifications:

$$\mathbf{a}_1 = .01, \qquad \mathbf{d} = .74, \qquad \mathbf{n} = 60.$$

In Table 2.3.1 (for $\mathbf{a}_1 = .01$), in the row $\mathbf{n} = 60$, columns $\mathbf{d} = .70$ and .80, we find respectively power of .93 and .98 between which linear interpolation gives power of approximately .95. Thus, the researcher is almost certain of detecting a mean loss of 4 lb at the $\mathbf{a}_1 = .01$ level, with $\mathbf{n} = 60$.

Note how a relatively small $\mathbf{d_4}'$ of .33 becomes a **d** for table entry of .74 which yields a high power value because of the effectiveness of "own-control" matching. Such large matching **r**'s are not infrequent in own-control designs in behavioral science.

## 2.4   SAMPLE SIZE TABLES

The tables in this section use values for the significance criterion, the ES to be detected, and the *desired power* to determine the sample size. They would therefore be of primary utility in the planning of experiments to provide a basis for the decision as to how many sampling units (**n**) are to be used. Although decisions about sample size in behavioral science are frequently made by appeal to tradition or precedent, ready availability of data, or intuition (Cohen, 1965, p. 97ff), unless Type II error rate considerations contribute to the decision, they can hardly be rational.

2.4.1   CASE 0: $\sigma_A = \sigma_B$, $\mathbf{n}_A = \mathbf{n}_B$. As was done in Section 2.3 for the power tables, the use of the sample size tables is first described for the conditions for which they were optimally designed, Case 0, where they yield the sample size, **n**, for each of two independent samples drawn from normal populations having equal variances. Their use in other cases is described later. Tables are used for **a**, **d**, and the desired power;

*1. Significance Criterion*, **a**. The same values of **a** are provided as for the power tables. For each of the following **a** levels, a table is provided: $a_1 = .01$ ($a_2 = .02$), $a_1 = .05$ ($a_2 = .10$), $a_1 = .10$ ($a_2 = .20$), $a_2 = .01$ ($a_1 = .005$), and $a_2 = .05$ ($a_1 = .025$).

*2. Effect Size*, **d**. This value is defined and interpreted as above [formulas (2.2.1, 2.2.2)] and used as in the power tables. The same provision is made: .10 (.10) .80 (.20) 1.40.

To find **n** for a value of **d** not provided, an adequate approximation is given by substituting in the following:

$$(2.4.1) \qquad\qquad n = \frac{n_{.10}}{100 d^2} + 1$$

where $n_{.10}$ is the necessary sample size for the given **a** and desired power at $d = .10$, and **d** is the nontabulated ES. Round the result to the nearest integer.[5]

*3. Desired Power.* The sample size tables list desired values of .25, .50, .60, 2/3, .70 (.05), .95, .99.

Some comment about the selection of the above values is in order. The .25 value is given only to help provide a frame of reference in sample size determination; it seems very unlikely that a behavioral scientist would normally *desire* only one chance in four of rejecting a null hypothesis. The values are about equally spaced between .50 and .99. An exception to this equality of power interval is the provision of power of 2/3. This was made so as to give the sample size at which the odds are two to one that a given **d** would be detected.

Entries for desired power values of .99, .95, and .90 are offered. This makes possible the setting of Type II error risk equal to the conventional Type I, or **a**, risks of .01, .05, and .10. There are conceivable research circumstances where, given an alternate-hypothetical value of **d**, the investigator may wish to equalize his Type I (**a**) and Type II (**b** = 1 − power) risks. The tables will accommodate this demand and provide the **n** values to accomplish this aim at conventional **a** levels.

---

[5] The $+1$ in the formula is optimal for tests at $a_2 = .05$ ($a_1 = .025$). Slightly greater accuracy is obtained if constants other than 1 are added at other **a** levels, as follows:
  $+1.5$ at $a_2 = .01$ ($a_1 = .005$) and $a_1 = .01$ ($a_2 = .02$),
  $+ .7$ at $a_1 = .05$ ($a_2 = .10$), and
  $+ .4$ at $a_1 = .10$ ($a_1 = .20$).
These constants are empirical and were determined by averaging discrepancies over the range power $\geq .70$, $.20 \leq d \leq 1.00$.

Table 2.4.1

n to detect d by t test

| | | | | | $a_1 = .01$ $(a_2 = .02)$ | | | | | | |
|---|---|---|---|---|---|---|---|---|---|---|---|
| | | | | | d | | | | | | |
| Power | .10 | .20 | .30 | .40 | .50 | .60 | .70 | .80 | 1.00 | 1.20 | 1.40 |
| .25 | 547 | 138 | 62 | 36 | 24 | 17 | 13 | 10 | 7 | 5 | 4 |
| .50 | 1083 | 272 | 122 | 69 | 45 | 31 | 24 | 18 | 12 | 9 | 7 |
| .60 | 1332 | 334 | 149 | 85 | 55 | 38 | 29 | 22 | 15 | 11 | 8 |
| 2/3 | 1552 | 382 | 170 | 97 | 62 | 44 | 33 | 25 | 17 | 12 | 9 |
| .70 | 1627 | 408 | 182 | 103 | 66 | 47 | 35 | 27 | 18 | 13 | 10 |
| .75 | 1803 | 452 | 202 | 114 | 74 | 52 | 38 | 30 | 20 | 14 | 11 |
| .80 | 2009 | 503 | 224 | 127 | 82 | 57 | 42 | 33 | 22 | 15 | 12 |
| .85 | 2263 | 567 | 253 | 143 | 92 | 64 | 48 | 37 | 24 | 17 | 13 |
| .90 | 2605 | 652 | 290 | 164 | 105 | 74 | 55 | 42 | 27 | 20 | 15 |
| .95 | 3155 | 790 | 352 | 198 | 128 | 89 | 66 | 51 | 33 | 23 | 18 |
| .99 | 4330 | 1084 | 482 | 272 | 175 | 122 | 90 | 69 | 45 | 31 | 23 |

| | | | | | $a_1 = .05$ $(a_2 = .10)$ | | | | | | |
|---|---|---|---|---|---|---|---|---|---|---|---|
| | | | | | d | | | | | | |
| Power | .10 | .20 | .30 | .40 | .50 | .60 | .70 | .80 | 1.00 | 1.20 | 1.40 |
| .25 | 189 | 48 | 21 | 12 | 8 | 6 | 5 | 4 | 3 | 2 | 2 |
| .50 | 542 | 136 | 61 | 35 | 22 | 16 | 12 | 9 | 6 | 5 | 4 |
| .60 | 721 | 181 | 81 | 46 | 30 | 21 | 15 | 12 | 8 | 6 | 5 |
| 2/3 | 862 | 216 | 96 | 55 | 35 | 25 | 18 | 14 | 9 | 7 | 5 |
| .70 | 942 | 236 | 105 | 60 | 38 | 27 | 20 | 15 | 10 | 7 | 6 |
| .75 | 1076 | 270 | 120 | 68 | 44 | 31 | 23 | 18 | 11 | 8 | 6 |
| .80 | 1237 | 310 | 138 | 78 | 50 | 35 | 26 | 20 | 13 | 9 | 7 |
| .85 | 1438 | 360 | 160 | 91 | 58 | 41 | 30 | 23 | 15 | 11 | 8 |
| .90 | 1713 | 429 | 191 | 108 | 69 | 48 | 36 | 27 | 18 | 13 | 10 |
| .95 | 2165 | 542 | 241 | 136 | 87 | 61 | 45 | 35 | 22 | 16 | 12 |
| .99 | 3155 | 789 | 351 | 198 | 127 | 88 | 65 | 50 | 32 | 23 | 17 |

| | | | | | $a_1 = .10$ $(a_2 = .20)$ | | | | | | |
|---|---|---|---|---|---|---|---|---|---|---|---|
| | | | | | d | | | | | | |
| Power | .10 | .20 | .30 | .40 | .50 | .60 | .70 | .80 | 1.00 | 1.20 | 1.40 |
| .25 | 74 | 19 | 9 | 5 | 3 | 3 | 2 | 2 | 2 | 2 | 2 |
| .50 | 329 | 82 | 37 | 21 | 14 | 10 | 7 | 5 | 4 | 3 | 2 |
| .60 | 471 | 118 | 53 | 30 | 19 | 14 | 10 | 8 | 5 | 4 | 3 |
| 2/3 | 586 | 147 | 65 | 37 | 24 | 17 | 12 | 10 | 6 | 4 | 3 |
| .70 | 653 | 163 | 73 | 41 | 27 | 19 | 14 | 11 | 7 | 5 | 4 |
| .75 | 766 | 192 | 85 | 48 | 31 | 22 | 16 | 13 | 8 | 6 | 4 |
| .80 | 902 | 226 | 100 | 57 | 36 | 26 | 19 | 14 | 10 | 7 | 5 |
| .85 | 1075 | 269 | 120 | 67 | 43 | 30 | 22 | 17 | 11 | 8 | 6 |
| .90 | 1314 | 329 | 146 | 82 | 53 | 37 | 27 | 21 | 14 | 10 | 7 |
| .95 | 1713 | 428 | 191 | 107 | 69 | 48 | 35 | 27 | 18 | 12 | 9 |
| .99 | 2604 | 651 | 290 | 163 | 104 | 73 | 53 | 41 | 26 | 18 | 14 |

**Table 2.4.1** *(continued)*

| | | | | | $a_2 = .01$ | $(a_1 = .005)$ | | | | | |
|---|---|---|---|---|---|---|---|---|---|---|---|
| | | | | | d | | | | | | |
| Power | .10 | .20 | .30 | .40 | .50 | .60 | .70 | .80 | 1.00 | 1.20 | 1.40 |
| .25 | 725 | 183 | 82 | 47 | 31 | 22 | 17 | 13 | 9 | 7 | 6 |
| .50 | 1329 | 333 | 149 | 85 | 55 | 39 | 29 | 22 | 15 | 11 | 9 |
| .60 | 1603 | 402 | 180 | 102 | 66 | 46 | 34 | 27 | 18 | 13 | 10 |
| 2/3 | 1810 | 454 | 203 | 115 | 74 | 52 | 39 | 30 | 20 | 14 | 11 |
| .70 | 1924 | 482 | 215 | 122 | 79 | 55 | 41 | 32 | 21 | 15 | 12 |
| .75 | 2108 | 528 | 236 | 134 | 86 | 60 | 45 | 35 | 23 | 17 | 13 |
| .80 | 2338 | 586 | 259 | 148 | 95 | 67 | 49 | 38 | 25 | 18 | 14 |
| .85 | 2611 | 654 | 292 | 165 | 106 | 74 | 55 | 43 | 28 | 20 | 15 |
| .90 | 2978 | 746 | 332 | 188 | 120 | 84 | 62 | 48 | 31 | 22 | 17 |
| .95 | 3564 | 892 | 398 | 224 | 144 | 101 | 74 | 57 | 37 | 26 | 20 |
| .99 | 4808 | 1203 | 536 | 302 | 194 | 136 | 100 | 77 | 50 | 35 | 26 |

| | | | | | $a_2 = .05$ | $(a_1 = .025)$ | | | | | |
|---|---|---|---|---|---|---|---|---|---|---|---|
| | | | | | d | | | | | | |
| Power | .10 | .20 | .30 | .40 | .50 | .60 | .70 | .80 | 1.00 | 1.20 | 1.40 |
| .25 | 332 | 84 | 38 | 22 | 14 | 10 | 8 | 6 | 5 | 4 | 3 |
| .50 | 769 | 193 | 86 | 49 | 32 | 22 | 17 | 13 | 9 | 7 | 5 |
| .60 | 981 | 246 | 110 | 62 | 40 | 28 | 21 | 16 | 11 | 8 | 6 |
| 2/3 | 1144 | 287 | 128 | 73 | 47 | 33 | 24 | 19 | 12 | 9 | 7 |
| .70 | 1235 | 310 | 138 | 78 | 50 | 35 | 26 | 20 | 13 | 10 | 7 |
| .75 | 1389 | 348 | 155 | 88 | 57 | 40 | 29 | 23 | 15 | 11 | 8 |
| .80 | 1571 | 393 | 175 | 99 | 64 | 45 | 33 | 26 | 17 | 12 | 9 |
| .85 | 1797 | 450 | 201 | 113 | 73 | 51 | 38 | 29 | 19 | 14 | 10 |
| .90 | 2102 | 526 | 234 | 132 | 85 | 59 | 44 | 34 | 22 | 16 | 12 |
| .95 | 2600 | 651 | 290 | 163 | 105 | 73 | 54 | 42 | 27 | 19 | 14 |
| .99 | 3675 | 920 | 409 | 231 | 148 | 103 | 76 | 58 | 38 | 27 | 20 |

However, in the judgment of the author, for most behavioral science research (although admitting of many exceptions), power values as large as .90–.99 would demand sample sizes so large as to exceed an investigator's resources. Even when, with much effort or at much cost, these large **n**'s can be attained, they are probably inefficient, given the nature of statistical inference and the sociology of science.

Why not seek power approaching 1.00, or equivalently, **b** risks close to zero? Why not use the simple principle, "the smaller the Type II error, the better"? For reasons that parallel the rejection of this principle as an operational principle for setting **a** levels. Other things equal, if **a** is made vanishingly small, power becomes quite small. Similarly, if **b** is made very small (desired power very large), other things being equal, required sample sizes become very large. The behavioral scientist must set desired power values as well as desired **a** significance criteria on the basis of the consideration of the seriousness of the consequences of the two kinds of errors and the cost of obtaining data. He cannot literally place a dollar value on the "cost" of each kind of error, as can the industrial quality control engineer who uses exactly the same formal statistical inferential procedures. He can, however, approximate this approach by subjectively weighing the gravity of these two possibilities and the cost of generating data (but see Overall & Dalal, 1965).

The view offered here is that more often than not, the behavioral scientist will decide that Type I errors, which result in false positive claims, are more serious and therefore to be more stringently guarded against than Type II errors, which result in false negative claims. The notion that failure to find is less serious than finding something that is not there accords with the conventional scientific view.

It is proposed here as a convention that, when the investigator has no other basis for setting the desired power value, the value .80 be used. This means that **b** is set at .20. This arbitrary but reasonable value is offered for several reasons (Cohen, 1965, pp. 98–99). The chief among them takes into consideration the implicit convention for **a** of .05. The **b** of .20 is chosen with the idea that the general relative seriousness of these two kinds of errors is of the order of .20/.05, i.e., that Type I errors are of the order of four times as serious as Type II errors. This .80 desired power convention is offered with the hope that it will be ignored whenever an investigator can find a basis in his substantive concerns in his specific research investigation to choose a value *ad hoc*.

Returning to the Case 0 use of the **n** tables and summarizing, the investigator finds (*a*) the table for the significance criterion (**a**) he is using, and looks for (*b*) the standardized difference between the population means (**d**) along the horizontal stub and (*c*) the desired power along the vertical stub. These determine **n**, the necessary size of *each* sample to detect **d** at the **a** significance criterion with the desired power.

**Illustrative Examples**

**2.8**   Reconsider example 2.1 for the Case 0 use of the power tables in which an experimental psychologist is studying the effect of opportunity to explore a maze on subsequent maze-learning in rats. As described there, initially she wished to detect an ES of **d** = .50 at $a_2$ = .05. Her plan to use **n** = 30 animals in each of her E and C groups resulted in a power estimate of .47. She will likely consider this value too low. Now let us assume that she wishes power to be .80 and wants to know the sample size necessary to accomplish this. The specifications thus are

$$\mathbf{a}_2 = .05, \qquad \mathbf{d} = .50, \qquad \text{power} = .80.$$

In Table 2.4.1 for $\mathbf{a}_2 = .05$, column $\mathbf{d} = .50$, row power $= .80$, $\mathbf{n}$ ($= \mathbf{n}_C = \mathbf{n}_E$ equals 64. She will need two samples of 64 animals each to have an .80 probability of detecting $\mathbf{d} = .50$ at $\mathbf{a}_2 = .05$. Thus, under these conditions, she will have to slightly more than double the planned $\mathbf{n}$ of 30 per group to go from power of .47 to power of .80.

If, on the other hand, she had reason to anticipate a higher $\mathbf{d}$, say of .80 (our conventional definition of a large ES), which she wished to detect with the same power at the same $\mathbf{a}$ level, then

$$\mathbf{a}_2 = .05, \qquad \mathbf{d} = .80, \qquad \text{power} = .80.$$

In the same Table 2.4.1 for $\mathbf{a}_2 = .05$, column $\mathbf{d} = .80$, row power $= .80$, she finds $\mathbf{n} = 26$ animals per group.

Alternatively, if she had reason to expect $\mathbf{d} = .20$ (our conventional definition of a small ES), for the same significance criterion and desired power, the specifications are:

$$\mathbf{a}_2 = .05, \qquad \mathbf{d} = .20, \qquad \text{power} = .80.$$

Again in Table 2.4.1 for $\mathbf{a}_2 = .05$, column $\mathbf{d} = .20$, the same row power $= .80$, $\mathbf{n}$ is 393 for *each* group.

This example illustrates dramatically the importance of putting oneself in the position to estimate ES in experimental planning. Depending on whether one posits $\mathbf{d} = .20$ or .80, for representative conditions (i.e., $\mathbf{a}_2 = .05$, power $= .80$), one needs two samples of 26 or 393 animals for the Case 0 design. It seems fairly apparent that experimental planning can hardly proceed in the absence of a prior rendering of judgment about the size of the effect one wishes to detect.

The researcher can, of course, reduce the $\mathbf{n}$ demanded by making his specifications less stringent with regard to either the significance level or the desired power (or both), if these are tolerable alternatives.

Thus, to take an extreme case with regard to the significance criterion, he can both increase his $\mathbf{a}$ risk to .10 and further define "the existence of the phenomenon" in directional terms, i.e., predict that $\mathbf{m}_E < \mathbf{m}_C$. Keeping the other specifications for the original problem, he has:

$$\mathbf{a}_1 = .10, \qquad \mathbf{d} = .50, \qquad \text{power} = .80.$$

In Table 2.4.1 for $\mathbf{a}_1 = .10$, for column $\mathbf{d} = .50$, row power $= .80$, he finds $\mathbf{n}$ ($= \mathbf{n}_C = \mathbf{n}_E$) $= 36$, compared with $\mathbf{n} = 64$ for $\mathbf{a}_2 = .05$ (same $\mathbf{d}$ and power).

Or, he can increase his **b** risk and settle for a 2:1 chance of detecting his assumed **d** = .50, i.e.,

$$\mathbf{a_2} = .05, \qquad \mathbf{d} = .50, \qquad \text{power} = 2/3.$$

In Table 2.4.1 for $\mathbf{a_2}$ = .05, for column **d** = .40, row power = 2/3, he finds **n** ( = $\mathbf{n_C}$ = $\mathbf{n_E}$) = 47, again compared with **n** = 64 for power = .80 (same **a** and **d**).

If he relaxes both **a** and desired power as above simultaneously, the specifications are now

$$\mathbf{a_1} = .10, \qquad \mathbf{d} = .50, \qquad \text{power} = 2/3.$$

In Table 2.4.1 for $\mathbf{a_1}$ = .10, for column **d** = .50 and row power = 2/3, he finds **n** ( = $\mathbf{n_C}$ = $\mathbf{n_E}$) = 24 compared with 64 for more stringent **a** and power (for the same **d**).

Experimental planning will frequently involve the study of the **n** demanded by various combinations of levels of **a**, desired power, and possibly **d**, with a final choice being determined by the specific circumstances of a given research (for illustration, see example 3.4 in the next chapter). If no acceptable combination yields an **n** within the resources of the investigator, the feasibility of more powerful designs (e.g., Case 4 for matched pairs) should be considered.

**2.9** Consider again the circumstances of the investigation of an endocrinological factor in schizophrenia, presented above in example 2.2. The design calls for a test of the significance of the difference between independent means of hospitalized schizophrenics and normal controls, and the investigator has large resources of patients and laboratory facilities. He anticipates a relatively small ES, namely **d** = .20, and wants to decide the necessary **n** for the research. He is prepared to use as a significance criterion $\mathbf{a_2}$ = .05, but in this instance wishes that his **b** (Type II) risk be of the same magnitude. That is, he wishes to incur no greater risk that he will fail to detect a hypothetical **d** = .20 than the risk that he will mistakenly conclude that a difference exists when **d** = 0. His specifications thus are

$$\mathbf{a_2} = .05, \qquad \mathbf{d} = .20, \qquad \text{power} = 1 - \mathbf{b} = 1 - .05 = .95.$$

In Table 2.4.1 for $\mathbf{a_2}$ = .05, column **d** = .20, row power = .95, he finds **n** ( = $\mathbf{n_A}$ = $\mathbf{n_B}$) = 651.

This example lends itself to illustrating the procedure of "proving" the null hypothesis (Section 1.5.5). Assume that this experiment is now carried out with **n** = 651 and that the investigator is prepared to consider **d** less than .20 to be negligible, hence **i** = **d** = .20. If the **t** test on the sample data yields a nonsignificant result, he can conclude that the population difference is negligible with a Type II risk of **b** no larger than .05 since were **d** .20 or larger, the probability of detecting it would have been at least .95.

2.4.2 CASE 1: $n_A \neq n_B$, $\sigma_A = \sigma_B$. Case 1 is not common when the sample size tables are used in experimental planning, since normally the planning will presume the selection of samples of equal size. Equal-sized samples are desirable, since it is demonstrable that with a given number of cases available for division into two samples for experimentation, equal division yields greater power than does unequal division.

There are, however, situations in which the size of one of the two samples is fixed in advance by circumstances. Perhaps the resources to apply to a given experimental treatment are limited to some fixed number, or perhaps no more than a given number can be withheld for use as control subjects. In such instances, the fixed sample size ($n_F$) will in general be different from the other sample, whose size is at the experimenter's discretion ($n_U$). The tables entries, as in Case 0, are **a, d**, and desired power, and **n** is sought. To find $n_U$, substitute the fixed **n** ($n_F$) and the **n** read from the table in

$$(2.4.2) \qquad\qquad n_U = \frac{n_F\, n}{2n_F - n},$$

where $n_F$ = the fixed sample size,
    **n** = the value read from the table, and
    $n_U$ = the necessary sample size for the other sample.

When $n_F \leq \frac{1}{2}n$, a zero or negative denominator results, and the problem is insoluble for the given specifications. One must either increase $n_F$ (usually not possible) or change desired power, **a**, or **d** so as to decrease **n**.

### Illustrative Example

**2.10** An educational psychologist plans research which will compare the effectiveness of a computer-based program for teaching reading to illiterates with a standard lecture method. He wishes to detect a **d** = .30 (i.e., between "slight" and "moderate") and is only interested in testing whether the computer-based method (C) yields higher criterion scores than the standard method (S), i.e., a directional (one-tailed) test. He sets his significance criterion at .05 ($=a_1$) and wishes power to be .75. That is, if the C method is superior to the S method by **d** = .30, he is prepared to run a risk of .25 ($=$**b**) of failing to get significant results, compared to the .05 risk he runs of concluding C's superiority when the means are equal. Now, if there were no restrictions of time or equipment availability, this would be a Case 0 problem with the specifications

$$\mathbf{a}_1 = .05, \qquad \mathbf{d} = .30, \qquad \text{power} = .75.$$

In Table 2.4.1 for $\mathbf{a}_1 = .05$, column $\mathbf{d} = .30$, row power $= .75$, he would find $\mathbf{n} = (\mathbf{n}_C = \mathbf{n}_S) = 120$, i.e., samples of 120 cases are needed in each group.

But now consider the real possibility that limitations in time and availability of equipment make it impossible for him to have more than 80 subjects in the computer group, while he is relatively unrestricted in regard to the sample size for the standard group. Given the fixed $\mathbf{n}_F$ of 80, how many cases does he need in the standard group $(\mathbf{n}_U)$ to meet the same specifications?

In formula (2.4.2), with $\mathbf{n}_F = 80$ and $\mathbf{n} = 120$ (from Table 2.4.1 at $\mathbf{a}_1 = .05$), he finds

$$\mathbf{n}_U = \frac{(80)(120)}{2(80) - 120} = 240.$$

Thus, the specifications for $\mathbf{a}$, $\mathbf{d}$, and power would be met with a fixed sample size of 80 in the C group, if he has 240 subjects in the standard group.

2.4.3   CASE 2: $\sigma_A \neq \sigma_B$, $\mathbf{n}_A = \mathbf{n}_B$. The **n** tables are used in Case 2 in exactly the same way as in Case 0. The inequality of population $\sigma$ values results only in a standardization of the difference in population means by the root mean square of the population variances [formula (2.3.2)] instead of the common population standard deviation. This has no effect on the use of the **n** tables. Only **d** is affected, and only in its interpretation via **U** measures; its interpretation in terms of **r** and $\mathbf{r}^2$ remain unaffected. See the discussion of the use of the power tables for Case 2, Section 2.3.3.

**Illustrative Example**

**2.11**   A clinical psychologist plans a study of the orienting reflex in which she will compare means of process paranoid schizophrenics (S) and employee controls (C). On the basis of past findings, she expects that the S group will show greater variability than the C group, but it is a mean difference she wishes to detect the $\mathbf{a}_2 = .05$ level with power of .90.

In considering setting her ES, she may proceed in either of the following ways (among others):

1.   She may hypothesize that the ES of S vs. C population membership is such that it accounts for about 10% of the variance of the combined populations. She notes from Table 2.2.1 that when $\mathbf{ar}^2 = .109$, $\mathbf{d} = .7$. Note that the fact that the *within*-population variances of S and C are assumed to differ does not affect the validity of the $\mathbf{r}^2$ interpretation. Her specifications then are

$$\mathbf{a_2} = .05, \qquad \mathbf{d} = .7, \qquad \text{power} = .90.$$

In Table 2.4.1 for $\mathbf{a_2} = .05$, column $\mathbf{d} = .7$, row power $= .90$, she finds $\mathbf{n}$ $(=\mathbf{n_S} = \mathbf{n_C}) = 44$ cases.

2. She may she the value of $\mathbf{d} = .70$ (or any other), not on the basis of its $\mathbf{r}^2$ equivalent, but directly. That is, she may hypothesize that the standardized difference between the population means is .70. Since she is assuming that $\sigma_S^2 \neq \sigma_C^2$, the standardizing unit cannot be the common within-population standard deviation, but is instead the square root of the mean of the two variances, i.e., $\sqrt{(\sigma_S^2 + \sigma_C^2)/2}$ [formula (2.3.2)].

2.4.4 CASE 3: ONE SAMPLE OF $\mathbf{n}$ OBSERVATIONS. In using the $\mathbf{n}$ tables for the one-sample $\mathbf{t}$ test, the only departure from Case 0 is that which was discussed in connection with the power tables for Case 3, i.e., the appropriate value of $\mathbf{d}$ for table entry. The reader is referred to Section 2.3.4. for the relevant discussion of the details. Briefly, if one is testing, with a single sample, the null hypothesis that the population mean has some specified value, $\mathbf{H_0:m} = \mathbf{c}$, and scales the ES in the usual way as a standardized difference, namely [formula (2.3.3)]

$$\mathbf{d_3'} = \frac{\mathbf{m} - \mathbf{c}}{\sigma},$$

one uses the $\mathbf{n}$ tables for the value of $\mathbf{d} = \mathbf{d_3'}\sqrt{2}$. The size of $\mathbf{n}$ will be underestimated, but only to a trivial degree, unless it is quite small (e.g., less than 10 or 15), when prudence might dictate using $\mathbf{n} + 1$, instead of $\mathbf{n}$ cases.

**Illustrative Example**

**2.12** A political scientist plans to appraise the status of the attitude toward the United Nations of the urban population of a new African republic. He will use an orally administered Thurstone Attitude Scale which has the property that a neutral response is scaled 6 (on an 11-point scale). His null hypothesis, then, is $\mathbf{H_0: m} = 6$. Since he wishes to be able to conclude that the average is either "pro" or "anti," he plans a nondirectional test and wishes to use a stringent significance criterion, namely $\mathbf{a_2} = .01$. He also seeks the assurance of relatively high power, .90. Furthermore, he wants to be in a position to conclude that the population in question is, on the average, only trivially different from neutral if, when the data are in, he does not find $\mathbf{t}$ to be significant. He defines such a trivial difference (i) as one no greater than a departure of .10 of the population mean from 6 $( = \mathbf{c})$, expressed in population standard deviation units. But this .10 value is $d_3'$ [formula (2.3.3)], the Case 3 ES measure, not **d**. To find **d**, $d_3'$ must be multiplied by $\sqrt{2}$ [formula (2.3.4)]. The result is $\mathbf{d} = .10\sqrt{2} = .1414$. The specifications are

$$\mathbf{a_2} = .01, \qquad \mathbf{d} = .1414, \qquad \text{power} = .90.$$

In Table 2.4.1 for $\mathbf{a_2} = .01$, his **d** value is not tabled. Following the procedure of Section 2.4.1, formula (2.4.1), he finds row power = .90 and column $\mathbf{d} = .10$, in order to find $\mathbf{n}_{.10} = 2978$. He then substitutes this value and $\mathbf{d} = .1414$ in formula (2.4.1) to find

$$\mathbf{n} = \frac{2978}{100(.1414)^2} + 1 = 1490.$$

Thus, he will need to draw a random sample of 1490 urban dwellers to assure with .90 probability the detection at the $\mathbf{a_2} = .01$ level of a .10 standard deviation departure of the population **m** from neutrality (a value of 6). If he should find, when the sample data are analyzed, that **t** is not significant, he may conclude with Type II error risk $\mathbf{b} = 1 - .90 = .10$ that the departure from neutrality in the population is negligible (Section 1.5.5).

2.4.5   CASE 4: ONE SAMPLE OF **n** DIFFERENCES BETWEEN PAIRED OBSERVATIONS. Here, again, the consideration involved in using the **n** tables are exactly the same as for the power tables and involve the determination of **d**. The issues are discussed in detail in Section 2.3.5, to which the reader is referred. See also Section 11.2 for a more general treatment.

Summarizing for convenience, if the investigator has no basis for estimating the population matching **r** between the **X**, **Y** pairs, he has no recourse but to work with their difference, **Z** ($=\mathbf{X} - \mathbf{Y}$) in the fashion of Case 3. That is, he indexes the effect size as [formula (2.3.5)]

$$\mathbf{d_z'} = \frac{\mathbf{m_z}}{\sigma_\mathbf{z}},$$

with the standard deviation of the difference scores as the unit in which the the mean difference is expressed, and enters the **n** tables with $\mathbf{d} = \mathbf{d_z'}\sqrt{2}$, using formula (2.4.1) for "interpolation" when necessary.

If the investigator has a basis for estimating the matching **r**, he can define [formula (2.3.8)]

$$\mathbf{d_4'} = \frac{\mathbf{m_X} - \mathbf{m_Y}}{\sigma},$$

which is exactly the same index as the **d** of independent samples (2.2.1) and (2.2.2), and use the **n** tables with [formula (2.3.9)] for

$$d = \frac{d_4'}{\sqrt{1-r}} .$$

The **n** read from the tables [or the tables plus formula (2.4.1)] is the necessary number of *pairs* to detect $d_z'$ or $d_4'$ (for which we enter with **d**) at the **a** significance criterion with the desired power. The Case 4 **n** (as was true for the Case 3 **n**) is, in principle, an underestimate, but unless **n** is quite small, the degree of underestimation is so small that it can be ignored.

**Illustrative Examples**

**2.13** In a child development study of maternal attitude toward children with cerebral palsy, data are to be gathered in the following way. Each mother to be selected has a child with cerebral palsy (P) and at least one other child within 3 years of age who is free of the disease (C). The mothers are to complete a series of attitude scales for each of their two children separately. For each scale, a comparison is planned between $m_P$ and $m_C$. Each mother's attitude toward her P child is "controlled" by her attitude toward her C child. The plan is to use $a_2 = .05$ as the significance criterion and power of .80. A conventional definition of a medium effect size, $d_4' = .50$, is posited for each scale. Note that $d_4'$ is simply the $m_P - m_C$ difference, standardized by the common within-population standard deviation [or, if $\sigma_P \neq \sigma_C$, their root mean square, $\sigma'$, formula (2.3.2)]. What sample size of mothers is necessary for these specifications?

For table entry, we require **d** from formula (2.3.9) and hence an estimate of **r**, the population correlation between attitude scale scores toward P and those toward C of such mothers, i.e., the within mother between child pairs **r**. The investigator, drawing on relevant evidence from the research literature and on the judgment that all sources of individual differences in attitude between mothers (e.g., differences in education, personality factors, response style) are contributing to this correlation, estimates **r** (probably conservatively) as .40. Thus $d = .50/\sqrt{(1 - .40)} = .50/.7746 = .645$. The specifications are

$$a_2 = .05, \quad d = .645, \quad \text{power} = .80.$$

As will generally be the case in Case 4 applications, the necessary **d** value is not tabulated and formula (2.4.1) is used. In Table 2.4.1 for $a_2 = .05$, one finds for row power $= .80$ in column $d = .10$, the $n_{.10}$ value of 1571, and substitutes it together with **d** in formula (2.4.1):

$$n = \frac{1571}{100(.645)^2} + 1 = 38.8.$$

Thus, a sample of 39 mothers is required. Note that if the research design had involved comparisons of the means of independent samples of P mothers with comparable C mothers (or equivalently if **r** were zero), 64 mothers of each type would have been needed (for the specifications $a_2 = .05$, power = .80, **d** = .50).

**2.14**  A neuropsychologist plans an investigation of the effect of leg amputation on various aspects of sensory threshold and discrimination above the amputation (A). He plans to control each A observation by measurement of the amputee subject on the same area on the contralateral side (C). He specifies a two-tailed test with Type I error risk of .02 ( $= a_2$) and Type II error risk of .10 ( $=b$, hence, power $= .90$). In specifying the ES, he may reason along either of the following lines:

1.  He considers the distribution of the differences between the paired measures, $A - C = Z$. He anticipates that the mean **Z** value for the population is of the order of .35 of a standard deviation of such differences (midway between operationally defined small and medium ES), i.e., $d_z' = m_z/\sigma_z = .35$ [formula (2.3.5)]. For table entry, he requires [formula (2.3.4)] $d = d_z'\sqrt{2} = .35(1.414) = .495$. His specifications thus are

$$a_2 = .02, \qquad d = .495, \qquad \text{power} = .90.$$

In Table 2.4.1 for $a_1 = .01$ ($a_2 = .02$) at row power $= .90$, if he is content to use **d** $= .50$, he finds[6] **n** $= 105$. This is the number of amputee subjects (i.e., pairs of observations) he needs.

2.  Alternately, he may prefer to work with the standard deviation of the separate measures, $\sigma$ ( $= \sigma_A = \sigma_C$) as unit,[7] and conceive his ES as [formula (2.3.8)] $d_4' = m_A - m_C/\sigma = .35$ (say). He must also posit a value of the population correlation coefficient between measures on the two limbs, **r**. In considering how to estimate this **r**, he may have information from normal (N) subjects that estimates this value for them as $r_N = .70$. It seems reasonable to him that the effect of amputation may well be to reduce this correlation to a value in the range .40–.60, for his sample. To find the values of **d**, he substitutes in formula (2.3.9):

for **r** $= .40$,      $d = .35/\sqrt{(1 - .40)} = .452$,

for **r** $= .60$,      $d = .35/\sqrt{(1 - .60)} = .553$.

---

[6] Otherwise, he uses formula (2.4.1), for which he reads out of the table $n_{.10} = 2605$ and, substituting it and **d** $= .495$, finds **n** $= 107$ (or 108, see footnote 5).

[7] If there is reason to believe that $\sigma_A \neq \sigma_C$ (for example, $\sigma_A > \sigma_C$ is not unlikely), we revert to a Case 2 definition, and use [formula (2.3.2)] $\sigma' = \sqrt{(\sigma_A^2 + \sigma_C^2)/2}$ in place of $\sigma$ in the definition of $d_4'$, with no effect on what follows.

Summarizing these specifications:

$$\mathbf{a}_2 = .02, \qquad \mathbf{d} = \frac{.452}{.553}, \qquad \text{power} = .90.$$

These $\mathbf{d}$ values will require the use of formula (2.4.1). In Table 2.4.1 for $\mathbf{a}_1 = .01$ ($\mathbf{a}_2 = .02$), for row power $= .90$, and column $\mathbf{d} = .10$, he finds $\mathbf{n}_{.10} = 2605$, and substituting

for $\mathbf{d} = .452$ (i.e., $\mathbf{r} = .40$), $\mathbf{n} = 129$,
for $\mathbf{d} = .553$ (i.e., $\mathbf{r} = .60$), $\mathbf{n} = 86$.

Note how critical is the effect on $\mathbf{n}$ of the value of $\mathbf{r}$ posited. Since $\mathbf{n}$ varies inversely with $\mathbf{d}^2$, and $\mathbf{d}^2$ varies inversely with $1 - \mathbf{r}$, the increase in the required $\mathbf{n}$ from a smaller correlation $\mathbf{r}_S$ to a larger one $\mathbf{r}_L$ will require an increase by a factor of $(1 - \mathbf{r}_S)/(1 - \mathbf{r}_L)$, in the case above, $(1 - .40)/(1 - .60)$ $= 1.50$, i.e., a 50% increase in $\mathbf{n}$.

This may suggest that the route to $\mathbf{d}$ by means of $\mathbf{d}_4'$ (which is equivalent to the Case 0 definition of $\mathbf{d}$), because of its critical dependence on $\mathbf{r}$, is less desirable than the previous alternative, which only requires the setting of ES in terms of $\mathbf{d}_Z$, and avoids the necessity of positing a value for $\mathbf{r}$. This would, however, be a mistaken conclusion, since the decision about ES in terms of $\mathbf{d}_Z'$ carries with it an *implicit* value of $\mathbf{r}$, as can be seen from the relationship [formula (2.3.7)] $\sigma_Z = \sigma\sqrt{2(1 - \mathbf{r})}$ [where $\sigma$ is either the common population standard deviation or $\sigma'$ from formula (2.3.2)]. Thus, if one proceeds to $\mathbf{d}$ from $\mathbf{d}_Z'$ in order to avoid the estimation of $\mathbf{r}$, which is necessary to proceed to $\mathbf{d}$ from $\mathbf{d}_4'$, one has *implicitly* posited (by simple algebra)

$$(2.3.10) \qquad\qquad \mathbf{r} = 1 - \tfrac{1}{2}\left(\frac{\mathbf{d}_4'}{\mathbf{d}_Z'}\right)^2.$$

Thus, if the investigator would want to set $\mathbf{d}_4'$ at (let us say, for concreteness) .4, but because he has no idea of $\mathbf{r}$, instead elects to set $\mathbf{d}_Z'$ at .6, he has in effect unwittingly assumed $\mathbf{r}$ to be

$$1 - \tfrac{1}{2}\left(\frac{.4}{.6}\right)^2 = .78,$$

i.e., a definite value. The point being emphasized is that $\mathbf{r}$ is inevitably a part of the $\mathbf{d}$ value, and one can estimate it either explicitly or implicitly. There are circumstances where the paired differences, $\mathbf{Z}$, represent a "natural" basis of study with which the investigator has some familiarity. In such cases he more readily expresses the ES as $\mathbf{d}_Z'$, and the fact that an $\mathbf{r}$ is implicit in his value of $\mathbf{d}$ is only of academic interest. But, as we have seen, the use of $\mathbf{Z}$ to evade the estimation of $\mathbf{r}$ does not succeed; a definite value for **r** is merely being posited implicitly, rather than explicitly. It appears obviously preferable that the researcher at least know, by means of formula (2.3.10), what **r** is being implicitly posited when he uses $\mathbf{d_z}'$, or employ the usually more natural approach via $\mathbf{d_4}'$ and come to terms with the problem of explicitly estimating **r** for formula (2.3.9).

**2.15**   An experimenter in a psychology laboratory is organizing a study to compare the effects of two reinforcement schedules on trials to response acquisition, using white rats. The design she will employ will utilize pairs of animals both of which come from the same litter and are free of obvious defects; she will randomly assign one to the A group and the other to the B group. She will consider the phenomenon she is interested in to be the superiority of the B over the A schedule, that is, more trials for A than B, and moreover wants to keep her Type I risk quite small. She then chooses $\mathbf{a_1} = .01$. The ES anticipated is moderate, as indexed by $\mathbf{d_4}' = .50$. On the basis of past work, she estimates the between litter-mates learning ability correlation as $\mathbf{r} = .65$. Her effective **d**, therefore, is [formula (2.3.9)] $.50 \sqrt{1/(1 - .65)} = .845$. Finally, she wishes to have a probability of .95 of detecting this (assumed) large effect. Thus, summarzing,

$$\mathbf{a_1} = .01, \quad \mathbf{d} = .845, \quad \text{power} = .95.$$

Recourse must be taken to formula (2.4.1). In Table 2.4.1 for $\mathbf{a_1} = .01$, row power = .95, $\mathbf{n_{.10}} = 3155$ and in formula (2.4.1)

$$\mathbf{n} = \frac{3155}{100(.845)^2} + 1 = 45.$$

Thus, 45 litter pairs will be needed.

## 2.5   The Use of the Tables for Significance Testing

2.5.1   General Introduction. As noted above in Section 1.5, provision has been made in the power tables to facilitate significance testing. Here, our focus shifts from research planning to the appraisal of research results, and from the consideration of the alternate-hypothetical state of affairs in the population to the palpable characteristics of the sample and their bearing on the null hypothesis.

Accordingly, we redefine our ES index, **d**, so that its elements are sample results, rather than population parameters, and call it $\mathbf{d_s}$. For all tests of the difference between means of independent samples,

$(2.5.1)$[8]
$$\mathbf{d_s} = \frac{\overline{\mathbf{X}}_A - \overline{\mathbf{X}}_B}{\mathbf{s}},$$

---

[8] It has been shown by Hedges (1981) and Kraemer (1983), in the context of the use of $\mathbf{d_s}$ in meta-analysis that the absolute value of $\mathbf{d_s}$ is positively biased by a factor of approximately ($4df$ − 1)/($4df$ − 4), which is of little consequence except for small samples. However, because the relationships with **t** given below are purely algebraic, this in no way affects its use in significance testing.

where $\overline{\mathbf{X}}_A$ and $\overline{\mathbf{X}}_B$ = the two sample means, and

$\mathbf{s}$ = the usual pooled within sample estimate of the population standard deviation,

that is,

(2.5.2)
$$\mathbf{s} = \sqrt{\frac{\sum(\mathbf{X}_A - \overline{\mathbf{X}}_A)^2 + \sum(\mathbf{X}_B - \overline{\mathbf{X}}_B)^2}{\mathbf{n}_A + \mathbf{n}_B - 2}},$$

Note that we have defined $\mathbf{s}$ quite generally so that it will hold for all cases involving two independent samples, whether or not sample sizes are equal.

Formula (2.5.1) should be interpreted literally for a directional (one-tailed) test and as an absolute difference [i.e., without sign, as in formula (2.2.2)] for the nondirectional (two-tailed) test.

Thus, $\mathbf{d}_s$ is the standardized mean difference for the sample. It is simply related to the $\mathbf{t}$ statistic by

(2.5.3)
$$\mathbf{d}_s = \mathbf{t}\sqrt{\frac{\mathbf{n}_A + \mathbf{n}_B}{\mathbf{n}_A \mathbf{n}_B}},$$

(2.5.4)
$$\mathbf{t} = \mathbf{d}_s\sqrt{\frac{\mathbf{n}_A \mathbf{n}_B}{\mathbf{n}_A + \mathbf{n}_B}}.$$

The value of $\mathbf{d}_s$ necessary for significance is called $\mathbf{d}_c$, i.e., the criterion value of $\mathbf{d}_s$. The second column of each of the power tables 2.3, headed $\mathbf{d}_c$, carries these values as a function of $\mathbf{n}$. Using these values, the investigator need not compute $\mathbf{t}$; the standardized difference between his sample means, $\mathbf{d}_s$, is compared with the tabled $\mathbf{d}_c$ values for his sample size. If the obtained $\mathbf{d}_s$ value equals or exceeds $\mathbf{d}_c$, his results are significant at the $\mathbf{a}$ value for that table; otherwise, they are not significant.

The advantages of using this approach are twofold:

1.   The value $\mathbf{s}$ is approximately the mean of the separate sample standard deviations. The latter are almost always computed, and often known approximately even prior to computation, so that the sample $\mathbf{d}_s$ can be approximated at a glance once the sample means are determined. If such an approximate value of $\mathbf{d}_s$ is materially different from the tabulated $\mathbf{d}_c$ value, the significance decision can be made without any computation. Thus, the $\mathbf{d}_c$ values can be used for a quick check on the significance of results.

2.   A second advantage lies in the convenience of having the $\mathbf{d}_c$ values for many values of $\mathbf{n}$. Most $\mathbf{t}$ tables provide criterion values of $\mathbf{t}$ for relatively few values for degrees of freedom; each power table provides $\mathbf{d}_c$ values for 68 entries of $\mathbf{n}$ between 8 and 1000.

In general, these advantages are probably not great. They are judged, however, to be useful with sufficient frequency to warrant the inclusion of the $\mathbf{d_c}$ values in the power tables.

The $\mathbf{d_s}$ concept has virtues which should be noted quite apart from its use in significance testing. In general, the equivalents of **d** in terms of non-overlap (**U**), correlation (**r**), and proportion of variance accounted for ($\mathbf{r^2}$), described for the population in Section 2.2, also hold for the sample, subject to the restrictions described there and in section 2.3. One simply uses Table 2.2.1 with $\mathbf{d_c}$ as **d**. The **U** measures will hold only to the extent to which the samples approach the conditions of normal distribution, equal variability, and equal sample size, on which these measures are predicated. The (point biserial) **r** and $\mathbf{r^2}$ equivalents, on the other hand, have no such restrictions. Further, their systematic use as an accompaniment to significance testing will frequently prove illuminating and has been advocated as a routine procedure (Cohen, 1965, pp. 101–104). Finally, formula (2.5.4) makes quite explicit the fact that a significance decision (from **t**) is a function both of the sample effect size (how much) and **n**, the amount of evidence brought to bear on the null hypothesis. Behavioral scientists too often use evidence in regard to significance (e.g., **t** values) as arbiters with which to judge the size of the effect or degree of relationship (e.g., as estimates of **d** values and their equivalents). The formula starkly exposes this error.

2.5.2   SIGNIFICANCE TESTING IN CASE 0. In Case 0, the use of the $\mathbf{d_c}$ values in the power tables 2.3 is quite straightforward. The investigator computes (or estimates) his sample $\mathbf{d_c}$ value and enters the appropriate power table for his **a**, in the row for his **n** ( $=\mathbf{n_A}=\mathbf{n_B}$), and checks to see whether his $\mathbf{d_s}$ equals or exceeds the tabled $\mathbf{d_c}$ value. Whether significant or not, he may then wish to express his $\mathbf{d_c}$ in terms of one or more of the **U** indices, **r**, or $\mathbf{r^2}$, using Table 2.2.1, or for greater accuracy, formulas (2.2.3)–(2.2.6).

**Illustrative Example**

**2.16**   Consider the conditions stated initially for example 2.1. Whatever the details of his expected ES (given there as **d** = .50), the experiment has been run at $\mathbf{a_2}$ = .05 with two independent experimental and control samples of 30 cases each. He computes his sample result as a standardized difference between means [$\mathbf{d_s}$, formula (2.5.1)] and finds that it equals .46. His specifications are simply

$$\mathbf{a_2} = .05, \qquad \mathbf{n} = 30, \qquad \mathbf{d_s} = .46.$$

In Table 2.3.5 for $\mathbf{a_2}$ = .05 and **n** = 30, $\mathbf{d_c}$ = .52. Since his $\mathbf{d_s}$ value is smaller than $d_c$, his observed difference is not significant at $a_2 = .05$. (He learns incidentally that with samples of 30 cases, it takes a difference between means of about half a standard deviation to reach significance at $a_2 = .05$.)

He may go on to refer to Table 2.2.1 [or, for greater accuracy, formula (2.2.6)] from which he learns that the point biserial $r$ between E versus C group membership and number of trials to learning is about .22 which, in turn, means that about .05 ($= r^2$) of the total among rat variance in trials is associated with group membership, *in his sample*.

If, for the purpose of reporting in the literature, he wants the $t$ value, it is very readily found for Case 0, where formula (2.5.4) simplifies (since $n_E = n_C = n$) to

$$(2.5.5) \qquad\qquad t = d_s \sqrt{\frac{n}{2}}$$

which is here

$$t = .46\sqrt{15} = 1.78.$$

This example can be used as an illustration of approximate "at-a-glance" significance decisions. Assume, instead, that he finds the following sample means and standard deviations ($n = 30$, $a_2 = .05$ criterion):

$$X_E = 10.8, \qquad X_C = 12.1,$$

$$s_E = 3.81, \qquad s_C = 4.24.$$

One notes at a glance that $s$ is approximately 4 and the difference between means, 1.3. The latter is only about a third of $s$, hence $d_s \approx .33$, clearly less than the $d_c = .52$ for the specified conditions.

2.5.3   SIGNIFICANCE TESTING IN CASE 1, $n_A \neq n_B$. The inequality of the sample sizes in a $t$ test for independent means provides no new problems in the use of $d_c$. Formula (2.5.2) for $s$, the standardizing unit for the sample mean difference, is written for the (more general) case which provides for differing values of $n_A$ and $n_B$. In entering the tables, the value of $n$ to be used is the harmonic mean of $n_A$ and $n_B$, which we have already described above when Case 1 was first discussed in Section 2.3.2 [formula (2.3.1)]:

$$n' = \frac{2n_A n_B}{n_A + n_B}.$$

The tabulated $d_c$ value for Case 1 is an overestimate, but a very slight one unless $n'$ is both absolutely small (say less than 20) and much smaller than $(n_A + n_B)/2$ (see Section 2.3.2).

**Illustrative Example**

**2.17**  Reconsider the conditions of example 2.3. Assume that the experiment has been performed, and the psychologists are appraising the results of their directional hypothesis at $a_1 = .05$ that the new psychotherapeutic technique B ($n_B = 60$) yields a higher mean criterion rating than the standard technique A ($n_A = 90$). Using the sample means (which differ in the predicted direction) and **s**, they find $d_s = .32$ [formula (2.5.1)]. They also compute [formula (2.3.1)]

$$\mathbf{n}' = \frac{2(90)(60)}{90 + 60} = 72.$$

Their specifications thus are

$$a_1 = .05, \qquad n' = 72, \qquad d_s = .32.$$

In Table 2.3.2 for $a_1 = .05$ at $n' = 72$, $d_c = .28$. The $d_s$ value of .32 exceeds the criterion value, so they conclude that the mean for the new method is significantly higher than that of the old (at $a_1 = .05$) on the rating criterion.

If they had instead computed **t**, they would have found it to equal 1.92. If they then wanted to have a $d_s$ value (for example, to express their results in terms of a **U** value, or **r**, or $r^2$), they can find it from formula (2.5.3):

$$\mathbf{d_s} = 1.92\sqrt{\frac{90 + 60}{(90)(60)}} = .32.$$

Or, alternatively, if they first compute $d_s$ and requires the **t** value, they can find it from formula (2.5.4).

2.5.4  SIGNIFICANCE TESTING IN CASE 2: $\sigma_A \neq \sigma_B$, $n_A = n_B$. Case 2 specifies that the standard deviations of the two *populations* are not equal. It is included here to stress two facts. One is that the *sample* standard deviations are virtually never equal but that this does not matter in the relationships discussed above in Section 2.5.1. The other is that even if the *population* standard deviations are judged to be unequal (for example, on the basis of a variance ratio test), the relationship between $d_s$ and **t** nevertheless holds, since it is purely algebraic, and further, that the interpretation of $d_s$ in terms of **r** and $r^2$ continues to hold (but not in terms of the **U** indices).

An issue not to be confused with that of the **t**–$d_s$–**r** relationships is the question of the validity of the **t** test under conditions of population variance heterogeneity. As discussed above in Section 2.3.3, provided that the sample sizes are approximately equal, the validity of the **t** test is hardly affected by any but relatively extreme population variance discrepancies. Thus, the $d_c$ values will remain approximately valid under nonextreme Case 2 conditions.

**Illustrative Example**

**2.18**   Consider again the wage survey by the labor economist of example 2.4. When the survey of men and women workers' ($n = 100$) weekly wages is completed, he proceeds to compare their means at the prespecified $a_2 = .01$ level. His expected population difference $\sigma_A \neq \sigma_B$ is reflected in the sample, where one variance is about twice the other (a highly significant difference with $n$'s of 100). He nevertheless proceeds to determine the $d_s$ value as (say) .40. His specifications are:

$$a_2 = .01, \qquad n = 100, \qquad d_s = .40.$$

In Table 2.3.4. (for $a_2 = .01$) with $n = 100$, he finds $d_c = .37$. He concludes, at $a_2 = .01$, that there is a sex difference in mean wages in the population sampled, since $d_s$ exceeds $d_c$. Since the effect of $\sigma_A \neq \sigma_B$ on the validity of the test is trivial for large *and equal* samples (Scheffé, 1959, p. 340) his conclusion is valid.

Note, incidentally, that the $d_s$ turned out to be smaller than the **d** value he had posited in planning the experiment (see example 2.4). His smaller $d_s$ is nevertheless significant because of the large power he had had against the ES of **d** = .50, namely .82. A good reason to seek high power is, of course, the real possibility that the $d_s$, when found, will prove materially smaller than the **d** expected in the planning. This leaves a margin for error, either judgmental or sampling, in the setting of **d**.

2.5.5 SIGNIFICANCE TESTING IN CASE 3: ONE SAMPLE OF n OBSERVATIONS. For those circumstances in which the null hypothesis takes the form: A single sample of **n** observations comes from a normal population whose mean is **c**, one must take into account the construction of the Tables 2.3, including the $d_c$ values. The reader is reminded that the latter proceeded on the assumption of *two*-sample tests, with, therefore, the sampling error variance of two means. Thus, it is necessary in one-sample tests to adjust the tabulated $d_c$ value. This proceeds very simply: To find the proper criterion value for one-sample tests, $d_c'$, one finds:

$$(2.5.6) \qquad\qquad d_c' = d_c \sqrt{\tfrac{1}{2}} \quad \text{or} \quad .707 d_c.$$

This value is an underestimate, but a very slight one unless **n** is less than 30 (see Section 2.3.4).

As for the observed $d_s$ value for Case 3, we follow the principle expressed in Section 2.5.1 and merely define $d_s$ as we defined $d_3'$ with sample values substituted for the population values of formula (2.3.3):

$$(2.5.7) \qquad\qquad \mathbf{d_s'} = \frac{\overline{\mathbf{X}} - \mathbf{c}}{\mathbf{s}}.$$

The prime is used to indicate that a one-sample test is involved. The relationship between $\mathbf{d_s'}$ and $\mathbf{t}$ as given in formulas (2.5.3) and (2.5.4) must be revised for one-sample tests, as follows:

$$(2.5.8) \qquad\qquad \mathbf{d_s't} = \sqrt{\frac{1}{\mathbf{n}}},$$

$$(2.5.9) \qquad\qquad \mathbf{t} = \mathbf{d_s'}\sqrt{\mathbf{n}}.$$

The first of these formulae may be useful when a **t** has been computed and a standardized sample ES index is desired; the second is of use when the **t** value is needed (e.g., for reporting results in an article).

Formula (2.5.9) [as well as formulas (2.5.4) and (2.5.5)] makes patent the dependence of the significance decision on both effect size in the sample ($\mathbf{d_s'}$) and the amount of evidence provided by the sample (**n**).

### Illustrative Example

**2.19** In example 2.5, an experimenter was planning a test on the effect of rearing rats in total darkness on their weight gain from birth to 90 days. The test is of the departure, in either direction, from an established standard value of 70 ( = **c**). The sample used was of 60 cases, and the test was planned and performed at $\mathbf{a_2} = .10$. He finds the sample mean gain to be $\overline{\mathbf{X}} = 68.8$ and the standard deviation to be $\mathbf{s} = 8.1$. From formula (2.5.7), he finds $\mathbf{d_s'} = (-).15$. His specifications are:

$$\mathbf{a_2} = .10, \qquad \mathbf{n} = 60, \qquad \mathbf{d_s'} = .15.$$

In Table 2.3.6 for $\mathbf{a_2} = .10$, $\mathbf{n} = 60$, he finds $\mathbf{d_c} = .30$. Since this is a one-sample test, he goes on to find $\mathbf{d_c'} = .30\sqrt{\tfrac{1}{2}} = .21$. Comparing his observed $\mathbf{d_s'}$ with the criterion $\mathbf{d_c'}$, he concludes that the sample mean departure from 70 is not significant at $\mathbf{a_2} = .10$.

2.5.6   SIGNIFICANCE TESTING IN CASE 4: ONE SAMPLE OF **n** DIFFERENCES BETWEEN PAIRED OBSERVATIONS. The significance test of the difference between means of paired observations is a special case of the one-sample test (Case 3) where $\mathbf{c} = 0$ (see discussion in Section 2.3.5). That is, the computations proceed by taking the **X**, **Y** pairs, of which there are **n**, and finding the differences, $\mathbf{X} - \mathbf{Y} = \mathbf{Z}$. The result is a single sample of **n Z** observations. From this point one proceeds as in Case 3, the null hypothesis being that the population mean of these **Z** values is 0. Once the sample data are being analyzed, the issue of the population (or sample) **r** between **X** and **Y**, discussed in the power and sample size sections on Case 4 (Sections 2.3.5. and 2.4.5), plays no role in the computations of significance.

For case 4, we define $d_s'$ as in formula (2.5.6), calling the variable **Z** instead of **X** and treating **c** as 0, i.e.,

$$(2.5.10) \qquad\qquad d_s' = \frac{\overline{Z}}{s}.$$

where **s** is the sample standard deviation of the **Z** values.

Note that this is the exact sample analog of formula (2.3.5).

Also as in Case 3, we must make the adjustment of the tables $d_c$ value, to allow for sampling error variance of only one mean, (here, a mean difference) instead of the two on which the tables are based. This requires multiplying $d_s'$ by $\sqrt{\frac{1}{2}}$ [formula (2.5.6)] to find the Case 4 criterion, $d_c'$.

As in Case 3, the relationship between $d_s'$ and t as given in formulas (2.5.8) and (2.5.9) hold for Case 4. Thus, one can simply translate a $d_s'$ value into t, if the latter value is required, or a t value into $d_s'$, if one wants to express the size of the mean difference in the sample in standardized terms, that is, in terms of the standard deviation of the differences.

Finally, and again as in Case 3, the $d_c'$ value is slightly underestimated, but to a degree which can be safely ignored unless **n** is small.

### Illustrative Example

**2.20** In example 2.6, an educational researcher was planning an experimental comparison of two programed texts in algebra by assigning the members of 50 IQ-matched pairs at random to the two texts, and, following instruction, testing their achievement. Assume that the experiment has been performed and the data marshalled for the significance test, to be performed at $a_2 = .05$, as specified in the plans.

The test is of the significance of the departure of the mean difference, $\overline{Z} = (\overline{X} - \overline{Y})$, from zero, which is equivalent to a test of $\overline{X} - \overline{Y} = 0$. He finds $\overline{Z} = -2.78$, **s** (of the **Z**'s) $= 8.22$, and entering these in formula (2.5.10), $d_s' = (-).34$. (Since the test is nondirectional, the negative sign does not enter, other than to indicate the $\overline{X}$ is less than $\overline{Y}$.) His specifications are:

$$a_2 = .05, \qquad n = 50, \qquad d_s' = .34.$$

In Table 2.3.5 for $a_2 = .05$, $n = 50$, he finds $d_c = .40$. Since this is a one-sample test, he needs to find $d_c' = .40\sqrt{\frac{1}{2}} = .28$. Comparing his observed

**d**$_s$' value of .34 with the criterion **d**$_c$' value of .28, he concludes that his departure from no difference of 2.78 (in favour of the **X** program) is significant at
**a**$_2$ = .05. If a value of **t** is required, it can be found from formula (2.5.9)
as **t** = .34$\sqrt{50}$ = 2.40.

CHAPTER 3

# The Significance of a Product Moment $r_s$

## 3.1 INTRODUCTION AND USE

Behavioral scientists generally, and particularly psychologists with substantive interests in individual differences in personality, attitude, and ability, frequently take recourse to correlational anlysis as an investigative tool in both pure and applied studies. By far the most frequently used statistical method of expression of the relationship between two variables is the Pearson product-moment correlation coefficient, **r**.

**r** is an index of linear relationship, the slope of the best-fitting straight line for a bivariate (**X**, **Y**) distribution where the **X** and **Y** variables have each been standardized to the same variability. Its limits are $-1.00$ to $+1.00$. The purpose of this handbook precludes the use of space for a detailed consideration of the interpretations and assumptions of **r**. For this, the reader is referred to a general textbook, such as Cohen & Cohen (1983), Hays (1981), or Blalock (1972).

When used as a purely descriptive measure of degree of linear relationship between two variables, no assumptions need be made with regard to the shape of the marginal population distribution of **X** and **Y**, nor of the distribution of **Y** for any given value of **X** (or vice versa), nor of equal variability of **Y** for different values of **X** (homoscedasticity). However, when significance tests come to be employed, assumptions of normality and homoscedasticity are formally invoked. Despite this, it should be noted that, as in the case of the **t** test with means, moderate assumption failure here, particularly with large **n**, will not seriously affect the validity of significance tests, nor of the power estimates associated with them.

75

In this chapter we consider inference from a single correlation coefficient, $r_s$, obtained from a sample of n pairs (**X**, **Y**) of observations. There is only one population parameter involved, namely **r**, the population correlation coefficient. It is possible to test the null hypothesis that the population **r** equals *any* value **c** (discussed in Chapter 4). In most instances, however, the behavioral scientist is interested in whether there is *any* (linear) relationship between two variables, and this translates into the null hypothesis, $H_0$: **r** = 0. Thus, in common statistical parlance, a significant $r_s$ is one which leads to a rejection of the null hypothesis that the population **r** is zero. It is around this null hypothesis that this chapter and its tables are oriented. (For the test on a difference between two **r**'s, see Chapter 4.)

The significance test of $r_s$ may proceed by means of the **t** distribution, as follows:

$$(3.1.1) \qquad\qquad t = \frac{r_s\sqrt{n-2}}{\sqrt{1-r_s^2}}$$

where **n** is the number of (**X**, **Y**) pairs in the sample, and the appropriate **t** distribution is that for **n** − 2 degrees of freedom.[1] As in tests on means, the **t** criterion for rejection depends on the **a** (significance) level and the directionality of the test:

1. If *either* a positive or a negative value of $r_s$ is considered (*a priori*) evidence against the null hypothesis, the test is nondirectional, i.e., two tailed.

2. If the sign of $r_s$ is specified in advance, that is, if only positive (or only negative) correlation is deemed relevant for rejecting the null hypothesis, the test is directional, i.e., one tailed.

A word about regression coefficients. When one variable of the **X**, **Y** pair, conventionally **Y**, can be looked upon as dependent upon **X**, one may speak of the regression of **Y** on **X**. The slope of the best-fitting line for predicting **Y** from **X**, when each is in its *original* ("raw") unit of measurement, is called the regression coefficient, $\mathbf{B_{YX}}$. $\mathbf{B_{YX}}$ is simply the *un*standardized slope of **Y** on **X** and can be written simply as a function of **r** and the two standard deviations, $\sigma_X$ and $\sigma_Y$:

$$(3.1.2) \qquad\qquad \mathbf{B_{YX}} = r\,\frac{\sigma_Y}{\sigma_X} \;;$$

[1] In the power tables, minimum values of $r_s$ necessary for significance, given **a** and **n**, are provided in the criterion **r** ($r_c$) column. This obviates the necessity in most instances of computing **t** from formula (3.1.1) and interpolating for **df** in **t** tables. See Section 3.5 which describes this procedure in detail.

thus

(3.1.3)                       $$r = B_{YX} \frac{\sigma_X}{\sigma_Y}.$$

$B_{YX}$, being the slope of the regression line, indicates how many units of change in **Y** are produced by a unit change in **X**, where the units are the "raw" values of the respective variables. In problems where such dependencies can be assumed, and where the units in which **X** and **Y** are measured are inherently meaningful (e.g., dollars, population densities), regression coefficients are often preferred to correlation coefficients. Also, regression coefficients remain constant under changes in the variability of **X**, while correlation coefficients do not.

A test of the significance of **B**, i.e., that it departs from zero in the population, is automatically provided from the test of **r**. A glance at formula (3.1.2) shows that **B** is zero if and only if **r** is zero.[2] The researcher accustomed to regression formulations in the two-variable case where **X**, **Y** pairs are sampled need only translate his problem (including the effect size) into correlation terms and proceed. (Tests on *partial* regression coefficients are discussed in Chapter 9.)

## 3.2   THE EFFECT SIZE: **r**

The ES index offers no difficulty here (but see Section 11.1). The requirements for an ES index include that it be a pure (dimensionless) number, one not dependent on the units of the measurement scale(s). The population correlation co-efficient, **r**, serves this purpose.

Thus, a general formulation of the power estimation problem is: One is going to test the significance ($H_0$: **r** = 0) of a sample $r_s$ value at the **a** significance criterion with **n** pairs of observations; if the population **r** is some specified value (thus, the ES), what is the power of the test (the probability of rejecting the null hypothesis)? Tables 3.3 would be used to find the power value.

Similarly, a general formulation of the sample size estimation problem is: One plans to test the significance ($H_0$: **r** = 0) of a sample $r_s$ value at the **a** significance criterion and wishes to detect some specified population **r** (this being the ES); he then specifies the desired power (probability of rejecting the null hypothesis). How many pairs of observations, **n**, would be necessary? Table 3.4 would be used to find the value of **n**.

---

[2] The reader may object that **B** is zero when $\sigma_Y$ is zero whatever the value of **r**. However, when $\sigma_Y$ is zero, **r** is indeterminate, that is, it is not meaningful to talk of correlation when one of the variables does not vary.

3.2.1   r AS PV AND THE SIZE OF CORRELATIONAL EFFECTS.   One conceptually useful way to approach an understanding of **r** is to consider $r^2$ (as
already noted in Chapter 2).[3] The square of the correlation coefficient is
the proportion of variance (PV) in either of the two variables which may be
predicted by (or accounted for, or attributed to) the variance of the other,
using a straight-line relationship (Cohen & Cohen, 1983). Concretely, given
an **r** of .50 between IQ and course grades, $r^2 = .25$, so that 25% of the
variance in course grades for the members of this population may be attributed
to differences among them in IQ. (Of course, the attribution of causality is a
logical or scientific issue, and not one of statistical inference, as such.) Note,
incidentally, that the descriptive use of $r^2$ (as that of **r**) is not dependent on
assumptions of normality or homoscedasticity.

Measures of proportion of variance are usually more immediately
comprehensible than other indices in that, being relative amounts, they
come closer to the behavioral scientist's verbal formulations of relative magnitude of association. They have the additional virtue of providing a common
basis for the expression of different measures of relationships, e.g., standardized difference between means (**d**), variation among means (correlation
ratio), as well as **r**.

The only difficulty arising from the use of PV measures lies in the fact that
in many, perhaps most, of the areas of behavioral science, they turn out to
be so small! For example, workers in personality-social psychology, both
pure and applied (i.e., clinical, educational, personnel), normally encounter
correlation coefficients above the .50–.60 range only when the correlations
are measurement reliability coefficients. In PV terms, this effective upper
limit implies something of the order of one-quarter or one-third of variance
accounted for. The fact is that the state of development of much of behavioral
science is such that not very much variance in the dependent variable is
predictable. This is essentially merely another way of stating the obvious:
that the behavioral sciences collectively are not as far advanced as the
physical sciences. In the latter, we can frequently account for upwards of
99% of dependent variable variance, for example, in classical mechanics.[4]
Thus, when we consider **r** = .50 a large ES (see below), the implication that
.25 of the variance accounted for is a large proportion must be understood
*relatively*, not absolutely.

---

[3] Another possibly useful way to understand **r** is as a proportion of common elements
between variables. The implicit model for this interpretation is not compelling for most behavioral science applications (behavioral genetics may be one exception). See Ozer (1985) for a
contrary view and "Effect Size" in Chapter 11 for further discussion of r and $r^2$.

[4] This is one way to understand the reason for the fact that applied statistical analysis
flourishes in the biological and social sciences and has only limited specialized applications
in pure physical science.

The question, "relative to what?" is not answerable concretely. The frame of reference is the writer's subjective averaging of PVs from his reading of the research literature in behavioral science. Since no one reads a stratified random probability sample of the behavioral science literature (whose definition alone would be no mean task), this average may be biased in a "soft" direction, i.e., towards personality–social psychology, sociology, and cultural anthropology and away from experimental and physiological psychology.

The preceding serves as an introduction to operational definitions of "small," "medium," and "large" ES as expressed in terms of **r**, offered as a convention. The same diffidence is felt here as in Section 2.2 (and other such sections in later chapters). A reader who finds that what is here defined as "large" is too small (or too large) to meet what his area of behavioral science would consider appropriate standards is urged to make more suitable operational definitions. What are offered below are definitions for use when no others suggest themselves, or as conventions.

SMALL EFFECT SIZE: $r = .10$. An **r** of .10 in a population is indeed small. The implied PV is $r^2 = .01$, and there seems little question but that relationships of that order in **X**, **Y** pairs in a population would not be perceptible on the basis of casual observation. But is it too small?

It probably is not. First of all, it is comparable to the definition of a small ES for a mean difference (Chapter 2), which was $d = .2$, implying point biserial $r = .10$ (for populations of equal size). More important than this, however, is the writer's conviction that many relationships pursued in "soft" behavioral science are of this order of magnitude. Thurstone once said that in psychology we measure men by their shadows. As the behavioral scientist moves from his theoretical constructs, among which there are hypothetically strong relationships, to their operational realizations in measurement and subject manipulation, very much "noise" (measurement unreliability, lack of fidelity to the construct) is likely to accompany the variables. (See Section 11.3 for a discussion of psychometric reliability and power analysis.) This, in turn, will attenuate the correlation in the population between the constructs as *measured*. Thus, if two constructs in theory (hence perfectly measured) can be expected to correlate .25, and the actual measurement of each is correlated .63 with its respective pure construct, the observed correlation between the two *fallible* measures of the construct would be reduced to .25 (.63) (.63) = .10. Since the above values are not unrealistic, it follows that often (perhaps more often than we expect), we are indeed seeking to reject null hypotheses about $r_s$ when **r** is some value near .10.

We can offer no exemplification with known instances of population **r**'s of the order of .10, by the very nature of the problem. In fields where correlation coefficients are used, one rarely if ever encounters low $r_s$'s on samples large enough to yield standard errors small enough to distinguish them from $r$'s of zero.

MEDIUM EFFECT SIZE: $r = .30$. When $r = .30$, $r^2 = PV = .09$, so that our definition of a medium effect in linear correlation implies that 9% of the variance of the dependent variable is attributable to the independent variable. It is shown later that this level of ES is comparable to that of medium ES in differences between two means.

Many of the correlation coefficients encountered in behavioral science are of this order of magnitude, and, indeed, this degree of relationship would be perceptible to the naked eye of a reasonably sensitive observer. If we appeal to fields which use psychological tests, we find, for example, that Guilford and Fruchter write that "the validity coefficient (r with criterion) of a single test may be expected in the range from .00 to .60, with most indices in the lower half of that range [1978, p. 87]."

When one considers correlations among tests of diverse abilities, average $r$'s run rather higher than .30. However, for example, for adolescents, correlations among representative tests of creativity average to almost exactly .30, and creativity tests have an average $r$ with IQ of just below .30 (Getzels & Jackson, 1962, p. 20). In another area, scores on the two major variables of personality self-description, neuroticism (or trait anxiety) and extraversion correlate about $-.30$ in college students and in psychiatric populations (Jensen, 1965). In still another area, about 40% of the correlation coefficients among the nine clinical scales of the Minnesota Multiphasic Personality Inventory which are reported in the literature are in the .25–.35 range. Broadly speaking, it seems justifiable to identify as a medium ES in correlation, a value at the midpoint of the range of correlations between discriminably different psychological variables.

LARGE EFFECT SIZE: $r = .50$. The definition of a large correlational ES as $r = .50$ leads to $r^2 = .25$ of the variance of either variable being associated linearly with variance in the other. Its comparability with the definition of large ES in mean differences ($d = .8$) will be demonstrated below. Here, we may simply note that it falls around the upper end of the range of (nonreliability) $r$'s one encounters in those fields of behavioral science which use them extensively, e.g., differential, personality–social, personnel, educational, clinical, and counseling psychology. Thus, Ghiselli writing in an applied psychology framework states "the practical upper limit of predictive effectiveness . . . [is] . . . a validity coefficient of the order of .50 [1964, p. 61]." Guilford's figure, as noted above, is similar. We appeal to the mental-personality-social measurement field for our criterion because of its very heavy use of linear correlation, both historically and contemporaneously. One can, of course, find higher values of $r$ in behavioral science. Reliability coefficients of tests, particularly of the equivalence variety, will generally run much higher. Also, if effects in highly controlled "hard" psychology (e.g., psychophysics) are studied by means of **r**'s, they would frequently be distinctly higher than .50. But they are not generally so studied. It seems reasonable that the frame of reference used for conventional definitions of correlational ES should arise from the fields which most heavily use correlations.

The example which comes most readily to mind of this .50 level of correlation is from educational psychology, which gave birth to many of the concepts and technology of correlation methods in behavioral science (e.g., Galton, Spearman). Correlations between IQs or total scores from other comprehensive aptitude batteries correlate with school grades at values which cluster around .50. In contrast, when one looks at near-maximum correlation coefficients of personality measures with comparable real-life criteria, the values one encounters fall at the order of a medium ES, i.e., **r** = .30.

Thus, when a investigator anticipates a degree of correlation between two different variables "about as high as they come," this would by our definition be a large effect, **r** = .50.

3.2.2 COMPARABILITY OF ES FOR **r** WITH **d**. It is patently desirable that effect sizes given a qualitative label, e.g., "medium," when studied by means of one design or parameter, be comparable to effects given the same label when studied by another. An attempt has been made for the operationally defined small, medium, and large ES to be comparable across the different ES parameters necessitated by the variety of tests discussed in this book.

Strict comparability, defined in exact mathematical terms, poses numerous difficulties. First, several alternative definitions are possible. Consider PV, which seems a likely candidate. When a variable is measured on an ordered equal-interval scale, so that the variance concept is meaningful, we can express ES in terms of proportion of variance, as was done above and in Chapter 2. But when the dependent variable is a nominal scale, we can no longer define variance and PV but would need to move to its generalization, multivariance or generalized variance, and enter the world of set correlation. (We do, in fact, do so in Chapter 10, but the going is rough.) Or, we would need to invoke from information theory the even more general (and much less less familiar) concept of amount of information or uncertainty. If we decide to forego nominal scale comparability and try to use PV as a "strictly" comparable base for ES for interval scales, we encounter two further difficulties. One is that we would need to specify alternate models which would lead to varying PV's. For example, in Section 2.2 we defined the populations as distinct "points" and therefore, the relevant **r** as the point biserial **r** ($r_p$). So conceived, PV $= r_p^2$. But if our model is changed so that the populations are adjacent along a scale so that when combined they define a normal distribution (e.g., an adult male population defined by a median cut into "tall" and "short" men), the correlation with height of some dependent variable would be given by the biserial $r(r_b)$ (Cohen & Cohen, 1983, pp. 66–67), so that PV $= r_b^2$. But since $r_b$ is greater than $r_p$, their squares and hence their PVs would differ. Thus, the "same" difference between means would, depending on the nature of the model assumption, lead to different proportions of variance.

A further problem would arise in that, having somehow defined strictly comparable ES in PV terms, when the latter were then translated into more familiar measures, awkward values which are not convenient multiples would result. Thus, if a medium PV were defined as .10, this would lead to $d = .667$ (under the conditions defined in Section 2.2) and $r = .316$.

We are prepared to be content with less formal bases for comparability than purely mathematical ones, utilizing the "state of the science" in relevant areas of behavioral science, as we have done above. But we wish to be guided in our operational definitions by quantitative considerations, here specifically correlational comparability.

In Section 2.2, the $d$ criteria for small, medium, and large ES were stated and translated into *point* biserial $r$ ($r_p$) and $r_p^2$. The use of $r_p$ assumes that population membership ($\mathbf{X}$) is two-valued and "point" in character. The $t$ test for $r$, which concerns us in this chapter, presumes normal distributions on both $\mathbf{X}$ and $\mathbf{Y}$. Comparability in PV would demand that the biserial $r$ ($r_b$), for which a normal distribution is assumed to underlie the $\mathbf{X}$ dichotomy, should be the basis of comparison. With populations of equal size (i.e., forming the dichotomy at the median),

(3.2.1)                              $r_b = 1.253 r_p.$

Thus, if we translate the $d$ criteria to $r_p$ (Table 2.2.1) and then, by means of formula (3.2.1) to $r_b$, and compare the latter with the ES criteria set forth above for $r$, we find the following:

| ES | d | $r_p \times 1.253 = r_b$ | r |
|---|---|---|---|
| Small | .20 | .100 | .125 | .10 |
| Medium | .50 | .243 | .304 | .30 |
| Large | .80 | .371 | .465 | .50 |

Comparing the $r_b$ equivalent to the $r$ criteria of the present chapter, we find what are judged to be reasonably close values for small and large ES and almost exact equality at the very important medium ES level. Thus, the terms "small," "medium," and "large" mean about the same thing in correlation terms as we go from consideration of mean differences to consideration of **r**'s.

## 3.3 POWER TABLES

The tables in this section yield power values when, in addition to the significance criterion and ES $= r$, the sample size is specified. Thus, these power tables will find their greatest use in determining the power of a test of the significance of a sample $r_s$, *after* the data are gathered and the test is made. They can also be used in experimental planning by varying **n**, or ES ($= r$), or **a** to determine the consequence which such alternatives have on power.

Specifically, the power tables yield power values for the **t** test of $H_0$: $r = 0$, i.e., for the test of the significance of a product moment $r_s$, determined on a sample of **n** pairs of observations **X**, **Y** at the **a** significance criterion. The tables give values for **a**, **r**, and **n**:

*1. Significance Criterion*, **a**. Tables are provided for the following values of **a**: $a_1 = .01$, $a_1 = .05$, $a_1 = .10$; $a_2 = .01$, $a_2 = .05$, $a_2 = .10$, the subscripts referring to one- and two-tailed tests. Since power at $a_1$ is to an adequate approximation equal to power at $a_2 = 2a_1$ for power greater than .10, one can determine power at $a_2 = .02$ (from the $a_1 = .01$ table), $a_2 = .20$ (from $a_1 = .10$), $a_1 = .005$ (from $a_2 = .01$), and $a_1 = .025$ (from $a_2 = .05$).

*2. Effect Size, ES.* The ES index here is simply **r**, the population product-moment correlation coefficient. In directional (one-tailed) tests ($a_1$), **r** is understood as either positive or negative, depending on the direction posited in the alternate hypotheses, e.g., $H_1$: $r = -.30$. In nondirectional (two-tailed) tests, **r** is understood as absolute, e.g., "given a level of population $r = .30$, whether positive or negative. . . ."

Provision is made for $r = .10$ (.10) .90. Conventional definitions of ES have been offered above, as follows:

small:   $r = .10$,
medium: $r = .30$,
large:   $r = .50$.

*3. Sample Size*, **n**. This is the number of *pairs* of observations **X**, **Y** in the sample. Provision is made for $n = 8$ (1) 40 (2) 60 (4) 100 (20) 200 (50) 500 (100) 1000.

The values in the body of the table are the power of the test times 100, i.e., the percentage of tests carried out under the given conditions which will result in the rejection of the null hypothesis, $H_0$: $r = 0$. The values are rounded to the *nearest* unit and are accurate to within $\pm 1$ as tabled (i.e., to within .01).

Table 3.3.1

Power of t test of r = 0 at $a_1$ = .01

| n | $r_c$ | .10 | .20 | .30 | .40 | .50 | .60 | .70 | .80 | .90 |
|---|---|---|---|---|---|---|---|---|---|---|
| | | | | | | r | | | | |
| 8 | 789 | 02 | 03 | 05 | 08 | 13 | 22 | 37 | 60 | 88 |
| 9 | 750 | 02 | 03 | 06 | 10 | 16 | 27 | 44 | 69 | 93 |
| 10 | 715 | 02 | 03 | 06 | 11 | 19 | 32 | 52 | 76 | 96 |
| 11 | 685 | 02 | 04 | 07 | 13 | 22 | 37 | 58 | 82 | 98 |
| 12 | 658 | 02 | 04 | 08 | 14 | 25 | 42 | 64 | 86 | 99 |
| 13 | 634 | 02 | 05 | 09 | 16 | 28 | 46 | 69 | 90 | 99 |
| 14 | 612 | 02 | 05 | 10 | 18 | 31 | 51 | 74 | 92 | * |
| 15 | 592 | 02 | 05 | 10 | 20 | 34 | 55 | 78 | 94 | |
| 16 | 574 | 02 | 06 | 11 | 22 | 38 | 59 | 81 | 96 | |
| 17 | 558 | 03 | 06 | 12 | 23 | 41 | 63 | 84 | 97 | |
| 18 | 543 | 03 | 06 | 13 | 25 | 43 | 66 | 86 | 98 | |
| 19 | 529 | 03 | 06 | 14 | 27 | 46 | 69 | 89 | 98 | |
| 20 | 516 | 03 | 07 | 15 | 29 | 49 | 72 | 91 | 99 | |
| 21 | 503 | 03 | 07 | 16 | 31 | 52 | 75 | 92 | 99 | |
| 22 | 492 | 03 | 07 | 17 | 32 | 54 | 77 | 94 | 99 | |
| 23 | 482 | 03 | 08 | 18 | 34 | 56 | 79 | 95 | * | |
| 24 | 472 | 03 | 08 | 18 | 36 | 59 | 81 | 95 | | |
| 25 | 462 | 03 | 08 | 19 | 37 | 61 | 83 | 96 | | |
| 26 | 453 | 03 | 09 | 20 | 39 | 63 | 85 | 97 | | |
| 27 | 445 | 03 | 09 | 21 | 41 | 65 | 87 | 98 | | |
| 28 | 437 | 03 | 09 | 22 | 43 | 67 | 88 | 98 | | |
| 29 | 430 | 03 | 10 | 23 | 44 | 69 | 89 | 98 | | |
| 30 | 423 | 03 | 10 | 24 | 46 | 71 | 91 | 99 | | |
| 31 | 416 | 04 | 11 | 25 | 47 | 73 | 92 | 99 | | |
| 32 | 409 | 04 | 11 | 26 | 49 | 75 | 93 | 99 | | |
| 33 | 403 | 04 | 11 | 27 | 51 | 76 | 93 | 99 | | |
| 34 | 397 | 04 | 12 | 28 | 52 | 78 | 94 | 99 | | |
| 35 | 392 | 04 | 12 | 29 | 54 | 79 | 95 | * | | |
| 36 | 386 | 04 | 12 | 30 | 55 | 80 | 95 | | | |
| 37 | 381 | 04 | 13 | 30 | 56 | 82 | 96 | | | |
| 38 | 376 | 04 | 13 | 31 | 58 | 83 | 96 | | | |
| 39 | 371 | 04 | 13 | 32 | 59 | 84 | 97 | | | |
| 40 | 367 | 04 | 14 | 33 | 61 | 85 | 97 | | | |
| 42 | 358 | 04 | 15 | 35 | 63 | 87 | 98 | | | |
| 44 | 350 | 05 | 15 | 37 | 66 | 89 | 98 | | | |
| 46 | 342 | 05 | 16 | 39 | 68 | 90 | 99 | | | |
| 48 | 335 | 05 | 17 | 41 | 70 | 92 | 99 | | | |

Table 3.3.1 *(continued)*

| n | $r_c$ | .10 | .20 | .30 | .40 | .50 | .60 | .70 | .80 | .90 |
|---|---|---|---|---|---|---|---|---|---|---|
| | | | | | | | | r | | |
| 50 | 328 | 05 | 18 | 42 | 72 | 93 | 99 | * | * | * |
| 52 | 322 | 05 | 18 | 44 | 74 | 94 | 99 | | | |
| 54 | 316 | 05 | 19 | 46 | 76 | 95 | * | | | |
| 56 | 310 | 06 | 20 | 48 | 78 | 96 | | | | |
| 58 | 305 | 06 | 21 | 49 | 80 | 96 | | | | |
| 60 | 300 | 06 | 21 | 51 | 81 | 97 | | | | |
| 64 | 290 | 06 | 23 | 54 | 84 | 98 | | | | |
| 68 | 282 | 06 | 25 | 57 | 87 | 98 | | | | |
| 72 | 274 | 07 | 26 | 60 | 89 | 99 | | | | |
| 76 | 266 | 07 | 28 | 63 | 90 | 99 | | | | |
| 80 | 260 | 07 | 29 | 66 | 92 | 99 | | | | |
| 84 | 253 | 08 | 31 | 68 | 93 | * | | | | |
| 88 | 248 | 08 | 33 | 70 | 94 | | | | | |
| 92 | 242 | 08 | 34 | 73 | 95 | | | | | |
| 96 | 237 | 09 | 36 | 75 | 96 | | | | | |
| 100 | 232 | 09 | 37 | 76 | 97 | | | | | |
| 120 | 212 | 11 | 45 | 85 | 99 | | | | | |
| 140 | 196 | 12 | 52 | 90 | * | | | | | |
| 160 | 184 | 14 | 59 | 94 | | | | | | |
| 180 | 173 | 16 | 65 | 96 | | | | | | |
| 200 | 164 | 18 | 70 | 98 | | | | | | |
| 250 | 147 | 23 | 81 | 99 | | | | | | |
| 300 | 134 | 28 | 88 | * | | | | | | |
| 350 | 124 | 32 | 93 | | | | | | | |
| 400 | 116 | 37 | 96 | | | | | | | |
| 450 | 110 | 42 | 98 | | | | | | | |
| 500 | 104 | 46 | 99 | | | | | | | |
| 600 | 095 | 55 | * | | | | | | | |
| 700 | 088 | 63 | | | | | | | | |
| 800 | 082 | 69 | | | | | | | | |
| 900 | 078 | 75 | | | | | | | | |
| 1000 | 074 | 80 | | | | | | | | |

* Power values below this point are greater than .995.

Table 3.3.2

Power of t test of r = 0 at $a_1$ = .05

| n | $r_c$ | .10 | .20 | .30 | .40 | .50 | .60 | .70 | .80 | .90 |
|---|---|---|---|---|---|---|---|---|---|---|
| 8 | 621 | 08 | 12 | 18 | 26 | 37 | 52 | 68 | 85 | 97 |
| 9 | 582 | 08 | 13 | 20 | 29 | 42 | 57 | 74 | 90 | 99 |
| 10 | 549 | 08 | 14 | 22 | 32 | 46 | 62 | 79 | 93 | 99 |
| 11 | 521 | 09 | 15 | 23 | 35 | 50 | 67 | 83 | 95 | * |
| 12 | 497 | 09 | 15 | 25 | 38 | 54 | 71 | 87 | 97 | |
| 13 | 476 | 09 | 16 | 26 | 40 | 57 | 74 | 89 | 98 | |
| 14 | 458 | 10 | 17 | 28 | 43 | 60 | 78 | 91 | 98 | |
| 15 | 441 | 10 | 18 | 30 | 45 | 63 | 81 | 93 | 99 | |
| 16 | 426 | 10 | 19 | 31 | 48 | 66 | 83 | 95 | 99 | |
| 17 | 412 | 10 | 19 | 33 | 50 | 69 | 85 | 96 | * | |
| 18 | 400 | 11 | 20 | 34 | 52 | 71 | 87 | 97 | | |
| 19 | 389 | 11 | 21 | 36 | 54 | 73 | 89 | 97 | | |
| 20 | 378 | 11 | 22 | 37 | 56 | 75 | 90 | 98 | | |
| 21 | 369 | 11 | 22 | 39 | 58 | 77 | 92 | 98 | | |
| 22 | 360 | 11 | 23 | 40 | 60 | 79 | 93 | 99 | | |
| 23 | 352 | 12 | 24 | 41 | 62 | 81 | 94 | 99 | | |
| 24 | 344 | 12 | 24 | 42 | 64 | 83 | 95 | 99 | | |
| 25 | 337 | 12 | 25 | 44 | 65 | 84 | 95 | 99 | | |
| 26 | 330 | 12 | 26 | 45 | 67 | 85 | 97 | * | | |
| 27 | 323 | 13 | 26 | 46 | 68 | 86 | 96 | | | |
| 28 | 317 | 13 | 27 | 47 | 70 | 88 | 97 | | | |
| 29 | 311 | 13 | 28 | 49 | 71 | 89 | 97 | | | |
| 30 | 306 | 13 | 28 | 50 | 72 | 90 | 98 | | | |
| 31 | 301 | 13 | 29 | 51 | 74 | 90 | 98 | | | |
| 32 | 296 | 14 | 30 | 52 | 75 | 91 | 98 | | | |
| 33 | 291 | 14 | 30 | 53 | 76 | 92 | 99 | | | |
| 34 | 287 | 14 | 31 | 54 | 77 | 93 | 99 | | | |
| 35 | 283 | 14 | 32 | 55 | 78 | 93 | 99 | | | |
| 36 | 279 | 14 | 32 | 56 | 79 | 94 | 99 | | | |
| 37 | 275 | 15 | 33 | 57 | 80 | 95 | 99 | | | |
| 38 | 271 | 15 | 33 | 58 | 81 | 95 | 99 | | | |
| 39 | 267 | 15 | 34 | 59 | 82 | 95 | * | | | |
| 40 | 264 | 15 | 35 | 60 | 83 | 96 | | | | |
| 42 | 257 | 16 | 36 | 62 | 85 | 97 | | | | |
| 44 | 251 | 16 | 37 | 64 | 86 | 97 | | | | |
| 46 | 246 | 16 | 38 | 66 | 88 | 98 | | | | |
| 48 | 240 | 17 | 39 | 67 | 89 | 98 | | | | |

Table 3.3.2 *(continued)*

| | | | | | r | | | | |
|---|---|---|---|---|---|---|---|---|---|
| n | $r_c$ | .10 | .20 | .30 | .40 | .50 | .60 | .70 | .80 | .90 |
| 50 | 235 | 17 | 41 | 69 | 90 | 98 | * | * | * | * |
| 52 | 231 | 17 | 42 | 71 | 91 | 99 | | | |
| 54 | 226 | 18 | 43 | 72 | 92 | 99 | | | |
| 56 | 222 | 18 | 44 | 73 | 93 | 99 | | | |
| 58 | 218 | 19 | 45 | 75 | 94 | 99 | | | |
| 60 | 214 | 19 | 46 | 76 | 94 | 99 | | | |
| 64 | 207 | 20 | 48 | 79 | 95 | * | | | |
| 68 | 201 | 20 | 50 | 81 | 96 | | | | |
| 72 | 195 | 21 | 52 | 83 | 97 | | | | |
| 76 | 190 | 22 | 54 | 85 | 98 | | | | |
| 80 | 185 | 22 | 56 | 86 | 98 | | | | |
| 84 | 181 | 23 | 58 | 88 | 99 | | | | |
| 88 | 176 | 24 | 59 | 89 | 99 | | | | |
| 92 | 173 | 24 | 61 | 90 | 99 | | | | |
| 96 | 169 | 25 | 63 | 91 | 99 | | | | |
| 100 | 165 | 26 | 64 | 92 | 99 | | | | |
| 120 | 151 | 29 | 71 | 96 | * | | | | |
| 140 | 140 | 32 | 77 | 98 | | | | | |
| 160 | 130 | 35 | 82 | 99 | | | | | |
| 180 | 123 | 38 | 86 | 99 | | | | | |
| 200 | 117 | 41 | 89 | * | | | | | |
| 250 | 104 | 47 | 94 | | | | | | |
| 300 | 095 | 54 | 97 | | | | | | |
| 350 | 088 | 59 | 98 | | | | | | |
| 400 | 082 | 64 | 99 | | | | | | |
| 450 | 078 | 68 | * | | | | | | |
| 500 | 074 | 72 | | | | | | | |
| 600 | 067 | 79 | | | | | | | |
| 700 | 062 | 84 | | | | | | | |
| 800 | 058 | 88 | | | | | | | |
| 900 | 055 | 91 | | | | | | | |
| 1000 | 052 | 94 | | | | | | | |

*   Power values below this point are greater than .995.

Table 3.3.3

Power of t test of r = 0 at $a_1$ = .10

| n | $r_c$ | .10 | .20 | .30 | .40 | .50 | .60 | .70 | .80 | .90 |
|---|---|---|---|---|---|---|---|---|---|---|
| 8 | 507 | 15 | 22 | 30 | 41 | 53 | 67 | 81 | 92 | 99 |
| 9 | 472 | 15 | 23 | 32 | 44 | 58 | 72 | 85 | 95 | 99 |
| 10 | 443 | 16 | 24 | 34 | 47 | 61 | 76 | 88 | 97 | * |
| 11 | 419 | 16 | 25 | 36 | 50 | 65 | 79 | 91 | 98 | |
| 12 | 398 | 17 | 26 | 38 | 53 | 68 | 83 | 93 | 99 | |
| 13 | 380 | 17 | 27 | 40 | 55 | 71 | 85 | 95 | 99 | |
| 14 | 365 | 17 | 28 | 42 | 58 | 74 | 87 | 96 | 99 | |
| 15 | 351 | 18 | 29 | 44 | 60 | 76 | 89 | 97 | * | |
| 16 | 338 | 18 | 30 | 45 | 62 | 79 | 90 | 98 | | |
| 17 | 327 | 19 | 31 | 47 | 64 | 81 | 92 | 98 | | |
| 18 | 317 | 19 | 32 | 49 | 66 | 82 | 93 | 98 | | |
| 19 | 308 | 19 | 33 | 50 | 68 | 84 | 94 | 99 | | |
| 20 | 299 | 20 | 34 | 52 | 70 | 86 | 95 | 99 | | |
| 21 | 291 | 20 | 35 | 53 | 72 | 87 | 96 | 99 | | |
| 22 | 284 | 20 | 36 | 54 | 73 | 88 | 97 | 99 | | |
| 23 | 277 | 21 | 36 | 56 | 75 | 89 | 97 | * | | |
| 24 | 271 | 21 | 37 | 57 | 76 | 90 | 98 | | | |
| 25 | 265 | 21 | 38 | 58 | 78 | 91 | 98 | | | |
| 26 | 260 | 22 | 39 | 59 | 79 | 92 | 98 | | | |
| 27 | 255 | 22 | 40 | 61 | 80 | 93 | 99 | | | |
| 28 | 250 | 22 | 40 | 62 | 81 | 94 | 99 | | | |
| 29 | 245 | 23 | 41 | 63 | 82 | 94 | 99 | | | |
| 30 | 241 | 23 | 42 | 64 | 83 | 95 | 99 | | | |
| 31 | 237 | 23 | 43 | 65 | 84 | 95 | 99 | | | |
| 32 | 233 | 23 | 43 | 66 | 85 | 96 | 99 | | | |
| 33 | 229 | 24 | 44 | 67 | 86 | 96 | 99 | | | |
| 34 | 225 | 24 | 45 | 68 | 87 | 97 | * | | | |
| 35 | 222 | 24 | 45 | 69 | 88 | 97 | | | | |
| 36 | 219 | 24 | 46 | 70 | 88 | 97 | | | | |
| 37 | 216 | 25 | 47 | 71 | 89 | 98 | | | | |
| 38 | 213 | 25 | 48 | 72 | 90 | 98 | | | | |
| 39 | 210 | 25 | 48 | 73 | 90 | 98 | | | | |
| 40 | 207 | 25 | 49 | 74 | 91 | 98 | | | | |
| 42 | 202 | 26 | 50 | 75 | 92 | 99 | | | | |
| 44 | 197 | 26 | 51 | 77 | 93 | 99 | | | | |
| 46 | 192 | 27 | 53 | 78 | 94 | 99 | | | | |
| 48 | 188 | 27 | 54 | 79 | 94 | 99 | | | | |

Table 3.3.3 *(continued)*

| n | $r_c$ | .10 | .20 | .30 | .40 | .50 | .60 | .70 | .80 | .90 |
|---|---|---|---|---|---|---|---|---|---|---|
| | | | | | | | | r | | |
| 50 | 184 | 28 | 55 | 81 | 95 | 99 | * | * | * | * |
| 52 | 181 | 28 | 56 | 82 | 96 | * | | | | |
| 54 | 177 | 29 | 57 | 83 | 96 | | | | | |
| 56 | 174 | 29 | 58 | 84 | 97 | | | | | |
| 58 | 171 | 30 | 59 | 85 | 97 | | | | | |
| 60 | 168 | 30 | 60 | 86 | 97 | | | | | |
| 64 | 162 | 31 | 62 | 88 | 98 | | | | | |
| 68 | 157 | 32 | 64 | 89 | 98 | | | | | |
| 72 | 153 | 33 | 66 | 90 | 99 | | | | | |
| 76 | 149 | 34 | 68 | 92 | 99 | | | | | |
| 80 | 145 | 35 | 70 | 93 | 99 | | | | | |
| 84 | 141 | 36 | 71 | 94 | * | | | | | |
| 88 | 138 | 36 | 73 | 95 | | | | | | |
| 92 | 135 | 37 | 74 | 95 | | | | | | |
| 96 | 132 | 38 | 75 | 96 | | | | | | |
| 100 | 129 | 39 | 76 | 96 | | | | | | |
| 120 | 118 | 42 | 82 | 98 | | | | | | |
| 140 | 109 | 46 | 86 | 99 | | | | | | |
| 160 | 102 | 49 | 90 | * | | | | | | |
| 180 | 096 | 52 | 92 | | | | | | | |
| 200 | 091 | 55 | 94 | | | | | | | |
| 250 | 081 | 62 | 97 | | | | | | | |
| 300 | 074 | 67 | 99 | | | | | | | |
| 350 | 069 | 72 | 99 | | | | | | | |
| 400 | 064 | 76 | * | | | | | | | |
| 450 | 061 | 80 | | | | | | | | |
| 500 | 057 | 83 | | | | | | | | |
| 600 | 052 | 88 | | | | | | | | |
| 700 | 048 | 91 | | | | | | | | |
| 800 | 045 | 94 | | | | | | | | |
| 900 | 043 | 96 | | | | | | | | |
| 1000 | 041 | 97 | | | | | | | | |

* Power values below this point are greater than .995.

Table 3.3.4

Power of t test of r = 0 at $a_2$ = .01

| n | $r_c$ | .10 | .20 | .30 | .40 | .50 | .60 | .70 | .80 | .90 |
|---|---|---|---|---|---|---|---|---|---|---|
| 8 | 834 | 01 | 02 | 03 | 05 | 08 | 14 | 26 | 47 | 80 |
| 9 | 798 | 01 | 02 | 03 | 06 | 10 | 18 | 32 | 56 | 88 |
| 10 | 765 | 01 | 02 | 04 | 07 | 12 | 22 | 40 | 65 | 93 |
| 11 | 735 | 01 | 02 | 04 | 08 | 15 | 27 | 46 | 73 | 96 |
| 12 | 708 | 01 | 02 | 05 | 09 | 17 | 31 | 52 | 79 | 97 |
| 13 | 684 | 01 | 03 | 05 | 10 | 20 | 35 | 58 | 84 | 99 |
| 14 | 661 | 01 | 03 | 06 | 12 | 22 | 40 | 64 | 87 | 99 |
| 15 | 641 | 01 | 03 | 06 | 13 | 25 | 44 | 68 | 90 | * |
| 16 | 623 | 01 | 03 | 07 | 14 | 28 | 48 | 73 | 93 | |
| 17 | 606 | 01 | 03 | 08 | 16 | 30 | 52 | 77 | 95 | |
| 18 | 590 | 01 | 04 | 08 | 17 | 33 | 56 | 80 | 96 | |
| 19 | 575 | 02 | 04 | 09 | 19 | 36 | 59 | 83 | 97 | |
| 20 | 561 | 02 | 04 | 09 | 20 | 38 | 62 | 85 | 98 | |
| 21 | 549 | 02 | 04 | 10 | 21 | 41 | 66 | 88 | 98 | |
| 22 | 537 | 02 | 04 | 11 | 23 | 43 | 68 | 90 | 99 | |
| 23 | 526 | 02 | 04 | 12 | 25 | 46 | 71 | 91 | 99 | |
| 24 | 515 | 02 | 05 | 12 | 26 | 49 | 74 | 93 | 99 | |
| 25 | 505 | 02 | 05 | 13 | 28 | 51 | 76 | 94 | * | |
| 26 | 496 | 02 | 05 | 14 | 30 | 53 | 78 | 95 | | |
| 27 | 487 | 02 | 06 | 14 | 31 | 55 | 80 | 96 | | |
| 28 | 479 | 02 | 06 | 15 | 33 | 57 | 82 | 96 | | |
| 29 | 471 | 02 | 06 | 16 | 34 | 60 | 84 | 97 | | |
| 30 | 463 | 02 | 06 | 17 | 36 | 62 | 85 | 98 | | |
| 31 | 456 | 02 | 07 | 17 | 37 | 64 | 87 | 98 | | |
| 32 | 449 | 02 | 07 | 18 | 39 | 66 | 88 | 98 | | |
| 33 | 442 | 02 | 07 | 19 | 40 | 67 | 89 | 99 | | |
| 34 | 436 | 02 | 07 | 20 | 42 | 69 | 90 | 99 | | |
| 35 | 430 | 02 | 08 | 20 | 43 | 71 | 91 | 99 | | |
| 36 | 424 | 02 | 08 | 21 | 45 | 72 | 92 | 99 | | |
| 37 | 417 | 02 | 08 | 22 | 47 | 74 | 93 | 99 | | |
| 38 | 413 | 02 | 08 | 23 | 48 | 76 | 94 | * | | |
| 39 | 408 | 02 | 09 | 24 | 49 | 77 | 95 | | | |
| 40 | 403 | 02 | 09 | 25 | 50 | 78 | 95 | | | |
| 42 | 393 | 03 | 09 | 26 | 53 | 81 | 96 | | | |
| 44 | 384 | 03 | 10 | 28 | 56 | 83 | 97 | | | |
| 46 | 376 | 03 | 11 | 29 | 58 | 85 | 98 | | | |
| 48 | 368 | 03 | 11 | 31 | 61 | 87 | 98 | | | |

Table 3.3.4 *(continued)*

| n | $r_c$ | .10 | .20 | .30 | .40 | .50 | .60 | .70 | .80 | .90 |
|---|---|---|---|---|---|---|---|---|---|---|
| | | | | | | *r* | | | | |
| 50 | 361 | 03 | 12 | 33 | 63 | 89 | 99 | * | * | * |
| 52 | 354 | 03 | 12 | 34 | 66 | 90 | 99 | | | |
| 54 | 348 | 03 | 13 | 36 | 68 | 91 | 99 | | | |
| 56 | 341 | 03 | 14 | 38 | 70 | 93 | 99 | | | |
| 58 | 336 | 03 | 14 | 39 | 72 | 94 | * | | | |
| 60 | 330 | 03 | 15 | 41 | 74 | 94 | | | | |
| 64 | 320 | 04 | 16 | 44 | 77 | 96 | | | | |
| 68 | 310 | 04 | 17 | 47 | 80 | 97 | | | | |
| 72 | 302 | 04 | 19 | 50 | 83 | 98 | | | | |
| 76 | 294 | 04 | 20 | 53 | 85 | 98 | | | | |
| 80 | 286 | 04 | 21 | 56 | 87 | 99 | | | | |
| 84 | 280 | 05 | 23 | 59 | 89 | 99 | | | | |
| 88 | 273 | 05 | 24 | 61 | 91 | 99 | | | | |
| 92 | 267 | 05 | 25 | 64 | 92 | * | | | | |
| 96 | 262 | 05 | 27 | 66 | 94 | | | | | |
| 100 | 256 | 06 | 29 | 69 | 95 | | | | | |
| 120 | 234 | 07 | 35 | 78 | 98 | | | | | |
| 140 | 217 | 08 | 42 | 85 | 99 | | | | | |
| 160 | 203 | 09 | 49 | 90 | * | | | | | |
| 180 | 192 | 11 | 55 | 94 | | | | | | |
| 200 | 182 | 12 | 61 | 96 | | | | | | |
| 250 | 163 | 16 | 73 | 99 | | | | | | |
| 300 | 149 | 20 | 82 | * | | | | | | |
| 350 | 138 | 24 | 89 | | | | | | | |
| 400 | 129 | 28 | 93 | | | | | | | |
| 450 | 121 | 32 | 96 | | | | | | | |
| 500 | 115 | 37 | 97 | | | | | | | |
| 600 | 105 | 45 | 99 | | | | | | | |
| 700 | 097 | 53 | * | | | | | | | |
| 800 | 091 | 60 | | | | | | | | |
| 900 | 086 | 67 | | | | | | | | |
| 1000 | 081 | 72 | | | | | | | | |

*   Power values below this point are greater than .995.

Table 3.3.5

Power of t test of r = 0 at $a_2$ = .05

| n | $r_c$ | .10 | .20 | .30 | .40 | .50 | .60 | .70 | .80 | .90 |
|---|---|---|---|---|---|---|---|---|---|---|
| 8 | 707 | 06 | 07 | 11 | 16 | 25 | 37 | 54 | 75 | 94 |
| 9 | 666 | 06 | 08 | 12 | 19 | 29 | 43 | 62 | 82 | 97 |
| 10 | 632 | 06 | 08 | 13 | 21 | 33 | 49 | 68 | 87 | 98 |
| 11 | 602 | 06 | 09 | 14 | 23 | 36 | 54 | 73 | 91 | 99 |
| 12 | 576 | 06 | 09 | 16 | 26 | 40 | 58 | 78 | 93 | 99 |
| 13 | 553 | 06 | 10 | 17 | 28 | 44 | 63 | 82 | 95 | * |
| 14 | 532 | 06 | 10 | 18 | 30 | 47 | 66 | 85 | 96 | |
| 15 | 514 | 06 | 11 | 19 | 32 | 50 | 70 | 88 | 98 | |
| 16 | 497 | 07 | 11 | 21 | 35 | 53 | 73 | 90 | 98 | |
| 17 | 482 | 07 | 12 | 22 | 37 | 56 | 76 | 92 | 99 | |
| 18 | 468 | 07 | 12 | 23 | 39 | 59 | 79 | 94 | 99 | |
| 19 | 456 | .07 | 13 | 24 | 41 | 62 | 81 | 95 | 99 | |
| 20 | 444 | 07 | 14 | 25 | 43 | 64 | 83 | 96 | * | |
| 21 | 433 | 07 | 14 | 27 | 45 | 66 | 85 | 96 | | |
| 22 | 423 | 07 | 15 | 28 | 47 | 69 | 87 | 97 | | |
| 23 | 413 | 07 | 15 | 29 | 49 | 71 | 89 | 98 | | |
| 24 | 404 | .07 | 16 | 30 | 51 | 73 | 90 | 98 | | |
| 25 | 396 | 08 | 16 | 31 | 53 | 75 | 91 | 99 | | |
| 26 | 388 | 08 | 17 | 33 | 54 | 76 | 92 | 99 | | |
| 27 | 381 | 08 | 17 | 34 | 56 | 78 | 93 | 99 | | |
| 28 | 374 | 08 | 18 | 35 | 58 | 80 | 94 | 99 | | |
| 29 | 367 | 08 | 18 | 36 | 59 | 81 | 95 | 99 | | |
| 30 | 361 | 08 | 19 | 37 | 61 | 83 | 95 | * | | |
| 31 | 355 | 08 | 19 | 38 | 62 | 84 | 96 | | | |
| 32 | 349 | 08 | 20 | 39 | 64 | 85 | 97 | | | |
| 33 | 344 | 09 | 20 | 40 | 65 | 86 | 97 | | | |
| 34 | 339 | 09 | 21 | 42 | 67 | 87 | 97 | | | |
| 35 | 334 | 09 | 21 | 43 | 68 | 88 | 98 | | | |
| 36 | 329 | 09 | 22 | 44 | 69 | 89 | 98 | | | |
| 37 | 325 | 09 | 22 | 45 | 70 | 90 | 98 | | | |
| 38 | 320 | 09 | 23 | 46 | 72 | 91 | 99 | | | |
| 39 | 316 | 09 | 23 | 47 | 73 | 91 | 99 | | | |
| 40 | 312 | 09 | 24 | 48 | 74 | 92 | 99 | | | |
| 42 | 304 | 10 | 25 | 50 | 76 | 93 | 99 | | | |
| 44 | 297 | 10 | 26 | 52 | 78 | 94 | 99 | | | |
| 46 | 291 | 10 | 27 | 54 | 80 | 95 | * | | | |
| 48 | 285 | 10 | 28 | 55 | 82 | 96 | | | | |

Table 3.3.5 *(continued)*

| n | $r_c$ | .10 | .20 | .30 | .40 | .50 | .60 | .70 | .80 | .90 |
|---|---|---|---|---|---|---|---|---|---|---|
| | | | | | | | | | r | |
| 50 | 279 | 11 | 29 | 57 | 83 | 97 | * | * | * | * |
| 52 | 273 | 11 | 30 | 59 | 85 | 97 | | | | |
| 54 | 268 | 11 | 31 | 61 | 86 | 98 | | | | |
| 56 | 263 | 11 | 32 | 62 | 87 | 98 | | | | |
| 58 | 259 | 12 | 33 | 64 | 89 | 98 | | | | |
| 60 | 254 | 12 | 34 | 65 | 90 | 99 | | | | |
| 64 | 246 | 12 | 36 | 68 | 91 | 99 | | | | |
| 68 | 239 | 13 | 38 | 71 | 93 | 99 | | | | |
| 72 | 232 | 13 | 39 | 73 | 94 | * | | | | |
| 76 | 226 | 14 | 41 | 76 | 95 | | | | | |
| 80 | 220 | 14 | 43 | 78 | 96 | | | | | |
| 84 | 215 | 15 | 45 | 80 | 97 | | | | | |
| 88 | 210 | 15 | 47 | 82 | 98 | | | | | |
| 92 | 205 | 16 | 48 | 83 | 98 | | | | | |
| 96 | 201 | 16 | 50 | 85 | 98 | | | | | |
| 100 | 197 | 17 | 52 | 86 | 99 | | | | | |
| 120 | 179 | 19 | 59 | 92 | * | | | | | |
| 140 | 166 | 22 | 66 | 95 | | | | | | |
| 160 | 155 | 24 | 72 | 97 | | | | | | |
| 180 | 146 | 27 | 77 | 98 | | | | | | |
| 200 | 139 | 29 | 81 | 99 | | | | | | |
| 250 | 124 | 35 | 89 | * | | | | | | |
| 300 | 113 | 41 | 94 | | | | | | | |
| 350 | 105 | 46 | 97 | | | | | | | |
| 400 | 098 | 52 | 98 | | | | | | | |
| 450 | 092 | 56 | 99 | | | | | | | |
| 500 | 088 | 61 | 99 | | | | | | | |
| 600 | 080 | 69 | * | | | | | | | |
| 700 | 074 | 76 | | | | | | | | |
| 800 | 069 | 81 | | | | | | | | |
| 900 | 065 | 85 | | | | | | | | |
| 1000 | 062 | 89 | | | | | | | | |

*   Power values below this point are greater than .995.

**Table 3.3.6**

Power of t test of r = 0 at $a_2$ = .10

| | | | | | | r | | | | |
|---|---|---|---|---|---|---|---|---|---|---|
| n | $r_c$ | .10 | .20 | .30 | .40 | .50 | .60 | .70 | .80 | .90 |
| 8 | 621 | 11 | 14 | 19 | 27 | 38 | 52 | 68 | 85 | 97 |
| 9 | 582 | 11 | 15 | 21 | 30 | 42 | 57 | 74 | 90 | 99 |
| 10 | 549 | 11 | 15 | 22 | 33 | 46 | 62 | 79 | 93 | 99 |
| 11 | 521 | 12 | 16 | 24 | 35 | 50 | 67 | 83 | 95 | * |
| 12 | 497 | 12 | 17 | 25 | 38 | 54 | 71 | 87 | 97 | |
| 13 | 476 | 12 | 17 | 27 | 40 | 57 | 74 | 89 | 98 | |
| 14 | 458 | 12 | 18 | 28 | 43 | 60 | 78 | 91 | 98 | |
| 15 | 441 | 12 | 19 | 30 | 45 | 63 | 81 | 93 | 99 | |
| 16 | 426 | 12 | 19 | 31 | 48 | 66 | 83 | 95 | 99 | |
| 17 | 412 | 13 | 20 | 33 | 50 | 69 | 85 | 96 | * | |
| 18 | 400 | 13 | 21 | 34 | 52 | 71 | 87 | 97 | | |
| 19 | 389 | 13 | 22 | 36 | 54 | 73 | 89 | 97 | | |
| 20 | 378 | 13 | 22 | 37 | 56 | 75 | 90 | 98 | | |
| 21 | 369 | 13 | 23 | 39 | 58 | 77 | 92 | 98 | | |
| 22 | 360 | 13 | 24 | 40 | 60 | 79 | 93 | 99 | | |
| 23 | 352 | 14 | 24 | 41 | 62 | 81 | 94 | 99 | | |
| 24 | 344 | 14 | 25 | 42 | 64 | 83 | 95 | 99 | | |
| 25 | 337 | 14 | 26 | 44 | 65 | 84 | 95 | 99 | | |
| 26 | 330 | 14 | 26 | 45 | 67 | 85 | 96 | * | | |
| 27 | 323 | 14 | 27 | 46 | 68 | 86 | 96 | | | |
| 28 | 317 | 14 | 27 | 47 | 70 | 88 | 97 | | | |
| 29 | 311 | 15 | 28 | 49 | 71 | 89 | 97 | | | |
| 30 | 306 | 15 | 29 | 50 | 72 | 90 | 98 | | | |
| 31 | 301 | 15 | 29 | 51 | 74 | 90 | 98 | | | |
| 32 | 296 | 15 | 30 | 52 | 75 | 91 | 98 | | | |
| 33 | 291 | 15 | 31 | 53 | 76 | 92 | 99 | | | |
| 34 | 287 | 15 | 31 | 54 | 77 | 93 | 99 | | | |
| 35 | 283 | 16 | 32 | 55 | 78 | 93 | 99 | | | |
| 36 | 279 | 16 | 32 | 56 | 79 | 94 | 99 | | | |
| 37 | 275 | 16 | 33 | 57 | 80 | 95 | 99 | | | |
| 38 | 271 | 16 | 34 | 58 | 81 | 95 | 99 | | | |
| 39 | 267 | 16 | 34 | 59 | 82 | 95 | * | | | |
| 40 | 264 | 16 | 35 | 60 | 83 | 96 | | | | |
| 42 | 257 | 17 | 36 | 62 | 85 | 97 | | | | |
| 44 | 251 | 17 | 37 | 64 | 86 | 97 | | | | |
| 46 | 246 | 17 | 38 | 66 | 88 | 98 | | | | |
| 48 | 240 | 18 | 39 | 67 | 89 | 98 | | | | |

Table 3.3.6 *(continued)*

| n | $r_c$ | | .10 | .20 | .30 | .40 | .50 | .60 | .70 | .80 | .90 |
|---|---|---|---|---|---|---|---|---|---|---|---|
| | | **r** | | | | | | | | | |
| 50 | 235 | | 18 | 41 | 69 | 90 | 98 | * | * | * | * |
| 52 | 231 | | 18 | 42 | 71 | 91 | 99 | | | | |
| 54 | 226 | | 19 | 43 | 72 | 92 | 99 | | | | |
| 56 | 222 | | 19 | 44 | 73 | 93 | 99 | | | | |
| 58 | 218 | | 19 | 45 | 75 | 94 | 99 | | | | |
| 60 | 214 | | 20 | 46 | 76 | 94 | 99 | | | | |
| 64 | 207 | | 20 | 48 | 79 | 95 | * | | | | |
| 68 | 201 | | 21 | 50 | 81 | 96 | | | | | |
| 72 | 195 | | 22 | 52 | 83 | 97 | | | | | |
| 76 | 190 | | 22 | 54 | 85 | 98 | | | | | |
| 80 | 185 | | 23 | 56 | 86 | 98 | | | | | |
| 84 | 181 | | 24 | 58 | 88 | 99 | | | | | |
| 88 | 176 | | 24 | 59 | 89 | 99 | | | | | |
| 92 | 173 | | 25 | 61 | 90 | 99 | | | | | |
| 96 | 169 | | 26 | 63 | 91 | 99 | | | | | |
| 100 | 165 | | 27 | 64 | 92 | 99 | | | | | |
| 120 | 151 | | 29 | 71 | 96 | * | | | | | |
| 140 | 140 | | 32 | 77 | 98 | | | | | | |
| 160 | 130 | | 35 | 82 | 99 | | | | | | |
| 180 | 123 | | 38 | 86 | 99 | | | | | | |
| 200 | 117 | | 41 | 89 | * | | | | | | |
| 250 | 104 | | 47 | 94 | | | | | | | |
| 300 | 095 | | 54 | 97 | | | | | | | |
| 350 | 088 | | 59 | 98 | | | | | | | |
| 400 | 082 | | 64 | 99 | | | | | | | |
| 450 | 078 | | 68 | * | | | | | | | |
| 500 | 074 | | 72 | | | | | | | | |
| 600 | 067 | | 79 | | | | | | | | |
| 700 | 062 | | 84 | | | | | | | | |
| 800 | 058 | | 88 | | | | | | | | |
| 900 | 055 | | 91 | | | | | | | | |
| 1000 | 052 | | 94 | | | | | | | | |

* Power values below this point are greater than .995.

**Illustrative Examples**

3.1  A personality psychologist has performed an experiment in which he obtained paired measures on a sample of 50 subjects. One of these variables is a questionnaire score on extraversion, the other a neurophysiological measure which his theory posits should relate to the former. His hypothesis is formulated as nondirectional and he selects $a_2 = .05$ as his significance criterion. Although his theory dictates a strong relationship, unreliability and lack of high construct validity of his measures (e.g., social desirability variance in his questionnaire measure) lead him to expect only a medium ES, hence he posits $r = .30$ ($PV = r^2 = .09$). What is the power of the test of the significance of $r_s$ he performs? His specifications are

$$a_2 = .05, \qquad r = .30, \qquad n = 50.$$

In Table 3.3.5 (for $a_2 = .05$), column $r = .30$, row $n = 50$, power $= .57$. Thus, a significance test with 50 subjects at an $a_2 = .05$ criterion has not much more than a 50–50 chance of rejecting the null hypothesis when the population $r = .30$.

It may be argued that a theory which leads to so nonobvious a prediction as the correlation of measured electrical events in the nervous system with responses to complex social and intrapersonal questionnaire items combined in a certain specific way, should at least predict the *direction* of the association. Indeed it does—it predicts a positive correlation. If the investigator would have been prepared to renounce all interest in discovering an unanticipated *negative* correlation (if such, despite his theory, should be the case), he would have formulated his null and alternate hypothesis directionally ($H_0$: $r \leq 0$, $H_1$: $r = + .30$) and, leaving his other conditions unchanged, may have instead used a one-tailed significance criterion, thus:

$$a_1 = .05, \qquad r = .30, \qquad n = 50.$$

In Table 3.3.2 for $a_1 = .05$ (instead of Table 3.3.5 for $a_2 = .05$), column $r = .30$, row $n = 50$, power $= .69$. The use of a directional instead of a non-directional test under these conditions (of **a**, **r**, and **n**) would result in his chance of rejecting the null hypothesis being improved from .57 to .69. Note that the formulation of this illustration is *not* intended to suggest any manipulation of the directionality of the test *after* the data are gathered. This is properly formulated in advance and maintained. However, these tables may be used in experimental planning for seeking an optimum strategy. This could include the decision as to whether to state the hypothesis directionally or nondirectionally and would lead to such comparisons as the above. If we take this to be the case in the above example, the psychologist would then need to decide whether, under the given conditions, the gain in power from .57 to .69 is worth forgoing the possibility of concluding that **r** is negative. This decision will be made, of course, on substantive and not statistical grounds.

**3.2**  An educational psychologist is consulted by the dean responsible for admission at a small college with regard to the desirability of supplementing their criterion for admission by using a personality questionnaire. The plan is to administer the test to entering freshmen and determine whether scores on this test (**X**) correlate with freshman year grade point average (**Y**). Following discussion it is determined that it can be assumed that for entering freshmen, **X** is not correlated with the selection criterion, so that its correlation with **Y**, if any, represents incremental validity beyond present selection practices.  The decision is made that if **r** = .10, then it is worth adding to the selection procedure. Each annual freshmen class numbers about 500. The educational psychologist first seeks to determine power under these conditions if the decision to proceed is made at the $a_2 = .01$ and $a_2 = .05$ criteria. Her specifications are

$$a_2 = .01, \quad r = .10, \quad n = 500,$$
$$a_2 = .05, \quad r = .10, \quad n = 500.$$

In Table 3.3.4 for $a_2 = .01$, with column **r** = .10 and row **n** = 500, power = .37. Then in Table 3.3.5 (for $a_2 = .05$) for the same column and row, power = .61.

The educational psychologist finds herself dissatisfied with these results, since, even with the $a_2 = .05$ risk, she has only a three in five chance of detecting **r** = .10. She checks the consequence of $a_2 = .10$ (Table 3.3.6) for these conditions and finds power = .72, the same as for $a_1 = .10$ (Table 3.3.2). Thus, even if she were to use an $a_2 = .10$ criterion (which she and the dean judge to be too large a risk in this situation), or an $a_1 = .05$ criterion (which would mean eliminating the possibility of a valid conclusion that **r** is of sign opposite from the one anticipated), she would have power of not quite three in four. Since even liberalizing conditions which are unacceptable in the situation yield power values not as high as desired, she turns to other possibilities.

The psychologist considers an experimental plan which involves combining the data for two successive years, so that **n** will equal about 1000. The conditions now are

$$a_2 = .01, \quad r = .10, \quad n = 1000,$$
$$a_2 = .05, \quad r = .10, \quad n = 1000.$$

She uses Table 3.3.4 (for $a_2 = .01$), with column r = .10 and row n = 1000, and finds power = .72. Then, she considers Table 3.3.5 (for $a_2 = .05$) and finds power = 89. She suggests to the dean that if two successive years' admissions can be used (resulting in an additional year's delay) and that if the alpha risk of $a_2 = .05$ is acceptably small, that a population $r = .10$ can be detected with probability of almost nine in ten. The dean might well find this procedure acceptable.

It may be noted that if **X** has a higher correlation with **Y** in the population, say $r = .20$, the various conditions posited above yield power values as follows:

|  | n = 500 | n = 1000 |
|---|---|---|
| (Table 3.3.4)   $a_2 = .01$ | .97 | >.995 |
| (Table 3.3.5)   $a_2 = .05$ | .99 | >.995 |
| (Table 3.3.6)   $a_2 = .10$ ($a_1 = .05$) | >.995 | >.995 |

It is obvious that if **r** is as large as .20, it hardly matters what alpha criterion is chosen, and, moreover, it would certainly not pay to delay an additional year to bring **n** from 500 to 1000. This illustrates how crucial the ES decision may be in experimental planning.

**3.3**   An industrial psychologist is asked to perform an investigation of the relationship between weekly wages (which vary as a function of training and experience) and work output for a given job. The client's purpose is to decide on wage and qualification policy in a new venture. The economics of the situation are such that if an additional dollar a week in wage (**X**) is accompanied by as much as an additional 4 units (**Y**) of work output, it would be advantageous to hire the best qualified workers who will require the maximum salary. The ES is thus formulated in terms of a regression coefficient $B_{YX} = 4$. The industrial psychologist can obtain appropriate data on **n** = 120 workers and plans to perform a one-tailed test at the .01 level. The one-tailed test is justified on the grounds that the situation does not require distinguishing between a zero and a negative relationship in the null hypothesis—either will lead to the same decision (see Section 1.2 and Cohen, 1965, pp. 106–111, and ref.).

Since the ES is a regression coefficient, in order to use Tables 3.3 and 3.4.1, it must be converted into **r**. For this, values or estimates of the relevant population standard deviations of **X** and **Y** are needed. Assume these values are available, and are $\sigma_X = 8$ and $\sigma_Y = 80$. Thus, from formula (3.1.3),

$$r = B_{YX} \frac{\sigma_X}{\sigma_Y} = (4) \frac{8}{80} = .40.$$

Thus, the specifications are

$$a_1 = .01, \qquad r = .40, \qquad n = 120.$$

In Table 3.3.1 (for $a_1 = .01$), with column $r = .40$ and row $n = 120$, power $= .99$. Thus, if the relationship in the population is such that a dollar increase in weekly pay is associated with an increase of 4 work units (which, given $\sigma_Y$ and $\sigma_X$, implies $r = .40$), then, with $n = 120$, the probability that he will reject the null hypothesis at the $a_1 = .01$ criterion is .99. Note that these conditions happen to yield equality of alpha and beta risks at .01, a result which can, of course, be directly sought. For this, the sample size Tables (3.4.1) are somewhat more convenient.

## 3.4 SAMPLE SIZE TABLES

The tables in this section list values for the significance criterion, the $r$ ( $=$ ES) to be detected, and the *desired power*. The number of paired observations ($X$, $Y$) required in the sample, $n$, is then completely determined. These tables are designed primarily for use in the planning of experiments, during which the decision on sample size is made. As already noted (Section 2.4), a rational decision on sample size requires, after the significance criterion and ES are formulated, attention to the question: How much power (or how little Type II error risk) is desired?

The use of these tables is subject to the same assumptions of normality and homoscedasticity as those applying to the power tables in the previous section (see Section 3.1). Tables give values for $a$, $r$, and desired power:

*1. Significance Criterion*, $a$. The same values of $a$ are provided as for the power tables. Five tables are provided, one for each of the following nonparenthetic $a$ levels: $a_1 = .01$ ($a_2 = .02$), $a_1 = .05$ ($a_2 = .10$), $a_1 = .10$ ($a_2 = .20$), $a_2 = .01$ ($a_1 = .005$), and $a_2 = .05$ ($a_1 = .025$).

*2. Effect Size, ES*. The population $r$ serves as ES. For problems in which the effect size is expressed as a regression coefficient, it is converted to $r$ by means of formula (3.1.3). The same provision for $r$ is made as in the power tables: .10 (.10) .90. For $r$ values other than the nine provided, the following formula, rounding to the nearest integer, provides an excellent approximation[5]:

$$(3.4.1) \qquad n = n_{.10} \left( \frac{.100}{z} \right)^2 + 2,$$

where $n_{.10}$ is the necessary sample size for the given $a$ and desired power at $r = .10$ (obtained from the table), and $z$ is the Fisher $z$ transformation for

[5] A check on formula (3.4.1) was made by applying it to the 96 values for $a_1 = .005$, .025, .050, and .010, $r = .20$ (.10) .90 at power levels .50, .80, and .99. The mean discrepancy from the *rounded* values of Tables 3.4 was $+.01$, with a standard deviation of .46. No discrepancy exceeded 1.1. Since rounding error alone would result in a standard deviation of discrepancies of .29, the approximation is more than adequate.

the nontabled **r** value. The constant .100 is the value of the **z** transformation when **r** = .10. Discussion of the Fisher **z** transformation is found in many statistics textbooks (e.g., Hays, 1981). The next chapter contains an **r** to **z** transformation table (4.2.2).

*3. Desired Power.* As in Chapter 2, provision is made for desired power values of .25, .50, .60, $\frac{2}{3}$, .70 (.05), .95, .99. For discussion of the basis for selecting these values, the provision for equalizing **a** and **b** risks, and the rationale of a proposed convention of desired power of .80, see Section 2.4.

Summarizing the use of the **n** tables which follow, the investigator finds (*a*) the table for the significance criterion (**a**) he is using, and locates (*b*) the population **r** along the horizontal stub and (*c*) the desired power along the vertical stub. **n**, the necessary sample size to detect **r** at the **a** significance criterion with the desired power, is then determined. If the **r** value in his specifications is not provided in the tables, he (*a*) finds the table for the significance criterion he is using, and (*b*) enters it in column **r** = .10 and row for desired power, and reads out $n_{.10}$. He then finds in Table 4.2.2 of the next chapter the Fisher **z** value for his **r**, and enters it and $n_{.10}$ in formula (3.4.1) to compute **n**.

It should be noted that these tables are not valid under conditions of range restriciton such as may occur in personnel selection. See Schmidt, Hunter, and Urry (1976), Raju, Edwards, and LoVerde (1985), Alexander, Carson, Alliger, and Barrett (1985), and their references.

## Illustrative Examples

**3.4** Reconsider the conditions of example 3.1, in which a personality psychologist is concerned with the relationship between a neurophysiological measure and a questionnaire score on extraversion. As originally described, he wishes to detect an ES of **r** = .30 at $a_2$ = .05. His plan to use **n** = 50 subjects resulted in a power estimate of .57. He will almost certainly consider this value too low. Assume that he wishes power to be at the conventional .80 value and wants to know the sample size necessary for this. The specifications are

$$a_2 = .05, \qquad r = .30, \qquad power = .80.$$

In Table 3.4.1 for $a_2$ = .05, column **r** = .30, row power = .80, he finds **n** = 85. Thus, with these specifications of **a** and **r**, he will require 85 subjects to achieve power of .80.

What if this psychologist had instead anticipated a strong relationship between the two variables, **r** = .50 (our operational definition of a large ES), using the same **a** and power:

$$a_2 = .05, \qquad r = .50, \qquad power = .80.$$

**Table 3.4.1**
n to detect r by t test

| | | | | | | | | | |
|---|---|---|---|---|---|---|---|---|---|
| | $a_1 = .01$ ($a_2 = .02$) | | | | | | | | |
| | | | | | r | | | | |
| Power | .10 | .20 | .30 | .40 | .50 | .60 | .70 | .80 | .90 |
| .25 | 274 | 69 | 31 | 18 | 12 | 9 | 7 | 5 | 4 |
| .50 | 541 | 135 | 59 | 31 | 20 | 14 | 10 | 7 | 5 |
| .60 | 664 | 165 | 72 | 39 | 24 | 16 | 11 | 8 | 6 |
| 2/3 | 758 | 188 | 82 | 44 | 28 | 18 | 13 | 9 | 6 |
| .70 | 810 | 201 | 88 | 48 | 29 | 19 | 13 | 9 | 6 |
| .75 | 897 | 222 | 97 | 53 | 32 | 21 | 14 | 10 | 7 |
| .80 | 1000 | 247 | 108 | 59 | 36 | 23 | 16 | 11 | 7 |
| .85 | 1126 | 278 | 121 | 66 | 40 | 26 | 17 | 12 | 8 |
| .90 | 1296 | 320 | 139 | 76 | 45 | 29 | 20 | 13 | 8 |
| .95 | 1570 | 387 | 168 | 91 | 55 | 35 | 23 | 16 | 10 |
| .99 | 2153 | 530 | 229 | 124 | 75 | 47 | 31 | 20 | 13 |
| | $a_1 = .05$ ($a_2 = .10$) | | | | | | | | |
| | | | | | r | | | | |
| Power | .10 | .20 | .30 | .40 | .50 | .60 | .70 | .80 | .90 |
| .25 | 97 | 24 | 12 | 8 | 6 | 4 | 4 | 3 | 3 |
| .50 | 272 | 69 | 30 | 17 | 11 | 8 | 6 | 5 | 4 |
| .60 | 361 | 91 | 40 | 22 | 14 | 10 | 7 | 5 | 4 |
| 2/3 | 431 | 108 | 47 | 26 | 16 | 11 | 8 | 6 | 4 |
| .70 | 470 | 117 | 52 | 28 | 18 | 12 | 8 | 6 | 4 |
| .75 | 537 | 134 | 59 | 32 | 20 | 13 | 9 | 7 | 5 |
| .80 | 617 | 153 | 68 | 37 | 22 | 15 | 10 | 7 | 5 |
| .85 | 717 | 178 | 78 | 43 | 26 | 17 | 12 | 8 | 6 |
| .90 | 854 | 211 | 92 | 50 | 31 | 20 | 13 | 9 | 6 |
| .95 | 1078 | 266 | 116 | 63 | 39 | 25 | 16 | 11 | 7 |
| .99 | 1570 | 387 | 168 | 91 | 55 | 35 | 23 | 15 | 10 |
| | $a_1 = .10$ ($a_2 = .20$) | | | | | | | | |
| | | | | | r | | | | |
| Power | .10 | .20 | .30 | .40 | .50 | .60 | .70 | .80 | .90 |
| .25 | 39 | 11 | 6 | 4 | 3 | 3 | 3 | 3 | 3 |
| .50 | 166 | 42 | 19 | 11 | 7 | 5 | 4 | 3 | 3 |
| .60 | 237 | 60 | 27 | 15 | 10 | 7 | 5 | 4 | 3 |
| 2/3 | 294 | 74 | 33 | 18 | 12 | 8 | 6 | 4 | 4 |
| .70 | 327 | 82 | 36 | 20 | 13 | 9 | 6 | 5 | 4 |
| .75 | 383 | 96 | 42 | 23 | 14 | 10 | 7 | 5 | 4 |
| .80 | 451 | 113 | 49 | 27 | 17 | 11 | 8 | 6 | 4 |
| .85 | 537 | 134 | 58 | 32 | 19 | 13 | 9 | 6 | 4 |
| .90 | 656 | 163 | 72 | 39 | 24 | 16 | 11 | 7 | 5 |
| .95 | 854 | 211 | 92 | 50 | 31 | 20 | 13 | 9 | 6 |
| .99 | 1296 | 320 | 139 | 76 | 45 | 29 | 19 | 13 | 8 |

**Table 3.4.1** (continued)

| | | | | $a_2 = .01$ ($a_1 = .005$) | | | | | |
|---|---|---|---|---|---|---|---|---|---|
| | | | | | r | | | | |
| Power | .10 | .20 | .30 | .40 | .50 | .60 | .70 | .80 | .90 |
| .25 | 362 | 91 | 40 | 23 | 15 | 11 | 8 | 6 | 5 |
| .50 | 662 | 164 | 72 | 39 | 24 | 16 | 12 | 8 | 6 |
| .60 | 797 | 198 | 87 | 47 | 29 | 19 | 13 | 9 | 7 |
| 2/3 | 901 | 223 | 97 | 53 | 32 | 21 | 15 | 10 | 7 |
| .70 | 958 | 237 | 103 | 56 | 34 | 23 | 15 | 11 | 7 |
| .75 | 1052 | 260 | 113 | 62 | 37 | 25 | 17 | 11 | 8 |
| .80 | 1163 | 287 | 125 | 68 | 41 | 27 | 18 | 12 | 8 |
| .85 | 1299 | 320 | 139 | 76 | 45 | 30 | 20 | 13 | 9 |
| .90 | 1481 | 365 | 158 | 86 | 51 | 34 | 22 | 15 | 9 |
| .95 | 1773 | 436 | 189 | 102 | 62 | 40 | 26 | 17 | 11 |
| .99 | 2390 | 588 | 254 | 137 | 82 | 52 | 34 | 23 | 13 |

| | | | | $a_2 = .05$ ($a_1 = .025$) | | | | | |
|---|---|---|---|---|---|---|---|---|---|
| | | | | | r | | | | |
| Power | .10 | .20 | .30 | .40 | .50 | .60 | .70 | .80 | .90 |
| .25 | 167 | 42 | 20 | 12 | 8 | 6 | 5 | 4 | 3 |
| .50 | 385 | 96 | 42 | 24 | 15 | 10 | 7 | 6 | 4 |
| .60 | 490 | 122 | 53 | 29 | 18 | 12 | 9 | 6 | 5 |
| 2/3 | 570 | 142 | 63 | 34 | 21 | 14 | 10 | 7 | 5 |
| .70 | 616 | 153 | 67 | 37 | 23 | 15 | 10 | 7 | 5 |
| .75 | 692 | 172 | 75 | 41 | 25 | 17 | 11 | 8 | 6 |
| .80 | 783 | 194 | 85 | 46 | 28 | 18 | 12 | 9 | 6 |
| .85 | 895 | 221 | 97 | 52 | 32 | 21 | 14 | 10 | 6 |
| .90 | 1047 | 259 | 113 | 62 | 37 | 24 | 16 | 11 | 7 |
| .95 | 1294 | 319 | 139 | 75 | 46 | 30 | 19 | 13 | 8 |
| .99 | 1828 | 450 | 195 | 105 | 64 | 40 | 27 | 18 | 11 |

The same table (Table 3.4.1 for $a_2 = .05$) for column $r = .50$, row power $= .80$ yields $n = 28$.

At the other extreme of our operational definitions, suppose he hypothesized $r = .10$ (a small ES), keeping the other specifications constant:

$$a_2 = .05, \qquad r = .10, \qquad power = .80.$$

In Table 3.4.1 for $a_2 = .05$, for $r = .10$ and power $= .80$, $n = 783$.

Again we see how crucial anticipated ES is to the decision about sample size. Over our range from large to medium to small ES, the $n$'s required go from 28 to 85 to 783. Reversing the argument, it is apparent that a decision about sample size *implies* some value for $r$ (given $a$ and desired power). Many experiments are undertaken as if the experimenter were anticipating a *very* large ES, since presumably he would not bother to do the experiment if he thought he had a low probability of rejecting the null hypothesis.

Another point incidentally illustrated here is the nonlinearity of the r scale: At any given desired power level, equal increments in r do *not* produce equal or even proportional decrements in necessary n (as is implicit in formula (3.4.1), i.e., n varies approximately as the square of the reciprocal of the z value).

Experimental planning may involve preparing tables in which, for alternative power levels, the n's necessary under varying alternative ES values and alternative a criteria are assembled from Table 3.4.1 and scrutinized in the light of the substantive issues of the research. A possible table for this example is shown in Table 3.4.2.

**Table 3.4.2**
An Example of a Sample Size Planning Table

| | Power | | | | | | | | |
| | .70 | | | .80 | | | .90 | | |
| | ES = r | | | ES = r | | | ES = r | | |
| | .20 | .30 | .40 | .20 | .30 | .40 | .20 | .30 | .40 |
|---|---|---|---|---|---|---|---|---|---|
| $a_1 = .01$ | 201 | 88 | 48 | 247 | 108 | 59 | 320 | 139 | 76 |
| $a_1 = .05$ | 117 | 52 | 28 | 153 | 68 | 37 | 211 | 92 | 50 |
| $a_1 = .10$ | 82 | 36 | 20 | 113 | 49 | 27 | 163 | 72 | 39 |
| $a_2 = .01$ | 237 | 103 | 56 | 287 | 125 | 68 | 365 | 158 | 86 |
| $a_2 = .05$ | 153 | 67 | 37 | 194 | 85 | 46 | 259 | 113 | 62 |

An experimenter with such a table before him is in a position to make a choice of an experimental plan which is consonant both with his knowledge and informed hunches of his substantive field and with statistical analytic issues. Thus, he might decide after reviewing the table that he is prepared to expend the money and effort involved in running 85 or 86 subjects, but would prefer the 85 subjects called for when he posits r = .30 at power = .80 for $a_2 = .05$ rather than the 86 called for when, with more stringent $a_2 = .01$ and greater power = .90, he must posit r = .40; he may not consider the risk of assuming r so high worth the a and power advantage. He may consider least desirable the plan which calls for n = 82, which allows for a distinctly smaller ES or r = .20, but at the cost of less power (.70) and a large, one-tailed Type I risk ($a_1 = .10$) or equivalently an even larger two-tailed Type I risk ($a_2 = .20$).

**3.5**  A social psychologist is planning an experiment in which college students selected with regard to a personality questionnaire measure (**Y**) will be subjected to various alternative communications in a study of attitude change. Before this is undertaken, however, he considers it important that it be demonstrable that his measure (**Y**) *not* be related to a questionnaire measure of social desirability (**X**). He finds himself in the apparent position of having to prove the null hypothesis that $r = 0$, which is formally impossible.

However, instead of demanding of himself the impossible proof that $r = 0$, he may revise this to an attempt to demonstrate that $r$ is trivially small, which is probably all that is ever meant by "no" relationship in behavioral science (see Section 1.5.5). He may consider an $r$ no greater absolutely than .10 as meeting this criterion in this context. It now becomes possible to mount an experiment from which the conclusion that $r$ is trivially small may properly be drawn. He sets up as the ES he wishes to detect $r = .10$. To assure himself a good chance of detecting this value if it should obtain, he demands relatively high power, say .90. Assume he is prepared to run a large risk that he will mistakenly reject $r = 0$ by setting $a_2 = .10$. He now seeks the **n** which will satisfy these specifications, which, summarized, are

$$a_2 = .10, \qquad r = .10, \qquad \text{power} = .90.$$

Table 3.4.1 for $a_1 = .05$ ($a_2 = .10$), for column $r = .10$, row power = .90, yields n = 854. (Since both **X** and **Y** are obtained by group procedures, this large sample may well be within his resources.[6])

Assume that the data are collected and he finds $r_s = .04$, which is not significant at $a_2 = .10$. He can conclude that the population $r$ is effectively zero. This is because, if the population $r$ is as large as .10, it is unlikely (**b** = 1 − power = 1 − .90 = .10) that he would have failed to find $r_s$ significant.

In this way, experiments can be organized which can accomplish what is really sought when we attempt to "prove null hypotheses." What we have done instead is to mitigate the null hypothesis to mean "trivially small" and set up this small value as the ES (alternate hypothesis) in an experiment which has enough power to detect it. If we then fail to reject the literal null hypothesis, we can conclude that the effect is negligible.

---

[6] An alternative design for the overall study, which does not depend on this **r** being trivially small (but makes other assumptions), would be a factorial design (**Y** levels by communications) analysis of covariance in which the attitude change measure would be the dependent variable and the social desirability control measure (**X**) would be the covariate or "adjusting" variable. See Chapter 9.

**3.6**   A research clinical psychologist is preparing an investigation of rate of decay of the orienting reflex (OR) in various psychopathological patient groups. An issue arises as to whether the OR is appreciably related to amount of confusion as rated by trained observers (C). In the context of the study, she decides that if the proportion of variance in OR associated with C is as large as .10, she wants to perform a preliminary experiment at the $a_2$ = .10 level which will have power of .90 to detect it. Since PV = $r^2$ = .10, ES = r = $\sqrt{.10}$ = .32, a value not provided in Table 3.4.1. She thus takes recourse to formula (3.4.1), which requires $n_{.10}$ (from Table 3.4.1 for $a_2$ = .10) and z, the Fisher z transformation of an r of .32. The latter is found in Table 4.2.2 of the next chapter to be z = .332. $n_{.10}$ is found in Table 3.4.1 for $a_2$ = .10 in column r = .10, row power = .90, as 854. Entering these values in formula (3.4.1),

$$n = 854\left(\frac{.100}{.332}\right)^2 + 2 = 79.5.$$

Thus, if she is to have a .90 probability of detecting r = .32 (PV = $r^2$ = .10) at the $a_2$ = .10 level, she will need a sample n of 80 cases.

If, on reconsideration, she decides she would prefer to use more stringent $a_2$ = .05 level and is prepared to operate with .85 power to detect the same PV = .10, all that changes is the $n_{.10}$ value. She uses Table 3.4.1 for $a_2$ = .05, r = .10, power = .85, and finds $n_{.10}$ = 895. Substituting in formula (3.4.1),

$$n = 895\left(\frac{.100}{.332}\right)^2 + 2 = 83.1,$$

a slightly larger value.

## 3.5   THE USE OF THE TABLES FOR SIGNIFICANCE TESTING OF r

Although the major purpose of this handbook is the exposition and facilitation of power analysis, the power tables contain criterion values of the ES *in the sample* necessary to reach statistical significance. These values facilitate the testing of null hypotheses when the sample results are determined.

The power tables in this chapter (Tables 3.3.1–3.3.5) contain, in the $r_c$ column, the sample $r_s$ necessary to attain the significance level of the table for the sample size of the row in which it appears. The $r_c$ is taken as absolute (of either sign) for nondirectional (two-tailed) tests, and as of the appropriate sign in directional (one-tailed) tests. These values are of the same kind as appear in some statistical texts, but provide many more values, both for **a** and for **n**.

**Illustrative Examples**

**3.7**  Consider the analysis of the data arising from the experiment relating extraversion to a neurophysiological measure given in example 3.1. Assume that the data have been collected as planned, and the sample $r_s$ is found to equal $-.241$. The specifications for the significance test are

$$a_2 = .05, \qquad n = 50, \qquad r_s = -.241.$$

Table 3.3.5 (for $a_2 = .05$) is used for $n = 50$, and the $r_c$ value is found to equal .279. Since .241 (the sign is ignored because the test is two-tailed) is smaller than $r_c$, the null hypothesis is not rejected.

**3.8**  Reconsider the condition of example 3.2, where the validity of a personality questionnaire to predict freshman grade point average is under study. Assume that prior to data collection, the decision is made to test the null hypothesis at $a_2 = .05$ and $n = 500$. When the data are collected, $r_s$ is found to equal .136. Thus,

$$a_2 = .05, \qquad n = 500, \qquad r_s = .136.$$

In Table 3.3.5 (for $a_2 = .05$) at $n = 500$, the criterion value $r_c$ is found to be .088. Since $r_s$ exceeds this, the null hypothesis is rejected, and it is concluded that there is a (nonzero) relationship between the questionnaire measure and grade point average.

**3.9**  The industrial psychologist in example 3.3 designed an experiment using 120 paired observations to determine whether a regression coefficient of wages on work unit output was significant at $a_1 = .01$. In that example, it was demonstrated how the regression coefficient could be converted to an $r$ and the tables of this chapter could be applied. In planning, his alternate hypothesis was $r = .40$. When the sample data were analyzed, the $r_s$ was found to equal $+.264$. The following specifications, then, are the conditions for his test of the null hypothesis that population $r = 0$:

$$a_1 = .01, \qquad n = 120, \qquad r_s = +.264.$$

He uses Table 3.3.1 (for $a_1 = .01$) at row $n = 120$ and finds that $r_c = .212$. Since his sample $r_s$ exceeds the $a_1 = .01$ criterion value .212, *and is of the proper sign* (since the test was directional), the null hypothesis is rejected.

Note that rejecting $H_0: r = 0$ means rejecting $H_0: B = 0$, i.e., if the correlation is not zero, neither is the regression coefficient (as discussed in Section 3.1).

Note, too, that although the sample $r_s$ of .264 is much smaller than the anticipated population $r$ of .40 which figured in the experimental planning, it is nevertheless significantly different from zero. (This comes about because the power of the experiment to detect an $r = .40$ was very high, .99.) The rejection of the null hypothesis does *not* warrant the conclusion that the specified alternate hypothesis (anticipated ES) is true, only that the null hypothesis is false (subject of course to the Type I risk). See Cohen (1973) in this regard.

CHAPTER 4

# Differences between Correlation Coefficients

## 4.1 INTRODUCTION AND USE

This chapter is concerned with the testing under various specified conditions of hypotheses concerning differences between population correlation coefficients. The previous chapter was devoted to a frequently occurring special case of this issue, namely, the difference between a population $r$ and zero. In the present chapter, other cases are considered: the difference between two population $r$'s when a sample is available from each (Cases 0 and 1), and the difference between a population $r$ and any specified hypothetical value (Case 2).

Interest in relationships in behavioral sciences transcends the simple question of whether a relationship exists (Chapter 3). Whether the degree of relationship between two variables is greater in one natural population or given experimental condition than it is in another, is an issue that arises with some frequency. A related issue involves the question of whether, in a population or condition, the degree of relationship differs from some specified value, not necessarily zero. Tests of these issues are available through Fisher's $z$ transformation of $r$ (e.g., Cohen & Cohen, 1983, pp. 53–55, 62; Hays, 1981, 466–467; Blalock, 1972, 401–407), and the power analyses in this chapter relate to these tests.

The above informal statement requires closer specification. By "relationship," linear correlation indexed by the Pearson product-moment correlation coefficient, $r$, is intended. The usual normality and homoscedasticity assumptions are formally assumed for the $r$'s involved (Cohen & Cohen, 1983), but even with considerable departure from these assumptions, the validity of

**109**

tabled **a** and power values is not greatly affected, particularly for large samples.

The material in this chapter will be organized into "cases," according to the specific hypothesis and sample(s) employed:

*Case 0.* $r_s$ values from equal size samples to test $r_1 = r_2$.

*Case 1.* The same hypothesis, but $n_1 \neq n_2$.

*Case 2.* One sample drawn from a population to test $r = c$.

A word about differences between independent regression coefficients. As such, the procedures and tables of this chapter do not provide a basis for power analysis of the test of $H_0 : B_1 - B_2 = 0$. (Note, however, that if the standard deviations of **X** and **Y** can be assumed equal over the two populations, the test of the equality of **r**'s is equivalent to the test of equality of **B**'s.) The more general test can be analyzed by the method of Chapter 9.

### 4.2 THE EFFECT SIZE INDEX: q

The detectability of a difference in magnitude between population **r**'s is not a simple function of the difference. That is, if we were to define $j = r_1 - r_2$ and try to use **j** as our ES, we would soon discover that the detectability of **j**, under fixed conditions of **a** and **n**, would *not* be constant, but would depend on where along the **r** scale the difference **j** occurred. As a concrete example, when

1. $r_1 = .50$ and $r_2 = .25$, $j = .50 - .25 = .25$; and when

2. $r_1 = .90$ and $r_2 = .65$, $j = .90 - .65 = .25$ also.

But for these two *equal* differences of $j = .25$, given $a_2 = .05$ and $n = 35$ (for example), the power to detect the first difference $(.50 - .25)$ is only .22, while the power for the second $(.90 - .65)$ is .80. Thus, **r** does not supply a scale of equal units of detectability, and so the difference between **r**'s is not an appropriate ES index.

The Fisher **z** transformation of **r** provides a solution to the problem. When **r**'s are transformed by the relationship

(4.2.1)
$$z = \tfrac{1}{2} \log_e \frac{1 + r}{1 - r},$$

equal differences between **z**'s are equally detectable. Thus, we define as our ES index

(4.2.2)
$$q = z_1 - z_2 \qquad \text{(directional)}$$
$$= | z_1 - z_2 | \qquad \text{(nondirectional)}.$$

Thus, unlike $r_1 - r_2$, $z_1 - z_2 = q$ gives values whose detectability does *not* depend on whether the $z$'s (and hence the $r$'s) are both small or both large. The power and sample size tables of this chapter provide entry for $q = .10$ (.10) .80 (.20) 1.40.

To facilitate the conversion of $r_1 - r_2$ to $z_1 - z_2 = q$ values, Tables 4.2.1 and 4.2.2 have been provided. Table 4.2.1 yields $q$ values as a function of $r_1 - r_2$; Table 4.2.2 is the usual $r$ to $z$ transformation table.

**Table 4.2.1**

$r_1$ values as a function of $r_2$ and $q = z_1 - z_2$

| $r_2$ | .10 | .20 | .30 | .40 | .50 | .60 | .70 | .80 | 1.00 | 1.20 | 1.40 |
|---|---|---|---|---|---|---|---|---|---|---|---|
| .00 | 10 | 20 | 29 | 38 | 46 | 54 | 60 | 66 | 762 | 834 | 885 |
| .05 | 15 | 25 | 34 | 42 | 50 | 57 | 64 | 69 | 782 | 848 | 896 |
| .10 | 20 | 29 | 38 | 46 | 54 | 60 | 66 | 72 | 801 | 862 | 905 |
| .15 | 25 | 34 | 42 | 50 | 57 | 64 | 69 | 74 | 818 | 874 | 914 |
| .20 | 29 | 38 | 46 | 54 | 61 | 67 | 72 | 76 | 834 | 886 | 922 |
| .25 | 34 | 43 | 50 | 58 | 64 | 69 | 74 | 78 | 850 | 897 | 930 |
| .30 | 39 | 47 | 54 | 61 | 67 | 72 | 77 | 80 | 864 | 907 | 937 |
| .35 | 43 | 51 | 58 | 64 | 70 | 75 | 79 | 82 | 878 | 916 | 943 |
| .40 | 48 | 55 | 62 | 68 | 73 | 77 | 81 | 84 | 890 | 925 | 949 |
| .45 | 53 | 59 | 66 | 71 | 76 | 79 | 83 | 86 | 902 | 933 | 955 |
| .50 | 57 | 63 | 69 | 74 | 78 | 82 | 85 | 87 | 914 | 941 | 960 |
| .55 | 62 | 67 | 73 | 77 | 81 | 84 | 87 | 89 | 924 | 949 | 965 |
| .60 | 66 | 71 | 76 | 80 | 83 | 86 | 88 | 90 | 935 | 956 | 970 |
| .65 | 70 | 75 | 79 | 83 | 86 | 88 | 90 | 92 | 944 | 962 | 975 |
| .70 | 75 | 79 | 82 | 85 | 88 | 90 | 92 | 93 | 953 | 968 | 979 |
| .75 | 79 | 83 | 85 | 88 | 90 | 92 | 93 | 94 | 962 | 974 | 983 |
| .80 | 83 | 86 | 89 | 90 | 92 | 94 | 95 | 96 | 970 | 980 | 987 |
| .85 | 88 | 90 | 91 | 93 | 94 | 95 | 96 | 97 | 978 | 985 | 990 |
| .90 | 92 | 93 | 94 | 95 | 96 | 97 | 97 | 98 | 986 | 990 | 994 |
| .95 | 96 | 97 | 97 | 98 | 98 | 98 | 99 | 99 | 993 | 995 | 997 |

Table 4.2.1 is generally more convenient for use in power analysis and when $r_1$ and $r_2$ are of the same sign. Assume both positive and $r_1 > r_2$. Given $r_2$, the smaller, read across to $r_1$, the larger. When $r_1$ is found, it is used to determine $q$, the column heading, which is the difference between the $z$ transformations of the $r$'s, i.e., $q = z_1 - z_2$. For example, if you wished to detect a difference between population $r$'s of .25 ($= r_2$) and .50 ($= r_1$), the table provides the difference $q$ between their respective $z$ values, as follows: Locate in the first

Table 4.2.2
Transformation of Product Moment r to z

| r | z | r | z | r | z | r | z |
|---|---|---|---|---|---|---|---|
| .00 | .000 | .25 | .255 | .50 | .549 | .75 | 0.973 |
| .01 | .010 | .26 | .266 | .51 | .563 | .76 | 0.996 |
| .02 | .020 | .27 | .277 | .52 | .576 | .77 | 1.020 |
| .03 | .030 | .28 | .288 | .53 | .590 | .78 | 1.045 |
| .04 | .040 | .29 | .299 | .54 | .604 | .79 | 1.071 |
| .05 | .050 | .30 | .310 | .55 | .618 | .80 | 1.099 |
| .06 | .060 | .31 | .321 | .56 | .633 | .81 | 1.127 |
| .07 | .070 | .32 | .332 | .57 | .648 | .82 | 1.157 |
| .08 | .080 | .33 | .343 | .58 | .662 | .83 | 1.188 |
| .09 | .090 | .34 | .354 | .59 | .678 | .84 | 1.221 |
| .10 | .100 | .35 | .365 | .60 | .693 | .85 | 1.256 |
| .11 | .110 | .36 | .377 | .61 | .709 | .86 | 1.293 |
| .12 | .121 | .37 | .388 | .62 | .725 | .87 | 1.333 |
| .13 | .131 | .38 | .400 | .63 | .741 | .88 | 1.376 |
| .14 | .141 | .39 | .412 | .64 | .758 | .89 | 1.422 |
| .15 | .151 | .40 | .424 | .65 | .775 | .90 | 1.472 |
| .16 | .161 | .41 | .436 | .66 | .793 | .91 | 1.528 |
| .17 | .172 | .42 | .448 | .67 | .811 | .92 | 1.589 |
| .18 | .182 | .43 | .460 | .68 | .829 | .93 | 1.658 |
| .19 | .192 | .44 | .472 | .69 | .848 | .94 | 1.738 |
| .20 | .203 | .45 | .485 | .70 | .867 | .95 | 1.832 |
| .21 | .213 | .46 | .497 | .71 | .887 | .96 | 1.946 |
| .22 | .224 | .47 | .510 | .72 | .908 | .97 | 2.092 |
| .23 | .234 | .48 | .523 | .73 | .929 | .98 | 2.298 |
| .24 | .245 | .49 | .536 | .74 | .950 | .99 | 2.647 |

column the value $r_2 = .25$, then read across to $r_1 = .50$, and at the top of the column, find **q** $= .30$.

Since one cannot have both convenient multiples of .10 for **q** and simultaneously convenient multiples of .05 for both $r_1$ and $r_2$, the use of Table 4.2.1 may require interpolation in **q**. Thus, for $r_1 = .25$, $r_1 = .60$, entry in the row for $r_2 = .25$ yields **q** $= .40$ for $r_1 = .58$ and **q** $= .50$ for $r_1 = .64$. Linear interpolation gives the approximate value of **q** $= .433$.

Alternatively, for exact values of **q**, Table 4.2.2 may be used to locate $r_1 = .60$ and $r_2 = .25$ and their respective **z** values found: $z_1 = .693$, $z_2 = .255$. Then, **q** $= .693 - .255 = .438$. Note that in either case, interpolation would be needed when this nontabled **q** value is used in the power tables (but not for sample size determination[1]).

Table 4.2.2 would also be used when $r_1$ and $r_2$ are of different sign. For example, for $r_1 = +.60$ and $r_2 = -.25$, the respective **z** values are found from Table 4.2.2 as $z_1 = +.693$ and $z_2 = -.255$. Then **q** $= z_1 - z_2 = +.693 - (-.255) = .948$.

Finally, Table 4.2.2 will be necessary to find $q_s$ when the power tables are used for significance testing, as described in Section 4.5.

In practice, the need to use nontabled values of **q** in power and sample size determination will not arise frequently. This is because one rarely has so highly specified an alternate hypothesis in terms of $r_1$ and $r_2$ values that one must find power or sample size for a value of **q** which is not tabled. A less exact specification of the $r_1 - r_2$ difference permits the use of the nearest tabled value of **q** in Table 4.2.1 and the later tables of this chapter. Indeed, the even less exact procedure of defining **q** as "small," "medium," or "large" with the operational definitions proposed below will suffice for many purposes.

4.2.1 "SMALL," "MEDIUM," AND "LARGE" DIFFERENCES IN CORRELATION. To provide the behavioral scientist with a frame of reference in which to appraise differences in degree of correlation, we attach specific values of **q** to the adjectives "small," "medium," and "large" to serve as operational definitions which are offered as conventions. This conforms to the general plan which has been followed with each type of statistical test in this handbook. Again, the reader is urged to avoid the use of these conventions, if he can, in favor of exact values provided by theory. However, it is less likely here than, say, in testing differences between means, that contemporary theory will lead to exact alternative-hypothetical values of **q**.

EQUAL UNITS AND AMOUNTS OF RELATIONSHIP. Differences in "amounts" of relationship expressed in Fisher **z**'s, i.e., **q** values, are not generally

---

[1] As will be seen below, determining **n** from the sample size table (Table 4.4.1) requires no interpolation. For nontabled values of **q**, formula (4.4.1) is used.

familiar to behavioral scientists. Indeed, the intuitive concept "amount" of relationship requires specification for it to be useful. It is frequently pointed out in textbooks in applied statistics that r is an index number, not a measurement on a linear scale of equal units, and that in consequence equal changes in r do not represent equal changes in amount of relationship at different points along the range of possible values. (It has already been stated above that equal differences in population r's are not equally detectable.)

There are, however, simple functions of r which more closely accord with intuitive notions about amounts of relationship so that differences in these functions are equal in some acceptable sense.

One of these functions has already been encountered. Given an r for a population of X,Y pairs, $r^2$, the "coefficient of determination," is the proportion of variance (PV) in either variable which is linearly accounted for by the other. Thus, the quantity $r_1^2 - r_2^2$ represents amount of change in the proportion of variance accounted for; equal amounts of PV change can be meaningfully understood as equal amounts of change in amount of relationship, anywhere along the r scale. In this sense, the $r_1, r_2$ pairs .38, .10 and .88, .80 represent equal differences in amount of relationship, since in both pairs, $r_1^2 - r_2^2 = .134$—the larger $r_1$ of each pair accounts for 13.4% more variance than the smaller; similarly the pairs .60, .00 and .92, .70 ($r_1^2 - r_2^2 = .36$).

Another of those conversion functions is the complement of the coefficient of alienation, $1 - \sqrt{1 - r^2}$, expressed as percent and called E, the "index of forecasting efficiency" (Guilford & Fruchter, 1978, pp.356–358). E indexes the amount of reduction in errors of prediction relative to the case where r = 0, when errors of prediction are measured by their standard deviation about the linearly predicted value. This standard deviation, called the "standard error of estimate," is reduced as r increases, and when r = ± 1, becomes zero, so that E = 100%. When a pair of r's is converted to a pair of E's, the index $E_1 - E_2$, in the sense of amount of reduction in error standard deviation, represents another meaningful rendition of the concept "differences in amount of relationship" which is independent of where on the r scale the difference occurs. In this sense, the $r_1, r_2$ pairs .38, .10 and .53, .40 represent (approximately) equal differences in amount of relationship, since in both pairs, $E_1 - E_2 = 7\%$—the larger $r_1$ of each pair results in an additional 7% reduction of standard error of estimate over the smaller r; similarly the pairs .50, .25 and .64, .50 (where $E_1 - E_2 = 10\%$).

The difference functions $r_1^2 - r_2^2$ and $E_1 - E_2$ are not equivalent, yet each offers a reasonable rendition of "equal differences in amount of relationship." Our ES index, $q = z_1 - z_2$ was chosen on the criterion of equal detectability, rather than equal amounts. Fortunately, over the most frequently encountered values of the correlation scale, equal q values yield not grossly unequal values of either $r_1^2 - r_2^2$ or $E_1 - E_2$. Thus equal detectability over much of the correlation scale represents approximately equal "differences in amount of relationship" as rendered either by difference in proportion of variance accounted for or by percent reduction in the standard error of estimate. In the description of our operational definitions of "small," "medium," and "large" **q** values, each will be interpreted in the latter terms and the range of approximate constancy will be described for each.

SMALL EFFECT SIZE: **q** = .10. A small difference between correlations is defined as **q** = .10. The following pairs of **r**'s illustrate this amount of difference: .00, .10; .20, .29; .40, .48; .60, .66; .80, .83; .90, .92; .95, .96 (Table 4.2.1).

When the smaller $r_2$ falls between .25 and .80, a **q** = .10 implies $r_1^2 - r_2^2$ falling in the range .05–.08. (Outside these **r**$_2$ limits, $r_1^2 - r_2^2$ is below .05). Thus one can generally think of a small difference in correlation as one for which the population of larger **r** has an **X**, **Y** percentage shared variance 5–8 % larger than that of the population with the smaller **r**.

In terms of difference between amounts of relationship expressed in fore- casting efficiency terms for $r_2$ between .25 and .95, **q** = .10 implies $E_1 - E_2$ values of 3–5%. (For $r_2$ outside these limits, $E_1 - E_2$ is smaller than 3%.)

MEDIUM EFFECT SIZE: **q** = .30. With **q** = .30 taken to define a med- ium ES, we find (Table 4.2.1) the following pairs of **r**'s illustrating this amount of difference: .00, .29; .20, .46; .40, .62; .60, .76; .80, .89; .90, .94; .95, .97.

When the smaller $r_2$ falls between .15 and .75, **q** = .30 implies a difference between $r^2$ falling between .15–.23. Taking a narrower range of $r_2$ between .25 and .70, $r_1^2 - r_2^2$ falls between .18–.23. Thus, over the middle of the correlation scale, a medium difference in correlation can be understood as one for which the population of larger **r** has a percentage of shared variance between **X** and **Y** which is about 20 % larger than that of the smaller **r**. Outside these ranges of $r_2$, the shared variance difference is less; for low $r_2$, it reaches a minimum value (for $r_2 = .00$, $r_1 = .29$) of .084.

Interpreted in forecasting efficiency terms, for $r_2$ between .25 and .90, **q** = .30 implies $E_1 - E_2$ values of 10–15%, values outside these $r_2$ limits again yielding smaller discrepancies in $E_1 - E_2$.

LARGE EFFECT SIZE: **q** = .50. A large difference in **r**'s is operationally defined as one which yields **q** = .50. Pairs of **r**'s illustrating this degree of difference are: .00, .46; .20, .61; .40, .73; .60, .83; .80, .92; .90, .96; and .95, .98 (Table 4.2.1). Here it becomes particularly obvious how different is our approach via **q** from the simple difference $r_1 - r_2$.

Large differences, so defined, mean $r_1^2 - r_2^2$ values falling in the range .28 to .38 when $r_2$ (the smaller) falls between the limits .10–.70, or, taking a slightly narrower range for $r_2$ of .20 to .65, PV differences of .32 to .38. Thus, a large difference in $r$'s in the middle of the scale is taken to mean one which involves about a third of the total variance.

In terms of difference in forecasting efficiency, when $r_2$ lies between .20 and .80, $E_1 - E_2$ is within the limits of 20–25%. If the latter seems small to the reader, it should be pointed out that a substantial reduction of the standard error of estimate from its maximum value when $r = 0$ requires very large values of $r$. Thus, for example, when one considers the definition in Chapter 3 of a large ES, $r = .50$, one finds that its $E$ value is only 13.4%. For $E$ to be as much as 50%, $r$ must be .866. Thus, a difference between $E$'s of 20–25% should be consonant with the intuitive conception of a large difference between amounts of correlation.

*Comparison with Definitions for Significance Test of* $r$. We can reinterpret the operational definitions of "small," "medium," and "large" ES of Chapter 3 on significance testing of a single $r$ in the light of the $q$ of the present chapter. Since $q = z_1 - z_2$, and $r_2 = 0$ transforms to $z_2 = 0$, given the definitions of Chapter 3 of ES $= r = .10$, .30, and .50, these become respectively $q = .10$, .31, and .55. They are thus approximately comparable with the $q$ values .10, .30, and .50 of the present chapter. However, the set $r = .10$, .30, .50 yields smaller values when expressed as $r^2$ and $E$ differences from zero than those of the middle range described above. Thus the ES definitions for *differences* in relationship expressed as shared variance or reduction in error of prediction are larger than the ES definitions for significance testing of a single $r$.

### 4.3  Power Tables

When the significance criterion, ES, and sample size are specified, the tables in this section can be used to determine power values. Their major use will thus be after a research is performed or at least planned. They can, of course, also be used in research planning by varying $n$, ES, or $a$, or all three, to see the consequences to power of such alternatives.

4.3.1  CASE 0: $n_1 = n_2$. The power tables are designed to yield conveniently power values for the normal curve test of the difference between the Fisher transformations of the $r$'s ($q = z_1 - z_2$) of two independent samples of equal size. This is designated Case 0; other cases are described and illustrated in later sections. Tables give values for $a$, $q$, and $n$:

*1. Significance Criterion,* $a$. Six tables are provided for the following values of $a$: $a_1 = .01$, $a_1 = .05$, $a_1 = .10$, $a_2 = .01$, $a_2 = .05$, $a_2 = .10$, where the subscripts refer to one- and two-tailed tests. Since power at $a_1$ is to an adequate approximation equal to power at $a_2 = 2a_1$ for power greater than

Table 4.3.1

Power of Normal Curve Test of $r_1 = r_2$
via Fisher z transormation at $a_1$ = .01

| n | $q_c$ | .10 | .20 | .30 | .40 | .50 | .60 | .70 | .80 | 1.00 | 1.20 | 1.40 |
|---|---|---|---|---|---|---|---|---|---|---|---|---|
| 8 | 1.471 | 02 | 02 | 03 | 05 | 06 | 08 | 11 | 14 | 23 | 33 | 46 |
| 9 | 1.343 | 02 | 02 | 04 | 05 | 07 | 10 | 13 | 17 | 28 | 40 | 54 |
| 10 | 1.243 | 02 | 03 | 04 | 06 | 08 | 11 | 15 | 20 | 32 | 47 | 62 |
| 11 | 1.163 | 02 | 03 | 04 | 06 | 09 | 13 | 18 | 23 | 37 | 53 | 68 |
| 12 | 1.097 | 02 | 03 | 05 | 07 | 10 | 15 | 20 | 26 | 42 | 59 | 74 |
| 13 | 1.040 | 02 | 03 | 05 | 08 | 11 | 16 | 22 | 30 | 46 | 64 | 79 |
| 14 | .992 | 02 | 03 | 05 | 08 | 12 | 18 | 25 | 33 | 51 | 69 | 83 |
| 15 | .950 | 02 | 03 | 06 | 09 | 14 | 20 | 27 | 36 | 55 | 73 | 86 |
| 16 | .912 | 02 | 03 | 06 | 10 | 15 | 21 | 29 | 39 | 59 | 77 | 89 |
| 17 | .879 | 02 | 04 | 06 | 10 | 16 | 23 | 32 | 42 | 63 | 80 | 92 |
| 18 | .849 | 02 | 04 | 07 | 11 | 17 | 25 | 34 | 45 | 66 | 83 | 93 |
| 19 | .822 | 02 | 04 | 07 | 12 | 18 | 26 | 36 | 47 | 69 | 86 | 95 |
| 20 | .798 | 02 | 04 | 07 | 12 | 19 | 28 | 39 | 50 | 72 | 88 | 96 |
| 21 | .775 | 02 | 04 | 08 | 13 | 20 | 30 | 41 | 53 | 75 | 90 | 97 |
| 22 | .755 | 02 | 04 | 08 | 14 | 22 | 32 | 43 | 56 | 78 | 92 | 98 |
| 23 | .736 | 02 | 05 | 08 | 14 | 23 | 33 | 46 | 58 | 80 | 93 | 98 |
| 24 | .718 | 02 | 05 | 09 | 15 | 24 | 35 | 48 | 60 | 82 | 94 | 99 |
| 25 | .701 | 02 | 05 | 09 | 16 | 25 | 37 | 50 | 63 | 84 | 95 | 99 |
| 26 | .686 | 02 | 05 | 10 | 16 | 26 | 39 | 52 | 65 | 86 | 96 | 99 |
| 27 | .672 | 02 | 05 | 10 | 17 | 28 | 40 | 54 | 67 | 87 | 97 | 99 |
| 28 | .658 | 02 | 05 | 10 | 18 | 29 | 42 | 56 | 69 | 89 | 97 | * |
| 29 | .645 | 02 | 05 | 11 | 19 | 30 | 44 | 58 | 71 | 90 | 98 | |
| 30 | .633 | 03 | 06 | 11 | 20 | 31 | 45 | 60 | 73 | 91 | 98 | |
| 31 | .622 | 03 | 06 | 11 | 20 | 32 | 47 | 62 | 75 | 92 | 98 | |
| 32 | .611 | 03 | 06 | 12 | 21 | 34 | 48 | 63 | 76 | 93 | 99 | |
| 33 | .601 | 03 | 06 | 12 | 22 | 35 | 50 | 65 | 78 | 94 | 99 | |
| 34 | .591 | 03 | 06 | 13 | 23 | 36 | 52 | 67 | 79 | 95 | 99 | |
| 35 | .582 | 03 | 06 | 13 | 23 | 37 | 53 | 68 | 81 | 95 | 99 | |
| 36 | .573 | 03 | 07 | 13 | 24 | 38 | 54 | 70 | 82 | 96 | 99 | |
| 37 | .564 | 03 | 07 | 14 | 25 | 40 | 56 | 71 | 83 | 96 | * | |
| 38 | .556 | 03 | 07 | 14 | 26 | 41 | 57 | 73 | 85 | 97 | | |
| 39 | .548 | 03 | 07 | 15 | 26 | 42 | 59 | 74 | 86 | 97 | | |
| 40 | .541 | 03 | 07 | 15 | 27 | 43 | 60 | 75 | 87 | 98 | | |
| 42 | .527 | 03 | 07 | 16 | 29 | 45 | 63 | 78 | 89 | 98 | | |
| 44 | .514 | 03 | 08 | 17 | 30 | 48 | 65 | 80 | 90 | 99 | | |
| 46 | .502 | 03 | 08 | 18 | 32 | 50 | 68 | 82 | 92 | 99 | | |
| 48 | .490 | 03 | 08 | 18 | 33 | 52 | 70 | 84 | 93 | 99 | | |

Table 4.3.1 *(continued)*

| n | $q_c$ | .10 | .20 | .30 | .40 | .50 | .60 | .70 | .80 | 1.00 | 1.20 | 1.40 |
|---|---|---|---|---|---|---|---|---|---|---|---|---|
| | | | | | | q | | | | | | |
| 50 | .480 | 03 | 09 | 19 | 35 | 54 | 72 | 86 | 94 | 99 | * | * |
| 52 | .470 | 03 | 09 | 20 | 36 | 56 | 74 | 87 | 95 | * | | |
| 54 | .461 | 03 | 09 | 21 | 38 | 58 | 76 | 89 | 96 | | | |
| 56 | .452 | 04 | 10 | 22 | 39 | 60 | 78 | 90 | 96 | | | |
| 58 | .444 | 04 | 10 | 23 | 41 | 62 | 79 | 91 | 97 | | | |
| 60 | .434 | 04 | 10 | 23 | 42 | 63 | 81 | 92 | 97 | | | |
| 64 | .421 | 04 | 11 | 25 | 45 | 67 | 84 | 94 | 98 | | | |
| 68 | .408 | 04 | 12 | 27 | 48 | 70 | 86 | 95 | 99 | | | |
| 72 | .396 | 04 | 12 | 29 | 51 | 73 | 88 | 96 | 99 | | | |
| 76 | .385 | 04 | 13 | 30 | 54 | 76 | 90 | 97 | 99 | | | |
| 80 | .375 | 04 | 14 | 32 | 56 | 78 | 92 | 98 | * | | | |
| 84 | .365 | 05 | 15 | 34 | 59 | 80 | 93 | 98 | | | | |
| 88 | .357 | 05 | 15 | 36 | 61 | 82 | 94 | 99 | | | | |
| 92 | .349 | 05 | 16 | 37 | 63 | 84 | 95 | 99 | | | | |
| 96 | .341 | 05 | 17 | 39 | 66 | 86 | 96 | 99 | | | | |
| 100 | .334 | 05 | 18 | 41 | 68 | 88 | 97 | 99 | | | | |
| 120 | .304 | 06 | 21 | 49 | 77 | 93 | 99 | * | | | | |
| 140 | .281 | 07 | 25 | 56 | 84 | 97 | * | | | | | |
| 160 | .263 | 07 | 29 | 63 | 89 | 98 | | | | | | |
| 180 | .247 | 08 | 33 | 69 | 92 | 99 | | | | | | |
| 200 | .234 | 09 | 37 | 74 | 95 | * | | | | | | |
| 250 | .206 | 12 | 47 | 86 | 99 | | | | | | | |
| 300 | .191 | 13 | 54 | 91 | 99 | | | | | | | |
| 350 | .177 | 16 | 62 | 95 | * | | | | | | | |
| 400 | .165 | 18 | 69 | 97 | | | | | | | | |
| 450 | .156 | 20 | 75 | 98 | | | | | | | | |
| 500 | .148 | 23 | 80 | 99 | | | | | | | | |
| 600 | .135 | 27 | 87 | * | | | | | | | | |
| 700 | .125 | 32 | 92 | | | | | | | | | |
| 800 | .117 | 37 | 95 | | | | | | | | | |
| 900 | .110 | 42 | 97 | | | | | | | | | |
| 1000 | .104 | 46 | 98 | | | | | | | | | |

* Power values below this point are greater than .995.

Table 4.3.2

Power of Normal Curve Test of $r_1 = r_2$
via Fisher z transformation at $a_1 = .05$

| n | $q_c$ | | | | | | q | | | | | |
|---|---|---|---|---|---|---|---|---|---|---|---|---|
| | | .10 | .20 | .30 | .40 | .50 | .60 | .70 | .80 | 1.00 | 1.20 | 1.40 |
| 8 | 1.040 | 07 | 09 | 12 | 16 | 20 | 24 | 30 | 35 | 47 | 60 | 71 |
| 9 | .950 | 07 | 10 | 13 | 17 | 22 | 27 | 33 | 40 | 54 | 67 | 78 |
| 10 | .879 | 07 | 10 | 14 | 19 | 24 | 30 | 37 | 44 | 59 | 73 | 83 |
| 11 | .822 | 07 | 11 | 15 | 20 | 26 | 33 | 40 | 48 | 64 | 77 | 88 |
| 12 | .776 | 08 | 11 | 16 | 21 | 28 | 36 | 44 | 52 | 68 | 82 | 91 |
| 13 | .736 | 08 | 12 | 16 | 23 | 30 | 38 | 47 | 56 | 72 | 85 | 93 |
| 14 | .701 | 08 | 12 | 17 | 24 | 32 | 41 | 50 | 59 | 76 | 88 | 95 |
| 15 | .672 | 08 | 12 | 18 | 25 | 34 | 43 | 53 | 62 | 79 | 90 | 96 |
| 16 | .645 | 08 | 13 | 19 | 27 | 36 | 45 | 56 | 65 | 82 | 92 | 97 |
| 17 | .622 | 08 | 13 | 20 | 28 | 37 | 48 | 58 | 68 | 84 | 94 | 98 |
| 18 | .606 | 09 | 14 | 20 | 29 | 39 | 50 | 61 | 71 | 86 | 95 | 99 |
| 19 | .582 | 09 | 14 | 21 | 30 | 41 | 52 | 63 | 73 | 88 | 96 | 99 |
| 20 | .564 | 09 | 14 | 22 | 32 | 43 | 54 | 65 | 75 | 90 | 97 | 99 |
| 21 | .548 | 09 | 15 | 23 | 33 | 44 | 56 | 67 | 77 | 91 | 97 | 99 |
| 22 | .534 | 09 | 15 | 24 | 34 | 46 | 58 | 70 | 79 | 92 | 98 | * |
| 23 | .520 | 09 | 16 | 24 | 35 | 47 | 60 | 71 | 81 | 94 | 98 | |
| 24 | .508 | 09 | 16 | 25 | 36 | 49 | 62 | 73 | 83 | 94 | 99 | |
| 25 | .496 | 09 | 16 | 26 | 38 | 51 | 64 | 75 | 84 | 95 | 99 | |
| 26 | .485 | 10 | 17 | 27 | 39 | 52 | 65 | 77 | 86 | 96 | 99 | |
| 27 | .475 | 10 | 17 | 27 | 40 | 53 | 67 | 78 | 87 | 97 | 99 | |
| 28 | .465 | 10 | 17 | 28 | 41 | 55 | 68 | 80 | 88 | 97 | * | |
| 29 | .456 | 10 | 18 | 29 | 42 | 56 | 70 | 81 | 89 | 98 | | |
| 30 | .448 | 10 | 18 | 29 | 43 | 58 | 71 | 82 | 90 | 98 | | |
| 31 | .440 | 10 | 18 | 30 | 44 | 59 | 73 | 84 | 91 | 98 | | |
| 32 | .432 | 10 | 19 | 31 | 45 | 60 | 74 | 85 | 92 | 98 | | |
| 33 | .425 | 10 | 19 | 31 | 46 | 61 | 75 | 86 | 93 | 99 | | |
| 34 | .418 | 11 | 20 | 32 | 47 | 63 | 76 | 87 | 93 | 99 | | |
| 35 | .411 | 11 | 20 | 33 | 48 | 64 | 77 | 88 | 94 | 99 | | |
| 36 | .405 | 11 | 20 | 33 | 49 | 65 | 79 | 88 | 95 | 99 | | |
| 37 | .399 | 11 | 21 | 34 | 50 | 66 | 80 | 89 | 95 | 99 | | |
| 38 | .393 | 11 | 21 | 35 | 51 | 67 | 81 | 90 | 96 | 99 | | |
| 39 | .388 | 11 | 21 | 35 | 52 | 68 | 82 | 91 | 96 | * | | |
| 40 | .382 | 11 | 22 | 36 | 53 | 69 | 83 | 91 | 96 | | | |
| 42 | .372 | 11 | 22 | 37 | 55 | 71 | 84 | 93 | 97 | | | |
| 44 | .363 | 12 | 23 | 39 | 57 | 73 | 86 | 94 | 98 | | | |
| 46 | .355 | 12 | 24 | 40 | 58 | 75 | 87 | 95 | 98 | | | |
| 48 | .347 | 12 | 24 | 41 | 60 | 77 | 89 | 95 | 98 | | | |

Table 4.3.2 *(continued)*

| n | $q_c$ | .10 | .20 | .30 | .40 | .50 | .60 | .70 | .80 | 1.00 | 1.20 | 1.40 |
|---|---|---|---|---|---|---|---|---|---|---|---|---|
| 50 | .339 | 12 | 25 | 42 | 62 | 78 | 90 | 96 | 99 | * | * | * |
| 52 | .332 | 13 | 26 | 44 | 63 | 80 | 91 | 97 | 99 | | | |
| 54 | .326 | 13 | 26 | 45 | 65 | 81 | 92 | 97 | 99 | | | |
| 56 | .320 | 13 | 27 | 46 | 66 | 82 | 93 | 97 | 99 | | | |
| 58 | .314 | 13 | 28 | 47 | 67 | 84 | 93 | 98 | 99 | | | |
| 60 | .308 | 13 | 28 | 48 | 69 | 85 | 94 | 98 | * | | | |
| 64 | .298 | 14 | 29 | 50 | 71 | 87 | 95 | 99 | | | | |
| 68 | .289 | 14 | 31 | 53 | 74 | 89 | 96 | 99 | | | | |
| 72 | .280 | 14 | 32 | 55 | 76 | 90 | 97 | 99 | | | | |
| 76 | .272 | 15 | 33 | 57 | 78 | 92 | 98 | * | | | | |
| 80 | .265 | 15 | 34 | 59 | 80 | 93 | 98 | | | | | |
| 84 | .258 | 16 | 35 | 60 | 82 | 94 | 99 | | | | | |
| 88 | .252 | 16 | 37 | 62 | 83 | 95 | 99 | | | | | |
| 92 | .247 | 16 | 38 | 64 | 85 | 95 | 99 | | | | | |
| 96 | .241 | 16 | 39 | 66 | 86 | 96 | 99 | | | | | |
| 100 | .236 | 17 | 41 | 68 | 87 | 97 | 99 | | | | | |
| 120 | .231 | 19 | 45 | 74 | 92 | 99 | * | | | | | |
| 140 | .199 | 21 | 50 | 80 | 95 | 99 | | | | | | |
| 160 | .186 | 22 | 55 | 84 | 97 | * | | | | | | |
| 180 | .175 | 24 | 59 | 88 | 98 | | | | | | | |
| 200 | .166 | 26 | 63 | 91 | 99 | | | | | | | |
| 250 | .146 | 30 | 73 | 96 | * | | | | | | | |
| 300 | .135 | 34 | 79 | 98 | | | | | | | | |
| 350 | .125 | 37 | 84 | 99 | | | | | | | | |
| 400 | .117 | 40 | 88 | * | | | | | | | | |
| 450 | .110 | 44 | 91 | | | | | | | | | |
| 500 | .104 | 47 | 93 | | | | | | | | | |
| 600 | .095 | 53 | 96 | | | | | | | | | |
| 700 | .088 | 59 | 98 | | | | | | | | | |
| 800 | .082 | 64 | 99 | | | | | | | | | |
| 900 | .078 | 68 | * | | | | | | | | | |
| 1000 | .074 | 72 | | | | | | | | | | |

* Power values below this point are greater than .995

Table 4.3.3

Power of Normal Curve Test of $r_1 = r_2$
via Fisher z transformation at $a_1 = .10$

| | | | | | | | q | | | | | |
|---|---|---|---|---|---|---|---|---|---|---|---|---|
| n | $q_c$ | .10 | .20 | .30 | .40 | .50 | .60 | .70 | .80 | 1.00 | 1.20 | 1.40 |
| 8 | .811 | 13 | 17 | 21 | 26 | 31 | 37 | 43 | 49 | 62 | 73 | 82 |
| 9 | .740 | 13 | 17 | 22 | 28 | 34 | 40 | 47 | 54 | 67 | 79 | 87 |
| 10 | .685 | 14 | 18 | 24 | 30 | 36 | 44 | 51 | 59 | 72 | 83 | 91 |
| 11 | .641 | 14 | 19 | 25 | 31 | 39 | 47 | 55 | 62 | 76 | 87 | 94 |
| 12 | .604 | 14 | 20 | 26 | 33 | 41 | 50 | 58 | 66 | 80 | 90 | 95 |
| 13 | .573 | 14 | 20 | 27 | 35 | 43 | 52 | 61 | 69 | 83 | 92 | 97 |
| 14 | .547 | 15 | 21 | 28 | 37 | 46 | 55 | 64 | 72 | 86 | 94 | 98 |
| 15 | .523 | 15 | 21 | 29 | 38 | 48 | 57 | 67 | 75 | 88 | 95 | 98 |
| 16 | .503 | 15 | 22 | 30 | 40 | 50 | 60 | 69 | 78 | 90 | 96 | 99 |
| 17 | .484 | 15 | 23 | 31 | 41 | 52 | 62 | 72 | 80 | 91 | 97 | 99 |
| 18 | .468 | 16 | 23 | 32 | 43 | 53 | 64 | 74 | 82 | 93 | 98 | 99 |
| 19 | .453 | 16 | 24 | 33 | 44 | 55 | 66 | 76 | 84 | 94 | 98 | * |
| 20 | .440 | 16 | 24 | 34 | 45 | 57 | 68 | 78 | 85 | 95 | 99 | |
| 21 | .427 | 16 | 25 | 35 | 47 | 59 | 70 | 79 | 87 | 96 | 99 | |
| 22 | .416 | 17 | 25 | 36 | 48 | 60 | 71 | 81 | 88 | 96 | 99 | |
| 23 | .405 | 17 | 26 | 37 | 49 | 62 | 73 | 82 | 89 | 97 | 99 | |
| 24 | .396 | 17 | 26 | 38 | 51 | 63 | 75 | 84 | 90 | 97 | * | |
| 25 | .387 | 17 | 27 | 39 | 52 | 65 | 76 | 85 | 92 | 98 | | |
| 26 | .378 | 17 | 27 | 40 | 53 | 66 | 77 | 86 | 92 | 98 | | |
| 27 | .370 | 17 | 28 | 40 | 54 | 67 | 79 | 87 | 93 | 99 | | |
| 28 | .363 | 18 | 28 | 41 | 55 | 69 | 80 | 88 | 94 | 99 | | |
| 29 | .355 | 18 | 29 | 42 | 56 | 70 | 81 | 89 | 95 | 99 | | |
| 30 | .349 | 18 | 29 | 43 | 57 | 71 | 82 | 90 | 95 | 99 | | |
| 31 | .343 | 18 | 30 | 44 | 59 | 72 | 83 | 91 | 96 | 99 | | |
| 32 | .337 | 18 | 30 | 44 | 60 | 73 | 84 | 92 | 96 | 99 | | |
| 33 | .331 | 19 | 31 | 45 | 61 | 74 | 85 | 92 | 97 | * | | |
| 34 | .326 | 19 | 31 | 46 | 62 | 75 | 86 | 93 | 97 | | | |
| 35 | .320 | 19 | 31 | 47 | 62 | 76 | 87 | 94 | 97 | | | |
| 36 | .316 | 19 | 32 | 47 | 63 | 77 | 88 | 94 | 98 | | | |
| 37 | .311 | 19 | 32 | 48 | 64 | 78 | 88 | 95 | 98 | | | |
| 38 | .307 | 19 | 33 | 49 | 65 | 79 | 89 | 95 | 98 | | | |
| 39 | .302 | 20 | 33 | 50 | 66 | 80 | 90 | 95 | 98 | | | |
| 40 | .298 | 20 | 34 | 50 | 67 | 81 | 90 | 96 | 98 | | | |
| 42 | .290 | 20 | 35 | 52 | 69 | 82 | 91 | 96 | 99 | | | |
| 44 | .283 | 20 | 35 | 53 | 70 | 84 | 92 | 97 | 99 | | | |
| 46 | .277 | 21 | 36 | 54 | 72 | 85 | 93 | 98 | 99 | | | |
| 48 | .270 | 21 | 37 | 56 | 73 | 86 | 94 | 98 | 99 | | | |

Table 4.3.3. (continued)

| n | $q_c$ | q | | | | | | | | | | |
|---|---|---|---|---|---|---|---|---|---|---|---|---|
| | | .10 | .20 | .30 | .40 | .50 | .60 | .70 | .80 | 1.00 | 1.20 | 1.40 |
| 50 | .264 | 21 | 38 | 57 | 74 | 87 | 95 | 98 | * | * | * | * |
| 52 | .259 | 22 | 39 | 58 | 76 | 88 | 95 | 99 | | | | |
| 54 | .254 | 22 | 39 | 59 | 77 | 89 | 96 | 99 | | | | |
| 56 | .249 | 22 | 40 | 60 | 78 | 90 | 96 | 99 | | | | |
| 58 | .244 | 22 | 41 | 61 | 79 | 91 | 97 | 99 | | | | |
| 60 | .240 | 23 | 42 | 63 | 80 | 92 | 97 | 99 | | | | |
| 64 | .232 | 23 | 43 | 65 | 82 | 93 | 98 | * | | | | |
| 68 | .225 | 24 | 44 | 67 | 84 | 94 | 98 | | | | | |
| 72 | .218 | 24 | 46 | 68 | 86 | 95 | 99 | | | | | |
| 76 | .212 | 25 | 47 | 70 | 87 | 96 | 99 | | | | | |
| 80 | .207 | 25 | 48 | 72 | 88 | 97 | 99 | | | | | |
| 84 | .201 | 26 | 50 | 73 | 90 | 97 | 99 | | | | | |
| 88 | .197 | 26 | 51 | 75 | 91 | 98 | * | | | | | |
| 92 | .192 | 27 | 52 | 76 | 92 | 98 | | | | | | |
| 96 | .188 | 27 | 53 | 78 | 93 | 98 | | | | | | |
| 100 | .184 | 28 | 54 | 79 | 93 | 99 | | | | | | |
| 120 | .168 | 30 | 60 | 84 | 96 | 99 | | | | | | |
| 140 | .155 | 32 | 65 | 89 | 98 | * | | | | | | |
| 160 | .145 | 35 | 69 | 92 | 99 | | | | | | | |
| 180 | .136 | 37 | 73 | 94 | 99 | | | | | | | |
| 200 | .129 | 39 | 76 | 96 | * | | | | | | | |
| 250 | .113 | 44 | 84 | 98 | | | | | | | | |
| 300 | .105 | 47 | 88 | 99 | | | | | | | | |
| 350 | .097 | 51 | 91 | * | | | | | | | | |
| 400 | .091 | 55 | 94 | | | | | | | | | |
| 450 | .086 | 58 | 96 | | | | | | | | | |
| 500 | .081 | 62 | 97 | | | | | | | | | |
| 600 | .074 | 67 | 99 | | | | | | | | | |
| 700 | .069 | 72 | 99 | | | | | | | | | |
| 800 | .064 | 76 | * | | | | | | | | | |
| 900 | .061 | 80 | | | | | | | | | | |
| 1000 | .057 | 83 | | | | | | | | | | |

* Power values below this point are greater than .995.

## Table 4.3.4

Power of Normal Curve Test of $r_1 = r_2$
via Fisher z transformation at $a_2 = .01$

| n | $q_c$ | .10 | .20 | .30 | .40 | .50 | .60 | .70 | .80 | 1.00 | 1.20 | 1.40 |
|---|---|---|---|---|---|---|---|---|---|---|---|---|
| 8 | 1.629 | 01 | 01 | 02 | 03 | 04 | 05 | 07 | 09 | 16 | 25 | 36 |
| 9 | 1.487 | 01 | 01 | 02 | 03 | 04 | 06 | 09 | 12 | 20 | 31 | 44 |
| 10 | 1.377 | 01 | 02 | 02 | 03 | 05 | 07 | 10 | 14 | 24 | 37 | 52 |
| 11 | 1.288 | 01 | 02 | 02 | 04 | 06 | 08 | 12 | 16 | 28 | 43 | 59 |
| 12 | 1.215 | 01 | 02 | 03 | 04 | 06 | 10 | 14 | 19 | 32 | 49 | 65 |
| 13 | 1.152 | 01 | 02 | 03 | 05 | 07 | 11 | 16 | 22 | 37 | 54 | 71 |
| 14 | 1.098 | 01 | 02 | 03 | 05 | 08 | 12 | 17 | 24 | 41 | 59 | 76 |
| 15 | 1.052 | 01 | 02 | 03 | 06 | 09 | 13 | 19 | 27 | 45 | 64 | 80 |
| 16 | 1.010 | 01 | 02 | 04 | 06 | 10 | 15 | 21 | 30 | 49 | 69 | 84 |
| 17 | .973 | 01 | 02 | 04 | 06 | 11 | 16 | 23 | 32 | 53 | 73 | 87 |
| 18 | .940 | 01 | 02 | 04 | 07 | 11 | 18 | 26 | 35 | 56 | 76 | 90 |
| 19 | .911 | 01 | 02 | 04 | 07 | 12 | 19 | 28 | 38 | 60 | 79 | 92 |
| 20 | .884 | 01 | 02 | 04 | 08 | 13 | 20 | 30 | 40 | 63 | 82 | 93 |
| 21 | .859 | 01 | 02 | 05 | 08 | 14 | 22 | 32 | 43 | 66 | 85 | 95 |
| 22 | .836 | 01 | 03 | 05 | 09 | 15 | 23 | 34 | 46 | 69 | 87 | 96 |
| 23 | .815 | 01 | 03 | 05 | 09 | 16 | 25 | 36 | 48 | 72 | 89 | 97 |
| 24 | .795 | 01 | 03 | 05 | 10 | 17 | 26 | 38 | 51 | 75 | 91 | 98 |
| 25 | .777 | 01 | 03 | 06 | 11 | 18 | 28 | 40 | 53 | 77 | 92 | 98 |
| 26 | .760 | 01 | 03 | 06 | 11 | 19 | 29 | 42 | 55 | 79 | 93 | 99 |
| 27 | .744 | 01 | 03 | 06 | 12 | 20 | 31 | 44 | 58 | 81 | 94 | 99 |
| 28 | .728 | 01 | 03 | 07 | 12 | 21 | 32 | 46 | 60 | 83 | 95 | 99 |
| 29 | .714 | 02 | 03 | 07 | 13 | 27 | 34 | 48 | 62 | 85 | 96 | 99 |
| 30 | .701 | 02 | 03 | 07 | 13 | 23 | 36 | 50 | 64 | 86 | 97 | 99 |
| 31 | .688 | 02 | 03 | 07 | 14 | 24 | 37 | 52 | 66 | 88 | 97 | * |
| 32 | .676 | 02 | 04 | 07 | 15 | 25 | 39 | 54 | 68 | 89 | 98 | |
| 33 | .665 | 02 | 04 | 08 | 15 | 26 | 40 | 55 | 70 | 90 | 98 | |
| 34 | .654 | 02 | 04 | 08 | 16 | 27 | 42 | 57 | 72 | 91 | 98 | |
| 35 | .644 | 02 | 04 | 08 | 16 | 28 | 43 | 59 | 73 | 92 | 99 | |
| 36 | .634 | 02 | 04 | 09 | 17 | 29 | 44 | 61 | 75 | 93 | 99 | |
| 37 | .625 | 02 | 04 | 09 | 18 | 30 | 46 | 62 | 76 | 94 | 99 | |
| 38 | .616 | 02 | 04 | 09 | 18 | 31 | 47 | 64 | 78 | 95 | 99 | |
| 39 | .607 | 02 | 04 | 10 | 19 | 32 | 49 | 65 | 79 | 95 | 99 | |
| 40 | .599 | 02 | 04 | 10 | 20 | 34 | 50 | 67 | 81 | 96 | * | |
| 42 | .583 | 02 | 05 | 11 | 21 | 36 | 53 | 70 | 82 | 97 | | |
| 44 | .569 | 02 | 05 | 11 | 22 | 38 | 56 | 72 | 85 | 97 | | |
| 46 | .556 | 02 | 05 | 12 | 24 | 40 | 58 | 75 | 87 | 98 | | |
| 48 | .543 | 02 | 05 | 12 | 25 | 42 | 61 | 77 | 89 | 98 | | |

Table 4.3.4 *(continued)*

| n | $q_c$ | .10 | .20 | .30 | .40 | .50 | .60 | .70 | .80 | 1.00 | 1.20 | 1.40 |
|---|---|---|---|---|---|---|---|---|---|---|---|---|
| | | | | | | q | | | | | | |
| 50 | .531 | 02 | 05 | 13 | 26 | 44 | 63 | 79 | 90 | 99 | * | * |
| 52 | .520 | 02 | 06 | 14 | 28 | 46 | 65 | 81 | 92 | 99 | | |
| 54 | .510 | 02 | 06 | 14 | 29 | 48 | 68 | 83 | 93 | 99 | | |
| 56 | .501 | 02 | 06 | 15 | 30 | 50 | 69 | 85 | 94 | 99 | | |
| 58 | .491 | 02 | 06 | 16 | 32 | 52 | 72 | 86 | 95 | * | | |
| 60 | .482 | 02 | 07 | 16 | 33 | 54 | 73 | 88 | 95 | | | |
| 64 | .467 | 02 | 07 | 18 | 36 | 57 | 77 | 90 | 97 | | | |
| 68 | .452 | 02 | 08 | 19 | 38 | 61 | 80 | 92 | 98 | | | |
| 72 | .438 | 02 | 08 | 21 | 41 | 64 | 83 | 94 | 98 | | | |
| 76 | .426 | 03 | 09 | 22 | 44 | 67 | 85 | 95 | 99 | | | |
| 80 | .415 | 03 | 09 | 24 | 46 | 70 | 87 | 96 | 99 | | | |
| 84 | .405 | 03 | 10 | 25 | 49 | 73 | 89 | 97 | 99 | | | |
| 88 | .395 | 03 | 10 | 27 | 51 | 75 | 91 | 98 | * | | | |
| 92 | .386 | 03 | 11 | 28 | 54 | 78 | 92 | 98 | | | | |
| 96 | .378 | 03 | 11 | 30 | 56 | 80 | 94 | 99 | | | | |
| 100 | .370 | 03 | 12 | 31 | 58 | 82 | 95 | 99 | | | | |
| 120 | .337 | 04 | 15 | 39 | 69 | 89 | 98 | * | | | | |
| 140 | .311 | 04 | 18 | 46 | 77 | 94 | 99 | | | | | |
| 160 | .291 | 05 | 21 | 53 | 83 | 97 | * | | | | | |
| 180 | .274 | 05 | 24 | 60 | 88 | 98 | | | | | | |
| 200 | .260 | 06 | 28 | 66 | 92 | 99 | | | | | | |
| 250 | .228 | 07 | 38 | 79 | 97 | * | | | | | | |
| 300 | .211 | 09 | 44 | 86 | 99 | | | | | | | |
| 350 | .196 | 11 | 52 | 92 | * | | | | | | | |
| 400 | .183 | 12 | 60 | 95 | | | | | | | | |
| 450 | .172 | 14 | 66 | 97 | | | | | | | | |
| 500 | .163 | 16 | 72 | 98 | | | | | | | | |
| 600 | .149 | 20 | 81 | * | | | | | | | | |
| 700 | .138 | 24 | 88 | | | | | | | | | |
| 800 | .129 | 28 | 92 | | | | | | | | | |
| 900 | .122 | 32 | 95 | | | | | | | | | |
| 1000 | .115 | 37 | 97 | | | | | | | | | |

* Power values below this point are greater than .995.

Table 4.3.5

Power of Normal Curve Test of $r_1 = r_2$
via Fisher z transformation at $a_2 = .05$

| n | $q_c$ | | | | | | q | | | | | |
|---|-------|-----|-----|-----|-----|-----|-----|-----|-----|------|------|------|
| | | .10 | .20 | .30 | .40 | .50 | .60 | .70 | .80 | 1.00 | 1.20 | 1.40 |
| 8 | 1.240 | 05 | 06 | 08 | 10 | 12 | 16 | 20 | 24 | 35 | 48 | 60 |
| 9 | 1.132 | 05 | 06 | 08 | 11 | 14 | 18 | 23 | 28 | 41 | 55 | 68 |
| 10 | 1.048 | 05 | 07 | 09 | 12 | 15 | 20 | 26 | 32 | 46 | 61 | 75 |
| 11 | .980 | 05 | 07 | 09 | 13 | 17 | 22 | 29 | 36 | 52 | 67 | 80 |
| 12 | .924 | 06 | 07 | 10 | 14 | 19 | 25 | 32 | 40 | 56 | 72 | 84 |
| 13 | .877 | 06 | 07 | 10 | 15 | 20 | 27 | 35 | 43 | 61 | 77 | 88 |
| 14 | .836 | 06 | 08 | 11 | 16 | 22 | 29 | 38 | 47 | 65 | 80 | 91 |
| 15 | .800 | 06 | 08 | 11 | 17 | 23 | 31 | 40 | 50 | 69 | 84 | 93 |
| 16 | .769 | 06 | 08 | 12 | 17 | 25 | 33 | 43 | 53 | 72 | 86 | 95 |
| 17 | .741 | 06 | 08 | 12 | 18 | 26 | 35 | 46 | 56 | 75 | 89 | 96 |
| 18 | .716 | 06 | 09 | 13 | 19 | 28 | 38 | 48 | 59 | 78 | 91 | 97 |
| 19 | .693 | 06 | 09 | 14 | 20 | 29 | 40 | 51 | 62 | 81 | 92 | 98 |
| 20 | .672 | 06 | 09 | 14 | 21 | 30 | 42 | 53 | 65 | 83 | 94 | 98 |
| 21 | .653 | 06 | 09 | 15 | 22 | 32 | 44 | 56 | 67 | 85 | 95 | 99 |
| 22 | .636 | 06 | 09 | 15 | 23 | 33 | 46 | 58 | 69 | 87 | 96 | 99 |
| 23 | .620 | 06 | 10 | 16 | 24 | 35 | 48 | 60 | 72 | 88 | 97 | 99 |
| 24 | .605 | 06 | 10 | 16 | 25 | 36 | 49 | 62 | 74 | 90 | 97 | * |
| 25 | .591 | 06 | 10 | 17 | 26 | 38 | 51 | 64 | 76 | 91 | 98 | |
| 26 | .578 | 06 | 10 | 18 | 27 | 39 | 53 | 66 | 77 | 92 | 98 | |
| 27 | .566 | 06 | 11 | 18 | 28 | 41 | 55 | 68 | 79 | 93 | 99 | |
| 28 | .554 | 06 | 11 | 19 | 29 | 42 | 56 | 70 | 81 | 94 | 99 | |
| 29 | .544 | 07 | 11 | 19 | 30 | 44 | 58 | 71 | 82 | 95 | 99 | |
| 30 | .534 | 07 | 11 | 20 | 31 | 45 | 60 | 73 | 84 | 96 | 99 | |
| 31 | .524 | 07 | 12 | 20 | 32 | 46 | 61 | 75 | 85 | 96 | 99 | |
| 32 | .515 | 07 | 12 | 21 | 33 | 48 | 63 | 76 | 86 | 97 | * | |
| 33 | .506 | 07 | 12 | 21 | 34 | 49 | 64 | 77 | 87 | 97 | | |
| 34 | .498 | 07 | 12 | 22 | 35 | 51 | 66 | 79 | 88 | 98 | | |
| 35 | .490 | 07 | 13 | 22 | 36 | 52 | 67 | 80 | 89 | 98 | | |
| 36 | .483 | 07 | 13 | 23 | 37 | 53 | 68 | 81 | 90 | 98 | | |
| 37 | .475 | 07 | 13 | 24 | 38 | 54 | 70 | 82 | 91 | 98 | | |
| 38 | .469 | 07 | 13 | 24 | 39 | 55 | 71 | 83 | 92 | 99 | | |
| 39 | .462 | 07 | 14 | 25 | 40 | 56 | 72 | 84 | 92 | 99 | | |
| 40 | .456 | 07 | 14 | 25 | 41 | 58 | 73 | 85 | 93 | 99 | | |
| 42 | .444 | 07 | 14 | 26 | 42 | 60 | 75 | 87 | 94 | 99 | | |
| 44 | .433 | 07 | 15 | 27 | 44 | 62 | 78 | 89 | 95 | 99 | | |
| 46 | .423 | 08 | 15 | 29 | 46 | 64 | 79 | 90 | 96 | * | | |
| 48 | .413 | 08 | 16 | 30 | 48 | 66 | 81 | 91 | 97 | | | |

Table 4.3.5 *(continued)*

| | | q | | | | | | | | | | |
|---|---|---|---|---|---|---|---|---|---|---|---|---|
| n | $q_c$ | .10 | .20 | .30 | .40 | .50 | .60 | .70 | .80 | 1.00 | 1.20 | 1.40 |
| 50 | .404 | 08 | 16 | 31 | 49 | 68 | 83 | 92 | 97 | * | * | * |
| 52 | .396 | 08 | 17 | 32 | 51 | 70 | 84 | 93 | 98 | | | |
| 54 | .388 | 08 | 17 | 33 | 52 | 71 | 36 | 94 | 93 | | | |
| 56 | .381 | 08 | 18 | 34 | 54 | 73 | 87 | 95 | 98 | | | |
| 58 | .374 | 08 | 18 | 35 | 55 | 75 | 33 | 96 | 99 | | | |
| 60 | .367 | 08 | 19 | 36 | 57 | 76 | 89 | 96 | 99 | | | |
| 64 | .355 | 09 | 20 | 38 | 60 | 79 | 91 | 97 | 99 | | | |
| 68 | .344 | 09 | 21 | 40 | 63 | 81 | 93 | 98 | * | | | |
| 72 | .334 | 09 | 22 | 42 | 65 | 84 | 94 | 98 | | | | |
| 76 | .324 | 09 | 23 | 44 | 68 | 86 | 95 | 99 | | | | |
| 80 | .316 | 10 | 24 | 46 | 70 | 87 | 96 | 99 | | | | |
| 84 | .308 | 10 | 25 | 48 | 72 | 89 | 97 | 99 | | | | |
| 88 | .301 | 10 | 26 | 50 | 74 | 90 | 97 | * | | | | |
| 92 | .294 | 10 | 27 | 52 | 76 | 92 | 98 | | | | | |
| 96 | .287 | 10 | 28 | 53 | 78 | 93 | 98 | | | | | |
| 100 | .281 | 11 | 29 | 55 | 80 | 94 | 99 | | | | | |
| 120 | .256 | 12 | 33 | 63 | 86 | 97 | * | | | | | |
| 140 | .237 | 13 | 38 | 70 | 91 | 99 | | | | | | |
| 160 | .221 | 14 | 43 | 76 | 94 | 99 | | | | | | |
| 180 | .208 | 16 | 47 | 81 | 96 | * | | | | | | |
| 200 | .198 | 17 | 51 | 85 | 98 | | | | | | | |
| 250 | .173 | 20 | 62 | 92 | 99 | | | | | | | |
| 300 | .161 | 23 | 68 | 96 | * | | | | | | | |
| 350 | .149 | 26 | 75 | 98 | | | | | | | | |
| 400 | .139 | 29 | 80 | 99 | | | | | | | | |
| 450 | .131 | 32 | 85 | 99 | | | | | | | | |
| 500 | .124 | 35 | 88 | * | | | | | | | | |
| 600 | .113 | 41 | 93 | | | | | | | | | |
| 700 | .105 | 46 | 96 | | | | | | | | | |
| 800 | .098 | 51 | 98 | | | | | | | | | |
| 900 | .093 | 56 | 99 | | | | | | | | | |
| 1000 | .088 | 61 | 99 | | | | | | | | | |

* Power values below this point are greater than .995.

Table 4.3.6

Power of Normal Curve Test of $r_1 = r_2$
via Fisher z transformation at $a_2 = .10$

| n | $q_c$ | .10 | .20 | .30 | .40 | .50 | .60 | .70 | .80 | 1.00 | 1.20 | 1.40 |
|---|---|---|---|---|---|---|---|---|---|---|---|---|
| 8 | 1.040 | 10 | 12 | 14 | 17 | 20 | 25 | 30 | 35 | 48 | 60 | 71 |
| 9 | .950 | 11 | 12 | 15 | 18 | 22 | 28 | 33 | 40 | 54 | 67 | 78 |
| 10 | .879 | 11 | 12 | 15 | 19 | 24 | 30 | 37 | 44 | 59 | 73 | 83 |
| 11 | .822 | 11 | 13 | 16 | 20 | 26 | 33 | 40 | 48 | 64 | 77 | 88 |
| 12 | .776 | 11 | 13 | 17 | 22 | 28 | 36 | 44 | 52 | 68 | 82 | 91 |
| 13 | .736 | 11 | 13 | 18 | 23 | 30 | 38 | 47 | 56 | 72 | 85 | 93 |
| 14 | .701 | 11 | 14 | 18 | 24 | 32 | 41 | 50 | 59 | 76 | 88 | 95 |
| 15 | .672 | 11 | 14 | 19 | 26 | 34 | 43 | 53 | 62 | 79 | 90 | 96 |
| 16 | .645 | 11 | 14 | 20 | 27 | 36 | 45 | 56 | 65 | 82 | 92 | 97 |
| 17 | .622 | 11 | 15 | 20 | 28 | 38 | 48 | 58 | 68 | 84 | 94 | 98 |
| 18 | .606 | 11 | 15 | 21 | 29 | 39 | 50 | 61 | 71 | 86 | 95 | 99 |
| 19 | .582 | 11 | 15 | 22 | 31 | 41 | 52 | 63 | 73 | 88 | 96 | 99 |
| 20 | .564 | 11 | 16 | 23 | 32 | 43 | 54 | 65 | 75 | 90 | 97 | 99 |
| 21 | .548 | 12 | 16 | 23 | 33 | 44 | 56 | 67 | 77 | 91 | 97 | 99 |
| 22 | .534 | 12 | 16 | 24 | 34 | 46 | 58 | 70 | 79 | 92 | 98 | * |
| 23 | .520 | 12 | 17 | 25 | 35 | 48 | 60 | 71 | 81 | 94 | 98 | |
| 24 | .508 | 12 | 17 | 25 | 37 | 49 | 67 | 73 | 83 | 94 | 99 | |
| 25 | .496 | 12 | 17 | 26 | 38 | 51 | 64 | 75 | 84 | 95 | 99 | |
| 26 | .485 | 12 | 18 | 27 | 39 | 52 | 65 | 77 | 86 | 96 | 99 | |
| 27 | .475 | 12 | 18 | 27 | 40 | 54 | 67 | 78 | 87 | 97 | 99 | |
| 28 | .465 | 12 | 18 | 28 | 41 | 55 | 68 | 80 | 88 | 97 | * | |
| 29 | .456 | 12 | 19 | 29 | 42 | 56 | 70 | 81 | 89 | 98 | | |
| 30 | .448 | 12 | 19 | 30 | 43 | 58 | 71 | 82 | 90 | 98 | | |
| 31 | .440 | 12 | 19 | 30 | 44 | 59 | 73 | 84 | 91 | 98 | | |
| 32 | .432 | 12 | 20 | 31 | 45 | 60 | 74 | 85 | 92 | 98 | | |
| 33 | .425 | 13 | 20 | 32 | 46 | 61 | 75 | 86 | 93 | 99 | | |
| 34 | .418 | 13 | 20 | 32 | 47 | 63 | 76 | 87 | 93 | 99 | | |
| 35 | .411 | 13 | 21 | 33 | 48 | 64 | 77 | 88 | 94 | 99 | | |
| 36 | .405 | 13 | 21 | 34 | 49 | 65 | 79 | 88 | 95 | 99 | | |
| 37 | .399 | 13 | 21 | 34 | 50 | 66 | 80 | 89 | 95 | 99 | | |
| 38 | .393 | 13 | 22 | 35 | 51 | 67 | 81 | 90 | 96 | 99 | | |
| 39 | .388 | 13 | 22 | 36 | 52 | 68 | 82 | 91 | 96 | * | | |
| 40 | .382 | 13 | 22 | 36 | 53 | 69 | 83 | 91 | 96 | | | |
| 42 | .372 | 13 | 23 | 38 | 55 | 71 | 84 | 93 | 97 | | | |
| 44 | .363 | 13 | 24 | 39 | 57 | 73 | 86 | 94 | 98 | | | |
| 46 | .355 | 14 | 24 | 40 | 58 | 75 | 87 | 95 | 98 | | | |
| 48 | .347 | 14 | 25 | 41 | 60 | 77 | 89 | 95 | 98 | | | |

Table 4.3.6 (continued)

| n | $q_c$ | q .10 | .20 | .30 | .40 | .50 | .60 | .70 | .80 | 1.00 | 1.20 | 1.40 |
|---|---|---|---|---|---|---|---|---|---|---|---|---|
| 50 | .339 | 14 | 25 | 43 | 62 | 78 | 90 | 96 | 99 | * | * | * |
| 52 | .332 | 14 | 26 | 44 | 63 | 80 | 91 | 97 | 99 | | | |
| 54 | .326 | 14 | 26 | 45 | 65 | 81 | 92 | 97 | 99 | | | |
| 56 | .320 | 14 | 27 | 46 | 66 | 82 | 93 | 97 | 99 | | | |
| 58 | .314 | 15 | 28 | 47 | 67 | 84 | 93 | 98 | 99 | | | |
| 60 | .308 | 15 | 29 | 48 | 69 | 85 | 94 | 98 | * | | | |
| 64 | .298 | 15 | 30 | 51 | 71 | 87 | 95 | 99 | | | | |
| 68 | .289 | 15 | 31 | 53 | 74 | 89 | 96 | 99 | | | | |
| 72 | .280 | 16 | 32 | 55 | 76 | 90 | 97 | 99 | | | | |
| 76 | .272 | 16 | 33 | 57 | 78 | 92 | 98 | * | | | | |
| 80 | .265 | 16 | 35 | 59 | 80 | 93 | 98 | | | | | |
| 84 | .258 | 17 | 36 | 60 | 82 | 94 | 99 | | | | | |
| 88 | .252 | 17 | 37 | 62 | 83 | 95 | 99 | | | | | |
| 92 | .247 | 17 | 38 | 64 | 85 | 95 | 99 | | | | | |
| 96 | .241 | 17 | 39 | 66 | 86 | 96 | 99 | | | | | |
| 100 | .236 | 18 | 41 | 68 | 87 | 97 | 99 | | | | | |
| 120 | .231 | 20 | 45 | 74 | 92 | 99 | * | | | | | |
| 140 | .199 | 21 | 50 | 80 | 95 | 99 | | | | | | |
| 160 | .186 | 23 | 55 | 84 | 97 | * | | | | | | |
| 180 | .175 | 25 | 59 | 88 | 98 | | | | | | | |
| 200 | .166 | 26 | 63 | 91 | 99 | | | | | | | |
| 250 | .146 | 31 | 73 | 96 | * | | | | | | | |
| 300 | .135 | 34 | 79 | 98 | | | | | | | | |
| 350 | .125 | 37 | 84 | 99 | | | | | | | | |
| 400 | .117 | 40 | 88 | * | | | | | | | | |
| 450 | .110 | 44 | 91 | | | | | | | | | |
| 500 | .104 | 47 | 93 | | | | | | | | | |
| 600 | .095 | 53 | 96 | | | | | | | | | |
| 700 | .088 | 59 | 98 | | | | | | | | | |
| 800 | .082 | 64 | 99 | | | | | | | | | |
| 900 | .078 | 68 | * | | | | | | | | | |
| 1000 | .074 | 72 | | | | | | | | | | |

* Power values below this point are greater than .995.

(say) .10, the tables can also be used for power at $a_2 = .02, a_2 = .20, a_1 = .005$, and $a_1 = .025$.

2. *Effect Size*, ES. This is the difference between Fisher z-transformed r's, **q**, whose properties are described in Section 4.2. Tables 4.2.1 and 4.2.2 facilitate the conversion of $r_1, r_2$ pairs into **q** values. Provision in the power tables is made for $q = .10 \,(.10)\, .80 \,(.20)\, 1.40$. Conventional definitions of ES have been offered, as follows:

small: $q = .10$, medium: $q = .30$, large: $q = .50$.

3. *Sample Size*, **n**. This is the size of each of the two samples whose $r_s$'s are being compared. Provision is made for $n = 8 \,(1)\, 40 \,(2)\, 60 \,(4)\, 100 \,(20)$ 200 (50) 500 (100) 1000.

The values in the body of the table are the power of the test $\times 100$, i.e., the percentage of tests carried out under the given conditions which will result in the rejection of the null hypothesis. They are rounded to the nearest unit and are accurate to within $\pm 1$ as tabled.

## Illustrative Examples

**4.1** A marriage counselor has been studying the issue of personality similarity as a factor in the quality of marriage relationships. She has gathered data on several personality questionnaire variables from 60 husband–wife pairs in marriages rated as harmonious (Group 1) and from another 60 pairs with marital difficulties (Group 2). The study design involves the determination of the husband–wife correlation in each group for each personality variable, followed by a test of the significance of the difference between the two groups' $r_s$'s (for each variable), i.e., $H_0{:}r_1 = r_2$. Her significance criterion is $a_2 = .05$. Given that the ES is $q = .30$ (the optional definition of a medium difference), what is the power of each test? The specifications are

$$a_2 = .05, \qquad q = .30, \qquad n_1 = n_2 = n = 60.$$

To find the test's power, in Table 4.3.5 for $a_2 = .05$, column $q = .30$, and row $n = 60$, power $= .36$. Thus, the probability of a significant ($a_2 = .05$) result is only slightly greater than one in three if the two populations differ in degree of relationship by $q = .30$ (e.g., population r values of .20, .46, or .40, .62 or .60, .76 from Table 4.2.1, or, if of opposite sign, e.g., $-.15, .15$ or $-.10$, $+.20$).

If one posits large ($q = .50$) instead of medium ES, one finds in the same table and row, but for column $q = .50$, power $= .76$. Only if one is seeking to detect an ES of $q = .60–.70$ does power increase to the low nineties, but this ES implies r pairs such as .20, .70 or .40, .80 or opposite sign pairs of the order of $-.30, +.30$ or $-.10, +.50$.

**4.2** A theory of psychopathology yields the derivation that the correla-ation between two variables $X$, $Y$, should be higher for paranoid schizo-phrenics than for catatonic schizophrenics. A research psychiatrist gathers the relevant data for 180 cases in each diagnostic group, in order to perform a one-tailed significance test at $a_1 = .01$. On the several alternative hypotheses that the difference in $r$ is small ($q = .10$), medium ($q = .30$), and large ($q = .50$), what is the power in each instance? Specifications are

$$a_1 = .01, \qquad q = \begin{matrix} .10 \\ .30, \\ .50 \end{matrix} \qquad n_1 = n_2 = n = 180.$$

In Table 4.3.1 for $a_1 = .01$, row $n = 180$, and for columns $q = .10, .30$, and .50, one finds respectively power values of .08, .69, and .99. The extreme spread of these power values strongly suggests the importance of deciding how large the anticipated ES is (at least at this level of $n$). Depending on the ES, the experiment has either a poor, fairly good, or virtually certain proba-bility of a significant result. If the result is not significant, the only con-clusion that can be drawn is that the difference in degree of relationship between the populations favoring the paranoid schizophrenics, if any, is not large. Were the degree of relationship large, with power of .99 to detect a large effect, it would likely have been found. A medium or small difference may well exist; the latter possibility, in particular, is quite consonant with the results. Of course, given nonsignificant results, the investigator cannot con-clude that a difference exists, whatever the *a priori* power.

**4.3.2** CASE 1: $n_1 \neq n_2$. The tables will yield power values when, under the conditions for a valid test of the significance of the difference between two population $r$'s, samples of different sizes are drawn. In such cases, compute

(4.3.1) $$n' = \frac{2(n_1 - 3)(n_2 - 3)}{n_1 + n_2 - 6} + 3,$$

and use the $n'$ value in the $n$ column of the table. Unless one of the $n$'s is very small ($<10$), the power value found is an exact value.[2] Also, all of the interpretative material of Section 4.3.1 on differences between degrees of relationship holds for Case 1.

**Illustrative Example**

**4.3** A psycholinguist has developed and used in a series of researches a certain procedure ($P_2$) for measuring speech disruption whose population reliability (i.e., correlation between parallel forms) is estimated as falling in the .75–.85 range. For theoretical and practical reasons, he designs an alter-

---

[2] That is, it is as exact as the Case 0 value, i.e., accurate within $\pm 1$.

native procedure ($P_1$) whose reliability compared to $P_2$ he wishes to assess. For practical reasons he is interested in the possibility that $r_1 > r_2$, but difference in the other direction would also be quite meaningful to theory. Thus a nondirectional test is indicated, and he elects to use $a_2 = .05$. If $r_2$ is approximately .80, he is interested in the possibility that $r_1$ is about .10 away (particularly if it is about .90). Reference to Table 4.2.1 indicates that the $r$ pairs .75, .88; .80, .90; and .85, .93, all of which define an ES = $q$ = .40 (i.e., between medium and large), represent the magnitude involved. Now, he has accumulated data on the original procedure for $n_2 = 260$, and uses the new procedure on an independent sample of $n_1 = 51$. What is the power of the test?

$$a_2 = .05, \qquad q = .40, \qquad n_1 = 51 \neq 260 = n_2.$$

With unequal $n$, he finds [from formula (4.3.1)]

$$n' = \frac{2\,(51 - 3)(260 - 3)}{51 + 260 - 6} + 3 = \frac{2\,(48)(257)}{305} + 3 = 84.$$

In Table 4.3.5 for $a_2 = .05$, column $q = .40$, and row $n' = n = 84$, power = .72. Thus, his chances are (not quite) three in four of detecting a difference of $q = .40$, given these conditions.

Note the implication of $n'$. His samples of 51 and 260, a total of 311 cases, yields as much power as two equal samples of 84 cases, a total of 168 cases. As previously noted in two-sample comparisons, for a given total number cases, optimal power for any specified conditions occurs when the total number is divided equally. That is, an equal division of his 311 cases would yield two samples of 155 cases, for which the power would be .93 (interpolating in Table 4.3.5), instead of the value of .72 for the actual unequal division.

4.3.3   CASE 2: ONE SAMPLE OF $n$ OBSERVATIONS TO TEST $r = c$. Thus far we have considered the power of the normal curve test via the difference between Fisher's transformations of $r$'s of two independent samples, where the null hypothesis is $r_1 = r_2$. The same transformation and test can be used to test the departure of the $r$ of a single population from some specified value $c$. The null hypothesis for the one-sample test is $r = c$. The test is employed when, given a sample of $n$ cases, the investigator's purpose is to determine whether the data are consonant with the hypothesis that the population $r$ is .50 or .90 or $-.25$ or any other value. It is thus the general case of which the test of Chapter 3 that $r$ is zero is a special case.

Although the special case $r = c = 0$ arises frequently in behavioral science, the $r = c \neq 0$ form is also encountered. It will be found useful in psychometric technology where experience has led to certain expectations or standards for values of reliability and validity coefficients which would then serve as values for $c$. In behavioral genetics or other areas of behavioral science where strong theory exists, derivations from theory may also yield specific values of $c$ whose statistical testing brings important information.

For the one-sample case (Case 2), we define our ES as for the other cases, i.e., as the difference between $z$-transformed $r$'s, but whereas in formula (4.2.2), $r_2 \rightarrow z_2$ is an estimable population parameter, here it is a constant, so that for Case 2

(4.3.2)  $\quad q_2' = z_1 - z_c \qquad$ (directional)

$\qquad\qquad = |z_1 - z_c| \qquad$ (nondirectional),

where $z_1$ = the Fisher $z$ transformation of the alternative-hypothetical $r$ as before and

$\quad z_c$ = the Fisher $z$ transformation of the null-hypothetical $c$.

There is no conceptual change: $q_2'$ is the difference between the (alternate) population value ($r_1$) and the value specified by the null hypothesis ($c$) expressed, as before, in units of the $z$ transformation. The interpretation of $q_2'$ proceeds exactly as described in Section 4.2 with regard to Table 4.2.1, $r^2$, and $E$, and the operational definitions of small, medium, and large ES.

The tables, however, are not applied to the value $q_2'$ since they are constructed for Case 0, where there are *two* sample statistics ($z_1$ and $z_2$) which *each* contribute sampling error variance to the observed sample difference, for a total variance of $2/(n - 3)$. Here only one sample contributes sampling error variance, yielding half the amount, $1/(n - 3)$. This is simply allowed for by finding

(4.3.3)                            $$q = q_2' \sqrt{2}.$$

The $q$ value is sought in the tables, while $q_2'$ is the ES index which is interpreted. This procedure is exact.[3]

If $q_2'$ is chosen as a convenient multiple of .10, $q$ will in general not be a multiple of .10. Thus the operational definitions of ES for $q_2'$ of .10, .30, and .50 become, for the one sample test, $q = .14, .42$, and .71. Linear interpolation between power values will provide values which are sufficiently close (within .01 or .02) for most purposes.

### Illustrative Example

**4.4**  A social psychologist has developed a considerable body of data on attitudes toward the mentally ill. One of his scales yields an alternate-form correlation coefficient which he can estimate as being very close to .60 in the population. He has prepared a revision of this scale to improve its reliability but must weigh an improvement of reliability against the loss of comparability of a revised scale. He decides that if he could raise the population

---

[3] Unlike the one-sample test of a mean (Section 2.3.4) which proceeds by a $t$ test with its dependence on varying $n$ and $df$, the present test uses the normal curve for all $n$, and no overestimation of power occurs when the tables are used for the one-sample test of $r$.

reliability (correlation) to the middle seventies, say .76 (see Table 4.2.1), it would warrant the replacement of the original scale. Thus, he will perform a one-sample test to determine whether he can conclude that the revision is superior. As formulated, he has no interest in the possibility that the revision has lower reliability; thus his test is one-tailed (directional), and he selects as his significance criterion $a_1 = .05$. He administers the revised scale to a sample of 50 subjects.

The null hypothesis he is testing is, therefore, $r \leq .60$ with an alternative hypothesis (or ES) of $r = .76$. Informally stated, his research questions are: Does the revised scale have reliability in the population better than .60? For the power analysis, he asks: If it is as high as .76, what is the probability that I will conclude that it is better than .60 with $n = 50$ at $a_1 = .05$?

Reference to Table 4.2.1 shows that the .60, .76 values of $r$ yield $q_2' = .30$ (and incidentally, why the author chose the value .76). Note that $q_2' = .30$ represents a medium effect. For table entry, we need $q = .30\sqrt{2} = .424$. Summarizing the specifications

$$a_1 = .05, \qquad q = .424, \qquad n = 50.$$

In Table 4.3.2 for $a_1 = .05$ and row $n = 50$, he finds power in columns $q = .40$ and .50 to be .62 and .78, respectively. Linear interpolation between these values yields power at $q = .424$ of $(.424 - .40)(.78 - .62)/.10 + .62 = .66$. Thus, if $r = .76$, his $a_1 = .05$ test for $n = 50$ has a two in three chance of getting a significant result, warranting the conclusion that $r > .60$. Note that no mention has been made of the sample $r_s$; this is irrelevant to the power analysis, which may (or better, should) be performed prior to the data collection.

## 4.4 SAMPLE SIZE TABLES

The tables in this section list values of the significance criterion, the ES to be detected, and the *desired power*. One then finds the necessary sample size. Their primary utility lies in the planning of experiments to provide a basis for the decision as to the number of sampling units (**n**) to use.

4.4.1 CASE 0: $n_1 = n_2$. The use of the sample size tables first described is that for which they were optimally designed, Case 0, where they yield the sample size, **n**, for each of two independent samples whose population $r$'s are to be compared. The description of their use in two other cases follows this subsection. Tables are entered with **a**, **q**, and desired power.

*1. Significance Criterion*, **a**. The same values of **a** are provided as in the power tables, a table for each of the following: $a_1 = .01$ ($a_2 = .02$), $a_1 = .05$ ($a_2 = .10$), $a_1 = .10$ ($a_2 = .20$), $a_2 = .01$ ($a_1 = .005$), and $a_2 = .05$ ($a_1 = .025$).

*2. Effect Size*, **q**. This value is defined and interpreted as above [formula

Table 4.4.1

n to detect q = $z_1 - z_2$ by Fisher
z Transformation of r

| | | | | | $a_1 = .01$ ($a_2 = .02$) | | | | | | |
| | | | | | | q | | | | | |
| Power | .10 | .20 | .30 | .40 | .50 | .60 | .70 | .80 | 1.00 | 1.20 | 1.40 |
|---|---|---|---|---|---|---|---|---|---|---|---|
| .25 | 549 | 139 | 64 | 37 | 25 | 18 | 14 | 12 | 8 | 7 | 6 |
| .50 | 1085 | 274 | 123 | 71 | 46 | 33 | 25 | 20 | 14 | 11 | 9 |
| .60 | 1334 | 336 | 151 | 86 | 56 | 40 | 30 | 24 | 16 | 12 | 10 |
| 2/3 | 1523 | 383 | 172 | 98 | 64 | 45 | 34 | 27 | 18 | 14 | 11 |
| .70 | 1628 | 409 | 184 | 105 | 68 | 48 | 36 | 28 | 19 | 14 | 11 |
| .75 | 1804 | 453 | 203 | 116 | 75 | 53 | 40 | 31 | 21 | 16 | 12 |
| .80 | 2010 | 505 | 226 | 128 | 83 | 59 | 44 | 34 | 23 | 17 | 13 |
| .85 | 2265 | 568 | 254 | 144 | 93 | 66 | 49 | 38 | 26 | 19 | 15 |
| .90 | 2606 | 654 | 292 | 166 | 107 | 75 | 56 | 44 | 29 | 21 | 16 |
| .95 | 3157 | 792 | 353 | 200 | 129 | 91 | 67 | 52 | 35 | 25 | 19 |
| .99 | 4333 | 1085 | 484 | 274 | 176 | 123 | 91 | 71 | 46 | 33 | 25 |

| | | | | | $a_1 = .05$ ($a_2 = .10$) | | | | | | |
| | | | | | | q | | | | | |
| Power | .10 | .20 | .30 | .40 | .50 | .60 | .70 | .80 | 1.00 | 1.20 | 1.40 |
|---|---|---|---|---|---|---|---|---|---|---|---|
| .25 | 191 | 50 | 24 | 15 | 11 | 8 | 7 | 6 | 5 | 4 | 4 |
| .50 | 544 | 138 | 63 | 37 | 25 | 18 | 14 | 11 | 8 | 7 | 6 |
| .60 | 724 | 183 | 83 | 48 | 32 | 23 | 18 | 14 | 10 | 8 | 7 |
| 2/3 | 865 | 218 | 99 | 57 | 37 | 27 | 21 | 16 | 12 | 9 | 7 |
| .70 | 944 | 238 | 108 | 62 | 41 | 29 | 22 | 18 | 12 | 10 | 8 |
| .75 | 1079 | 272 | 123 | 70 | 46 | 33 | 25 | 20 | 14 | 10 | 9 |
| .80 | 1240 | 312 | 140 | 80 | 52 | 37 | 28 | 22 | 15 | 12 | 9 |
| .85 | 1441 | 362 | 163 | 93 | 61 | 43 | 32 | 25 | 17 | 13 | 10 |
| .90 | 1716 | 431 | 193 | 110 | 72 | 51 | 38 | 30 | 20 | 15 | 12 |
| .95 | 2167 | 544 | 243 | 138 | 90 | 63 | 47 | 37 | 25 | 18 | 14 |
| .99 | 3157 | 792 | 353 | 200 | 129 | 91 | 67 | 52 | 35 | 25 | 19 |

| | | | | | $a_1 = .10$ ($a_2 = .20$) | | | | | | |
| | | | | | | q | | | | | |
| Power | .10 | .20 | .30 | .40 | .50 | .60 | .70 | .80 | 1.00 | 1.20 | 1.40 |
|---|---|---|---|---|---|---|---|---|---|---|---|
| .25 | 77 | 21 | 11 | 8 | 6 | 5 | 4 | 4 | 4 | -- | -- |
| .50 | 331 | 85 | 39 | 24 | 16 | 12 | 10 | 8 | 6 | 5 | 5 |
| .60 | 474 | 121 | 55 | 32 | 22 | 16 | 13 | 10 | 8 | 6 | 5 |
| 2/3 | 589 | 150 | 68 | 40 | 26 | 19 | 15 | 12 | 9 | 7 | 6 |
| .70 | 655 | 166 | 75 | 44 | 29 | 21 | 16 | 13 | 10 | 8 | 6 |
| .75 | 768 | 194 | 88 | 51 | 34 | 24 | 19 | 15 | 11 | 8 | 7 |
| .80 | 905 | 228 | 103 | 59 | 39 | 28 | 21 | 17 | 12 | 9 | 8 |
| .85 | 1078 | 272 | 122 | 70 | 46 | 33 | 25 | 20 | 14 | 10 | 8 |
| .90 | 1317 | 331 | 149 | 85 | 56 | 39 | 30 | 24 | 16 | 12 | 10 |
| .95 | 1716 | 431 | 193 | 110 | 72 | 51 | 38 | 30 | 20 | 15 | 12 |
| .99 | 2606 | 654 | 292 | 166 | 107 | 75 | 56 | 44 | 29 | 21 | 16 |

Table 4.4.1 *(continued)*

| Power | .10 | .20 | .30 | .40 | .50 | .60 | .70 | .80 | 1.00 | 1.20 | 1.40 |
|---|---|---|---|---|---|---|---|---|---|---|---|
| | | | | $a_2 = .01$ ($a_1 = .005$) | | | | | | | |
| | | | | | | $q$ | | | | | |
| .25 | 726 | 184 | 83 | 48 | 32 | 23 | 18 | 14 | 10 | 8 | 7 |
| .50 | 1330 | 335 | 150 | 86 | 56 | 40 | 30 | 24 | 16 | 12 | 10 |
| .60 | 1604 | 403 | 181 | 103 | 67 | 47 | 36 | 28 | 19 | 14 | 11 |
| 2/3 | 1811 | 455 | 204 | 116 | 75 | 53 | 40 | 31 | 21 | 16 | 12 |
| .70 | 1925 | 484 | 217 | 123 | 80 | 56 | 42 | 33 | 22 | 16 | 13 |
| .75 | 2116 | 531 | 238 | 135 | 88 | 62 | 46 | 36 | 24 | 18 | 14 |
| .80 | 2339 | 587 | 263 | 149 | 96 | 68 | 51 | 39 | 26 | 19 | 15 |
| .85 | 2613 | 655 | 293 | 166 | 107 | 75 | 56 | 44 | 29 | 21 | 16 |
| .90 | 2979 | 747 | 334 | 189 | 122 | 86 | 64 | 49 | 33 | 24 | 18 |
| .95 | 3566 | 894 | 399 | 226 | 146 | 102 | 76 | 59 | 39 | 28 | 21 |
| .99 | 4809 | 1205 | 537 | 303 | 195 | 137 | 101 | 78 | 51 | 36 | 28 |

| Power | .10 | .20 | .30 | .40 | .50 | .60 | .70 | .80 | 1.00 | 1.20 | 1.40 |
|---|---|---|---|---|---|---|---|---|---|---|---|
| | | | | $a_2 = .05$ ($a_1 = .025$) | | | | | | | |
| | | | | | | $q$ | | | | | |
| .25 | 333 | 86 | 40 | 24 | 16 | 12 | 10 | 8 | 6 | 5 | 5 |
| .50 | 771 | 195 | 88 | 51 | 34 | 24 | 19 | 15 | 11 | 8 | 7 |
| .60 | 983 | 248 | 112 | 64 | 42 | 30 | 23 | 18 | 13 | 10 | 8 |
| 2/3 | 1146 | 289 | 130 | 74 | 49 | 35 | 26 | 21 | 14 | 11 | 9 |
| .70 | 1237 | 312 | 140 | 80 | 52 | 37 | 28 | 22 | 15 | 12 | 9 |
| .75 | 1391 | 350 | 157 | 90 | 59 | 42 | 31 | 25 | 17 | 13 | 10 |
| .80 | 1573 | 395 | 177 | 101 | 66 | 47 | 35 | 28 | 19 | 14 | 11 |
| .85 | 1799 | 452 | 203 | 115 | 75 | 53 | 40 | 31 | 21 | 15 | 12 |
| .90 | 2104 | 528 | 236 | 134 | 87 | 61 | 46 | 36 | 24 | 18 | 14 |
| .95 | 2602 | 653 | 292 | 165 | 107 | 75 | 56 | 44 | 29 | 21 | 16 |
| .99 | 3677 | 922 | 411 | 233 | 150 | 105 | 78 | 60 | 40 | 29 | 22 |

(4.2.2)] and used as in the power tables. The same provision is made: .10 (.10) .80 (.20) 1.40.

To find **n** for a value of **q** not tabled, a good approximation is given by substituting in

$$(4.4.1) \qquad n = \frac{n_{.10} - 3}{100q^2} + 3,$$

where $n_{.10}$ is the necessary sample size for the given **a** and desired power at **q** = .10, and **q** is the nontabled ES. Round to the nearest integer.

*3. Desired Power.* Provision is made for entering the sample size tables with desired power values of .25, .50, .60, 2/3, .70 (.05) .95, .99. See the discussion in Section 2.4.1 on the selection of these values and considerations affecting choice in a given investigation. The suggestion of desired power =

.80 to serve as a convention, in the absence of other bases for choice, is reiterated here.

Summarizing the Case 0 procedure, the investigator finds (a) the table for the significance criterion (**a**) he is using, and looks for (b) the difference in **z**-transformed **r**'s (**q**) along the horizontal stub and (c) the desired power along the vertical stub. He then finds **n**, the necessary size of *each* sample to detect **q** at the **a** significance criterion with the desired power.

### Illustrative Examples

**4.5**   Reconsider example 4.1, where a research study in personality similarity between spouses as a factor in the quality of marital relationships is described. In its initial formulation, a medium difference in correlation, i.e., ES = **q** = .30 was posited, and the significance criterion of $a_2 = .05$ was to be used. If power of .80 is desired, what is the sample size necessary? The specifications thus are

$$a_2 = .05, \quad q = .30, \quad \text{power} = .80.$$

In Table 4.4.1 for $a_2 = .05$, column **q** = .30, and row power = .80, **n** = 177. The investigator will thus need samples of good and poor marital pairs with 177 couples in each in order to detect a **q** = .30 difference in **z**-transformed correlations at the $a_2 = .05$ level. If she reconsiders her specifications and is content to posit **q** = .50 instead, the sample size required in each group is 66.

**4.6**   In example 4.2, a study testing for a higher correlation of a given pair of variables in paranoid than in catatonic schizophrenics was described. The significance criterion is $a_1 = .01$. Assume that the psychiatrist is content with power of .75 and poses the question: How many cases are required, assuming successively that **q** = .10, .30, and .50?

$$a_1 = .01, \quad q = \begin{matrix} .10 \\ .30 \\ .50 \end{matrix}, \quad \text{power} = .75.$$

In the section of Table 4.4.1 for $a_1 = .01$ and row power = .75, the values in columns **q** = .10, .30, .50 are found to be 1804, 203, and 75, respectively. She may then decide that she is content to try to detect a medium effect and plan to collect samples of 203 cases of each schizophrenic type. Alternatively, she may reconsider her significance criterion. If she sets it at $a_1 = .05$, she finds from Table 4.4.1 (specifications otherwise the same) **n**'s of 1079, 123, and 46 for the three **q** levels; if she sets it at $a_1 = .10$, she finds in the next section of the table 768, 88, and 34. Her explorations in sample size requirements can be summarized in tabular form:

**n** FOR DESIRED POWER $= .75$

| | | | q | |
|---|---|---|---|---|
| | | .10 | .30 | .50 |
| Significance | .01 | 1804 | 203 | 75 |
| level $a_1$ | .05 | 1079 | 123 | 46 |
| | .10 | 768 | 88 | 34 |

Depending on her resources for data gathering and the theory being tested, she can make a choice among these possibilities, or investigate others (non-directional **a, q** of .20, .40).

4.4.2   CASE 1: $n_1 \neq n_2$. One does not ordinarily *plan* to use samples of unequal size (since equal sample sizes are optimal), but Case 1 can occur in planning when a value of $r_s$ is already available from a given sample or one sample's size is necessarily fixed by circumstances, so that the researcher's freedom in setting sample size is restricted to only one of the two samples. With one sample size fixed at $n_F$, this value will generally differ from that of the other sample, whose size is at the researcher's disposal ($n_U$). As in Case 0, given **a, q**, and desired power, Table 4.4.1 gives values for **n**. To find $n_U$, substitute the fixed sample size ($n_F$) and the **n** read from the table in

$$(4.4.2) \qquad\qquad n_U = \frac{n_F(n + 3) - 6n}{2n_F - n - 3}.$$

(See Section 2.4.2 when denominator is zero or negative.)

**Illustrative Example**

4.7   Return to consider again the situation described in example 4.3. The issue is whether a new procedure ($P_2$) has a significantly different ($a_2 = .05$) parallel form correlation from that of an older procedure ($P_1$). The ES to be detected is $q = .40$, and a sample is already available to estimate the correlation of $P_1$, with $n_F = 260$. Assuming that he desires power of .90, what sample size $n_U$ does he require for the test?

If he were unconstrained in the choice of **n** for both samples, i.e., if Case 0 conditions prevailed, his specifications would simply be

$$a_2 = .05, \qquad q = .40, \qquad \text{power} = .90.$$

In the section of Table 4.4.1 for $a_2 = .05$, with column $q = .40$ and row power $= .90$, one finds that samples of 134 cases each would be required. But in this instance, he already has one sample whose size is fixed at $n_F = 260$.

Thus, the other sample need only contain (substituting $n_F = 260$ and $n = 134$ in formula (4.4.2))

$$n_U = \frac{260(134 + 3) - 6(134)}{2(260) - 134 - 3} = 91 \text{ cases.}$$

Thus, the availability of a sample of $n_F = 260$ cases makes it possible for him to satisfy his specifications (attain power of .90 to detect $q = .40$ at $a_2 = .05$) with a sample for the new procedure of 91 cases.

4.4.3   CASE 2: ONE SAMPLE OF $n$ OBSERVATIONS TO TEST $r = c$. In using the $n$ tables for the one-sample test, the only departure from Case 0 is that which was discussed in connection with the power tables for Case 2, the proper value of $q$ to be sought in the table (see Section 4.3.3 for details). Briefly, if one is testing with a single sample the null hypothesis that the population $r$ has some specified value, i.e., $H_0 : r = c$, and scales his ES in the usual way, as a difference between $z$-transformed values of $r_1$ and $c$, namely $q_2' = z_1 - z_c$, then $n$ value is determined for $q = q_2' \sqrt{2}$. If the resultant $q$ is not tabled (a likely occurrence), he takes recourse to the procedure described in connection with formula (4.4.1).

**Illustrative Example**

**4.8**   We return to example 4.4, where a social psychologist, engaged in an attitude-scale revision effort, plans a test at $a_1 = .05$ of $H_0 : r \leq .60$ against the alternate $H_1 : r_1 = .76$. Instead of assuming a sample size and determining the resulting power, as was done in problem 4.4, let us here assume that he seeks the sample size necessary for power to be .95. Note that this is an instance in which the investigator wishes the two kinds of errors to be equal, i.e., Type I $= .05$, Type II $= b = 1 - .95 = .05$.

As before, for $r$'s of .60 and .76, the difference in $z$ units (Table 4.2.1) is .30, which is $q_2'$. To use the table we require $q = .30 \sqrt{2} = .4243$, as in problem 4.4. Thus, the specifications are

$$a_1 = .05, \quad q = .4243, \quad \text{power} = .95.$$

Since $q = .4243$ is not tabled, we follow the procedure described in Section 4.4.1. In the part of Table 4.4.1 for $a_1 = .05$, row power $= .95$, and column $q = .10$, find $n_{.10}, = 2167$. Then substitute $n_{.10} = 2167$ and $q = .4243$ in formula (4.4.1) for the required $n$:

$$n = \frac{2167 - 3}{100 \, (.4243)^2} + 3 = 123.$$

Thus if $r = .76$, a one-sample test of $H_0 : r = .60$ performed at the $a_1 = .05$ level will have .95 probability of a significant result if the sample $n$ is 123.

## 4.5 THE USE OF THE TABLES FOR SIGNIFICANCE TESTING

4.5.1. GENERAL INTRODUCTION. Provision has been made in the power tables to facilitate significance testing. Power analysis is largely concerned with the planning of experiments and thus with the alternate-hypothetical ES. Once the experiment is performed, attention turns to the assessment of the null hypothesis in the light of the sample data.

We accordingly redefine our ES index, $q$, so that its elements are sample statistics, rather than population values, and call it $q_s$. For cases 0 and 1, where the $r$'s of two independent samples are being compared, the sample $r_s$ values are transformed into sample Fisher $z_s$ values, and

$$(4.5.1) \qquad q_s = z_{s_1} - z_{s_2} \qquad \text{(directional)}$$
$$= \left| z_{s_1} - z_{s_2} \right| \qquad \text{(nondirectional)}.$$

Thus, $q_s$ is simply the difference in sample $z$ values. It is related to the unit normal curve deviate (or "critical ratio") $x$, by[4]

$$(4.5.2) \qquad q_s = x \sqrt{\frac{n_1 + n_2 - 6}{(n_1 - 3)(n_2 - 3)}} \, ,$$

$$(4.5.3) \qquad x = q_s \sqrt{\frac{(n_1 - 3)(n_2 - 3)}{n_1 + n_2 - 6}} \, .$$

The relationships are stated here for the more general situation where the sample $n$'s need not be equal. They simplify for the Case 0, equal $n$ condition (see below).

The value of $q_s$ necessary for significance is called $q_c$, i.e., the criterion value of $q_s$. The second column of the power Tables 4.3, headed $q_c$, carries these values as a function of $n$. Using these values, the investigator need not compute the normal curve deviate $x$. He simply finds the $z$ transformations of his sample $r_s$'s in Table 4.2.2, then finds their difference, $q_s$, and compares it with the tabled $q_c$ value for his sample size. If the obtained $q_s$ value equals or exceeds $q_c$, his obtained difference is significant at the $a$ value for that table; otherwise, it is not.

4.5.2 SIGNIFICANCE TESTING IN CASE 0, $n_1 = n_2 = n$. In Case 0, where $n_1 = n_2 = n$, the relationships between $q_s$ and the normal deviate $x$ are simplified:

$$(4.5.4) \qquad q_s = x \sqrt{\frac{2}{n - 3}} \, ,$$

$$(4.5.5) \qquad x = q_s \sqrt{\frac{n - 3}{2}} \, .$$

---

[4] The unit normal curve deviate is frequently represented by the symbol $z$. We use $x$ here to avoid confusion.

[Formula (4.5.4) was used in the computation of the $q_c$ values of the power tables, $x$ being the normal curve deviate for the $a$ criterion.]

The Case 0 use of the $q_c$ values is quite straightforward: The investigator looks up the $z_s$ values for the two $r_s$'s in Table 4.2.2, finds their difference, $q_s$ [formula (4.5.1)], and uses the appropriate power table depending on $a$, in the row for his $n( =n_1 =n_2)$, checking whether his $q_s$ value equals or exceeds the tabulated $q_c$ value.


**Illustrative Example**

**4.9**   Consider the conditions of example 4.1, where a marriage counselor is studying the difference in husband–wife correlation on a series of personality variables between 60 marriages rated as harmonious (Group 1) and 60 having marital difficulties (Group 2). The significance criterion is $a_2 = .05$. When the data are analyzed, it is found for a specific variable **A** that $r_{s_1}$ is .42 and $r_{s_2}$ is .16. She looks up the $z$ transformation of these $r_s$'s and finds $z_{s_1}$ = .448 and $z_{s_2}$ = .161. Thus, $q_s$ = .448 − .161 = .287. Her specifications, thus are

$$a_2 = .05, \qquad n = 60, \qquad q_s = .287.$$

In Table 4.3.5 (for $a_2 = .05$) for row $n = 60$, she finds under $q_c$ the value .367. Since her $q_s$ is smaller than $q_c$, her observed difference is not significant at $a_2 = .05$. [From formula (4.5.5), $x = .287 \sqrt{(60 - 3)/2} = 1.53$.]

Assume now that for another variable B, she finds $r_{s_1} = .35, r_{s_2} = -.14$. Transformed by means of Table 4.2.2, these $r$ values yield, respectively, $z_{s_1} = .365, z_{s_2} = -.141$. By formula (4.5.1) for nondirectional tests,

$$q_s = |.365 - (-.141)| = |.506| = .506.$$

The specifications remain the same as for variable **A**, except that now $q_s = .506$. Since this exceeds the $q_c = .367$, the difference in correlation for variable **B** is significant at $a_2 = .05$. [From formula (4.5.5), $x = .506 \sqrt{(60 - 3)/2} = 2.70$.]

Consider now the results for a third variable, **C**. Assume she finds $r_{s_1} = -.20, r_{s_2} = -.06$. Transformed, these $r$ values yield, respectively, $z_{s_1} = -.203, z_{s_2} = -.060$. By formula (4.5.1) for nondirectional tests,

$$q_s = |-.203 - (-.060)| = |-.143| = .143,$$

which is less than $q_c = .367$ and hence not significant at $a_2 = .05$. [From formula (4.5.5), $x = .143 \sqrt{(60 - 3)/2} = .76$.]

**4.10** Example 4.2 described a study in clinical psychiatry which depended on comparing at the $a_1 = .01$ level correlations of two variables between (a) paranoid and (b) catatonic schizophrenics, $r_{s_1}$ being predicted the larger. When samples of $n = 180$ are analyzed, it is found that $r_{s_1} = .60$, $r_{s_2} = .36$. When transformed, these yield $z_{s_1} = .693$ and $z_{s_2} = .377$. Thus $q_s = .693 - .377 = .316$. The specifications are

$$a_1 = .01, \qquad n = 180, \qquad q_s = .316.$$

Table 4.3.1 (for $a_1 = .01$) for row $n = 180$ and column $q_c$, yields the value .247. Since $q_s$ (.316) exceeds the criterion value (.247), it can be concluded at $a_1 = .01$ that the relationship is significantly larger for the paranoids. [If desired, $x$ can be found from formula (4.5.5) to be $.316\sqrt{(180 - 3)/2}$ = 2.97.] Note that if the $r_s$'s for paranoids and catatonics were reversed, i.e., if the sample results were contrary to the predicted direction, no $q$ values need be determined—the difference, being contrary to the predicted direction in a directional test, is nonsignificant whatever its magnitude.

To make another point, we assume instead that $r_{s_1}, r_{s_2}$ turn out to be $+ .15, - .14$ so that $z_{s_1}, z_{s_2}$ are .151, $- .141$, and $q_s = .151 - (- .141) = .292$. Now, since $q_s = .292$ is greater than $q_c = .247$, the difference between $r_s$'s is significant, i.e., we conclude that $r_1$ is (algebraically) greater than $r_2$. Note that this is true despite the fact that neither is significantly different (at the same $a_1 = .01$ level) from zero. (In Chapter 3, Table 3.3.1, $r_c$ for $n = 180$ is .173, which neither value exceeds.) Thus, two-sample values departing *in opposite directions* from zero may be significantly different from each other while neither is significantly different from zero. There is no contradiction if nonsignificance is properly interpreted as the data not warranting the rejection of the null hypothesis. Thus, the results of each sample do not warrant the conclusion that its population $r$ is not zero, but, together, they do warrant the conclusion that the population $r$'s differ (subject, of course, to the Type I error).

4.5.3. SIGNIFICANCE TESTING IN CASE 1, $n_1 \neq n_2$. The fact of inequality of sample sizes in significance testing using the tabled $q_c$ values requires only finding the harmonic mean of the $(n - 3)$'s, $n'$, as described in Section 4.3.2 [formula (4.3.1)]:

$$n' = \frac{2(n_1 - 3)(n_2 - 3)}{n_1 + n_2 - 6} + 3.$$

In using Tables 4.3, values of $n'$ are substituted for $n$. Otherwise, exactly the same procedure is followed as in Case 0.

If the normal curve deviate value $x$ is desired, it is found using formula (4.5.3), or, if $n'$ has been found, it is computationally simpler to substitute $n'$ for $n$ in formula (4.5.5).

**Illustrative Example**

**4.11**    Example 4.3 describes an investigation in psycholinguistics designed to improve the reliability (parallel forms correlation) of a speech disruption measure. The statistical test takes the form of comparing the $r_s$'s for the new ($P_1$) and old ($P_2$) procedure at the $a_2 = .05$ significance level. Assume he finds $r_{s_1} = .89$ for $n_1 = 51$ and $r_{s_2} = .79$ for $n_2 = 260$. The transformed values are found to be $z_{s_1} = 1.422$ and $z_{s_2} = 1.071$, so that

$$q = |1.422 - 1.071| = |.351| = .351.$$

To use the table, find $n'$ from formula (4.3.1):

$$n' = \frac{2(51 - 3)(260 - 3)}{51 + 260 - 6} + 3 = 84$$

(as before in example 4.3).

The specifications for significance testing of the sample difference are:

$$a_1 = .05, \qquad n' = 84, \qquad q_s = .351.$$

Table 4.3.5 for $a_2 = .05$, row $n = 84$, and column $q_c$, yields .308. Since $q_s$ exceeds $q_c$, the difference in sample correlations is significant. (If desired, **x** may be found from formula (4.5.5) as $.351\sqrt{(84 - 3)/2} = 2.23$.)

Note that in planning (example 4.3), an ES of $q = .40$ was posited. Despite the fact that the observed difference $q_s = .351$ fell short of this, it was nevertheless significant. As has been noted previously, this can only occur when, for the planning specifications, power exceeds .50. (In this example, it was .72.)

4.5.4   SIGNIFICANCE TESTING IN CASE 2: ONE SAMPLE, $H_0 : r = c$. When the null hypothesis takes the form: The $r$ of a population of paired values from which a sample of $n$ observations has been randomly drawn equals $c$, an adjustment must be made of the tabled $q_c$ value. Since the tables were constructed for Case 0 conditions (two samples of equal size), they are designed to allow for sampling error variance of two $z_s$'s, while in Case 2 there is only one. To find the proper criterion for one-sample tests of $r = c$, one finds

(4.5.6)                     $$q_c' = q_c\sqrt{\tfrac{1}{2}} = .707q_c,$$

where $q_c$ is the tabulated value for $n$.

As for the observed $q_s$ value for Case 2, we follow the principle expressed in (4.5.1), and simply define $q_s'$ as we defined $q_2'$ [formula (4.3.2)], merely substituting the sample value of $z_s$ for the population parameter $z_1$:

(4.5.7)                   $q_s' = z_s - z_c$        (directional)

                         $= |z_s - z_c|$    (nondirectional)

The prime is used to denote that a one-sample test is involved. The relationships between $q_s'$ and the normal deviate $x$ for this case are now

(4.5.8)                        $$q_s' = x \sqrt{\frac{1}{n-3}} ,$$

(4.5.9)                        $$x = q_s' \sqrt{n-3}.$$

Formula (4.5.9) can be used if the exact value of the normal deviate ("critical ratio") is desired, e.g., for reporting results for publication.

**Illustrative Example**

**4.12**   In example 4.4, which was concerned with an attempt to improve the reliability of an attitude scale, a test of $H_0$: $r \leq .60$ at $a_1 = .05$ (i.e., predicting $r > .60$) with a sample of $n = 50$ was described. When the data are collected, the social psychologist finds $r_s = .72$. Can he safely conclude that the new scale has a population reliability coefficient (alternate form correlation) greater than .60? He converts these two values of $r_s$ to $z_s$, and finds their difference:

$$q_s' = .908 - .693 = .215.$$

This is the sample ES. His specifications, then, are

$$a_1 = .05, \qquad n = 50, \qquad q_s' = .215.$$

In Table 4.3.2 (for $a_1 = .05$) with row $n = 50$, he finds in column $q_c$, .339. This would be the criterion for a two-sample test. For this one-sample case, he goes on to find [formula (4.5.6)] $q_c' = .339\sqrt{\frac{1}{2}} = (.707)(.339) = .240$. This is the relevant criterion value, and since $q_s' = .215$ is less than $q_c' = .240$, he *cannot* conclude at $a_1 = .05$ that the population reliability of the new procedure exceeds .60.

If he wishes to determine the exact normal curve deviate value $x$ which would result from the test, he finds [formula (4.5.9)] $x = .215\sqrt{50-3} = .147$.

# CHAPTER 5

# The Test That a Proportion Is .50 and the Sign Test

## 5.1 INTRODUCTION AND USE

It arises with some frequency in behavioral science that a null hypothesis takes the form that the fraction of a population of potential observations having some defined characteristic is one-half, i.e., $H_0$: $P = .50$. Examples come to mind from areas as diverse as political science (opinion or political polling), experimental psychology (learning theory, psychophysics), and behavior genetics. Thus, for example, the question as to whether or not there is majority support in the electorate for a course of action by the national administration could be approached by polling a suitably drawn sample and testing the null hypothesis that the proportion of the population in favor is .50; rejection of this null hypothesis leads to the conclusion. As another example, the ability of an experimental subject to detect a near-threshold stimulus which is presented on a random half of a series of trials can be assessed by testing the null hypothesis that on a very long series he would be correct in his judgments of present–absent on $P = .50$ of the trials. The finding that the sample $P$ is greater than .50 and significant would lead to the conclusion that he is (at least on some trials) making the perceptual discrimination. Research in extrasensory perception involving the calling of the side of a coin or the color of the suit of a playing card would test null hypotheses of the same form.

The fact that in many human populations the sexes are about equally divided leads to the relevance of the $P = .50$ test in studies of sex differences. Thus, if an investigator is interested in the relationship between sex and a definable characteristic (say, falling into a given psychiatric diagnostic group or a political party), he can draw a random sample of a group having the characteristic and test the null hypothesis that the proportion of males is .50. Departure from .50 is taken as evidence for a sex difference in incidence of the characteristic, and therefore a relationship between sex and the characteristic.

The widest application of the test of $H_0$: $P = .50$ arises in the form of the nonparametric "Sign Test" (Siegel, 1956, pp. 68–75). Consider the following circumstances. We have a population of $X$, $Y$ paired observations, and we are concerned with the relative magnitude of the $X$'s and $Y$'s. If we can merely say for each pair in a sample whether $X$ is greater than $Y$ (so that $X - Y$ is *positive*) or $X$ is less than $Y$ (so that $X - Y$ is *negative*), we have a basis for deciding whether the X population is stochastically larger or smaller than the Y population. By "stochastically larger (smaller)" we simply mean that in more than half of the $X$, $Y$ pairs in the population, $X$ is larger (smaller) than $Y$. Under these circumstances, the null hypothesis that the X and Y populations are stochastically equal is simply $H_0$: $P = .50$, where $P$ is the proportion of pairs in which $X$ (or $Y$) is larger.

Note that no assumption need be made about the shape of either the $X$ or the $Y$ distributions, or of their joint (bivariate) distribution. Indeed, it is not even necessary that the values of the variables be expressed in metric (i.e., interval or ratio scale) form: only "larger than" or "smaller than" judgments are required. Thus, the test is distribution-free, and since no estimation of population parameters are called for, nonparametric as well.

If stronger assumptions are permitted, specifically, if it can be assumed that $X - Y = Z$ values are normally distributed and with equal variance, then the $t$ test for dependent means of Section 2.3.5 is appropriate, and, for equal specifications, more powerful. Further, with large samples, moderate failure of these assumptions is tolerable. The investigator may nevertheless choose to perform the less powerful sign test as a "shortcut" or "approximate" test (Welkowitz, Ewen, & Cohen, 1982, Chapter 17).

This test can equally be used for a test of the difference between correlated or dependent proportions (Hays, 1973, pp. 740–742). If we assess $X$ and $Y$ as having some attribute present (1) or absent (0), then our $X$, $Y$ pairs are either (1, 0), (0, 1), (1, 1), or (0, 0). We then discard the instances of the latter two possibilities, where we cannot make a judgment of "greater than." Now, if the proportions having the attribute differ between $X$ and $Y$, then $P$, the proportion of differing $X$, $Y$ pairs in which $X$ is greater than $Y$, will depart from .50. Thus, the null hypothesis is again $P = .50$, and the methods of this chapter can be applied.

The statistical term for the test model under consideration is the "symmetrical binomial cumulative distribution." It is frequently referred to by this name in the statistical literature [see MacKinnon (1959, 1961) for some useful tables]. "Symmetrical" is used for $\mathbf{P} = 1 - \mathbf{P} = .50$; tests of other values of **P** proceed by means of other binomial cumulative distributions (see Hays, 1973, pp. 185–197). The methods of the next chapter may be used to test the more general hypothesis $\mathbf{H_0}: \mathbf{P} = \mathbf{k}$, where **k** is any proportion.

## 5.2    The Effect Size Index: **g**

We index departure from $\mathbf{P} = .50$ simply by the distance in units of proportion from .50, i.e.,

(5.2.1)              $\mathbf{g} = \mathbf{P} - .50$ or $.50 - \mathbf{P}$        (directional),

and

              $\mathbf{g} = |\mathbf{P} - .50|$                (nondirectional).

In this form, our null hypothesis is that $\mathbf{g} = 0$. A test of $\mathbf{H_0}: \mathbf{P} = .50$ when $\mathbf{P_1}$ is actually .60 represents an alternate hypothesis or ES of $\mathbf{g} = .60 - .50 = .10$. Unlike some of the other ES indices in this book, **g** is fortunately expressed in a unit which is immediately comprehensible to the behavioral scientist.

5.2.1    "SMALL," "MEDIUM," AND "LARGE" VALUES OF **g**. We offer as conventions operational definitions of qualitatively defined levels of ES here with, if anything, greater diffidence than in the previous chapters (see particularly the general discussion in Section 1.4). Since **g** is so transparently clear a unit, it is expected that workers in any given substantive area of the behavioral sciences will very frequently be able to set relevant ES values without the proposed conventions, or set up conventions of their own which are suited to their area of inquiry.

They are offered here for whatever use they may afford researchers in areas where effect sizes are obscure, for use with the sign test where experience in an area may not provide a guide, and for the sake of symmetry of exposition. One further reason lies in a larger effort to make behavioral scientists using statistical inference more aware of the sizes of the effects they are studying. It must be reiterated, however, that a basis for positing **g** which comes from theory or experience should automatically take precedence over these conventions.

SMALL EFFECT SIZE: $\mathbf{g} = .05$. With $\mathbf{g} = .05$ as the definition, we are considering a division of the population of .55:.45 as a small departure from the null (.50:.50). This may be considered either too large or too small a criterion, depending on the reader's perspective.

For a *normally distributed* population of differences, the division between the highest .55 and the lowest .45 of them comes at about one-eighth (.126) of their standard deviation away from their mean (see discussion of $U_3$, Section 2.2 and Table 2.2.1). If such a division obtained in a sign test, with .55 positive and .45 negative, the mean of the positive differences would be .85, and of the negative differences $(-).75$, when expressed in units of the (total) standard deviation of the differences. This may well seem like very little, less than "small," particularly when one considers that at $P = .50$, these tail means are .80 and $- .80$.

On the other hand, consider political polling. In a presidential election, a candidate who garners 55% of the popular vote is said to have won by a landslide. (In only 11 of the 28 presidential elections since 1872 did the popular plurality candidate get more than 55% of the vote; in only 4, more than 60%.) In opinion polling on closely divided issues (where it is most relevant), a .55:.45 division is sizable. Another relevant fact: the well-known excess of women over men among the aged amounts to a female–male sex ratio of .547:.453 in the population aged 65 and over (for the year 1970). Also the difference in vocabulary knowledge between adult siblings of opposite sex is such that in about 55% of the pairs who differ, the female will be superior [estimated from Wechsler (1958, p. 147)].

Thus, the $g = .05$ criterion for a small departure may be too large or too small from some specific viewpoint; it seems, however, a reasonable criterion for general use.

MEDIUM EFFECT SIZE: $g = .15$. A .65:.35 split is offered as a conventional definition of a medium departure from .50:.50. This is a 13:7 ratio, i.e., approximately 2:1. (If exactly 2 to 1 is desired, it is provided in the tables at $g = \frac{1}{6}$.)

In a normal distribution of differences, the highest .65 are cut off at .385 of a standard deviation away from the mean. Interpreted as a sign test with .65 positive differences, the mean of these differences is .96, while that of the negative differences is $(-).77$ (in standard units). Thus, if adult mixed-sex sibling pairs were given a standard Arithmetic Reasoning test, in about two-thirds of the cases where the siblings differed, the brothers would get the larger score [estimated from Wechsler (1958, p. 147)].

In more familiar terms, and returning to divisions in the popular vote in presidential elections, there never has been a division as extreme as .65:.35 since popular vote totals became available (1872). (The largest proportion polled up to 1972 was .608 by Roosevelt in 1936. Ironically, this was the year of the Literary Digest Poll debacle, when Landon's election was predicted by a socioeconomically biased sample.)

An instance of a division of the order of $g = .15$ can be drawn from mortality statistics. If one were to collect very large and equal random samples of black and white births inthe East South Central States, those dying before the age of one year would contain almost twice as many blacks as whites (.643:.357).[1]

Another instance of a medium effect size is the sex difference in incidence of manic-depressive psychosis: Authorities generally agree that the diagnosis is made about twice as frequently in females than in males, hence $P \cong .67$ and $g \cong .67 - .50 = .17$ (see Campbell, 1953, p. 70).

For another example, consider again *normally distributed* populations of differences between adult brother–sister pairs with regard to two intelligence subtest variables, arthmetic reasoning and a speeded digit-symbol substitution task. In the arithmetic subtest, in approximately .64 of the pairs, the brothers would obtain the higher score, and in the digit-symbol subtest, in the same proportion of the pairs the sisters would show superior performance (estimated from Wechsler (1958, p. 147)]. Thus, $g \approx .14$ in both instances, a medium departure.

LARGE EFFECT SIZE $g = .25$. We operationally define as a large ES a .75:.25, or 3:1 split. In line with our orientation in setting the ES conventions, this should be a departure from .50:.50 which is fairly obvious to the observer's naked eye, yet not so large as to render statistical analysis wholly superfluous (see Section 1.4).

In a normally distributed population of differences, the largest .75 of them are cut off at .674 of a standard deviation below the mean. When interpreted as a sign test with .75 positive differences, the mean of the positive differences would be 1.10 and the mean of the negative differences $(-).60$ (in standard units). Thus, there would be a half standard deviation separation between the means of the positive and negative tail segments.[2]

It is difficult to come by well-known examples to illustrate a departure from the null of $g = .25$, i.e., .75:.25 population splits where .50:.50 represents "no effect." For example, as already noted, no recorded popular vote for the U.S. presidency has approached this size, and no brother–sister difference in the area of human abilities, such as were used to illustrate small and medium ES are known which are of this magnitude.

An obvious example can be drawn from Mendelian genetic ratios. For the simple case of single gene complete dominance inheritance, the matings of heterozygous parents yield offspring .25 of whom would manifest the recessive character. Thus, the ratio among phenotypes showing to

---

[1] Computed from Bureau of the Census (1975, Table 89, p. 63).

[2] The reader should not confuse this with the medium ES of $d = .5$ separation between means of different *whole* normal populations, standardized by their common *within* population standard deviation, used in connection with the **t** test (see Section 2.2). Here tail segments of a *single* normal population are involved, and the standardizing unit is the total standard deviation, a much larger unit than the within-population standard deviation.

not showing the recessive trait would be .25:.75, thus a departure of .25 from a null hypothesis which posits equal incidence of the two phenotypes.

One can find populations that split .75:.25, but they are not compelling examples unless there is a reasonable basis for stating a .50:.50 null hypothesis. For example, the proportion of adult males in the U.S. who are unmarried is close to .25, but to consider this a $g = .25$ departure from .50:.50 seems forced in the absence of any particular reason to posit an equiprobable null hypothesis for single/not single. Or, in other words, what effect is there none of if the proportion of single men were .50?

The area of sex differences has provided some useful illustrations of small and medium ES. On can find examples of large sex differences, but they are larger than our $g = .25$ criterion. Thus, when one identifies the sex distribution in samples of school children who are stutterers or behavior problems or who are diagnosed as reading disability cases or color blind, the departure from a no sex effect .50 incidence for boys is typically at least .30 (i.e., .80:.20), color blindness (usually a sex-linked recessive character) rising to about $g = .40$ (i.e., .90:.10).

One example of a $g = .25$ sex difference can be offered: If one were to draw large and equal samples of male and female arrests from police blotters in U.S. cities of over 2500 population, and then to identify the arrests for auto theft, 75% of them would be males!

## 5.3   POWER TABLES

The tables in this section yield power values when, in addition to the significance criterion and ES ($= g$), the sample size is specified. They should therefore be used in finding the power of the test of $H_0$: $P = .50$ (or $g = 0$), after the data are gathered. They can also be used in planning experiments by varying $n$, ES, or $a$, or all three, to determine the consequence to power of such alternative specifications. The tables give values for "nearest" $a$, $g$, and $n$:

*1. Significance Criterion*, $a$. Since frequencies are discrete, the (exact) binomial test cannot be performed at a constant conventional value of $a$, such as .05 or .01. For example, when a population $P = .50$, and a random sample of $n = 10$ cases is drawn, the probability ($a_2$) of a 10:0 or 0:10 distribution in the sample is .002, of a 9:1 or 1:9 distribution is .021, and of an 8:2 or 2:8 distribution is .109. No tests *at* $a_2 = .01$, .05, or .10 are possible because intermediate values for frequences between 10 and 9 and between 9 and 8 are not possible. Thus, for each value of $n$ in each power table, the exact value of $a_1$ or $a_2$ for the test is given. This is generally[3] the *nearest* available value to the conventional .01, .05, and .10 criteria.

Tables are provided for the following "nearest" values of $a$: $a_1 \approx .01$, $a_1 \approx .05$, $a_1 \approx .10$; $a_2 \approx .01$, $a_2 \approx .05$, $a_2 \approx .10$, the subscripts referring to one- and two-tailed tests. Since power at $a_1$ closely approximates power at $a_2 = 2a_1$, for power greater than .10, one can also determine power at $a_2 \approx .02$ (from the $a_1 \approx .01$ table), $a_2 \approx .20$ (from $a_1 \approx .10$), $a_1 \approx .005$ (from $a_2 \approx .01$, and $a_1 \approx .025$ (from $a_2 \approx .05$). In each instance one simply doubles or halves the exact values for $a_1$ or $a_2$ given in the table. These will, however, not necessarily be the nearest possible values to those desired.

*2. Effect Size, ES.* The ES index here is **g**, the discrepancy in the population from the null-hypothetical **P** = .50. In directional (one-tailed) tests ($a_1$), **g** is understood as either positive or negative, depending on the direction posited in the alternate hypothesis, e.g., $H_1$: $g = -.15$ (i.e., $P_1 = .35$). In nondirectional (two-tailed) tests, **g** is understood as absolute, e.g., "given a departure from .50 or .15, whether positive or negative. . . ."

Provision is made for $g = .05$ (.05) .40, and also $\frac{1}{6}$. Conventional definitions have been offered above, as follows:

small: $g = .05$ (.55:.45)

medium: $g = .15$ (.65:.35),

large: $g = .25$ (.75:.25).

*3. Sample Size, n.* This is the number of observations in the sample. Depending on the nature of the application of the test, observations may be single, or as in the "Sign Test," paired. Provision is made for $n = 8$ (1) 40 (2) 60 (4) 100 (20) 200 (50) 500 (100) 1000.

The values in the body of the table are the power of the test times 100, i.e., the percent of tests carried out under the given conditions which will result in the rejection of the null hypothesis, $H_0$: $P = .50$ at the exact level of **a** given in the third column. The values are accurate to two places, as given. For a few values of **n** (250, 350, and 450), exact binomial values are not available in published tables and the normal approximation was used. (Also, see Cohen, 1970.)

(For the meaning and use of **v**, see Section 5.5).

---

[3] An occasional exception is made in order to provide more values. For example, when $n = 16$, a break of 12:4 or 4:12 is significant at $a_2 = .077$. This is given in Table 5.3.5 for $a_2 \approx .05$. A break of 11:4 or 4:11 is significant at $a_2 = .210$ and is given in Table 5.3.6 for $a_2 \approx .10$, even though .077 is closer to .10 than .210 is. This exception avoids duplicating the information in that line of the table in Table 5.3.6 and instead provides an additional line of values.

Table 5.3.1

Power of Sign Test (P = .50) at $a_1 \approx .01$

| n | v | $a_1$ | .05 | .10 | .15 | 1/6 | .20 | .25 | .30 | .35 | .40 |
|---|---|---|---|---|---|---|---|---|---|---|---|
| 8 | 8 | 004 | 01 | 02 | 03 | 04 | 06 | 10 | 17 | 27 | 43 |
| 9 | 9 | 002 | 00 | 01 | 02 | 03 | 04 | 08 | 13 | 23 | 39 |
| 10 | 9 | 011 | 02 | 05 | 09 | 10 | 15 | 24 | 38 | 54 | 74 |
| 11 | 10 | 006 | 01 | 03 | 06 | 08 | 11 | 20 | 32 | 49 | 70 |
| 12 | 11 | 003 | 01 | 02 | 04 | 05 | 09 | 16 | 27 | 44 | 66 |
| 13 | 11 | 011 | 03 | 06 | 11 | 14 | 20 | 32 | 50 | 69 | 87 |
| 14 | 12 | 006 | 02 | 04 | 08 | 11 | 16 | 28 | 45 | 65 | 84 |
| 15 | 13 | 004 | 01 | 03 | 06 | 08 | 13 | 24 | 40 | 60 | 82 |
| 16 | 13 | 011 | 03 | 07 | 13 | 17 | 25 | 40 | 60 | 79 | 93 |
| 17 | 14 | 006 | 02 | 05 | 10 | 13 | 20 | 35 | 55 | 76 | 92 |
| 18 | 15 | 004 | 01 | 03 | 08 | 10 | 16 | 31 | 50 | 72 | 90 |
| 19 | 15 | 010 | 03 | 07 | 15 | 19 | 28 | 47 | 67 | 86 | 96 |
| 20 | 16 | 006 | 02 | 05 | 12 | 15 | 24 | 41 | 63 | 83 | 96 |
| 21 | 16 | 013 | 04 | 10 | 20 | 25 | 36 | 57 | 77 | 92 | 99 |
| 22 | 17 | 008 | 03 | 07 | 16 | 21 | 31 | 52 | 73 | 90 | 98 |
| 23 | 18 | 005 | 02 | 05 | 13 | 17 | 27 | 47 | 69 | 88 | 98 |
| 24 | 18 | 011 | 04 | 10 | 21 | 26 | 39 | 61 | 81 | 94 | 99 |
| 25 | 19 | 007 | 03 | 07 | 17 | 22 | 34 | 56 | 78 | 93 | 99 |
| 26 | 19 | 014 | 05 | 12 | 26 | 32 | 46 | 69 | 87 | 97 | * |
| 27 | 20 | 010 | 03 | 10 | 22 | 28 | 41 | 64 | 84 | 96 | |
| 28 | 21 | 006 | 02 | 07 | 18 | 23 | 36 | 60 | 82 | 95 | |
| 29 | 21 | 012 | 04 | 12 | 26 | 33 | 48 | 71 | 89 | 98 | |
| 30 | 22 | 008 | 03 | 09 | 22 | 29 | 43 | 67 | 87 | 97 | |
| 31 | 23 | 005 | 02 | 07 | 19 | 25 | 39 | 63 | 85 | 97 | |
| 32 | 23 | 010 | 04 | 12 | 27 | 34 | 50 | 74 | 91 | 98 | |
| 33 | 24 | 007 | 03 | 09 | 23 | 30 | 45 | 70 | 89 | 98 | |
| 34 | 24 | 012 | 05 | 14 | 31 | 39 | 55 | 79 | 94 | 99 | |
| 35 | 25 | 008 | 04 | 11 | 27 | 34 | 51 | 76 | 93 | 99 | |
| 36 | 26 | 006 | 03 | 09 | 23 | 30 | 47 | 73 | 91 | 99 | |
| 37 | 26 | 010 | 04 | 13 | 31 | 39 | 57 | 81 | 95 | 99 | |
| 38 | 27 | 007 | 03 | 11 | 27 | 35 | 52 | 78 | 94 | 99 | |
| 39 | 27 | 012 | 05 | 16 | 36 | 44 | 62 | 85 | 96 | * | |
| 40 | 28 | 008 | 04 | 13 | 31 | 40 | 58 | 82 | 96 | | |
| 42 | 29 | 010 | 05 | 15 | 35 | 44 | 63 | 86 | 97 | | |
| 44 | 30 | 011 | 05 | 17 | 39 | 49 | 67 | 89 | 98 | | |
| 46 | 31 | 013 | 06 | 19 | 43 | 53 | 71 | 91 | 99 | | |
| 48 | 33 | 007 | 04 | 14 | 35 | 45 | 64 | 88 | 98 | | |

Table 5.3.1 *(continued)*

| n | v | a₁ | .05 | .10 | .15 | 1/6 | .20 | .25 | .30 | .35 | .40 |
|---|---|---|---|---|---|---|---|---|---|---|---|
| 50 | 34 | 008 | 04 | 16 | 39 | 49 | 68 | 90 | 99 | * | * |
| 52 | 35 | 009 | 05 | 18 | 43 | 53 | 72 | 92 | 99 | | |
| 54 | 36 | 010 | 06 | 20 | 46 | 56 | 76 | 94 | 99 | | |
| 56 | 37 | 011 | 06 | 22 | 49 | 60 | 79 | 95 | * | | |
| 58 | 38 | 012 | 07 | 24 | 53 | 63 | 81 | 96 | | | |
| 60 | 40 | 007 | 04 | 18 | 45 | 56 | 76 | 95 | | | |
| 64 | 42 | 008 | 06 | 22 | 52 | 63 | 82 | 97 | | | |
| 68 | 44 | 010 | 07 | 25 | 58 | 69 | 86 | 98 | | | |
| 72 | 46 | 012 | 08 | 29 | 63 | 74 | 89 | 99 | | | |
| 76 | 49 | 008 | 06 | 25 | 59 | 70 | 88 | 99 | | | |
| 80 | 51 | 009 | 07 | 29 | 64 | 75 | 91 | 99 | | | |
| 84 | 53 | 011 | 08 | 32 | 69 | 79 | 93 | 99 | | | |
| 88 | 55 | 012 | 09 | 36 | 73 | 83 | 95 | * | | | |
| 92 | 58 | 008 | 07 | 31 | 70 | 80 | 94 | | | | |
| 96 | 60 | 009 | 08 | 35 | 73 | 84 | 95 | | | | |
| 100 | 62 | 010 | 10 | 38 | 77 | 86 | 97 | | | | |
| 120 | 73 | 011 | 12 | 47 | 85 | 93 | 99 | | | | |
| 140 | 84 | 011 | 13 | 54 | 91 | 96 | * | | | | |
| 160 | 95 | 011 | 15 | 60 | 94 | 98 | | | | | |
| 180 | 106 | 010 | 17 | 65 | 96 | 99 | | | | | |
| 200 | 117 | 010 | 18 | 69 | 98 | 99 | | | | | |
| 250** | 144 | 010 | 22 | 80 | 99 | * | | | | | |
| 300** | 171 | 009 | 26 | 87 | * | | | | | | |
| 350** | 197 | 010 | 33 | 93 | | | | | | | |
| 400 | 224 | 009 | 36 | 95 | | | | | | | |
| 450** | 250 | 010 | 42 | 98 | | | | | | | |
| 500 | 277 | 009 | 45 | 98 | | | | | | | |
| 600 | 329 | 010 | 55 | * | | | | | | | |
| 700 | 381 | 011 | 63 | | | | | | | | |
| 800 | 433 | 011 | 70 | | | | | | | | |
| 900 | 485 | 011 | 76 | | | | | | | | |
| 1000 | 537 | 010 | 80 | | | | | | | | |

* Power values below this point are greater than .995.

** Normal approximation.

Table 5.3.2

Power of Sign Test (P = .50) at $a_1 \approx .05$

| n | v | $a_1$ | .05 | .10 | .15 | 1/6 | .20 | .25 | .30 | .35 | .40 |
|---|---|---|---|---|---|---|---|---|---|---|---|
| 8 | 7 | 035 | 06 | 11 | 17 | 20 | 26 | 37 | 50 | 66 | 81 |
| 9 | 8 | 020 | 04 | 07 | 12 | 14 | 20 | 30 | 44 | 60 | 77 |
| 10 | 8 | 055 | 10 | 17 | 26 | 30 | 38 | 53 | 68 | 82 | 93 |
| 11 | 9 | 033 | 06 | 12 | 20 | 23 | 31 | 46 | 62 | 78 | 91 |
| 12 | 9 | 073 | 13 | 23 | 35 | 39 | 49 | 65 | 79 | 91 | 97 |
| 13 | 10 | 046 | 09 | 17 | 28 | 32 | 42 | 58 | 75 | 88 | 97 |
| 14 | 11 | 029 | 06 | 12 | 20 | 26 | 36 | 52 | 70 | 85 | 96 |
| 15 | 11 | 059 | 12 | 22 | 35 | 40 | 52 | 69 | 84 | 94 | 99 |
| 16 | 12 | 038 | 09 | 17 | 29 | 34 | 45 | 63 | 80 | 92 | 98 |
| 17 | 12 | 072 | 15 | 26 | 42 | 48 | 60 | 77 | 89 | 97 | * |
| 18 | 13 | 048 | 11 | 21 | 35 | 41 | 53 | 72 | 87 | 96 | 99 |
| 19 | 14 | 032 | 08 | 16 | 30 | 35 | 47 | 67 | 84 | 95 | 99 |
| 20 | 14 | 058 | 13 | 25 | 42 | 48 | 61 | 79 | 91 | 98 | * |
| 21 | 15 | 039 | 10 | 20 | 36 | 42 | 55 | 74 | 89 | 97 | |
| 22 | 15 | 067 | 15 | 29 | 47 | 54 | 67 | 84 | 94 | 99 | |
| 23 | 16 | 047 | 12 | 24 | 41 | 48 | 62 | 80 | 93 | 98 | |
| 24 | 17 | 032 | 09 | 19 | 36 | 42 | 56 | 77 | 91 | 98 | |
| 25 | 17 | 054 | 13 | 27 | 47 | 54 | 68 | 85 | 95 | 99 | |
| 26 | 18 | 038 | 10 | 23 | 41 | 48 | 63 | 82 | 94 | 99 | |
| 27 | 18 | 061 | 15 | 31 | 52 | 59 | 73 | 89 | 97 | * | |
| 28 | 19 | 044 | 12 | 26 | 46 | 54 | 68 | 86 | 96 | 99 | |
| 29 | 19 | 068 | 17 | 34 | 56 | 64 | 77 | 92 | 98 | * | |
| 30 | 20 | 049 | 14 | 29 | 51 | 58 | 73 | 89 | 97 | | |
| 31 | 21 | 035 | 11 | 25 | 46 | 53 | 69 | 87 | 97 | | |
| 32 | 21 | 055 | 15 | 32 | 55 | 63 | 77 | 92 | 98 | | |
| 33 | 22 | 040 | 12 | 28 | 50 | 58 | 73 | 90 | 98 | | |
| 34 | 22 | 061 | 17 | 35 | 59 | 67 | 81 | 94 | 99 | | |
| 35 | 23 | 045 | 13 | 31 | 54 | 62 | 77 | 92 | 99 | | |
| 36 | 23 | 066 | 18 | 38 | 63 | 71 | 84 | 95 | 99 | | |
| 37 | 24 | 049 | 15 | 33 | 58 | 66 | 81 | 94 | 99 | | |
| 38 | 25 | 036 | 12 | 29 | 53 | 62 | 77 | 93 | 99 | | |
| 39 | 25 | 054 | 16 | 36 | 62 | 70 | 84 | 96 | 99 | | |
| 40 | 26 | 040 | 13 | 32 | 57 | 66 | 81 | 95 | 99 | | |
| 42 | 27 | 044 | 15 | 34 | 61 | 69 | 84 | 96 | 99 | | |
| 44 | 28 | 048 | 16 | 37 | 64 | 72 | 86 | 97 | * | | |
| 46 | 29 | 052 | 17 | 40 | 67 | 75 | 88 | 98 | | | |
| 48 | 30 | 056 | 18 | 42 | 70 | 78 | 90 | 98 | | | |

Table 5.3.2 *(continued)*

| n | v | $a_1$ | .05 | .10 | .15 | 1/6 | .20 | .25 | .30 | .35 | .40 |
|---|---|---|---|---|---|---|---|---|---|---|---|
| 50 | 31 | 059 | 20 | 45 | 73 | 80 | 92 | 99 | * | * | * |
| 52 | 32 | 063 | 21 | 47 | 75 | 82 | 93 | 99 | | | |
| 54 | 34 | 038 | 15 | 38 | 68 | 77 | 90 | 98 | | | |
| 56 | 35 | 041 | 16 | 41 | 71 | 79 | 91 | 99 | | | |
| 58 | 36 | 043 | 17 | 43 | 73 | 81 | 93 | 99 | | | |
| 60 | 37 | 046 | 18 | 45 | 75 | 83 | 94 | 99 | | | |
| 64 | 39 | 052 | 20 | 49 | 79 | 86 | 95 | * | | | |
| 68 | 41 | 057 | 23 | 53 | 83 | 89 | 97 | | | | |
| 72 | 44 | 038 | 18 | 47 | 79 | 87 | 96 | | | | |
| 76 | 46 | 042 | 20 | 51 | 83 | 89 | 97 | | | | |
| 80 | 48 | 046 | 22 | 55 | 85 | 92 | 98 | | | | |
| 84 | 50 | 051 | 24 | 58 | 88 | 93 | 98 | | | | |
| 88 | 52 | 055 | 25 | 61 | 90 | 95 | 99 | | | | |
| 92 | 54 | 059 | 27 | 64 | 91 | 96 | 99 | | | | |
| 96 | 57 | 041 | 22 | 59 | 90 | 95 | 99 | | | | |
| 100 | 59 | 044 | 24 | 62 | 91 | 96 | 99 | | | | |
| 120 | 70 | 041 | 26 | 68 | 95 | 98 | * | | | | |
| 140 | 80 | 054 | 34 | 78 | 98 | 99 | | | | | |
| 160 | 91 | 048 | 35 | 81 | 99 | * | | | | | |
| 180 | 102 | 043 | 35 | 84 | 99 | | | | | | |
| 200** | 112 | 052 | 42 | 89 | * | | | | | | |
| 250** | 139 | 050 | 45 | 93 | | | | | | | |
| 300** | 165 | 047 | 52 | 97 | | | | | | | |
| 350** | 191 | 050 | 59 | 98 | | | | | | | |
| 400** | 217 | 049 | 64 | 99 | | | | | | | |
| 450** | 243 | 050 | 68 | * | | | | | | | |
| 500 | 269 | 049 | 72 | | | | | | | | |
| 600 | 321 | 047 | 78 | | | | | | | | |
| 700 | 372 | 052 | 85 | | | | | | | | |
| 800 | 424 | 048 | 88 | | | | | | | | |
| 900 | 475 | 051 | 92 | | | | | | | | |
| 1000 | 527 | 047 | 93 | | | | | | | | |

*  Values below this point are greater than .995, unless other values are specified.
** Normal approximation.

**Table 5.3.3**

Power of Sign Test (P = .50) at $a_1 \approx .10$

| n | v | $a_1$ | .05 | .10 | .15 | 1/6 | .20 | .25 | .30 | .35 | .40 |
|---|---|-------|-----|-----|-----|-----|-----|-----|-----|-----|-----|
| 8 | 6 | 145 | 22 | 32 | 43 | 47 | 55 | 68 | 80 | 89 | 96 |
| 9 | 7 | 090 | 15 | 23 | 34 | 38 | 46 | 60 | 74 | 86 | 95 |
| 10 | 7 | 172 | 27 | 38 | 51 | 56 | 65 | 78 | 88 | 95 | 99 |
| 11 | 8 | 113 | 19 | 30 | 43 | 47 | 57 | 71 | 84 | 93 | 98 |
| 12 | 8 | 194 | 30 | 44 | 58 | 63 | 72 | 84 | 93 | 98 | * |
| 13 | 9 | 133 | 23 | 35 | 50 | 55 | 65 | 79 | 90 | 97 | 99 |
| 14 | 10 | 090 | 17 | 28 | 42 | 48 | 58 | 74 | 87 | 95 | 99 |
| 15 | 10 | 151 | 26 | 40 | 56 | 62 | 72 | 85 | 94 | 98 | * |
| 16 | 11 | 105 | 20 | 33 | 49 | 55 | 66 | 81 | 92 | 98 | |
| 17 | 11 | 166 | 29 | 45 | 62 | 67 | 78 | 89 | 96 | 99 | |
| 18 | 12 | 119 | 23 | 37 | 55 | 61 | 72 | 86 | 95 | 99 | |
| 19 | 13 | 084 | 17 | 31 | 48 | 54 | 67 | 83 | 93 | 98 | |
| 20 | 13 | 132 | 25 | 42 | 60 | 66 | 77 | 90 | 97 | 99 | |
| 21 | 14 | 095 | 20 | 35 | 54 | 60 | 72 | 87 | 96 | 99 | |
| 22 | 14 | 143 | 28 | 45 | 65 | 71 | 81 | 93 | 98 | * | |
| 23 | 15 | 105 | 22 | 39 | 59 | 65 | 77 | 90 | 97 | * | |
| 24 | 16 | 076 | 17 | 33 | 53 | 59 | 73 | 88 | 96 | 99 | |
| 25 | 16 | 115 | 24 | 42 | 63 | 70 | 81 | 93 | 98 | * | |
| 26 | 17 | 084 | 19 | 36 | 57 | 64 | 77 | 91 | 98 | | |
| 27 | 17 | 124 | 26 | 46 | 67 | 73 | 84 | 95 | 99 | | |
| 28 | 18 | 092 | 21 | 40 | 62 | 69 | 81 | 93 | 99 | | |
| 29 | 18 | 132 | 28 | 49 | 70 | 77 | 87 | 96 | 99 | | |
| 30 | 19 | 100 | 23 | 43 | 65 | 72 | 84 | 95 | 99 | | |
| 31 | 20 | 075 | 19 | 38 | 60 | 68 | 81 | 94 | 99 | | |
| 32 | 20 | 108 | 25 | 46 | 69 | 76 | 87 | 96 | 99 | | |
| 33 | 21 | 081 | 21 | 41 | 64 | 71 | 84 | 95 | 99 | | |
| 34 | 21 | 115 | 27 | 49 | 72 | 79 | 89 | 97 | * | | |
| 35 | 22 | 088 | 22 | 44 | 68 | 75 | 86 | 96 | 99 | | |
| 36 | 22 | 121 | 29 | 52 | 75 | 81 | 91 | 98 | * | | |
| 37 | 23 | 094 | 24 | 46 | 71 | 78 | 89 | 97 | | | |
| 38 | 23 | 128 | 30 | 54 | 77 | 84 | 92 | 98 | | | |
| 39 | 24 | 100 | 26 | 49 | 74 | 80 | 91 | 98 | | | |
| 40 | 25 | 077 | 21 | 44 | 69 | 77 | 88 | 97 | | | |
| 42 | 26 | 082 | 23 | 47 | 72 | 80 | 90 | 98 | | | |
| 44 | 27 | 087 | 24 | 49 | 75 | 82 | 92 | 99 | | | |
| 46 | 28 | 092 | 26 | 52 | 77 | 84 | 93 | 99 | | | |
| 48 | 29 | 097 | 27 | 54 | 79 | 86 | 94 | 99 | | | |

Table 5.3.3 (continued)

| n | v | a₁ | .05 | .10 | .15 | 1/6 | .20 | .25 | .30 | .35 | .40 |
|---|---|---|---|---|---|---|---|---|---|---|---|
| | | | | | | | **g** | | | | |

| n | v | $a_1$ | .05 | .10 | .15 | 1/6 | .20 | .25 | .30 | .35 | .40 |
|---|---|---|---|---|---|---|---|---|---|---|---|
| 50 | 30 | 101 | 29 | 56 | 81 | 87 | 95 | 99 | * | * | * |
| 52 | 31 | 106 | 30 | 58 | 83 | 89 | 96 | * | | | |
| 54 | 32 | 110 | 31 | 60 | 85 | 90 | 97 | | | | |
| 56 | 33 | 114 | 33 | 62 | 86 | 91 | 97 | | | | |
| 58 | 34 | 119 | 34 | 64 | 88 | 92 | 98 | | | | |
| 60 | 36 | 078 | 26 | 56 | 83 | 89 | 96 | | | | |
| 64 | 38 | 084 | 28 | 59 | 86 | 91 | 97 | | | | |
| 68 | 40 | 091 | 31 | 63 | 88 | 93 | 98 | | | | |
| 72 | 42 | 097 | 33 | 66 | 90 | 95 | 99 | | | | |
| 76 | 44 | 103 | 35 | 69 | 92 | 96 | 99 | | | | |
| 80 | 46 | 109 | 37 | 72 | 93 | 97 | 99 | | | | |
| 84 | 48 | 115 | 39 | 74 | 95 | 97 | * | | | | |
| 88 | 51 | 083 | 33 | 69 | 93 | 97 | 99 | | | | |
| 92 | 53 | 087 | 35 | 72 | 94 | 97 | * | | | | |
| 96 | 55 | 092 | 36 | 74 | 95 | 98 | | | | | |
| 100 | 57 | 097 | 38 | 76 | 96 | 98 | | | | | |
| 120 | 68 | 085 | 39 | 80 | 98 | 99 | | | | | |
| 140 | 78 | 102 | 47 | 87 | 99 | * | | | | | |
| 160 | 89 | 089 | 47 | 89 | 99 | | | | | | |
| 180 | 99 | 102 | 53 | 93 | * | | | | | | |
| 200** | 110 | 089 | 53 | 93 | | | | | | | |
| 250** | 136 | 100 | 60 | 97 | | | | | | | |
| 300** | 162 | 092 | 66 | 98 | | | | | | | |
| 350** | 187 | 100 | 74 | 99 | | | | | | | |
| 400** | 213 | 106 | 77 | * | | | | | | | |
| 450** | 239 | 100 | 80 | | | | | | | | |
| 500 | 265 | 097 | 83 | | | | | | | | |
| 600 | 316 | 103 | 88 | | | | | | | | |
| 700 | 367 | 106 | 92 | | | | | | | | |
| 800 | 419 | 095 | 94 | | | | | | | | |
| 900 | 470 | 097 | 96 | | | | | | | | |
| 1000 | 521 | 097 | 97 | | | | | | | | |

*  Values below this point are greater than .995, unless other values are specified.

** Normal approximation.

Table 5.3.4

Power of Sign Test (P = .50) at $a_2 \approx .01$

| n | v | $a_2$ | .05 | .10 | .15 | 1/6 | .20 | .25 | .30 | .35 | .40 |
|---|---|---|---|---|---|---|---|---|---|---|---|
| | | | | | | g | | | | | |
| 8 | 8 | 008 | 01 | 02 | 03 | 04 | 06 | 10 | 17 | 27 | 43 |
| 9 | 9 | 004 | 01 | 01 | 02 | 03 | 04 | 08 | 12 | 23 | 39 |
| 10 | 10 | 002 | 00 | 01 | 01 | 02 | 03 | 06 | 11 | 20 | 35 |
| 11 | 10 | 012 | 02 | 03 | 06 | 08 | 11 | 20 | 32 | 49 | 70 |
| 12 | 11 | 006 | 01 | 02 | 04 | 05 | 09 | 16 | 27 | 44 | 66 |
| 13 | 12 | 003 | 01 | 01 | 03 | 04 | 06 | 13 | 23 | 40 | 62 |
| 14 | 12 | 013 | 02 | 04 | 08 | 11 | 16 | 28 | 45 | 65 | 84 |
| 15 | 13 | 007 | 01 | 03 | 06 | 08 | 13 | 24 | 40 | 60 | 82 |
| 16 | 14 | 004 | 01 | 02 | 05 | 06 | 10 | 20 | 35 | 56 | 79 |
| 17 | 14 | 013 | 02 | 05 | 10 | 13 | 20 | 35 | 55 | 76 | 92 |
| 18 | 15 | 008 | 01 | 03 | 08 | 10 | 16 | 31 | 50 | 72 | 90 |
| 19 | 16 | 004 | 01 | 02 | 06 | 08 | 13 | 26 | 46 | 68 | 88 |
| 20 | 16 | 012 | 02 | 05 | 12 | 15 | 24 | 41 | 63 | 83 | 96 |
| 21 | 17 | 007 | 01 | 04 | 09 | 12 | 20 | 37 | 59 | 80 | 95 |
| 22 | 18 | 004 | 01 | 03 | 07 | 10 | 16 | 32 | 54 | 77 | 94 |
| 23 | 18 | 011 | 02 | 05 | 13 | 17 | 27 | 47 | 69 | 88 | 98 |
| 24 | 19 | 007 | 01 | 04 | 10 | 14 | 23 | 42 | 66 | 86 | 97 |
| 25 | 19 | 015 | 03 | 07 | 17 | 22 | 34 | 56 | 78 | 94 | 99 |
| 26 | 20 | 009 | 02 | 06 | 14 | 19 | 30 | 52 | 75 | 92 | 99 |
| 27 | 21 | 006 | 01 | 04 | 11 | 15 | 26 | 47 | 71 | 90 | 99 |
| 28 | 21 | 013 | 03 | 07 | 18 | 23 | 36 | 60 | 82 | 95 | * |
| 29 | 22 | 008 | 02 | 06 | 15 | 20 | 32 | 56 | 79 | 94 | 99 |
| 30 | 23 | 005 | 01 | 04 | 12 | 17 | 28 | 51 | 76 | 93 | 99 |
| 31 | 23 | 011 | 02 | 07 | 19 | 25 | 39 | 63 | 85 | 97 | * |
| 32 | 24 | 007 | 02 | 06 | 16 | 21 | 34 | 59 | 83 | 96 | |
| 33 | 24 | 014 | 03 | 09 | 23 | 30 | 45 | 70 | 89 | 98 | |
| 34 | 25 | 009 | 02 | 07 | 20 | 26 | 41 | 66 | 87 | 98 | |
| 35 | 26 | 006 | 02 | 06 | 17 | 22 | 36 | 63 | 85 | 97 | |
| 36 | 26 | 011 | 03 | 09 | 23 | 30 | 47 | 73 | 91 | 99 | |
| 37 | 27 | 008 | 02 | 07 | 20 | 27 | 42 | 69 | 90 | 98 | |
| 38 | 27 | 014 | 03 | 11 | 27 | 35 | 52 | 78 | 94 | 99 | |
| 39 | 28 | 009 | 02 | 11 | 24 | 31 | 48 | 75 | 93 | 99 | |
| 40 | 29 | 006 | 02 | 09 | 21 | 27 | 44 | 72 | 91 | 99 | |
| 42 | 30 | 008 | 02 | 09 | 24 | 32 | 50 | 77 | 94 | 99 | |
| 44 | 31 | 010 | 03 | 10 | 28 | 36 | 55 | 81 | 96 | * | |
| 46 | 32 | 011 | 03 | 12 | 31 | 40 | 60 | 85 | 97 | | |
| 48 | 33 | 013 | 04 | 14 | 35 | 45 | 64 | 88 | 98 | | |

**Table 5.3.4** *(continued)*

| n | v | $a_2$ | | | | | g | | | | |
|---|---|---|---|---|---|---|---|---|---|---|---|
| | | | .05 | .10 | .15 | 1/6 | .20 | .25 | .30 | .35 | .40 |
| 50 | 35 | 007 | 02 | 10 | 28 | 37 | 57 | 84 | 97 | * | * |
| 52 | 36 | 008 | 03 | 11 | 31 | 41 | 61 | 87 | 98 | | |
| 54 | 37 | 009 | 03 | 13 | 35 | 45 | 66 | 89 | 99 | | |
| 56 | 38 | 010 | 04 | 14 | 38 | 49 | 69 | 91 | 99 | | |
| 58 | 39 | 012 | 04 | 16 | 42 | 52 | 73 | 93 | 99 | | |
| 60 | 40 | 013 | 05 | 18 | 45 | 56 | 76 | 95 | * | | |
| 64 | 43 | 008 | 03 | 15 | 41 | 52 | 74 | 94 | 99 | | |
| 68 | 45 | 010 | 04 | 18 | 47 | 59 | 80 | 96 | * | | |
| 72 | 47 | 013 | 05 | 21 | 53 | 65 | 84 | 98 | | | |
| 76 | 50 | 008 | 04 | 18 | 50 | 62 | 82 | 97 | | | |
| 80 | 52 | 010 | 05 | 21 | 55 | 67 | 86 | 98 | | | |
| 84 | 54 | 012 | 05 | 25 | 60 | 72 | 90 | 99 | | | |
| 88 | 57 | 007 | 04 | 21 | 57 | 69 | 88 | 99 | | | |
| 92 | 59 | 009 | 05 | 24 | 62 | 74 | 91 | 99 | | | |
| 96 | 61 | 010 | 06 | 27 | 66 | 78 | 93 | * | | | |
| 100 | 63 | 012 | 07 | 31 | 70 | 81 | 95 | | | | |
| 120 | 75 | 008 | 06 | 32 | 75 | 86 | 97 | | | | |
| 140 | 86 | 009 | 07 | 40 | 84 | 92 | 99 | | | | |
| 160 | 97 | 009 | 09 | 47 | 89 | 95 | * | | | | |
| 180 | 108 | 009 | 10 | 53 | 93 | 97 | | | | | |
| 200 | 119 | 009 | 11 | 59 | 95 | 99 | | | | | |
| 250** | 146 | 010 | 15 | 72 | 99 | * | | | | | |
| 300 | 173 | 009 | 19 | 81 | * | | | | | | |
| 350** | 200 | 010 | 23 | 87 | | | | | | | |
| 400 | 226 | 011 | 29 | 93 | | | | | | | |
| 450** | 253 | 010 | 32 | 95 | | | | | | | |
| 500 | 279 | 011 | 38 | 97 | | | | | | | |
| 600 | 332 | 010 | 45 | 99 | | | | | | | |
| 700 | 385 | 009 | 52 | * | | | | | | | |
| 800 | 437 | 010 | 60 | | | | | | | | |
| 900 | 489 | 010 | 67 | | | | | | | | |
| 1000 | 541 | 010 | 73 | | | | | | | | |

* Values below this point are greater than .995, unless other values are specified.

** Normal approximation.

**Table 5.3.5**

Power of Sign Test (P = .50) at $a_2 \approx$ .05

| n | v | $a_2$ | .05 | .10 | .15 | 1/6 | .20 | .25 | .30 | .35 | .40 |
|---|---|-------|-----|-----|-----|-----|-----|-----|-----|-----|-----|
| 8 | 7 | 070 | 08 | 11 | 17 | 20 | 26 | 37 | 50 | 66 | 81 |
| 9 | 8 | 039 | 05 | 07 | 12 | 14 | 20 | 30 | 44 | 60 | 77 |
| 10 | 9 | 021 | 03 | 05 | 09 | 10 | 15 | 24 | 38 | 54 | 74 |
| 11 | 9 | 065 | 08 | 12 | 20 | 24 | 31 | 46 | 62 | 78 | 91 |
| 12 | 10 | 039 | 05 | 09 | 15 | 18 | 25 | 39 | 56 | 74 | 89 |
| 13 | 11 | 022 | 03 | 06 | 11 | 14 | 20 | 33 | 50 | 69 | 87 |
| 14 | 11 | 057 | 07 | 13 | 22 | 26 | 36 | 52 | 70 | 85 | 96 |
| 15 | 12 | 035 | 05 | 09 | 17 | 21 | 30 | 46 | 65 | 82 | 94 |
| 16 | 12 | 077 | 10 | 17 | 29 | 34 | 45 | 63 | 80 | 92 | 98 |
| 17 | 13 | 049 | 07 | 13 | 24 | 28 | 39 | 57 | 76 | 90 | 98 |
| 18 | 14 | 031 | 05 | 10 | 19 | 23 | 33 | 52 | 72 | 88 | 97 |
| 19 | 14 | 064 | 09 | 17 | 30 | 35 | 47 | 67 | 84 | 95 | 99 |
| 20 | 15 | 041 | 06 | 13 | 25 | 30 | 42 | 62 | 80 | 93 | 99 |
| 21 | 16 | 027 | 04 | 10 | 20 | 25 | 36 | 57 | 77 | 92 | 99 |
| 22 | 16 | 052 | 08 | 16 | 30 | 36 | 49 | 70 | 87 | 96 | * |
| 23 | 17 | 035 | 06 | 12 | 25 | 31 | 44 | 65 | 84 | 95 | 99 |
| 24 | 17 | 064 | 10 | 19 | 36 | 42 | 56 | 77 | 91 | 98 | * |
| 25 | 18 | 043 | 07 | 15 | 31 | 37 | 51 | 73 | 89 | 97 | |
| 26 | 19 | 029 | 05 | 12 | 26 | 32 | 46 | 69 | 87 | 97 | |
| 27 | 19 | 052 | 08 | 19 | 36 | 43 | 58 | 79 | 93 | 99 | |
| 28 | 20 | 036 | 06 | 15 | 31 | 38 | 53 | 75 | 91 | 98 | |
| 29 | 20 | 061 | 10 | 22 | 41 | 48 | 64 | 83 | 95 | 99 | |
| 30 | 21 | 043 | 07 | 18 | 36 | 43 | 59 | 80 | 94 | 99 | |
| 31 | 22 | 029 | 06 | 14 | 31 | 38 | 54 | 77 | 93 | 99 | |
| 32 | 22 | 050 | 09 | 21 | 40 | 48 | 64 | 85 | 96 | 99 | |
| 33 | 23 | 035 | 07 | 17 | 36 | 43 | 60 | 82 | 95 | 99 | |
| 34 | 23 | 058 | 10 | 23 | 45 | 53 | 69 | 88 | 97 | * | |
| 35 | 24 | 041 | 08 | 20 | 40 | 48 | 65 | 86 | 97 | | |
| 36 | 24 | 065 | 11 | 26 | 49 | 58 | 74 | 91 | 98 | | |
| 37 | 25 | 047 | 09 | 22 | 45 | 53 | 70 | 89 | 98 | | |
| 38 | 26 | 034 | 07 | 19 | 40 | 48 | 66 | 87 | 97 | | |
| 39 | 26 | 053 | 10 | 25 | 49 | 57 | 74 | 91 | 98 | | |
| 40 | 27 | 038 | 08 | 21 | 44 | 53 | 70 | 90 | 98 | | |
| 42 | 28 | 044 | 09 | 24 | 48 | 57 | 74 | 92 | 99 | | |
| 44 | 29 | 049 | 10 | 26 | 52 | 61 | 78 | 94 | 99 | | |
| 46 | 30 | 054 | 11 | 29 | 56 | 65 | 81 | 95 | 99 | | |
| 48 | 31 | 059 | 12 | 31 | 59 | 68 | 84 | 96 | * | | |

Table 5.3.5 *(continued)*

| n | v | $a_2$ | .05 | .10 | .15 | 1/6 | .20 | .25 | .30 | .35 | .40 |
|---|---|---|---|---|---|---|---|---|---|---|---|
| 50 | 32 | 065 | 13 | 34 | 62 | 71 | 86 | 97 | * | * | * |
| 52 | 34 | 036 | 09 | 26 | 54 | 64 | 81 | 96 | | | |
| 54 | 35 | 040 | 10 | 28 | 57 | 67 | 84 | 97 | | | |
| 56 | 36 | 044 | 11 | 30 | 60 | 70 | 86 | 97 | | | |
| 58 | 37 | 048 | 11 | 33 | 63 | 73 | 88 | 98 | | | |
| 60 | 38 | 052 | 12 | 35 | 66 | 76 | 90 | 98 | | | |
| 64 | 40 | 060 | 14 | 39 | 71 | 80 | 92 | 99 | | | |
| 68 | 43 | 038 | 11 | 34 | 67 | 77 | 91 | 99 | | | |
| 72 | 45 | 044 | 12 | 38 | 72 | 81 | 93 | 99 | | | |
| 76 | 47 | 050 | 14 | 42 | 76 | 84 | 95 | * | | | |
| 80 | 49 | 057 | 16 | 46 | 80 | 87 | 96 | | | | |
| 84 | 52 | 038 | 12 | 41 | 76 | 85 | 96 | | | | |
| 88 | 54 | 042 | 14 | 44 | 80 | 88 | 97 | | | | |
| 92 | 56 | 047 | 15 | 48 | 83 | 90 | 98 | | | | |
| 96 | 58 | 052 | 17 | 51 | 85 | 92 | 98 | | | | |
| 100 | 60 | 057 | 18 | 54 | 87 | 93 | 99 | | | | |
| 120 | 71 | 055 | 21 | 61 | 92 | 97 | * | | | | |
| 140 | 82 | 052 | 22 | 67 | 95 | 98 | | | | | |
| 160 | 93 | 048 | 24 | 72 | 97 | 99 | | | | | |
| 180 | 104 | 044 | 25 | 76 | 98 | 99 | | | | | |
| 200 | 114 | 056 | 31 | 83 | 99 | * | | | | | |
| 250** | 141 | 050 | 35 | 89 | * | | | | | | |
| 300 | 167 | 057 | 43 | 94 | | | | | | | |
| 350** | 194 | 050 | 46 | 96 | | | | | | | |
| 400 | 220 | 051 | 52 | 98 | | | | | | | |
| 450** | 246 | 050 | 58 | 99 | | | | | | | |
| 500 | 272 | 054 | 62 | * | | | | | | | |
| 600 | 325 | 045 | 67 | | | | | | | | |
| 700 | 377 | 054 | 74 | | | | | | | | |
| 800 | 428 | 052 | 81 | | | | | | | | |
| 900 | 480 | 049 | 85 | | | | | | | | |
| 1000 | 531 | 054 | 89 | | | | | | | | |

* Values below this point are greater than .995, unless other values are specified.

** Normal approximation.

**Table 5.3.6**

Power of Sign Test (P = .50) at $a_2 \approx .10$

| | | | | | | | g | | | | |
|---|---|---|---|---|---|---|---|---|---|---|---|
| n | v | $a_2$ | .05 | .10 | .15 | 1/6 | .20 | .25 | .30 | .35 | .40 |
| 8 | 6 | 289 | 31 | 37 | 45 | 49 | 56 | 68 | 80 | 90 | 96 |
| 9 | 7 | 180 | 20 | 26 | 35 | 39 | 47 | 60 | 74 | 86 | 95 |
| 10 | 8 | 109 | 13 | 18 | 27 | 30 | 38 | 53 | 68 | 82 | 93 |
| 11 | 8 | 227 | 25 | 32 | 44 | 48 | 57 | 61 | 84 | 93 | 98 |
| 12 | 9 | 146 | 17 | 24 | 35 | 40 | 49 | 65 | 79 | 91 | 97 |
| 13 | 10 | 092 | 11 | 18 | 28 | 32 | 42 | 58 | 75 | 88 | 97 |
| 14 | 10 | 180 | 21 | 30 | 43 | 48 | 59 | 74 | 87 | 95 | 99 |
| 15 | 11 | 118 | 15 | 23 | 35 | 41 | 52 | 69 | 84 | 94 | 99 |
| 16 | 11 | 210 | 25 | 35 | 50 | 55 | 66 | 81 | 92 | 98 | * |
| 17 | 12 | 143 | 18 | 27 | 42 | 48 | 60 | 77 | 89 | 97 | * |
| 18 | 13 | 096 | 13 | 21 | 36 | 41 | 53 | 72 | 87 | 96 | 99 |
| 19 | 13 | 167 | 21 | 32 | 48 | 54 | 67 | 83 | 93 | 98 | * |
| 20 | 14 | 115 | 15 | 26 | 42 | 48 | 61 | 79 | 91 | 98 | |
| 21 | 15 | 078 | 11 | 20 | 36 | 42 | 55 | 74 | 89 | 97 | |
| 22 | 15 | 134 | 18 | 30 | 48 | 54 | 67 | 84 | 94 | 99 | |
| 23 | 16 | 093 | 13 | 24 | 41 | 48 | 62 | 80 | 93 | 98 | |
| 24 | 16 | 152 | 20 | 34 | 53 | 60 | 73 | 88 | 96 | 99 | |
| 25 | 17 | 108 | 15 | 28 | 47 | 54 | 68 | 85 | 95 | 99 | |
| 26 | 18 | 076 | 11 | 23 | 41 | 48 | 63 | 82 | 94 | 99 | |
| 27 | 18 | 122 | 17 | 31 | 52 | 59 | 73 | 89 | 97 | * | |
| 28 | 19 | 087 | 13 | 26 | 46 | 54 | 68 | 86 | 96 | 99 | |
| 29 | 19 | 136 | 19 | 35 | 56 | 64 | 77 | 92 | 98 | * | |
| 30 | 20 | 099 | 15 | 29 | 51 | 58 | 73 | 89 | 97 | | |
| 31 | 21 | 071 | 11 | 25 | 46 | 53 | 69 | 87 | 97 | | |
| 32 | 21 | 110 | 17 | 33 | 55 | 63 | 77 | 92 | 98 | | |
| 33 | 22 | 080 | 13 | 28 | 50 | 58 | 73 | 90 | 98 | | |
| 34 | 22 | 121 | 18 | 36 | 59 | 67 | 81 | 94 | 99 | | |
| 35 | 23 | 090 | 15 | 31 | 54 | 62 | 77 | 92 | 99 | | |
| 36 | 23 | 132 | 20 | 39 | 63 | 71 | 84 | 95 | 99 | | |
| 37 | 24 | 099 | 16 | 34 | 58 | 66 | 81 | 94 | 99 | | |
| 38 | 25 | 073 | 13 | 29 | 53 | 62 | 77 | 93 | 99 | | |
| 39 | 25 | 108 | 18 | 37 | 62 | 70 | 84 | 96 | 99 | | |
| 40 | 26 | 081 | 14 | 32 | 57 | 66 | 81 | 95 | 99 | | |
| 42 | 27 | 088 | 15 | 35 | 61 | 69 | 84 | 96 | 99 | | |
| 44 | 28 | 096 | 17 | 37 | 64 | 72 | 86 | 97 | * | | |
| 46 | 29 | 104 | 18 | 40 | 67 | 75 | 88 | 98 | | | |
| 48 | 30 | 111 | 20 | 42 | 70 | 78 | 90 | 98 | | | |

Table 5.3.6 *(continued)*

| n | v | $a_2$ | g | | | | | | | | |
|---|---|---|---|---|---|---|---|---|---|---|---|
| | | | .05 | .10 | .15 | 1/6 | .20 | .25 | .30 | .35 | .40 |
| 50 | 31 | 119 | 21 | 45 | 73 | 80 | 92 | 99 | * | * | * |
| 52 | 32 | 126 | 22 | 47 | 75 | 82 | 93 | 99 | | | |
| 54 | 34 | 076 | 16 | 38 | 68 | 77 | 90 | 98 | | | |
| 56 | 35 | 081 | 17 | 41 | 71 | 79 | 91 | 99 | | | |
| 58 | 36 | 087 | 18 | 43 | 73 | 81 | 93 | 99 | | | |
| 60 | 37 | 092 | 19 | 45 | 75 | 83 | 94 | 99 | | | |
| 64 | 39 | 103 | 21 | 49 | 79 | 86 | 95 | * | | | |
| 68 | 41 | 114 | 23 | 53 | 83 | 89 | 97 | | | | |
| 72 | 44 | 076 | 18 | 47 | 79 | 87 | 96 | | | | |
| 76 | 46 | 085 | 20 | 51 | 83 | 89 | 97 | | | | |
| 80 | 48 | 093 | 22 | 55 | 85 | 92 | 98 | | | | |
| 84 | 50 | 101 | 24 | 58 | 88 | 93 | 98 | | | | |
| 88 | 52 | 109 | 26 | 61 | 90 | 95 | 99 | | | | |
| 92 | 54 | 117 | 28 | 64 | 91 | 96 | 99 | | | | |
| 96 | 57 | 082 | 23 | 59 | 90 | 95 | 99 | | | | |
| 100 | 59 | 089 | 24 | 62 | 91 | 96 | 99 | | | | |
| 120 | 70 | 082 | 26 | 68 | 95 | 98 | * | | | | |
| 140 | 80 | 108 | 34 | 78 | 98 | 99 | | | | | |
| 160 | 91 | 097 | 35 | 81 | 99 | * | | | | | |
| 180 | 102 | 086 | 36 | 84 | 99 | | | | | | |
| 200 | 112 | 104 | 42 | 89 | * | | | | | | |
| 250** | 139 | 100 | 45 | 93 | | | | | | | |
| 300 | 165 | 094 | 52 | 97 | | | | | | | |
| 350** | 191 | 100 | 59 | 98 | | | | | | | |
| 400 | 217 | 099 | 64 | 99 | | | | | | | |
| 450** | 243 | 100 | 68 | * | | | | | | | |
| 500 | 269 | 098 | 72 | | | | | | | | |
| 600 | 321 | 094 | 78 | | | | | | | | |
| 700 | 372 | 104 | 85 | | | | | | | | |
| 800 | 424 | 097 | 88 | | | | | | | | |
| 900 | 475 | 102 | 92 | | | | | | | | |
| 1000 | 527 | 094 | 93 | | | | | | | | |

* Values below this point are greater than .995, unless other values are specified.

** Normal approximation.

**Illustrative Examples**

**5.1**  A class in political science at a large state university undertakes a research project, as follows: There are about to be student government elections, and the class attempts to forecast the result by polling a random sample of 100 students who indicate they will vote. Two candidate slates are in contention, and, among other questions, respondents are asked their slate preference. A test is to be performed at the $a_2 \approx .05$ level of the null hypothesis that either slate will poll .50 of the votes. Assuming that, in fact, the present split in the student body is .55:.45, i.e., that $g = .55 - .50 = .05$, what is the power of the test? The specifications are;:

$$a_2 \approx .05, \quad \cdot g = .05, \quad n = 100.$$

In Table 5.3.5 (for $a_2 \approx .05$), one finds that the closest exact value to $a_2 = .05$ for $n = 100$ is $a_2 = .057$. At that level, for column $g = .05$, power equals .18. Thus, if the population split is .55:.45, there is only an 18% chance of detecting this slight edge at the $a_2 = .057$ level with $n = 100$.

Other things equal, what is the probability that a .60:.40 population split is detectable?

$$a_2 = .057, \quad g = .10, \quad n = 100.$$

In row $n = 100$ of Table 5.3.5 in column $g = .10$, one finds power of .54. Thus, there is only about an even chance of detecting a .60:.40 disparity in preference for the two slates with $n = 100$ at $a_2 = .057$. Under these conditions, apparently, a sample of 100 cases is insufficient for useful forecasting, unless **P** departs a great deal from .50. Note that one must posit $g = .15$, a population .65:.35 split 'hence a "landslide") for the power of the test to be usefully large (i.e., .87).

**5.2**  An experimental psychologist undertakes an investigation in which he randomly assigns the two members of 24 litter pairs of rats to an E (impoverished environment) and C (control) condition. At maturity, each of the pairs is brought together and a panel of three observers renders judgments as to which of the two is the more aggressive, a majority vote being determining. These circumstances call for a sign test. The null hypothesis is that $P_E \leq .50$, to be tested at $a_1 \approx .05$, against the directional alternative that $P_E > .50$, that is, that more of the E members would be judged aggressive, this being the expectation derived from his theory. The latter leads him to expect a strong effect, which he operationally defines as "large," i.e., $g = .25$. Thus, his exact alternate hypothesis is that the population $P_E = .50 + .25 = .75$. Given the latter, what is the power of the test? The specifications are:

$$a_1 \approx .05, \quad g = .25, \quad n = 24.$$

Note that although there are 48 animals involved, the observational unit is the pair, which can yield a positive $(E > C)$ or a negative $(E < C)$ difference in dominance, hence $n = 24$.

In Table 5.3.2 for $a_1 \approx .05$, one notes first that for row $n = 24$, the nearest to the .05 exact value of $a_1 = .032$. (The next most stringent criterion for $a_1$ at $n = 24$ is .076—see Table 5.3.3.) Reading over to column $g = .25$, one finds his power to be .77. Thus, if the effect is that large, he has a fairly good chance (about 3 in 4) of rejecting the null.

However, if the observational judgment about aggressiveness is difficult to make, as evidenced, for example, by many split decisions among the judges, he might reason that the large effect expected from theory may be attenuated by measurement (judgment) error, and that perhaps he should not expect more than a 2:1 rather than a 3:1 predominance of E members being judged the more aggressive, hence $g = P_E - .50 = \frac{2}{3} - \frac{1}{2} = \frac{1}{6}$. For this alternate hypothesis, that is for $g = \frac{1}{6}$ along row $n = 24$ (where $a_1 = .032$), the power = only .42. He might consider liberalizing his $a_1$ criterion, since the discreteness has forced him to use $a_1 = .032$ when he was prepared to work at $a_1 = .05$. He revises his specifications to

$$a_1 \approx .10, \qquad g = \tfrac{1}{6}, \qquad n = 24.$$

In Table 5.3.3 for $a_1 \approx .10$, he finds (as noted before) that at $n = 24$ he can work at the exact value $a_1 = .076$, which is not very far from his originally intended $a_1 = .05$ level. Reading over to $g = \frac{1}{6}$, he finds power = .59, which he may still find inadequate for his purpose.

**5.3** An educational psychologist has designed an experiment to decide which of two alternative frame sequences more effectively teaches a small unit of plane geometry in a programed textbook. A group of 300 subjects was formed into 150 pairs, the members of each matched for available mathematical aptitude score, sex, and class. They were assigned textbooks differing only in whether the A or B version of the unit was included in their program. When the text was completed, the students were given a criterion problem and the "passers" were determined. The test performed involved finding whether the (correlated) proportions of passers in the A and B groups differ (Hays, 1973, pp. 740–742), or, equivalently, whether, out of the pairs whose outcomes (pass or fail) *differ* ($n_d$), the proportion who had the A versions differ from .50. Note that this number cannot be known in advance, but varies inversely with the degree of between pair correlation, i.e., the stronger the relationship between pair members, necessarily the fewer pairs will have differing outcomes. He wishes to be able to reject the null hypothesis if, in the population, there is a .60:.40 split among those pairs who have differing outcomes, thus $g = .10$. As stated, the test is non-directional, and he has set $a_2 \approx .05$. He finds, after the experiment is completed, that in 60 of the 150 pairs, the pass–fail outcomes of the two members of the pair differ, i.e., $n_d = 60$. What is the power of the test? The specifications are:

$$a_2 \approx .05, \qquad g = .10, \qquad n = 60.$$

In Table 5.3.5 (for $a_2 \approx .05$) for $n = 60$, he first finds that the exact $a_2$ value for the test at that $n$ is .052. In column $g = .10$, he finds power $= .35$. He might well consider this power value inadequate for his purpose. He reconsiders the plan.

It occurs to him that he can liberalize his significance driterion, since a Type I error in this situation is relatively tolerable. Thus:

$$a_2 \approx .10, \qquad g = .10, \qquad n = 60.$$

Now, in Table 5.3.6 (for $a_2 \approx .10$) for $n = 60$, he first finds that the exact $a_2$ value is .092, and for $g = .10$, finds power $= .45$. This still leaves him with a less than equiprobable chance of rejecting the null for these specifications.

He then decides to consider even further liberalization of his significance criterion: He can test at $a_2 \approx .20$ by using the $a_1 \approx .10$ criterion on a two-sided basis:

$$a_2 \approx .20, \qquad g = .10, \qquad n = 60.$$

In Table 5.3.3 for $a_1 \approx .10$, but used in a way that makes $a_2 \approx .20$, he first finds that for $n = 60$, the exact $a_1$ value is .078, so for his intended use, $a_2 = 2(.078) = .156$. For $g = .10$, he finds power $= .56$.

Although by progressively liberalizing his $a_2$ criterion from .052 to .156, he has increased power from .35 to .56, he may well decide that the latter value is still inadequate. If he cannot reasonably expect $g > .10$, his only recourse within this design is to increase $n$.

## 5.4   SAMPLE SIZE TABLES

The tables in this section give values for the significance criterion, the $g$ ($= ES$) to be detected, and the desired power. The sample size, $n$ (i.e., the number which is the base of the sample proportion to be tested), is then determined. These tables are designed primarily for use in making the decision about sample size during the planning of experiments. As Section 2.4 points out, a rational decision on sample size requires, once a significance criterion and ES are formulated, attention to the question: how much power (how little Type II error risk) is desired?

**Table 5.4.1**

n to detect g in the Sign Test (P = .50)

| Power | \| \| \| \| \| \| \| \| | | | | | | | |
|---|---|---|---|---|---|---|---|---|

### $a_1$ = .01 ($a_2$ = .02)

| Power | .05 | .10 | .15 | 1/6 | .20 | .25 | .30 | .35 | .40 |
|---|---|---|---|---|---|---|---|---|---|
| .25 | 274 | 69 | 32 | 27 | 19 | 14 | 11 | 7 | 7 |
| .50 | 541 | 135 | 60 | 49 | 32 | 22 | 17 | 14 | 11 |
| .60 | 665 | 166 | 73 | 59 | 42 | 27 | 19 | 14 | 11 |
| 2/3 | 759 | 189 | 83 | 67 | 47 | 30 | 19 | 17 | 11 |
| .70 | 811 | 202 | 89 | 72 | 49 | 32 | 22 | 17 | 11 |
| .75 | 899 | 223 | 98 | 79 | 54 | 34 | 25 | 17 | 14 |
| .80 | 1001 | 248 | 109 | 88 | 60 | 37 | 27 | 19 | 14 |
| .85 | 1127 | 279 | 122 | 98 | 67 | 42 | 30 | 19 | 17 |
| .90 | 1297 | 321 | 140 | 112 | 77 | 50 | 32 | 22 | 17 |
| .95 | 1571 | 388 | 169 | 135 | 92 | 56 | 37 | 27 | 19 |
| .99 | 2154 | 530 | 230 | 184 | 124 | 75 | 50 | 35 | 25 |

### $a_1$ = .05 ($a_2$ = .10)

| Power | .05 | .10 | .15 | 1/6 | .20 | .25 | .30 | .35 | .40 |
|---|---|---|---|---|---|---|---|---|---|
| .25 | 95 | 28 | 13 | 13 | 8 | 8 | 5 | 5 | 5 |
| .50 | 271 | 68 | 30 | 28 | 18 | 13 | 8 | 8 | 5 |
| .60 | 360 | 90 | 42 | 35 | 23 | 16 | 11 | 8 | 8 |
| 2/3 | 430 | 107 | 47 | 37 | 28 | 18 | 13 | 11 | 8 |
| .70 | 469 | 116 | 51 | 44 | 30 | 18 | 13 | 11 | 8 |
| .75 | 536 | 133 | 58 | 49 | 35 | 23 | 13 | 11 | 8 |
| .80 | 616 | 152 | 67 | 53 | 37 | 23 | 16 | 13 | 8 |
| .85 | 716 | 177 | 77 | 62 | 44 | 28 | 18 | 13 | 11 |
| .90 | 853 | 210 | 91 | 73 | 50 | 33 | 23 | 16 | 11 |
| .95 | 1077 | 265 | 115 | 92 | 62 | 40 | 28 | 18 | 13 |
| .99 | 1568 | 385 | 166 | 133 | 89 | 54 | 35 | 26 | 18 |

### $a_1$ = .10 ($a_2$ = .20)

| Power | .05 | .10 | .15 | 1/6 | .20 | .25 | .30 | .35 | .40 |
|---|---|---|---|---|---|---|---|---|---|
| .25 | 39 | 14 | 9 | 7 | 7 | 4 | 4 | 4 | 4 |
| .50 | 164 | 46 | 21 | 19 | 14 | 9 | 7 | 4 | 4 |
| .60 | 235 | 59 | 28 | 21 | 17 | 9 | 9 | 7 | 4 |
| 2/3 | 292 | 73 | 35 | 28 | 19 | 14 | 9 | 7 | 7 |
| .70 | 325 | 81 | 37 | 30 | 21 | 14 | 9 | 7 | 7 |
| .75 | 381 | 94 | 44 | 35 | 26 | 17 | 12 | 9 | 7 |
| .80 | 449 | 111 | 48 | 39 | 28 | 19 | 14 | 9 | 7 |
| .85 | 535 | 132 | 57 | 48 | 35 | 21 | 14 | 9 | 7 |
| .90 | 654 | 161 | 70 | 56 | 39 | 26 | 19 | 12 | 9 |
| .95 | 852 | 209 | 90 | 72 | 49 | 30 | 21 | 14 | 9 |
| .99 | 1293 | 317 | 136 | 109 | 73 | 44 | 28 | 21 | 14 |

**Table 5.4.1** *(continued)*

| | | | | $a_2 = .01$ $(a_1 = .005)$ | | | | | |
| | | | | g | | | | | |
| Power | .05 | .10 | .15 | 1/6 | .20 | .25 | .30 | .35 | .40 |
|---|---|---|---|---|---|---|---|---|---|
| .25 | 363 | 92 | 44 | 34 | 26 | 18 | 12 | 8 | 8 |
| .50 | 663 | 166 | 74 | 60 | 42 | 26 | 18 | 12 | 12 |
| .60 | 800 | 199 | 88 | 71 | 49 | 34 | 24 | 12 | 12 |
| 2/3 | 903 | 225 | 99 | 80 | 55 | 34 | 26 | 15 | 15 |
| .70 | 960 | 239 | 105 | 85 | 58 | 39 | 26 | 15 | 15 |
| .75 | 1054 | 262 | 115 | 93 | 64 | 39 | 26 | 15 | 15 |
| .80 | 1165 | 289 | 127 | 102 | 70 | 44 | 32 | 15 | 15 |
| .85 | 1301 | 322 | 141 | 114 | 78 | 49 | 34 | 24 | 18 |
| .90 | 1483 | 367 | 160 | 129 | 88 | 54 | 37 | 26 | 18 |
| .95 | 1775 | 438 | 191 | 153 | 104 | 64 | 44 | 32 | 21 |
| .99 | 2392 | 589 | 255 | 205 | 139 | 84 | 55 | 39 | 26 |

| | | | | $a_2 = .05$ $(a_1 = .025)$ | | | | | |
| | | | | g | | | | | |
| Power | .05 | .10 | .15 | 1/6 | .20 | .25 | .30 | .35 | .40 |
|---|---|---|---|---|---|---|---|---|---|
| .25 | 166 | 44 | 20 | 17 | 12 | 9 | 6 | 6 | 6 |
| .50 | 384 | 96 | 44 | 37 | 25 | 17 | 12 | 9 | 6 |
| .60 | 489 | 122 | 54 | 44 | 32 | 20 | 15 | 9 | 9 |
| 2/3 | 570 | 142 | 62 | 50 | 37 | 25 | 17 | 12 | 9 |
| .70 | 616 | 153 | 67 | 54 | 37 | 25 | 17 | 12 | 9 |
| .75 | 692 | 172 | 75 | 61 | 44 | 28 | 17 | 15 | 9 |
| .80 | 783 | 194 | 85 | 68 | 49 | 30 | 20 | 15 | 12 |
| .85 | 895 | 221 | 97 | 78 | 53 | 32 | 25 | 17 | 12 |
| .90 | 1047 | 259 | 113 | 90 | 61 | 40 | 28 | 17 | 15 |
| .95 | 1294 | 319 | 138 | 111 | 75 | 49 | 32 | 23 | 17 |
| .99 | 1827 | 449 | 194 | 155 | 105 | 63 | 42 | 30 | 20 |

As was pointed out above in Section 5.3, the use of the exact binomial test precludes the use of exact conventional significance criteria because of the discreteness of sample frequencies. In order to avoid the cumbersomeness of supplying the exact **a** values for each value of **n** read from the table, the values of **n** read from the table are to be interpreted as follows:

*1. n Less than 50.* The exact **a** value which was used is *no greater than* the stated value; it is the (discrete) value of **a** below the stated value. Thus, the actual **a** values for, say, the table for $a_2 = .05$ are more or less below .05. Accordingly, the power values, being for actual **a** generally less than nominal **a**, will be (slightly) lower than would be the case if the exact values could be used.

*2. n of 50 or More.* The normal approximation to the binomial was used, and the **n** values are the *nearest* integral number (as is true throughout the book), not the next largest.

Tables give values for **a**, **g**, and desired power.

*1. Significance Criterion,* **a**. The same values are provided as for the power tables, but as just noted, are for exact values not exceeding the nominal value when the value of **n** read from the table is less than 50. Five tables are provided, one for each of the following nonparenthetic **a** levels: $a_1 = .01$ ($a_2 = .02$), $a_1 = .05$ ($a_2 = .10$), $a_1 = .10$ ($a_2 = .20$), $a_2 = .01$ ($a_1 = .005$), and $a_2 = .05$ ($a_1 = .025$).

*2. Effect Size, ES.* The difference between the alternative-hypothetical value of **P** and $.50 = g$, the ES index. The same provision for **g** is made as in the power tables: .05 (.05) .40 and $\frac{1}{6}$. For **g** values other than the nine provided, the following formula, rounding to the nearest integer, provides a good approximation:

$$(5.4.1) \qquad\qquad n = \frac{n_{.05}}{400g^2} - K,$$

where $n_{.05}$ is the necessary sample size for the given **a** and desired power at $g = .05$ (obtained from the table), and **K** is a constant which varies with the desired power, as follows[4]:

| Power: | .50 | .60 | $\frac{2}{3}$ | .70 | .80 | .85 | .90 | .95 | .99 |
|---|---|---|---|---|---|---|---|---|---|
| K: | 0 | 0.5 | 1.0 | 1.5 | 2.5 | 3.0 | 3.5 | 6.0 | 9.0 |

*3. Desired Power.* As in the previous chapters, provision is made for desired power values of .25, .50, .60, $\frac{2}{3}$, .70 (.05), .95, .99. For discussion of the basis for selecting these values, the provision for equalizing **a** and **b** risks, and the rationale of a proposed convention of desired power of .80, see Section 2.4.

Summarizing the use of the following **n** tables, the investigator finds (*a*) the table for the significance criterion (**a**) he is using, locates (*b*) the population (alternate-hypothetical) value of **g** and (*c*) the desired power along the vertical stub. He then finds **n**, the necessary sample size to detect **g** at (when $n < 50$, no more than) the **a** significance criterion with the desired power. If the **g** value in his specifications is not provided, he locates the value for

---

[4] The approximation is the normal approximation, thus the **n** found will be the estimated value *at* the **a** value necessary for the desired power. It will thus be comparable in its interpretation to the tabled values of $n \geq 50$, i.e., the *nearest* number, not the next largest, as is the case with tabled values of $n < 50$.

$n_{.05}$ in the relevant **a** table in column **g** = .05 and the row for desired power. This is used, together with the value of **K** for the desired power, in formula (5.4.1) to compute **n**.

**Illustrative Examples**

**5.4** Consider again the situation described in example 5.1, where a political science class undertakes a project involving polling a sample of the college student body with regard to student government elections. As described there originally, they wish to detect a .55:.45 division between two slates (hence, **g** = .05) at $a_2$ = .05. Their original intention to use **n** = 100 respondents who would express a preference led to power of .18. We may safely assume that this value is found inadequate. Assume now that they wish to have power at the proposed conventional value of .80 and seek the necessary sample size to achieve this. The specifications are:

$$a_2 = .05, \qquad g = .05, \qquad power = .80.$$

In Table 5.4.1 in the section for $a_2$ = .05, column **g** = .05, row power = .80, one finds **n** = 783. This is a very large sample, indeed, far larger than the originally intended **n** = 100. It thus takes many cases to detect a small ES (**g** = .05) with conventional desired power of .80.

If they posit instead that the division in the student population may be as large as .60:.40 (hence, **g** = .60 − .50 = .10), a value which falls between the operational definitions of small and medium ES for this test, what is the sample size required? The new specifications:

$$a_2 = .05, \qquad g = .10, \qquad power = .80.$$

In the same line (power = .80) of the same table (Table 4.5.1. in the section for $a_2$ = .05), for column **g** = .10, one finds **n** = 194.

**5.5** The experimental psychologist of example 5.2 was studying the effects of an impoverished early environment on the aggressiveness of rats. Using litter pairs (one E and one C), the plan is, following the experimental manipulation, to have judgments rendered as to which pair member is the more aggressive. He intends a directional sign test at about $a_1$ = .05, predicting that the E member will be more frequently judged the more aggressive. Assume that although he anticipates a large *true* effect, because of expected judge unreliability, he posits as an alternate hypothesis $g = P_E - .50 = \frac{2}{3} - \frac{1}{2} = \frac{1}{6}$. He desires power to be .80. What is the required **n**? The specifications are

$$a_1 = .05, \qquad g = \tfrac{1}{6}, \qquad power = .80.$$

In the section of Table 5.4.1 for $a_1 = .05$ in column $g = \frac{1}{6}$ for row desired power $= .80$, he finds $n = 53$ litter pairs. Since $n > 50$, a normal curve test is envisaged.

Assume that this is a much larger experiment than he had planned to mount. He wonders how much reduction in $n$ would occur if he reduced his desired power to .70, keeping the other specifications unchanged, i.e.,

$$a_1 = .05, \qquad g = \tfrac{1}{6}, \qquad \text{power} = .70.$$

In the $a_1 = .05$ section of Table 5.4.1, in column $g = \frac{1}{6}$, he now reads from row power $= .70$ that the necessary $n$ is 44. Since $n < 50$, the specification is for an exact binomial sign test at $a_1 \le .05$ and power $\ge .70$. To find the exact value of $a_1$ and power, he uses the *power* table for $a_1 \approx .05$, Table 5.3.2 for $n = 44$. He finds there in column $a_1$ that the exact value is .048 at which criterion column $g = \frac{1}{6}$ gives exact power .72.

This $n$ is still rather large for his resources. While in the power Table 5.3.2, he glances upward along the $a_1$ column and notices that if he slightly liberalizes his $a_1$ criterion to .054 and applies it with $n = 39$, $g = \frac{1}{6}$, power $= .70$. Thus, he can save 5 $(= 44 - 39)$ litter pairs by working at $a_1 = .054$ instead of .048 and with power of .70 instead of .72, differences he might well consider trivial.

He glances a little further up the $a_1$ column and notes that if he further liberalizes his $a_1$ criterion to .066 this value can be used in a test where $n = 36$, at $g = \frac{1}{6}$, power $= .71$. He thus has essentially the same power at a saving of three more pairs, if he is prepared to use the $a_1 = .066$ significance criterion.

He decides that he is quite prepared for $a_1$ to exceed .05, but is uncomfortable about the $(1 - .71 =)$ .29 Type II (b) risk. In studying the test at $n = 36$, he notes that the risk ratio, .29:.066, is such that he runs about a 4 times larger risk of failing to obtain significance if $g = \frac{1}{6}$ than of getting a spuriously significant result if $g \le 0$ (i.e., if the directional null hypothesis is true). Although, as was suggested in Section 2.4, such a ratio is consonant with the conventional scientific caution, an investigator's knowledge about the place of his specific research effort in his research context requires (certainly permits) that he set values for **a** and **b** and thus their ratio. Our experimental psychologist determines that he wishes to reduce the risk ratio, and is quite prepared to liberalize his $a_1$ criterion in order to increase his power to about .80. He thus changes his specifications to

$$a_1 = .10, \qquad g = \tfrac{1}{6}, \qquad \text{power} = .80.$$

Using again the sample size Table 5.4.1, but in the section for $a_1 = .10$, for column $g = \frac{1}{6}$, row power $= .80$, he finds $n = 39$. Since $n \le 50$, the table assumes an exact binomial test, so $a_1 \le .10$ and power $\ge .80$. To determine exact values, he turns to power Table 5.3.3 (for $a_1 \approx .10$) and, for row $n = 39$, sees that the exact $a_1 = .100$ and the exact power at $g = \frac{1}{6}$ is .80. (It is, of course, a coincidence that his specifications are met exactly.) His risk ratio is now $b = 1 - .80 = .20$ to $a_1 = .100$, exactly 2 to 1. He may proceed on the basis of these specifications, or seek others in the vicinity of $n = 39$, e.g., at $n = 38$, where power is .84 and the two risks are almost equal, .16 : .128, or if he does not wish to exceed $a_1 = .10$, at $n = 40$ where the risk ratio is .23 : .077, or at $n = 37$ where it is .22 to .094.

**5.6**   The test of the null hypothesis that $P = .50$ (or $g = 0$) as applied to a test of correlated proportions was illustrated in problem 5.3. In that problem, an education psychologist was comparing two alternate pro-gramed frame sequences in a unit of plane geometry, by forming matched pairs of students, supplying them with one or the other sequence, and determining whether they passed a criterion problem. For the test, only the pairs whose pass–fail outcomes differ are relevant, since the null hypothesis formulation is that among such pairs, $P = .50$ of them come from sequence A (or B).

If, as described initially in problem 5.3, he expects a .60 : .40 split among the pairs with differing outcomes ($g = .10$), plans to use the $a_2 = .05$ signifi-cance criterion, and wishes power to be .75, his specifications are

$$a_2 = .05, \qquad g = .10, \qquad \text{power} = .75.$$

In the $a_2 = .05$ section of Table 5.4.1 with column $g = .10$ and row power $= .75$, he finds $n = 172$. Since this represents the number of pairs of *differing* outcome, which he anticipates to be one-third of the total number of pairs, this means that these specifications require that he have a total of $3(172) = 516$ pairs or 1032 subjects in all. Assuming classes of 30 students, this would require some 35 classes in plane geometry!

Assume the validity of the exclamation point, specifically that in the entire city there are only 26 classes in plane geometry, and that furthermore, he is not sure he can get the cooperation of every last one of the teachers involved. He reconsiders his specifications, and, as in problem 5.3, realizes that the nature of the decision is such that he can afford a larger Type I error criterion, so he changes his specifications to

$$a_2 = .10, \qquad g = .10, \qquad \text{power} = .75.$$

In the section of Table 5.4.1 for $a_2 = .10$ in column $g = .10$, row power $= .75$, he finds $n = 133$. This means a total of 399 pairs on the expected one-third of total differing in outcome, or 788 students, or 26–27 classes. He *knows* that there will be some defections from the 26 classes in the city's high schools, so he decided to liberalize his $a$ criterion to $a_2 = .20$. He

reasons that in this situation, failure to detect the alternate-hypothetical
.60:.40 discrepancy is almost as serious as a mistaken conclusion of the
superiority of one sequence over the other. Since he is committed to a
$1 - .75 = .25$ ($= \mathbf{b}$) risk of the former, he decides to raise the latter to .20
($= \mathbf{a_2}$). What sample size is now demanded? The specifications are

$$\mathbf{a_2} = .20, \qquad \mathbf{g} = .10, \qquad \text{power} = .75.$$

In Table 5.4.1 the subtable for $\mathbf{a_2} = .20$ is used and for column $\mathbf{g} = .10$
and row power $= .75$, $\mathbf{n} = 94$, the number of differing pairs required. This,
in turn, requires in all $3(94) = 282$ pairs—or 564 students—a total of 19 classes
which is close to the total number he can expect to get.

In the above example, we have manipulated only the significance criterion.
In other problems where there is a fixed maximum $\mathbf{n}$ permitted by the resources (which, of course is true, in principle, for all research problems),
other specifications instead of (or in addition to) the significance criterion
may be more appropriately modified. Thus, some of the specifications which
result in about the same required $\mathbf{n}$ from Table 5.4.1 are tabulated.

| $\mathbf{a_2}$ | $\mathbf{g}$ | Power | $\mathbf{n}$ |
|------|------|-------|-----|
| .01 | $\frac{1}{6}$ | .75 | 92 |
| .02 | .15 | .75 | 98 |
| .02 | $\frac{1}{6}$ | .85 | 98 |
| .05 | .10 | .50 | 96 |
| .05 | .15 | .85 | 97 |
| .10 | .10 | .60 | 90 |
| .10 | .15 | .90 | 91 |
| .10 | $\frac{1}{6}$ | .95 | 92 |
| .20 | .15 | .95 | 90 |

The investigator must weigh the alternative specifications for *his* problem from such a sample size table, and decide his best strategy. It was
implicitly assumed in this problem that the investigator could not reasonably
anticipate $\mathbf{g}$ greater than .10, nor was he prepared to tolerate less than 3:1
odds that, given a .60:.40 split, he would be able to make a definitive decision favoring the A or B sequences. This then left him to consider the significance criterion, which, given the nature of the problem, we saw he could
liberalize.

**5.7** A psychiatrist plans an experiment involving a single neurotic
subject to determine whether, *for this subject*, psychoanalytic sessions following
ingestion of a very small dosage of LSD are more productive than those
following placebo. His purpose is to decide, after the experimental series,

either to continue the psychoanalysis with LSD or without it (strictly, with placebo). The design is to determine randomly which of the sessions in each successive pair is to be an LSD session, the other to be placebo. Transcripts of the tape-recorded sessions are to be submitted to a panel of judges who must render a blind consensus judgment as to which session of each pair is the more productive.

He reasons that unless in the population[5] there is a superiority of the order of 4:1 favoring LSD sessions, he would just as soon not decide in its favor; hence he expects a population split of .80:.20, or $g = .80 - .50 = .30$. As formulated, the test is nondirectional and he decides that the significance criterion be $a_1 = .05$. Finally, if $g$ is in fact .30, he wants to be fairly sure that he will reject the null and fixes the desired power at .90. How many session pairs does he require for these specifications, which are, in summary

$$a_1 = .05, \qquad g = .30, \qquad \text{power} = .90.$$

In Table 5.4.1 in the section for $a_1 = .05$ with column $g = .30$ and row power $= .90$, he finds $n = 23$. He will thus need 23 *pairs* of sessions to satisfy the specifications. Since the $n$ is less than 50, he can determine the exact conditions of the binomial test by referring to the *power* table for the $a_1 = .05$ level, Table 5.3.2. In that table with $n = 23$, he sees that for the binomial test, the exact $a_1$ value is .047 at which, given $g = .30$, power $= .93$. He might look at other $n$ values in the vicinity to see if they yield paired values of exact $a_1$ and exact power which he prefers to those at $n = 23$ (for example, at $n = 22$, $a_1 = .067$ with power $= .94$; at $n = 24$, $a_1 = .032$ with power $= .91$, etc.).[6]

It is insufficiently appreciated in many areas of the behavioral sciences that statistical investigations can be usefully undertaken with single subjects. The $n$ of a study is the number of observations or instances, not necessarily the number of organisms or sets of organisms. Naturally, in investigations of single subjects, the populations to which generalizations can be made or inferences drawn are made up of instances or observations of *that* subject and cannot validly transcend him to populations of subjects. Still, such single subject experiments and their logically limited conclusions can be of either practical utility (as in the above example) or heuristic importance. For a

---

[5] The population here is, as is so often the case in behavioral sciences, an abstraction. It may be thought of as all the session pairs that might occur under the conditions specified.

[6] There is an alternative statistical-design strategy for problems of this kind which may well be superior to the preset fixed $n$ described in this problem. "Sequential" tests proceed by assessing each experimental unit (usually a subject, but here, a session) as it becomes available and deciding whether to draw a conclusion or observe another experimental unit. Such tests require special procedures originally described by Wald (1947) and, less technically, by Fiske and Jones (1954).

treatment of the rationale, method, and some applications of single subject studies see Davidson and Costello (1969).

**5.8**   Assume that a certain mathematical model in signal detection predicts a proportion of success over a given series of trials to be .68, hence $g = .18$, while the null hypothesis is that $P = .50$. What is the **n** required, if the psychologist wishes power at .95 for a directional test at $a_1 = .05$, that is, equal **a** and **b** risks at .05? The specifications are

$$a_1 = .05, \qquad g = .18, \qquad power = .95.$$

Since $g = .18$ is not tabled, the psychologist must take recourse to formula (5.4.1), which requires $n_{.05}$, the **n** required under the conditions stated when $g = .05$.

In Table 5.4.1 in the section for $a_1 = .05$, at row power $= .95$, he finds in column $g = .05$ the value $1077 = n_{.05}$. Substituting that value, $g = .18$, and the value for **K** for power $= .95$ provided with formula (5.4.1), he finds

$$n = \frac{1077}{400(.18)^2} - 6.0 = 83.1 - 6.0 = 77.1.$$

Thus, the normal (or chi square) approximation test will yield a probability of .95 of rejecting $H_0: P = .50$ if the actual $P = .68$ when $n = 77$. (Note that since the test is directional, the standard normal curve deviate required for significance at the .05 level is $\geq 1.65$. If the equivalent chi square form of the test is used, the criterion is the one tabled for one **df** $(u = 1)$ at $a = .10$, namely 2.706.)


## 5.5   THE USE OF THE TABLES FOR SIGNIFICANCE TESTING

As was the case in previous chapters, the power tables provide a significance criterion column to facilitate the performance of the statistical test of the null hypothesis after the data are collected. This is particularly useful for the test of this chapter, since it obviates the necessity of using a separate set of tables for the binomial function.

For any given **n**, the significance criterion in the test of $H_0: P = .50$ is simply the number of observations in the larger (or smaller) subgroup defined with regard to the presence or absence of the characteristic under study (e.g., males, success, positive differences, etc.). If this number departs sufficiently from $\frac{1}{2}n$, the null hypothesis is rejected.

The power tables in this chapter (Tables 5.3.1–5.3.5) contain, in the **v** column, the number of observations in the larger portion of the sample necessary to attain the exact significance level (given in column **a**) for the sample size of the row in which it appears. For nondirectional (two-tailed) tests, **v** is simply the number in the larger portion; for directional (one-tailed) tests, it is assumed that the test has been oriented so that the predicted direction is the one in which the larger portion occurs, since no matter how extreme the departure from .50, if it is in the wrong direction in a one-tailed test, the result is not significant.

Except for the three values of **n** double-asterisked in Tables 5.3.1–5.3.5, all the values given for **v** are exactly the minimum number needed to reject the null hypothesis ($P = .50$, $g = 0$) at the exact significance criterion given in the next column (**a**) using the symmetrical binomial test. At $n = 250$, 350, and 450, the value **v** is that required by the normal (or equivalently chi square) approximation to the binomial.

## Illustrative Examples

**5.9**   Consider the analysis of the data arising from the political science class project to forecast the result of a student government election using a sample of 100 voters at $a_2 \approx .05$. When the sample results are tallied, it is found that one of the two slates has garnered 57 ($= v_s$) of the 100 votes. The specifications for the significance test are

$$a_2 \approx .05, \qquad n = 100, \qquad v_s = 57.$$

In Table 5.3.5 for $a_2 \approx .05$ at row $n = 100$ it is first found that the nearest exact value to $a_2$ of .05 is at .057 (from column $a_2$). For significance at $a_2 = .057$, in the same row, it is found that the larger portion must contain $v = 60$ cases. Since 57 is less than 60, the departure from $P_s = .50$ is insufficient for rejection at $a_2 = .057$.

Let us consider the same situation from the perspective of problem 5.4, where it was finally decided, on the basis of a power analysis, that **n** should equal 194. Assume, instead, that the survey is accomplished with $n = 200$ voter respondents, at the $a_2 \approx .05$ level as before, and that one of the two slates has $v_s = 116$ adherents. The specifications for the test of significance now are:

$$a_2 \approx .05, \qquad n = 200, \qquad v_s = 116.$$

The same table (5.3.5 for $a_2 \approx .05$) is used for row $n = 200$, and now the exact $a_2$ value equals .056 (from column $a_2$). In the same row, the criterion for significance (at the $a_2 = .056$ level) is found in column **v** to be 114. Since 116 exceeds this (minimum necessary) value, the null hypothesis is rejected at the .056 level, and the class concludes that the slate in question has a majority of the voting population.

**5.10** Reconsider the circumstances of example 5.2, where an experimental psychologist was studying the effect on litter pairs of an early impoverished environment (versus control) on aggressiveness. Assume that the experiment was carried out as planned, and that it was found that 17 ($=v_s$) of the 24 E rats were judged more aggressive (in the predicted direction). Is this significantly different from the 12 expected on the null hypothesis? The specifications are

$$a_1 \approx .05, \quad n = 24, \quad v_s = 17.$$

In Table 5.3.2. (for $a_1 \approx .05$) for row $n = 24$, he finds first that the nearest $a_2$ exact value to .05 is (in column $a_1$) .032, at which level he requires a minimum of 17 ($=v$) pairs in which the E rat was judged the more aggressive. Since there are 17 ($=v_s$) in this group, his results are significant, and he can reject the null hypothesis at $a_1 = .032$ (see example 5.12 below).

**5.11** The educational psychologist in example 5.3 was studying which of two frame sequences more effectively taught a unit of plane geometry. Using matched pairs of students, he found that 60 (of the original 150) pairs were made up of members one of whom had passed and the other of whom had failed the criterion problem. Assume, as originally specified in example 5.3, that the test was planned to be performed at the $a_2 \approx .05$, and that it was found that the students in sequence A who passed the criterion problem while their matches failed numbered 35. The specifications for the significance test are

$$a_2 \approx .05, \quad n = 60, \quad v_s = 35.$$

In Table 5.3.5 (for $a_2 \approx .05$) for $n = 60$, he finds first that the exact $a_2$ value nearest .05 is .052, and for significance at that level he requires $v = 38$. Since his observed $v_s$ falls short of that value, he cannot reject the null hypothesis and conclude superiority for sequence A.

When this problem was revisited in example 5.6, the educational psychologist eventually decided that his needs would be better met by using the $a_2 \approx .20$ level. Assume that, on the basis of power considerations, he uses an initial sample size that results in his having 96 pairs of subjects with differing outcomes on the criterion. Let us say that he finds that of these there are 59 for which those with sequence A passed (while their matches on B failed). Does this lead to rejection of the $P = .50$ null hypothesis? The test specifications are

$$a_2 \approx .20, \quad n = 96, \quad v_s = 59.$$

Although there is no power table headed ". . . at $a_2 \approx .20$," the values for $v$ are the same as those given for $a_1 \approx .10$. Accordingly, in Table 5.3.3

for row $n = 96$, he finds in column $a_1$ that a test is available at $a_1 = .092$. He can treat it as providing a test at $2a_1 = .184 = a_2$. At this level, if the larger portion has $v = 55$ or more cases of the 96, he can conclude that the frame sequence of that portion is superior. Since sequence A superior pairs numbered 59, the null hypothesis is rejected and the superiority of sequence A affirmed at the .184 significance level.

**5.12**   In example 5.7, a psychiatrist was planning a study of the effects of LSD in a single patient on the productivity of psychoanalytic sessions by randomly assigning LSD or placebo to successive pairs of sessions. His planning specifications ($a_1 = .05$, $g = .30$, power = .90) led to the determination that he required $n = 23$ pairs of sessions. Assume that he has now performed the experiment as planned and finds that his judges have decided that in 16 of the paired sessions, the session preceded by LSD was more productive than the one preceded by placebo. Does this warrant rejecting the null hypothesis? The specifications are

$$a_1 \approx .05, \qquad n = 23, \qquad v_s = 16.$$

In Table 5.3.2 for $a_1 \approx .05$ and row $n = 23$, he finds that $v = 16$ (for exact $a_1 = .047$). In other words, when the population $P = .50$, he will obtain a 16:7 (or more extreme) break in the predicted direction .047 of the time in random sampling. Since his $v_s$ is included in the critical region (i.e., 16–23 out of 23), he rejects the null and concludes that *for this patient*, LSD leads to more productive sessions than placebo.

Note that his sample proportion is $16/23 = .70$, which is less than the .80 he hypothesized in the alternative hypothesis, yet this result led to a proper rejection of the null hypothesis. This can occur whenever the power planned for exceeds .50. This makes it clear that the rejection of the null hypothesis ($P = .50$) does not carry the implication that the alternate hypothesis ($P = .80$ or $g = .30$) is necessarily true. His sample value of .70 is not consistent with $P = .50$ (at $a_1 = .047$), but is consistent with many values of $P$, including in this instance .80.

CHAPTER 6

# Differences between Proportions

## 6.1 Introduction and Use

This chapter is concerned with the testing of hypotheses concerning differences between independent population proportions ($P$). Chapter 5 was devoted to a frequently occurring related issue, namely, the difference between a population proportion and .50. In the present chapter, other cases are considered: the difference between two independent population $P$'s when a random sample is available from each, and the difference between a population $P$ and any specified hypothetical value.

A proportion is a special case of an arithmetic mean, one in which the measurement scale has only two possible values, zero for the absence of a characteristic and one for its presence. Thus, one can describe a population as having a proportion of males of .62, or, with equal validity (if not equal stylistic grace), as having a mean "male-ness" of .62, the same value necessarily coming about when one scores each male 1, each nonmale 0, and finds the mean. It follows, then, that the same kinds of inferential issues arise for this special kind of mean as arise for means in general.

When one considers a difference between independent population proportions it becomes apparent that one can just as well think of the issue in terms of a relationship between two variables. Thus, if the $P$ of Republicans in a given population above a certain income level is .30 and the $P$ of Democrats above that level is .20, it is a matter of convenience or habit of thought whether this is viewed as a difference between Republicans and Democrats in income or as a relationship between political affiliation and income. It is apparent, then, that differences between proportions (as, indeed, between means) can be viewed in correlational terms.

**179**

It is possible to approach the testing of hypotheses about proportions by different statistical techniques, including the classical normal curve test using a "critical ratio" applied directly to the proportions (Edwards, 1972, pp. 42–44; Guilford & Fruchter, 1978, pp. 159–161; Blalock, 1972, pp. 228–232), by a chi-square contingency test (see Chapter 7 and references), by a special case of the hypergeometric probability distribution ("Fisher's Exact Method") for 2 × 2 tables (Hays, 1981, pp. 552–554; Owen, 1962, pp. 479–496), or by means of a normal curve test applied to the arcsine transformation of the proportions. Despite its unfamiliarity, it is the last of these alternatives that provides the basis for the approach of this chapter because of certain advantages it has, particularly from the viewpoint of power analysis. However, the results from using any of these procedures will be the same to a close approximation, particularly when samples are not small (Cohen, 1970).

The types of tests on proportions which the methods of this chapter facilitate are organized into cases, according to the specific hypothesis and sample(s) employed:

*Case 0.* $P_s$ values from equal size samples to test $P_1 = P_2$.

*Case 1.* The same hypothesis, but $n_1 \neq n_2$.

*Case 2.* One sample drawn from a population to test $P = c$.

## 6.2   THE ARCSINE TRANSFORMATION AND THE EFFECT SIZE INDEX: h

$P_s$ shares with the product moment $r_s$ the difficulty that the standard deviation of the sampling distributions depend upon their population parameters, which are unknown. A consequence of this is that the detectability of a difference in magnitude between either population $P$'s or $r$'s is not a simple function of the difference. This problem and its resolution for differences in $r$'s was discussed in Section 4.2 (*q.v.*). The same problem with $P$'s has a similar resolution.

If we were to define $j = P_1 - P_2$, and try to use $j$ as our ES, we would soon discover that the detectability of some given value of $j$, under given fixed conditions of $a$ and $n$, would *not* be constant, but would vary depending upon where along the scale of $P$ between zero and one the value $j$ occurred. Concretely, when

1. $P_1 = .65$ and $P_2 = .45$, $j = .65 - .45 = .20$; and when

2. $P_1 = .25$ and $P_2 = .05$, $j = .25 - .05 = .20$ also.

But for these two *equal* differences of $j = .20$, given $a_2 = .05$ and $n = 46$ (for

**Table 6.2.1**

$P_1$ values as a function of $P_2$ and $h = \phi_1 - \phi_2$

| $P_2$ | $h = \phi_1 - \phi_2$ | | | | | | | | | | | |
|---|---|---|---|---|---|---|---|---|---|---|---|---|
| | .10 | .20 | .30 | .40 | .50 | .60 | .70 | .80 | .90 | 1.00 | 1.10 | 1.20 |
| .05 | 07 | 10 | 13 | 17 | 21 | 25 | 30 | 34 | 39 | 44 | 49 | 54 |
| .10 | 13 | 17 | 21 | 25 | 29 | 34 | 39 | 44 | 49 | 54 | 59 | 63 |
| .15 | 19 | 23 | 27 | 32 | 36 | 41 | 46 | 51 | 56 | 61 | 66 | 71 |
| .20 | 24 | 29 | 33 | 38 | 43 | 48 | 53 | 58 | 63 | 67 | 72 | 76 |
| .25 | 29 | 34 | 39 | 44 | 49 | 54 | 59 | 64 | 68 | 73 | 77 | 81 |
| .30 | 35 | 40 | 44 | 49 | 54 | 59 | 64 | 69 | 73 | 78 | 82 | 85 |
| .35 | 40 | 45 | 50 | 55 | 60 | 65 | 69 | 74 | 78 | 82 | 86 | 89 |
| .40 | 45 | 50 | 55 | 60 | 65 | 69 | 74 | 78 | 82 | 86 | 89 | 92 |
| .45 | 50 | 55 | 60 | 65 | 69 | 74 | 78 | 82 | 86 | 89 | 92 | 95 |
| .50 | 55 | 60 | 65 | 69 | 74 | 78 | 82 | 86 | 89 | 92 | 95 | 97 |
| .55 | 60 | 65 | 69 | 74 | 78 | 82 | 86 | 89 | 92 | 95 | 97 | 98 |
| .60 | 65 | 70 | 74 | 78 | 82 | 86 | 89 | 92 | 95 | 97 | 98 | 99 |
| .65 | 70 | 74 | 78 | 82 | 86 | 89 | 92 | 95 | 97 | 98 | 99 | * |
| .70 | 74 | 79 | 83 | 86 | 90 | 92 | 95 | 97 | 98 | 99 | * | |
| .75 | 79 | 83 | 87 | 90 | 93 | 95 | 97 | 98 | 99 | * | | |
| .80 | 84 | 87 | 91 | 93 | 96 | 97 | 99 | * | * | | | |
| .85 | 88 | 91 | 94 | 96 | 98 | 99 | * | | | | | |
| .90 | 93 | 95 | 97 | 99 | * | * | | | | | | |
| .95 | 97 | 98 | 99 | * | | | | | | | | |

* Values below this point are greater than .995.

example), the power to detect the first difference $(.65 - .45)$ is .48, while the power for the second $(.25 - .05)$ is .82. Thus, **P** does not provide a scale of equal units of detectability, hence the difference between **P**'s is not an appropriate ES index.

As was the case with **r**, a nonlinear transformation of **P** provides a solution to the problem. When **P**'s are transformed by the relationship.[1]

(6.2.1)                  $\phi = 2 \arcsin \sqrt{P}$,

equal differences between $\phi$'s are equally detectable. Thus, we define as the ES index for a difference in proportions

(6.2.2)          $h = \phi_1 - \phi_2$       (directional)

                $= |\phi_1 - \phi_2|$    (nondirectional).

[1] The use of the symbol $\phi$ for the arcsin transformation should not be confused with its use elsewhere in this book to represent the fourfold point product-moment correlation coefficient.

Thus, unlike $P_1 - P_2$, $\phi_1 - \phi_2 = h$ gives values whose detectability does *not* depend on whether the $\phi$'s (and hence the $P$'s) fall around the middle or on one side of their possible range. The power and sample size tables in this chapter provide values for $h = .10$ (.10) 1.20.

Tables 6.2.1 and 6.2.2 provide the necessary conversion of $P_1 - P_2$ to $\phi_1 - \phi_2 = h$ values. Table 6.2.1 gives $h$ values as a function of $P_1 - P_2$; Table 6.2.2 is a $P$ to $\phi$ transformation table.

Table 6.2.1 is likely to be more convenient for use in power analysis, and when the tabled $h$ values are sufficient. It provides direct conversion of $P_1 - P_2$ to $\phi_1 - \phi_2 = h$ values for tabled $h$. Taking $P_1 > P_2$, locate at the left $P_2$, the smaller $P$, and read horizontally to $P_1$, the larger. When $P_1$ is found, determine the heading of the column which is $h$, the difference between the arcsine transformations of the $P$'s, that is, $\phi_1 - \phi_2$. For example, with $P$'s of .35 ($= P_2$) and .50 ($= P_1$), the table provides the difference $h$ between their respective $\phi$ values, as follows: Find in the first column $P_2 = .35$ and read across to $P_1 = .50$; then read up to the head of that column, where you find $h = .30$.

Since one cannot have both convenient multiples of .10 for $h$ and simultaneously convenient multiples of .05 for both $P_1$ and $P_2$, the use of Table 6.2.1 may require interpolation in $h$. Thus, for $P_2 = .25$ and $P_1 = .50$, values in the row for $P_2 = .25$ indicate that $h = .50$ for $P_1 = .49$ and $h = .60$ for $P_1 = .54$. Linear interpolation gives the approximate value of $h = .52$.

Alternatively, for exact values of $h$, $P_1 = .50$ and $P_2 = .25$ may be located in Table 6.2.2 and their respective $\phi$ values found: $\phi_1 = 1.571$, $\phi_2 = 1.047$. Then, $h = 1.571 - 1.047 = .524$. Note that with the resulting nontabled $h$ value, interpolation would be required in order to use it in the power tables (but not for sample size determination[2]).

Table 6.2.2 will also be useful for finding $h_s$ when the power tables are used for significance testing, as described in Section 6.5.

In practice, the need to use nontabled values of $h$ in power and sample size determination will not arise frequently. This is because one rarely has so highly specified an alternate hypothesis in terms of $P_1$ and $P_2$ that one must find power or sample size for a value of $h$ which is not tabled. A looser specification of the $P_1 - P_2$ difference permits the use of the nearest tabled value of $h$ in Table 6.2.1 and the later tables in this chapter. Indeed, the even looser procedure of defining $h$ as "small," "medium," or "large," with the operational definitions proposed below, will suffice for most purposes.

---

[2] As will be seen below, determining $n$ from the sample size Table (4.4.1) requires no interpolation. For nontabled values of $h$, formula (6.4.1) is used.

**Table 6.2.2**

Transformations of Proportion (P) to $\phi$**

| P | $\phi$ | P | $\phi$ | P | $\phi$ | P | $\phi$ |
|---|---|---|---|---|---|---|---|
| .00 | .000* | .25 | 1.047 | .50 | 1.571 | .75 | 2.094 |
| .01 | .200 | .26 | 1.070 | .51 | 1.591 | .76 | 2.118 |
| .02 | .284 | .27 | 1.093 | .52 | 1.611 | .77 | 2.141 |
| .03 | .348 | .28 | 1.115 | .53 | 1.631 | .78 | 2.165 |
| .04 | .403 | .29 | 1.137 | .54 | 1.651 | .79 | 2.190 |
| .05 | .451 | .30 | 1.159 | .55 | 1.671 | .80 | 2.214 |
| .06 | .495 | .31 | 1.181 | .56 | 1.691 | .81 | 2.240 |
| .07 | .536 | .32 | 1.203 | .57 | 1.711 | .82 | 2.265 |
| .08 | .574 | .33 | 1.224 | .58 | 1.731 | .83 | 2.292 |
| .09 | .609 | .34 | 1.245 | .59 | 1.752 | .84 | 2.319 |
| .10 | .644 | .35 | 1.266 | .60 | 1.772 | .85 | 2.346 |
| .11 | .676 | .36 | 1.287 | .61 | 1.793 | .86 | 2.375 |
| .12 | .707 | .37 | 1.308 | .62 | 1.813 | .87 | 2.404 |
| .13 | .738 | .38 | 1.328 | .63 | 1.834 | .88 | 2.434 |
| .14 | .767 | .39 | 1.349 | .64 | 1.855 | .89 | 2.465 |
| .15 | .795 | .40 | 1.369 | .65 | 1.875 | .90 | 2.498 |
| .16 | .823 | .41 | 1.390 | .66 | 1.897 | .91 | 2.532 |
| .17 | .850 | .42 | 1.410 | .67 | 1.918 | .92 | 2.568 |
| .18 | .876 | .43 | 1.430 | .68 | 1.939 | .93 | 2.606 |
| .19 | .902 | .44 | 1.451 | .69 | 1.961 | .94 | 2.647 |
| .20 | .927 | .45 | 1.471 | .70 | 1.982 | .95 | 2.691 |
| .21 | .952 | .46 | 1.491 | .71 | 2.004 | .96 | 2.739 |
| .22 | .976 | .47 | 1.511 | .72 | 2.026 | .97 | 2.793 |
| .23 | 1.000 | .48 | 1.531 | .73 | 2.049 | .98 | 2.858 |
| .24 | 1.024 | .49 | 1.551 | .74 | 2.071 | .99 | 2.941 |
| | | | | | | 1.00 | 3.142* |

*For observed $P_s = 0$, $\phi_0 = 2$ arcsin $1/4n$;
for observed $P_s = 1$, $\phi_1 = 3.142 - \phi_0$ (Owen, 1962, p. 293).
**This table is abridged from Table 9.9 in Owen, D. B., *Handbook of Statistical Tables*. Reading, Mass.: Addison-Wesley, 1962. Reproduced with the permission of the publisher. (Courtesy of the U.S. Atomic Energy Commission.)

6.2.1 "SMALL," "MEDIUM," AND "LARGE" DIFFERENCES BETWEEN PROPORTIONS. To provide the investigator with a frame of reference for the appraisal of differences between proportions, we define the adjectives "small," "medium," and "large" in terms of specific values of **h** at these levels to serve as conventions, as has been done with each type of statistical test discussed in this handbook. As before, the reader is counseled to avoid the use of these conventions, if he can, in favor of exact values provided by theory or experience in the specific area in which he is working.

As noted above, in working with **h**, we use an index of ES which provides units which are equal in detectability, rather than equal in units of raw differences in proportion (i.e., $j = P_1 - P_2$). This means that for any given value of **h**, the value of **j** varies depending on whether **j** occurs symmetrically about .50 as a midpoint between $P_1$ and $P_2$, where it is at its largest, or toward either tail ($P_2$ near zero or $P_1$ near one), where it is at its smallest. If we restrict ourselves to the part of the **P** scale between .05 and .95, the range of **j** is tolerably small. Thus, we do not have to pay a large price in consistency of interpretation of **h** in terms of $P_1 - P_2 = j$ for the convenience of using an equal power unit. In the description of each conventional level of ES which follows, the range of **j** values for each value of **h** will be described.

SMALL EFFECT SIZE: **h** = .20. A small difference between proportions is defined as a difference between their arcsine transformation values of .20. The following pairs of **P**'s illustrate this amount of difference: .05, .10; .20, .29; .40, .50; .60, .70; .80, .87; .90, .95 (Table 6.2.1). The ($P_1$, $P_2$) pairs yielding any value of **h** are symmetric about **P** = .50 (where $\phi = 1.571$); also, **j** is largest when $P_1$ and $P_2$ are symmetrical about .50. Thus, for **h** = .20, **j** reaches its maximum of .100 when the **P**s are .45 and .55. The minimum value of **j** is not useful, since it approaches zero as $P_1$ approaches one or $P_2$ approaches zero. If we stay within a **P** range .05–.95, the minimum value of **j** is .052. Summarizing then, a small difference between proportions, **h** = .20, means a raw difference **j** which varies from .05 near either extreme to .10 around the middle of the **P** scale. As can be seen from the values of **P** given above, and from Table 6.2.2, between .20 and .80, **j** equals .09 or .10 when **h** = .20.

As has already been noted, a difference between populations 1 and 2 in the proportions having attribute **X** can alternatively be viewed as a relationship between population membership (1 versus 2) and having–not having **X**. This relationship can be indexed by the product-moment correlation coefficient **r**, which, when applied to dichotomous variables, is frequently called the phi or four-fold point correlation coefficient. When the two populations are equally numerous, the value of this **r** implied by **h** = .20 varies narrowly from .095 (for **P**'s of .05–.10 or .90–.95) to .100 (for **P**'s of

.45–.55).[3] This is quite consistent with the definition of a small **r** given in Section 3.2.

In summary, a small difference in proportions is a difference of about .10 (down to .05 near the extremes) and is equivalent to an **r** of about .10.

MEDIUM EFFECT SIZE: **h** = .50. With **h** = .50 taken to define a medium ES, we find (from Table 6.2.1) the following pairs of **P**'s illustrating this amount of difference: .05, .21; .20, .43; .40, .65; .60, .82; .80, .96. The difference **j** reaches its maximum of .248 for **P** values of .376 and .624. Within a restricted .05–.95 scale for **P**, the minimum value of **j** is .160 (**P**'s of .050 and .210 or .790 and .950). Over a broad range of midscale values, say between .20 and .80, a medium difference between proportions is a **j** of .23 to .25.

Expressed in terms of **r**, this is equivalent to a value of .238 to .248. This is lower than our operational definition of a medium ES for **r** in general, which was .30, but quite consistent with the more relevant point biserial **r** or $\eta$ (see Sections 3.2, 8.2).

Thus, a medium difference in proportions is a raw difference of about .20 to .25 over most of the scale and is equivalent to an **r** between population and attribute of about .25.

LARGE EFFECT SIZE: **h** = .80. A large difference in proportions is operationally defined as one which yields **h** = $\phi_1 - \phi_2$ = .80. Pairs of **P**'s illustrative of this degree of difference are: .05, .34; .20, .58; .40, .78; .60, .92; .80, .996. The maximum difference is .390 and occurs for **P**'s of .305 and .695. For **P**'s between .05 and .95, the smallest difference is .293 (for **P**'s of .050 and .343 or .657 and .950). Over a wide range of midscale values (**P**'s between .12 and .88), a large difference between proportions is .35 to .39.

Again, when this difference in proportions is translated into a fourfold product moment **r**, the value ranges between .37 and .39. Note, again, that this value is smaller than the ES for a large **r** defined in Section 3.2, which was .50.

Thus, a large ES in differences between proportions is defined as being about .35 to .39, and implying an **r** between population membership and presence–absence of the attribute of about .37–.39.

For a further consideration of the interpretation of the difference between proportions (**j**) as a measure of effect size, see Section 11.1 "Effect Size" in Chapter 11 and Rosenthal and Rubin (1982).

## 6.3 POWER TABLES

When the significance criterion, ES, and sample size are specified, the tables in this section can be used to determine power values. Thus, they will receive their major use after a research is performed, or at least after

[3] The equality of the maximum **j** for a given value of **h** with the **r** for this maximum (both .100 here) is no accident. For *any* value of **h**, this equality holds. When two proportions are symmetrical about .50, their difference equals the fourfold point **r**.

Table 6.3.1

Power of Normal Curve Test of $P_1 = P_2$
via Arcsine Transformation at $a_1 = .01$

| | | h | | | | | | | | | | | |
| --- | --- | --- | --- | --- | --- | --- | --- | --- | --- | --- | --- | --- | --- |
| n | $h_c$ | .10 | .20 | .30 | .40 | .50 | .60 | .70 | .80 | .90 | 1.00 | 1.10 | 1.20 |
| 10 | 1.040 | 02 | 03 | 05 | 08 | 11 | 16 | 22 | 30 | 38 | 46 | 55 | 64 |
| 11 | .992 | 02 | 03 | 05 | 08 | 12 | 18 | 25 | 33 | 41 | 51 | 60 | 69 |
| 12 | .950 | 02 | 03 | 06 | 09 | 14 | 20 | 27 | 36 | 45 | 55 | 64 | 73 |
| 13 | .912 | 02 | 03 | 06 | 10 | 15 | 21 | 29 | 39 | 49 | 59 | 68 | 77 |
| 14 | .879 | 02 | 04 | 06 | 10 | 16 | 23 | 32 | 42 | 52 | 63 | 72 | 80 |
| 15 | .849 | 02 | 04 | 07 | 11 | 17 | 25 | 34 | 45 | 56 | 66 | 75 | 83 |
| 16 | .823 | 02 | 04 | 07 | 12 | 18 | 26 | 36 | 47 | 59 | 69 | 78 | 86 |
| 17 | .798 | 02 | 04 | 07 | 12 | 19 | 28 | 39 | 50 | 62 | 72 | 81 | 88 |
| 18 | .775 | 02 | 04 | 08 | 13 | 20 | 30 | 41 | 53 | 65 | 75 | 83 | 90 |
| 19 | .755 | 02 | 04 | 08 | 14 | 22 | 32 | 43 | 56 | 67 | 77 | 86 | 91 |
| 20 | .736 | 02 | 05 | 08 | 14 | 23 | 33 | 46 | 58 | 70 | 80 | 88 | 93 |
| 21 | .718 | 02 | 05 | 09 | 15 | 24 | 35 | 48 | 60 | 72 | 82 | 89 | 94 |
| 22 | .701 | 02 | 05 | 09 | 16 | 25 | 37 | 50 | 63 | 75 | 84 | 91 | 95 |
| 23 | .686 | 02 | 05 | 10 | 17 | 26 | 39 | 52 | 65 | 77 | 86 | 92 | 96 |
| 24 | .672 | 02 | 05 | 10 | 17 | 28 | 40 | 54 | 67 | 79 | 87 | 93 | 97 |
| 25 | .658 | 02 | 05 | 10 | 18 | 29 | 42 | 56 | 69 | 80 | 89 | 94 | 97 |
| 26 | .645 | 02 | 05 | 11 | 19 | 30 | 44 | 58 | 71 | 82 | 90 | 95 | 98 |
| 27 | .633 | 03 | 06 | 11 | 20 | 31 | 45 | 60 | 73 | 84 | 91 | 96 | 98 |
| 28 | .622 | 03 | 06 | 11 | 20 | 32 | 47 | 62 | 75 | 85 | 92 | 96 | 98 |
| 29 | .611 | 03 | 06 | 12 | 21 | 34 | 48 | 63 | 76 | 86 | 93 | 97 | 99 |
| 30 | .601 | 03 | 06 | 12 | 22 | 35 | 50 | 65 | 78 | 88 | 94 | 97 | 99 |
| 31 | .591 | 03 | 06 | 13 | 23 | 36 | 51 | 67 | 79 | 89 | 95 | 98 | 99 |
| 32 | .582 | 03 | 06 | 13 | 23 | 37 | 53 | 68 | 81 | 90 | 95 | 98 | 99 |
| 33 | .573 | 03 | 07 | 13 | 24 | 38 | 54 | 70 | 82 | 91 | 96 | 98 | 99 |
| 34 | .564 | 03 | 07 | 14 | 25 | 40 | 56 | 71 | 83 | 92 | 96 | 99 | * |
| 35 | .556 | 03 | 07 | 14 | 26 | 41 | 57 | 73 | 85 | 92 | 97 | 99 | |
| 36 | .548 | 03 | 07 | 15 | 26 | 42 | 59 | 74 | 86 | 93 | 97 | 99 | |
| 37 | .541 | 03 | 07 | 15 | 27 | 43 | 60 | 75 | 87 | 94 | 98 | 99 | |
| 38 | .534 | 03 | 07 | 15 | 28 | 44 | 61 | 77 | 88 | 94 | 98 | 99 | |
| 39 | .527 | 03 | 07 | 16 | 29 | 45 | 63 | 78 | 89 | 95 | 98 | 99 | |
| 40 | .520 | 03 | 08 | 16 | 30 | 46 | 64 | 79 | 89 | 96 | 98 | * | |
| 42 | .508 | 03 | 08 | 17 | 31 | 49 | 66 | 81 | 91 | 96 | 99 | | |
| 44 | .496 | 03 | 08 | 18 | 33 | 51 | 69 | 83 | 92 | 97 | 99 | | |
| 46 | .485 | 03 | 09 | 19 | 34 | 53 | 71 | 85 | 93 | 98 | 99 | | |
| 48 | .475 | 03 | 09 | 20 | 36 | 55 | 73 | 86 | 94 | 98 | 99 | | |

Table 6.3.1 *(continued)*

| n | $h_c$ | .10 | .20 | .30 | .40 | .50 | .60 | .70 | .80 | .90 | 1.00 | 1.10 | 1.20 |
|---|---|---|---|---|---|---|---|---|---|---|---|---|---|
| 50 | .465 | 03 | 09 | 20 | 37 | 57 | 75 | 88 | 95 | 99 | * | * | * |
| 52 | .456 | 03 | 10 | 21 | 39 | 59 | 77 | 89 | 96 | 99 | | | |
| 54 | .448 | 04 | 10 | 22 | 40 | 61 | 79 | 91 | 97 | 99 | | | |
| 56 | .440 | 04 | 10 | 23 | 42 | 63 | 80 | 92 | 97 | 99 | | | |
| 58 | .432 | 04 | 11 | 24 | 43 | 64 | 82 | 93 | 98 | 99 | | | |
| 60 | .425 | 04 | 11 | 25 | 45 | 66 | 83 | 93 | 98 | * | | | |
| 64 | .411 | 04 | 12 | 26 | 47 | 69 | 86 | 95 | 99 | | | | |
| 68 | .399 | 04 | 12 | 28 | 50 | 72 | 88 | 96 | 99 | | | | |
| 72 | .388 | 04 | 13 | 30 | 53 | 75 | 90 | 97 | 99 | | | | |
| 76 | .377 | 04 | 14 | 32 | 56 | 78 | 91 | 98 | * | | | | |
| 80 | .368 | 05 | 14 | 33 | 58 | 80 | 93 | 98 | | | | | |
| 84 | .359 | 05 | 15 | 35 | 60 | 82 | 94 | 99 | | | | | |
| 88 | .351 | 05 | 16 | 37 | 63 | 84 | 95 | 99 | | | | | |
| 92 | .343 | 05 | 17 | 39 | 65 | 86 | 96 | 99 | | | | | |
| 96 | .336 | 05 | 17 | 40 | 67 | 87 | 97 | 99 | | | | | |
| 100 | .329 | 05 | 18 | 42 | 69 | 89 | 97 | * | | | | | |
| 120 | .300 | 06 | 22 | 50 | 78 | 94 | 99 | | | | | | |
| 140 | .278 | 07 | 26 | 57 | 85 | 97 | * | | | | | | |
| 160 | .260 | 08 | 30 | 64 | 89 | 98 | | | | | | | |
| 180 | .245 | 08 | 33 | 70 | 93 | 99 | | | | | | | |
| 200 | .233 | 09 | 37 | 75 | 95 | * | | | | | | | |
| 250 | .208 | 11 | 46 | 85 | 98 | | | | | | | | |
| 300 | .190 | 14 | 55 | 91 | 99 | | | | | | | | |
| 350 | .176 | 16 | 63 | 95 | * | | | | | | | | |
| 400 | .165 | 18 | 69 | 97 | | | | | | | | | |
| 450 | .155 | 20 | 75 | 99 | | | | | | | | | |
| 500 | .147 | 23 | 80 | 99 | | | | | | | | | |
| 600 | .134 | 28 | 87 | * | | | | | | | | | |
| 700 | .124 | 32 | 92 | | | | | | | | | | |
| 800 | .116 | 37 | 95 | | | | | | | | | | |
| 900 | .110 | 42 | 97 | | | | | | | | | | |
| 1000 | .104 | 46 | 98 | | | | | | | | | | |

* Power values below this point are greater than .995.

Table 6.3.2

Power of Normal Curve Test of $P_1 = P_2$
via ArcsineTransformation at $a_1 = .05$

| n | $h_c$ | .10 | .20 | .30 | .40 | .50 | .60 | .70 | .80 | .90 | 1.00 | 1.10 | 1.20 |
|---|---|---|---|---|---|---|---|---|---|---|---|---|---|
| | | | | | | | | **h** | | | | | |
| 10 | .736 | 08 | 12 | 17 | 23 | 30 | 38 | 47 | 56 | 64 | 72 | 79 | 85 |
| 11 | .701 | 08 | 12 | 17 | 24 | 32 | 41 | 50 | 59 | 68 | 76 | 83 | 88 |
| 12 | .672 | 08 | 12 | 18 | 25 | 34 | 43 | 53 | 62 | 71 | 79 | 85 | 90 |
| 13 | .645 | 08 | 13 | 19 | 27 | 36 | 45 | 56 | 65 | 74 | 82 | 88 | 92 |
| 14 | .622 | 08 | 13 | 20 | 28 | 37 | 48 | 58 | 68 | 77 | 84 | 90 | 94 |
| 15 | .601 | 09 | 14 | 21 | 29 | 39 | 50 | 61 | 71 | 79 | 86 | 91 | 95 |
| 16 | .582 | 09 | 14 | 21 | 30 | 41 | 52 | 63 | 73 | 82 | 88 | 93 | 96 |
| 17 | .564 | 09 | 14 | 22 | 32 | 43 | 54 | 65 | 75 | 84 | 90 | 94 | 97 |
| 18 | .548 | 09 | 15 | 23 | 33 | 44 | 56 | 68 | 77 | 85 | 91 | 95 | 97 |
| 19 | .534 | 09 | 15 | 24 | 34 | 46 | 58 | 70 | 79 | 87 | 92 | 96 | 98 |
| 20 | .520 | 09 | 16 | 24 | 35 | 47 | 60 | 72 | 81 | 89 | 94 | 97 | 98 |
| 21 | .508 | 09 | 16 | 25 | 36 | 49 | 62 | 73 | 83 | 90 | 94 | 97 | 99 |
| 22 | .496 | 09 | 16 | 26 | 38 | 51 | 64 | 75 | 84 | 91 | 95 | 98 | 99 |
| 23 | .485 | 10 | 17 | 27 | 39 | 52 | 65 | 77 | 86 | 92 | 96 | 98 | 99 |
| 24 | .475 | 10 | 17 | 27 | 40 | 53 | 67 | 78 | 87 | 93 | 97 | 98 | 99 |
| 25 | .465 | 10 | 17 | 28 | 41 | 55 | 68 | 80 | 88 | 94 | 97 | 99 | * |
| 26 | .456 | 10 | 18 | 29 | 42 | 56 | 70 | 81 | 89 | 95 | 98 | 99 | |
| 27 | .448 | 10 | 18 | 29 | 43 | 58 | 71 | 82 | 90 | 95 | 98 | 99 | |
| 28 | .440 | 10 | 18 | 30 | 44 | 59 | 73 | 84 | 91 | 96 | 98 | 99 | |
| 29 | .432 | 10 | 19 | 31 | 45 | 60 | 74 | 85 | 92 | 96 | 98 | 99 | |
| 30 | .425 | 10 | 19 | 31 | 46 | 61 | 75 | 86 | 93 | 97 | 99 | * | |
| 31 | .418 | 11 | 20 | 32 | 47 | 63 | 76 | 87 | 93 | 97 | 99 | | |
| 32 | .411 | 11 | 20 | 33 | 48 | 64 | 77 | 88 | 94 | 97 | 99 | | |
| 33 | .405 | 11 | 20 | 33 | 49 | 65 | 79 | 88 | 95 | 98 | 99 | | |
| 34 | .399 | 11 | 21 | 34 | 50 | 66 | 80 | 89 | 95 | 98 | 99 | | |
| 35 | .393 | 11 | 21 | 35 | 51 | 67 | 81 | 90 | 96 | 98 | 99 | | |
| 36 | .388 | 11 | 21 | 35 | 52 | 68 | 82 | 91 | 96 | 99 | * | | |
| 37 | .382 | 11 | 22 | 36 | 53 | 69 | 83 | 91 | 96 | 99 | | | |
| 38 | .377 | 11 | 22 | 37 | 54 | 70 | 83 | 92 | 97 | 99 | | | |
| 39 | .372 | 12 | 22 | 37 | 55 | 71 | 84 | 93 | 97 | 99 | | | |
| 40 | .368 | 12 | 23 | 38 | 56 | 72 | 85 | 93 | 97 | 99 | | | |
| 42 | .359 | 12 | 23 | 39 | 57 | 74 | 87 | 94 | 98 | 99 | | | |
| 44 | .351 | 12 | 24 | 41 | 59 | 76 | 88 | 95 | 98 | * | | | |
| 46 | .343 | 12 | 25 | 42 | 61 | 77 | 89 | 96 | 99 | | | | |
| 48 | .336 | 13 | 25 | 43 | 62 | 79 | 90 | 96 | 99 | | | | |

Table 6.3.2 *(continued)*

| n | $h_c$ | h | | | | | | | | | | | |
|---|---|---|---|---|---|---|---|---|---|---|---|---|---|
| | | .10 | .20 | .30 | .40 | .50 | .60 | .70 | .80 | .90 | 1.00 | 1.10 | 1.20 |
| 50 | .329 | 13 | 26 | 44 | 64 | 80 | 91 | 97 | 99 | * | * | * | * |
| 52 | .323 | 13 | 27 | 45 | 65 | 82 | 92 | 97 | 99 | | | | |
| 54 | .317 | 13 | 27 | 47 | 67 | 83 | 93 | 98 | 99 | | | | |
| 56 | .311 | 13 | 28 | 48 | 68 | 84 | 94 | 98 | * | | | | |
| 58 | .305 | 14 | 28 | 49 | 69 | 85 | 94 | 98 | | | | | |
| 60 | .300 | 14 | 29 | 50 | 71 | 86 | 95 | 99 | | | | | |
| 64 | .291 | 14 | 30 | 52 | 73 | 88 | 96 | 99 | | | | | |
| 68 | .282 | 14 | 32 | 54 | 75 | 90 | 97 | 99 | | | | | |
| 72 | .274 | 15 | 33 | 56 | 77 | 91 | 97 | 99 | | | | | |
| 76 | .267 | 15 | 34 | 58 | 79 | 92 | 98 | * | | | | | |
| 80 | .260 | 16 | 35 | 60 | 81 | 94 | 98 | | | | | | |
| 84 | .254 | 16 | 36 | 62 | 83 | 94 | 99 | | | | | | |
| 88 | .248 | 16 | 38 | 63 | 84 | 95 | 99 | | | | | | |
| 92 | .243 | 17 | 39 | 65 | 86 | 96 | 99 | | | | | | |
| 96 | .237 | 17 | 40 | 67 | 87 | 97 | 99 | | | | | | |
| 100 | .233 | 17 | 41 | 68 | 88 | 97 | * | | | | | | |
| 120 | .212 | 19 | 46 | 75 | 93 | 99 | | | | | | | |
| 140 | .197 | 21 | 51 | 81 | 96 | 99 | | | | | | | |
| 160 | .184 | 23 | 56 | 85 | 97 | * | | | | | | | |
| 180 | .173 | 24 | 60 | 89 | 98 | | | | | | | | |
| 200 | .164 | 26 | 64 | 91 | 99 | | | | | | | | |
| 250 | .147 | 30 | 72 | 96 | * | | | | | | | | |
| 300 | .134 | 34 | 79 | 98 | | | | | | | | | |
| 350 | .124 | 38 | 84 | 99 | | | | | | | | | |
| 400 | .116 | 41 | 88 | * | | | | | | | | | |
| 450 | .110 | 44 | 91 | | | | | | | | | | |
| 500 | .104 | 47 | 94 | | | | | | | | | | |
| 600 | .095 | 53 | 97 | | | | | | | | | | |
| 700 | .088 | 59 | 98 | | | | | | | | | | |
| 800 | .082 | 64 | 99 | | | | | | | | | | |
| 900 | .078 | 68 | * | | | | | | | | | | |
| 1000 | .074 | 72 | | | | | | | | | | | |

* Power values below this point are greater than .995.

**Table 6.3.3**

Power of Normal Curve Test of $P_1 = P_2$
via Arcsine Transformation at $a_1 = .10$

| n | $h_c$ | h .10 | .20 | .30 | .40 | .50 | .60 | .70 | .80 | .90 | 1.00 | 1.10 | 1.20 |
|---|---|---|---|---|---|---|---|---|---|---|---|---|---|
| 10 | .573 | 15 | 20 | 27 | 35 | 44 | 52 | 61 | 69 | 77 | 83 | 88 | 92 |
| 11 | .547 | 15 | 21 | 28 | 37 | 46 | 55 | 64 | 72 | 80 | 86 | 90 | 94 |
| 12 | .523 | 15 | 21 | 29 | 38 | 48 | 57 | 67 | 75 | 82 | 88 | 92 | 95 |
| 13 | .503 | 15 | 22 | 30 | 40 | 50 | 60 | 69 | 78 | 84 | 90 | 94 | 96 |
| 14 | .484 | 15 | 23 | 31 | 41 | 52 | 62 | 72 | 80 | 86 | 91 | 95 | 97 |
| 15 | .468 | 16 | 23 | 32 | 43 | 53 | 64 | 74 | 82 | 88 | 93 | 96 | 98 |
| 16 | .453 | 16 | 24 | 33 | 44 | 55 | 66 | 76 | 84 | 90 | 94 | 97 | 98 |
| 17 | .440 | 16 | 24 | 34 | 45 | 57 | 68 | 78 | 85 | 91 | 95 | 97 | 99 |
| 18 | .427 | 16 | 25 | 35 | 47 | 59 | 70 | 79 | 87 | 92 | 96 | 98 | 99 |
| 19 | .416 | 17 | 25 | 36 | 48 | 60 | 71 | 81 | 88 | 93 | 96 | 98 | 99 |
| 20 | .405 | 17 | 26 | 37 | 49 | 62 | 73 | 82 | 89 | 94 | 97 | 99 | 99 |
| 21 | .396 | 17 | 26 | 38 | 51 | 63 | 75 | 84 | 90 | 95 | 97 | 99 | * |
| 22 | .386 | 17 | 27 | 39 | 52 | 65 | 76 | 85 | 91 | 96 | 98 | 99 | |
| 23 | .378 | 17 | 27 | 40 | 53 | 66 | 77 | 86 | 92 | 96 | 98 | 99 | |
| 24 | .370 | 17 | 28 | 40 | 54 | 67 | 79 | 87 | 93 | 97 | 99 | 99 | |
| 25 | .362 | 18 | 28 | 41 | 55 | 69 | 80 | 88 | 94 | 97 | 99 | * | |
| 26 | .355 | 18 | 29 | 42 | 56 | 70 | 81 | 89 | 95 | 98 | 99 | | |
| 27 | .349 | 18 | 29 | 43 | 57 | 71 | 82 | 90 | 95 | 98 | 99 | | |
| 28 | .342 | 18 | 30 | 44 | 59 | 72 | 83 | 91 | 96 | 98 | 99 | | |
| 29 | .337 | 18 | 30 | 44 | 60 | 73 | 84 | 92 | 96 | 98 | 99 | | |
| 30 | .331 | 19 | 31 | 45 | 61 | 74 | 85 | 92 | 97 | 99 | * | | |
| 31 | .326 | 19 | 31 | 46 | 62 | 75 | 86 | 93 | 97 | 99 | | | |
| 32 | .320 | 19 | 32 | 47 | 62 | 76 | 87 | 94 | 97 | 99 | | | |
| 33 | .316 | 19 | 32 | 47 | 63 | 77 | 88 | 94 | 98 | 99 | | | |
| 34 | .311 | 19 | 32 | 48 | 64 | 78 | 88 | 95 | 98 | 99 | | | |
| 35 | .306 | 19 | 33 | 49 | 65 | 79 | 89 | 95 | 98 | 99 | | | |
| 36 | .302 | 20 | 33 | 50 | 66 | 80 | 90 | 95 | 98 | 99 | | | |
| 37 | .298 | 20 | 34 | 50 | 67 | 81 | 90 | 96 | 98 | * | | | |
| 38 | .294 | 20 | 34 | 51 | 68 | 82 | 91 | 96 | 99 | | | | |
| 39 | .290 | 20 | 35 | 52 | 69 | 82 | 91 | 96 | 99 | | | | |
| 40 | .287 | 20 | 35 | 52 | 69 | 83 | 92 | 97 | 99 | | | | |
| 42 | .280 | 21 | 36 | 54 | 71 | 84 | 93 | 97 | 99 | | | | |
| 44 | .273 | 21 | 37 | 55 | 72 | 86 | 94 | 98 | 99 | | | | |
| 46 | .267 | 21 | 37 | 56 | 74 | 87 | 94 | 98 | 99 | | | | |
| 48 | .262 | 21 | 38 | 57 | 75 | 88 | 95 | 98 | * | | | | |

Table 6.3.3 *(continued)*

| n | $h_c$ | .10 | .20 | .30 | .40 | .50 | .60 | .70 | .80 | .90 | 1.00 | 1.10 | 1.20 |
|---|---|---|---|---|---|---|---|---|---|---|---|---|---|
| 50 | .256 | 22 | 39 | 59 | 76 | 89 | 96 | 99 | * | * | * | * | * |
| 52 | .251 | 22 | 40 | 60 | 78 | 90 | 96 | 99 | | | | | |
| 54 | .247 | 22 | 40 | 61 | 79 | 91 | 97 | 99 | | | | | |
| 56 | .242 | 23 | 41 | 62 | 80 | 91 | 97 | 99 | | | | | |
| 58 | .238 | 23 | 42 | 63 | 81 | 92 | 97 | 99 | | | | | |
| 60 | .234 | 23 | 43 | 64 | 82 | 93 | 98 | 99 | | | | | |
| 64 | .227 | 24 | 44 | 66 | 84 | 94 | 98 | * | | | | | |
| 68 | .220 | 24 | 45 | 68 | 85 | 95 | 99 | | | | | | |
| 72 | .214 | 25 | 47 | 70 | 87 | 96 | 99 | | | | | | |
| 76 | .208 | 25 | 48 | 71 | 88 | 96 | 99 | | | | | | |
| 80 | .203 | 26 | 49 | 73 | 89 | 97 | 99 | | | | | | |
| 84 | .198 | 26 | 51 | 75 | 91 | 97 | * | | | | | | |
| 88 | .193 | 27 | 52 | 76 | 91 | 98 | | | | | | | |
| 92 | .189 | 27 | 53 | 77 | 92 | 98 | | | | | | | |
| 96 | .185 | 28 | 54 | 79 | 93 | 99 | | | | | | | |
| 100 | .181 | 28 | 55 | 80 | 94 | 99 | | | | | | | |
| 120 | .165 | 31 | 61 | 85 | 97 | * | | | | | | | |
| 140 | .153 | 33 | 65 | 89 | 98 | | | | | | | | |
| 160 | .143 | 35 | 69 | 92 | 99 | | | | | | | | |
| 180 | .135 | 37 | 73 | 94 | 99 | | | | | | | | |
| 200 | .128 | 39 | 76 | 96 | * | | | | | | | | |
| 250 | .115 | 44 | 83 | 98 | | | | | | | | | |
| 300 | .105 | 48 | 88 | 99 | | | | | | | | | |
| 350 | .097 | 52 | 91 | * | | | | | | | | | |
| 400 | .091 | 55 | 94 | | | | | | | | | | |
| 450 | .085 | 59 | 96 | | | | | | | | | | |
| 500 | .081 | 62 | 97 | | | | | | | | | | |
| 600 | .074 | 67 | 99 | | | | | | | | | | |
| 700 | .069 | 72 | 99 | | | | | | | | | | |
| 800 | .064 | 76 | * | | | | | | | | | | |
| 900 | .060 | 80 | | | | | | | | | | | |
| 1000 | .057 | 83 | | | | | | | | | | | |

* Power values below this point are greater than .995.

**Table 6.3.4**

Power of Normal Curve Test of $P_1 = P_2$
via ArcsineTransformation at $a_2 = .01$

| n | $h_c$ | .10 | .20 | .30 | .40 | .50 | .60 | .70 | .80 | .90 | 1.00 | 1.10 | 1.20 |
|---|-------|-----|-----|-----|-----|-----|-----|-----|-----|-----|------|------|------|
| 10 | 1.152 | 01 | 02 | 03 | 05 | 07 | 11 | 16 | 22 | 29 | 37 | 45 | 54 |
| 11 | 1.098 | 01 | 02 | 03 | 05 | 08 | 12 | 18 | 24 | 32 | 41 | 50 | 59 |
| 12 | 1.052 | 01 | 02 | 03 | 06 | 09 | 13 | 19 | 27 | 36 | 45 | 55 | 64 |
| 13 | 1.010 | 01 | 02 | 03 | 06 | 10 | 15 | 21 | 30 | 39 | 49 | 59 | 69 |
| 14 | .973 | 01 | 02 | 04 | 06 | 11 | 16 | 23 | 32 | 42 | 53 | 63 | 73 |
| 15 | .940 | 01 | 02 | 04 | 07 | 11 | 18 | 26 | 35 | 46 | 56 | 67 | 76 |
| 16 | .911 | 01 | 02 | 04 | 07 | 12 | 19 | 28 | 38 | 49 | 60 | 70 | 79 |
| 17 | .884 | 01 | 02 | 04 | 08 | 13 | 20 | 30 | 40 | 52 | 63 | 74 | 82 |
| 18 | .859 | 01 | 02 | 05 | 08 | 14 | 22 | 32 | 43 | 55 | 66 | 77 | 85 |
| 19 | .836 | 01 | 03 | 05 | 09 | 15 | 23 | 34 | 45 | 58 | 69 | 79 | 87 |
| 20 | .815 | 01 | 03 | 05 | 09 | 16 | 25 | 36 | 48 | 61 | 72 | 82 | 89 |
| 21 | .795 | 01 | 03 | 05 | 10 | 17 | 26 | 38 | 51 | 63 | 75 | 84 | 91 |
| 22 | .777 | 01 | 03 | 06 | 11 | 18 | 28 | 40 | 53 | 66 | 77 | 86 | 92 |
| 23 | .760 | 01 | 03 | 06 | 11 | 19 | 29 | 42 | 55 | 68 | 79 | 88 | 93 |
| 24 | .744 | 01 | 03 | 06 | 12 | 20 | 31 | 44 | 58 | 71 | 81 | 89 | 94 |
| 25 | .728 | 01 | 03 | 06 | 12 | 21 | 32 | 46 | 60 | 73 | 83 | 91 | 95 |
| 26 | .714 | 02 | 03 | 07 | 13 | 22 | 34 | 48 | 62 | 75 | 85 | 92 | 96 |
| 27 | .701 | 02 | 03 | 07 | 13 | 23 | 36 | 50 | 64 | 77 | 86 | 93 | 97 |
| 28 | .688 | 02 | 03 | 07 | 14 | 24 | 37 | 52 | 66 | 79 | 88 | 94 | 97 |
| 29 | .676 | 02 | 04 | 08 | 15 | 25 | 39 | 54 | 68 | 80 | 89 | 95 | 98 |
| 30 | .665 | 02 | 04 | 08 | 15 | 26 | 40 | 55 | 70 | 82 | 90 | 95 | 98 |
| 31 | .654 | 02 | 04 | 08 | 16 | 27 | 42 | 57 | 72 | 83 | 91 | 96 | 98 |
| 32 | .644 | 02 | 04 | 08 | 16 | 28 | 43 | 59 | 73 | 85 | 92 | 97 | 99 |
| 33 | .634 | 02 | 04 | 09 | 17 | 29 | 44 | 61 | 75 | 86 | 93 | 97 | 99 |
| 34 | .625 | 02 | 04 | 09 | 18 | 30 | 46 | 62 | 77 | 87 | 94 | 97 | 99 |
| 35 | .616 | 02 | 04 | 09 | 18 | 31 | 47 | 64 | 78 | 88 | 95 | 98 | 99 |
| 36 | .607 | 02 | 04 | 10 | 19 | 32 | 49 | 65 | 79 | 89 | 95 | 98 | 99 |
| 37 | .599 | 02 | 04 | 10 | 20 | 34 | 50 | 67 | 81 | 90 | 96 | 98 | * |
| 38 | .591 | 02 | 04 | 10 | 20 | 35 | 52 | 68 | 82 | 91 | 96 | 99 | |
| 39 | .583 | 02 | 05 | 11 | 21 | 36 | 53 | 70 | 83 | 92 | 97 | 99 | |
| 40 | .576 | 02 | 05 | 11 | 22 | 37 | 54 | 71 | 84 | 93 | 97 | 99 | |
| 42 | .562 | 02 | 05 | 11 | 23 | 39 | 57 | 74 | 86 | 94 | 98 | 99 | |
| 44 | .549 | 02 | 05 | 12 | 24 | 41 | 59 | 76 | 88 | 95 | 98 | * | |
| 46 | .537 | 02 | 05 | 13 | 26 | 43 | 62 | 78 | 90 | 96 | 99 | | |
| 48 | .526 | 02 | 06 | 13 | 27 | 45 | 64 | 80 | 91 | 97 | 99 | | |

Table 6.3.4 *(continued)*

| n | $h_c$ | .10 | .20 | .30 | .40 | .50 | .60 | .70 | .80 | .90 | 1.00 | 1.10 | 1.20 |
|---|---|---|---|---|---|---|---|---|---|---|---|---|---|
| 50 | .515 | 02 | 06 | 14 | 28 | 47 | 66 | 82 | 92 | 97 | 99 | * | * |
| 52 | .505 | 02 | 06 | 15 | 30 | 49 | 69 | 84 | 93 | 98 | 99 | | |
| 54 | .496 | 02 | 06 | 15 | 31 | 51 | 71 | 86 | 94 | 98 | * | | |
| 56 | .487 | 02 | 06 | 16 | 32 | 53 | 73 | 87 | 95 | 99 | | | |
| 58 | .478 | 02 | 07 | 17 | 34 | 55 | 74 | 88 | 96 | 99 | | | |
| 60 | .470 | 02 | 07 | 18 | 35 | 56 | 76 | 90 | 96 | 99 | | | |
| 64 | .455 | 02 | 07 | 19 | 38 | 60 | 79 | 92 | 97 | 99 | | | |
| 68 | .442 | 02 | 08 | 20 | 40 | 63 | 82 | 93 | 98 | * | | | |
| 72 | .429 | 02 | 08 | 22 | 43 | 66 | 85 | 95 | 99 | | | | |
| 76 | .418 | 03 | 09 | 23 | 46 | 69 | 87 | 96 | 99 | | | | |
| 80 | .407 | 03 | 09 | 25 | 48 | 72 | 89 | 97 | 99 | | | | |
| 84 | .397 | 03 | 10 | 26 | 51 | 75 | 91 | 98 | * | | | | |
| 88 | .388 | 03 | 11 | 28 | 53 | 77 | 92 | 98 | | | | | |
| 92 | .380 | 03 | 11 | 29 | 55 | 79 | 93 | 99 | | | | | |
| 96 | .372 | 03 | 12 | 31 | 58 | 81 | 94 | 99 | | | | | |
| 100 | .364 | 03 | 12 | 33 | 60 | 83 | 95 | 99 | | | | | |
| 120 | .333 | 04 | 15 | 40 | 70 | 90 | 98 | * | | | | | |
| 140 | .308 | 04 | 18 | 47 | 78 | 95 | 99 | | | | | | |
| 160 | .288 | 05 | 22 | 54 | 84 | 97 | * | | | | | | |
| 180 | .272 | 05 | 25 | 61 | 89 | 98 | | | | | | | |
| 200 | .258 | 06 | 28 | 66 | 92 | 99 | | | | | | | |
| 250 | .230 | 07 | 37 | 78 | 97 | * | | | | | | | |
| 300 | .210 | 09 | 45 | 86 | 99 | | | | | | | | |
| 350 | .195 | 11 | 53 | 92 | * | | | | | | | | |
| 400 | .182 | 12 | 60 | 95 | | | | | | | | | |
| 450 | .172 | 14 | 66 | 97 | | | | | | | | | |
| 500 | .163 | 16 | 72 | 98 | | | | | | | | | |
| 600 | .149 | 20 | 81 | * | | | | | | | | | |
| 700 | .138 | 24 | 88 | | | | | | | | | | |
| 800 | .129 | 28 | 92 | | | | | | | | | | |
| 900 | .121 | 32 | 95 | | | | | | | | | | |
| 1000 | .115 | 37 | 97 | | | | | | | | | | |

* Power values below this point are greater than .995.

**Table 6.3.5**

Power of Normal Curve Test of $P_1 = P_2$
via Arcsine Transformation at $a_2 = .05$

| | | | | | | | h | | | | | | |
|---|---|---|---|---|---|---|---|---|---|---|---|---|---|
| n | $h_c$ | .10 | .20 | .30 | .40 | .50 | .60 | .70 | .80 | .90 | 1.00 | 1.10 | 1.20 |
| 10 | .877 | 06 | 07 | 10 | 15 | 20 | 27 | 35 | 43 | 52 | 61 | 69 | 77 |
| 11 | .836 | 06 | 08 | 11 | 16 | 22 | 29 | 38 | 47 | 56 | 65 | 73 | 80 |
| 12 | .800 | 06 | 08 | 11 | 17 | 23 | 31 | 40 | 50 | 60 | 69 | 77 | 84 |
| 13 | .769 | 06 | 08 | 12 | 17 | 25 | 33 | 43 | 53 | 63 | 72 | 80 | 86 |
| 14 | .741 | 06 | 08 | 12 | 18 | 26 | 36 | 46 | 56 | 66 | 75 | 83 | 89 |
| 15 | .716 | 06 | 09 | 13 | 19 | 28 | 38 | 48 | 59 | 69 | 78 | 85 | 91 |
| 16 | .693 | 06 | 09 | 14 | 20 | 29 | 40 | 51 | 62 | 72 | 81 | 88 | 92 |
| 17 | .672 | 06 | 09 | 14 | 21 | 31 | 42 | 53 | 65 | 75 | 83 | 89 | 94 |
| 18 | .653 | 06 | 09 | 15 | 22 | 32 | 44 | 56 | 67 | 77 | 85 | 91 | 95 |
| 19 | .636 | 06 | 09 | 15 | 23 | 34 | 46 | 58 | 69 | 79 | 87 | 92 | 96 |
| 20 | .620 | 06 | 10 | 16 | 24 | 35 | 48 | 60 | 72 | 81 | 89 | 94 | 97 |
| 21 | .605 | 06 | 10 | 16 | 25 | 37 | 49 | 62 | 74 | 83 | 90 | 95 | 97 |
| 22 | .591 | 06 | 10 | 17 | 26 | 38 | 51 | 64 | 76 | 85 | 91 | 95 | 98 |
| 23 | .578 | 06 | 10 | 17 | 27 | 39 | 53 | 66 | 77 | 86 | 92 | 96 | 98 |
| 24 | .566 | 06 | 11 | 18 | 28 | 41 | 55 | 68 | 79 | 88 | 93 | 97 | 99 |
| 25 | .554 | 06 | 11 | 19 | 29 | 42 | 56 | 70 | 81 | 89 | 94 | 97 | 99 |
| 26 | .544 | 07 | 11 | 19 | 30 | 44 | 58 | 71 | 82 | 90 | 95 | 98 | 99 |
| 27 | .533 | 07 | 11 | 20 | 31 | 45 | 60 | 73 | 84 | 91 | 96 | 98 | 99 |
| 28 | .524 | 07 | 12 | 20 | 32 | 46 | 61 | 75 | 85 | 92 | 96 | 98 | 99 |
| 29 | .515 | 07 | 12 | 21 | 33 | 48 | 63 | 76 | 86 | 93 | 97 | 99 | * |
| 30 | .506 | 07 | 12 | 21 | 34 | 49 | 64 | 77 | 87 | 94 | 97 | 99 | |
| 31 | .498 | 07 | 12 | 22 | 35 | 50 | 66 | 79 | 88 | 94 | 98 | 99 | |
| 32 | .490 | 07 | 13 | 22 | 36 | 52 | 67 | 80 | 89 | 95 | 98 | 99 | |
| 33 | .483 | 07 | 13 | 23 | 37 | 53 | 69 | 81 | 90 | 96 | 98 | 99 | |
| 34 | .475 | 07 | 13 | 23 | 38 | 54 | 70 | 82 | 91 | 96 | 98 | 99 | |
| 35 | .469 | 07 | 13 | 24 | 39 | 55 | 71 | 83 | 92 | 96 | 99 | * | |
| 36 | .462 | 07 | 14 | 24 | 40 | 56 | 72 | 84 | 92 | 97 | 99 | | |
| 37 | .456 | 07 | 14 | 25 | 41 | 58 | 73 | 85 | 93 | 97 | 99 | | |
| 38 | .450 | 07 | 14 | 26 | 41 | 59 | 74 | 86 | 94 | 98 | 99 | | |
| 39 | .444 | 07 | 14 | 26 | 42 | 60 | 75 | 87 | 94 | 98 | 99 | | |
| 40 | .438 | 07 | 15 | 27 | 43 | 61 | 77 | 88 | 95 | 98 | 99 | | |
| 42 | .428 | 07 | 15 | 28 | 45 | 63 | 79 | 89 | 96 | 98 | * | | |
| 44 | .418 | 08 | 16 | 29 | 47 | 65 | 80 | 91 | 96 | 99 | | | |
| 46 | .409 | 08 | 16 | 30 | 48 | 67 | 82 | 92 | 97 | 99 | | | |
| 48 | .400 | 08 | 17 | 31 | 50 | 69 | 84 | 93 | 97 | 99 | | | |

Table 6.3.5 *(continued)*

| n | $h_c$ | .10 | .20 | .30 | .40 | .50 | .60 | .70 | .80 | .90 | 1.00 | 1.10 | 1.20 |
|---|---|---|---|---|---|---|---|---|---|---|---|---|---|
| 50 | .392 | 08 | 17 | 32 | 52 | 71 | 85 | 94 | 98 | 99 | * | * | * |
| 52 | .384 | 08 | 18 | 33 | 53 | 72 | 86 | 95 | 98 | * | | | |
| 54 | .377 | 08 | 18 | 34 | 55 | 74 | 88 | 95 | 99 | | | | |
| 56 | .370 | 08 | 18 | 35 | 56 | 75 | 89 | 96 | 99 | | | | |
| 58 | .364 | 08 | 19 | 37 | 58 | 77 | 90 | 96 | 99 | | | | |
| 60 | .358 | 09 | 19 | 38 | 59 | 78 | 91 | 97 | 99 | | | | |
| 64 | .346 | 09 | 20 | 40 | 62 | 81 | 92 | 98 | 99 | | | | |
| 68 | .336 | 09 | 21 | 42 | 65 | 83 | 94 | 98 | * | | | | |
| 72 | .327 | 09 | 22 | 44 | 67 | 85 | 95 | 99 | | | | | |
| 76 | .318 | 09 | 23 | 46 | 69 | 87 | 96 | 99 | | | | | |
| 80 | .310 | 10 | 24 | 48 | 72 | 89 | 97 | 99 | | | | | |
| 84 | .302 | 10 | 25 | 49 | 74 | 90 | 97 | * | | | | | |
| 88 | .295 | 10 | 26 | 51 | 76 | 91 | 98 | | | | | | |
| 92 | .289 | 10 | 27 | 53 | 77 | 92 | 98 | | | | | | |
| 96 | .283 | 11 | 28 | 55 | 79 | 93 | 99 | | | | | | |
| 100 | .277 | 11 | 29 | 56 | 81 | 94 | 99 | | | | | | |
| 120 | .253 | 12 | 34 | 64 | 87 | 97 | * | | | | | | |
| 140 | .234 | 14 | 39 | 71 | 92 | 99 | | | | | | | |
| 160 | .219 | 16 | 43 | 77 | 95 | 99 | | | | | | | |
| 180 | .207 | 16 | 48 | 81 | 97 | * | | | | | | | |
| 200 | .196 | 17 | 52 | 85 | 98 | | | | | | | | |
| 250 | .175 | 20 | 61 | 92 | 99 | | | | | | | | |
| 300 | .160 | 23 | 69 | 96 | * | | | | | | | | |
| 350 | .148 | 26 | 75 | 98 | | | | | | | | | |
| 400 | .139 | 29 | 81 | 99 | | | | | | | | | |
| 450 | .131 | 32 | 85 | 99 | | | | | | | | | |
| 500 | .124 | 35 | 89 | * | | | | | | | | | |
| 600 | .113 | 41 | 93 | | | | | | | | | | |
| 700 | .105 | 46 | 96 | | | | | | | | | | |
| 800 | .098 | 52 | 98 | | | | | | | | | | |
| 900 | .092 | 56 | 99 | | | | | | | | | | |
| 1000 | .088 | 61 | 99 | | | | | | | | | | |

* Power values below this point are greater than .995.

**Table 6.3.6**

Power of Normal Curve Test of $P_1 = P_2$
via Arcsine Transformation at $a_2 = .10$

| n | $h_c$ | | | | | | | h | | | | | |
|---|---|---|---|---|---|---|---|---|---|---|---|---|---|
| | | .10 | .20 | .30 | .40 | .50 | .60 | .70 | .80 | .90 | 1.00 | 1.10 | 1.20 |
| 10 | .736 | 11 | 13 | 18 | 23 | 30 | 38 | 47 | 56 | 64 | 72 | 79 | 85 |
| 11 | .701 | 11 | 14 | 18 | 24 | 32 | 41 | 50 | 59 | 68 | 76 | 83 | 88 |
| 12 | .672 | 11 | 14 | 19 | 26 | 34 | 43 | 53 | 62 | 71 | 79 | 85 | 90 |
| 13 | .645 | 11 | 14 | 20 | 27 | 36 | 45 | 56 | 65 | 74 | 82 | 88 | 92 |
| 14 | .622 | 11 | 15 | 20 | 28 | 38 | 48 | 58 | 68 | 77 | 84 | 90 | 94 |
| 15 | .601 | 11 | 15 | 21 | 29 | 39 | 50 | 61 | 71 | 79 | 86 | 91 | 95 |
| 16 | .582 | 11 | 15 | 22 | 31 | 41 | 52 | 63 | 73 | 82 | 88 | 93 | 96 |
| 17 | .564 | 11 | 16 | 23 | 32 | 43 | 54 | 65 | 75 | 84 | 90 | 94 | 97 |
| 18 | .548 | 12 | 16 | 23 | 33 | 44 | 56 | 68 | 77 | 85 | 91 | 95 | 97 |
| 19 | .534 | 12 | 16 | 24 | 34 | 46 | 58 | 70 | 79 | 87 | 92 | 96 | 98 |
| 20 | .520 | 12 | 17 | 25 | 35 | 48 | 60 | 72 | 81 | 89 | 94 | 97 | 98 |
| 21 | .508 | 12 | 17 | 25 | 37 | 49 | 62 | 73 | 83 | 90 | 94 | 97 | 99 |
| 22 | .496 | 12 | 17 | 26 | 38 | 51 | 64 | 75 | 84 | 91 | 95 | 98 | 99 |
| 23 | .485 | 12 | 18 | 27 | 39 | 52 | 65 | 77 | 86 | 92 | 96 | 98 | 99 |
| 24 | .475 | 12 | 18 | 28 | 40 | 54 | 67 | 78 | 87 | 93 | 97 | 98 | 99 |
| 25 | .465 | 12 | 18 | 28 | 41 | 55 | 68 | 80 | 88 | 94 | 97 | 99 | * |
| 26 | .456 | 12 | 19 | 29 | 42 | 56 | 70 | 81 | 89 | 95 | 98 | 99 | |
| 27 | .448 | 12 | 19 | 30 | 43 | 58 | 71 | 82 | 90 | 95 | 98 | 99 | |
| 28 | .440 | 12 | 19 | 30 | 44 | 59 | 73 | 84 | 91 | 96 | 98 | 99 | |
| 29 | .432 | 12 | 20 | 31 | 45 | 60 | 74 | 85 | 92 | 96 | 98 | 99 | |
| 30 | .425 | 13 | 20 | 32 | 46 | 61 | 75 | 86 | 93 | 97 | 99 | * | |
| 31 | .418 | 13 | 20 | 32 | 47 | 63 | 76 | 87 | 93 | 97 | 99 | | |
| 32 | .411 | 13 | 21 | 33 | 48 | 64 | 77 | 88 | 94 | 97 | 99 | | |
| 33 | .405 | 13 | 21 | 34 | 49 | 65 | 79 | 88 | 95 | 98 | 99 | | |
| 34 | .399 | 13 | 21 | 34 | 50 | 66 | 80 | 89 | 95 | 98 | 99 | | |
| 35 | .393 | 13 | 22 | 35 | 51 | 67 | 81 | 90 | 96 | 98 | 99 | | |
| 36 | .388 | 13 | 22 | 36 | 52 | 68 | 82 | 91 | 96 | 99 | * | | |
| 37 | .382 | 13 | 22 | 36 | 53 | 69 | 83 | 91 | 96 | 99 | | | |
| 38 | .377 | 13 | 23 | 37 | 54 | 70 | 83 | 92 | 97 | 99 | | | |
| 39 | .372 | 13 | 23 | 38 | 55 | 71 | 84 | 93 | 97 | 99 | | | |
| 40 | .368 | 13 | 23 | 38 | 56 | 72 | 85 | 93 | 97 | 99 | | | |
| 42 | .359 | 14 | 24 | 39 | 57 | 74 | 87 | 94 | 98 | 99 | | | |
| 44 | .351 | 14 | 24 | 41 | 59 | 76 | 88 | 95 | 98 | * | | | |
| 46 | .343 | 14 | 25 | 42 | 61 | 77 | 89 | 96 | 99 | | | | |
| 48 | .336 | 14 | 26 | 43 | 62 | 79 | 90 | 96 | 99 | | | | |

**Table 6.3.6** *(continued)*

|   |   | h |   |   |   |   |   |   |   |   |   |   |   |
|---|---|---|---|---|---|---|---|---|---|---|---|---|---|
| n | $h_c$ | .10 | .20 | .30 | .40 | .50 | .60 | .70 | .80 | .90 | 1.00 | 1.10 | 1.20 |
| 50 | .329 | 14 | 26 | 44 | 64 | 80 | 91 | 97 | 99 | * | * | * | * |
| 52 | .323 | 14 | 27 | 45 | 65 | 82 | 92 | 97 | 99 |   |   |   |   |
| 54 | .317 | 15 | 28 | 47 | 67 | 83 | 93 | 98 | 99 |   |   |   |   |
| 56 | .311 | 15 | 28 | 48 | 68 | 84 | 94 | 98 | * |   |   |   |   |
| 58 | .305 | 15 | 29 | 49 | 69 | 85 | 94 | 98 |   |   |   |   |   |
| 60 | .300 | 15 | 29 | 50 | 71 | 86 | 95 | 99 |   |   |   |   |   |
| 64 | .291 | 15 | 31 | 52 | 73 | 88 | 96 | 99 |   |   |   |   |   |
| 68 | .282 | 16 | 32 | 54 | 75 | 90 | 97 | 99 |   |   |   |   |   |
| 72 | .274 | 16 | 33 | 56 | 77 | 91 | 97 | 99 |   |   |   |   |   |
| 76 | .267 | 16 | 34 | 58 | 79 | 92 | 98 | * |   |   |   |   |   |
| 80 | .260 | 17 | 35 | 60 | 81 | 94 | 98 |   |   |   |   |   |   |
| 84 | .254 | 17 | 37 | 62 | 83 | 94 | 99 |   |   |   |   |   |   |
| 88 | .248 | 17 | 38 | 64 | 84 | 95 | 99 |   |   |   |   |   |   |
| 92 | .243 | 18 | 39 | 65 | 86 | 96 | 99 |   |   |   |   |   |   |
| 96 | .237 | 18 | 40 | 67 | 87 | 97 | 99 |   |   |   |   |   |   |
| 100 | .233 | 18 | 41 | 68 | 88 | 97 | * |   |   |   |   |   |   |
| 120 | .212 | 20 | 46 | 75 | 93 | 99 |   |   |   |   |   |   |   |
| 140 | .197 | 22 | 51 | 81 | 96 | 99 |   |   |   |   |   |   |   |
| 160 | .184 | 23 | 56 | 85 | 97 | * |   |   |   |   |   |   |   |
| 180 | .173 | 25 | 60 | 89 | 98 |   |   |   |   |   |   |   |   |
| 200 | .164 | 26 | 64 | 91 | 99 |   |   |   |   |   |   |   |   |
| 250 | .147 | 30 | 72 | 96 | * |   |   |   |   |   |   |   |   |
| 300 | .134 | 34 | 79 | 98 |   |   |   |   |   |   |   |   |   |
| 350 | .124 | 38 | 84 | 99 |   |   |   |   |   |   |   |   |   |
| 400 | .116 | 41 | 88 | * |   |   |   |   |   |   |   |   |   |
| 450 | .110 | 44 | 91 |   |   |   |   |   |   |   |   |   |   |
| 500 | .104 | 48 | 94 |   |   |   |   |   |   |   |   |   |   |
| 600 | .095 | 54 | 97 |   |   |   |   |   |   |   |   |   |   |
| 700 | .088 | 59 | 98 |   |   |   |   |   |   |   |   |   |   |
| 800 | .082 | 64 | 99 |   |   |   |   |   |   |   |   |   |   |
| 900 | .078 | 68 | * |   |   |   |   |   |   |   |   |   |   |
| 1000 | .074 | 72 |   |   |   |   |   |   |   |   |   |   |   |

* Power values below this point are greater than .995.

it is planned. They can, of course, also be used in research planning by varying **n**, ES or **a**, or all three to see how their variation affects power.

6.3.1   CASE 0: $n_1 = n_2$. The power tables of this chapter are designed to yield directly power values for the normal curve test of the difference between **P**'s of two independent samples of equal size (via the arcsine transformation). This is designated Case 0. Other cases are described and illustrated in succeeding sections. Tables are entered with **a**, **h**, and **n**.

*1. Significance Criterion*, **a**. Six tables are provided for the following values of **a**: $a_1 = .01,, .05, .10$ and $a_2 = .01, .05,$ and $.10$, where the subscripts refer to one- and two-tailed tests. since power at $a_1$ is to a close approximation equal to power at $a_2 = 2a_1$ for power greater than (say) .10, the tables can also be used for power at $a_2 = .02$, $a_2 = .20$, $a_1 = .005$, and $a_1 = .025$.

*2. Effect Size*, ES. This is the difference between arcsine-transformed **P**'s, i.e., $\phi_1 - \phi_2 = h$, whose properties are described in Section 6.2. Table 6.2.1 facilitates the conversion of $P_1$, $P_2$ pairs into **h** values. The tables provide for $h = .10 (.10) 1.20$. Conventional or operational definitions of ES have been offered, as follows:

small:     **h** = .20,

medium: **h** = .50,

large:     **h** = .80.

*3. Sample Size*, **n**. This is the size of each of the two samples whose proportions are being compared. Provision is made for **n** = 10 (1) 40 (2) 60 (4) 100 (20) 200 (50) 500 (100) 1000.

The values in the table are the power of the test times 100, i.e., the percent of tests carried out under the given conditions which will result in the rejection of the null hypothesis. They are rounded to the nearest unit and are accurate to within ±1 as tabulated.

**Illustrative Examples**

**6.1**   A social psychologist is interested in the cross-cultural generalizability of the finding in the United States that first-born and only child *S*s (A) more frequently than later-born *S*s (B) prefer waiting with others to waiting alone while anticipating an anxiety provoking experience. In a non-Western culture, he performs a replicating experiment for which he obtains the cooperation of 80 *S*'s of each birth order type, 160 in all. The prior work in the U.S. suggests that about two-thirds of the A's prefer waiting "together" while only about half of the B's do. On the expectation of a difference of similar magnitude in the other culture, even though both **P**'s might rise or fall under his particular conditions, he posits an ES of about the same size, namely $h = .30$ (actually, $h = \phi_{.67} - \phi_{.50} = 1.918 - 1.571 = .347$ from Table 6.2.2). He plans a directional test of $\mathbf{H_0}$: $\mathbf{P_A} = \mathbf{P_B}$ at $\mathbf{a_1} = .05$. What is the power of the test? The specification summary is

$$\mathbf{a_1} = .05, \qquad \mathbf{h} = .30, \qquad \mathbf{n_A} = \mathbf{n_B} = \mathbf{n} = 80.$$

In Table 6.3.2 for $\mathbf{a_1} = .05$, column $\mathbf{h} = .30$, and row $\mathbf{n} = 80$, he finds power $= .60$. Thus, he works with only $3 : 2$ odds of obtaining a significant ($\mathbf{a_1} = .05$) result if the populations in the new culture have proportions whose $\phi$'s differ by .30 in favor of the A sample. Note that $\mathbf{h} = .30$ when the following pairs of proportions are compared: .10 and .21, .25 and .39, .40 and .55, .60 and .78, .75 and .87, .90 and .97, as well as .50 and .65, the values approximated by the original experiments.

On the reasonable assumption that the psychologist finds the power value of .60 unsatisfactorily low, he would need to change his plans, either by increasing **n** or by increasing **a**, preferably the former. This assumes, of course, that the experiment has not yet been run. If it has, and his results were nonsignificant, he could not readily conclude that the U.S. finding did not generalize, since even if **h** were .30 in the new culture, his **b** risk was much too large $(1 - .60 = .40)$ for such a conclusion. If, on the other hand, the results *were* significant, although he can conclude that $\mathbf{P_A} > \mathbf{P_B}$, he cannot conclude that the population difference in terms of **h** *was* .30 (although his results are consistent with **h** being .30, and, of course, other values).

**6.2**   A clinical psychologist plans a research in which patients, upon admission to a mental hospital, are randomly assigned to two admission wards of different treatment atmospheres, one "custodial–authoritarian" (C), the other "therapeutic–democratic" (T). Among other criteria, she plans six months after admission, to compare the proportions that have been discharged. The issue, then, is the effect of the atmosphere of the initial ward placement on length of stay in the hospital. The hospital admits about 50 patients a month, and she plans to assign randomly to C and T conditions for a four-month period, yielding two samples of about 100 cases each. She reviews Table 6.2.1 and decides that the ES she expects is given by $h = .40$, since the pairs of proportions which differ by this amount around the middle of the scale of **P** (where from experience she expects the results to lie) are .40 and .60, .45 and .65, .50 and .69, and .55 and .74. The test will be performed at $\mathbf{a_2} = .05$. She wishes to assess the power of the eventual test of the significance of the difference between $\mathbf{P_C}$ and $\mathbf{P_T}$. In summary, the specifications are

$$\mathbf{a_2} = .05, \qquad \mathbf{h} = .40, \qquad \mathbf{n_C} = \mathbf{n_T} = \mathbf{n} = 100.$$

To find the power of this test, use Table 6.3.5 (for $a_2 = .05$) with column $h = .40$, row $n = 100$; power is .81. She thus has about four chances in five of concluding (at the .05 level) that the atmosphere difference has consequence to length of stay *if* the difference in proportions amounts to $h = .40$. If either (*a*) she wishes a better probability than .81 under these specifications, or (*b*) she wants to assure high power if the difference in proportions were smaller, say $h = .30$, she might consider running her experiment longer in order to get more $S$'s. If she can run a fifth month for a total of about 250 $S$s, under condition (*a*) above the specifications are:

$$a_2 = .05, \qquad h = .40, \qquad n_C = n_T = n = 125.$$

In Table 6.3.5, again for column $h = .40$, and roughly interpolating between the rows $n = 120$ and $n = 140$, we find power with this larger $n$ to be about .88 (i.e., one-quarter of the way between .87 and .92), a better than 7:1 chance of rejecting the null hypothesis if $h = .40$. Or, assuming the (*b*) condition, the specifications become

$$a_2 = .05, \qquad h = .30, \qquad n_C = n_T = n = 125.$$

When we move to the left one column in Table 6.3.5, i.e., to $h = .30$, roughly interpolating again between the rows $n = 120$ and $n = 140$, we find power to be about .66 (i.e., one-quarter of the way between .61 and .71). This value may well give her pause. If $h$ is as small as .30, she would have to run about seven months (so that $n = 180$) to get power of .81 at $a_2 = .05$.

6.3.2   CASE 1: $n_1 \neq n_2$. The tables will yield valid power values for tests on differences between population proportions when samples of different sizes are drawn. In such cases, find the harmonic mean of $n_1$ and $n_2$, i.e.,

$$(6.3.1) \qquad\qquad n' = \frac{2n_1 n_2}{n_1 + n_2}$$

and use the $n$ column of the power table for $n'$. The results of this procedure are exact,[4] provided that neither $n$ is very small ($< 10$).

**Illustrative Example**

6.3   In example 6.1 we described a cross-cultural research on the experimental hypothesis that first-born and only children (A) have a preference for waiting with others rather than alone relative to the later born (B) while anticipating an experience that is contemplated with anxiety. There, we posited that the social psychologist obtained the cooperation of 80 $S$s of

---

[4] That is, as exact as the Case 0 value, generally within $\pm 1$ as tabulated.

each birth-order type. It was found there that if $h = .30$, the probability of finding a difference significant at $a_1 = .05$ was .60. That example was somewhat artificial, in that in canvassing people to volunteer for the experiment, it is likely that the number of first and only born volunteers would not equal the number of later born volunteers, since there are more of the latter in most populations, particularly in a non-Western culture. If, for example, 80 A's and 245 B's volunteered, it would be a mistake to accept only 80 of the B's in order to keep the sample $n$'s equal. The mistake lies in the loss of power through reduced total $n$. What is the power of the test using all the volunteers? Keeping the other conditions the same, the specifications are

$$a_1 = .05, \qquad h = .30, \qquad n_A = 80 \neq 245 = n_B.$$

With unequal $n$'s, one finds [from (6.3.1)]

$$n' = \frac{2(80)(245)}{80 + 245} = 120.6.$$

Using Table 6.3.2 for $a_1 = .05$, as before, and column $h = .30$, but now row $n = 120$, one finds that power $= .75$, in contrast with the value of .60 obtained for $n_A = n_B = 80$.

**6.4** A proposition derivable from psychoanalytic theory holds that the incidence of homosexuality should be higher in female paranoid schizophrenics (P) than in females bearing other psychiatric diagnoses (O). A clinical psychologist has records available for 85 P's and 450 O's. On the expectation that the difference in relative incidence or proportion of cases in which homosexuality is found in the case records of the two populations is "medium," i.e., $h = .50$, what is the power of a (directional) test of $H_0: P_P \leq P_O$ at $a_1 = .01$? The specifications are

$$a_1 = .01, \qquad h = .50, \qquad n_P = 85 \neq 450 = n_O.$$

For unequal $n$'s, first find [from formula (6.3.1)]

$$n' = \frac{2(85)(450)}{85 + 450} = 143.0.$$

Using Table 6.3.1 (for $a_1 = .01$) for column $h = .50$, row $n = 140$, one finds power $= .97$.

The psychologist formulated the test as directional, since the theory's prediction was not merely that there would be a difference, but that $P_P > P_O$. Theories normally do predict the direction of differences. However, if, in fact, it turned out that the sample proportions differed in the direction *opposite* to prediction, no conclusion could be drawn no matter how great the difference. (See Section 1.2 and Cohen, 1965, pp. 106–111.) It is instructive to inquire here what the power would be if a nondirectional test, which permits conclusions in either direction, were performed. The specifications are to be otherwise held constant, i.e.,

$$\mathbf{a_2} = .01, \qquad \mathbf{h} = .50, \qquad \mathbf{n'} = 143.$$

In Table 6.3.4 (for $\mathbf{a_2} = .01$) for column $\mathbf{h} = .50$, row $\mathbf{n} = 140$, we find power $= .95$, in contrast to the $\mathbf{a_1} = .01$ power value of $.97$. The clinical psychologist might well decide that the loss in power is trivial, and that it is worth formulating the problem in nondirectional (two-tailed) terms to make possible the converse conclusion.[5]

### 6.3.3   CASE 2: ONE SAMPLE OF $\mathbf{n}$ OBSERVATIONS TO TEST $\mathbf{P} = \mathbf{c}$. 

Thus far we have been considering the power of the test of the difference between proportions of two independent samples, where the null hypothesis is $\mathbf{P_1} = \mathbf{P_2}$. Essentially the same test procedure can be used to test the departure of the $\mathbf{P}$ in a single population from some specified value $\mathbf{c}$. $\mathbf{H_0}$ for the one-sample test is $\mathbf{P} = \mathbf{c}$. The test is employed when, given a random sample of $\mathbf{n}$ cases, the investigator's purpose is to determine whether the data are consonant with the hypothesis that the population $\mathbf{P}$ is $.62$ or $.90$ or any other value. It is thus the general case of which the test that $\mathbf{P} = .50$ of the preceding chapter is a special case.[6]

Although the special case $\mathbf{P} = \mathbf{c} = .50$ occurs quite widely in behavioral science (including particularly the "Sign Test"), the case of $\mathbf{P} = \mathbf{c} \neq .50$ is not as frequently found. Increasingly, however, the use of mathematical models provides ever stronger and more precise hypotheses, which are frequently cast in a form which predicts values of $\mathbf{P}$ not generally equal to $.50$. The rejection or affirmation of such hypotheses may proceed by use of the tables provided in this chapter.

For Case 2 we define the ES as for the other cases, that is, as the difference between arcsine-transformed $\mathbf{P}$'s. However, in formula (6.2.2), $\mathbf{P_2} \rightarrow \phi_2$ is an estimable population parameter. Here it is a constant, so that for Case 2

(6.3.2)              $\mathbf{h_2'} = \phi_1 - \phi_c$     (directional)

                          $= |\phi_1 - \phi_c|$     (nondirectional),

where $\phi_1 =$ the arcsine transformation of $\mathbf{P_1}$ as before, and

$\phi_c =$ the arcsine transformation of $\mathbf{c}$.

---

[5] It should be noted that the smallness of the power difference is due to the fact that the power values are close to 1.00.

[6] As in the case where $\mathbf{H_0}: \mathbf{P} = .50$, the test of $\mathbf{H_0}: \mathbf{P} = \mathbf{c}$ can be performed exactly by means of tables for the binomial distribution. The present procedure, however, requires no additional tables and provides an excellent approximation unless $\mathbf{n}$ is quite small.

There is no conceptual change in the ES; $h_2'$ is the difference between the (alternate) population value $P_1$ and the value specified by the null hypothesis, $c$, expressed in units of the arcsine transformation of formula (6.2.1). and Table 6.2.2. The interpretation of $h_2'$ proceeds exactly as described in Section 6.2 with regard to Table 6.2.1 and the operational definition of small, medium, and large ES.

The power and sample size tables, however, cannot be used directly with $h_2'$ since they are constructed for Case 0, where there are *two* sample statistics *each* of which contributes sampling error variance for a total of $2/n$. Here, there is only one sample contributing sampling error variance, yielding half the amount, $1/n$. This is simply allowed for by finding

$$(6.3.3) \qquad h = h_2' \sqrt{2} = 1.414\, h_2'.$$

The value $h$ is sought in the tables, while $h_2'$ is the ES index which is interpreted.

If $h_2'$ is chosen as a convenient multiple of .10, $h$ will in general not be such a multiple. Thus, the proposed operational definitions of ES for $h_2'$ of .20, .50, and .80 become, for table entry, .28, .71, and 1.13. Linear interpolation between columns will provide values which are sufficiently close (within .01 or .02) for most purposes.


## Illustrative Example

**6.5** A mathematical model predicts that a certain response will occur in $(H_0\colon P_1 = c =)$ .40 of the animals subjected to a certain set of conditions. An experimental psychologist plans to test this model using $n = 60$ animals and as the significance criterion $a_2 = .05$. Assuming that the model is incorrect, and that the population rate is actually .50, what would be the power of this test?

The ES is found directly from Table 6.2.1, where, from .40 (column $P_2$) to .50 amounts to a difference in $\phi$'s of .20. This value is for $h_2'$. For entry into the power table, we require [from (6.3.3)], $h = h_2' \sqrt{2} = .20\, \sqrt{2} = .28$. Thus, the specifications are

$$a_2 = .05, \qquad h = .28, \qquad n = 60.$$

In Table 6.3.5 (for $a_2 = .05$), row $n = 60$, for column $h = .20$, power is .19 and for $h = .30$, power is .38. Interpolating linearly between these values, we approximate the power as $.19 + (.38 - .19)(.28 - .20)/(.30 - .20) = .34$. Thus, even if a discrepancy of .50–.40 in the parameter existed, the experiment as planned would have only about one chance in three of detecting it. It is apparent that if this experimental plan is followed, and the result is a nonsignificant departure of the sample **P** value, the psychologist would be making an error to conclude that the results were confirmatory of the model. Our alternate hypothetical value of .50 would likely be considered a large discrepancy in this context, and failing to reject the model when there was only a one-third chance of doing so, given a large true departure from it, can hardly be considered confirmatory.

The above results hold to a sufficient approximation whether the test is to be performed by means of the arcsine transformation (as described in Section 6.5), or the exact binomial, or the approximations to the latter provided by either the normal curve test using proportions or the equivalent $\chi^2$ " goodness of fit" test on frequencies.

### 6.4   SAMPLE SIZE TABLES

The tables in this section list the significance criterion, the ES to be detected, and the *desired power*. One then can find the necessary sample size. Their primary utility lies in the planning of experiments to provide a basis for the decision as to the sample size to use.

6.4.1    CASE 0: $n_1 = n_2$. The use of the sample size tables is first described for the application for which they were optimally designed, Case 0, where they yield the sample size, **n**, for each of two independent samples whose populations **P**'s are to be compared. The description of their use in two other cases follows this subsection. Tables give values for **a**, **h**, and desired power:

*1. Significance Criterion*, **a**. The same **a** values are provided as in the power tables by means of a table for each of the following: $a_1 = .01$ ($a_2 = .02$), $a_1 = .05$ ($a_2 = .10$), $a_1 = .10$ ($a_2 = .20$), $a_2 = .01$ ($a_1 = .005$), and $a_2 = .05$ ($a_1 = .025$).

*2. Effect Size*. **h** is defined and interpreted as above [formula (6.2.2)] and used as in the power tables. The same provision is made: $h = .10$ (.10) 1.20.

To find **n** for a value of **h** not tabled, substitute in

$$(6.4.1) \qquad\qquad n = \frac{n_{.10}}{100h^2},$$

where $n_{.10}$ is the necessary sample size for the given **a** and desired power at $h = .10$ (read from the table) and **h** is the nontabled ES. Round to the nearest integer.

*3. Desired Power*. Provision is made for desired power values of .25, .50, .60, 2/3, .70 (.05) .95, .99. (See Section 2.4.1 for a discussion of the basis for the selection of these values, and the proposal that power = .80 serve as a convention in the absence of another basis for a choice. )

Table 6.4.1

n to detect $h = \phi_1 - \phi_2$ via Arcsine Transformation

### $a_1 = .01\ (a_2 = .02)$

| Power | .10 | .20 | .30 | .40 | .50 | .60 | .70 | .80 | .90 | 1.00 | 1.10 | 1.20 |
|---|---|---|---|---|---|---|---|---|---|---|---|---|
| .25 | 546 | 136 | 61 | 34 | 22 | 15 | 11 | 9 | 7 | 5 | 5 | 4 |
| .50 | 1082 | 271 | 120 | 68 | 43 | 30 | 22 | 17 | 13 | 11 | 9 | 8 |
| .60 | 1331 | 333 | 148 | 83 | 53 | 37 | 27 | 21 | 16 | 13 | 11 | 9 |
| 2/3 | 1520 | 380 | 169 | 95 | 61 | 42 | 31 | 24 | 19 | 15 | 13 | 11 |
| .70 | 1625 | 406 | 181 | 102 | 65 | 45 | 33 | 25 | 20 | 16 | 13 | 11 |
| .75 | 1801 | 450 | 200 | 113 | 72 | 50 | 37 | 28 | 22 | 18 | 15 | 13 |
| .80 | 2007 | 502 | 223 | 125 | 80 | 56 | 41 | 31 | 25 | 20 | 17 | 14 |
| .85 | 2262 | 565 | 251 | 141 | 90 | 63 | 46 | 35 | 28 | 23 | 19 | 16 |
| .90 | 2603 | 651 | 289 | 163 | 104 | 72 | 53 | 41 | 32 | 26 | 22 | 18 |
| .95 | 3154 | 789 | 350 | 197 | 126 | 88 | 64 | 49 | 39 | 32 | 26 | 22 |
| .99 | 4330 | 1082 | 481 | 271 | 173 | 120 | 88 | 68 | 53 | 43 | 36 | 30 |

### $a_1 = .05\ (a_2 = .10)$

| Power | .10 | .20 | .30 | .40 | .50 | .60 | .70 | .80 | .90 | 1.00 | 1.10 | 1.20 |
|---|---|---|---|---|---|---|---|---|---|---|---|---|
| .25 | 188 | 47 | 21 | 12 | 8 | 5 | 4 | 3 | 2 | 2 | 2 | 1 |
| .50 | 541 | 135 | 60 | 34 | 22 | 15 | 11 | 8 | 7 | 5 | 4 | 4 |
| .60 | 721 | 180 | 80 | 45 | 29 | 20 | 15 | 11 | 9 | 7 | 6 | 5 |
| 2/3 | 862 | 215 | 96 | 54 | 34 | 24 | 18 | 13 | 11 | 9 | 7 | 6 |
| .70 | 941 | 235 | 105 | 59 | 38 | 26 | 19 | 15 | 12 | 9 | 8 | 7 |
| .75 | 1076 | 269 | 120 | 67 | 43 | 30 | 22 | 17 | 13 | 11 | 9 | 7 |
| .80 | 1237 | 309 | 137 | 77 | 49 | 34 | 25 | 19 | 15 | 12 | 10 | 9 |
| .85 | 1438 | 359 | 160 | 90 | 58 | 40 | 29 | 22 | 18 | 14 | 12 | 10 |
| .90 | 1713 | 428 | 190 | 107 | 69 | 48 | 35 | 27 | 21 | 17 | 14 | 12 |
| .95 | 2164 | 541 | 240 | 135 | 87 | 60 | 44 | 34 | 27 | 22 | 18 | 15 |
| .99 | 3154 | 789 | 350 | 197 | 126 | 88 | 64 | 49 | 39 | 32 | 26 | 22 |

### $a_1 = .10\ (a_2 = .20)$

| Power | .10 | .20 | .30 | .40 | .50 | .60 | .70 | .80 | .90 | 1.00 | 1.10 | 1.20 |
|---|---|---|---|---|---|---|---|---|---|---|---|---|
| .25 | 74 | 18 | 8 | 5 | 3 | 2 | 2 | 1 | 1 | 1 | 1 | 1 |
| .50 | 328 | 82 | 36 | 21 | 13 | 9 | 7 | 5 | 4 | 3 | 3 | 2 |
| .60 | 471 | 118 | 52 | 29 | 19 | 13 | 10 | 7 | 6 | 5 | 4 | 3 |
| 2/3 | 586 | 147 | 65 | 37 | 23 | 16 | 12 | 9 | 7 | 6 | 5 | 4 |
| .70 | 652 | 163 | 72 | 41 | 26 | 18 | 13 | 10 | 8 | 7 | 5 | 5 |
| .75 | 765 | 191 | 85 | 48 | 31 | 21 | 16 | 12 | 9 | 8 | 6 | 5 |
| .80 | 902 | 225 | 100 | 56 | 36 | 25 | 18 | 14 | 11 | 9 | 7 | 6 |
| .85 | 1075 | 269 | 119 | 67 | 43 | 30 | 22 | 17 | 13 | 11 | 9 | 7 |
| .90 | 1314 | 328 | 146 | 82 | 53 | 36 | 27 | 21 | 16 | 13 | 11 | 9 |
| .95 | 1713 | 428 | 190 | 107 | 69 | 48 | 35 | 27 | 21 | 17 | 14 | 12 |
| .99 | 2603 | 651 | 289 | 163 | 104 | 72 | 53 | 41 | 32 | 26 | 22 | 18 |

**Table 6.4.1** *(continued)*

| Power | .10 | .20 | .30 | .40 | .50 | .60 | .70 | .80 | .90 | 1.00 | 1.10 | 1.20 |
|---|---|---|---|---|---|---|---|---|---|---|---|---|
| | | | | $a_2 = .01$ ($a_1 = .005$) h | | | | | | | | |
| .25 | 723 | 181 | 80 | 45 | 29 | 20 | 15 | 11 | 9 | 7 | 6 | 5 |
| .50 | 1327 | 332 | 147 | 83 | 53 | 37 | 27 | 21 | 16 | 13 | 11 | 9 |
| .60 | 1601 | 400 | 178 | 100 | 64 | 44 | 33 | 25 | 20 | 16 | 13 | 11 |
| 2/3 | 1808 | 452 | 201 | 113 | 72 | 50 | 37 | 28 | 22 | 18 | 15 | 13 |
| .70 | 1922 | 481 | 214 | 120 | 77 | 53 | 39 | 30 | 24 | 19 | 16 | 13 |
| .75 | 2113 | 528 | 235 | 132 | 85 | 59 | 43 | 33 | 26 | 21 | 17 | 15 |
| .80 | 2336 | 584 | 260 | 146 | 93 | 65 | 48 | 36 | 29 | 23 | 19 | 16 |
| .85 | 2610 | 652 | 290 | 163 | 104 | 72 | 53 | 41 | 32 | 26 | 22 | 18 |
| .90 | 2976 | 744 | 331 | 186 | 119 | 83 | 61 | 46 | 37 | 30 | 25 | 21 |
| .95 | 3563 | 891 | 396 | 223 | 143 | 99 | 73 | 56 | 44 | 36 | 29 | 25 |
| .99 | 4806 | 1202 | 534 | 300 | 192 | 134 | 98 | 75 | 59 | 48 | 40 | 33 |

| Power | .10 | .20 | .30 | .40 | .50 | .60 | .70 | .80 | .90 | 1.00 | 1.10 | 1.20 |
|---|---|---|---|---|---|---|---|---|---|---|---|---|
| | | | | $a_2 = .05$ ($a_1 = .025$) h | | | | | | | | |
| .25 | 330 | 83 | 37 | 21 | 13 | 9 | 7 | 5 | 4 | 3 | 3 | 2 |
| .50 | 768 | 192 | 85 | 48 | 31 | 21 | 16 | 12 | 9 | 8 | 6 | 5 |
| .60 | 980 | 245 | 109 | 61 | 39 | 27 | 20 | 15 | 12 | 10 | 8 | 7 |
| 2/3 | 1143 | 286 | 127 | 71 | 46 | 32 | 23 | 18 | 14 | 11 | 9 | 8 |
| .70 | 1234 | 309 | 137 | 77 | 49 | 34 | 25 | 19 | 15 | 12 | 10 | 9 |
| .75 | 1388 | 347 | 154 | 87 | 56 | 39 | 28 | 22 | 17 | 14 | 11 | 10 |
| .80 | 1570 | 392 | 174 | 98 | 63 | 44 | 32 | 25 | 19 | 16 | 13 | 11 |
| .85 | 1796 | 449 | 200 | 112 | 72 | 50 | 37 | 28 | 22 | 18 | 15 | 12 |
| .90 | 2101 | 525 | 233 | 131 | 84 | 58 | 43 | 33 | 26 | 21 | 17 | 15 |
| .95 | 2599 | 650 | 289 | 162 | 104 | 72 | 53 | 41 | 32 | 26 | 21 | 18 |
| .99 | 3674 | 919 | 408 | 230 | 147 | 102 | 75 | 57 | 45 | 37 | 30 | 26 |

The Case 0 procedure involves finding (*a*) the table for the significance criterion (**a**) being used, then finding (*b*) the difference in arcsine-transformed **P**'s (**h**) along the horizontal stub and (*c*) the desired power along the vertical stub. This gives **n**, the necessary size for *each* sample to detect **h** at the **a** significance level with the desired power.

## Illustrative Example

**6.6**  Consider again the research in example 6.1, where there is described a crosscultural test of the experimental hypothesis that, in circumstances which arouse anxiety, *S*s who were first-born or only children more frequently prefer to wait with others than do *S*s who were later born. It was found there that if the population proportions differed by $h = .30$, a test of the null hypothesis at $a_1 = .05$ using samples of 80 cases in each group, would have only a .60 probability of rejection (power). If power of .80 is desired, what sample sizes should be used? The specifications are

$$a_1 = .05, \qquad h = .30, \qquad \text{power} = .80.$$

Table 6.4.1 for $a_1 = .05$, column $h = .30$, and row power $= .80$ yields $n = 137$. The social psychologist would thus need samples of 137 each of the two kinds of $S$s in order to have a probability of .80 of rejecting the null hypothesis if the population $P$'s differed by $h = .30$.

6.4.2 CASE 1: $n_1 \neq n_2$. Although in manipulative experiments one does not ordinarily plan to use samples of unequal size (since the equal $n$ condition is optimal), unequal $n$'s can occur in planning when a sample proportion is already available for one population or when the size of one sample is necessarily fixed by other circumstances. In such an eventuality, the investigator is free to set the size of only one of the two samples. With one sample size fixed at $n_F$, the problem is to determine the necessary size of the sample whose size is at the investigator's disposal ($n_U$). Table 6.4.1 is used as in Case 0 with $a$, $h$, and desired power, and $n$ is determined. In order to find $n_U$, substitute the fixed sample size ($n_F$) and the $n$ read from Table 6.4.1 in

$$(6.4.2) \qquad n_U = \frac{n\, n_F}{2n_F - n}.$$

(See Section 2.4.2 when denominator is zero or negative.)

**Illustrative Example**

6.7 A psychopharmacologist plans to study the efficacy of a new drug for first psychiatric admissions bearing a given admission diagnosis. He wishes to compare the discharge rate four months from admission of patients treated with this drug (E) with that of patients currently treated by other means (C). He wishes to detect with power of .90 a small difference, in either direction from the rate for C patients, accepting the proposed convention of a small difference of $h = .20$. He plans the test at the $a_2 = .01$ criterion. From past records of $n_F = 1600$ patients bearing the diagnosis, he has available a sample $P_C$. His specifications summary is

$$a_2 = .01, \qquad h = .20, \qquad \text{power} = .90.$$

In the section of Table 6.4.1. for $a_2 = .01$, column $h = .20$, and row power $= .90$, he finds $n = 744$. Thus, his specifications are met by two samples, each of 744 cases. But he already has one sample of $n_F = 1600$ cases for the C group. To find how many patients he requires in the E group, he substitutes in formula (6.4.2) to find

$$n_U = \frac{744(1600)}{2(1600) - 744} = 485 \text{ cases}.$$

Thus, the availability of a sample of $n_F = 1600$ cases makes it possible for him to satisfy his specifications (attain power of .90 to detect $h = .20$ at $a_2 = .01$) with a sample for the new drug of 485 cases.

6.4.3   CASE 2: ONE SAMPLE OF n OBSERVATIONS TO TEST $P = c$. In using the **n** tables for the one-sample test, the only departure from Case 0 is that which was discussed for the use of the power tables for Case 2, namely the proper value of **h** to use the tables (see Section 6.3.3). Briefly, to test with a single sample the null hypothesis that a population **P** has some specified value, i.e., $H_0$: $P = c$, and the ES is indexed in the usual way, as a difference between arcsine transformed values of the alternate, $P_1$, and **c**, namely $h_2' = \phi_1 - \phi_2$, entry into the **n** tables is made with $h = h_2' \sqrt{2}$. If, as is probable, the resultant **h** is not tabled, recourse is taken to formula (6.4.1).

**Illustrative Example**

**6.8**   Return to example 6.5, where an experimental psychologist was testing a derivation from a mathematical model that a population response rate was $P = .40$. With a test to be performed at $a_2 = .05$, given that the true parameter differs from .40 by $ES = h_2' = .20$, how large a sample of animals does he need to attain power of .95? He sets this high power requirement because he wishes to interpret *non*significance as confirmatory of the model (Section 1.5.5).

Since there is only one sample **P** yielding sampling error, as described in Section 6.3.3, for the table entry he requires [formula (6.4.1)] $h = h_2' \sqrt{2} = .20 \sqrt{2} = .2828$. Thus, the specifications are

$$a_2 = .05, \qquad h = .2828, \qquad \text{power} = .95.$$

Since $h = .2828$ is not tabled, he follows the procedure described in Section 6.4.1. Use the part of Table 6.4.1 for $a_2 = .05$, row power $= .95$, and column $h = .10$ to find $n_{.10} = 2599$. Then substitute $n_{.10} = 2599$ and $h = .2828$ in formula (6.4.1) for the required **n**:

$$n = \frac{2599}{100(.2828)^2} = 325.$$

Thus, if $P = .50$, a one-sample test of $H_0: P = .40$ performed at the $a_2 = .05$ level, in order to have .95 probability of rejection of $H_0$, must have sample $n = 325$. (This is much larger than the $n = 60$ experiment originally posited, but a nonsignificant result from the latter would have been inconclusive.)

## 6.5 THE USE OF THE TABLES FOR SIGNIFICANCE TESTING

6.5.1 GENERAL INTRODUCTION. As a convenience to the researcher, provision has been made in the power tables to facilitate significance testing. Power analysis is primarily relevant to the planning of experiments and thus with the alternate-hypothetical ES. Once the experiment is performed and the data are in, attention turns to the assessment of the null hypothesis in the light of the sample data.

For significance testing, we redefine our ES index, $h$, so that its elements are observed sample statistics rather than hypothetical population parameters, and call it $h_s$. For Cases 0 and 1, where the $P$'s of two independent samples are being compared, the sample $P_s$ values are transformed by the arcsine function, and

$$(6.5.1) \qquad h_s = \phi_{s_1} - \phi_{s_2} \qquad \text{(directional)}$$

$$= |\phi_{s_1} - \phi_{s_2}| \qquad \text{(nondirectional)}.$$

Thus, $h_s$ is simply the difference in sample $\phi$ values. It is related to the unit normal curve deviate (or "critical ratio") $x$, by

$$(6.5.2) \qquad h_s = x \sqrt{\frac{n_1 + n_2}{n_1 n_2}},$$

$$(6.5.3) \qquad x = h_s \sqrt{\frac{n_1 n_2}{n_1 + n_2}}.$$

These formulas are stated generally, so that the sample $n$'s need not be equal. They simplify for the Case 0 condition of equal $n$ (see below).

.The value of $h_s$ necessary for significance is called $h_c$, i.e., the criterion value of $h_s$. The second column of the power tables 6.3, headed $h_c$, carries these values as a function of $n$. Using these values, the normal curve deviate $x$ need not be computed. One simply finds the sample difference in arcsine transformed $\phi$'s using Table 6.2.2, and compares it with the tabled $h_c$ value for his sample size. If the obtained $h_s$ value equals or exceeds $h_c$, his obtained difference is significant at the $a$ level for that table; otherwise, it is not.

6.5.2  SIGNIFICANCE TESTING IN CASE 0, $n_1 = n_2 = n$. When the sample sizes are equal, the relationship between $h_s$ and the normal deviate $x$ are simplified:

(6.5.4)
$$h_s = x \sqrt{\frac{2}{n}},$$

(6.5.5)
$$x = h_s \sqrt{\frac{n}{2}}.$$

[Formula (6.5.4) was used for the computation of the tables, $q_c$ values, $x$ being taken as the normal curve deviate for the $a$ criterion.]

Use of the $h_c$ values in Case 0 is straightforward: the investigator looks up the arcsine $P = \phi$ values for the two $P_s$'s in Table 6.2.2, finds their difference, $h_s$, and enters the appropriate power table depending on $a$, in the row for his $n$ ($= n_1 = n_2$), and checks whether his $h_s$ value equals or exceeds the tabled $h_c$ value.

**Illustrative Example**

**6.9**  Reconsider the research described in example 6.2, where a clinical psychologist was planning a study to compare the relative treatment effectiveness of two ward atmospheres (T and C) by comparing the proportions of 100 cases originally admitted to each ward who are discharged within six months. Now assume that the experiment is performed as planned and the sample proportions discharged turn out to be .41 for the C condition and .57 for the T condition. Is this difference significant at the planned $a_2 = .05$ level? First, she looks up the $\phi$ transformation of these $P_s$'s in Table 6.2.2, and finds them to be respectively, 1.390 and 1.711. Thus, $h_s = |1.711 - 1.390| = .321$. Therefore, the specifications are:

$$a_2 = .05, \qquad n = 100, \qquad h_s = .321.$$

In Table 6.3.5 (for $a_2 = .05$) for row $n = 100$, she finds under $h_c$ the value .277. Since her $h_s$ value exceeds $h_c$, her observed difference is significant. This determination may be sufficient for her purposes, but if she wants the exact normal deviate value, $x$, she can substitute in formula (6.5.5) and find $x = .321 \sqrt{100/2} = 2.27$.

6.5.3  SIGNIFICANCE TESTING IN CASE 1, $n_1 \neq n_2$. Inequality of sample sizes in significance testing using the tabled $h_c$ values requires only finding the harmonic mean of the two $n$'s, $n'$, as described in Section 6.3.2 [formula (6.3.1)]:

$$n' = \frac{2n_1 n_2}{n_1 + n_2}.$$

The Tables 6.3 are applied, using $n'$ for $n$. The procedure is otherwise exactly the same as for Case 0.

If the normal curve deviate value $x$ is desired, it is found using formula (6.5.3), or, if $n'$ has already been found, more simply by substituting $n'$ for $n$ in formula (6.5.5).

**Illustrative Example**

**6.10** Example 6.3, which in turn referred to example 6.1, described a cross-cultural test of the experimental hypothesis that, under anxiety conditions, first-born and only children (A) more frequently than later-born (B) prefer to wait with others. As revised in example 6.3, sample sizes of $n_A = 80$ and $n_B = 245$ are available for a test at $a_1 = .05$. Assume now that when the experiment is run, he finds the sample proportions preferring to wait with others to be $56/80 = .70$ for the A sample and $159/245 = .65$ for the B sample. Since the difference is in the predicted direction $(P_A > P_B)$, the test proceeds. The $P_s$'s are transformed to $\phi$'s by finding in Table 6.2.2 the values respectively of 1.982 and 1.875. Their difference, $h_s = 1.982 - 1.875 = .107$, is found. For use in the table, find $n'$ from formula (6.3.1) (as in example 6.3):

$$n' = \frac{2(80)(245)}{80 + 245} = 120.6.$$

The specifications for significance testing of the sample difference are:

$$a_1 = .05, \qquad n' = 120.6, \qquad h_s = .107.$$

Table 6.3.2 (for $a_1 = .05$) for row $n = 120$ and column $h_c$ yields .212 Since $h_s$ is smaller than the criterion $h_c$, the difference is not significant at $a_1 = .05$.[7] Thus, the research provides no warrant for concluding the generalizability of the United States finding to this culture.

6.5.4 SIGNIFICANCE TESTING IN CASE 2: ONE SAMPLE, $H_0$: $P = c$. When the null hypothesis takes the form: "For a population from which a sample of $n$ observations is randomly drawn, the $P$ having a given characteristic equals $c$," an adjustment must be made of the tabled $h_c$ value. This is because the tables were constructed for Case 0 conditions and hence allow for

---

[7] When $n'$ is not tabulated, and intermediate $h_c$ values are desired, linear interpolation will usually provide an adequate approximation. If greater accuracy is desired, either $h_c$ or $x$ can be solved by using formulas (6.5.2) and (6.5.3).

sampling error variance of two $P_s$'s, while in Case 2 there is only one. The proper criterion for one sample tests of $P = c$ is

(6.5.6) $$h_c' = h_c \sqrt{\tfrac{1}{2}} = .707 h_c,$$

where $h_c$ is the tabulated value for $n$.

As for the observed $h_s$ value for Case 2, we follow the principle expressed in (6.5.1) and simply define $h_s'$ as we defined $h_2'$ [formula (6.3.2)], merely substituting the sample value of $\phi_s$ for the population parameter $\phi_1$:

(6.5.7) $$h_s' = \phi_s - \phi_c \quad \text{(directional)}$$
$$= |\phi_s - \phi_c| \quad \text{(nondirectional)}.$$

The prime is used to denote a one-sample test. The relationships between $h_s'$ and the normal deviate $x$ for the case are now

(6.5.8) $$h_s' = x \sqrt{\frac{1}{n}},$$

(6.5.9) $$x = h_s' \sqrt{n}.$$

Formula (6.5.9) can be used if the exact normal deviate ("critical ratio") is desired, e.g., for reporting results for publication.

### Illustrative Example

**6.11** Assume that the experimental psychologist of example 6.5, following the power analysis described therein, actually performs the experiment to test $H_0$: $P = .40$, but uses instead the more liberal rejection criterion of $a_2 = .20$ and a larger sample size of $n = 100$, both of these changes in specifications serving to make it easier to detect departures from, and hence reject, the model. (The reader can determine as an exercise that, if in fact, $P = .50$, then power is now approximately .75.) Given these new conditions, he finds that the sample proportion of animals giving the response is $47/100 = .47$. Can he conclude from this result that the null hypothesis is false, i.e., that the value predicted by the mathematical model, .40, is incorrect?

He finds the arcsine transformations of these two values from Table 6.2.2 to be 1.511 (for .47) and 1.369 (for .40), and their difference [formula (6.5.7)]$h_s' = |1.511 - 1.369| = .142$. This is the sample ES. His specifications, then, are

$$a_2 = .20, \qquad n = 100, \qquad h_s' = .142.$$

Table 6.3.3 (for $a_1 = .10$, but used here for $a_2 = .20$), with row $n = 100$ and column $h_c$, gives the value .181. This would be the criterion for a two-sample test where each $n = 100$. For this one-sample case, he goes on to find [formula (6.5.6)] $h_c' = .181\sqrt{\tfrac{1}{2}} = (.707)(.181) = .128$. This is the relevant criterion value, and since the sample $h_s' = .142$ exceeds it, the null hypothesis of $P = c = .40$ is rejected. The experiment, thus, casts serious doubt on the validity of the model.

If he wishes to determine the exact normal deviate value $x$ which would result from this test, he finds [formula (6.5.9)] $x = .142\sqrt{100} = 1.42$.

# CHAPTER 7

# Chi-Square Tests for Goodness of Fit and Contingency Tables

## 7.1 INTRODUCTION AND USE

This chapter is concerned with the most frequent application of the chi-square ($\chi^2$) distribution in behavioral science applications, namely to sets of frequencies or proportions. Two types of circumstances may be distinguished:

*1. Case 0: Goodness of Fit Tests.* Here a single array of categories of sample frequencies or proportions is tested against a prespecified set which comprise the null hypothesis (Edwards, 1972, pp. 53–55; Hays, 1981, pp. 537–544).

*2. Case 1: Contingency Tests.* Here observed frequencies are each classified simultaneously by means of two different variables or principles of classification, i.e., in a two-way table. The joint frequencies are tested against a null hypothesis which specifies no association between the two bases of classification (see the following: Hays, 1981, pp. 544–552; Edwards, 1972, pp. 55–65; Blalock, 1972, pp. 275–314).

The chi-square test on frequencies is quite general in its applicability to problems in data analysis in behavioral science, in both manipulative experiments and survey analysis. It is particularly appropriate with variables expressed as nominal scales or unordered categories, e.g., religion, marital status, experimental condition, etc.

When used for frequency comparisons, the chi-square test is a non-parametric test, since it compares entire distributions rather than para-meters (means, variances) of distributions. Thus, other than the need to avoid very small hypothetical frequencies (see Hays, 1981, pp. 521), the test is relatively free of constraining assumptions.

Milligan (1980) shows how the tables of this chapter can be used for determining power for the analysis of multidimensional contingency tables using the loglinear model.

In the following section, the two types of tests will be described in greater detail in the context of the ES index.

## 7.2   THE EFFECT SIZE INDEX: w

We require for an ES index a "pure" number which increases with the degree of discrepancy between the distribution specified by the alternate hypothesis and that which represents the null hypothesis. We achieve "pure-ness" here by working with *relative* frequencies, i.e., proportions. In both cases, there are "cells"; categories in Case 0 and joint categories in Case 1. For each cell, there are two population proportions, one given by the null hypothesis, the other by the alternate. The ES index, w, measures the dis-crepancy between these paired proportions over the cells in the following way:

$$(7.2.1) \qquad w = \sqrt{\sum_{i=1}^{m} \frac{(P_{1i} - P_{0i})^2}{P_{0i}}},$$

where $P_{0i}$ = the proportion in cell i posited by the null hypothesis,

   $P_{1i}$ = the proportion in cell i posited by the alternate hypothesis and reflects the effect for that cell, and

   m = the number of cells.

Thus, for each cell, the difference between the two hypothetical P's is squared and divided by the null-specified $P_0$; the resulting values are then added over the cells, and the square root taken.

Note the identity in structure of formula (7.2.1) with that of the standard computing formula for $\chi^2$ with frequencies; in w, proportions are used in place of frequencies (for generality), and the population values replace the sample values.[1] Indeed, if the *sample* proportions are used in the formula

---

[1] The technically oriented reader will note that w is simply the square root of the noncentrality parameter, lambda, divided by the total sample size.

in place of the $P_{1i}$'s, and the resulting **w'** is squared and multiplied by **N**, the total sample size, the result is the sample $\chi^2$ value.

**w** varies from zero, when the paired **P**'s in all cells are equal and hence there is no effect and the null hypothesis is true, to an upper limit which depends on the nature of the problem, as is detailed below.

The structure of $\chi^2$ tests on distributions (hence **w**) is "naturally" non-directional. Only when there is **u** = 1 degree of freedom in $\chi^2$, are there only two directions in which discrepancies between null and alternate can occur. With more than 1 **df**, departures can occur in many directions. The results of all these departures from the null are included in the upper tail rejection region, and, as normally used, $\chi^2$ tests do not discriminate among these and are therefore nondirectional. The tests will be so treated here.

7.2.1 CASE 0: **w** AND GOODNESS OF FIT. The null hypothesis for goodness of fit tests is simply:

$$\mathbf{H_0 : P_{01}, P_{02}, P_{03}, \ldots, P_{0m}}, \quad \left( \sum_{i=1}^{m} \mathbf{P_{0i}} = 1 \right),$$

i.e., a specified distribution of proportions in **m** cells, summing to unity. A population of independent observations is posited as falling into **m** mutually exclusive and exhaustive classes with a specified proportion in each.

The source of such null-hypothetical distributions varies in different behavioral science applications. One common example is a test of the hypothesis that a population is normally distributed on a continuous variable **X**. Then, $\mathbf{H_0}$ is the array of proportions in successive step intervals of **X** which would accord with the form of the normal distribution (Hays, 1981, 542–544). For **m** = 9 intervals, the successive $\mathbf{P_{0i}}$ values might be: $\mathbf{H_0}$: .020, .051, .118, .195, .232, .195, .118, .051, .020.

In some areas of behavioral science, a strong theory may yield predicted distributions of populations over relevant classes, or cells. For example, a behavioral geneticist may be enabled by Mendelian theory to predict the ratio of four behavior types resulting from cross-breeding to be 1:3:3:9. The theory would be expressed in proportions in the $\mathbf{H_0}$: .0625, .1875, .1875, .5626 (Edwards, 1972, p. 54f).

Another source of $\mathbf{H_0}$ might be an empirical distribution determined for the population in the past, as in census data. A contemporary sample could be tested against such an $\mathbf{H_0}$ in a study of social or economic change.

The logical structure of many experiments, e.g., those resulting in decisions or the expression of preference among **m** alternatives, suggests a null hypothesis of equiprobability: $\mathbf{H_0 : P_{01} = P_{02} = P_{03} = \cdots = P_{0m}} = 1/\mathbf{m}$. Thus, a study of consumer preference among **m** = 4 advertising displays would posit $\mathbf{H_0 : P_{0i}} = .25$ for **i** = 1, 2, 3, 4.

The test for equiprobability can be seen as a generalization of the test $H_0$: $P = .50$ to which Chapter 5 was devoted. In the present context, the test of Chapter 5 is the test for equiprobability when $m = 2$, where $g = \frac{1}{2}w$.

Furthermore, the Case 0 circumstance for $\chi^2$ tests of frequencies for $m = 2$ is an alternative procedure to the Chapter 6, Case 2 test that the proportion of a population having a given characteristic equals some specified value $c$. In present terms, the same hypothesis is stated as $H_0$: $P_{01} = c$, $P_{02} = 1 - c$.

By whichever of the above relevant approaches an $H_0$ set of $P_{0i}$'s is established, the alternative hypothesis is expressed by a paired set of $P_{1i}$'s and the departure or ES defined by $w$ of formula (7.2.1). It is clear that with no departure, the numerator of each cell's contribution is zero, hence $w = 0$ when there is no effect, i.e., the null hypothesis is true. In general, the maximum value of $w$ in Case 0 applications is infinity. This occurs when the null hypothesis specifies that for any given cell, $P_0 = 0$. If zero values for the $P_{0i}$ are ruled out as inadmissible, $w$ can become as large as we like by defining any $P_0$ value as very small (relative to its fixed paired $P_1$ value).

For the special circumstances of equiprobability in $m$ cells, the maximum value of $w$ is $\sqrt{m - 1}$. Thus, for the $m = 4$ advertising displays, the maximum possible value of $w$, which occurs when all respondents prefer one display, is $\sqrt{4 - 1} = \sqrt{3} = 1.73$.

Despite the general upper limit of infinity, in practice, for sample sizes large enough to yield valid results with the $\chi^2$ test, it is not generally necessary to make provision for $w$ greater than .90 (a long way, indeed, from infinity!).

In Case 0 tests, in general, the degrees of freedom ($u$) for $\chi^2$ is simply $m - 1$. An exception to this rule occurs where additional degrees of freedom are "lost" because of additional parameter estimation. In the normal curve fitting test, for example, where the sample yields estimates of the mean and standard deviation, each estimate costs an additional degree of freedom, so that $u = m - 3$. In the other examples given above, $u$ is always $m - 1$.

In a later section, operationally defined values of $w$ for "small," "medium," and "large" ES will be offered.

7.2.2   CASE 1: $w$ AND CONTINGENCY TESTS. The most frequent application of $\chi^2$ in behavioral science is to what are variously called "contingency," "independence," or "association" tests. They can also be viewed as tests of the equality of two or more distributions over a set of two or more categories.

Consider a circumstance where there are two variables or classification schemes, each made up of mutually exclusive and exhaustive categories.

Call one of the variables **R**, made up of **r** $\geq 2$ categories, and the other **K**, made up of **k** $\geq 2$ categories. If all the members of a population are simultaneously characterized with regard to their category assignment on **R** and **K**, the results can be expressed in a two-way table of dimension **r** $\times$ **k**, with **rk** cells. In each cell, we can write the proportion of observations in the population which it contains. From such a table, one can determine whether **R** is associated with (or contingent upon, or not independent of) **K** in the population, or, equivalently, whether the **r** subpopulations on the **R** variable having differing distributions over the **k** categories of **K**.[2]

For concreteness, consider the cross-classification Table (7.2.1) in which a sub-population has been jointly characterized with regard to sex = **R** (**r** = 2) and political preference = **K** (**k** = 3). Note that the marginal (i.e., total) distribution for sex is .60, .40, and that for political preference .45, .45, .10.

TABLE 7.2.1

$P_1$ VALUES IN A JOINT DISTRIBUTION OF SEX AND
POLITICAL PREFERENCE

|  | Dem. | Rep. | Ind. | Sex marginal |
|---|---|---|---|---|
| Men | .22 | .35 | .03 | .60 |
| Women | .23 | .10 | .07 | .40 |
| Preference marginal | .45 | .45 | .10 | 1.00 |

Note that although the marginal ratio of men to women is .60 : .40 or 3 : 2, the ratio for Republicans is 3.5 : 1, and the Democrats are made up about equally of men and women (i.e., 1 : 1). Similarly, one might note that although there are equal marginal proportions of Democrats and Republicans, there are more Republicans than Democrats among the men and the preference is reversed among the women. This inequality of ratios within a column (or row) of the table with the column (or row) marginal ratios constitutes evidence that **R** and **K** are not independent of each other, or that they are associated.

A formal way to describe this association proceeds by asking the question, "Given the two marginal distributions in this population, what cell values would constitute independence (or no association)?" This is readily found for each cell by multiplying its row marginal proportion by its column marginal proportion. Consider the proportion of men-Democrats which

---

[2] **R** and **K** can be interchanged; the relationships are symmetrical.

would evidence no association: Since .60 of the population are men, and .45 of the population are Democrats, the condition of no association would lead us to expect $(.60)(.45) = .27$ of the population being men-Democrats. The other no-association cell proportions are similarly computed and are given in Table 7.2.2. Note that this operation has resulted in within row (or column) ratios being equal to the row (or column) marginal ratios. In the circumstance described in Table 7.2.2, in contrast to that in Table 7.2.1, given the knowledge of a person's sex, one can make no better a guess as to political preference than doing so without such knowledge. The converse is also true, since the association is symmetric.

TABLE 7.2.2

$P_0$ (No Association) Values in a Joint Distribution
of Sex and Political Preference

|  | Dem. | Rep. | Ind. | Sex marginal |
|---|---|---|---|---|
| Men | .27 | .27 | .06 | .60 |
| Women | .18 | .18 | .04 | .40 |
| Preference marginal | .45 | .45 | .10 | 1.00 |

Although the above has been described in terms of association between **R** and **K**, it could also be understood as an inquiry into whether the different **R** groups (the two sexes) have the same proportional distribution over the various categories of **K** (political preference). In Table 7.2.1, they clearly do not, while in the no-association condition described in Table 7.2.2, they do.[3]

In the analysis of contingency tables, the null hypothesis conventionally tested is that of no association. Thus, for the issue of association between sex and political preference, the null hypothesis is represented by the $P_0$ values in the cells of Table 7.2.2. Small departures from these values would represent weak association (or dependence), large departures strong association. The degree of departure or ES index is given by **w**, as defined in formula (7.2.1). It is applied in **r** × **k** contingency tables in the same way as in goodness of fit tests. Each of the **rk** = **m** cells has a null-hypothetical $P_0$ value given by the product of the marginal proportions (such as in Table 7.2.2) and an alternate-hypothetical $P_1$ value reflecting the association posited

---

[3] Again we note that **R** and **K** can be interchanged.

(as in Table 7.2.1). For the problem considered, using the values in these tables,

$$\mathbf{w} = \sqrt{\sum_{i=1}^{rk=6} \frac{(\mathbf{P}_{1i} - \mathbf{P}_{0i})^2}{\mathbf{P}_{0i}}} = \sqrt{\frac{(.22 - .27)^2}{.27} + \frac{(.35 - .27)^2}{.27} + \cdots + \frac{(.07 - .04)^2}{.04}}$$

$$= \sqrt{.0093 + .0237 + .0150 + .0139 + .0356 + .0225}$$

$$= \sqrt{.1200} = .346.$$

Thus $\mathbf{w} = .346$ indexes the amount of departure from no association, or the degree of association between sex and political preference in this population. Equivalently it can be understood as indexing the difference between men and women in their distribution over political preference.

In Case 1 tests, the number of degrees of freedom associated with the $\chi^2$ for an $\mathbf{r} \times \mathbf{k}$ contingency table is given by

(7.2.2)                          $$\mathbf{u} = (\mathbf{r} - 1)(\mathbf{k} - 1).$$

For the $2 \times 3$ table under consideration, $\mathbf{u} = (2 - 1)(3 - 1) = (1)(2) = 2$. Because the marginals of both rows and columns are fixed, it is *not* the number of cells less one, as in Case 0.[4]

In contingency tables, the maximum value of $\mathbf{w}$ depends upon $\mathbf{r}$, $\mathbf{k}$, and the marginal conditions. If $\mathbf{r}$ and $\mathbf{k}$ are assigned so that $\mathbf{r}$ is not larger than $\mathbf{k}$ (this will be assumed throughout) and no restriction is put on the marginals, maximum $\mathbf{w}$ is $\sqrt{\mathbf{r} - 1}$. Thus, in the example, no $\mathbf{P}_1$ values can be written which yield $\mathbf{w}$ greater than $\sqrt{2 - 1} = 1$. If for both marginals the classes have equal proportions, i.e., $1/\mathbf{r}$ for one set and $1/\mathbf{k}$ for the other, maximum $\mathbf{w} = \sqrt{\mathbf{r}(\mathbf{r} - 1)/\mathbf{k}}$.

**w** AND OTHER MEASURES OF ASSOCIATION.   Although $\mathbf{w}$ is a useful ES index in the power analysis of contingency tables, as a measure of association it lacks familiarity and convenience. As noted above, its maximum is $\sqrt{\mathbf{r} - 1}$; hence $\mathbf{w}$ varies with the size of the smaller of the table's two dimensions.

There are several indices of association for $\mathbf{r} \times \mathbf{k}$ contingency tables which are familiar to behavioral scientists and which are simply related to $\mathbf{w}$. These will be briefly described, and formulas relating them to $\mathbf{w}$ will be given. In Table 7.2.3, for the convenience of the reader, the equivalent values for these other indices are given for the values of $\mathbf{w}$ provided in the power and sample size tables in this chapter. The formulas and table make possible indexing ES in terms of these other measures.

---

[4] For example, note that in Table 7.2.1, after one has specified the 2 ($=\mathbf{u}$) values .22 and .35, all the other cell values are determined by the requirement that they sum to the row and column totals.

TABLE 7.2.3

EQUIVALENTS OF **w** IN TERMS OF **C**, $\phi$, AND $\phi'$

| w | C | r = 2* | 3 | 4 | 5 | 6 |
|---|---|--------|---|---|---|---|
| | | | | $\phi'$ | | |
| .10 | .100 | .10 | .071 | .058 | .050 | .045 |
| .20 | .196 | .20 | .141 | .115 | .100 | .089 |
| .30 | .287 | .30 | .212 | .173 | .150 | .134 |
| .40 | .371 | .40 | .283 | .231 | .200 | .179 |
| .50 | .447 | .50 | .354 | .289 | .250 | .224 |
| .60 | .514 | .60 | .424 | .346 | .300 | .268 |
| .70 | .573 | .70 | .495 | .404 | .350 | .313 |
| .80 | .625 | .80 | .566 | .462 | .400 | .358 |
| .90 | .669 | .90 | .636 | .520 | .450 | .402 |

* This column gives the equivalents in terms of $\phi$, the product-moment correlation coefficient for the fourfold ($2 \times 2$) table.

*Contingency Coefficient*, **C**. The most widely used measure of association in contingency tables is **C**, Pearson's coefficient of contingency (Hays, 1981, p. 558). The relationship among **C**, $\chi^2$, and **w** is given by

$$(7.2.3) \qquad \mathbf{C} = \sqrt{\frac{\chi^2}{\chi^2 + \mathbf{N}}} = \sqrt{\frac{\mathbf{w}^2}{\mathbf{w}^2 + 1}}$$

(The first expression gives the *sample* **C** value, the second that of the population.)

For the population data of Table 7.2.1, for example, where $\mathbf{w}^2 = .346^2 = .12$, the **C** value equals $\sqrt{.12/(.12 + 1)} = \sqrt{.12/1.12} = .33$.

To express **w** in terms of **C**,

$$(7.2.4) \qquad \mathbf{w} = \sqrt{\frac{\mathbf{C}^2}{1 - \mathbf{C}^2}}.$$

**C** = 0 when **w** = 0, indicating no association. The maximum value of **C** is not 1, but increases towards 1, as maximum **w** increases. We have seen that maximum **w** equals $\sqrt{\mathbf{r} - 1}$. Therefore, substituting in (7.2.3), maximum **C** = $\sqrt{(\mathbf{r} - 1)/\mathbf{r}}$. For example, a $2 \times \mathbf{k}$ table ($\mathbf{k} \geq 2$) has a maximum **C** of $\sqrt{(2 - 1)/2} = \sqrt{\frac{1}{2}} = .71$, while a $5 \times \mathbf{k}$ table ($\mathbf{k} \geq 5$) has a maximum **C** of $\sqrt{(5 - 1)/5} = \sqrt{4/5} = .89$. This varying upper limit dependency on **r** is generally considered a deficiency in the measure, becoming particularly awkward when one wishes to compare **C** values coming from tables of different size.

Note the relationship between **w** and **C** in Table 7.2.3. As **w** increases, **C** increases, but with progressively smaller increments.

$\phi$, *The Fourfold Point Correlation Coefficient.* Among contingency tables, the most frequently analyzed in behavioral science is the 2 × 2 table. In 2 × 2 tables, one can conceive of each of the **R** and **K** dichotomous dimensions as scaled 0 for one category and 1 for the other (or any other distinct values) and compute a product-moment correlation coefficient between the two dimensions. In such circumstances the correlation coefficient[5] is called $\phi$ (see Cohen & Cohen, 1983, pp. 65–66; Guilford & Fruchter, 1981, pp. 316–318). Its relationship to **w** is one of identity:

$$(7.2.5) \qquad \phi = \sqrt{\frac{\chi^2}{\mathbf{N}}} = \mathbf{w}.$$

(The first expression is the *sample* $\phi$ value, the second that of the population.)

Since $\phi$ is a bonafide product moment correlation coefficient, $\phi^2$ is interpretable as the proportion of variance (PV) shared by the two variables **R** and **K** (see Chapter 3; also Chapters 2, 4, 6, 11). Thus, for the 2 × 2 table, $\mathbf{w}^2$ gives directly the PV shared by the two dichotomies.

*Cramér's $\phi'$.* A useful generalization of $\phi$ for contingency tables of any dimensionality is provided by Cramér's statistic $\phi'$ (Hays, 1981, p. 557; Blalock, 1972, p. 297);

$$(7.2.6) \qquad \phi' = \sqrt{\frac{\chi^2}{\mathbf{N}(\mathbf{r} - 1)}} = \frac{\mathbf{w}}{\sqrt{\mathbf{r} - 1}},$$

where **r** is, as before, not greater than **k**. (Again, the first expression gives the sample value and the second the population value.) **w** in terms of $\phi'$ and **r** is given by

$$(7.2.7) \qquad \mathbf{w} = \phi'\sqrt{\mathbf{r} - 1}.$$

Naturally, $\phi'$ cannot be interpreted as a product-moment correlation, since neither **R** nor **K** is, in general, metric or even ordered. But it does have a range between zero and a uniform upper limit of one. The latter is true because, as we have seen, the upper limit of **w** in a contingency table is $\sqrt{\mathbf{r} - 1}$.

---

[5] Not to be confused with the same symbol, $\phi$, to indicate the arcsine transformation of **P** in Chapter 6.

That $\phi'$ is a generalization of $\phi$ can be seen when we note that for a $2 \times 2$ table, $r = 2$; formula (7.2.6) then gives $\phi' = w/\sqrt{2-1} = w \ (=\phi)$. This is why the $\phi$ equivalents of Table 7.2.3 are given under $\phi'$ for $r = 2$. The latter is more general, since it applies not only to $2 \times 2$ tables but to $2 \times k$ tables. For example, for the association between sex and political preference in Table 7.2.1, a $2 \times 3$ table, $\phi' = .346/\sqrt{2-1} = .346$.

7.2.3  "SMALL," "MEDIUM," AND "LARGE" $w$ VALUES. Since $w$ is not a familiar index, it becomes particularly important to have some guide to its magnitude for the purpose of power analysis or the estimation of necessary sample size or both. The best guide here, as always, is the development of some sense of magnitude *ad hoc*, for a particular problem or a particular field. Since it is a function of proportions, the investigator should generally be able to express the size of the effect he wishes to be able to detect by writing a set of alternate-hypothetical proportions for either Case 0 or Case 1, and, with the null-hypothetical proportions, compute $w$. Some experimentation along these lines should provide one with a "feel" for $w$.

As in the other chapters, values of $w$ for "small," "medium," and "large" ES are offered to serve as conventions for these qualitative adjectives. Their use requires particular caution, since, apart from their possible inaptness in any given substantive context, what is subjectively the "same" degree of departure (Case 0) or degree of association (Case 1) may yield varying $w$ as the size of $r$, $k$, or $u$ (degrees of freedom) changes, and conversely. Note, for example, in Table 7.2.3, that for constant $e$, $\phi'$ decreases as $r$ increases. The investigator is best advised to use the conventional definitions as a general frame of reference for ES and not to take them too literally.

SMALL EFFECT SIZE: $w = .10$. For Case 0 goodness of fit applications, $w = .10$ for the following $H_0$, $H_1$ pairs, where in each instance $H_0$ posits equiprobability for the $m$ cells, and the $H_1$ values are placed at equal intervals and symmetrically about $1/m$:

| $m =$ | 2 | $H_0$: | .50 | .50 |
| | | $H_1$: | .45 | .55 | (same as $g = .05$; see Section 5.2) |

| $m =$ | 3 | $H_0$: | .333 | .333 | .333 |
| | | $H_1$: | .293 | .333 | .374 |

| $m =$ | 4 | $H_0$: | .250 | .250 | .250 | .250 |
| | | $H_1$: | .216 | .239 | .261 | .284 |

| $m =$ | 5 | $H_0$: | .200 | .200 | .200 | .200 | .200 |
| | | $H_1$: | .172 | .186 | .200 | .214 | .228 |

| $m =$ | 10 | $H_0$: | .100 | .100 | .100 | .100 | .100 | .100 | .100 | .100 | .100 | .100 |
| | | $H_1$: | .084 | .088 | .091 | .095 | .098 | .102 | .105 | .109 | .112 | .116 |

The illustration of Case 1 instances of **w** = .10 would demand the presentation of several cumbersome contingency tables. Instead, attention is called to Table 7.2.3, where equivalents of **w** = .10 for **C**, $\phi$, and $\phi'$ are given. Note that what is defined as a small degree of association implies a **C** of .100, and for a 2 × 2 table, a $\phi$ also of .100. For larger tables, Cramér's $\phi'$ decreases, so that when the smaller dimension (of **r** categories) is 6, $\phi' = .045$.

MEDIUM EFFECT SIZE: **w** = .30. To illustrate a medium ES in Case 0 applications, the following **H₀**, **H₁** pairs are presented in all of which **w** = .30:

**m** = 2  **H₀**: .50  .50
**H₁**: .35  .65  (same as **g** = .15; see Section 5.2)

**m** = 3  **H₀**: .333  .333  .333
**H₁**: .211  .333  .456

**m** = 4  **H₀**: .250  .250  .250  .250
**H₁**: .149  .216  .284  .351

**m** = 5  **H₀**: .200  .200  .200  .200  .200
**H₁**: .115  .158  .200  .242  .285

**m** = 10  **H₀**: .100  .100  .100  .100  .100  .100  .100  .100  .100  .100
**H₁**: .053  .063  .074  .084  .095  .105  .116  .126  .137  .147

For contingency tables (Case 1) we note, as before, the equivalences from Table 7.2.3. Equivalent to **w** = .30 are **C** = .287 and the fourfold $\phi$ = **w** = .10. For $\phi'$ in larger tables, constant **w** = .30 implies diminishing values, e.g., $\phi' = .134$ for **r** = 6.

The **P₁** values relating sex to political preference of Table 7.2.1 yielded an **w** = .346, slightly above our operational definition of a medium effect.

LARGE EFFECT SIZE: **w** = .50. As before, we here illustrate the large ES for Case 0 by a series of **H₀**, **H₁** pairs for each of which **w** = .50:

**m** = 2  **H₀**: .50  .50
**H₁**: .25  .75  (same as **g** = .25; see Section 5.2)

**m** = 3  **H₀**: .333  .333  .333
**H₁**: .129  .333  .537

**m** = 4  **H₀**: .250  .250  .250  .250
**H₁**: .082  .194  .306  .418

**m** = 5  **H₀**: .200  .200  .200  .200  .200
**H₁**: .059  .129  .200  .271  .341

**m** = 10  **H₀**: .100  .100  .100  .100  .100  .100  .100  .100  .100 . 100
**H₁**: .022  .039  .056  .074  .091  .109  .126  .143  .161  .178

For contingency tables, a large degree of association as defined here implies $C = .447$ and for the $2 \times 2$ table, $\phi = w = .50$ (Table 7.2.3). For larger tables, the $\phi'$ values decrease with constant $w = .50$ as $r$ increases, e.g., for $r = 6$, $\phi' = .224$.

SOME FURTHER COMMENTS ON ES AND $w$. The Case 0 illustrations above were all for $H_1$ of an equally spaced departure from an $H_0$ of equiprobability. This was done for the sake of simplicity, but should not mislead the reader. *Any* full set of proportions can be tested as an $H_0$, and $w$ will index the departure of *any* $H_1$ from it. Thus, when we define $w = .30$ as a medium departure of $H_1$ from $H_0$, or ES, any discrepancy yielding $w = .30$ is so defined. For example, for $m = 4$, the following $H_0$, $H_1$ pair also represents an ES of $w = .30$ and their detectability by means of a $\chi^2$ test is the same as for the $m = 4$ illustration above:

$$H_0: \quad .250 \quad .250 \quad .250 \quad .250$$
$$H_1: \quad .380 \quad .207 \quad .207 \quad .207$$

This is a $w = .30$ departure from equiprobability in which the effect is concentrated in the first category, the remainder being equiprobable.

The following pair illustrates yet another $w = .30$ departure from equiprobability for $m = 4$, one in which the effect is divided equally between the first two categories, and between the last two:

$$H_0: \quad .250 \quad .250 \quad .250 \quad .250$$
$$H_1: \quad .325 \quad .325 \quad .175 \quad .175$$

Since the departure from $H_0$ may occur in many ways, and since $H_0$ may itself occasionally represent other than an equiprobable distribution, clearly any given value of $w$ may arise from a multiplicity of patterns of discrepancies. It is the size of $w$ which is important. An investigator may specify an $H_0$ appropriate to his purpose, and posit an $H_1$ which he believes to be the true state of nature. He then obtains some specific $w$, say .30. He may be wrong about the specific $H_1$ set of $P_1$ values he has posited, but the power (or sample size) he determines from the tables for $w = .30$ will hold for *any* $H_1$ which yields $w = .30$. Thus, however they may have come about, his inference can be viewed as testing $H_0: w = 0$ against $H_1: w = .30$.

We reiterate a word of caution about the use of constant $w$ values to define a given level of departure, such as the operational definitions of "small," "medium," and "large" ES as applied to Case 1 contingency tests. It was noted several times above that constant $w$ implies a decreasing value for $\phi'$ as table size (specifically $r$) increases (see Table 7.2.3).[6] If an investigator thinks of amount of association in terms of $\phi'$, then clearly he cannot use the

---

[6] This is also true for a measure of association not discussed here. Tschuprow's $T$ (Blalock, 1972, p. 296). The remarks about $\phi$ in this context hold also for $T$.

operational definitions suggested above, or any other pegged to a constant **w**. Thus, for example, if he is prepared to define a "large" amount of association as a $\phi' = .40$, this implies varying **w** depending on **r**: it would be **w** = .40 for a 2 × **k** table, **w** = .57 for a 3 × **k** table, $\cdots$ **w** = .89 for a 6 × **k** table [formula (7.2.7) and Table 7.2.3].

## 7.3  POWER TABLES

The power tables for this section are given on pages 228–248.

The 42 tables in this section are used when an overall sample size **N** is specified together with the degrees of freedom (**u**), the significance criterion **a**, and the ES, **w**; the tables then yield power values. As throughout this handbook, power tables find their major use after an experiment has been performed. They can also be used in experimental planning by varying **N** (and/or ES, and/or **a**) to study the consequences to power of such alternatives.

Tables list values for **a**, **u**, **w**, and **N**:

*1. Significance Criterion*, **a**. Since $\chi^2$ is naturally nondirectional (see above, Section 7.2), 14 tables (for varying **u**) are provided at each of the **a** levels .01, .05, and .10.

*2. Degrees of Freedom*, **u**. At each **a** level, a table is provided for each of the following 14 values of **u**: 1 (1) 10, 12 (4) 24. They have been selected so as to cover most problems involving $\chi^2$ comparisons of proportions (or frequencies) likely to be encountered in practice. In particular, since for **r** × **k** contingency tables, **u** = (**r** − 1)(**k** − 1), the larger values of **u** (12, 16, 20, 24) were chosen so as to have many factors. Thus, tables whose **r** × **k** are 2 × 25, 3 × 13, 4 × 9, and 5 × 7 all have **u** = 24. When necessary, linear interpolation between **u** values in the 10–24 range will yield quite adequate approximations.

*3. Effect Size*, **w**. For either Case 0 or Case 1 applications, **w** as defined in formula (7.2.1) provides the ES index. Provision is made for finding nine values of **w**: .10, (.10) .90. As a frame of reference for ES magnitude, conventional definitions have been offered above, as follows:

small:    **w** = .10,
medium:  **w** = .30,
large:    **w** = .50.

*4. Sample Size*, **N**. This is the *total* number of cases in the comparison. Provision is made for **N** = 25 (5) 50 (10) 100 (20) 200 (50) 400 (100) 1000.

Table 7.3.1

Power of $\chi^2$ test at $a = .01$, $u = 1$

| N | .10 | .20 | .30 | .40 | .50 | .60 | .70 | .80 | .90 |
|---|-----|-----|-----|-----|-----|-----|-----|-----|-----|
| | | | | | w | | | | |
| 25 | 02 | 06 | 14 | 28 | 47 | 66 | 82 | 92 | 97 |
| 30 | 02 | 07 | 17 | 36 | 56 | 76 | 90 | 96 | 99 |
| 35 | 02 | 08 | 21 | 42 | 65 | 83 | 94 | 98 | * |
| 40 | 03 | 10 | 25 | 48 | 72 | 89 | 97 | 99 | |
| 45 | 03 | 11 | 29 | 54 | 78 | 93 | 98 | * | |
| 50 | 03 | 12 | 32 | 60 | 83 | 95 | 99 | | |
| 60 | 04 | 15 | 40 | 70 | 90 | 98 | * | | |
| 70 | 04 | 18 | 47 | 78 | 95 | 99 | | | |
| 80 | 05 | 21 | 54 | 84 | 97 | * | | | |
| 90 | 05 | 25 | 61 | 89 | 98 | | | | |
| 100 | 06 | 28 | 66 | 92 | 99 | | | | |
| 120 | 07 | 36 | 76 | 96 | * | | | | |
| 140 | 08 | 42 | 83 | 98 | | | | | |
| 160 | 10 | 48 | 89 | 99 | | | | | |
| 180 | 11 | 54 | 93 | * | | | | | |
| 200 | 12 | 60 | 95 | | | | | | |
| 250 | 16 | 72 | 98 | | | | | | |
| 300 | 20 | 81 | * | | | | | | |
| 350 | 24 | 88 | | | | | | | |
| 400 | 28 | 92 | | | | | | | |
| 500 | 37 | 97 | | | | | | | |
| 600 | 45 | 99 | | | | | | | |
| 700 | 53 | * | | | | | | | |
| 800 | 60 | | | | | | | | |
| 900 | 66 | | | | | | | | |
| 1000 | 72 | | | | | | | | |

Table 7.3.2

Power of $\chi^2$ test at $a = .01$, $u = 2$

| N | .10 | .20 | .30 | .40 | .50 | .60 | .70 | .80 | .90 |
|---|-----|-----|-----|-----|-----|-----|-----|-----|-----|
| | | | | | w | | | | |
| 25 | 02 | 04 | 10 | 20 | 36 | 55 | 73 | 87 | 95 |
| 30 | 02 | 05 | 12 | 27 | 45 | 66 | 83 | 93 | 98 |
| 35 | 02 | 06 | 14 | 32 | 54 | 75 | 89 | 97 | 99 |
| 40 | 02 | 07 | 18 | 37 | 61 | 82 | 94 | 98 | * |
| 45 | 02 | 07 | 21 | 43 | 68 | 87 | 96 | 99 | |
| 50 | 02 | 08 | 24 | 49 | 74 | 91 | 98 | * | |
| 60 | 03 | 11 | 30 | 59 | 84 | 96 | 99 | | |
| 70 | 03 | 13 | 37 | 68 | 90 | 98 | * | | |
| 80 | 03 | 15 | 43 | 76 | 94 | 99 | | | |
| 90 | 04 | 18 | 49 | 82 | 97 | * | | | |
| 100 | 04 | 20 | 55 | 87 | 98 | | | | |
| 120 | 05 | 27 | 66 | 93 | 99 | | | | |
| 140 | 06 | 32 | 75 | 97 | * | | | | |
| 160 | 07 | 37 | 82 | 98 | | | | | |
| 180 | 07 | 43 | 87 | 99 | | | | | |
| 200 | 08 | 49 | 91 | * | | | | | |
| 250 | 11 | 61 | 97 | | | | | | |
| 300 | 14 | 72 | 99 | | | | | | |
| 350 | 17 | 80 | * | | | | | | |
| 400 | 20 | 87 | | | | | | | |
| 500 | 27 | 94 | | | | | | | |
| 600 | 35 | 98 | | | | | | | |
| 700 | 42 | 99 | | | | | | | |
| 800 | 49 | * | | | | | | | |
| 900 | 55 | | | | | | | | |
| 1000 | 61 | | | | | | | | |

Table 7.3.3

Power of $\chi^2$ test at $a = .01$, $u = 3$

| N | .10 | .20 | .30 | .40 | .50 | .60 | .70 | .80 | .90 |
|---|---|---|---|---|---|---|---|---|---|
| 25 | 01 | 03 | 08 | 16 | 30 | 48 | 66 | 82 | 92 |
| 30 | 02 | 04 | 10 | 22 | 38 | 59 | 77 | 90 | 96 |
| 35 | 02 | 05 | 12 | 26 | 46 | 68 | 85 | 95 | 99 |
| 40 | 02 | 05 | 14 | 31 | 54 | 76 | 91 | 97 | 99 |
| 45 | 02 | 06 | 17 | 36 | 61 | 82 | 94 | 99 | * |
| 50 | 02 | 07 | 19 | 42 | 68 | 87 | 97 | 99 | |
| 60 | 02 | 08 | 25 | 52 | 78 | 94 | 99 | * | |
| 70 | 03 | 10 | 31 | 61 | 86 | 97 | * | | |
| 80 | 03 | 12 | 36 | 69 | 91 | 99 | | | |
| 90 | 03 | 14 | 42 | 76 | 95 | 99 | | | |
| 100 | 03 | 16 | 48 | 82 | 97 | * | | | |
| 120 | 04 | 22 | 59 | 90 | 99 | | | | |
| 140 | 05 | 26 | 68 | 95 | * | | | | |
| 160 | 05 | 31 | 76 | 97 | | | | | |
| 180 | 06 | 36 | 82 | 99 | | | | | |
| 200 | 07 | 42 | 87 | 99 | | | | | |
| 250 | 09 | 54 | 95 | * | | | | | |
| 300 | 11 | 65 | 98 | | | | | | |
| 350 | 14 | 74 | 99 | | | | | | |
| 400 | 16 | 82 | * | | | | | | |
| 500 | 22 | 91 | | | | | | | |
| 600 | 29 | 96 | | | | | | | |
| 700 | 35 | 98 | | | | | | | |
| 800 | 42 | 99 | | | | | | | |
| 900 | 48 | * | | | | | | | |
| 1000 | 54 | | | | | | | | |

Table 7.3.4

Power of $\chi^2$ test at $a = .01$, $u = 4$

| N | .10 | .20 | .30 | .40 | .50 | .60 | .70 | .80 | .90 |
|---|---|---|---|---|---|---|---|---|---|
| 25 | 01 | 03 | 07 | 14 | 26 | 43 | 61 | 77 | 89 |
| 30 | 01 | 03 | 08 | 18 | 34 | 53 | 72 | 87 | 95 |
| 35 | 02 | 04 | 10 | 22 | 41 | 63 | 81 | 93 | 98 |
| 40 | 02 | 04 | 12 | 27 | 49 | 71 | 88 | 96 | 99 |
| 45 | 02 | 05 | 14 | 32 | 56 | 78 | 92 | 98 | * |
| 50 | 02 | 06 | 16 | 37 | 62 | 84 | 95 | 99 | |
| 60 | 02 | 07 | 21 | 46 | 74 | 91 | 98 | * | |
| 70 | 02 | 09 | 26 | 55 | 82 | 96 | 99 | | |
| 80 | 02 | 10 | 32 | 64 | 89 | 98 | * | | |
| 90 | 03 | 12 | 37 | 71 | 93 | 99 | | | |
| 100 | 03 | 14 | 43 | 77 | 96 | * | | | |
| 120 | 03 | 18 | 53 | 87 | 98 | | | | |
| 140 | 04 | 22 | 63 | 93 | * | | | | |
| 160 | 04 | 27 | 71 | 96 | | | | | |
| 180 | 05 | 32 | 78 | 98 | | | | | |
| 200 | 06 | 37 | 84 | 99 | | | | | |
| 250 | 07 | 49 | 93 | * | | | | | |
| 300 | 09 | 60 | 97 | | | | | | |
| 350 | 12 | 69 | 99 | | | | | | |
| 400 | 14 | 77 | * | | | | | | |
| 500 | 19 | 89 | | | | | | | |
| 600 | 25 | 95 | | | | | | | |
| 700 | 31 | 98 | | | | | | | |
| 800 | 37 | 99 | | | | | | | |
| 900 | 43 | * | | | | | | | |
| 1000 | 49 | | | | | | | | |

Table 7.3.6

## Power of $\chi^2$ test at $a = .01$, $u = 6$

| N | .10 | .20 | .30 | .40 | .50 | .60 | .70 | .80 | .90 |
|---|---|---|---|---|---|---|---|---|---|
| | | | | | w | | | | |
| 25 | 01 | 02 | 05 | 11 | 21 | 35 | 53 | 70 | 84 |
| 30 | 01 | 03 | 07 | 14 | 27 | 45 | 64 | 81 | 92 |
| 35 | 01 | 03 | 08 | 18 | 34 | 54 | 74 | 89 | 96 |
| 40 | 01 | 04 | 10 | 21 | 41 | 63 | 82 | 93 | 98 |
| 45 | 02 | 04 | 11 | 25 | 47 | 71 | 88 | 96 | 99 |
| 50 | 02 | 05 | 13 | 30 | 54 | 77 | 92 | 98 | * |
| 60 | 02 | 06 | 17 | 38 | 66 | 87 | 97 | * | |
| 70 | 02 | 07 | 21 | 47 | 76 | 93 | 99 | | |
| 80 | 02 | 08 | 25 | 55 | 83 | 96 | * | | |
| 90 | 02 | 10 | 30 | 63 | 89 | 98 | | | |
| 100 | 02 | 11 | 35 | 70 | 93 | 99 | | | |
| 120 | 03 | 14 | 45 | 81 | 97 | * | | | |
| 140 | 03 | 18 | 54 | 89 | 99 | | | | |
| 160 | 03 | 21 | 63 | 93 | * | | | | |
| 180 | 04 | 25 | 71 | 96 | | | | | |
| 200 | 05 | 30 | 77 | 98 | | | | | |
| 250 | 06 | 41 | 89 | * | | | | | |
| 300 | 07 | 51 | 95 | | | | | | |
| 350 | 09 | 61 | 98 | | | | | | |
| 400 | 11 | 70 | 99 | | | | | | |
| 500 | 15 | 83 | * | | | | | | |
| 600 | 19 | 91 | | | | | | | |
| 700 | 24 | 96 | | | | | | | |
| 800 | 30 | 98 | | | | | | | |
| 900 | 35 | 99 | | | | | | | |
| 1000 | 41 | * | | | | | | | |

Table 7.3.5

## Power of $\chi^2$ test at $a = .01$, $u = 5$

| N | .10 | .20 | .30 | .40 | .50 | .60 | .70 | .80 | .90 |
|---|---|---|---|---|---|---|---|---|---|
| | | | | | w | | | | |
| 25 | 01 | 03 | 06 | 12 | 23 | 38 | 56 | 74 | 86 |
| 30 | 01 | 03 | 07 | 16 | 30 | 49 | 68 | 84 | 93 |
| 35 | 01 | 03 | 09 | 20 | 37 | 58 | 78 | 91 | 97 |
| 40 | 02 | 04 | 10 | 24 | 44 | 67 | 85 | 95 | 99 |
| 45 | 02 | 04 | 12 | 28 | 51 | 74 | 90 | 97 | 99 |
| 50 | 02 | 05 | 14 | 33 | 58 | 80 | 94 | 99 | * |
| 60 | 02 | 06 | 19 | 44 | 70 | 89 | 98 | * | |
| 70 | 02 | 07 | 23 | 51 | 79 | 94 | 99 | | |
| 80 | 02 | 09 | 28 | 59 | 86 | 97 | * | | |
| 90 | 02 | 10 | 33 | 67 | 91 | 99 | | | |
| 100 | 03 | 12 | 38 | 74 | 94 | 99 | | | |
| 120 | 03 | 16 | 49 | 84 | 98 | * | | | |
| 140 | 03 | 20 | 58 | 91 | 99 | | | | |
| 160 | 04 | 24 | 67 | 95 | * | | | | |
| 180 | 04 | 28 | 74 | 97 | | | | | |
| 200 | 05 | 33 | 80 | 99 | | | | | |
| 250 | 07 | 44 | 91 | * | | | | | |
| 300 | 08 | 55 | 96 | | | | | | |
| 350 | 10 | 65 | 98 | | | | | | |
| 400 | 12 | 74 | 99 | | | | | | |
| 500 | 17 | 86 | * | | | | | | |
| 600 | 22 | 93 | | | | | | | |
| 700 | 27 | 97 | | | | | | | |
| 800 | 33 | 99 | | | | | | | |
| 900 | 38 | 99 | | | | | | | |
| 1000 | 44 | * | | | | | | | |

Table 7.3.7

Power of $\chi^2$ test at $a = .01$, $u = 7$

| N | | | | | w | | | | |
|---|---|---|---|---|---|---|---|---|---|
| | .10 | .20 | .30 | .40 | .50 | .60 | .70 | .80 | .90 |
| 25 | 01 | 02 | 05 | 10 | 19 | 32 | 49 | 67 | 81 |
| 30 | 01 | 03 | 06 | 13 | 25 | 42 | 61 | 78 | 90 |
| 35 | 01 | 03 | 07 | 16 | 31 | 51 | 71 | 87 | 95 |
| 40 | 01 | 03 | 08 | 19 | 37 | 60 | 79 | 92 | 98 |
| 45 | 02 | 04 | 10 | 23 | 44 | 67 | 86 | 95 | 99 |
| 50 | 02 | 04 | 12 | 27 | 50 | 74 | 90 | 98 | * |
| 60 | 02 | 05 | 15 | 35 | 62 | 85 | 96 | 99 | |
| 70 | 02 | 06 | 19 | 44 | 72 | 91 | 98 | * | |
| 80 | 02 | 07 | 23 | 52 | 81 | 95 | 99 | | |
| 90 | 02 | 08 | 28 | 60 | 87 | 98 | * | | |
| 100 | 02 | 10 | 32 | 67 | 91 | 99 | | | |
| 120 | 03 | 13 | 42 | 78 | 96 | * | | | |
| 140 | 03 | 16 | 51 | 87 | 99 | | | | |
| 160 | 03 | 19 | 60 | 92 | * | | | | |
| 180 | 04 | 23 | 67 | 95 | | | | | |
| 200 | 04 | 27 | 74 | 98 | | | | | |
| 250 | 05 | 37 | 87 | * | | | | | |
| 300 | 07 | 48 | 94 | | | | | | |
| 350 | 08 | 58 | 97 | | | | | | |
| 400 | 10 | 67 | 99 | | | | | | |
| 500 | 13 | 81 | * | | | | | | |
| 600 | 18 | 90 | | | | | | | |
| 700 | 22 | 95 | | | | | | | |
| 800 | 27 | 98 | | | | | | | |
| 900 | 32 | 99 | | | | | | | |
| 1000 | 37 | * | | | | | | | |

Table 7.3.8

Power of $\chi^2$ test at $a = .01$, $u = 8$

| N | | | | | w | | | | |
|---|---|---|---|---|---|---|---|---|---|
| | .10 | .20 | .30 | .40 | .50 | .60 | .70 | .80 | .90 |
| 25 | 01 | 02 | 04 | 09 | 17 | 30 | 46 | 64 | 79 |
| 30 | 01 | 02 | 05 | 12 | 23 | 39 | 58 | 75 | 88 |
| 35 | 01 | 03 | 07 | 15 | 29 | 48 | 68 | 84 | 94 |
| 40 | 01 | 03 | 08 | 18 | 35 | 57 | 77 | 91 | 97 |
| 45 | 01 | 03 | 09 | 21 | 41 | 64 | 84 | 95 | 99 |
| 50 | 02 | 04 | 11 | 25 | 47 | 72 | 89 | 97 | 99 |
| 60 | 02 | 05 | 14 | 33 | 59 | 83 | 95 | 99 | * |
| 70 | 02 | 06 | 17 | 41 | 70 | 90 | 98 | * | |
| 80 | 02 | 07 | 21 | 49 | 78 | 95 | 99 | | |
| 90 | 02 | 08 | 25 | 57 | 85 | 97 | * | | |
| 100 | 02 | 09 | 30 | 64 | 90 | 99 | | | |
| 120 | 02 | 12 | 39 | 75 | 96 | * | | | |
| 140 | 03 | 15 | 48 | 84 | 98 | | | | |
| 160 | 03 | 18 | 57 | 91 | 99 | | | | |
| 180 | 03 | 21 | 64 | 95 | * | | | | |
| 200 | 04 | 25 | 72 | 97 | | | | | |
| 250 | 05 | 35 | 85 | 99 | | | | | |
| 300 | 06 | 45 | 93 | * | | | | | |
| 350 | 07 | 55 | 97 | | | | | | |
| 400 | 09 | 64 | 99 | | | | | | |
| 500 | 12 | 78 | * | | | | | | |
| 600 | 16 | 88 | | | | | | | |
| 700 | 20 | 94 | | | | | | | |
| 800 | 25 | 97 | | | | | | | |
| 900 | 30 | 99 | | | | | | | |
| 1000 | 35 | 99 | | | | | | | |

Table 7.3.9

Power of $\chi^2$ test at $a = .01$, $u = 9$

| N | .10 | .20 | .30 | .40 | .50 | .60 | .70 | .80 | .90 |
|---|-----|-----|-----|-----|-----|-----|-----|-----|-----|
| 25 | 01 | 02 | 04 | 08 | 16 | 28 | 44 | 61 | 77 |
| 30 | 01 | 02 | 05 | 11 | 21 | 36 | 55 | 73 | 87 |
| 35 | 01 | 03 | 06 | 13 | 27 | 45 | 66 | 82 | 93 |
| 40 | 01 | 03 | 07 | 16 | 33 | 54 | 74 | 89 | 97 |
| 45 | 01 | 03 | 08 | 20 | 39 | 62 | 82 | 94 | 98 |
| 50 | 01 | 04 | 10 | 23 | 45 | 69 | 87 | 96 | 99 |
| 60 | 02 | 04 | 13 | 31 | 57 | 80 | 94 | 99 | * |
| 70 | 02 | 05 | 16 | 38 | 67 | 88 | 98 | * | |
| 80 | 02 | 06 | 20 | 46 | 76 | 94 | 99 | | |
| 90 | 02 | 07 | 24 | 54 | 83 | 97 | * | | |
| 100 | 02 | 08 | 28 | 61 | 88 | 98 | | | |
| 120 | 02 | 11 | 36 | 73 | 95 | * | | | |
| 140 | 03 | 13 | 45 | 82 | 98 | | | | |
| 160 | 03 | 16 | 54 | 89 | 99 | | | | |
| 180 | 03 | 20 | 62 | 94 | * | | | | |
| 200 | 04 | 23 | 69 | 96 | | | | | |
| 250 | 05 | 33 | 83 | 99 | | | | | |
| 300 | 06 | 42 | 91 | * | | | | | |
| 350 | 07 | 52 | 96 | | | | | | |
| 400 | 08 | 61 | 98 | | | | | | |
| 500 | 11 | 76 | * | | | | | | |
| 600 | 15 | 86 | | | | | | | |
| 700 | 19 | 93 | | | | | | | |
| 800 | 23 | 96 | | | | | | | |
| 900 | 28 | 98 | | | | | | | |
| 1000 | 33 | 99 | | | | | | | |

Table 7.3.10

Power of $\chi^2$ test at $a = .01$, $u = 10$

| N | .10 | .20 | .30 | .40 | .50 | .60 | .70 | .80 | .90 |
|---|-----|-----|-----|-----|-----|-----|-----|-----|-----|
| 25 | 01 | 02 | 04 | 08 | 15 | 26 | 41 | 58 | 74 |
| 30 | 01 | 02 | 05 | 10 | 20 | 34 | 53 | 71 | 85 |
| 35 | 01 | 03 | 06 | 13 | 25 | 43 | 63 | 81 | 92 |
| 40 | 01 | 03 | 07 | 15 | 31 | 51 | 72 | 88 | 96 |
| 45 | 01 | 03 | 08 | 18 | 36 | 59 | 80 | 92 | 98 |
| 50 | 01 | 03 | 09 | 22 | 42 | 66 | 85 | 96 | 99 |
| 60 | 02 | 04 | 12 | 29 | 54 | 78 | 93 | 99 | * |
| 70 | 02 | 05 | 15 | 36 | 64 | 87 | 97 | * | |
| 80 | 02 | 06 | 18 | 44 | 74 | 93 | 99 | | |
| 90 | 02 | 07 | 22 | 51 | 81 | 96 | * | | |
| 100 | 02 | 08 | 26 | 58 | 87 | 98 | | | |
| 120 | 02 | 10 | 34 | 71 | 94 | 99 | | | |
| 140 | 03 | 13 | 43 | 81 | 97 | * | | | |
| 160 | 03 | 15 | 51 | 88 | 99 | | | | |
| 180 | 03 | 18 | 59 | 92 | * | | | | |
| 200 | 03 | 22 | 66 | 96 | | | | | |
| 250 | 04 | 31 | 81 | 99 | | | | | |
| 300 | 05 | 40 | 90 | * | | | | | |
| 350 | 06 | 49 | 95 | | | | | | |
| 400 | 08 | 58 | 98 | | | | | | |
| 500 | 11 | 74 | * | | | | | | |
| 600 | 14 | 84 | | | | | | | |
| 700 | 18 | 91 | | | | | | | |
| 800 | 22 | 96 | | | | | | | |
| 900 | 26 | 98 | | | | | | | |
| 1000 | 31 | 99 | | | | | | | |

Table 7.3.11

Power of $\chi^2$ test at a = .01, u = 12

| N | .10 | .20 | .30 | .40 | .50 | .60 | .70 | .80 | .90 |
|---|---|---|---|---|---|---|---|---|---|
| 25 | 01 | 02 | 03 | 07 | 13 | 23 | 37 | 54 | 70 |
| 30 | 01 | 02 | 04 | 09 | 17 | 31 | 48 | 66 | 82 |
| 35 | 01 | 02 | 05 | 11 | 22 | 39 | 59 | 77 | 89 |
| 40 | 01 | 03 | 06 | 14 | 27 | 47 | 68 | 85 | 94 |
| 45 | 01 | 03 | 07 | 16 | 33 | 55 | 76 | 90 | 97 |
| 50 | 01 | 03 | 08 | 19 | 38 | 62 | 82 | 94 | 99 |
| 60 | 01 | 04 | 10 | 26 | 49 | 74 | 91 | 98 | * |
| 70 | 02 | 04 | 13 | 32 | 60 | 84 | 96 | 99 | |
| 80 | 02 | 05 | 16 | 40 | 69 | 90 | 98 | * | |
| 90 | 02 | 06 | 20 | 47 | 77 | 94 | 99 | | |
| 100 | 02 | 07 | 23 | 54 | 83 | 97 | * | | |
| 120 | 02 | 09 | 31 | 66 | 92 | 99 | | | |
| 140 | 03 | 11 | 39 | 77 | 96 | * | | | |
| 160 | 03 | 14 | 47 | 85 | 99 | | | | |
| 180 | 03 | 16 | 55 | 90 | * | | | | |
| 200 | 03 | 19 | 62 | 94 | * | | | | |
| 250 | 04 | 27 | 77 | 99 | | | | | |
| 300 | 05 | 36 | 87 | * | | | | | |
| 350 | 06 | 45 | 94 | | | | | | |
| 400 | 07 | 54 | 97 | | | | | | |
| 500 | 09 | 69 | 99 | | | | | | |
| 600 | 12 | 81 | * | | | | | | |
| 700 | 16 | 89 | | | | | | | |
| 800 | 19 | 94 | | | | | | | |
| 900 | 23 | 97 | | | | | | | |
| 1000 | 27 | 99 | | | | | | | |

Table 7.3.12

Power of $\chi^2$ test at a = .01, u = 16

| N | .10 | .20 | .30 | .40 | .50 | .60 | .70 | .80 | .90 |
|---|---|---|---|---|---|---|---|---|---|
| 25 | 01 | 02 | 03 | 06 | 11 | 19 | 31 | 46 | 63 |
| 30 | 01 | 02 | 04 | 07 | 14 | 25 | 41 | 59 | 75 |
| 35 | 01 | 02 | 04 | 09 | 18 | 32 | 51 | 70 | 85 |
| 40 | 01 | 02 | 05 | 11 | 22 | 40 | 60 | 79 | 91 |
| 45 | 01 | 02 | 06 | 13 | 27 | 47 | 69 | 86 | 95 |
| 50 | 01 | 03 | 07 | 16 | 32 | 54 | 76 | 91 | 97 |
| 60 | 01 | 03 | 09 | 21 | 42 | 67 | 86 | 96 | 99 |
| 70 | 01 | 04 | 11 | 27 | 52 | 78 | 93 | 99 | * |
| 80 | 02 | 04 | 13 | 33 | 62 | 86 | 97 | * | |
| 90 | 02 | 05 | 16 | 40 | 71 | 91 | 99 | | |
| 100 | 02 | 06 | 19 | 46 | 77 | 95 | 99 | | |
| 120 | 02 | 07 | 25 | 59 | 88 | 98 | * | | |
| 140 | 02 | 09 | 32 | 70 | 94 | * | | | |
| 160 | 02 | 11 | 40 | 79 | 97 | | | | |
| 180 | 02 | 13 | 47 | 86 | 99 | | | | |
| 200 | 03 | 16 | 54 | 91 | * | | | | |
| 250 | 03 | 22 | 71 | 97 | | | | | |
| 300 | 04 | 30 | 82 | 99 | | | | | |
| 350 | 05 | 38 | 90 | * | | | | | |
| 400 | 06 | 46 | 95 | | | | | | |
| 500 | 08 | 62 | 99 | | | | | | |
| 600 | 10 | 75 | * | | | | | | |
| 700 | 13 | 84 | | | | | | | |
| 800 | 16 | 91 | | | | | | | |
| 900 | 19 | 95 | | | | | | | |
| 1000 | 22 | 97 | | | | | | | |

Table 7.3.13

Power of $\chi^2$ test at $a = .01$, $u = 20$

| N | | | | | w | | | | |
|---|---|---|---|---|---|---|---|---|---|
| | .10 | .20 | .30 | .40 | .50 | .60 | .70 | .80 | .90 |
| 25 | 01 | 02 | 03 | 05 | 09 | 16 | 27 | 41 | 57 |
| 30 | 01 | 02 | 03 | 06 | 12 | 22 | 36 | 53 | 70 |
| 35 | 01 | 02 | 04 | 08 | 15 | 28 | 45 | 64 | 80 |
| 40 | 01 | 02 | 05 | 09 | 19 | 35 | 54 | 74 | 88 |
| 45 | 01 | 02 | 05 | 11 | 23 | 41 | 63 | 81 | 93 |
| 50 | 01 | 02 | 06 | 13 | 27 | 48 | 70 | 87 | 96 |
| 60 | 01 | 03 | 07 | 18 | 37 | 61 | 83 | 95 | 99 |
| 70 | 01 | 03 | 09 | 23 | 46 | 73 | 91 | 98 | * |
| 80 | 01 | 04 | 11 | 29 | 56 | 81 | 95 | 99 | |
| 90 | 02 | 05 | 13 | 35 | 64 | 88 | 98 | * | |
| 100 | 02 | 05 | 16 | 41 | 72 | 92 | 99 | | |
| 120 | 02 | 06 | 22 | 53 | 84 | 97 | * | | |
| 140 | 02 | 08 | 28 | 64 | 91 | 99 | | | |
| 160 | 02 | 09 | 35 | 74 | 96 | * | | | |
| 180 | 02 | 11 | 41 | 81 | 98 | | | | |
| 200 | 02 | 13 | 48 | 87 | 99 | | | | |
| 250 | 03 | 19 | 64 | 96 | * | | | | |
| 300 | 04 | 26 | 77 | 99 | | | | | |
| 350 | 04 | 33 | 85 | * | | | | | |
| 400 | 05 | 41 | 92 | | | | | | |
| 500 | 07 | 56 | 98 | | | | | | |
| 600 | 08 | 69 | * | | | | | | |
| 700 | 11 | 80 | | | | | | | |
| 800 | 13 | 87 | | | | | | | |
| 900 | 16 | 92 | | | | | | | |
| 1000 | 19 | 96 | | | | | | | |

Table 7.3.14

Power of $\chi^2$ test at $a = .01$, $u = 24$

| N | | | | | w | | | | |
|---|---|---|---|---|---|---|---|---|---|
| | .10 | .20 | .30 | .40 | .50 | .60 | .70 | .80 | .90 |
| 25 | 01 | 02 | 02 | 04 | 08 | 14 | 23 | 36 | 51 |
| 30 | 01 | 02 | 03 | 06 | 10 | 19 | 32 | 48 | 65 |
| 35 | 01 | 02 | 03 | 07 | 13 | 24 | 40- | 59 | 76 |
| 40 | 01 | 02 | 04 | 08 | 17 | 30 | 49 | 69 | 84 |
| 45 | 01 | 02 | 04 | 10 | 20 | 37 | 58 | 77 | 92 |
| 50 | 01 | 02 | 05 | 12 | 23 | 43 | 65 | 84 | 94 |
| 60 | 01 | 03 | 06 | 15 | 33 | 56 | 78 | 93 | 98 |
| 70 | 01 | 03 | 08 | 20 | 42 | 68 | 88 | 97 | * |
| 80 | 01 | 03 | 10 | 25 | 51 | 77 | 93 | 99 | |
| 90 | 01 | 04 | 12 | 30 | 59 | 84 | 97 | * | |
| 100 | 02 | 04 | 14 | 36 | 67 | 90 | 98 | | |
| 120 | 02 | 06 | 19 | 48 | 80 | 96 | * | | |
| 140 | 02 | 07 | 24 | 59 | 89 | 99 | | | |
| 160 | 02 | 08 | 30 | 69 | 94 | * | | | |
| 180 | 02 | 10 | 37 | 77 | 97 | | | | |
| 200 | 02 | 12 | 43 | 84 | 99 | | | | |
| 250 | 03 | 17 | 59 | 94 | * | | | | |
| 300 | 03 | 22 | 73 | 98 | | | | | |
| 350 | 04 | 29 | 83 | 99 | | | | | |
| 400 | 04 | 36 | 90 | * | | | | | |
| 500 | 06 | 51 | 97 | | | | | | |
| 600 | 07 | 64 | 99 | | | | | | |
| 700 | 09 | 75 | * | | | | | | |
| 800 | 12 | 84 | | | | | | | |
| 900 | 14 | 90 | | | | | | | |
| 1000 | 17 | 94 | | | | | | | |

Table 7.3.15

Power of $\chi^2$ test at a = .05, u = 1

| N | w .10 | .20 | .30 | .40 | .50 | .60 | .70 | .80 | .90 |
|---|---|---|---|---|---|---|---|---|---|
| 25 | 08 | 17 | 32 | 52 | 70 | 85 | 94 | 98 | 99 |
| 30 | 08 | 19 | 38 | 59 | 78 | 91 | 97 | 99 | * |
| 35 | 09 | 22 | 43 | 66 | 84 | 94 | 99 | * | |
| 40 | 09 | 24 | 47 | 71 | 89 | 97 | 99 | | |
| 45 | 10 | 27 | 52 | 76 | 92 | 98 | * | | |
| 50 | 11 | 29 | 56 | 81 | 94 | 99 | | | |
| 60 | 12 | 34 | 64 | 87 | 97 | * | | | |
| 70 | 13 | 39 | 71 | 92 | 99 | | | | |
| 80 | 15 | 43 | 76 | 95 | 99 | | | | |
| 90 | 16 | 47 | 81 | 97 | * | | | | |
| 100 | 17 | 52 | 85 | 98 | | | | | |
| 120 | 19 | 59 | 91 | 99 | | | | | |
| 140 | 22 | 66 | 94 | * | | | | | |
| 160 | 24 | 71 | 97 | | | | | | |
| 180 | 27 | 76 | 98 | | | | | | |
| 200 | 29 | 81 | 99 | | | | | | |
| 250 | 35 | 89 | * | | | | | | |
| 300 | 41 | 93 | | | | | | | |
| 350 | 46 | 96 | | | | | | | |
| 400 | 52 | 98 | | | | | | | |
| 500 | 61 | 99 | | | | | | | |
| 600 | 69 | * | | | | | | | |
| 700 | 75 | | | | | | | | |
| 800 | 81 | | | | | | | | |
| 900 | 85 | | | | | | | | |
| 1000 | 89 | | | | | | | | |

Table 7.3.16

Power of $\chi^2$ test at a = .05, u = 2

| N | w .10 | .20 | .30 | .40 | .50 | .60 | .70 | .80 | .90 |
|---|---|---|---|---|---|---|---|---|---|
| 25 | 07 | 13 | 25 | 42 | 60 | 77 | 89 | 96 | 99 |
| 30 | 07 | 15 | 29 | 49 | 69 | 85 | 94 | 98 | * |
| 35 | 08 | 17 | 34 | 55 | 76 | 90 | 97 | 99 | |
| 40 | 08 | 19 | 38 | 61 | 82 | 93 | 98 | * | |
| 45 | 09 | 21 | 42 | 67 | 86 | 96 | 99 | | |
| 50 | 09 | 23 | 46 | 72 | 90 | 97 | * | | |
| 60 | 10 | 26 | 54 | 80 | 94 | 99 | | | |
| 70 | 11 | 30 | 61 | 86 | 97 | * | | | |
| 80 | 12 | 34 | 67 | 90 | 99 | | | | |
| 90 | 12 | 38 | 72 | 93 | 99 | | | | |
| 100 | 13 | 42 | 77 | 96 | * | | | | |
| 120 | 15 | 49 | 85 | 98 | | | | | |
| 140 | 17 | 55 | 90 | 99 | | | | | |
| 160 | 19 | 61 | 93 | * | | | | | |
| 180 | 21 | 67 | 96 | | | | | | |
| 200 | 23 | 72 | 97 | | | | | | |
| 250 | 27 | 82 | 99 | | | | | | |
| 300 | 32 | 88 | * | | | | | | |
| 350 | 37 | 93 | | | | | | | |
| 400 | 42 | 96 | | | | | | | |
| 500 | 50 | 99 | | | | | | | |
| 600 | 58 | * | | | | | | | |
| 700 | 66 | | | | | | | | |
| 800 | 72 | | | | | | | | |
| 900 | 77 | | | | | | | | |
| 1000 | 82 | | | | | | | | |

Table 7.3.17

Power of $\chi^2$ at a = .05, u = 3

| N | .10 | .20 | .30 | .40 | .50 | .60 | .70 | .80 | .90 |
|---|---|---|---|---|---|---|---|---|---|
| | | | | | | | | w | |
| 25 | 07 | 12 | 21 | 36 | 54 | 71 | 85 | 93 | 98 |
| 30 | 07 | 13 | 25 | 42 | 62 | 80 | 90 | 97 | 99 |
| 35 | 07 | 15 | 29 | 49 | 70 | 86 | 95 | 99 | * |
| 40 | 07 | 16 | 32 | 55 | 76 | 90 | 97 | 99 | |
| 45 | 08 | 18 | 36 | 60 | 81 | 94 | 99 | * | |
| 50 | 08 | 19 | 40 | 65 | 86 | 96 | 99 | | |
| 60 | 09 | 22 | 47 | 74 | 92 | 98 | 99 | | |
| 70 | 09 | 26 | 54 | 81 | 95 | 99 | * | | |
| 80 | 10 | 29 | 60 | 86 | 98 | * | | | |
| 90 | 11 | 32 | 66 | 90 | 99 | | | | |
| 100 | 12 | 36 | 71 | 93 | 99 | | | | |
| 120 | 13 | 42 | 80 | 97 | * | | | | |
| 140 | 15 | 49 | 86 | 99 | | | | | |
| 160 | 16 | 55 | 90 | 99 | | | | | |
| 180 | 18 | 60 | 94 | * | | | | | |
| 200 | 19 | 65 | 96 | | | | | | |
| 250 | 23 | 76 | 99 | | | | | | |
| 300 | 27 | 84 | * | | | | | | |
| 350 | 32 | 90 | | | | | | | |
| 400 | 36 | 93 | | | | | | | |
| 500 | 44 | 98 | | | | | | | |
| 600 | 52 | 99 | | | | | | | |
| 700 | 59 | * | | | | | | | |
| 800 | 65 | | | | | | | | |
| 900 | 71 | | | | | | | | |
| 1000 | 76 | | | | | | | | |

Table 7.3.18

Power of $\chi^2$ test at a = .05, u = 4

| N | .10 | .20 | .30 | .40 | .50 | .60 | .70 | .80 | .90 |
|---|---|---|---|---|---|---|---|---|---|
| | | | | | | | | w | |
| 25 | 06 | 11 | 19 | 32 | 50 | 66 | 81 | 91 | 97 |
| 30 | 07 | 12 | 22 | 38 | 57 | 75 | 88 | 96 | 99 |
| 35 | 07 | 13 | 26 | 44 | 65 | 82 | 93 | 98 | * |
| 40 | 07 | 14 | 29 | 50 | 72 | 88 | 96 | 99 | |
| 45 | 07 | 16 | 32 | 55 | 77 | 92 | 98 | * | |
| 50 | 08 | 17 | 36 | 60 | 82 | 94 | 99 | | |
| 60 | 08 | 20 | 43 | 70 | 89 | 98 | * | | |
| 70 | 09 | 23 | 49 | 77 | 94 | 99 | | | |
| 80 | 09 | 26 | 55 | 83 | 96 | * | | | |
| 90 | 10 | 29 | 61 | 88 | 98 | | | | |
| 100 | 11 | 32 | 66 | 91 | 99 | | | | |
| 120 | 12 | 38 | 75 | 96 | * | | | | |
| 140 | 13 | 44 | 82 | 98 | | | | | |
| 160 | 14 | 50 | 88 | 99 | | | | | |
| 180 | 16 | 55 | 92 | * | | | | | |
| 200 | 17 | 60 | 94 | | | | | | |
| 250 | 21 | 72 | 98 | | | | | | |
| 300 | 24 | 80 | 99 | | | | | | |
| 350 | 28 | 87 | * | | | | | | |
| 400 | 32 | 91 | | | | | | | |
| 500 | 40 | 96 | | | | | | | |
| 600 | 47 | 99 | | | | | | | |
| 700 | 54 | * | | | | | | | |
| 800 | 60 | | | | | | | | |
| 900 | 66 | | | | | | | | |
| 1000 | 72 | | | | | | | | |

Table 7.3.19

Power of $\chi^2$ test at a = .05, u = 5

| N | .10 | .20 | .30 | .40 | .50 | .60 | .70 | .80 | .90 |
|---|---|---|---|---|---|---|---|---|---|
| | | | | | w | | | | |
| 25 | 06 | 10 | 17 | 29 | 45 | 62 | 78 | 89 | 95 |
| 30 | 06 | 11 | 20 | 35 | 53 | 72 | 86 | 94 | 98 |
| 35 | 07 | 12 | 23 | 40 | 61 | 79 | 91 | 97 | 99 |
| 40 | 07 | 13 | 26 | 46 | 68 | 85 | 95 | 99 | * |
| 45 | 07 | 14 | 30 | 51 | 74 | 89 | 97 | 99 | |
| 50 | 07 | 16 | 33 | 56 | 79 | 93 | 98 | * | |
| 60 | 08 | 18 | 39 | 66 | 87 | 97 | 99 | | |
| 70 | 08 | 21 | 45 | 73 | 92 | 99 | * | | |
| 80 | 09 | 24 | 51 | 80 | 95 | 99 | | | |
| 90 | 09 | 26 | 57 | 85 | 97 | * | | | |
| 100 | 10 | 29 | 62 | 89 | 98 | | | | |
| 120 | 11 | 35 | 72 | 94 | * | | | | |
| 140 | 12 | 40 | 79 | 97 | | | | | |
| 160 | 13 | 46 | 85 | 99 | | | | | |
| 180 | 14 | 51 | 89 | 99 | | | | | |
| 200 | 16 | 56 | 93 | * | | | | | |
| 250 | 19 | 68 | 97 | | | | | | |
| 300 | 22 | 77 | 99 | | | | | | |
| 350 | 26 | 84 | * | | | | | | |
| 400 | 29 | 89 | | | | | | | |
| 500 | 36 | 95 | | | | | | | |
| 600 | 43 | 98 | | | | | | | |
| 700 | 50 | 99 | | | | | | | |
| 800 | 56 | * | | | | | | | |
| 900 | 62 | | | | | | | | |
| 1000 | 68 | | | | | | | | |

Table 7.3.20

Power of $\chi^2$ test at a = .05, u = 6

| N | .10 | .20 | .30 | .40 | .50 | .60 | .70 | .80 | .90 |
|---|---|---|---|---|---|---|---|---|---|
| | | | | | w | | | | |
| 25 | 06 | 09 | 16 | 27 | 42 | 59 | 75 | 87 | 94 |
| 30 | 06 | 10 | 19 | 32 | 50 | 68 | 83 | 93 | 98 |
| 35 | 06 | 11 | 22 | 38 | 57 | 76 | 89 | 96 | 99 |
| 40 | 07 | 12 | 24 | 43 | 64 | 82 | 94 | 98 | * |
| 45 | 07 | 14 | 27 | 48 | 70 | 87 | 96 | 99 | |
| 50 | 07 | 15 | 30 | 53 | 76 | 91 | 98 | * | |
| 60 | 07 | 17 | 36 | 62 | 84 | 96 | 99 | | |
| 70 | 08 | 19 | 42 | 70 | 90 | 98 | * | | |
| 80 | 08 | 22 | 48 | 77 | 94 | 99 | | | |
| 90 | 09 | 24 | 54 | 82 | 96 | * | | | |
| 100 | 09 | 27 | 59 | 87 | 98 | | | | |
| 120 | 10 | 32 | 68 | 93 | 99 | | | | |
| 140 | 11 | 38 | 76 | 96 | * | | | | |
| 160 | 12 | 43 | 82 | 98 | | | | | |
| 180 | 14 | 48 | 87 | 99 | | | | | |
| 200 | 15 | 53 | 91 | * | | | | | |
| 250 | 18 | 64 | 96 | | | | | | |
| 300 | 21 | 74 | 99 | | | | | | |
| 350 | 24 | 81 | * | | | | | | |
| 400 | 27 | 87 | | | | | | | |
| 500 | 34 | 94 | | | | | | | |
| 600 | 40 | 97 | | | | | | | |
| 700 | 47 | 99 | | | | | | | |
| 800 | 53 | * | | | | | | | |
| 900 | 59 | | | | | | | | |
| 1000 | 64 | | | | | | | | |

Table 7.3.21

Power of $\chi^2$ test at $a = .05$, $u = 7$

| N | | | | | w | | | | |
|---|---|---|---|---|---|---|---|---|---|
| | .10 | .20 | .30 | .40 | .50 | .60 | .70 | .80 | .90 |
| 25 | 06 | 09 | 15 | 25 | 39 | 56 | 72 | 85 | 93 |
| 30 | 06 | 10 | 18 | 30 | 47 | 65 | 81 | 92 | 97 |
| 35 | 06 | 11 | 20 | 35 | 55 | 73 | 88 | 96 | 99 |
| 40 | 06 | 12 | 23 | 40 | 61 | 80 | 92 | 98 | * |
| 45 | 07 | 13 | 26 | 45 | 68 | 85 | 95 | 99 | |
| 50 | 07 | 14 | 28 | 50 | 73 | 89 | 97 | 99 | |
| 60 | 07 | 16 | 34 | 59 | 82 | 95 | 99 | * | |
| 70 | 08 | 18 | 40 | 67 | 88 | 98 | * | | |
| 80 | 08 | 20 | 45 | 74 | 93 | 99 | | | |
| 90 | 09 | 23 | 51 | 80 | 96 | * | | | |
| 100 | 09 | 25 | 56 | 85 | 97 | | | | |
| 120 | 10 | 30 | 65 | 92 | 99 | | | | |
| 140 | 11 | 35 | 73 | 96 | * | | | | |
| 160 | 12 | 40 | 80 | 98 | | | | | |
| 180 | 13 | 45 | 85 | 99 | | | | | |
| 200 | 14 | 50 | 89 | 99 | | | | | |
| 250 | 16 | 61 | 96 | * | | | | | |
| 300 | 19 | 71 | 98 | | | | | | |
| 350 | 22 | 79 | 99 | | | | | | |
| 400 | 25 | 85 | * | | | | | | |
| 500 | 31 | 93 | | | | | | | |
| 600 | 38 | 97 | | | | | | | |
| 700 | 44 | 99 | | | | | | | |
| 800 | 50 | 99 | | | | | | | |
| 900 | 56 | * | | | | | | | |
| 1000 | 61 | | | | | | | | |

Table 7.3.22

Power of $\chi^2$ test at $a = .05$, $u = 8$

| N | | | | | w | | | | |
|---|---|---|---|---|---|---|---|---|---|
| | .10 | .20 | .30 | .40 | .50 | .60 | .70 | .80 | .90 |
| 25 | 06 | 09 | 14 | 24 | 37 | 53 | 70 | 83 | 92 |
| 30 | 06 | 09 | 17 | 28 | 45 | 63 | 79 | 90 | 96 |
| 35 | 06 | 10 | 18 | 33 | 52 | 71 | 86 | 95 | 98 |
| 40 | 06 | 11 | 21 | 38 | 59 | 78 | 91 | 97 | 99 |
| 45 | 07 | 12 | 24 | 43 | 65 | 83 | 94 | 99 | * |
| 50 | 07 | 13 | 27 | 48 | 71 | 88 | 96 | 99 | |
| 60 | 07 | 15 | 32 | 57 | 80 | 94 | 99 | * | |
| 70 | 07 | 17 | 37 | 65 | 87 | 97 | * | | |
| 80 | 08 | 19 | 43 | 72 | 92 | 99 | | | |
| 90 | 08 | 21 | 48 | 78 | 95 | 99 | | | |
| 100 | 09 | 24 | 53 | 83 | 97 | * | | | |
| 120 | 09 | 28 | 63 | 90 | 99 | | | | |
| 140 | 10 | 33 | 71 | 95 | * | | | | |
| 160 | 11 | 38 | 78 | 97 | | | | | |
| 180 | 12 | 43 | 83 | 99 | | | | | |
| 200 | 13 | 48 | 88 | 99 | | | | | |
| 250 | 16 | 59 | 95 | * | | | | | |
| 300 | 18 | 68 | 98 | | | | | | |
| 350 | 21 | 77 | 99 | | | | | | |
| 400 | 24 | 83 | * | | | | | | |
| 500 | 30 | 92 | | | | | | | |
| 600 | 36 | 96 | | | | | | | |
| 700 | 42 | 98 | | | | | | | |
| 800 | 48 | 99 | | | | | | | |
| 900 | 53 | * | | | | | | | |
| 1000 | 59 | | | | | | | | |

Table 7.3.23

Power of $\chi^2$ test at $a = .05$, $u = 9$

| N | .10 | .20 | .30 | .40 | .50 | .60 | .70 | .80 | .90 |
|---|-----|-----|-----|-----|-----|-----|-----|-----|-----|
| 25 | 06 | 08 | 14 | 23 | 35 | 51 | 67 | 81 | 91 |
| 30 | 06 | 09 | 16 | 27 | 43 | 60 | 77 | 89 | 96 |
| 35 | 06 | 10 | 18 | 32 | 50 | 69 | 84 | 94 | 98 |
| 40 | 06 | 11 | 20 | 36 | 56 | 76 | 90 | 97 | 99 |
| 45 | 06 | 12 | 23 | 41 | 63 | 82 | 93 | 98 | * |
| 50 | 07 | 13 | 25 | 45 | 68 | 86 | 96 | 99 | |
| 60 | 07 | 14 | 30 | 54 | 78 | 93 | 98 | * | |
| 70 | 07 | 16 | 36 | 62 | 85 | 96 | 99 | | |
| 80 | 08 | 18 | 41 | 70 | 90 | 98 | * | | |
| 90 | 08 | 20 | 46 | 76 | 94 | 99 | | | |
| 100 | 08 | 23 | 51 | 81 | 96 | * | | | |
| 120 | 09 | 27 | 60 | 89 | 99 | | | | |
| 140 | 10 | 32 | 69 | 94 | * | | | | |
| 160 | 11 | 36 | 76 | 97 | | | | | |
| 180 | 12 | 41 | 82 | 98 | | | | | |
| 200 | 13 | 45 | 86 | 99 | | | | | |
| 250 | 15 | 56 | 94 | * | | | | | |
| 300 | 17 | 66 | 97 | | | | | | |
| 350 | 20 | 74 | 99 | | | | | | |
| 400 | 23 | 81 | * | | | | | | |
| 500 | 28 | 90 | | | | | | | |
| 600 | 34 | 95 | | | | | | | |
| 700 | 40 | 98 | | | | | | | |
| 800 | 45 | 99 | | | | | | | |
| 900 | 51 | * | | | | | | | |
| 1000 | 56 | | | | | | | | |

Table 7.3.24

Power of $\chi^2$ test at $a = .05$, $u = 10$

| N | .10 | .20 | .30 | .40 | .50 | .60 | .70 | .80 | .90 |
|---|-----|-----|-----|-----|-----|-----|-----|-----|-----|
| 25 | 06 | 08 | 13 | 21 | 34 | 49 | 65 | 79 | 89 |
| 30 | 06 | 09 | 15 | 26 | 41 | 58 | 75 | 87 | 95 |
| 35 | 06 | 10 | 17 | 30 | 48 | 67 | 83 | 93 | 98 |
| 40 | 06 | 10 | 19 | 35 | 54 | 74 | 88 | 96 | 99 |
| 45 | 06 | 11 | 22 | 39 | 60 | 80 | 92 | 98 | * |
| 50 | 07 | 12 | 24 | 43 | 66 | 85 | 95 | 99 | |
| 60 | 07 | 14 | 29 | 52 | 76 | 92 | 98 | * | |
| 70 | 07 | 16 | 34 | 60 | 83 | 96 | 99 | | |
| 80 | 08 | 18 | 39 | 67 | 89 | 98 | * | | |
| 90 | 08 | 19 | 44 | 74 | 93 | 99 | | | |
| 100 | 08 | 21 | 49 | 79 | 96 | * | | | |
| 120 | 09 | 26 | 58 | 87 | 98 | | | | |
| 140 | 10 | 30 | 67 | 93 | 99 | | | | |
| 160 | 10 | 35 | 74 | 96 | * | | | | |
| 180 | 11 | 39 | 80 | 98 | | | | | |
| 200 | 12 | 43 | 85 | 99 | | | | | |
| 250 | 14 | 54 | 93 | * | | | | | |
| 300 | 17 | 64 | 97 | | | | | | |
| 350 | 19 | 72 | 99 | | | | | | |
| 400 | 21 | 79 | * | | | | | | |
| 500 | 27 | 89 | | | | | | | |
| 600 | 32 | 95 | | | | | | | |
| 700 | 38 | 98 | | | | | | | |
| 800 | 43 | 99 | | | | | | | |
| 900 | 49 | * | | | | | | | |
| 1000 | 54 | | | | | | | | |

Table 7.3.25

Power of $\chi^2$ test at a = .05, u = 12

| N | .10 | .20 | .30 | .40 | .50 | .60 | .70 | .80 | .90 |
|---|-----|-----|-----|-----|-----|-----|-----|-----|-----|
| 25 | 06 | 08 | 12 | 20 | 31 | 45 | 61 | 76 | 87 |
| 30 | 06 | 09 | 14 | 24 | 38 | 54 | 71 | 85 | 93 |
| 35 | 06 | 09 | 16 | 28 | 44 | 63 | 79 | 90 | 97 |
| 40 | 06 | 10 | 18 | 32 | 50 | 70 | 86 | 95 | 99 |
| 45 | 06 | 11 | 20 | 36 | 57 | 77 | 90 | 97 | 99 |
| 50 | 06 | 11 | 22 | 40 | 62 | 82 | 94 | 98 | * |
| 60 | 07 | 13 | 27 | 48 | 72 | 90 | 97 | * | |
| 70 | 07 | 14 | 31 | 56 | 80 | 94 | 99 | | |
| 80 | 07 | 16 | 36 | 64 | 87 | 97 | * | | |
| 90 | 08 | 18 | 41 | 70 | 91 | 99 | | | |
| 100 | 08 | 20 | 45 | 76 | 94 | 99 | | | |
| 120 | 09 | 24 | 54 | 85 | 98 | * | | | |
| 140 | 09 | 28 | 63 | 90 | 99 | | | | |
| 160 | 10 | 32 | 70 | 95 | * | | | | |
| 180 | 11 | 36 | 77 | 97 | | | | | |
| 200 | 11 | 40 | 82 | 98 | | | | | |
| 250 | 13 | 50 | 91 | * | | | | | |
| 300 | 15 | 60 | 96 | | | | | | |
| 350 | 18 | 69 | 98 | | | | | | |
| 400 | 20 | 76 | 99 | | | | | | |
| 500 | 25 | 87 | * | | | | | | |
| 600 | 30 | 93 | | | | | | | |
| 700 | 35 | 97 | | | | | | | |
| 800 | 40 | 98 | | | | | | | |
| 900 | 45 | 99 | | | | | | | |
| 1000 | 50 | * | | | | | | | |

Table 7.3.26

Power of $\chi^2$ test at a = .05, u = 16

| N | .10 | .20 | .30 | .40 | .50 | .60 | .70 | .80 | .90 |
|---|-----|-----|-----|-----|-----|-----|-----|-----|-----|
| 25 | 06 | 07 | 11 | 17 | 27 | 40 | 55 | 70 | 82 |
| 30 | 06 | 08 | 13 | 21 | 33 | 48 | 65 | 80 | 90 |
| 35 | 06 | 09 | 14 | 24 | 39 | 56 | 74 | 87 | 95 |
| 40 | 06 | 09 | 16 | 28 | 45 | 64 | 81 | 92 | 97 |
| 45 | 06 | 10 | 18 | 31 | 50 | 71 | 86 | 95 | 99 |
| 50 | 06 | 10 | 19 | 35 | 56 | 76 | 91 | 97 | * |
| 60 | 06 | 12 | 23 | 43 | 66 | 85 | 96 | 99 | |
| 70 | 07 | 13 | 27 | 50 | 75 | 92 | 98 | * | |
| 80 | 07 | 14 | 31 | 57 | 82 | 95 | 99 | | |
| 90 | 07 | 16 | 36 | 64 | 87 | 97 | * | | |
| 100 | 07 | 17 | 40 | 70 | 91 | 99 | | | |
| 120 | 08 | 21 | 48 | 80 | 96 | * | | | |
| 140 | 09 | 24 | 56 | 87 | 98 | | | | |
| 160 | 09 | 28 | 64 | 92 | 99 | | | | |
| 180 | 10 | 31 | 71 | 95 | * | | | | |
| 200 | 10 | 35 | 76 | 97 | | | | | |
| 250 | 12 | 45 | 87 | 99 | | | | | |
| 300 | 14 | 54 | 94 | * | | | | | |
| 350 | 15 | 62 | 97 | | | | | | |
| 400 | 17 | 70 | 99 | | | | | | |
| 500 | 21 | 82 | * | | | | | | |
| 600 | 26 | 90 | | | | | | | |
| 700 | 30 | 95 | | | | | | | |
| 800 | 35 | 97 | | | | | | | |
| 900 | 40 | 99 | | | | | | | |
| 1000 | 45 | 99 | | | | | | | |

Table 7.3.27

Power of $\chi^2$ test at $a = .05$, $u = 20$

| N | .10 | .20 | .30 | .40 | .50 | .60 | .70 | .80 | .90 |
|---|-----|-----|-----|-----|-----|-----|-----|-----|-----|
| 25 | 05 | 07 | 10 | 16 | 24 | 36 | 50 | 65 | 79 |
| 30 | 06 | 08 | 12 | 19 | 29 | 44 | 60 | 75 | 87 |
| 35 | 06 | 08 | 13 | 22 | 35 | 51 | 69 | 83 | 93 |
| 40 | 06 | 09 | 14 | 25 | 40 | 59 | 78 | 89 | 96 |
| 45 | 06 | 09 | 16 | 28 | 46 | 66 | 83 | 93 | 98 |
| 50 | 06 | 10 | 18 | 31 | 51 | 72 | 87 | 96 | 99 |
| 60 | 06 | 11 | 21 | 38 | 61 | 82 | 94 | 99 | * |
| 70 | 06 | 12 | 24 | 45 | 70 | 89 | 97 | * | |
| 80 | 07 | 13 | 28 | 52 | 78 | 93 | 99 | | |
| 90 | 07 | 14 | 32 | 59 | 84 | 96 | * | | |
| 100 | 07 | 16 | 36 | 65 | 88 | 98 | | | |
| 120 | 08 | 19 | 44 | 75 | 94 | 99 | | | |
| 140 | 08 | 22 | 51 | 83 | 98 | * | | | |
| 160 | 09 | 25 | 59 | 89 | 99 | | | | |
| 180 | 09 | 28 | 66 | 93 | * | | | | |
| 200 | 10 | 31 | 72 | 96 | | | | | |
| 250 | 11 | 40 | 84 | 99 | | | | | |
| 300 | 13 | 49 | 91 | * | | | | | |
| 350 | 14 | 57 | 96 | | | | | | |
| 400 | 16 | 65 | 98 | | | | | | |
| 500 | 19 | 78 | * | | | | | | |
| 600 | 23 | 87 | | | | | | | |
| 700 | 27 | 92 | | | | | | | |
| 800 | 31 | 96 | | | | | | | |
| 900 | 36 | 98 | | | | | | | |
| 1000 | 40 | 99 | | | | | | | |

Table 7.3.28

Power of $\chi^2$ test at $a = .05$, $u = 24$

| N | .10 | .20 | .30 | .40 | .50 | .60 | .70 | .80 | .90 |
|---|-----|-----|-----|-----|-----|-----|-----|-----|-----|
| 25 | 05 | 07 | 10 | 15 | 22 | 33 | 46 | 60 | 74 |
| 30 | 06 | 07 | 11 | 17 | 27 | 40 | 56 | 71 | 84 |
| 35 | 06 | 08 | 12 | 20 | 32 | 47 | 65 | 80 | 91 |
| 40 | 06 | 08 | 13 | 23 | 37 | 54 | 72 | 86 | 95 |
| 45 | 06 | 09 | 15 | 26 | 42 | 61 | 79 | 91 | 97 |
| 50 | 06 | 09 | 16 | 29 | 47 | 67 | 84 | 94 | 99 |
| 60 | 06 | 10 | 19 | 35 | 57 | 78 | 92 | 98 | * |
| 70 | 06 | 11 | 22 | 42 | 66 | 86 | 96 | 99 | |
| 80 | 06 | 12 | 26 | 48 | 74 | 91 | 98 | * | |
| 90 | 07 | 13 | 29 | 54 | 80 | 95 | 99 | | |
| 100 | 07 | 15 | 33 | 60 | 85 | 97 | * | | |
| 120 | 07 | 17 | 40 | 71 | 92 | 99 | | | |
| 140 | 08 | 20 | 47 | 80 | 96 | * | | | |
| 160 | 08 | 23 | 54 | 86 | 98 | | | | |
| 180 | 09 | 26 | 61 | 91 | 99 | | | | |
| 200 | 09 | 29 | 67 | 94 | * | | | | |
| 250 | 10 | 37 | 80 | 98 | | | | | |
| 300 | 12 | 45 | 89 | * | | | | | |
| 350 | 13 | 53 | 94 | | | | | | |
| 400 | 15 | 60 | 97 | | | | | | |
| 500 | 18 | 74 | 99 | | | | | | |
| 600 | 21 | 83 | * | | | | | | |
| 700 | 25 | 90 | | | | | | | |
| 800 | 29 | 94 | | | | | | | |
| 900 | 33 | 97 | | | | | | | |
| 1000 | 37 | 98 | | | | | | | |

# Table 7.3.29

Power of $\chi^2$ test at a = .10, u = 1

| N | .10 | .20 | .30 | .40 | .50 | .60 | .70 | .80 | .90 |
|---|---|---|---|---|---|---|---|---|---|
| 25 | 14 | 26 | 44 | 64 | 80 | 91 | 97 | 99 | * |
| 30 | 15 | 29 | 50 | 71 | 86 | 95 | 99 | * | |
| 35 | 16 | 32 | 55 | 76 | 91 | 97 | * | | |
| 40 | 17 | 35 | 60 | 81 | 94 | 98 | | | |
| 45 | 17 | 38 | 64 | 85 | 96 | 99 | | | |
| 50 | 18 | 41 | 68 | 88 | 97 | * | | | |
| 60 | 20 | 46 | 75 | 93 | 99 | | | | |
| 70 | 22 | 51 | 81 | 96 | 99 | | | | |
| 80 | 23 | 56 | 85 | 97 | * | | | | |
| 90 | 25 | 60 | 88 | 98 | | | | | |
| 100 | 26 | 64 | 91 | 99 | | | | | |
| 120 | 29 | 71 | 95 | * | | | | | |
| 140 | 32 | 76 | 97 | | | | | | |
| 160 | 35 | 81 | 98 | | | | | | |
| 180 | 38 | 85 | 99 | | | | | | |
| 200 | 41 | 88 | * | | | | | | |
| 250 | 48 | 94 | | | | | | | |
| 300 | 54 | 97 | | | | | | | |
| 350 | 59 | 98 | | | | | | | |
| 400 | 64 | 99 | | | | | | | |
| 500 | 72 | * | | | | | | | |
| 600 | 79 | | | | | | | | |
| 700 | 84 | | | | | | | | |
| 800 | 88 | | | | | | | | |
| 900 | 91 | | | | | | | | |
| 1000 | 94 | | | | | | | | |

# Table 7.3.30

Power of $\chi^2$ test at a = .10, u = 2

| N | .10 | .20 | .30 | .40 | .50 | .60 | .70 | .80 | .90 |
|---|---|---|---|---|---|---|---|---|---|
| 25 | 13 | 22 | 36 | 54 | 72 | 85 | 94 | 98 | 99 |
| 30 | 13 | 24 | 41 | 61 | 79 | 91 | 97 | 99 | * |
| 35 | 14 | 26 | 46 | 67 | 84 | 94 | 98 | * | |
| 40 | 15 | 29 | 50 | 73 | 89 | 97 | 99 | | |
| 45 | 15 | 31 | 55 | 77 | 92 | 98 | * | | |
| 50 | 16 | 33 | 59 | 81 | 94 | 99 | | | |
| 60 | 17 | 38 | 66 | 87 | 97 | * | | | |
| 70 | 18 | 42 | 72 | 92 | 99 | | | | |
| 80 | 19 | 46 | 77 | 95 | 99 | | | | |
| 90 | 21 | 50 | 82 | 97 | * | | | | |
| 100 | 22 | 54 | 85 | 98 | * | | | | |
| 120 | 24 | 61 | 91 | 99 | | | | | |
| 140 | 26 | 67 | 94 | * | | | | | |
| 160 | 29 | 73 | 97 | | | | | | |
| 180 | 31 | 77 | 98 | | | | | | |
| 200 | 33 | 81 | 99 | | | | | | |
| 250 | 39 | 89 | * | | | | | | |
| 300 | 44 | 93 | | | | | | | |
| 350 | 49 | 96 | | | | | | | |
| 400 | 54 | 98 | | | | | | | |
| 500 | 63 | 99 | | | | | | | |
| 600 | 70 | * | | | | | | | |
| 700 | 76 | | | | | | | | |
| 800 | 81 | | | | | | | | |
| 900 | 85 | | | | | | | | |
| 1000 | 89 | | | | | | | | |

Table 7.3.32

Power of $\chi^2$ test at $a = .10$, $u = 4$

| N | .10 | .20 | .30 | .40 | .50 | .60 | .70 | .80 | .90 |
|---|-----|-----|-----|-----|-----|-----|-----|-----|-----|
| 25 | 12 | 18 | 29 | 44 | 61 | 77 | 88 | 95 | 98 |
| 30 | 12 | 20 | 33 | 51 | 69 | 84 | 93 | 98 | 99 |
| 35 | 13 | 22 | 37 | 57 | 76 | 89 | 96 | 99 | * |
| 40 | 13 | 23 | 41 | 62 | 81 | 93 | 98 | * | |
| 45 | 13 | 25 | 45 | 67 | 86 | 95 | 99 | | |
| 50 | 14 | 27 | 48 | 72 | 89 | 97 | 99 | | |
| 60 | 15 | 31 | 55 | 80 | 94 | 99 | * | | |
| 70 | 16 | 34 | 62 | 85 | 97 | * | | | |
| 80 | 16 | 38 | 67 | 90 | 98 | | | | |
| 90 | 17 | 41 | 72 | 93 | 99 | | | | |
| 100 | 18 | 44 | 77 | 95 | | | | | |
| 120 | 20 | 51 | 84 | 98 | | | | | |
| 140 | 22 | 57 | 89 | 99 | | | | | |
| 160 | 23 | 62 | 93 | * | | | | | |
| 180 | 25 | 67 | 95 | | | | | | |
| 200 | 27 | 72 | 97 | | | | | | |
| 250 | 31 | 81 | 99 | | | | | | |
| 300 | 36 | 88 | * | | | | | | |
| 350 | 40 | 92 | | | | | | | |
| 400 | 44 | 95 | | | | | | | |
| 500 | 52 | 98 | | | | | | | |
| 600 | 60 | 99 | | | | | | | |
| 700 | 66 | * | | | | | | | |
| 800 | 72 | | | | | | | | |
| 900 | 77 | | | | | | | | |
| 1000 | 81 | | | | | | | | |

Table 7.3.31

Power of $\chi^2$ test at $a = .10$, $u = 3$

| N | .10 | .20 | .30 | .40 | .50 | .60 | .70 | .80 | .90 |
|---|-----|-----|-----|-----|-----|-----|-----|-----|-----|
| 25 | 12 | 20 | 32 | 48 | 66 | 81 | 91 | 97 | 99 |
| 30 | 13 | 22 | 36 | 55 | 73 | 87 | 95 | 99 | * |
| 35 | 13 | 24 | 41 | 61 | 79 | 92 | 97 | 99 | |
| 40 | 14 | 26 | 45 | 67 | 85 | 95 | 99 | * | |
| 45 | 14 | 28 | 49 | 72 | 89 | 97 | 99 | | |
| 50 | 15 | 30 | 53 | 76 | 92 | 98 | * | | |
| 60 | 16 | 33 | 60 | 83 | 96 | 99 | | | |
| 70 | 17 | 37 | 66 | 88 | 98 | * | | | |
| 80 | 18 | 41 | 72 | 92 | 99 | | | | |
| 90 | 19 | 45 | 77 | 95 | 99 | | | | |
| 100 | 20 | 48 | 81 | 97 | * | | | | |
| 120 | 22 | 55 | 87 | 99 | | | | | |
| 140 | 24 | 61 | 92 | 99 | | | | | |
| 160 | 26 | 67 | 95 | * | | | | | |
| 180 | 28 | 72 | 97 | | | | | | |
| 200 | 30 | 76 | 98 | | | | | | |
| 250 | 34 | 85 | 99 | | | | | | |
| 300 | 39 | 90 | * | | | | | | |
| 350 | 44 | 94 | | | | | | | |
| 400 | 48 | 97 | | | | | | | |
| 500 | 57 | 99 | | | | | | | |
| 600 | 64 | * | | | | | | | |
| 700 | 71 | | | | | | | | |
| 800 | 76 | | | | | | | | |
| 900 | 81 | | | | | | | | |
| 1000 | 85 | | | | | | | | |

## Table 7.3.34

Power of $\chi^2$ test at $a$ = .10, $u$ = 6

|  | w | | | | | | | | |
| N | .10 | .20 | .30 | .40 | .50 | .60 | .70 | .80 | .90 |
|---|---|---|---|---|---|---|---|---|---|
| 25 | 12 | 17 | 26 | 39 | 55 | 71 | 84 | 92 | 97 |
| 30 | 12 | 18 | 29 | 45 | 63 | 79 | 90 | 96 | 99 |
| 35 | 12 | 19 | 32 | 50 | 70 | 85 | 94 | 98 | * |
| 40 | 13 | 21 | 36 | 56 | 75 | 89 | 97 | 99 | |
| 45 | 13 | 22 | 39 | 61 | 80 | 93 | 98 | * | |
| 50 | 13 | 24 | 43 | 66 | 85 | 95 | 99 | | |
| 60 | 14 | 27 | 49 | 74 | 91 | 98 | * | | |
| 70 | 15 | 30 | 55 | 80 | 95 | 99 | | | |
| 80 | 15 | 33 | 61 | 85 | 97 | * | | | |
| 90 | 16 | 36 | 66 | 89 | 98 | | | | |
| 100 | 17 | 39 | 71 | 92 | 99 | | | | |
| 120 | 18 | 45 | 79 | 96 | * | | | | |
| 140 | 19 | 50 | 85 | 98 | | | | | |
| 160 | 21 | 56 | 89 | 99 | | | | | |
| 180 | 22 | 61 | 93 | * | | | | | |
| 200 | 24 | 66 | 95 | | | | | | |
| 250 | 28 | 75 | 98 | | | | | | |
| 300 | 31 | 83 | 99 | | | | | | |
| 350 | 35 | 89 | * | | | | | | |
| 400 | 39 | 92 | | | | | | | |
| 500 | 46 | 97 | | | | | | | |
| 600 | 53 | 99 | | | | | | | |
| 700 | 60 | * | | | | | | | |
| 800 | 66 | | | | | | | | |
| 900 | 71 | | | | | | | | |
| 1000 | 75 | | | | | | | | |

## Table 7.3.33

Power of $\chi^2$ test at $a$ = .10, $u$ = 5

|  | w | | | | | | | | |
| N | .10 | .20 | .30 | .40 | .50 | .60 | .70 | .80 | .90 |
|---|---|---|---|---|---|---|---|---|---|
| 25 | 12 | 17 | 27 | 41 | 58 | 74 | 86 | 94 | 98 |
| 30 | 12 | 19 | 31 | 47 | 66 | 81 | 92 | 97 | 99 |
| 35 | 12 | 20 | 35 | 53 | 72 | 87 | 95 | 99 | * |
| 40 | 13 | 22 | 38 | 59 | 78 | 91 | 97 | 99 | |
| 45 | 13 | 24 | 42 | 64 | 83 | 94 | 99 | * | |
| 50 | 14 | 25 | 45 | 69 | 87 | 96 | 99 | | |
| 60 | 14 | 28 | 52 | 76 | 92 | 98 | * | | |
| 70 | 15 | 32 | 58 | 83 | 96 | 99 | | | |
| 80 | 16 | 35 | 64 | 88 | 98 | * | | | |
| 90 | 17 | 38 | 69 | 91 | 99 | | | | |
| 100 | 17 | 41 | 74 | 94 | 99 | | | | |
| 120 | 19 | 47 | 81 | 97 | * | | | | |
| 140 | 20 | 53 | 87 | 99 | | | | | |
| 160 | 22 | 59 | 91 | 99 | | | | | |
| 180 | 24 | 64 | 94 | * | | | | | |
| 200 | 25 | 69 | 96 | | | | | | |
| 250 | 29 | 78 | 99 | | | | | | |
| 300 | 33 | 85 | * | | | | | | |
| 350 | 37 | 90 | | | | | | | |
| 400 | 41 | 94 | | | | | | | |
| 500 | 49 | 98 | | | | | | | |
| 600 | 56 | 99 | | | | | | | |
| 700 | 63 | * | | | | | | | |
| 800 | 69 | | | | | | | | |
| 900 | 74 | | | | | | | | |
| 1000 | 78 | | | | | | | | |

Table 7.3.35

Power of $\chi^2$ test at a = .10, u = 7

|  |  |  |  |  | w |  |  |  |  |
|---|---|---|---|---|---|---|---|---|---|
| N | .10 | .20 | .30 | .40 | .50 | .60 | .70 | .80 | .90 |
| 25 | 11 | 16 | 24 | 37 | 52 | 68 | 82 | 91 | 96 |
| 30 | 12 | 17 | 28 | 43 | 59 | 76 | 88 | 95 | 99 |
| 35 | 12 | 19 | 31 | 48 | 67 | 83 | 93 | 98 | 99 |
| 40 | 12 | 20 | 34 | 53 | 73 | 88 | 96 | 99 | * |
| 45 | 13 | 21 | 37 | 58 | 78 | 91 | 98 | * |  |
| 50 | 13 | 23 | 40 | 63 | 81 | 94 | 99 |  |  |
| 60 | 14 | 26 | 47 | 71 | 89 | 97 | * |  |  |
| 70 | 14 | 28 | 53 | 78 | 93 | 99 |  |  |  |
| 80 | 15 | 31 | 58 | 83 | 96 | * |  |  |  |
| 90 | 15 | 34 | 63 | 88 | 98 |  |  |  |  |
| 100 | 16 | 37 | 68 | 91 | 99 |  |  |  |  |
| 120 | 17 | 43 | 76 | 95 | * |  |  |  |  |
| 140 | 19 | 48 | 83 | 98 |  |  |  |  |  |
| 160 | 20 | 53 | 88 | 99 |  |  |  |  |  |
| 180 | 21 | 58 | 91 | * |  |  |  |  |  |
| 200 | 23 | 63 | 94 |  |  |  |  |  |  |
| 250 | 26 | 73 | 98 |  |  |  |  |  |  |
| 300 | 30 | 81 | * |  |  |  |  |  |  |
| 350 | 33 | 87 |  |  |  |  |  |  |  |
| 400 | 37 | 91 |  |  |  |  |  |  |  |
| 500 | 44 | 96 |  |  |  |  |  |  |  |
| 600 | 51 | 98 |  |  |  |  |  |  |  |
| 700 | 57 | 99 |  |  |  |  |  |  |  |
| 800 | 63 | * |  |  |  |  |  |  |  |
| 900 | 68 |  |  |  |  |  |  |  |  |
| 1000 | 73 |  |  |  |  |  |  |  |  |

Table 7.3.36

Power of $\chi^2$ test at a = .10, u = 8

|  |  |  |  |  | w |  |  |  |  |
|---|---|---|---|---|---|---|---|---|---|
| N | .10 | .20 | .30 | .40 | .50 | .60 | .70 | .80 | .90 |
| 25 | 11 | 16 | 23 | 35 | 50 | 66 | 80 | 88 | 96 |
| 30 | 12 | 17 | 26 | 41 | 58 | 74 | 87 | 94 | 98 |
| 35 | 12 | 18 | 30 | 46 | 65 | 81 | 92 | 97 | 99 |
| 40 | 12 | 19 | 33 | 51 | 71 | 86 | 95 | 99 | * |
| 45 | 12 | 21 | 36 | 56 | 76 | 90 | 97 | 99 |  |
| 50 | 13 | 22 | 39 | 61 | 81 | 93 | 98 | * |  |
| 60 | 13 | 24 | 45 | 69 | 88 | 97 | 99 |  |  |
| 70 | 14 | 27 | 50 | 76 | 92 | 99 | * |  |  |
| 80 | 14 | 30 | 56 | 82 | 95 | 99 |  |  |  |
| 90 | 15 | 33 | 61 | 86 | 97 | * |  |  |  |
| 100 | 16 | 35 | 66 | 90 | 98 |  |  |  |  |
| 120 | 17 | 41 | 74 | 95 | * |  |  |  |  |
| 140 | 18 | 46 | 81 | 97 |  |  |  |  |  |
| 160 | 19 | 51 | 86 | 99 |  |  |  |  |  |
| 180 | 21 | 56 | 90 | 99 |  |  |  |  |  |
| 200 | 22 | 61 | 93 | * |  |  |  |  |  |
| 250 | 25 | 71 | 97 |  |  |  |  |  |  |
| 300 | 28 | 79 | 99 |  |  |  |  |  |  |
| 350 | 32 | 85 | * |  |  |  |  |  |  |
| 400 | 35 | 90 |  |  |  |  |  |  |  |
| 500 | 42 | 95 |  |  |  |  |  |  |  |
| 600 | 49 | 98 |  |  |  |  |  |  |  |
| 700 | 55 | 99 |  |  |  |  |  |  |  |
| 800 | 61 | * |  |  |  |  |  |  |  |
| 900 | 66 |  |  |  |  |  |  |  |  |
| 1000 | 71 |  |  |  |  |  |  |  |  |

Table 7.3.37

Power of $\chi^2$ test at $a$ = .10, $u$ = 9

| | | | | | w | | | | |
|---|---|---|---|---|---|---|---|---|---|
| N | .10 | .20 | .30 | .40 | .50 | .60 | .70 | .80 | .90 |
| 25 | 11 | 15 | 23 | 34 | 48 | 64 | 78 | 88 | 95 |
| 30 | 12 | 16 | 25 | 39 | 56 | 72 | 85 | 94 | 98 |
| 35 | 12 | 18 | 28 | 44 | 62 | 79 | 91 | 97 | 99 |
| 40 | 12 | 19 | 31 | 49 | 69 | 85 | 94 | 98 | * |
| 45 | 12 | 20 | 34 | 54 | 74 | 89 | 97 | 99 | |
| 50 | 13 | 21 | 37 | 58 | 79 | 92 | 98 | * | |
| 60 | 13 | 24 | 43 | 67 | 86 | 96 | 99 | | |
| 70 | 14 | 26 | 48 | 74 | 91 | 98 | * | | |
| 80 | 14 | 29 | 54 | 80 | 95 | 99 | | | |
| 90 | 15 | 31 | 59 | 85 | 97 | * | | | |
| 100 | 15 | 34 | 64 | 88 | 98 | | | | |
| 120 | 16 | 39 | 72 | 94 | 99 | | | | |
| 140 | 18 | 44 | 79 | 97 | * | | | | |
| 160 | 19 | 49 | 85 | 98 | | | | | |
| 180 | 20 | 54 | 89 | 99 | | | | | |
| 200 | 21 | 58 | 92 | * | | | | | |
| 250 | 24 | 69 | 97 | | | | | | |
| 300 | 27 | 77 | 99 | | | | | | |
| 350 | 31 | 84 | * | | | | | | |
| 400 | 34 | 88 | | | | | | | |
| 500 | 40 | 95 | | | | | | | |
| 600 | 47 | 98 | | | | | | | |
| 700 | 53 | 99 | | | | | | | |
| 800 | 58 | * | | | | | | | |
| 900 | 64 | | | | | | | | |
| 1000 | 69 | | | | | | | | |

Table 7.3.38

Power of $\chi^2$ test at $a$ = .10, $u$ = 10

| | | | | | w | | | | |
|---|---|---|---|---|---|---|---|---|---|
| N | .10 | .20 | .30 | .40 | .50 | .60 | .70 | .80 | .90 |
| 25 | 11 | 15 | 22 | 33 | 46 | 62 | 76 | 87 | 94 |
| 30 | 11 | 16 | 25 | 38 | 54 | 70 | 84 | 93 | 97 |
| 35 | 12 | 17 | 27 | 42 | 60 | 77 | 90 | 96 | 99 |
| 40 | 12 | 18 | 30 | 47 | 67 | 83 | 92 | 98 | * |
| 45 | 12 | 19 | 33 | 52 | 72 | 88 | 96 | 99 | |
| 50 | 12 | 20 | 36 | 57 | 77 | 91 | 98 | * | |
| 60 | 13 | 23 | 41 | 65 | 85 | 96 | 99 | | |
| 70 | 13 | 25 | 47 | 72 | 90 | 98 | * | | |
| 80 | 14 | 28 | 52 | 78 | 94 | 99 | | | |
| 90 | 14 | 30 | 57 | 83 | 96 | * | | | |
| 100 | 15 | 33 | 62 | 87 | 98 | | | | |
| 120 | 16 | 38 | 70 | 93 | 99 | | | | |
| 140 | 17 | 42 | 77 | 96 | * | | | | |
| 160 | 18 | 47 | 83 | 98 | | | | | |
| 180 | 19 | 52 | 88 | 99 | | | | | |
| 200 | 20 | 57 | 91 | * | | | | | |
| 250 | 23 | 67 | 96 | | | | | | |
| 300 | 26 | 75 | 99 | | | | | | |
| 350 | 29 | 82 | * | | | | | | |
| 400 | 33 | 87 | | | | | | | |
| 500 | 39 | 94 | | | | | | | |
| 600 | 45 | 97 | | | | | | | |
| 700 | 51 | 99 | | | | | | | |
| 800 | 57 | * | | | | | | | |
| 900 | 62 | | | | | | | | |
| 1000 | 67 | | | | | | | | |

## Table 7.3.39

Power of $\chi^2$ test at a = .10, u = 12

| N | | | | | w | | | | |
|---|---|---|---|---|---|---|---|---|---|
| | .10 | .20 | .30 | .40 | .50 | .60 | .70 | .80 | .90 |
| 25 | 11 | 14 | 21 | 31 | 44 | 58 | 73 | 85 | 92 |
| 30 | 11 | 15 | 23 | 35 | 51 | 67 | 81 | 91 | 97 |
| 35 | 11 | 16 | 26 | 40 | 57 | 74 | 87 | 95 | 98 |
| 40 | 12 | 17 | 28 | 44 | 63 | 80 | 92 | 97 | 99 |
| 45 | 12 | 18 | 31 | 49 | 69 | 85 | 95 | 99 | * |
| 50 | 12 | 19 | 33 | 53 | 74 | 89 | 97 | 99 | |
| 60 | 13 | 22 | 39 | 61 | 82 | 94 | 99 | * | |
| 70 | 13 | 24 | 44 | 69 | 88 | 97 | | | |
| 80 | 14 | 26 | 49 | 75 | 92 | 99 | | | |
| 90 | 14 | 28 | 54 | 80 | 95 | 99 | | | |
| 100 | 14 | 31 | 58 | 85 | 97 | * | | | |
| 120 | 15 | 35 | 67 | 91 | 99 | | | | |
| 140 | 16 | 40 | 74 | 95 | * | | | | |
| 160 | 17 | 44 | 80 | 97 | | | | | |
| 180 | 18 | 49 | 85 | 99 | | | | | |
| 200 | 19 | 53 | 89 | 99 | | | | | |
| 250 | 22 | 63 | 95 | * | | | | | |
| 300 | 25 | 72 | 98 | | | | | | |
| 350 | 28 | 79 | 99 | | | | | | |
| 400 | 31 | 85 | * | | | | | | |
| 500 | 36 | 92 | | | | | | | |
| 600 | 42 | 96 | | | | | | | |
| 700 | 48 | 98 | | | | | | | |
| 800 | 53 | 99 | | | | | | | |
| 900 | 58 | * | | | | | | | |
| 1000 | 63 | | | | | | | | |

## Table 7.3.40

Power of $\chi^2$ test at a = .10, u = 16

| N | | | | | w | | | | |
|---|---|---|---|---|---|---|---|---|---|
| | .10 | .20 | .30 | .40 | .50 | .60 | .70 | .80 | .90 |
| 25 | 11 | 14 | 19 | 28 | 39 | 53 | 67 | 80 | 90 |
| 30 | 11 | 15 | 21 | 32 | 46 | 61 | 76 | 88 | 95 |
| 35 | 11 | 15 | 23 | 36 | 52 | 69 | 83 | 93 | 97 |
| 40 | 11 | 16 | 26 | 40 | 58 | 75 | 88 | 96 | 99 |
| 45 | 12 | 17 | 28 | 44 | 63 | 81 | 92 | 98 | 99 |
| 50 | 12 | 18 | 30 | 48 | 68 | 85 | 95 | 99 | * |
| 60 | 12 | 20 | 35 | 56 | 77 | 92 | 98 | * | |
| 70 | 13 | 22 | 39 | 63 | 84 | 95 | 99 | | |
| 80 | 13 | 24 | 44 | 70 | 89 | 98 | | | |
| 90 | 13 | 26 | 49 | 75 | 93 | 99 | | | |
| 100 | 14 | 28 | 53 | 80 | 95 | 99 | | | |
| 120 | 15 | 32 | 61 | 88 | 98 | * | | | |
| 140 | 15 | 36 | 69 | 93 | 99 | | | | |
| 160 | 16 | 40 | 75 | 96 | * | | | | |
| 180 | 17 | 44 | 81 | 98 | | | | | |
| 200 | 18 | 48 | 85 | 99 | | | | | |
| 250 | 20 | 58 | 93 | * | | | | | |
| 300 | 23 | 66 | 97 | | | | | | |
| 350 | 25 | 74 | 99 | | | | | | |
| 400 | 28 | 80 | 99 | | | | | | |
| 500 | 33 | 89 | * | | | | | | |
| 600 | 38 | 94 | | | | | | | |
| 700 | 43 | 97 | | | | | | | |
| 800 | 48 | 99 | | | | | | | |
| 900 | 53 | 99 | | | | | | | |
| 1000 | 58 | * | | | | | | | |

Table 7.3.41

Power of $\chi^2$ test at $a$ = .10, $u$ = 20

| N | .10 | .20 | .30 | .40 | .50 | .60 | .70 | .80 | .90 |
|---|-----|-----|-----|-----|-----|-----|-----|-----|-----|
| w | | | | | | | | | |
| 25 | 11 | 13 | 18 | 26 | 36 | 49 | 63 | 76 | 86 |
| 30 | 11 | 14 | 20 | 29 | 42 | 57 | 72 | 84 | 93 |
| 35 | 11 | 15 | 22 | 33 | 48 | 64 | 79 | 90 | 96 |
| 40 | 11 | 16 | 24 | 37 | 53 | 71 | 85 | 94 | 98 |
| 45 | 11 | 16 | 26 | 40 | 59 | 77 | 90 | 97 | 99 |
| 50 | 12 | 17 | 28 | 44 | 64 | 82 | 93 | 98 | * |
| 60 | 12 | 19 | 32 | 52 | 73 | 89 | 97 | 99 | |
| 70 | 12 | 20 | 36 | 59 | 80 | 94 | 99 | * | |
| 80 | 13 | 22 | 40 | 65 | 86 | 97 | 99 | | |
| 90 | 13 | 24 | 45 | 71 | 90 | 98 | * | | |
| 100 | 13 | 26 | 49 | 76 | 93 | 99 | | | |
| 120 | 14 | 29 | 57 | 84 | 97 | * | | | |
| 140 | 15 | 33 | 64 | 90 | 99 | | | | |
| 160 | 16 | 37 | 71 | 94 | * | | | | |
| 180 | 16 | 40 | 77 | 97 | | | | | |
| 200 | 17 | 44 | 82 | 98 | | | | | |
| 250 | 19 | 53 | 90 | * | | | | | |
| 300 | 21 | 62 | 95 | | | | | | |
| 350 | 23 | 70 | 98 | | | | | | |
| 400 | 26 | 76 | 99 | | | | | | |
| 500 | 30 | 86 | * | | | | | | |
| 600 | 35 | 92 | | | | | | | |
| 700 | 40 | 96 | | | | | | | |
| 800 | 44 | 98 | | | | | | | |
| 900 | 49 | 99 | | | | | | | |
| 1000 | 53 | * | | | | | | | |

Table 7.3.42

Power of $\chi^2$ test at $a$ = .10, $u$ = 24

| N | .10 | .20 | .30 | .40 | .50 | .60 | .70 | .80 | .90 |
|---|-----|-----|-----|-----|-----|-----|-----|-----|-----|
| w | | | | | | | | | |
| 25 | 11 | 13 | 17 | 24 | 34 | 46 | 59 | 72 | 84 |
| 30 | 11 | 14 | 19 | 27 | 39 | 53 | 68 | 81 | 91 |
| 35 | 11 | 14 | 21 | 31 | 45 | 61 | 76 | 88 | 95 |
| 40 | 11 | 15 | 22 | 34 | 50 | 67 | 82 | 92 | 97 |
| 45 | 11 | 16 | 24 | 38 | 55 | 73 | 87 | 95 | 99 |
| 50 | 11 | 16 | 26 | 41 | 60 | 78 | 91 | 97 | 99 |
| 60 | 12 | 18 | 30 | 48 | 69 | 86 | 96 | 99 | * |
| 70 | 12 | 19 | 34 | 55 | 77 | 92 | 98 | * | |
| 80 | 12 | 20 | 38 | 61 | 83 | 97 | 99 | | |
| 90 | 13 | 22 | 42 | 66 | 88 | 98 | * | | |
| 100 | 13 | 24 | 46 | 72 | 92 | 99 | | | |
| 120 | 14 | 27 | 53 | 81 | 96 | * | | | |
| 140 | 14 | 31 | 61 | 88 | 98 | | | | |
| 160 | 15 | 34 | 67 | 92 | 99 | | | | |
| 180 | 16 | 38 | 73 | 95 | * | | | | |
| 200 | 16 | 41 | 78 | 97 | | | | | |
| 250 | 18 | 50 | 88 | 99 | | | | | |
| 300 | 20 | 58 | 94 | * | | | | | |
| 350 | 22 | 66 | 97 | | | | | | |
| 400 | 24 | 72 | 99 | | | | | | |
| 500 | 28 | 83 | * | | | | | | |
| 600 | 32 | 90 | | | | | | | |
| 700 | 37 | 96 | | | | | | | |
| 800 | 41 | 98 | | | | | | | |
| 900 | 46 | 99 | | | | | | | |
| 1000 | 50 | * | | | | | | | |

Note that although all the tables begin at $N = 25$, for the Case 0 and Case 1 application of $\chi^2$ of this chapter, samples of this size will yield tests of dubious validity as $u$ increases. See Section 7.4 for discussion and references on this point.

The values in the body of the tables are the power times 100, i.e., the percent of tests carried out under the specified conditions which will result in the rejection of the null hypothesis. They are rounded to the nearest unit, and they are generally accurate to within $\pm 1$ as tabled.

7.3.1   CASE 0: GOODNESS OF FIT TESTS. By the way of review: In Case 0, the $H_0$ is a set of proportions ($P_{0i}$) in $m$ categories which reflect no effect in a way appropriate to the problem. The $H_1$ is another set of proportions ($P_{1i}$) in the $m$ categories which collectively reflect the effect. Each category contributes a value ($P_{1i} - P_{0i})^2/P_{0i}$ to a total, whose square root, $w$, indexes the ES. The $u$ for a given problem is $m - 1$, unless there are further constraints due to parameter estimation, as e.g., in fitting a normal distribution, where $u = m - 3$ (see Section 7.2.1 and references).

**Illustrative Examples**

**7.1**   A market researcher is seeking to determine the relative preference by consumers among four different package designs for a new product. He arranges to have a panel of 100 consumers each select the single design he prefers over the rest. He performs a $\chi^2$ test at $a = .05$ on the preference distribution against a null hypothesis of equal preference, i.e.,

$$\begin{array}{ccccc} & A & B & C & D \\ H_0: & .25 & .25 & .25 & .25 \end{array}$$

What is the power of this test, if in fact, in the population, the actual distribution is

$$\begin{array}{ccccc} & A & B & C & D \\ H_1: & .3750 & .2083 & .2083 & .2083 \; ? \end{array}$$

First, one finds $w$ for this alternative [formula (7.2.1)]:

$$w = \sqrt{\frac{(.3750 - .2500)^2}{.2500} + \frac{3(.2083 - .2500)^2}{.2500}} = .289.$$

The degrees of freedom, $u$, for this application is $m - 1 = 3$, there being only one constraint on the freedom of the category $P$ values to vary, namely the requirement that they sum to 1.00. Thus, the summary of his specifications is

$$a = .05, \quad u = 3, \quad w = .289, \quad N = 100.$$

In Table 7.3.17 for **a** = .05 and **u** = 3 at row **N** = 100, we find power for column **w** = .20 to be .36 and for **w** = .30 to be .71. Linear interpolation yields (approximate) power of

$$.36 + \frac{(.289 - .20)}{(.30 - .20)} (.71 - .36) = .36 + .31 = .67.$$

Thus, if **H**₁ is true, or for any other **H**₁ which yields a **w** = .289, the market researcher has about a 2 in 3 chance of rejecting the null hypothesis of equal preference in the population among the four designs.

**7.2** A psychometrician needs to determine whether a population distribution of scores on a psychological test under development is normal. He secures a random sample of 200 Ss, and by methods described by Hays (1981, pp. 542–544) determines that for 9 step intervals of his score distribution, a normal distribution would have the following proportions in successive intervals:

**H₀:**  .020  .051  .118  .195  .232  .195  .118  .051  .020

After experimenting with several alternate population distributions, he concludes that he wishes to be able to detect a departure from normality of **w** = .20. Since the burden of "proof" of normality is his, he selects **a** = .10 as his significance criterion in order to be lenient in his rejection of the null hypothesis of normality. Under these conditions, what is the power of his $\chi^2$ test for goodness of fit to normality?

To determine the **u**, consider that in the fitting of the normal distribution to his sample values, in addition to the usual constraint of summation of the proportions to .100, he has estimated from his sample two population parameters, the mean and standard deviation. Thus, his degrees of freedom are **u** = **m** − 3 = 9 − 3 = 6.

The specifications for the power of the $\chi^2$ test are:

**a** = .10,     **u** = 6,     **w** = .20,     **N** = 200.

In Table 7.3.34 (for **a** = .10, **u** = 6) for column **w** = .20, row **N** = 200, he finds power = .66. Under the circumstances, he might consider that, given a departure of **w** = .20 from normality, a probability of rejection of normality of only .66 might not be sufficient.

**7.3.2**  CASE 1: CONTINGENCY TESTS. In Case 1, we deal with a two-way table of variables **R** and **K** which has **rk** = **m** cells, each containing a proportion of the population. The **m** null-hypothetical proportions **P₀ᵢ** are those which reflect no association between **R** and **K** and are found as products of the marginal proportions, as in Table 7.2.2. The alternate-hypothetical proportions $P_{0i}$ are another set which then necessarily reflect some association, of greater or lesser degree. The amount of association or departure from $H_0$ is found as in Case 0, i.e., each of the **m** cells contributes a value $(P_{1i} - P_{0i})^2/P_{0i}$ to a total whose square root is **w**. The **u** for a given problem is $(r - 1)(k - 1)$. Such problems can be viewed equally as concerning association between **R** and **K** or as concerning differences among the **r** subpopulations in distributions over the **k** categories (or **k** subpopulations over the **r** categories).

## Illustrative Examples

**7.3** A political scientist is studying the relationship between sex and political preference (Democrat, Republican, Independent) for a certain population. Assume that she knows, or can estimate, the marginals, i.e., the proportions of men and women voters, and the proportions of each political preference in the population. She has available a sample of **N** = 140 voters for the $\chi^2$ contingency test, which she performs at the **a** = .01 significance level. Her null hypothesis is expressed by the $P_{0i}$ in Table 7.2.2 above, which reflects no association between voter sex and politial preference or, equivalently, no sex difference in political preference distribution. The degrees of freedom for the test, $u = (2 - 1)(3 - 1) = 2$. If the joint proportions in the population are the $P_{1i}$ of Table 7.2.1, what is the power of the test? It has been shown above (Section 6.2) that the ES of the departure of the $P_{1i}$ from the $P_{0i}$ is **w** = .346. Then,

$$a = .01, \quad u = 2, \quad w = .346, \quad N = 140.$$

Table 7.3.2 (for **a** = .01) at **u** = 2, **N** = 140, power for **w** = .30 is .75 and for **w** = .40, .97. Linear interpolation gives the (approximate) power for **w** = .346 as

$$.75 + \frac{(.346 - .30)}{(.40 - .30)} (.97 - .75) = .85.$$

Thus, if the population proportions are as in Table 7.2.1, or for any other set of values yielding **w** = .346, the probability of rejecting the hypothesis of no association at **a** = .01 using 140 respondents is .85.

**7.4** A clinical psychologist is studying the predictive validity of a new psychodiagnostic procedure administered to patients upon admission to a psychiatric hospital, using as a criterion final psychiatric diagnosis. Assume that 80 patients are classified into the diagnostic categories "brain damaged," "functional psychotic," and "psychoneurotic," both by the psychodiagnostic procedure and by the final diagnosis. The contingency table for assessing predictive validity will thus be a $3 \times 3$ table, with $\mathbf{u} = (3 - 1)(3 - 1) = 4$. If the degree of association in the population is indexed by a Cramér $\phi'$ of .20, what is the power of a $\chi^2$ test using $\mathbf{a} = .05$ as the significance criterion?

To be used in the power tables, the $\phi'$ must be converted into its $\mathbf{w}$ equivalent. From formula (7.2.7), noting that $\mathbf{r}(=\mathbf{k}) = 3$, we find $\mathbf{w} = .20\sqrt{3 - 1} = .283$. The specifications, then, are:

$$\mathbf{a} = .05, \qquad \mathbf{u} = 4, \qquad \mathbf{w} = .283, \qquad \mathbf{N} = 80.$$

In Table 7.3.18 (for $\mathbf{a} = .05$, $\mathbf{u} = 4$) for row $\mathbf{N} = 80$, we find power at $\mathbf{w} = .20$ to be .26 and at $\mathbf{w} = .30$ to be .55. Interpolating linearly for $\mathbf{w} = .283$, power is found to be approximately

$$.26 + \frac{(.283 - .20)}{(.30 - .20)} (.55 - .26) = .50.$$

Thus, at the level of association of $\phi' = .20$ posited for the population, it is a "toss-up" whether a contingency test significant at $\mathbf{a} = .05$ will result with $\mathbf{N} = 80$.

**7.5**   A community psychiatry research team undertakes an inquiry into the association between religious-ethnic group ($\mathbf{r} = 5$) and type of diagnosis given ($\mathbf{k} = 6$) in a statewide population of child clinic referrals. Data are available for $\mathbf{N} = 400$ referrals. If the degree of association is small ($\mathbf{w} = .10$; $\mathbf{C} = .100$; $\phi' = .050$ from Table 7.2.3), what is the power of a $\chi^2$ test performed at the 0.1 level? For this large table, $\mathbf{u}$ is equal to $(5 - 1)(6 - 1) = 20$. The specifications, in summary form, are

$$\mathbf{a} = .01, \qquad \mathbf{u} = 20, \qquad \mathbf{w} = .10, \qquad \mathbf{N} = 400.$$

In Table 7.3.13 for $\mathbf{a} = .01$ and $\mathbf{u} = 20$, column $\mathbf{w} = .10$, and row $\mathbf{N} = 400$, we find power to be .05(!). Note that even if the lenient $\mathbf{a} = .10$ criterion is used instead (Table 7.3.41), power is still only .26. If the actual association is "medium" $\mathbf{w} = .30$, and from Table 7.2.3, $\mathbf{C} = .287$, $\phi' = .150$), at $\mathbf{a} = .01$, power is .92 and at $\mathbf{a} = .05$, power is .98.

## 7.4   SAMPLE SIZE TABLES

The sample size tables for this section are given on pages 253–267.

The tables in this section give values for the significance criterion ($\mathbf{a}$), the degrees of freedom ($\mathbf{u}$), the ES to be detected ($\mathbf{w}$), and the *desired power*. The necessary total sample size $\mathbf{N}$ then may be found. As with the other sample size tables in this handbook, they will be used primarily in the planning of experiments where they provide a basis for the decision as to the sample size to use.

## TABLE 7.4.1

### N TO DETECT w BY $\chi^2$ AT a $= .01$, u $= 1, 2, 3$

|        | u = 1 w |       |       |       |       |       |       |       |       |
|--------|------|------|------|------|------|------|------|------|------|
| Power  | .10  | .20  | .30  | .40  | .50  | .60  | .70  | .80  | .90  |
| .25    | 362  | 90   | 40   | 23   | 14   | 10   | 7    | 6    | 4    |
| .50    | 664  | 166  | 74   | 41   | 27   | 18   | 14   | 10   | 8    |
| .60    | 800  | 200  | 89   | 50   | 32   | 22   | 16   | 13   | 10   |
| 2/3    | 904  | 226  | 100  | 56   | 36   | 25   | 18   | 14   | 11   |
| .70    | 961  | 240  | 107  | 60   | 38   | 27   | 20   | 15   | 12   |
| .75    | 1056 | 264  | 117  | 66   | 42   | 29   | 22   | 17   | 13   |
| .80    | 1168 | 292  | 130  | 73   | 47   | 32   | 24   | 18   | 14   |
| .85    | 1305 | 326  | 145  | 82   | 52   | 36   | 27   | 20   | 16   |
| .90    | 1488 | 372  | 165  | 93   | 60   | 41   | 30   | 23   | 18   |
| .95    | 1781 | 445  | 198  | 111  | 71   | 49   | 36   | 28   | 22   |
| .99    | 2403 | 601  | 267  | 150  | 96   | 67   | 49   | 38   | 30   |

|        | u = 2 w |       |       |       |       |       |       |       |       |
|--------|------|------|------|------|------|------|------|------|------|
| Power  | .10  | .20  | .30  | .40  | .50  | .60  | .70  | .80  | .90  |
| .25    | 467  | 117  | 52   | 29   | 19   | 13   | 10   | 7    | 6    |
| .50    | 819  | 205  | 91   | 51   | 33   | 23   | 17   | 13   | 10   |
| .60    | 975  | 244  | 108  | 61   | 39   | 27   | 20   | 15   | 12   |
| 2/3    | 1092 | 273  | 121  | 68   | 44   | 30   | 22   | 17   | 13   |
| .70    | 1157 | 289  | 129  | 72   | 46   | 32   | 24   | 18   | 14   |
| .75    | 1264 | 316  | 140  | 79   | 51   | 35   | 26   | 20   | 16   |
| .80    | 1388 | 347  | 154  | 87   | 56   | 39   | 28   | 22   | 17   |
| .85    | 1540 | 385  | 171  | 96   | 62   | 43   | 31   | 24   | 19   |
| .90    | 1743 | 436  | 194  | 109  | 70   | 48   | 36   | 27   | 22   |
| .95    | 2065 | 516  | 229  | 129  | 83   | 57   | 42   | 32   | 25   |
| .99    | 2742 | 685  | 305  | 171  | 110  | 76   | 56   | 43   | 34   |

|        | u = 3 w |       |       |       |       |       |       |       |       |
|--------|------|------|------|------|------|------|------|------|------|
| Power  | .10  | .20  | .30  | .40  | .50  | .60  | .70  | .80  | .90  |
| .25    | 544  | 136  | 60   | 34   | 22   | 15   | 11   | 8    | 7    |
| .50    | 931  | 233  | 103  | 58   | 37   | 26   | 19   | 15   | 11   |
| .60    | 1101 | 275  | 122  | 69   | 44   | 31   | 22   | 17   | 14   |
| 2/3    | 1227 | 307  | 136  | 77   | 49   | 34   | 25   | 19   | 15   |
| .70    | 1297 | 324  | 144  | 81   | 52   | 36   | 26   | 20   | 16   |
| .75    | 1412 | 353  | 157  | 88   | 56   | 39   | 29   | 22   | 17   |
| .80    | 1546 | 386  | 172  | 97   | 62   | 43   | 32   | 24   | 19   |
| .85    | 1709 | 427  | 190  | 107  | 68   | 47   | 35   | 27   | 21   |
| .90    | 1925 | 481  | 214  | 120  | 77   | 53   | 39   | 30   | 24   |
| .95    | 2267 | 567  | 252  | 142  | 91   | 63   | 46   | 35   | 28   |
| .99    | 2983 | 746  | 331  | 186  | 119  | 83   | 61   | 47   | 37   |

TABLE 7.4.2

**N** TO DETECT **w** BY $\chi^2$ AT **a** $= .01$, **u** $= 4, 5, 6$

| | | | | | | | | | |
|---|---|---|---|---|---|---|---|---|---|
| | | | | $\dfrac{u = 4}{w}$ | | | | | |
| Power | .10 | .20 | .30 | .40 | .50 | .60 | .70 | .80 | .90 |
| .25 | 607 | 152 | 67 | 38 | 24 | 17 | 12 | 9 | 7 |
| .50 | 1023 | 256 | 114 | 64 | 41 | 28 | 21 | 16 | 13 |
| .60 | 1204 | 301 | 134 | 75 | 48 | 33 | 25 | 19 | 15 |
| 2/3 | 1338 | 335 | 149 | 84 | 54 | 37 | 27 | 21 | 17 |
| .70 | 1412 | 353 | 157 | 88 | 56 | 39 | 29 | 22 | 17 |
| .75 | 1534 | 383 | 170 | 96 | 61 | 43 | 31 | 24 | 19 |
| .80 | 1648 | 412 | 183 | 103 | 66 | 46 | 34 | 26 | 20 |
| .85 | 1847 | 462 | 205 | 115 | 74 | 51 | 38 | 29 | 23 |
| .90 | 2074 | 518 | 230 | 130 | 83 | 58 | 42 | 32 | 26 |
| .95 | 2433 | 608 | 270 | 152 | 97 | 68 | 50 | 38 | 30 |
| .99 | 3180 | 795 | 353 | 199 | 127 | 88 | 65 | 50 | 39 |
| | | | | $\dfrac{u = 5}{w}$ | | | | | |
| Power | .10 | .20 | .30 | .40 | .50 | .60 | .70 | .80 | .90 |
| .25 | 663 | 166 | 74 | 41 | 27 | 18 | 14 | 10 | 8 |
| .50 | 1103 | 276 | 123 | 59 | 44 | 31 | 23 | 17 | 14 |
| .60 | 1294 | 323 | 144 | 81 | 52 | 36 | 26 | 20 | 16 |
| 2/3 | 1434 | 359 | 159 | 90 | 57 | 40 | 29 | 22 | 18 |
| .70 | 1512 | 378 | 168 | 94 | 60 | 42 | 31 | 24 | 19 |
| .75 | 1640 | 410 | 182 | 102 | 66 | 46 | 33 | 26 | 20 |
| .80 | 1787 | 447 | 199 | 112 | 71 | 50 | 36 | 28 | 22 |
| .85 | 1966 | 492 | 218 | 123 | 79 | 55 | 40 | 31 | 24 |
| .90 | 2203 | 551 | 245 | 138 | 88 | 61 | 45 | 34 | 27 |
| .95 | 2576 | 644 | 286 | 161 | 103 | 72 | 53 | 40 | 32 |
| .99 | 3350 | 837 | 372 | 209 | 134 | 93 | 68 | 52 | 41 |
| | | | | $\dfrac{u = 6}{w}$ | | | | | |
| Power | .10 | .20 | .30 | .40 | .50 | .60 | .70 | .80 | .90 |
| .25 | 713 | 178 | 79 | 45 | 29 | 20 | 15 | 11 | 9 |
| .50 | 1175 | 294 | 131 | 73 | 47 | 33 | 24 | 18 | 15 |
| .60 | 1374 | 343 | 153 | 86 | 55 | 38 | 28 | 21 | 17 |
| 2/3 | 1521 | 380 | 169 | 95 | 61 | 42 | 31 | 24 | 19 |
| .70 | 1601 | 400 | 178 | 100 | 64 | 44 | 33 | 25 | 20 |
| .75 | 1734 | 434 | 193 | 108 | 69 | 48 | 35 | 27 | 21 |
| .80 | 1887 | 472 | 210 | 118 | 75 | 52 | 39 | 29 | 23 |
| .85 | 2073 | 518 | 230 | 130 | 83 | 58 | 42 | 32 | 26 |
| .90 | 2318 | 580 | 258 | 145 | 93 | 64 | 47 | 36 | 29 |
| .95 | 2704 | 676 | 300 | 169 | 108 | 75 | 55 | 42 | 33 |
| .99 | 3502 | 876 | 389 | 219 | 140 | 97 | 71 | 55 | 43 |

TABLE 7.4.3

$N$ TO DETECT $w$ BY $\chi^2$ AT $a = .01$, $u = 7, 8, 9$

|  |  |  |  | $\frac{u = 7}{w}$ |  |  |  |  |  |
|---|---|---|---|---|---|---|---|---|---|
| Power | .10 | .20 | .30 | .40 | .50 | .60 | .70 | .80 | .90 |
| .25 | 758 | 190 | 84 | 47 | 30 | 21 | 15 | 12 | 9 |
| .50 | 1241 | 310 | 138 | 78 | 50 | 34 | 25 | 19 | 15 |
| .60 | 1447 | 362 | 161 | 90 | 58 | 40 | 30 | 23 | 18 |
| 2/3 | 1599 | 400 | 178 | 100 | 64 | 44 | 33 | 25 | 20 |
| .70 | 1683 | 421 | 187 | 105 | 67 | 47 | 34 | 26 | 21 |
| .75 | 1820 | 455 | 202 | 114 | 73 | 51 | 37 | 28 | 22 |
| .80 | 1979 | 495 | 220 | 124 | 79 | 55 | 40 | 31 | 24 |
| .85 | 2171 | 543 | 241 | 136 | 87 | 60 | 44 | 34 | 27 |
| .90 | 2424 | 606 | 269 | 151 | 97 | 67 | 49 | 38 | 30 |
| .95 | 2821 | 705 | 313 | 176 | 113 | 78 | 58 | 44 | 35 |
| .99 | 3641 | 910 | 405 | 228 | 146 | 101 | 74 | 57 | 45 |

|  |  |  |  | $\frac{u = 8}{w}$ |  |  |  |  |  |
|---|---|---|---|---|---|---|---|---|---|
| Power | .10 | .20 | .30 | .40 | .50 | .60 | .70 | .80 | .90 |
| .25 | 801 | 200 | 89 | 50 | 32 | 22 | 16 | 13 | 10 |
| .50 | 1302 | 325 | 145 | 81 | 52 | 36 | 27 | 20 | 16 |
| .60 | 1515 | 379 | 168 | 95 | 61 | 42 | 31 | 24 | 19 |
| 2/3 | 1673 | 418 | 186 | 105 | 67 | 46 | 34 | 26 | 21 |
| .70 | 1759 | 440 | 195 | 110 | 70 | 49 | 36 | 27 | 22 |
| .75 | 1900 | 475 | 211 | 119 | 76 | 53 | 39 | 30 | 23 |
| .80 | 2064 | 516 | 229 | 129 | 83 | 57 | 42 | 32 | 25 |
| .85 | 2261 | 565 | 251 | 141 | 90 | 63 | 46 | 35 | 28 |
| .90 | 2521 | 630 | 280 | 158 | 101 | 70 | 51 | 39 | 31 |
| .95 | 2929 | 732 | 325 | 183 | 117 | 81 | 60 | 46 | 36 |
| .99 | 3769 | 942 | 419 | 236 | 151 | 105 | 77 | 59 | 47 |

|  |  |  |  | $\frac{u = 9}{w}$ |  |  |  |  |  |
|---|---|---|---|---|---|---|---|---|---|
| Power | .10 | .20 | .30 | .40 | .50 | .60 | .70 | .80 | .90 |
| .25 | 840 | 210 | 93 | 53 | 34 | 23 | 17 | 13 | 10 |
| .50 | 1359 | 340 | 151 | 85 | 54 | 38 | 28 | 21 | 17 |
| .60 | 1579 | 395 | 175 | 99 | 63 | 44 | 32 | 25 | 19 |
| 2/3 | 1741 | 435 | 193 | 109 | 70 | 48 | 36 | 27 | 21 |
| .70 | 1830 | 457 | 203 | 114 | 73 | 51 | 37 | 29 | 23 |
| .75 | 1975 | 494 | 219 | 123 | 79 | 55 | 40 | 31 | 24 |
| .80 | 2143 | 536 | 238 | 134 | 86 | 60 | 44 | 33 | 26 |
| .85 | 2346 | 586 | 260 | 147 | 94 | 65 | 48 | 37 | 29 |
| .90 | 2612 | 653 | 290 | 163 | 104 | 73 | 53 | 41 | 32 |
| .95 | 3030 | 758 | 337 | 189 | 121 | 84 | 62 | 47 | 37 |
| .99 | 3889 | 972 | 432 | 243 | 156 | 108 | 79 | 61 | 48 |

TABLE 7.4.4

**N** TO DETECT **w** BY $\chi^2$ AT **a** $= .01$, **u** $= 10, 12, 16$

| | | | | $u = 10$ |  |  |  |  |  |
| | | | | $w$ | | | | | |
| Power | .10 | .20 | .30 | .40 | .50 | .60 | .70 | .80 | .90 |
|---|---|---|---|---|---|---|---|---|---|
| .25 | 877 | 219 | 97 | 55 | 35 | 24 | 18 | 14 | 11 |
| .50 | 1413 | 353 | 157 | 88 | 57 | 39 | 29 | 22 | 17 |
| .60 | 1639 | 410 | 182 | 102 | 66 | 46 | 33 | 26 | 20 |
| 2/3 | 1805 | 451 | 201 | 113 | 72 | 50 | 37 | 28 | 22 |
| .70 | 1896 | 474 | 211 | 119 | 76 | 53 | 39 | 30 | 23 |
| .75 | 2046 | 511 | 227 | 128 | 82 | 57 | 42 | 32 | 25 |
| .80 | 2218 | 554 | 246 | 139 | 89 | 62 | 45 | 35 | 27 |
| .85 | 2425 | 606 | 269 | 152 | 97 | 67 | 49 | 38 | 30 |
| .90 | 2698 | 675 | 300 | 169 | 108 | 75 | 55 | 42 | 33 |
| .95 | 3126 | 781 | 347 | 195 | 125 | 87 | 64 | 49 | 39 |
| .99 | 4002 | 1001 | 445 | 250 | 160 | 111 | 82 | 63 | 49 |

| | | | | $u = 12$ |  |  |  |  |  |
| | | | | $w$ | | | | | |
| Power | .10 | .20 | .30 | .40 | .50 | .60 | .70 | .80 | .90 |
|---|---|---|---|---|---|---|---|---|---|
| .25 | 995 | 249 | 111 | 62 | 40 | 28 | 20 | 16 | 12 |
| .50 | 1513 | 378 | 168 | 95 | 61 | 42 | 31 | 24 | 19 |
| .60 | 1750 | 438 | 194 | 109 | 70 | 49 | 36 | 27 | 22 |
| 2/3 | 1925 | 481 | 214 | 120 | 77 | 53 | 39 | 30 | 24 |
| .70 | 2020 | 505 | 224 | 126 | 81 | 56 | 41 | 32 | 25 |
| .75 | 2177 | 544 | 242 | 136 | 87 | 60 | 44 | 34 | 27 |
| .80 | 2356 | 589 | 262 | 147 | 94 | 65 | 48 | 37 | 29 |
| .85 | 2573 | 643 | 286 | 161 | 103 | 71 | 53 | 40 | 32 |
| .90 | 2858 | 714 | 318 | 179 | 114 | 79 | 58 | 45 | 35 |
| .95 | 3302 | 826 | 367 | 206 | 132 | 92 | 67 | 52 | 41 |
| .99 | 4211 | 1053 | 468 | 263 | 168 | 117 | 86 | 66 | 52 |

| | | | | $u = 16$ |  |  |  |  |  |
| | | | | $w$ | | | | | |
| Power | .10 | .20 | .30 | .40 | .50 | .60 | .70 | .80 | .90 |
|---|---|---|---|---|---|---|---|---|---|
| .25 | 1072 | 268 | 119 | 67 | 43 | 30 | 22 | 17 | 13 |
| .50 | 1690 | 422 | 188 | 106 | 68 | 47 | 34 | 26 | 21 |
| .60 | 1948 | 487 | 216 | 121 | 78 | 54 | 40 | 30 | 24 |
| 2/3 | 2137 | 534 | 237 | 134 | 85 | 59 | 44 | 33 | 26 |
| .70 | 2240 | 560 | 249 | 140 | 90 | 62 | 46 | 35 | 28 |
| .75 | 2408 | 602 | 268 | 150 | 96 | 67 | 49 | 38 | 30 |
| .80 | 2601 | 650 | 289 | 163 | 104 | 72 | 53 | 41 | 32 |
| .85 | 2834 | 709 | 315 | 177 | 113 | 79 | 58 | 44 | 35 |
| .90 | 3139 | 785 | 349 | 196 | 126 | 87 | 64 | 49 | 39 |
| .95 | 3614 | 903 | 402 | 226 | 145 | 100 | 74 | 56 | 45 |
| .99 | 4580 | 1145 | 509 | 286 | 183 | 127 | 93 | 72 | 57 |

TABLE 7.4.5

**N** TO DETECT **w** BY $\chi^2$ AT **a** = .01, **u** = 20, 24

| Power | .10 | .20 | .30 | .40 | .50 | .60 | .70 | .80 | .90 |
|---|---|---|---|---|---|---|---|---|---|
| | | | | | $u = 20$ $w$ | | | | |
| .25 | 1181 | 295 | 131 | 74 | 47 | 33 | 24 | 18 | 15 |
| .50 | 1845 | 461 | 205 | 115 | 74 | 51 | 38 | 29 | 23 |
| .60 | 2121 | 530 | 236 | 133 | 85 | 59 | 43 | 33 | 26 |
| 2/3 | 2322 | 581 | 258 | 145 | 93 | 65 | 47 | 36 | 29 |
| .70 | 2432 | 608 | 270 | 152 | 97 | 68 | 50 | 38 | 30 |
| .75 | 2611 | 653 | 290 | 163 | 104 | 73 | 53 | 41 | 32 |
| .80 | 2816 | 704 | 313 | 176 | 113 | 78 | 57 | 44 | 35 |
| .85 | 3063 | 766 | 340 | 191 | 123 | 85 | 63 | 48 | 38 |
| .90 | 3385 | 846 | 376 | 212 | 135 | 94 | 69 | 53 | 42 |
| .95 | 3886 | 972 | 432 | 243 | 155 | 108 | 79 | 61 | 48 |
| .99 | 4903 | 1226 | 545 | 306 | 196 | 136 | 100 | 77 | 61 |

| Power | .10 | .20 | .30 | .40 | .50 | .60 | .70 | .80 | .90 |
|---|---|---|---|---|---|---|---|---|---|
| | | | | | $u = 24$ $w$ | | | | |
| .25 | 1280 | 320 | 142 | 80 | 51 | 36 | 26 | 20 | 16 |
| .50 | 1986 | 496 | 221 | 124 | 79 | 55 | 41 | 31 | 25 |
| .60 | 2278 | 569 | 253 | 142 | 91 | 63 | 46 | 36 | 28 |
| 2/3 | 2490 | 622 | 277 | 156 | 100 | 69 | 51 | 39 | 31 |
| .70 | 2606 | 651 | 290 | 163 | 104 | 72 | 53 | 41 | 32 |
| .75 | 2794 | 699 | 310 | 175 | 112 | 78 | 57 | 44 | 34 |
| .80 | 3010 | 753 | 334 | 188 | 120 | 84 | 61 | 47 | 37 |
| .85 | 3269 | 817 | 363 | 204 | 131 | 91 | 67 | 51 | 40 |
| .90 | 3607 | 902 | 401 | 225 | 144 | 100 | 74 | 56 | 45 |
| .95 | 4132 | 1033 | 459 | 258 | 165 | 115 | 84 | 65 | 51 |
| .99 | 5193 | 1298 | 577 | 325 | 208 | 144 | 106 | 81 | 64 |

TABLE 7.4.6

**N** TO DETECT **w** BY $\chi^2$ AT **a** $= .05$, **u** $= 1, 2, 3$

| Power | $\dfrac{u = 1}{w}$ | | | | | | | | |
|---|---|---|---|---|---|---|---|---|---|
| | .10 | .20 | .30 | .40 | .50 | .60 | .70 | .80 | .90 |
| .25 | 165 | 41 | 18 | 10 | 7 | 5 | 3 | 3 | 2 |
| .50 | 384 | 96 | 43 | 24 | 15 | 11 | 8 | 6 | 5 |
| .60 | 490 | 122 | 54 | 31 | 20 | 14 | 10 | 8 | 6 |
| 2/3 | 571 | 142 | 63 | 36 | 23 | 16 | 12 | 9 | 7 |
| .70 | 617 | 154 | 69 | 39 | 25 | 17 | 13 | 10 | 8 |
| .75 | 694 | 175 | 77 | 43 | 28 | 19 | 14 | 11 | 9 |
| .80 | 785 | 196 | 87 | 49 | 31 | 22 | 16 | 12 | 10 |
| .85 | 898 | 224 | 100 | 56 | 36 | 25 | 18 | 14 | 11 |
| .90 | 1051 | 263 | 117 | 66 | 42 | 29 | 21 | 16 | 13 |
| .95 | 1300 | 325 | 144 | 81 | 52 | 36 | 27 | 20 | 16 |
| .99 | 1837 | 459 | 204 | 115 | 73 | 51 | 37 | 29 | 23 |

| Power | $\dfrac{u = 2}{w}$ | | | | | | | | |
|---|---|---|---|---|---|---|---|---|---|
| | .10 | .20 | .30 | .40 | .50 | .60 | .70 | .80 | .90 |
| .25 | 226 | 56 | 25 | 14 | 9 | 6 | 5 | 4 | 3 |
| .50 | 496 | 124 | 55 | 31 | 20 | 14 | 10 | 8 | 6 |
| .60 | 621 | 155 | 69 | 39 | 25 | 17 | 13 | 10 | 8 |
| 2/3 | 717 | 179 | 80 | 45 | 29 | 20 | 15 | 11 | 9 |
| .70 | 770 | 193 | 86 | 48 | 31 | 21 | 16 | 12 | 10 |
| .75 | 859 | 215 | 95 | 54 | 34 | 24 | 18 | 13 | 11 |
| .80 | 964 | 241 | 107 | 60 | 39 | 27 | 20 | 15 | 12 |
| .85 | 1092 | 273 | 121 | 68 | 44 | 30 | 22 | 17 | 13 |
| .90 | 1265 | 316 | 141 | 79 | 51 | 35 | 26 | 20 | 16 |
| .95 | 1544 | 386 | 172 | 97 | 62 | 43 | 32 | 24 | 19 |
| .99 | 2140 | 535 | 238 | 134 | 86 | 59 | 44 | 33 | 26 |

| Power | $\dfrac{u = 3}{w}$ | | | | | | | | |
|---|---|---|---|---|---|---|---|---|---|
| | .10 | .20 | .30 | .40 | .50 | .60 | .70 | .80 | .90 |
| .25 | 258 | 65 | 29 | 16 | 10 | 7 | 5 | 4 | 3 |
| .50 | 576 | 144 | 64 | 36 | 23 | 16 | 12 | 9 | 7 |
| .60 | 715 | 179 | 79 | 45 | 29 | 20 | 15 | 11 | 9 |
| 2/3 | 820 | 205 | 91 | 51 | 33 | 23 | 17 | 13 | 10 |
| .70 | 879 | 220 | 98 | 55 | 35 | 24 | 18 | 14 | 11 |
| .75 | 976 | 244 | 108 | 61 | 39 | 27 | 20 | 15 | 12 |
| .80 | 1090 | 273 | 121 | 68 | 44 | 30 | 22 | 17 | 13 |
| .85 | 1230 | 308 | 137 | 77 | 49 | 34 | 25 | 19 | 15 |
| .90 | 1417 | 354 | 157 | 89 | 57 | 39 | 29 | 22 | 17 |
| .95 | 1717 | 429 | 191 | 107 | 69 | 48 | 35 | 27 | 21 |
| .99 | 2352 | 588 | 261 | 147 | 94 | 65 | 48 | 37 | 29 |

## TABLE 7.4.7

**N** TO DETECT **w** BY $\chi^2$ AT **a** = .05, **u** = 4, 5, 6

| | | | | | $\dfrac{u = 4}{w}$ | | | | |
|---|---|---|---|---|---|---|---|---|---|
| Power | .10 | .20 | .30 | .40 | .50 | .60 | .70 | .80 | .90 |
| .25 | 308 | 77. | 34 | 19 | 12 | 9 | 6 | 5 | 4 |
| .50 | 642 | 160 | 71 | 40 | 26 | 18 | 13 | 10 | 8 |
| .60 | 792 | 198 | 88 | 50 | 32 | 22 | 16 | 12 | 10 |
| 2/3 | 911 | 228 | 101 | 57 | 36 | 25 | 19 | 14 | 11 |
| .70 | 968 | 242 | 108 | 61 | 39 | 27 | 20 | 15 | 12 |
| .75 | 1072 | 268 | 119 | 67 | 43 | 30 | 22 | 17 | 13 |
| .80 | 1194 | 298 | 133 | 75 | 48 | 33 | 24 | 19 | 15 |
| .85 | 1342 | 336 | 149 | 84 | 54 | 37 | 27 | 21 | 17 |
| .90 | 1540 | 385 | 171 | 96 | 62 | 43 | 31 | 24 | 19 |
| .95 | 1857 | 464 | 206 | 116 | 74 | 52 | 38 | 29 | 23 |
| .99 | 2524 | 631 | 280 | 158 | 101 | 70 | 52 | 39 | 31 |

| | | | | | $\dfrac{u = 5}{w}$ | | | | |
|---|---|---|---|---|---|---|---|---|---|
| Power | .10 | .20 | .30 | .40 | .50 | .60 | .70 | .80 | .90 |
| .25 | 341 | 85 | 38 | 21 | 14 | 9 | 7 | 5 | 4 |
| .50 | 699 | 175 | 78 | 44 | 28 | 19 | 14 | 11 | 9 |
| .60 | 859 | 215 | 95 | 54 | 34 | 24 | 18 | 13 | 11 |
| 2/3 | 979 | 245 | 109 | 61 | 39 | 27 | 20 | 15 | 12 |
| .70 | 1045 | 261 | 116 | 65 | 42 | 29 | 21 | 16 | 13 |
| .75 | 1155 | 289 | 128 | 72 | 46 | 32 | 24 | 18 | 14 |
| .80 | 1283 | 321 | 143 | 80 | 51 | 36 | 26 | 20 | 16 |
| .85 | 1439 | 360 | 160 | 90 | 58 | 40 | 29 | 22 | 18 |
| .90 | 1647 | 412 | 183 | 103 | 66 | 46 | 34 | 26 | 20 |
| .95 | 1978 | 494 | 220 | 124 | 79 | 55 | 40 | 31 | 24 |
| .99 | 2673 | 668 | 297 | 167 | 107 | 74 | 55 | 42 | 33 |

| | | | | | $\dfrac{u = 6}{w}$ | | | | |
|---|---|---|---|---|---|---|---|---|---|
| Power | .10 | .20 | .30 | .40 | .50 | .60 | .70 | .80 | .90 |
| .25 | 370 | 92 | 41 | 23 | 15 | 10 | 8 | 6 | 5 |
| .50 | 750 | 188 | 83 | 47 | 30 | 21 | 15 | 12 | 9 |
| .60 | 919 | 230 | 102 | 57 | 37 | 25 | 19 | 14 | 11 |
| 2/3 | 1044 | 261 | 116 | 65 | 42 | 29 | 21 | 16 | 13 |
| .70 | 1114 | 279 | 124 | 70 | 45 | 31 | 23 | 17 | 14 |
| .75 | 1229 | 307 | 137 | 77 | 49 | 34 | 25 | 19 | 15 |
| .80 | 1362 | 341 | 151 | 85 | 54 | 38 | 28 | 21 | 17 |
| .85 | 1526 | 381 | 170 | 95 | 61 | 42 | 31 | 24 | 19 |
| .90 | 1742 | 435 | 194 | 109 | 70 | 48 | 36 | 27 | 22 |
| .95 | 2086 | 521 | 232 | 130 | 83 | 58 | 43 | 33 | 26 |
| .99 | 2805 | 701 | 312 | 175 | 112 | 78 | 57 | 44 | 35 |

TABLE 7.4.8

**N** TO DETECT **w** BY $\chi^2$ AT **a** = .05, **u** = 7, 8, 9

| | | | | | $\frac{u = 7}{w}$ | | | | |
|---|---|---|---|---|---|---|---|---|---|
| Power | .10 | .20 | .30 | .40 | .50 | .60 | .70 | .80 | .90 |
| .25 | 397 | 99 | 44 | 25 | 16 | 11 | 8 | 6 | 5 |
| .50 | 797 | 199 | 89 | 50 | 32 | 22 | 16 | 12 | 10 |
| .60 | 973 | 243 | 108 | 61 | 39 | 27 | 20 | 15 | 12 |
| 2/3 | 1104 | 276 | 123 | 69 | 44 | 31 | 23 | 17 | 14 |
| .70 | 1177 | 294 | 131 | 74 | 47 | 33 | 24 | 18 | 15 |
| .75 | 1296 | 324 | 144 | 81 | 52 | 36 | 26 | 20 | 16 |
| .80 | 1435 | 359 | 159 | 90 | 57 | 40 | 29 | 22 | 18 |
| .85 | 1604 | 401 | 178 | 100 | 64 | 45 | 33 | 25 | 20 |
| .90 | 1828 | 457 | 203 | 114 | 73 | 51 | 37 | 29 | 23 |
| .95 | 2184 | 546 | 243 | 136 | 87 | 61 | 45 | 34 | 27 |
| .99 | 2925 | 731 | 325 | 183 | 117 | 81 | 60 | 46 | 36 |

| | | | | | $\frac{u = 8}{w}$ | | | | |
|---|---|---|---|---|---|---|---|---|---|
| Power | .10 | .20 | .30 | .40 | .50 | .60 | .70 | .80 | .90 |
| .25 | 422 | 105 | 47 | 26 | 17 | 12 | 9 | 7 | 5 |
| .50 | 840 | 210 | 93 | 53 | 34 | 23 | 17 | 13 | 10 |
| .60 | 1024 | 256 | 114 | 64 | 41 | 28 | 21 | 16 | 13 |
| 2/3 | 1160 | 290 | 129 | 72 | 46 | 32 | 24 | 18 | 14 |
| .70 | 1235 | 309 | 137 | 77 | 49 | 34 | 25 | 19 | 15 |
| .75 | 1359 | 340 | 151 | 85 | 54 | 38 | 28 | 21 | 17 |
| .80 | 1502 | 376 | 167 | 94 | 60 | 42 | 31 | 23 | 19 |
| .85 | 1677 | 419 | 186 | 105 | 67 | 47 | 34 | 26 | 21 |
| .90 | 1908 | 477 | 212 | 119 | 76 | 53 | 39 | 30 | 24 |
| .95 | 2274 | 569 | 253 | 142 | 91 | 63 | 46 | 36 | 28 |
| .99 | 3036 | 759 | 337 | 189 | 121 | 84 | 62 | 47 | 37 |

| | | | | | $\frac{u = 9}{w}$ | | | | |
|---|---|---|---|---|---|---|---|---|---|
| Power | .10 | .20 | .30 | .40 | .50 | .60 | .70 | .80 | .90 |
| .25 | 445 | 111 | 49 | 28 | 18 | 12 | 9 | 7 | 5 |
| .50 | 881 | 220 | 98 | 55 | 35 | 24 | 18 | 14 | 11 |
| .60 | 1071 | 268 | 119 | 67 | 43 | 30 | 22 | 17 | 13 |
| 2/3 | 1212 | 303 | 135 | 76 | 48 | 34 | 25 | 19 | 15 |
| .70 | 1289 | 322 | 143 | 81 | 52 | 36 | 26 | 20 | 16 |
| .75 | 1417 | 354 | 157 | 89 | 57 | 39 | 29 | 22 | 17 |
| .80 | 1565 | 391 | 174 | 98 | 63 | 43 | 32 | 24 | 19 |
| .85 | 1745 | 436 | 194 | 109 | 70 | 48 | 36 | 27 | 22 |
| .90 | 1983 | 496 | 220 | 124 | 79 | 55 | 40 | 31 | 24 |
| .95 | 2359 | 590 | 262 | 147 | 94 | 66 | 48 | 37 | 29 |
| .99 | 3139 | 785 | 349 | 196 | 126 | 87 | 64 | 49 | 39 |

TABLE 7.4.9

$N$ TO DETECT $w$ BY $\chi^2$ AT $a = .05$, $u = 10, 12, 16$

| | | | | | $u = 10$ | | | | |
| | | | | | $w$ | | | | |
| Power | .10 | .20 | .30 | .40 | .50 | .60 | .70 | .80 | .90 |
|---|---|---|---|---|---|---|---|---|---|
| .25 | 467 | 117 | 52 | 29 | 19 | 13 | 10 | 7 | 6 |
| .50 | 919 | 230 | 102 | 57 | 37 | 26 | 19 | 14 | 11 |
| .60 | 1115 | 279 | 124 | 60 | 45 | 31 | 23 | 17 | 14 |
| 2/3 | 1260 | 315 | 140 | 79 | 50 | 35 | 26 | 20 | 16 |
| .70 | 1340 | 335 | 149 | 84 | 54 | 37 | 27 | 21 | 17 |
| .75 | 1472 | 368 | 164 | 92 | 59 | 41 | 30 | 23 | 18 |
| .80 | 1624 | 406 | 180 | 102 | 65 | 45 | 33 | 25 | 20 |
| .85 | 1809 | 452 | 201 | 113 | 72 | 50 | 37 | 28 | 22 |
| .90 | 2053 | 513 | 228 | 128 | 82 | 57 | 42 | 32 | 25 |
| .95 | 2438 | 610 | 271 | 152 | 98 | 68 | 50 | 38 | 30 |
| .99 | 3236 | 809 | 360 | 202 | 129 | 90 | 66 | 51 | 40 |

| | | | | | $u = 12$ | | | | |
| | | | | | $w$ | | | | |
| Power | .10 | .20 | .30 | .40 | .50 | .60 | .70 | .80 | .90 |
|---|---|---|---|---|---|---|---|---|---|
| .25 | 508 | 127 | 56 | 32 | 20 | 14 | 10 | 8 | 6 |
| .50 | 990 | 248 | 110 | 62 | 40 | 28 | 20 | 15 | 12 |
| .60 | 1198 | 299 | 133 | 75 | 48 | 33 | 24 | 19 | 15 |
| 2/3 | 1351 | 338 | 150 | 84 | 54 | 38 | 28 | 21 | 17 |
| .70 | 1435 | 359 | 159 | 90 | 57 | 40 | 29 | 22 | 18 |
| .75 | 1574 | 393 | 175 | 98 | 63 | 44 | 32 | 25 | 19 |
| .80 | 1734 | 433 | 193 | 108 | 69 | 48 | 35 | 27 | 21 |
| .85 | 1928 | 482 | 214 | 120 | 77 | 54 | 39 | 30 | 24 |
| .90 | 2183 | 546 | 243 | 136 | 87 | 61 | 45 | 34 | 27 |
| .95 | 2586 | 646 | 287 | 162 | 103 | 72 | 53 | 40 | 32 |
| .99 | 3416 | 854 | 380 | 214 | 137 | 95 | 70 | 53 | 42 |

| | | | | | $u = 16$ | | | | |
| | | | | | $w$ | | | | |
| Power | .10 | .20 | .30 | .40 | .50 | .60 | .70 | .80 | .90 |
|---|---|---|---|---|---|---|---|---|---|
| .25 | 581 | 145 | 65 | 36 | 23 | 16 | 12 | 9 | 7 |
| .50 | 1116 | 279 | 124 | 70 | 45 | 31 | 23 | 17 | 14 |
| .60 | 1343 | 336 | 149 | 84 | 54 | 37 | 27 | 21 | 17 |
| 2/3 | 1511 | 378 | 168 | 94 | 60 | 42 | 31 | 24 | 19 |
| .70 | 1603 | 401 | 178 | 100 | 64 | 45 | 33 | 25 | 20 |
| .75 | 1753 | 438 | 195 | 110 | 70 | 49 | 36 | 27 | 22 |
| .80 | 1927 | 482 | 214 | 120 | 77 | 54 | 39 | 30 | 24 |
| .85 | 2137 | 534 | 237 | 134 | 85 | 59 | 44 | 33 | 26 |
| .90 | 2412 | 603 | 268 | 151 | 96 | 67 | 49 | 38 | 30 |
| .95 | 2845 | 711 | 316 | 178 | 114 | 79 | 58 | 44 | 35 |
| .99 | 3733 | 933 | 415 | 233 | 149 | 104 | 76 | 58 | 46 |

TABLE 7.4.10

**N** TO DETECT **w** BY $\chi^2$ AT **a** $= .05$, **u** $= 20, 24$

| | | | | | u = 20 | | | | |
| | | | | | w | | | | |
| Power | .10 | .20 | .30 | .40 | .50 | .60 | .70 | .80 | .90 |
|---|---|---|---|---|---|---|---|---|---|
| .25 | 646 | 161 | 72 | 40 | 26 | 18 | 13 | 10 | 8 |
| .50 | 1226 | 307 | 136 | 77 | 49 | 34 | 25 | 19 | 15 |
| .60 | 1471 | 368 | 163 | 92 | 59 | 41 | 30 | 23 | 18 |
| 2/3 | 1651 | 413 | 183 | 103 | 66 | 46 | 34 | 26 | 20 |
| .70 | 1750 | 437 | 194 | 109 | 70 | 49 | 36 | 27 | 22 |
| .75 | 1911 | 478 | 212 | 119 | 76 | 53 | 39 | 30 | 24 |
| .80 | 2096 | 524 | 233 | 131 | 84 | 58 | 43 | 33 | 26 |
| .85 | 2320 | 580 | 258 | 145 | 93 | 64 | 47 | 36 | 29 |
| .90 | 2613 | 653 | 290 | 163 | 105 | 73 | 53 | 41 | 32 |
| .95 | 3072 | 768 | 341 | 192 | 123 | 85 | 63 | 48 | 38 |
| .99 | 4010 | 1002 | 446 | 251 | 160 | 111 | 82 | 63 | 50 |

| | | | | | u = 24 | | | | |
| | | | | | w | | | | |
| Power | .10 | .20 | .30 | .40 | .50 | .60 | .70 | .80 | .90 |
|---|---|---|---|---|---|---|---|---|---|
| .25 | 704 | 176 | 78 | 44 | 28 | 20 | 14 | 11 | 9 |
| .50 | 1326 | 331 | 147 | 83 | 53 | 37 | 27 | 21 | 16 |
| .60 | 1587 | 397 | 176 | 99 | 63 | 44 | 32 | 25 | 20 |
| 2/3 | 1778 | 444 | 198 | 111 | 71 | 49 | 36 | 28 | 22 |
| .70 | 1882 | 470 | 209 | 118 | 75 | 52 | 38 | 29 | 23 |
| .75 | 2053 | 513 | 228 | 128 | 82 | 57 | 42 | 32 | 25 |
| .80 | 2249 | 562 | 250 | 141 | 90 | 62 | 46 | 35 | 28 |
| .85 | 2484 | 621 | 276 | 155 | 99 | 59 | 51 | 39 | 31 |
| .90 | 2794 | 698 | 310 | 175 | 112 | 78 | 57 | 44 | 34 |
| .95 | 3276 | 819 | 364 | 205 | 131 | 91 | 67 | 51 | 40 |
| .99 | 4259 | 1065 | 473 | 266 | 170 | 118 | 87 | 67 | 53 |

TABLE 7.4.11

**N** TO DETECT **w** BY $\chi^2$ AT **a** $= .10$, **u** $= 1, 2, 3$

| | | | | | u = 1 w | | | | |
|---|---|---|---|---|---|---|---|---|---|
| Power | .10 | .20 | .30 | .40 | .50 | .60 | .70 | .80 | .90 |
| .25 | 91 | 23 | 10 | 6 | 4 | 3 | 2 | 1 | 1 |
| .50 | 270 | 68 | 30 | 17 | 11 | 8 | 6 | 4 | 3 |
| .60 | 360 | 90 | 40 | 23 | 14 | 10 | 7 | 6 | 4 |
| 2/3 | 430 | 108 | 48 | 27 | 17 | 12 | 9 | 7 | 5 |
| .70 | 470 | 118 | 52 | 29 | 19 | 13 | 10 | 7 | 6 |
| .75 | 538 | 134 | 60 | 34 | 22 | 15 | 11 | 8 | 7 |
| .80 | 618 | 155 | 69 | 39 | 25 | 17 | 13 | 10 | 8 |
| .85 | 719 | 180 | 80 | 45 | 29 | 20 | 15 | 11 | 9 |
| .90 | 856 | 214 | 95 | 53 | 34 | 24 | 17 | 13 | 11 |
| .95 | 1082 | 271 | 120 | 68 | 43 | 30 | 22 | 17 | 13 |
| .99 | 1577 | 394 | 175 | 99 | 63 | 44 | 32 | 25 | 19 |

| | | | | | u = 2 w | | | | |
|---|---|---|---|---|---|---|---|---|---|
| Power | .10 | .20 | .30 | .40 | .50 | .60 | .70 | .80 | .90 |
| .25 | 127 | 32 | 14 | 8 | 5 | 4 | 3 | 2 | 2 |
| .50 | 356 | 89 | 40 | 22 | 14 | 10 | 7 | 6 | 4 |
| .60 | 465 | 116 | 52 | 29 | 19 | 13 | 9 | 7 | 6 |
| 2/3 | 550 | 137 | 61 | 34 | 22 | 15 | 11 | 9 | 7 |
| .70 | 597 | 149 | 66 | 37 | 24 | 17 | 12 | 9 | 7 |
| .75 | 677 | 169 | 75 | 42 | 27 | 19 | 14 | 11 | 8 |
| .80 | 771 | 193 | 86 | 48 | 31 | 21 | 16 | 12 | 10 |
| .85 | 888 | 222 | 99 | 55 | 36 | 25 | 18 | 14 | 11 |
| .90 | 1046 | 261 | 116 | 65 | 42 | 29 | 21 | 16 | 13 |
| .95 | 1302 | 326 | 145 | 81 | 52 | 36 | 27 | 20 | 16 |
| .99 | 1856 | 464 | 206 | 116 | 74 | 52 | 38 | 29 | 23 |

| | | | | | u = 3 w | | | | |
|---|---|---|---|---|---|---|---|---|---|
| Power | .10 | .20 | .30 | .40 | .50 | .60 | .70 | .80 | .90 |
| .25 | 155 | 39 | 17 | 10 | 6 | 4 | 3 | 2 | 2 |
| .50 | 418 | 104 | 46 | 26 | 17 | 12 | 9 | 7 | 5 |
| .60 | 541 | 135 | 60 | 34 | 22 | 15 | 11 | 8 | 7 |
| 2/3 | 636 | 159 | 71 | 40 | 25 | 18 | 13 | 10 | 8 |
| .70 | 688 | 172 | 76 | 43 | 28 | 19 | 14 | 11 | 8 |
| .75 | 776 | 194 | 86 | 49 | 31 | 22 | 16 | 12 | 10 |
| .80 | 880 | 220 | 98 | 55 | 35 | 24 | 18 | 14 | 11 |
| .85 | 1008 | 252 | 112 | 63 | 40 | 28 | 21 | 16 | 12 |
| .90 | 1180 | 295 | 131 | 74 | 47 | 33 | 24 | 18 | 15 |
| .95 | 1457 | 364 | 162 | 91 | 58 | 40 | 30 | 23 | 18 |
| .99 | 2051 | 513 | 228 | 128 | 82 | 57 | 42 | 32 | 25 |

TABLE 7.4.12

**N** TO DETECT **w** BY $\chi^2$ AT **a** = .10, **u** = 4, 5, 6

| | u = 4 | | | | | | | | |
| | | | | | w | | | | |
| Power | .10 | .20 | .30 | .40 | .50 | .60 | .70 | .80 | .90 |
| --- | --- | --- | --- | --- | --- | --- | --- | --- | --- |
| .25 | 178 | 44 | 20 | 11 | 7 | 5 | 4 | 3 | 2 |
| .50 | 469 | 117 | 52 | 29 | 19 | 13 | 10 | 7 | 6 |
| .60 | 604 | 151 | 67 | 38 | 24 | 17 | 12 | 9 | 7 |
| 2/3 | 706 | 176 | 78 | 44 | 28 | 20 | 14 | 11 | 9 |
| .70 | 763 | 191 | 85 | 48 | 31 | 21 | 16 | 12 | 9 |
| .75 | 857 | 214 | 95 | 54 | 34 | 24 | 17 | 13 | 11 |
| .80 | 968 | 242 | 108 | 61 | 39 | 27 | 20 | 15 | 12 |
| .85 | 1105 | 276 | 123 | 69 | 44 | 31 | 23 | 17 | 14 |
| .90 | 1288 | 322 | 143 | 81 | 52 | 36 | 26 | 20 | 16 |
| .95 | 1583 | 396 | 176 | 99 | 63 | 44 | 32 | 25 | 20 |
| .99 | 2209 | 552 | 245 | 138 | 88 | 61 | 45 | 35 | 27 |

| | u = 5 | | | | | | | | |
| | | | | | w | | | | |
| Power | .10 | .20 | .30 | .40 | .50 | .60 | .70 | .80 | .90 |
| --- | --- | --- | --- | --- | --- | --- | --- | --- | --- |
| .25 | 198 | 50 | 22 | 12 | 8 | 6 | 4 | 3 | 2 |
| .50 | 514 | 128 | 57 | 32 | 21 | 14 | 10 | 8 | 6 |
| .60 | 658 | 164 | 73 | 41 | 26 | 18 | 13 | 10 | 8 |
| 2/3 | 766 | 192 | 85 | 48 | 31 | 21 | 16 | 12 | 9 |
| .70 | 827 | 207 | 92 | 52 | 33 | 23 | 17 | 13 | 10 |
| .75 | 927 | 232 | 103 | 58 | 37 | 26 | 19 | 14 | 11 |
| .80 | 1045 | 261 | 116 | 65 | 42 | 29 | 21 | 16 | 13 |
| .85 | 1189 | 297 | 132 | 74 | 48 | 33 | 24 | 19 | 15 |
| .90 | 1382 | 345 | 154 | 86 | 55 | 38 | 28 | 22 | 17 |
| .95 | 1691 | 423 | 188 | 106 | 68 | 47 | 35 | 26 | 21 |
| .99 | 2344 | 586 | 260 | 147 | 94 | 65 | 48 | 37 | 29 |

| | u = 6 | | | | | | | | |
| | | | | | w | | | | |
| Power | .10 | .20 | .30 | .40 | .50 | .60 | .70 | .80 | .90 |
| --- | --- | --- | --- | --- | --- | --- | --- | --- | --- |
| .25 | 216 | 54 | 24 | 14 | 9 | 6 | 4 | 3 | 3 |
| .50 | 553 | 138 | 61 | 35 | 22 | 15 | 11 | 9 | 7 |
| .60 | 706 | 176 | 78 | 44 | 28 | 20 | 14 | 11 | 9 |
| 2/3 | 820 | 205 | 91 | 51 | 33 | 23 | 17 | 13 | 10 |
| .70 | 884 | 221 | 98 | 55 | 35 | 25 | 18 | 14 | 11 |
| .75 | 990 | 247 | 110 | 62 | 40 | 27 | 20 | 15 | 12 |
| .80 | 1113 | 278 | 124 | 70 | 45 | 31 | 23 | 17 | 14 |
| .85 | 1264 | 316 | 140 | 79 | 51 | 35 | 26 | 20 | 16 |
| .90 | 1465 | 366 | 163 | 92 | 59 | 41 | 30 | 23 | 18 |
| .95 | 1787 | 447 | 199 | 112 | 71 | 50 | 36 | 28 | 22 |
| .99 | 2465 | 616 | 274 | 154 | 99 | 68 | 50 | 39 | 30 |

TABLE 7.4.13

$N$ TO DETECT $w$ BY $\chi^2$ AT $a = .10$, $u = 7, 8, 9$

|  | | | | | $u = 7$ | | | | |
|  | | | | | $w$ | | | | |
| Power | .10 | .20 | .30 | .40 | .50 | .60 | .70 | .80 | .90 |
|---|---|---|---|---|---|---|---|---|---|
| .25 | 233 | 58 | 26 | 15 | 9 | 6 | 5 | 4 | 3 |
| .50 | 590 | 147 | 66 | 37 | 24 | 16 | 12 | 9 | 7 |
| .60 | 750 | 187 | 83 | 47 | 30 | 21 | 15 | 12 | 9 |
| 2/3 | 870 | 217 | 97 | 54 | 35 | 24 | 18 | 14 | 11 |
| .70 | 936 | 234 | 104 | 59 | 37 | 26 | 19 | 15 | 12 |
| .75 | 1047 | 262 | 116 | 65 | 42 | 29 | 21 | 16 | 13 |
| .80 | 1175 | 294 | 131 | 73 | 47 | 33 | 24 | 18 | 15 |
| .85 | 1332 | 333 | 148 | 83 | 53 | 37 | 27 | 21 | 16 |
| .90 | 1541 | 385 | 171 | 96 | 62 | 43 | 31 | 24 | 19 |
| .95 | 1875 | 469 | 208 | 117 | 75 | 52 | 38 | 29 | 23 |
| .99 | 2574 | 644 | 286 | 161 | 103 | 72 | 53 | 40 | 32 |

|  | | | | | $u = 8$ | | | | |
|  | | | | | $w$ | | | | |
| Power | .10 | .20 | .30 | .40 | .50 | .60 | .70 | .80 | .90 |
|---|---|---|---|---|---|---|---|---|---|
| .25 | 249 | 62 | 28 | 16 | 10 | 7 | 5 | 4 | 3 |
| .50 | 624 | 156 | 69 | 39 | 25 | 17 | 13 | 10 | 8 |
| .60 | 791 | 198 | 88 | 49 | 32 | 22 | 16 | 12 | 10 |
| 2/3 | 916 | 229 | 102 | 57 | 37 | 25 | 19 | 14 | 11 |
| .70 | 985 | 246 | 109 | 62 | 39 | 27 | 20 | 15 | 12 |
| .75 | 1099 | 275 | 122 | 69 | 44 | 31 | 22 | 17 | 14 |
| .80 | 1232 | 308 | 137 | 77 | 49 | 34 | 25 | 19 | 15 |
| .85 | 1395 | 349 | 155 | 87 | 56 | 39 | 28 | 22 | 17 |
| .90 | 1611 | 403 | 179 | 101 | 64 | 45 | 33 | 25 | 20 |
| .95 | 1955 | 489 | 217 | 122 | 78 | 54 | 40 | 31 | 24 |
| .99 | 2676 | 669 | 297 | 167 | 107 | 74 | 55 | 42 | 33 |

|  | | | | | $u = 9$ | | | | |
|  | | | | | $w$ | | | | |
| Power | .10 | .20 | .30 | .40 | .50 | .60 | .70 | .80 | .90 |
|---|---|---|---|---|---|---|---|---|---|
| .25 | 263 | 66 | 29 | 16 | 11 | 7 | 5 | 4 | 3 |
| .50 | 655 | 164 | 73 | 41 | 26 | 18 | 13 | 10 | 8 |
| .60 | 829 | 207 | 92 | 52 | 33 | 23 | 17 | 13 | 10 |
| 2/3 | 958 | 240 | 106 | 60 | 38 | 27 | 20 | 15 | 12 |
| .70 | 1030 | 258 | 114 | 64 | 41 | 29 | 21 | 16 | 13 |
| .75 | 1148 | 287 | 128 | 72 | 46 | 32 | 23 | 18 | 14 |
| .80 | 1286 | 322 | 143 | 80 | 51 | 36 | 26 | 20 | 16 |
| .85 | 1454 | 364 | 162 | 91 | 58 | 40 | 30 | 23 | 18 |
| .90 | 1677 | 419 | 186 | 105 | 67 | 47 | 34 | 26 | 21 |
| .95 | 2031 | 508 | 226 | 127 | 81 | 56 | 41 | 32 | 25 |
| .99 | 2770 | 692 | 308 | 173 | 111 | 77 | 57 | 43 | 34 |

TABLE 7.4.14

**N** TO DETECT **w** BY $\chi^2$ AT **a** $= .10$, **u** $= 10, 12, 16$

| | | | | $\begin{array}{c}u = 10\\ \hline w\end{array}$ | | | | |
|---|---|---|---|---|---|---|---|---|
| Power | .10 | .20 | .30 | .40 | .50 | .60 | .70 | .80 | .90 |
| .25 | 277 | 69 | 31 | 17 | 11 | 8 | 6 | 4 | 3 |
| .50 | 685 | 171 | 76 | 43 | 27 | 19 | 14 | 11 | 8 |
| .60 | 865 | 216 | 96 | 54 | 35 | 24 | 18 | 14 | 11 |
| 2/3 | 999 | 250 | 111 | 62 | 40 | 28 | 20 | 16 | 12 |
| .70 | 1073 | 268 | 119 | 67 | 43 | 30 | 22 | 17 | 13 |
| .75 | 1195 | 299 | 133 | 75 | 48 | 33 | 24 | 19 | 15 |
| .80 | 1337 | 334 | 149 | 84 | 53 | 37 | 27 | 21 | 17 |
| .85 | 1510 | 377 | 168 | 94 | 60 | 42 | 31 | 24 | 19 |
| .90 | 1739 | 435 | 193 | 109 | 70 | 48 | 35 | 27 | 21 |
| .95 | 2102 | 525 | 234 | 131 | 84 | 58 | 43 | 33 | 26 |
| .99 | 2858 | 715 | 318 | 179 | 114 | 79 | 58 | 45 | 35 |

| | | | | $\begin{array}{c}u = 12\\ \hline w\end{array}$ | | | | |
|---|---|---|---|---|---|---|---|---|
| Power | .10 | .20 | .30 | .40 | .50 | .60 | .70 | .80 | .90 |
| .25 | 303 | 76 | 34 | 19 | 12 | 8 | 6 | 5 | 4 |
| .50 | 740 | 185 | 82 | 46 | 30 | 21 | 15 | 12 | 9 |
| .60 | 931 | 233 | 103 | 58 | 37 | 26 | 19 | 15 | 11 |
| 2/3 | 1073 | 268 | 119 | 67 | 43 | 30 | 22 | 17 | 13 |
| .70 | 1152 | 288 | 128 | 72 | 46 | 32 | 24 | 18 | 14 |
| .75 | 1281 | 320 | 142 | 80 | 51 | 36 | 26 | 20 | 16 |
| .80 | 1430 | 358 | 159 | 89 | 57 | 40 | 29 | 22 | 18 |
| .85 | 1612 | 403 | 179 | 101 | 64 | 45 | 33 | 25 | 20 |
| .90 | 1853 | 463 | 206 | 116 | 74 | 51 | 38 | 29 | 23 |
| .95 | 2233 | 558 | 248 | 140 | 89 | 62 | 46 | 35 | 28 |
| .99 | 3022 | 756 | 336 | 189 | 121 | 84 | 62 | 47 | 37 |

| | | | | $\begin{array}{c}u = 16\\ \hline w\end{array}$ | | | | |
|---|---|---|---|---|---|---|---|---|
| Power | .10 | .20 | .30 | .40 | .50 | .60 | .70 | .80 | .90 |
| .25 | 348 | 87 | 39 | 22 | 14 | 10 | 7 | 5 | 4 |
| .50 | 838 | 210 | 93 | 52 | 34 | 23 | 17 | 13 | 10 |
| .60 | 1049 | 262 | 117 | 66 | 42 | 29 | 21 | 16 | 13 |
| 2/3 | 1205 | 301 | 134 | 75 | 48 | 33 | 25 | 19 | 15 |
| .70 | 1291 | 323 | 143 | 81 | 52 | 36 | 26 | 20 | 16 |
| .75 | 1432 | 358 | 159 | 90 | 57 | 40 | 29 | 22 | 18 |
| .80 | 1595 | 399 | 177 | 100 | 64 | 44 | 33 | 25 | 20 |
| .85 | 1793 | 448 | 199 | 112 | 72 | 50 | 37 | 28 | 22 |
| .90 | 2054 | 513 | 228 | 128 | 82 | 57 | 42 | 32 | 25 |
| .95 | 2464 | 616 | 274 | 154 | 99 | 68 | 50 | 38 | 30 |
| .99 | 3310 | 828 | 368 | 207 | 132 | 92 | 68 | 52 | 41 |

## TABLE 7.4.15

**N** TO DETECT **w** BY $\chi^2$ AT **a** $= .10$, **u** $= 20, 24$

| Power | u = 20 w | | | | | | | | |
|---|---|---|---|---|---|---|---|---|---|
| | .10 | .20 | .30 | .40 | .50 | .60 | .70 | .80 | .90 |
| .25 | 388 | 97 | 43 | 24 | 16 | 11 | 8 | 6 | 5 |
| .50 | 924 | 231 | 103 | 58 | 37 | 26 | 19 | 14 | 11 |
| .60 | 1153 | 288 | 128 | 72 | 46 | 32 | 24 | 18 | 14 |
| 2/3 | 1321 | 330 | 147 | 83 | 53 | 37 | 27 | 21 | 16 |
| .70 | 1414 | 353 | 157 | 88 | 57 | 39 | 29 | 22 | 17 |
| .75 | 1565 | 391 | 174 | 98 | 63 | 43 | 32 | 24 | 19 |
| .80 | 1740 | 435 | 193 | 109 | 70 | 48 | 36 | 27 | 21 |
| .85 | 1951 | 488 | 217 | 122 | 78 | 54 | 40 | 30 | 24 |
| .90 | 2230 | 557 | 248 | 139 | 89 | 62 | 46 | 35 | 28 |
| .95 | 2666 | 667 | 296 | 167 | 107 | 74 | 54 | 42 | 33 |
| .99 | 3562 | 891 | 396 | 223 | 142 | 99 | 73 | 56 | 44 |

| Power | u = 24 w | | | | | | | | |
|---|---|---|---|---|---|---|---|---|---|
| | .10 | .20 | .30 | .40 | .50 | .60 | .70 | .80 | .90 |
| .25 | 425 | 106 | 47 | 27 | 17 | 12 | 9 | 7 | 5 |
| .50 | 1002 | 250 | 111 | 63 | 40 | 28 | 20 | 16 | 12 |
| .60 | 1246 | 311 | 138 | 78 | 50 | 35 | 25 | 19 | 15 |
| 2/3 | 1425 | 356 | 158 | 89 | 57 | 40 | 29 | 22 | 18 |
| .70 | 1524 | 381 | 169 | 95 | 61 | 42 | 31 | 24 | 19 |
| .75 | 1685 | 421 | 187 | 105 | 67 | 47 | 34 | 26 | 21 |
| .80 | 1870 | 468 | 208 | 117 | 75 | 52 | 38 | 29 | 23 |
| .85 | 2094 | 524 | 233 | 131 | 84 | 58 | 43 | 33 | 26 |
| .90 | 2388 | 597 | 265 | 149 | 96 | 66 | 49 | 37 | 29 |
| .95 | 2848 | 712 | 316 | 178 | 114 | 79 | 58 | 44 | 35 |
| .99 | 3788 | 947 | 421 | 237 | 152 | 105 | 77 | 59 | 47 |

For typographic convenience, the 42 tables are arranged generally three to a table number, by **a** levels and successively tabled **u** values within each **a** level. The subtable for the relevant **a**, **u** combination is found and entered with **w** and desired power. The same provisions for **a**, **u**, and **w** are made as for the power tables in Section 7.3, as follows:

*1. Significance Criterion,* **a**. Table sets are provided for nondirectional **a** of .01, .05, and .10, each set made up of tables for the values of **u**.

*2. Degrees of Freedom,* **u**. For each **a** level, tables are provided in succession for the 14 values of **u** = 1 (1) 10, 12 (4) 24.

*3. Effect Size,* **w**. **w** is defined by formula (7.2.1) and interpreted as described in Section 7.2. As before, 9 values of **w** are given: .10 (.10), .90.

For **w** values not tabled, find **N** by

$$(7.4.1) \qquad\qquad \mathbf{N} = \frac{\mathbf{N}_{.10}}{100\mathbf{w}^2},$$

where $\mathbf{N}_{.10}$ is the necessary sample size for the given **a**, **u**, and desired power at **w** = .10 (read from the table), and **w** is the nontabulated ES. Round to the nearest integer. This formula may be used not only for **w** values in the range covered by the table, but also for **w** less than .10 or greater than .90.

*4. Desired Power.* Provision is made for desired power values of .25, .50, .60, 2/3, .70 (.05), .95, .99. See Section 2.4.1 for the basis for selection of these values, and a discussion of the proposal that .80 serve as a convention for desired power in the absence of another basis for a choice.

A caveat is necessary at this point. Some values of **N** are given in the tables which are quite small (i.e., large **w** and **a**, small **u** and power). These are not to be taken as a sanction for the use of $\chi^2$ tests where the null-hypothetical frequencies ($\mathbf{P}_{0i}\mathbf{N}$) become very small, since such tests are of questionable validity. These small **N** values are given for the sake of completeness and for other applications of $\chi^2$, not illustrated here, which are not limited in this way. For useful guidance with regard to sample size requirements in $\chi^2$, the reader is referred to the textbooks cited in Section 7.2.

7.4.1  CASE 0: GOODNESS OF FIT. For Case 0 tests, one finds the subtable for the significance criterion (**a**) and degrees of freedom (**u**) which obtain, locates **w** and desired power, and finds **N**, the necessary total sample size. For nontabulated **w**, use formula (7.4.1).

## Illustrative Examples

**7.6** Reconsider the problem posed in example 7.2, where a psychometrician is testing by means of $\chi^2$ the conformity of a sample distribution of test scores to the normal curve for $m = 9$ step intervals, the latter constituting $H_0$. He wished a lenient ($a = .10$) test of $H_0$. Given that the population departure is $w = .20$, it was found that power was .66 for $N = 200$. On the assumption that the power is too small for a convincing " demonstration " (see Section 1.5.5) of normality, how many cases would he need for power to be .99?

Recalling that in such applications, $u = m - 3 = 6$, his specification summary is

$$a = .10, \qquad u = 6, \qquad w = .20, \qquad \text{power} = .99$$

He uses the last subtable of Table 7.4.12 for $a = .10$, $u = 6$, column $w = .20$, and row power $= .99$, and finds $N = 616$. With this sample size, he runs a **b** risk of only $1 - .99 = .01$ that, if the departure from normality is $w = .20$, he will fail to detect it at $a = .10$.

If this sample size is a great strain on his resources, he might consider settling for power $= .95$ (hence $b = .05$), where, from the same subtable, he finds the necessary $N$ to be 447.

**7.7** Consider example 7.1 again, now from the point of view of sample size decision as part of experimental planning. The market researcher wishes to detect a departure in the population from equal preference among $m = 4$ package designs by means of a $\chi^2$ test with $u = m - 1 = 3$, using an $a = .05$ significance criterion. The alternate hypothesis which was posited resulted in $w = .289$. From the power tables, it was found that, using $N = 100$, power was .67. If the conventional .80 power were desired, what $N$ would be required?

$$a = .05, \qquad u = 3, \qquad w = .289, \qquad \text{power} = .80.$$

Since $w = .289$ is not tabled, the use of formula (7.4.1) is required. For $N_{.10}$, the sample size needed to detect $w = .10$ with power $= .80$ for $a = .05$ and $u = 3$, we use the third subtable of Table 7.4.6 (for $a = .05$, $u = 3$) for column $w = .10$ and row power $= .80$, and find $N_{.10} = 1090$. Substituting in formula (7.4.1),

$$N = \frac{1090}{100(.289^2)} = 130.5.$$

Thus, 131 repondents will lead to a .80 probability of rejecting the null hypothesis of equal preference at $a = .05$, given that the population departure is indexed by $w = .289$.

7.4.2   CASE 1: CONTINGENCY TEST. As in Case 0, one finds the necessary total sample size **N** in Case 1 by finding the subtable for the significance criterion (**a**) and degrees of freedom $[\mathbf{u} = (\mathbf{k} - 1)(\mathbf{r} - 1)]$ which obtain, and seeking **w** and the power desired. Formula (7.4.1) is again used for non-tabulated **w**.

**Illustrative Examples**

**7.8**   In example 7.5, a community psychiatry research team was studying the relationship between religious-ethnic group membership (**r** = 5) and diagnosis (**k** = 6) for child clinic referrals. To detect **w** = .10 at the **a** = .01 significance level by a $\chi^2$ contingency test with $\mathbf{u} = (5 - 1)(6 - 1) = 20$, it was found that for **N** = 400, power was only .05. What sample size is required for conventional desired power of .80? The specification summary is

$$\mathbf{a} = .01, \qquad \mathbf{u} = 20, \qquad \mathbf{w} = .10, \qquad \text{power} = .80.$$

The first subtable for Table 7.4.5 (for **a** = .01, **u** = 20) for column **w** = .10 and row power = .80, is used to determine **N** = 2816.

Later in example 7.5, the same problem was considered using the less stringent **a** = .10 significance criterion. To find **N** for power of .80, in the first subtable of Table 7.4.15 (for **a** = .10, **u** = 20) locate column **w** = .10 and row power = .80, the result is **N** = 1740, still a very large **N**. In contrast, if a medium ES (**w** = .30) could have been posited, power = .80 at **a** = .01 would be attained with **N** = 313 (first subtable of Table 7.4.5).

**7.9**   Reconsider example 7.3, where a political scientist was studying the relationship between sex (**r** = 2) and political preference (**k** = 3). Assuming the degree of relationship given by the alternate-hypothetical $\mathbf{P}_{1i}$ of Table 7.2.1, and the null-hypothetical or no association $\mathbf{P}_{0i}$ of Table 7.2.2, **w** was found to equal .346. For the $\chi^2$ contingency test with $\mathbf{u} = (2 - 1)(3 - 1) = 2$, at the **a** = .01 level with **N** = 140 cases, power was found to be .55. Assume now that power is desired to be .99, so that **b** = .01 = **a**, i.e., that the Type I and Type II risks are equal and very small. What sample size is needed?

$$\mathbf{a} = .01, \qquad \mathbf{u} = 2, \qquad \mathbf{w} = .346, \qquad \text{power} = .99.$$

Since **w** = .346 is not tabulated, recourse will be taken to formula (7.4.1). To find the **N** needed to detect **w** = .346 for **a** = .01, **u** = 2, and power = .99, the second subtable of Table 7.4.1 (for **a** = .01, **u** = 2) is used for column **w** = .10 and row power = .99, and $\mathbf{N}_{.10} = 2742$ is found. Substituting in formula (7.4.1),

$$\mathbf{N} = \frac{2742}{100(.346^2)} = 229.0.$$

Thus 229 respondents are needed to yield $\mathbf{a} = \mathbf{b} = .01$ risks in a contingency test of this $2 \times 3$ table, given an ES of $\mathbf{w} = .346$.

Maintaining the $\mathbf{a} = \mathbf{b}$ requirement, but at .05, what $\mathbf{N}$ would be necessary?

$$\mathbf{a} = .05, \quad \mathbf{u} = 2, \quad \mathbf{w} = .346, \quad \text{power} = .95.$$

To find $\mathbf{N}_{.10}$, the second subtable of Table 7.4.6 (for $\mathbf{a} = .05$, $\mathbf{u} = 2$) is used for column $\mathbf{w} = .10$ and row power $= .95$, and 1544 is found. Substituting in formula (7.4.1),

$$\mathbf{N} = \frac{1544}{100(.346^2)} = 129.0.$$

The reduction in stringency from $\mathbf{a} = \mathbf{b} = .01$ to $\mathbf{a} = \mathbf{b} = .05$ results in a reduction in sample size demand from 229 to 129.

# CHAPTER 8

# The Analysis of
# Variance

## 8.1 INTRODUCTION AND USE

This chapter deals with an entire class of problems in tests of the equality of a set of **k** population means, where **k** equals two or more. The methods of this chapter can also be used for tests of the equality of sets of mean *differences*, as in tests of interactions. The test statistic is the **F** ratio, and the model is that of the test on means of "fixed effect" variates in the analysis of variance and covariance (Edwards, 1972; Winer, 1971; Hays, 1981). In its simplest form, it is a "one-way" ("randomized groups") design with equal **n** in each sample. The power and sample size tables in this chapter are designed for greatest simplicity in these applications (Case 0). More complicated designs involving fixed effects can also be power-analyzed with the help of these tables, as will be described below. In all cases, however, the null hypothesis states that the means or mean difference of specified ("fixed") populations are equal, or, equivalently, that "effects" defined as linear functions of means are all zero. Section 8.3.5 shows how power analysis on various tests of means, which will have been described in the context of the analysis of variance, can be performed in analogous analysis of covariance designs.

The tests here can be viewed as extensions of the tests of Chapter 2, where only two fixed population means are involved. Or, conversely, the **t** test on two means is, in fact, merely a special case of the **F** test on **k** means where **k** = 2, as is detailed in most statistics textbooks. As such, the same formal model assumptions are made: that the values in the **k** populations are normally distributed and have the same variance, $\sigma^2$. It is, however, well established that moderate violations of these assumptions have generally negligible effects on the validity of null hypothesis tests and power analyses. For evidence on the issue of the "robustness" of **F** tests with regard to both Type I and Type II error in the face of assumption violation, see Scheffé (1959, Chapter 10), and for a less technical summary, Cohen (1965, pp. 114–116).[1] Note that no assumption is made about the distribution of the **k** population means for fixed effects.

The **F** test on means for fixed effects can occur under a variety of circumstances for which the tables in this chapter may be used:

*Case 0.* One-way analysis of variance with **n**'s equal. This is the simplest design, where without other considerations, one compares **k** means based on samples of equal size.

*Case 1.* One-way analysis of variance with unequal **n**'s.

*Case 2.* Tests of main effects in factorial and other complex designs.

*Case 3.* Tests of interactions in factorial designs.

*Analysis of Covariance.* Each of the above cases has its analog in the analysis of covariance.

### 8.2   THE EFFECT SIZE INDEX: **f**

Our need for a pure number to index the degree of departure from no effect (i.e., **k** equal population means) is here satisfied in a way related to the solution in Chapter 2, where there were only two means. Recall that the difference in means was "standardized" by dividing it by the (common) within-population standard deviation, i.e.,

$$(2.2.1) \qquad\qquad \mathbf{d} = \frac{\mathbf{m}_1 - \mathbf{m}_2}{\sigma} .$$

Since both numerator and denominator are expressed in the (frequently arbitrary) original unit of measurement, their ratio, **d**, is a pure or dimensionless number.

With **k** ≥ 2 means such as we deal with here, we represent the spread of the means not by their range as above (except secondarily, see below), but by a quantity formally like a standard deviation, again dividing by the common standard deviation of the populations involved. It is thus

---

[1] Budescu and Applebaum (1981) have shown that when the F test is applied to samples from binomial and Poisson population distributions, the use of variance stabilizing transformations results in little change in significance level or, in most cases, power. Budescu (1982) reported that for normally distributed populations with heterogeneous variances, substituting for $\sigma$ in the denominator of Equation (8.2.1) the square root of the $n_i$-weighted population variance results in good power approximations.

Also, Koele (1982) shows how to calculate power for random and mixed models, and demonstrates that they have much lower power than that for fixed effects. Barcikowski (1973) provides tables for optimum sample size/number of levels for the random effects model.

$$(8.2.1) \qquad\qquad \mathbf{f} = \frac{\sigma_m}{\sigma} \, ,$$

where, for equal **n** (Cases 0 and 2),

$$(8.2.2) \qquad\qquad \sigma_m = \sqrt{\frac{\sum\limits_{i=1}^{k}(\mathbf{m}_i - \mathbf{m})^2}{k}} \, ,$$

the standard deviation of the population means expressed in original scale units. The values in the parentheses are the departures of the population means ($\mathbf{m}_i$) from the mean of the combined populations or the mean of the means for equal sample sizes (**m**), and are sometimes called the (fixed) "effects"; the $\sigma$'s of formulas (8.2.1) and (2.2.1) are the same, the standard deviation within the populations, also expressed in original scale units. **f** is thus also a pure number, the standard deviation of the standardized means. That is to say that if all the values in the combined populations were to be converted into **z** "standard" scores (Hays, 1973, p. 250f), using the within-population standard deviation, **f** is the standard deviation of these **k** mean **z** scores.

**f** can take on values between zero, when the population means are all equal (or the effects are all zero), and an indefinitely large number as $\sigma_m$ increases relative to $\sigma$.

The structure of **F** ratio tests on means, hence the index **f**, is "naturally" nondirectional (as was the index **w** of the preceding chapter). Only when there are two population means are there only two directions in which discrepancies between null and alternative hypotheses can occur. With $\mathbf{k} > 2$ means, departures can occur in many "directions." The result of all these departures from the null are included in the upper tail rejection region, and, as normally used, **F** tests do not discriminate among these and are therefore nondirectional.

**f** is related to an index $\phi$ used in standard treatments of power,[2] nomographs for which are widely reprinted in statistical testbooks (e.g., Winer, 1971; Scheffé, 1959) and books of tables (Owen, 1962). $\phi$ standardizes by the standard *error* of the sample mean and is thus (in part) a function of the size of each sample, **n**, while **f** is solely a descriptor of the population. Their relationship is given by

$$(8.2.3) \qquad\qquad \mathbf{f} = \frac{\phi}{\sqrt{\mathbf{n}}} \, ,$$

or

$$(8.2.4) \qquad\qquad \phi = \mathbf{f}\sqrt{\mathbf{n}}$$

---

[2] This use of the symbol $\phi$ is not to be confused with its other uses in the text, as the fourfold-point product-moment correlation in Chapter 7 or as the arcsine transformation of a proportion in Chapter 6.

The above description has, for the sake of simplicity, proceeded on the assumption that the sizes of the **k** samples are all the same. No change in the basic conception of **f** takes place when we use it to index the effect size for tests on means of samples of unequal size (Case 1) or as an ES measure for tests on interactions (Case 3). In these applications, the definition of **f** as the "standard deviation of standardized means" requires some further elaboration, which is left to the sections concerned with these cases.

The remainder of this section provides systems for the translation of **f** into (a) a range measure, **d**, and (b) correlation ratio and variance proportion measures, and offers operational definitions of "small," "medium," and "large" ES. Here, too, *the exposition proceeds on the assumption of equal n per sample* and is appropriate to the **F** test on means (Cases 0 and 2). In later discussion of Cases 1 and 3, qualifications will be offered, as necessary.

### 8.2.1   **f** AND THE STANDARDIZED RANGE OF POPULATION MEANS, **d**.

Although our primary ES index is **f**, the standard deviation of the standardized **k** population means, it may facilitate the use and understanding of this index to translate it to and from **d**, the range of standardized means, i.e., the distance between the smallest and largest of the **k** means:

$$(8.2.5) \qquad\qquad \mathbf{d} = \frac{\mathbf{m}_{max} - \mathbf{m}_{min}}{\sigma},$$

where $\mathbf{m}_{max}$ = the largest of the **k** means,

$\qquad$ $\mathbf{m}_{min}$ = the smallest of the **k** means, and

$\qquad\qquad$ $\sigma$ = the (common) standard deviation within the populations (as before).

Notice that in the case of **k** = 2 means (**n** equal), the **d** of (8.2.5.) becomes the **d** used as the ES index for the **t** test of Chapter 2. The relationship between **f** and **d** for 2 means is simply

$$(8.2.6) \qquad\qquad \mathbf{f} = \tfrac{1}{2}\mathbf{d},$$

i.e., the standard deviation of two values is simply half their difference, and therefore

$$(8.2.7) \qquad\qquad \mathbf{d} = 2\mathbf{f}.$$

As the number of means increases beyond two, the relationship between their standard deviation (**f**) and their range (**d**) depends upon exactly how the means are dispersed over their range. With **k** means, two (the largest and smallest) define **d**, but then the remaining **k** − 2 may fall variously over the **d** interval; thus, **f** is not uniquely determined without further specification of the pattern of separation of the means. We will identify three patterns and describe the relationship each one has to **f**, which is also, in general, a function of the number of means. The patterns are:

1. Minimum variability: one mean at each end of **d**, the remaining **k** − 2 means all at the midpoint.
2. Intermediate variability: the **k** means equally spaced over **d**.
3. Maximum variability: the means all at the end points of **d**.

For each of these patterns, there is a fixed relationship between **f** and **d** for any given number of means, **k**.

*Pattern 1.* For any given range of means, **d**, the minimum standard deviation, $f_1$, results when the remaining **k** − 2 means are concentrated at the mean of the means (0 when expressed in standard units), i.e., half-way between the largest and smallest. For Pattern 1,

$$(8.2.8) \qquad\qquad f_1 = d\sqrt{\frac{1}{2k}}$$

gives the value of **f** for **k** means when the range **d** is specified. For example, 7 (= **k**) means dispersed in Pattern 1 would have the (standardized) values − $\frac{1}{2}$**d**, 0, 0, 0, 0, 0, + $\frac{1}{2}$**d**. Their standard deviation would be

$$f_1 = d\sqrt{\frac{1}{2(7)}} = \sqrt{.071429} = .267d,$$

slightly more than one-quarter of the range. Thus, a set of 7 population means spanning half a within-population standard deviation would have **f** = .267(.5) = .13.

The above gives **f** as a function of **d**. The reciprocal relationship is required to determine what value of the range is implied by any given (e.g., tabled) value of **f** when Pattern 1 holds, and is

$$(8.2.9) \qquad\qquad d_1 = f\sqrt{2k}.$$

For example, for the 7 (= **k**) means dispersed in Pattern 1 above, their range would be

$$d_1 = f\sqrt{2(7)} = f\sqrt{14} = 3.74f.$$

A value of **f** = .50 for these means would thus imply a standardized range of 3.74(.50) = 1.87.

For the convenience of the user of this handbook, Table 8.2.1 gives the constants (**c** and **b**) relating **f** to **d** for this pattern and the others discussed below for **k** = 2(1) 16, 25, covering the power and sample size tables provided. Their use is illustrated later in the chapter.

Table 8.2.1

Constants for Transforming d to $f_j$ and f to $d_j$ for Patterns j = 1, 2, 3

| k | $f_j = c_j d$ | | | $d_j = b_j f$ | | |
|---|---|---|---|---|---|---|
| | $c_1$ | $c_2$ | $c_3$ | $b_1$ | $b_2$ | $b_3$ |
| 2 | .500 | .500 | .500 | 2.00 | 2.00 | 2.00 |
| 3 | .408 | .408 | .471 | 2.45 | 2.45 | 2.12 |
| 4 | .354 | .373 | .500 | 2.83 | 2.68 | 2.00 |
| 5 | .316 | .354 | .490 | 3.16 | 2.83 | 2.04 |
| 6 | .289 | .342 | .500 | 3.46 | 2.93 | 2.00 |
| 7 | .267 | .333 | .495 | 3.74 | 3.00 | 2.02 |
| 8 | .250 | .327 | .500 | 4.00 | 3.06 | 2.00 |
| 9 | .236 | .323 | .497 | 4.24 | 3.10 | 2.01 |
| 10 | .224 | .319 | .500 | 4.47 | 3.13 | 2.00 |
| 11 | .213 | .316 | .498 | 4.69 | 3.16 | 2.01 |
| 12 | .204 | .314 | .500 | 4.90 | 3.19 | 2.00 |
| 13 | .196 | .312 | .499 | 5.10 | 3.21 | 2.01 |
| 14 | .189 | .310 | .500 | 5.29 | 3.22 | 2.00 |
| 15 | .183 | .309 | .499 | 5.48 | 3.24 | 2.00 |
| 16 | .177 | .307 | .500 | 5.66 | .325 | 2.00 |
| . | . | . | . | . | . | . |
| . | . | . | . | . | . | . |
| . | . | . | . | . | . | . |
| 25 | .141 | .300 | .500 | 7.07 | 3.01 | 2.00 |

*Pattern 2.* A pattern of medium variability results when the **k** means are equally spaced over the range, and therefore at intervals of $d/(k-1)$. For Pattern 2, the **f** which results from any given range **d** is

(8.2.10)
$$f_2 = \frac{d}{2}\sqrt{\frac{k+1}{3(k-1)}} .$$

For example, for **k** = 7,

$$f_2 = \frac{d}{2}\sqrt{\frac{7+1}{3(7-1)}} = \frac{d}{2}\sqrt{\frac{8}{18}} = .333d,$$

i.e., 7 equally spaced means would have the values $-\frac{1}{2}d$, $-\frac{1}{3}d$, $-\frac{1}{6}d$, 0, $+\frac{1}{6}d$, $+\frac{1}{3}d$, and $+\frac{1}{2}d$, and a standard deviation equal to one-third of their range.

Note that this value for the same $k$ is larger than $f_1 = .267d$ for Pattern 1. For a range of half a within-population standard deviation, $f_2 = .333(.5) = .17$ (while comparably, $f_1 = .13$).

The reciprocal relationship for determining the range implied by a tabled (or any other) value of $f$ for Pattern 2 is

$$(8.2.11) \qquad\qquad d_2 = 2f\sqrt{\frac{3(k-1)}{k+1}}.$$

For 7 means in Pattern 2, their range would be

$$d_2 = 2f\sqrt{\frac{3(7-1)}{7+1}} = 2f\sqrt{\frac{18}{8}} = 3f.$$

Thus, a value of $f = .50$ for these equally spaced means would imply a standardized range of $3(.50) = 1.50)$.

Table 8.2.1 gives the relevant constants ($b_2$ and $c_2$) for varying $k$, making the solution of formulas (8.2.10) and (8.2.11) generally unnecessary.

*Pattern 3.* It is demonstrable and intuitively evident that for any given range the dispersion which yields the maximum standard deviation has the $k$ means falling at both extremes of the range. When $k$ is even, $\frac{1}{2}k$ fall at $-\frac{1}{2}d$ and the other $\frac{1}{2}k$ fall at $+\frac{1}{2}d$; when $k$ is odd, $(k+1)/2$ of the means fall at either end and the $(k-1)/2$ remaining means at the other. With this pattern, for all *even* numbers of means,

$$(8.2.12) \qquad\qquad f_3 = \tfrac{1}{2}d.$$

When $k$ is odd, and there is thus one more mean at one extreme than at the other,

$$(8.2.13) \qquad\qquad f_3 = d\frac{\sqrt{k^2-1}}{2k}.$$

For example, for $k = 7$ means in Pattern 3 (4 means at either $-\frac{1}{2}d$ or $+\frac{1}{2}d$, 3 means at the other), their standard deviation is

$$f_3 = d\frac{\sqrt{7^2-1}}{2(7)} = d\frac{\sqrt{48}}{14} = .495d.$$

Note that $f_3$ is larger (for $k = 7$) than $f_2 = .333d$ and $f_1 = .267d$. If, as before, we posit a range of half a within-population standard deviation, $f_3 = .495(.5) = .25$.

The reciprocal relationship used to determine the range implied by a given value of $f$ when $k$ is even is simply

$$(8.2.14) \qquad\qquad d_3 = 2f,$$

and when **k** is odd,

$$(8.2.15) \qquad\qquad \mathbf{d}_3 = \mathbf{f}\frac{2\mathbf{k}}{\sqrt{\mathbf{k}^2 - 1}}.$$

For the running example of **k** = 7 means, in Pattern 3 their range would be

$$\mathbf{d}_3 = \mathbf{f}\frac{2(7)}{\sqrt{7^2 - 1}} = \mathbf{f}\frac{14}{\sqrt{48}} = 2.02\mathbf{f},$$

so that if we posit, as before, a value of **f** = .50, for these 7 extremely placed means, **d**$_3$ = 2.02(.5) = 1.01, i.e., slightly more than a within-population standard deviation.

As can be seen from Table 8.2.1, there is not as much variability as a function of **k** in the relationship between **f** and **d** for Pattern 3 as for the others. **f**$_3$ is either (for **k** even) exactly or (for **k** odd) approximately $\frac{1}{2}$**d**, the minimum value being **f**$_3$ = .471**d** at **k** = 3.

This section has described and tabled the relationship between the primary ES index for the **F** test, **f**, the standard deviation of standardized means, and **d**, the standardized range of means, for three patterns of distribution of the **k** means. This makes it possible to use **d** as an alternate index of effect size, or equivalently, to determine the **d** implied by tabled or other values of **f**, and **f** implied by specified values of **d**. (The use of **d** will be illustrated in the problems of Sections 8.3 and 8.4) The reader is reminded that these relationships hold only for equal sample sizes (Cases 0 and 2).

8.2.2  **f**, THE CORRELATION RATIO, AND PROPORTION OF VARIANCE. Expressing **f** in terms of **d** provides one useful perspective on the appraisal of effect size with multiple means. Another frame of reference in which to understand **f** is described in this section, namely, in terms of correlation between population membership and the dependent variable, and in the related terms of the proportion of the total variance (PV) of the **k** populations combined which is accounted for by population membership.

Just as the **d** of this chapter is a generalization to **k** populations of the **d** used as an ES index for **t** tests on two means of Chapter 2, so is $\eta$ (eta), the correlation ratio, a similar generalization of the Pearson **r**, and $\eta^2$ a generalization of **r**$^2$, the proportion of variance (PV) accounted for by population membership.

To understand $\eta^2$, consider the set of **k** populations, all of the same variance, $\sigma^2$, but each with its own mean, **m**$_i$. The variance of the means

$\sigma_m{}^2$ is some quantity which differs from zero when the **k** means are not all equal. If we square both sides of formula (8.2.1), we note that

$$(8.2.16) \qquad\qquad f^2 = \frac{\sigma_m{}^2}{\sigma^2},$$

is the ratio of the variance of the means to the variance of the values within the populations.

Now consider that the populations are combined into a single "super-population" whose mean is **m** (the mean of the population $m_i$'s when the populations are considered equally numerous; otherwise, their mean when each $m_i$ is weighted by its population size). The variance of the "superpopulation," or total variance ($\sigma_t{}^2$), is larger than the within-population variance because it is augmented by the variance of the constituent population means. It is simply the sum of these two variances:

$$(8.2.17) \qquad\qquad \sigma_t{}^2 = \sigma^2 + \sigma_m{}^2.$$

We now define $\eta^2$ as the proportion of the total superpopulation variance made up by the variance of the population means:

$$(8.2.18) \qquad\qquad \eta^2 = \frac{\sigma_m{}^2}{\sigma_t{}^2} = \frac{\sigma_m{}^2}{\sigma^2 + \sigma_m{}^2}.$$

The combination of this formula with formula (8.2.16) and some simple algebraic manipulation yields

$$(8.2.19) \qquad\qquad \eta^2 = \frac{f^2}{1 + f^2},$$

and

$$(8.2.20) \qquad\qquad \eta = \sqrt{\frac{f^2}{1 + f^2}}.$$

Thus, a simple function of $f^2$ yields $\eta^2$, a measure of dispersion of the $m_i$ and hence of the implication of difference in population membership to the overall variability. When the population means are all equal, $\sigma_m{}^2$ and hence $f^2$ is zero, and $\eta^2 = 0$, indicating that none of the total variance is due to difference in population membership. As formula (8.2.18) makes clear, when all the cases in each population have the same value, $\sigma^2 = 0$, and all of the total variance is produced by the variance of the means, so that $\eta^2 = 1.00$. Table 8.2.2 provides $\eta^2$ and $\eta$ values as a function of **f**.

Note that $\eta^2$, like all measures of ES, describes a population state of affairs. It can also be computed on samples and its population value estimated therefrom. (See examples 8.17 and 8.19.) Depending on the basis of the estimation, the estimate is variously called $\eta^2$, $\epsilon^2$ (Peters and Van Voorhis, 1940, pp. 312–325, 353–357; Cureton, 1966, pp. 605–607), or estimated $\omega^2$ (Hays, 1981, pp. 349–366). In general, $\eta^2$ is presented in applied statistics textbooks only in connection with its use in the appraisal of the curvilinear regression of **Y** on **X**, where the populations are defined by equal segments along the **X** variable, and $\sigma_m{}^2$ is the variance of the **X**-segments' **Y** means. Although this is a useful application of $\eta^2$, it is a rather limited special case. For the broader view, see Hays (1973) (under $\omega^2$), Cohen (1965, pp. 104–105), Cohen & Cohen (1983, pp. 196–198) and Friedman (1968, 1982).

$\eta^2$ is literally a generalization of the (point-biserial) $r^2$ of Chapter 2 which gives the PV for the case where there are **k** = 2 populations. It is possible to express the relationship between the dependent variable **Y** and population membership **X** as a simple (i.e., zero-order) product moment $r^2$, when **X** is restricted to two possibilities, i.e., membership in A (**X** = 0) or membership in B(**X** = 1) (see Chapter 2). When we generalize **X** to represent a nominal scale of **k** possible alternative population memberships, $r^2$ no longer suffices, and the more general $\eta^2$ is used. It is interesting to note that if **k**-population membership is rendered as a set of independent variables (say, as dichotomous "dummy" variables), the simple $r^2$ generalizes to *multiple* $R^2$, which is demonstrably equal to $\eta^2$ (see Section 9.2.1).

We have interpreted $\eta^2$ as the PV associated with alternative membership in populations. A mathematically equivalent description of $\eta^2$ proceeds by the following contrast: Assume that we "predict" all the members of our populations as having the same **Y** value, the **m** of our superpopulation. The gross error of this "prediction" can be appraised by finding for each subject the discrepancy between his value and **m**, squaring this value, and adding such squared values over all subjects. Call this $E_t$. Another "prediction" can be made by assigning to each subject the mean of *his* population, $m_i$. Again, we determine the discrepancy between his actual value and this "prediction" ($m_i$), square and total over all subjects from all populations. Call this $E_p$. To the extent to which the **k** population means are spread, $E_p$ will be smaller than $E_t$.

(8.2.21)
$$\eta^2 = \frac{E_t - E_p}{E_t} = 1 - \frac{E_p}{E_t},$$

i.e., the proportionate amount *by which* errors are reduced by using own population mean ($m_i$) rather than superpopulation mean (**m**) as a basis for "prediction." Or, we can view these as alternative means of *characterizing* the members of our populations, and $\eta^2$ indexes the degree of increased incisiveness that results from using the $m_i$ rather than $m$.

The discussion has thus far proceeded with $\eta^2$, the PV measure. For purposes of morale, and to offer a scale which is comparable to that of the familiar product moment $r$, we can index ES by means of $\eta$, the correlation ratio, in addition to or instead of the lower value yielded by $\eta^2$. As can be seen from taking the square root in formula (8.2.18),, $\eta$ is the ratio of the *standard deviation* of population means to the *standard deviation* of the values in the superpopulation, i.e., the combined populations. Since standard devia-

Table 8.2.2

$\eta^2$ and $\eta$ as a Function of f; f as a Function of $\eta^2$ and $\eta$

| f | $\eta^2$ | $\eta$ | $\eta^2$ | f | $\eta$ | f |
|------|--------|-------|-------|-------|------|-------|
| .00 | .0000 | .000 | .00 | .000 | .00 | .000 |
| .05 | .0025 | .050 | .01 | .101 | .05 | .050 |
| .10 | .0099 | .100 | .02 | .143 | .10 | .101 |
| .15 | .0220 | .148 | .03 | .176 | .15 | .152 |
| .20 | .0385 | .196 | .04 | .204 | .20 | .204 |
| .25 | .0588 | .243 | .05 | .229 | .25 | .258 |
| .30 | .0826 | .287 | .06 | .253 | .30 | .314 |
| .35 | .1091 | .330 | .07 | .274 | .35 | .374 |
| .40 | .1379 | .371 | .08 | .295 | .40 | .436 |
| .45 | .1684 | .410 | .09 | .314 | .45 | .504 |
| .50 | .2000 | .447 | .10 | .333 | .50 | .577 |
| .55 | .2322 | .482 | .15 | .420 | .55 | .659 |
| .60 | .2647 | .514 | .20 | .500 | .60 | .750 |
| .65 | .2970 | .545 | .25 | .577 | .65 | .855 |
| .70 | .3289 | .573 | .30 | .655 | .70 | .980 |
| .75 | .3600 | .600 | .40 | .816 | .75 | 1.134 |
| .80 | .3902 | .625 | .50 | 1.000 | .80 | 1.333 |
| .85 | .4194 | .648 | .60 | 1.225 | .85 | 1.614 |
| .90 | .4475 | .669 | .70 | 1.528 | .90 | 2.065 |
| .95 | .4744 | .689 | .80 | 2.000 | .95 | 3.042 |
| 1.00 | .5000 | .707 | .90 | 3.000 | 1.00 | – |

tions are as respectable as variances, no special apology is required in working with $\eta$ rather than $\eta^2$.

In formulas (8.2.19) and (8.2.20), we have $\eta^2$ and $\eta$ as functions of **f**. This is useful for assessing the implication of a given value of **f** (in terms of which our tables are organized) to PV or correlation. The reciprocal relation, **f** as a function of $\eta$, is also useful when the investigator, thinking in PV or correlational terms, needs to determine the **f** they imply, e.g., in order to use the tables:

$$(8.2.22) \qquad\qquad \mathbf{f} = \sqrt{\frac{\eta^2}{1 - \eta^2}}$$

For the convenience of the user of this handbook, this formula is solved for various values of $\eta$ and $\eta^2$ and the results presented in Table 8.2.2.

Table 8.2.2 deserves a moment's attention. As discussed in the next section and in Section 11.1 (and, indeed, as noted in previous chapters, particularly Chapter 3), effect sizes in behavioral science are generally small, and, in terms of **f**, will generally be found in the .00–.40 range. With **f** small, $\mathbf{f}^2$ is smaller, and $1 + \mathbf{f}^2$, the denominator of $\eta^2$ [formula (8.2.19)] is only slightly greater than one. The result is that for small values of **f** such as are typically encountered, $\eta$ is approximately equal to **f**, being only slightly smaller, and therefore $\eta^2$ is similarly only slightly smaller than $\mathbf{f}^2$. Thus, in the range of our primary interest, **f** provides in itself an approximate correlation measure, and $\mathbf{f}^2$ an approximate PV measure. For very large effect sizes, say **f** $> .40$, **f** and $\eta$ diverge too much for this rough and ready approximation, and $\mathbf{f}^2$ and $\eta^2$ even more so.

8.2.3  "SMALL," "MEDIUM," AND "LARGE" **f** VALUES. It has already been suggested that values of **f** as large as .50 are not common in behavioral science, thus providing a prelude to the work of this section. Again, as in previous chapters, we take on the task of helping the user of this handbook to achieve a workable frame of reference for the ES index or measure of the alternate-hypothetical state of affairs, in this case **f**.

The optimal procedure for setting **f** in a given investigation is that the investigator, drawing on previous findings and theory in that area and his own scientific judgment, specify the **k** means and $\sigma$ he expects and compute the resulting **f** from these values by means of formulas (8.2.1) and (8.2.2). If this demand for specification is too strong, he may specify the range of means, **d**, from formula (8.2.5), choose one of the patterns of mean dispersion of Section 8.2.1, and use Table 8.2.1 to determine the implied value of **f**. On the same footing as this procedure, which may be used instead of or in conjunction with it, is positing the expected results in terms of the proportion of total variance associated with membership in the **k** populations, i.e., $\eta^2$. Formula (8.2.22) and Table 8.2.2 then provide the translation from $\eta^2$ to **f**. (In the case of **f** for interactions, see Section 8.3.4.)

All the above procedures are characterized by their use of magnitudes selected by the investigator to represent the situation of the *specific* research he is planning. When experience with a given research area or variable is insufficient to formulate alternative hypotheses as "strong" as these procedures demand, and to serve as a set of conventions or operational definitions, we define specific values of **f** for "small," "medium," and "large" effects. The reader is referred to Sections 1.4 and 2.2.3 for review of the considerations leading to the setting of ES conventions, and the advantages and disadvantages inherent in them. Briefly, we note here that these qualitative adjectives are relative, and, being general, may not be reasonably descriptive in any specific area. Thus, what a sociologist may consider a small effect size may well be appraised as medium by a clinical psychologist.

It must be reiterated here that however problematic the setting of an ES, it is a task which simply cannot be shirked. The investigator who insists that he has absolutely no way of knowing how large an ES to posit fails to appreciate that this necessarily means that he has no rational basis for deciding whether he needs to make ten observations or ten thousand.

Before presenting the operational definitions for **f**, a word about their consistency. They are fully consistent with the definitions of Chapter 2 for **k** = 2 populations in terms of **d**, which, as noted, is simply 2**f**. They are also generally consistent with the other ES indices which can be translated into PV measures (see Sections 3.2.2 and 6.2.1).

We continue, for the present, to conceive of the populations as being sampled with equal **n**'s.

SMALL EFFECT SIZE: **f** = .10. We define a small effect as a standard deviation of **k** population means one-tenth as large as the standard deviation of the observations within the populations. For **k** = 2 populations, this definition is exactly equivalent to the comparable definition of a small difference, **d** = 2(.10) = .20 of Chapter 2 [formula (8.2.7) and, more generally, Table 8.2.1]. As **k** increases, a given **f** implies a greater range for Patterns 1 and 2. Thus, with **k** = 6 means, one at each end of the range and the remaining 4 at the middle (Pattern 1), an **f** of .10 implies a range $d_1$ of 3.46(.10) = .35, while equal spacing (Pattern 2) implies a range $d_2$ of 2.93(.10) = .29. (The constants 3.46 and 2.93 are respectively the $b_1$ and $b_2$ values at **k** = 6 in Table 8.2.1.) When **f** = .10 occurs with the extreme Pattern 3, the $d_3$ is at (for **k** even) or slightly above (for **k** odd) 2**f** = .20 (Table 8.2.1). Thus, depending on **k** and the pattern of the means over the range, a small effect implies **d** at least .20, and, with large **k** disposed in Pattern 1, a small effect can be expressed in a $d_1$ of the order of .50 or larger (for example, see Table 8.2.1 in column $b_1$ for **k** ≥ 12).

When expressed in correlation and PV terms, the $f = .10$ definition of a small effect is fully consistent with the definitions of Chapters 2, 3, and 6 (various forms of product moment $r$). An $f = .10$ is equivalent to $\eta = .100$ and $\eta^2 = .0099$, about 1% of the total superpopulation variance accounted for by group membership. As already noted (particularly in Section 2.2.3), scientifically important (or at least meaningful) effects may be of this modest order of magnitude. The investigator who is inclined to disregard ES criteria for effects this small on the grounds that he would never be seeking to establish such small effects needs to be reminded that he is likely to be thinking in terms of theoretical constructs, which are implicitly measured without error. Any source of irrelevant variance in his measures (psychometric unreliability, dirty test tubes, lack of experimental control, or whatever) will serve to reduce his effect sizes *as measured*, so that what would be a medium or even large effect if one could use "true" measures may be attenuated to a small effect in practice (See Section 11.3 and Cohen, 1962, p. 151).

MEDIUM EFFECT SIZE: $f = .25$. A standard deviation of $k$ population means one-quarter as large as the standard deviation of the observations within the populations, is the operational definition of a medium effect size. With $k = 2$ populations, this accords with the $d = 2(.25) = .50$ definition of a medium difference between two means of Chapter 2, and this is a minimum value for the range over $k$ means. With increasing $k$ for either minimum (Pattern 1) or intermediate (Pattern 2) variability, the range implied by $f = .25$ increases from $d = .50$. For example, with $k = 7$ population means, if $k - 2 = 5$ of them are at the middle of the range and the remaining two at the endpoints of the range (Pattern 1), a medium $d_1 = 3.74(.25) = .94$ (Table 8.2.1 gives $b_1 = 3.74$ at $k = 7$). Thus, medium effect size for 7 means disposed in Pattern 1 implies a range of means of almost one standard deviation. If the seven means are spaced equally over the range (Pattern 2), a medium $d_2 = 3.00(.25) = .75$ (Table 8.2.1 gives $b_2 = 3.00$ for $k = 7$), i.e., a span of means of three-quarters of a within-population standard deviation. As a concrete example of this, consider the IQ's of seven populations made up of certain occupational groups, e.g., house painters, chauffeurs, auto mechanics, carpenters, butchers, riveters, and linemen. Assume a within-population standard deviation for IQ of 12 ($= \sigma$) and that their IQ means are equally spaced. Now, assume a medium ES, hence $f = .25$. (Expressed in IQ units, this would mean that the standard deviation of the seven IQ means would be $f\sigma = .25(12) = 3$.) The range of these means would be $d_2 = .75$ of the within-population $\sigma$. Expressed in units of IQ, this would be $d_2\sigma = .75(12) = 9$ IQ points, say from 98 to 107. (These values are about right [Berelson & Steiner, 1964, pp. 223–224], but of course any seven equally spaced values whose range is 9 would satisfy the criterion of a medium ES as defined here.)

Viewed from the perspective of correlation and proportion of variance accounted for, we note that $f = .25$ implies a correlation ratio ($\eta$) of .243 and a PV (here $\eta^2$) of .0588, i.e., not quite 6% of the total variance of the combined populations accounted for by population membership (Table 8.2.2). Again, note that this is identical with the correlational-PV criterion of a medium difference between two means (Section 2.2), necessarily so since in this limiting case $\eta = r$ (point biserial). It is also consistent with the definition of a medium difference between two proportions, when expressed as an $r$ (fourfold point or $\phi$ correlation), which equals .238 to .248 when, the proportions are in the interval .20 to .80 (Section 6.2). It is, however smaller than the criterion for a medium ES in hypotheses concerning the Pearson $r$ (Section 3.2), where the medium $r$ is .30 (and $r^2 = .09$).

LARGE EFFECT SIZE: $f = .40$. Our operational definition (or proposed convention) of a large spread of $k$ means is that the standard deviation of the means be .40 of the standard deviation of the observations within the populations. This is consistent with the criterion of a large difference between two means of $d = 2(.40) = .80$ (Section 2.2.2) and is the minimum range (since $k = 2$) which can be called large by this definition. With the means disposed in Pattern 1, a large span for 6 means is $d_1 = 3.46(.40) = 1.38$, for 7 means $d_1 = 3.74(.40) = 1.50$, for 8 means $d_1 = 4.00(.40) = 1.60$, etc., i.e., about $1\frac{1}{2}$ standard deviations ($b_1$ constants from Table 8.2.1). For equally spaced means (Pattern 2), this implies for 6 means, a range of $d_2 = 2.93(.40) = 1.17$, for 7 means a range of $d_2 = 3.00(.40) = 1.20$, and for 8 means a range of $d_2 = 3.06(.40) = 1.22$, etc., i.e., about $1\frac{1}{8}$ standard deviations ($b_2$ constants from Table 8.2.1). We use a similar illustration to that given for medium effect size, where for $k = 7$ occupation groups with equally spaced population mean IQs, we found the range $d_2 = b_2 f = 3.00(.25) = .75$, or, expressed in IQ units, $.75\sigma = .75(12) = 9.0$. Consider now a new set of 7 occupations: house painter, chauffeur, upholsterer, mechanic, lathe operator, machinist, laboratory assistant. Their mean IQ's, to have a large range, would need to cover uniformly the interval $d_2 = b_2 f = 3.00(.40) = 1.20$, or expressed in IQ units, again assuming that $\sigma = 12$, $1.20\sigma = 1.20(12) = 14.4$, say from 98 to 112 (Berelson & Steiner, 1964, pp. 223–224). Again note that any set of 7 occupation groups with IQ means spanning the same range would represent a large effect as defined here, wherever that range occurs.

In terms of correlation and proportion of variance accounted for, $f = .40$ implies a correlation ratio ($\eta$) of .371 and a PV (here $\eta^2$) of .1379, somewhat more than twice the PV for a medium effect ($\eta^2 = .0588$). Note the necessary consistency with the definition in correlation–PV terms of a large difference between two means ($\eta =$ point biserial $r$; see Section 2.2). This definition is also fully consistent with the definition of a large difference between two proportions, when expressed as an $r$ (fourfold point or $\phi$

correlation), which equals .37–.39 when the proportions fall between .20 and .80 (Section 6.2). However, it is smaller than the criterion for a large ES in hypotheses concerning the Pearson $r$, where large $r$ is defined as .50, $r^2 = PV = .25$ (Section 3.2).

## 8.3 POWER TABLES

The power tables for this section are given on pages 289–354; the text follows on page 355.

Table 8.3.1

Power of F test at a = .01, u = 1

| n | $F_c$ | .05 | .10 | .15 | .20 | .25 | .30 | .35 | .40 | .50 | .60 | .70 | .80 |
|---|---|---|---|---|---|---|---|---|---|---|---|---|---|
| 2 | 98.503 | 01 | 01 | 01 | 01 | 02 | 02 | 03 | 04 | 04 | 05 | 06 | 08 |
| 3 | 21.198 | 01 | 01 | 01 | 02 | 02 | 02 | 03 | 04 | 05 | 07 | 09 | 11 |
| 4 | 13.745 | 01 | 01 | 01 | 02 | 02 | 03 | 04 | 05 | 07 | 10 | 14 | 19 |
| 5 | 11.259 | 01 | 01 | 02 | 02 | 03 | 03 | 05 | 06 | 10 | 15 | 21 | 29 |
| 6 | 10.044 | 01 | 01 | 02 | 02 | 03 | 04 | 06 | 08 | 13 | 20 | 29 | 40 |
| 7 | 9.330 | 01 | 01 | 02 | 03 | 04 | 05 | 07 | 10 | 17 | 26 | 38 | 50 |
| 8 | 8.861 | 01 | 01 | 02 | 03 | 04 | 06 | 09 | 12 | 21 | 32 | 46 | 60 |
| 9 | 8.531 | 01 | 02 | 02 | 03 | 05 | 07 | 10 | 14 | 25 | 39 | 54 | 68 |
| 10 | 8.285 | 01 | 02 | 02 | 04 | 06 | 08 | 12 | 17 | 29 | 45 | 61 | 75 |
| 11 | 8.096 | 01 | 02 | 03 | 04 | 06 | 09 | 14 | 19 | 34 | 51 | 67 | 81 |
| 12 | 7.946 | 01 | 02 | 03 | 05 | 07 | 11 | 16 | 22 | 38 | 56 | 73 | 86 |
| 13 | 7.823 | 01 | 02 | 03 | 05 | 08 | 12 | 18 | 25 | 42 | 61 | 78 | 89 |
| 14 | 7.721 | 01 | 02 | 03 | 05 | 08 | 13 | 20 | 28 | 46 | 66 | 82 | 92 |
| 15 | 7.636 | 01 | 02 | 03 | 06 | 09 | 15 | 22 | 30 | 50 | 70 | 85 | 94 |
| 16 | 7.562 | 01 | 02 | 04 | 06 | 10 | 16 | 24 | 33 | 54 | 74 | 88 | 96 |
| 17 | 7.499 | 01 | 02 | 04 | 07 | 11 | 17 | 26 | 36 | 58 | 78 | 91 | 97 |
| 18 | 7.444 | 01 | 02 | 04 | 07 | 12 | 19 | 28 | 39 | 62 | 81 | 92 | 98 |
| 19 | 7.396 | 01 | 02 | 04 | 08 | 13 | 20 | 30 | 41 | 65 | 83 | 94 | 98 |
| 20 | 7.353 | 01 | 02 | 04 | 08 | 14 | 22 | 32 | 44 | 68 | 86 | 95 | 99 |
| 21 | 7.314 | 01 | 02 | 05 | 08 | 15 | 24 | 34 | 47 | 71 | 88 | 96 | 99 |
| 22 | 7.280 | 01 | 03 | 05 | 09 | 16 | 25 | 37 | 49 | 73 | 90 | 97 | 99 |
| 23 | 7.248 | 01 | 03 | 05 | 09 | 17 | 27 | 39 | 52 | 76 | 91 | 98 | * |
| 24 | 7.220 | 01 | 03 | 05 | 10 | 18 | 28 | 41 | 54 | 78 | 93 | 98 | |
| 25 | 7.194 | 01 | 03 | 06 | 10 | 19 | 30 | 43 | 57 | 80 | 94 | 99 | |
| 26 | 7.171 | 01 | 03 | 06 | 11 | 20 | 31 | 45 | 59 | 82 | 95 | 99 | |
| 27 | 7.149 | 01 | 03 | 06 | 12 | 21 | 33 | 47 | 61 | 84 | 96 | 99 | |
| 28 | 7.129 | 01 | 03 | 06 | 12 | 22 | 35 | 49 | 63 | 86 | 96 | 99 | |
| 29 | 7.110 | 01 | 03 | 07 | 13 | 23 | 36 | 50 | 65 | 87 | 97 | * | |
| 30 | 7.093 | 01 | 03 | 07 | 13 | 24 | 38 | 53 | 67 | 89 | 97 | | |
| 31 | 7.077 | 02 | 03 | 07 | 14 | 25 | 39 | 55 | 69 | 90 | 98 | | |
| 32 | 7.062 | 02 | 03 | 07 | 15 | 26 | 41 | 56 | 71 | 91 | 98 | | |
| 33 | 7.048 | 02 | 04 | 08 | 15 | 27 | 42 | 58 | 73 | 92 | 99 | | |
| 34 | 7.035 | 02 | 04 | 08 | 16 | 28 | 44 | 60 | 75 | 93 | 99 | | |
| 35 | 7.023 | 02 | 04 | 08 | 17 | 30 | 45 | 62 | 76 | 94 | 99 | | |
| 36 | 7.011 | 02 | 04 | 08 | 17 | 31 | 47 | 63 | 78 | 94 | 99 | | |
| 37 | 7.001 | 02 | 04 | 09 | 18 | 32 | 48 | 65 | 79 | 95 | 99 | | |
| 38 | 6.990 | 02 | 04 | 09 | 19 | 33 | 50 | 66 | 80 | 96 | 99 | | |
| 39 | 6.981 | 02 | 04 | 09 | 19 | 34 | 51 | 68 | 82 | 96 | * | | |

Table 8.3.1 (continued)

| n | $F_c$ | .05 | .10 | .15 | .20 | .25 | .30 | .35 | .40 | .50 | .60 | .70 | .80 |
|---|---|---|---|---|---|---|---|---|---|---|---|---|---|
| 40 | 6.971 | 02 | 04 | 10 | 20 | 35 | 53 | 69 | 83 | 97 | * | * | * |
| 42 | 6.954 | 02 | 04 | 10 | 21 | 37 | 55 | 72 | 85 | 97 | | | |
| 44 | 6.939 | 02 | 05 | 11 | 23 | 39 | 58 | 75 | 87 | 98 | | | |
| 46 | 6.925 | 02 | 05 | 11 | 24 | 41 | 60 | 77 | 89 | 98 | | | |
| 48 | 6.912 | 02 | 05 | 12 | 25 | 44 | 63 | 79 | 90 | 99 | | | |
| 50 | 6.901 | 02 | 05 | 13 | 27 | 46 | 65 | 81 | 92 | 99 | | | |
| 52 | 6.890 | 02 | 05 | 13 | 28 | 48 | 67 | 83 | 93 | 99 | | | |
| 54 | 6.880 | 02 | 06 | 14 | 30 | 50 | 70 | 85 | 94 | 99 | | | |
| 56 | 6.871 | 02 | 06 | 15 | 31 | 52 | 72 | 86 | 95 | * | | | |
| 58 | 6.862 | 02 | 06 | 16 | 33 | 54 | 73 | 88 | 95 | | | | |
| 60 | 6.854 | 02 | 06 | 16 | 34 | 56 | 75 | 89 | 96 | | | | |
| 64 | 6.840 | 02 | 07 | 18 | 37 | 59 | 79 | 91 | 97 | | | | |
| 68 | 6.828 | 02 | 07 | 19 | 40 | 63 | 82 | 93 | 98 | | | | |
| 72 | 6.817 | 02 | 08 | 21 | 42 | 66 | 84 | 95 | 99 | | | | |
| 76 | 6.807 | 02 | 08 | 22 | 45 | 69 | 87 | 96 | 99 | | | | |
| 80 | 6.798 | 02 | 09 | 24 | 48 | 72 | 89 | 97 | 99 | | | | |
| 84 | 6.790 | 03 | 09 | 25 | 50 | 74 | 90 | 97 | * | | | | |
| 88 | 6.783 | 03 | 10 | 27 | 53 | 77 | 92 | 98 | | | | | |
| 92 | 6.776 | 03 | 10 | 29 | 55 | 79 | 93 | 98 | | | | | |
| 96 | 6.770 | 03 | 11 | 30 | 57 | 81 | 94 | 99 | | | | | |
| 100 | 6.764 | 03 | 11 | 32 | 60 | 83 | 95 | 99 | | | | | |
| 120 | 6.742 | 03 | 14 | 40 | 70 | 90 | 98 | * | | | | | |
| 140 | 6.727 | 04 | 17 | 47 | 78 | 95 | 99 | | | | | | |
| 160 | 6.715 | 04 | 21 | 54 | 84 | 97 | * | | | | | | |
| 180 | 6.706 | 04 | 24 | 61 | 89 | 99 | | | | | | | |
| 200 | 6.699 | 05 | 28 | 67 | 92 | 99 | | | | | | | |
| 250 | 6.686 | 07 | 37 | 79 | 97 | * | | | | | | | |
| 300 | 6.677 | 08 | 45 | 87 | 99 | | | | | | | | |
| 350 | 6.671 | 10 | 53 | 92 | * | | | | | | | | |
| 400 | 6.667 | 11 | 60 | 95 | | | | | | | | | |
| 450 | 6.663 | 13 | 67 | 97 | | | | | | | | | |
| 500 | 6.661 | 15 | 73 | 99 | | | | | | | | | |
| 600 | 6.656 | 19 | 82 | * | | | | | | | | | |
| 700 | 6.653 | 24 | 88 | | | | | | | | | | |
| 800 | 6.651 | 28 | 93 | | | | | | | | | | |
| 900 | 6.649 | 32 | 95 | | | | | | | | | | |
| 1000 | 6.648 | 37 | 97 | | | | | | | | | | |

* Power values below this point are greater than .995.

Table 8.3.2

Power of F test at a = .01, u = 2

| n | $F_c$ | .05 | .10 | .15 | .20 | .25 | .30 | .35 | .40 | .50 | .60 | .70 | .80 |
|---|---|---|---|---|---|---|---|---|---|---|---|---|---|
| | | | | | | | | | | | | f | |
| 2 | 30.817 | 01 | 01 | 01 | 01 | 02 | 02 | 03 | 03 | 03 | 04 | 06 | 07 |
| 3 | 10.925 | 01 | 01 | 01 | 02 | 02 | 02 | 03 | 04 | 05 | 07 | 10 | 13 |
| 4 | 8.022 | 01 | 01 | 01 | 02 | 02 | 03 | 04 | 05 | 08 | 12 | 17 | 24 |
| 5 | 6.927 | 01 | 01 | 02 | 02 | 03 | 04 | 05 | 07 | 11 | 18 | 27 | 38 |
| 6 | 6.359 | 01 | 01 | 02 | 02 | 03 | 05 | 07 | 09 | 16 | 26 | 38 | 51 |
| 7 | 6.013 | 01 | 01 | 02 | 03 | 04 | 06 | 08 | 11 | 21 | 33 | 48 | 63 |
| 8 | 5.780 | 01 | 01 | 02 | 03 | 05 | 07 | 10 | 14 | 26 | 41 | 58 | 73 |
| 9 | 5.614 | 01 | 02 | 02 | 04 | 05 | 08 | 12 | 17 | 31 | 49 | 67 | 81 |
| 10 | 5.488 | 01 | 02 | 03 | 04 | 06 | 10 | 14 | 21 | 37 | 56 | 74 | 87 |
| 11 | 5.390 | 01 | 02 | 03 | 04 | 07 | 11 | 17 | 24 | 42 | 63 | 80 | 91 |
| 12 | 5.313 | 01 | 02 | 03 | 05 | 08 | 13 | 19 | 27 | 48 | 69 | 85 | 94 |
| 13 | 5.249 | 01 | 02 | 03 | 05 | 09 | 14 | 22 | 31 | 53 | 74 | 89 | 96 |
| 14 | 5.195 | 01 | 02 | 03 | 06 | 10 | 16 | 24 | 34 | 58 | 79 | 92 | 98 |
| 15 | 5.150 | 01 | 02 | 04 | 06 | 11 | 18 | 27 | 38 | 62 | 82 | 94 | 99 |
| 16 | 5.111 | 01 | 02 | 04 | 07 | 12 | 20 | 30 | 41 | 67 | 86 | 96 | 99 |
| 17 | 5.078 | 01 | 02 | 04 | 07 | 13 | 21 | 32 | 45 | 70 | 89 | 97 | 99 |
| 18 | 5.048 | 01 | 02 | 04 | 08 | 14 | 23 | 35 | 48 | 74 | 91 | 98 | * |
| 19 | 5.022 | 01 | 02 | 05 | 09 | 15 | 25 | 38 | 52 | 77 | 93 | 98 | |
| 20 | 4.999 | 01 | 02 | 05 | 09 | 17 | 27 | 40 | 55 | 80 | 94 | 99 | |
| 21 | 4.977 | 01 | 03 | 05 | 10 | 18 | 29 | 43 | 58 | 83 | 95 | 99 | |
| 22 | 4.959 | 01 | 03 | 05 | 10 | 19 | 31 | 46 | 61 | 85 | 96 | * | |
| 23 | 4.943 | 01 | 03 | 06 | 11 | 20 | 33 | 48 | 64 | 87 | 97 | | |
| 24 | 4.928 | 01 | 03 | 06 | 12 | 22 | 35 | 51 | 66 | 89 | 98 | | |
| 25 | 4.914 | 01 | 03 | 06 | 12 | 23 | 37 | 53 | 69 | 91 | 98 | | |
| 26 | 4.901 | 01 | 03 | 07 | 13 | 24 | 39 | 56 | 71 | 92 | 99 | | |
| 27 | 4.889 | 01 | 03 | 07 | 14 | 26 | 41 | 58 | 74 | 93 | 99 | | |
| 28 | 4.878 | 01 | 03 | 07 | 15 | 27 | 43 | 60 | 75 | 94 | 99 | | |
| 29 | 4.868 | 01 | 03 | 07 | 15 | 28 | 45 | 62 | 78 | 95 | 99 | | |
| 30 | 4.859 | 02 | 03 | 08 | 16 | 30 | 47 | 65 | 80 | 96 | * | | |
| 31 | 4.850 | 02 | 04 | 08 | 17 | 31 | 49 | 67 | 81 | 96 | | | |
| 32 | 4.842 | 02 | 04 | 08 | 18 | 33 | 51 | 69 | 83 | 97 | | | |
| 33 | 4.834 | 02 | 04 | 09 | 19 | 34 | 53 | 70 | 84 | 98 | | | |
| 34 | 4.827 | 02 | 04 | 09 | 19 | 35 | 54 | 72 | 86 | 98 | | | |
| 35 | 4.820 | 02 | 04 | 09 | 20 | 37 | 56 | 74 | 87 | 98 | | | |
| 36 | 4.814 | 02 | 04 | 10 | 21 | 38 | 58 | 76 | 88 | 99 | | | |
| 37 | 4.808 | 02 | 04 | 10 | 22 | 40 | 59 | 77 | 89 | 99 | | | |
| 38 | 4.802 | 02 | 04 | 10 | 23 | 41 | 61 | 79 | 90 | 99 | | | |
| 39 | 4.797 | 02 | 04 | 11 | 24 | 42 | 63 | 80 | 91 | 99 | | | |

Table 8.3.2 (continued)

| n | $F_c$ | .05 | .10 | .15 | .20 | .25 | .30 | .35 | .40 | .50 | .60 | .70 | .80 |
|---|---|---|---|---|---|---|---|---|---|---|---|---|---|
| 40 | 4.791 | 02 | 05 | 11 | 25 | 44 | 64 | 81 | 92 | 99 | * | * | * |
| 42 | 4.782 | 02 | 05 | 12 | 26 | 46 | 67 | 84 | 94 | * | | | |
| 44 | 4.774 | 02 | 05 | 13 | 28 | 49 | 70 | 86 | 95 | | | | |
| 46 | 4.766 | 02 | 05 | 14 | 30 | 51 | 73 | 88 | 96 | | | | |
| 48 | 4.760 | 02 | 05 | 14 | 32 | 54 | 75 | 90 | 97 | | | | |
| 50 | 4.753 | 02 | 06 | 15 | 33 | 56 | 77 | 91 | 97 | | | | |
| 52 | 4.747 | 02 | 06 | 16 | 35 | 59 | 79 | 92 | 98 | | | | |
| 54 | 4.742 | 02 | 06 | 17 | 37 | 61 | 81 | 93 | 98 | | | | |
| 56 | 4.737 | 02 | 06 | 18 | 39 | 63 | 83 | 94 | 99 | | | | |
| 58 | 4.732 | 02 | 07 | 19 | 40 | 65 | 85 | 95 | 99 | | | | |
| 60 | 4.728 | 02 | 07 | 20 | 42 | 67 | 86 | 96 | 99 | | | | |
| 64 | 4.720 | 02 | 08 | 22 | 46 | 71 | 89 | 97 | 99 | | | | |
| 68 | 4.713 | 02 | 08 | 24 | 49 | 75 | 91 | 98 | * | | | | |
| 72 | 4.707 | 02 | 09 | 26 | 52 | 78 | 93 | 99 | | | | | |
| 76 | 4.702 | 02 | 09 | 28 | 55 | 81 | 95 | 99 | | | | | |
| 80 | 4.697 | 03 | 10 | 30 | 58 | 83 | 96 | 99 | | | | | |
| 84 | 4.693 | 03 | 10 | 32 | 61 | 85 | 97 | * | | | | | |
| 88 | 4.689 | 03 | 11 | 34 | 64 | 88 | 97 | | | | | | |
| 92 | 4.685 | 03 | 12 | 36 | 67 | 89 | 98 | | | | | | |
| 96 | 4.682 | 03 | 13 | 38 | 69 | 91 | 98 | | | | | | |
| 100 | 4.678 | 03 | 13 | 40 | 72 | 92 | 99 | | | | | | |
| 120 | 4.666 | 04 | 17 | 49 | 82 | 97 | * | | | | | | |
| 140 | 4.657 | 04 | 21 | 58 | 89 | 99 | | | | | | | |
| 160 | 4.651 | 05 | 26 | 66 | 93 | 99 | | | | | | | |
| 180 | 4.645 | 05 | 30 | 73 | 96 | * | | | | | | | |
| 200 | 4.642 | 06 | 34 | 79 | 98 | | | | | | | | |
| 250 | 4.634 | 07 | 45 | 89 | 99 | | | | | | | | |
| 300 | 4.629 | 09 | 56 | 95 | * | | | | | | | | |
| 350 | 4.626 | 11 | 65 | 97 | | | | | | | | | |
| 400 | 4.623 | 13 | 72 | 99 | | | | | | | | | |
| 450 | 4.621 | 16 | 79 | * | | | | | | | | | |
| 500 | 4.620 | 18 | 84 | | | | | | | | | | |
| 600 | 4.617 | 24 | 91 | | | | | | | | | | |
| 700 | 4.616 | 29 | 95 | | | | | | | | | | |
| 800 | 4.614 | 35 | 98 | | | | | | | | | | |
| 900 | 4.613 | 40 | 99 | | | | | | | | | | |
| 1000 | 4.612 | 46 | 99 | | | | | | | | | | |

* Power values below this point are greater than .995.

Table 8.3.3

Power of F test at a = .01, u = 3

| n | F$_c$ | .05 | .10 | .15 | .20 | .25 | .30 | .35 | .40 | .50 | .60 | .70 | .80 |
|---|---|---|---|---|---|---|---|---|---|---|---|---|---|
| 2 | 16.694 | 01 | 01 | 01 | 01 | 02 | 02 | 02 | 03 | 04 | 05 | 06 | 07 |
| 3 | 7.591 | 01 | 01 | 01 | 02 | 02 | 03 | 03 | 04 | 06 | 08 | 12 | 16 |
| 4 | 5.953 | 01 | 01 | 01 | 02 | 02 | 03 | 04 | 06 | 09 | 15· | 22 | 31 |
| 5 | 5.292 | 01 | 01 | 02 | 02 | 03 | 04 | 06 | 08 | 14 | 23 | 34 | 48 |
| 6 | 4.938 | 01 | 01 | 02 | 03 | 04 | 05 | 08 | 11 | 20 | 32 | 47 | 63 |
| 7 | 4.718 | 01 | 01 | 02 | 03 | 04 | 06 | 10 | 14 | 26 | 42 | 59 | 75 |
| 8 | 4.568 | 01 | 02 | 02 | 03 | 05 | 08 | 12 | 17 | 32 | 51 | 69 | 84 |
| 9 | 4.460 | 01 | 02 | 02 | 04 | 06 | 10 | 15 | 21 | 39 | 59 | 78 | 90 |
| 10 | 4.378 | 01 | 02 | 03 | 04 | 07 | 11 | 17 | 25 | 45 | 67 | 84 | 94 |
| 11 | 4.313 | 01 | 02 | 03 | 05 | 08 | 13 | 20 | 29 | 52 | 74 | 89 | 97 |
| 12 | 4.262 | 01 | 02 | 03 | 05 | 09 | 15 | 23 | 34 | 58 | 79 | 92 | 98 |
| 13 | 4.219 | 01 | 02 | 03 | 06 | 10 | 17 | 27 | 38 | 63 | 84 | 95 | 99 |
| 14 | 4.183 | 01 | 02 | 04 | 07 | 12 | 19 | 30 | 42 | 68 | 88 | 97 | 99 |
| 15 | 4.153 | 01 | 02 | 04 | 07 | 13 | 22 | 33 | 46 | 73 | 91 | 98 | * |
| 16 | 4.126 | 01 | 02 | 04 | 08 | 14 | 24 | 36 | 50 | 77 | 93 | 99 | |
| 17 | 4.104 | 01 | 02 | 04 | 09 | 16 | 26 | 40 | 54 | 81 | 95 | 99 | |
| 18 | 4.084 | 01 | 02 | 05 | 09 | 17 | 29 | 43 | 58 | 84 | 96 | 99 | |
| 19 | 4.067 | 01 | 02 | 05 | 10 | 19 | 31 | 46 | 62 | 86 | 97 | * | |
| 20 | 4.051 | 01 | 03 | 05 | 11 | 20 | 33 | 49 | 65 | 89 | 98 | | |
| 21 | 4.038 | 01 | 03 | 06 | 11 | 22 | 36 | 52 | 68 | 91 | 99 | | |
| 22 | 4.025 | 01 | 03 | 06 | 12 | 23 | 38 | 55 | 71 | 92 | 99 | | |
| 23 | 4.013 | 01 | 03 | 06 | 13 | 25 | 40 | 58 | 74 | 94 | 99 | | |
| 24 | 4.003 | 01 | 03 | 07 | 14 | 26 | 43 | 61 | 77 | 95 | 99 | | |
| 25 | 3.993 | 01 | 03 | 07 | 15 | 28 | 45 | 63 | 79 | 96 | * | | |
| 26 | 3.984 | 01 | 03 | 07 | 16 | 30 | 48 | 66 | 81 | 97 | | | |
| 27 | 3.976 | 01 | 03 | 08 | 17 | 31 | 50 | 68 | 83 | 97 | | | |
| 28 | 3.969 | 02 | 03 | 08 | 18 | 33 | 52 | 71 | 85 | 98 | | | |
| 29 | 3.962 | 02 | 04 | 08 | 19 | 35 | 54 | 73 | 87 | 98 | | | |
| 30 | 3.955 | 02 | 04 | 09 | 20 | 36 | 56 | 75 | 88 | 99 | | | |
| 31 | 3.949 | 02 | 04 | 09 | 21 | 38 | 58 | 77 | 90 | 99 | | | |
| 32 | 3.944 | 02 | 04 | 10 | 22 | 40 | 60 | 79 | 91 | 99 | | | |
| 33 | 3.939 | 02 | 04 | 10 | 23 | 41 | 62 | 80 | 92 | 99 | | | |
| 34 | 3.934 | 02 | 04 | 10 | 24 | 43 | 64 | 82 | 93 | 99 | | | |
| 35 | 3.929 | 02 | 04 | 11 | 25 | 45 | 66 | 83 | 94 | * | | | |
| 36 | 3.925 | 02 | 04 | 11 | 26 | 46 | 68 | 85 | 94 | | | | |
| 37 | 3.921 | 02 | 05 | 12 | 27 | 48 | 70 | 86 | 95 | | | | |
| 38 | 3.917 | 02 | 05 | 12 | 28 | 49 | 71 | 87 | 96 | | | | |
| 39 | 3.914 | 02 | 05 | 13 | 29 | 51 | 73 | 88 | 96 | | | | |

Table 8.3.3 (continued)

| n | $F_c$ | .05 | .10 | .15 | .20 | .25 | .30 | .35 | .40 | .50 | .60 | .70 | .80 |
|---|---|---|---|---|---|---|---|---|---|---|---|---|---|
| 40 | 3.910 | 02 | 05 | 13 | 30 | 53 | 74 | 89 | 97 | * | * | * | * |
| 42 | 3.904 | 02 | 05 | 14 | 32 | 56 | 77 | 91 | 98 | | | | |
| 44 | 3.898 | 02 | 06 | 15 | 34 | 58 | 80 | 93 | 98 | | | | |
| 46 | 3.893 | 02 | 06 | 16 | 36 | 61 | 82 | 94 | 99 | | | | |
| 48 | 3.889 | 02 | 06 | 17 | 38 | 64 | 84 | 95 | 99 | | | | |
| 50 | 3.884 | 02 | 06 | 18 | 41 | 66 | 86 | 96 | 99 | | | | |
| 52 | 3.880 | 02 | 07 | 19 | 43 | 69 | 88 | 97 | 99 | | | | |
| 54 | 3.876 | 02 | 07 | 21 | 45 | 71 | 90 | 97 | * | | | | |
| 56 | 3.873 | 02 | 07 | 22 | 47 | 73 | 91 | 98 | | | | | |
| 58 | 3.870 | 02 | 08 | 23 | 49 | 75 | 92 | 98 | | | | | |
| 60 | 3.867 | 02 | 08 | 24 | 51 | 77 | 93 | 99 | | | | | |
| 64 | 3.862 | 02 | 09 | 26 | 55 | 81 | 95 | 99 | | | | | |
| 68 | 3.857 | 02 | 09 | 29 | 59 | 84 | 96 | 99 | | | | | |
| 72 | 3.853 | 03 | 10 | 31 | 62 | 87 | 97 | * | | | | | |
| 76 | 3.849 | 03 | 11 | 34 | 65 | 89 | 98 | | | | | | |
| 80 | 3.845 | 03 | 11 | 36 | 69 | 91 | 99 | | | | | | |
| 84 | 3.842 | 03 | 12 | 38 | 72 | 93 | 99 | | | | | | |
| 88 | 3.839 | 03 | 13 | 41 | 74 | 94 | 99 | | | | | | |
| 92 | 3.837 | 03 | 14 | 43 | 77 | 95 | 99 | | | | | | |
| 96 | 3.834 | 03 | 15 | 45 | 79 | 96 | * | | | | | | |
| 100 | 3.832 | 03 | 16 | 48 | 81 | 97 | | | | | | | |
| 120 | 3.824 | 04 | 21 | 59 | 90 | 99 | | | | | | | |
| 140 | 3.818 | 04 | 26 | 68 | 95 | * | | | | | | | |
| 160 | 3.813 | 05 | 31 | 76 | 97 | | | | | | | | |
| 180 | 3.810 | 06 | 36 | 82 | 99 | | | | | | | | |
| 200 | 3.807 | 07 | 42 | 87 | 99 | | | | | | | | |
| 250 | 3.802 | 09 | 54 | 95 | * | | | | | | | | |
| 300 | 3.798 | 11 | 66 | 98 | | | | | | | | | |
| 350 | 3.796 | 13 | 75 | 99 | | | | | | | | | |
| 400 | 3.794 | 16 | 82 | * | | | | | | | | | |
| 450 | 3.793 | 19 | 87 | | | | | | | | | | |
| 500 | 3.792 | 22 | 91 | | | | | | | | | | |
| 600 | 3.790 | 29 | 96 | | | | | | | | | | |
| 700 | 3.789 | 35 | 98 | | | | | | | | | | |
| 800 | 3.788 | 42 | 99 | | | | | | | | | | |
| 900 | 3.787 | 49 | * | | | | | | | | | | |
| 1000 | 3.787 | 55 | | | | | | | | | | | |

* Power values below this point are greater than .995.

Table 8.3.4

Power of F test at a = .01, u = 4

| | | | | | | | f | | | | | | |
|---|---|---|---|---|---|---|---|---|---|---|---|---|---|
| n | $F_c$ | .05 | .10 | .15 | .20 | .25 | .30 | .35 | .40 | .50 | .60 | .70 | .80 |
| 2 | 11.392 | 01 | 01 | 01 | 01 | 02 | 02 | 02 | 03 | 04 | 05 | 06 | 08 |
| 3 | 5.994 | 01 | 01 | 01 | 02 | 02 | 02 | 03 | 04 | 06 | 10 | 14 | 20 |
| 4 | 4.893 | 01 | 01 | 01 | 02 | 03 | 03 | 04 | 06 | 11 | 18 | 27 | 39 |
| 5 | 4.431 | 01 | 01 | 02 | 02 | 03 | 05 | 06 | 09 | 17 | 28 | 42 | 57 |
| 6 | 4.177 | 01 | 01 | 02 | 03 | 04 | 06 | 09 | 12 | 23 | 39 | 56 | 73 |
| 7 | 4.018 | 01 | 01 | 02 | 03 | 05 | 08 | 11 | 16 | 31 | 50 | 69 | 84 |
| 8 | 3.910 | 01 | 02 | 02 | 04 | 06 | 09 | 14 | 21 | 39 | 60 | 78 | 91 |
| 9 | 3.828 | 01 | 02 | 03 | 04 | 07 | 11 | 17 | 25 | 46 | 69 | 86 | 95 |
| 10 | 3.769 | 01 | 02 | 03 | 05 | 08 | 13 | 21 | 30 | 54 | 76 | 91 | 97 |
| 11 | 3.721 | 01 | 02 | 03 | 05 | 09 | 15 | 24 | 35 | 60 | 82 | 94 | 99 |
| 12 | 3.682 | 01 | 02 | 03 | 06 | 11 | 18 | 28 | 40 | 67 | 87 | 96 | 99 |
| 13 | 3.649 | 01 | 02 | 04 | 07 | 12 | 20 | 32 | 45 | 72 | 90 | 98 | * |
| 14 | 3.623 | 01 | 02 | 04 | 07 | 13 | 23 | 35 | 50 | 77 | 93 | 99 | |
| 15 | 3.601 | 01 | 02 | 04 | 08 | 15 | 26 | 39 | 54 | 81 | 95 | 99 | |
| 16 | 3.581 | 01 | 02 | 05 | 09 | 17 | 28 | 43 | 59 | 85 | 97 | * | |
| 17 | 3.564 | 01 | 02 | 05 | 10 | 18 | 31 | 47 | 63 | 88 | 98 | | |
| 18 | 3.549 | 01 | 03 | 05 | 11 | 20 | 34 | 50 | 67 | 90 | 98 | | |
| 19 | 3.536 | 01 | 03 | 06 | 11 | 22 | 37 | 54 | 70 | 92 | 99 | | |
| 20 | 3.524 | 01 | 03 | 06 | 12 | 24 | 39 | 57 | 74 | 94 | 99 | | |
| 21 | 3.514 | 01 | 03 | 06 | 13 | 26 | 42 | 60 | 77 | 95 | * | | |
| 22 | 3.504 | 01 | 03 | 07 | 14 | 27 | 45 | 64 | 80 | 96 | | | |
| 23 | 3.495 | 01 | 03 | 07 | 15 | 29 | 48 | 67 | 82 | 97 | | | |
| 24 | 3.487 | 01 | 03 | 07 | 16 | 31 | 50 | 69 | 84 | 98 | | | |
| 25 | 3.480 | 01 | 03 | 08 | 17 | 33 | 53 | 72 | 86 | 98 | | | |
| 26 | 3.473 | 01 | 03 | 08 | 19 | 35 | 55 | 74 | 88 | 99 | | | |
| 27 | 3.467 | 02 | 04 | 09 | 20 | 37 | 58 | 77 | 90 | 99 | | | |
| 28 | 3.462 | 02 | 04 | 09 | 21 | 39 | 60 | 79 | 91 | 99 | | | |
| 29 | 3.457 | 02 | 04 | 10 | 22 | 41 | 63 | 81 | 92 | 99 | | | |
| 30 | 3.452 | 02 | 04 | 10 | 23 | 43 | 65 | 83 | 93 | * | | | |
| 31 | 3.448 | 02 | 04 | 11 | 24 | 45 | 67 | 84 | 94 | | | | |
| 32 | 3.443 | 02 | 04 | 11 | 25 | 47 | 69 | 86 | 95 | | | | |
| 33 | 3.439 | 02 | 04 | 12 | 27 | 49 | 71 | 87 | 96 | | | | |
| 34 | 3.436 | 02 | 05 | 12 | 28 | 50 | 73 | 89 | 97 | | | | |
| 35 | 3.432 | 02 | 05 | 13 | 29 | 52 | 75 | 90 | 97 | | | | |
| 36 | 3.429 | 02 | 05 | 13 | 30 | 54 | 76 | 91 | 98 | | | | |
| 37 | 3.426 | 02 | 05 | 14 | 32 | 56 | 78 | 92 | 98 | | | | |
| 38 | 3.423 | 02 | 05 | 14 | 33 | 57 | 79 | 93 | 98 | | | | |
| 39 | 3.420 | 02 | 05 | 15 | 34 | 59 | 81 | 94 | 99 | | | | |

Table 8.3.4 (continued)

| n | $F_c$ | .05 | .10 | .15 | .20 | .25 | .30 | .35 | .40 | .50 | .60 | .70 | .80 |
|---|---|---|---|---|---|---|---|---|---|---|---|---|---|
| | | | | | | | | f | | | | | |
| 40 | 3.418 | 02 | 05 | 15 | 35 | 61 | 82 | 94 | 99 | * | * | * | * |
| 42 | 3.413 | 02 | 06 | 17 | 38 | 64 | 85 | 96 | 99 | | | | |
| 44 | 3.409 | 02 | 06 | 18 | 40 | 67 | 87 | 97 | 99 | | | | |
| 46 | 3.405 | 02 | 06 | 19 | 43 | 70 | 89 | 97 | * | | | | |
| 48 | 3.401 | 02 | 07 | 20 | 45 | 72 | 91 | 98 | | | | | |
| 50 | 3.398 | 02 | 07 | 22 | 48 | 75 | 92 | 98 | | | | | |
| 52 | 3.395 | 02 | 07 | 23 | 50 | 77 | 93 | 99 | | | | | |
| 54 | 3.392 | 02 | 08 | 24 | 52 | 79 | 94 | 99 | | | | | |
| 56 | 3.389 | 02 | 08 | 26 | 55 | 81 | 95 | 99 | | | | | |
| 58 | 3.386 | 02 | 09 | 27 | 57 | 83 | 96 | 99 | | | | | |
| 60 | 3.384 | 02 | 09 | 28 | 59 | 85 | 97 | * | | | | | |
| 64 | 3.380 | 02 | 10 | 31 | 63 | 88 | 98 | | | | | | |
| 68 | 3.376 | 03 | 11 | 34 | 67 | 90 | 98 | | | | | | |
| 72 | 3.373 | 03 | 11 | 37 | 71 | 92 | 99 | | | | | | |
| 76 | 3.371 | 03 | 12 | 39 | 74 | 94 | 99 | | | | | | |
| 80 | 3.368 | 03 | 13 | 42 | 77 | 95 | * | | | | | | |
| 84 | 3.366 | 03 | 14 | 45 | 80 | 96 | | | | | | | |
| 88 | 3.364 | 03 | 15 | 48 | 82 | 97 | | | | | | | |
| 92 | 3.361 | 03 | 16 | 50 | 84 | 98 | | | | | | | |
| 96 | 3.360 | 03 | 17 | 53 | 86 | 98 | | | | | | | |
| 100 | 3.358 | 03 | 19 | 55 | 88 | 99 | | | | | | | |
| 120 | 3.352 | 04 | 24 | 67 | 94 | * | | | | | | | |
| 140 | 3.347 | 05 | 30 | 76 | 98 | | | | | | | | |
| 160 | 3.344 | 06 | 37 | 84 | 99 | | | | | | | | |
| 180 | 3.341 | 06 | 43 | 89 | * | | | | | | | | |
| 200 | 3.339 | 07 | 49 | 93 | | | | | | | | | |
| 250 | 3.335 | 10 | 63 | 98 | | | | | | | | | |
| 300 | 3.332 | 12 | 74 | 99 | | | | | | | | | |
| 350 | 3.330 | 15 | 82 | * | | | | | | | | | |
| 400 | 3.329 | 19 | 89 | | | | | | | | | | |
| 450 | 3.328 | 22 | 93 | | | | | | | | | | |
| 500 | 3.327 | 26 | 96 | | | | | | | | | | |
| 600 | 3.326 | 34 | 98 | | | | | | | | | | |
| 700 | 3.325 | 42 | * | | | | | | | | | | |
| 800 | 3.324 | 49 | | | | | | | | | | | |
| 900 | 3.323 | 56 | | | | | | | | | | | |
| 1000 | 3.323 | 63 | | | | | | | | | | | |

* Power values below this point are greater than .995.

**Table 8.3.5**

Power of F test at a = .01, u = 5

| n | $F_c$ | .05 | .10 | .15 | .20 | .25 | .30 | .35 | .40 | .50 | .60 | .70 | .80 |
|---|-------|-----|-----|-----|-----|-----|-----|-----|-----|-----|-----|-----|-----|
| 2 | 8.746 | 01 | 01 | 01 | 01 | 02 | 02 | 02 | 03 | 04 | 05 | 07 | 09 |
| 3 | 5.064 | 01 | 01 | 01 | 02 | 02 | 03 | 03 | 04 | 07 | 11 | 17 | 24 |
| 4 | 4.248 | 01 | 01 | 02 | 02 | 03 | 04 | 05 | 07 | 12 | 21 | 32 | 46 |
| 5 | 3.895 | 01 | 01 | 02 | 02 | 03 | 05 | 07 | 10 | 19 | 33 | 49 | 66 |
| 6 | 3.699 | 01 | 01 | 02 | 03 | 04 | 07 | 10 | 14 | 28 | 45 | 64 | 80 |
| 7 | 3.576 | 01 | 01 | 02 | 03 | 05 | 08 | 13 | 19 | 36 | 57 | 76 | 90 |
| 8 | 3.489 | 01 | 02 | 02 | 04 | 07 | 10 | 16 | 24 | 45 | 67 | 85 | 95 |
| 9 | 3.426 | 01 | 02 | 03 | 05 | 08 | 13 | 20 | 30 | 53 | 76 | 91 | 98 |
| 10 | 3.388 | 01 | 02 | 03 | 05 | 09 | 15 | 24 | 35 | 61 | 83 | 95 | 99 |
| 11 | 3.339 | 01 | 02 | 03 | 06 | 10 | 18 | 28 | 41 | 68 | 88 | 97 | * |
| 12 | 3.309 | 01 | 02 | 04 | 07 | 12 | 21 | 32 | 46 | 74 | 92 | 98 | |
| 13 | 3.284 | 01 | 02 | 04 | 07 | 14 | 24 | 37 | 52 | 79 | 95 | 99 | |
| 14 | 3.263 | 01 | 02 | 04 | 08 | 15 | 27 | 41 | 57 | 84 | 97 | * | |
| 15 | 3.244 | 01 | 02 | 05 | 09 | 17 | 30 | 45 | 62 | 87 | 98 | | |
| 16 | 3.229 | 01 | 02 | 05 | 10 | 19 | 33 | 49 | 66 | 90 | 99 | | |
| 17 | 3.215 | 01 | 03 | 05 | 11 | 21 | 36 | 53 | 70 | 92 | 99 | | |
| 18 | 3.203 | 01 | 03 | 06 | 12 | 23 | 39 | 57 | 74 | 94 | 99 | | |
| 19 | 3.192 | 01 | 03 | 06 | 13 | 25 | 42 | 61 | 77 | 96 | * | | |
| 20 | 3.182 | 01 | 03 | 07 | 14 | 27 | 45 | 64 | 81 | 97 | | | |
| 21 | 3.174 | 01 | 03 | 07 | 15 | 30 | 48 | 68 | 83 | 98 | | | |
| 22 | 3.166 | 01 | 03 | 07 | 16 | 32 | 51 | 71 | 86 | 98 | | | |
| 23 | 3.159 | 01 | 03 | 08 | 18 | 34 | 54 | 74 | 88 | 99 | | | |
| 24 | 3.153 | 01 | 03 | 08 | 19 | 36 | 57 | 76 | 90 | 99 | | | |
| 25 | 3.147 | 01 | 04 | 09 | 20 | 38 | 60 | 79 | 91 | 99 | | | |
| 26 | 3.142 | 02 | 04 | 09 | 21 | 40 | 63 | 81 | 93 | * | | | |
| 27 | 3.137 | 02 | 04 | 10 | 23 | 43 | 65 | 83 | 94 | | | | |
| 28 | 3.133 | 02 | 04 | 10 | 24 | 45 | 67 | 85 | 95 | | | | |
| 29 | 3.129 | 02 | 04 | 11 | 25 | 47 | 70 | 87 | 96 | | | | |
| 30 | 3.125 | 02 | 04 | 11 | 27 | 49 | 72 | 88 | 97 | | | | |
| 31 | 3.121 | 02 | 04 | 12 | 28 | 51 | 74 | 90 | 97 | | | | |
| 32 | 3.118 | 02 | 05 | 12 | 29 | 53 | 76 | 91 | 98 | | | | |
| 33 | 3.115 | 02 | 05 | 13 | 31 | 55 | 78 | 92 | 98 | | | | |
| 34 | 3.112 | 02 | 05 | 14 | 32 | 57 | 80 | 93 | 98 | | | | |
| 35 | 3.109 | 02 | 05 | 14 | 34 | 59 | 81 | 94 | 99 | | | | |
| 36 | 3.107 | 02 | 05 | 15 | 35 | 61 | 83 | 95 | 99 | | | | |
| 37 | 3.104 | 02 | 05 | 16 | 36 | 63 | 84 | 95 | 99 | | | | |
| 38 | 3.102 | 02 | 06 | 16 | 38 | 64 | 86 | 96 | 99 | | | | |
| 39 | 3.100 | 02 | 06 | 17 | 39 | 66 | 87 | 97 | 99 | | | | |

Table 8.3.5 (continued)

| | | | | | | | $f$ | | | | | | |
|---|---|---|---|---|---|---|---|---|---|---|---|---|---|
| n | $F_c$ | .05 | .10 | .15 | .20 | .25 | .30 | .35 | .40 | .50 | .60 | .70 | .80 |
| 40 | 3.097 | 02 | 06 | 18 | 41 | 68 | 88 | 97 | * | * | * | * | * |
| 42 | 3.093 | 02 | 06 | 19 | 43 | 71 | 90 | 98 | | | | | |
| 44 | 3.090 | 02 | 07 | 20 | 46 | 74 | 92 | 98 | | | | | |
| 46 | 3.087 | 02 | 07 | 22 | 49 | 77 | 93 | 99 | | | | | |
| 48 | 3.084 | 02 | 07 | 23 | 52 | 79 | 94 | 99 | | | | | |
| 50 | 3.081 | 02 | 08 | 25 | 54 | 81 | 96 | 99 | | | | | |
| 52 | 3.079 | 02 | 08 | 26 | 57 | 84 | 96 | * | | | | | |
| 54 | 3.076 | 02 | 09 | 28 | 59 | 85 | 97 | | | | | | |
| 56 | 3.074 | 02 | 09 | 30 | 61 | 87 | 98 | | | | | | |
| 58 | 3.072 | 02 | 10 | 31 | 64 | 89 | 98 | | | | | | |
| 60 | 3.070 | 02 | 10 | 33 | 66 | 90 | 99 | | | | | | |
| 64 | 3.067 | 03 | 11 | 36 | 70 | 92 | 99 | | | | | | |
| 68 | 3.064 | 03 | 12 | 39 | 74 | 94 | 99 | | | | | | |
| 72 | 3.061 | 03 | 13 | 42 | 77 | 96 | * | | | | | | |
| 76 | 3.059 | 03 | 14 | 45 | 80 | 97 | | | | | | | |
| 80 | 3.057 | 03 | 15 | 48 | 83 | 98 | | | | | | | |
| 84 | 3.055 | 03 | 16 | 51 | 86 | 98 | | | | | | | |
| 88 | 3.053 | 03 | 18 | 54 | 88 | 99 | | | | | | | |
| 92 | 3.052 | 03 | 19 | 57 | 90 | 99 | | | | | | | |
| 96 | 3.050 | 04 | 20 | 60 | 91 | 99 | | | | | | | |
| 100 | 3.049 | 04 | 21 | 62 | 93 | * | | | | | | | |
| 120 | 3.044 | 04 | 28 | 74 | 97 | | | | | | | | |
| 140 | 3.040 | 05 | 35 | 83 | 99 | | | | | | | | |
| 160 | 3.037 | 06 | 42 | 89 | * | | | | | | | | |
| 180 | 3.035 | 07 | 49 | 93 | | | | | | | | | |
| 200 | 3.033 | 08 | 55 | 96 | | | | | | | | | |
| 250 | 3.030 | 11 | 70 | 99 | | | | | | | | | |
| 300 | 3.028 | 14 | 80 | * | | | | | | | | | |
| 350 | 3.026 | 18 | 88 | | | | | | | | | | |
| 400 | 3.025 | 22 | 93 | | | | | | | | | | |
| 450 | 3.024 | 26 | 96 | | | | | | | | | | |
| 500 | 3.023 | 30 | 98 | | | | | | | | | | |
| 600 | 3.022 | 39 | 99 | | | | | | | | | | |
| 700 | 3.022 | 47 | * | | | | | | | | | | |
| 800 | 3.021 | 56 | | | | | | | | | | | |
| 900 | 3.021 | 63 | | | | | | | | | | | |
| 1000 | 3.020 | 70 | | | | | | | | | | | |

* Power values below this point are greater than .995.

Table 8.3.6

Power of F test at a = .01, u = 6

| n | $F_c$ | | | | | | f | | | | | | |
|---|-------|-----|-----|-----|-----|-----|-----|-----|-----|-----|-----|-----|-----|
| | | .05 | .10 | .15 | .20 | .25 | .30 | .35 | .40 | .50 | .60 | .70 | .80 |
| 2 | 7.191 | 01 | 01 | 01 | 01 | 02 | 02 | 02 | 03 | 04 | 06 | 07 | 10 |
| 3 | 4.456 | 01 | 01 | 01 | 02 | 02 | 03 | 03 | 05 | 08 | 13 | 19 | 28 |
| 4 | 3.812 | 01 | 01 | 02 | 02 | 03 | 04 | 06 | 08 | 14 | 24 | 37 | 53 |
| 5 | 3.528 | 01 | 01 | 02 | 03 | 04 | 06 | 08 | 12 | 22 | 38 | 56 | 73 |
| 6 | 3.369 | 01 | 01 | 02 | 03 | 05 | 07 | 11 | 16 | 32 | 51 | 71 | 86 |
| 7 | 3.266 | 01 | 02 | 02 | 04 | 06 | 09 | 15 | 22 | 41 | 64 | 83 | 94 |
| 8 | 3.196 | 01 | 02 | 03 | 04 | 07 | 12 | 19 | 28 | 51 | 74 | 90 | 97 |
| 9 | 3.143 | 01 | 02 | 03 | 05 | 09 | 14 | 23 | 34 | 60 | 82 | 95 | 99 |
| 10 | 3.103 | 01 | 02 | 03 | 06 | 10 | 17 | 27 | 40 | 68 | 88 | 97 | * |
| 11 | 3.072 | 01 | 02 | 03 | 06 | 12 | 20 | 32 | 46 | 74 | 92 | 99 | |
| 12 | 3.047 | 01 | 02 | 04 | 07 | 13 | 23 | 37 | 52 | 80 | 95 | 99 | |
| 13 | 3.026 | 01 | 02 | 04 | 08 | 15 | 27 | 41 | 58 | 85 | 97 | * | |
| 14 | 3.008 | 01 | 02 | 05 | 09 | 17 | 30 | 46 | 63 | 89 | 98 | | |
| 15 | 2.992 | 01 | 02 | 05 | 10 | 20 | 34 | 51 | 68 | 92 | 99 | | |
| 16 | 2.979 | 01 | 02 | 05 | 11 | 22 | 37 | 55 | 72 | 94 | 99 | | |
| 17 | 2.968 | 01 | 03 | 06 | 12 | 24 | 41 | 59 | 76 | 95 | * | | |
| 18 | 2.957 | 01 | 03 | 06 | 13 | 26 | 44 | 63 | 80 | 97 | | | |
| 19 | 2.949 | 01 | 03 | 07 | 15 | 29 | 48 | 67 | 83 | 98 | | | |
| 20 | 2.941 | 01 | 03 | 07 | 16 | 31 | 51 | 71 | 86 | 98 | | | |
| 21 | 2.934 | 01 | 03 | 08 | 17 | 34 | 54 | 74 | 88 | 99 | | | |
| 22 | 2.928 | 01 | 03 | 08 | 19 | 36 | 57 | 77 | 90 | 99 | | | |
| 23 | 2.922 | 01 | 03 | 09 | 20 | 38 | 60 | 80 | 92 | 99 | | | |
| 24 | 2.917 | 02 | 04 | 09 | 21 | 41 | 63 | 82 | 93 | * | | | |
| 25 | 2.912 | 02 | 04 | 10 | 23 | 43 | 66 | 84 | 95 | | | | |
| 26 | 2.908 | 02 | 04 | 10 | 24 | 46 | 69 | 86 | 96 | | | | |
| 27 | 2.904 | 02 | 04 | 11 | 26 | 48 | 71 | 88 | 96 | | | | |
| 28 | 2.900 | 02 | 04 | 11 | 27 | 50 | 74 | 90 | 97 | | | | |
| 29 | 2.896 | 02 | 04 | 12 | 29 | 53 | 76 | 91 | 98 | | | | |
| 30 | 2.893 | 02 | 05 | 13 | 30 | 55 | 78 | 92 | 98 | | | | |
| 31 | 2.890 | 02 | 05 | 13 | 32 | 57 | 80 | 93 | 99 | | | | |
| 32 | 2.887 | 02 | 05 | 14 | 33 | 59 | 82 | 94 | 99 | | | | |
| 33 | 2.884 | 02 | 05 | 15 | 35 | 61 | 83 | 95 | 99 | | | | |
| 34 | 2.882 | 02 | 05 | 15 | 36 | 63 | 85 | 96 | 99 | | | | |
| 35 | 2.880 | 02 | 05 | 16 | 38 | 65 | 86 | 97 | 99 | | | | |
| 36 | 2.877 | 02 | 06 | 17 | 40 | 67 | 88 | 97 | * | | | | |
| 37 | 2.875 | 02 | 06 | 18 | 41 | 69 | 89 | 98 | | | | | |
| 38 | 2.873 | 02 | 06 | 18 | 43 | 71 | 90 | 98 | | | | | |
| 39 | 2.871 | 02 | 06 | 19 | 44 | 72 | 91 | 98 | | | | | |

Table 8.3.6 *(continued)*

| n | $F_c$ | .05 | .10 | .15 | .20 | .25 | .30 | .35 | .40 | .50 | .60 | .70 | .80 |
|---|---|---|---|---|---|---|---|---|---|---|---|---|---|
| 40 | 2.870 | 02 | 06 | 20 | 46 | 74 | 92 | 99 | * | * | * | * | * |
| 42 | 2.866 | 02 | 07 | 22 | 49 | 77 | 94 | 99 | | | | | |
| 44 | 2.863 | 02 | 07 | 23 | 52 | 80 | 95 | 99 | | | | | |
| 46 | 2.861 | 02 | 08 | 25 | 55 | 82 | 96 | * | | | | | |
| 48 | 2.858 | 02 | 08 | 27 | 57 | 85 | 97 | | | | | | |
| 50 | 2.856 | 02 | 09 | 28 | 60 | 87 | 98 | | | | | | |
| 52 | 2.854 | 02 | 09 | 30 | 63 | 88 | 98 | | | | | | |
| 54 | 2.852 | 02 | 10 | 32 | 65 | 90 | 99 | | | | | | |
| 56 | 2.850 | 02 | 10 | 33 | 68 | 91 | 99 | | | | | | |
| 58 | 2.848 | 02 | 11 | 35 | 70 | 93 | 99 | | | | | | |
| 60 | 2.847 | 02 | 11 | 37 | 72 | 94 | 99 | | | | | | |
| 64 | 2.844 | 03 | 12 | 40 | 76 | 95 | * | | | | | | |
| 68 | 2.841 | 03 | 13 | 44 | 80 | 97 | | | | | | | |
| 72 | 2.839 | 03 | 14 | 47 | 83 | 98 | | | | | | | |
| 76 | 2.837 | 03 | 16 | 51 | 86 | 98 | | | | | | | |
| 80 | 2.835 | 03 | 17 | 54 | 88 | 99 | | | | | | | |
| 84 | 2.834 | 03 | 18 | 57 | 90 | 99 | | | | | | | |
| 88 | 2.832 | 03 | 20 | 60 | 92 | 99 | | | | | | | |
| 92 | 2.831 | 04 | 21 | 63 | 93 | * | | | | | | | |
| 96 | 2.830 | 04 | 23 | 66 | 95 | | | | | | | | |
| 100 | 2.829 | 05 | 24 | 69 | 96 | | | | | | | | |
| 120 | 2.825 | 05 | 32 | 80 | 99 | | | | | | | | |
| 140 | 2.821 | 06 | 39 | 88 | * | | | | | | | | |
| 160 | 2.819 | 07 | 47 | 93 | | | | | | | | | |
| 180 | 2.817 | 08 | 54 | 96 | | | | | | | | | |
| 200 | 2.815 | 09 | 61 | 98 | | | | | | | | | |
| 250 | 2.813 | 12 | 76 | * | | | | | | | | | |
| 300 | 2.811 | 16 | 86 | | | | | | | | | | |
| 350 | 2.810 | 20 | 92 | | | | | | | | | | |
| 400 | 2.809 | 24 | 96 | | | | | | | | | | |
| 450 | 2.808 | 29 | 98 | | | | | | | | | | |
| 500 | 2.807 | 34 | 99 | | | | | | | | | | |
| 600 | 2.806 | 44 | * | | | | | | | | | | |
| 700 | 2.806 | 53 | | | | | | | | | | | |
| 800 | 2.805 | 62 | | | | | | | | | | | |
| 900 | 2.805 | 69 | | | | | | | | | | | |
| 1000 | 2.805 | 76 | | | | | | | | | | | |

* Power values below this point are greater than .995.

**Table 8.3.7**

Power of F test at a = .01, u = 8

| n | $F_c$ | .05 | .10 | .15 | .20 | .25 | .30 | .35 | .40 | .50 | .60 | .70 | .80 |
|---|-------|-----|-----|-----|-----|-----|-----|-----|-----|-----|-----|-----|-----|
| 2 | 5.467 | 01 | 01 | 01 | 01 | 02 | 02 | 02 | 03 | 05 | 06 | 09 | 12 |
| 3 | 3.705 | 01 | 01 | 01 | 02 | 02 | 03 | 04 | 06 | 10 | 16 | 25 | 37 |
| 4 | 3.256 | 01 | 01 | 02 | 02 | 03 | 05 | 07 | 09 | 18 | 31 | 47 | 65 |
| 5 | 3.053 | 01 | 01 | 02 | 03 | 04 | 06 | 10 | 14 | 28 | 47 | 67 | 84 |
| 6 | 2.936 | 01 | 01 | 02 | 03 | 05 | 09 | 14 | 20 | 40 | 63 | 82 | 93 |
| 7 | 2.861 | 01 | 02 | 02 | 04 | 07 | 11 | 18 | 27 | 51 | 75 | 91 | 98 |
| 8 | 2.808 | 01 | 02 | 03 | 05 | 08 | 14 | 23 | 34 | 61 | 84 | 96 | 99 |
| 9 | 2.770 | 01 | 02 | 03 | 06 | 10 | 18 | 28 | 42 | 71 | 90 | 98 | * |
| 10 | 2.740 | 01 | 02 | 03 | 07 | 12 | 21 | 34 | 49 | 78 | 94 | 99 | |
| 11 | 2.716 | 01 | 02 | 04 | 08 | 14 | 25 | 40 | 56 | 84 | 97 | * | |
| 12 | 2.697 | 01 | 02 | 04 | 09 | 17 | 29 | 45 | 62 | 89 | 98 | | |
| 13 | 2.681 | 01 | 02 | 05 | 10 | 19 | 33 | 51 | 68 | 92 | 99 | | |
| 14 | 2.667 | 01 | 02 | 05 | 11 | 22 | 37 | 56 | 74 | 95 | * | | |
| 15 | 2.656 | 01 | 03 | 06 | 12 | 24 | 42 | 61 | 78 | 96 | | | |
| 16 | 2.646 | 01 | 03 | 06 | 13 | 27 | 46 | 66 | 82 | 98 | | | |
| 17 | 2.638 | 01 | 03 | 07 | 15 | 30 | 50 | 70 | 86 | 98 | | | |
| 18 | 2.630 | 01 | 03 | 07 | 16 | 33 | 54 | 74 | 88 | 99 | | | |
| 19 | 2.624 | 01 | 03 | 08 | 18 | 35 | 57 | 77 | 91 | 99 | | | |
| 20 | 2.618 | 01 | 03 | 08 | 20 | 38 | 61 | 81 | 93 | * | | | |
| 21 | 2.612 | 01 | 03 | 09 | 21 | 41 | 64 | 83 | 94 | | | | |
| 22 | 2.608 | 01 | 04 | 10 | 23 | 44 | 68 | 86 | 96 | | | | |
| 23 | 2.603 | 02 | 04 | 10 | 25 | 47 | 71 | 88 | 97 | | | | |
| 24 | 2.599 | 02 | 04 | 11 | 26 | 50 | 74 | 90 | 97 | | | | |
| 25 | 2.596 | 02 | 04 | 12 | 28 | 52 | 76 | 92 | 98 | | | | |
| 26 | 2.592 | 02 | 04 | 12 | 30 | 55 | 79 | 93 | 98 | | | | |
| 27 | 2.589 | 02 | 05 | 13 | 32 | 58 | 81 | 94 | 99 | | | | |
| 28 | 2.586 | 02 | 05 | 14 | 34 | 60 | 83 | 95 | 99 | | | | |
| 29 | 2.583 | 02 | 05 | 15 | 35 | 63 | 85 | 96 | 99 | | | | |
| 30 | 2.581 | 02 | 05 | 15 | 37 | 65 | 87 | 97 | * | | | | |
| 31 | 2.579 | 02 | 05 | 16 | 39 | 67 | 88 | 97 | | | | | |
| 32 | 2.576 | 02 | 06 | 17 | 41 | 70 | 90 | 98 | | | | | |
| 33 | 2.574 | 02 | 06 | 18 | 43 | 72 | 91 | 98 | | | | | |
| 34 | 2.573 | 02 | 06 | 19 | 45 | 74 | 92 | 99 | | | | | |
| 35 | 2.571 | 02 | 06 | 20 | 46 | 75 | 93 | 99 | | | | | |
| 36 | 2.569 | 02 | 06 | 21 | 48 | 77 | 94 | 99 | | | | | |
| 37 | 2.567 | 02 | 07 | 22 | 50 | 79 | 95 | 99 | | | | | |
| 38 | 2.566 | 02 | 07 | 23 | 52 | 80 | 95 | 99 | | | | | |
| 39 | 2.564 | 02 | 07 | 24 | 54 | 82 | 96 | * | | | | | |

Table 8.3.7 *(continued)*

| n | $F_c$ | .05 | .10 | .15 | .20 | .25 | .30 | .35 | .40 | .50 | .60 | .70 | .80 |
|---|---|---|---|---|---|---|---|---|---|---|---|---|---|
| 40 | 2.563 | 02 | 07 | 25 | 55 | 83 | 97 | * | * | * | * | * | * |
| 42 | 2.561 | 02 | 08 | 27 | 58 | 86 | 97 | | | | | | |
| 44 | 2.558 | 02 | 08 | 29 | 62 | 88 | 98 | | | | | | |
| 46 | 2.556 | 02 | 09 | 31 | 65 | 90 | 99 | | | | | | |
| 48 | 2.554 | 02 | 10 | 33 | 68 | 92 | 99 | | | | | | |
| 50 | 2.553 | 02 | 10 | 35 | 70 | 93 | 99 | | | | | | |
| 52 | 2.551 | 02 | 11 | 37 | 73 | 94 | 99 | | | | | | |
| 54 | 2.550 | 02 | 11 | 39 | 75 | 95 | * | | | | | | |
| 56 | 2.548 | 03 | 12 | 41 | 78 | 96 | | | | | | | |
| 58 | 2.547 | 03 | 13 | 43 | 80 | 97 | | | | | | | |
| 60 | 2.546 | 03 | 13 | 45 | 82 | 97 | | | | | | | |
| 64 | 2.543 | 03 | 15 | 49 | 85 | 98 | | | | | | | |
| 68 | 2.541 | 03 | 16 | 53 | 88 | 99 | | | | | | | |
| 72 | 2.540 | 03 | 18 | 57 | 90 | 99 | | | | | | | |
| 76 | 2.538 | 03 | 20 | 61 | 92 | * | | | | | | | |
| 80 | 2.537 | 03 | 21 | 64 | 94 | | | | | | | | |
| 84 | 2.536 | 04 | 23 | 67 | 95 | | | | | | | | |
| 88 | 2.535 | 04 | 24 | 70 | 96 | | | | | | | | |
| 92 | 2.534 | 04 | 26 | 73 | 97 | | | | | | | | |
| 96 | 2.533 | 04 | 28 | 76 | 98 | | | | | | | | |
| 100 | 2.532 | 04 | 30 | 78 | 98 | | | | | | | | |
| 120 | 2.529 | 05 | 39 | 88 | * | | | | | | | | |
| 140 | 2.526 | 06 | 48 | 94 | | | | | | | | | |
| 160 | 2.524 | 07 | 57 | 97 | | | | | | | | | |
| 180 | 2.523 | 09 | 65 | 99 | | | | | | | | | |
| 200 | 2.521 | 10 | 72 | 99 | | | | | | | | | |
| 250 | 2.519 | 14 | 85 | * | | | | | | | | | |
| 300 | 2.518 | 19 | 92 | | | | | | | | | | |
| 350 | 2.517 | 25 | 97 | | | | | | | | | | |
| 400 | 2.516 | 30 | 99 | | | | | | | | | | |
| 450 | 2.516 | 36 | 99 | | | | | | | | | | |
| 500 | 2.515 | 42 | * | | | | | | | | | | |
| 600 | 2.515 | 53 | | | | | | | | | | | |
| 700 | 2.514 | 63 | | | | | | | | | | | |
| 800 | 2.514 | 72 | | | | | | | | | | | |
| 900 | 2.514 | 79 | | | | | | | | | | | |
| 1000 | 2.513 | 85 | | | | | | | | | | | |

* Power values below this point are greater than .995.

**Table 8.3.8**

Power of F test at a = .01, u = 10 ·

| n | $F_c$ | .05 | .10 | .15 | .20 | .25 | .30 | .35 | .40 | .50 | .60 | .70 | .80 |
|---|-------|-----|-----|-----|-----|-----|-----|-----|-----|-----|-----|-----|-----|
| 2 | 4.539 | 01 | 01 | 01 | 01 | 02 | 02 | 03 | 03 | 05 | 07 | 10 | 15 |
| 3 | 3.258 | 01 | 01 | 02 | 02 | 02 | 03 | 04 | 06 | 11 | 20 | 31 | 46 |
| 4 | 2.914 | 01 | 01 | 02 | 02 | 03 | 05 | 08 | 11 | 22 | 38 | 57 | 74 |
| 5 | 2.752 | 01 | 01 | 02 | 03 | 05 | 07 | 11 | 17 | 34 | 56 | 77 | 91 |
| 6 | 2.662 | 01 | 01 | 02 | 04 | 06 | 10 | 16 | 25 | 47 | 72 | 89 | 97 |
| 7 | 2.603 | 01 | 02 | 03 | 05 | 08 | 13 | 22 | 33 | 60 | 83 | 95 | 99 |
| 8 | 2.561 | 01 | 03 | 03 | 06 | 10 | 17 | 28 | 41 | 70 | 91 | 98 | * |
| 9 | 2.530 | 01 | 03 | 03 | 07 | 12 | 21 | 34 | 49 | 79 | 95 | 99 | |
| 10 | 2.506 | 01 | 03 | 04 | 08 | 14 | 25 | 40 | 57 | 86 | 97 | * | |
| 11 | 2.487 | 01 | 03 | 04 | 09 | 17 | 30 | 47 | 65 | 97 | 99 | | |
| 12 | 2.471 | 01 | 03 | 05 | 10 | 20 | 35 | 53 | 71 | 94 | 99 | | |
| 13 | 2.458 | 01 | 03 | 05 | 11 | 23 | 40 | 59 | 77 | 96 | * | | |
| 14 | 2.448 | 01 | 03 | 06 | 13 | 26 | 44 | 65 | 82 | 98 | | | |
| 15 | 2.439 | 01 | 03 | 06 | 14 | 29 | 49 | 70 | 86 | 99 | | | |
| 16 | 2.431 | 01 | 03 | 07 | 16 | 32 | 53 | 74 | 89 | 99 | | | |
| 17 | 2.424 | 01 | 03 | 08 | 18 | 35 | 58 | 78 | 91 | * | | | |
| 18 | 2.418 | 01 | 03 | 08 | 19 | 39 | 62 | 82 | 94 | | | | |
| 19 | 2.413 | 01 | 03 | 09 | 21 | 42 | 66 | 85 | 95 | | | | |
| 20 | 2.408 | 01 | 04 | 10 | 23 | 45 | 69 | 88 | 96 | | | | |
| 21 | 2.403 | 02 | 04 | 10 | 25 | 49 | 73 | 90 | 97 | | | | |
| 22 | 2.399 | 02 | 04 | 11 | 27 | 52 | 76 | 92 | 98 | | | | |
| 23 | 2.396 | 02 | 04 | 12 | 29 | 55 | 79 | 93 | 99 | | | | |
| 24 | 2.393 | 02 | 04 | 13 | 31 | 58 | 81 | 95 | 99 | | | | |
| 25 | 2.390 | 02 | 05 | 13 | 33 | 61 | 84 | 96 | 99 | | | | |
| 26 | 2.387 | 02 | 05 | 14 | 35 | 63 | 86 | 97 | * | | | | |
| 27 | 2.384 | 02 | 05 | 15 | 38 | 66 | 88 | 97 | | | | | |
| 28 | 2.382 | 02 | 05 | 16 | 40 | 69 | 90 | 98 | | | | | |
| 29 | 2.380 | 02 | 05 | 17 | 42 | 71 | 91 | 98 | | | | | |
| 30 | 2.378 | 02 | 06 | 18 | 44 | 73 | 92 | 99 | | | | | |
| 31 | 2.376 | 02 | 06 | 19 | 46 | 76 | 93 | 99 | | | | | |
| 32 | 2.374 | 02 | 06 | 20 | 48 | 78 | 94 | 99 | | | | | |
| 33 | 2.372 | 02 | 06 | 21 | 50 | 80 | 95 | 99 | | | | | |
| 34 | 2.371 | 02 | 07 | 22 | 52 | 81 | 96 | * | | | | | |
| 35 | 2.369 | 02 | 07 | 24 | 54 | 83 | 97 | | | | | | |
| 36 | 2.368 | 02 | 07 | 25 | 56 | 85 | 97 | | | | | | |
| 37 | 2.367 | 02 | 08 | 26 | 58 | 86 | 98 | | | | | | |
| 38 | 2.365 | 02 | 08 | 27 | 60 | 87 | 98 | | | | | | |
| 39 | 2.364 | 02 | 08 | 28 | 62 | 89 | 98 | | | | | | |

**Table 8.3.8** *(continued)*

| n | $F_c$ | | | | | | | | | | | | |
|---|---|---|---|---|---|---|---|---|---|---|---|---|---|
| | | | | | | | f | | | | | | |
| | | .05 | .10 | .15 | .20 | .25 | .30 | .35 | .40 | .50 | .60 | .70 | .80 |
| 40 | 2.363 | 02 | 08 | 29 | 63 | 90 | 99 | * | * | * | * | * | * |
| 42 | 2.361 | 02 | 09 | 32 | 67 | 92 | 99 | | | | | | |
| 44 | 2.359 | 02 | 10 | 34 | 70 | 93 | 99 | | | | | | |
| 46 | 2.358 | 02 | 10 | 36 | 73 | 95 | * | | | | | | |
| 48 | 2.356 | 02 | 11 | 39 | 76 | 96 | | | | | | | |
| 50 | 2.355 | 02 | 12 | 41 | 78 | 97 | | | | | | | |
| 52 | 2.353 | 03 | 12 | 43 | 81 | 97 | | | | | | | |
| 54 | 2.352 | 03 | 13 | 46 | 83 | 98 | | | | | | | |
| 56 | 2.351 | 03 | 14 | 48 | 85 | 98 | | | | | | | |
| 58 | 2.350 | 03 | 15 | 50 | 87 | 99 | | | | | | | |
| 60 | 2.349 | 03 | 16 | 53 | 88 | 99 | | | | | | | |
| 64 | 2.347 | 03 | 17 | 57 | 91 | 99 | | | | | | | |
| 68 | 2.346 | 03 | 19 | 61 | 93 | * | | | | | | | |
| 72 | 2.344 | 03 | 21 | 65 | 95 | | | | | | | | |
| 76 | 2.343 | 04 | 23 | 69 | 96 | | | | | | | | |
| 80 | 2.342 | 04 | 25 | 72 | 97 | | | | | | | | |
| 84 | 2.341 | 04 | 27 | 75 | 98 | | | | | | | | |
| 88 | 2.340 | 04 | 29 | 78 | 99 | | | | | | | | |
| 92 | 2.339 | 04 | 31 | 81 | 99 | | | | | | | | |
| 96 | 2.338 | 05 | 33 | 83 | 99 | | | | | | | | |
| 100 | 2.338 | 05 | 35 | 86 | 99 | | | | | | | | |
| 120 | 2.335 | 06 | 46 | 93 | * | | | | | | | | |
| 140 | 2.333 | 07 | 56 | 97 | | | | | | | | | |
| 160 | 2.331 | 08 | 65 | 99 | | | | | | | | | |
| 180 | 2.330 | 10 | 73 | * | | | | | | | | | |
| 200 | 2.329 | 12 | 79 | | | | | | | | | | |
| 250 | 2.327 | 17 | 91 | | | | | | | | | | |
| 300 | 2.326 | 23 | 96 | | | | | | | | | | |
| 350 | 2.326 | 29 | 99 | | | | | | | | | | |
| 400 | 2.325 | 36 | * | | | | | | | | | | |
| 450 | 2.325 | 42 | | | | | | | | | | | |
| 500 | 2.324 | 51 | | | | | | | | | | | |
| 600 | 2.324 | 61 | | | | | | | | | | | |
| 700 | 2.323 | 71 | | | | | | | | | | | |
| 800 | 2.323 | 80 | | | | | | | | | | | |
| 900 | 2.323 | 86 | | | | | | | | | | | |
| 1000 | 2.323 | 91 | | | | | | | | | | | |

* Power values below this point are greater than .995.

Table 8.3.9

Power of F test at a = .01, u = 12

| n | $F_c$ | .05 | .10 | .15 | .20 | .25 | .30 | .35 | .40 | .50 | .60 | .70 | .80 |
|---|-------|-----|-----|-----|-----|-----|-----|-----|-----|-----|-----|-----|-----|
| 2 | 3.960 | 01 | 01 | 01 | 01 | 02 | 02 | 03 | 04 | 05 | 08 | 12 | 18 |
| 3 | 2.958 | 01 | 01 | 01 | 02 | 03 | 04 | 05 | 07 | 13 | 23 | 37 | 54 |
| 4 | 2.679 | 01 | 01 | 02 | 03 | 04 | 06 | 09 | 13 | 26 | 44 | 65 | 82 |
| 5 | 2.548 | 01 | 01 | 02 | 03 | 05 | 08 | 13 | 20 | 40 | 64 | 84 | 95 |
| 6 | 2.472 | 01 | 02 | 02 | 04 | 07 | 12 | 19 | 29 | 54 | 79 | 94 | 99 |
| 7 | 2.422 | 01 | 02 | 03 | 05 | 09 | 15 | 25 | 38 | 67 | 89 | 98 | * |
| 8 | 2.387 | 01 | 02 | 03 | 06 | 11 | 20 | 32 | 48 | 78 | 95 | 99 | |
| 9 | 2.361 | 01 | 02 | 04 | 07 | 14 | 25 | 39 | 57 | 85 | 98 | * | |
| 10 | 2.340 | 01 | 02 | 04 | 08 | 17 | 30 | 47 | 65 | 91 | 99 | | |
| 11 | 2.325 | 01 | 02 | 05 | 10 | 20 | 35 | 54 | 72 | 94 | * | | |
| 12 | 2.312 | 01 | 02 | 05 | 11 | 23 | 40 | 60 | 78 | 97 | | | |
| 13 | 2.301 | 01 | 03 | 06 | 13 | 26 | 45 | 66 | 83 | 98 | | | |
| 14 | 2.292 | 01 | 03 | 06 | 15 | 30 | 51 | 72 | 87 | 99 | | | |
| 15 | 2.285 | 01 | 03 | 07 | 16 | 33 | 56 | 77 | 91 | 99 | | | |
| 16 | 2.278 | 01 | 03 | 08 | 18 | 37 | 60 | 81 | 93 | * | | | |
| 17 | 2.272 | 01 | 03 | 08 | 20 | 41 | 65 | 84 | 95 | | | | |
| 18 | 2.267 | 01 | 03 | 09 | 23 | 45 | 69 | 87 | 97 | | | | |
| 19 | 2.262 | 01 | 04 | 10 | 25 | 48 | 73 | 90 | 98 | | | | |
| 20 | 2.258 | 02 | 04 | 11 | 27 | 52 | 76 | 92 | 98 | | | | |
| 21 | 2.255 | 02 | 04 | 12 | 29 | 55 | 80 | 94 | 99 | | | | |
| 22 | 2.251 | 02 | 04 | 13 | 32 | 59 | 83 | 95 | 99 | | | | |
| 23 | 2.248 | 02 | 05 | 14 | 34 | 62 | 85 | 96 | 99 | | | | |
| 24 | 2.246 | 02 | 05 | 15 | 36 | 65 | 87 | 97 | * | | | | |
| 25 | 2.243 | 02 | 05 | 16 | 39 | 68 | 89 | 98 | | | | | |
| 26 | 2.241 | 02 | 05 | 17 | 41 | 71 | 91 | 98 | | | | | |
| 27 | 2.239 | 02 | 05 | 18 | 43 | 73 | 92 | 99 | | | | | |
| 28 | 2.237 | 02 | 06 | 19 | 46 | 76 | 94 | 99 | | | | | |
| 29 | 2.235 | 02 | 06 | 20 | 48 | 78 | 95 | 99 | | | | | |
| 30 | 2.233 | 02 | 06 | 21 | 50 | 80 | 96 | * | | | | | |
| 31 | 2.231 | 02 | 07 | 22 | 53 | 82 | 96 | | | | | | |
| 32 | 2.230 | 02 | 07 | 24 | 55 | 84 | 97 | | | | | | |
| 33 | 2.228 | 02 | 07 | 25 | 57 | 86 | 98 | | | | | | |
| 34 | 2.227 | 02 | 07 | 26 | 59 | 87 | 98 | | | | | | |
| 35 | 2.226 | 02 | 08 | 27 | 61 | 88 | 98 | | | | | | |
| 36 | 2.225 | 02 | 08 | 29 | 63 | 90 | 99 | | | | | | |
| 37 | 2.224 | 02 | 08 | 30 | 65 | 91 | 99 | | | | | | |
| 38 | 2.223 | 02 | 09 | 31 | 67 | 92 | 99 | | | | | | |
| 39 | 2.222 | 02 | 09 | 32 | 69 | 93 | 99 | | | | | | |

Table 8.3.9 *(continued)*

| n | $F_c$ | .05 | .10 | .15 | .20 | .25 | .30 | .35 | .40 | .50 | .60 | .70 | .80 |
|---|---|---|---|---|---|---|---|---|---|---|---|---|---|
| 40 | 2.221 | 02 | 09 | 34 | 71 | 94 | 99 | * | * | * | * | * | * |
| 42 | 2.219 | 02 | 10 | 36 | 74 | 95 | * | | | | | | |
| 44 | 2.217 | 02 | 11 | 39 | 77 | 96 | | | | | | | |
| 46 | 2.216 | 02 | 12 | 42 | 80 | 97 | | | | | | | |
| 48 | 2.215 | 02 | 12 | 44 | 82 | 98 | | | | | | | |
| 50 | 2.213 | 03 | 13 | 47 | 85 | 98 | | | | | | | |
| 52 | 2.212 | 03 | 14 | 50 | 87 | 99 | | | | | | | |
| 54 | 2.211 | 03 | 15 | 52 | 88 | 99 | | | | | | | |
| 56 | 2.210 | 03 | 16 | 55 | 90 | 99 | | | | | | | |
| 58 | 2.209 | 03 | 17 | 57 | 91 | * | | | | | | | |
| 60 | 2.209 | 03 | 18 | 59 | 93 | | | | | | | | |
| 64 | 2.207 | 03 | 20 | 64 | 95 | | | | | | | | |
| 68 | 2.206 | 03 | 22 | 68 | 96 | | | | | | | | |
| 72 | 2.204 | 04 | 24 | 72 | 97 | | | | | | | | |
| 76 | 2.203 | 04 | 26 | 76 | 98 | | | | | | | | |
| 80 | 2.202 | 04 | 29 | 79 | 99 | | | | | | | | |
| 84 | 2.202 | 04 | 31 | 82 | 99 | | | | | | | | |
| 88 | 2.201 | 04 | 33 | 84 | 99 | | | | | | | | |
| 92 | 2.200 | 05 | 36 | 87 | * | | | | | | | | |
| 96 | 2.199 | 05 | 38 | 89 | | | | | | | | | |
| 100 | 2.199 | 05 | 40 | 91 | | | | | | | | | |
| 120 | 2.197 | 07 | 52 | 96 | | | | | | | | | |
| 140 | 2.195 | 08 | 63 | 99 | | | | | | | | | |
| 160 | 2.194 | 10 | 72 | * | | | | | | | | | |
| 180 | 2.193 | 12 | 79 | | | | | | | | | | |
| 200 | 2.192 | 14 | 85 | | | | | | | | | | |
| 250 | 2.191 | 20 | 94 | | | | | | | | | | |
| 300 | 2.190 | 26 | 98 | | | | | | | | | | |
| 350 | 2.189 | 34 | 99 | | | | | | | | | | |
| 400 | 2.188 | 41 | * | | | | | | | | | | |
| 450 | 2.188 | 48 | | | | | | | | | | | |
| 500 | 2.188 | 55 | | | | | | | | | | | |
| 600 | 2.187 | 68 | | | | | | | | | | | |
| 700 | 2.187 | 78 | | | | | | | | | | | |
| 800 | 2.187 | 86 | | | | | | | | | | | |
| 900 | 2.186 | 91 | | | | | | | | | | | |
| 1000 | 2.186 | 94 | | | | | | | | | | | |

* Power values below this point are greater than .995.

Table 8.3.10

Power of F test at a = .01, u = 15

| | | | | | | | | f | | | | | |
|---|---|---|---|---|---|---|---|---|---|---|---|---|---|
| n | F$_c$ | .05 | .10 | .15 | .20 | .25 | .30 | .35 | .40 | .50 | .60 | .70 | .80 |
| 2 | 3.409 | 01 | 01 | 01 | 01 | 02 | 02 | 03 | 04 | 06 | 10 | 15 | 23 |
| 3 | 2.656 | 01 | 01 | 02 | 02 | 03 | 04 | 06 | 08 | 16 | 29 | 46 | 64 |
| 4 | 2.437 | 01 | 01 | 02 | 03 | 04 | 07 | 10 | 15 | 31 | 53 | 75 | 90 |
| 5 | 2.332 | 01 | 01 | 02 | 04 | 06 | 10 | 16 | 25 | 48 | 74 | 91 | 98 |
| 6 | 2.272 | 01 | 02 | 03 | 05 | 08 | 14 | 23 | 35 | 64 | 87 | 97 | * |
| 7 | 2.232 | 01 | 02 | 03 | 06 | 10 | 19 | 31 | 46 | 77 | 94 | 99 | |
| 8 | 2.203 | 01 | 02 | 03 | 07 | 13 | 24 | 39 | 56 | 86 | 98 | * | |
| 9 | 2.182 | 01 | 02 | 04 | 08 | 16 | 30 | 47 | 66 | 92 | 99 | | |
| 10 | 2.166 | 01 | 02 | 05 | 10 | 20 | 36 | 55 | 74 | 95 | * | | |
| 11 | 2.153 | 01 | 02 | 05 | 11 | 24 | 42 | 63 | 81 | 98 | | | |
| 12 | 2.143 | 01 | 03 | 06 | 13 | 28 | 48 | 69 | 86 | 99 | | | |
| 13 | 2.134 | 01 | 03 | 07 | 15 | 32 | 54 | 75 | 90 | 99 | | | |
| 14 | 2.127 | 01 | 03 | 07 | 17 | 36 | 59 | 80 | 93 | * | | | |
| 15 | 2.120 | 01 | 03 | 08 | 20 | 40 | 65 | 85 | 95 | | | | |
| 16 | 2.115 | 01 | 03 | 09 | 22 | 44 | 69 | 88 | 97 | | | | |
| 17 | 2.110 | 01 | 04 | 10 | 25 | 49 | 74 | 91 | 98 | | | | |
| 18 | 2.106 | 01 | 04 | 11 | 27 | 53 | 78 | 93 | 99 | | | | |
| 19 | 2.102 | 02 | 04 | 12 | 30 | 57 | 81 | 95 | 99 | | | | |
| 20 | 2.099 | 02 | 04 | 13 | 32 | 60 | 84 | 96 | 99 | | | | |
| 21 | 2.096 | 02 | 04 | 14 | 35 | 64 | 87 | 97 | * | | | | |
| 22 | 2.093 | 02 | 05 | 15 | 38 | 68 | 89 | 98 | | | | | |
| 23 | 2.091 | 02 | 05 | 16 | 41 | 71 | 91 | 99 | | | | | |
| 24 | 2.088 | 02 | 05 | 17 | 43 | 74 | 93 | 99 | | | | | |
| 25 | 2.086 | 02 | 06 | 19 | 46 | 77 | 94 | 99 | | | | | |
| 26 | 2.084 | 02 | 06 | 20 | 49 | 79 | 95 | * | | | | | |
| 27 | 2.083 | 02 | 06 | 21 | 51 | 81 | 96 | | | | | | |
| 28 | 2.081 | 02 | 07 | 23 | 54 | 84 | 97 | | | | | | |
| 29 | 2.079 | 02 | 07 | 24 | 56 | 86 | 98 | | | | | | |
| 30 | 2.078 | 02 | 07 | 25 | 59 | 87 | 98 | | | | | | |
| 31 | 2.077 | 02 | 08 | 27 | 61 | 89 | 99 | | | | | | |
| 32 | 2.076 | 02 | 08 | 28 | 63 | 90 | 99 | | | | | | |
| 33 | 2.074 | 02 | 08 | 30 | 66 | 92 | 99 | | | | | | |
| 34 | 2.073 | 02 | 09 | 31 | 68 | 93 | 99 | | | | | | |
| 35 | 2.072 | 02 | 09 | 33 | 70 | 94 | 99 | | | | | | |
| 36 | 2.071 | 02 | 09 | 34 | 72 | 95 | * | | | | | | |
| 37 | 2.070 | 02 | 10 | 36 | 74 | 95 | | | | | | | |
| 38 | 2.070 | 02 | 10 | 37 | 76 | 96 | | | | | | | |
| 39 | 2.069 | 02 | 11 | 39 | 77 | 97 | | | | | | | |

Table 8.3.10 (continued)

| n | $F_c$ | .05 | .10 | .15 | .20 | .25 | .30 | .35 | .40 | .50 | .60 | .70 | .80 |
|---|---|---|---|---|---|---|---|---|---|---|---|---|---|
| | | | | | | | f | | | | | | |
| 40 | 2.068 | 02 | 11 | 40 | 79 | 97 | * | * | * | * | * | * | * |
| 42 | 2.066 | 02 | 12 | 43 | 82 | 98 | | | | | | | |
| 44 | 2.065 | 02 | 13 | 46 | 85 | 99 | | | | | | | |
| 46 | 2.064 | 03 | 14 | 49 | 87 | 99 | | | | | | | |
| 48 | 2.063 | 03 | 15 | 52 | 89 | 99 | | | | | | | |
| 50 | 2.062 | 03 | 16 | 55 | 91 | 99 | | | | | | | |
| 52 | 2.061 | 03 | 17 | 58 | 92 | * | | | | | | | |
| 54 | 2.060 | 03 | 18 | 61 | 94 | | | | | | | | |
| 56 | 2.059 | 03 | 19 | 63 | 95 | | | | | | | | |
| 58 | 2.059 | 03 | 20 | 66 | 96 | | | | | | | | |
| 60 | 2.058 | 03 | 22 | 68 | 96 | | | | | | | | |
| 64 | 2.057 | 03 | 24 | 73 | 98 | | | | | | | | |
| 68 | 2.056 | 04 | 26 | 77 | 98 | | | | | | | | |
| 72 | 2.055 | 04 | 29 | 80 | 99 | | | | | | | | |
| 76 | 2.054 | 04 | 32 | 84 | 99 | | | | | | | | |
| 80 | 2.053 | 04 | 34 | 86 | * | | | | | | | | |
| 84 | 2.052 | 05 | 37 | 89 | | | | | | | | | |
| 88 | 2.052 | 05 | 40 | 91 | | | | | | | | | |
| 92 | 2.051 | 05 | 43 | 92 | | | | | | | | | |
| 96 | 2.051 | 06 | 45 | 94 | | | | | | | | | |
| 100 | 2.050 | 06 | 48 | 95 | | | | | | | | | |
| 120 | 2.048 | 07 | 61 | 98 | | | | | | | | | |
| 140 | 2.047 | 09 | 71 | * | | | | | | | | | |
| 160 | 2.046 | 11 | 80 | | | | | | | | | | |
| 180 | 2.045 | 14 | 87 | | | | | | | | | | |
| 200 | 2.044 | 16 | 91 | | | | | | | | | | |
| 250 | 2.043 | 24 | 97 | | | | | | | | | | |
| 300 | 2.042 | 32 | 99 | | | | | | | | | | |
| 350 | 2.042 | 40 | * | | | | | | | | | | |
| 400 | 2.041 | 48 | | | | | | | | | | | |
| 450 | 2.041 | 57 | | | | | | | | | | | |
| 500 | 2.041 | 64 | | | | | | | | | | | |
| 600 | 2.040 | 76 | | | | | | | | | | | |
| 700 | 2.040 | 86 | | | | | | | | | | | |
| 800 | 2.040 | 92 | | | | | | | | | | | |
| 900 | 2.040 | 95 | | | | | | | | | | | |
| 1000 | 2.040 | 98 | | | | | | | | | | | |

* Power values below this point are greater than .995.

Table 8.3.11

Power of F test at a = .01, u = 24

| n | $F_c$ | .05 | .10 | .15 | .20 | .25 | .30 | .35 | .40 | .50 | .60 | .70 | .80 |
|---|---|---|---|---|---|---|---|---|---|---|---|---|---|
| | | | | | | | f | | | | | | |
| 2 | 2.620 | 01 | 01 | 01 | 02 | 02 | 03 | 04 | 05 | 09 | 15 | 25 | 38 |
| 3 | 2.184 | 01 | 01 | 02 | 02 | 04 | 05 | 08 | 12 | 26 | 46 | 68 | 85 |
| 4 | 2.049 | 01 | 01 | 02 | 03 | 06 | 09 | 15 | 24 | 48 | 75 | 92 | 98 |
| 5 | 1.983 | 01 | 02 | 03 | 05 | 08 | 15 | 24 | 38 | 69 | 91 | 99 | * |
| 6 | 1.944 | 01 | 02 | 03 | 06 | 11 | 21 | 35 | 52 | 84 | 97 | * | |
| 7 | 1.918 | 01 | 02 | 04 | 08 | 15 | 29 | 46 | 66 | 92 | 99 | | |
| 8 | 1.900 | 01 | 02 | 04 | 10 | 20 | 37 | 57 | 76 | 97 | * | | |
| 9 | 1.886 | 01 | 02 | 05 | 12 | 25 | 45 | 67 | 85 | 99 | | | |
| 10 | 1.876 | 01 | 03 | 06 | 14 | 30 | 53 | 75 | 90 | * | | | |
| 11 | 1.867 | 02 | 03 | 07 | 17 | 36 | 60 | 82 | 94 | | | | |
| 12 | 1.860 | 02 | 03 | 08 | 20 | 41 | 67 | 87 | 96 | | | | |
| 13 | 1.854 | 02 | 03 | 09 | 23 | 47 | 73 | 91 | 98 | | | | |
| 14 | 1.850 | 02 | 04 | 10 | 26 | 53 | 79 | 94 | 99 | | | | |
| 15 | 1.846 | 02 | 04 | 11 | 30 | 58 | 83 | 96 | 99 | | | | |
| 16 | 1.842 | 02 | 04 | 13 | 33 | 63 | 87 | 97 | * | | | | |
| 17 | 1.839 | 02 | 04 | 14 | 37 | 68 | 90 | 98 | | | | | |
| 18 | 1.836 | 02 | 05 | 16 | 41 | 72 | 93 | 99 | | | | | |
| 19 | 1.833 | 02 | 05 | 17 | 44 | 76 | 95 | 99 | | | | | |
| 20 | 1.831 | 02 | 05 | 19 | 48 | 80 | 96 | * | | | | | |
| 21 | 1.829 | 02 | 06 | 20 | 51 | 83 | 97 | | | | | | |
| 22 | 1.827 | 02 | 06 | 22 | 55 | 86 | 98 | | | | | | |
| 23 | 1.826 | 02 | 07 | 24 | 58 | 88 | 99 | | | | | | |
| 24 | 1.824 | 02 | 07 | 26 | 62 | 90 | 99 | | | | | | |
| 25 | 1.823 | 02 | 07 | 28 | 65 | 92 | 99 | | | | | | |
| 26 | 1.821 | 02 | 08 | 30 | 68 | 93 | 99 | | | | | | |
| 27 | 1.820 | 02 | 08 | 32 | 71 | 95 | * | | | | | | |
| 28 | 1.819 | 02 | 09 | 34 | 73 | 96 | | | | | | | |
| 29 | 1.818 | 02 | 09 | 36 | 76 | 96 | | | | | | | |
| 30 | 1.817 | 02 | 10 | 38 | 78 | 97 | | | | | | | |
| 31 | 1.816 | 02 | 10 | 40 | 80 | 98 | | | | | | | |
| 32 | 1.815 | 02 | 11 | 42 | 82 | 98 | | | | | | | |
| 33 | 1.815 | 02 | 12 | 44 | 84 | 99 | | | | | | | |
| 34 | 1.814 | 02 | 12 | 46 | 86 | 99 | | | | | | | |
| 35 | 1.813 | 02 | 13 | 48 | 87 | 99 | | | | | | | |
| 36 | 1.813 | 02 | 13 | 50 | 89 | 99 | | | | | | | |
| 37 | 1.812 | 03 | 14 | 52 | 90 | 99 | | | | | | | |
| 38 | 1.811 | 03 | 15 | 54 | 91 | * | | | | | | | |
| 39 | 1.811 | 03 | 15 | 56 | 92 | | | | | | | | |

Table 8.3.11 *(continued)*

| n | $F_c$ | .05 | .10 | .15 | .20 | .25 | .30 | .35 | .40 | .50 | .60 | .70 | .80 |
|---|---|---|---|---|---|---|---|---|---|---|---|---|---|
| | | | | | | | | | | | | f | |
| 40 | 1.810 | 03 | 16 | 58 | 93 | * | * | * | * | * | * | * | * |
| 42 | 1.809 | 03 | 17 | 62 | 95 | | | | | | | | |
| 44 | 1.809 | 03 | 19 | 65 | 96 | | | | | | | | |
| 46 | 1.808 | 03 | 20 | 68 | 97 | | | | | | | | |
| 48 | 1.807 | 03 | 22 | 72 | 98 | | | | | | | | |
| 50 | 1.806 | 03 | 24 | 74 | 98 | | | | | | | | |
| 52 | 1.806 | 03 | 25 | 77 | 99 | | | | | | | | |
| 54 | 1.805 | 04 | 27 | 80 | 99 | | | | | | | | |
| 56 | 1.805 | 04 | 29 | 82 | 99 | | | | | | | | |
| 58 | 1.804 | 04 | 30 | 84 | * | | | | | | | | |
| 60 | 1.804 | 04 | 32 | 86 | | | | | | | | | |
| 64 | 1.803 | 04 | 36 | 89 | | | | | | | | | |
| 68 | 1.802 | 05 | 39 | 92 | | | | | | | | | |
| 72 | 1.802 | 05 | 43 | 94 | | | | | | | | | |
| 76 | 1.801 | 05 | 47 | 95 | | | | | | | | | |
| 80 | 1.800 | 06 | 50 | 97 | | | | | | | | | |
| 84 | 1.800 | 06 | 54 | 98 | | | | | | | | | |
| 88 | 1.800 | 06 | 57 | 98 | | | | | | | | | |
| 92 | 1.799 | 07 | 60 | 99 | | | | | | | | | |
| 96 | 1.799 | 07 | 64 | 99 | | | | | | | | | |
| 100 | 1.799 | 08 | 67 | 99 | | | | | | | | | |
| 120 | 1.797 | 10 | 79 | * | | | | | | | | | |
| 140 | 1.796 | 13 | 88 | | | | | | | | | | |
| 160 | 1.796 | 16 | 94 | | | | | | | | | | |
| 180 | 1.795 | 20 | 97 | | | | | | | | | | |
| 200 | 1.795 | 24 | 98 | | | | | | | | | | |
| 250 | 1.794 | 35 | * | | | | | | | | | | |
| 300 | 1.793 | 46 | | | | | | | | | | | |
| 350 | 1.793 | 57 | | | | | | | | | | | |
| 400 | 1.793 | 67 | | | | | | | | | | | |
| 450 | 1.793 | 75 | | | | | | | | | | | |
| 500 | 1.792 | 82 | | | | | | | | | | | |
| 600 | 1.792 | 92 | | | | | | | | | | | |
| 700 | 1.792 | 96 | | | | | | | | | | | |
| 800 | 1.792 | 99 | | | | | | | | | | | |
| 900 | 1.792 | 99 | | | | | | | | | | | |
| 1000 | 1.792 | * | | | | | | | | | | | |

* Power values below this point are greater than .995.

Table 8.3.12

Power of F test at a = .05, u = 1

| n | $F_c$ | .05 | .10 | .15 | .20 | .25 | .30 | .35 | .40 | .50 | .60 | .70 | .80 |
|---|-------|-----|-----|-----|-----|-----|-----|-----|-----|-----|-----|-----|-----|
| 2 | 18.513 | 05 | 05 | 06 | 06 | 07 | 07 | 08 | 09 | 10 | 12 | 14 | 16 |
| 3 | 7.709 | 05 | 05 | 06 | 07 | 08 | 09 | 10 | 12 | 16 | 20 | 26 | 32 |
| 4 | 5.987 | 05 | 06 | 06 | 07 | 09 | 11 | 13 | 16 | 23 | 30 | 39 | 48 |
| 5 | 5.318 | 05 | 06 | 07 | 08 | 11 | 13 | 16 | 20 | 29 | 39 | 50 | 61 |
| 6 | 4.965 | 05 | 06 | 07 | 09 | 12 | 15 | 20 | 24 | 35 | 47 | 60 | 71 |
| 7 | 4.747 | 05 | 06 | 08 | 10 | 14 | 18 | 23 | 28 | 41 | 55 | 68 | 79 |
| 8 | 4.600 | 05 | 06 | 08 | 11 | 15 | 20 | 26 | 32 | 47 | 62 | 75 | 85 |
| 9 | 4.494 | 05 | 07 | 09 | 12 | 17 | 22 | 29 | 36 | 52 | 68 | 80 | 89 |
| 10 | 4.414 | 05 | 07 | 09 | 13 | 18 | 25 | 32 | 40 | 57 | 73 | 85 | 93 |
| 11 | 4.351 | 05 | 07 | 10 | 14 | 20 | 27 | 35 | 44 | 62 | 77 | 88 | 95 |
| 12 | 4.301 | 05 | 07 | 10 | 15 | 22 | 29 | 38 | 47 | 66 | 81 | 91 | 97 |
| 13 | 4.260 | 05 | 07 | 11 | 16 | 23 | 32 | 41 | 51 | 70 | 84 | 93 | 98 |
| 14 | 4.225 | 05 | 08 | 11 | 17 | 25 | 34 | 44 | 54 | 73 | 87 | 95 | 98 |
| 15 | 4.196 | 06 | 08 | 12 | 18 | 26 | 36 | 47 | 57 | 76 | 89 | 96 | 99 |
| 16 | 4.171 | 06 | 08 | 12 | 19 | 28 | 38 | 49 | 60 | 79 | 91 | 97 | 99 |
| 17 | 4.149 | 06 | 08 | 13 | 20 | 30 | 40 | 52 | 63 | 82 | 93 | 98 | * |
| 18 | 4.130 | 06 | 08 | 14 | 21 | 31 | 42 | 54 | 66 | 84 | 94 | 98 | |
| 19 | 4.113 | 06 | 09 | 14 | 22 | 33 | 44 | 57 | 68 | 86 | 95 | 99 | |
| 20 | 4.098 | 06 | 09 | 15 | 23 | 34 | 46 | 59 | 70 | 88 | 96 | 99 | |
| 21 | 4.085 | 06 | 09 | 15 | 24 | 36 | 48 | 61 | 73 | 89 | 97 | 99 | |
| 22 | 4.073 | 06 | 09 | 16 | 26 | 37 | 50 | 63 | 75 | 91 | 97 | * | |
| 23 | 4.062 | 06 | 10 | 16 | 27 | 39 | 52 | 65 | 77 | 92 | 98 | | |
| 24 | 4.052 | 06 | 10 | 17 | 28 | 40 | 54 | 67 | 78 | 93 | 98 | | |
| 25 | 4.043 | 06 | 10 | 18 | 29 | 42 | 56 | 69 | 80 | 94 | 99 | | |
| 26 | 4.034 | 06 | 10 | 18 | 30 | 43 | 58 | 71 | 82 | 95 | 99 | | |
| 27 | 4.026 | 06 | 10 | 19 | 31 | 45 | 59 | 72 | 83 | 95 | 99 | | |
| 28 | 4.020 | 06 | 11 | 19 | 32 | 46 | 61 | 74 | 84 | 96 | 99 | | |
| 29 | 4.013 | 06 | 11 | 20 | 33 | 47 | 62 | 76 | 86 | 97 | 99 | | |
| 30 | 4.007 | 06 | 11 | 21 | 34 | 49 | 64 | 77 | 87 | 97 | * | | |
| 31 | 4.001 | 06 | 11 | 21 | 35 | 50 | 65 | 78 | 88 | 97 | | | |
| 32 | 3.996 | 06 | 12 | 22 | 36 | 51 | 67 | 80 | 89 | 98 | | | |
| 33 | 3.991 | 06 | 12 | 22 | 37 | 53 | 68 | 81 | 90 | 98 | | | |
| 34 | 3.986 | 07 | 12 | 23 | 38 | 54 | 69 | 82 | 91 | 98 | | | |
| 35 | 3.982 | 07 | 12 | 24 | 39 | 55 | 71 | 83 | 92 | 99 | | | |
| 36 | 3.978 | 07 | 13 | 24 | 40 | 56 | 72 | 84 | 92 | 99 | | | |
| 37 | 3.974 | 07 | 13 | 25 | 40 | 58 | 73 | 85 | 93 | 99 | | | |
| 38 | 3.970 | 07 | 13 | 25 | 41 | 59 | 74 | 86 | 94 | 99 | | | |
| 39 | 3.967 | 07 | 13 | 26 | 42 | 60 | 75 | 87 | 94 | 99 | | | |

Table 8.3.12 *(continued)*

| n | $F_c$ | .05 | .10 | .15 | .20 | .25 | .30 | .35 | .40 | .50 | .60 | .70 | .80 |
|---|---|---|---|---|---|---|---|---|---|---|---|---|---|
| 40 | 3.963 | 07 | 14 | 27 | 43 | 61 | 77 | 88 | 95 | 99 | * | * | * |
| 42 | 3.957 | 07 | 14 | 28 | 45 | 63 | 79 | 89 | 96 | * | | | |
| 44 | 3.952 | 07 | 15 | 29 | 47 | 65 | 80 | 91 | 96 | | | | |
| 46 | 3.947 | 07 | 15 | 30 | 49 | 67 | 82 | 92 | 97 | | | | |
| 48 | 3.942 | 07 | 16 | 31 | 50 | 69 | 84 | 93 | 97 | | | | |
| 50 | 3.938 | 07 | 16 | 32 | 52 | 71 | 85 | 94 | 98 | | | | |
| 52 | 3.934 | 08 | 17 | 33 | 53 | 73 | 87 | 95 | 98 | | | | |
| 54 | 3.931 | 08 | 17 | 34 | 55 | 74 | 88 | 95 | 99 | | | | |
| 56 | 3.928 | 08 | 18 | 36 | 57 | 76 | 89 | 96 | 99 | | | | |
| 58 | 3.924 | 08 | 18 | 37 | 58 | 77 | 90 | 97 | 99 | | | | |
| 60 | 3.922 | 08 | 19 | 38 | 60 | 79 | 91 | 97 | 99 | | | | |
| 64 | 3.916 | 08 | 20 | 40 | 62 | 81 | 93 | 98 | * | | | | |
| 68 | 3.912 | 08 | 21 | 42 | 65 | 83 | 94 | 98 | | | | | |
| 72 | 3.908 | 09 | 22 | 44 | 68 | 85 | 95 | 99 | | | | | |
| 76 | 3.904 | 09 | 23 | 46 | 70 | 87 | 96 | 99 | | | | | |
| 80 | 3.901 | 09 | 24 | 48 | 72 | 89 | 97 | 99 | | | | | |
| 84 | 3.898 | 09 | 25 | 50 | 74 | 90 | 97 | * | | | | | |
| 88 | 3.895 | 09 | 26 | 52 | 76 | 92 | 98 | | | | | | |
| 92 | 3.893 | 10 | 27 | 54 | 78 | 93 | 98 | | | | | | |
| 96 | 3.891 | 10 | 28 | 55 | 80 | 94 | 99 | | | | | | |
| 100 | 3.889 | 10 | 29 | 57 | 81 | 94 | 99 | | | | | | |
| 120 | 3.881 | 11 | 34 | 65 | 88 | 97 | * | | | | | | |
| 140 | 3.875 | 13 | 39 | 72 | 92 | 99 | | | | | | | |
| 160 | 3.871 | 14 | 44 | 77 | 95 | 99 | | | | | | | |
| 180 | 3.868 | 15 | 48 | 82 | 97 | * | | | | | | | |
| 200 | 3.865 | 16 | 52 | 86 | 98 | | | | | | | | |
| 250 | 3.860 | 20 | 62 | 92 | 99 | | | | | | | | |
| 300 | 3.857 | 23 | 70 | 96 | * | | | | | | | | |
| 350 | 3.855 | 26 | 76 | 98 | | | | | | | | | |
| 400 | 3.853 | 30 | 82 | 99 | | | | | | | | | |
| 450 | 3.852 | 33 | 86 | * | | | | | | | | | |
| 500 | 3.851 | 36 | 89 | | | | | | | | | | |
| 600 | 3.849 | 42 | 94 | | | | | | | | | | |
| 700 | 3.848 | 47 | 97 | | | | | | | | | | |
| 800 | 3.847 | 53 | 98 | | | | | | | | | | |
| 900 | 3.847 | 58 | 99 | | | | | | | | | | |
| 1000 | 3.846 | 62 | 99 | | | | | | | | | | |

* Power values below this point are greater than .995.

Table 8.3.13

Power of F test at a = .05, u = 2

| n | $F_c$ | .05 | .10 | .15 | .20 | .25 | .30 | .35 | .40 | .50 | .60 | .70 | .80 |
|---|---|---|---|---|---|---|---|---|---|---|---|---|---|
| 2 | 9.552 | 05 | 05 | 06 | 06 | 07 | 07 | 08 | 08 | 10 | 12 | 15 | 18 |
| 3 | 5.143 | 05 | 05 | 06 | 07 | 08 | 09 | 10 | 12 | 17 | 22 | 29 | 37 |
| 4 | 4.256 | 05 | 06 | 06 | 08 | 09 | 11 | 14 | 17 | 24 | 33 | 44 | 54 |
| 5 | 3.885 | 05 | 06 | 07 | 09 | 11 | 14 | 17 | 22 | 32 | 44 | 56 | 69 |
| 6 | 3.682 | 05 | 06 | 07 | 10 | 13 | 16 | 21 | 26 | 39 | 53 | 67 | 79 |
| 7 | 3.555 | 05 | 06 | 08 | 11 | 14 | 19 | 25 | 31 | 46 | 62 | 76 | 87 |
| 8 | 3.467 | 05 | 06 | 08 | 12 | 16 | 22 | 28 | 36 | 53 | 69 | 83 | 92 |
| 9 | 3.403 | 05 | 07 | 09 | 13 | 18 | 24 | 32 | 40 | 59 | 75 | 88 | 95 |
| 10 | 3.354 | 05 | 07 | 10 | 14 | 20 | 27 | 35 | 45 | 64 | 81 | 91 | 97 |
| 11 | 3.316 | 05 | 07 | 10 | 15 | 21 | 30 | 39 | 49 | 69 | 85 | 94 | 98 |
| 12 | 3.285 | 06 | 07 | 11 | 16 | 23 | 32 | 42 | 53 | 74 | 88 | 96 | 99 |
| 13 | 3.260 | 06 | 08 | 11 | 17 | 25 | 35 | 46 | 57 | 77 | 91 | 97 | 99 |
| 14 | 3.238 | 06 | 08 | 12 | 18 | 27 | 38 | 49 | 61 | 81 | 93 | 98 | * |
| 15 | 3.220 | 06 | 08 | 13 | 20 | 29 | 40 | 52 | 64 | 84 | 95 | 99 | |
| 16 | 3.205 | 06 | 08 | 13 | 21 | 31 | 43 | 55 | 67 | 86 | 96 | 99 | |
| 17 | 3.191 | 06 | 09 | 14 | 22 | 33 | 45 | 58 | 70 | 89 | 97 | 99 | |
| 18 | 3.179 | 06 | 09 | 14 | 23 | 34 | 48 | 61 | 73 | 90 | 98 | * | |
| 19 | 3.168 | 06 | 09 | 15 | 24 | 36 | 50 | 64 | 76 | 92 | 99 | | |
| 20 | 3.159 | 06 | 09 | 16 | 26 | 38 | 52 | 66 | 78 | 93 | 99 | | |
| 21 | 3.150 | 06 | 09 | 16 | 27 | 40 | 54 | 69 | 80 | 95 | 99 | | |
| 22 | 3.143 | 06 | 10 | 17 | 28 | 42 | 57 | 71 | 82 | 96 | 99 | | |
| 23 | 3.136 | 06 | 10 | 18 | 29 | 43 | 59 | 73 | 84 | 96 | * | | |
| 24 | 3.130 | 06 | 10 | 18 | 30 | 45 | 61 | 75 | 86 | 97 | | | |
| 25 | 3.124 | 06 | 10 | 19 | 32 | 47 | 63 | 77 | 87 | 98 | | | |
| 26 | 3.119 | 06 | 11 | 20 | 33 | 48 | 65 | 79 | 89 | 98 | | | |
| 27 | 3.114 | 06 | 11 | 20 | 34 | 50 | 66 | 80 | 90 | 98 | | | |
| 28 | 3.110 | 06 | 11 | 21 | 35 | 52 | 68 | 82 | 91 | 99 | | | |
| 29 | 3.105 | 06 | 12 | 22 | 36 | 53 | 70 | 83 | 92 | 99 | | | |
| 30 | 3.102 | 06 | 12 | 22 | 37 | 55 | 71 | 85 | 93 | 99 | | | |
| 31 | 3.098 | 07 | 12 | 23 | 39 | 56 | 73 | 86 | 94 | 99 | | | |
| 32 | 3.095 | 07 | 12 | 24 | 40 | 58 | 75 | 87 | 94 | 99 | | | |
| 33 | 3.091 | 07 | 13 | 24 | 41 | 59 | 76 | 88 | 95 | * | | | |
| 34 | 3.088 | 07 | 13 | 25 | 42 | 61 | 77 | 89 | 96 | | | | |
| 35 | 3.086 | 07 | 13 | 26 | 43 | 62 | 79 | 90 | 96 | | | | |
| 36 | 3.083 | 07 | 13 | 26 | 44 | 63 | 80 | 91 | 97 | | | | |
| 37 | 3.081 | 07 | 14 | 27 | 45 | 65 | 81 | 92 | 97 | | | | |
| 38 | 3.078 | 07 | 14 | 28 | 46 | 66 | 82 | 92 | 97 | | | | |
| 39 | 3.076 | 07 | 14 | 28 | 47 | 67 | 83 | 93 | 98 | | | | |

**Table 8.3.13** *(continued)*

| n | $F_c$ | .05 | .10 | .15 | .20 | .25 | .30 | .35 | .40 | .50 | .60 | .70 | .80 |
|---|---|---|---|---|---|---|---|---|---|---|---|---|---|
| 40 | 3.074 | 07 | 15 | 29 | 48 | 68 | 84 | 94 | 98 | * | * | * | * |
| 42 | 3.070 | 07 | 15 | 30 | 51 | 71 | 86 | 95 | 98 | | | | |
| 44 | 3.066 | 07 | 16 | 32 | 53 | 73 | 88 | 96 | 99 | | | | |
| 46 | 3.063 | 07 | 16 | 33 | 55 | 75 | 89 | 96 | 99 | | | | |
| 48 | 3.060 | 08 | 17 | 34 | 57 | 77 | 90 | 97 | 99 | | | | |
| 50 | 3.058 | 08 | 18 | 36 | 58 | 79 | 92 | 98 | 99 | | | | |
| 52 | 3.055 | 08 | 18 | 37 | 60 | 80 | 93 | 98 | * | | | | |
| 54 | 3.053 | 08 | 19 | 38 | 62 | 82 | 94 | 98 | | | | | |
| 56 | 3.051 | 08 | 19 | 40 | 64 | 83 | 94 | 99 | | | | | |
| 58 | 3.049 | 08 | 20 | 41 | 65 | 85 | 95 | 99 | | | | | |
| 60 | 3.047 | 08 | 21 | 42 | 67 | 86 | 96 | 99 | | | | | |
| 64 | 3.044 | 08 | 22 | 45 | 70 | 88 | 97 | 99 | | | | | |
| 68 | 3.041 | 09 | 23 | 47 | 73 | 90 | 98 | * | | | | | |
| 72 | 3.039 | 09 | 24 | 49 | 75 | 92 | 98 | | | | | | |
| 76 | 3.036 | 09 | 25 | 52 | 78 | 93 | 99 | | | | | | |
| 80 | 3.034 | 09 | 27 | 54 | 80 | 94 | 99 | | | | | | |
| 84 | 3.032 | 10 | 28 | 56 | 82 | 95 | 99 | | | | | | |
| 88 | 3.031 | 10 | 29 | 58 | 84 | 96 | 99 | | | | | | |
| 92 | 3.029 | 10 | 30 | 60 | 85 | 97 | * | | | | | | |
| 96 | 3.028 | 10 | 31 | 62 | 87 | 97 | | | | | | | |
| 100 | 3.026 | 11 | 32 | 64 | 88 | 98 | | | | | | | |
| 120 | 3.021 | 12 | 38 | 73 | 94 | 99 | | | | | | | |
| 140 | 3.018 | 14 | 44 | 79 | 97 | * | | | | | | | |
| 160 | 3.015 | 15 | 49 | 85 | 98 | | | | | | | | |
| 180 | 3.013 | 16 | 54 | 89 | 99 | | | | | | | | |
| 200 | 3.011 | 18 | 59 | 92 | * | | | | | | | | |
| 250 | 3.008 | 22 | 69 | 97 | | | | | | | | | |
| 300 | 3.006 | 25 | 78 | 99 | | | | | | | | | |
| 350 | 3.004 | 29 | 84 | * | | | | | | | | | |
| 400 | 3.003 | 33 | 89 | | | | | | | | | | |
| 450 | 3.002 | 36 | 92 | | | | | | | | | | |
| 500 | 3.002 | 40 | 95 | | | | | | | | | | |
| 600 | 3.001 | 47 | 98 | | | | | | | | | | |
| 700 | 3.000 | 53 | 99 | | | | | | | | | | |
| 800 | 3.000 | 59 | * | | | | | | | | | | |
| 900 | 2.999 | 65 | | | | | | | | | | | |
| 1000 | 2.999 | 70 | | | | | | | | | | | |

* Power values below this point are greater than .995.

Table 8.3.14

Power of F test at a = .05, u = 3

| n | $F_c$ | .05 | .10 | .15 | .20 | .25 | .30 | .35 | .40 | .50 | .60 | .70 | .80 |
|---|---|---|---|---|---|---|---|---|---|---|---|---|---|
| 2 | 6.591 | 05 | 05 | 06 | 06 | 07 | 07 | 08 | 09 | 11 | 13 | 17 | 20 |
| 3 | 4.066 | 05 | 05 | 06 | 07 | 08 | 09 | 11 | 13 | 18 | 25 | 33 | 42 |
| 4 | 3.490 | 05 | 06 | 07 | 08 | 10 | 12 | 15 | 18 | 27 | 38 | 50 | 62 |
| 5 | 3.239 | 05 | 06 | 07 | 09 | 12 | 15 | 19 | 24 | 36 | 50 | 64 | 76 |
| 6 | 3.098 | 05 | 06 | 08 | 10 | 13 | 18 | 23 | 29 | 44 | 60 | 75 | 86 |
| 7 | 3.009 | 05 | 06 | 08 | 11 | 15 | 21 | 27 | 35 | 52 | 69 | 83 | 92 |
| 8 | 2.947 | 05 | 07 | 09 | 12 | 17 | 24 | 31 | 40 | 59 | 77 | 89 | 96 |
| 9 | 2.901 | 05 | 07 | 09 | 14 | 19 | 27 | 36 | 46 | 66 | 82 | 93 | 98 |
| 10 | 2.867 | 05 | 07 | 10 | 15 | 21 | 30 | 40 | 51 | 71 | 87 | 96 | 99 |
| 11 | 2.839 | 06 | 07 | 11 | 16 | 24 | 33 | 44 | 55 | 76 | 91 | 97 | 99 |
| 12 | 2.817 | 06 | 08 | 11 | 17 | 26 | 36 | 48 | 60 | 81 | 93 | 98 | * |
| 13 | 2.798 | 06 | 08 | 12 | 19 | 28 | 39 | 52 | 64 | 84 | 95 | 99 | |
| 14 | 2.783 | 06 | 08 | 13 | 20 | 30 | 42 | 55 | 68 | 87 | 97 | 99 | |
| 15 | 2.770 | 06 | 08 | 13 | 21 | 32 | 45 | 59 | 71 | 90 | 98 | * | |
| 16 | 2.758 | 06 | 09 | 14 | 23 | 34 | 48 | 62 | 75 | 92 | 98 | | |
| 17 | 2.748 | 06 | 09 | 15 | 24 | 37 | 51 | 65 | 78 | 94 | 99 | | |
| 18 | 2.740 | 06 | 09 | 16 | 26 | 39 | 53 | 68 | 80 | 95 | 99 | | |
| 19 | 2.732 | 06 | 09 | 16 | 27 | 41 | 56 | 71 | 83 | 96 | 99 | | |
| 20 | 2.725 | 06 | 10 | 17 | 28 | 43 | 59 | 73 | 85 | 97 | * | | |
| 21 | 2.719 | 06 | 10 | 18 | 30 | 45 | 61 | 76 | 87 | 98 | | | |
| 22 | 2.714 | 06 | 10 | 18 | 31 | 47 | 63 | 78 | 88 | 98 | | | |
| 23 | 2.709 | 06 | 10 | 19 | 32 | 49 | 66 | 80 | 90 | 99 | | | |
| 24 | 2.704 | 06 | 11 | 20 | 34 | 51 | 68 | 82 | 91 | 99 | | | |
| 25 | 2.700 | 06 | 11 | 21 | 35 | 53 | 70 | 84 | 93 | 99 | | | |
| 26 | 2.696 | 06 | 11 | 22 | 37 | 54 | 72 | 85 | 94 | 99 | | | |
| 27 | 2.692 | 07 | 12 | 22 | 38 | 56 | 74 | 87 | 94 | 99 | | | |
| 28 | 2.689 | 07 | 12 | 23 | 39 | 58 | 75 | 88 | 95 | * | | | |
| 29 | 2.686 | 07 | 12 | 24 | 41 | 60 | 77 | 89 | 96 | | | | |
| 30 | 2.683 | 07 | 13 | 25 | 42 | 61 | 79 | 90 | 96 | | | | |
| 31 | 2.680 | 07 | 13 | 25 | 43 | 63 | 80 | 91 | 97 | | | | |
| 32 | 2.678 | 07 | 13 | 26 | 45 | 65 | 81 | 92 | 97 | | | | |
| 33 | 2.675 | 07 | 14 | 27 | 46 | 66 | 83 | 93 | 98 | | | | |
| 34 | 2.673 | 07 | 14 | 28 | 47 | 68 | 54 | 94 | 98 | | | | |
| 35 | 2.671 | 07 | 14 | 29 | 48 | 69 | 85 | 94 | 98 | | | | |
| 36 | 2.669 | 07 | 14 | 29 | 50 | 70 | 86 | 95 | 99 | | | | |
| 37 | 2.668 | 07 | 15 | 30 | 51 | 72 | 87 | 96 | 99 | | | | |
| 38 | 2.666 | 07 | 15 | 31 | 52 | 73 | 88 | 96 | 99 | | | | |
| 39 | 2.664 | 07 | 15 | 32 | 53 | 74 | 89 | 97 | 99 | | | | |

Table 8.3.14 (continued)

| n | $F_c$ | .05 | .10 | .15 | .20 | .25 | .30 | .35 | .40 | .50 | .60 | .70 | .80 |
|---|-------|-----|-----|-----|-----|-----|-----|-----|-----|-----|-----|-----|-----|
| 40 | 2.663 | 07 | 16 | 32 | 54 | 76 | 90 | 97 | 99 | * | * | * | * |
| 42 | 2.660 | 07 | 16 | 34 | 57 | 78 | 91 | 98 | * | | | | |
| 44 | 2.657 | 08 | 17 | 35 | 59 | 80 | 93 | 98 | | | | | |
| 46 | 2.655 | 08 | 18 | 37 | 61 | 82 | 94 | 99 | | | | | |
| 48 | 2.653 | 08 | 18 | 39 | 63 | 84 | 95 | 99 | | | | | |
| 50 | 2.651 | 08 | 19 | 40 | 65 | 85 | 96 | 99 | | | | | |
| 52 | 2.649 | 08 | 20 | 42 | 67 | 87 | 96 | 99 | | | | | |
| 54 | 2.648 | 08 | 20 | 43 | 69 | 88 | 97 | 99 | | | | | |
| 56 | 2.646 | 08 | 21 | 45 | 71 | 89 | 97 | * | | | | | |
| 58 | 2.645 | 08 | 22 | 46 | 72 | 90 | 98 | | | | | | |
| 60 | 2.643 | 09 | 22 | 47 | 74 | 91 | 98 | | | | | | |
| 64 | 2.641 | 09 | 24 | 50 | 77 | 93 | 99 | | | | | | |
| 68 | 2.639 | 09 | 25 | 53 | 80 | 95 | 99 | | | | | | |
| 72 | 2.637 | 09 | 27 | 56 | 82 | 96 | 99 | | | | | | |
| 76 | 2.635 | 10 | 28 | 58 | 84 | 97 | * | | | | | | |
| 80 | 2.633 | 10 | 29 | 61 | 86 | 97 | | | | | | | |
| 84 | 2.632 | 10 | 31 | 63 | 88 | 98 | | | | | | | |
| 88 | 2.631 | 10 | 32 | 65 | 90 | 98 | | | | | | | |
| 92 | 2.630 | 11 | 34 | 67 | 91 | 99 | | | | | | | |
| 96 | 2.629 | 11 | 35 | 69 | 92 | 99 | | | | | | | |
| 100 | 2.628 | 11 | 36 | 71 | 93 | 99 | | | | | | | |
| 120 | 2.624 | 13 | 43 | 80 | 97 | * | | | | | | | |
| 140 | 2.621 | 14 | 49 | 86 | 99 | | | | | | | | |
| 160 | 2.619 | 16 | 55 | 91 | 99 | | | | | | | | |
| 180 | 2.618 | 18 | 61 | 94 | * | | | | | | | | |
| 200 | 2.616 | 19 | 66 | 96 | | | | | | | | | |
| 250 | 2.614 | 24 | 77 | 99 | | | | | | | | | |
| 300 | 2.612 | 28 | 84 | * | | | | | | | | | |
| 350 | 2.611 | 32 | 90 | | | | | | | | | | |
| 400 | 2.611 | 37 | 93 | | | | | | | | | | |
| 450 | 2.610 | 41 | 96 | | | | | | | | | | |
| 500 | 2.609 | 45 | 98 | | | | | | | | | | |
| 600 | 2.609 | 53 | 99 | | | | | | | | | | |
| 700 | 2.608 | 60 | * | | | | | | | | | | |
| 800 | 2.608 | 66 | | | | | | | | | | | |
| 900 | 2.607 | 72 | | | | | | | | | | | |
| 1000 | 2.607 | 77 | | | | | | | | | | | |

* Power values below this point are greater than .995.

**Table 8.3.15**

Power of F test at a = .05, u = 4

| n | $F_c$ | .05 | .10 | .15 | .20 | .25 | .30 | .35 | .40 | .50 | .60 | .70 | .80 |
|---|---|---|---|---|---|---|---|---|---|---|---|---|---|
| | | | | | | | | | f | | | | |
| 2 | 5.192 | 05 | 05 | 06 | 07 | 08 | 08 | 09 | 10 | 13 | 15 | 19 | 24 |
| 3 | 3.478 | 05 | 05 | 06 | 07 | 09 | 10 | 12 | 14 | 20 | 28 | 38 | 48 |
| 4 | 3.056 | 05 | 06 | 07 | 08 | 10 | 13 | 16 | 20 | 30 | 42 | 56 | 69 |
| 5 | 2.866 | 05 | 06 | 07 | 09 | 12 | 16 | 21 | 26 | 40 | 55 | 70 | 83 |
| 6 | 2.759 | 05 | 06 | 08 | 10 | 14 | 19 | 25 | 32 | 49 | 66 | 81 | 91 |
| 7 | 2.690 | 05 | 06 | 09 | 12 | 16 | 22 | 30 | 39 | 58 | 76 | 88 | 96 |
| 8 | 2.642 | 05 | 07 | 09 | 13 | 19 | 26 | 35 | 45 | 65 | 83 | 93 | 98 |
| 9 | 2.606 | 05 | 07 | 10 | 14 | 21 | 29 | 40 | 51 | 72 | 88 | 96 | 99 |
| 10 | 2.579 | 06 | 07 | 10 | 16 | 23 | 33 | 44 | 56 | 78 | 92 | 98 | * |
| 11 | 2.558 | 06 | 08 | 11 | 17 | 26 | 37 | 49 | 61 | 82 | 94 | 99 | |
| 12 | 2.540 | 06 | 08 | 12 | 19 | 28 | 40 | 53 | 66 | 86 | 96 | 99 | |
| 13 | 2.525 | 06 | 08 | 13 | 20 | 31 | 43 | 57 | 70 | 89 | 98 | * | |
| 14 | 2.513 | 06 | 08 | 13 | 22 | 33 | 47 | 61 | 74 | 92 | 98 | | |
| 15 | 2.503 | 06 | 09 | 14 | 23 | 36 | 50 | 65 | 78 | 94 | 99 | | |
| 16 | 2.494 | 06 | 09 | 15 | 25 | 38 | 53 | 68 | 81 | 95 | 99 | | |
| 17 | 2.486 | 06 | 09 | 16 | 26 | 40 | 56 | 71 | 83 | 96 | * | | |
| 18 | 2.479 | 06 | 09 | 17 | 28 | 43 | 59 | 74 | 86 | 97 | | | |
| 19 | 2.473 | 06 | 10 | 17 | 30 | 45 | 62 | 77 | 88 | 98 | | | |
| 20 | 2.468 | 06 | 10 | 18 | 31 | 47 | 65 | 79 | 90 | 99 | | | |
| 21 | 2.463 | 06 | 10 | 19 | 33 | 50 | 67 | 82 | 91 | 99 | | | |
| 22 | 2.458 | 06 | 11 | 20 | 34 | 52 | 69 | 84 | 93 | 99 | | | |
| 23 | 2.454 | 06 | 11 | 21 | 36 | 54 | 72 | 85 | 94 | 99 | | | |
| 24 | 2.451 | 06 | 11 | 22 | 37 | 56 | 74 | 87 | 95 | * | | | |
| 25 | 2.447 | 06 | 12 | 23 | 39 | 58 | 76 | 89 | 96 | | | | |
| 26 | 2.444 | 07 | 12 | 23 | 40 | 60 | 78 | 90 | 96 | | | | |
| 27 | 2.441 | 07 | 12 | 24 | 42 | 62 | 80 | 91 | 97 | | | | |
| 28 | 2.439 | 07 | 13 | 25 | 43 | 64 | 81 | 92 | 98 | | | | |
| 29 | 2.436 | 07 | 13 | 26 | 45 | 66 | 83 | 93 | 98 | | | | |
| 30 | 2.434 | 07 | 13 | 27 | 46 | 67 | 84 | 94 | 98 | | | | |
| 31 | 2.432 | 07 | 14 | 28 | 48 | 69 | 86 | 95 | 99 | | | | |
| 32 | 2.430 | 07 | 14 | 29 | 49 | 71 | 87 | 96 | 99 | | | | |
| 33 | 2.428 | 07 | 14 | 30 | 51 | 72 | 88 | 96 | 99 | | | | |
| 34 | 2.427 | 07 | 15 | 30 | 52 | 74 | 89 | 97 | 99 | | | | |
| 35 | 2.425 | 07 | 15 | 31 | 54 | 75 | 90 | 97 | 99 | | | | |
| 36 | 2.424 | 07 | 15 | 32 | 55 | 76 | 91 | 97 | * | | | | |
| 37 | 2.422 | 07 | 16 | 33 | 56 | 78 | 92 | 98 | | | | | |
| 38 | 2.421 | 07 | 16 | 34 | 57 | 79 | 92 | 98 | | | | | |
| 39 | 2.419 | 07 | 16 | 35 | 59 | 80 | 93 | 98 | | | | | |

Table 8.3.15 *(continued)*

| n | $F_c$ | .05 | .10 | .15 | .20 | .25 | .30 | .35 | .40 | .50 | .60 | .70 | .80 |
|---|---|---|---|---|---|---|---|---|---|---|---|---|---|
| 40 | 2.418 | 07 | 17 | 36 | 60 | 81 | 94 | 99 | * | * | * | * | * |
| 42 | 2.416 | 08 | 18 | 37 | 62 | 83 | 95 | 99 | | | | | |
| 44 | 2.414 | 08 | 18 | 39 | 65 | 85 | 96 | 99 | | | | | |
| 46 | 2.412 | 08 | 19 | 41 | 67 | 87 | 97 | 99 | | | | | |
| 48 | 2.410 | 08 | 20 | 43 | 69 | 89 | 97 | * | | | | | |
| 50 | 2.409 | 08 | 21 | 44 | 71 | 90 | 98 | | | | | | |
| 52 | 2.407 | 08 | 21 | 46 | 73 | 91 | 98 | | | | | | |
| 54 | 2.406 | 08 | 22 | 48 | 75 | 92 | 99 | | | | | | |
| 56 | 2.405 | 09 | 23 | 49 | 77 | 93 | 99 | | | | | | |
| 58 | 2.404 | 09 | 24 | 51 | 78 | 94 | 99 | | | | | | |
| 60 | 2.403 | 09 | 24 | 52 | 80 | 95 | 99 | | | | | | |
| 64 | 2.401 | 09 | 26 | 55 | 83 | 96 | * | | | | | | |
| 68 | 2.399 | 09 | 28 | 58 | 85 | 97 | | | | | | | |
| 72 | 2.397 | 10 | 29 | 61 | 87 | 98 | | | | | | | |
| 76 | 2.396 | 10 | 31 | 64 | 89 | 98 | | | | | | | |
| 80 | 2.395 | 10 | 32 | 66 | 91 | 99 | | | | | | | |
| 84 | 2.394 | 11 | 34 | 69 | 92 | 99 | | | | | | | |
| 88 | 2.393 | 11 | 35 | 71 | 94 | 99 | | | | | | | |
| 92 | 2.392 | 11 | 37 | 73 | 95 | * | | | | | | | |
| 96 | 2.391 | 11 | 39 | 75 | 96 | | | | | | | | |
| 100 | 2.390 | 12 | 40 | 77 | 96 | | | | | | | | |
| 120 | 2.387 | 13 | 47 | 85 | 99 | | | | | | | | |
| 140 | 2.385 | 15 | 54 | 91 | 99 | | | | | | | | |
| 160 | 2.383 | 17 | 61 | 94 | * | | | | | | | | |
| 180 | 2.382 | 18 | 67 | 97 | | | | | | | | | |
| 200 | 2.381 | 20 | 72 | 98 | | | | | | | | | |
| 250 | 2.379 | 25 | 82 | * | | | | | | | | | |
| 300 | 2.378 | 29 | 89 | | | | | | | | | | |
| 350 | 2.377 | 34 | 94 | | | | | | | | | | |
| 400 | 2.376 | 39 | 96 | | | | | | | | | | |
| 450 | 2.376 | 44 | 98 | | | | | | | | | | |
| 500 | 2.376 | 49 | 99 | | | | | | | | | | |
| 600 | 2.375 | 57 | * | | | | | | | | | | |
| 700 | 2.374 | 65 | | | | | | | | | | | |
| 800 | 2.374 | 72 | | | | | | | | | | | |
| 900 | 2.374 | 78 | | | | | | | | | | | |
| 1000 | 2.374 | 82 | | | | | | | | | | | |

* Power values below this point are greater than .995.

**Table 8.3.16**

Power of F test at a = .05, u = 5

| n | $F_c$ | .05 | .10 | .15 | .20 | .25 | .30 | .35 | .40 | .50 | .60 | .70 | .80 |
|---|-------|-----|-----|-----|-----|-----|-----|-----|-----|-----|-----|-----|-----|
| | | | | | | f | | | | | | | |
| 2 | 4.387 | 05 | 05 | 06 | 07 | 08 | 08 | 09 | 10 | 13 | 17 | 21 | 26 |
| 3 | 3.106 | 05 | 06 | 06 | 07 | 09 | 11 | 13 | 15 | 22 | 31 | 42 | 53 |
| 4 | 2.773 | 05 | 06 | 07 | 08 | 11 | 14 | 17 | 22 | 33 | 47 | 61 | 75 |
| 5 | 2.621 | 05 | 06 | 07 | 10 | 13 | 17 | 22 | 29 | 44 | 61 | 76 | 88 |
| 6 | 2.534 | 05 | 06 | 08 | 11 | 15 | 21 | 27 | 35 | 54 | 72 | 86 | 94 |
| 7 | 2.478 | 05 | 07 | 09 | 12 | 18 | 24 | 33 | 42 | 63 | 81 | 92 | 98 |
| 8 | 2.438 | 05 | 07 | 09 | 14 | 20 | 28 | 38 | 49 | 71 | 87 | 96 | 99 |
| 9 | 2.409 | 05 | 07 | 10 | 15 | 23 | 32 | 43 | 55 | 77 | 92 | 98 | * |
| 10 | 2.391 | 06 | 07 | 11 | 17 | 25 | 36 | 48 | 61 | 83 | 95 | 99 | |
| 11 | 2.368 | 06 | 08 | 12 | 19 | 28 | 40 | 53 | 66 | 87 | 97 | 99 | |
| 12 | 2.354 | 06 | 08 | 13 | 20 | 31 | 44 | 58 | 71 | 90 | 98 | * | |
| 13 | 2.342 | 06 | 08 | 13 | 22 | 33 | 47 | 62 | 75 | 93 | 99 | | |
| 14 | 2.332 | 06 | 09 | 14 | 24 | 36 | 51 | 66 | 79 | 95 | 99 | | |
| 15 | 2.324 | 06 | 09 | 15 | 25 | 39 | 55 | 70 | 82 | 96 | * | | |
| 16 | 2.316 | 06 | 09 | 16 | 27 | 42 | 58 | 73 | 85 | 97 | | | |
| 17 | 2.310 | 06 | 10 | 17 | 29 | 44 | 61 | 76 | 88 | 98 | | | |
| 18 | 2.304 | 06 | 10 | 18 | 30 | 47 | 64 | 79 | 90 | 99 | | | |
| 19 | 2.299 | 06 | 10 | 19 | 32 | 49 | 67 | 82 | 92 | 99 | | | |
| 20 | 2.294 | 06 | 11 | 20 | 34 | 52 | 70 | 84 | 93 | 99 | | | |
| 21 | 2.290 | 06 | 11 | 21 | 36 | 54 | 72 | 86 | 94 | * | | | |
| 22 | 2.286 | 06 | 11 | 22 | 37 | 57 | 75 | 88 | 95 | | | | |
| 23 | 2.283 | 06 | 11 | 22 | 39 | 59 | 77 | 90 | 96 | | | | |
| 24 | 2.280 | 06 | 12 | 23 | 41 | 61 | 79 | 91 | 97 | | | | |
| 25 | 2.277 | 07 | 12 | 24 | 43 | 63 | 81 | 92 | 98 | | | | |
| 26 | 2.275 | 07 | 13 | 25 | 44 | 65 | 83 | 93 | 98 | | | | |
| 27 | 2.272 | 07 | 13 | 26 | 46 | 67 | 84 | 94 | 98 | | | | |
| 28 | 2.270 | 07 | 13 | 27 | 47 | 69 | 86 | 95 | 99 | | | | |
| 29 | 2.268 | 07 | 14 | 28 | 49 | 71 | 87 | 96 | 99 | | | | |
| 30 | 2.266 | 07 | 14 | 29 | 51 | 73 | 88 | 96 | 99 | | | | |
| 31 | 2.265 | 07 | 14 | 30 | 52 | 74 | 90 | 97 | 99 | | | | |
| 32 | 2.263 | 07 | 15 | 31 | 54 | 76 | 91 | 97 | * | | | | |
| 33 | 2.262 | 07 | 15 | 32 | 55 | 77 | 92 | 98 | | | | | |
| 34 | 2.260 | 07 | 16 | 33 | 57 | 79 | 93 | 98 | | | | | |
| 35 | 2.259 | 07 | 16 | 34 | 58 | 80 | 93 | 98 | | | | | |
| 36 | 2.257 | 07 | 16 | 35 | 60 | 81 | 94 | 99 | | | | | |
| 37 | 2.256 | 07 | 17 | 36 | 61 | 83 | 95 | 99 | | | | | |
| 38 | 2.255 | 07 | 17 | 37 | 62 | 84 | 95 | 99 | | | | | |
| 39 | 2.254 | 08 | 18 | 38 | 64 | 85 | 96 | 99 | | | | | |

Table 8.3.16 (continued)

| n | $F_c$ | .05 | .10 | .15 | .20 | .25 | .30 | .35 | .40 | .50 | .60 | .70 | .80 |
|---|---|---|---|---|---|---|---|---|---|---|---|---|---|
| 40 | 2.253 | 08 | 18 | 39 | 65 | 86 | 96 | 99 | * | * | * | * | * |
| 42 | 2.251 | 08 | 19 | 41 | 68 | 88 | 97 | * | | | | | |
| 44 | 2.249 | 08 | 20 | 43 | 70 | 89 | 98 | | | | | | |
| 46 | 2.248 | 08 | 21 | 45 | 72 | 91 | 98 | | | | | | |
| 48 | 2.246 | 08 | 21 | 47 | 74 | 92 | 99 | | | | | | |
| 50 | 2.245 | 08 | 22 | 48 | 76 | 93 | 99 | | | | | | |
| 52 | 2.244 | 09 | 23 | 50 | 78 | 94 | 99 | | | | | | |
| 54 | 2.243 | 09 | 24 | 52 | 80 | 95 | 99 | | | | | | |
| 56 | 2.242 | 09 | 25 | 54 | 82 | 96 | * | | | | | | |
| 58 | 2.241 | 09 | 26 | 55 | 83 | 96 | | | | | | | |
| 60 | 2.240 | 09 | 26 | 57 | 85 | 97 | | | | | | | |
| 64 | 2.238 | 09 | 28 | 60 | 87 | 98 | | | | | | | |
| 68 | 2.237 | 10 | 30 | 63 | 89 | 99 | | | | | | | |
| 72 | 2.235 | 10 | 32 | 66 | 91 | 99 | | | | | | | |
| 76 | 2.234 | 10 | 33 | 69 | 93 | 99 | | | | | | | |
| 80 | 2.233 | 11 | 35 | 72 | 94 | 99 | | | | | | | |
| 84 | 2.232 | 11 | 37 | 74 | 95 | * | | | | | | | |
| 88 | 2.232 | 11 | 39 | 76 | 96 | | | | | | | | |
| 92 | 2.231 | 12 | 40 | 78 | 97 | | | | | | | | |
| 96 | 2.230 | 12 | 42 | 80 | 97 | | | | | | | | |
| 100 | 2.229 | 12 | 44 | 82 | 98 | | | | | | | | |
| 120 | 2.227 | 14 | 52 | 89 | 99 | | | | | | | | |
| 140 | 2.225 | 16 | 59 | 94 | * | | | | | | | | |
| 160 | 2.224 | 18 | 66 | 97 | | | | | | | | | |
| 180 | 2.223 | 20 | 72 | 98 | | | | | | | | | |
| 200 | 2.222 | 23 | 77 | 99 | | | | | | | | | |
| 250 | 2.220 | 28 | 87 | * | | | | | | | | | |
| 300 | 2.219 | 33 | 93 | | | | | | | | | | |
| 350 | 2.218 | 39 | 96 | | | | | | | | | | |
| 400 | 2.218 | 44 | 98 | | | | | | | | | | |
| 450 | 2.217 | 49 | 99 | | | | | | | | | | |
| 500 | 2.217 | 54 | * | | | | | | | | | | |
| 600 | 2.217 | 63 | | | | | | | | | | | |
| 700 | 2.216 | 71 | | | | | | | | | | | |
| 800 | 2.216 | 77 | | | | | | | | | | | |
| 900 | 2.216 | 83 | | | | | | | | | | | |
| 1000 | 2.216 | 87 | | | | | | | | | | | |

* Power values below this point are greater than .995.

Table 8.3.17

Power of F test at a = .05, u = 6

| n | $F_c$ | .05 | .10 | .15 | .20 | .25 | .30 | .35 | .40 | .50 | .60 | .70 | .80 |
|---|-------|-----|-----|-----|-----|-----|-----|-----|-----|-----|-----|-----|-----|
| 2 | 3.866 | 05 | 05 | 06 | 07 | 08 | 08 | 09 | 11 | 14 | 18 | 23 | 29 |
| 3 | 2.848 | 05 | 06 | 06 | 08 | 09 | 11 | 13 | 16 | 24 | 34 | 46 | 51 |
| 4 | 2.573 | 05 | 06 | 07 | 09 | 11 | 14 | 18 | 23 | 36 | 51 | 66 | 80 |
| 5 | 2.445 | 05 | 06 | 08 | 10 | 13 | 18 | 24 | 31 | 48 | 66 | 81 | 91 |
| 6 | 2.372 | 05 | 06 | 08 | 11 | 16 | 22 | 30 | 38 | 58 | 77 | 90 | 96 |
| 7 | 2.324 | 05 | 07 | 09 | 13 | 19 | 26 | 35 | 46 | 68 | 85 | 95 | 99 |
| 8 | 2.291 | 05 | 07 | 10 | 15 | 21 | 30 | 41 | 53 | 76 | 91 | 98 | * |
| 9 | 2.266 | 06 | 07 | 11 | 16 | 24 | 35 | 47 | 60 | 82 | 94 | 99 | |
| 10 | 2.246 | 06 | 08 | 11 | 18 | 27 | 39 | 52 | 66 | 87 | 97 | * | |
| 11 | 2.231 | 06 | 08 | 12 | 20 | 30 | 43 | 57 | 71 | 90 | 98 | | |
| 12 | 2.219 | 06 | 08 | 13 | 22 | 33 | 47 | 62 | 76 | 93 | 99 | | |
| 13 | 2.209 | 06 | 09 | 14 | 23 | 36 | 51 | 67 | 80 | 95 | 99 | | |
| 14 | 2.200 | 06 | 09 | 15 | 25 | 39 | 55 | 71 | 83 | 97 | * | | |
| 15 | 2.193 | 06 | 09 | 16 | 27 | 42 | 59 | 74 | 86 | 98 | | | |
| 16 | 2.186 | 06 | 10 | 17 | 29 | 45 | 62 | 78 | 89 | 98 | | | |
| 17 | 2.181 | 06 | 10 | 18 | 31 | 48 | 66 | 81 | 91 | 99 | | | |
| 18 | 2.176 | 06 | 10 | 19 | 33 | 51 | 69 | 83 | 93 | 99 | | | |
| 19 | 2.171 | 06 | 11 | 20 | 35 | 53 | 72 | 86 | 94 | * | | | |
| 20 | 2.168 | 06 | 11 | 21 | 37 | 56 | 74 | 88 | 95 | | | | |
| 21 | 2.164 | 06 | 11 | 22 | 39 | 58 | 77 | 90 | 96 | | | | |
| 22 | 2.161 | 06 | 12 | 23 | 40 | 61 | 79 | 91 | 97 | | | | |
| 23 | 2.158 | 07 | 12 | 24 | 42 | 63 | 81 | 93 | 98 | | | | |
| 24 | 2.156 | 07 | 12 | 25 | 44 | 65 | 83 | 94 | 98 | | | | |
| 25 | 2.153 | 07 | 13 | 26 | 46 | 68 | 85 | 95 | 99 | | | | |
| 26 | 2.151 | 07 | 13 | 27 | 48 | 70 | 87 | 96 | 99 | | | | |
| 27 | 2.149 | 07 | 14 | 28 | 50 | 72 | 88 | 96 | 99 | | | | |
| 28 | 2.147 | 07 | 14 | 29 | 51 | 74 | 89 | 97 | 99 | | | | |
| 29 | 2.145 | 07 | 14 | 30 | 53 | 75 | 91 | 97 | * | | | | |
| 30 | 2.144 | 07 | 15 | 31 | 55 | 77 | 92 | 98 | | | | | |
| 31 | 2.142 | 07 | 15 | 33 | 56 | 79 | 93 | 98 | | | | | |
| 32 | 2.141 | 07 | 16 | 34 | 58 | 80 | 93 | 99 | | | | | |
| 33 | 2.140 | 07 | 16 | 35 | 60 | 82 | 94 | 99 | | | | | |
| 34 | 2.138 | 07 | 17 | 36 | 61 | 83 | 95 | 99 | | | | | |
| 35 | 2.137 | 07 | 17 | 37 | 63 | 84 | 96 | 99 | | | | | |
| 36 | 2.136 | 07 | 17 | 38 | 64 | 85 | 96 | 99 | | | | | |
| 37 | 2.135 | 08 | 18 | 39 | 66 | 87 | 97 | 99 | | | | | |
| 38 | 2.134 | 08 | 18 | 40 | 67 | 88 | 97 | * | | | | | |
| 39 | 2.133 | 08 | 19 | 41 | 68 | 89 | 97 | | | | | | |

Table 8.3.17 (continued)

| n | $F_c$ | .05 | .10 | .15 | .20 | .25 | .30 | .35 | .40 | .50 | .60 | .70 | .80 |
|---|---|---|---|---|---|---|---|---|---|---|---|---|---|
| | | | | | | | | | | f | | | |
| 40 | 2.132 | 08 | 19 | 42 | 70 | 89 | 98 | * | * | * | * | * | * |
| 42 | 2.131 | 08 | 20 | 44 | 72 | 91 | 98 | | | | | | |
| 44 | 2.129 | 08 | 21 | 46 | 75 | 92 | 99 | | | | | | |
| 46 | 2.128 | 08 | 22 | 48 | 77 | 94 | 99 | | | | | | |
| 48 | 2.126 | 08 | 23 | 50 | 79 | 95 | 99 | | | | | | |
| 50 | 2.125 | 09 | 24 | 52 | 81 | 96 | 99 | | | | | | |
| 52 | 2.124 | 09 | 25 | 54 | 82 | 96 | * | | | | | | |
| 54 | 2.123 | 09 | 26 | 56 | 84 | 97 | | | | | | | |
| 56 | 2.122 | 09 | 27 | 58 | 86 | 97 | | | | | | | |
| 58 | 2.122 | 09 | 27 | 60 | 87 | 98 | | | | | | | |
| 60 | 2.121 | 09 | 28 | 61 | 88 | 98 | | | | | | | |
| 64 | 2.119 | 10 | 30 | 65 | 91 | 99 | | | | | | | |
| 68 | 2.118 | 10 | 32 | 68 | 92 | 99 | | | | | | | |
| 72 | 2.117 | 10 | 34 | 71 | 94 | 99 | | | | | | | |
| 76 | 2.116 | 11 | 36 | 74 | 95 | * | | | | | | | |
| 80 | 2.115 | 11 | 38 | 76 | 96 | | | | | | | | |
| 84 | 2.114 | 12 | 40 | 78 | 97 | | | | | | | | |
| 88 | 2.114 | 12 | 42 | 81 | 98 | | | | | | | | |
| 92 | 2.113 | 12 | 44 | 83 | 98 | | | | | | | | |
| 96 | 2.112 | 13 | 45 | 84 | 99 | | | | | | | | |
| 100 | 2.112 | 13 | 47 | 86 | 99 | | | | | | | | |
| 120 | 2.110 | 15 | 56 | 92 | * | | | | | | | | |
| 140 | 2.108 | 17 | 64 | 96 | | | | | | | | | |
| 160 | 2.107 | 19 | 71 | 98 | | | | | | | | | |
| 180 | 2.106 | 21 | 76 | 99 | | | | | | | | | |
| 200 | 2.105 | 23 | 81 | * | | | | | | | | | |
| 250 | 2.104 | 29 | 90 | | | | | | | | | | |
| 300 | 2.103 | 35 | 95 | | | | | | | | | | |
| 350 | 2.102 | 40 | 98 | | | | | | | | | | |
| 400 | 2.102 | 46 | 99 | | | | | | | | | | |
| 450 | 2.102 | 52 | * | | | | | | | | | | |
| 500 | 2.101 | 57 | | | | | | | | | | | |
| 600 | 2.101 | 67 | | | | | | | | | | | |
| 700 | 2.100 | 75 | | | | | | | | | | | |
| 800 | 2.100 | 82 | | | | | | | | | | | |
| 900 | 2.100 | 87 | | | | | | | | | | | |
| 1000 | 2.100 | 91 | | | | | | | | | | | |

* Power values below this point are greater than .995.

Table 8.3.18

Power of F test at a = .05, u = 8

| n | $F_c$ | .05 | .10 | .15 | .20 | .25 | .30 | .35 | .40 | .50 | .60 | .70 | .80 |
|---|---|---|---|---|---|---|---|---|---|---|---|---|---|
| 2 | 3.230 | 05 | 05 | 06 | 07 | 08 | 09 | 10 | 11 | 15 | 20 | 26 | 34 |
| 3 | 2.510 | 05 | 06 | 06 | 08 | 10 | 12 | 15 | 18 | 28 | 40 | 53 | 67 |
| 4 | 2.305 | 05 | 06 | 07 | 09 | 12 | 16 | 21 | 27 | 42 | 59 | 75 | 87 |
| 5 | 2.208 | 05 | 06 | 08 | 11 | 15 | 20 | 27 | 35 | 55 | 74 | 88 | 96 |
| 6 | 2.152 | 05 | 07 | 09 | 12 | 18 | 25 | 34 | 44 | 66 | 84 | 95 | 99 |
| 7 | 2.115 | 05 | 07 | 10 | 14 | 21 | 30 | 41 | 53 | 76 | 91 | 98 | * |
| 8 | 2.089 | 06 | 07 | 10 | 16 | 24 | 35 | 47 | 60 | 83 | 95 | 99 | |
| 9 | 2.070 | 06 | 08 | 11 | 18 | 27 | 40 | 54 | 67 | 88 | 98 | * | |
| 10 | 2.055 | 06 | 08 | 12 | 20 | 31 | 45 | 60 | 73 | 92 | 99 | | |
| 11 | 2.043 | 06 | 08 | 13 | 22 | 34 | 49 | 65 | 79 | 95 | 99 | | |
| 12 | 2.033 | 06 | 09 | 14 | 24 | 38 | 54 | 70 | 83 | 97 | * | | |
| 13 | 2.025 | 06 | 09 | 15 | 26 | 41 | 58 | 74 | 87 | 98 | | | |
| 14 | 2.018 | 06 | 09 | 17 | 29 | 45 | 62 | 78 | 90 | 99 | | | |
| 15 | 2.013 | 06 | 10 | 18 | 31 | 48 | 66 | 82 | 92 | 99 | | | |
| 16 | 2.008 | 06 | 10 | 19 | 33 | 51 | 70 | 85 | 94 | * | | | |
| 17 | 2.004 | 06 | 10 | 20 | 35 | 54 | 73 | 87 | 95 | | | | |
| 18 | 2.000 | 06 | 11 | 21 | 37 | 57 | 76 | 90 | 97 | | | | |
| 19 | 1.996 | 06 | 11 | 22 | 40 | 60 | 79 | 91 | 97 | | | | |
| 20 | 1.993 | 06 | 12 | 23 | 42 | 63 | 82 | 93 | 98 | | | | |
| 21 | 1.990 | 07 | 12 | 25 | 44 | 66 | 84 | 94 | 99 | | | | |
| 22 | 1.988 | 07 | 13 | 26 | 46 | 68 | 86 | 95 | 99 | | | | |
| 23 | 1.986 | 07 | 13 | 27 | 48 | 71 | 88 | 96 | 99 | | | | |
| 24 | 1.984 | 07 | 13 | 28 | 50 | 73 | 89 | 97 | 99 | | | | |
| 25 | 1.982 | 07 | 14 | 29 | 52 | 75 | 91 | 98 | * | | | | |
| 26 | 1.980 | 07 | 14 | 31 | 54 | 77 | 92 | 98 | | | | | |
| 27 | 1.978 | 07 | 15 | 32 | 56 | 79 | 93 | 99 | | | | | |
| 28 | 1.977 | 07 | 15 | 33 | 58 | 81 | 94 | 99 | | | | | |
| 29 | 1.976 | 07 | 16 | 34 | 60 | 83 | 95 | 99 | | | | | |
| 30 | 1.974 | 07 | 16 | 36 | 62 | 84 | 96 | 99 | | | | | |
| 31 | 1.973 | 07 | 17 | 37 | 64 | 86 | 96 | 99 | | | | | |
| 32 | 1.972 | 07 | 17 | 38 | 65 | 87 | 97 | * | | | | | |
| 33 | 1.971 | 08 | 18 | 39 | 67 | 88 | 97 | | | | | | |
| 34 | 1.970 | 08 | 18 | 41 | 69 | 89 | 98 | | | | | | |
| 35 | 1.969 | 08 | 19 | 42 | 70 | 90 | 98 | | | | | | |
| 36 | 1.968 | 08 | 19 | 43 | 72 | 91 | 98 | | | | | | |
| 37 | 1.967 | 08 | 20 | 44 | 73 | 92 | 99 | | | | | | |
| 38 | 1.967 | 08 | 20 | 46 | 75 | 93 | 99 | | | | | | |
| 39 | 1.966 | 08 | 21 | 47 | 76 | 94 | 99 | | | | | | |

Table 8.3.18 *(continued)*

| n | $F_c$ | .05 | .10 | .15 | .20 | .25 | .30 | .35 | .40 | .50 | .60 | .70 | .80 |
|---|---|---|---|---|---|---|---|---|---|---|---|---|---|
| | | | | | | | | | | f | | | |
| 40 | 1.965 | 08 | 21 | 48 | 77 | 94 | 99 | * | * | * | * | * | * |
| 42 | 1.964 | 08 | 22 | 50 | 80 | 95 | 99 | | | | | | |
| 44 | 1.963 | 08 | 23 | 53 | 82 | 96 | * | | | | | | |
| 46 | 1.962 | 09 | 25 | 55 | 84 | 97 | | | | | | | |
| 48 | 1.961 | 09 | 26 | 57 | 86 | 98 | | | | | | | |
| 50 | 1.960 | 09 | 27 | 59 | 87 | 98 | | | | | | | |
| 52 | 1.959 | 09 | 28 | 61 | 89 | 99 | | | | | | | |
| 54 | 1.958 | 09 | 29 | 63 | 90 | 99 | | | | | | | |
| 56 | 1.957 | 09 | 30 | 65 | 91 | 99 | | | | | | | |
| 58 | 1.957 | 10 | 31 | 67 | 92 | 99 | | | | | | | |
| 60 | 1.956 | 10 | 32 | 69 | 93 | 99 | | | | | | | |
| 64 | 1.955 | 10 | 34 | 72 | 95 | * | | | | | | | |
| 68 | 1.954 | 11 | 37 | 75 | 96 | | | | | | | | |
| 72 | 1.953 | 11 | 39 | 78 | 97 | | | | | | | | |
| 76 | 1.952 | 12 | 41 | 81 | 98 | | | | | | | | |
| 80 | 1.952 | 12 | 43 | 83 | 98 | | | | | | | | |
| 84 | 1.951 | 12 | 45 | 85 | 99 | | | | | | | | |
| 88 | 1.950 | 13 | 48 | 87 | 99 | | | | | | | | |
| 92 | 1.950 | 13 | 50 | 89 | 99 | | | | | | | | |
| 96 | 1.949 | 14 | 52 | 90 | * | | | | | | | | |
| 100 | 1.949 | 14 | 54 | 92 | | | | | | | | | |
| 120 | 1.947 | 17 | 63 | 96 | | | | | | | | | |
| 140 | 1.946 | 19 | 71 | 98 | | | | | | | | | |
| 160 | 1.945 | 22 | 78 | 99 | | | | | | | | | |
| 180 | 1.944 | 24 | 83 | * | | | | | | | | | |
| 200 | 1.944 | 27 | 88 | | | | | | | | | | |
| 250 | 1.943 | 34 | 95 | | | | | | | | | | |
| 300 | 1.942 | 41 | 98 | | | | | | | | | | |
| 350 | 1.941 | 48 | 99 | | | | | | | | | | |
| 400 | 1.941 | 54 | * | | | | | | | | | | |
| 450 | 1.941 | 60 | | | | | | | | | | | |
| 500 | 1.940 | 66 | | | | | | | | | | | |
| 600 | 1.940 | 75 | | | | | | | | | | | |
| 700 | 1.940 | 82 | | | | | | | | | | | |
| 800 | 1.940 | 88 | | | | | | | | | | | |
| 900 | 1.940 | 92 | | | | | | | | | | | |
| 1000 | 1.939 | 95 | | | | | | | | | | | |

* Power values below this point are greater than .995.

Table 8.3.19

Power of F test at a = .05, u = 10

| n | $F_c$ | .05 | .10 | .15 | .20 | .25 | .30 | .35 | .40 | .50 | .60 | .70 | .80 |
|---|---|---|---|---|---|---|---|---|---|---|---|---|---|
| 2 | 2.854 | 05 | 05 | 06 | 07 | 08 | 09 | 10 | 12 | 16 | 23 | 30 | 39 |
| 3 | 2.258 | 05 | 06 | 07 | 09 | 11 | 13 | 17 | 21 | 32 | 46 | 62 | 76 |
| 4 | 2.133 | 05 | 06 | 07 | 10 | 13 | 17 | 23 | 30 | 47 | 65 | 81 | 92 |
| 5 | 2.053 | 05 | 06 | 08 | 11 | 16 | 22 | 30 | 40 | 61 | 80 | 92 | 98 |
| 6 | 2.008 | 05 | 07 | 09 | 13 | 19 | 28 | 38 | 50 | 73 | 90 | 97 | * |
| 7 | 1.978 | 05 | 07 | 10 | 15 | 23 | 33 | 45 | 59 | 82 | 95 | 99 | |
| 8 | 1.956 | 06 | 07 | 11 | 17 | 27 | 39 | 53 | 67 | 88 | 98 | * | |
| 9 | 1.940 | 06 | 08 | 12 | 20 | 31 | 44 | 60 | 74 | 93 | 99 | | |
| 10 | 1.928 | 06 | 08 | 13 | 22 | 34 | 50 | 66 | 80 | 96 | * | | |
| 11 | 1.913 | 06 | 09 | 14 | 24 | 38 | 55 | 71 | 84 | 97 | | | |
| 12 | 1.910 | 06 | 09 | 15 | 27 | 42 | 60 | 76 | 88 | 98 | | | |
| 13 | 1.903 | 06 | 09 | 17 | 29 | 46 | 65 | 81 | 91 | 99 | | | |
| 14 | 1.898 | 06 | 10 | 18 | 32 | 50 | 69 | 84 | 94 | * | | | |
| 15 | 1.893 | 06 | 10 | 19 | 34 | 53 | 73 | 87 | 95 | | | | |
| 16 | 1.889 | 06 | 11 | 20 | 37 | 57 | 76 | 90 | 97 | | | | |
| 17 | 1.885 | 06 | 11 | 22 | 39 | 60 | 79 | 92 | 98 | | | | |
| 18 | 1.882 | 06 | 12 | 23 | 42 | 64 | 82 | 94 | 98 | | | | |
| 19 | 1.879 | 06 | 12 | 24 | 44 | 67 | 85 | 95 | 99 | | | | |
| 20 | 1.877 | 07 | 12 | 26 | 47 | 69 | 87 | 96 | 99 | | | | |
| 21 | 1.874 | 07 | 13 | 27 | 49 | 72 | 89 | 97 | 99 | | | | |
| 22 | 1.872 | 07 | 13 | 29 | 51 | 75 | 91 | 98 | * | | | | |
| 23 | 1.870 | 07 | 14 | 30 | 54 | 77 | 92 | 98 | | | | | |
| 24 | 1.869 | 07 | 14 | 31 | 56 | 79 | 93 | 99 | | | | | |
| 25 | 1.867 | 07 | 15 | 33 | 58 | 81 | 94 | 99 | | | | | |
| 26 | 1.866 | 07 | 15 | 34 | 60 | 83 | 95 | 99 | | | | | |
| 27 | 1.864 | 07 | 16 | 36 | 62 | 85 | 96 | 99 | | | | | |
| 28 | 1.863 | 07 | 17 | 37 | 64 | 86 | 97 | * | | | | | |
| 29 | 1.862 | 07 | 17 | 38 | 66 | 88 | 97 | | | | | | |
| 30 | 1.861 | 07 | 18 | 40 | 68 | 89 | 98 | | | | | | |
| 31 | 1.860 | 08 | 18 | 41 | 70 | 90 | 98 | | | | | | |
| 32 | 1.859 | 08 | 19 | 43 | 72 | 91 | 99 | | | | | | |
| 33 | 1.858 | 08 | 19 | 44 | 73 | 92 | 99 | | | | | | |
| 34 | 1.857 | 08 | 20 | 45 | 75 | 93 | 99 | | | | | | |
| 35 | 1.856 | 08 | 21 | 47 | 76 | 94 | 99 | | | | | | |
| 36 | 1.856 | 08 | 21 | 48 | 78 | 95 | 99 | | | | | | |
| 37 | 1.855 | 08 | 22 | 49 | 79 | 95 | 99 | | | | | | |
| 38 | 1.854 | 08 | 22 | 51 | 81 | 96 | * | | | | | | |
| 39 | 1.854 | 08 | 23 | 52 | 82 | 96 | | | | | | | |

**Table 8.3.19** *(continued)*

| n | $F_c$ | .05 | .10 | .15 | .20 | .25 | .30 | .35 | .40 | .50 | .60 | .70 | .80 |
|---|---|---|---|---|---|---|---|---|---|---|---|---|---|
| | | | | | | | | | | $f$ | | | |
| 40 | 1.853 | 08 | 23 | 53 | 83 | 97 | * | * | * | * | * | * | * |
| 42 | 1.852 | 09 | 25 | 56 | 85 | 98 | | | | | | | |
| 44 | 1.851 | 09 | 26 | 58 | 87 | 98 | | | | | | | |
| 46 | 1.850 | 09 | 27 | 61 | 89 | 99 | | | | | | | |
| 48 | 1.849 | 09 | 28 | 63 | 90 | 99 | | | | | | | |
| 50 | 1.848 | 09 | 30 | 65 | 92 | 99 | | | | | | | |
| 52 | 1.848 | 10 | 31 | 67 | 93 | 99 | | | | | | | |
| 54 | 1.847 | 10 | 32 | 69 | 94 | * | | | | | | | |
| 56 | 1.846 | 10 | 33 | 71 | 95 | | | | | | | | |
| 58 | 1.846 | 10 | 35 | 73 | 96 | | | | | | | | |
| 60 | 1.845 | 10 | 36 | 75 | 96 | | | | | | | | |
| 64 | 1.845 | 11 | 38 | 78 | 97 | | | | | | | | |
| 68 | 1.844 | 11 | 41 | 81 | 98 | | | | | | | | |
| 72 | 1.843 | 12 | 43 | 84 | 99 | | | | | | | | |
| 76 | 1.842 | 12 | 46 | 86 | 99 | | | | | | | | |
| 80 | 1.842 | 13 | 48 | 88 | 99 | | | | | | | | |
| 84 | 1.841 | 13 | 51 | 90 | * | | | | | | | | |
| 88 | 1.841 | 14 | 53 | 92 | | | | | | | | | |
| 92 | 1.840 | 14 | 55 | 93 | | | | | | | | | |
| 96 | 1.840 | 15 | 57 | 94 | | | | | | | | | |
| 100 | 1.839 | 15 | 60 | 95 | | | | | | | | | |
| 120 | 1.838 | 18 | 69 | 98 | | | | | | | | | |
| 140 | 1.837 | 21 | 77 | 99 | | | | | | | | | |
| 160 | 1.836 | 24 | 84 | * | | | | | | | | | |
| 180 | 1.836 | 27 | 88 | | | | | | | | | | |
| 200 | 1.835 | 30 | 92 | | | | | | | | | | |
| 250 | 1.834 | 38 | 97 | | | | | | | | | | |
| 300 | 1.834 | 46 | 99 | | | | | | | | | | |
| 350 | 1.833 | 53 | * | | | | | | | | | | |
| 400 | 1.833 | 60 | | | | | | | | | | | |
| 450 | 1.833 | 66 | | | | | | | | | | | |
| 500 | 1.832 | 72 | | | | | | | | | | | |
| 600 | 1.832 | 81 | | | | | | | | | | | |
| 700 | 1.832 | 88 | | | | | | | | | | | |
| 800 | 1.832 | 92 | | | | | | | | | | | |
| 900 | 1.832 | 95 | | | | | | | | | | | |
| 1000 | 1.832 | 97 | | | | | | | | | | | |

* Power values below this point are greater than .995.

Table 8.3.20

Power of F test at a = .05, u = 12

| n | $F_c$ | .05 | .10 | .15 | .20 | .25 | .30 | .35 | .40 | .50 | .60 | .70 | .80 |
|---|-------|-----|-----|-----|-----|-----|-----|-----|-----|-----|-----|-----|-----|
| | | | | | | | f | | | | | | |
| 2 | 2.604 | 05 | 05 | 06 | 07 | 08 | 09 | 11 | 13 | 18 | 25 | 34 | 44 |
| 3 | 2.148 | 05 | 06 | 07 | 08 | 10 | 13 | 17 | 22 | 34 | 50 | 66 | 80 |
| 4 | 2.010 | 05 | 06 | 08 | 10 | 14 | 18 | 25 | 33 | 52 | 71 | 86 | 95 |
| 5 | 1.944 | 05 | 06 | 09 | 12 | 17 | 24 | 33 | 44 | 67 | 85 | 95 | 99 |
| 6 | 1.905 | 05 | 07 | 10 | 14 | 21 | 30 | 42 | 54 | 78 | 93 | 99 | * |
| 7 | 1.879 | 06 | 07 | 11 | 16 | 25 | 36 | 50 | 64 | 87 | 97 | * | |
| 8 | 1.860 | 06 | 08 | 12 | 19 | 29 | 43 | 58 | 72 | 92 | 99 | | |
| 9 | 1.847 | 06 | 08 | 13 | 21 | 33 | 49 | 65 | 79 | 95 | * | | |
| 10 | 1.836 | 06 | 08 | 14 | 24 | 38 | 55 | 71 | 85 | 98 | | | |
| 11 | 1.827 | 06 | 09 | 15 | 26 | 42 | 60 | 77 | 89 | 99 | | | |
| 12 | 1.821 | 06 | 09 | 17 | 29 | 46 | 65 | 81 | 92 | 99 | | | |
| 13 | 1.815 | 06 | 10 | 18 | 32 | 51 | 70 | 85 | 94 | * | | | |
| 14 | 1.810 | 06 | 10 | 19 | 35 | 55 | 74 | 88 | 96 | | | | |
| 15 | 1.806 | 06 | 11 | 21 | 37 | 58 | 78 | 91 | 97 | | | | |
| 16 | 1.802 | 06 | 11 | 22 | 40 | 62 | 81 | 93 | 98 | | | | |
| 17 | 1.799 | 06 | 12 | 24 | 43 | 66 | 84 | 95 | 99 | | | | |
| 18 | 1.796 | 07 | 12 | 25 | 46 | 69 | 87 | 96 | 99 | | | | |
| 19 | 1.794 | 07 | 13 | 27 | 48 | 72 | 89 | 97 | 99 | | | | |
| 20 | 1.792 | 07 | 13 | 28 | 51 | 75 | 91 | 98 | * | | | | |
| 21 | 1.790 | 07 | 14 | 30 | 54 | 77 | 92 | 98 | | | | | |
| 22 | 1.788 | 07 | 14 | 31 | 56 | 80 | 94 | 99 | | | | | |
| 23 | 1.786 | 07 | 15 | 33 | 59 | 82 | 95 | 99 | | | | | |
| 24 | 1.785 | 07 | 15 | 34 | 61 | 84 | 96 | 99 | | | | | |
| 25 | 1.784 | 07 | 16 | 36 | 63 | 86 | 97 | * | | | | | |
| 26 | 1.782 | 07 | 17 | 37 | 65 | 88 | 97 | | | | | | |
| 27 | 1.781 | 07 | 17 | 39 | 68 | 89 | 98 | | | | | | |
| 28 | 1.780 | 07 | 18 | 41 | 70 | 90 | 98 | | | | | | |
| 29 | 1.779 | 08 | 18 | 42 | 72 | 92 | 99 | | | | | | |
| 30 | 1.778 | 08 | 19 | 44 | 73 | 93 | 99 | | | | | | |
| 31 | 1.777 | 08 | 20 | 45 | 75 | 94 | 99 | | | | | | |
| 32 | 1.776 | 08 | 20 | 47 | 77 | 94 | 99 | | | | | | |
| 33 | 1.776 | 08 | 21 | 48 | 78 | 95 | 99 | | | | | | |
| 34 | 1.775 | 08 | 22 | 50 | 80 | 96 | * | | | | | | |
| 35 | 1.774 | 08 | 22 | 51 | 81 | 96 | | | | | | | |
| 36 | 1.774 | 08 | 23 | 53 | 83 | 97 | | | | | | | |
| 37 | 1.773 | 08 | 24 | 54 | 84 | 97 | | | | | | | |
| 38 | 1.773 | 08 | 24 | 55 | 85 | 98 | | | | | | | |
| 39 | 1.772 | 09 | 25 | 57 | 86 | 98 | | | | | | | |

Table 8.3.20 *(continued)*

| | | | | | | | | | | | | | | f |
|---|---|---|---|---|---|---|---|---|---|---|---|---|---|---|
| n | $F_c$ | .05 | .10 | .15 | .20 | .25 | .30 | .35 | .40 | .50 | .60 | .70 | .80 | |
| 40 | 1.771 | 09 | 26 | 58 | 87 | 98 | * | * | * | * | * | * | * | |
| 42 | 1.771 | 09 | 27 | 61 | 89 | 99 | | | | | | | | |
| 44 | 1.770 | 09 | 28 | 63 | 91 | 99 | | | | | | | | |
| 46 | 1.769 | 09 | 30 | 66 | 92 | 99 | | | | | | | | |
| 48 | 1.768 | 10 | 31 | 68 | 94 | * | | | | | | | | |
| 50 | 1.768 | 10 | 32 | 71 | 95 | | | | | | | | | |
| 52 | 1.767 | 10 | 34 | 73 | 96 | | | | | | | | | |
| 54 | 1.766 | 10 | 35 | 75 | 96 | | | | | | | | | |
| 56 | 1.766 | 11 | 36 | 77 | 97 | | | | | | | | | |
| 58 | 1.766 | 11 | 38 | 78 | 97 | | | | | | | | | |
| 60 | 1.765 | 11 | 39 | 80 | 98 | | | | | | | | | |
| 64 | 1.764 | 11 | 42 | 83 | 99 | | | | | | | | | |
| 68 | 1.763 | 12 | 45 | 86 | 99 | | | | | | | | | |
| 72 | 1.763 | 12 | 47 | 88 | 99 | | | | | | | | | |
| 76 | 1.762 | 13 | 50 | 90 | * | | | | | | | | | |
| 80 | 1.762 | 14 | 53 | 92 | | | | | | | | | | |
| 84 | 1.761 | 14 | 55 | 93 | | | | | | | | | | |
| 88 | 1.761 | 15 | 58 | 95 | | | | | | | | | | |
| 92 | 1.760 | 15 | 60 | 96 | | | | | | | | | | |
| 96 | 1.760 | 16 | 62 | 96 | | | | | | | | | | |
| 100 | 1.760 | 16 | 65 | 97 | | | | | | | | | | |
| 120 | 1.759 | 19 | 74 | 99 | | | | | | | | | | |
| 140 | 1.758 | 23 | 82 | * | | | | | | | | | | |
| 160 | 1.757 | 26 | 88 | | | | | | | | | | | |
| 180 | 1.756 | 29 | 92 | | | | | | | | | | | |
| 200 | 1.756 | 33 | 95 | | | | | | | | | | | |
| 250 | 1.755 | 41 | 98 | | | | | | | | | | | |
| 300 | 1.755 | 50 | * | | | | | | | | | | | |
| 350 | 1.754 | 58 | | | | | | | | | | | | |
| 400 | 1.754 | 65 | | | | | | | | | | | | |
| 450 | 1.754 | 71 | | | | | | | | | | | | |
| 500 | 1.754 | 77 | | | | | | | | | | | | |
| 600 | 1.753 | 86 | | | | | | | | | | | | |
| 700 | 1.753 | 91 | | | | | | | | | | | | |
| 800 | 1.753 | 95 | | | | | | | | | | | | |
| 900 | 1.753 | 97 | | | | | | | | | | | | |
| 1000 | 1.753 | 98 | | | | | | | | | | | | |

* Power values below this point are greater than .995.

Table 8.3.21

Power of F test at a = .05, u = 15

| n | $F_c$ | .05 | .10 | .15 | .20 | .25 | .30 | .35 | .40 | .50 | .60 | .70 | .80 |
|---|-------|-----|-----|-----|-----|-----|-----|-----|-----|-----|-----|-----|-----|
| 2 | 2.352 | 05 | 05 | 06 | 07 | 08 | 10 | 12 | 14 | 20 | 28 | 39 | 51 |
| 3 | 1.992 | 05 | 06 | 07 | 09 | 11 | 15 | 19 | 25 | 39 | 57 | 74 | 87 |
| 4 | 1.880 | 05 | 06 | 08 | 11 | 15 | 20 | 28 | 37 | 58 | 78 | 92 | 98 |
| 5 | 1.826 | 05 | 07 | 09 | 13 | 19 | 27 | 38 | 50 | 74 | 91 | 98 | * |
| 6 | 1.794 | 05 | 07 | 10 | 15 | 23 | 34 | 47 | 61 | 85 | 96 | * | |
| 7 | 1.772 | 06 | 07 | 11 | 18 | 28 | 41 | 56 | 71 | 92 | 99 | | |
| 8 | 1.757 | 06 | 08 | 12 | 21 | 33 | 48 | 65 | 79 | 96 | * | | |
| 9 | 1.745 | 06 | 08 | 14 | 24 | 38 | 55 | 72 | 85 | 98 | | | |
| 10 | 1.736 | 06 | 09 | 15 | 27 | 43 | 61 | 78 | 90 | 99 | | | |
| 11 | 1.729 | 06 | 09 | 17 | 30 | 47 | 67 | 83 | 93 | * | | | |
| 12 | 1.724 | 06 | 10 | 18 | 33 | 52 | 72 | 87 | 96 | | | | |
| 13 | 1.719 | 06 | 10 | 20 | 36 | 57 | 77 | 90 | 97 | | | | |
| 14 | 1.715 | 06 | 11 | 21 | 39 | 61 | 81 | 93 | 98 | | | | |
| 15 | 1.711 | 06 | 11 | 23 | 42 | 65 | 84 | 95 | 99 | | | | |
| 16 | 1.708 | 06 | 12 | 25 | 45 | 69 | 87 | 96 | 99 | | | | |
| 17 | 1.706 | 07 | 12 | 26 | 48 | 72 | 90 | 97 | * | | | | |
| 18 | 1.704 | 07 | 13 | 28 | 51 | 76 | 92 | 98 | | | | | |
| 19 | 1.702 | 07 | 14 | 30 | 54 | 78 | 93 | 99 | | | | | |
| 20 | 1.700 | 07 | 14 | 31 | 57 | 81 | 95 | 99 | | | | | |
| 21 | 1.698 | 07 | 15 | 33 | 60 | 84 | 96 | 99 | | | | | |
| 22 | 1.696 | 07 | 16 | 35 | 63 | 86 | 97 | * | | | | | |
| 23 | 1.695 | 07 | 16 | 37 | 65 | 88 | 97 | | | | | | |
| 24 | 1.694 | 07 | 17 | 39 | 68 | 89 | 98 | | | | | | |
| 25 | 1.693 | 07 | 17 | 40 | 70 | 91 | 98 | | | | | | |
| 26 | 1.692 | 07 | 18 | 42 | 72 | 92 | 99 | | | | | | |
| 27 | 1.691 | 08 | 19 | 44 | 74 | 93 | 99 | | | | | | |
| 28 | 1.690 | 08 | 20 | 46 | 76 | 94 | 99 | | | | | | |
| 29 | 1.689 | 08 | 20 | 47 | 78 | 95 | * | | | | | | |
| 30 | 1.688 | 08 | 21 | 49 | 80 | 96 | | | | | | | |
| 31 | 1.687 | 08 | 22 | 51 | 82 | 97 | | | | | | | |
| 32 | 1.687 | 08 | 22 | 52 | 83 | 97 | | | | | | | |
| 33 | 1.686 | 08 | 23 | 54 | 84 | 98 | | | | | | | |
| 34 | 1.686 | 08 | 24 | 56 | 86 | 98 | | | | | | | |
| 35 | 1.685 | 09 | 25 | 57 | 87 | 98 | | | | | | | |
| 36 | 1.684 | 09 | 25 | 59 | 88 | 99 | | | | | | | |
| 37 | 1.684 | 09 | 26 | 60 | 89 | 99 | | | | | | | |
| 38 | 1.683 | 09 | 27 | 62 | 90 | 99 | | | | | | | |
| 39 | 1.683 | 09 | 28 | 63 | 91 | 99 | | | | | | | |

Table 8.3.21 (continued)

| n | $F_c$ | .05 | .10 | .15 | .20 | .25 | .30 | .35 | .40 | .50 | .60 | .70 | .80 |
|---|---|---|---|---|---|---|---|---|---|---|---|---|---|
| 40 | 1.683 | 09 | 28 | 65 | 92 | 99 | * | * | * | * | * | * | * |
| 42 | 1.682 | 09 | 30 | 68 | 93 | * | | | | | | | |
| 44 | 1.681 | 10 | 32 | 70 | 95 | | | | | | | | |
| 46 | 1.680 | 10 | 33 | 73 | 96 | | | | | | | | |
| 48 | 1.680 | 10 | 35 | 75 | 97 | | | | | | | | |
| 50 | 1.679 | 10 | 36 | 77 | 97 | | | | | | | | |
| 52 | 1.679 | 11 | 38 | 79 | 98 | | | | | | | | |
| 54 | 1.678 | 11 | 39 | 81 | 98 | | | | | | | | |
| 56 | 1.678 | 11 | 41 | 83 | 99 | | | | | | | | |
| 58 | 1.677 | 11 | 43 | 84 | 99 | | | | | | | | |
| 60 | 1.677 | 12 | 44 | 86 | 99 | | | | | | | | |
| 64 | 1.676 | 12 | 47 | 89 | 99 | | | | | | | | |
| 68 | 1.676 | 13 | 50 | 91 | * | | | | | | | | |
| 72 | 1.675 | 13 | 53 | 93 | | | | | | | | | |
| 76 | 1.675 | 14 | 56 | 94 | | | | | | | | | |
| 80 | 1.674 | 15 | 59 | 95 | | | | | | | | | |
| 84 | 1.674 | 15 | 62 | 96 | | | | | | | | | |
| 88 | 1.674 | 16 | 64 | 97 | | | | | | | | | |
| 92 | 1.673 | 17 | 67 | 98 | | | | | | | | | |
| 96 | 1.673 | 17 | 69 | 98 | | | | | | | | | |
| 100 | 1.673 | 18 | 71 | 99 | | | | | | | | | |
| 120 | 1.672 | 21 | 81 | * | | | | | | | | | |
| 140 | 1.671 | 25 | 88 | | | | | | | | | | |
| 160 | 1.670 | 29 | 92 | | | | | | | | | | |
| 180 | 1.670 | 33 | 96 | | | | | | | | | | |
| 200 | 1.670 | 37 | 97 | | | | | | | | | | |
| 250 | 1.669 | 47 | 99 | | | | | | | | | | |
| 300 | 1.669 | 56 | * | | | | | | | | | | |
| 350 | 1.668 | 64 | | | | | | | | | | | |
| 400 | 1.668 | 72 | | | | | | | | | | | |
| 450 | 1.668 | 78 | | | | | | | | | | | |
| 500 | 1.668 | 83 | | | | | | | | | | | |
| 600 | 1.667 | 91 | | | | | | | | | | | |
| 700 | 1.667 | 95 | | | | | | | | | | | |
| 800 | 1.667 | 97 | | | | | | | | | | | |
| 900 | 1.667 | 99 | | | | | | | | | | | |
| 1000 | 1.667 | 99 | | | | | | | | | | | |

* Power values below this point are greater than .995.

Table 8.3.22

Power of F test at a = .05, u = 24

| | | | | | | | $f$ | | | | | | |
|---|---|---|---|---|---|---|---|---|---|---|---|---|---|
| n | $F_c$ | .05 | .10 | .15 | .20 | .25 | .30 | .35 | .40 | .50 | .60 | .70 | .80 |
| 2 | 1.964 | 05 | 06 | 06 | 08 | 09 | 11 | 14 | 17 | 26 | 39 | 53 | 69 |
| 3 | 1.737 | 05 | 06 | 07 | 10 | 13 | 18 | 24 | 32 | 52 | 73 | 88 | 96 |
| 4 | 1.663 | 05 | 07 | 09 | 12 | 18 | 26 | 37 | 49 | 74 | 91 | 98 | * |
| 5 | 1.627 | 05 | 07 | 10 | 15 | 24 | 35 | 49 | 64 | 88 | 98 | * | |
| 6 | 1.605 | 06 | 08 | 12 | 19 | 30 | 45 | 61 | 76 | 95 | * | | |
| 7 | 1.590 | 06 | 08 | 13 | 22 | 36 | 54 | 71 | 85 | 98 | | | |
| 8 | 1.580 | 06 | 09 | 15 | 26 | 43 | 62 | 79 | 91 | 99 | | | |
| 9 | 1.572 | 06 | 09 | 17 | 30 | 49 | 69 | 86 | 95 | * | | | |
| 10 | 1.566 | 06 | 10 | 19 | 34 | 55 | 76 | 90 | 97 | | | | |
| 11 | 1.561 | 06 | 11 | 21 | 38 | 61 | 81 | 94 | 99 | | | | |
| 12 | 1.557 | 06 | 11 | 23 | 42 | 66 | 86 | 96 | 99 | | | | |
| 13 | 1.554 | 06 | 12 | 25 | 47 | 71 | 89 | 98 | * | | | | |
| 14 | 1.551 | 07 | 13 | 27 | 51 | 76 | 92 | 98 | | | | | |
| 15 | 1.549 | 07 | 13 | 29 | 54 | 80 | 94 | 99 | | | | | |
| 16 | 1.546 | 07 | 14 | 32 | 58 | 83 | 96 | 99 | | | | | |
| 17 | 1.545 | 07 | 15 | 34 | 62 | 86 | 97 | * | | | | | |
| 18 | 1.543 | 07 | 16 | 36 | 65 | 89 | 98 | | | | | | |
| 19 | 1.542 | 07 | 16 | 38 | 69 | 91 | 99 | | | | | | |
| 20 | 1.540 | 07 | 17 | 41 | 72 | 92 | 99 | | | | | | |
| 21 | 1.539 | 07 | 18 | 43 | 75 | 94 | 99 | | | | | | |
| 22 | 1.538 | 08 | 19 | 45 | 77 | 95 | * | | | | | | |
| 23 | 1.537 | 08 | 20 | 48 | 80 | 96 | | | | | | | |
| 24 | 1.536 | 08 | 21 | 50 | 82 | 97 | | | | | | | |
| 25 | 1.536 | 08 | 22 | 52 | 84 | 98 | | | | | | | |
| 26 | 1.535 | 08 | 23 | 54 | 86 | 98 | | | | | | | |
| 27 | 1.534 | 08 | 24 | 57 | 87 | 99 | | | | | | | |
| 28 | 1.533 | 08 | 25 | 59 | 89 | 99 | | | | | | | |
| 29 | 1.533 | 09 | 25 | 61 | 90 | 99 | | | | | | | |
| 30 | 1.532 | 09 | 26 | 63 | 92 | 99 | | | | | | | |
| 31 | 1.532 | 09 | 27 | 65 | 93 | * | | | | | | | |
| 32 | 1.531 | 09 | 28 | 66 | 94 | | | | | | | | |
| 33 | 1.531 | 09 | 29 | 68 | 94 | | | | | | | | |
| 34 | 1.531 | 09 | 30 | 70 | 95 | | | | | | | | |
| 35 | 1.530 | 09 | 31 | 72 | 96 | | | | | | | | |
| 36 | 1.530 | 10 | 32 | 73 | 96 | | | | | | | | |
| 37 | 1.529 | 10 | 34 | 75 | 97 | | | | | | | | |
| 38 | 1.529 | 10 | 35 | 76 | 97 | | | | | | | | |
| 39 | 1.529 | 10 | 36 | 78 | 98 | | | | | | | | |

Table 8.3.22 (continued)

| | | | | | | | f | | | | | | |
|---|---|---|---|---|---|---|---|---|---|---|---|---|---|
| n | $F_c$ | .05 | .10 | .15 | .20 | .25 | .30 | .35 | .40 | .50 | .60 | .70 | .80 |
| 40 | 1.529 | 10 | 37 | 79 | 98 | * | * | * | * | * | * | * | * |
| 42 | 1.528 | 11 | 39 | 82 | 99 | | | | | | | | |
| 44 | 1.528 | 11 | 41 | 84 | 99 | | | | | | | | |
| 46 | 1.527 | 11 | 43 | 86 | 99 | | | | | | | | |
| 48 | 1.527 | 12 | 45 | 88 | * | | | | | | | | |
| 50 | 1.526 | 12 | 47 | 90 | | | | | | | | | |
| 52 | 1.526 | 12 | 49 | 91 | | | | | | | | | |
| 54 | 1.526 | 13 | 51 | 92 | | | | | | | | | |
| 56 | 1.525 | 13 | 53 | 93 | | | | | | | | | |
| 58 | 1.525 | 13 | 55 | 94 | | | | | | | | | |
| 60 | 1.525 | 14 | 57 | 95 | | | | | | | | | |
| 64 | 1.524 | 14 | 60 | 97 | | | | | | | | | |
| 68 | 1.524 | 15 | 64 | 98 | | | | | | | | | |
| 72 | 1.523 | 16 | 67 | 98 | | | | | | | | | |
| 76 | 1.523 | 17 | 70 | 99 | | | | | | | | | |
| 80 | 1.523 | 18 | 73 | 99 | | | | | | | | | |
| 84 | 1.523 | 18 | 76 | 99 | | | | | | | | | |
| 88 | 1.522 | 19 | 79 | * | | | | | | | | | |
| 92 | 1.522 | 20 | 81 | | | | | | | | | | |
| 96 | 1.522 | 21 | 83 | | | | | | | | | | |
| 100 | 1.522 | 22 | 85 | | | | | | | | | | |
| 120 | 1.521 | 26 | 92 | | | | | | | | | | |
| 140 | 1.520 | 31 | 96 | | | | | | | | | | |
| 160 | 1.520 | 36 | 98 | | | | | | | | | | |
| 180 | 1.520 | 41 | 99 | | | | | | | | | | |
| 200 | 1.519 | 47 | * | | | | | | | | | | |
| 250 | 1.519 | 59 | | | | | | | | | | | |
| 300 | 1.519 | 70 | | | | | | | | | | | |
| 350 | 1.519 | 78 | | | | | | | | | | | |
| 400 | 1.518 | 85 | | | | | | | | | | | |
| 450 | 1.518 | 90 | | | | | | | | | | | |
| 500 | 1.518 | 94 | | | | | | | | | | | |
| 600 | 1.518 | 98 | | | | | | | | | | | |
| 700 | 1.518 | 99 | | | | | | | | | | | |
| 800 | 1.518 | * | | | | | | | | | | | |
| 900 | 1.518 | | | | | | | | | | | | |
| 1000 | 1.518 | | | | | | | | | | | | |

* Power values below this point are greater than .995.

Table 8.3.23

Power of F test at a = .10, u = 1

| n | $F_c$ | .05 | .10 | .15 | .20 | .25 | .30 | .35 | .40 | .50 | .60 | .70 | .80 |
|---|---|---|---|---|---|---|---|---|---|---|---|---|---|
| 2 | 8.526 | 10 | 11 | 12 | 13 | 13 | 14 | 15 | 17 | 20 | 23 | 27 | 30 |
| 3 | 4.545 | 10 | 11 | 12 | 13 | 15 | 17 | 19 | 22 | 28 | 35 | 42 | 50 |
| 4 | 3.776 | 10 | 11 | 13 | 14 | 17 | 20 | 23 | 27 | 36 | 45 | 55 | 64 |
| 5 | 3.458 | 10 | 11 | 13 | 16 | 19 | 23 | 27 | 32 | 43 | 55 | 66 | 76 |
| 6 | 3.285 | 10 | 12 | 14 | 17 | 21 | 26 | 31 | 37 | 50 | 63 | 74 | 83 |
| 7 | 3.177 | 10 | 12 | 15 | 19 | 23 | 29 | 35 | 42 | 56 | 69 | 80 | 89 |
| 8 | 3.102 | 10 | 12 | 15 | 20 | 25 | 32 | 39 | 47 | 62 | 75 | 85 | 92 |
| 9 | 3.048 | 10 | 13 | 16 | 21 | 28 | 35 | 43 | 51 | 66 | 80 | 89 | 95 |
| 10 | 3.007 | 10 | 13 | 17 | 23 | 30 | 37 | 46 | 55 | 71 | 83 | 92 | 97 |
| 11 | 2.975 | 11 | 13 | 18 | 24 | 32 | 40 | 49 | 58 | 75 | 87 | 94 | 98 |
| 12 | 2.949 | 11 | 14 | 19 | 25 | 34 | 43 | 52 | 62 | 78 | 89 | 96 | 99 |
| 13 | 2.927 | 11 | 14 | 19 | 27 | 36 | 45 | 55 | 65 | 81 | 91 | 97 | 99 |
| 14 | 2.909 | 11 | 14 | 20 | 28 | 37 | 48 | 58 | 68 | 83 | 93 | 98 | 99 |
| 15 | 2.894 | 11 | 15 | 21 | 29 | 39 | 50 | 60 | 70 | 86 | 95 | 98 | * |
| 16 | 2.881 | 11 | 15 | 22 | 31 | 41 | 52 | 63 | 73 | 88 | 96 | 99 | |
| 17 | 2.869 | 11 | 15 | 23 | 32 | 43 | 54 | 65 | 75 | 89 | 97 | 99 | |
| 18 | 2.859 | 11 | 16 | 23 | 33 | 45 | 56 | 68 | 77 | 91 | 97 | 99 | |
| 19 | 2.850 | 11 | 16 | 24 | 34 | 46 | 58 | 70 | 79 | 92 | 98 | * | |
| 20 | 2.843 | 11 | 16 | 25 | 36 | 48 | 60 | 72 | 81 | 93 | 98 | | |
| 21 | 2.836 | 11 | 17 | 26 | 37 | 50 | 62 | 73 | 83 | 94 | 99 | | |
| 22 | 2.829 | 11 | 17 | 26 | 38 | 51 | 64 | 75 | 84 | 95 | 99 | | |
| 23 | 2.823 | 11 | 18 | 27 | 39 | 53 | 66 | 77 | 86 | 96 | 99 | | |
| 24 | 2.818 | 12 | 18 | 28 | 40 | 54 | 67 | 78 | 87 | 96 | 99 | | |
| 25 | 2.813 | 12 | 18 | 29 | 42 | 56 | 69 | 80 | 86 | 97 | 99 | | |
| 26 | 2.809 | 12 | 19 | 29 | 43 | 57 | 70 | 81 | 89 | 97 | * | | |
| 27 | 2.805 | 12 | 19 | 30 | 44 | 58 | 72 | 83 | 90 | 98 | | | |
| 28 | 2.801 | 12 | 19 | 31 | 45 | 60 | 73 | 84 | 91 | 98 | | | |
| 29 | 2.797 | 12 | 20 | 32 | 46 | 61 | 74 | 85 | 92 | 98 | | | |
| 30 | 2.794 | 12 | 20 | 32 | 47 | 62 | 76 | 86 | 93 | 99 | | | |
| 31 | 2.791 | 12 | 20 | 33 | 48 | 63 | 77 | 87 | 93 | 99 | | | |
| 32 | 2.788 | 12 | 21 | 34 | 49 | 65 | 78 | 88 | 94 | 99 | | | |
| 33 | 2.786 | 12 | 21 | 34 | 50 | 66 | 79 | 89 | 95 | 99 | | | |
| 34 | 2.783 | 12 | 21 | 35 | 51 | 67 | 80 | 90 | 95 | 99 | | | |
| 35 | 2.781 | 13 | 22 | 36 | 52 | 68 | 81 | 90 | 96 | 99 | | | |
| 36 | 2.779 | 13 | 22 | 36 | 53 | 69 | 82 | 91 | 96 | * | | | |
| 37 | 2.777 | 13 | 22 | 37 | 54 | 70 | 83 | 92 | 96 | | | | |
| 38 | 2.775 | 13 | 23 | 38 | 55 | 71 | 84 | 92 | 97 | | | | |
| 39 | 2.773 | 13 | 23 | 38 | 56 | 72 | 85 | 93 | 97 | | | | |

Table 8.3.23 (continued)

| n | $F_c$ | f | | | | | | | | | | | |
|---|---|---|---|---|---|---|---|---|---|---|---|---|---|
| | | .05 | .10 | .15 | .20 | .25 | .30 | .35 | .40 | .50 | .60 | .70 | .80 |
| 40 | 2.771 | 13 | 24 | 39 | 57 | 73 | 85 | 93 | 97 | * | * | * | * |
| 42 | 2.768 | 13 | 24 | 40 | 59 | 75 | 87 | 94 | 98 | | | | |
| 44 | 2.765 | 13 | 25 | 42 | 60 | 77 | 88 | 95 | 98 | | | | |
| 46 | 2.762 | 14 | 26 | 43 | 62 | 78 | 90 | 96 | 99 | | | | |
| 48 | 2.760 | 14 | 26 | 44 | 63 | 80 | 91 | 96 | 99 | | | | |
| 50 | 2.758 | 14 | 27 | 45 | 65 | 81 | 92 | 97 | 99 | | | | |
| 52 | 2.756 | 14 | 28 | 47 | 66 | 82 | 92 | 97 | 99 | | | | |
| 54 | 2.754 | 14 | 28 | 48 | 68 | 84 | 93 | 98 | 99 | | | | |
| 56 | 2.752 | 14 | 29 | 49 | 69 | 85 | 94 | 98 | * | | | | |
| 58 | 2.750 | 15 | 30 | 50 | 71 | 86 | 95 | 98 | | | | | |
| 60 | 2.749 | 15 | 30 | 51 | 72 | 87 | 95 | 99 | | | | | |
| 64 | 2.746 | 15 | 31 | 53 | 74 | 89 | 96 | 99 | | | | | |
| 68 | 2.743 | 16 | 33 | 56 | 76 | 90 | 97 | 99 | | | | | |
| 72 | 2.741 | 16 | 34 | 58 | 78 | 92 | 98 | 99 | | | | | |
| 76 | 2.739 | 16 | 35 | 59 | 80 | 93 | 98 | * | | | | | |
| 80 | 2.738 | 17 | 36 | 61 | 82 | 94 | 99 | | | | | | |
| 84 | 2.736 | 17 | 38 | 63 | 84 | 95 | 99 | | | | | | |
| 88 | 2.735 | 17 | 39 | 65 | 85 | 96 | 99 | | | | | | |
| 92 | 2.733 | 18 | 40 | 67 | 86 | 96 | 99 | | | | | | |
| 96 | 2.732 | 18 | 41 | 68 | 88 | 97 | 99 | | | | | | |
| 100 | 2.731 | 18 | 42 | 70 | 89 | 97 | * | | | | | | |
| 120 | 2.727 | 20 | 48 | 76 | 93 | 99 | | | | | | | |
| 140 | 2.724 | 22 | 53 | 82 | 96 | 99 | | | | | | | |
| 160 | 2.721 | 24 | 57 | 86 | 98 | * | | | | | | | |
| 180 | 2.719 | 25 | 62 | 89 | 99 | | | | | | | | |
| 200 | 2.718 | 27 | 65 | 92 | 99 | | | | | | | | |
| 250 | 2.716 | 31 | 74 | 96 | * | | | | | | | | |
| 300 | 2.714 | 35 | 80 | 98 | | | | | | | | | |
| 350 | 2.713 | 39 | 85 | 99 | | | | | | | | | |
| 400 | 2.712 | 42 | 89 | * | | | | | | | | | |
| 450 | 2.711 | 46 | 92 | | | | | | | | | | |
| 500 | 2.711 | 49 | 94 | | | | | | | | | | |
| 600 | 2.710 | 55 | 97 | | | | | | | | | | |
| 700 | 2.709 | 61 | 98 | | | | | | | | | | |
| 800 | 2.709 | 66 | 99 | | | | | | | | | | |
| 900 | 2.708 | 70 | * | | | | | | | | | | |
| 1000 | 2.708 | 74 | | | | | | | | | | | |

* Power values below this point are greater than .995.

Table 8.3.24

Power of F test at a = .10, u = 2

| n | $F_c$ | .05 | .10 | .15 | .20 | .25 | .30 | .35 | .40 | .50 | .60 | .70 | .80 |
|---|---|---|---|---|---|---|---|---|---|---|---|---|---|
| | | | | | | | | | | | | f | |
| 2 | 5.462 | 10 | 11 | 12 | 13 | 13 | 14 | 15 | 17 | 20 | 23 | 27 | 32 |
| 3 | 3.463 | 10 | 11 | 12 | 14 | 15 | 17 | 20 | 22 | 29 | 36 | 45 | 53 |
| 4 | 3.006 | 10 | 11 | 13 | 15 | 17 | 20 | 24 | 28 | 38 | 48 | 59 | 70 |
| 5 | 2.807 | 10 | 12 | 13 | 16 | 20 | 24 | 29 | 34 | 46 | 59 | 71 | 81 |
| 6 | 2.695 | 10 | 12 | 14 | 18 | 22 | 27 | 33 | 40 | 54 | 68 | 80 | 89 |
| 7 | 2.624 | 10 | 12 | 15 | 19 | 24 | 30 | 37 | 45 | 61 | 75 | 86 | 93 |
| 8 | 2.575 | 11 | 13 | 16 | 21 | 27 | 34 | 41 | 50 | 67 | 81 | 90 | 96 |
| 9 | 2.538 | 11 | 13 | 17 | 22 | 29 | 37 | 45 | 55 | 72 | 85 | 94 | 98 |
| 10 | 2.511 | 11 | 13 | 18 | 24 | 31 | 40 | 49 | 59 | 76 | 89 | 96 | 99 |
| 11 | 2.489 | 11 | 14 | 18 | 25 | 33 | 43 | 53 | 63 | 80 | 92 | 97 | 99 |
| 12 | 2.471 | 11 | 14 | 19 | 27 | 36 | 46 | 56 | 67 | 84 | 94 | 98 | * |
| 13 | 2.456 | 11 | 14 | 20 | 28 | 38 | 49 | 60 | 70 | 86 | 95 | 99 | |
| 14 | 2.444 | 11 | 15 | 21 | 30 | 40 | 51 | 63 | 73 | 89 | 97 | 99 | |
| 15 | 2.434 | 11 | 15 | 22 | 31 | 42 | 54 | 66 | 76 | 91 | 97 | * | |
| 16 | 2.425 | 11 | 16 | 23 | 32 | 44 | 56 | 68 | 79 | 92 | 98 | | |
| 17 | 2.417 | 11 | 16 | 24 | 34 | 46 | 59 | 71 | 81 | 94 | 99 | | |
| 18 | 2.410 | 11 | 16 | 24 | 35 | 48 | 61 | 73 | 83 | 95 | 99 | | |
| 19 | 2.404 | 11 | 17 | 25 | 37 | 50 | 63 | 75 | 85 | 96 | 99 | | |
| 20 | 2.398 | 12 | 17 | 26 | 38 | 52 | 65 | 77 | 87 | 97 | * | | |
| 21 | 2.393 | 12 | 17 | 27 | 39 | 53 | 67 | 79 | 88 | 97 | | | |
| 22 | 2.389 | 12 | 18 | 28 | 41 | 55 | 69 | 81 | 90 | 98 | | | |
| 23 | 2.385 | 12 | 18 | 29 | 42 | 57 | 71 | 83 | 91 | 98 | | | |
| 24 | 2.381 | 12 | 19 | 29 | 43 | 59 | 73 | 84 | 92 | 99 | | | |
| 25 | 2.378 | 12 | 19 | 30 | 45 | 60 | 74 | 86 | 93 | 99 | | | |
| 26 | 2.375 | 12 | 19 | 31 | 46 | 62 | 76 | 87 | 94 | 99 | | | |
| 27 | 2.372 | 12 | 20 | 32 | 47 | 63 | 78 | 88 | 95 | 99 | | | |
| 28 | 2.369 | 12 | 20 | 33 | 48 | 65 | 79 | 89 | 95 | 99 | | | |
| 29 | 2.367 | 12 | 20 | 33 | 50 | 66 | 80 | 90 | 96 | * | | | |
| 30 | 2.365 | 12 | 21 | 34 | 51 | 68 | 82 | 91 | 96 | | | | |
| 31 | 2.363 | 13 | 21 | 35 | 52 | 69 | 83 | 92 | 97 | | | | |
| 32 | 2.361 | 13 | 22 | 36 | 53 | 70 | 84 | 93 | 97 | | | | |
| 33 | 2.359 | 13 | 22 | 37 | 54 | 71 | 85 | 93 | 98 | | | | |
| 34 | 2.357 | 13 | 22 | 37 | 55 | 73 | 86 | 94 | 98 | | | | |
| 35 | 2.355 | 13 | 23 | 38 | 56 | 74 | 87 | 95 | 98 | | | | |
| 36 | 2.354 | 13 | 23 | 39 | 57 | 75 | 88 | 95 | 98 | | | | |
| 37 | 2.352 | 13 | 24 | 40 | 59 | 76 | 89 | 96 | 99 | | | | |
| 38 | 2.351 | 13 | 24 | 40 | 60 | 77 | 89 | 96 | 99 | | | | |
| 39 | 2.350 | 13 | 24 | 41 | 61 | 78 | 90 | 96 | 99 | | | | |

**Table 8.3.24** (continued)

| n | $F_c$ | .05 | .10 | .15 | .20 | .25 | .30 | .35 | .40 | .50 | .60 | .70 | .80 |
|---|---|---|---|---|---|---|---|---|---|---|---|---|---|
| | | | | | | | | | | | | | $f$ |
| 40 | 2.348 | 13 | 25 | 42 | 62 | 79 | 91 | 97 | 99 | * | * | * | * |
| 42 | 2.346 | 14 | 25 | 43 | 64 | 81 | 92 | 97 | 99 | | | | |
| 44 | 2.344 | 14 | 26 | 45 | 65 | 82 | 93 | 98 | * | | | | |
| 46 | 2.342 | 14 | 27 | 46 | 67 | 84 | 94 | 98 | | | | | |
| 48 | 2.341 | 14 | 28 | 48 | 69 | 85 | 95 | 99 | | | | | |
| 50 | 2.339 | 14 | 28 | 49 | 71 | 87 | 96 | 99 | | | | | |
| 52 | 2.338 | 15 | 29 | 50 | 72 | 88 | 96 | 99 | | | | | |
| 54 | 2.336 | 15 | 30 | 52 | 74 | 89 | 97 | 99 | | | | | |
| 56 | 2.335 | 15 | 31 | 53 | 75 | 90 | 97 | 99 | | | | | |
| 58 | 2.334 | 15 | 31 | 54 | 76 | 91 | 98 | * | | | | | |
| 60 | 2.333 | 15 | 32 | 55 | 78 | 92 | 98 | | | | | | |
| 64 | 2.331 | 16 | 33 | 58 | 80 | 93 | 98 | | | | | | |
| 68 | 2.329 | 16 | 35 | 60 | 82 | 95 | 99 | | | | | | |
| 72 | 2.328 | 17 | 36 | 62 | 84 | 96 | 99 | | | | | | |
| 76 | 2.326 | 17 | 38 | 65 | 86 | 96 | 99 | | | | | | |
| 80 | 2.325 | 17 | 39 | 67 | 88 | 97 | * | | | | | | |
| 84 | 2.324 | 18 | 40 | 69 | 89 | 98 | | | | | | | |
| 88 | 2.323 | 18 | 42 | 70 | 90 | 98 | | | | | | | |
| 92 | 2.322 | 18 | 43 | 72 | 92 | 99 | | | | | | | |
| 96 | 2.321 | 19 | 44 | 74 | 93 | 99 | | | | | | | |
| 100 | 2.321 | 19 | 45 | 75 | 93 | 99 | | | | | | | |
| 120 | 2.318 | 21 | 52 | 82 | 97 | * | | | | | | | |
| 140 | 2.315 | 23 | 57 | 87 | 98 | | | | | | | | |
| 160 | 2.314 | 25 | 62 | 91 | 99 | | | | | | | | |
| 180 | 2.313 | 27 | 67 | 94 | * | | | | | | | | |
| 200 | 2.312 | 29 | 71 | 96 | | | | | | | | | |
| 250 | 2.310 | 33 | 80 | 98 | | | | | | | | | |
| 300 | 2.309 | 37 | 86 | 99 | | | | | | | | | |
| 350 | 2.308 | 42 | 90 | * | | | | | | | | | |
| 400 | 2.307 | 46 | 94 | | | | | | | | | | |
| 450 | 2.307 | 49 | 96 | | | | | | | | | | |
| 500 | 2.306 | 53 | 97 | | | | | | | | | | |
| 600 | 2.306 | 60 | 99 | | | | | | | | | | |
| 700 | 2.305 | 66 | * | | | | | | | | | | |
| 800 | 2.305 | 71 | | | | | | | | | | | |
| 900 | 2.305 | 76 | | | | | | | | | | | |
| 1000 | 2.304 | 80 | | | | | | | | | | | |

* Power values below this point are greater than .995.

Table 8.3.25

Power of F test at a = .10, u = 3

| n | $F_c$ | .05 | .10 | .15 | .20 | .25 | .30 | .35 | .40 | .50 | .60 | .70 | .80 |
|---|---|---|---|---|---|---|---|---|---|---|---|---|---|
| | | | | | | | | f | | | | | |
| 2 | 4.191 | 10 | 11 | 12 | 12 | 13 | 15 | 16 | 17 | 20 | 25 | 29 | 35 |
| 3 | 2.924 | 10 | 11 | 12 | 14 | 15 | 18 | 20 | 23 | 31 | 39 | 49 | 59 |
| 4 | 2.606 | 10 | 11 | 13 | 15 | 18 | 21 | 25 | 30 | 41 | 53 | 65 | 76 |
| 5 | 2.462 | 10 | 12 | 14 | 17 | 20 | 25 | 30 | 37 | 50 | 64 | 77 | 87 |
| 6 | 2.381 | 10 | 12 | 15 | 18 | 23 | 29 | 35 | 43 | 59 | 73 | 85 | 93 |
| 7 | 2.327 | 11 | 12 | 15 | 20 | 26 | 32 | 40 | 49 | 66 | 81 | 91 | 96 |
| 8 | 2.291 | 11 | 13 | 16 | 22 | 28 | 36 | 45 | 54 | 72 | 86 | 94 | 98 |
| 9 | 2.264 | 11 | 13 | 17 | 23 | 31 | 40 | 49 | 59 | 78 | 90 | 97 | 99 |
| 10 | 2.243 | 11 | 14 | 18 | 25 | 33 | 43 | 54 | 64 | 82 | 93 | 98 | * |
| 11 | 2.226 | 11 | 14 | 19 | 27 | 36 | 46 | 58 | 68 | 86 | 95 | 99 | |
| 12 | 2.213 | 11 | 14 | 20 | 28 | 38 | 50 | 61 | 72 | 89 | 97 | 99 | |
| 13 | 2.202 | 11 | 15 | 21 | 30 | 41 | 53 | 65 | 76 | 91 | 98 | * | |
| 14 | 2.192 | 11 | 15 | 22 | 31 | 43 | 56 | 68 | 79 | 93 | 98 | | |
| 15 | 2.184 | 11 | 16 | 23 | 33 | 45 | 59 | 71 | 82 | 95 | 99 | | |
| 6 | 2.177 | 11 | 16 | 24 | 35 | 48 | 61 | 74 | 84 | 96 | 99 | | |
| 7 | 2.171 | 11 | 16 | 25 | 36 | 50 | 64 | 77 | 86 | 97 | * | | |
| 18 | 2.166 | 11 | 17 | 26 | 38 | 52 | 66 | 79 | 88 | 98 | | | |
| 19 | 2.162 | 12 | 17 | 27 | 39 | 54 | 69 | 81 | 90 | 98 | | | |
| 20 | 2.157 | 12 | 18 | 28 | 41 | 56 | 71 | 83 | 91 | 99 | | | |
| 21 | 2.154 | 12 | 18 | 29 | 43 | 58 | 73 | 85 | 93 | 99 | | | |
| 22 | 2.150 | 12 | 18 | 29 | 44 | 60 | 75 | 86 | 94 | 99 | | | |
| 23 | 2.147 | 12 | 19 | 30 | 46 | 62 | 77 | 88 | 95 | 99 | | | |
| 24 | 2.144 | 12 | 19 | 31 | 47 | 64 | 79 | 89 | 95 | * | | | |
| 25 | 2.142 | 12 | 20 | 32 | 48 | 66 | 80 | 90 | 96 | | | | |
| 26 | 2.139 | 12 | 20 | 33 | 50 | 67 | 82 | 91 | 97 | | | | |
| 27 | 2.137 | 12 | 21 | 34 | 51 | 69 | 83 | 91 | 97 | | | | |
| 28 | 2.135 | 12 | 21 | 35 | 53 | 70 | 84 | 93 | 98 | | | | |
| 29 | 2.133 | 13 | 21 | 36 | 54 | 72 | 86 | 94 | 98 | | | | |
| 30 | 2.132 | 13 | 22 | 37 | 55 | 73 | 87 | 95 | 98 | | | | |
| 31 | 2.130 | 13 | 22 | 38 | 57 | 75 | 88 | 95 | 99 | | | | |
| 32 | 2.129 | 13 | 23 | 39 | 58 | 76 | 89 | 96 | 99 | | | | |
| 33 | 2.127 | 13 | 23 | 39 | 59 | 77 | 90 | 96 | 99 | | | | |
| 34 | 2.126 | 13 | 23 | 40 | 60 | 78 | 91 | 97 | 99 | | | | |
| 35 | 2.124 | 13 | 24 | 41 | 61 | 79 | 91 | 97 | 99 | | | | |
| 36 | 2.123 | 13 | 24 | 42 | 63 | 81 | 92 | 98 | 99 | | | | |
| 37 | 2.122 | 13 | 25 | 43 | 64 | 82 | 93 | 98 | * | | | | |
| 38 | 2.121 | 14 | 25 | 44 | 65 | 83 | 93 | 98 | | | | | |
| 39 | 2.120 | 14 | 26 | 45 | 66 | 84 | 94 | 98 | | | | | |

Table 8.3.25 *(continued)*

| n | $F_c$ | .05 | .10 | .15 | .20 | .25 | .30 | .35 | .40 | .50 | .60 | .70 | .80 |
|---|---|---|---|---|---|---|---|---|---|---|---|---|---|
| 40 | 2.119 | 14 | 26 | 45 | 67 | 84 | 94 | 99 | * | * | * | * | * |
| 42 | 2.118 | 14 | 27 | 47 | 69 | 86 | 95 | 99 | | | | | |
| 44 | 2.116 | 14 | 28 | 49 | 71 | 88 | 96 | 99 | | | | | |
| 46 | 2.115 | 14 | 28 | 50 | 73 | 89 | 97 | 99 | | | | | |
| 48 | 2.113 | 15 | 29 | 52 | 75 | 90 | 97 | * | | | | | |
| 50 | 2.112 | 15 | 30 | 53 | 76 | 91 | 98 | | | | | | |
| 52 | 2.111 | 15 | 31 | 55 | 78 | 92 | 98 | | | | | | |
| 54 | 2.110 | 15 | 32 | 56 | 79 | 93 | 99 | | | | | | |
| 56 | 2.109 | 15 | 33 | 58 | 81 | 94 | 99 | | | | | | |
| 58 | 2.108 | 16 | 33 | 59 | 82 | 95 | 99 | | | | | | |
| 60 | 2.107 | 16 | 34 | 60 | 83 | 95 | 99 | | | | | | |
| 64 | 2.106 | 16 | 36 | 63 | 85 | 96 | 99 | | | | | | |
| 68 | 2.104 | 17 | 37 | 66 | 88 | 97 | * | | | | | | |
| 72 | 2.103 | 17 | 39 | 68 | 89 | 98 | | | | | | | |
| 76 | 2.102 | 17 | 41 | 70 | 91 | 98 | | | | | | | |
| 80 | 2.101 | 18 | 42 | 72 | 92 | 99 | | | | | | | |
| 84 | 2.101 | 18 | 44 | 74 | 93 | 99 | | | | | | | |
| 88 | 2.100 | 19 | 45 | 76 | 94 | 99 | | | | | | | |
| 92 | 2.099 | 19 | 46 | 78 | 95 | 99 | | | | | | | |
| 96 | 2.098 | 20 | 48 | 80 | 96 | * | | | | | | | |
| 100 | 2.098 | 20 | 49 | 81 | 96 | | | | | | | | |
| 120 | 2.096 | 22 | 56 | 87 | 99 | | | | | | | | |
| 140 | 2.094 | 24 | 62 | 92 | 99 | | | | | | | | |
| 160 | 2.093 | 26 | 68 | 95 | * | | | | | | | | |
| 180 | 2.092 | 28 | 72 | 97 | | | | | | | | | |
| 200 | 2.091 | 30 | 77 | 98 | | | | | | | | | |
| 250 | 2.089 | 35 | 85 | 99 | | | | | | | | | |
| 300 | 2.088 | 40 | 91 | * | | | | | | | | | |
| 350 | 2.088 | 45 | 94 | | | | | | | | | | |
| 400 | 2.087 | 50 | 97 | | | | | | | | | | |
| 450 | 2.087 | 54 | 98 | | | | | | | | | | |
| 500 | 2.087 | 58 | 99 | | | | | | | | | | |
| 600 | 2.086 | 65 | * | | | | | | | | | | |
| 700 | 2.086 | 71 | | | | | | | | | | | |
| 800 | 2.086 | 77 | | | | | | | | | | | |
| 900 | 2.085 | 81 | | | | | | | | | | | |
| 1000 | 2.085 | 85 | | | | | | | | | | | |

* Power values below this point are greater than .995.

Table 8.3.26

Power of F test at a = .10, u = 4

| | | f | | | | | | | | | | | |
|---|---|---|---|---|---|---|---|---|---|---|---|---|---|
| n | $F_c$ | .05 | .10 | .15 | .20 | .25 | .30 | .35 | .40 | .50 | .60 | .70 | .80 |
| 2 | 3.520 | 10 | 11 | 11 | 12 | 13 | 15 | 16 | 18 | 21 | 26 | 32 | 38 |
| 3 | 2.605 | 10 | 11 | 12 | 14 | 16 | 18 | 21 | 25 | 33 | 43 | 53 | 64 |
| 4 | 2.361 | 10 | 11 | 13 | 15 | 18 | 22 | 27 | ·32 | 44 | 57 | 70 | 81 |
| 5 | 2.249 | 10 | 12 | 14 | 17 | 21 | 26 | 32 | 39 | 54 | 69 | 82 | 91 |
| 6 | 2.184 | 10 | 12 | 15 | 19 | 24 | 31 | 38 | 46 | 63 | 79 | 89 | 96 |
| 7 | 2.142 | 11 | 13 | 16 | 21 | 27 | 35 | 43 | 53 | 71 | 85 | 94 | 98 |
| 8 | 2.113 | 11 | 13 | 17 | 23 | 30 | 39 | 48 | 59 | 77 | 90 | 97 | 99 |
| 9 | 2.091 | 11 | 13 | 18 | 24 | 33 | 43 | 53 | 64 | 82 | 94 | 98 | * |
| 10 | 2.074 | 11 | 14 | 19 | 26 | 36 | 47 | 58 | 69 | 87 | 96 | 99 | |
| 11 | 2.061 | 11 | 14 | 20 | 28 | 38 | 50 | 62 | 73 | 90 | 97 | * | |
| 12 | 2.050 | 11 | 15 | 21 | 30 | 41 | 54 | 66 | 77 | 92 | 98 | | |
| 13 | 2.041 | 11 | 15 | 22 | 32 | 44 | 57 | 70 | 81 | 94 | 99 | | |
| 14 | 2.034 | 11 | 16 | 23 | 34 | 46 | 60 | 73 | 84 | 96 | 99 | | |
| 15 | 2.027 | 11 | 16 | 24 | 35 | 49 | 63 | 76 | 86 | 97 | * | | |
| 16 | 2.022 | 11 | 16 | 25 | 37 | 51 | 66 | 79 | 88 | 98 | | | |
| 17 | 2.017 | 11 | 17 | 26 | 39 | 54 | 69 | 81 | 90 | 98 | | | |
| 18 | 2.012 | 12 | 17 | 27 | 41 | 56 | 71 | 84 | 92 | 99 | | | |
| 19 | 2.009 | 12 | 18 | 28 | 42 | 58 | 74 | 86 | 93 | 99 | | | |
| 20 | 2.005 | 12 | 18 | 29 | 44 | 61 | 76 | 87 | 94 | 99 | | | |
| 21 | 2.002 | 12 | 19 | 30 | 46 | 63 | 78 | 89 | 95 | * | | | |
| 22 | 1.999 | 12 | 19 | 31 | 47 | 65 | 80 | 90 | 96 | | | | |
| 23 | 1.997 | 12 | 20 | 32 | 49 | 67 | 82 | 92 | 97 | | | | |
| 24 | 1.994 | 12 | 20 | 33 | 51 | 69 | 83 | 93 | 97 | | | | |
| 25 | 1.992 | 12 | 21 | 34 | 52 | 70 | 85 | 94 | 98 | | | | |
| 26 | 1.990 | 12 | 21 | 35 | 54 | 72 | 86 | 95 | 98 | | | | |
| 27 | 1.989 | 13 | 21 | 36 | 55 | 74 | 87 | 95 | 99 | | | | |
| 28 | 1.987 | 13 | 22 | 37 | 57 | 75 | 89 | 96 | 99 | | | | |
| 29 | 1.986 | 13 | 22 | 38 | 58 | 77 | 90 | 97 | 99 | | | | |
| 30 | 1.984 | 13 | 23 | 39 | 60 | 78 | 91 | 97 | 99 | | | | |
| 31 | 1.983 | 13 | 23 | 40 | 61 | 79 | 92 | 97 | 99 | | | | |
| 32 | 1.982 | 13 | 24 | 41 | 62 | 81 | 92 | 98 | * | | | | |
| 33 | 1.980 | 13 | 24 | 42 | 64 | 82 | 93 | 98 | | | | | |
| 34 | 1.979 | 13 | 25 | 43 | 65 | 83 | 94 | 98 | | | | | |
| 35 | 1.978 | 13 | 25 | 44 | 66 | 84 | 94 | 99 | | | | | |
| 36 | 1.977 | 14 | 26 | 45 | 67 | 85 | 95 | 99 | | | | | |
| 37 | 1.977 | 14 | 26 | 46 | 69 | 86 | 96 | 99 | | | | | |
| 38 | 1.976 | 14 | 26 | 47 | 70 | 87 | 96 | 99 | | | | | |
| 39 | 1.975 | 14 | 27 | 48 | 71 | 88 | 96 | 99 | | | | | |

Table 8.3.26 (continued)

| n | $F_c$ | .05 | .10 | .15 | .20 | .25 | .30 | .35 | .40 | .50 | .60 | .70 | .80 |
|---|---|---|---|---|---|---|---|---|---|---|---|---|---|
| 40 | 1.974 | 14 | 27 | 49 | 72 | 89 | 97 | 99 | * | * | * | * | * |
| 42 | 1.973 | 14 | 28 | 51 | 74 | 90 | 97 | * | | | | | |
| 44 | 1.971 | 14 | 29 | 52 | 76 | 91 | 98 | | | | | | |
| 46 | 1.970 | 15 | 30 | 54 | 78 | 93 | 98 | | | | | | |
| 48 | 1.969 | 15 | 31 | 56 | 79 | 94 | 99 | | | | | | |
| 50 | 1.968 | 15 | 32 | 57 | 81 | 94 | 99 | | | | | | |
| 52 | 1.967 | 15 | 33 | 59 | 83 | 95 | 99 | | | | | | |
| 54 | 1.966 | 16 | 34 | 61 | 84 | 96 | 99 | | | | | | |
| 56 | 1.966 | 16 | 35 | 62 | 85 | 96 | * | | | | | | |
| 58 | 1.965 | 16 | 36 | 64 | 86 | 97 | | | | | | | |
| 60 | 1.964 | 16 | 37 | 65 | 88 | 97 | | | | | | | |
| 64 | 1.963 | 17 | 38 | 68 | 90 | 98 | | | | | | | |
| 68 | 1.962 | 17 | 40 | 70 | 91 | 99 | | | | | | | |
| 72 | 1.961 | 18 | 42 | 73 | 93 | 99 | | | | | | | |
| 76 | 1.960 | 18 | 44 | 75 | 94 | 99 | | | | | | | |
| 80 | 1.959 | 19 | 45 | 77 | 95 | * | | | | | | | |
| 84 | 1.959 | 19 | 47 | 79 | 96 | | | | | | | | |
| 88 | 1.958 | 19 | 48 | 81 | 97 | | | | | | | | |
| 92 | 1.957 | 20 | 50 | 83 | 97 | | | | | | | | |
| 96 | 1.957 | 20 | 52 | 84 | 98 | | | | | | | | |
| 100 | 1.956 | 21 | 53 | 86 | 98 | | | | | | | | |
| 120 | 1.954 | 23 | 60 | 91 | 99 | | | | | | | | |
| 140 | 1.953 | 25 | 67 | 95 | * | | | | | | | | |
| 160 | 1.952 | 28 | 73 | 97 | | | | | | | | | |
| 180 | 1.951 | 30 | 77 | 98 | | | | | | | | | |
| 200 | 1.951 | 32 | 82 | 99 | | | | | | | | | |
| 250 | 1.950 | 38 | 89 | * | | | | | | | | | |
| 300 | 1.949 | 43 | 94 | | | | | | | | | | |
| 350 | 1.948 | 49 | 97 | | | | | | | | | | |
| 400 | 1.948 | 53 | 98 | | | | | | | | | | |
| 450 | 1.947 | 58 | 99 | | | | | | | | | | |
| 500 | 1.947 | 62 | * | | | | | | | | | | |
| 600 | 1.947 | 70 | | | | | | | | | | | |
| 700 | 1.947 | 76 | | | | | | | | | | | |
| 800 | 1.946 | 82 | | | | | | | | | | | |
| 900 | 1.946 | 86 | | | | | | | | | | | |
| 1000 | 1.946 | 89 | | | | | | | | | | | |

* Power values below this point are greater than .995.

**Table 8.3.27**

Power of F test at a = .10, u = 5

| n | $F_c$ | .05 | .10 | .15 | .20 | .25 | .30 | .35 | .40 | .50 | .60 | .70 | .80 |
|---|---|---|---|---|---|---|---|---|---|---|---|---|---|
| | | | | | | | | | | | | f | |
| 2 | 3.108 | 10 | 11 | 11 | 12 | 13 | 15 | 16 | 18 | 22 | 28 | 34 | 41 |
| 3 | 2.394 | 10 | 11 | 12 | 14 | 16 | 19 | 22 | 26 | 35 | 46 | 58 | 69 |
| 4 | 2.196 | 10 | 11 | 13 | 16 | 19 | 23 | 28 | 34 | 47 | 62 | 75 | 85 |
| 5 | 2.103 | 10 | 12 | 14 | 18 | 22 | 28 | 34 | 42 | 58 | 74 | 86 | 94 |
| 6 | 2.049 | 10 | 12 | 15 | 20 | 25 | 32 | 40 | 49 | 68 | 83 | 93 | 97 |
| 7 | 2.014 | 11 | 13 | 16 | 22 | 28 | 37 | 46 | 56 | 75 | 89 | 96 | 99 |
| 8 | 1.990 | 11 | 13 | 17 | 23 | 32 | 41 | 52 | 63 | 81 | 93 | 98 | * |
| 9 | 1.971 | 11 | 14 | 18 | 26 | 35 | 46 | 57 | 68 | 86 | 96 | 99 | |
| 10 | 1.957 | 11 | 14 | 19 | 28 | 38 | 50 | 62 | 73 | 90 | 97 | * | |
| 11 | 1.946 | 11 | 14 | 21 | 30 | 41 | 54 | 66 | 78 | 93 | 99 | | |
| 12 | 1.937 | 11 | 15 | 22 | 32 | 44 | 57 | 70 | 81 | 95 | 99 | | |
| 13 | 1.929 | 11 | 15 | 23 | 34 | 47 | 61 | 74 | 84 | 96 | * | | |
| 14 | 1.923 | 11 | 16 | 24 | 36 | 50 | 64 | 77 | 87 | 97 | | | |
| 15 | 1.917 | 11 | 16 | 25 | 38 | 52 | 67 | 80 | 90 | 98 | | | |
| 16 | 1.912 | 11 | 17 | 26 | 40 | 55 | 70 | 83 | 92 | 99 | | | |
| 17 | 1.908 | 12 | 17 | 27 | 41 | 58 | 73 | 85 | 93 | 99 | | | |
| 18 | 1.905 | 12 | 18 | 29 | 43 | 60 | 76 | 87 | 95 | 99 | | | |
| 19 | 1.902 | 12 | 18 | 30 | 45 | 62 | 78 | 89 | 96 | * | | | |
| 20 | 1.899 | 12 | 19 | 31 | 47 | 65 | 80 | 91 | 96 | | | | |
| 21 | 1.896 | 12 | 19 | 32 | 49 | 67 | 82 | 92 | 97 | | | | |
| 22 | 1.894 | 12 | 20 | 33 | 51 | 69 | 84 | 93 | 98 | | | | |
| 23 | 1.891 | 12 | 20 | 34 | 52 | 71 | 86 | 94 | 98 | | | | |
| 24 | 1.890 | 12 | 21 | 35 | 54 | 73 | 87 | 95 | 99 | | | | |
| 25 | 1.888 | 12 | 21 | 36 | 56 | 75 | 88 | 96 | 99 | | | | |
| 26 | 1.886 | 13 | 22 | 38 | 57 | 76 | 90 | 97 | 99 | | | | |
| 27 | 1.885 | 13 | 22 | 39 | 59 | 78 | 91 | 97 | 99 | | | | |
| 28 | 1.883 | 13 | 23 | 40 | 61 | 79 | 92 | 98 | 99 | | | | |
| 29 | 1.882 | 13 | 23 | 41 | 62 | 81 | 93 | 98 | * | | | | |
| 30 | 1.881 | 13 | 24 | 42 | 64 | 82 | 94 | 98 | | | | | |
| 31 | 1.880 | 13 | 24 | 43 | 65 | 83 | 94 | 99 | | | | | |
| 32 | 1.879 | 13 | 25 | 44 | 66 | 85 | 95 | 99 | | | | | |
| 33 | 1.878 | 13 | 25 | 45 | 68 | 86 | 96 | 99 | | | | | |
| 34 | 1.877 | 14 | 26 | 46 | 69 | 87 | 96 | 99 | | | | | |
| 35 | 1.876 | 14 | 26 | 47 | 70 | 88 | 97 | 99 | | | | | |
| 36 | 1.875 | 14 | 27 | 48 | 72 | 89 | 97 | 99 | | | | | |
| 37 | 1.874 | 14 | 27 | 49 | 73 | 90 | 97 | * | | | | | |
| 38 | 1.874 | 14 | 28 | 50 | 74 | 90 | 98 | | | | | | |
| 39 | 1.873 | 14 | 28 | 51 | 75 | 91 | 98 | | | | | | |

Table 8.3.27 *(continued)*

| n | $F_c$ | .05 | .10 | .15 | .20 | .25 | .30 | .35 | .40 | .50 | .60 | .70 | .80 |
|---|---|---|---|---|---|---|---|---|---|---|---|---|---|
| 40 | 1.872 | 14 | 29 | 52 | 76 | 92 | 98 | * | * | * | * | * | * |
| 42 | 1.871 | 14 | 30 | 54 | 78 | 93 | 99 | | | | | | |
| 44 | 1.870 | 15 | 31 | 56 | 80 | 94 | 99 | | | | | | |
| 46 | 1.869 | 15 | 32 | 58 | 82 | 95 | 99 | | | | | | |
| 48 | 1.868 | 15 | 33 | 60 | 83 | 96 | 99 | | | | | | |
| 50 | 1.867 | 15 | 34 | 61 | 85 | 96 | * | | | | | | |
| 52 | 1.866 | 16 | 35 | 63 | 86 | 97 | | | | | | | |
| 54 | 1.866 | 16 | 36 | 65 | 88 | 98 | | | | | | | |
| 56 | 1.865 | 16 | 37 | 66 | 89 | 98 | | | | | | | |
| 58 | 1.864 | 16 | 38 | 68 | 90 | 98 | | | | | | | |
| 60 | 1.864 | 17 | 39 | 69 | 91 | 99 | | | | | | | |
| 64 | 1.863 | 17 | 41 | 72 | 93 | 99 | | | | | | | |
| 68 | 1.862 | 18 | 43 | 75 | 94 | 99 | | | | | | | |
| 72 | 1.861 | 18 | 45 | 77 | 95 | * | | | | | | | |
| 76 | 1.860 | 19 | 46 | 79 | 96 | | | | | | | | |
| 80 | 1.860 | 19 | 48 | 81 | 97 | | | | | | | | |
| 84 | 1.859 | 20 | 50 | 83 | 98 | | | | | | | | |
| 88 | 1.858 | 20 | 52 | 85 | 98 | | | | | | | | |
| 92 | 1.858 | 21 | 54 | 86 | 98 | | | | | | | | |
| 96 | 1.858 | 21 | 55 | 88 | 99 | | | | | | | | |
| 100 | 1.857 | 22 | 57 | 89 | 99 | | | | | | | | |
| 120 | 1.855 | 24 | 64 | 94 | * | | | | | | | | |
| 140 | 1.854 | 27 | 71 | 97 | | | | | | | | | |
| 160 | 1.853 | 29 | 77 | 98 | | | | | | | | | |
| 180 | 1.853 | 32 | 81 | 99 | | | | | | | | | |
| 200 | 1.852 | 34 | 85 | * | | | | | | | | | |
| 250 | 1.851 | 40 | 92 | | | | | | | | | | |
| 300 | 1.851 | 46 | 96 | | | | | | | | | | |
| 350 | 1.850 | 52 | 98 | | | | | | | | | | |
| 400 | 1.850 | 57 | 99 | | | | | | | | | | |
| 450 | 1.849 | 62 | * | | | | | | | | | | |
| 500 | 1.849 | 66 | | | | | | | | | | | |
| 600 | 1.849 | 74 | | | | | | | | | | | |
| 700 | 1.849 | 80 | | | | | | | | | | | |
| 800 | 1.849 | 84 | | | | | | | | | | | |
| 900 | 1.848 | 89 | | | | | | | | | | | |
| 1000 | 1.848 | 92 | | | | | | | | | | | |

* Power values below this point are greater than .995.

Table 8.3.28

Power of F test at a = .10, u = 6

| | | | | | | | f | | | | | | |
|---|---|---|---|---|---|---|---|---|---|---|---|---|---|
| n | $F_c$ | .05 | .10 | .15 | .20 | .25 | .30 | .35 | .40 | .50 | .60 | .70 | .80 |
| 2 | 2.827 | 10 | 11 | 11 | 12 | 13 | 14 | 17 | 19 | 23 | 29 | 36 | 44 |
| 3 | 2.243 | 10 | 11 | 12 | 14 | 16 | 19 | 23 | 27 | 37 | 49 | 61 | 73 |
| 4 | 2.075 | 10 | 11 | 13 | 16 | 20 | 24 | 30 | 36 | 50 | 66 | 79 | 89 |
| 5 | 1.996 | 10 | 12 | 14 | 18 | 23 | 29 | 36 | 45 | 62 | 78 | 89 | 96 |
| 6 | 1.950 | 11 | 12 | 15 | 20 | 26 | 34 | 43 | 53 | 71 | 86 | 95 | 99 |
| 7 | 1.919 | 11 | 13 | 17 | 22 | 30 | 39 | 49 | 60 | 79 | 92 | 98 | * |
| 8 | 1.898 | 11 | 13 | 18 | 24 | 33 | 44 | 55 | 66 | 85 | 95 | 99 | |
| 9 | 1.882 | 11 | 14 | 19 | 27 | 37 | 48 | 61 | 72 | 89 | 97 | * | |
| 10 | 1.870 | 11 | 14 | 20 | 29 | 40 | 53 | 66 | 74 | 93 | 99 | | |
| 11 | 1.860 | 11 | 15 | 21 | 31 | 43 | 57 | 70 | 81 | 95 | 99 | | |
| 12 | 1.852 | 11 | 15 | 23 | 33 | 46 | 61 | 74 | 85 | 97 | * | | |
| 13 | 1.846 | 11 | 16 | 24 | 35 | 50 | 64 | 78 | 88 | 98 | | | |
| 14 | 1.840 | 11 | 16 | 25 | 38 | 53 | 68 | 81 | 90 | 98 | | | |
| 15 | 1.835 | 11 | 17 | 26 | 40 | 56 | 71 | 84 | 92 | 99 | | | |
| 16 | 1.831 | 12 | 17 | 27 | 42 | 58 | 74 | 86 | 94 | 99 | | | |
| 17 | 1.827 | 12 | 18 | 29 | 44 | 61 | 77 | 88 | 95 | * | | | |
| 18 | 1.824 | 12 | 18 | 30 | 46 | 64 | 79 | 90 | 96 | | | | |
| 19 | 1.821 | 12 | 19 | 31 | 48 | 66 | 82 | 92 | 97 | | | | |
| 20 | 1.819 | 12 | 19 | 32 | 50 | 68 | 84 | 93 | 98 | | | | |
| 21 | 1.817 | 12 | 20 | 34 | 52 | 71 | 85 | 94 | 98 | | | | |
| 22 | 1.815 | 12 | 20 | 35 | 54 | 73 | 87 | 95 | 99 | | | | |
| 23 | 1.813 | 12 | 21 | 36 | 56 | 75 | 89 | 96 | 99 | | | | |
| 24 | 1.811 | 13 | 21 | 37 | 57 | 77 | 90 | 97 | 99 | | | | |
| 25 | 1.810 | 13 | 22 | 38 | 59 | 78 | 91 | 97 | 99 | | | | |
| 26 | 1.808 | 13 | 23 | 40 | 61 | 80 | 92 | 98 | * | | | | |
| 27 | 1.807 | 13 | 23 | 41 | 63 | 82 | 93 | 98 | | | | | |
| 28 | 1.806 | 13 | 24 | 42 | 64 | 83 | 94 | 99 | | | | | |
| 29 | 1.805 | 13 | 24 | 43 | 66 | 84 | 95 | 99 | | | | | |
| 30 | 1.803 | 13 | 25 | 44 | 67 | 86 | 96 | 99 | | | | | |
| 31 | 1.802 | 13 | 25 | 46 | 69 | 87 | 96 | 99 | | | | | |
| 32 | 1.802 | 14 | 26 | 47 | 70 | 88 | 97 | 99 | | | | | |
| 33 | 1.801 | 14 | 26 | 48 | 71 | 89 | 97 | * | | | | | |
| 34 | 1.800 | 14 | 27 | 49 | 73 | 90 | 97 | | | | | | |
| 35 | 1.799 | 14 | 27 | 50 | 74 | 91 | 98 | | | | | | |
| 36 | 1.798 | 14 | 28 | 51 | 75 | 91 | 98 | | | | | | |
| 37 | 1.798 | 14 | 29 | 52 | 76 | 92 | 98 | | | | | | |
| 38 | 1.797 | 14 | 29 | 53 | 78 | 93 | 99 | | | | | | |
| 39 | 1.797 | 14 | 30 | 54 | 79 | 94 | 99 | | | | | | |

Table 8.3.28 *(continued)*

| n | $F_c$ | .05 | .10 | .15 | .20 | .25 | .30 | .35 | .40 | .50 | .60 | .70 | .80 |
|---|---|---|---|---|---|---|---|---|---|---|---|---|---|
| 40 | 1.796 | 15 | 30 | 55 | 80 | 94 | 99 | * | * | * | * | * | * |
| 42 | 1.795 | 15 | 31 | 57 | 82 | 95 | 99 | | | | | | |
| 44 | 1.794 | 15 | 32 | 59 | 84 | 96 | 99 | | | | | | |
| 46 | 1.793 | 15 | 33 | 61 | 85 | 97 | * | | | | | | |
| 48 | 1.792 | 16 | 35 | 63 | 87 | 97 | | | | | | | |
| 50 | 1.791 | 16 | 36 | 65 | 88 | 98 | | | | | | | |
| 52 | 1.791 | 16 | 37 | 67 | 89 | 98 | | | | | | | |
| 54 | 1.790 | 16 | 38 | 68 | 91 | 99 | | | | | | | |
| 56 | 1.790 | 17 | 39 | 70 | 92 | 99 | | | | | | | |
| 58 | 1.789 | 17 | 40 | 71 | 92 | 99 | | | | | | | |
| 60 | 1.789 | 17 | 41 | 73 | 93 | 99 | | | | | | | |
| 64 | 1.788 | 18 | 43 | 76 | 95 | * | | | | | | | |
| 68 | 1.787 | 18 | 45 | 78 | 96 | | | | | | | | |
| 72 | 1.786 | 19 | 47 | 81 | 97 | | | | | | | | |
| 76 | 1.785 | 19 | 49 | 83 | 98 | | | | | | | | |
| 80 | 1.785 | 20 | 51 | 85 | 98 | | | | | | | | |
| 84 | 1.784 | 20 | 53 | 86 | 99 | | | | | | | | |
| 88 | 1.784 | 21 | 55 | 88 | 99 | | | | | | | | |
| 92 | 1.783 | 21 | 57 | 89 | 99 | | | | | | | | |
| 96 | 1.783 | 22 | 58 | 91 | 99 | | | | | | | | |
| 100 | 1.783 | 22 | 60 | 92 | * | | | | | | | | |
| 120 | 1.781 | 25 | 68 | 96 | | | | | | | | | |
| 140 | 1.780 | 28 | 75 | 98 | | | | | | | | | |
| 160 | 1.779 | 31 | 80 | 99 | | | | | | | | | |
| 180 | 1.779 | 33 | 85 | * | | | | | | | | | |
| 200 | 1.778 | 36 | 89 | | | | | | | | | | |
| 250 | 1.778 | 43 | 94 | | | | | | | | | | |
| 300 | 1.777 | 49 | 97 | | | | | | | | | | |
| 350 | 1.777 | 55 | 99 | | | | | | | | | | |
| 400 | 1.776 | 60 | * | | | | | | | | | | |
| 450 | 1.776 | 66 | | | | | | | | | | | |
| 500 | 1.776 | 70 | | | | | | | | | | | |
| 600 | 1.776 | 78 | | | | | | | | | | | |
| 700 | 1.775 | 84 | | | | | | | | | | | |
| 800 | 1.775 | 89 | | | | | | | | | | | |
| 900 | 1.775 | 92 | | | | | | | | | | | |
| 1000 | 1.775 | 94 | | | | | | | | | | | |

* Power values below this point are greater than .995.

**Table 8.3.29**

Power of F test at a = .10, u = 8

| | | | | | | | f | | | | | | |
|---|---|---|---|---|---|---|---|---|---|---|---|---|---|
| n | $F_c$ | .05 | .10 | .15 | .20 | .25 | .30 | .35 | .40 | .50 | .60 | .70 | .80 |
| 2 | 2.469 | 10 | 11 | 11 | 12 | 14 | 15 | 17 | 20 | 25 | 33 | 41 | 50 |
| 3 | 2.038 | 10 | 11 | 13 | 15 | 17 | 21 | 25 | 30 | 41 | 55 | 68 | 80 |
| 4 | 1.909 | 10 | 12 | 14 | 17 | 21 | 26 | 32 | 40 | 56 | 72 | 85 | 93 |
| 5 | 1.847 | 10 | 12 | 15 | 19 | 25 | 32 | 40 | 49 | 68 | 84 | 94 | 98 |
| 6 | 1.811 | 11 | 13 | 16 | 21 | 29 | 37 | 48 | 58 | 78 | 91 | 98 | * |
| 7 | 1.787 | 11 | 13 | 17 | 24 | 33 | 43 | 55 | 66 | 85 | 95 | 99 | |
| 8 | 1.770 | 11 | 14 | 19 | 26 | 36 | 48 | 61 | 73 | 90 | 98 | * | |
| 9 | 1.757 | 11 | 14 | 20 | 29 | 40 | 53 | 67 | 79 | 94 | 99 | | |
| 10 | 1.747 | 11 | 15 | 21 | 31 | 44 | 58 | 72 | 83 | 96 | 99 | | |
| 11 | 1.740 | 11 | 15 | 23 | 34 | 48 | 63 | 76 | 87 | 98 | * | | |
| 12 | 1.733 | 11 | 16 | 24 | 36 | 51 | 67 | 80 | 90 | 99 | | | |
| 13 | 1.728 | 11 | 16 | 26 | 39 | 55 | 71 | 84 | 93 | 99 | | | |
| 14 | 1.723 | 11 | 17 | 27 | 41 | 58 | 74 | 87 | 94 | 99 | | | |
| 15 | 1.720 | 12 | 18 | 28 | 44 | 61 | 77 | 89 | 96 | * | | | |
| 16 | 1.716 | 12 | 18 | 30 | 46 | 64 | 80 | 91 | 97 | | | | |
| 17 | 1.713 | 12 | 19 | 31 | 48 | 67 | 83 | 93 | 98 | | | | |
| 18 | 1.711 | 12 | 19 | 33 | 51 | 70 | 85 | 94 | 98 | | | | |
| 19 | 1.709 | 12 | 20 | 34 | 53 | 72 | 87 | 95 | 99 | | | | |
| 20 | 1.707 | 12 | 20 | 35 | 55 | 75 | 89 | 96 | 99 | | | | |
| 21 | 1.705 | 12 | 21 | 37 | 57 | 77 | 91 | 97 | 99 | | | | |
| 22 | 1.703 | 13 | 22 | 38 | 59 | 79 | 92 | 98 | * | | | | |
| 23 | 1.702 | 13 | 22 | 40 | 61 | 81 | 93 | 98 | | | | | |
| 24 | 1.700 | 13 | 23 | 41 | 63 | 83 | 94 | 99 | | | | | |
| 25 | 1.699 | 13 | 24 | 42 | 65 | 84 | 95 | 99 | | | | | |
| 26 | 1.698 | 13 | 24 | 44 | 67 | 86 | 96 | 99 | | | | | |
| 27 | 1.697 | 13 | 25 | 45 | 69 | 87 | 96 | 99 | | | | | |
| 28 | 1.696 | 13 | 25 | 46 | 70 | 88 | 97 | * | | | | | |
| 29 | 1.695 | 13 | 26 | 48 | 72 | 90 | 97 | | | | | | |
| 30 | 1.694 | 14 | 27 | 49 | 74 | 91 | 98 | | | | | | |
| 31 | 1.693 | 14 | 27 | 50 | 75 | 92 | 98 | | | | | | |
| 32 | 1.692 | 14 | 28 | 52 | 76 | 92 | 99 | | | | | | |
| 33 | 1.692 | 14 | 29 | 53 | 78 | 93 | 99 | | | | | | |
| 34 | 1.691 | 14 | 29 | 54 | 79 | 94 | 99 | | | | | | |
| 35 | 1.691 | 14 | 30 | 55 | 80 | 95 | 99 | | | | | | |
| 36 | 1.690 | 14 | 30 | 56 | 81 | 95 | 99 | | | | | | |
| 37 | 1.689 | 15 | 31 | 58 | 83 | 96 | 99 | | | | | | |
| 38 | 1.689 | 15 | 32 | 59 | 84 | 96 | * | | | | | | |
| 39 | 1.688 | 15 | 32 | 60 | 85 | 97 | | | | | | | |

**Table 8.3.29** *(continued)*

| n | $F_c$ | .05 | .10 | .15 | .20 | .25 | .30 | .35 | .40 | .50 | .60 | .70 | .80 |
|---|---|---|---|---|---|---|---|---|---|---|---|---|---|
| | | | | | | | | | | | | | |
| 40 | 1.688 | 15 | 33 | 61 | 86 | 97 | * | * | * | * | * | * | * |
| 42 | 1.687 | 15 | 34 | 63 | 87 | 98 | | | | | | | |
| 44 | 1.686 | 16 | 35 | 65 | 89 | 98 | | | | | | | |
| 46 | 1.686 | 16 | 37 | 67 | 90 | 99 | | | | | | | |
| 48 | 1.685 | 16 | 38 | 69 | 92 | 99 | | | | | | | |
| | | | | | | | | | | | | | |
| 50 | 1.684 | 16 | 39 | 71 | 93 | 99 | | | | | | | |
| 52 | 1.684 | 17 | 40 | 73 | 94 | 99 | | | | | | | |
| 54 | 1.683 | 17 | 42 | 75 | 94 | 99 | | | | | | | |
| 56 | 1.683 | 17 | 43 | 76 | 95 | * | | | | | | | |
| 58 | 1.682 | 18 | 44 | 78 | 96 | | | | | | | | |
| | | | | | | | | | | | | | |
| 60 | 1.682 | 18 | 45 | 79 | 96 | | | | | | | | |
| 64 | 1.681 | 18 | 48 | 82 | 97 | | | | | | | | |
| 68 | 1.681 | 19 | 50 | 84 | 98 | | | | | | | | |
| 72 | 1.680 | 20 | 52 | 86 | 99 | | | | | | | | |
| 76 | 1.679 | 20 | 54 | 88 | 99 | | | | | | | | |
| | | | | | | | | | | | | | |
| 80 | 1.679 | 21 | 56 | 90 | 99 | | | | | | | | |
| 84 | 1.679 | 21 | 58 | 91 | 99 | | | | | | | | |
| 88 | 1.678 | 22 | 60 | 93 | * | | | | | | | | |
| 92 | 1.678 | 23 | 62 | 94 | | | | | | | | | |
| 96 | 1.677 | 23 | 64 | 95 | | | | | | | | | |
| | | | | | | | | | | | | | |
| 100 | 1.677 | 24 | 66 | 95 | | | | | | | | | |
| 120 | 1.676 | 27 | 74 | 98 | | | | | | | | | |
| 140 | 1.675 | 30 | 81 | 99 | | | | | | | | | |
| 160 | 1.675 | 33 | 86 | * | | | | | | | | | |
| 180 | 1.674 | 36 | 90 | | | | | | | | | | |
| | | | | | | | | | | | | | |
| 200 | 1.674 | 39 | 93 | | | | | | | | | | |
| 250 | 1.673 | 47 | 97 | | | | | | | | | | |
| 300 | 1.673 | 54 | 99 | | | | | | | | | | |
| 350 | 1.672 | 61 | * | | | | | | | | | | |
| 400 | 1.672 | 66 | | | | | | | | | | | |
| 450 | 1.672 | 72 | | | | | | | | | | | |
| | | | | | | | | | | | | | |
| 500 | 1.672 | 76 | | | | | | | | | | | |
| 600 | 1.671 | 84 | | | | | | | | | | | |
| 700 | 1.671 | 89 | | | | | | | | | | | |
| 800 | 1.671 | 93 | | | | | | | | | | | |
| 900 | 1.671 | 96 | | | | | | | | | | | |
| 1000 | 1.671 | 97 | | | | | | | | | | | |

* Power values below this point are greater than .995.

Table 8.3.30

Power of F test at a = .10, u = 10

| n | $F_c$ | .05 | .10 | .15 | .20 | .25 | .30 | .35 | .40 | .50 | .60 | .70 | .80 |
|---|---|---|---|---|---|---|---|---|---|---|---|---|---|
| | | | | | | | f | | | | | | |
| 2 | 2.248 | 10 | 11 | 12 | 13 | 14 | 16 | 18 | 21 | 27 | 36 | 45 | 51 |
| 3 | 1.904 | 10 | 11 | 13 | 15 | 18 | 22 | 26 | 32 | 45 | 60 | 74 | 85 |
| 4 | 1.799 | 10 | 12 | 14 | 17 | 22 | 28 | 35 | 43 | 61 | 78 | 90 | 96 |
| 5 | 1.747 | 11 | 12 | 15 | 20 | 26 | 34 | 44 | 54 | 74 | 89 | 96 | 99 |
| 6 | 1.717 | 11 | 13 | 17 | 23 | 31 | 41 | 52 | 63 | 83 | 95 | 99 | * |
| 7 | 1.697 | 11 | 13 | 18 | 25 | 35 | 47 | 59 | 71 | 90 | 98 | * | |
| 8 | 1.683 | 11 | 14 | 20 | 28 | 39 | 53 | 66 | 78 | 94 | 99 | | |
| 9 | 1.672 | 11 | 15 | 21 | 31 | 44 | 58 | 72 | 84 | 96 | * | | |
| 10 | 1.664 | 11 | 15 | 23 | 34 | 48 | 63 | 77 | 88 | 98 | | | |
| 11 | 1.657 | 11 | 16 | 24 | 37 | 52 | 68 | 82 | 91 | 99 | | | |
| 12 | 1.652 | 11 | 16 | 26 | 39 | 56 | 72 | 85 | 93 | 99 | | | |
| 13 | 1.648 | 11 | 17 | 27 | 42 | 59 | 76 | 88 | 95 | * | | | |
| 14 | 1.644 | 12 | 18 | 29 | 45 | 63 | 79 | 91 | 97 | | | | |
| 15 | 1.641 | 12 | 18 | 30 | 47 | 66 | 82 | 93 | 98 | | | | |
| 16 | 1.638 | 12 | 19 | 32 | 50 | 69 | 85 | 94 | 98 | | | | |
| 17 | 1.635 | 12 | 20 | 33 | 53 | 72 | 87 | 96 | 99 | | | | |
| 18 | 1.633 | 12 | 20 | 35 | 55 | 75 | 89 | 97 | 99 | | | | |
| 19 | 1.631 | 12 | 21 | 37 | 57 | 78 | 91 | 98 | * | | | | |
| 20 | 1.630 | 12 | 22 | 38 | 60 | 80 | 93 | 98 | | | | | |
| 21 | 1.628 | 13 | 22 | 40 | 62 | 82 | 94 | 99 | | | | | |
| 22 | 1.627 | 13 | 23 | 41 | 64 | 84 | 95 | 99 | | | | | |
| 23 | 1.625 | 13 | 24 | 43 | 66 | 86 | 96 | 99 | | | | | |
| 24 | 1.624 | 13 | 24 | 44 | 68 | 87 | 97 | 99 | | | | | |
| 25 | 1.623 | 13 | 25 | 46 | 70 | 89 | 97 | * | | | | | |
| 26 | 1.622 | 13 | 26 | 47 | 72 | 90 | 98 | | | | | | |
| 27 | 1.621 | 14 | 26 | 49 | 74 | 91 | 98 | | | | | | |
| 28 | 1.620 | 14 | 27 | 50 | 76 | 92 | 98 | | | | | | |
| 29 | 1.620 | 14 | 28 | 52 | 77 | 93 | 99 | | | | | | |
| 30 | 1.619 | 14 | 28 | 53 | 79 | 94 | 99 | | | | | | |
| 31 | 1.618 | 14 | 29 | 55 | 80 | 95 | 99 | | | | | | |
| 32 | 1.618 | 14 | 30 | 56 | 81 | 95 | 99 | | | | | | |
| 33 | 1.617 | 14 | 31 | 57 | 83 | 96 | 99 | | | | | | |
| 34 | 1.616 | 15 | 31 | 59 | 84 | 96 | * | | | | | | |
| 35 | 1.616 | 15 | 32 | 60 | 85 | 97 | | | | | | | |
| 36 | 1.615 | 15 | 33 | 61 | 86 | 97 | | | | | | | |
| 37 | 1.615 | 15 | 33 | 62 | 87 | 98 | | | | | | | |
| 38 | 1.615 | 15 | 34 | 64 | 88 | 98 | | | | | | | |
| 39 | 1.614 | 15 | 35 | 65 | 89 | 98 | | | | | | | |

Table 8.3.30 *(continued)*

| n | $F_c$ | .05 | .10 | .15 | .20 | .25 | .30 | .35 | .40 | .50 | .60 | .70 | .80 |
|---|---|---|---|---|---|---|---|---|---|---|---|---|---|
| | | | | | | | | | | | | **f** | |
| 40 | 1.614 | 15 | 35 | 66 | 90 | 98 | * | * | * | * | * | * | * |
| 42 | 1.613 | 16 | 37 | 68 | 91 | 99 | | | | | | | |
| 44 | 1.612 | 16 | 38 | 70 | 93 | 99 | | | | | | | |
| 46 | 1.612 | 16 | 40 | 72 | 94 | 99 | | | | | | | |
| 48 | 1.611 | 17 | 41 | 74 | 95 | * | | | | | | | |
| 50 | 1.611 | 17 | 42 | 76 | 95 | | | | | | | | |
| 52 | 1.610 | 17 | 44 | 78 | 96 | | | | | | | | |
| 54 | 1.610 | 18 | 45 | 80 | 97 | | | | | | | | |
| 56 | 1.609 | 18 | 46 | 81 | 97 | | | | | | | | |
| 58 | 1.609 | 18 | 48 | 83 | 98 | | | | | | | | |
| 60 | 1.609 | 19 | 49 | 84 | 98 | | | | | | | | |
| 64 | 1.608 | 19 | 52 | 86 | 99 | | | | | | | | |
| 68 | 1.607 | 20 | 54 | 89 | 99 | | | | | | | | |
| 72 | 1.607 | 21 | 56 | 90 | 99 | | | | | | | | |
| 76 | 1.607 | 21 | 59 | 92 | * | | | | | | | | |
| 80 | 1.606 | 22 | 61 | 93 | | | | | | | | | |
| 84 | 1.606 | 23 | 63 | 94 | | | | | | | | | |
| 88 | 1.605 | 23 | 66 | 95 | | | | | | | | | |
| 92 | 1.605 | 24 | 68 | 96 | | | | | | | | | |
| 96 | 1.605 | 25 | 70 | 97 | | | | | | | | | |
| 100 | 1.605 | 25 | 71 | 97 | | | | | | | | | |
| 120 | 1.604 | 29 | 79 | 99 | | | | | | | | | |
| 140 | 1.603 | 32 | 86 | * | | | | | | | | | |
| 160 | 1.603 | 36 | 90 | | | | | | | | | | |
| 180 | 1.602 | 39 | 93 | | | | | | | | | | |
| 200 | 1.602 | 43 | 96 | | | | | | | | | | |
| 250 | 1.601 | 51 | 99 | | | | | | | | | | |
| 300 | 1.601 | 59 | * | | | | | | | | | | |
| 350 | 1.600 | 66 | | | | | | | | | | | |
| 400 | 1.600 | 72 | | | | | | | | | | | |
| 450 | 1.600 | 77 | | | | | | | | | | | |
| 500 | 1.600 | 81 | | | | | | | | | | | |
| 600 | 1.600 | 88 | | | | | | | | | | | |
| 700 | 1.600 | 93 | | | | | | | | | | | |
| 800 | 1.599 | 96 | | | | | | | | | | | |
| 900 | 1.599 | 98 | | | | | | | | | | | |
| 1000 | 1.599 | 99 | | | | | | | | | | | |

* Power values below this point are greater than .995.

Table 8.3.31

Power of F test at a = .10, u = 12

| n | $F_c$ | .05 | .10 | .15 | .20 | .25 | .30 | .35 | .40 | .50 | .60 | .70 | .80 |
|---|---|---|---|---|---|---|---|---|---|---|---|---|---|
| | | | | | | | | f | | | | | |
| 2 | 2.097 | 10 | 11 | 11 | 13 | 15 | 17 | 19 | 22 | 29 | 39 | 49 | 61 |
| 3 | 1.809 | 10 | 11 | 13 | 15 | 19 | 23 | 28 | 34 | 49 | 65 | 79 | 89 |
| 4 | 1.719 | 10 | 12 | 14 | 18 | 23 | 30 | 38 | 47 | 66 | 82 | 93 | 98 |
| 5 | 1.675 | 11 | 12 | 16 | 21 | 28 | 37 | 47 | 58 | 78 | 92 | 98 | * |
| 6 | 1.649 | 11 | 13 | 17 | 24 | 33 | 44 | 56 | 68 | 87 | 97 | 99 | |
| 7 | 1.631 | 11 | 14 | 19 | 27 | 37 | 50 | 64 | 76 | 93 | 99 | * | |
| 8 | 1.619 | 11 | 14 | 20 | 30 | 42 | 56 | 70 | 82 | 96 | * | | |
| 9 | 1.610 | 11 | 15 | 22 | 33 | 47 | 62 | 76 | 87 | 98 | | | |
| 10 | 1.603 | 11 | 16 | 24 | 36 | 51 | 68 | 81 | 91 | 99 | | | |
| 11 | 1.597 | 11 | 16 | 25 | 39 | 56 | 72 | 86 | 94 | 99 | | | |
| 12 | 1.592 | 11 | 17 | 27 | 42 | 60 | 77 | 89 | 96 | * | | | |
| 13 | 1.588 | 12 | 18 | 29 | 45 | 64 | 80 | 92 | 97 | | | | |
| 14 | 1.585 | 12 | 18 | 31 | 48 | 67 | 84 | 94 | 98 | | | | |
| 15 | 1.582 | 12 | 19 | 32 | 51 | 71 | 86 | 95 | 99 | | | | |
| 16 | 1.580 | 12 | 20 | 34 | 54 | 74 | 89 | 96 | 99 | | | | |
| 17 | 1.578 | 12 | 20 | 36 | 56 | 77 | 91 | 97 | * | | | | |
| 18 | 1.576 | 12 | 21 | 37 | 59 | 79 | 92 | 98 | | | | | |
| 19 | 1.574 | 13 | 22 | 39 | 62 | 82 | 94 | 99 | | | | | |
| 20 | 1.573 | 13 | 23 | 41 | 64 | 84 | 95 | 99 | | | | | |
| 21 | 1.571 | 13 | 23 | 43 | 66 | 86 | 96 | 99 | | | | | |
| 22 | 1.570 | 13 | 24 | 44 | 69 | 88 | 97 | * | | | | | |
| 23 | 1.569 | 13 | 25 | 46 | 71 | 89 | 97 | | | | | | |
| 24 | 1.568 | 13 | 26 | 48 | 73 | 91 | 98 | | | | | | |
| 25 | 1.567 | 13 | 26 | 49 | 75 | 92 | 98 | | | | | | |
| 26 | 1.566 | 14 | 27 | 51 | 77 | 93 | 99 | | | | | | |
| 27 | 1.565 | 14 | 28 | 52 | 78 | 94 | 99 | | | | | | |
| 28 | 1.565 | 14 | 29 | 54 | 80 | 95 | 99 | | | | | | |
| 29 | 1.564 | 14 | 29 | 55 | 81 | 95 | 99 | | | | | | |
| 30 | 1.563 | 14 | 30 | 57 | 83 | 96 | * | | | | | | |
| 31 | 1.563 | 14 | 31 | 58 | 84 | 97 | | | | | | | |
| 32 | 1.562 | 15 | 32 | 60 | 85 | 97 | | | | | | | |
| 33 | 1.562 | 15 | 32 | 61 | 87 | 98 | | | | | | | |
| 34 | 1.561 | 15 | 33 | 63 | 88 | 98 | | | | | | | |
| 35 | 1.561 | 15 | 34 | 64 | 89 | 98 | | | | | | | |
| 36 | 1.560 | 15 | 35 | 65 | 90 | 99 | | | | | | | |
| 37 | 1.560 | 15 | 35 | 67 | 90 | 99 | | | | | | | |
| 38 | 1.560 | 16 | 36 | 68 | 91 | 99 | | | | | | | |
| 39 | 1.559 | 16 | 37 | 69 | 92 | 99 | | | | | | | |

Table 8.3.31 *(continued)*

| | | | | | | | | | | | | | f |
|---|---|---|---|---|---|---|---|---|---|---|---|---|---|
| n | $F_c$ | .05 | .10 | .15 | .20 | .25 | .30 | .35 | .40 | .50 | .60 | .70 | .80 |
| 40 | 1.559 | 16 | 38 | 70 | 93 | 99 | * | * | * | * | * | * | * |
| 42 | 1.558 | 16 | 39 | 73 | 94 | 99 | | | | | | | |
| 44 | 1.558 | 17 | 41 | 75 | 95 | * | | | | | | | |
| 46 | 1.557 | 17 | 42 | 77 | 96 | | | | | | | | |
| 48 | 1.557 | 17 | 44 | 79 | 97 | | | | | | | | |
| 50 | 1.556 | 18 | 45 | 81 | 97 | | | | | | | | |
| 52 | 1.556 | 18 | 47 | 82 | 98 | | | | | | | | |
| 54 | 1.555 | 18 | 48 | 84 | 98 | | | | | | | | |
| 56 | 1.555 | 19 | 50 | 85 | 99 | | | | | | | | |
| 58 | 1.555 | 19 | 51 | 86 | 99 | | | | | | | | |
| 60 | 1.554 | 19 | 53 | 88 | 99 | | | | | | | | |
| 64 | 1.554 | 20 | 55 | 90 | 99 | | | | | | | | |
| 68 | 1.553 | 21 | 58 | 92 | * | | | | | | | | |
| 72 | 1.553 | 22 | 60 | 93 | | | | | | | | | |
| 76 | 1.553 | 22 | 63 | 95 | | | | | | | | | |
| 80 | 1.552 | 23 | 65 | 96 | | | | | | | | | |
| 84 | 1.552 | 24 | 68 | 96 | | | | | | | | | |
| 88 | 1.552 | 24 | 70 | 97 | | | | | | | | | |
| 92 | 1.551 | 25 | 72 | 98 | | | | | | | | | |
| 96 | 1.551 | 26 | 74 | 98 | | | | | | | | | |
| 100 | 1.551 | 27 | 76 | 99 | | | | | | | | | |
| 120 | 1.550 | 31 | 84 | * | | | | | | | | | |
| 140 | 1.549 | 34 | 89 | | | | | | | | | | |
| 160 | 1.549 | 38 | 93 | | | | | | | | | | |
| 180 | 1.549 | 42 | 96 | | | | | | | | | | |
| 200 | 1.548 | 46 | 97 | | | | | | | | | | |
| 250 | 1.548 | 55 | 99 | | | | | | | | | | |
| 300 | 1.548 | 63 | * | | | | | | | | | | |
| 350 | 1.547 | 70 | | | | | | | | | | | |
| 400 | 1.547 | 76 | | | | | | | | | | | |
| 450 | 1.547 | 81 | | | | | | | | | | | |
| 500 | 1.547 | 85 | | | | | | | | | | | |
| 600 | 1.547 | 91 | | | | | | | | | | | |
| 700 | 1.547 | 95 | | | | | | | | | | | |
| 800 | 1.546 | 97 | | | | | | | | | | | |
| 900 | 1.546 | 99 | | | | | | | | | | | |
| 1000 | 1.546 | 99 | | | | | | | | | | | |

* Power values below this point are greater than .995.

**Table 8.3.32**

Power of F test at a = .10, u = 15

| | | | | | | | f | | | | | | |
|---|---|---|---|---|---|---|---|---|---|---|---|---|---|
| n | $F_c$ | .05 | .10 | .15 | .20 | .25 | .30 | .35 | .40 | .50 | .60 | .70 | .80 |
| 2 | 1.940 | 10 | 11 | 12 | 13 | 15 | 17 | 20 | 24 | 32 | 43 | 55 | 67 |
| 3 | 1.707 | 10 | 11 | 13 | 16 | 20 | 24 | 30 | 38 | 54 | 71 | 85 | 93 |
| 4 | 1.633 | 10 | 12 | 15 | 19 | 25 | 32 | 41 | 51 | 72 | 87 | 96 | 99 |
| 5 | 1.596 | 11 | 13 | 16 | 22 | 30 | 40 | 52 | 63 | 84 | 95 | 99 | * |
| 6 | 1.574 | 11 | 13 | 18 | 25 | 35 | 48 | 61 | 74 | 91 | 98 | * | |
| 7 | 1.560 | 11 | 14 | 20 | 29 | 41 | 55 | 69 | 81 | 96 | 99 | | |
| 8 | 1.549 | 11 | 15 | 22 | 32 | 46 | 62 | 76 | 87 | 98 | * | | |
| 9 | 1.541 | 11 | 15 | 23 | 36 | 51 | 68 | 82 | 92 | 99 | | | |
| 10 | 1.535 | 11 | 16 | 25 | 39 | 56 | 73 | 86 | 95 | * | | | |
| 11 | 1.531 | 12 | 17 | 27 | 43 | 61 | 78 | 90 | 97 | | | | |
| 12 | 1.527 | 12 | 18 | 29 | 46 | 65 | 82 | 93 | 98 | | | | |
| 13 | 1.523 | 12 | 18 | 31 | 49 | 69 | 85 | 95 | 99 | | | | |
| 14 | 1.521 | 12 | 19 | 33 | 52 | 73 | 88 | 96 | 99 | | | | |
| 15 | 1.518 | 12 | 20 | 35 | 56 | 76 | 91 | 97 | * | | | | |
| 16 | 1.516 | 12 | 21 | 37 | 59 | 79 | 93 | 98 | | | | | |
| 17 | 1.514 | 12 | 22 | 39 | 62 | 82 | 94 | 99 | | | | | |
| 18 | 1.513 | 13 | 22 | 41 | 64 | 85 | 96 | 99 | | | | | |
| 19 | 1.511 | 13 | 23 | 43 | 67 | 87 | 97 | 99 | | | | | |
| 20 | 1.510 | 13 | 24 | 45 | 70 | 89 | 97 | * | | | | | |
| 21 | 1.509 | 13 | 25 | 46 | 72 | 90 | 98 | | | | | | |
| 22 | 1.508 | 13 | 26 | 48 | 74 | 92 | 98 | | | | | | |
| 23 | 1.507 | 13 | 26 | 50 | 76 | 93 | 99 | | | | | | |
| 24 | 1.506 | 14 | 27 | 52 | 78 | 94 | 99 | | | | | | |
| 25 | 1.505 | 14 | 28 | 54 | 80 | 95 | 99 | | | | | | |
| 26 | 1.504 | 14 | 29 | 56 | 82 | 96 | * | | | | | | |
| 27 | 1.504 | 14 | 30 | 57 | 83 | 97 | | | | | | | |
| 28 | 1.503 | 14 | 31 | 59 | 85 | 97 | | | | | | | |
| 29 | 1.503 | 15 | 32 | 61 | 86 | 98 | | | | | | | |
| 30 | 1.502 | 15 | 32 | 62 | 88 | 98 | | | | | | | |
| 31 | 1.502 | 15 | 33 | 64 | 89 | 98 | | | | | | | |
| 32 | 1.501 | 15 | 34 | 65 | 90 | 99 | | | | | | | |
| 33 | 1.501 | 15 | 35 | 67 | 91 | 99 | | | | | | | |
| 34 | 1.500 | 15 | 36 | 68 | 92 | 99 | | | | | | | |
| 35 | 1.500 | 16 | 37 | 70 | 93 | 99 | | | | | | | |
| 36 | 1.500 | 16 | 38 | 71 | 93 | 99 | | | | | | | |
| 37 | 1.499 | 16 | 39 | 72 | 94 | * | | | | | | | |
| 38 | 1.499 | 16 | 39 | 74 | 95 | | | | | | | | |
| 39 | 1.499 | 16 | 40 | 75 | 95 | | | | | | | | |

Table 8.3.32 (continued)

| n | $F_c$ | .05 | .10 | .15 | .20 | .25 | .30 | .35 | .40 | .50 | .60 | .70 | .80 |
|---|---|---|---|---|---|---|---|---|---|---|---|---|---|
| | | | | | | | | | f | | | | |
| 40 | 1.498 | 17 | 41 | 76 | 96 | * | * | * | * | * | * | * | * |
| 42 | 1.498 | 17 | 43 | 78 | 97 | | | | | | | | |
| 44 | 1.497 | 17 | 45 | 80 | 97 | | | | | | | | |
| 46 | 1.497 | 18 | 46 | 82 | 98 | | | | | | | | |
| 48 | 1.496 | 18 | 48 | 84 | 98 | | | | | | | | |
| 50 | 1.496 | 18 | 49 | 86 | 99 | | | | | | | | |
| 52 | 1.496 | 19 | 51 | 87 | 99 | | | | | | | | |
| 54 | 1.495 | 19 | 53 | 88 | 99 | | | | | | | | |
| 56 | 1.495 | 20 | 54 | 90 | 99 | | | | | | | | |
| 58 | 1.495 | 20 | 56 | 91 | * | | | | | | | | |
| 60 | 1.494 | 20 | 57 | 92 | | | | | | | | | |
| 64 | 1.494 | 21 | 60 | 94 | | | | | | | | | |
| 68 | 1.494 | 22 | 63 | 95 | | | | | | | | | |
| 72 | 1.493 | 23 | 66 | 96 | | | | | | | | | |
| 76 | 1.493 | 24 | 68 | 97 | | | | | | | | | |
| 80 | 1.493 | 24 | 71 | 98 | | | | | | | | | |
| 84 | 1.492 | 25 | 73 | 98 | | | | | | | | | |
| 88 | 1.492 | 26 | 75 | 99 | | | | | | | | | |
| 92 | 1.492 | 27 | 77 | 99 | | | | | | | | | |
| 96 | 1.492 | 28 | 79 | 99 | | | | | | | | | |
| 100 | 1.491 | 29 | 81 | 99 | | | | | | | | | |
| 120 | 1.491 | 33 | 88 | * | | | | | | | | | |
| 140 | 1.490 | 37 | 93 | | | | | | | | | | |
| 160 | 1.490 | 42 | 96 | | | | | | | | | | |
| 180 | 1.490 | 46 | 98 | | | | | | | | | | |
| 200 | 1.489 | 50 | 99 | | | | | | | | | | |
| 250 | 1.489 | 60 | * | | | | | | | | | | |
| 300 | 1.489 | 68 | | | | | | | | | | | |
| 350 | 1.488 | 75 | | | | | | | | | | | |
| 400 | 1.488 | 81 | | | | | | | | | | | |
| 450 | 1.488 | 86 | | | | | | | | | | | |
| 500 | 1.488 | 90 | | | | | | | | | | | |
| 600 | 1.488 | 95 | | | | | | | | | | | |
| 700 | 1.488 | 97 | | | | | | | | | | | |
| 800 | 1.488 | 99 | | | | | | | | | | | |
| 900 | 1.488 | 99 | | | | | | | | | | | |
| 1000 | 1.488 | * | | | | | | | | | | | |

* Power values below this point are greater than .995.

Table 8.3.33

Power of F test at a = .10, u = 24

| n | $F_c$ | .05 | .10 | .15 | .20 | .25 | .30 | .35 | .40 | .50 | .60 | .70 | .80 |
|---|---|---|---|---|---|---|---|---|---|---|---|---|---|
| 2 | 1.689 | 10 | 11 | 12 | 14 | 16 | 19 | 23 | 28 | 40 | 54 | 69 | 81 |
| 3 | 1.536 | 10 | 12 | 14 | 17 | 22 | 29 | 37 | 46 | 66 | 84 | 94 | 99 |
| 4 | 1.485 | 11 | 12 | 16 | 21 | 29 | 39 | 51 | 63 | 84 | 96 | 99 | * |
| 5 | 1.460 | 11 | 13 | 18 | 26 | 36 | 49 | 63 | 76 | 93 | 99 | * | |
| 6 | 1.445 | 11 | 14 | 20 | 30 | 43 | 58 | 73 | 85 | 98 | * | | |
| 7 | 1.434 | 11 | 15 | 22 | 34 | 50 | 67 | 82 | 92 | 99 | | | |
| 8 | 1.427 | 11 | 16 | 25 | 39 | 56 | 74 | 88 | 95 | * | | | |
| 9 | 1.422 | 11 | 17 | 27 | 43 | 62 | 80 | 92 | 98 | | | | |
| 10 | 1.417 | 12 | 18 | 29 | 48 | 68 | 85 | 95 | 99 | | | | |
| 11 | 1.414 | 12 | 19 | 32 | 52 | 73 | 89 | 97 | 99 | | | | |
| 12 | 1.411 | 12 | 20 | 35 | 56 | 78 | 92 | 98 | * | | | | |
| 13 | 1.409 | 12 | 21 | 37 | 60 | 81 | 94 | 99 | | | | | |
| 14 | 1.407 | 12 | 22 | 40 | 64 | 85 | 96 | 99 | | | | | |
| 15 | 1.405 | 13 | 23 | 42 | 67 | 88 | 97 | * | | | | | |
| 16 | 1.404 | 13 | 24 | 45 | 71 | 90 | 98 | | | | | | |
| 17 | 1.402 | 13 | 25 | 47 | 74 | 92 | 99 | | | | | | |
| 18 | 1.401 | 13 | 26 | 50 | 77 | 94 | 99 | | | | | | |
| 19 | 1.400 | 13 | 27 | 52 | 79 | 95 | 99 | | | | | | |
| 20 | 1.399 | 14 | 28 | 54 | 82 | 96 | * | | | | | | |
| 21 | 1.399 | 14 | 29 | 57 | 84 | 97 | | | | | | | |
| 22 | 1.398 | 14 | 30 | 59 | 86 | 98 | | | | | | | |
| 23 | 1.397 | 14 | 31 | 61 | 88 | 98 | | | | | | | |
| 24 | 1.397 | 15 | 32 | 63 | 89 | 99 | | | | | | | |
| 25 | 1.396 | 15 | 33 | 65 | 91 | 99 | | | | | | | |
| 26 | 1.395 | 15 | 35 | 67 | 92 | 99 | | | | | | | |
| 27 | 1.395 | 15 | 36 | 59 | 93 | 99 | | | | | | | |
| 28 | 1.395 | 15 | 37 | 71 | 94 | * | | | | | | | |
| 29 | 1.394 | 16 | 38 | 73 | 95 | | | | | | | | |
| 30 | 1.394 | 16 | 39 | 74 | 95 | | | | | | | | |
| 31 | 1.393 | 16 | 40 | 76 | 96 | | | | | | | | |
| 32 | 1.393 | 16 | 41 | 77 | 97 | | | | | | | | |
| 33 | 1.393 | 17 | 42 | 79 | 97 | | | | | | | | |
| 34 | 1.393 | 17 | 43 | 80 | 98 | | | | | | | | |
| 35 | 1.392 | 17 | 45 | 82 | 98 | | | | | | | | |
| 36 | 1.392 | 17 | 46 | 83 | 98 | | | | | | | | |
| 37 | 1.392 | 17 | 47 | 84 | 99 | | | | | | | | |
| 38 | 1.392 | 18 | 48 | 85 | 99 | | | | | | | | |
| 39 | 1.391 | 18 | 49 | 86 | 99 | | | | | | | | |

Table 8.3.33 (continued)

| | | | | | | | f | | | | | | |
|---|---|---|---|---|---|---|---|---|---|---|---|---|---|
| n | $F_c$ | .05 | .10 | .15 | .20 | .25 | .30 | .35 | .40 | .50 | .60 | .70 | .80 |
| 40 | 1.391 | 18 | 50 | 87 | 99 | * | * | * | * | * | * | * | * |
| 42 | 1.391 | 19 | 52 | 89 | 99 | | | | | | | | |
| 44 | 1.391 | 19 | 54 | 91 | * | | | | | | | | |
| 46 | 1.390 | 20 | 56 | 92 | | | | | | | | | |
| 48 | 1.390 | 20 | 58 | 93 | | | | | | | | | |
| 50 | 1.389 | 21 | 60 | 94 | | | | | | | | | |
| 52 | 1.389 | 21 | 62 | 95 | | | | | | | | | |
| 54 | 1.389 | 22 | 64 | 96 | | | | | | | | | |
| 56 | 1.389 | 22 | 66 | 97 | | | | | | | | | |
| 58 | 1.389 | 23 | 67 | 97 | | | | | | | | | |
| 60 | 1.388 | 23 | 69 | 98 | | | | | | | | | |
| 64 | 1.388 | 24 | 72 | 98 | | | | | | | | | |
| 68 | 1.388 | 25 | 75 | 99 | | | | | | | | | |
| 72 | 1.388 | 26 | 78 | 99 | | | | | | | | | |
| 76 | 1.387 | 27 | 80 | * | | | | | | | | | |
| 80 | 1.387 | 29 | 83 | | | | | | | | | | |
| 84 | 1.387 | 30 | 85 | | | | | | | | | | |
| 88 | 1.387 | 31 | 87 | | | | | | | | | | |
| 92 | 1.387 | 32 | 88 | | | | | | | | | | |
| 96 | 1.386 | 33 | 90 | | | | | | | | | | |
| 100 | 1.386 | 34 | 91 | | | | | | | | | | |
| 120 | 1.386 | 40 | 96 | | | | | | | | | | |
| 140 | 1.385 | 45 | 98 | | | | | | | | | | |
| 160 | 1.385 | 51 | 99 | | | | | | | | | | |
| 180 | 1.385 | 56 | * | | | | | | | | | | |
| 200 | 1.385 | 61 | | | | | | | | | | | |
| 250 | 1.384 | 72 | | | | | | | | | | | |
| 300 | 1.384 | 80 | | | | | | | | | | | |
| 350 | 1.384 | 87 | | | | | | | | | | | |
| 400 | 1.384 | 91 | | | | | | | | | | | |
| 450 | 1.384 | 94 | | | | | | | | | | | |
| 500 | 1.384 | 97 | | | | | | | | | | | |
| 600 | 1.384 | 99 | | | | | | | | | | | |
| 700 | 1.384 | * | | | | | | | | | | | |
| 800 | 1.384 | | | | | | | | | | | | |
| 900 | 1.384 | | | | | | | | | | | | |
| 1000 | 1.384 | | | | | | | | | | | | |

* Power values below this point are greater than .995.

The 33 tables in this section yield power values for the **F** test when, in addition to the significance criterion (**a**) and ES (**f**), the degrees of freedom for the numerator of the **F** ratio (**u**) and sample size (**n**) are specified. They are most directly used to appraise the power of **F** tests in a completed research *post hoc*, but can, of course, be similarly used for a research *plan*, the details of which (e.g., significance criterion, sample size) can be varied to study consequences to power.

The tables give values for **a**, **u**, **f**, and **n**:

*1. Significance Criterion*, **a**. Since **F** is naturally nondirectional (see above, Section 8.1), 11 tables (for varying **u**) are provided at each of the **a** levels, .01, .05, and .10.

*2. Degrees of Freedom of the Numerator of the **F** Ratio*, **u**. At each significance criterion, a table is provided for each of the following 11 values of **u**: 1 (1) 6 (2) 12, 15, 24. For cases 0, 1, and 2, all of which involve a comparison of **k** = **u** + 1 means, the number of means which can be compared using the tables is thus **k** = 2 (1) 7 (2) 13, 16, and 25. For tests on interactions (Case 3), **u** is the interaction **df**, and equals (**k** − 1)(**r** − 1), or (**k** − 1)(**r** − 1)(**p** − 1), etc., where **k**, **r**, **p** are the number of levels of interacting main effects. Thus, **u** = 12 for the interaction of a 4 × 5 or a 3 × 7 or a 2 × 13 factorial design or the three-way interaction of a 2 × 4 × 5, a 2 × 3 × 7, or a 3 × 3 × 4 factorial design.

For missing values of **u** (7, 9, 11, etc.), linear interpolation between tables will yield quite adequate approximations.

*3. Effect Size*, **f**. Provision is made for 12 values of **f**: .05 (.05) .40 (.10) .80. For Cases 0 and 2, **f** is simply defined as the standard deviation of standardized means [formula (8.2.1)]. Its definition is generalized for unequal **n** (Case 1) and for interactions (Case 3), and the relevant formulas are given in the sections dealing with those cases. For all applications, conventional levels have been proposed (Section 8.2.3), as follows:

small: **f** = .10,

medium: **f** = .25,

large: **f** = .40.

*4. Sample Size*, **n**. This is, for Cases 0 and 2, the **n** for *each* of the **k** sample means being compared. For the other cases, **n** is a function of the sizes of the samples or "cells" involved; see Sections 8.3.2, 8.3.4. The power tables provide for **n** = 2 (1) 40 (2) 60 (4) 100 (20) 200 (50) 500 (100) 1000. Here, too, linear interpolation is quite adequate.

The values in the body of the tables are power times 100, i.e., the percent of tests carried out under the specified conditions which will result in rejection of the null hypothesis. They are rounded to the nearest unit and are generally accurate to within one unit as tabled.

8.3.1   CASE 0: **k** MEANS WITH EQUAL **n**. The simplest case is the one-way analysis of variance of **k** samples, *each* with the same number of observations, **n** (Case 0). The **F** test is based on $u = k - 1$ numerator **df**, and $k(n - 1)$ denominator **df**. The power tables were designed for Case 0 conditions, and this section describes and illustrates their use under these conditions. Later sections describe their application with unequal **n**'s (Case 1), in factorial and other designs (Case 2), and for tests of interactions (Case 3).

In Case 0, the investigator posits an alternate hypothesis or ES in terms of **f**, the standard deviation of standardized means, by one or more of the following procedures:

1. By hypothesizing the **k** varying population means expressed in the raw unit of measurement, finding the standard deviation of these means, and dividing this by the estimated within-population standard deviation. This is a literal application of formula (8.2.1). (See example 8.8 in Section 8.3.4.)

2. By hypothesizing the range of the **k** means (**d**) and their pattern, and using the formulas of Section 8.2.1. or the $c_i$ values of Table 8.2.1 to convert **d** to **f**.

3. By hypothesizing the ES as a proportion of the total variance for which population membership accounts ($\eta^2$) or as a correlation ratio ($\eta$), and using the formulas of Section 8.2.2 [particularly formula (8.2.22)] or Table 8.2.2 to convert $\eta$ or $\eta^2$ to **f**.

4. With experience, or perhaps by using the proposed operational definitions of small, medium, and large **f** values as a framework, he can work directly with **f**, i.e., simply directly specify his alternate hypothesis or ES by selecting an appropriate value of **f**.

Since the specification of a value of **f** which correctly reflects the investigator's ES expectations is crucial, cross-checking among the above routes is recommended. Thus, for example, having reached an **f** by specifying an $\eta^2$, it would be worthwhile to determine what range of means (**d**) for a given anticipated pattern that value of **f** implies, and to ascertain whether this **d** is consistent with expectation.

Once **f** is selected, the rest is simple in Case 0 applications. Find the table for the **a** and $u \, (= k - 1)$ of the problem and locate **n**, the common sample size, and **f**. This determines their power ($\times 100$). For nontabulated **f** or **u**, linear interpolation is reasonably accurate.

**Illustrative Examples**

**8.1** An educational psychologist performs an experiment in which $k = 4$ different teaching methods are to be contrasted. A total of $N = 80$ pupils are randomly assigned to samples of $n = 20$ pupils per methods group and are tested on an achievement criterion test following instruction. The resulting data are tested by an overall $F$ test of a one-way analysis of variance design, using an $a = .05$ significance criterion.

In setting the ES which she expects in the population (i.e., the alternate hypothesis), she believes that the 4 means should span a range $d$ of three-quarters of a within-population standard deviation. This judgment is based on past experience and knowledge of the characteristics of the teaching methods. On this basis, she further expects that the four means will be about equally spaced along this range, thus in Pattern 2 (Section 8.2.1). From Table 8.2.1, she reads that for $k = 4$ in Pattern 2, $f = .373d$, so that, given an anticipated $d = .75$, $f = .373(.75) = .280$. Having reached this value, she cross-checks by noting [from formula (8.2.19)] that this implies an $\eta^2 = f^2/(1 + f^2) = .280^2/(1 + .280^2) = .0727$, i.e., about $7\frac{1}{4}\%$ of the measure's total variance is accounted for by group membership, or in correlation ratio terms, $\eta = \sqrt{.0727} = .270$. She observes further that $f = .280$ is just slightly above the operational definition of a medium ES ($f = .25$). She accepts the results of this cross-checking as consonant with her expectations. The necessary specifications for determining the power of the $F$ test are complete. Note that in a one-way analysis of variance on $k$ "levels," the numerator $df$ are $u = k - 1 = 3$. Thus,

$$a = .05, \qquad u = 3, \qquad f = .28, \qquad n = 20.$$

In Table 8.3.14 for $a = .05$ and $u = 3$, at row $n = 20$, she finds power for column $f = .25$ to be .43 and for $f = .30$ to be .59. Linear interpolation yields (approximate) power of

$$.43 + \frac{(.28 - .25)}{(.30 - .25)}(.59 - .43) = .43 + .10 = .53.$$

Thus, if the standard deviation of the 4 standardized population means, $f$, is .28 of a within-population standard deviation, with $n = 20$ cases per sample, the $F$ test has had only a .53 probability of rejecting the null hypothesis at the .05 level. Note that the operative condition is the value of $f$ of .28, whether the range and pattern of population means was as predicted or whether another range and pattern, which would yield the same $f$, applied.

An experiment whose power is as low as .53 for detecting its anticipated ES is relatively inconclusive when it fails to reject the null hypothesis. Given a population $f = .28$, rather than $f = 0$ as posited by the null hypothesis, it is a "toss-up" whether his results will be significant at the **a** and **n** conditions which obtain. Note that even if the **a** criterion were liberalized to .10, linear interpolation in Table 8.3.25 (for **a** = .10, **u** = 3) between **f** = .25 and .30 gives approximate power at **n** = 20 of only .56 + .09 = .65.

This problem has been presented as if the experiment were already completed (or at least committed), with a *post hoc* determination of power under the given conditions. See problem 8.9 below for a consideration of this problem as one of experimental *planning*, where, under stated conditions, the purpose is the determination of sample size to attain a specified power.

**8.2**   A large scale research on mental hospital treatment programs of chronic schizophrenics is undertaken by a psychiatric research team. A pool of **N** = 600 suitable patients is randomly divided into 3 (=**k**) equal samples, each assigned to a different building, and in each building a different microsocial system of roles, functions, responsibilities, and rewards of staff and patients is instituted following training. After a suitable interval, patients are assessed by the research team by means of behavior rating scales. The social-scientific "cost" of mistakenly rejecting the null hypothesis leads the team to decide on **a** = .01. The team is split, however, on the question of how large an effect the difference in the three systems will have, some expecting that 5% of behavior rating variance will be accounted for by system membership, the others expecting 10%. Hence $\eta^2 = .05$ or .10. In their discussion, they agree in their expectation that the population means are at equal intervals, hence in Pattern 2 (but note that for **k** = 3, Pattern 2 and Pattern 1 are the same). From Table 8.2.2, they note that at $\eta^2 = .05$, **f** = .229, and at $\eta^2 = .10$, **f** = .333. They determine, using the constants of Table 8.2.1, that the span of means for Pattern 2 for **f** = .229 is $d_2 = 2.45(.229) = .56$, and for **f** = .333, $d_2 = 2.45(.333) = .82$. Thus the proponents of $\eta^2 = .05$ expect a spread of the three means of a little more than half a within-population standard deviation, while the $\eta^2 = .10$ faction expect a spread of almost five-sixths of a $\sigma$. This translation brings them no closer to agreement. What is the power of the eventual **F** test under each of these two alternative hypotheses?

$$a = .01, \qquad u = k - 1 = 2, \qquad f = \begin{cases} .23 \\ .33 \end{cases}, \qquad n = 200.$$

In Table 8.3.2 (for **a** = .01, **u** = 2) at row **n** = 200, they find that at **f** = .20, power is .98, and at **f** = .25, power is greater than .995. This means they need have no dispute—if the **f** = .23 ($\eta^2 = .05$) faction is right, power is about .99; if the **f** = .33 ($\eta^2 = .10$) faction is right, power is greater than .995. If either is correct, they are virtually certain to reject the null hypothesis at **a** = .01 with the **F** test.

In a circumstance like this, where there is "power to spare" (and assuming that the $\eta^2 = .05$ "pessimists" are not substantially overestimating the ES), there may be an opportunity to capitalize on these riches by enlarging on the experimental issues. For example, assume that there was a fourth microsocial system that had been a candidate for inclusion in the experiment and that adequate physical and staff resources are available for its inclusion. It might then be worth exploring the statistical power consequences of dividing the available 600 chronic patients into $k = 4$ equal groups. Assuming no change in the conditions, and for the same $f$ values, interpolation in Table 8.3.3 (for $a = .01$, $k - 1 = u = 3$) shows that at $n = 140$ (150 is not tabulated), power at $f = .23$ is about .97 and at $f = .33$, power again exceeds .995. Thus, this experiment could be enlarged at no substantial loss in power, assuming $f$ is not materially lower than .23. But note that if $f$ is really .15, the original $k = 3$, $n = 200$ experiment has still creditable power of .79 (Table 8.3.2), but the power of the revised $k = 4$, $n = 150$ experiment is only about .72 (interpolating between $n = 140$ and 160 in Table 8.3.3).

### 8.3.2   CASE 1: $k$ MEANS WITH UNEQUAL $n$.

When the sample sizes ($n_i$) drawn up from the $k$ populations whose means ($m_i$) are being compared are not all the same, no fundamental conceptual change occurs, but further attention to the definition of $f$ is required and procedures for power analysis require accommodation from those of Case 0.

$f$ was defined as the standard deviation of standardized means, $\sigma_m/\sigma$ [formula (8.2.1)], where $\sigma_m$ was given for equal $n$ in formula (8.2.2) as

$$\sigma_m = \sqrt{\frac{\sum_{i=1}^{k}(m_i - m)^2}{k}}.$$

When $n$'s are not equal, it is no longer true that the reference point from which the "effects" are calculated, $m$, is a simple mean of the $k$ population means, i.e., $m = \sum m_i/k$, but rather a *weighted* mean of these means, the weight of each $m_i$ being $p_i$, the proportion of the total $N = \sum n_i$ which its sample $n_i$ comprises. Thus, for Case 1

(8.3.1)                          $$m = \frac{\sum n_i m_i}{N} = \sum p_i m_i.$$

The $m$ for equal $n$ is a special case of this formula, where all the $p_i = n/N = n/kn = 1/k$.

Similarly, in computing the standard deviations of the means, $\sigma_m$, the separate effects of the **k** populations, $m_i - m$, must be weighted by their proportionate sample sizes:

$$(8.3.2) \qquad \sigma_m = \sqrt{\frac{\sum_{i=1}^{k} n_i(m_i - m)^2}{N}} = \sqrt{\sum_{i=1}^{k} p_i(m_i - m)^2} \, .$$

Here, too, the formula given for $\sigma_m$ for equal **n** in the previous section (8.2.2) is a special case of formula (8.3.2), where all $p_i = 1/k$.

Thus, with the understanding that for unequal **n** each population mean "counts" to the extent of the relative proportion of its sample size, no change in the definition of **f** is required; it is the standard deviation of the (weighted) standardized means.

The implication of this weighting requires comment. If the populations whose means are extreme, i.e., have large $(m_i - m)^2$, also have large **n**'s relative to the others, **f** will be larger than with equal **n**; conversely, if extreme populations have small **n**'s, **f** will be smaller, This suggests that in circumstances where the researcher has reason to believe that certain of the **k** populations will provide particularly discrepant means, dividing the total **N** unequally with larger sample **n**'s drawn from these populations will increase **f** (over equal **n**), and thereby increase power.

This statistical fact, however, cannot necessarily be taken as a mandate to so design experiments. Its utilization depends on whether the purpose of the research is solely to (*a*) test with a view to reject the null hypothesis of equal population means, or whether it (*b*) seeks to reflect a "natural" population state of affairs. When there is no "natural" population, as when the populations are of different experimental manipulations of randomly assigned subjects, as in a true experiment, we are perforce in situation (*a*). When a natural population exists, our purpose may be either (*a*) or (*b*).

An illustration should clarify the distinction. In an experiment where the effect on a dependent variable of three different experimental conditions is under scrutiny, each condition is a systematic artificial creation of the experimenter. The populations are hypothetical collections of results of a given condition being applied to all subjects. Consider, by way of contrast, a survey research designed to inquire into differences among Protestants, Catholics, and Jews in scores on a scale of attitude toward the United Nations (AUN). Here there are also three populations, but population membership is not an artificial creation of the manipulative efforts of the investigator. These are natural populations, and their properties as *populations* include their relative sizes in their combined superpopulation. There is now a choice with regard to how sampling is to proceed. The investigator can draw a random sample of **N** cases of the total population and administer the AUN scale to all **N** cases, then sort them into religious groups. The proportions in each religious group will then not be equal, but reflect (within sampling error) the relative sizes of the religious affiliation populations. Alternatively, having decided to study a total of **N** cases, he can draw *equal* samples from each religion.

Now, assume that the Jews yield a small **p**, and that their AUN population mean is quite extreme. In the former sampling plan, the **f**, based on the small weight given the Jews, would be smaller than the **f** obtained with equal sample sizes, where the mean of the Jews would be weighted equally with the others. The larger **f** would have associated with it a larger $\eta^2$ (as well as greater power). But if $\eta^2$ is to be interpreted as giving the proportion of AUN variance associated with religion in the general population, i.e., *in the natural population*, where there are relatively few Jews, it is the first sampling plan and the smaller $\eta^2$ which is appropriate. The $\eta^2$ from equal sampling would have to be interpreted as the proportion of AUN variance associated with (artificially) equiprobable religious group membership. The equal-sampling $\eta^2$ is not objectionable if the investigator wishes to consider membership in a given religious group as an abstract effect quite apart from the relative frequency with which that effect (i.e., that religious group) occurs in the population, but it clearly cannot be referred to the natural population with its varying group frequencies.

On the other hand, assume that the purpose of the investigator is solely to determine *whether* religious population means differ on AUN, i.e., to determine the status of the overall null hypothesis. Thus, no issue as to the interpretation of $\eta^2$ need arise. On this assumption, if his alternate hypothesis gives him confidence that the population mean of the Jews will be discrepant, he may advantageously oversample Jews by having their **n** equal (or even draw a *larger* sample of Jews than of the other groups) in order to make **f** larger (if his alternate hypothesis is valid), and thus increase his power.

As has already been implied, the weighting of the population means does not change the meaning of $\eta^2$ nor disturb its relationship to **f**. Thus, formulas (8.2.16)–(8.2.22) and Table 8.2.2 all obtain for Case 1. This is *not* the case for the translation between **f** and **d** measures of range in the various patterns detailed in Section 8.2.1 [formulas (8.2.5)–(8.2.15) and Table 8.2.1]. The assumption throughout that material is one of equal sample sizes, and it is clear that any given **d** value for some pattern of **k** means will lead to differing **f**'s depending upon how the varying $p_i$ are assigned to the $m_i$. The proposed conventions in regard to small, medium, and large **f** values continue to be applicable for Case 1 (except, of course, for their explication in terms of **d** values).

Finally, in Case 1, where there is no common **n** value to use in the power tables, one enters with their arithmetic mean:

$$(8.3.3) \qquad n = \frac{\sum\limits_{i=1}^{k} n_i}{k} = \frac{N}{k}.$$

Aside from the use of the mean sample size, the procedure for the use of Table 8.3 is identical with that of Case 0.

### Illustrative Examples

**8.3**  A university political science class has designed a poll to inquire into student opinion about the relative responsibilities and rights of local, state, and federal governments. An index score on centralism (CI) is derived and its relationship to various respondent characteristics is studied. One such characteristic is academic area, i.e., science, humanities, social science, etc., of which there are **k** = 6 in all. Data are available on a random sample of 300 respondents drawn from the university student roster. In considering the ES that they anticipate, they note that since they intend to generalize to the natural population of the college and are sampling accordingly, they will have unequal sample sizes and their conception of **f** must take into account the differential weighting of effects in the $\sigma_m$ of formula (8.3.2). So computed, they posit **f** at .15. They note ruefully that they expect the greatest effects [departures from the grand weighted mean of formula (8.3.1)] to come from the smallest academic area samples, and that if they had sampled the academic areas equally, they could anticipate an **f** of .20. However, sampling academic areas equally would result in inequalities on the "breaks" of the data which are to be studied, e.g., sex, political party affiliation, ethnic background. In any case, their interest lies in the correlates of CI in the "natural" university population.

What is the power at **a** = .05 under the conditions which obtain, namely

$$\mathbf{a} = .05, \qquad \mathbf{u} = \mathbf{k} - 1 = 5, \qquad \mathbf{f} = .15, \qquad \mathbf{n} = \mathbf{N}/\mathbf{k} = 50.$$

Note that **n** is entered at the average sample size, $300/6 = 50$. Table 8.3.16 (for **a** = .05, **u** = 5) for row **n** = 50, column **f** = .15, indicates that power = .48. Clearly, the *a priori* probability of the **F** test's rejecting the null hypothesis given under these conditions is not very high.

Assume that it is undesirable to increase **a** to .10 (which would increase power to .61—see Table 8.3.27) or to draw a larger sample; is there some other possible strategem to improve the prognosis for this significance test? The following might be acceptable: The division of the cases into as many as six academic areas might be reconsidered, given the partially arbitrary nature of such a partitioning. The class might discover that a somewhat less fine discrimination into three more broadly defined academic areas such as science, humanities–arts, and engineering might be acceptable. Assume that under these conditions f [still based on the $\sigma_m$ of formula (8.3.1)] is again computed to be about .15. The revised plan has the conditions

$$a = .05, \qquad u = 3 - 1 = 2, \qquad f = .15, \qquad n = 300/3 = 100.$$

In Table 8.3.13 for $a = .05$ and $u = 2$, $n = 100$, and $f = .15$, power $= .64$, a distinct improvement over the .48 value of the previous plan. If this process can, without doing violence to the issue, be carried a step further to a partitioning into two areas, and *if* the same f can be assumed, Table 8.3.12 (for $a = .05$, $u = 1$) gives power at $n = 300/2 = 150$ for $f = .15$ of about .74 (by linear interpolation). It must again be stressed that all this reasoning takes place without recourse to the data which are to be analyzed, i.e., we are in the area of planning the data analysis.

Thus, when there is some freedom available in the partitioning of a sample into groups, power considerations may advantageously enter into the decision. With f (and total **N**) constant, fewer groups and hence smaller **u** with larger **n** will result in increased power. Although f will not in general remain constant over changes in partitioning, this too may become a useful lever in planning analyses, since some partitions of the total sample will lead to larger anticipated f values, and hence greater power, than others. Therefore, when alternative partitions are possible, the investigator should seek the one whose combined effect on **u** and expected f is such as to maximize power. See problems 8.13 and 8.14 for further discussion.

**8.4**  As part of an inquiry into the differential effectiveness of psychiatric hospitals in a national system, an analysis is to be performed on the issue as to whether the psychiatric nurses in the various hospitals differ from hospital to hospital with regard to scores on an attitude scale of Social Restrictiveness (Cohen & Struening, 1963; 1964). There are **k** = 12 psychiatric hospitals of wide geographic distribution which have supplied quasi-random samples of their nursing personnel of varying sizes, depending upon administrative considerations and the size of their nursing staffs. The total **N** = 326, so that the average **n** per hospital is 326/12 = 27.2. The investigators anticipate that the ES of hospital on attitude is of medium size, i.e., that **f** = .25. They note that the f in question includes the differential weighting of the $\sigma_m$ of formula (8.2.3), but since they have no reason to expect any relationship between the size of a hospital mean's discrepancy from the grand mean (i.e., the hospital's "effect") and the size of its sample, there is no need to modify the conception of a medium ES being operationalized by **f** = .25.

What is the power of the **F** test on means at $a = .05$? The conditions of the test, in summary, are

$$a = .05, \quad u = k - 1 = 11, \quad f = .25, \quad n = 27.$$

There are no tables for $u = 11$, so that interpolation between Tables 8.3.19 (for $a = .05$, $u = 10$) and 8.3.20 (for $a = .05$, $u = 12$) is necessary. Table 8.3.19 for row $n = 27$ and column $f = .25$ yields power of .85. Table 8.3.20 for the same $n$ and $f$ gives power of .89. Linear interpolation between these values yields a power estimate of .87. Thus, given that the (weighted) standard deviation of the standardized means of the populations of nurses in these 12 hospitals is .25, the probability that **F** will meet the $a = .05$ criterion is .87, a value that would probably be deemed quite satisfactory.

8.3.3  CASE 2: FIXED MAIN EFFECTS IN FACTORIAL AND COMPLEX DESIGNS. In any experimental design of whatever structural complexity, a "fixed main effect" can be subjected to approximate power analysis with the aid of the tables of this chapter. In factorial, randomized blocks, split-plot, Latin square (etc.) designs, the **F** test on a fixed main effect involving **k** levels is a test of the equality of the **k** population means, whatever other fixed or random main or interaction effects may be included in the design (Winer, 1971; Hays, 1973; Edwards, 1972). We will illustrate the principles involved in this extension by examining power analysis of a main effect in a fixed factorial design. Except for a minor complication due to denominator **df**, and some qualification in the interpretation of $\eta^2$, this test proceeds as in Cases 0 and 1 above.

Consider, for example, an $I \times J$ factorial design, where there are $i = 3$ levels of **I**, $j = 4$ levels of **J**, and each of the $ij = 12$ cells contains $n_c = 10$ observations. The structure of the analysis in the usual model which includes interaction is:

| Effect | df |
|---|---|
| **I** | $u_I = i - 1 = 2$ |
| **J** | $u_J = j - 1 = 3$ |
| $I \times J$ | $u_{I \times J} = (i-1)(j-1) = 6$ |
| Within cell (error) | $ij(n_c - 1) = 12(9) = 108$ |
| Total | $ijn_c - 1 = 119$ |

Now, consider the null hypothesis for the **J** effect, i.e., that the 4 population means of $J_1$ through $J_4$ are equal. The 4 sample means for **J** are each computed on $n_j = in_c = 3(10) = 30$ observations. (Similarly, each of the 3 means for **I** is computed on $n_i = jn_c = 4(10) = 40$ observations.) The minor complication arises at the point where one wants to determine the power of the test on **J** by applying the appropriate $u_j = 3$ table at $n = n_j = 30$. This procedure is equivalent to ignoring the fact that the **I** main effect and **I** × **J** interaction exist in the design, i.e., a Case 0 test of 4 means, each of $n = 30$. But the latter test has for its **F**-ratio *denominator* (within cell, or error) **df**, $4(30 - 1) = 116$. More generally, the denominator **df** presumed in the calculation of the table entries is, for **k** means each of **n** cases, $k(n - 1) = (u + 1)(n - 1)$. Thus, in this case, the table's value is based on 3 and 116 **df**, while the **F** test to be performed is for 3 and 108**df**.

To cope with this problem of the discrepancy in denominator (error) **df** between the presumption of a single source of nonerror variance of one-way design on which the tables are based and the varying numbers of sources of nonerror variance (main effects, interactions) of factorial and other complex designs, for all tests of effects in the latter, we adjust the **n** used for table entry to

$$(8.3.4) \qquad n' = \frac{\text{denominator } \mathbf{df}}{u + 1} + 1.$$

The denominator **df** for a factorial design is the total **N** minus the total number of cells, and **u** is the **df** of the effect in question, as exemplified above for the **I** × **J** factorial design. Concretely, the **J** effect is tested as if it were based on samples of size

$$n' = \frac{108}{3 + 1} + 1 = 28,$$

which together with the **f** value posited for the **J** effect, is used for entry into the appropriate table (for **a** and **u**) to determine power.

What happens to the interpretation of **f** when the basis of classification **K** into **k** levels is present together with others, as it is in factorial design? However complicated the factorial design, i.e., no matter how many other factors (**I**, **J**, etc.) and interactions (**K** × **I**, **K** × **J**, **K** × **I** × **J**, etc.) may be involved, the definition of **f** for the **k** means of **K** remains the same—the standard deviation of the **k** standardized means, where the standardization is by the common within (cell) population standard deviation [formulas (8.2.1) and (8.2.2)]. Thus, there is no need to adjust one's conception of **f** for a set of **k** means when one moves from the one-way analysis of variance (Cases 0 and 1) to the case where additional bases of partitioning of the data exist. Furthermore, the translation between **f** and the **d** measures considered in 7.2.1 is also not affected. It is, however, necessary to consider the interpretation of $\eta^2$ in Case 2.

In Section 8.2.2, $\eta^2$ was defined as the proportion of the total variance made up by the variance of the means [formula 8.2.18)]. The total variance, in turn, was simply the sum of the within-population variance and the variance of the means [formula (8.2.17)]. The framework of that exposition was the analysis of variance into two components, between-populations and within-populations. In factorial design, the total variance is made up not only of the within (cell) population variance and the variance of the means of the levels of the factor under study, but also the variances of the means of the other factor(s) and also of the interactions. Therefore, the variance base of $\eta^2$ of formula (8.2.18), namely $\sigma^2 + \sigma_m{}^2$, is no longer the total variance, and the formulas involving $\eta$ and $\eta^2$ [(8.2.19), (8.2.20), (8.2.22)] and Table 8.2.2 require the reinterpretation of $\eta$ as a *partial* correlation ratio, and $\eta^2$ as a proportion, not of the total variance, but of the total from which there has been excluded (partialled out) the variance due to the other factor(s) and interactions.

This can be made concrete by reference to the $I \times J$ ($3 \times 4$) factorial illustration. Consider the four population means of the levels of $J$ and assume their $f_J$ is .30. Assume further that $f_I$ is .50 and $f_{I \times I}$ is .20. When $\eta^2$ for $J$ is computed from formula (8.2.19) (or looked up in Table 8.2.2):

$$\eta^2 = \frac{f^2}{1 + f^2} = \frac{.30^2}{1 + .30^2} = .0826,$$

the results for $J$ clearly are not in the slightest affected by the size of the $I$ or $I \times J$ effects. The $\eta^2$ for $J$ in this design might be written in the conventional notation of partial correlation, with $Y$ as the dependent variable under study, as $\eta^2_{YJ \cdot I, I \times J}$, i.e., the proportion of the $Y$ variance associated with $J$ population membership, when variance due to $I$ and to $I \times J$ is excluded from consideration. Thus, given $f_J = .30$, the variance of the $J$ means accounts for .0826 of the quantity made up of itself plus the within-cell population variance.

In higher order factorial designs, the $\eta^2$ computed from an $f$ for a given source $J$ might be represented as $\eta^2_{YJ \cdot \text{all other}}$, the "all other" meaning all the other sources of total variance, main effects, and interactions. Each source's "size" may be assessed by such a partial PV. Because of their construction, however, they do not cumulate to a meaningful total.

The proposed operational definitions of small, medium, and large ES in terms of $f$ have their usual meaning. When assessing power in testing the effects of the above $I \times J$ factorial, $f_I$ and $f_J$ (and also $f_{I \times J}$—see Section 8.3.4) can each be set quite independently of the others (because of their partial nature), by using the operational definitions or by whatever other means suit the investigator. They can, for example, be set by stating the alternative-hypothetical *cell* means and σ, and computing the resulting **f** values for all effects (illustrated in example 8.9 of the next section).

The scope of the present treatment precludes a detailed discussion of the power analysis of fixed effects in complex designs other than the factorial. Such analyses can be accomplished using the tables of this chapter if the following principles are kept in mind:

1. The basic ES index, **f**, represents the standard deviation of *standardized* means, the standardization being accomplished by division by the appropriate σ. We have seen that for fixed factorial designs, σ is the square root of the within *cell* population variance. In other designs, and more generally, σ is the square root of the variance being estimated by the denominator ("error") mean square of the **F** test which is to be performed. For example, in repeated measurements designs using multiple groups of subjects ("split plot" designs), there are at least two error terms, (a) a "subjects within groups" or between-subjects error, and (b) an interaction term involving subjects, or within-subject error. In the definition of **f** for any source (i.e., set of means), the standardization or scaling of the $\sigma_m$ will come from either (a) or (b), depending on whether the source is a between or a within source, just as will their **F** ratio denominators (Winer, 1971).

2. The adjustment to **n′** of formula (8.3.4) calls for the denominator **df**, i.e., the **df** for the actual error term of the **F** ratio that is appropriate for the test of that source of variance in that design. For example, consider the test of the treatment effect in an unreplicated 6 × 6 Latin square (Edwards, 1972, pp. 285–317). Six treatment means, each based on **n** = 6 observations, are to be compared, so **u** = 5. Since the Latin square residual (error) mean square, which is the denominator of the **F** ratio, is based on $(n - 1)(n - 2) = 20$ **df**, the **n′** for table entry is, from (8.3.4), $20/(6 + 1) + 1 = 3.86$. Power would then be found by linear interpolation between **n** = 3 and 4 at the **f** value posited in the power table for **u** = 5 for the specified **a** level.

### Illustrative Examples

**8.5** An experimental psychologist has designed an experiment to investigate the effect of genetic strain (**I**) at **i** = 3 levels and conditions of irradiation (**J**) at **j** = 4 levels on maze learning in rats. He draws 24 animals randomly from a supply of each genetic strain and apportions each strain sample randomly and equally to the four conditions, so that his 3 × 4 = 12 cells each contain a maze score for each of $n_c$ = 6 animals for a total **N** of 12(6) = 72 animals. The denominator **df** for the **F** tests in this analysis is therefore 72 − 12 = 60. He expects a medium ES for **I** and a large

ES for **J**, and following the operational definitions of Section 8.2.3, sets $f_i = .25$ and $f_j = .40$. Note that these values are standardized by the within cell population and each of the main effects is independent of the other. (The question of the **I** × **J** interaction is considered in the next section under Case 3.) What is the power of these two main effect **F** tests at the **a** = .05 criterion?

For the test on the equality of the mean maze scores for the 3 strains (**I**), **u** = **i** = 2, and each mean is taken over 24 animals. However, for table entry, we require the **n'** of formula (8.3.4): $60/(2 + 1) + 1 = 21$. Thus, the specifications are:

$$a = .05, \qquad u = 2, \qquad f = .25, \qquad n' = 21.$$

Table 8.3.13 (**a** = .05, **u** = 2) at row **n** = 21 and column **f** = .25 indicates power of .40. The chances of detecting a medium effect in strain differences for these specifications are only two in five.

For a test of equality of means of the four irradiation conditions (**J**), **u** = **j** − 1 = 3, and each mean is taken over 18 animals. Again it is **n'** of formula (8.3.4) that is required, and it is $60/(3 + 1) + 1 = 16$. The specification summary for the test on **J** is thus:

$$a = .05, \qquad u = 3, \qquad f = .40, \qquad n' = 16.$$

In Table 8.3.14 (**a** = 05, **u** = 3), at row **n** = 16 and column **f** = .40, he finds power = .75. The power of the test on irradiation conditions (**J**), given the large effect anticipated, is distinctly better than that for genetic strains (**I**); a probability of .75 of rejecting the null hypothesis means .75/.25, or three to one odds for rejection under these specifications.

**8.6**   An experiment in developmental social psychology is designed to study the effect of sex of experimenter (**S** at **s** = 2 levels), age of subject (**A** at **a** = 3 levels), instruction conditions (**C**, at **c** = 4), and their interactions (which are considered in the next section) on the persuasibility of elementary school boys. A total **N** of 120 subjects is assigned randomly (within age groups and equally) to the 2 × 3 × 4 = 24 cells of the design; thus, there are 5 cases in each cell. Expectations from theory and previous research lead the experimenter to posit, for each effect, the following ES for the three effects: $f_S = .10$, $f_A = .25$, and $f_C = .40$. (Note that these **f** values imply *partial* $\eta^2$, respectively, of .01, .06, and .14.) Using as a significance criterion **a** = .05, what is the power of each of the main effects **F** tests?

This is a 2 × 3 × 4 fixed factorial design, and although we will not here consider the power testing of the four interaction effects (**S** × **A**, **S** × **C**, **A** × **C**, and **S** × **A** × **C**), they are part of the model (see Illustrative Example 8.7 in Section 8.3.4). The correct **df** for the denominator (within cell mean square) of all the **F** tests is $120 - 24 = 96$.

For the test of the **S** effect, $u = 2 - 1 = 1$, and although each mean is based on 60 cases, the **n'** for table entry is $96/(1 + 1) + 1 = 49$. Thus, the specifications are

$$a = .05, \qquad u = 1, \qquad f = .10, \qquad n' = 49.$$

In Table 8.3.12 for $a = .05$ and $u = 1$, at column $f = .10$, for both rows $n = 48$ and 50, power is given as .16. The probability of detecting $f = .10$ (a conventionally small effect) is very poor.

For the three age groups (hence $u = 2$), the **n'** obtained by formula (8.3.4) is $96/(2 + 1) + 1 = 33$. The specifications for the determination of the power of the **F** test on the **A** main effect are thus:

$$a = .05, \qquad u = 2, \qquad f = .25, \qquad n' = 33.$$

In Table 8.3.13 ($a = .05$, $u = 2$), at row $n = 33$ and column $f = .25$, power $= .59$. Note that $f = .25$ is our conventional definition of a medium effect.

Finally, the test of the means of the four instruction conditions (hence $u = 3$) has for its **n'** $96/(3 + 1) + 1 = 25$. The specification summary:

$$a = .05, \qquad u = 3, \qquad f = .40, \qquad n' = 25.$$

Table 8.3.14 at row $n = 25$, column $f = .40$ yields power of .93. Under these conditions, the **b** (Type II) error $(1 - \text{power})$ is about the same as the **a** (Type I) error, but note that a large effect has been posited.

In summary, the experimenter has a very poor (.16) expectation of detecting the small **S** effect, a no better than fair (.59) chance of detecting the medium **A** effect, and an excellent (.93) chance of finding a significant **C** effect, assuming the validity of his alternate hypotheses (i.e., his **f** values), $a = .05$, and $N = 120$. As an exercise, the reader may determine that changing the specifications to 6 cases per cell ($N = 144$), and leaving the other specifications unchanged, the tabled power values become .19 for **S**, .70 for **A**, and .97 for **C**. Note the inconsequential improvement this 20% increase in the size of the experiment has for the **S** and **C** effects, although bringing **A** from power of .59 to .70 might be worthwhile. Reaching significant power for **S** seems hopeless, but we have repeatedly seen that very large samples are required to obtain good power to detect small effects.

8.3.4 CASE 3: TESTS OF INTERACTIONS. A detailed exposition of interaction effects in experimental design is beyond the scope of this handbook; the reader is referred to one of the standard treatments (e.g., Hays, 1981; Winer, 1971; Edwards, 1972). We assume throughout equal $n_c$ in the cells of the factorial.

For our present purposes, we note that an **R** × **C** interaction can be understood in the following ways:

1. Differences in effects between two levels of **R**, say $R_i$ and $R_k$ ($i, k = 1, 2, 3, \ldots, r$; $i < k$) with regard to differences in pairs of **C**, say $C_j - C_p$ ($j, p = 1, 2, 3, \ldots, c$; $j < p$). More simply, a contribution to an **R** × **C** interaction would be a difference between two levels of **R** with regard to a difference between two levels of **C**. Thus, if in the population, the sex difference (males minus females) in conditioning to sound ($C_j$) is algebraically larger than the sex difference in conditioning to electric shock ($C_p$), a sex by conditioning stimulus (**R** × **C**) interaction would be said to exist. A first-order interaction (**R** × **C**) is equivalent to differences between differences; a second-order interaction (**R** × **C** × **H**) equivalent to differences between differences of differences; etc. (see example 8.8 below).

2. Equivalently, a first-order interaction (**R** × **C**) can be thought of as a residual effect after the separate main effects of **R** and **C** have been taken out or allowed for. Thus, after any systematic (averaged over stimulus) sex difference in conditioning is allowed for, and any systematic (averaged over sex) difference in conditioning stimulus is also allowed for, if there remains any variation in the sex-stimulus cells, a sex by conditioning stimulus (**R** × **C**) interaction would be said to exist. A second-order interaction (**R** × **C** × **H**) would be said to exist if there was residual variation after the **R**, **C**, **H**, **R** × **C**, **R** × **H**, and **C** × **H** effects were removed, etc.

3. A third equivalent conception of an **R** × **C** interaction implied by either of the above is simply that the effect of **R** varies from one level of **C** to another (and conversely). Thus, a nonzero sex by conditioning stimulus interaction means (and is meant by): The effect of a given stimulus (relative to others) varies between sexes or depends upon which sex is under consideration. This, in turn, means that there is a *joint* effect of sex and stimulus over and above any separate (main) effect of the two variables. Equivalently, the effect of each is *conditional* on the other.

To index the size of an interaction, we use **f** defined in a way which is a generalization of the basic definition set forth in equations (8.2.1) and (8.2.2). First we return to the second conception of an **R** × **C** interaction above, where we spoke of a "residual effect" after the main effects of **R** and **C** have been taken out. Consider the cell defined by the $i$th level of **R** and the $j$th level of **C**, the $ij$th cell of the table, which contains in all **rc** cells. That cell's population mean is $m_{ij}$. Its value depends on (*a*) the main effect of $R_i$, i.e., $m_i. - m$, the departure of the population mean of level **i** of **R**, (*b*) the main effect of $C_j$, i.e., $m_{.j} - m$, the departure of the population mean of level **j** of **C**, (*c*) the value of **m**, and (*d*) the *interaction effect* for that cell, $x_{ij}$, the quantity in which we are particularly interested. Simple algebra leads to the following definition of $x_{ij}$ in terms of the cell mean ($m_{ij}$), the main effect means $m_i.$, $m_j$ ), and the total population mean (**m**):

$$(8.3.5) \qquad x_{ij} = m_{ij} - m_{i.} - m_{.j} + m.$$

When a cell has $x_{ij} = 0$, it has no interaction effect, i.e., its mean is accounted for by the $R_i$ and $C_j$ main effects and the total population mean. When all the **rc** cells have **x** values of zero, the $R \times C$ interaction is zero. Thus, the degree of *variability* of the **x** values about their (necessarily) zero mean is indicative of the size of the $R \times C$ interaction.

Thus, as a measure of the size of the interaction of the $R \times C$ factorial design, we use the standard deviation of the $x_{ij}$ values in the **rc** cells. As an exact analogy to our (raw) measure of the size of a main effect, $\sigma_m$ of formula (8.2.2), we find

$$(8.3.6) \qquad \sigma_x = \sqrt{\frac{\sum x_{ij}^2}{rc}},$$

the square root of the mean of the squared interaction effect values for the **rc** cells.

To obtain a standardized ES measure of interaction, we proceed as before to divide by $\sigma$, the within-cell population standard deviation, to obtain **f**:

$$(8.3.7) \qquad f = \frac{\sigma_x}{\sigma}.$$

The **f** for an interaction of formula (8.3.7) can be interpreted in the same way as throughout this chapter, as a measure of variability and hence size of (interaction) effects, whose mean is zero, standardized by the common within (cell) population standard deviation. Because it is the same measure, it can be understood:

1. in the framework which relates it to $\eta$ and the proportion of variance of Section 8.2.2, as modified in terms of partial $\eta$ for Case 2 in Section 8.3.3; or

2. By using the operational definitions of small, medium, and large **f** values of Section 8.2.3 (even though the discussion in these sections was

particularized in terms of the variability of means, rather than of interaction effects); or

3. By writing the alternate-hypothetical cell means and computing the **x** values and $\sigma_x$ and **f** by formulas (8.3.5)–(8.3.7). (This latter procedure is illustrated in example 8.9 below.)

For the sake of simplicity of exposition, the above discussion has been of **f** for a two-way (first-order) interaction. The generalization of **f** for higher-order interactions is fairly straightforward. For example, given a three-way interaction, $\mathbf{R} \times \mathbf{C} \times \mathbf{H}$, with **R** at **r** levels, **C** at **c** levels, and **H** at **h** levels, there are now **rch** cells. Consider the cell defined by the **i**th level of **R**, the **j**th level of **C**, and the **k**th level of **H**. Its interaction effect is

$$\mathbf{x_{ijk}} = \mathbf{m_{ijk}} - \mathbf{m_i} - \mathbf{m_j} - \mathbf{m_k} - \mathbf{x_{ij}} - \mathbf{x_{ik}} - \mathbf{x_{jk}} + 2\mathbf{m},$$

where the $\mathbf{x_{ij}}$, $\mathbf{x_{ik}}$, and $\mathbf{x_{jk}}$ are the two-way interaction effects as defined in formula (8.3.4). Analogous to formula (8.3.6), the raw variability measure is

$$(8.3.8) \qquad \sigma_x = \sqrt{\frac{\sum \mathbf{x}_{ijk}^2}{\mathbf{rch}}},$$

i.e., the square root of the mean of the squared interaction effect values for the **rch** cells. It is then standardized by formula (8.3.7) to give **f**, the ES for a three-way interaction.

The number of degrees of freedom (**u**) for an interaction is the product of the **df**s of its constituent factors: $(\mathbf{r} - 1)(\mathbf{c} - 1)$ for a two-way interaction, $(\mathbf{r} - 1)(\mathbf{c} - 1)(\mathbf{h} - 1)$ for a three-way interaction, etc.

For the reasons discussed in the preceding section on main effects, the test on interactions in factorial designs require that **n′** be used for table entry. Formula (8.3.4) is again used with the same denominator **df** as for the main effects and with **u** the appropriate **df** for the interaction.

In summary, power determination for interaction tests proceeds as follows: **u** is the **df** for the interaction and, together with the significance criterion **a**, determines the relevant power table. The table is then entered with **f**, which is determined by using one or more of the methods detailed above or by using the ES conventions, and **n′**, a function of the denominator **df** and **u** (8.3.4). The power value is then read from the table. Linear interpolation for **f**, **n**, and **u** (between tables) is used where necessary and provides a good approximation.

## Illustrative Examples

**8.7**  Reconsider the experiment described in example 8.6, an inquiry in developmental social psychology in which the factors were sex of experimenter (**S** at **s** = 2 levels), age of subject (**A** at **a** = 3 levels), and instruction conditions (**C** at **c** = 4 levels), i.e., a 2 × 3 × 4 factorial design, and the dependent variable a measure of persuasibility. There are **n** = 5 subjects in each of the 24 cells of the design, a total **N** of 120, and the denominator **df** is 120 − 24 = 96. For convenience, we restate the specifications and resulting tabled power value for each of the main effect **F** tests:

> **S:**   $a = .05$,   $u = 1$,   $f = .10$,   $n' = .49$;   power = .16
> **A:**   $a = .05$,   $u = 2$,   $f = .25$,   $n' = .33$;   power = .59
> **C:**   $a = .05$,   $u = 3$,   $f = .40$,   $n' = .25$;   power = .93

Consider first the interaction of sex of experimenter by age of subject (**S** × **A**), which is posited to be of medium size, i.e., $f = .25$, and the same significance criterion, $a = .05$, is to be used. Note that this interaction concerns the residuals in the 2 × 3 table which results when the 4 levels of **C** are collapsed. The **df** for this interaction is therefore $u = (2 − 1)(3 − 1) = 2$. All the effects in this fixed factorial design, including the **S** × **A** effect, use as their error term the within-cell mean square, hence the denominator **df**, as noted above, is 120 − 24 = 96. This latter value and **u** are used in formula (8.3.4) to determine $n'$ for table entry: $n' = 96/(2 + 1) + 1 = 33$. The specifications for the power of the **S** × **A** effect are thus:

$$a = .05, \qquad u = 2, \qquad f = .25, \qquad n' = 33.$$

In Table 8.3.13 for $a = .05$ and $u = 2$, with row $n = 33$ and column $f = .25$, the power of the test is found as .59, a rather unimpressive value. Note that this is exactly the same value as was found for the **A** main effect, which is necessarily the case, since the specifications are the same. For **A**, we also used $a = .05$ and $f = .25$, and its **u** is also 2. Since **S** × **A** and **A** (as well as the other effects) also share the same denominator **df**, their $n'$ values are also necessarily the same.

Let us also specify $a = .05$ and $f = .25$ for the **S** × **C** interaction. It is based on the 2 × 4 table which results when the three levels of **A** are collapsed, and its **u** is therefore $(2 − 1)(4 − 1) = 3$. With the same denominator **df** of 96, the $n'$ for this effect is $96/(3 + 1) + 1 = 25$. Thus,

$$a = .05, \qquad u = 3, \qquad f = .25, \qquad n' = 25,$$

and Table 8.3.14 (for $a = .05$, $u = 3$) gives at row $n = 33$ and column $f = .25$ the power value .53. For the specifications for **a** and **f** the power is even poorer than for the **S** × **A** interaction. This is because the increase in **u** results in a decrease in $n'$.

The **A** × **C** interaction is defined by the 3 × 4 table that results when the sex of experimenters is ignored, and its **u** is therefore $(3 − 1)(4 − 1) = 6$. For this **u** and denominator **df** = 96, the **n'** here is $96/(6 + 1) + 1 = 14.7$. For the sake of comparability, we again posit **a** = .05 and **f** = .25. The specifications for the test of the **A** × **C** interaction, then, are:

$$\mathbf{a} = .05, \qquad \mathbf{u} = 6, \qquad \mathbf{f} = .25, \qquad \mathbf{n'} = 14.7.$$

In Table 8.3.17 (**a** = .05, **u** = 6), column **f** = .25 gives power values of .39 at **n** = 14 and .42 at **n** = 15; linear interpolation gives power of .41 for **n'** = 14.7. Note that, although the specifications remain **a** = .05 and **f** = .25, since **u** is now 6, the resulting drop in **n'** has produced a reduction in power relative to the other two two-way interactions.

Finally, the three-way **S** × **A** × **C** interaction has **u** = $(2 - 1)(3 - 1)$ $(4 - 1) = 6$, the same as for the **A** × **C** interaction, and thus the same **n'** = $96/(6 + 1) + 1 = 14.7$. If we posit, as before, **a** = .05, and **f** = .25, the specifications are exactly the same as for the **A** × **C** interaction,

$$\mathbf{a} = .05, \qquad \mathbf{u} = 6, \qquad \mathbf{f} = .25, \qquad \mathbf{n'} = 14.7,$$

and necessarily the same power of .41 is found (Table 8.3.17).

Because the **df** for interactions are products of the **df**s of their constituent main effect factors (e.g., for **A** × **C**, **u** = 2 × 3 = 6), the interactions in a factorial design will generally have larger **u** values than do the main effects, and, given the structure of the formula for **n'** (8.3.4), their **n'** values will generally be smaller than those for the main effects. This in turn means that, for any given size of effect (**f**) and significance criterion (**a**), the power of the interaction tests in a factorial design will, on the average, be smaller than that of main effects (excepting 2$^K$ designs, where they will be the same). This principle is even more clearly illustrated in the next example.

**8.8**   Consider an **A** × **B** × **C** fixed factorial design, 3 × 4 × 5 (= 60 cells), with three observations in each cell, so that **N** = 60 × 3 = 180. The within-cell error term for the denominator of the **F** tests will thus have 180 − 60 = 120 **df**. To help the reader get a feel for the power of main effect and interaction tests in factorial design as a function of **f**, **a**, **u**, and the **n'** of formula (8.3.4), tabled power values for the **F** tests in this experiment are given in Table 8.3.34 for the conventional **f** values for small, medium, and large ES at **a** = .01, .05, and .10. Note that although this is a rather large experiment, for many combinations of the parameters, the power values are low. Study of the table shows that

1. Unless a large ES of **f** = .40 is posited, power is generally poor. Even at **f** = .40, when **a** = .01 governs the test, two of the two-way interactions have power less than .80, and for the triple interaction it is only .49. It seems clear that unless unusually large experiments are undertaken, tests of small effects have abysmally low power, and those for medium interaction effects for **u** > 4

have poor power even at **a** = .10.

2. For a medium ES of **f** = .25, only the main effect tests at **a** = .10 have power values that give better than two to one odds for rejecting the null hypothesis. At **a** = .05, power ranges from poor to hopeless, and at .01, not even the tests of main effects have power as large as .50.

TABLE 8.3.34

POWER AS A FUNCTION OF **f**, **a**, **u**, AND **n'** IN A $3 \times 4 \times 5$ DESIGN
WITH $\mathbf{n_c} = 3$ AND DENOMINATOR **df** = 120

| Effect | u | n' | **a** = .01 | .05 | .10 | .01 | .05 | .10 | .01 | .05 | .10 |
|--------|---|-----|-----|-----|-----|-----|-----|-----|-----|-----|-----|
| | | | **f** = .10 | | | **f** = .25 | | | **f** = .40 | | |
| **A** | 2 | 41 | 05 | 15 | 25 | 45 | 70 | 80 | 93 | 98 | 99 |
| **B** | 3 | 31 | 04 | 13 | 22 | 38 | 63 | 75 | 90 | 97 | 99 |
| **C** | 4 | 25 | 03 | 12 | 21 | 33 | 58 | 70 | ·86 | 96 | 98 |
| **A** × **B** | 6 | 18.1 | 03 | 10 | 18 | 26 | 51 | 64 | 80 | 93 | 97 |
| **A** × **C** | 8 | 14.3 | 02 | 09 | 17 | 23 | 46 | 59 | 75 | 91 | 95 |
| **B** × **C** | 12 | 10.2 | 02 | 08 | 16 | 18 | 39 | 52 | 66 | 86 | 92 |
| **A** × **B** × **C** | 24 | 5.8 | 02 | 08 | 14 | 10 | 29 | 42 | 49 | 74 | 83 |

3. For ESs no larger than what is conventionally defined as small (**f** = .10), there is little point in carrying out the experiment: even at the most lenient **a** = .10 criterion, the largest power value is .25.

4. At the popular **a** = .05 level, only at **f** = .40 are the power values high (excepting even here the .74 value for the **A** × **B** × **C** effect).

5. The table clearly exemplifies the principle of lower power values for interactions, progressively so as the order of the interaction increases (or, more exactly, as **u** increases). For example, only for **f** = .40 at **a** = .10 does the power value for **A** × **B** × **C** exceed .80.

The preparation and study of such tables in experimental planning and post hoc power analysis is strongly recommended. The reader is invited, as an exercise, to compute such a table for a $3 \times 4$ design with 15 observations per cell, and hence the same **N** = 180 as above. Comparison of this table with Table 8.3.34 should help clarify the implications of few cells (hence smaller **u**, larger denominator **df**, and larger **n'** values) to power.

Because of the relative infirmity of tests of interactions due to their often large **u**, the research planner should entertain the possibility of setting, a priori, larger **a** values for the interaction tests than for the tests of main effects, usually .10 rather than .05. The price paid in credibility when the null hypothesis for an interaction is rejected may well be worth the increase in power thus attained. This decision must, of course, be made on the basis not only of the design and ES parameters which obtain, but also with the substantive issues of the research kept in mind.

**8.9**  A psychologist designs an experiment in which he will study the effects of age (**R**) at $r = 2$ levels, nature of contingency of reinforcement (**C**) at $c = 4$ levels, and their interaction (**R** $\times$ **C**) on a dependent learning variable. There are to be 12 subjects in each of the $rc = 8$ cells, and $\mathbf{a} = .05$ throughout.

We will use this example to illustrate the direct specification of the alternate hypothesis and hence the ES. Assume that the area has been well studied and the psychologist has a "strong" theory, so that he can estimate the within-cell population standard deviation $\sigma = 8$, and further, he can state as an alternative to the overall null hypothesis specific hypothetical values for each of the eight cell's population means, the $\mathbf{m}_{ij}$. The latter then imply the **R** means ($\mathbf{m}_{i.}$), the **C** means ($\mathbf{m}_{.j}$), and the grand mean $\mathbf{m}$. They are as follows:

|        | $C_1$ | $C_2$ | $C_3$ | $C_4$ | $m_i.$    |
|--------|-------|-------|-------|-------|-----------|
| $R_1$  | 41    | 34    | 30    | 27    | 33        |
| $R_2$  | 33    | 24    | 22    | 29    | 27        |
| $m_{.j}$ | 37    | 29    | 26    | 28    | $30 = m$  |

These values, in raw form, comprise his ES for the effects of **R**, **C**, and **R** $\times$ **C**. Their conversion to **f** values for the main effects is quite straightforward. Applying formula (8.2.2) for **R** and **C**,

$$\sigma_{m_R} = \sqrt{\frac{(33 - 30)^2 + (27 - 30)^2}{2}} = \sqrt{9} = 3,$$

and

$$\sigma_{m_C} = \sqrt{\frac{(37 - 30)^2 + (29 - 30)^2 + (26 - 30)^2 + (28 - 30)^2}{4}} = \sqrt{17.5} = 4.183.$$

When these are each standardized by dividing by the within-population $\sigma = 8$ [formula (8.2.1)], he finds

$$\mathbf{f_R} = 3/8 = .375$$

and

$$f_C = 4.183/8 = .523.$$

For the $R \times C$ interaction ES, he finds the interaction effects for each cell using formula (8.3.4)

$$x_{ij} = m_{ij} - m_{i.} - m_{.j} + m.$$

Thus,

$$x_{11} = 41 - 33 - 37 + 30 = +1$$

$$x_{12} = 34 - 33 - 29 + 30 = +2$$

$$\vdots \quad \vdots \quad \vdots \quad \vdots \quad \vdots \quad \vdots$$

$$x_{24} = 29 - 27 - 28 + 30 = +4$$

These $x_{ij}$ values for the $2 \times 4$ table of means are

|       | $C_1$ | $C_2$ | $C_3$ | $C_4$ |
|-------|-------|-------|-------|-------|
| $R_1$ | +1    | +2    | +1    | −4    |
| $R_2$ | −1    | −2    | −1    | +4    |

Note that they are so defined that they must sum to zero in every row and column; these constraints are what result in the df for the $R \times C$ interaction being $u = (r - 1)(c - 1)$; in this case, $u = 3$.

Applying formula (8.3.6) to these values,

$$\sigma_x = \sqrt{\frac{\sum x_{ij}^2}{rc}} = \sqrt{\frac{(+1)^2 + (+2)^2 + (+1)^2 + \cdots + (+4)^2}{2(4)}}$$

$$= \sqrt{\frac{44}{8}} = 2.345.$$

Standardizing to find $f$ [formula (8.3.7)],

$$f_{R \times C} = \sigma_x/\sigma = 2.345/8 = .293.$$

Thus, his alternative-hypothetical cell population means, together with an estimate of $\sigma$, have provided an $f$ for the $R \times C$ effect (as well as for the main effects).

One of the ways in which to understand interactions, described in the introduction to this section, was as differences among differences. This is readily illustrated for this problem. Return to the cell means and consider such quantities as $m_{1j} - m_{2j}$, i.e., the difference (with sign) between the means of $A_1$ and $A_2$ for each level of **C**. They are, respectively, $(41 - 33 =)$ $+8$, $(34 - 24 =) +10$, $+8$, and $-2$. Were these four values $(+8, +10, +8,$ and $-2)$ all equal, there would be zero interaction. Calling these values $D_j$ and their mean $\bar{D}$ (here $+6$) for simplicity, $\sigma_x$ can be found for a $2 \times c$ table by

$$\sigma_x = \sqrt{\frac{\sum_{j=1}^{c} (D_j - \bar{D})^2}{4c}}$$

$$= \sqrt{\frac{(+8 - 6)^2 + (+10 - 6)^2 + (+8 - 6)^2 + (-2 - 6)^2}{4(4)}}$$

$$= \sqrt{\frac{88}{16}} = 2.345,$$

as before.

Since there are 8 $(= rc)$ cells with 12 subjects in each for a total $N = 96$, the denominator **df** for the **F** tests of the main effects and the interaction is $96 - 8 = 88$. For the interaction test, $u = (2 - 1)(4 - 1) = 3$; therefore, the $n'$ for table entry from formula (8.3.4) is $88/(3 + 1) + 1 = 23$. The specifications for the test on the $R \times C$ interaction are thus:

$$a = .05, \qquad u = 3, \qquad f = .293, \qquad n' = 23.$$

In Table 8.3.14 (for $a = .05$, $u = 3$) at row $n' = 23$, we find power at $f = .25$ to be .49 and at $f = .30$ to be .66. Linear interpolation for $f = .293$ gives the approximate power value of .64. The power for the main effects:

**R**:      $a = .05$,    $u = 3$,    $f = .375$,    $n' = 45$,    power = .94;

**C**:      $a = .05$,    $u = 3$,    $f = .523$,    $n' = 23$,    power = .99.

Power under these specifications for **R** and **C** is very good, but is only .64 for the interaction, despite the fact that its **f** of .293 is larger than a conventionally defined medium effect and that the experiment is fairly large. Since the interaction is likely to be the central issue in this experiment, the power of .64 is hardly adequate. To increase it, the experimenter should weigh the alternatives of increasing the size of the experiment or using the more modest $a = .10$ for the interaction test. If, for example, he increases the cell size from 12 to 17, the total **N** becomes 136, the denominator **df** $= 136 - 8 = 128$, and $n'$ for $R \times C$ is $128/(3 + 1) + 1 = 33$. The specifications then are

$$a = .05, \qquad u = 3, \qquad f = .293, \qquad n' = 33,$$

and power is found (by interpolation) to be .81. The size of the experiment must be increased by 42% to raise the power of the interaction test from .64 to .81. On the other hand, increasing the **a** to .10 for the experiment as originally planned, i.e., for

$$\mathbf{a} = .10, \qquad \mathbf{u} = 3, \qquad \mathbf{f} = .293, \qquad \mathbf{n'} = 23,$$

power is found to be .75.

8.3.5 THE ANALYSIS OF COVARIANCE. With a simple conceptual adjustment of frame of reference, all the previous material in this chapter can be applied to power analysis in the analysis of covariance.

In the analysis of covariance (with a single covariate), each member of the population has, in addition to a value **Y** (the variable of interest or dependent variable) a value on another variable, **X**, called the concomitant or adjusting variable, or covariate. A covariance design is a procedure for statistically controlling for **X** by means of a regression adjustment so that one can study **Y** freed of that portion of its variance linearly associated with **X**. In addition to the assumptions of the analysis of variance, the method of covariance adjustment also assumes that the regression coefficients in the separate populations are equal. Detailed discussion of the analysis of covariance is beyond the scope of this treatment; the reader is referred to one of the standard texts: Blalock (1972), Winer (1971).

Instead of analyzing **Y**, the analysis of covariance analyzes **Y′**, a regression-adjusted or statistically controlled value, which is

$$(8.3.9) \qquad \mathbf{Y'} = \mathbf{Y} - \mathbf{b}(\mathbf{X} - \overline{\mathbf{X}}),$$

where **b** is the (common) regression coefficient of **Y** on **X** in each of the populations and $\overline{\mathbf{X}}$ is the grand population mean of the concomitant variable. **Y′** is also called a residual, since it is the departure of the **Y** value from the **YX** regression line common to the various populations.

The analysis of covariance is essentially the analysis of variance of the **Y′** measures. Given this, if one reinterprets the preceding material in this chapter as referring to means and variances of the adjusted or residual **Y′** values, it is all applicable to the analysis of covariance.

For example, the basic formula for **f** (8.2.1) is $\sigma_m/\sigma$. For covariance analysis, $\sigma_m$ is the standard deviation of the **k** population's *adjusted* means of **Y′**, that is, **m′**, and $\sigma$ is the (common) standard deviation of the **Y′** values within the populations. The **d** measure of Section 8.2.1 is the difference between the largest and smallest of the **k** *adjusted* means divided by the within-population standard deviation of the **Y′** values. The use and interpretation of $\eta^2$ as a proportion of variance and $\eta$ as a correlation ratio now refers to **Y'**, the dependent variable **Y** freed from that portion of its variance linearly associated with **X**. And so on.

An academic point: In the analysis of covariance, the denominator **df** is reduced by one (due to the estimation of the regression coefficient **b**). This discrepancy from the denominator **df** on which the tabled power values are based is of no practical consequence in most applications, say when $(u + 1)(n - 1)$ is as large as 15 or 20.

The analysis of covariance can proceed with multiple covariates **X**$_i$ ($i = 1, 2, \ldots, p$) as readily, in principle, as with one. The adjustment proceeds by multiple linear regression, so that

$$(8.3.10) \quad \mathbf{Y}' = \mathbf{Y} - \mathbf{b}_1(\mathbf{X}_1 - \overline{\mathbf{X}}_1) - \mathbf{b}_2(\mathbf{X}_2 - \overline{\mathbf{X}}_2) - \cdots - \mathbf{b}_p(\mathbf{X}_p - \overline{\mathbf{X}}_p).$$

Whether **Y'** comes about from one or several adjusting variables, it remains conceptually the same. The loss in denominator **df** is now **p** instead of 1, but unless **p** is large and **N** is small (say less than 40), the resulting overestimation of the tabled power values is not material.

The procedural emphasis should not be permitted to obscure the fact that the analysis of covariance designs when appropriately used yield greater power, in general, than analogous analysis of variance designs. This is fundamentally because the within-population $\sigma$ of the *adjusted* **Y'** variable will be smaller than $\sigma$ of the unadjusted **Y** variable. Specifically, where **r** is the population coefficient between **X** and **Y**, $\sigma_y' = \sigma_y\sqrt{1 - r^2}$. Since $\sigma$ is the denominator of **f** [formula (8.2.1)] and since the numerator undergoes no such systematic change (it may, indeed, increase), the *effective* **f** in an analysis of covariance will be larger than **f** in the analysis of variance of **Y**. This is true, of course, only for the proper use of the analysis of covariance, for discussion of which the reader is referred to the references cited above.

No illustrative examples are offered here because all of the eight examples which precede can be reconsidered in a covariance framework by merely assuming for each the existence of one or more relevant covariates. Each problem then proceeds with adjusted (**Y'**) values in place of the unadjusted (**Y**) values in which they are couched.

A very general approach to the analysis of covariance (and also the analysis of variance) is provided by multiple regression/correlation analysis, as described by Cohen and Cohen (1983). Some insight into this method and a treatment of its power-analytic procedures are given in Chapter 9.

## 8.4  SAMPLE SIZE TABLES

The sample size tables for this section are given on pages 381–389; the text follows on page 390.

## Table 8.4.1

n to detect f by F test at a = .01
for u = 1, 2, 3, 4

### u = 1

| Power | .05 | .10 | .15 | .20 | .25 | .30 | .35 | .40 | .50 | .60 | .70 | .80 |
|---|---|---|---|---|---|---|---|---|---|---|---|---|
| | | | | | f | | | | | | | |
| .10 | 336 | 85 | 39 | 22 | 15 | 11 | 9 | 7 | 5 | 4 | 4 | 3 |
| .50 | 1329 | 333 | 149 | 85 | 55 | 39 | 29 | 22 | 15 | 11 | 9 | 7 |
| .70 | 1924 | 482 | 215 | 122 | 79 | 55 | 41 | 32 | 21 | 15 | 12 | 9 |
| .80 | 2338 | 586 | 259 | 148 | 95 | 67 | 49 | 38 | 25 | 18 | 14 | 11 |
| .90 | 2978 | 746 | 332 | 188 | 120 | 84 | 62 | 48 | 31 | 22 | 17 | 13 |
| .95 | 3564 | 892 | 398 | 224 | 144 | 101 | 74 | 57 | 37 | 26 | 20 | 16 |
| .99 | 4808 | 1203 | 536 | 302 | 194 | 136 | 100 | 77 | 50 | 35 | 26 | 21 |

### u = 2

| Power | .05 | .10 | .15 | .20 | .25 | .30 | .35 | .40 | .50 | .60 | .70 | .80 |
|---|---|---|---|---|---|---|---|---|---|---|---|---|
| | | | | | f | | | | | | | |
| .10 | 307 | 79 | 36 | 21 | 14 | 10 | 8 | 6 | 5 | 4 | 3 | 3 |
| .50 | 1093 | 275 | 123 | 70 | 45 | 32 | 24 | 19 | 13 | 9 | 7 | 6 |
| .70 | 1543 | 387 | 173 | 98 | 63 | 44 | 33 | 26 | 17 | 12 | 10 | 8 |
| .80 | 1851 | 464 | 207 | 117 | 76 | 53 | 39 | 30 | 20 | 14 | 11 | 9 |
| .90 | 2325 | 582 | 260 | 147 | 95 | 66 | 49 | 38 | 25 | 18 | 14 | 11 |
| .95 | 2756 | 690 | 308 | 174 | 112 | 78 | 58 | 45 | 29 | 21 | 16 | 12 |
| .99 | 3658 | 916 | 408 | 230 | 148 | 103 | 76 | 59 | 38 | 27 | 20 | 16 |

### u = 3

| Power | .05 | .10 | .15 | .20 | .25 | .30 | .35 | .40 | .50 | .60 | .70 | .80 |
|---|---|---|---|---|---|---|---|---|---|---|---|---|
| | | | | | f | | | | | | | |
| .10 | 278 | 71 | 32 | 19 | 13 | 9 | 7 | 6 | 4 | 3 | 3 | 2 |
| .50 | 933 | 234 | 105 | 59 | 38 | 27 | 20 | 16 | 11 | 8 | 6 | 5 |
| .70 | 1299 | 326 | 146 | 83 | 53 | 37 | 28 | 22 | 14 | 10 | 8 | 7 |
| .80 | 1548 | 388 | 175 | 98 | 63 | 44 | 33 | 25 | 17 | 12 | 9 | 8 |
| .90 | 1927 | 483 | 215 | 122 | 78 | 55 | 41 | 31 | 21 | 15 | 11 | 9 |
| .95 | 2270 | 568 | 253 | 143 | 92 | 64 | 48 | 37 | 24 | 17 | 13 | 10 |
| .99 | 2986 | 747 | 333 | 188 | 121 | 84 | 62 | 48 | 31 | 22 | 17 | 13 |

### u = 4

| Power | .05 | .10 | .15 | .20 | .25 | .30 | .35 | .40 | .50 | .60 | .70 | .80 |
|---|---|---|---|---|---|---|---|---|---|---|---|---|
| | | | | | f | | | | | | | |
| .10 | 253 | 64 | 29 | 17 | 12 | 8 | 7 | 5 | 4 | 3 | 3 | 2 |
| .50 | 820 | 206 | 92 | 52 | 34 | 24 | 18 | 14 | 10 | 7 | 6 | 5 |
| .70 | 1128 | 283 | 127 | 72 | 46 | 33 | 24 | 19 | 13 | 9 | 7 | 6 |
| .80 | 1341 | 336 | 150 | 85 | 55 | 38 | 29 | 22 | 15 | 11 | 8 | 7 |
| .90 | 1661 | 416 | 186 | 105 | 68 | 47 | 35 | 27 | 18 | 13 | 10 | 8 |
| .95 | 1948 | 488 | 218 | 123 | 79 | 55 | 41 | 32 | 21 | 15 | 11 | 9 |
| .99 | 2546 | 640 | 286 | 160 | 103 | 76 | 53 | 41 | 27 | 19 | 14 | 11 |

Table 8.4.2

n to detect f by F test at a = .01
for u = 5, 6, 8, 10

### u = 5

| Power | .05 | .10 | .15 | .20 | .25 | .30 | .35 | .40 | .50 | .60 | .70 | .80 |
|---|---|---|---|---|---|---|---|---|---|---|---|---|
| .10 | 233 | 59 | 27 | 16 | 11 | 8 | 6 | 5 | 4 | 3 | 2 | 2 |
| .50 | 737 | 185 | 82 | 47 | 30 | 22 | 16 | 13 | 9 | 6 | 5 | 4 |
| .70 | 1009 | 253 | 113 | 64 | 41 | 29 | 22 | 17 | 11 | 8 | 6 | 5 |
| .80 | 1193 | 299 | 134 | 76 | 49 | 34 | 26 | 20 | 13 | 10 | 7 | 6 |
| .90 | 1469 | 368 | 164 | 93 | 60 | 42 | 31 | 24 | 16 | 12 | 9 | 7 |
| .95 | 1719 | 431 | 192 | 109 | 70 | 49 | 36 | 28 | 18 | 13 | 10 | 8 |
| .99 | 2235 | 560 | 249 | 141 | 91 | 63 | 47 | 36 | 24 | 17 | 13 | 10 |

### u = 6

| Power | .05 | .10 | .15 | .20 | .25 | .30 | .35 | .40 | .50 | .60 | .70 | .80 |
|---|---|---|---|---|---|---|---|---|---|---|---|---|
| .10 | 218 | 55 | 25 | 15 | 10 | 7 | 6 | 5 | 3 | 3 | 2 | 2 |
| .50 | 673 | 169 | 76 | 43 | 28 | 20 | 15 | 12 | 8 | 6 | 5 | 4 |
| .70 | 917 | 230 | 103 | 58 | 38 | 27 | 20 | 15 | 10 | 8 | 6 | 5 |
| .80 | 1080 | 271 | 121 | 68 | 44 | 31 | 23 | 18 | 12 | 9 | 7 | 6 |
| .90 | 1326 | 332 | 148 | 84 | 54 | 38 | 28 | 22 | 14 | 10 | 8 | 6 |
| .95 | 1547 | 388 | 173 | 98 | 63 | 44 | 33 | 25 | 17 | 12 | 9 | 7 |
| .99 | 2003 | 502 | 224 | 126 | 81 | 57 | 42 | 33 | 21 | 15 | 11 | 9 |

### u = 8

| Power | .05 | .10 | .15 | .20 | .25 | .30 | .35 | .40 | .50 | .60 | .70 | .80 |
|---|---|---|---|---|---|---|---|---|---|---|---|---|
| .10 | 194 | 49 | 23 | 13 | 9 | 6 | 5 | 4 | 3 | 3 | 2 | 2 |
| .50 | 580 | 146 | 65 | 37 | 24 | 17 | 13 | 10 | 7 | 5 | 4 | 3 |
| .70 | 785 | 197 | 88 | 50 | 32 | 23 | 17 | 13 | 9 | 7 | 5 | 4 |
| .80 | 918 | 230 | 103 | 58 | 38 | 27 | 20 | 15 | 10 | 8 | 6 | 5 |
| .90 | 1122 | 281 | 126 | 71 | 46 | 32 | 24 | 19 | 12 | 9 | 7 | 6 |
| .95 | 1303 | 327 | 146 | 83 | 53 | 37 | 28 | 22 | 14 | 10 | 8 | 6 |
| .99 | 1676 | 420 | 187 | 106 | 68 | 48 | 36 | 27 | 18 | 13 | 10 | 8 |

### u = 10

| Power | .05 | .10 | .15 | .20 | .25 | .30 | .35 | .40 | .50 | .60 | .70 | .80 |
|---|---|---|---|---|---|---|---|---|---|---|---|---|
| .10 | 176 | 45 | 21 | 12 | 8 | 6 | 5 | 4 | 3 | 2 | 2 | 2 |
| .50 | 515 | 129 | 58 | 33 | 21 | 15 | 12 | 9 | 6 | 5 | 4 | 3 |
| .70 | 691 | 173 | 78 | 44 | 29 | 20 | 15 | 12 | 8 | 6 | 5 | 4 |
| .80 | 810 | 203 | 91 | 51 | 33 | 23 | 18 | 14 | 9 | 7 | 5 | 4 |
| .90 | 982 | 246 | 110 | 62 | 40 | 28 | 21 | 16 | 11 | 8 | 6 | 5 |
| .95 | 1138 | 285 | 127 | 72 | 47 | 33 | 24 | 19 | 12 | 9 | 7 | 6 |
| .99 | 1456 | 365 | 163 | 92 | 60 | 42 | 31 | 24 | 16 | 11 | 9 | 7 |

## Table 8.4.3

n to detect f by F test at a = .01
for u = 12, 15, 24

### u = 12

| Power | .05 | .10 | .15 | .20 | .25 | .30 | .35 | .40 | .50 | .60 | .70 | .80 |
|---|---|---|---|---|---|---|---|---|---|---|---|---|
| .10 | 162 | 41 | 19 | 11 | 8 | 5 | 4 | 4 | 3 | 2 | 2 | 2 |
| .50 | 467 | 117 | 53 | 30 | 20 | 14 | 10 | 8 | 6 | 4 | 3 | 3 |
| .70 | 623 | 157 | 70 | 40 | 26 | 18 | 14 | 11 | 7 | 5 | 3 | 3 |
| .80 | 726 | 182 | 82 | 46 | 30 | 21 | 16 | 12 | 8 | 6 | 5 | 4 |
| .90 | 881 | 221 | 99 | 56 | 36 | 25 | 19 | 15 | 10 | 7 | 6 | 5 |
| .95 | 1017 | 255 | 114 | 65 | 42 | 29 | 22 | 17 | 11 | 8 | 6 | 5 |
| .99 | 1297 | 325 | 145 | 83 | 53 | 37 | 28 | 21 | 14 | 10 | 8 | 6 |

### u = 15

| Power | .05 | .10 | .15 | .20 | .25 | .30 | .35 | .40 | .50 | .60 | .70 | .80 |
|---|---|---|---|---|---|---|---|---|---|---|---|---|
| .10 | 147 | 37 | 17 | 10 | 7 | 5 | 4 | 3 | 2 | 2 | 2 | -- |
| .50 | 413 | 104 | 47 | 27 | 17 | 12 | 9 | 7 | 5 | 4 | 3 | 3 |
| .70 | 548 | 138 | 62 | 35 | 23 | 16 | 12 | 10 | 6 | 5 | 4 | 3 |
| .80 | 632 | 159 | 71 | 41 | 26 | 19 | 14 | 11 | 7 | 5 | 4 | 4 |
| .90 | 769 | 193 | 86 | 49 | 32 | 22 | 17 | 13 | 9 | 6 | 5 | 4 |
| .95 | 885 | 222 | 99 | 56 | 36 | 26 | 19 | 15 | 10 | 7 | 6 | 4 |
| .99 | 1125 | 282 | 126 | 72 | 46 | 32 | 24 | 19 | 12 | 9 | 7 | 5 |

### u = 24

| Power | .05 | .10 | .15 | .20 | .25 | .30 | .35 | .40 | .50 | .60 | .70 | .80 |
|---|---|---|---|---|---|---|---|---|---|---|---|---|
| .10 | 118 | 30 | 14 | 8 | 6 | 4 | 3 | 3 | 2 | 2 | -- | -- |
| .50 | 318 | 80 | 36 | 21 | 14 | 10 | 7 | 6 | 4 | 3 | 3 | 2 |
| .70 | 417 | 105 | 47 | 27 | 17 | 12 | 9 | 7 | 5 | 4 | 3 | 3 |
| .80 | 485 | 121 | 55 | 31 | 20 | 15 | 11 | 8 | 6 | 4 | 3 | 3 |
| .90 | 578 | 145 | 65 | 37 | 24 | 17 | 13 | 10 | 7 | 5 | 4 | 3 |
| .95 | 662 | 166 | 74 | 42 | 27 | 19 | 14 | 11 | 8 | 6 | 4 | 4 |
| .99 | 831 | 209 | 92 | 53 | 34 | 24 | 18 | 14 | 9 | 7 | 5 | 4 |

**Table 8.4.4**

n to detect f by F test at a = .05
for u = 1, 2, 3, 4

### u = 1

f

| Power | .05 | .10 | .15 | .20 | .25 | .30 | .35 | .40 | .50 | .60 | .70 | .80 |
|---|---|---|---|---|---|---|---|---|---|---|---|---|
| .10 | 84 | 22 | 10 | 6 | 5 | 4 | 3 | 3 | 2 | -- | -- | -- |
| .50 | 769 | 193 | 86 | 49 | 32 | 22 | 17 | 13 | 9 | 7 | 5 | 4 |
| .70 | 1235 | 310 | 138 | 78 | 50 | 35 | 26 | 20 | 13 | 10 | 7 | 6 |
| .80 | 1571 | 393 | 175 | 99 | 64 | 45 | 33 | 26 | 17 | 12 | 9 | 7 |
| .90 | 2102 | 526 | 234 | 132 | 85 | 59 | 44 | 34 | 22 | 16 | 12 | 9 |
| .95 | 2600 | 651 | 290 | 163 | 105 | 73 | 54 | 42 | 27 | 19 | 14 | 11 |
| .99 | 3675 | 920 | 409 | 231 | 148 | 103 | 76 | 58 | 38 | 27 | 20 | 15 |

### u = 2

f

| Power | .05 | .10 | .15 | .20 | .25 | .30 | .35 | .40 | .50 | .60 | .70 | .80 |
|---|---|---|---|---|---|---|---|---|---|---|---|---|
| .10 | 84 | 22 | 10 | 6 | 5 | 4 | 3 | 3 | 2 | -- | -- | -- |
| .50 | 662 | 166 | 74 | 42 | 27 | 19 | 15 | 11 | 8 | 6 | 5 | 4 |
| .70 | 1028 | 258 | 115 | 65 | 42 | 29 | 22 | 17 | 11 | 8 | 6 | 5 |
| .80 | 1286 | 322 | 144 | 81 | 52 | 36 | 27 | 21 | 14 | 10 | 8 | 6 |
| .90 | 1682 | 421 | 188 | 106 | 68 | 48 | 35 | 27 | 18 | 13 | 10 | 8 |
| .95 | 2060 | 515 | 230 | 130 | 83 | 58 | 43 | 33 | 22 | 15 | 12 | 9 |
| .99 | 2855 | 714 | 318 | 179 | 115 | 80 | 59 | 46 | 29 | 21 | 16 | 12 |

### u = 3

f

| Power | .05 | .10 | .15 | .20 | .25 | .30 | .35 | .40 | .50 | .60 | .70 | .80 |
|---|---|---|---|---|---|---|---|---|---|---|---|---|
| .10 | 79 | 21 | 10 | 6 | 4 | 3 | 3 | 2 | 2 | -- | -- | -- |
| .50 | 577 | 145 | 65 | 37 | 24 | 16 | 13 | 10 | 7 | 5 | 4 | 3 |
| .70 | 881 | 221 | 99 | 56 | 36 | 25 | 19 | 15 | 10 | 7 | 6 | 5 |
| .80 | 1096 | 274 | 123 | 69 | 45 | 31 | 23 | 18 | 12 | 9 | 7 | 5 |
| .90 | 1415 | 354 | 158 | 89 | 58 | 40 | 30 | 23 | 15 | 11 | 8 | 7 |
| .95 | 1718 | 430 | 192 | 108 | 70 | 49 | 36 | 28 | 18 | 13 | 10 | 8 |
| .99 | 2353 | 589 | 262 | 148 | 95 | 66 | 49 | 38 | 24 | 17 | 13 | 10 |

### u = 4

f

| Power | .05 | .10 | .15 | .20 | .25 | .30 | .35 | .40 | .50 | .60 | .70 | .80 |
|---|---|---|---|---|---|---|---|---|---|---|---|---|
| .10 | 74 | 19 | 9 | 6 | 4 | 3 | 2 | 2 | -- | -- | -- | -- |
| .50 | 514 | 129 | 58 | 33 | 21 | 15 | 11 | 9 | 6 | 5 | 4 | 3 |
| .70 | 776 | 195 | 87 | 49 | 32 | 22 | 17 | 13 | 9 | 6 | 5 | 4 |
| .80 | 956 | 240 | 107 | 61 | 39 | 27 | 20 | 16 | 10 | 8 | 6 | 5 |
| .90 | 1231 | 309 | 138 | 78 | 50 | 35 | 26 | 20 | 13 | 10 | 7 | 6 |
| .95 | 1486 | 372 | 166 | 94 | 60 | 42 | 31 | 24 | 16 | 11 | 9 | 7 |
| .99 | 2021 | 506 | 225 | 127 | 82 | 57 | 42 | 33 | 21 | 15 | 11 | 9 |

**Table 8.4.5**

n to detect f by F test at a = .05
for u = 5, 6, 8, 10

|  |  |  |  | **u = 5** |  |  |  |  |  |  |  |  |
|  |  |  |  | **f** |  |  |  |  |  |  |  |  |

| Power | .05 | .10 | .15 | .20 | .25 | .30 | .35 | .40 | .50 | .60 | .70 | .80 |
|-------|-----|-----|-----|-----|-----|-----|-----|-----|-----|-----|-----|-----|
| .10 | 69 | 18 | 9 | 5 | 4 | 3 | 2 | 2 | -- | -- | -- | -- |
| .50 | 467 | 117 | 53 | 30 | 19 | 14 | 10 | 8 | 6 | 4 | 3 | 3 |
| .70 | 698 | 175 | 78 | 44 | 29 | 20 | 15 | 12 | 8 | 6 | 5 | 4 |
| .80 | 856 | 215 | 96 | 54 | 35 | 25 | 18 | 14 | 9 | 7 | 5 | 4 |
| .90 | 1098 | 275 | 123 | 69 | 45 | 31 | 23 | 18 | 12 | 9 | 7 | 5 |
| .95 | 1320 | 331 | 148 | 83 | 54 | 38 | 28 | 22 | 14 | 10 | 8 | 6 |
| .99 | 1783 | 447 | 199 | 112 | 72 | 50 | 37 | 29 | 19 | 13 | 10 | 8 |

|  |  |  |  | **u = 6** |  |  |  |  |  |  |  |  |
|  |  |  |  | **f** |  |  |  |  |  |  |  |  |

| Power | .05 | .10 | .15 | .20 | .25 | .30 | .35 | .40 | .50 | .60 | .70 | .80 |
|-------|-----|-----|-----|-----|-----|-----|-----|-----|-----|-----|-----|-----|
| .10 | 66 | 17 | 8 | 5 | 4 | 3 | 2 | 2 | -- | -- | -- | -- |
| .50 | 429 | 108 | 49 | 28 | 18 | 13 | 10 | 8 | 5 | 4 | 3 | 3 |
| .70 | 638 | 160 | 72 | 41 | 26 | 18 | 14 | 11 | 7 | 5 | 4 | 4 |
| .80 | 780 | 195 | 87 | 50 | 32 | 22 | 17 | 13 | 9 | 6 | 5 | 4 |
| .90 | 995 | 250 | 112 | 63 | 41 | 29 | 21 | 16 | 11 | 8 | 6 | 5 |
| .95 | 1192 | 299 | 133 | 75 | 49 | 34 | 25 | 20 | 13 | 9 | 7 | 6 |
| .99 | 1604 | 402 | 179 | 101 | 65 | 46 | 34 | 26 | 17 | 12 | 9 | 7 |

|  |  |  |  | **u = 8** |  |  |  |  |  |  |  |  |
|  |  |  |  | **f** |  |  |  |  |  |  |  |  |

| Power | .05 | .10 | .15 | .20 | .25 | .30 | .35 | .40 | .50 | .60 | .70 | .80 |
|-------|-----|-----|-----|-----|-----|-----|-----|-----|-----|-----|-----|-----|
| .10 | 60 | 16 | 7 | 5 | 3 | 2 | 2 | -- | -- | -- | -- | -- |
| .50 | 374 | 94 | 42 | 24 | 16 | 11 | 8 | 7 | 5 | 4 | 3 | 2 |
| .70 | 548 | 138 | 61 | 35 | 23 | 16 | 12 | 9 | 6 | 5 | 4 | 3 |
| .80 | 669 | 168 | 75 | 42 | 27 | 19 | 14 | 11 | 8 | 6 | 4 | 4 |
| .90 | 848 | 213 | 95 | 54 | 35 | 24 | 18 | 14 | 9 | 7 | 5 | 4 |
| .95 | 1012 | 254 | 113 | 64 | 41 | 29 | 22 | 17 | 11 | 8 | 6 | 5 |
| .99 | 1351 | 338 | 151 | 86 | 55 | 39 | 29 | 22 | 14 | 10 | 8 | 6 |

|  |  |  |  | **u = 10** |  |  |  |  |  |  |  |  |
|  |  |  |  | **f** |  |  |  |  |  |  |  |  |

| Power | .05 | .10 | .15 | .20 | .25 | .30 | .35 | .40 | .50 | .60 | .70 | .80 |
|-------|-----|-----|-----|-----|-----|-----|-----|-----|-----|-----|-----|-----|
| .10 | 55 | 14 | 7 | 4 | 3 | 2 | 2 | -- | -- | -- | -- | -- |
| .50 | 335 | 84 | 38 | 21 | 14 | 10 | 8 | 6 | 4 | 3 | 3 | 2 |
| .70 | 488 | 123 | 55 | 31 | 20 | 14 | 11 | 8 | 6 | 4 | 3 | 3 |
| .80 | 591 | 148 | 66 | 38 | 24 | 17 | 13 | 10 | 7 | 5 | 4 | 3 |
| .90 | 747 | 187 | 84 | 48 | 31 | 22 | 16 | 13 | 8 | 6 | 5 | 4 |
| .95 | 888 | 223 | 99 | 56 | 36 | 26 | 19 | 15 | 10 | 7 | 5 | 4 |
| .99 | 1177 | 295 | 132 | 75 | 48 | 34 | 25 | 19 | 13 | 9 | 7 | 6 |

**Table 8.4.6**

n to detect f by F test at a = .05
for u = 12, 15, 24

### u = 12
#### f

| Power | .05 | .10 | .15 | .20 | .25 | .30 | .35 | .40 | .50 | .60 | .70 | .80 |
|---|---|---|---|---|---|---|---|---|---|---|---|---|
| .10 | 51 | 13 | 7 | 4 | 3 | 2 | 2 | -- | -- | -- | -- | -- |
| .50 | 306 | 77 | 35 | 20 | 13 | 9 | 7 | 6 | 4 | 3 | 3 | 2 |
| .70 | 443 | 111 | 50 | 28 | 18 | 13 | 10 | 8 | 5 | 4 | 3 | 3 |
| .80 | 534 | 134 | 60 | 34 | 22 | 16 | 12 | 9 | 6 | 5 | 4 | 3 |
| .90 | 673 | 169 | 75 | 43 | 28 | 20 | 15 | 11 | 8 | 6 | 4 | 4 |
| .95 | 796 | 200 | 89 | 51 | 33 | 23 | 17 | 13 | 9 | 6 | 5 | 4 |
| .99 | 1052 | 264 | 118 | 67 | 43 | 30 | 22 | 17 | 11 | 8 | 6 | 5 |

### u = 15
#### f

| Power | .05 | .10 | .15 | .20 | .25 | .30 | .35 | .40 | .50 | .60 | .70 | .80 |
|---|---|---|---|---|---|---|---|---|---|---|---|---|
| .10 | 47 | 12 | 6 | 4 | 3 | 2 | --- | -- | -- | -- | -- | -- |
| .50 | 272 | 69 | 31 | 18 | 12 | 8 | 6 | 5 | 4 | 3 | 2 | 2 |
| .70 | 391 | 98 | 44 | 25 | 16 | 12 | 9 | 7 | 5 | 4 | 3 | 2 |
| .80 | 471 | 118 | 53 | 30 | 20 | 14 | 10 | 8 | 6 | 4 | 3 | 3 |
| .90 | 588 | 148 | 66 | 38 | 24 | 17 | 13 | 10 | 7 | 5 | 4 | 3 |
| .95 | 697 | 175 | 78 | 44 | 29 | 20 | 15 | 12 | 8 | 6 | 4 | 4 |
| .99 | 915 | 229 | 102 | 58 | 38 | 26 | 20 | 15 | 10 | 7 | 6 | 4 |

### u = 24
#### f

| Power | .05 | .10 | .15 | .20 | .25 | .30 | .35 | .40 | .50 | .60 | .70 | .80 |
|---|---|---|---|---|---|---|---|---|---|---|---|---|
| .10 | 38 | 10 | 5 | 3 | 2 | --- | --- | -- | -- | -- | -- | -- |
| .50 | 213 | 54 | 24 | 14 | 9 | 7 | 5 | 4 | 3 | 2 | 2 | -- |
| .70 | 303 | 76 | 34 | 20 | 13 | 9 | 7 | 5 | 4 | 3 | 2 | 2 |
| .80 | 363 | 91 | 41 | 23 | 15 | 11 | 8 | 6 | 4 | 3 | 3 | 2 |
| .90 | 457 | 115 | 51 | 29 | 19 | 13 | 10 | 8 | 5 | 4 | 3 | 3 |
| .95 | 525 | 132 | 59 | 34 | 22 | 15 | 11 | 9 | 6 | 4 | 4 | 3 |
| .99 | 680 | 171 | 76 | 44 | 28 | 20 | 15 | 11 | 8 | 6 | 4 | 4 |

**Table 8.4.7**

n to detect f by F test at a = .10
for u = 1, 2, 3, 4

|  | | | | | | $u = 1$ | | | | | | |
|  | | | | | | f | | | | | | |

| Power | .05 | .10 | .15 | .20 | .25 | .30 | .35 | .40 | .50 | .60 | .70 | .80 |
|---|---|---|---|---|---|---|---|---|---|---|---|---|
| .50 | 542 | 136 | 61 | 35 | 22 | 16 | 12 | 9 | 6 | 5 | 4 | 3 |
| .70 | 942 | 236 | 105 | 60 | 38 | 27 | 20 | 15 | 10 | 7 | 6 | 5 |
| .80 | 1237 | 310 | 138 | 78 | 50 | 35 | 26 | 20 | 13 | 9 | 7 | 6 |
| .90 | 1713 | 429 | 191 | 108 | 69 | 48 | 36 | 27 | 18 | 13 | 10 | 8 |
| .95 | 2165 | 542 | 241 | 136 | 87 | 61 | 45 | 35 | 22 | 16 | 12 | 9 |
| .99 | 3155 | 789 | 351 | 198 | 127 | 88 | 65 | 50 | 32 | 23 | 17 | 13 |

|  | | | | | | $u = 2$ | | | | | | |
|  | | | | | | f | | | | | | |

| Power | .05 | .10 | .15 | .20 | .25 | .30 | .35 | .40 | .50 | .60 | .70 | .80 |
|---|---|---|---|---|---|---|---|---|---|---|---|---|
| .50 | 475 | 119 | 53 | 30 | 20 | 14 | 11 | 8 | 6 | 4 | 3 | 3 |
| .70 | 797 | 200 | 89 | 50 | 32 | 23 | 17 | 13 | 9 | 6 | 5 | 4 |
| .80 | 1029 | 258 | 115 | 65 | 41 | 29 | 22 | 17 | 11 | 8 | 6 | 5 |
| .90 | 1395 | 349 | 156 | 88 | 57 | 40 | 29 | 23 | 15 | 11 | 8 | 6 |
| .95 | 1738 | 435 | 194 | 109 | 70 | 49 | 36 | 28 | 18 | 13 | 10 | 8 |
| .99 | 2475 | 619 | 276 | 155 | 100 | 70 | 51 | 33 | 21 | 15 | 11 | 9 |

|  | | | | | | $u = 3$ | | | | | | |
|  | | | | | | f | | | | | | |

| Power | .05 | .10 | .15 | .20 | .25 | .30 | .35 | .40 | .50 | .60 | .70 | .80 |
|---|---|---|---|---|---|---|---|---|---|---|---|---|
| .50 | 419 | 105 | 47 | 27 | 18 | 12 | 9 | 7 | 5 | 4 | 3 | 3 |
| .70 | 690 | 173 | 77 | 43 | 28 | 20 | 15 | 11 | 8 | 6 | 4 | 4 |
| .80 | 883 | 221 | 99 | 56 | 36 | 25 | 19 | 15 | 10 | 7 | 5 | 4 |
| .90 | 1180 | 296 | 132 | 74 | 48 | 34 | 25 | 19 | 13 | 9 | 7 | 5 |
| .95 | 1458 | 365 | 163 | 92 | 59 | 41 | 30 | 24 | 15 | 11 | 8 | 7 |
| .99 | 2051 | 513 | 229 | 129 | 83 | 58 | 43 | 33 | 21 | 15 | 11 | 9 |

|  | | | | | | $u = 4$ | | | | | | |
|  | | | | | | f | | | | | | |

| Power | .05 | .10 | .15 | .20 | .25 | .30 | .35 | .40 | .50 | .60 | .70 | .80 |
|---|---|---|---|---|---|---|---|---|---|---|---|---|
| .50 | 376 | 95 | 43 | 24 | 16 | 11 | 9 | 7 | 5 | 4 | 3 | 3 |
| .70 | 612 | 154 | 68 | 38 | 25 | 18 | 13 | 10 | 7 | 5 | 4 | 3 |
| .80 | 773 | 193 | 87 | 49 | 32 | 22 | 17 | 13 | 9 | 6 | 5 | 4 |
| .90 | 1031 | 258 | 115 | 65 | 42 | 29 | 22 | 17 | 11 | 8 | 6 | 5 |
| .95 | 1267 | 317 | 141 | 80 | 51 | 36 | 27 | 21 | 13 | 10 | 7 | 6 |
| .99 | 1768 | 443 | 197 | 111 | 71 | 50 | 37 | 28 | 19 | 13 | 10 | 8 |

**Table 8.4.8**

n to detect f by F test at a = .10
for u = 5, 6, 8, 10

### u = 5
### f

| Power | .05 | .10 | .15 | .20 | .25 | .30 | .35 | .40 | .50 | .60 | .70 | .80 |
|---|---|---|---|---|---|---|---|---|---|---|---|---|
| .50 | 343 | 86 | 39 | 22 | 14 | 10 | 8 | 6 | 4 | 3 | 3 | 2 |
| .70 | 551 | 139 | 61 | 35 | 23 | 16 | 12 | 9 | 6 | 5 | 4 | 3 |
| .80 | 693 | 174 | 77 | 44 | 28 | 20 | 15 | 12 | 8 | 6 | 4 | 4 |
| .90 | 922 | 231 | 103. | 58 | 37 | 26 | 20 | 15 | 10 | 7 | 6 | 4 |
| .95 | 1128 | 283 | 126 | 71 | 46 | 32 | 24 | 18 | 12 | 9 | 7 | 5 |
| .99 | 1564 | 392 | 175 | 98 | 63 | 44 | 33 | 25 | 16 | 12 | 9 | 7 |

### u = 6
### f

| Power | .05 | .10 | .15 | .20 | .25 | .30 | .35 | .40 | .50 | .60 | .70 | .80 |
|---|---|---|---|---|---|---|---|---|---|---|---|---|
| .50 | 317 | 80 | 36 | 20 | 13 | 9 | 7 | 6 | 4 | 3 | 3 | 2 |
| .70 | 506 | 127 | 57 | 32 | 21 | 15 | 11 | 9 | 6 | 4 | 3 | 3 |
| .80 | 635 | 159 | 71 | 40 | 26 | 18 | 14 | 11 | 7 | 5 | 4 | 3 |
| .90 | 838 | 210 | 94 | 53 | 34 | 24 | 18 | 14 | 9 | 7 | 5 | 4 |
| .95 | 1022 | 256 | 114 | 65 | 42 | 29 | 22 | 17 | 11 | 8 | 6 | 5 |
| .99 | 1408 | 353 | 157 | 89 | 57 | 40 | 30 | 23 | 15 | 11 | 8 | 6 |

### u = 8
### f

| Power | .05 | .10 | .15 | .20 | .25 | .30 | .35 | .40 | .50 | .60 | .70 | .80 |
|---|---|---|---|---|---|---|---|---|---|---|---|---|
| .50 | 278 | 70 | 32 | 18 | 12 | 9 | 6 | 5 | 4 | 3 | 2 | 2 |
| .70 | 436 | 110 | 49 | 28 | 18 | 13 | 10 | 8 | 5 | 4 | 3 | 3 |
| .80 | 545 | 137 | 61 | 35 | 23 | 16 | 12 | 9 | 6 | 5 | 4 | 3 |
| .90 | 717 | 180 | 80 | 46 | 29 | 21 | 15 | 12 | 8 | 6 | 4 | 4 |
| .95 | 870 | 218 | 97 | 55 | 36 | 25 | 19 | 14 | 9 | 7 | 5 | 4 |
| .99 | 1190 | 298 | 133 | 75 | 49 | 34 | 25 | 19 | 13 | 9 | 7 | 5 |

### u = 10
### f

| Power | .05 | .10 | .15 | .20 | .25 | .30 | .35 | .40 | .50 | .60 | .70 | .80 |
|---|---|---|---|---|---|---|---|---|---|---|---|---|
| .50 | 250 | 63 | 28 | 16 | 11 | 8 | 6 | 5 | 3 | 3 | 2 | 2 |
| .70 | 390 | 98 | 44 | 25 | 16 | 11 | 9 | 7 | 5 | 4 | 3 | 2 |
| .80 | 482 | 121 | 54 | 31 | 20 | 14 | 11 | 8 | 6 | 4 | 3 | 3 |
| .90 | 633 | 159 | 71 | 40 | 26 | 18 | 14 | 11 | 7 | 5 | 4 | 3 |
| .95 | 765 | 192 | 86 | 49 | 31 | 22 | 16 | 13 | 8 | 6 | 5 | 4 |
| .99 | 1040 | 261 | 116 | 66 | 42 | 30 | 22 | 17 | 11 | 8 | 6 | 5 |

Table 8.4.9

n to detect f by F test at a = .10
for u = 12, 15, 24

### u = 12
f

| Power | .05 | .10 | .15 | .20 | .25 | .30 | .35 | .40 | .50 | .60 | .70 | .80 |
|-------|-----|-----|-----|-----|-----|-----|-----|-----|-----|-----|-----|-----|
| .50 | 229 | 58 | 26 | 15 | 10 | 7 | 5 | 4 | 3 | 2 | 2 | 2 |
| .70 | 355 | 89 | 40 | 23 | 15 | 11 | 8 | 6 | 4 | 3 | 3 | 2 |
| .80 | 437 | 110 | 49 | 28 | 18 | 13 | 10 | 8 | 5 | 4 | 3 | 3 |
| .90 | 571 | 143 | 64 | 36 | 24 | 17 | 12 | 10 | 6 | 5 | 4 | 3 |
| .95 | 688 | 173 | 77 | 44 | 28 | 20 | 15 | 11 | 8 | 5 | 4 | 4 |
| .99 | 931 | 233 | 104 | 59 | 38 | 27 | 20 | 15 | 10 | 7 | 5 | 4 |

### u = 15
f

| Power | .05 | .10 | .15 | .20 | .25 | .30 | .35 | .40 | .50 | .60 | .70 | .80 |
|-------|-----|-----|-----|-----|-----|-----|-----|-----|-----|-----|-----|-----|
| .50 | 205 | 52 | 23 | 13 | 9 | 6 | 5 | 4 | 3 | 2 | 2 | 2 |
| .70 | 315 | 79 | 35 | 20 | 13 | 9 | 7 | 6 | 4 | 3 | 2 | 2 |
| .80 | 386 | 97 | 43 | 25 | 16 | 12 | 9 | 7 | 5 | 4 | 3 | 2 |
| .90 | 502 | 126 | 56 | 32 | 21 | 15 | 11 | 9 | 6 | 4 | 3 | 3 |
| .95 | 603 | 151 | 68 | 38 | 25 | 17 | 13 | 10 | 7 | 5 | 4 | 3 |
| .99 | 812 | 203 | 91 | 51 | 33 | 23 | 17 | 13 | 9 | 6 | 5 | 4 |

### u = 24
f

| Power | .05 | .10 | .15 | .20 | .25 | .30 | .35 | .40 | .50 | .60 | .70 | .80 |
|-------|-----|-----|-----|-----|-----|-----|-----|-----|-----|-----|-----|-----|
| .50 | 161 | 41 | 18 | 11 | 7 | 5 | 4 | 3 | 2 | 2 | -- | -- |
| .70 | 246 | 62 | 27 | 16 | 10 | 7 | 6 | 5 | 3 | 2 | 2 | 2 |
| .80 | 298 | 75 | 34 | 19 | 12 | 9 | 7 | 5 | 4 | 3 | 2 | 2 |
| .90 | 382 | 96 | 43 | 25 | 16 | 11 | 8 | 7 | 5 | 3 | 3 | 2 |
| .95 | 456 | 114 | 52 | 30 | 19 | 13 | 10 | 8 | 5 | 4 | 3 | 3 |
| .99 | 607 | 152 | 68 | 39 | 25 | 17 | 13 | 10 | 7 | 5 | 4 | 3 |

The tables in this section list values for the significance criterion (**a**), the numerator degrees of freedom (**u**), the ES to be detected (**f**), and the *desired power*. The required size per sample, **n**, may then be determined. The chief use of these tables is in the planning of experiments where they provide a basis for decisions about sample size requirements.

The 33 tables are laid out generally four to a table number, by **a** levels and successively tabled **u** values within each **a** level. The subtable for the required **a**, **u** combination is found and **f** and desired power are located. The same provisions for **a**, **u**, and **f** are made as for the tables in Section 8.3, as follows:

*1. Significance Criterion*, **a**. Table sets are provided for nondirectional **a** of .01, .05, and .10, each set made up of tables for varying values of **u**.

*2. Numerator Degrees of Freedom*, **u**. For each **a** level, tables are provided in succession for the 11 values of **u** = 1 (1) 6 (2) 12, 15, 24. Since the number of means to be compared is **k** = **u** + 1, the tables can be used directly for sets of means numbering **k** = 2 (1) 7 (2) 13, 16, and 25, and for interactions whose **df** equal the above 11 values of **u**. For missing values of **u** (7, 9, 11, etc.), linear interpolation between tables will yield adequate approximations to the desired **n**.

*3. Effect Size*, **f**. **f** was defined and interpreted for equal **n** in Sections 8.2, and generalized for unequal **n** in Section 8.3.2 and for interactions in Section 8.3.4. As in the power tables, provision is made in the sample size tables for the 12 values: .05 (.05) .40 (.10) .80. Conventional levels have been proposed (Section 8.2.3), as follows: small ES: **f** = .10, medium ES: **f** = .25, and large ES: **f** = .40. (No values of **n** less than 2 are given, since there would then be no within-population variance estimate from the data.)

To find **n** for a value of **f** not tabled, substitute in

(8.4.1)
$$n = \frac{n_{.05}}{400f^2} + 1,$$

where $n_{.05}$ is the necessary sample size for the given **a**, **u**, and desired power at **f** = .05 (read from the table), and **f** is the nontabled ES. Round to the nearest integer.

*4. Desired Power.* Provision is made for desired power values of .10 (except at **a** = .10 where it would be meaningless), .50, .70, .80, .90, .95, .99. See 2.4.1 for the rationale for selecting such values for tabling, and particularly for a discussion of the proposal that .80 serve as a convention for desired power in the absence of another basis for a choice.

8.4.1 CASE 0: **k** MEANS WITH EQUAL **n**. The sample size tables were designed for this, the simplest case. Find the subtable for the significance criterion (**a**) and numerator **df** (**k** − 1 = **u**) which obtain and locate **f** and desired power, to determine **n**, the necessary size per each sample mean. For nontabled **f**, use the tables to find $n_{.05}$ and substitute in formula (8.4.1).

**Illustrative Examples**

**8.10** Reconsider the educational experiment on the differential effectiveness of **k** = 4 teaching methods to equal sized samples of **n** = 20 (example 8.1). Using **a** = .05 as the significance criterion, and **f** = .28, it was found that power was approximately .53. Now we recast this as a problem in experimental planning, where we wish to determine the sample size necessary to achieve a specified power value, say .80. Initially, to illustrate the simplicity of the use of the sample size tables for tabled values of **f**, we change her specification of **f** to .25, our operational definition of a medium ES. Summarizing, the conditions for determining **n** for this test are

$$\mathbf{a} = .05, \quad \mathbf{u} = \mathbf{k} - 1 = 3, \quad \mathbf{f} = .25, \quad \text{power} = .80.$$

In the third subtable of Table 8.4.4 (for **a** = .05, **u** = 3) with column **f** = .25, and row power = .80, we find that we need **n** = 45 cases in each of the 4 method groups. Thus, slightly scaling down her ES from .28 to .25, she needs 4(45) = 180 = **N** to have .80 probability of a significant result at **a** = .05.

Since her **f** was originally .28, we illustrate the determination of **n** for this nontabled value, leaving the other specifications unchanged:

$$\mathbf{a} = .05, \quad \mathbf{u} = 3, \quad \mathbf{f} = .28, \quad \text{power} = .80.$$

For nontabled **f**, we use formula (8.4.1). For $n_{.05}$, the sample size needed to detect **f** = .05 for **a** = .05, **u** = 3 with power = .80, we use the same subtable as above, the third subtable of Table 8.4.4 (for **a** = .05, **u** = 3) with column **f** = .05 and row power = .80 and find $n_{.05}$ = 1096. Substituting in formula (8.4.1),

$$n = \frac{1096}{400(.28^2)} + 1 = \frac{1096}{31.36} + 1 = 35.9.$$

Thus, she would need 36 cases in each of the 4 groups to have power of .80 to detect **f** = .28 at **a** = .05. (This value of **n** is, as it should be, smaller than that which resulted when a smaller **f** of .25 was posited above.)

**8.11** We reconsider the social psychiatric research of example 8.2, now as a problem in experimental planning. A pool of suitable in-patients is to be randomly assigned to $k = 3$ equal samples, and each subjected to a different microsocial system. Following this treatment, criterion measures will then be **F**-tested at $a = .01$. Temporarily, we revise the team's two proposed ES measures (the basis for which is described in example 8.2), $f = .229$ and .333, to a range of four tabled values: $f = .20, .25, .30, .35$. It is desired that power be .90 and we seek the **n** required for each of these specifications, which, in summary, are

$$a = .01, \quad u = k - 1 = 2, \quad f = \begin{cases} .20 \\ .25 \\ .30 \\ .35 \end{cases}, \quad \text{power} = .90.$$

We use the second subtable of Table 8.4.1 (for $a = .01$, $u = 2$) at row power $= .90$ and columns $f = .20, .25, .30$, and .35 and find the respective *per sample* **n**'s of 147, 95, 66, and 49. Thus, for these conditions, an **f** of .20 requires three times as large an experiment as an **f** of .35. Note that in terms of proportion of variance, the respective $\eta^2$ for these values are .0385 and .1091 (Table 8.2.2).

Having illustrated the direct table look-up afforded by tabled **f** values, we turn to the actual **f** values posited by the two factions on the research team in the original example, .229 and .333. These nontabled values require the use of formula (8.4.1). The specifications are

$$a = .01, \quad u = 2, \quad f = \begin{cases} .229 \\ .333 \end{cases}, \quad \text{power} = .90.$$

For $n_{.05}$, the sample size needed to detect $f = .05$ for $a = .01$, $u = 2$, with power .90, we use the second subtable of Table 8.4.1 (for $a = .01$, $u = 2$) with column $f = .05$ and row power $= .90$ and find $n_{.05} = 2325$. Substituting it and $f = .229$ in formula (8.4.1),

$$n = \frac{2325}{400(.229^2)} + 1 = 111.8,$$

and for $f = .333$,

$$n = \frac{2325}{400(.333^2)} + 1 = 53.8.$$

Thus, if the "weak effect" faction ($f = .229$) is correct, samples of 112 cases are required, while if the "strong effect" faction ($f = .333$) is correct, only 54, less than half that number, are required per sample.

If they compromise by splitting the difference in **n** and use $(111 + 53)/2 =$

82 cases, we can solve formula (8.4.1) for **f**, the "detectable effect size,"[3] for given **a**, desired power, and **n**:

$$(8.4.2) \qquad f = \sqrt{\frac{n_{.05}}{400(n-1)}}$$

$$= \sqrt{\frac{2325}{400(81)}} = .268.$$

The interpretation of this result is that for an **F** test at **a** = .01 of three means each based on 82 cases to have power of .90, the population ES must be **f** = .268. Since the relationship involved is not linear, splitting the difference in **n** does not split the difference on **f**. The latter would be **f** = (.229 + .333)/2 = .281. If the latter was the basis for compromise, the experiment would demand, applying formula (8.4.1) to these specifications,

$$n = \frac{2325}{400(.281^2)} + 1 = 74.6,$$

or 75 cases.

There is yet a third way of splitting the difference, i.e., between the .05 and .10 proportion of variance of criterion accounted for by experimental group membership, $\eta^2$. If the compromise is effected on this basis, $\eta^2$ = (.05 + .10)/2 = .075. Then, from formula (8.2.22),

$$f = \sqrt{\frac{.075}{1 - .075}} = .285.$$

Substituting this value of **f** with the $n_{.05}$ = 2325 for these conditions in formula (8.4.1),

$$n = \frac{2325}{400(.285^2)} + 1 = 72.6,$$

or 73 cases, which hardly differs from the **n** demanded by averaging the **f**'s (75). This will generally be the case unless the two **f**'s are very widely separated.

8.4.2 CASE 2: **k** MEANS WITH UNEQUAL **n**. Sample size decisions for research planning in Case 2 offer no special problems. One must keep in mind

---

[3] The concept "detectable effect size" transcends its applications here. It is useful in *post hoc* power analysis, particularly in the assessment of failures to reject the null hypothesis and in summarizing the results of a series of experiments bearing on the same issue. See Cohen (1965, p. 100; 1970, p. 828).

that with unequal $n_i$, **f** is the standard deviation of the $p_i$-*weighted* standardized means, as described in Section 8.3.2. When the sample size tables are applied with the usual specifications, the **n** indicated in Case 2 is the *average* sample size of the **k** samples, i.e., $n = N/k$. Similarly, for nontabled **f**, the **n** found from formula (8.4.1) is the average sample size.

The unequal $n_i$ case arises in research planning in various circumstances.

1. In political opinion, market research, or other surveys, where a total natural population is sampled and constitutent populations are of varying frequency, e.g., religious affiliations (as illustrated in Section 8.3.2), socioeconomic categories, etc. (See example 8.12 below.).

2. In experiments where one or more samples of fixed size are to be used, and the size of one or more samples is open to the determination of the experimenter. For example, scheduling problems may dictate that a control sample is to have 50 cases, but the sample sizes of two experimental groups can be determined using considerations of desired power.

3. In some experiments, it may be desired that a reference or control sample have larger **n** than the other **k** − 1 samples.  (See example 8.12 below.)

In each of these circumstances, the average **n** which is read from the tables [or computed from formula (8.4.1)] is multiplied by **k** to yield the total **N**.

### Illustrative Examples

**8.12**   To illustrate Case 1 in surveys of natural populations, return to example 8.3, where a political science class designs an opinion survey of college students on government centralism. A source of variance to be studied is the academic areas of respondents of which there are 6 (= **k**). The **f** for the anticipated unequal $n_i$ is posited at .15, and **a** = .05. Now, instead of treating this as a completed or committed experiment (where total **N** was set at 300 and power then found to be .48), let us ask what **N** is required to attain power of .80. The specifications are

$$\mathbf{a} = .05, \qquad \mathbf{u} = \mathbf{k} - 1 = 5, \qquad \mathbf{f} = .15, \qquad \text{power} = .80.$$

In the first subtable of Table 8.4.5 (for **a** = .05, **u** = 5) at column **f** = 15 and row power = .80, **n** = 96. This is the average size necessary for the 6 academic area samples. The quantity we need is the total sample size, **N** = 6(96) = 576.

Example 8.3 went on to consider the effect on power of a reduction of **k** from 6 to 3 more broadly defined academic areas. Paralleling this, we determine **N** needed for **k** = 3, keeping the other specifications unchanged:

$$\mathbf{a} = .05, \quad \mathbf{u} = \mathbf{k} - 1 = 2, \quad \mathbf{f} = .15, \quad \text{power} = .80.$$

From the second subtable of Table 8.4.4 (for **a** = .05, **u** = 2) for column **f** = .15, row power = .80, we find **n** = 144, so that **N** = 3(144) = 432. Note that going from 6 to 3 groups results here in a 25% reduction of the **N** demanded (from 576 to 432). Of course, we assumed **f** to remain the same, which would probably not be the case.

**8.13** A psychophysiologist is planning an experiment in which he will study the effect of two drugs (A and B) on neural regeneration relative to a control (C). He plans that $\mathbf{n_A} = \mathbf{n_B}$ (which we call $\mathbf{n_E}$) but $\mathbf{n_C}$ is to be 40% larger, i.e., $\mathbf{n_C} = 1.4\mathbf{n_E}$. He posits that the three within-population-standardized mean differences will be $(\mathbf{m_A} - \mathbf{m}) = -.5, (\mathbf{m_B} - \mathbf{m}) = +.5$, and $(\mathbf{m_C} - \mathbf{m}) = 0$, that **a** = .05, and he wishes power to be .90. To determine the necessary sample size, he must first find the **f** implied by his alternate-hypothetical means. His total sample size is

$$\mathbf{N} = \mathbf{n_E} + \mathbf{n_E} + 1.4\mathbf{n_E} = 3.4\mathbf{n_E} \ ,$$

so

$$\mathbf{P_A} = \mathbf{P_B} = \frac{\mathbf{n_E}}{\mathbf{N}} = \frac{\mathbf{n_E}}{3.4\mathbf{n_E}} = .294$$

and

$$\mathbf{P_C} = \frac{1.4\mathbf{n_E}}{\mathbf{N}} = \frac{1.4\mathbf{n_E}}{3.4\mathbf{n_E}} = .412.$$

Combining formulas (8.3.1), (8.3.2), and (8.2.1),[4]

$$(8.4.3) \quad \mathbf{f} = \sqrt{\sum \mathbf{P_i} \left( \frac{\mathbf{m_i} - \mathbf{m}}{\sigma} \right)^2}$$

$$= \sqrt{.294(-.5^2) + .294(+.5^2) + .412(0^2)} = \sqrt{.1470} = .38.$$

Collecting the specifications,

$$\mathbf{a} = .05, \quad \mathbf{u} = \mathbf{k} - 1 = 2, \quad \mathbf{f} = .38, \quad \text{power} = .90.$$

---

[4] Although the means are equally spaced, we cannot use the **d** procedures of Section 8.2.1, which are predicated on equal **n**.

Since $f$ is not tabled, we proceed to find the average $n$ by formula (8.4.1), which calls for $n_{.05}$, the $n$ required for these specifications of $a$, $u$, and power when $f = .05$. In the second subtable of Table 8.4.4, $a = .05$ and $u = 2$, row power $= .90$, and $f = .05$, $n_{.05} = 1682$. Applying formula (8.4.1),

$$n = \frac{1682}{400(.38^2)} + 1 = 30.1.$$

But this $n$ is for Case 1, the *average* $n$ per sample. The total $N = 3(30.1) = 90.3$. The sample sizes are unequal portions of this, as specified: The sample size of groups A and B are each $.294(90.3) = 27$ and of group C is $.412(90.3) = 37$. Thus, with sample sizes respectively for A, B, and C of 27, 27, and 37, he will have a .90 probability that his $F$ test on the 3 sample means will meet the .05 significance criterion, given that $f = .38$.

### 8.4.3   Cases 2 and 3: Fixed Main and Interaction Effects in Factorial and Complex Designs.

In factorial design, the power values of tests of both main and interaction effects are determined by the design's denominator $df$, which in turn depends upon a single given cell sample size ($n_c$). It is therefore convenient to present sample size determination for all the effects together for any given design. (In other complex designs, i.e., those with more than one source of nonerror variance, the same methods apply, although there may be different denominator $df$s for different effects.) The reader is referred to Sections 8.3.3 and 8.3.4 for discussions of interaction effects and the interpretation of $\eta$ and $\eta^2$ as partial values.

The procedure for using the tables to determine the sample size required by an effect is essentially the same as for Cases 0 and 1. The sample size table (for specified $a$ and $u$) is entered with $f$ and the desired power, and the $n$ is read from the table. However, this $n$ must be understood as the $n'$ of formula (8.3.4), a function of the denominator $df$ and the $df$ for the effect, $u$. The *cell* sample size implied by the $n'$ value read from the table is then found from

(8.4.4)     $$n_c = \frac{(n' - 1)(u + 1)}{\text{number of cells}} + 1,$$

where $u$ is the $df$ for the effect being analyzed, and "number of cells" is the number of (the highest order of) cells in the analysis, e.g., for all main and interaction effects in an $R \times C \times H$ design it is $rch$. We assume throughout that all cells have the same $n_c$. The $n_c$ thus computed need not be an integer. It is therefore rounded up to the next higher integer (or down, if it is very close to the lower integer) to determine the cell sample size that must actually be employed. Multiplying this integral $n_c$ value by the number of cells in the design then gives the actual total $N$ required by the specifications for the effect in question.

When **f** is not a tabled value, one proceeds as in Cases 0 and 1 to find **n** by formula (8.4.1). This is again **n'**, and one proceeds as above to determine $n_c$ and **N**.

Since the tests of the various effects in a factorial (or other complex) design will demand different **N**s, these must then be resolved into a single **N** which will then be used in the experiment.

### Illustrative Examples

**8.14** Reconsider example 8.6, now as a problem in sample size determination to achieve specified power. The experiment is concerned with the effects on persuasibility in elementary school boys of sex of experimenter (**S**), age of subject (**A**), and instruction conditions (**C**), in respectively a $2 \times 3 \times 4$ ( $= 24$ cells) factorial design. The ES posited for the three main effects are $f_S = .10$, $f_A = .25$ and $f_C = .40$ and for all interaction tests, **f** = .25; all the tests are to be performed at **a** = .05. Assume that power of .80 is desired for all of the tests, subject to reconsideration and reconciliation of the differing **N**'s which will result.

For the **S** effect, the specifications are thus:

$$a = .05, \quad u = 2 - 1 = 1, \quad f = .10, \quad \text{power} = .80.$$

In the first subtable of Table 8.4.4 for **a** = .05, **u** = 1, with column **f** = .10 and power = .80, we find the value 394. Treating it as **n'**, we then find from formula (8.4.4) that the cell sample size implied by **n'** is

$$n_c = \frac{(394 - 1)(1 + 1)}{24} + 1 = (33.75) = 34,$$

and the actual total **N** required for the **S** effect by these specifications is $24(34) = 816$ (!). Although conceivable, it seems unlikely that an experiment of this size would be attempted. Note that **f** = .10 operationally defines a small ES, and we have seen in previous chapters that to have power of .80 to detect small ES requires very large sample sizes. This virtually restricts such attempts to large scale survey research of the type used in political polling and to sociological, market, and economic research.

Consider now the **N** demanded by the specifications for the age effect, which are

$$a = .05, \quad u = 3 - 1 = 2, \quad f = .25, \quad \text{power} = .80.$$

In the second subtable of Table 8.4.4, for **a** = .05 and **u** = 2, with column

$f = .25$, and row power $= .80$, we find the $n$ ($= n'$) value of 52. Substituting in (8.4.4), $n_c = (52 - 1)(2 + 1)/24 + 1 = (7.38 =) 8$, hence the actual total $N = 24(8) = 192$. This more modest $n$ demand is primarily due to positing $f = .25$ (medium ES).

Finally, we find $n$ required for the test on **C**, as specified:

$$a = .05, \qquad u = 4 - 1 = 3, \qquad f = .40, \qquad \text{power} = .80.$$

The third subtable of Table 8.4.4 (for $a = .05$, $u = 3$) at $f = .40$, power $= .80$, yields the value 18 for $n$ ($= n'$). $n_c = (18 - 1)(3 + 1)/24 + 1 = (3.8 =) 4$, so the total $N$ required is $24(4) = 96$. This relatively small required $N$ is primarily a consequence of positing $f = .40$, a large ES.

Taking stock at this point, the three tests of the main effects, of varying specifications, have led to varying $N$ demands of 816 for **S**, 192 for **A**, and 96 for **C**.

Turning now to the tests of the interactions, they all share the same $a = .05$, $f = .25$, and the power desired specified at .80. They differ only in their $u$ values, but this means that they will differ in $n'$ and therefore $N$:

For **S** $\times$ **A**, $u = (2 - 1)(3 - 1) = 2$. The specifications are the same as for the **A** main effect ($a = .05$, $u = 2$, $f = .25$, power $= .80$), so the results are the same: eight cases per cell, hence $N = 192$.

For **S** $\times$ **C**, $u = (2 - 1)(4 - 1) = 3$. From the third subtable of Table 8.4.4 ($a = .05$, $u = 3$), for power $= .80$ when $f = .25$, the value $n' = 45$ is found. Formula (8.4.4) then gives $n_c = (45 - 1)(3 + 1)/24 + 1 = (8.33 =) 9$, and $N = 24(9) = 216$.

For **A** $\times$ **C**, $u = (3 - 1)(4 - 1) = 6$. The second subtable of Table 8.4.5 ($a = .05$, $u = 6$) gives $n' = 32$ for power $= .80$, $f = .25$. Formula (8.4.4) then gives $n_c = (32 - 1)(6 + 1)/24 + 1 = (10.04 =) 10$ (We round down here since 10.04 is only trivially larger than 10.) $N$ is therefore $24(10) = 240$.

Finally, for the test of the **S** $\times$ **A** $\times$ **C** interaction effect, $u = (2 - 1)(3 - 1)(4 - 1) = 6$, and the specifications are the same as for **A** $\times$ **C**, therefore $n_c = 10$ and $N = 240$.

We have thus had an array of $N$ values demanded by the three main and four interaction effects ranging from 96 to 816, and some choice must be made. Table 8.4.10 summarizes the specifications and resulting sample size demands for the seven tests of this $2 \times 3 \times 4$ factorial design. Surveying the results of this analysis, the researcher planning this experiment may reason as follows:

The central issues in this research are the interactions, so the fact that adequate power for the small **S** effect is beyond practical reach (816 cases in a manipulative experiment is virtually unheard of) is not fatal. If an experiment as large as $N = 240$ can be mounted, power of at least .80 at $a = .05$ can be attained for the ES values specified. The actual power values for all the tests are then determined by the methods of Sections 8.3.3 and 8.3.4. They turn out to be: **S** .31, **A** .91, **C** >.995, **S** × **A** .92, **S** × **C** .88, **A** × **C** .80, and **S** × **A** × **C** .80.

TABLE 8.4.10

SAMPLE SIZE DEMANDS FOR THE MAIN AND INTERACTION EFFECTS IN THE
**S** × **A** × **C** (2 × 3 × 4) FACTORIAL DESIGN

| Effect | Specifications | | | | | |
|---|---|---|---|---|---|---|
|  | **a** | **u** | **f** | Power | $n_c$ | **N** |
| **S** | .05 | 1 | .10 | .80 | 34 | 816 |
| **A** | .05 | 2 | .25 | .80 | 8 | 192 |
| **C** | .05 | 3 | .40 | .80 | 4 | 96 |
| **S** × **A** | .05 | 2 | .25 | .80 | 8 | 192 |
| **S** × **C** | .05 | 3 | .25 | .80 | 9 | 216 |
| **A** × **C** | .05 | 6 | .25 | .80 | 10 | 240 |
| **S** × **A** × **C** | .05 | 6 | .25 | .80 | 10 | 240 |

Alternatively, it may well be the case that **N** = 240 exceeds the resources of the researcher, but after studying Table 8.4.10 he decides that he can (barely) manage eight cases per cell and **N** = 192; this will provide adequate power for **A**, **C**, and **S** × **A** (**S** is hopeless, anyway). The actual power values with **N** = 192 for the tests of the interactions are then determined to be: **S** × **A** .84, **S** × **C** .79, **A** × **C** .68, and **S** × **A** × **C** .68. The planner may be willing to settle for these values and proceed with **N** = 192.

On the other hand, we may judge that the two-to-one odds for rejection in the **F** tests of the **A** × **C** and **S** × **A** × **C** interactions are not good enough. He may be willing to decide, a priori, that he is prepared to test these interactions at **a** = .10. Note that he need not shift to **a** = .10 for the other tests. He is simply prepared to offer a somewhat less credible rejection of these two null hypotheses if it should turn out that the increase in power is sufficient to make it worthwhile. These tests will thus have the same specifications: **a** = .10, **u** = 6, **f** = .25, and, since **N** = 192, denominator **df** = 192 − 24 = 168, and **n′** = 168/(6 + 1) + 1 = 25. Looking up **n** = 25 at **f** = .25 in Table 8.3.28 (for **a** = .10, **u** = 6), he finds power = .78. He may then consider whether he prefers power of .68 at **a** = .05 or power of .78 at **a** = .10 for these two tests, a not very happy pair of alternatives. (A factor in his decision may be his judgment as to whether **f** = .25 is a possibly overoptimistic estimation of the true ES. If so, he had better opt for the **a** = .10 alternative since, at **a** = .05, power would be less than .68).

There is another device available in research planning to bring sample size

demands into conformity with available resources, already illustrated in problem 8.3. One should consider dropping the number of levels of a research
factor in order to reduce the size of **u**, particularly in interactions. In this
illustration, if only two age groups are used, **u** = 3 for **A** × **C** and **S** × **A** × **C**.
For **N** = 192, now in 2 × 2 × 4 = 16 cells (hence, **n**$_c$ = 12), the denominator
**df** will be 192 − 16 = 176, and **n**′ will be 176/(3 + 1) = 1 = 45. For **a** = .05
and **u** = 3, Table 8.3.14 gives power = .81 at **f** = .25 for **n** = 45. This appears
to be the preferred resolution of the problem in this illustration. In other circumstances an entire research factor may be dropped in the interests of increasing power or decreasing sample size demand for the remainder of the
experiment.

   **8.15**   We return to example 8.9 which described a learning experiment of
the effects of age (**R**) at **r** = 2 levels and contingency of reinforcement (**C**) at
**c** = 4 levels on a measure of learning, so that there are 2 × 4 = 8 cells. Although **f** may be specified by using the operational definition conventions,
example 8.9 illustrated how **f** values for the main effects and interaction are
arrived at by positing values for the alternate-hypothetical cell means and
within-population σ and computing them from these values. We found there
that **f** for **R** was .375, for **C** .523, and for **R** × **C** .293. The problem is now
recast into one in which sample size is to be determined, given the desired
power and the other specifications. Assume initially that all three tests are to
be performed at **a** = .05 and that the power desired is at least .80.
   For the test of the **R** (age) effect, the specification summary is thus:

$$\mathbf{a} = .05, \qquad \mathbf{u} = \mathbf{r} - 1 = 1, \qquad \mathbf{f} = .375, \qquad \text{power} = .80.$$

Since **f** = .375 is not a tabled value, we proceed by means of formulas (8.4.1)
and (8.4.4). In the first subtable of Table 8.4.4 (**a** = .05, **u** = 1), at power =
.80, the value at **f** = .05 is 1571. Thus, from (8.4.1),

$$\mathbf{n}' = \frac{1571}{400(.375^2)} + 1 = 28.93,$$

and then applying formula (8.4.4),

$$\mathbf{n}_c = \frac{(28.93 - 1)(1 + 1)}{8} + 1 = (7.98 =) \, 8,$$

so that each of the eight cells will have eight cases, and **N** = 64 cases are
required for the test of the **R** effect.
   For the test of the reinforcement contingency (**C**) effect, the specifications
are:

$$\mathbf{a} = .05, \qquad \mathbf{u} = \mathbf{c} - 1 = 3, \qquad \mathbf{f} = .523, \qquad \text{power} = .80.$$

The third subtable of Table 8.4.4 ($a = .05$, $u = 3$), gives $n_{.05} = 1096$ for power $= .80$. Formula (8.4.1) then gives, for $f = .523$,

$$n' = \frac{1096}{400(.523^2)} + 1 = 11.02$$

and formula (8.4.4) gives

$$n_c = \frac{(11.02 - 1)(3 + 1)}{8} + 1 = (6.01 =) 6,$$

so that $N = 8 \times 6 = 48$, a substantially smaller demand for the test of the **C** effect.

The specifications for the test of the **R** $\times$ **C** interaction effect are:

$$a = .05, \qquad u = (r - 1)(c - 1) = 3, \qquad f = .293, \qquad \text{power} = .80,$$

and, since **a**, **u**, and power are the same as for the **R** main effect, the $n_{.05} = 1096$ is the same. For $f = .293$,

$$n' = \frac{1096}{400(.293^2)} + 1 = 32.92,$$

and

$$n_c = \frac{(32.92 - 1)(3 + 1)}{8} + 1 = (16.96 =) 17$$

so $N = 8 \times 17 = 136$ for the **R** $\times$ **C** test.

So again, as will so often be the case for interactions, the sample size demand is large relative to those for the main effects. If the experimenter is prepared to mount that large an experiment, power for testing the interaction effect will be .80, and it will be much better than that for the main effects:

**R**: $a = .05$, $u = 1$, $f = .375$, $n' = (136 - 8)/(1 + 1) + 1 = 65$.

From Table 8.3.12, power $= .99$.

**C**: $a = .05$, $u = 3$, $f = .523$, $n' = (136 - 8)/(3 + 1) + 1 = 33$.

From Table 8.3.14, power $> .995$.

If the experimenter finds $N = 136$ a larger experiment than he can manage, he may investigate the consequence to the **N** required by switching to an $a = .10$ criterion for the **R** $\times$ **C** test. For this change in the specifications, $n_{.05}$ for $a = .10$, $u = 3$ (third subtable of Table 8.4.7) is 883, $n' = 26.71$, $n_c = 14$ and $N = 112$.

As another possibility, he may retain $a = .05$, but settle for power $= .70$ for the **R** $\times$ **C** test. From Table 8.4.4 for $a = .05$, $u = 3$, $n_{.05}$ is found to be

881, so **n'** is computed as 26.66, $n_c$ as 14 and **N** $= 112$. Thus, for the reduction in **N** from 136 to 112, he may either use the lenient **a** $= .10$ criterion with power $= .80$, or the conventional **a** $= .05$ but with power $= .70$.

Finally, as in the preceding problem, he may consider giving up one of the reinforcement conditions so that there are only $2 \times 3 = 6$ cells and the **u** for **R** $\times$ **C** is reduced to $(2 - 1)(3 - 1) = 2$. If the choice of which condition to omit may be made on purely statistical grounds, the table of alternate-hypothetical population means presented in problem 8.9 above suggests that $C_3$ is the best candidate. Note that the omission of the means for $C_3$ will change all three **f** values. The **f** for **R** $\times$ **C** increases to .328 (and is slightly decreased for the main effects). For the revised $2 \times 3$ design, then, the specifications for **R** $\times$ **C** are:

$$\textbf{a} = .05, \qquad \textbf{u} = 2, \qquad \textbf{f} = .328, \qquad \text{power} = .80,$$

and via formulas (8.4.1) and (8.4.4), $n_c$ is found to be 16 and **N** $= 6 \times 16 = 96$. (The reader may wish to check the above as an exercise.) Thus, by removing the condition that makes the least contribution to the interaction, its **f** is increased (from .293 to .328), its **u** is decreased, and the result is that for **a** $= .05$ and power $= .80$, 96 rather than 136 cases are required. The experimenter might well decide to follow this course.

This and the preceding problem tell a morality tale about research design. The possibility of studying many issues within a single experiment, so well described in the standard textbooks on experimental design and the analysis of variance, should be accompanied by a warning that the power of the resulting tests will be inadequate unless **N** is (usually unrealistically) large or the ESs are (also usually unrealistically) large. Recall that this principle is not re-

TABLE 8.4.11

**n** PER GROUP AND TOTAL **N** AS A FUNCTION OF **k** FOR **k** GROUPS UNDER THE CONDITIONS **a** $= .05$ AND POWER $= .80$ FOR **f** $= .25$

| k | u | n | N |
|---|---|---|---|
| 2 | 1 | 64 | 128 |
| 3 | 2 | 52 | 156 |
| 4 | 3 | 45 | 180 |
| 5 | 4 | 39 | 195 |
| 6 | 5 | 35 | 210 |
| 7 | 6 | 32 | 224 |
| 9 | 8 | 27 | 243 |
| 11 | 10 | 24 | 264 |
| 13 | 12 | 22 | 286 |
| 16 | 15 | 20 | 320 |
| 25 | 24 | 15 | 375 |

stricted to factorial or other complex designs; a simple one-way analysis of variance on **k** groups will, unless **f** is large, require relatively large **N** (as illustrated in problem 8.3). Consider the standard conditions **a** = .05, **f** = .25 (medium ES), and desired power = .80 for a one-way design with **k** groups. Table 8.4.11 shows now the required **n** per group and total **N** (= **nk**) vary as **k** increases (the **n** values are simply read from Tables 8.4.4–8.4.6). Although the required sample size *per group* decreases as **k** increases, the total **N** increases with **k**. Although for a medium ES 150 subjects provide adequate power to appraise two or three treatments, that number is not sufficient for six or seven. The reader might find it instructive to construct and study tables like 8.4.11 for other values of **f** and **a**.

8.4.5    THE ANALYSIS OF COVARIANCE. As was discussed in the section on the use of the power tables in the analysis of covariance (8.3.5), no special procedural change takes place from analogous analysis of variance designs. What changes is the conception of the dependent variable, which becomes **Y′**, a regression-adjusted or statistically controlled value [defined in formula (8.3.9)], whose use may result in a larger ES than the use of the unadjusted **Y**. Population means, variances, ranges, etc., now merely refer to this adjusted variable in place of the unadjusted variable of the analysis of variance. For more detail, see Section 8.3.5. See also the alternative approach to data-analytic problems of this kind by means of multiple regression/correlation analysis in Chapter 9.

Thus, sample size estimation in the analysis of covariance proceeds in exactly the same way as in analogous analysis of variance designs.

## 8.5    THE USE OF THE TABLES FOR SIGNIFICANCE TESTING

8.5.1    INTRODUCTION. As is the case in most of the chapters in this handbook, provision for facilitating significance testing has been made in the power tables as a convenience to the reader. While power analysis is primarily relevant to experimental planning and has as an important parameter the alternative-hypothetical population ES, once the research data are collected, attention turns to the assessment of the null hypothesis in the light of the data (Cohen, 1973). (See Section 1.5, and for some of the advantages of the corollary approach in **t** tests, Section 2.5.)

Because of the discrepancy between the actual denominator **df** in a factorial or other complex design and the one-way design (Cases 0 and 1) assumed in the construction of the tables, it does not pay to undertake the adjustments that would be necessary to use the tabled values of **F**$_c$ for significance testing in Cases 2 and 3, since **F** tables are widely available in statistical textbooks and specialized collections (e.g., Owen, 1962). Accordingly, we do not discuss or exemplify the use of the **F**$_c$ values in the power

tables in this handbook for significance testing of fixed main effects or interactions (Cases 2 and 3).

For significance testing, the function of the data of interest to us in the
Case 0 and 1 applications of this chapter is the **F** ratio for the relevant null
hypothesis which is found in the sample, $F_s$.

In each power table (8.3) for a given significance criterion **a** and numerator
**df, u,** the second column contains $F_c$, the minimum **F** necessary for significance at the **a** level for that **u**. The $F_c$ values vary with **n,** the relevant sample
size. Significance testing proceeds by simply comparing the computed $F_s$
with the tabled $F_c$.

8.5.2   SIGNIFICANCE TESTING IN CASE 0: **k** MEANS WITH EQUAL **n**. Find
the power table for the significance criterion (**a**) and numerator **df,** $u = k - 1$,
which obtain. Enter with **n,** the size per sample mean, and read out $F_c$. If
the computed $F_s$ equals or exceeds the tabulated $F_c$, the null hypothesis is
rejected.

**Illustrative Examples**

**8.16**   Assume that the educational experiment described in 8.1 has been
performed: a comparison (at **a** = .05) of the differential effectiveness of
**k** = 4 teaching methods, for each of which there is a random sample of
**n** = 20. Whatever the history of the planning of this experiment, including
most particularly the anticipated ES (**f** = .280), what is *now* relevant is the
**F** value (between groups mean square/within groups mean square) computed from the 4(20) = 80 achievement scores found in the completed experiment, $F_s$. Assume $F_s$ is found to equal 2.316. Thus, the specifications for the
significance test are

$$a = .05, \qquad u = k - 1 = 3, \qquad n = 20, \qquad F_s = 2.316.$$

To determine the significance status of the results, checking column
$F_c$ of Table 8.3.14 (**a** = .05, **u** = 3) for **n** = 20 gives $F_c = 2.725$. Since the
computed $F_s$ of 2.316 is smaller than the criterion value, the results are not
significant at **a** = .05, i.e., the data do not warrant the conclusion that the
population achievement means of the four teaching methods differ.

**8.17**   In example 8.2, a power analysis of an experiment in social psychiatry was described in which **k** = 3 equal samples of **n** = 200 each were
subjected to different microsocial systems. Consider the experiment completed and the data analyzed. In planning the experiment, it was found that
for the population ES values which were posited, at **a** = .01, power would

be very large. This is, however, not relevant to the significance-testing procedure. Assume that the $F_s$ is found to equal 4.912. What is the status of the null hypotheses on the three population means? The relevant specifications are

$$a = .01, \quad u = k - 1 = 2, \quad n = 200, \quad F_s = 4.912.$$

Table 8.3.2 (for $a = .01$ and $u = 2$) with row $n = 200$ yields $F_c = 4.642$. Since $F_s$ exceeds this value, the null hypothesis is rejected, and it is concluded (at $a = .01$) that the three population means are not all equal. Note that one does *not* conclude that the population ES of the power specifications (in this case there were two values, $\eta^2 = .05$ and $.10$, or $f = .23$ and $.33$) necessarily obtains. In fact, the *sample* $\eta^2$ is $uF_s/[uF_s + (u + 1)(n - 1)] = .016$ and the best estimate of the population $\eta^2$ is $.013$ $(= \epsilon^2)$. See section 8.2.2 above and Cohen (1965, pp. 101–106 and ref.).

8.5.2   SIGNIFICANCE TESTING IN CASE 1: **k** MEANS WITH UNEQUAL **n**. When the sample **n**'s are not all equal, the significance testing procedure is as in Case 0 except that one enters the table with their arithmetic mean, i.e., **N/k** [formula (8.3.3)]. This will generally not yield a tabled value of **n**, but the **n** scale is such that on the rare occasions when it is necessary, linear interpolation between $F_c$ values is quite adequate.

**Illustrative Examples**

**8.18**   Example 8.3 described an opinion poll on government centralism on a college campus in which there would be a comparison among means of $k = 6$ academic area groups of unequal size, with a total sample size of approximately 300. The **F** test is to be performed at $a = .05$. Assume that when the survey is concluded, the actual total $N = 293$, and $F_s = 2.405$. Since $N = 293$, the **n** needed for entry is $N/k = 293/6 = 48.8$. What is the status of the null hypothesis of equal population means, for these specifications, i.e.,

$$a = .05, \quad u = k - 1 = 5, \quad n = 48.8, \quad F_s = 2.405.$$

In Table 8.3.16 (for $a = .05$, $u = 5$) see column $F_c$. There is no need for interpolation, since, using the conservative **n** of 48, $F_c = 2.246$, which is exceeded by $F_s = 2.405$. Therefore, the null hypothesis is rejected, and it can be concluded that the academic area population means on the centralism index are not all equal. (Note again the irrelevance to conclusions about the null hypothesis of the alternate-hypothetical ES of the power analysis described in example 8.3. )

**8.19**   In example 8.4, samples of varying **n** of psychiatric nurses from **k** = 12 hospitals were to be studied with regard to differences in mean scores on an attitude scale of Social Restrictiveness towards psychiatric patients. The total **N** = 326, so the average **n** per hospital is **N**/**k** = 27.2. The significance criterion is **a** = .05. When the data are analyzed, the **F**$_s$ of the test of **H**$_0$: **m**$_1$ = **m**$_2$ = ... = **m**$_{12}$ equals 3.467. The specifications for the significance test, thus, are

$$\mathbf{a} = .05, \qquad \mathbf{u} = \mathbf{k} - 1 = 11, \qquad \mathbf{n} = 27.2, \qquad \mathbf{F}_s = 3.467.$$

There are no tables for **u** = 11. Although we can linearly interpolate between **F**$_c$ values for **u** = 10 and **u** = 12 to find **F**$_c$ for **u** = 11, it would only be necessary to do so if **F**$_s$ fell between these two **F**$_c$ values. The **F**$_c$ value for the smaller **u** (here 10) will always be larger than that of the larger **u** (here 12). Thus, if **F**$_s$ exceeds the **F**$_c$ for **u** = 10, it must be significant, and if **F**$_s$ is smaller than **F**$_c$ for **u** = 12, it must be nonsignificant. Accordingly, we use Table 8.3.19 (for **a** = .05, **u** = 10) with row **n** = 27, and find **F**$_c$ = 1.864. Since **F**$_s$ = 3.467 is greater than this value, we conclude that the null hypothesis is rejected at **a** = .05. Again we call to the reader's attention that we do *not* conclude that the population ES used in the power analysis of example 8.4 necessarily obtains (Cohen, 1973). That value was **f** = .25, hence (Table 8.2.2) the population $\eta^2$ posited was .0588. For the sample, $\eta^2$ is .1083 and $\epsilon^2$, the best estimate of the population $\eta^2$, is .0771 (Section 8.2.2).

# CHAPTER 9

# Multiple Regression and Correlation Analysis

## 9.1 INTRODUCTION AND USE

During the past decade, under the impetus of the computer revolution and increasing sophistication in statistics and research design among behavioral scientists, multiple regression and correlation analysis (MRC) has come to be understood as an exceedingly flexible data-analytic procedure remarkably suited to the variety and types of problems encountered in behavioral research (Cohen & Cohen, 1983; Pedhazur, 1982; McNeil, Kelly & McNeil, 1975; Ward & Jennings, 1973). Although long a part of the content of statistics textbooks, it had been relegated to the limited role of studying linear relationships among quantitative variables, usually in the applied technology of social science. For example, in psychology it was largely employed in the forecasting of success or outcome using psychological tests and ratings as predictors in personnel selection, college admission, psychodiagnosis, and the like. In its "new look," fixed model MRC is a highly general data-analytic system that can be employed whenever a quantitative "dependent variable" (**Y**) is to be studied in its relationship to one or more research factors of interest, where each research factor (**A**, **B**, etc.) is a *set* made up of one or more "independent variables" (IVs). The form of the relationship is not constrained: it may be straight-line or curvilinear, general or conditional, whole or partial. The nature of the research factors is also not constrained: they may be quantitative or qualitative (nominal scales), main effects or interactions, variates of direct interest, or covariates to be partialled (as in the analysis of covariance). Research factors and their constituent IVs may be correlated with each other or uncorrelated (as in the factorial designs discussed in the preceding chapter), naturally occurring properties like sex or religion or IQ or, alternatively, experimentally manipulated "treatments." In short, virtually any information may be represented as a research factor and its relationship to (or effect on) **Y** studied by MRC.[1]

The details of the methods of representation and study of research factors in general MRC are obviously beyond the scope of this chapter. The reader is referred to Cohen & Cohen (1983), which provides a comprehensive exposition of the system. Its major features will, however, be conveyed in the course of describing and exemplifying its power analysis.

One of the interesting properties of general MRC, already implied, is that its generality is such as to incorporate the analysis of variance and the analysis of covariance as special cases (Cohen, 1968; Cohen & Cohen, 1983; Overall & Spiegel, 1969; Overall, Spiegel, & Cohen, 1975). Being more general, however, it allows greater scope in data analyses. For example, it can represent in sets of IVs interactions of quantitative as well as qualitative (nominal) variables and can employ as covariates variables that are curvilinearly related, variables with missing data, and nominal scales. An important advantage when one leaves the beaten path of simple experimental designs is that any data structure containing a dependent variable can be fully analyzed using any "canned" multiple regression computer program.

The statistical assumptions are those of all fixed model least-squares procedures that use the **F** (or **t**) distribution: the IVs are taken to be fixed, and for each combination of values of the IVs, the **Y** observations are assumed to be independent, normally distributed, and of constant variance across combinations. These **F** tests are, however, "robust" (Scheffé, 1959, Chapter 10; Cohen, 1983, pp. 112–114), so that moderate departures from these assumptions will have generally little effect on the validity of null hypothesis tests and power analyses.

The **F** test in fixed MRC analysis can be understood as a test of the null hypothesis that the proportion of the variance in **Y** accounted for by some source ($PV_S$) is zero in the population. It can be most generally written

(9.1.1) $$F = \frac{PV_S/u}{PV_E/v} \qquad (df = u, v),$$

where $PV_S$ is the proportion of **Y** variance accounted for by that source (S) in the sample; $PV_E$ is the proportion of error (E) or residual variance; **u** is the

---

[1]See Chapter 10 for power analysis in set correlation, a multivariate generalization of MRC.

number of IVs for the source, hence the **df** for the numerator; **v** is the number of **df** for the error variance, i.e., the denominator **df**.

As written, (9.1.1) contains in both numerator and denominator a proportion of **Y** variance divided by its **df**, hence a normalized mean square. Thus, as in the analysis of variance, **F** is a ratio of mean squares, each based on a given number of **df**. We shall shortly see that the PVs are functions of squared multiple correlations ($R^2$s).

It is useful to rewrite equation (9.1.1) as

(9.1.2)  $$F = \frac{PV_S}{PV_E} \times \frac{v}{u} \qquad (df = u, v).$$

The left-hand term is a measure of effect size (ES) in the sample, the proportion of **Y** variance accounted for by the source in question relative to the proportion of error, a signal-to-noise ratio. The right-hand term carries information about the size of the experiment (**N**) and the number of variables required to represent the source. The degree of significance, as always, is a multiplicative function of effect size and experiment size. The power of the test is the same type of function, but now it is the *population* ES that is involved.

Dependent on how the source and error are defined, the formulas for **F** given above are variously specialized, and, in parallel, so are their respective power-analytic procedures. Three cases may be distinguished:

*Case 0.* A set **B**, made up of **u** variables, is related to **Y**, and $R^2_{Y \cdot B}$ is determined; its complement, $1 - R^2_{Y \cdot B}$, is the error variance proportion. The null hypothesis is that the population value of $R^2_{Y \cdot B}$ is zero.

*Case 1.* The proportion of **Y** variance accounted for by a set **B**, *over and above* what is accounted for by another set **A**, is determined. This quantity is given by $R^2_{Y \cdot A, B} - R^2_{Y \cdot A}$. The source of **Y** variance under test may be represented as **B · A**, i.e., set **B** from which set **A** has been partialled, or, the *unique* contribution of set **B** in accounting for **Y** variance. The null hypothesis is that **B · A** accounts for no **Y** variance in the population. In Case 1, the error variance proportion is $1 - R^2_{Y \cdot A, B}$.

*Case 2.* As in Case 1, the source of variance under test is **B · A**, its sample value is $R^2_{Y \cdot A, B} - R^2_{Y \cdot A}$, and the null hypothesis holds that the latter value is zero in the population. In Case 2, however, there are yet other variables (set **C**) employed in the definition of the error term, which is now $1 - R^2_{Y \cdot A, B, C}$. It will be shown that this is the most general case—Cases 0 and 1 (and others) may be derived from it as special cases.

## 9.2   THE EFFECT SIZE INDEX: $f^2$

Since the same **F** sampling distribution is used here as in the analysis of variance, the same ES index, **f**, is employed. However, since the MRC system proceeds more naturally with PVs, i.e., squared correlation values, it is more convenient to work directly with $f^2$ rather than **f**. We emphasize, however, that the index is fundamentally the same, and that the properties and relationships described for **f** in the context of Chapter 8, e.g., as a standard deviation of standardized means, continue to hold here.

The left-hand term of the general **F** formula (9.1.2) above is defined on the sample, but if we instead define it on the population, it becomes the general formula for $f^2$, thus

$$(9.2.1) \qquad\qquad f^2 = \frac{PV_S}{PV_E},$$

a population signal-to-noise ratio. For each of the Cases 0, 1, and 2, the source/error population variances are differently operationalized, as they are in the **F** tests, but they have the same conceptual meaning.

In the simple Case 0 applications, with the source of **Y** variance of interest defined as set **B**, only a single population parameter is involved: $PV_S$ is $R^2_{Y \cdot B}$, $PV_E$ is $1 - R^2_{Y \cdot B}$, so

$$(9.2.2) \qquad\qquad f^2 = \frac{R^2_{Y \cdot B}}{1 - R^2_{Y \cdot B}}.$$

Thus, if the alternate hypothesis for a set **B** comprised of **u** variables is that $R^2_{Y \cdot B} = .20$, then the ES employed in power and sample size analyses is $.20/(1 - .20) = .25$.

In Case 1 applications, it is the partialled **B** · **A** that is the source of interest, so the $PV_S$ is $R^2_{Y \cdot A,B} - R^2_{Y \cdot A}$. Since the proportion $R^2_{Y \cdot A,B}$ of the **Y** variance in the population has been accounted for by sets **A** and **B**, $PV_E = 1 - R^2_{Y \cdot A,B}$ (Model I error; see Cohen & Cohen, 1983, pp. 155–158); thus, (9.2.1) specializes to

$$(9.2.3) \qquad\qquad f^2 = \frac{R^2_{Y \cdot A,B} - R^2_{Y \cdot A}}{1 - R^2_{Y \cdot A,B}}.$$

Note that two population $R^2$s must be posited to determine $f^2$ (but see the next section.) If it is assumed that set **A** accounts for $.30\ (= R^2_{Y \cdot A})$ of the **Y** variance, and that sets **A** and **B** account together for $.45\ (= R^2_{Y \cdot A,B})$ of the **Y** variance, then **B** · **A** (or **B** *uniquely*) accounts for $.15\ (= R^2_{Y \cdot A,B} - R^2_{Y \cdot A})$ of the **Y** variance; $.55\ (= 1 - R^2_{Y \cdot A,B})$ is the Case 1 error variance proportion, and $f^2 = .15/.55 = .2727$.

Finally, in Case 2 applications, the same **B · A** source of **Y** variance is under scrutiny, so $PV_S$ is again $R^2_{Y·A,B} - R^2_{Y·A}$. But the "noise" is further reduced by the other variables, comprising a set **C**, so $PV_E = 1 - R^2_{Y·A,B,C}$ (Model II error, Cohen & Cohen, 1983, pp. 158–160). With the PVs thus specified, formula (9.2.1) becomes

$$(9.2.4) \qquad f^2 = \frac{R^2_{Y·A,B} - R^2_{Y·A}}{1 - R^2_{Y·A,B,C}}.$$

Here, three population parameter $R^2$ values must be posited (or, at least the difference between two for the numerator and a third for the denominator) in order to determine $f^2$. Thus, if as before, set **B** accounts uniquely (relative to set **A**) for .15 ($= R^2_{Y·A,B} - R^2_{Y·A} = .45 - .30$) of the **Y** variance, and $R^2_{Y·A,B,C} = .60$, then the Model II error is $1 - R^2_{Y·A,B,C} = .40$, and $f^2 = .15/.40 = .3750$. Note that for the same proportion of **Y** variance accounted for by **B · A**, $f^2$ in Case 2 cannot be smaller than in Case 1 and will generally be larger. This is because $R^2_{Y·A,B,C}$ is generally larger than $R^2_{Y·A,B}$, and in any case cannot be smaller.

9.2.1   $f^2$, $R^2$, SEMIPARTIAL AND PARTIAL $R^2$, AND $\eta^2$. We have seen above that $f^2$ for a set **B** is, in general, a function of $R^2$ values and that in Case 0 it is simply $R^2_{Y·B}/(1 - R^2_{Y·B})$. If this relationship is inverted, one can determine what value of $R^2_{Y·B}$ is implied by any given value of $f^2$ in Case 0:

$$(9.2.5) \qquad R^2_{Y·B} = \frac{f^2}{1 + f^2}.$$

If this relationship seems familiar, it is because the right-hand expression is identically what was given in the formula for $\eta^2$ in Chapter 8 (8.2.19). As was briefly noted there, when group membership (a nominal scale) is rendered as a set of IVs (set **B** here), the proportion of **Y** variance it accounts for is $R^2_{Y·B}$. Thus, as an example of the generality of the MRC system, we see that the $\eta^2$ of the one-way analysis of variance is a special case of $R^2$.

But set **B** need not, of course, represent group membership. It may carry any kind of information (e.g., linear and nonlinear aspects of quantitative research factors), and $R^2_{Y·B}$ is interpreted as the PV in **Y** for which it accounts (Cohen & Cohen, 1983, Chapter 4–7).

In Cases 1 and 2, the $PV_S$ is $R^2_{Y·A,B} - R^2_{Y·A}$, the proportion of **Y** variance accounted for by **B · A**. So conceived, it may be symbolized as $R^2_{Y·(B·A)}$, a squared multiple *semipartial* (or *part*) correlation. Thus, as above, if $R^2_{Y·A} = .30$ and $R^2_{Y·A,B} = .45$, then the increment due to **B** over **A** is $R^2_{Y·A,B} - R^2_{Y·A} = .15 = R^2_{Y·(B·A)}$. The notation and conception are analogous to those for single variables; as the subscripts indicate, it relates **Y** to **B · A**. It is a *semi-partial* $R^2$ because **A** is partialled from **B**, but not from **Y**. When **A** is partialled from both **B** and **Y**, the resulting coefficient is a squared multiple *partial* correlation, symbolized as $R^2_{YB \cdot A}$, whose formula is

$$(9.2.6) \qquad R^2_{YB \cdot A} = \frac{R^2_{Y \cdot A, B} - R^2_{Y \cdot A}}{1 - R^2_{Y \cdot A}} = \frac{R^2_{Y \cdot (B \cdot A)}}{1 - R^2_{Y \cdot A}}.$$

Instead of expressing the **Y** variance due to **B** · **A** as a proportion of the *total* **Y** variance, as does the semipartial $R^2$, the partial $R^2$ expresses it as a proportion of that part of the total **Y** variance not accounted for by set **A**, i.e., of $1 - R^2_{Y \cdot A}$. Thus, with $R^2_{Y \cdot A, B} - R^2_{Y \cdot A} = .45 - .30 = .15 = R^2_{Y \cdot (B \cdot A)}$, $R^2_{YB \cdot A} = .15/(1 - .30) = .2143$. Another and perhaps most useful conception of $R^2_{YB \cdot A}$ is that it is the proportion of **Y** variance accounted for by set **B** (on the average) in subsets of the cases in the population having the same scores on the variables in set **A**; therefore, it is $R^2_{Y \cdot B}$ when set **A** is "held constant," or "statistically controlled." Thus, the interpretation of multiple partial correlation follows, for sets, the same interpretation as for partial correlations for single variables.

In Case 1 circumstances, when an investigator can express his alternate hypothesis in terms of a value for $R^2_{YB \cdot A}$, that is the only parameter necessary to determine $f^2$. Some simple algebraic manipulation demonstrates that the Case 1 $f^2$ can be written as

$$(9.2.7) \qquad f^2 = \frac{R^2_{YB \cdot A}}{1 - R^2_{YB \cdot A}},$$

i.e., exactly as for Case 0, but substituting the $R^2_{YB \cdot A}$ for $R^2_{Y \cdot B}$. For the $R^2_{YB \cdot A} = .2143$ exemplified above, (9.2.7) gives $.2143/(1 - .2143) = .2727$, the same $f^2$ as was found from (9.2.3).

If (9.2.7) is inverted, one obtains the partial $R^2$ implied by $f^2$ in a Case 1 application,

$$(9.2.8) \qquad R^2_{YB \cdot A} = \frac{f^2}{1 + f^2},$$

exactly the same expression as for $R^2_{Y \cdot B}$ in Case 0, formula (9.2.5). Note that these relationships are the same as between $f^2$ and partial $\eta^2$ (Section 8.3.3), thus demonstrating that partial $\eta^2$ is merely a special case of partial $R^2$, just as $\eta^2$ is a special case of $R^2$.

9.2.2   "SMALL," "MEDIUM," AND "LARGE" $f^2$ VALUES.   In MRC applications, the natural means of expressing alternate hypotheses is in terms of proportions of variance in **Y** (the dependent variable) accounted for by the source under study, i.e., as an $R^2$, partial $R^2$, or semipartial $R^2$. These may then be translated into $f^2$ values using the formulas of the preceding section. Since, as we have seen throughout this book, PV constitutes a quasi-universal and fairly readily understood measure of strength of relationship or effect size when the dependent variable is an interval, ratio, or dichotomous scale, the need to think in terms of $f^2$ is reduced, and with it, the need to rely on conventional operational definitions of "small," "medium," and "large" values for $f^2$. We nevertheless offer such conventions for the frame of reference that they provide, and for use in power surveys and other methodological investigations. We reiterate the caveat that they can represent only a crude guide in as diverse a colleciton of areas as fall under the rubric of behavioral science.

The values for $f^2$ that follow are somewhat larger than strict equivalence with the operational definitions for the other tests in this book would dictate. For example, when there is only 1 ($= \mathbf{u}$) independent variable, the **F** test for $R^2$ specializes to $t^2$ of the **t** test for **r**, whose ES operational definitions are respectively .10, .30, and .50 (Section 3.2.1), hence, for $r^2$, .01, .09, and .25. These in turn yield $f^2$ values (for Case 0), respectively, of .01, .10, and .33 (from formula 9.2.2), each smaller than the respective $f^2$ value given below. The reason for somewhat higher standards for $f^2$ for the operational definitions in MRC is the expectation that the number of IVs in typical applications will be several (if not many). It seems intuitively evident that, for example, if $f^2 = .10$ defines a "medium" $r^2$ ($= .09$), it is reasonable for $f^2 = .15$ to define a "medium" $R^2$ (or partial $R^2$) of .15 when several IVs are involved.

SMALL EFFECT SIZE: $f^2 = .02$. Translated into $R^2$ (9.2.5) or partial $R^2$ for Case 1 (9.1.8), this gives $.02/(1 + .02) = .0196$. We thus define a small effect as one that accounts for 2% of the **Y** variance (in contrast with 1% for **r**), and translate to an $\mathbf{R} = \sqrt{.0196} = .14$ (compared to .10 for **r**). This is a modest enough amount, just barely escaping triviality and (alas!) all too frequently in practice represents the true order of magnitude of the effect being tested. The discussion under "Small Effect Size" in Section 3.2.1 is relevant here: what may be a moderate theoretical ES may easily, in a "noisy" research, be no larger than what is defined here as small.

MEDIUM EFFECT SIZE: $f^2 = .15$. In PV terms, this amounts to an $R^2$ or partial $R^2$ of $.15/(1 + .15) = .13$, hence **R** or partial $\mathbf{R} = .36$ (compared to $r = .30$ for a medium ES). It may seem that 13% is a paltry amount of variance to define as "medium" when a set made up of several variables is used, but keep in mind that we are defining population values—these are not subject to the inflation (least squares overfitting) which requires correction for shrinkage of a sample $R^2$ (Cohen & Cohen, 1983, pp. 105–107). In any case, if an investigator finds this criterion too small (or, for that matter, too large) for an area in which he is experienced, he clearly has no need for conventions —he should specify the $R^2$ (or partial $R^2$) appropriate to his substantive content and type of **F** test, and determine the $f^2$ from the relevant formula in the preceding material.

LARGE EFFECT SIZE:   $f^2 = .35$. This translates into PV = .26 for $R^2$ and partial $R^2$, which in terms of correlation, gives .51 (slightly larger than the $r = .50$ defining a "large mount" of correlation). This value seems about right for defining a large effect in the middle of the range of fields we cover. It will undoubtedly be often found to be small in sociology, economics, and psychophysics on the one hand, and too large in personality, clinical, and social psychology on the other. As always, this criterion is a compromise that should be rejected when it seems unsuited to the substantive content of any given investigation.

## 9.3   POWER TABLES

The determination of power as a function of the other parameters proceeds differently in this chapter than in those preceding. Whereas for the other tests, the power tables were entered with the ES index and sample size, here the noncentrality parameter of the noncentral **F** distribution, $\lambda$, is used. $\lambda$ is a simple function of the ES index and the numerator and denominator **df**, respectively **u** and **v**:

$$(9.3.1) \qquad \lambda = f^2 (u + v + 1).$$

We have seen that $f^2$ and the error model differ in the three cases, so each case has its own function of population $R^2$ values for $f^2$ and its own function of **N** and number of IVs (**u**) for **v**. These will be made explicit as each case is discussed.

The three tables in this section yield power values for the **F** tests on the proportion of **Y** variance accounted for by a set of **u** variables **B** (or a partialled set, **B·A**). To read out power, the tables are entered with **a**, $\lambda$, **u**, and **v**.

1. *Significance Criterion,* **a**. Tables 9.3.1 and 9.3.2 are for **a** = .01 and .05, respectively.

2. $\lambda$, *the Noncentrality Parameter.* $\lambda$ is tabled over the most useful range for typical MRC applications. Power values are provided at the following 15 $\lambda$ values: 2 (2) 20 (4) 40. Since $\lambda$ is a continuous function, interpolation will generally be necessary. Linear interpolation is quite adequate for virtually all purposes, and, because of the intervals tabled, can frequently be done by mental arithmetic. (For interpolation when $\lambda < 2$, note that at $\lambda = 0$, for all values of **u**, power = **a**.)

3. *Degrees of Freedom of the Numerator of the* **F** *Ratio,* **u**. This is also the number of variables in the set **B** which represents the source of variance under study. Each table provides entries for the following 23 values of **u**: 1 (1) 15, 18, 20, 24, 30, 40, 48, 60, 120. (The larger values are rarely used in

MRC.) When necessary, linear interpolation will yield good approximations.

4. *Degrees of Freedom of the Denominator of the* **F** *Ratio,* **v.** For each value of **u**, power entries for the following four values of **v** are provided: 20, 60, 120, and $\infty$. Interpolation between **v** values should be linear in the reciprocals of **v**, specifically in 1/20, 1/60, 1/120, and 0, respectively.

In a typical problem, power is to be found for a given $\lambda$ for a given **v**, where **v** falls between $v_L$ and $v_U$, the lower and upper values tabled in 9.3.1 and 9.3.2, e.g., $v_L = 60$, $v_U = 120$. The power values Power $_L$ and Power $_U$ are obtained for $\lambda$ at $v_L$ and at $v_U$ by linear interpolation. Then, to obtain power for the given **v**, substitute in

$$(9.3.2) \quad \text{Power} = \text{Power}_L + \frac{1/v_L - 1/v}{1/v_L - 1/v_U} (\text{Power}_U - \text{Power}_L).$$

Note that for $v_U = \infty$, $1/v_U = 0$, so that for $v > 120$, the denominator of (9.3.2) = $1/120 - 0 = .0833$.

As throughout this manual, the values in the table are power times 100, the percent of significance tests performed on random samples (under the conditions specified for **a**, **u**, **v**, and $\lambda$) which will yield a value of **F** that results in rejecting the null hypothesis. They are rounded to the nearest unit and are accurate to within one unit as tabled.

9.3.1  CASE 0: TEST OF $R^2$.   The simplest case is one in which a set **B**, made up of a number (**u**) of independent variables, is correlated with a dependent variable **Y**, and $R^2_{Y \cdot B}$, the PV of **Y** accounted for by the set **B**, is determined. The null hypothesis is simply that the population $R^2_{Y \cdot B}$ is zero. Specializing the general **F** test of formula (9.1.2) for Case 0, $PV_S$ is the sample $R^2_{Y \cdot B}$, $PV_E = 1 - R^2_{Y \cdot B}$, and $N = u + v + 1$.

For the power analysis, only the alternate-hypothetical population $R^2_{Y \cdot B}$ is required, since $f^2 = R^2_{Y \cdot B}/(1 - R^2_{Y \cdot B})$, as given in (9.2.2). (Alternatively, a conventional $f^2$ value may be used.) Thus, formula (9.3.1) becomes for Case 0

$$(9.3.3) \quad \lambda = \frac{R^2_{Y \cdot B}}{1 - R^2_{Y \cdot B}} \times N.$$

Since in the MRC system virtually any information can be represented as a set of IVs, the MRC Case 0 test is a very general test which, in addition to its conventional application with multiple quantitative IVs, subsumes a great variety of other test procedures as special cases. Some examples:

1. The **u** variables of set **B** may represent group membership in $u + 1 = k$ groups, so the one-way analysis of variance **F** test for equal (Chapter 8, Case 0) or unequal (Chapter 8, Case 1) sample sizes are special cases. As

**Table 9.3.1**
Power of the F Test as a Function of λ, **u**, and **v**
a = .01

| u | v | 2 | 4 | 6 | 8 | 10 | 12 | 14 | 16 | 18 | 20 | 24 | 28 | 32 | 36 | 40 |
|---|---|---|---|---|---|----|----|----|----|----|----|----|----|----|----|----|
| 1 | 20 | 10 | 23 | 37 | 51 | 63 | 73 | 80 | 86 | 90 | 94 | 97 | 99 | * | | |
|   | 60 | 12 | 26 | 42 | 57 | 69 | 79 | 86 | 91 | 94 | 96 | 99 | * | | | |
|   | 120 | 12 | 27 | 44 | 58 | 71 | 80 | 87 | 92 | 95 | 97 | 99 | * | | | |
|   | ∞ | 12 | 28 | 45 | 60 | 72 | 81 | 88 | 92 | 95 | 97 | 99 | * | | | |
| 2 | 20 | 06 | 15 | 26 | 37 | 48 | 58 | 67 | 75 | 81 | 86 | 93 | 96 | 98 | 99 | * |
|   | 60 | 08 | 18 | 30 | 45 | 57 | 68 | 76 | 83 | 88 | 92 | 97 | 99 | 99 | * | |
|   | 120 | 08 | 19 | 33 | 47 | 59 | 70 | 78 | 85 | 90 | 93 | 97 | 99 | * | | |
|   | ∞ | 08 | 20 | 35 | 49 | 61 | 72 | 80 | 87 | 91 | 94 | 98 | 99 | * | | |
| 3 | 20 | 05 | 11 | 20 | 29 | 39 | 48 | 57 | 65 | 72 | 78 | 87 | 93 | 96 | 98 | 99 |
|   | 60 | 06 | 14 | 25 | 37 | 49 | 60 | 69 | 77 | 83 | 88 | 94 | 97 | 99 | * | |
|   | 120 | 06 | 15 | 27 | 39 | 51 | 62 | 72 | 79 | 85 | 90 | 95 | 98 | 99 | * | |
|   | ∞ | 07 | 16 | 29 | 42 | 54 | 65 | 74 | 82 | 87 | 91 | 96 | 98 | * | | |
| 4 | 20 | 04 | 09 | 16 | 23 | 32 | 41 | 49 | 57 | 64 | 71 | 81 | 89 | 93 | 96 | 98 |
|   | 60 | 05 | 12 | 21 | 31 | 42 | 53 | 62 | 71 | 78 | 83 | 91 | 96 | 98 | 99 | * |
|   | 120 | 05 | 13 | 23 | 34 | 45 | 56 | 66 | 74 | 81 | 86 | 93 | 97 | 98 | * | |
|   | ∞ | 06 | 14 | 25 | 37 | 49 | 60 | 69 | 77 | 84 | 89 | 95 | 98 | 99 | * | |
| 5 | 20 | 03 | 07 | 13 | 20 | 27 | 35 | 43 | 50 | 58 | 64 | 76 | 84 | 90 | 93 | 96 |
|   | 60 | 04 | 10 | 18 | 28 | 37 | 48 | 57 | 66 | 73 | 79 | 88 | 94 | 97 | 98 | 99 |
|   | 120 | 04 | 11 | 20 | 30 | 41 | 51 | 61 | 70 | 77 | 83 | 91 | 95 | 98 | 99 | * |
|   | ∞ | 05 | 12 | 22 | 33 | 44 | 55 | 65 | 74 | 80 | 86 | 93 | 97 | 99 | 99 | * |
| 6 | 20 | 03 | 06 | 11 | 17 | 23 | 30 | 37 | 45 | 52 | 58 | 70 | 79 | 86 | 91 | 95 |
|   | 60 | 04 | 09 | 16 | 24 | 34 | 43 | 52 | 61 | 69 | 75 | 85 | 92 | 96 | 98 | 99 |
|   | 120 | 04 | 10 | 17 | 27 | 37 | 47 | 57 | 66 | 73 | 79 | 89 | 94 | 97 | 99 | * |
|   | ∞ | 05 | 11 | 19 | 30 | 41 | 51 | 61 | 70 | 77 | 83 | 91 | 96 | 98 | 99 | * |

a = .01

λ

| | | | | | | | | | | | | | | | | |
|---|---|---|---|---|---|---|---|---|---|---|---|---|---|---|---|---|
| 7 | 20 | 03 | 05 | 09 | 15 | 20 | 26 | 33 | 40 | 46 | 53 | 65 | 74 | 82 | 88 | 92 |
| | 60 | 04 | 08 | 14 | 22 | 30 | 39 | 48 | 57 | 64 | 71 | 82 | 90 | 94 | 97 | 99 |
| | 120 | 04 | 09 | 16 | 24 | 34 | 43 | 53 | 62 | 69 | 76 | 86 | 93 | 96 | 96 | 99 |
| | ∞ | 04 | 10 | 18 | 27 | 37 | 48 | 58 | 67 | 74 | 81 | 90 | 95 | 98 | 99 | * |
| 8 | 20 | 02 | 05 | 08 | 13 | 18 | 23 | 29 | 36 | 42 | 48 | 60 | 70 | 78 | 84 | 89 |
| | 60 | 03 | 07 | 13 | 20 | 27 | 36 | 44 | 53 | 61 | 67 | 79 | 87 | 93 | 96 | 98 |
| | 120 | 03 | 08 | 14 | 22 | 31 | 40 | 49 | 58 | 66 | 73 | 84 | 91 | 95 | 98 | 99 |
| | ∞ | 04 | 09 | 16 | 25 | 35 | 45 | 55 | 64 | 72 | 78 | 88 | 94 | 97 | 99 | 99 |
| 9 | 20 | 02 | 04 | 07 | 11 | 16 | 21 | 26 | 32 | 38 | 44 | 55 | 65 | 74 | 81 | 86 |
| | 60 | 03 | 06 | 11 | 18 | 25 | 33 | 41 | 49 | 57 | 64 | 76 | 85 | 91 | 95 | 97 |
| | 120 | 03 | 07 | 13 | 20 | 29 | 37 | 46 | 55 | 63 | 70 | 81 | 89 | 94 | 97 | 98 |
| | ∞ | 04 | 08 | 15 | 23 | 33 | 42 | 52 | 61 | 69 | 76 | 86 | 93 | 96 | 98 | 99 |
| 10 | 20 | 02 | 04 | 06 | 10 | 14 | 19 | 24 | 29 | 34 | 40 | 51 | 61 | 70 | 77 | 83 |
| | 60 | 02 | 06 | 10 | 16 | 23 | 30 | 38 | 46 | 54 | 61 | 73 | 83 | 89 | 94 | 96 |
| | 120 | 02 | 07 | 12 | 19 | 27 | 35 | 44 | 52 | 60 | 67 | 79 | 87 | 93 | 96 | 98 |
| | ∞ | 03 | 08 | 14 | 22 | 31 | 40 | 49 | 58 | 66 | 74 | 84 | 91 | 96 | 98 | 99 |
| 11 | 20 | 02 | 04 | 07 | 10 | 13 | 17 | 22 | 26 | 31 | 37 | 47 | 57 | 66 | 74 | 80 |
| | 60 | 03 | 05 | 10 | 15 | 21 | 29 | 36 | 44 | 51 | 58 | 71 | 80 | 87 | 92 | 95 |
| | 120 | 03 | 06 | 11 | 17 | 25 | 33 | 41 | 50 | 58 | 65 | 77 | 86 | 92 | 95 | 97 |
| | ∞ | 03 | 07 | 13 | 20 | 29 | 38 | 47 | 56 | 64 | 71 | 83 | 90 | 95 | 97 | 99 |
| 12 | 20 | 02 | 03 | 05 | 08 | 12 | 15 | 20 | 24 | 29 | 34 | 44 | 53 | 62 | 70 | 77 |
| | 60 | 02 | 05 | 09 | 14 | 20 | 26 | 33 | 41 | 48 | 55 | 68 | 78 | 85 | 91 | 94 |
| | 120 | 02 | 06 | 11 | 17 | 24 | 31 | 38 | 47 | 55 | 62 | 75 | 84 | 90 | 95 | 97 |
| | ∞ | 03 | 07 | 12 | 19 | 27 | 36 | 45 | 54 | 62 | 69 | 81 | 89 | 94 | 97 | 99 |
| 13 | 20 | 02 | 04 | 06 | 08 | 11 | 14 | 18 | 22 | 26 | 31 | 40 | 50 | 59 | 67 | 74 |
| | 60 | 02 | 05 | 08 | 13 | 18 | 25 | 32 | 39 | 46 | 52 | 65 | 76 | 84 | 89 | 93 |
| | 120 | 02 | 05 | 10 | 15 | 22 | 29 | 37 | 45 | 53 | 60 | 72 | 82 | 89 | 93 | 96 |
| | ∞ | 03 | 06 | 11 | 18 | 26 | 35 | 44 | 52 | 60 | 68 | 80 | 88 | 93 | 96 | 98 |

*(Continued)*

**Table 9.3.1** (Continued)

| u | v | | | | | | | | λ | | | | | | | | |
|---|---|---|---|---|---|---|---|---|---|---|---|---|---|---|---|---|---|
| | | 2 | 4 | 6 | 8 | 10 | 12 | 14 | 16 | 18 | 20 | 24 | 28 | 32 | 36 | 40 |
| 14 | 20 | 02 | 04 | 05 | 08 | 10 | 13 | 17 | 20 | 24 | 29 | 38 | 47 | 55 | 63 | 70 |
| | 60 | 02 | 05 | 08 | 12 | 17 | 23 | 30 | 36 | 43 | 50 | 62 | 73 | 82 | 88 | 92 |
| | 120 | 03 | 05 | 09 | 14 | 21 | 28 | 35 | 43 | 50 | 58 | 70 | 80 | 88 | 92 | 96 |
| | ∞ | 03 | 06 | 11 | 17 | 25 | 33 | 42 | 50 | 59 | 66 | 78 | 87 | 92 | 96 | 98 |
| 15 | 20 | 02 | 03 | 05 | 07 | 09 | 12 | 15 | 19 | 23 | 27 | 35 | 44 | 52 | 60 | 67 |
| | 60 | 02 | 04 | 07 | 11 | 16 | 22 | 28 | 34 | 41 | 47 | 60 | 71 | 80 | 86 | 91 |
| | 120 | 02 | 05 | 09 | 13 | 19 | 26 | 33 | 41 | 48 | 55 | 68 | 78 | 86 | 90 | 95 |
| | ∞ | 02 | 06 | 10 | 16 | 24 | 32 | 40 | 49 | 57 | 64 | 77 | 86 | 92 | 95 | 98 |
| 18 | 20 | 02 | 03 | 04 | 06 | 08 | 10 | 13 | 15 | 18 | 22 | 29 | 36 | 44 | 51 | 59 |
| | 60 | 02 | 04 | 06 | 10 | 14 | 18 | 23 | 29 | 35 | 41 | 53 | 64 | 74 | 81 | 87 |
| | 120 | 02 | 04 | 07 | 11 | 17 | 22 | 29 | 36 | 43 | 49 | 62 | 73 | 82 | 88 | 93 |
| | ∞ | 02 | 05 | 09 | 14 | 21 | 28 | 36 | 44 | 52 | 59 | 72 | 82 | 89 | 94 | 96 |
| 20 | 20 | 02 | 03 | 04 | 05 | 07 | 09 | 11 | 14 | 16 | 19 | 25 | 32 | 39 | 46 | 53 |
| | 60 | 02 | 04 | 06 | 09 | 12 | 16 | 21 | 26 | 32 | 37 | 49 | 60 | 70 | 78 | 84 |
| | 120 | 02 | 04 | 07 | 10 | 15 | 20 | 26 | 32 | 39 | 46 | 59 | 70 | 79 | 86 | 91 |
| | ∞ | 02 | 05 | 08 | 13 | 19 | 26 | 33 | 41 | 49 | 56 | 69 | 80 | 87 | 92 | 96 |
| 24 | 20 | 02 | 03 | 04 | 05 | 06 | 07 | 09 | 11 | 13 | 15 | 20 | 26 | 32 | 38 | 44 |
| | 60 | 02 | 03 | 05 | 07 | 10 | 14 | 17 | 22 | 26 | 31 | 42 | 52 | 62 | 71 | 78 |
| | 120 | 02 | 03 | 06 | 09 | 13 | 17 | 22 | 28 | 34 | 40 | 52 | 63 | 73 | 81 | 87 |
| | ∞ | 02 | 04 | 07 | 12 | 17 | 23 | 29 | 37 | 44 | 51 | 64 | 75 | 84 | 90 | 94 |
| 30 | 20 | 02 | 02 | 03 | 04 | 05 | 06 | 07 | 08 | 10 | 12 | 15 | 19 | 24 | 29 | 34 |
| | 60 | 02 | 03 | 04 | 06 | 08 | 11 | 14 | 17 | 21 | 25 | 34 | 43 | 52 | 61 | 69 |
| | 120 | 02 | 03 | 05 | 07 | 10 | 14 | 18 | 22 | 27 | 33 | 44 | 55 | 65 | 73 | 80 |
| | ∞ | 02 | 04 | 06 | 10 | 14 | 19 | 25 | 31 | 37 | 44 | 57 | 69 | 79 | 86 | 91 |

| | | | | | | | | | | | | | | | | |
|---|---|---|---|---|---|---|---|---|---|---|---|---|---|---|---|---|
| 40 | 20 | 02 | 02 | 03 | 03 | 04 | 05 | 05 | 06 | 07 | 08 | 11 | 13 | 16 | 20 | 23 |
| | 60 | 02 | 02 | 03 | 05 | 06 | 08 | 10 | 12 | 15 | 18 | 24 | 32 | 39 | 47 | 55 |
| | 120 | 02 | 03 | 04 | 06 | 08 | 10 | 13 | 17 | 20 | 24 | 33 | 41 | 52 | 61 | 70 |
| | ∞ | 02 | 03 | 05 | 08 | 11 | 15 | 20 | 25 | 31 | 37 | 49 | 60 | 71 | 79 | 86 |
| 48 | 20 | 02 | 02 | 02 | 03 | 03 | 04 | 04 | 05 | 06 | 07 | 08 | 11 | 13 | 15 | 18 |
| | 60 | 02 | 02 | 03 | 04 | 05 | 06 | 08 | 10 | 12 | 14 | 19 | 25 | 32 | 39 | 45 |
| | 120 | 02 | 02 | 03 | 04 | 06 | 08 | 11 | 14 | 17 | 20 | 28 | 36 | 45 | 53 | 62 |
| | ∞ | 02 | 03 | 05 | 07 | 10 | 13 | 17 | 21 | 26 | 32 | 43 | 54 | 65 | 74 | 81 |
| 60 | 20 | 01 | 02 | 02 | 03 | 03 | 03 | 04 | 04 | 05 | 05 | 07 | 08 | 10 | 11 | 13 |
| | 60 | 01 | 02 | 03 | 03 | 04 | 05 | 06 | 08 | 09 | 11 | 14 | 19 | 24 | 29 | 35 |
| | 120 | 01 | 02 | 03 | 04 | 05 | 07 | 08 | 11 | 13 | 15 | 21 | 28 | 35 | 43 | 51 |
| | ∞ | 01 | 02 | 04 | 06 | 08 | 11 | 14 | 18 | 22 | 27 | 37 | 47 | 58 | 67 | 75 |
| 120 | 20 | 01 | 02 | 02 | 02 | 02 | 02 | 02 | 03 | 03 | 03 | 03 | 04 | 04 | 05 | 06 |
| | 60 | 01 | 02 | 02 | 02 | 02 | 03 | 03 | 04 | 04 | 05 | 06 | 08 | 09 | 11 | 13 |
| | 120 | 01 | 02 | 02 | 02 | 03 | 04 | 04 | 05 | 06 | 07 | 09 | 12 | 15 | 18 | 22 |
| | ∞ | 01 | 02 | 03 | 04 | 05 | 06 | 08 | 10 | 12 | 15 | 20 | 27 | 35 | 43 | 51 |

*Power values here and to the right are > .995.

**Table 9.3.2**
Power of the **F** Test as a Function of λ, **u**, and **v**
a = .05

| u | v | 2 | 4 | 6 | 8 | 10 | 12 | 14 | 16 | 18 | 20 | 24 | 28 | 32 | 36 | 40 |
|---|---|---|---|---|---|----|----|----|----|----|----|----|----|----|----|----|
| 1 | 20 | 27 | 48 | 64 | 77 | 85 | 91 | 95 | 97 | 98 | 99 | * | | | | |
|   | 60 | 29 | 50 | 67 | 79 | 88 | 92 | 96 | 98 | 99 | 99 | * | | | | |
|   | 120 | 29 | 51 | 68 | 80 | 88 | 93 | 96 | 98 | 99 | 99 | * | | | | |
|   | ∞ | 29 | 52 | 69 | 81 | 89 | 93 | 96 | 98 | 99 | 99 | * | | | | |
| 2 | 20 | 20 | 36 | 52 | 65 | 75 | 83 | 88 | 92 | 95 | 97 | 99 | * | | | |
|   | 60 | 22 | 40 | 56 | 69 | 79 | 87 | 91 | 95 | 97 | 98 | * | | | | |
|   | 120 | 22 | 41 | 57 | 71 | 80 | 87 | 92 | 95 | 97 | 98 | * | | | | |
|   | ∞ | 23 | 42 | 58 | 72 | 82 | 88 | 93 | 96 | 97 | 99 | * | | | | |
| 3 | 20 | 17 | 30 | 44 | 56 | 67 | 75 | 82 | 87 | 91 | 94 | 97 | 99 | * | | |
|   | 60 | 19 | 34 | 49 | 62 | 73 | 81 | 87 | 92 | 95 | 97 | 98 | * | | | |
|   | 120 | 19 | 35 | 50 | 64 | 75 | 83 | 89 | 93 | 95 | 97 | 99 | * | | | |
|   | ∞ | 19 | 36 | 52 | 65 | 76 | 84 | 90 | 93 | 96 | 98 | 99 | * | | | |
| 4 | 20 | 15 | 26 | 38 | 49 | 60 | 69 | 76 | 83 | 87 | 91 | 95 | 98 | 99 | * | |
|   | 60 | 17 | 30 | 44 | 57 | 68 | 77 | 83 | 89 | 92 | 95 | 98 | 99 | * | | |
|   | 120 | 17 | 31 | 46 | 58 | 70 | 78 | 85 | 90 | 93 | 96 | 98 | 99 | * | | |
|   | ∞ | 17 | 32 | 47 | 60 | 72 | 80 | 87 | 91 | 94 | 96 | 99 | * | | | |
| 5 | 20 | 13 | 23 | 34 | 44 | 54 | 63 | 71 | 78 | 83 | 87 | 93 | 96 | 98 | 99 | * |
|   | 60 | 15 | 27 | 40 | 52 | 63 | 72 | 80 | 86 | 90 | 93 | 97 | 99 | * | | |
|   | 120 | 16 | 29 | 41 | 54 | 65 | 75 | 82 | 87 | 91 | 94 | 98 | 99 | * | | |
|   | ∞ | 16 | 29 | 43 | 56 | 68 | 77 | 84 | 89 | 93 | 95 | 98 | 99 | * | | |
| 6 | 20 | 12 | 21 | 30 | 40 | 50 | 59 | 66 | 73 | 79 | 84 | 91 | 95 | 97 | 99 | * |
|   | 60 | 14 | 25 | 37 | 48 | 59 | 68 | 76 | 83 | 87 | 91 | 96 | 98 | 99 | * | |
|   | 120 | 14 | 27 | 39 | 50 | 62 | 71 | 79 | 85 | 89 | 93 | 97 | 99 | 99 | * | |
|   | ∞ | 15 | 27 | 40 | 53 | 64 | 74 | 81 | 87 | 91 | 94 | 97 | 99 | * | | |

| | | | | | | | | | | | | | | | | |
|---|---|---|---|---|---|---|---|---|---|---|---|---|---|---|---|---|
| 7 | 20 | 11 | 19 | 28 | 37 | 46 | 54 | 62 | 69 | 75 | 80 | 88 | 93 | 96 | 98 | 99 |
| | 60 | 17 | 24 | 35 | 45 | 56 | 65 | 73 | 80 | 85 | 89 | 94 | 97 | 99 | 99 | * |
| | 120 | 13 | 25 | 37 | 47 | 59 | 68 | 76 | 82 | 87 | 91 | 96 | 98 | 99 | * | |
| | ∞ | 14 | 25 | 38 | 50 | 61 | 71 | 79 | 85 | 89 | 93 | 97 | 99 | 99 | * | |
| 8 | 20 | 10 | 18 | 26 | 34 | 42 | 50 | 58 | 65 | 71 | 76 | 85 | 91 | 94 | 97 | 98 |
| | 60 | 12 | 23 | 33 | 43 | 52 | 62 | 70 | 77 | 83 | 87 | 93 | 97 | 98 | 99 | * |
| | 120 | 12 | 24 | 35 | 45 | 55 | 65 | 73 | 80 | 85 | 89 | 95 | 98 | 99 | * | |
| | ∞ | 13 | 24 | 36 | 48 | 59 | 68 | 77 | 83 | 88 | 92 | 96 | 99 | 99 | * | |
| 9 | 20 | 10 | 17 | 24 | 32 | 39 | 47 | 54 | 61 | 68 | 73 | 82 | 88 | 93 | 96 | 97 |
| | 60 | 11 | 21 | 31 | 41 | 50 | 58 | 67 | 74 | 80 | 85 | 92 | 96 | 98 | 99 | * |
| | 120 | 11 | 22 | 33 | 44 | 53 | 62 | 71 | 78 | 83 | 88 | 94 | 97 | 99 | * | |
| | ∞ | 13 | 23 | 34 | 45 | 56 | 66 | 74 | 81 | 86 | 90 | 95 | 98 | 99 | * | |
| 10 | 20 | 09 | 16 | 23 | 30 | 37 | 44 | 51 | 58 | 64 | 70 | 79 | 86 | 91 | 94 | 96 |
| | 60 | 10 | 20 | 30 | 39 | 48 | 56 | 65 | 72 | 78 | 83 | 90 | 95 | 97 | 99 | 99 |
| | 120 | 11 | 21 | 31 | 42 | 51 | 60 | 69 | 75 | 81 | 86 | 93 | 96 | 98 | 99 | * |
| | ∞ | 12 | 21 | 32 | 43 | 54 | 64 | 72 | 79 | 85 | 89 | 94 | 98 | 99 | * | |
| 11 | 20 | 09 | 15 | 21 | 27 | 34 | 41 | 48 | 55 | 61 | 67 | 76 | 84 | 89 | 93 | 96 |
| | 60 | 11 | 18 | 27 | 36 | 45 | 54 | 62 | 70 | 76 | 81 | 89 | 94 | 97 | 98 | 99 |
| | 120 | 11 | 19 | 29 | 39 | 49 | 58 | 67 | 74 | 80 | 85 | 91 | 96 | 98 | 99 | * |
| | ∞ | 12 | 21 | 31 | 42 | 52 | 62 | 70 | 78 | 83 | 89 | 94 | 97 | 99 | 99 | * |
| 12 | 20 | 08 | 14 | 20 | 27 | 33 | 39 | 45 | 52 | 58 | 64 | 74 | 81 | 87 | 91 | 94 |
| | 60 | 09 | 18 | 28 | 36 | 44 | 52 | 59 | 67 | 73 | 79 | 87 | 93 | 96 | 98 | 99 |
| | 120 | 10 | 20 | 30 | 40 | 48 | 56 | 63 | 72 | 78 | 83 | 90 | 95 | 97 | 99 | 99 |
| | ∞ | 11 | 20 | 30 | 40 | 50 | 60 | 69 | 76 | 82 | 87 | 93 | 97 | 98 | 99 | * |
| 13 | 20 | 09 | 13 | 19 | 24 | 30 | 37 | 43 | 49 | 55 | 61 | 71 | 79 | 85 | 90 | 93 |
| | 60 | 10 | 16 | 24 | 33 | 41 | 50 | 58 | 65 | 71 | 77 | 86 | 92 | 95 | 97 | 99 |
| | 120 | 10 | 18 | 26 | 36 | 45 | 54 | 62 | 70 | 76 | 81 | 89 | 94 | 97 | 98 | 99 |
| | ∞ | 11 | 19 | 29 | 40 | 50 | 59 | 67 | 75 | 81 | 85 | 92 | 96 | 98 | 99 | * |

*(Continued)*

**Table 9.3.2** *(Continued)*

| u | v | 2 | 4 | 6 | 8 | 10 | 12 | 14 | 16 | 18 | 20 | 24 | 28 | 32 | 36 | 40 |
|---|---|---|---|---|---|----|----|----|----|----|----|----|----|----|----|----|
| 14 | 20 | 09 | 13 | 18 | 23 | 29 | 35 | 41 | 47 | 52 | 58 | 68 | 76 | 83 | 88 | 92 |
|    | 60 | 10 | 16 | 23 | 31 | 40 | 48 | 56 | 63 | 69 | 75 | 84 | 90 | 94 | 97 | 98 |
|    | 120 | 10 | 17 | 25 | 34 | 43 | 52 | 61 | 68 | 74 | 80 | 88 | 93 | 97 | 98 | 99 |
|    | ∞ | 11 | 19 | 28 | 38 | 48 | 58 | 65 | 73 | 79 | 84 | 91 | 96 | 98 | 99 | * |
| 15 | 20 | 08 | 12 | 17 | 22 | 27 | 33 | 39 | 44 | 50 | 55 | 65 | 74 | 81 | 86 | 90 |
|    | 60 | 09 | 15 | 22 | 30 | 38 | 46 | 54 | 61 | 67 | 73 | 83 | 89 | 94 | 96 | 98 |
|    | 120 | 10 | 16 | 24 | 33 | 42 | 51 | 59 | 66 | 73 | 78 | 87 | 92 | 96 | 98 | 99 |
|    | ∞ | 10 | 18 | 27 | 37 | 47 | 56 | 64 | 72 | 78 | 83 | 91 | 95 | 97 | 99 | 99 |
| 18 | 20 | 08 | 11 | 15 | 19 | 24 | 29 | 34 | 39 | 44 | 49 | 58 | 67 | 74 | 80 | 85 |
|    | 60 | 09 | 14 | 20 | 27 | 34 | 41 | 48 | 55 | 62 | 68 | 78 | 85 | 91 | 94 | 97 |
|    | 120 | 09 | 15 | 22 | 30 | 38 | 46 | 54 | 61 | 68 | 74 | 83 | 90 | 94 | 97 | 98 |
|    | ∞ | 10 | 17 | 25 | 34 | 43 | 52 | 60 | 68 | 76 | 80 | 88 | 93 | 97 | 98 | 99 |
| 20 | 20 | 08 | 11 | 14 | 18 | 22 | 26 | 31 | 36 | 40 | 45 | 54 | 63 | 70 | 77 | 82 |
|    | 60 | 08 | 13 | 19 | 25 | 31 | 38 | 45 | 52 | 58 | 64 | 75 | 83 | 89 | 93 | 96 |
|    | 120 | 09 | 14 | 21 | 28 | 36 | 43 | 51 | 58 | 65 | 71 | 81 | 88 | 93 | 96 | 98 |
|    | ∞ | 09 | 16 | 24 | 32 | 41 | 50 | 58 | 65 | 72 | 78 | 87 | 92 | 96 | 98 | 99 |
| 24 | 20 | 07 | 10 | 13 | 16 | 19 | 23 | 27 | 31 | 35 | 39 | 47 | 55 | 62 | 69 | 75 |
|    | 60 | 08 | 12 | 17 | 22 | 28 | 34 | 40 | 46 | 52 | 58 | 69 | 78 | 84 | 89 | 93 |
|    | 120 | 08 | 13 | 19 | 25 | 32 | 39 | 46 | 53 | 60 | 66 | 76 | 84 | 90 | 94 | 96 |
|    | ∞ | 09 | 15 | 21 | 29 | 37 | 46 | 54 | 61 | 68 | 74 | 83 | 90 | 94 | 97 | 98 |
| 30 | 20 | 07 | 09 | 11 | 14 | 16 | 19 | 22 | 25 | 29 | 32 | 39 | 45 | 53 | 59 | 65 |
|    | 60 | 08 | 11 | 15 | 19 | 24 | 29 | 34 | 40 | 45 | 51 | 61 | 70 | 78 | 84 | 89 |
|    | 120 | 08 | 12 | 16 | 22 | 28 | 34 | 40 | 46 | 53 | 59 | 69 | 78 | 85 | 90 | 94 |
|    | ∞ | 08 | 13 | 19 | 26 | 33 | 41 | 48 | 56 | 62 | 69 | 79 | 87 | 92 | 95 | 97 |

λ

| | | | | | | | | | | | | | | | | |
|---|---|---|---|---|---|---|---|---|---|---|---|---|---|---|---|---|
| 40 | 20 | 07 | 08 | 10 | 11 | 13 | 15 | 18 | 20 | 22 | 25 | 30 | 35 | 41 | 47 | 52 |
| | 60 | 07 | 10 | 12 | 16 | 19 | 23 | 27 | 32 | 36 | 41 | 50 | 59 | 67 | 74 | 80 |
| | 120 | 07 | 10 | 14 | 18 | 23 | 28 | 33 | 38 | 44 | 49 | 60 | 69 | 77 | 83 | 88 |
| | ∞ | 08 | 12 | 17 | 22 | 29 | 35 | 42 | 49 | 55 | 61 | 72 | 81 | 87 | 92 | 95 |
| 48 | 20 | 07 | 08 | 09 | 10 | 12 | 14 | 15 | 17 | 19 | 21 | 25 | 30 | 35 | 39 | 44 |
| | 60 | 07 | 09 | 11 | 14 | 17 | 20 | 24 | 28 | 31 | 35 | 44 | 52 | 59 | 67 | 73 |
| | 120 | 07 | 10 | 13 | 16 | 20 | 24 | 29 | 34 | 39 | 44 | 54 | 63 | 71 | 78 | 83 |
| | ∞ | 08 | 11 | 15 | 21 | 26 | 32 | 38 | 45 | 51 | 57 | 68 | 76 | 84 | 89 | 93 |
| 60 | 20 | 07 | 08 | 09 | 10 | 12 | 13 | 14 | 16 | 18 | 19 | 23 | 26 | 30 | 34 | 38 |
| | 60 | 07 | 08 | 10 | 12 | 15 | 17 | 20 | 23 | 26 | 29 | 36 | 43 | 50 | 57 | 63 |
| | 120 | 07 | 09 | 11 | 14 | 17 | 21 | 25 | 28 | 33 | 37 | 46 | 54 | 62 | 70 | 76 |
| | ∞ | 07 | 10 | 14 | 18 | 23 | 28 | 34 | 39 | 45 | 51 | 62 | 71 | 79 | 85 | 90 |
| 120 | 20 | 06 | 07 | 08 | 08 | 09 | 10 | 10 | 11 | 12 | 12 | 14 | 15 | 17 | 19 | 20 |
| | 60 | 06 | 07 | 08 | 09 | 10 | 11 | 12 | 13 | 15 | 16 | 19 | 23 | 26 | 30 | 34 |
| | 120 | 06 | 07 | 08 | 10 | 11 | 13 | 15 | 17 | 19 | 21 | 26 | 31 | 36 | 41 | 47 |
| | ∞ | 06 | 08 | 11 | 13 | 16 | 19 | 23 | 24 | 31 | 35 | 43 | 52 | 60 | 68 | 74 |

*Power values here and to the right are > .995.

already noted, the $\eta^2$ of Chapter 8 equals the $R^2_{Y \cdot B}$ when group membership has been coded as IVs, by any of several methods, to yield set **B** (Cohen & Cohen, 1983, Chapter 5). The MRC approach will produce exactly the same power-analytic results since it is not a different method, but rather a generalization. See examples 9.3–9.5 for a demonstration of this point.

2. When **Y** is related to some quantitative variable **W**, several methods are available for representing **W** in such a way as to allow for possible nonlinearity of the relationship. Among these are methods that represent **W** as a set of variables (Cohen & Cohen, 1983, Chapter 6). The method of "power polynomials," for example, may represent the construct **W** as the set of IVs: **X**, $X^2$, and $X^3$. These 3 ($=$ **u**) variables, then, comprise set **B**, and $R^2_{Y \cdot B}$ is the proportion of **Y** variance accounted for by the construct **W**, not constrained by the presumption that the relationship is straight-line ("linear"). See example 9.2.

In Case 0 applications, the power of the **F** test is determined by entering the table for the given **a** significance criterion at the block **u** for the number of variables in set **B**, in the row **v** for the denominator **df** and with λ as computed from (9.3.3), linearly interpolating, as necessary.

### Illustrative Examples

**9.1**   Consider a conventional application of MRC, in which a personnel psychologist seeks to determine the efficacy of the prediction of sales success in a sample of 95 ($=$ **N**) applicants for sales positions using as IVs age, education, amount of prior sales experience, and scores on a verbal aptitude test and extraversion questionnaire. These 5 ($=$ **u**) variables comprise set **B**. What is the power of the **F** test at **a** $=$ .05 if the population $R^2_{Y \cdot B}$ is .10?

When $R^2_{Y \cdot B} = .10$, $f^2 = .10/(1 - .10) = .1111$. For **N** $=95$ and **u** $= 5$, the error **df**, **v** $= ($**N** $-$ **u** $- 1 = 95 - 5 - 1 =) 89$. Thus, from (9.3.1) or (9.3.3), λ $= .1111 \times 95 = 10.6$.

The specification summary thus is

$$\mathbf{a} = .05, \qquad \mathbf{u} = 5, \qquad \mathbf{v} = 89, \qquad \lambda = 10.6.$$

Entering Table 9.3.2 (for **a** $= .05$) at block **u** $= 5$ for **v** $= 60$, power at λ $= 10$ is .62 and at λ $= 12$ is .72. Linear interpolation finds the power at **v** $= 60$ for λ $= 10.6$ to be .66. Similarly, linear interpolation at **v** $= 120$ between λ $= 10$ (.65) and λ $= 12$ (.75) finds power for λ $= 10.6$ to be .68. Finally, using equation (9.3.2) for inverse linear interpolation of our **v** $= 89$ between .66 (for **v** $= 60$) and .68 (for **v** $= 120$) gives:

$$.66 + \frac{1/60 - 1/89}{1/60 - 1/120} \ (.68 - .66) = .67.$$

As is frequently the case, we could just as well have done this double interpolation by eye and estimated the interpolated power value within .01 of the computed value. Such "guestimated" interpolated power values are usually of quite sufficient accuracy. Thus, if these five IVs together account for 10% of the variance in sales success in the population, the odds are only two to one that a sample of 95 cases will yield a sample $R^2$ that is significant at $a = .05$.

**9.2** A sociologist is investigating the correlates of scores on a scale of attitude toward socialized medicine (ASM) in a sample of 90 adult males ranging in age from 25 to 75. One such correlate is age. He assumes a medium ES, $f^2 = .15$, i.e., he expects that age accounts for some $.15/(1 + .15) = 13\%$ of the ASM ($= Y$) variance in the population sampled, although not necessarily linearly. To provide for the possibility of a curvilinear relationship, he generates a polynomial in the first three powers of age (Cohen & Cohen, 1983, pp. 224–232), i.e., he represents the construct age as a set of variables made up of age ($X$), age-squared ($X^2$), and age-cubed ($X^3$) and then performs an MRC analysis, using these 3 ($= u$) IVs as the set **B**. Since many other correlates of ASM are to be studied, in the interests of minimizing the rate of spurious rejections of the null hypotheses "investigationwise" (Cohen & Cohen, 1983, pp. 166–176), $a = .01$ is to be used throughout. The parameters are now completely specified: formula (9.3.2) gives $v = 90 - 3 - 1 = 86$, and formula (9.3.1) or (9.3.3) gives $\lambda = .15(90) = 13.5$. Thus,

$$a = .01 \qquad u = 3, \qquad v = 86, \qquad \lambda = 13.5.$$

In block $u = 3$ of Table 9.3.1 (for $a = .01$), linear interpolation between $\lambda = 12$ and 14 for $v = 60$ (.60 and .69) gives .68 and for $v = 120$ (.62 and .72) gives .70, so interpolation via (9.3.2) between .68 and .70 (or inspection) gives power $= .69$.

**9.3** A laboratory experiment in social psychology is performed in which subjects are observed in the presence of 1, 2, 3, or 4 ($= p$) peers and some quantitative response variable ($Y$) is noted. A total of $N = 90$ subjects are run in each of the four experimental conditions (note, incidentally, that the sample $n$s cannot be equal). These data may be analyzed by the analysis of variance, but also by MRC. Set **B** may carry the information about the experimental condition in any one of several ways, e.g., by power polynomials as in the preceding example ($p, p^2, p^3$), or by orthogonal polynomial coding into three variables, etc. (Cohen & Cohen, 1983, Chapter 6). With $u = 3$, however represented, the same $R^2_{Y \cdot B}$ and therefore $f^2$ will result. For $u = 3$, $a = .01$, and selecting $f^2 = .15$ as in example 9.2, the specifications are all the same (since $v = 90 - 3 - 1 = 86$ again, and $\lambda = .15[90] = 13.5$), so necessarily, the same power of .69 is found.

The primary point of this example is to underscore the fact that the MRC system may be applied to the data arising from manipulative experiments as readily as to those arising from nonexperimental surveys as in the preceding example, in contradiction to the longstanding association of MRC with the latter in the culture of the behavioral and biological sciences.

**9.4**   This example is offered to demonstrate explicitly the fact that Case 0 MRC applications subsume, as a special case, the one-way analysis of variance, and therefore yield the same results. Example 8.4 in the preceding chapter described a research on the differential effectiveness of 12 ( $=$ **k**) psychiatric hospitals, a phase of which involved a comparison between the means of the psychiatric nurses in the hospitals on an attitude scale of Social Restrictiveness. The total **N** $= 326$, **a** $= .05$, and **f** was posited as .25; the data were there analyzed as a one-way analysis of variance.

These data could just as well be analyzed by MRC. Using any of the simple coding techniques for representing group membership (i.e., a nominal scale) described in Cohen & Cohen (1983, Chapter 5), one would create a set (**B**) of **k** $- 1 = 11 = $ **u** artificial variates on which the 326 nurses would be "scored." An MRC could then be performed with **Y** the Social Restrictiveness score and the 11 variables carrying the information of the hospital from which each score came as a set of IVs, and $R^2_{Y \cdot B}$ determined and **F**-tested. No special analytic attention need be paid to the inequality of sample sizes from hospital to hospital.

The **f** used as an ES in the analysis of variance was defined as the standard deviation of standardized means. This again is a special case of **f** as interpreted in the MRC context. In the context of the analysis of variance, it yields $\eta^2$ as a PV measure, given in formula (8.2.19), by finding $f^2/(1 + f^2)$. But, as we have seen, this too is the formula for $R^2$ as a function of **f** in Case 0, given in (9.2.5). Positing **f** $= .25$ in example 8.4 is equivalent to positing $\eta^2 = R^2_{Y \cdot B} = .25^2/(1 + .25^2) + .0588$, not quite 6% of the attitude score variance accounted for by hospitals.

Since **f** $= .25$, $f^2 = .0625$. **N** $= 326$ and the error **df** from (9.3.2) is **v** $= 326 - 11 - 1 = 314$. Thus, (9.3.1) gives $\lambda = .0625(326) = 20.4$. The specification summary for the **F** test of $R^2_{Y \cdot B}$ is

$$\textbf{a} = .05, \qquad \textbf{u} = 11, \qquad \textbf{v} = 314, \qquad \lambda = 20.4.$$

Table 9.3.2 (for **a** $= .05$) gives in block **u** $= 11$ for **v** $= 120$ power $= .85$ and .91 for $\lambda = 20$ and 24, respectively; linear interpolation gives power for $\lambda = 20.4$ to be .86. Similarly, at **v** $= \infty$, linear interpolation between .89 and .94 gives power $= .90$. Finally, inverse linear interpolation for **v** $= 314$ between .86 and .90 via Equation (9.3.2) gives power $= .88$. The power found for these specifications in example 8.4 was .87.

In practice, errors in the approximation of noncentral **F** (Section 10.8.2), rounding, and interpolation may lead to discrepancies between the two procedures of one or two units, but they are theoretically identical.

**9.5**   As further illustration of the point, we do as a Case 0 MRC power analysis example 8.1 of the preceding chapter: an educational experiment in which **k** = 4 teaching methods are each applied to **n** = 20 randomly assigned pupils (so total **N** = 80) and their means on a criterion achievement test are compared at **a** = .05. By the route described there, **f** = .28 is posited.

For an MRC analysis, teaching methods are represented as a nominal scale by means of a set (**B**) of **u** = **k** − 1 = 3 IVs. Since $f^2 = .28^2 = .0784$, error **df** (Case 0) **v** = 80 − 3 − 1 = 76 and **N** = 80, the λ value from (9.3.1) or (9.3.3) is .0784(80) = 6.3. The specification summary:

$$a = .05, \qquad u = 3, \qquad v = 76, \qquad \lambda = 6.3.$$

Linear interpolation in Table 9.3.2 (for **a** = .05) in block **u** = 3 in line **v** = 60 for λ = 6.3 between λ = 6 and 8 (power = .49 and .62, respectively) gives power = .51 and in line **v** = 120 (power = .50 and .64, respectively) gives power = .52: inverse interpolation for **v** = 76 between .51 and .52 via (9.3.2) gives power = .51. Chapter 8 gave power = .53, the discrepancy being due to approximation/rounding/interpolation.

Note that in this and the two preceding examples, the actual analysis employed may be the analysis of variance; because of their equivalence, the MRC power analysis may nevertheless be applied, and will give the correct power for the analysis of variance.

**9.6**   As another example of the generality of the MRC system of data analysis, reconsider the significance test of a simple product moment **r** between two variables **X** and **Y**. It may be treated as the special case of a Case 0 MRC, where set **B** contains only one IV, **X**, hence $R^2_{Y \cdot B} = r^2$, and **u** = 1.

Chapter 3 was devoted to the test of **r**, and example 3.1 concerned a research study in personality psychology in which, for **N** = 50 subjects, scores on an extraversion questionnaire and a neurophysiological measure were obtained and correlated. The test was a nondirectional **t** test performed at $a_2$ = .05, where the alternate hypothesis was specified as **r** = .30. The power of the test for these specifications was found to be .57.

Analyzed as a Case 0 MRC test, we note first that **F** tests are naturally nondirectional so the $a_2$ = **a** = .05. Substituting $r^2$ for $R^2_{Y \cdot B}$ in (9.2.2) gives

(9.3.4)
$$f^2 = \frac{r^2}{1 - r^2},$$

so $f^2 = .30^2/(1 - .30^2) = .09/.91 = .0989$. Since $u = 1$ and $N = 50$, the error $df$ $v = 50 - 1 - 1 = 48$, and $\lambda = .0989(50) = 4.9$. Thus, the specifications to test $H_0$: $r = 0$ by Case 0 of MRC are:

$$a = .05, \qquad u = 1, \qquad v = 48 \qquad \lambda = 4.9.$$

Table 9.3.2 (for $a = .05$) for $u = 1$ in row $v = 20$ gives power of .48 and .64 for $\lambda = 4$ and 6, respectively. Linear interpolation yields power $= .55$ at $\lambda = 4.9$; similarly, in row $v = 60$, linear interpolation between .50 and .67 gives power $= .58$ at $\lambda = 4.9$. Inverse linear interpolation (9.3.2) for $v = 48$ between .55 at $v = 20$ and .58 at $v = 60$ yields power for $\lambda = 4.9$, $u = 1$, and $v = 48$ equal to .58. (The power value found in example 3.1, analyzed by the method of Chapter 3, was .57.)

**9.7**   As yet another example of the generality of MRC, return to Chapter 2, where the **t** test for two means was presented. It was shown there that the point biserial **r** between group membership and **Y** could be written as a function of **d**, the standardized difference between the two means (Section 2.2.2). Point biserial $r^2$ is a special case of $r^2$ and thus also a special case of $R^2_{Y \cdot B}$ where set **B** contains a single (dichotomous) IV, so $u = 1$. (An alternative route to the same point proceeds from specializing the one-way analysis of variance of the **k** groups for $k = 2$, utilizing the relationship between **f** and **d**, and then invoking point biserial $r^2 = \eta^2 = R^2_{Y \cdot B}$.) One can then find the point biserial $r^2$ from **d** by formula (2.2.7), and then $f^2$ from formula (9.3.4); or, with some algebraic manipulation, one can find $f^2$ for the two-group case directly by

$$(9.3.5) \qquad\qquad f^2 = pqd^2,$$

where **p** is the proportion of the total **N** in either of the two samples, and $q = 1 - p$. For sample of the same size, $p = q = .5$, so (9.3.5) simplifies further to

$$(9.3.6) \qquad\qquad f^2 = \frac{d^2}{4} \ .$$

To illustrate the MRC Case 0 approach to the test of the difference between two independent means, return to example 2.3, where two samples of cases in a psychological service center have been treated by a standard (A) and innovative (B) psychotherapeutic technique. The **t** test is performed for $d = .6$, and $n_A = 90$, $n_B = 60$. We will redo the second version of 2.3, where $a_2 = .05$. $N = 150$, $p = 90/150 = .60$, $q = 1 - .60, = .40$. Formula (9.3.5) then gives $f^2 = .60(.40)(.6^2) = .0864$. With $u = 1$, the (Case 0) $v = 150 - 1 - 1 = 148$. The value of $\lambda$ is thus $.0864(150) = 13.0$. In summary,

$$a = .05, \qquad u = 1, \qquad v = 148, \qquad \lambda = 13.0.$$

Table 9.3.2 (for $a = .05$) gives in block $u = 1$ for both $v = 120$ and $v = \infty$, power $= .93$ at $\lambda = 12$ and $.96$ at $\lambda = 14$, and, rounding down, linear interpolation for $\lambda = 13$ gives power $= .94$.

This example was used in Chapter 2 to illustrate that chapter's Case 1 — two independent samples of unequal size. Actually all the cases in Chapter 2 may be analyzed by MRC methods; the one outlined above will apply to Cases 0 and 2 in Chapter 2 as well.

Note that it does not matter whether the data analyst actually performs the usual $t$ test in the usual way. Being equivalent, the power analysis as Case 0 MRC correctly gives the power of the $t$ test.

### 9.3.2 CASE 1: TEST OF $R^2_{Y \cdot A,B} - R^2_{Y \cdot A}$, MODEL 1 ERROR.

The source of $Y$ variance under test is the proportion accounted by set $B$ (comprised of $u$ IVs) over and above what is accounted for by set $A$ (comprised of $w$ variables). $H_0$ states that its population value is zero. Recall that this quantity, computed as $R^2_{Y \cdot A,B} - R^2_{Y \cdot A}$, may be symbolized as $R^2_{Y \cdot (B \cdot A)}$, the squared semipartial (or part) multiple correlation, and may be thought of as the proportion of the $Y$ variance accounted for by $B \cdot A$, or *uniquely* by $B$ relative to $A$. It constitutes a generalization of the methods used to control *statistically* for ("hold constant," "partial out") a source of $Y$ variance (set $A$) whose operation is undesirable for substantive reasons. When used for this purpose, a causal model is implied in which whatever causality exists runs from set $A$ to set $B$ and not vice versa (Cohen & Cohen, 1983, pp. 423–425). One reason for its use then is to remove set $A$'s $Y$ variance to void its spurious attribution to set $B$, or its attenuation of the $Y$, $B$ relationship. A quite distinct and important second reason for its use is to reduce the proportion of $Y$ variance which makes up the error term by removing from it the variance that can be accounted for by set $A$, thus resulting in an increase in the power of the statistical test. Special cases of this statistical control procedure include simple partial correlation with one or more variables partialled and the analysis of covariance.

In Case 1, the error variance has had excluded from it not only the $Y$ variance accounted for by set $B$, but also whatever additional variance set $A$ accounts for, i.e., it is $1 - R^2_{Y \cdot A,B}$, which (to distinguish it from Case 2) is designated as Model I error. Since set $B$ contains $u$ variables and set $A$ contains $w$ variables, $R^2_{Y \cdot A,B}$ is based on $u + w$ variables, and the Model I error $df$ is

$$(9.3.7) \qquad\qquad v = N - u - w - 1.$$

Case 1 power analysis proceeds by positing $R^2_{Y \cdot A}$, $R^2_{Y \cdot A,B}$, and their difference, which is the quantity under test. Formula (9.2.3) divides this quantity by the Model I error to give $f^2$ for Case 1. Alternatively, $f^2$ can be found as a function of $R^2_{YB \cdot A}$ from formula (9.2.7). Multiplying $f^2$ by $u + v + 1$ gives $\lambda$ (Eq. 9.3.1); thus

$$(9.3.8) \qquad \lambda = \frac{R^2_{Y \cdot A,B} - R^2_{Y \cdot A}}{1 \times R^2_{Y \cdot A,B}} \times (u + v + 1),$$

or, as a function of the squared multiple *partial* correlation,

$$(9.3.9) \qquad \lambda = \frac{R^2_{YB \cdot A}}{1 - R^2_{YB \cdot A}} \times (u + v + 1).$$

The table for the **a** specified (9.3.1 or 9.3.2) is entered in the block **u** and power is found by linear interpolation of $\lambda$ between the columns and inverse interpolation of **v** between the rows using (9.3.2), exactly as in Case 0.

CASE 1–1.   A frequently occurring special case of Case 1 is the test of the null hypothesis that a given single IV makes no unique contribution to the population $R^2$, i.e., accounts for no **Y** variance that is not accounted for by the remaining IVs, which comprise set **A**. Case 1 is then specialized for a set **B** containing only 1 ($= u$) IV.

If we call this variable **X**, then the numerator for $f^2$ of formula (9.2.3) specializes to the squared semipartial (or part) correlation of **Y** with **X·A**, $r^2_{Y \cdot (X \cdot A)}$, the increase in $R^2$ that occurs when **X** is added to the other variables. The alternate formula (9.2.7) for $f^2$ gives it now as a function of the squared partial correlation $r^2_{YX \cdot A}$. Since it is conceptually and computationally convenient to work with such PV measures, it is important to note that the results of the significance test using **F** for the PV are *identical* with the **t** test performed on the raw score ($B_{YX \cdot A}$) or standardized ($\beta_{YX \cdot A}$) partial regression coefficient for **X**, which is the significance test value usually reported in computer output. Since the tests of all these alternative ways of expressing **X**s unique contribution to **Y** are equivalent, the power analysis of the test of the PV for **X** by means of the specialization of formulas (9.2.3) or (9.2.7) is at the same time a power analysis of the test of **X**'s partial regression coefficient. The latter null hypothesis is that the population's $B_{YX \cdot A}$ (or $\beta_{YX \cdot A}$) $= 0$, i.e., that **X** makes no contribution to the multiple regression equation that estimates **Y**.

### Illustrative Examples

**9.8**   As part of the sociological investigation of correlates of attitudes toward socialized medicine (ASM) described in example 9.2, the effect of education (set **B**) on ASM ($=$ **Y**) is also under scrutiny in the sample of 90 adult males. It seems clear, however, that since there has been a progressive increase in the educational level over the last half century, on the average, older subjects have had less education (i.e., age and education are correlated), and some of the observed relationship of education to ASM may be due to this contaminating effect of age. (Note that the causal direction is from age to education, not vice versa.) It would then be desirable to partial out the effect of age, i.e., to remove from the ASM variance that portion of it for which age can account, so as to hold age constant statistically in relating ASM to education. Age is thus here designated as set **A**, the set to be partialled, and the source of variance of focal interest is **B·A**. Since error variance will be $1 - R^2_{Y·A,B}$, we have the conditions of Case 1.

Age as set **A** is defined and has the same parameters as in example 9.2 (where it was set **B**): for the reasons given there, it is represented by three variables as a power polynomial, hence it has (**w** $=$ ) 3 **df**, and its $f^2$ is .15, so $R^2_{Y·A} = .13$ from (9.2.5). Assume that the sociologist anticipates the possibility of curvilinearity in the relationships of years of education and considers it adequate to represent education as two polynomial terms in set **B** (education and education-squared), so **u** $= 2$.

To set a value for the Case 1 $f^2$ for **B·A**, the sociologist may proceed in any of the following ways:

1. By positing the increase in $R^2$ when set **B** is added to set **A**, explicitly as the semipartial $R^2_{Y·(B·A)}$ ($= R^2_{Y·A,B} - R^2_{Y·A}$), or implicitly by positing $R^2_{Y·A,B}$ (since the value for $R^2_{Y·A}$ is already set). $f^2$ may then be found by formula (9.2.3). For example, he may posit an increase in $R^2_{Y·A,B}$ over $R^2_{Y·A}$ of .12, therefore $R^2_{Y·A,B} = .25$, and $f^2$ for **B·A** is $.12/(1 - .25) = .16$.

2. By estimating the partial $R^2_{YB·A}$ of formula (9.2.6), and then entering it in formula (9.2.8) to find $f^2$. For example, he may decide that he expects that .14 of the **Y** variance that is not age-related is accounted for by education controlled for age, **B·A**, i.e., $R^2_{YB·A} = .14$. Therefore, $f^2 = .14/(1 - .14) = .1628$.

3. He may simply select an operationally defined ES, e.g., $f^2 = .15$ ("medium").

Assume he selects the first alternative: $f^2 = .16$. With **u** $= 2$, **w** $= 3$, and **N** $= 90$, formula (9.3.7) gives **v** $= 90 - 2 - 3 - 1 = 84$; then formula (9.3.1) gives $\lambda = .16 (2 + 84 + 1) = 13.9$. The specifications for the test of the null hypothesis that $R^2_{Y·(B·A)}$ (or $R^2_{YB·A}$) equals zero in the population, i.e., that any observed relationship of education to ASM can be wholly accounted for by the concomitant effects of age, using Model I error (Case 1) are:

$$\mathbf{a} = .01, \quad \mathbf{u} = 2, \quad \mathbf{v} = 84, \quad \lambda = 13.9.$$

Table 9.3.1 (for $\mathbf{a} = .01$) in block $\mathbf{u} = 2$ gives at $\lambda = 12, 14$, for row $\mathbf{v} = 60$, power $= .68, .76$, and for row $\mathbf{v} = 120$, power $= .70, .78$. By linear interpolation, for $\lambda = 13.9$, power $= .76$ at $\mathbf{v} = 60$ and $.78$ at $\mathbf{v} = 120$. Equation (9.3.2) (or inspection) then gives power $= .77$ at $\mathbf{v} = 84$.

The provision for curvilinearity in the case of both education and age should not mislead the reader into the belief that quantitative variables are routinely so treated in MRC. Such is not the case. It is appropriate in this example because of the nature of these variables — variables scored in units of time are frequently related curvilinearly to other variables. This tends, incidentally, also to be the case for variables measured in monetary units and in frequencies and percentages (see Cohen & Cohen, 1983, Chapter 6).

**9.9**   Let us return again to the research in instructional methods originally presented in example 8.1 as a one-way analysis of variance, and then redone as a Case 0 application of MRC in example 9.5. Set **B** represented membership in one of four methods groups (hence, $\mathbf{u} = 3$), total $\mathbf{N} = 80$, $\mathbf{a} = .05$, and **Y** was a postexperiment achievement test score.

Now, **f** was set at .28, which in turn implies that $R^2_{Y \cdot B} = .28^2/1 + .28^2)$ $= .07$ (from formula (9.2.5)), and power was found to be .51. Thus, only some 7% of the postexperiment achievement variance is expected to be accounted for by the methods effect, with only a "fifty-fifty" chance of attaining a significant **F**-test result. The reason for the relatively weak effect (and poor power) is that many factors which operate to produce variance (individual differences) in **Y** are not controlled. Chief among these is the *pre*experiment achievement levels of the pupils. If this source of variance were removed from **Y**, what remains would be that portion of the post variance that is not predictable from prescores, hence the variance of (regressed) *change*. Another way of stating this is that the prescores are being "held constant," or that the postscore **Y** is being "adjusted" for differences in prescore both within and between methods groups. The latter is the formulation of the *analysis of covariance*. It is thus proposed that the design be changed from a one-way analysis of variance to a one-way analysis of covariance, using the prescore as the covariate. This is a Case 1 application of MRC, with set **A** containing the prescore as a single variate. (It is presumed that the post-on-pre regression is linear, else there would be required some nonlinear representation of the prescore.)

One approach to determining the Case 1 $\mathbf{f}^2$ is first to estimate the proportion of (within-group) **Y** variance accounted for by the covariate. Assuming that $\mathbf{r} = .60$ is a reasonable estimate of pre-post correlation, $\mathbf{r}^2$ and hence $R^2_{Y \cdot A}$ equals .36. Since cases are randomly assigned to method groups, it may be assumed that this variance is simply additive with that due to methods,

$R^2_{Y \cdot B}$; therefore, $R^2_{Y \cdot A,B}$ is posited to be $.36 + .07 = .43$. The ingredients for the Case 1 $f^2$ for set **B** are thus all assembled, and can be entered in formula (9.2.3): $(.43 - .36)/(1 - .43) = .07/.57 = .1228$ (compared with .0784 for Case 0 $f^2$ in the original). The error **df** will be somewhat smaller since for Case 1, formula (9.3.7) also debits **w** from **N**: $v = N - u - w - 1 = 80 - 3 - 2 - 1 = 74$ (compared to 76 in the original). The result, by formula (9.3.1) is $\lambda = .1228(78) = 9.6$. The summary of the specifications:

$$a = .05, \qquad u = 3, \qquad v = 74, \qquad \lambda = 9.6.$$

Table 9.3.2 (for $a = .05$) gives in block $u = 3$ for row $v = 60$ at $\lambda = 8$, 10, power of .62, .73, and for row $v = 120$, power of .64 and .75. The linearly interpolated power values for $\lambda = 9.6$ are .71 for $v = 60$ and .73 for $v = 120$. Equation (9.3.2) then gives power $= .72$, a rather substantial improvement over the .51 found when the total **Y** (post) variance was analyzed.

The reason for the improved power is the reduction in the $PV_E$ from $1 - R^2_{Y \cdot B}$ of Case 0 (the analysis of variance) to $1 - R^2_{Y \cdot A,B}$ of Case 1 (the analysis of covariance). As can be seen from the example, this is a powerful (!) data-analytic device which should be employed when possible. The potential increase in power provides sufficient motivation for partialling procedures in general and the analysis of covariance in particular, but, interestingly enough, receives little emphasis in textbook expositions of the analysis of covariance or in its use. Rather the emphasis is on the "adjustment" of the groups' **Y** means to take into account differences in their means of covariates, which differences would otherwise leave ambiguous the **Y** differences observed. This type of application, in which an effort is made at statistical and post hoc "equation" of groups on relevant concomitant variables, will be illustrated in the next example. Note that randomization (as in the present example) *assures* that the *population* $R^2$s between covariates and group membership are zero—there *are* no expected group differences. Indeed, that is the very purpose of randomization. When the analysis of covariance is used in randomized experiments, the adjusted **Y** means differ from the unadjusted means only because of sampling error, hence typically only trivially. The purpose here is not to adjust the means but rather to reduce the error variance, and thereby increase power.

A detailed exposition of the use of MRC in the analysis of covariance and its generalization is beyond the scope of this treatment. For example, the analysis of covariance presumes that the regression of **Y** on set **A** is the same in each of the groups being compared; this hypothesis is tested in MRC by creating a new set of IVs which carries the interaction of sets **A** and **B** and testing the significance of its unique contribution. The reader is referred to Chapters 8 and 10 in Cohen & Cohen (1983).

**9.10**   Let us return yet again to the sociological survey of attitudes toward socialized medicine (ASM) described in examples 9.2 and 9.8. An important hypothesis concerns difference in ASM among the five ethnic groups into which the $N = 90$ cases are classified. Since these groups differ with regard to age and education, however, a simple comparison among them on ASM may yield differences (or *non*differences) that are a consequence of their age and/or educational differences, and hence, on the causal model that is being entertained, spurious. An analysis of covariance may be undertaken, then, to adjust the ethnic group differences for age and education.

As an MRC Case 1 application, set **B** is now made up of IVs that represent ethnic group membership (with $u = 5 - 1 = 4$), and age and education together comprise the set **A** to be partialled or adjusted for. Age and education are represented polynomially to allow for curvilinearity (see examples 9.2 and 9.8) using three and two IVs respectively, hence set **A** contains 5 ( = **w**) IVs. In example 9.8, it was posited that they yield a population $R^2$ of .25, hence, as set **A** is redefined here, $R^2_{Y \cdot A} = .25$. If it is expected that the addition of ethnic group membership (set **B**) to age and education (set **A**) results in an $R^2_{Y \cdot A,B} = .30$, then, by formula (9.2.4), $f^2 = (.30 - .25)/(1 - .30) = .05/.70 = .0714$. The error **df** in Case 1 is $v = N - u - w - 1 = 90 - 4 - 5 - 1 = 80$. Formula (9.3.1) or (9.3.8) thus gives $\lambda = .0714(85) = 6.1$, and the specifications are:

$$a = .01, \qquad u = 4, \qquad v = 80, \qquad \lambda = 6.1.$$

Interpolation in Table 9.3.1 in block $u = 4$ in row $v = 60$ for $\lambda = 6.1$ gives power $= .22$ and in row $v = 120$ gives power $= .24$; (9.3.2) then gives for $v = 80$, power $= .24$. Thus, the expected *unique* contribution of ethnicity in accounting for ASM variance, $R^2_{Y \cdot (B \cdot A)} = .05$, is not likely to be detected in this research. Even if the **N** were twice as large, $v = 180 - 4 - 5 - 1 = 170$, $\lambda = .0714(175) = 12.5$, and power would still be only .61.

Note the important distinction between proportion of ASM variance accounted for by ethnicity, $R^2_{Y \cdot B}$, and the proportion of ASM variance accounted for by ethnicity partialling (holding constant, allowing for differences in) age and education, i.e., the *net* contribution of ethnicity, $R^2_{Y \cdot (B \cdot A)}$. The former may well be larger than .05 (or smaller when "suppression" is operating). It is in any case a different quantity and a different null hypothesis is being tested, exactly the difference between the analysis of variance and the analysis of covariance. Whatever **Y** variance is shared by the covariates (set **A**) and ethnic group membership (set **B**) is attributed to **A** (or, at least, denied to **B**) in the causal model being employed.

**9.11** Three different methods of infant day care are subjected to a comparative evaluation by means of a longitudinal quasi-experiment, using cognitive, affective, and health outcomes over a two-year period as criteria. There are available three different centers for the study, and the methods are assigned to the centers consistent with the wishes of their respective boards of directors. This is indeed a far cry from a randomized experiment, yet it is consistent with the realities of much evaluative field research, which must be done with dirty test-tubes, or not at all. Such a research can hardly produce definitive conclusions, yet, when carefully done, can yield results of limited but useful generalizability.

The largest threat to the validity of the findings lies in the fact that the children, not having been randomly assigned from a single population to the centers, cannot be assumed to be similar upon entry. Nor is it reasonable to suppose that they are *like* random samples from the *same* population since the social ecology of urban settings will make it very likely that selective factors are operating to make children in any given center representative of an at least somewhat different portion of the total child population than children in another center. Since these differences may bear on the outcome, they are a contaminant — the dirt in the test-tubes which, since it cannot be removed, should at least be allowed for to the extent possible. This is accomplished by the device of partialling from the outcome data variables carrying relevant ingoing child characteristics in regard to which the groups to be compared differ. In the language of the analysis of covariance, the criterion means will be "adjusted" to allow for differences in these ingoing characteristics represented as covariates.

Let us assume that the factors that require control and for which data are available are socioeconomic status (defined as family income and mother's education), family composition (including head of household and number of older siblings), ethnic group membership, and age of entry. These comprise set **A**, made up of 8 ($=$ **w**) IVs. Set **B** carries the information of method (or center), made up of 2 ($=$ **k** $-$ 1 $=$ **u**) IVs which identify the group membership of each child. Data are available on a total of **N** $=$ 148 in the three centers. Because there will be a relatively large number of outcome criteria, each serving successively as **Y**, **a** $=$ .01 is used throughout in order to hold down the investigationwise Type I error rate (Cohen & Cohen, 1983, pp. 166–169).

For one of the criteria, it is expected that methods will account for about 10% of the **Y** variance remaining after the variance associated with the covariates has been removed, i.e., $R^2_{YB \cdot A} = .10$. From this parameter, the $f^2$ for Case 1 can be found from formula (9.2.7): $f^2 = .10/(1 - .10) = .1111$. Since **u** $=$ 2, and **w** $=$ 8, from formula (9.3.7) for the Case 1 error **df**, **v** $=$ 148 $-$ 2 $-$ 8 $-$ 1 $=$ 137. Formula (9.3.1) or (9.3.9) then gives $\lambda =$

.1111(140) = 15.6. The specification summary for the null hypothesis that, after allowing for the **Y** variance due to the covariates, methods account for no **Y** variance, or, equivalently, that the three covariance-adjusted population methods means do not differ is:

$$a = .01, \qquad u = 2, \qquad v = 137, \qquad \lambda = 15.6.$$

Table 9.3.1 gives in block **u** = 2 for row **v** = 120 at $\lambda$ = 14, 16, power = .78, .85, and for **v** = $\infty$, power = .80, .87. Linear interpolation for $\lambda$ = 15.6 gives for **v** = 120, $\infty$, power = .84, .86; Equation (9.3.2) then gives for **v** = 137, power = .84. Thus, if $f^2$ = .10, the probability is .84 (or the odds are better than 5:1) that the sample data will yield an **F** ratio for this test that is significant at **a** = .01.

**9.12**   Return to the personnel psychologist of example 9.1, who was working with five IVs in the development of a selection procedure for sales applicants. Data for three of the IVs (age, education, prior experience) are readily obtained from the application blank, but the other two (verbal aptitude, extraversion) are psychological test scores whose acquisition is costly. He considers the plan of using as a criterion for omitting these two IVs from the selection procedure their failure to yield a significant (**a** = .05) increase in the PV accounted for by the other three IVs in the sample of **N** = 95 cases. He would not, however, wish to do so if, in the population, they add as much as 4% of the **Y** variance beyond what is accounted for by the three application blank IVs.

As a Case 1 MRC application, set **A** is made up of the 3 (= **w**) application blank variables, and set **B** of the 2 (= **u**) psychological test variables. It was posited in example 9.1 that the PV accounted for by all five IVs was .10 (= $R^2_{Y \cdot A,B}$). The null hypothesis here is that $R^2_{Y \cdot A,B} - R^2_{Y \cdot A} = R^2_{Y \cdot (A \cdot B)} = 0$, and the alternate hypothesis posits it as .04. For Case 1, the $f^2$ value from formula (9.2.3) is .04/(1 − .10) = .0444, the error **df** is **v** = 95 − 2 − 3 − 1 = 89, and formula (9.3.1) or (9.3.8) gives $\lambda$ = .0444(92) = 4.1. What is the probability that, if the two test variables together uniquely account for .04 of the **Y** variance, the null hypothesis will be rejected at **a** = .05, and they will thus be retained in the selection procedure?

$$a = .05, \qquad u = 2, \qquad v = 89, \qquad \lambda = 4.1.$$

Performing the necessary double interpolation in Table 9.3.2 for **u** = 2, **v** = 89 and $\lambda$ = 4.1 gives the probability of rejecting that null hypothesis as .42. The (Type II error) risk is thus (**b** = 1 − .42 =).58, much too great to use the significance of the sample $R^2_{Y \cdot (B \cdot A)}$ as the basis for excluding the two psychological tests since that is the risk of losing as much as 4% of the **Y** variance on this basis. Prudence would dictate the rejection of this plan.

The personnel psychologist may then consider another plan: if *either* of the two psychological test variables fails to have a significant (**a** = .05) partial regression coefficient in the multiple regression equation based on all five IVs, exclude it from the selection procedure. He would however not wish to do so if it accounted uniquely for 3% of the **Y** variance in the population. This is the special Case 1–1, the test of the unique contribution of a single IV, **X**. Thus, he wishes to guard against the alternative hypothesis that $r^2_{Y(X \cdot A)} = .03$, where set **A** is made up of the remaining 4 (= **w**) IVs, and set **B** contains only **X**. As before, it is assumed that $R^2_{Y \cdot A,B} = .10$, so $f^2$ from formula (9.2.3) is $.03/(1 - .10) = .0333$, **u** = 1, and **v** from formula (9.3.7) is $95 - 1 - 4 - 1 = 89$ (again; although sets **A** and **B** change in their definition, for all these hypotheses, the $PV_E$ remains constant at $1 - .10 = .90$ and its **df**, **v**, remains constant at 89). Formula (9.3.1) gives $\lambda = .0333 \, (1 + 89 + 1) = 3.0$. The specifications are thus:

$$\mathbf{a} = .05, \quad \mathbf{u} = 1, \quad \mathbf{v} = 89, \quad \lambda = 3.0,$$

and Table 9.3.2 gives in block **u** = 1, by linear interpolation and Eq. (9.3.2) for $\lambda = 3.0$, the power value for the test of either of the two psychological test IVs as .40. The Type II error risk is .60 of accepting the null hypothesis for either the verbal aptitude or extraversion tests when it uniquely contributes 3% of the population criterion variance. This is even a poorer procedure than when the two were considered jointly, using 4% as the alternative hypothesis. It seems clear that for this sample size (and the other parameters) decisions to drop variables from a multiple regression equation on grounds of nonsignificance are exceedingly risky.

This example is intended to sound a strong cautionary note against the common practice of regressing a (frequently large) group of IVs simultaneously on some dependent variable and then excluding those (usually a majority of the group) which make no significant contribution. This strategy is heavily exploited in automatic "stepwise" regression procedures. For a detailed appraisal of this method and some generally superior strategies, see Cohen & Cohen (1983, pp. 120–125, 137–139).

### 9.3.3 CASE 2: TEST OF $R^2_{Y \cdot A,B} - R^2_{Y \cdot A}$, MODEL 2 ERROR.

Recall that Case 2 differs from Case 1 *only* in regard to the error term employed in the **F** test. Both test the null hypothesis that set **B** accounts for no **Y** variance beyond what is accounted for by set **A**, i.e., $H_0 : R^2_{Y \cdot (A \cdot B)} = R^2_{Y \cdot A,B} - R^2_{Y \cdot A} = 0$, but while Case 1 uses as its $PV_E$ the term $1 - R^2_{Y \cdot A,B}$, Case 2 uses $1 - R^2_{Y \cdot A,B,C}$ (Model 2 error). Set **C** is a group of IVs, **z** in number, whose **Y** variance is also removed from error.

Case 2 MRC applies to a wide variety of research designs ranging from standard stereotyped factorial analysis of variance and analysis of covariance designs to ad hoc designs whose analysis is determined by the details of the causal models which are assumed. What they all have in common is that the source of **Y** variance under test is defined as **B·A**, while, in addition to sets **A** and **B**, other variables that are not involved in the definition of the source of interest are used to reduce the $PV_E$; these are designated as set **C**. The data analyst employing this Model 2 error is simply taking advantage of the opportunity afforded by the availability of the **z** variables in set **C** to attempt to increase power by reducing error, a centrally important goal of research design. This attempt will succeed when the reduction in $PV_E$, namely $R^2_{Y \cdot A,B,C} - R^2_{Y \cdot A,B}$, is large enough to offset the loss of the **z** additional **df** from the error term, whose **df** is now

$$(9.3.10) \qquad v = N - u - w - z - 1.$$

A more concise exposition of general MRC analysis would simply offer what we call Case 2 as the general case, and derive Cases 0 and 1 (and others) as special cases. When set **C** is taken as an empty set, $R^2_{Y \cdot A,B,C} = R^2_{Y \cdot A,B}$, **z** = 0, and Case 1 results. If set **A** is empty as well, Case 0 results. Another possibility is for only set **A** to be empty.

Another direction of specialization is to instances where sets **A** and **B** share no variance in **Y** (i.e., are orthogonal): $R^2_{Y \cdot A,B} = R^2_{Y \cdot A} + R^2_{Y \cdot B}$, thus $R^2_{Y \cdot A,B} - R^2_{Y \cdot A} = R^2_{Y \cdot B}$ (already illustrated for Case 1 in example 9.9). Such instances include orthogonal factorial and Latin square analysis of variance and analysis of covariance designs, repeated measurement, split-plot, and other complex orthogonal designs. It is important to note that in the MRC approach, the orthogonal case is a special case; nonorthogonality requires no special contortions in the analysis (Cohen & Cohen, 1983).

**9.13**  An investigation is undertaken of the factors associated with length of stay (**Y**) of patients admitted to a large psychiatric hospital. Three groups of IVs are to be related to **Y**:**D**, five variables carrying demographic and socioeconomic information; **H**, five variables descriptive of features of the patient's psychiatric history; and **S**,scores on four symptom scales on admission. The causal model employed treats the group **D** as causally prior to the other two groups and group **H** as prior to **S**. The causal hierarchy dictates that **Y** will be related to **D**, to **H·D**,and to **S·H,D**. Since all of these sources are expected to account for nontrivial PVs, the error term should include them all, although the null hypothesis for **D** and **H·D** do not involve all three — thus the conditions for Case 2 are met. Assume **N** = 200 and **a** = .01 throughout.

The alternate-hypothetical values posited for the three sources are as follows: of the total **Y** variance, **D** accounts for .10, **H·D** for .06, and **S·D, H** for .04. These PVs are additive to the **Y** variance accounted for by the three groups of variables, $R^2_{Y·D,H,S} = .20$. They are also the numerators in the expressions of $f^2$.

Consider first the test of **H·D**. If we let group **H** = set **B** ($u = 3$), group **D** = set **A** ($w = 5$), and group **S** = set **C** ($z = 4$), then the Model 2 $PV_E$, $1 - R^2_{Y·A,B,C} = 1 - .20 = .80$, and its **df** from formula (9.3.10) is $v = 200 - 3 - 5 - 4 - 1 = 187$. The $f^2$ for **H·D** in Case 2 is given by (9.2.4) as $.06/.80 = .075$, so $\lambda = .075(191) = 14.3$ by (9.3.1). The specifications for the **F** test of the null hypothesis on **H·D** are

$$a = .01, \quad u = 3, \quad v = 187, \quad \lambda = 14.3,$$

and Table 9.3.1 (for $a = .01$) in block $u = 3$ gives power $= .74$ by interpolation at $\lambda = 14.3$.

Consider next the test of **D**, for which $R^2_{Y·D}$ was posited to be .10. If this were a Case 0 test, $PV_E$ from formula (9.2.2) would give $.10/90 = .1111$. To treat it as Case 2, we redefine the meaning in the $f^2$ formula for Case 2 (9.2.4) of sets **A**, **B**, and **C**. Now let set **A** be empty (hence $w = 0$), let set **B** contain group **D** ($u = 5$), and let set **C** contain both groups **H** and **S** (hence $z = 3 + 4 = 7$). With set **A** empty, the numerator of (9.2.4), $R^2_{Y·A,B} - R^2_{Y·A} = R^2_{Y·B} - 0 = R^2_{Y·D} = .10$, and the denominator $PV_E$, $1 - R^2_{Y·A,B,C} = 1 - R^2_{Y·B,C} = 1 - R^2_{Y·D,H,S} = .80$. The Case 2 $f^2$ is $.10/.80 = .125$, necessarily larger than for Case 0 since **Y** variance due to **H** and **S** have also been removed from the $PV_E$. Formula (9.3.10) gives the Case 2 error **df**, $v = 200 - 5 - 0 - 7 - 1 = 187$, as before. $\lambda = .125(193) = 24.1$, so for the **F** test of $R^2_{Y·D}$:

$$a = .01, \quad u = 5, \quad v = 187, \quad \lambda = 24.1,$$

and Table 9.3.1, block $u = 5$, gives power $= 92$ for $\lambda = 24.1$ by linear interpolation and (9.3.2).

Consider finally the test of **S·D, H**. This may be used here to illustrate the point made above that Case 1 is a special case of Case 2. To treat this as Case 2, let set **A** include groups **D** and **H** (so $w = 5 + 3 = 8$), let set **B** be group **S** ($u = 4$), and let set **C** be empty, since no variables in addition to those of sets **A** and **B** are used in the error term. The Case $f^2$ formula (9.2.4) for **S·D, H** ($= $ **B·A**) is $.04/(1 - .20) = .05$, and $v = 200 - 4 - 8 - 1 = 187$, both the same as for Case 1. $\lambda$ is now $.05(192) = 9.6$. The summary of the specifications is

$$a = .01, \quad u = 4, \quad v = 187, \quad \lambda = 9.6,$$

and Table 9.3.1 gives the interpolated power value in block $u = 4$ as .44, a rather disappointing value. If the significance criterion is relaxed to $a = .05$, Table 9.3.2 gives in block $u = 4$, interpolating for $\lambda = 9.6$, power $= .69$— still rather lower than one would wish.

**9.14**   In examples 8.6 and 8.7, the power analysis of a $2 \times 3 \times 4$ factorial design analysis of variance on persuasibility (**Y**) in developmental social psychology was described. We shall maintain the same conditions, including the same $N = 120$, but now stipulate that the cell sizes are neither constant nor proportional, varying from three to seven due to the exigencies of scheduling and subject availability. It is now a *nonorthogonal* factorial design, and its analysis as a Case 2 MRC problem will be demonstrated.

Sex of experimenter (**S**, at two levels), age of subject (renamed **G** here to avoid confusion, at three levels) and instruction conditions (**K** here, at four levels) are the three factors, and the two-way interactions (**S** $\times$ **G**, **S** $\times$ **K**, **G** $\times$ **K**) and three-way interaction (**S** $\times$ **G** $\times$ **K**) are the sources of **Y** variance of interest. In MRC analysis, the number of IVs required to represent fully the information of a nominal scale (factor) is one fewer than the number of variables, so the three factors (main effects) are represented respectively by 1, 2, and 3 IVs. To represent interaction, each of the IVs of each factor involved is multiplied by each IV of each other factor. The resulting group of product IVs, after variance due to their constituent factors had been partialled, represent the interaction (Cohen & Cohen, 1983, Chapter 8).

For example, the **Y** variance due to the **G** $\times$ **K** interaction is determined as follows: Construct the product IVs by multiplying each of the two IVs that carry the **G** information by each of the three IVs that carry the **K** information, column by column in the data matrix; the resulting 6 IVs (**GK**) contain the **G** $\times$ **K** information, but they carry information from **G** and **K** as well. The proportion of **Y** variance due to **G** $\times$ **K** is then found by partialling that due to **G** and **K**, literally as $R^2_{Y \cdot G \times K} = R^2_{Y \cdot G,K,GK} - R^2_{Y \cdot G,K}$. Note that this satisfies our paradigm for the numerator of $f^2$ for Case 2: let set **B** be the $6 (= u)$ **GK** product IVs, and let set **A** carry both the two IVs for **G** and the three IVs for **K** (so $w = 5$); the result is the PV that is due to **B**$\cdot$**A**.

The Case 2 PV$_E$ is the residual when *all* the available sources **Y** variance has been removed. These are, in addition to **G**, **K**, and **G** $\times$ **K**, the other components of the three-way factorial design model: they are, each followed parenthetically by the number of IVs (hence **df**) representing them: **S** (1), **S** $\times$ **G**(2), **S** $\times$ **K**(3), and **S** $\times$ **G** $\times$ **K**(6), exactly as in the analysis of variance. These latter constitute set **C** for this analysis of **G** $\times$ **K**, with its **df** $= 1 + 2 + 3 + 6 = 12 = z$. The error **df** for Case 2 is thus $v = 120 - 6 - 5 - 12 - 1 = 96$, as it was in examples 8.6 and 8.7. Note that $u + w + z = (6 + 5 + 12 =) 23$, one fewer than the total number of cells ($2 \times 3 \times 4 = 24$). The full complement of IVs to represent all the main effects and interactions of a factorial design is always the number of cells minus one. Each of the IVs carries information about a specific aspect of one of the main or interaction effects.

Now assume that the value posited for $R^2_{Y \cdot A,B,C}$, based on all 23 IVs, is .325, so that $PV_E = 1 - .325 = .675$. Assume further that $R^2_{Y \cdot A,B} - R^2_{Y \cdot A}$ ($= R^2_{Y \cdot G \times K}$) is posited as .042. Then the Case 2 $f^2$ for $G \times K$ from formula (9.2.4) is .0625 (approximately). (These values were chosen here so that they would agree with $f = .25$ for the $G \times K$ [there called $A \times C$] interaction in example 8.7). From formula (9.3.1), $\lambda = .0625(103) = 6.4$. The specifications for the power of the test of $G \times K$, with 6 df, are thus

$$a = .05, \quad u = 6, \quad v = 96, \quad \lambda = 6.4,$$

and Table 9.3.2 gives, in block $u = 6$ for column $\lambda = 6.4$, power = .42, in close agreement with the value .41 found in example 8.7 for the same specifications (recall that they are theoretically identical).

Consider now the test for a main effect. In nonorthogonal designs the souces of variance are correlated with each other. When, as here, no causal hierarchy is presupposed, a factor's "gross" effect (e.g., $R^2_{Y \cdot K}$) is contaminated by those of the other factors, and requires "purification," i.e., partialling. Thus, the pure $K$ effects is $K \cdot S, G$. If we now let set $B$ be $K$ (with $u = 3$), and set $A$ be the combined $S$ and $G$ (with $w = 1 + 2 = 3$), then the PV for pure $K$ is given by the numerator of the Case 2 formula for $f^2$ (9.2.4). We assign to it the alternate-hypothetical value of .108 (selected in this example for consistency with example 8.6). Set $C$ now contains the remaining sources of $Y$ variance, the four interaction groups (made up, in all, of 17 IVs). the $PV_E$, $1 - R^2_{Y \cdot A,B,C}$, remains the same for all the tests; it was posited above to equal .675, based on $v = 96$. thus, the $f^2$ for $K \cdot S, G$ is .16, and $\lambda = .16(100) = 16.0$. The specification summary:

$$a = .05, \quad u = 3, \quad v = 96, \quad \lambda = 16.0.$$

In block $u = 3$ of Table 9.3.2 at $\lambda = 16$, for both $v = 120$ and $v = \infty$, power is given as .93 (making the use of [9.3.2] unnecessary). This agrees exactly with the value found for the same specifications for the conditions effect in example 8.6.

In complex problems such as this, the specification of the many alternate-hypothetical $R^2$s necessary to compute the $f^2$s for the effects can be avoided if the researcher is prepared to work directly with $f^2$, using conventional or other values. Direct specification of $f^2$ makes the determination of the power of the test of a given main effect or interaction a procedure that can be completed in a minute or two. Following this procedure, the reader may, as an exercise, use the present methods to find the power of the other effects in this problem, using the $f$ values specified in examples 8.6 and 8.7, and check the agreement with the results given there. As a somewhat more difficult problem, determine the various $R^2$ values implied by the $f^2$ values.

**9.15** Another occasion for the use of Case 2 MRC arises in connection with the analysis of the shape of the regression of **Y** on some quantitative research factor by means of power (or orthogonal) polynomials. In example 9.2, a study of the relationship between attitude toward socialized medicine (ASM = **Y**) and age in a sample of 90 adult male subjects was described. The focus there was on age as a construct, with no attention paid to the details of the shape of the relationship. To assure that the amount of variance in ASM accounted for by age was not to be constrained by the presumption of linearity, a third order polynomial was used, i.e., the 3 (= **u**) IVs age (**X**), age-squared (**X**$^2$), and age-cubed (**X**$^3$) defined the construct age, and were used as a set (**B**) in an MRC Case 0 analysis. It was posited that its $f^2 = .15$ (hence $R^2_{Y \cdot B} = .13$). The present focus is on the shape of this relationship, components of which are carried by each of the three IVs. Specifically, the sociologist believes that the regression of ASM on age has a substantial (negative) linear component such that younger respondents score generally higher on ASM than do older ones. Specifically, he posits that of the 13% of the ASM variance that he assumes is being accounted for by the three IVs, 8% may be accounted for by a straight line, i.e., by (linear) age (**X**): $r^2_{YX} = .08$, and the remainder (.05) jointly by the quadratic and cubic curvilinear components of age, **X**$^2$ and **X**$^3$, that bend that straight line to improve the fit. Although the latter do not figure in defining the source of variance of interest, which is **X**, the .05 of the **Y** variance for which they presumably account should not be included in the $PV_E$. We thus have the conditions for Case 2. (Note that in the standard significance test for $r_{YX}$, which is a Case 0 test, the error term, $1 - r^2_{YX}$, would be inflated by the PV due to **X**$^2$ and **X**$^3$, .05.)

Let the single variable **X** constitute set **B** (hence **u** = 1), and **X**$^2$ and **X**$^3$ together made up set **c** (hence **z** = 2). Since nothing is to be partialled from **X**, let set **A** be empty (hence **w** = 0). Substituting in the Case 2 formula for $f^2$ (9.2.4), the $f^2$ for **X** is $.08/(1 - .13) = .0920$. The error **df** is, from (9.3.10), **v** = 90 − 1 − 0 − 2 − 1 = 86 (as in example 9.2). Thus, from (9.3.1), $\lambda = .0920(88) = 8.1$. Using the same **a** = .01 criterion as before, the specification summary for the power of the test on the linear component of age, **X**, is

$$\mathbf{a} = .01, \quad \mathbf{u} = 1, \quad \mathbf{v} = 86, \quad \lambda = 8.1.$$

Interpolation in block **u** = 1 in Table 9.3.1 for $\lambda = 8.1$ gives power = .59. This is hardly a satisfactory level of power. It might be prudent to plan instead that this test be performed at **a** = .05, which, upon entering **u** = 1 and $\lambda = 8.1$ in Table 9.3.2 for **a** = .05, gives power = 80.

Now consider the test of the null hypothesis that there is in fact no curvilinearity in the regression of ASM on age. The curvilinearity is carried by $X^2$ and $X^3$, which we now designate as set **B**, but they also carry variance in **X**, which must be partialled from them (Cohen & Cohen, 1983, pp. 224–232). Let **X** constitute the set to be partialled **A**. Consistent with the PV of .13 for all three variables and .08 for **X**, we are assigning a PV to $X^2$ and $X^3$ together of .05. Since no further IVs are operating here (but see the further evolution of this problem in examples 9.8 and 9.10), there is no set **C**, so the power analysis may proceed as Case 1, or as we have seen as the special case of Case 2 where set **C** is empty. In either case, the $f^2$ for the two IVs of set **B** is $.05/(1 - .13) = .0575$, **u** = 2, **w** = 1, and **v** = 90 − 2 − 1 − 1 = 86 (as before). Thus $\lambda = .0575(89) = 5.1$. Continuing to use **a** = .05, the specification summary of this test of the null hypothesis on curvilinearity is:

$$a = .05, \qquad u = 2, \qquad v = 86, \qquad \lambda = 5.1$$

In Table 9.3.2, in block **u** = 2, linear interpolation of $\lambda = 5.1$ gives power = .50. Thus, in the presence in the population of substantial curvilinearity, the probability of so concluding is a "fifty-fifty" proposition. Not very good.

The investigator may now consider the possibility that all of the .05 of the **Y** variance accounted for nonlinearly resides in the quadratic term ($X^2$), and none of it in the cubic ($X^3$). This is not at all unreasonable, since the nonlinear relationship encountered in the "soft" behavioral sciences frequently yield trivially small contributions beyond the quadratic; the cubic term has been included here "just in case." Thus, let set **B** contain only $X^2$ (hence **u** = 1). We let set **A** contain **X**, which must be partialled from $X^2$ to define the unique quadratic contribution (hence, **w** = 1). Set **C** carries $X^3$ (hence **z** = 1), which we still plan to include in the analysis since it may well carry some variance and reduce the error term. This is a Case 2 MRC test: $f^2$ = $.05/(1 - .13) = .0575$ (as before), **v** = 90 − 1 − 1 − 1 − 1 = 86 (as before), so that $\lambda = .0575(88) = 5.1$. But **u** = 1 now, instead of 2, which, all other things equal, will yield greater power:

$$a = .05, \qquad u = 1, \qquad v = 86, \qquad \lambda = 5.1.$$

In Table 9.3.2, in block **u** = 1, interpolation of $\lambda = 5.1$ gives power = .60. Although better than .50, even assigning every shred of the assumed .05 curvilinear variance to $X^2$ does not result in a strong test. Apparently, a powerful test of curvilinearity is not available without increasing **N** (for this presumed ES).

Because of its high degree of generality, many further examples of Case 2 MRC analysis may be contrived. The elements are fairly simple: set **B** is the source of **Y** variance of interest, set **A** is made up of the IVs to be partialled (if any), and set **C** contains additional variables (if any) used to further reduce error variance. This structure includes virtually all the significance tests encountered in experimental designs of any degree of complexity. Additional applications and examples are given in Cohen & Cohen (1983, Chapters 4, 8, 10, and 11).

### 9.4   λ TABLES AND THE DETERMINATION OF SAMPLE SIZE

The determination of the sample size necessary to attain some desired amount of power (given the other parameters) proceeds by inverting the process of the preceding section, in which power was determined as a function of **N**. Unlike the sample size tables in the other chapters, the tables in this section give values of the noncentrality parameter $\lambda$; these are then used to find the necessary **N**.

A problem arises in that the relationship between $\lambda$ and power depends on **v**, which in turn is a function of **N**, which is what we are trying to determine. The problem can be solved by iteration: we select as a trial value of **v** one of those provided in the tables, use its $\lambda$ value for the desired power, and compute **N** with one of the formulas provided. Then, if the computed **N** implies **v** substantially different from our trial value, we repeat the computation using the new **v** value.

The basic formula (9.3.1) is rewritten as

(9.4.1)
$$\mathbf{v} = \frac{\lambda}{\mathbf{f}^2} - \mathbf{u} - 1.$$

**v** is the error (or denominator) **df**, made up of **N** and, negatively, the number of IVs employed in the determination of the $PV_E$, which varies depending on the case. It is then a simple matter to rewrite (9.4.1) to yield the requisite **N** as a function of $\lambda/\mathbf{f}^2$ and the number of **df** "lost" in the determination of $PV_E$. In the sections that follow, the **N** formulas are given for the three cases. The two tables that follow yield $\lambda$ values necessary to attain a given power for the **F** test of the null hypothesis for set **B** (made up of **v** variables) using the **a** significance criterion. The provisions for the parameters **a**, **u**, and **v** are the same as for the power tables in Section 9.3, as follows:

1. *Significance criterion, **a**.*   Tables 9.4.1 and 9.4.2 give $\lambda$ values respectively for **a** = .01 and .05.

2. *Degrees of Freedom of the Numerator of the **F** Ratio, **u**.*   This is simultaneously the number of IVs in set **B**. Each table gives $\lambda$ values over the range of power for the following 23 values of **u**: 1(1), 15, 18, 24, 30, 40, 48, 60, 120. Since all values of **u** up to 15 are given, it will only rarely be necessary to resort to interpolation (which may be linear).

3. *Degrees of Freedom of the Denominator of the **F** Ratio, **v**.*   For each

of the values of **u**, λ values for the desired power are provided for the same four values of **v** as in Section 9.3: 20, 60, 120, and ∞. Note that the λ values for the four values of **v** for any given level of desired power do not vary greatly, so that for many applications, a trial value of λ for **v** = 120 will yield an **N** of sufficient accuracy. Interpolation between λ values for a given **v** is linear in the reciprocals of the **v**'s; this would be necessary for "exact" values of λ. For the lower and upper tabled **v** values between which **v** falls ($v_L$, $v_U$) andtheir respective values λ values ($λ_L$, $λ_U$), the interpolated value of λ for the given **v** is

(9.4.2)
$$λ = λ_L - \frac{1/v_L - 1/v}{1/v_L - 1/v_U} (λ_L - λ_U).$$

4. *Desired Power.*   The tables provide for the power values: .25, .50, .60, 2/3, .70(.05).95, and .99. Section 2.4.1 for a discussion of the basis for the choice of desired power values, and of the proposal that power = .80 serve as a convention in the absence of another basis for a choice.

   9.4.1   CASE 0: TEST OF $R^2$.   For the simple case where the significance test is on $R^2_{Y \cdot B}$, and only the **u** variables of set **B** are employed in defining the error variance, the error df, **v** = **N** − **u** − 1. Substituting this in (9.4.1) above and solving for **N** gives

(9.4.3)
$$N = \frac{λ}{f^2}.$$

If the Case 0 $f^2$ is spelled out in PV terms (9.2.2) and substituted,

(9.4.4)
$$N = \frac{λ(1 - R^2_{Y \cdot B})}{R^2_{Y \cdot B}}.$$

   To determine **N**, enter the table for the **a** specified in the row for the number of IVs, **u**, and the column for the desired power, and read out λ for a trial value of **v**. λ is then entered into (9.4.3) when the effect size is expressed as $f^2$ or (9.4.4) when the effect size is expressed as a function of $R^2_{Y \cdot B}$ (9.2.2), and **N** for the trial **v** is computed. Since **v** = **N** − **u** − 1, the computed value of **N** will imply a value for **v** different from the trial **v**. If the disparity is great, one may repeat the process to obtain a new value of λ by interpolation using (9.4.2). One can reiterate this process with the new value of **N**, although this degree of accuracy is rarely needed in practice. The procedure is illustrated in the examples.

### Illustrative Examples

**9.16**  Recall the personnel psychologist in example 9.1 who was working with a selection battery made up of 5 ($= \mathbf{u}$) variables (set **B**), which he posited accounted for .10 ($= \mathbf{R}^2_{Y \cdot B}$) of the criterion variance in the population. Using the significance criterion $\mathbf{a} = .05$ for a sample of 95 ($= \mathbf{N}$) cases, it was found that the power of the **F** test on the sample $\mathbf{R}^2_{Y \cdot B}$ was .66. What must **N** be for the power of the test to be .80? The specifications are thus:

$$\mathbf{a} = .05, \qquad \mathbf{u} = 5, \qquad \mathbf{R}^2_{Y \cdot B} = .10, \qquad \text{power} = .80.$$

Table 9.4.2 (for $\mathbf{a} = .05$) gives in block $\mathbf{u} = 5$, column power $= .80$, $\lambda = 13.3$ for $\mathbf{v} = 120$, which we take as a trial value. Substituting in Equation (9.4.4),

$$\mathbf{N} = \frac{13.3\,(1 - .10)}{.10} = 120$$

which, since $\mathbf{v} = \mathbf{N} - \mathbf{u} - 1$, implies that $\mathbf{v} = 120 - 5 - 1 = 114$. The disparity between the $\mathbf{v} = 120$ value for which he obtained $\lambda = 13.3$ and the implied value of 114 is quite small (i.e., less than 10%), and for practical purposes the inexact computed **N** of 120 would generally be adequate. If he nevertheless wished the "exact" **N**, he would reiterate by means of (9.4.2): He seeks $\lambda$ for 114. Substituting for $\mathbf{v}_L$, $\mathbf{v}_U$ (60, 120) the values in Table 9.4.2 for $\lambda_L$, $\lambda_U$ (14.0, 13.3), he obtains

$$\lambda = 14.0 - \frac{1/60 - 1/114}{1/60 - 1/120}\,(14.0 - 13.3) = 13.3.$$

Thus, when rounded to one decimal place, there is no difference between the interpolated $\lambda$ value for $\mathbf{v} = 114$ and the tabled $\lambda$ value for $\mathbf{v} = 120$; the originally computed $\mathbf{N} = 120$ value stands.

**9.17**  The sociologist investigating correlates of attitude toward socialized medicine in a sample of 90 cases (example 9.2) found that at $\mathbf{a} = .01$, using a third-order polynomial representation of age (set **B**, $\mathbf{u} = 3$), and assuming that $\mathbf{f}^2 = .15$, had power of .69 for the **F** test of the sample $\mathbf{R}^2_{Y \cdot B}$. What **N** would be necessary for power of .80? The specifications are:

$$\mathbf{a} = .01, \qquad \mathbf{u} = 3, \qquad \mathbf{f}^2 = .15, \qquad \text{power} = .80.$$

Table 9.4.1 (for $\mathbf{a} = .01$) in block $\mathbf{u} = 3$ for column power $= .80$ gives for the trial value of $\mathbf{v} = 120$, $\lambda = 16.1$. Substituting in (9.4.3) gives $\mathbf{N} =$

16.1/.15 = 107, which implies **v** = 107 − 3 − 1 = 103. A more accurate value for **N** requires reiteration by interpolating for λ between **v** = 60 and **v** = 120 with Equation (9.4.2):

$$\lambda = 16.9 - \frac{1/60 - 1/103}{1/60 - 1/120} \ (16.9 - 16.1) = 16.2,$$

for which **N** = 16.2/.15 = 108, barely different from the previous value. Obviously no further iteration is necessary.

**9.18**   A clinical psychologist is planning a research on the prediction of success in psychotherapy from demographic, psychological test and projective technique data routinely gathered at intake. This collection of predictive factors (set **B**) are expressed as 20 (= **u**) IVs. She posits that they will account for some .16 (= $R^2_{Y \cdot B}$) of the variance in consensus ratings of success (**Y**), and wishes to ascertain the sample size necessary for the **F** test at **a** = .05 to have power = .90. Thus,

$$\mathbf{a} = .05, \qquad \mathbf{u} = 20, \qquad R^2_{Y \cdot B} = .16, \qquad \text{power} = .90.$$

Table 9.4.2, in block **v** = 20 for power = .90 gives for the trial value of **v** = 120 (again), λ = 29.6. Substituting in (9.4.4) gives **N** = 29.6 (1 − .16)/.16 = 155, which implies **v** = 155 − 20 − 1 = 134. Reiterating, we find with Equation (9.4.2) that for **v** = 134, interpolating between **v** = 120 and ∞, that

$$\lambda = 29.6 - \frac{1/120 - 1/134}{1/120} \ (29.6 - 26.1) = 29.2,$$

which via (9.4.4) yields **N** = 29.2 (1 − .16)/.16 = 153. Since this hardly differs from the previous value, no further iteration is necessary. She finds this **N** rather large given the expected rate of case acquisition.

She then reconsiders the problem. She knows that there is much redundancy among the 20 IVs, and that some of them are only marginally relevant to **Y**. She notices that the λ tables clearly show that for any given level of power, as **u** increases, λ increases and thus (since λ is a positive linear function of **N**) **N** increases. She decides to reduce her 20 IVs to four by some combination of a priori judgment and factor analysis. She expects that, having captured much of the criterion relevant variance in the reduced set of IVs, the population $R^2_{Y \cdot B}$ will only be reduced to .12. The revised specifications are:

$$\mathbf{a} = .05, \qquad \mathbf{u} = 4, \qquad R^2_{Y \cdot B} = .12, \qquad \text{power} = .90.$$

**Table 9.4.1**

λ values of the **F** Test as a Function of Power, **u**, and **v**

**a** = .01

| u | v | | Power | | | | | | | | | | |
|---|---|---|---|---|---|---|---|---|---|---|---|---|---|
| | | .25 | .50 | .60 | 2/3 | .70 | .75 | .80 | .85 | .90 | .95 | .99 |
| 1 | 20 | 4.3 | 7.8 | 9.4 | 10.7 | 11.3 | 12.5 | 13.8 | 15.4 | 17.6 | 21.1 | 28.5 |
| | 60 | 3.9 | 7.0 | 8.4 | 9.5 | 10.0 | 11.0 | 12.2 | 13.6 | 15.6 | 18.7 | 25.2 |
| | 120 | 3.8 | 6.8 | 8.1 | 9.2 | 9.8 | 10.7 | 11.9 | 13.3 | 15.1 | 18.1 | 24.5 |
| | ∞ | 3.6 | 6.6 | 8.0 | 9.0 | 9.6 | 10.6 | 11.7 | 13.0 | 14.9 | 17.8 | 24.0 |
| 2 | 20 | 5.9 | 10.3 | 12.3 | 13.8 | 14.6 | 16.0 | 17.6 | 19.5 | 22.1 | 26.2 | 34.9 |
| | 60 | 5.0 | 8.8 | 10.5 | 11.7 | 12.4 | 13.6 | 14.9 | 16.5 | 18.7 | 22.2 | 29.5 |
| | 120 | 4.9 | 8.4 | 10.0 | 11.2 | 11.9 | 13.0 | 14.3 | 15.9 | 18.0 | 21.3 | 28.0 |
| | ∞ | 4.7 | 8.2 | 9.8 | 10.9 | 11.8 | 12.6 | 13.9 | 15.4 | 17.4 | 20.6 | 27.4 |
| 3 | 20 | 7.2 | 12.3 | 14.6 | 16.3 | 17.3 | 18.8 | 20.6 | 22.8 | 25.7 | 30.4 | 40.1 |
| | 60 | 6.0 | 10.2 | 12.0 | 13.4 | 14.2 | 15.4 | 16.9 | 18.7 | 21.1 | 24.9 | 32.8 |
| | 120 | 5.7 | 9.7 | 11.4 | 12.8 | 13.5 | 14.7 | 16.1 | 17.8 | 20.1 | 23.7 | 31.2 |
| | ∞ | 5.4 | 9.3 | 11.0 | 12.3 | 13.0 | 14.1 | 15.5 | 17.1 | 19.2 | 22.7 | 29.8 |
| 4 | 20 | 8.4 | 14.2 | 16.7 | 18.6 | 19.7 | 21.4 | 23.4 | 25.8 | 29.0 | 34.1 | 44.7 |
| | 60 | 6.7 | 11.3 | 13.4 | 14.9 | 15.7 | 17.0 | 18.6 | 20.6 | 23.1 | 27.1 | 35.6 |
| | 120 | 6.4 | 10.7 | 12.6 | 14.1 | 14.8 | 16.1 | 17.6 | 19.4 | 21.8 | 25.7 | 33.6 |
| | ∞ | 6.1 | 10.1 | 12.0 | 13.4 | 14.1 | 15.3 | 16.7 | 18.5 | 20.7 | 24.3 | 31.8 |
| 5 | 20 | 9.5 | 15.9 | 18.7 | 20.8 | 21.9 | 23.8 | 25.9 | 28.6 | 32.1 | 37.6 | 49.1 |
| | 60 | 7.5 | 12.4 | 14.6 | 16.2 | 17.0 | 18.5 | 20.2 | 22.2 | 24.9 | 29.2 | 38.1 |
| | 120 | 7.0 | 11.7 | 13.7 | 15.2 | 16.0 | 17.4 | 18.9 | 20.9 | 23.4 | 27.4 | 35.7 |
| | ∞ | 6.6 | 11.0 | 12.9 | 14.3 | 15.1 | 16.4 | 17.9 | 19.7 | 22.0 | 25.8 | 33.5 |
| 6 | 20 | 10.5 | 17.5 | 20.5 | 22.8 | 24.0 | 26.1 | 28.4 | 31.3 | 35.0 | 41.0 | 53.3 |
| | 60 | 8.1 | 13.4 | 15.7 | 17.4 | 18.3 | 19.8 | 21.6 | 23.8 | 26.6 | 31.1 | 40.4 |
| | 120 | 7.6 | 12.5 | 14.6 | 16.2 | 17.1 | 18.5 | 20.2 | 22.2 | 24.8 | 29.0 | 37.7 |
| | ∞ | 7.1 | 11.8 | 13.7 | 15.2 | 16.0 | 17.3 | 18.9 | 20.7 | 23.2 | 27.0 | 35.0 |

| | | | | | | | | | | | | |
|---|---|---|---|---|---|---|---|---|---|---|---|---|
| 7 | 20 | 11.5 | 19.1 | 22.4 | 24.8 | 26.1 | 28.3 | 30.8 | 33.9 | 37.9 | 44.2 | 57.4 |
| | 60 | 8.8 | 14.3 | 16.7 | 18.5 | 19.5 | 21.1 | 23.0 | 25.2 | 28.2 | 32.9 | 42.5 |
| | 120 | 8.1 | 13.3 | 15.5 | 17.2 | 18.1 | 19.6 | 21.3 | 23.4 | 26.1 | 30.5 | 39.4 |
| | ∞ | 7.6 | 12.4 | 14.5 | 16.0 | 16.8 | 18.2 | 19.8 | 21.7 | 24.2 | 28.2 | 36.4 |
| 8 | 20 | 12.5 | 20.7 | 24.1 | 26.7 | 28.1 | 30.5 | 33.1 | 36.4 | 40.7 | 47.4 | 61.3 |
| | 60 | 9.4 | 15.2 | 17.7 | 19.6 | 20.6 | 22.3 | 24.2 | 26.6 | 29.7 | 34.6 | 44.6 |
| | 120 | 8.6 | 14.0 | 16.4 | 18.1 | 19.0 | 20.6 | 22.3 | 24.5 | 27.4 | 31.9 | 41.0 |
| | ∞ | 8.0 | 13.0 | 15.1 | 16.7 | 17.6 | 19.0 | 20.6 | 22.6 | 25.2 | 29.3 | 37.7 |
| 9 | 20 | 13.5 | 22.2 | 25.9 | 28.6 | 30.1 | 32.6 | 35.4 | 38.9 | 43.4 | 50.5 | 65.1 |
| | 60 | 9.9 | 16.1 | 18.7 | 20.7 | 21.7 | 23.5 | 25.5 | 27.9 | 31.1 | 36.2 | 46.6 |
| | 120 | 9.1 | 14.7 | 17.1 | 18.9 | 19.9 | 21.5 | 23.4 | 25.6 | 28.5 | 33.2 | 42.7 |
| | ∞ | 8.4 | 13.6 | 15.8 | 17.4 | 18.3 | 19.8 | 21.4 | 23.5 | 26.1 | 30.3 | 38.9 |
| 10 | 20 | 14.5 | 23.7 | 27.6 | 30.5 | 32.1 | 34.7 | 37.7 | 41.3 | 46.1 | 53.6 | 69.0 |
| | 60 | 10.5 | 16.9 | 19.7 | 21.7 | 22.8 | 24.6 | 26.7 | 29.2 | 32.5 | 37.8 | 48.5 |
| | 120 | 9.6 | 15.4 | 17.9 | 19.8 | 20.8 | 22.4 | 24.3 | 26.6 | 29.7 | 34.4 | 44.2 |
| | ∞ | 8.8 | 14.1 | 16.4 | 18.1 | 19.0 | 20.5 | 22.2 | 24.3 | 27.0 | 31.3 | 40.0 |
| 11 | 20 | 15.4 | 25.2 | 29.3 | 32.4 | 34.0 | 36.8 | 39.9 | 43.7 | 48.7 | 56.6 | 72.8 |
| | 60 | 11.0 | 19.5 | 22.6 | 24.9 | 26.1 | 28.2 | 30.6 | 33.5 | 37.2 | 43.2 | 55.3 |
| | 120 | 10.0 | 16.1 | 18.6 | 20.5 | 21.6 | 23.3 | 25.2 | 27.6 | 30.7 | 35.6 | 45.7 |
| | ∞ | 9.1 | 14.6 | 17.0 | 18.7 | 19.6 | 21.1 | 22.9 | 25.0 | 27.8 | 32.2 | 41.1 |
| 12 | 20 | 16.4 | 26.6 | 31.0 | 34.2 | 35.9 | 38.8 | 42.1 | 46.1 | 51.4 | 59.6 | 76.5 |
| | 60 | 11.6 | 18.5 | 21.4 | 23.6 | 24.8 | 26.7 | 29.0 | 31.7 | 35.2 | 40.8 | 52.1 |
| | 120 | 10.5 | 16.7 | 19.4 | 21.3 | 22.4 | 24.1 | 26.2 | 28.6 | 31.8 | 36.8 | 47.1 |
| | ∞ | 9.5 | 15.1 | 17.5 | 19.3 | 20.2 | 21.8 | 23.6 | 25.7 | 28.6 | 33.0 | 42.1 |
| 13 | 20 | 17.3 | 28.1 | 32.7 | 36.0 | 37.8 | 40.8 | 44.3 | 48.5 | 54.0 | 62.6 | 80.2 |
| | 60 | 12.1 | 19.3 | 22.3 | 24.5 | 25.7 | 27.8 | 30.1 | 32.9 | 36.5 | 42.2 | 53.9 |
| | 120 | 10.9 | 17.3 | 20.0 | 22.0 | 23.1 | 24.9 | 27.0 | 29.5 | 32.8 | 37.9 | 48.4 |
| | ∞ | 9.8 | 15.6 | 18.0 | 19.8 | 20.8 | 22.4 | 24.2 | 26.4 | 29.3 | 33.8 | 43.1 |

*(Continued)*

**Table 9.4.1** *(Continued)*

| u | v | | | | | | Power | | | | | |
|---|---|---|---|---|---|---|---|---|---|---|---|---|
| | | .25 | .50 | .60 | 2/3 | .70 | .75 | .80 | .85 | .90 | .95 | .99 |
| 14 | 20 | 18.3 | 29.5 | 34.3 | 37.8 | 39.7 | 42.9 | 46.5 | 50.8 | 56.6 | 65.5 | 83.8 |
| | 60 | 12.6 | 20.0 | 23.2 | 25.5 | 26.7 | 28.8 | 31.2 | 34.0 | 37.8 | 43.7 | 55.6 |
| | 120 | 11.3 | 17.9 | 20.7 | 22.8 | 23.9 | 25.7 | 27.9 | 30.4 | 33.8 | 39.0 | 49.8 |
| | ∞ | 10.1 | 16.0 | 18.5 | 20.4 | 21.3 | 23.0 | 24.8 | 27.1 | 30.3 | 34.6 | 44.0 |
| 15 | 20 | 19.2 | 31.0 | 36.0 | 39.6 | 41.6 | 44.9 | 48.7 | 53.2 | 59.1 | 68.5 | 87.5 |
| | 60 | 13.1 | 20.8 | 24.0 | 26.4 | 27.7 | 29.8 | 32.2 | 35.2 | 39.0 | 45.1 | 57.4 |
| | 120 | 11.7 | 18.5 | 21.4 | 23.5 | 24.7 | 26.5 | 28.7 | 31.3 | 34.8 | 40.1 | 51.1 |
| | ∞ | 10.4 | 16.5 | 19.0 | 20.9 | 21.9 | 23.5 | 25.4 | 27.7 | 30.7 | 35.4 | 44.9 |
| 18 | 20 | 22.0 | 35.3 | 40.9 | 45.0 | 47.2 | 50.9 | 55.1 | 60.1 | 66.8 | 77.2 | 98.4 |
| | 60 | 14.6 | 22.9 | 26.4 | 29.0 | 30.4 | 32.7 | 35.3 | 38.5 | 42.7 | 49.1 | 62.3 |
| | 120 | 12.8 | 20.2 | 23.3 | 25.5 | 26.7 | 28.8 | 31.1 | 33.9 | 37.5 | 43.2 | 54.8 |
| | ∞ | 11.3 | 17.7 | 20.4 | 22.3 | 23.4 | 25.1 | 27.1 | 29.5 | 32.7 | 37.5 | 47.5 |
| 20 | 20 | 23.8 | 38.1 | 44.1 | 48.5 | 50.9 | 54.8 | 59.3 | 64.8 | 71.9 | 83.0 | 105.6 |
| | 60 | 15.5 | 24.4 | 28.1 | 30.8 | 32.2 | 34.6 | 37.4 | 40.7 | 45.1 | 51.8 | 65.6 |
| | 120 | 13.6 | 21.3 | 24.5 | 26.8 | 28.1 | 30.2 | 32.6 | 35.5 | 39.3 | 45.2 | 57.2 |
| | ∞ | 11.8 | 18.5 | 21.2 | 23.2 | 24.3 | 26.1 | 28.2 | 30.6 | 33.9 | 38.9 | 49.0 |
| 24 | 20 | 27.4 | 43.7 | 50.5 | 55.5 | 58.2 | 62.7 | 67.8 | 73.9 | 81.9 | 94.4 | 119.8 |
| | 60 | 17.4 | 27.1 | 31.2 | 34.1 | 35.7 | 38.3 | 41.3 | 45.0 | 49.7 | 57.0 | 71.9 |
| | 120 | 15.0 | 23.4 | 26.8 | 29.4 | 30.7 | 33.0 | 35.6 | 38.7 | 42.7 | 49.0 | 61.8 |
| | ∞ | 12.8 | 19.9 | 22.8 | 24.9 | 26.1 | 27.9 | 30.1 | 32.7 | 36.1 | 41.3 | 51.9 |
| 30 | 20 | 32.8 | 52.1 | 60.1 | 65.9 | 69.1 | 74.3 | 80.3 | 87.5 | 96.8 | 111.4 | 141.0 |
| | 60 | 20.1 | 31.1 | 35.7 | 39.0 | 40.8 | 43.7 | 47.1 | 51.1 | 56.4 | 64.5 | 81.0 |
| | 120 | 14.5 | 23.4 | 27.1 | 29.7 | 31.2 | 33.6 | 36.3 | 39.6 | 43.9 | 50.6 | 64.0 |
| | ∞ | 14.1 | 21.8 | 24.9 | 27.2 | 28.4 | 30.4 | 32.7 | 35.5 | 39.1 | 44.6 | 55.9 |

| | | | | | | | | | | | | |
|---|---|---|---|---|---|---|---|---|---|---|---|---|
| 40 | 20 | 41.7 | 65.9 | 75.9 | 83.2 | 87.1 | 93.6 | 101.0 | 109.9 | 121.5 | 139.5 | 176.1 |
| | 60 | 24.4 | 37.5 | 42.9 | 46.8 | 48.9 | 52.4 | 56.3 | 61.0 | 67.1 | 76.6 | 95.7 |
| | 120 | 20.0 | 30.9 | 35.3 | 38.5 | 40.2 | 43.1 | 46.3 | 50.1 | 55.2 | 62.9 | 78.5 |
| | ∞ | 16.1 | 24.5 | 28.0 | 30.5 | 31.8 | 34.0 | 36.6 | 39.6 | 43.5 | 49.5 | 61.6 |
| 48 | 20 | 48.8 | 76.9 | 88.5 | 96.9 | 101.4 | 108.9 | 117.5 | 127.7 | 141.2 | 161.9 | 203.9 |
| | 60 | 27.8 | 42.5 | 48.5 | 52.9 | 55.2 | 59.1 | 63.5 | 68.7 | 75.5 | 86.0 | 107.0 |
| | 120 | 22.6 | 34.4 | 39.2 | 42.7 | 44.6 | 47.7 | 51.2 | 55.4 | 60.9 | 69.3 | 86.2 |
| | ∞ | 17.5 | 26.5 | 30.2 | 32.9 | 34.3 | 36.6 | 39.3 | 42.5 | 46.6 | 52.9 | 65.6 |
| 60 | 20 | 59.4 | 93.4 | 107.3 | 117.4 | 122.9 | 131.9 | 142.2 | 154.5 | 170.5 | 195.4 | 245.6 |
| | 60 | 32.9 | 50.0 | 56.9 | 62.0 | 64.7 | 69.1 | 74.1 | 80.2 | 88.0 | 100.0 | 124.0 |
| | 120 | 26.2 | 39.6 | 45.1 | 49.0 | 51.1 | 54.6 | 58.5 | 63.3 | 69.4 | 78.8 | 97.5 |
| | ∞ | 19.4 | 29.2 | 33.2 | 36.0 | 37.6 | 40.1 | 43.0 | 46.4 | 50.8 | 57.6 | 71.1 |
| 120 | 20 | 112.3 | 175.3 | 201.0 | 219.6 | 229.7 | 246.2 | 265.0 | 287.5 | 316.8 | 362.0 | 453.3 |
| | 60 | 57.3 | 86.1 | 97.7 | 106.0 | 110.5 | 117.7 | 126.0 | 135.8 | 148.4 | 167.9 | 206.4 |
| | 120 | 42.9 | 63.9 | 72.2 | 78.2 | 81.5 | 86.8 | 92.7 | 99.8 | 109.0 | 123.0 | 150.6 |
| | ∞ | 26.7 | 39.6 | 44.7 | 48.4 | 50.4 | 53.7 | 57.4 | 61.7 | 67.4 | 76.1 | 93.3 |

**Table 9.4.2**

λ Values of the **F** Test as a Function of Power, **u**, and **v**

**a** = .05

| u | v | .25 | .50 | .60 | 2/3 | .70 | .75 | .80 | .85 | .90 | .95 | .99 |
|---|---|-----|-----|-----|-----|-----|-----|-----|-----|-----|-----|-----|
| 1 | 20 | 1.9 | 4.1 | 5.3 | 6.2 | 6.7 | 7.5 | 8.5 | 9.7 | 11.4 | 14.1 | 20.1 |
|   | 60 | 1.7 | 3.9 | 4.9 | 5.8 | 6.2 | 7.0 | 7.9 | 9.1 | 10.6 | 13.2 | 18.7 |
|   | 120 | 1.7 | 3.8 | 4.9 | 5.7 | 6.2 | 6.9 | 7.8 | 9.0 | 10.5 | 13.0 | 18.4 |
|   | ∞ | 1.6 | 3.8 | 4.9 | 5.7 | 6.2 | 6.9 | 7.8 | 9.0 | 10.5 | 13.0 | 18.4 |
| 2 | 20 | 2.6 | 5.7 | 7.1 | 8.2 | 8.9 | 9.9 | 11.1 | 12.6 | 14.6 | 17.9 | 24.9 |
|   | 60 | 2.3 | 5.1 | 6.4 | 7.4 | 8.0 | 8.9 | 10.0 | 11.3 | 13.2 | 16.1 | 22.4 |
|   | 120 | 2.3 | 5.0 | 6.3 | 7.2 | 7.8 | 8.7 | 9.7 | 11.1 | 12.8 | 15.7 | 21.8 |
|   | ∞ | 2.2 | 5.0 | 6.2 | 7.2 | 7.7 | 8.6 | 9.6 | 10.9 | 12.7 | 15.4 | 21.4 |
| 3 | 20 | 3.2 | 6.9 | 8.6 | 9.9 | 10.6 | 11.8 | 13.2 | 14.9 | 17.2 | 20.9 | 28.7 |
|   | 60 | 2.8 | 6.0 | 7.5 | 8.6 | 9.3 | 10.3 | 11.5 | 13.0 | 15.0 | 18.3 | 25.1 |
|   | 120 | 2.7 | 5.8 | 7.3 | 8.4 | 9.0 | 10.0 | 11.1 | 12.6 | 14.5 | 17.7 | 24.3 |
|   | ∞ | 2.7 | 5.8 | 7.2 | 8.2 | 8.8 | 9.8 | 10.9 | 12.3 | 14.2 | 17.2 | 23.5 |
| 4 | 20 | 3.8 | 8.0 | 9.9 | 11.4 | 12.2 | 13.5 | 15.0 | 16.9 | 19.5 | 23.5 | 32.1 |
|   | 60 | 3.3 | 6.8 | 8.5 | 9.7 | 10.4 | 11.5 | 12.8 | 14.4 | 16.6 | 20.1 | 27.4 |
|   | 120 | 3.1 | 6.6 | 8.1 | 9.3 | 10.0 | 11.0 | 12.3 | 13.9 | 16.0 | 19.3 | 26.3 |
|   | ∞ | 3.1 | 6.4 | 7.9 | 9.1 | 9.7 | 10.7 | 11.9 | 13.4 | 15.4 | 18.6 | 25.2 |
| 5 | 20 | 4.4 | 9.0 | 11.1 | 12.7 | 13.6 | 15.0 | 16.7 | 18.8 | 21.6 | 26.0 | 35.2 |
|   | 60 | 3.7 | 7.5 | 9.3 | 10.6 | 11.3 | 12.6 | 14.0 | 15.7 | 18.0 | 21.7 | 29.4 |
|   | 120 | 3.5 | 7.2 | 8.9 | 10.1 | 10.8 | 12.0 | 13.3 | 15.0 | 17.2 | 20.7 | 28.1 |
|   | ∞ | 3.4 | 7.0 | 8.6 | 9.8 | 10.5 | 11.6 | 12.8 | 14.4 | 16.5 | 19.8 | 26.7 |
| 6 | 20 | 4.9 | 10.0 | 12.3 | 14.0 | 15.0 | 16.5 | 18.4 | 20.6 | 23.6 | 28.3 | 38.2 |
|   | 60 | 4.0 | 8.2 | 10.1 | 11.5 | 12.2 | 13.5 | 15.0 | 16.9 | 19.3 | 23.1 | 31.2 |
|   | 120 | 3.8 | 7.8 | 9.6 | 10.9 | 11.6 | 12.8 | 14.3 | 16.0 | 18.3 | 22.0 | 29.7 |
|   | ∞ | 3.6 | 7.5 | 9.2 | 10.4 | 11.1 | 12.3 | 13.6 | 15.3 | 17.4 | 20.9 | 28.0 |

Power

| | | | | | | | | | | | | |
|---|---|---|---|---|---|---|---|---|---|---|---|---|
| 7 | 20 | 5.4 | 11.0 | 13.4 | 15.3 | 16.3 | 18.0 | 19.9 | 22.3 | 25.5 | 30.5 | 41.0 |
| | 60 | 4.4 | 8.8 | 10.8 | 12.3 | 13.1 | 14.5 | 16.0 | 17.9 | 20.5 | 24.5 | 33.0 |
| | 120 | 4.1 | 8.3 | 10.2 | 11.6 | 12.4 | 13.6 | 15.1 | 16.9 | 19.4 | 23.2 | 31.2 |
| | ∞ | 3.9 | 8.0 | 9.7 | 11.0 | 11.8 | 13.0 | 14.4 | 16.0 | 18.3 | 21.8 | 29.2 |
| 8 | 20 | 5.9 | 11.9 | 14.5 | 16.5 | 17.6 | 19.4 | 21.5 | 24.0 | 27.4 | 32.7 | 43.8 |
| | 60 | 4.7 | 9.4 | 11.5 | 13.0 | 13.9 | 15.3 | 17.0 | 19.0 | 21.6 | 25.8 | 34.6 |
| | 120 | 4.4 | 8.8 | 10.8 | 12.2 | 13.1 | 14.4 | 15.9 | 17.8 | 20.3 | 24.3 | 32.6 |
| | ∞ | 4.2 | 8.4 | 10.2 | 11.6 | 12.3 | 13.6 | 15.0 | 16.8 | 19.1 | 22.7 | 30.4 |
| 9 | 20 | 6.4 | 12.8 | 15.6 | 17.7 | 18.9 | 20.8 | 23.0 | 25.7 | 29.2 | 34.8 | 46.6 |
| | 60 | 5.0 | 10.0 | 12.2 | 13.8 | 14.7 | 16.2 | 17.9 | 20.0 | 22.7 | 27.1 | 36.2 |
| | 120 | 4.7 | 9.3 | 11.4 | 12.9 | 13.7 | 15.1 | 16.7 | 18.7 | 21.3 | 25.4 | 33.9 |
| | ∞ | 4.2 | 8.8 | 10.7 | 12.1 | 12.9 | 14.2 | 15.6 | 17.4 | 19.8 | 23.6 | 31.4 |
| 10 | 20 | 6.9 | 13.7 | 16.7 | 18.9 | 20.1 | 22.1 | 24.4 | 27.3 | 31.0 | 37.0 | 49.2 |
| | 60 | 5.3 | 10.5 | 12.8 | 14.5 | 15.4 | 17.0 | 18.7 | 20.9 | 23.8 | 28.3 | 37.7 |
| | 120 | 5.0 | 9.8 | 11.9 | 13.5 | 14.3 | 15.8 | 17.4 | 19.5 | 22.1 | 26.4 | 35.2 |
| | ∞ | 4.4 | 9.2 | 11.2 | 12.6 | 13.4 | 14.7 | 16.8 | 18.1 | 20.5 | 24.4 | 32.4 |
| 11 | 20 | 7.3 | 14.6 | 17.7 | 20.0 | 21.3 | 23.4 | 25.9 | 28.9 | 32.8 | 39.0 | 51.9 |
| | 60 | 5.6 | 11.0 | 13.4 | 15.2 | 16.1 | 17.7 | 19.6 | 21.8 | 24.8 | 29.5 | 39.2 |
| | 120 | 5.2 | 10.2 | 12.4 | 14.0 | 14.9 | 16.4 | 18.1 | 20.2 | 23.0 | 27.3 | 36.4 |
| | ∞ | 4.9 | 9.6 | 11.6 | 13.1 | 13.9 | 15.2 | 17.3 | 18.7 | 21.2 | 25.1 | 33.3 |
| 12 | 20 | 7.8 | 15.4 | 18.7 | 21.2 | 22.5 | 24.8 | 27.3 | 30.5 | 34.6 | 41.1 | 54.5 |
| | 60 | 5.9 | 11.6 | 14.0 | 15.9 | 16.9 | 18.5 | 20.4 | 22.7 | 25.8 | 30.6 | 40.6 |
| | 120 | 5.4 | 10.6 | 12.9 | 14.6 | 15.5 | 17.1 | 18.8 | 21.0 | 23.8 | 28.3 | 37.5 |
| | ∞ | 5.1 | 9.9 | 12.0 | 13.5 | 14.4 | 15.7 | 17.8 | 19.3 | 21.8 | 25.9 | 34.2 |
| 13 | 20 | 8.3 | 16.3 | 19.8 | 22.4 | 23.7 | 26.1 | 28.7 | 32.0 | 36.3 | 43.1 | 57.1 |
| | 60 | 6.2 | 12.1 | 14.6 | 16.5 | 17.5 | 19.2 | 21.2 | 23.6 | 26.8 | 31.7 | 42.0 |
| | 120 | 5.7 | 11.1 | 13.4 | 15.1 | 16.1 | 17.6 | 19.5 | 21.7 | 24.6 | 29.2 | 38.6 |
| | ∞ | 5.3 | 10.2 | 12.4 | 13.9 | 14.8 | 16.2 | 17.8 | 19.8 | 22.4 | 26.5 | 35.0 |

*(Continued)*

**Table 9.4.2** *(Continued)*

| u | v | .25 | .50 | .60 | 2/3 | .70 | .75 | .80 | .85 | .90 | .95 | .99 |
|---|---|-----|-----|-----|-----|-----|-----|-----|-----|-----|-----|-----|
| 14 | 20 | 8.7 | 17.1 | 20.8 | 23.5 | 24.9 | 27.4 | 30.2 | 33.6 | 38.0 | 45.1 | 59.6 |
|    | 60 | 6.5 | 12.6 | 15.2 | 17.2 | 18.2 | 20.0 | 22.0 | 24.5 | 27.7 | 32.8 | 43.4 |
|    | 120 | 5.9 | 11.5 | 13.9 | 15.7 | 16.6 | 18.2 | 20.1 | 22.4 | 25.3 | 30.0 | 39.7 |
|    | ∞ | 5.5 | 10.6 | 12.7 | 14.3 | 15.2 | 16.7 | 18.3 | 20.4 | 23.0 | 27.2 | 35.8 |
| 15 | 20 | 9.2 | 18.0 | 21.8 | 24.6 | 26.1 | 28.7 | 31.6 | 35.1 | 39.8 | 47.1 | 62.2 |
|    | 60 | 6.7 | 13.1 | 15.8 | 17.8 | 18.9 | 20.7 | 22.8 | 25.3 | 28.7 | 33.9 | 44.7 |
|    | 120 | 6.1 | 11.9 | 14.3 | 16.2 | 17.2 | 18.8 | 20.7 | 23.1 | 26.1 | 30.9 | 40.8 |
|    | ∞ | 5.6 | 10.9 | 13.1 | 14.7 | 15.6 | 17.1 | 18.8 | 20.9 | 23.6 | 27.8 | 36.6 |
| 18 | 20 | 10.5 | 20.5 | 24.8 | 27.9 | 29.6 | 32.5 | 35.7 | 39.7 | 44.9 | 53.0 | 69.8 |
|    | 60 | 7.5 | 14.5 | 17.4 | 19.6 | 20.8 | 22.8 | 25.0 | 27.8 | 31.4 | 37.0 | 48.6 |
|    | 120 | 6.8 | 13.0 | 15.7 | 17.6 | 18.7 | 20.5 | 22.5 | 25.0 | 28.2 | 33.3 | 43.8 |
|    | ∞ | 6.1 | 11.7 | 14.1 | 15.8 | 16.8 | 18.3 | 20.1 | 22.3 | 25.2 | 29.6 | 38.8 |
| 20 | 20 | 11.4 | 22.2 | 26.8 | 30.1 | 32.0 | 35.0 | 38.5 | 42.7 | 48.3 | 57.0 | 74.8 |
|    | 60 | 8.1 | 15.4 | 18.5 | 20.8 | 22.1 | 24.1 | 26.5 | 29.4 | 33.2 | 39.1 | 51.2 |
|    | 120 | 7.2 | 13.7 | 16.5 | 18.6 | 19.7 | 21.6 | 23.7 | 26.3 | 29.6 | 34.9 | 45.8 |
|    | ∞ | 6.4 | 12.3 | 14.7 | 16.5 | 17.5 | 19.1 | 21.0 | 23.2 | 26.1 | 30.7 | 40.1 |
| 24 | 20 | 13.2 | 25.5 | 30.7 | 34.5 | 36.6 | 40.0 | 43.9 | 48.7 | 54.9 | 64.7 | 84.7 |
|    | 60 | 9.1 | 17.2 | 20.6 | 23.1 | 24.5 | 26.7 | 29.3 | 32.5 | 36.6 | 43.0 | 56.0 |
|    | 120 | 8.0 | 15.1 | 18.2 | 20.4 | 21.6 | 23.6 | 25.9 | 28.6 | 32.3 | 37.9 | 49.5 |
|    | ∞ | 7.0 | 13.3 | 15.9 | 17.8 | 18.8 | 20.5 | 22.5 | 24.8 | 27.9 | 32.8 | 42.6 |
| 30 | 20 | 15.9 | 30.4 | 36.5 | 41.0 | 43.4 | 47.4 | 52.0 | 57.6 | 64.9 | 76.2 | 99.4 |
|    | 60 | 10.5 | 19.8 | 23.6 | 26.6 | 28.0 | 30.5 | 33.4 | 36.9 | 41.5 | 48.6 | 63.1 |
|    | 120 | 9.1 | 17.1 | 20.5 | 22.9 | 24.3 | 26.5 | 29.0 | 32.0 | 36.0 | 42.2 | 54.7 |
|    | ∞ | 7.8 | 14.6 | 17.4 | 19.5 | 20.6 | 22.4 | 24.5 | 27.1 | 30.4 | 35.5 | 45.9 |

Power

| | | | | | | | | | | | | |
|---|---|---|---|---|---|---|---|---|---|---|---|---|
| 40 | 20 | 20.2 | 38.5 | 46.1 | 51.7 | 54.7 | 59.7 | 65.4 | 72.3 | 81.3 | 95.3 | 123.7 |
| | 60 | 12.9 | 23.9 | 28.5 | 31.9 | 33.7 | 36.7 | 40.1 | 44.1 | 49.5 | 57.8 | 74.5 |
| | 120 | 10.9 | 20.2 | 24.1 | 26.9 | 28.4 | 31.0 | 33.8 | 37.3 | 41.8 | 48.8 | 63.0 |
| | ∞ | 9.0 | 16.6 | 19.7 | 22.5 | 23.2 | 25.2 | 27.6 | 30.3 | 33.9 | 39.5 | 50.8 |
| 48 | 20 | 23.7 | 44.9 | 53.8 | 60.2 | 63.7 | 69.5 | 76.0 | 84.0 | 94.3 | 110.4 | 143.0 |
| | 60 | 14.7 | 27.1 | 32.3 | 36.0 | 38.1 | 41.4 | 45.2 | 49.7 | 55.6 | 64.8 | 83.3 |
| | 120 | 12.2 | 22.5 | 26.8 | 29.9 | 31.6 | 34.3 | 37.5 | 41.3 | 46.2 | 53.8 | 69.1 |
| | ∞ | 9.8 | 18.0 | 21.3 | 23.8 | 25.1 | 27.2 | 29.7 | 32.6 | 36.5 | 42.4 | 54.3 |
| 60 | 20 | 26.6 | 51.7 | 62.0 | 69.6 | 73.7 | 80.4 | 88.2 | 97.4 | 109.5 | 128.3 | 166.3 |
| | 60 | 19.9 | 35.0 | 41.1 | 45.5 | 47.9 | 51.9 | 56.3 | 61.7 | 68.7 | 79.4 | 101.0 |
| | 120 | 14.2 | 26.0 | 30.9 | 34.4 | 36.3 | 39.4 | 42.9 | 47.1 | 52.7 | 61.2 | 78.2 |
| | ∞ | 10.9 | 19.9 | 23.5 | 26.2 | 27.6 | 29.9 | 32.6 | 35.8 | 39.9 | 46.3 | 59.0 |
| 120 | 20 | 49.9 | 96.4 | 115.4 | 129.3 | 136.8 | 156.7 | 163.1 | 179.9 | 201.7 | 235.5 | 303.9 |
| | 60 | 30.5 | 55.3 | 65.2 | 72.4 | 76.3 | 82.6 | 89.7 | 98.3 | 109.3 | 126.2 | 159.9 |
| | 120 | 23.5 | 42.2 | 49.7 | 55.1 | 58.0 | 62.7 | 68.1 | 74.5 | 82.8 | 95.5 | 120.7 |
| | ∞ | 15.2 | 27.2 | 32.0 | 35.5 | 37.3 | 40.4 | 43.9 | 48.0 | 53.4 | 61.6 | 78.1 |

Table 9.4.2 gives for block $u = 4$, power $= .90$, at a trial value $v = 120$, $\lambda = 16.0$. Formula (9.4.4) now gives $N = 16.0\,(1 - .12)/.12 = 117$. Reiterating would produce little if any change. This tactic has thus resulted in a reduction in $N$ demand from 153 to 117, that is, by 24%.

The increase in $\lambda$, and therefore with $N$ as $u$ increases, which is apparent in the tables, is a statistical expression of the principle of parsimony in the philosophy of science. The fact that computers can easily cope with large numbers of IVs in MRC should not mislead the researcher into the belief that his investigation can. Not only does power suffer (or the $N$ demand increase) when $u$ is large, but the rate of spurious rejections of null hypotheses (experimentwise $a$) increases as well (Cohen & Cohen, 1983, pp. 166–169).

**9.19**  A behavioral scientist, working in a relatively uncharted area, plans to relate a set of 5 IVs to a dependent variable using MRC. With no clear idea of what the population $R^2_{Y \cdot B}$ is likely to be, he determines the nec‹ essary $N$ for a range of possible $R^2_{Y \cdot B}$ values. Using power $= .80$, and $a = .01$ and $.05$, he consults Tables 9.3.1 and 9.3.2 and using Equations (9.4.2) and (9.4.4) generates the following table of $N$'s:

| $R^2_{Y \cdot B}$ | .02 | .05 | .10 | .15 | .20 | .25 | .30 | .35 |
|---|---|---|---|---|---|---|---|---|
| $a = .01$ | 884 | 347 | 166 | 108 | 77 | 60 | 50 | 41 |
| $a = .05$ | 632 | 248 | 121 | 78 | 57 | 44 | 36 | 30 |

Let us assume that, upon reviewing this table, he narrows down the problem by deciding to use $a = .05$ as his criterion. He then may reconsider his sense of the likely magnitude of $R^2_{Y \cdot B}$ and decide, somewhat uncertainly, to posit it to be .10 (let us say), and use $N = 120$.

A Bayesian-inspired alternative procedure is worth consideration. Instead of expressing his alternative hypothesis as a point ($R^2_{Y \cdot B} = .10$), he may express it as a distribution of subjective probabilities among the $R^2_{Y \cdot B}$ by assigning $P$ (probability) values to the alternative $R^2_{Y \cdot B}$ possibilities such that the $P$ values add up to 1.00. He has enough of an idea of the likely strength of the effect to consider some values of $R^2_{Y \cdot B}$ to be much more likely than others, and even to scale these in this manner. For simplicity, let us assume that he rules out completely (assigns $P = 0$ to) $R^2_{Y \cdot B}$ values outside the range of .05 to .15, and within that range, assigns $P_{.05} = .3$, $P_{.10} = .5$, and $P_{.15} = .2$. He then uses the $P_i$ as weights to yield a value of $N$, e.g.,

$$(9.4.4) \qquad\qquad N = \Sigma\, P_i N_i,$$

which, for these data and subjective $P_i$s, yields $N = .3(248) + .5(120) + .2(78) = 150$. A similar procedure may be used in subjectively weighting power values as a function of a fixed $N$ over a range of ESs into a single estimate of power. Of course, these Bayesian-like procedures may be used for any statistical test, not just those of MRC.

Finally, however one proceeds in the end, the generation of tables of **N** such as the above is recommended for coping with the problem of making decisions about **N** in experimental planning.

**9.20**  In example 9.5, a Case 0 MRC power analysis was performed on a teaching methods problem, previously analyzed by the analysis of variance methods of Chapter 8 in example 8.1. The original specifications yielded power = .51 (.52 in example 8.1) for four groups (hence **u** = 3) of 20 cases each (hence **N** = 80), at **a** = .05 with **f** = .28. When redone as an analysis of variance problem in determining the sample size necessary for power = .80 (example 8.10), it was found that the **n** per group would be 35.9 (= 36), so **N** = 143.6 (= 144). Redoing this now as a Case 0 MRC problem in determining **N**, the specifications are:

$$a = .05, \quad u = 3, \quad f^2 = .0784, \quad \text{power} = .80.$$

Table 9.4.2 gives for **u** = 3, power = .80, at trial **v** = 120, $\lambda$ = 11.1. Formula (9.4.3) gives **N** = 11.1/.0784 = 142, which does not change on iteration using (9.4.2), and is in good agreement with the value found in example 8.10.

**9.4.2**  CASE 1: TEST OF $R^2_{Y \cdot A,B} - R^2_{Y \cdot A}$, MODEL 1 ERROR.  In the test of the increase in $R^2$ that occurs when set **B** (containing **u** IVs) is added to set **A** (containing **w** IVs), the $PV_E$ is $1 - R^2_{Y \cdot A,B} - R^2_{Y \cdot A}$, and its **df** given by formula (9.3.7) as **v** = **N** − **u** − **w** − 1. Substituting this in formula (9.4.1) and solving for **N** gives

$$(9.4.6) \qquad\qquad N = \frac{\lambda}{f^2} + w.$$

If $f^2$ is expressed as a function of $R^2_{Y \cdot A}$ and $R^2_{Y \cdot A,B}$ as given for Case 1 in (9.2.3),

$$(9.4.7) \qquad\qquad N = \frac{\lambda(1 - R^2_{Y \cdot A,B})}{R^2_{Y \cdot A,B} - R^2_{Y \cdot A}} + w.$$

Expressing the Case 1 $f^2$ as a function of the squared multiple *partial* correlations, $R^2_{YB \cdot A}$, as given by formula (9.2.7), gives

$$(9.4.8) \qquad\qquad N = \frac{\lambda(1 - R^2_{YB \cdot A})}{R^2_{YB \cdot A}} + w.$$

As in Case 0, $\lambda$ is found by entering Table 9.4.1 (for $a = .01$) or Table (9.4.2) (for $a = .05$) in block $u$ (the number of IVs in set $B$) and the column for the specified power. For $v$ we select a trial value, usually $v = 120$, enter the trial $\lambda$ in one of the above three formulas for $N$, and iterate if necessary using Formula (9.4.2), as illustrated in the previous examples.

For the special Case 1-1, where a single IV, $X$, makes up set $B$, $N$ from the above formulas gives the necessary sample size for the $t$ (or $F$) test of any of the partial correlation or regression coefficients of $X$.

### Illustrative Examples

**9.21**   The sociological investigation of attitude toward socialized medicine addressed itself in example 9.8 to the power of the $F$ test of education from which age has been partialled, using $a = .01$, $N = 90$, and positing $f^2 = .16$. Because of anticipated curvilinear relationships, both education and age were represented as power polynomials, education (set $B$) as a quadratic ($u = 2$), and age (set $A$) as a cubic ($w = 3$). For those specifications, the power for the test of $B \cdot A$ was found to be .77. What $N$ would be necessary for power to be .80? The specification summary is:

$$a = .01, \qquad u = 2, \qquad f^2 = .16, \qquad \text{power} = .80.$$

Table 9.4.1 (for $a = .01$) gives in block $u = 2$, power $= .80$, $\lambda = 14.2$ at trial $v = 120$. Substituting in Equation (9.4.6) gives $N = 14.2/.16 + 3 = 92$, which implies via (9.3.7) that $v = 92 - 2 - 3 - 1 = 86$. Reiterating with (9.4.2) yields $\lambda = 14.5$ and thus $N = 14.5/.16 + 3 = 94$, which is four more cases than originally planned for the .03 increase in power.

Now consider that in the same investigation, in example 9.17 for the Case 0 test on age, the specifications ($a = .01$, $u = 3$, $f^2 = .15$, power $= .80$) resulted in $N = 108$ cases. For this $N$, the power for the test on education partialling age may be found by determining from formula (9.3.8) that $\lambda = .16(3 + 102 + 1) = 17.0$, which, from power Table 9.3.1 yields for $u = 2$, $v = 102$, by interpolation, power $= .87$.

**9.22**   In another phase of the same sociological investigation of ASM correlates described in example 9.10, the effect of ethnic group membership, controlling (adjusting) for age and education (represented polynomially) was under scrutiny. This is an analysis of covariance since set $B$ is comprised of 4 ($= u$) artificial variates carrying information about group membership (in one of five groups). Set $A$ now contains the 5 ($= w$) covariate IVs carrying age and education information. It was posited that the covariates accounted for .25 ($= R^2_{Y \cdot A}$) of the ASM variance, to which ethnic group membership added another .05, thus $R^2_{Y \cdot A,B} - R^2_{Y \cdot A} = .05$, $R^2_{Y \cdot A,B} = .30$, and the Case 1 $f^2$ of (9.2.3) is $.05/(1 - .30) = .0714$. When to these specifications are added **a** = .01 and **N** = 90, it was found that the power of the **F** test on ethnicity partialling age and education (i.e., the overall **F** test on the adjusted ethnic group means of the analysis of covariance) was only .24, far less than had been found for age (example 9.2) and for education with age partialled (example 9.8). Apparently sample sizes of about 100 are too small to provide a good chance of demonstrating unique ("pure") ethnic group differences for the ES which is anticipated. Well, how large must **N** be for this test to have power = .80? The specifications are:

$$a = .01, \qquad u = 4, \qquad f^2 = .0714, \qquad \text{power} = .80.$$

Table 9.4.1 in block **u** = 4 for column power = .80 gives λ = 17.6 for a trial **v** = 120. Then (9.4.6) gives **N** = 17.6/.0714 + 5 = 251. This implies (9.3.7) **v** = 251 − 4 − 5 − 1 = 241. Reiteration with (9.4.2) yields λ = 17.1, hence (9.4.6) **N** = 17.1/.0714 + 5 = 244. This is a rather large sample, and it helps not a bit to use the alternative formula (9.4.7)—it gives, as it must, the same result. This test demands $2\frac{1}{2}$ times the **N** required by the other, and if **N** cannot be so increased, either the investigator must reconcile himself to a poor chance of detecting the ethnic group differences in ASM or the specifications must be changed. The only feasible possibility is a shift of **a** = .01 to .05. In Table 9.4.2 for **u** = 4, trial **v** = 120, power = .80, we find λ = 12.3, which yields **N** = 12.3/.0714 + 5 = 177, which by (9.4.2) iterates to **N** = 176. This is a substantial reduction from 244, but still twice the number for .80 power in the other two tests.

**9.23**   In the study described in example 9.11, three different methods of infant day care assigned to different centers were to be compared on various outcome criteria after controlling for socioeconomic status, family composition, ethnic group membership, and age at entry (set **A**, **w** = 8). Set **B** contains the 2 (= **u**) IVs which code group (method, center) membership. For a given criterion, the ES for methods was expressed as a squared multiple partial correlation: $R^2_{YB \cdot A}$ = .10, i.e., 10% of the set **A**-adjusted criterion variance was expected to be accounted for by method group membership. As described there, **N** was fixed and power then found. Now we assume that the planning, including the decision as to **N**, is done in advance (as it ideally should be). Assume that **a** = .01, and that the power desired is .90. The complete specifications are thus:

$$a = .01, \qquad u = 2, \qquad R^2_{YB \cdot A} = .10, \qquad \text{power} = .90.$$

In Table 9.4.1, for **u** = 2, power = .90, we find λ = 18.0 for the trial **v** = 120. Since ES is expressed as $R^2_{Y \cdot B}$, Equation (9.4.8) is used: **N** = 18.0 (1 − .10)/.10 + 8 = 170, which iterates to 169.

In investigations involving many dependent variables, hypotheses, and significance tests on a single sample, the power analyses of the tests will result in varying **N** demands. These will need to be reconciled by taking into account the relative importance of the tests, and the available resources in terms of subjects, time, and cost. In this process, it may be necessary (as we have already seen) to reconsider some of the specifications, particularly **a** and the power desired (see Cohen & Cohen, 1983, p. 162).

**9.24** Return yet once more to the problem in personnel selection of examples 9.1 and 9.12. In the latter, a strategy was considered for dropping two of the five IVs in the regression equation in the interests of reducing selection costs by testing whether they significantly (**a** = .05) increase the sample $R^2$ provided by the other three, dropping them if they fail to do so. This is a Case 1 MRC test, with set **B** made up of the 2 ( = **u**) IVs under scrutiny, and set **A** of the other 3 ( = **w**). It was posited that all five had a population PV of .10 ( = $R^2_{Y \cdot A,B}$), and that set **B** uniquely accounted for .04 ( = $R^2_{Y \cdot (B \cdot A)}$) of that amount. It was found that **N** = 95 resulted in such low power (.42) that this planned strategy would be a poor one.

We now ask what **N** would be required to make the nonsignificance of **B·A** an effective basis for the decision to omit the two variables. To determine this, we need to decide how large a risk he would be prepared to run of dropping the two variables when they, in fact, added .04 to $R^2$. This is a Type II error — **b** is the rate of failing to reject a false null hypothesis. Assume he decides **b** = .10, so the power desired is .90. Now the specifications are complete:

$$\mathbf{a} = .05, \qquad \mathbf{u} = 2, \qquad R^2_{Y \cdot (A \cdot B)} = .04 \qquad \text{power} = .90.$$
$$1 - R^2_{Y \cdot A,B} = .90,$$

Table 9.4.2 gives $\lambda$ = 12.8 for **u** = 2, trial **v** = 120, power = .90. Formula (9.4.7) then gives **N** = 12.8 (.90)/.04 + 3 = 291. Reiterating with **v** = 291 − 2 − 3 − 1 = 285 via (9.4.2) gives $\lambda$ = 12.7 and **N** = 289. He must then do a cost-benefit analysis to decide whether the cost of the research on **N** = 291 cases warrants the saving to be realized by dropping the two variables with that degree of confidence (.90) that as much as .04 of the criterion variance will not be lost. A lesser degree of confidence, say power = .80, leads to $\lambda$ = 9.7, and **N** = 220. This is more data for his cost-benefit analysis: is the saving of 32% (relative to **N** = 291) worth rejection odds of only four to one (compared to nine to one)?

Later in example 9.12, an alternate strategy of dropping either (or both) of the two IVs on grounds of nonsignificance (**a** = .05) was considered, positing that it (**X**) accounted for .03 ( = $r^2_{Y(X \cdot A)}$) of the **Y** variance uniquely among the five predictors, while the total PV accounted for was .10 ( =

$R^2_{Y \cdot A,B}$), as before. This is Case 1-1, since set **B** contains only 1 (= **u**) IV, set **A** now containing the other 4 (= **w**). It was found that for **N** = 95, power was only .33 for the two **t** (or **F**) tests. Again, we invert the problem and ask what **N** would be required for power to be .90. The specifications:

$$a = .05, \quad u = 1, \quad r^2_{Y(X \cdot A)} = .03 \quad \text{power} = .90.$$
$$1 - R^2_{Y \cdot A,B} = .90,$$

In block **u** = 1 of Table 9.4.2, for both **v** = 120 and **v** = ∞, λ = 10.5 at power = .90. Thus, **N** = 10.5 (.90)/.04 + 3 = 319 (with no iteration necessary). Even for power = .80, for both **v** = 120 and **v** = ∞, λ = 7.8, so **N** = 7.8 (.90)/.04 + 3 = 238.

The strategy described here parallels that which may be used to "prove" the null hypothesis (see Section 1.5.5). Of course, $H_0$ cannot literally be proved. It is usually a statement that the ES is (exactly) zero, and nothing short of a sample of infinite size, hence the population, can prove such a statement. But in many circumstances, all that is intended by "proving" the null hypothesis is that the ES is not necessarily zero but small enough to be negligible, i.e., no larger than **i** (Section 1.5.5). How large **i** is will vary with the substantive context. Assume, for example, that ES is expressed as $f^2$, and that the context is such as to consider $f^2$ no larger than .02 to be negligible; thus **i** = .02. Then, one sets a large value for power, say .95, hence the Type II error probability, **b** = .05. If one then sets **a** at some conventionally small value, say .05, and specifies the appropriate value for **u** (say 3), the specifications for the necessary **N** are complete, i.e.:

$$a = .05, \quad u = 3, \quad f^2 = .02, \quad \text{power} = .95 \quad (b = .05).$$

For a trial value of **v** = ∞, Table 9.4.2 gives for **v** = 3 and power = .95, λ = 17.2, hence (for Case 0) **N** = 860, which iterates to **N** = 863. If one then draws that large a sample, and performs the **F** test, if it proves to be not significant, then one can accept as "proven," not the $H_0 : f^2 = 0$, but rather the proposition that $f^2$ is negligibly small, i.e., not as large as .02 (= **i**), since if it were that large, the probability of rejecting it was .95. Thus, the risk of failing to reject it, the Type II error is **b** = .05. By such means, we can take as "proven" the hypothesis that ES is negligibly small, <**i**, at the **b** level of confidence (not literally the null hypothesis at the **a** level of confidence).

For the somewhat arbitrary specifications used above, the **N** required was at least (depending on **w** and **z**) 863. However, for any reasonably small value of **i** and reasonably large power, the necessary **N** for such a demonstration will always be large by the usual standards of most areas of behavioral science. But that is what it takes to "prove" the null hypothesis. The frequently encountered statements in research reports that something has "no effect on" or is "not related to" something else, on the strength of a nonsignificant result with $N = 30$ or 50, or 100, are clearly unwarranted, even when "no" is qualified, as intended, to mean negligible. They are yet further symptoms of the relative neglect of power analysis in research inference in the behavioral sciences.

9.4.3    CASE 2: TEST OF $R^2_{Y \cdot A,B} - R^2_{Y \cdot A}$, MODEL 2 ERROR.    The determination of $N$ proceeds here exactly as in Case 1, except that $PV_E$ is now $1 - R^2_{Y \cdot A,B,C}$; set $C$ is recruited to reduce $PV_E$, while not involved in the definition of the source of $Y$ variance being tested. Since Model 2 error $df$ is now $v = N - u - w - z - 1$, substituting in the general formula (9.4.1) and solving for $N$ gives

$$(9.4.9) \qquad\qquad N = \frac{\lambda}{f^2} + w + z.$$

Expressing Case 2 $f^2$ as a function of the three $R^2$s involved then gives

$$(9.4.10) \qquad\qquad N = \frac{\lambda(1 - R^2_{Y \cdot A,B,C})}{R^2_{Y \cdot A,B} - R^2_{Y \cdot A}} + w + z.$$

As in Case 0 and 1, $\lambda$ is found by entering the table for the specified $a$ in block $u$ (the number of IVs in set B) and the column for the specified power. For $v$ we select a trial value (usually $v = 120$, since it is the middle value of the span that covers most research). $\lambda$ is then entered in either (9.4.9) or (9.4.10) to find $N$, and, if necessary, the process is iterated using (9.4.2).

### Illustrative Examples

**9.25**    In the research on factors associated with a length of stay $(Y)$ in a psychiatric hospital (example 9.13), three groups of variables in a causal hierarchy were to be considered: five demographic-socioeconomic IVs $(D)$, three psychiatric history variables $(H)$, and four symptom scale scores determined at time of admission $(S)$. The tests to be performed were for $D$, $H \cdot D$, and $S \cdot D$, $H$, this pattern reflecting the presumed causal priority of the three factors. Since the $PV_E$ is $1 - R^2_{Y \cdot D,H,S}$, the tests of $D$ and $H \cdot D$ are Case 2 tests. The significance criterion is $a = .01$ throughout.

It was posited that $D$ accounted for .10 of the $Y$ variance, $H \cdot D$ for .06, and $S \cdot D, H$ for .04. The additivity of semipartial $R^2$s in this type of hierarchical pattern implies that $R^2_{Y \cdot D,H,S} = .10 + .06 + .04 = .20$, so the Model 2 $PV_E = 1 - .20 = .80$ throughout. For the test on $H \cdot D$ (letting $H = $ set $B$, $D = $ set $A$, and $S = $ set $C$), the $f^2$ from formula (9.2.4) is $.06/.80 = .075$. When

$N = 200$, it was found that the power of the test on **H**·**D** was .74. To find the $N$ necessary for power to be .80, the specifications are:

$$a = .01, \qquad u = 3, \qquad f^2 = .075 \qquad \text{power} = .80.$$

For these specifications, Table 9.4.1 gives $\lambda = 16.1$ for a trial $v = 120$. Equation (9.4.9) then gives $N = 16.1/.075 + 5 + 4 = 224$, which through iteration becomes $N = 220$.

The test of **D** is also a Case 2 test, since neither **H** nor **S** enter in the numerator of the F ratio, but are both involved in determining the $PV_E$, i.e., the $3 + 4 = 7 (= z)$ IVs of these two groups comprise set **C**, while, since no partialling is involved in **D** (set **B**), set **A** is empty. The Case 2 $f^2$ for **D** is thus $.10/.80 = .125$. For $N = 200$, it was found that the power of the test of **D** was .92. What $N$ would be required for power to be .95?

$$a = .01, \qquad u = 5, \qquad f^2 = .125, \qquad \text{power} = .95.$$

Table 9.3.1 gives (for $u = 5$, power $= .95$) $\lambda = 27.4$ for $v = 120$, so (9.4.9) then gives $N = 27.4/.125 + 0 + 7 = 226$; iteration yields $\lambda = 26.7$ and $N = 221$.

When the power of the test on **S**·**D**, **H** was found in example 9.13, given its small ES ($f^2 = .05$), with $N = 200$, it was found to be only .44 at $a = .01$ and .69 at $a = .05$. Raising $N$ from 200 to 221 increases $\lambda$ from 9.6 to 10.4 and increases power at $a = .01$ and .05 respectively to .49 and .72 (interpolating in block $u = 4$ in Tables 9.3.1 and 9.3.2.) Assume then that the test of **S**·**D**, **H** is to be performed at $a = .05$. $N = 221$ gives power of .72 — what $N$ is required to raise this to .80?

$$a = .05, \qquad u = 4, \qquad f^2 = .05, \qquad \text{power} = .80.$$

For these specifications, Table 9.4.2 gives $\lambda = 12.3$, which is iterated to 12.1. This is a Case 1 test: Formula (9.4.6) gives $N = 12.1/.05 + 8 = 250$. (This may also be treated as a special case of Case 2 with set **C** empty, with the same result — see example 9.13.) Thus, if the test on **S**·**D**, **H** is important to the investigation, and if the circumstances permit this increase in **N**, it would be clearly very desirable to do so.

**9.26**  Example 9.14 described the power analysis of a $2 \times 3 \times 4$ (**S** $\times$ **G** $\times$ **K**) factorial design with unequal cell frequencies as a Case 2 MRC problem. It had previously been power-analyzed as an orthogonal factorial design analysis of variance in example 8.6 and 8.7 and the determination of **N** for two of the **F** tests was demonstrated in example 8.14. We now consider for these two tests the determination of **N** when considered as Case 2 of an

MRC analysis. Repetition of the details of how interaction IVs are created and how the sets are defined is omitted here — the reader is referred to example 9.14 for these; only the highlights and specifications are given.

Fixed factorial designs are traditionally analyzed with all main effects and interaction sources of Y variance removed from error, so $PV_E$ is the complement of the PV accounted for by all $u + w + z = 23 (= 2 \times 3 \times 4 - 1)$ IVs which collectively carry the cell membership information. For the test on the $G \times K$ interaction, whose $f^2$ was posited as .0625 and $u = 6$, the power at $a = .05$ was found to be .40 when (total) $N = 120$ was assumed. To attain a conventional power of .80 for this test, what $N$ would be required? The relevant specifications are:

$$a = .05, \quad u = 6, \quad f^2 = .0625, \quad \text{power} = .80.$$

In Table 9.4.2, for $u = 6$ and power $= .80$, at trial $v = 120$, $\lambda = 14.3$. Substitution in (9.4.9) gives $N = 14.3/.0625 + 5 + 12 = 246$, which upon iteration (9.4.2) becomes $N = 241$ (in close agreement with $N = 240$ found for this test in example 8.14). This large $N$ is partly a consequence of the large df for $G \times K$, $u = 6$. Were $u = 1$, the necessary $N$ would be 143. (See the discussion of the power of tests of interactions in examples 8.7 and 8.8).

The $K$ main effect (literally $K \cdot S$, $G$ in a nonorthogonal design), with $u = 3$ was posited to have $f^2 = .16$ in example 9.14 (as it was in example 8.7). At $a = .05$, with $N = 120$, its $F$ test was found to have power $= .92$. If only this test were considered, the experiment could be reduced in size if one were content to have power $= .80$. By how much?

$$a = .05, \quad u = 3, \quad f^2 = .16, \quad \text{power} = .80.$$

This works out to a $\lambda = 11.1$ at the trial $v = 120$, which iterates to $\lambda = 11.4$ and, via (9.4.9), $N = 11.4/.16 + 5 + 15 = 91$, a reduction of 32% in $N$. (Unfortunately, this is not the only test to consider — we saw above that the $G \times K$ test requires 241 cases.)

**9.27** As the final example, we cope with the problem of setting $N$ to provide an adequate test of the curvilinearity of a regression. In example 9.15, we returned to the sociological investigation of the relationship of attitude toward socialized medicine (ASM $= Y$) to age to determine the power of tests which would appraise the shape of this relationship. Age was represented polynomially as $X$, $X^2$, and $X^3$, and it posited that this group of 3 IVs accounted for .13 of the ASM variance (hence $PV_E = .87$). It was also posited that $X$ alone (linear age) could account for .08 of the ASM variance, the balance (.05) requiring the curvilinear aspects $X^2$ and $X^3$. When $N$ was taken as 90, at $a = .01$ it was found that the test of the linear component of age had power of only .59, but that at $a = .05$, it reached a satisfactory power of .80.

The analysis of the curvilinear components proved to be another matter entirely. Treating $X^2$ and $X^3$ as set **B** ($u = 2$), and **X** as set **A**, $R^2_{Y \cdot A,B} - R^2_{Y \cdot A} = .13 - .08 = .05$, and $f^2 = .0575$; at $a = .05$, $u = 2$, for $N = 90$, power was only .50. Even when all the .05 curvilinear variance was assigned to $X^2$ (actually $X^2 \cdot X$), so that $u$ was reduced from 2 to 1, power for $N = 90$ at $a = .05$ was still only .60.

What **N** would be required for the **F** test of the $X^2$, $X^3$ pair to give power $= .80$?

$$a = .05, \qquad u = 2, \qquad f^2 = .0575, \qquad \text{power} = .80.$$

Table 9.4.2 gives for these specifications $\lambda = 9.7$ which is unchanged by iteration, so (9.4.9) yields $N = 9.7/.0575 + 1 + 1 = 171$, about twice the **N** originally considered.

Even if all the curvilinearity is assigned to $X^2$, **u** becomes 1, and for power $= .80$, **N** works out to 139.

The amount of curvilinearity of ASM on age posited here is not negligible — it would be readily perceived, for example, in a scatter diagram. Yet it would take an **N** of $150 - 200$ for adequate power to demonstrate it statistically.

# CHAPTER 10

# Set Correlation and Multivariate Methods

## 10.1 INTRODUCTION AND USE

The introduction to the preceding chapter described how multiple regression and correlation analysis (MRC) has come in recent years to be understood as a flexible data-analytic procedure because of its generality. The examples in that chapter demonstrated that it subsumed as special cases not only simple correlation and regression, but also the analysis of variance (ANOVA) and the analysis of covariance (ANCOVA). Moreover, its generality makes possible novel analytic forms, for example, the Analysis of Partial Variance (see, for example, Cohen & Cohen, 1983, pp. 403–406, and example 9.8).

As a data-analytic system, MRC is general because it is a realization of the univariate general linear model, univariate because however many independent variables it may employ, it deals with only one dependent variable at a time. The *multivariate* general linear model is a further generalization that deals with sets of dependent variables simultaneously. Each standard univariate method, e.g., ANOVA, ANCOVA, has its analogous multivariate method, multivariate analysis of variance (MANOVA), and multivariate analysis of covariance (MANCOVA). In the mathematics, the **N** values of a single variable are replaced by the **N** *sets* (vectors) of values of a group of variables and the latter are treated simultaneously by matrix-algebraic operations.

Set correlation (SC) is a realization of the multivariate general linear model and thus a generalization of multiple correlation (Cohen, 1982). Cohen & Cohen (1983) and Pedhazur (1982) serve as general references to

MRC as a general (univariate) data-analytic system. SC can employ all the coding devices, error models, and analytic strategies of MRC not only for independent variables, but also for dependent variables. Most important, the use of partialling (residualization) of sets by other sets, used for a variety of purposes in MRC for independent variables, becomes available for the dependent variables as well in SC.

The fact that SC is a multivariate generalization of MRC, which is in turn a generalization of the standard univariate methods, makes of SC a flexible data-analytic tool that subsumes contemporary standard methods as special cases and makes possible the generation of novel procedures that are uniquely appropriate to the special circumstances cast up in research in behavioral science.

An extensive exposition of SC is obviously beyond the scope of this chapter. The reader will need to refer to the basic reference, Cohen (1982), which is reprinted in Cohen & Cohen (1983, Appendix 4). Unbiased (shrunken) estimators of measures of set correlation are given by Cohen & Nee (1984). A personal computer program for SC, SETCOR, is a SYSTAT supplementary module (Cohen, 1989), and a Fortran IV program for SC is described by Cohen & Nee (1983).

Although this chapter is oriented toward SC, which provides its framework, the power-analytic procedures for the standard multivariate methods are covered as special cases.

10.1.1   MULTIVARIATE $R^2_{Y,X}$. Many measures of association between two sets of variables have been proposed (Cramer & Nicewander, 1979; Cohen, 1982). Of these, $R^2_{Y,X}$, the multivariate $R^2$ between a set $Y$ made up of $k_Y$ variables and a set $X$ made up of $k_X$ variables, a direct generalization of multiple $R^2$, provides the basis for the effect size measure used in this chapter. Using determinants of correlation matrices,

$$(10.1.1)\quad R^2_{Y,X} = 1 - \frac{|\boldsymbol{R}_{YX}|}{|\boldsymbol{R}_Y|\,|\boldsymbol{R}_X|},$$

where   $\boldsymbol{R}_{YX}$ is the full correlation matrix of the $Y$ and $X$ variables,
   $\boldsymbol{R}_Y$ is the matrix of correlations among the variables of set $Y$, and
   $\boldsymbol{R}_X$ is the matrix of correlations among the variables of set $X$.

This equation also holds when covariance or sums of products matrices replace the correlation matrices.

$R^2_{Y,X}$ may also be written as a function of the $q$ squared canonical correlations ($CR^2$) where $q = \min(k_Y, k_X)$, the number of variables in the smaller of the two sets:

(10.1.2)      $R^2_{Y.X} = 1 - (1 - CR^2_1)(1 - CR^2_2) \ldots (1 - CR^2_q).$

$R^2_{Y.X}$ is a generalization of the simple bivariate $r^2_{yx}$, and is properly interpreted as the proportion of the generalized variance or multivariance of set **Y** accounted for by set **X** (or vice versa, because like all product-moment correlation coefficients, it is symmetrical). Multivariance is the generalization of the univariate concept of variance to a set of variables and is defined as the determinant of the set's variance-covariance matrix. One may interpret proportions of multivariance much as one does proportions of variance of a single variable. Indeed, in the multivariate context of this chapter, the term "variance" when applied to a set of variables should be understood to mean "generalized variance" or "multivariance." $R^2_{Y.X}$ may also be interpreted geometrically as the degree of overlap of the spaces defined by the two sets, and is therefore invariant over nonsingular transformations (rotations) of the two sets, so that, for example, $R^2_{Y.X}$ does not change with changes in the coding of nominal scales. See Cohen (1982) for the justification of these statements and a discussion of these and other properties of $R^2_{Y.X}$.

Sets **Y** and **X** are to be understood as generic. Set **Y** may be a set of dependent variables **D**, or a set of dependent variables **D** from which another set **C** has been partialled, represented as **D•C**. Similarly, set **X** may be a set of independent variables **B**, or a set of independent variables **B** from which another set **A** has been partialled, **B•A**. Note that because the number of variables in set **X**, $k_X$, is not affected by partialling, $k_X = k_B$ for all types of association. Similarly, $k_y$ always equals $k_D$.

There are thus five types of association possible in SC:

|  | Set **Y**-Dependent |  | Set **X**-Independent |
|---|---|---|---|
| Whole: | set **D** | with | set **B** |
| Partial: | set **D•A** | with | set **B•A** |
| **Y** semipartial: | set **D•C** | with | set **B** |
| **X** semipartial: | set **D** | with | set **B•A** |
| Bipartial: | set **D•C** | with | set **B•A** |

Following an SC analysis, further analytic detail is provided by output for MRC analyses for each generic **y** variable on the set of generic **x** variables (and the reverse), **y** and **x** being single variables in their respective sets. Thus, it is for the individual variables, partialled or whole depending on the type of association, that the regression and correlation results are provided.

10.1.2   SIGNIFICANCE TESTING: WILKS **L** AND THE RAO **F** TEST. There are several approaches to testing the null hypothesis in multivariate analysis (Olson, 1976). Stevens (1986) provides an excellent discussion of these (and of multivariate analysis, generally) and concludes that the major alternatives are of comparable power and robustness (Olson, 1974). I have chosen the approach using Wilks' **L** (or lambda) and the Rao **F** test because it is a generalization of the conventional **F** test for proportion of variance in MRC (9.1.2), because in several cases **L** is the complement of $R^2_{Y,X}$, and because it is reasonably robust (Cohen, 1982).

A fundamental function for significance testing and effect size measurement in multivariate analysis is Wilks' (1932) lambda or likelihood ratio,

$$(10.1.3) \qquad\qquad L = \frac{|E|}{|E + H|} \quad ,$$

where   **E** is an error matrix, and
         **H** is an hypothesis matrix.

Like $R^2_{Y,X}$, **L** is invariant over changes in the scaling of the matrix elements: In conventional MANOVA and MANCOVA, these matrices are expressed in terms of sums of squares and products, and in SC, as covariance or correlation matrices. The values for **H** and **E** depend on the type of association and error model used (Cohen & Cohen, 1983; Cohen, 1982):

Model 1 error.   The residual variance remaining in set **Y** after the variance associated with sets **B** and **A** (when **A** exists) is removed. (This is exemplified for MRC in Cases 0 and 1 in Section 9.1.)

Model 2 error.   The residual variance of Model 1 error is reduced by removing from it the variance associated with a set **G** of independent variables not involved in the hypothesis. Error Model 2 is traditionally used, for example, when within cell error is used to test a main effect or interaction in ANOVA or MANCOVA (Sections 9.3.3, 10.3.5, 10.3.6).

Cohen (1982, Table 2) gives the matrix expressions for **H** and the error matrices of the two models for all five types of association. When Model 1 error is used, for all but the bipartial type of association, it can be shown that

$$(10.1.4) \qquad\qquad L = 1 - R^2_{Y,X},$$

so that **L** is simply the complement of the proportion of set **Y**'s generalized variance accounted for by set **X**; **L** thus measures degree of association backwards: small values of **L** imply strong association, and conversely.

Once **L** is determined for a sample, Rao's **F** test (1975) may be applied in order to test the null hypothesis that there is no linear association between sets **X** and **Y** (Cohen, 1982; Cohen & Nee, 1983; Eber & Cohen, 1987). As adapted for SC, the test is quite general, covering all five types of association and both error models. As should be the case, when $k_Y$ (or $k_X$) = 1, where multivariate $R^2_{Y,X}$ specializes to multiple $R^2_{y \cdot x}$ (or $R^2_{x \cdot y}$), the Rao **F** test specializes to the standard null hypothesis **F** test for a proportion of variance in MRC (9.1.2). For this case, and for the case where the smaller set is made up of no more than two variables, the Rao **F** test is exact; otherwise, it provides a good approximation.

$$(10.1.5) \qquad \mathbf{F} = (\mathbf{L}^{-1/\mathbf{S}} - 1)\frac{\mathbf{v}}{\mathbf{u}},$$

where

$$(10.1.6) \qquad \mathbf{u} = \text{numerator } \mathbf{df} = \mathbf{k_Y}\,\mathbf{k_X},$$

$$(10.1.7) \qquad \mathbf{v} = \text{denominator } \mathbf{df} = \mathbf{ms} + 1 - \mathbf{u}/2, \text{ where}$$

$$(10.1.8) \qquad \mathbf{m} = \mathbf{N} - \max{(\mathbf{k_C}, \mathbf{k_A} + \mathbf{k_G})} - (\mathbf{k_Y} + \mathbf{k_X} + 3)/2, \text{ and}$$

$$(10.1.9) \qquad \mathbf{s} = \sqrt{\frac{\mathbf{k^2_Y}\,\mathbf{k^2_X} - 4}{\mathbf{k^2_Y} + \mathbf{k^2_X} - 5}},$$

except that when $\mathbf{k^2_Y}\,\mathbf{k_X}^2 = 4$, $\mathbf{s} = 1$. For partial $\mathbf{R^2_{Y,X}}$, set $\mathbf{A}$ = set $\mathbf{C}$, so $\mathbf{k_A} = \mathbf{k_C}$ is the number of variables in the set that is being partialled, and for whole $\mathbf{R^2_{Y,X}}$, neither set $\mathbf{A}$ nor set $\mathbf{C}$ exists. Set $\mathbf{G}$ is the set of variables used for Model 2 error reduction (see Cohen, 1982, and Section 10.3). Recall that $\mathbf{k_Y}$ is $\mathbf{k_D}$ and $\mathbf{k_X}$ is $\mathbf{k_B}$ (because partialling has no effect on the number of variables), and that $\mathbf{k_C}$, $\mathbf{k_A}$, and $\mathbf{k_G}$ are zero when the set does not exist for the type of association or error model in question.

The statistical assumptions generalize from those described in Section 9.1 for a test of a variance proportion: the variables in set $\mathbf{X}$ are taken as fixed and those of set $\mathbf{Y}$ are assumed to be multivariate normal, but the test is fairly robust against assumption failure (Olson, 1974).[1]

Note that all of the foregoing has been concerned with testing the null hypothesis using the *sample* $\mathbf{R^2_{Y,X}}$ value and *sample* values of hypothesis and error matrices given in formula (10.1.3). The value reported in standard multivariate computer output as Wilks' $\mathbf{L}$ (lambda) is the likelihood ratio of determinants of observed sample results, subject to significance testing.

---

[1]Although this test assumes multivariate normality for the $\mathbf{Y}$ set, preliminary Monte Carlo results suggest that the test is quite robust for samples of 60 or more, even for discrete binary or trinary distributions.

10.1.3   SAMPLE AND POPULATION VALUES OF $R^2_{Y,X}$. Working in SC, one quickly discovers that sample values of $R^2_{Y,X}$ tend to run high. This is partly because, like all squared correlations (multiple $R^2$, simple $r^2$), it is positively biased; that is, on the average, it overestimates its population value. When the population $R^2_{Y,X} = 0$, the average or expected sample $R^2_{Y,X}$ is a function solely of the numerator (**u**) and denominator (**v**) degrees of freedom of the **F** test and the **s**:

$$(10.1.10) \qquad \mathbf{Exp_0}\,(R^2_{Y,X}) = 1 - \left(\frac{v}{v+u}\right)^2$$

(Cohen & Nee, 1984). It can be seen that as the product of the set sizes **u** increases relative to **v** (which is dominated by the sample size), $\mathbf{Exp_0}\,(R^2_{Y,X})$ increases. For example, consider the case of whole association between sets of $k_Y = 4$ and $k_X = 5$ variables for a sample of $N = 60$ cases. From Equation (10.1.9) (or Table 10.2.1 below), **s** = 3.32, **u** = 4 (5) = 20, and from (10.1.7) and (10.1.8), **v** = 170. Now, from (10.1.10), $\mathbf{Exp_0}(R^2_{Y,X}) = 1 - (170/(170 + 20))^{3.32} = .31$. This means that even when the population $R^2_{Y,X} = 0$, the average $R^2_{Y,X}$ value of 60-case samples drawn from the population will be .31, an apparently impressive value. If $N = 100$, **u** and **s** remain as before, but **v** is now 303, and $\mathbf{Exp_0}\,(R\,(R^2_{Y,X}) = .19$, still an apparently large value.

When the population $R^2_{Y,X} > 0$, too, sample $R^2_{Y,X}$'s exaggerate the proportion of variance accounted for, on the average. Cohen & Nee (1984, p. 911) provide a "shrinkage" formula for sample $R^2_{Y,X}$, that is, an almost unbiased estimate of the population value,

$$(10.1.11) \qquad R^2_{Y,X} = 1 - (1 - R^2_{Y,X})\left(\frac{v+u}{v}\right)^s.$$

Solving this equation for $R^2_{Y,X}$, we obtain an approximation of the expected (average) value of the sample $R^2_{Y,X}$ for a given value of the population $R^2_{Y,X}$:

$$(10.1.12) \qquad \mathbf{Exp_1}\,(R^2_{Y,X}) = 1 - (1 - R^2_{Y,X})\left(\frac{v}{v+u}\right)^s.$$

Thus, for example, for the previous specifications ($k_y = 4$, $k_x = 5$, $N = 60$, which led to **u** = 20, **v** = 170, **s** = 3.32), when the population $R^2_{Y,X} = .20$, the average sample $R^2_{Y,X} = 1 - (1 - .20)\,(170\,/(170 + 20))^{3.32} = .45$. Changing **N** to 100 (which makes **v** = 303) results in an average sample $R^2_{Y,X} = .35$. If we posit a population $R^2_{Y,X} = .10$, then for $N = 60$, $\mathbf{Exp_1}\,(R^2_{Y,X}) = .38$, and for $N = 100$, it equals .27. Small wonder that sample $R^2_{Y,X}$'s run high. The moral is that analysts should not be seduced by the relatively large sample $R^2_{Y,X}$'s they are likely to encounter to expect that population $R^2_{Y,X}$'s are similarly large. The sample $R^2_{Y,X}$ is a biased estimate of its population value, potentially strongly so, and much more so than is the multiple $R^2$. Incidentally, Equations (10.1.10), (10.1.11), and (10.1.12) specialize to the correct values for multiple $R^2$, and simple $r^2$. For example, for multiple $R^2$, $k_Y = 1$, $k_X = u$, so $s = 1$ and $v = N - k_X - 1$), so (10.1.11) becomes the standard Wherry shrinkage formula for $R^2$ (Cohen & Cohen, 1983, pp. 105–106).

However, the tendency for $R^2_{Y,X}$'s to be high is not entirely a consequence of the positive bias of sample values. Multivariate $R^2_{Y,X}$ is cumulative in the same sense as multiple $R^2$ is cumulative: just as a multiple $R^2$ must be at least as large as the largest $r^2$ between the (single) dependent variable and the $k_X$ independent variables, so must $R^2_{Y,X}$ be at least as large as the largest of the $k_Y$ multiple $R^2$ between the $k_Y$ variables and the set of $k_X$ variables or the $k_X$ multiple $R^2$ between the $k_X$ variables and the set of $k_Y$ variables. The addition of a variable can never result in the reduction of either multiple $R^2$ or multivariate $R^2_{Y,X}$, and will almost always result in an increase. Such, however, is not the case for $f^2$ in SC, as the next section shows.

## 10.2   THE EFFECT SIZE INDEX: $f^2$

Since SC is a generalization of univariate methods, we can generalize the $f$ of ANOVA and $f^2$ of MRC for use as the effect size (ES) measure in SC. The last section was concerned with sample results. Now, as has been the case throughout this book, we define the ES *in the population*.

First, we restate Wilks' likelihood ratio:

$$(10.2.1) \qquad\qquad L = \frac{|E|}{|E + H|},$$

but specify that $E$ and $H$ now refer to population error and hypothesis matrices.

Then, we generalize the $f^2$ signal to noise ratio as our ES measure:

$$(10.2.2) \qquad \begin{aligned} f^2 &= L^{-1/S} - 1 \\ &= \frac{\sqrt[s]{|E + H|} - \sqrt[s]{|E|}}{\sqrt[s]{|E|}}; \end{aligned}$$

the latter form makes it apparent that it is a signal to noise ratio. Note the parallel to MRC: $f^2$ defined on the population is the ES portion of the F test of equation (10.1.5). That equation (10.2.2) is in fact a generalization of the $f^2$ of MRC can be seen when we specialize it for the MRC case where set Y contains a single variable: when $k_Y = 1$, whatever the value of $k_X$, we see from (10.1.9) that $s = 1$. If $s = 1$ and equation (10.1.4) are then substituted in (10.2.2), the Model 1 error equations for $f^2$ in MRC, (9.2.2) and (9.2.3), result.

**10.2.1  $f^2$, s, L, AND $R^2_{Y,X}$.**   The relationship between $f^2$ and $R^2_{Y,X}$ is complex. First, $f^2$ is a function of the $s^{th}$ root of **L**, where **s** is the function of $k_Y$ and $k_X$ given in Equation (10.1.9) (and is not in general an integer). Second, **L** is a function of the determinants of the population hypothesis and error matrices (10.2.1), and these vary with type of association and error model (formulas given in Cohen, 1982, Table 5). Since $R^2_{Y,X}$ is a relatively accessible proportion of variance measure, and because in simple cases, **L** is the complement of $R^2_{Y,X}$ (10.1.4), it is conceptually useful to seek an understanding of $f^2$ by means of these "$R^2$-complementary" cases.

First consider **s**. Table 10.2.1 provides solutions of equation (10.1.9) for some values of $k_Y$ and $k_X$; it gives **s** as a function of the sizes of the two sets. Since (10.1.5) is symmetrical in $k_Y$ and $k_X$, the two are interchangeable. Recall that $q = \min(k_Y, k_X)$. When **q** equals 1 (as in MRC) or 2, $s = q$. For $q > 2$, $s < q$. With **q** held constant, as the larger set increases, **s** approaches **q**. Note particularly that the size of the smaller set strongly influences the value of **s**.

In turn, **s** strongly influences the effect size, $f^2$, as can be seen in formula (10.2.1). Table 10.2.2 shows how $f^2$ varies as a function of **s** and **L**. The table also gives the $R^2_{Y,X}$ values for the $R^2$-complementary cases. (Remember that these are *population* $R^2_{Y,X}$ values, smaller than the sample values one encounters in practice—see Section 10.1.) Note how for values of $R^2_{Y,X} < .10$, $f^2$ becomes very small when **s** increases to 4 or 5; i.e., when the smaller set contains 5 variables (see Table 10.2.1). Even fairly robust $R^2_{Y,X}$ values of .25 to .50 dwindle to quite modest $f^2$ values when **s** is as large as 5 and to rather small values when **s** is as large as 10.

Thus, Tables 10.2.1 and 10.2.2 teach us the first lesson about power in multivariate analysis: there is a price to be paid in ES magnitude in the employment of multiple dependent variables with multiple independent variables. When set **X** accounts for what appears to be a substantial proportion of the (generalized) variance of set **Y**, say = .30, if set **Y** contains 5 variables and set **X** no fewer, $s \approx 4$, and $f^2 = .09$ or less. Note that for the same proportion of variance, when there is only one dependent variable, i.e., in the (univariate) multiple correlation case, no matter how many variables in set **X**, $s = 1$, and $f^2 = .43$, a value *larger* than the $R^2_{Y,X}$ of .30. Note further that when $k_Y (= q)$ goes from 1 to 2, for the same .30 proportion of variance, $f^2$ drops to .20.

Large set sizes have a negative effect on power not only through their effect on $f^2$, but also through their effect on **u**, the numerator **df**. As noted

**Table 10.2.1**
s as a Function of $k_y$ and $k_x$

| $k_x$ | $k_y$=1 | 2 | 3 | 4 | 5 | 6 | 7 | 8 | 9 | 10 | 12 | 14 | 16 | 20 | 30 | 50 |
|---|---|---|---|---|---|---|---|---|---|---|---|---|---|---|---|---|
| 1 | 1 | | | | | | | | | | | | | | | |
| 2 | 1 | 2 | | | | | | | | | | | | | | |
| 3 | 1 | 2 | 2.43 | | | | | | | | | | | | | |
| 4 | 1 | 2 | 2.65 | 3.06 | | | | | | | | | | | | |
| 5 | 1 | 2 | 2.76 | 3.32 | 3.71 | | | | | | | | | | | |
| 6 | 1 | 2 | 2.83 | 3.49 | 4.00 | 4.39 | | | | | | | | | | |
| 7 | 1 | 2 | 2.87 | 3.62 | 4.21 | 4.69 | 5.08 | | | | | | | | | |
| 8 | 1 | 2 | 2.90 | 3.69 | 4.36 | 4.92 | 5.39 | 5.77 | | | | | | | | |
| 9 | 1 | 2 | 2.92 | 3.75 | 4.47 | 5.10 | 5.63 | 6.08 | 6.46 | | | | | | | |
| 10 | 1 | 2 | 2.94 | 3.79 | 4.56 | 5.24 | 5.83 | 6.34 | 6.78 | 7.16 | | | | | | |
| 12 | 1 | 2 | 2.95 | 3.85 | 4.68 | 5.44 | 6.12 | 6.74 | 7.28 | 7.76 | 8.56 | | | | | |
| 14 | 1 | 2 | 2.97 | 3.89 | 4.76 | 5.57 | 6.32 | 7.01 | 7.64 | 8.21 | 9.18 | 9.96 | | | | |
| 16 | 1 | 2 | 2.97 | 3.91 | 4.81 | 5.67 | 6.47 | 7.21 | 7.90 | 8.54 | 9.66 | 10.59 | 11.37 | | | |
| 20 | 1 | 2 | 2.98 | 3.94 | 4.88 | 5.79 | 6.64 | 7.47 | 8.43 | 8.99 | 10.34 | 11.52 | 12.54 | 14.18 | | |
| 30 | 1 | 2 | 2.99 | 3.98 | 4.94 | 5.90 | 6.83 | 7.75 | 8.64 | 9.51 | 11.17 | 12.72 | 14.15 | 16.67 | 21.24 | |
| 50 | 1 | 2 | 3.00 | 3.99 | 4.98 | 5.96 | 6.94 | 7.91 | 8.87 | 9.82 | 11.68 | 13.49 | 15.25 | 18.58 | 25.74 | 35.37 |

**Table 10.2.2**
$f^2$ as a function of **s** and **L** or $R^2_{Y,X}$

| | | | | $R^2_{Y,X}$ | | | | |
|---|---|---|---|---|---|---|---|---|
| | .04 | .06 | .08 | .10 | .12 | .15 | .20 | .25 |
| | | | | **L** | | | | |
| **s** | .96 | .94 | .92 | .90 | .88 | .85 | .80 | .75 |
| 1 | 04 | 06 | 09 | 11 | 14 | 18 | 25 | 33 |
| 2 | 02 | 03 | 04 | 05 | 07 | 08 | 12 | 15 |
| 2.5 | 02 | 03 | 03 | 04 | 05 | 07 | 09 | 12 |
| 3 | 01 | 02 | 03 | 04 | 04 | 06 | 08 | 10 |
| 3.5 | 01 | 02 | 02 | 03 | 04 | 05 | 07 | 09 |
| 4 | 01 | 02 | 02 | 03 | 03 | 04 | 06 | 07 |
| 4.5 | 01 | 01 | 02 | 02 | 03 | 04 | 05 | 07 |
| 5 | 01 | 01 | 02 | 02 | 03 | 03 | 05 | 06 |
| 5.5 | 01 | 01 | 02 | 02 | 02 | 03 | 04 | 05 |
| 6 | 01 | 01 | 01 | 02 | 02 | 03 | 04 | 05 |
| 6.5 | 01 | 01 | 01 | 02 | 02 | 03 | 03 | 05 |
| 7 | 01 | 01 | 01 | 02 | 02 | 02 | 03 | 04 |
| 8 | 01 | 01 | 01 | 01 | 02 | 02 | 03 | 04 |
| 9 | 00 | 01 | 01 | 01 | 01 | 02 | 03 | 03 |
| 10 | 00 | 01 | 01 | 01 | 01 | 02 | 02 | 03 |
| 12 | 00 | 01 | 01 | 01 | 01 | 01 | 02 | 02 |
| 15 | 00 | 00 | 01 | 01 | 01 | 01 | 01 | 02 |
| 20 | 00 | 00 | 00 | 01 | 01 | 01 | 01 | 01 |
| 30 | 00 | 00 | 00 | 00 | 00 | 01 | 01 | 01 |
| | | | | $R^2_{Y,X}$ | | | | |
| | .30 | .40 | .50 | .60 | .70 | .80 | .90 | |
| | | | | **L** | | | | |
| **s** | .70 | .60 | .50 | .40 | .30 | .20 | .10 | |
| 1 | 43 | 67 | 100 | 150 | 233 | 400 | 900 | |
| 2 | 20 | 29 | 41 | 58 | 83 | 124 | 216 | |
| 2.5 | 15 | 23 | 32 | 44 | 62 | 90 | 151 | |
| 3 | 13 | 19 | 26 | 36 | 49 | 71 | 115 | |
| 3.5 | 11 | 16 | 22 | 30 | 41 | 58 | 93 | |
| 4 | 09 | 14 | 19 | 26 | 35 | 50 | 78 | |
| 4.5 | 08 | 12 | 17 | 23 | 31 | 43 | 67 | |
| 5 | 07 | 11 | 15 | 20 | 27 | 38 | 58 | |
| 5.5 | 07 | 10 | 13 | 18 | 24 | 34 | 52 | |
| 6 | 06 | 09 | 12 | 16 | 22 | 31 | 47 | |
| 6.5 | 06 | 08 | 11 | 15 | 20 | 28 | 43 | |
| 7 | 05 | 08 | 10 | 14 | 19 | 26 | 39 | |
| 8 | 05 | 07 | 09 | 12 | 16 | 22 | 33 | |
| 9 | 04 | 06 | 08 | 11 | 14 | 20 | 29 | |
| 10 | 04 | 05 | 07 | 10 | 13 | 17 | 26 | |
| 12 | 03 | 04 | 06 | 08 | 11 | 14 | 21 | |
| 15 | 02 | 03 | 05 | 06 | 08 | 11 | 17 | |
| 20 | 02 | 03 | 04 | 05 | 06 | 08 | 12 | |

with regard to the power tables in Chapter 9, power decreases as **u** increases. Now in SC, as Equation (10.1.6) shows, **u** is equal to the *product* of the two set sizes. Thus, the effect of having many variables in either set takes its toll in power not only through the increase in **s** with its attendant decrease in $f^2$, but also through the increase in **u**. Multivariate or otherwise, the same old principle applies — the fewer variables the better — less is more (Cohen & Cohen, 1983, pp. 169–171).

10.2.2   "SMALL," "MEDIUM," AND "LARGE" $f^2$ VALUES.   The simplicity and familiarity of univariate ES measures has made the setting, explanation, and exemplification of operational or conventional definitions of small, medium, and large ES in the earlier chapters a comparatively easy task. With its dependence on set sizes and Wilks' **L** or $R^2_{Y,X}$, $f^2$ is neither simple nor familiar, nor is there much literature available from which to draw examples.

In the interest of consistency and continuity, we shall employ the same values as were used in the operational definitions for MRC. The implications of this are most readily perceived in the $R^2$-complementary cases. We have seen in Table 2.2.2 how a given $R^2_{Y,X}$ results in diminishing values of $f^2$ as **s** increases. Now, the relationship will be reversed and we shall see, for example, how $f^2$ for MRC (in the present context, where **s** = 1) implies a smaller (possibly much smaller) proportion of variance ($R^2_{Y,X}$) than the same $f^2$ in SC, where, with at least two variables in each set, **s** ≥ 2 (see Table 10.2.1).

The value of **L** or $R^2_{Y,X}$ implied by any given $f^2$ can be found by rewriting (10.2.2) as

(10.2.3) $$\mathbf{L} = (f^2 + 1)^{-\mathbf{S}}$$

which, when **L** = 1 − $R^2_{Y,X}$ becomes

(10.2.4) $$R^2_{Y,X} = 1 - (f^2 + 1)^{-\mathbf{S}}.$$

Table 10.2.3 gives the solution of these equations: the $R^2_{Y,X}$ (or 1 − **L**) values implied by $f^2$ as **s** increases. As the size of the smaller set, and therefore **s**, increases, any given level of the effect size, $f^2$, implies increasing $R^2_{Y,X}$. Table 10.2.3 will facilitate our understanding of the operational definitions of small, medium, and large $f^2$ values in terms of the implied $R^2_{Y,X}$ (and 1 − **L**) values.

Small Effect Size: $f^2$ = .02. In MRC, this implies $R^2$ = (.0196 =) .02 (see Section 9.2.2), as can be seen for **s** = 1 in Table 10.2.3. In SC, for 2 dependent variables (**s** = 2), $f^2$ = .02 implies $R^2_{Y,X}$ = .04, still small, but twice as large as for MRC. For large sets, let us say, for example, when $k_Y$ = 6 and $k_X$ = 8, **s** ≈ 5 and $f^2$ = .02 implies $R^2_{Y,X}$ = .10.

Medium Effect Size: $f^2 = .15$. While in MRC (where $s = 1$), this implies $R^2 = .13$, even for a modest $s = 2$, $f^2 = .15$ implies $R^2_{Y.X} = .25$ (Table 10.2.3). We are not accustomed to thinking of .25 of the variance amounting to only a medium ES—for a simple bivariate $r^2$, that was defined as a *large* effect (see Section 3.2.1). For large set sizes, say, when $s = 5$, $f^2 = .15$ implies $R^2_{Y.X} = .50$. Again we see how severely a proportion of variance is discounted under the stress of large set sizes.

Large Effect Size: $f^2 = .35$. In MRC, this implies $R^2 = .26$. In SC, for $s = 2$, $f^2 = .35$ implies $R^2_{Y.X} = .45$. Consider a somewhat larger value of $s$: for example when $s = 4$, which occurs when $k_Y = 5$, $k_X = 6$ (Table 10.2.1), $f^2 = .35$ implies $R^2_{Y.X} = .70$. When $s \approx 7$ (say, for $k_Y = 8$, $k_X = 14$, or for $k_Y = 7$, $k_X = 50$ or more, see Table 10.2.1), a large effect implies $R^2_{Y.X} = .88$.

I am even more diffident in offering the above operational definitions for $f^2$ in SC than for the other ESs in this book. Because of the novelty of SC and the neglect of the issue of the size of multivariate effects in standard methods, the definitions offered stem from no more reliable a source than my intuition. With the accumulation of experience, they may well require revision (I suspect downward).

Although Tables 10.2.1, 10.2.2, and 10.2.3 may be of some incidental use in facilitating calculation, they are offered primarily to help the reader get a feel for how set sizes influence $s$ and how $s$, in turn, mediates the relationship between the effect size measure, $f^2$, and $R^2_{Y.X}$ (in the $R^2$–complementary cases) and $L$. They should be of some use in making decisions in research planning.

10.2.3   SETTING $f^2$.   There are several alternative routes by which one can arrive at the $f^2$ value needed for power and sample size analysis:

1. *Using the Correlation Matrix and the SC program.*   The idea is to fool the SC program (Cohen & Nee, 1983; Eber & Cohen, 1987) into finding $f^2$ (as well as the degrees of freedom) for the power analysis. First, posit the alternate-hypothetical population matrix of correlation coefficients for all the variables in the analysis and enter them into the program as if they were sample results. Then, for problems where power is to be determined (Section 10.3), enter the specified value for $N$. When the program is run for the relevant type of association, it will produce a (phony) $F$ ratio and the (correct) degrees of freedom ($u$ and $v$). Since the $L^{-1/s} - 1$ term of (10.1.5) equals the $f^2$ given as (10.2.2), simple algebraic manipulation yields

(10.2.5) $$f^2 = F \frac{u}{v}.$$

Since power is fully determined by $f^2$, $u$, and $v$ (and $a$), this procedure will generally be preferred.

**Table 10.2.3**
$R^2_{Y,X}$ or $1 - L$ as a function of $f^2$ and s

| s | $f^2$ | | | | | | |
|---|---|---|---|---|---|---|---|
| | .02 | .05 | .10 | .15 | .20 | .25 | .30 |
| 1 | 02 | 05 | 09 | 13 | 17 | 20 | 23 |
| 2 | 04 | 09 | 17 | 24 | 31 | 36 | 41 |
| 2.5 | 05 | 11 | 21 | 29 | 37 | 43 | 48 |
| 3 | 06 | 14 | 25 | 34 | 42 | 49 | 54 |
| 3.5 | 07 | 16 | 28 | 39 | 47 | 54 | 60 |
| 4 | 08 | 18 | 32 | 43 | 52 | 59 | 65 |
| 4.5 | 09 | 20 | 35 | 47 | 56 | 63 | 69 |
| 5 | 09 | 22 | 38 | 50 | 60 | 67 | 73 |
| 5.5 | 10 | 24 | 41 | 54 | 63 | 71 | 76 |
| 6 | 11 | 25 | 44 | 57 | 67 | 74 | 79 |
| 6.5 | 12 | 27 | 46 | 60 | 69 | 77 | 82 |
| 7 | 13 | 29 | 49 | 62 | 72 | 79 | 84 |
| 8 | 15 | 32 | 53 | 67 | 77 | 83 | 88 |
| 9 | 16 | 36 | 58 | 72 | 81 | 87 | 91 |
| 10 | 18 | 39 | 61 | 75 | 84 | 89 | 93 |
| 12 | 21 | 44 | 68 | 81 | 89 | 93 | 96 |
| 15 | 26 | 52 | 76 | 88 | 94 | 96 | 98 |
| 20 | 33 | 62 | 85 | 94 | 97 | 99 | 99 |
| 30 | 45 | 77 | 94 | 98 | 100 | 100 | 100 |

| s | $f^2$ | | | | | | |
|---|---|---|---|---|---|---|---|
| | .35 | .40 | .50 | .60 | .70 | .80 | .90 |
| 1 | 26 | 29 | 33 | 38 | 41 | 44 | 47 |
| 2 | 45 | 49 | 56 | 61 | 65 | 69 | 72 |
| 2.5 | 53 | 57 | 64 | 69 | 73 | 77 | 80 |
| 3 | 59 | 64 | 70 | 76 | 80 | 83 | 85 |
| 3.5 | 65 | 69 | 76 | 81 | 84 | 87 | 89 |
| 4 | 70 | 74 | 80 | 85 | 88 | 90 | 92 |
| 4.5 | 74 | 78 | 84 | 88 | 91 | 93 | 94 |
| 5 | 78 | 81 | 87 | 90 | 93 | 95 | 96 |
| 5.5 | 81 | 84 | 89 | 92 | 95 | 96 | 97 |
| 6 | 83 | 87 | 91 | 94 | 96 | 97 | 98 |
| 6.5 | 86 | 89 | 93 | 95 | 97 | 98 | 98 |
| 7 | 88 | 91 | 94 | 96 | 98 | 98 | 99 |
| 8 | 91 | 93 | 96 | 98 | 99 | 99 | 99 |
| 9 | 93 | 95 | 97 | 99 | 99 | 99 | 100 |
| 10 | 95 | 97 | 98 | 99 | 100 | 100 | 100 |
| 12 | 97 | 98 | 99 | 100 | 100 | 100 | 100 |
| 15 | 99 | 99 | 100 | 100 | 100 | 100 | 100 |
| 20 | 100 | 100 | 100 | 100 | 100 | 100 | 100 |
| 30 | 100 | 100 | 100 | 100 | 100 | 100 | 100 |

Decimal points omitted. Read as X.XX.
$R^2_{Y,X}$ holds only for $R^2$-complementary cases. See text.

    When the problem is determining **N** (Section 10.4), simply supply the SC program with the correlation matrix as above together with an arbitrary value for $N$, say, $N = 1000$. Substituting the $F$, $u$, and $v$ produced by the program in (10.2.5) will yield the proper $f^2$.

   2.   *Using $R^2_{Y \cdot X}$.* For Model 1 error, use the following $L$ formulas for whole, partial, $Y$ semipartial, and $X$ semipartial association, respectively:

$$(10.2.6) \qquad\qquad L_W = 1 - R^2_{D \cdot B}$$

$$(10.2.7) \qquad\qquad L_P = 1 - R^2_{D \cdot A, B \cdot A}$$

$$(10.2.8) \qquad\qquad L_{YS} = 1 - R^2_{D \cdot C, B}$$

$$(10.2.9) \qquad\qquad L_{XS} = 1 - R^2_{D \cdot A, B \cdot A}.$$

Thus, $L$ is simply the complement of the appropriate $R^2_{Y \cdot X}$ in these cases, and $f^2$ is found from (10.2.2); i.e., as $L^{-1/S} - 1$. Note that the bipartial $f^2$ cannot be found by this $R^2$–complement route, and that to determine the $X$ semipartial $f^2$ by this procedure, it is the $R^2_{Y \cdot X}$ for the *partial* $R^2$ that is required, as is the case in MRC.

   With Model 2 error, set $G$ reduces the error variance from $|E_1|$ to $|E_2|$. Let $g$ express this reduction as a proportion, i.e.,

$$(10.2.10) \qquad\qquad g = |E_2|/|E_1|.$$

   The $f^2$ for Model 2 error is adequately approximated by dividing the Model 1 $f^2$ by $g$, thus

$$(10.2.11) \qquad\qquad f^2_2 = f^2_1/g.$$

   For example, assume that the type of association involved is $Y$ semipartial, and $f^2_1$ for Model 1 error is found from (10.2.8) and (10.2.2) to equal .12. The investigator estimates that the Model 2 error variance is .80 ($= g$) as large as the Model 1 error variance. The Model 2 $f^2_2$ is therefore $.12/.80 = .15$.

   This procedure avoids the necessity for positing each entry of what may well be a large correlation matrix in favor of positing a single $R^2_{Y \cdot X}$. But this road to $f^2$ may well be a rocky one, particularly when Model 2 error is to be employed.

   3.   *Using the operational ES definitions.*   In Section 10.2.2, values of $f^2$ of .02, .15, and .35 were proposed to operationally (or conventionally) define small, medium, and large ES, respectively, in SC. They were offered with at least as much diffidence as throughout this handbook. One would prefer, when possible, to use $f^2$ values specific to the problem at hand. The

operational definitions are most useful when there has been little multivariate analysis in the area under study to provide rough guidance in the sizes of effects than can be expected. They also serve usefully as conventions.

Analysts are of course not restricted to the values .02, .15, and .35. They can, for example, set $f^2 = .10$ as a "small to medium" ES, or .25 as a "medium to large" ES, or .50 as a "very large" ES.

It is generally helpful to check the implications of any given $f^2$ that the analyst plans to specify. For example, if one is considering setting $f^2$ at the medium .15 value, one should check the $R^2_{Y,X}$ (or $L$) that it implies, given the $s$ value that obtains, using Table 10.2.3. Conversely, if one has provisionally set $R^2_{Y,X}$, one should consider the magnitude of the $f^2$ that is implied relative to the operational definitions.

Despite the extent of commitment that it seems to entail, the first method, that of writing the full correlation matrix, is generally preferred. What commends it is the fact that it requires familiar product-moment correlations rather than either proportions of generalized variance ($R^2_{Y,X}$'s) or multivariate signal to noise ratios.

## 10.3   DETERMINING POWER

In Chapter 9, we saw that power in MRC is a function of the ES ($f^2$), the numerator ($u$) and denominator ($v$) degrees of freedom of the $F$ ratio, and the criterion for statistical significance ($a$). Under the pressure of this many parameters, unlike the earlier chapters, the power tables were written not for entry of the ES measure ($f^2$), but rather for $\lambda$, the noncentrality parameter of the noncentral $F$ distribution (see Equation 9.3.1):

$$(10.3.1) \qquad \lambda = f^2 (u + v + 1).$$

Note that $\lambda$ combines multiplicatively $f^2$, the size of the effect in the first term, with the amount of information about the effect in the second term, which depends heavily on $N$. $\lambda$, with its accompanying degrees of freedom and $a$, give the power value.

Because the Rao $F$ ratio is a generalization of the ordinary $F$ ratio, we can use the power tables of Chapter 9, Tables 9.3.1 and 9.3.2, for determining power in SC. Recall from Section 10.1.1 that

$$(10.1.6) \qquad u = \text{numerator } df = k_Y k_X,$$

and

$$(10.1.7) \qquad v = \text{demonimator } df = ms + 1 - u/2,$$

where

(10.1.8)      $m = N - \max(k_C, k_A + k_G) - (k_Y + k_X + 3)/2.$

Given $f^2$, $u$ and $v$, $\lambda$ is computed using (10.3.1). Then Table 9.3.1 (for $a = .01$) or Table 9.3.2 (for $a = .05$) is entered and power is read out, interpolating as necessary (see Section 9.3 for details).

### 10.3.1   WHOLE ASSOCIATION: QUANTITATIVE WITH QUANTITATIVE.

**Illustrative Examples**

**10.1**   A psychologist is interested in studying the relationship between the cognitive and personality domains. The plan is to obtain 4 cognitive and 5 personality trait measures from a sample of 60 introductory psychology students. Although there exists some fuzzy theory that suggests some specific between-domain pairwise relationships, the researcher decides to accept the discipline that a "significant" individual pairwise correlation is only to be accepted as such if there is a significant ($a = .01$) relationship between the two sets.

I strongly endorse this practice. Consider that there will be a total of (4 (5) =) 20 between-set $r$'s. To merely "harvest" and interpret those followed by asterisks on the computer output as "significant" (as is encouraged by some statistical computer packages) may well be an exercise in capitalization on chance. SC (and multivariate techniques in general) provides a formal significance test on the overall association. It is a prudent practice to provide some "protection" for the validity of positive conclusions about individual pairs (much as is done by Fisher's protected $t$ test) by setting as a condition for interpreting *any* of the pairwise $r$'s as significant that the multivariate $R^2_{Y,X}$ between *sets* be significant.

Our psychologist employs the first method for setting $f^2$: The matrix of population $r$'s that is posited is given as Table 10.3.1. This matrix is entered (as if it were a sample matrix) in the SC computer program for the whole type of association (sets **D** with **B**) and $N = 60$. The program duly reports that $R^2_{Y,X} = .3810$ (which is not required for our immediate purpose) and the (phony) $F = 1.323$ for $u = 20$ and $v = 170$ degrees of freedom.[2] Substituting in (10.2.5), $f^2 = 1.323 (20/170) = .1556$, completing the ingredients for (10.3.1) to find $\lambda$ as $.1556 (20 + 170 + 1) = 29.7$. The specifications for the determination of power are thus:

---

[2]Error **df** (**v**) for the Rao **F** test are always greater than **N** when the smaller set contains at least 2 variables, and as **s** increases, much greater. Also, note that **v** is not, in general, an integer, but is rounded to the nearest whole number.

$$\mathbf{a} = .01 \qquad \mathbf{u} = 20 \qquad \mathbf{v} = 170 \qquad \lambda = 29.7.$$

Recall that the power tables and the interpolation formula (9.3.2) in Chapter 9 are used in this chapter. (See Chapter 9 for the details of their use.) Entering Table 9.3.1 (for $\mathbf{a} = .01$) in block $\mathbf{u} = 20$, and interpolation between $\lambda = 28$ and 30 and between $\mathbf{v} = 120$ and $\infty$ gives power $= .77$. Given the investment in this research, this may well be considered a little short of ideal. Therefore, the psychologist determines what the power would be for $\mathbf{N} = 70$. Although this can be done as before with the SC program, because neither $\mathbf{f}^2$ nor $\mathbf{u}$ changes, all that is needed is the new $\mathbf{v}$. For this, $\mathbf{s}$ is needed, which, reading from Table 10.2.1, for $\mathbf{k_Y} = \mathbf{k_D} = 4$ and $\mathbf{k_X} = \mathbf{k_B} = 5$, is found to be 3.32. Then, from (10.1.8), $\mathbf{m} = 70 - (4 + 5 + 3)/2 = 63$, and from (10.1.7), $\mathbf{v} = 63 (3.32) + 1 - 20/2 = 203$. The new $\lambda = .1556 (20 + 203 + 1) = 34.9$ and the specifications are now:

$$\mathbf{a} = .01 \qquad \mathbf{u} = 20 \qquad \mathbf{v} = 203 \qquad \lambda = 34.9,$$

and interpolation in Table 9.3.1 gives power $= .87$. The researcher might well decide to scrape up another 10 subjects.

An interesting aspect of the relationship between univariate and multivariate power may be pursued here. Assume that the population $\mathbf{r}$'s are exactly as were posited in Table 10.3.1. Note that the highest of the 20 pairwise $\mathbf{r}$'s between a cognitive and a personality measure is .3, which obtained for three pairs. If we go back to Chapter 3 and check the power to detect a population $\mathbf{r}$ of .3 for $\mathbf{N} = 70$ at the $\mathbf{a_2} = .05$ level, we find it to be only .72 (Table 3.3.5). Thus, the probability of detecting any given one of the three as significant is not very high, and the probability of finding all three significant is approximately $(.72^3) = .37$. In the light of this, perhaps our psy-

**Table 10.3.1**
Population Correlation Matrix for 4 Cognitive and 5 Personality Measures

|       | Cognitive | | | | Personality | | | | |
|-------|-----|-----|-----|-----|-----|-----|-----|-----|-----|
|       | $d_1$ | $d_2$ | $d_3$ | $d_4$ | $b_1$ | $b_2$ | $b_3$ | $b_4$ | $b_5$ |
| $d_1$ | 1.0 |     |     |     |     |     |     |     |     |
| $d_2$ | .3  | 1.0 |     |     |     |     |     |     |     |
| $d_3$ | .4  | .5  | 1.0 |     |     |     |     |     |     |
| $d_4$ | .5  | .5  | .4  | 1.0 |     |     |     |     |     |
| $b_1$ | .1  | .0  | .2  | .2  | 1.0 |     |     |     |     |
| $b_2$ | .0  | .0  | .0  | .3  | .2  | 1.0 |     |     |     |
| $b_3$ | .0  | .2  | .1  | .2  | .3  | .3  | 1.0 |     |     |
| $b_4$ | .3  | .2  | .2  | .3  | .4  | .4  | .4  | 1.0 |     |
| $b_5$ | .2  | .0  | .0  | .2  | .4  | .3  | .3  | .5  | 1.0 |

chologist should consider using an even larger sample size to improve the power to detect individual $r$'s as significant.

This problem also illustrates the cumulative property of $R^2_{Y,X}$, one of the reasons that it tends to run high. In Table 10.3.1, the 20 individual population correlations between sets are quite modest: three .3s, eight .2s, and the rest .0s and .1s. Yet $R^2_{Y,X} = .3810$, an apparently impressive value.

We should note, however, that $R^2_{Y,X}$ depends not only on the between-set but also on the within-set correlations, and does so in a very complex way. For example, for the same between-set correlations in Table 10.3.1, if we were to posit instead a uniform $r = 0$ for all the 16 within-set correlations, then $R^2_{Y,X} = .55$; for within-set $r = .3$, $R^2_{Y,X} = .34$; for $r = .5$, $R^2_{Y,X} = .44$; for $r = .7$, $R^2_{Y,X} = .80$! What we see here is the operation of multivariate suppression, a rather complicated form of the phenomenon encountered in MRC. What is clear, however, is that in positing population correlations, the within-set correlations are important in determining $R^2_{Y,X}$, upon which $f^2$ and therefore $\lambda$ depend.

This problem is also instructive with regard to the relationship between $R^2_{Y,X}$ and $f^2$ and our operational definitions of effect sizes. We found $f^2 = .1556$, almost identically the operational definition of a medium ES in SC. While $R^2_{Y,X} = .3810$ may have suggested a stronger relationship, the set sizes and resulting $s = 3.32$ produced an $f^2$ less than half as large as $R^2_{Y,X}$.

Finally, the reader is reminded that the $R^2_{Y,X}$ of .3810 is a (hypothesized) *population* value. A *sample* $R^2_{Y,X}$ of .3810 in a sample of 60 for the present parameters would be quite unimpressive, because by Equation (10.1.11) we would estimate its population value as (i.e., "shrink" it to) .10. Another way to be unimpressed by the sample $R^2_{Y,X}$ of .3810 is to compute the expected value of the sample $R^2_{Y,X}$ when the population $R^2_{Y,X} = 0$; for the present parameters, Equation (10.1.10) gives $Exp_0 (R^2_{Y,X}) = .31$, as noted in Section 10.1.3.

**10.2**  A psychiatric epidemiologist has plans to generate a data base of $(N =) 100$ delinquent adolescents in community mental health treatment centers which will contain measures reflecting frequency of $(k_Y =) 8$ types of offense (e.g., mugging, assault, vandalism, etc.) and ratings on $(k_X =) 6$ psychopathology dimensions (e.g., anxiety, depression, oppositional disorder, etc.). Since in the course of this investigation multiple significance tests will be performed, in order to hold down the experimentwise a level, $a = .01$ is to be used for this and subsequent tests. She uses the second method of arriving at $f^2$, and posits that the population $R^2_{Y,X} = .25$ between the two sets.

The type of association is whole, so from (10.2.6), $L_W = 1 - .25 = .75$. From Table 10.2.1 she finds that for sets of 6 and 8 variables, $s = 4.92$ (remember that because of symmetry, $k_Y$ and $k_X$ are interchangeable). Then, from (10.2.2) $f^2 = .75^{-1/4.92} - 1 = .0602$. From (10.1.6) $u = 8 (6) = 48$, from (10.1.8) $m = 100 - (8 + 6 + 3)/2 = 91.5$, so from (10.1.7) $v = 91.5$ (4.92) $+1 - 48/2 = 427$. We can now find from (10.3.1) the noncentrality parameter $\lambda = .0602 \, (48 + 427 + 1) = 28.7$. The specification summary is:

$$\mathbf{a} = .01 \qquad \mathbf{u} = 48 \qquad \mathbf{v} = 427 \qquad \lambda = 28.7.$$

Using the interpolation formula (9.3.2) in Table 9.3.1 (for $\mathbf{a} = .01$) in block $\mathbf{u} = 48$ between $\lambda = 28$ and 30 and between 120 and $\infty$ gives power $= .51$. Even using a questionable $\mathbf{a} = .05$ criterion, the same procedure with the values of Table 9.3.2 gives power of only .74. (See example 10.17.)

If you are surprised by the poor power for a good-sized sample and what seems like a chunky $\mathbf{R}^2_{Y,X} = .25$, note that under the press of the large set sizes and resulting $\mathbf{s} = 4.92$, the effect size $\mathbf{f}^2$ of .06 is quite modest. The positive effect on $\lambda$ of the large $\mathbf{v}$ is offset by the lower power that accompanies large $\mathbf{u}$ in the power tables.

**10.3**  Our epidemiologist of the preceding example reconsiders her plans. If the large set sizes are the problem, she can deal with them by reducing them either in advance by an *a priori* combination and exclusion on theoretical grounds, or after the data are collected, by factor or cluster analysis. Assume that this process results in $\mathbf{k}_Y = 3$ and $\mathbf{k}_X = 2$. She estimates that with the reduction of information that would result, for these new measures $\mathbf{R}^2_{Y,X} = .20$ (down from .25). Now, from Table 10.2.1, $\mathbf{s} = 2$ (down from (4.92), and (10.2.2) gives $\mathbf{f}^2 = .80^{-.5} - 1 = .1180$ (up from .0602). For the **df, u** $= 2 \, (3) = 6$ (down from 48), $\mathbf{m} = 100 - 100 - (2 + 3 + 3)/2 = 96$, so $\mathbf{v} = 96 \, (2) + 1 - 6/2 = 190$ (down from 427). From (10.3.1) we can now find $\lambda = .1180 \, (6 + 190 + 1) = 23.2$. The new specifications are:

$$\mathbf{a} = .01 \qquad \mathbf{u} = 6 \qquad \mathbf{v} = 190 \qquad \lambda = 23.2.$$

Note that although $\lambda$, too, is down (from 28.7), it makes an enormous difference that we now enter Table 9.3.1 for $\mathbf{u} = 6$ rather than 48: interpolating with (9.3.2), we find power for the revised specifications of .88, compared to .51 before. This is obviously a far more viable result. Even if the posited $\mathbf{R}^2_{Y,X} = .20$ was overestimated (which has been known to happen), and the population $\mathbf{R}^2_{Y,X}$ is actually only .175, $\mathbf{f}^2$ works out to .1010, and because the **df** remain the same, $\lambda$ becomes 19.9 and power .80, a quite tolerable level. (See example 10.18.)

**10.4**  A clinical psychologist plans a research to investigate the relationship between 3 ($= \mathbf{k}_X$) physiologically based measures of anxiety and 2 ($\mathbf{k}_Y$) behaviorally based anxiety scales in an available clinic sample of 38 ($= \mathbf{N}$) cases, and intends to use the $\mathbf{a} = .05$ significance criterion. He posits the (alternative-hypothetical) population matrix shown in Table 10.3.2 in order to determine the $f^2$ and **df** for the analysis.

He enters this matrix in a computer program for SC together with the **N** = 38 (as if they were sample data) and the output gives $R^2_{Y,X}$ = .2653 (which is not needed for the power calculation), and **F** = 1.833, **u** = 6, and **v** = 66. From the latter, he finds from (10.2.5) that $f^2$ = 1.833 (6/66) = .1666, and then from (10.31.1) that $\lambda$ = .1666 (6 + 66 + 1) = 12.2. Following are the specifications:

$$\mathbf{a} = .05 \qquad \mathbf{u} = 6 \qquad \mathbf{v} = 66 \qquad \lambda = 12.2.$$

Interpolating in Table 9.3.2 (for **a** = .05) gives power = .69.

He finds this value disappointing. Moreover, it occurs to him that slight changes in the actual population matrix from those of Table 10.3.2 might reduce the $R^2_{Y,X}$ and therefore the $f^2$ and $\lambda$, with the result that the actual power might well be less than .69.

He then considers that as he conceives the population matrix (Table 10.3.2), the relationships of the physiologically based measures to the second anxiety scale are not as strong as with the first, and that dropping $d_2$ might actually increase power. Note that with a single dependent variable, he now has that special case of SC that is MRC, and so could analyze the problem using the methods of the preceding chapter. However, let's have him proceed with the SC method. He drops $d_2$ and runs the SC program on the remaining variables with $k_Y$ = 1 and $k_X$ = 3.

He now finds $R^2_{Y,X}$ = .2008, **F** = 2.847, **u** = 3, and **v** = 34. Using (10.2.5), he finds $f^2$ = 2.847 (3)/34 = .2512, or equivalently, using equation (9.2.2) in Chapter 9, $f^2$ = .2008/(1 − .2008) = .2513. From (10.3.1), $\lambda$ = .2512 (3 + 34 + 1) = 9.5. His new specifications are:

$$\mathbf{a} = .05 \qquad \mathbf{u} = 3 \qquad \mathbf{v} = 34 \qquad \lambda = 9.5,$$

**Table 10.3.2**
Population Correlation Matrix for 2 Behavioral and 3 Physiological Measures of Anxiety

|  | Behavioral | | Physiological | | |
| --- | --- | --- | --- | --- | --- |
|  | $d_1$ | $d_2$ | $b_1$ | $b_2$ | $b_3$ |
| $d_1$ | 1.0 | | | | |
| $d_2$ | .3 | 1.0 | | | |
| $b_1$ | .4 | .1 | 1.0 | | |
| $b_2$ | .3 | .0 | .3 | 1.0 | |
| $b_3$ | .2 | .2 | .4 | .6 | 1.0 |

and, interpolating in Table 9.3.2, he finds power to be .68, slightly less than it was for the original problem.

Why did his effort to attain greater power fail? In dropping $d_2$, despite the fact that it was the more weakly related variable, $R^2_{Y,X}$ dropped from .2653 to .2512, and although $f^2$ increased from .1666 to .2512, the decrease in $v$ in (10.3.1) for $\lambda$ reduced it too sharply to be offset by the decrease in $u$. The reader might find it useful to track these changes in detail.

The bottom line here is that our psychologist can either follow his original plan with 38 cases and .69 power, or seek an increase in $N$. With $N = 50$, power works out to .85, which the reader may seek to confirm as an exercise. (Also, see example 10.19.)

### 10.3.2  WHOLE ASSOCIATION: CATEGORICAL WITH QUANTITATIVE; K-GROUP MANOVA.

I wish to emphasize that in this and later sections where standard multivariate methods are illustrated using SC, the standard methods are simply special cases of SC. It is conventional in MANOVA, as in ANOVA, to use sums of squares/products matrices rather than variance/covariance matrices. These differ, however, only by a multiplicative constant, and because it is ratios of matrix determinants that define $R^2_{Y,X}$ and $f^2$, the constant factors out, so we can use either. The SC results are thus not approximations but rather *exactly* those of the standard methods. (For an alternative method of power analysis in MANOVA, see Stevens, 1986, pp. 139–143, 187–190.)

From the perspective of SC, the standard one-way K-group multivariate analysis of variance (MANOVA) is simply a whole association in which one set (usually $D$) is made up of quantitative variables and the other (usually $B$), represents membership in one of $K$ groups. The latter, a categorical or nominal scale, is coded using whichever coding method is appropriate to the problem (Cohen & Cohen, 1983, Chapter 5). Thus, $k_Y = k_D$ and $k_X = K - 1$, where $K$ is the number of groups.

It should also be pointed out that K-group discriminant analysis, employed to generate linear functions of a set of variables that maximally discriminate among the groups, shares the same null hypothesis, assumptions, and significance test with K-group MANOVA, and hence the same power analysis.

Investigators may use any of the methods of Section 10.2.3 for setting $f^2$. For example, they may posit a population $R^2_{Y,X}$, determine $s$ from Equation (10.1.9) or Table 10.2.1, and then $f^2$ from Table 10.2.2. Alternatively, they may posit a value of $f^2$, either *ad hoc* or using a conventional definition (Section 10.2.2), checking Table 10.2.3 for the $R^2_{Y,X}$ it implies. The set sizes and $N$ determine $u$ and $v$ using Equations (10.1.6-8), and $\lambda$ is found, as always, from Equation (10.3.1). Then $\lambda$ is entered with $u$ and $v$ in Table 9.3.1 ($a = .01$) or Table 9.3.2 ($a = .05$), and power is read out, interpolating as necessary.

## Illustrative Examples

**10.5**   An experimental psychologist plans a learning study using a control and three experimental groups of 20, 10, 10, and 10 cases, respectively (total $N = 50$), with a time score and an error score constituting the dependent variable set. He may use any method for coding the set $X$ group membership variables and obtain the same setwise results, but follow-up tests of each experimental group vs. the control group will be facilitated if dummy variable coding is used (see Cohen & Cohen, 1983, Chapter 5 and example 10.9). He estimates that in the population, he can account for $R^2_{Y,X} = .15$ of the (multi)variance of the two scores in a MANOVA at the .05 level. For $k_Y = 2$, $k_X = K - 1 = 3$, Table 10.2.1 gives $s = 2$, and Equation (10.2.2) gives $f^2 = .0847$. From Equation (10.1.6), $u = 2(3) = 6$, from (10.1.8), $m = 50 - (2 + 3 + 3)/2 = 46$, so from (10.1.7) $v = 46(2) + 1 - 6/2 = 90$. Finally, Equation (10.3.1) gives $\lambda = .0847(6 + 90 + 1) = 8.2$. The specification summary is:

$$a = .05 \qquad u = 6 \qquad v = 90 \qquad \lambda = 8.2.$$

Entering Table 9.3.2 (for $a = .05$) in block $u = 6$, and interpolating for $v = 90$ and $\lambda = 8.2$ via (9.3.2) gives power $= .51$, a fifty-fifty proposition. Note that although 15% of the variance is a sizable chunk by univariate standards, when it is expressed as $f^2$ for $s = 2$, it comes to only .0847, a value that falls almost exactly between the operational definitions of small and medium. It is instructive to note how it compares with the $f^2$ that would result if there were only one dependent varible, i.e., if this were a multiple correlation (or a univariate analysis of variance). For $s = 1$, the $R^2_{Y,X}$ of .15 yields $f^2 = .1765$; for these specifications, $\lambda = 8.8$, not much different from before, but it is evaluated at $u = 3$, $v = 46$, and Table 9.3.2 gives power $= .66$, distinctly higher than for two dependent variables. This makes sense intuitively: if an additional variable in either set leads to no increase in $R^2_{Y,X}$, it simply "dilutes" the power.

Power would, of course, improve if the psychologist could posit an $R^2_{Y,X} = .25$. Then Equation (10.2.2) gives $f^2 = .1547$ and (10.3.1) gives $\lambda = 15.0$. The specifications would now be:

$$a = .05 \qquad u + 6 \qquad v = 90 \qquad \lambda = 15.0,$$

and interpolating in Table 9.3.2 gives power $= .81$. On the other hand, if the population $R^2_{Y,X}$ should be .10, then $f^2 = .0541$, $\lambda = 5.2$, and power works out to .35.

See example 10.9 below for the power analysis of individual contrasts, and example 10.20 for finding $N$ as a function of power.

**10.6**  MANOVA is frequently used for a set of $k_Y$ variables as a preliminary test to prevent escalation of the experimentwise **a** error. If significant, the investigator then performs an ANOVA on each of the $k_Y$ variables, much in the spirit of Fisher's protected **t** test (Cliff, 1987, p. 411).

An advertising researcher plans a study of the differences among users of four brands of detergents in ratings of 12 product characteristics, for which a total sample of 120 cases is available. She plans first to do a MANOVA at **a** = .05 on the $k_Y$ = 12 variables in the interest of experimentwise Type I error control. She posits that, in the population, $R^2_{Y,X}$ = .15 of the multivariance of the set of characteristics will be accounted for by the $K - 1 = k_X$ = 3 variables needed to code brand membership for the four groups. For $k_Y$ = 12, $k_X$ = 3, we find from Table 10.2.1 that **s** = 2.95 (remember that **s** is symmetric in $k_Y$ and $k_X$), and Equation (10.2.2) gives $f^2$ = .0566. From Equations (10.1.6-8), **u** = 36, **m** = 111, so **v** = 310. We find from Equation (10.3.1) that $\lambda$ = .0566 (36 + 310 + 1) = 19.6. The specification summary is:

$$a = .05 \qquad u = 36 \qquad v = 310 \qquad \lambda = 19.6.$$

Entering Table 9.3.2 (for **a** = .05), we must interpolate using Equation (9.3.2) not only for $\lambda$ between 18 and 20 and **v** between 120 and $\infty$, but then, between those results, inversely for **u** between 30 and 40. The result is power = .58.

This is not very good. If she proceeds on this basis, unless $R^2_{Y,X}$ is actually greater than .15 or she is lucky, she may well not get the significant MANOVA result she needs to prudently test for brand group differences in the individual characteristics. She realizes, however, that there is likely to be a considerable amount of redundancy in the ratings of the 12 characteristics. Redundancy among dependent variables in multivariate analysis is as deleterious to power as is redundancy among independent variables in MRC. (Remember the special-case nature of the latter and the symmetry of SC.) Accordingly, she expects that a factor-analytic reduction to three or four common factors might well exhaust the reliable information in the 12 scales. She assumes that she can generate three factor scores from the data and perform the analysis on the basis of these summary scores rather than the 12 scales. What would the power of the MANOVA on the three summary scores be?

She posits $R^2_{Y,X}$ = .15, N = 120, and $k_X$ = 3 as before, but now $k_Y$ = 3 (instead of 12). Table 10.2.1 gives **s** = 2.43 (instead of 2.95), and Equation (10.2.2) gives $f^2$ = .0692, some 22% larger than the .0566 found before, **u** = 9 (instead of 36), and **v** = 280. $\lambda$ = .0692 (9 + 280 + 1) = 20.1. The new specifications are:

$$a = .05 \qquad u = 9 \qquad v = 280 \qquad \lambda = 20.1.$$

Table 9.3.2 is now entered for $u = 9$ (instead of 36), and power is now found to be .89, a far and happy cry from the .58 of the previous specifications. Let's hold the other specifications ($R^2_{Y,X} = .15$, $N = 120$, and $k_X = 3$) constant, and see how power varies as a function of $k_Y$:

| $k_Y$ | 1 | 2 | 3 | 4 | 5 | 6 | 8 | 10 | 12 | 16 |
|---|---|---|---|---|---|---|---|---|---|---|
| Power | .98 | .94 | .89 | .84 | .81 | .77 | .70 | .64 | .58 | .50 |

Although the rate at which power declines as $k_Y$ (or $k_X$) increases will vary as a function of the values chosen for the other parameters, the rate we see here is fairly representative of what occurs in practice.

Now assuming that her MANOVA will prove significant, what is the power for the tests of brand group differences on the three individual summary scores? First, note that these tests are now univariate anovas, or, equivalently, MRC analyses. Given the generality of SC, however, we can continue the power analysis of this special case exactly as we performed the other. She can not, of course, assume that she can expect to account for .15 of the variance of individual scores. Let's say she now posits $R^2_{Y,X} =$ multiple $R^2 = .05$. Since $k_Y = 1$, $s = 1$, $f^2 = .05/(1 - .05) = .0526$, $u = 3$, and $v = (120 - 3 - 1 = ) 116$. Therefore, $\lambda = .0526 (3 + 116 + 1) = 6.3$. Summarizing,

$$a = .05 \qquad u = 3 \qquad v = 116 \qquad \lambda = 6.3.$$

From Table 9.3.2, power works out to .52. This phase of the study is obviously underpowered. She will need either to increase her $N$ or hope that the population $R^2_{Y,X}$ for the individual summary scores is substantially larger than .05. (See the denouement in example 10.21.)

### 10.3.2.1 2-GROUP MANOVA.
Hotelling (1931) offered the $T^2$ test as a multivariate generalization of the Student t test, i.e., a test of the hypothesis that two groups have equal means on all the $k_Y$ variables in the $Y$ set. When $T^2$ is determined from a sample, multiplication by $(v - 2)/v$, where $v = N - 2$, produces $F$ for 1 and $v$ degrees of freedom. This obviously parallels the univariate $t^2 = F$ relationship. Thus, we do not need tables for the $T^2$ distribution because we can treat it as a special case of the $F$ distribution, just as we strictly do not need tables for the $t$ distribution.

It is nevertheless instructive to pursue the 2-group case. Mahalanobis' (1936) generalized distance, $D^2$, is a generalization of $d^2$, where $d$ is the standardized difference between population means that was employed as the effect size measure in Chapter 2 (2.2.1) (Flury & Riedwyl, 1986). If we square both sides of the Chapter 2 Equation (2.2.7) that relates the product moment $r$ to $d$, we obtain

(10.3.2)
$$r^2 = \frac{d^2}{d^2 + [1/p\,(1-p)]},$$

where $p$ is the proportion of the combined populations in either of the populations (see Section 2.2.2).

In the 2-group case of MANOVA, the special case of $R^2_{Y,X}$ where $k_X = K - 1 = 1$, $R^2_{Y,X}$ becomes the multiple $R^2_{X \cdot Y}$ between the single group membership variable $x$, which we can score 0,1, and the $Y$ set of $k_Y$ variables. (It may seem strange to have set $Y$ as "independent" variables and a single $x$ variable the "dependent" variable, but recall the symmetry of the $X$ and $Y$ sets in SC.) It can be demonstrated that (10.3.2) generalizes to

(10.3.3)
$$R^2_{X \cdot Y} = \frac{D^2}{D^2 + [1/p\,(1-p)]}.$$

Thus, if the investigator can posit the effect size as a Mahalanobis $D^2$, he can readily translate it into proportion of variance terms. Alternatively, if he is prepared to posit the ES in proportion of variance terms, he can assess the $D^2$ which is implied. Also, because one-way MANOVAs are $R^2$–complementary, he can transform freely among $R^2$, $D^2$, and $\lambda$. Note also that for this case, $f^2 = R^2/(1-R^2)$.

Finally, the significance test for a 2-group discriminant analysis is the same as for a 2-group MANOVA, therefore the power analysis is the same. The discriminant analysis is performed to determine the weights for the linear combination of the variables in the $Y$ set that maximally discriminates between the two groups. The computer programs for SC (Cohen & Nee, 1983; Eber & Cohen, 1987) provide these weights: they are the standardized regression coefficients of the multiple $R^2_{X \cdot Y}$.

### Illustrative Example

**10.7**   A neuropsychologist plans a study of the difference between patients with Alzheimer disease and normal controls of similar age on six variables derived from CAT scan measurements. He has available records for 50 patients and 40 controls, and will use the $a = .05$ significance criterion. For his ES estimate, in addition to the methods for setting $f^2$ described in Section 10.2.3, he may posit Mahalanobis' $D^2$ and (for $p = 50/90$) find $R^2_{Y,X}$ (= $R^2_{X \cdot Y}$) from Equation (10.3.3); because the $R^2_{Y,X}$ here is a multiple $R^2$, $s = 1$, and $f^2 = R^2_{Y,X}/(1-R^2_{Y,X})$.

As already noted, it generally would be salutary to use more than one of the above approaches, checking one against another, to zero in on an $f^2$ that he finds compelling.

Assume he ends up positing $R^2_{Y,X} = .125$, so $f^2 = .125/(1 - .125) = .1429$. $u = 6$, $v = (90 - 6 - 1 =) 83$, and therefore $\lambda = .1429 (6 + 83 + 1) = 12.9$. The summary:

$$a = .05 \qquad u = 6 \qquad v = 83 \qquad \lambda = 12.9.$$

Interpolating with (9.3.1) in Table 9.3.2 in block $u = 6$ for $v = 83$ and $\lambda = 12.9$ gives power $= .73$. Not too bad.

The follow-up tests on the individual CAT scan measures may be accomplished by ordinary 2-sample $t$ tests, and their power analysis may be accomplished by the methods of Chapter 2. Continuing, however, in our general SC framework, he posits an $R^2_{Y,X}$ (in this special case actually an $r^2_{pb}$) of .05, thus an $f^2 = .05/(1 - .05) = .0526$. $u = 1$, $v = 90 - 2 = 88$, and $\lambda = .0526 (1 + 88 + 1) = 4.7$. The specifications for an individual summary score's test are:

$$a = .05 \qquad u = 1 \qquad v = 88 \qquad \lambda = 4.7,$$

and Table 9.3.2 gives an interpolated value for power $= .57$. That's not very good.

However, he selected the $R^2_{Y,X} = .05$ value out of the blue. Let's treat this as an ordinary $t$ test and use the methods of Chapter 2 to fix on an ES. In terms of $d$, if we posit a medium ES of $d = .5$ and apply (10.3.2), with $p = .556$, then

$$r^2 = \frac{.5^2}{.5^2 + (1/(.556)(.444))} = .0581,$$

so the $R^2_{Y,X} = .05$ value we chose was somewhat smaller than what Chapter 2 defines as a medium difference between means. If we recalculate power for $R^2_{Y,X} = .0581$, $f^2 = .0581/(1 - .0581) = .0617$, $\lambda = .0617(1 + 88 + 1) = 5.6$, and power is found from Table 9.4.1 to be .64. If you go back to Chapter 2 and use the unequal sample procedure of Section 2.3.2 (Case 1), for $d = .5$ and $n' = 44.4$, you also get power $= .64$ — the results agree as they should, barring rounding error. (See example 10.22 for finding $N$'s necessary for power $= .80$.)

If the neuropsychologist plans a discriminant analysis, no separate power analysis is necessary because he has already determined the power of the overall test of the groups' mean differences on the six variables for the relevant specifications (.73). With the sample data in hand, assuming that a significant $R^2_{Y \cdot X}$ has been achieved in an SC (or MRC) analysis, the regression coefficients of the six variables on the Alzheimer–control (0,1) variable may be used as (standardized) weights that will maximize the difference between groups.

### 10.3.3 THE ANALYSIS OF PARTIAL VARIANCE AND THE ANALYSIS OF COVARIANCE.

In SC, partial association is defined as the $R^2_{Y \cdot X}$ between **D·A** and **B·A**, that is, between sets **D** and **B**, from both of which a set **A** has been partialled. It is thus a generalization to sets of variables of the familiar bivariate partial $r^2$, and of the multiple partial $R^2$ of MRC. In its general form, it is the multivariate generalization of "the analysis of partial variance" — APV (Cohen & Cohen, 1983, Chapter 10 and pp. 512–515).

There are two consequences of partialling set **A**. The first is the removal from set **D** of what would otherwise be error variance, thus generally increasing the power of the test. It is used for this purpose in experiments in which there is random assignment and thus no expected correlation between sets **A** and **B**. The second is that partialling set **A** from sets **D** and **B** assures that all the variables in the partialled sets **D** and **B** correlate zero with all the variables in the set **A**. This being the case, none of the variance shared by **D·A** and **B·A** can be a consequence of variability in the variables in set **A**. In a causal framework, to the extent to which **A** causes **D** and **B**, the degree of association observed between **D·A** and **B·A** can *not* be due to the causal effect of the variables in set **A**. This is the sense in which one "statistically controls" set **A** in the association between sets **D** and **B**. For example, a strong correlation found between weight and interest in the opposite sex in elementary school boys does not warrant the conclusion, "fat boys are lovers." If one were to partial age and height from the two variables, their partial (residual, net) correlation would likely approximate zero.

In SC's APV, there is no constraint on the nature of sets **B**, **D**, and **A** — they may be nominal scales, linear or nonlinear (e.g., polynomial) functions of quantitative variables or combinations thereof, in short, they may contain information in any form so one can partial anything from anything. From the perspective of the generality of SC, the multivariate analysis of covariance (MANCOVA) is that special case of partial association in which sets **D** and **A** are quantitative and set **B** is a nominal scale describing group membership. (See Sections 10.3.3.1 and 10.3.6.)

There is, however, in APV as in the analysis of covariance, the presumption that the relationship between sets **A** and **D** be the same for all sets of values for **B**, that is, that the relationship between sets **A** and **D** not be conditional on the values of set **B**. More formally, it is that the regressions of the variables in **D** on the set **A** variables be the same for all combinations of set **B** values. This is a generalization of the "homogeneity of regression" or "parallelism of slopes" assumption of the analysis of covariance that is tested by assessing the interaction of groups by covariates (Cohen & Cohen, 1983). In SC, this is generalized by assessing the set **B** by set **A** interaction.

### Illustrative Example

**10.8** A psychologist plans an investigation of the relationship between ability and memory, for which he has $k_Y = 3$ memory measures, $k_X = 2$ ability measures, and a sample of $N = 100$ cases; his **a** is to be .01. Since both age and education are likely to account for variance in these measures, he plans to partial them out of both sets. Further, because both age and education may well be nonlinearly related, he plans to make provision for this possibility by also including their squares (or, preferably the squares of their deviations from their respective means — see Centering, Cohen & Cohen, 1983, pp. 237–238). Thus, the set **A** that is to be partialled will contain ($k_A =$) 4 variables. He posits that the population $R^2_{Y,X}$ between sets **D·A** and **B·A** is .25.

For $k_Y = 3$, $k_X = 2$, from Table 10.2.1, $s = 2$. Then, from (10.2.7), $L_p = 1 - .25 = .75$, and from (10.2.2), $f^2 = .75^{-1/2} - 1 = .1547$. From (10.1.6), $u = 2(3) = 6$, from (10.1.8) $m = 100 - 4 - (2 + 3 + 3)/2 = 92$, so from (10.1.7) $v = 92(2) + 1 - 6/3 = 182$. With the necessary ingredients at hand, he can find from (10.3.1) $\lambda = .1547(6 + 182 + 1) = 29.2$, so the specifications for the determination of power are:

$$a = .01 \qquad u = 6 \qquad v = 182 \qquad \lambda = 29.2.$$

Interpolating with (9.3.2) in Table 9.3.1 (for $a = .01$) gives power $= .93$, a most reassuring value.

However, if the relationship between the memory measures and the ability measures are different for different sets of values of age and education, that is, if there is evidence for an age/ed × ability interaction, then the homogeneity of regression assumption fails, and the results of the analysis are ambiguous. He therefore needs to assess the power of the test of this interaction.

It is now necessary that he redefine the meaning of sets **B** and **A**. When the time comes to analyze his data he will construct a product set made up of the 8 variables that result when each of the 4 age/ed variables is multiplied by each of the 2 ability measures, so $k_B = k_X = 8$. The interaction is this product set from which the age/ed and ability sets are partialled, so the total number of variables to be partialled, $k_A = 4 + 2 = 6$. He wishes to be able to detect a partial $R^2_{Y,X}$ for this interaction if it is as large as .10, and to improve his power to detect such a hypothesized interaction, will use the $a = .05$ criterion.

For $k_Y = 3$ and $k_X = 8$, $s = 2.90$ and $u = 3(8) = 24$.[3] With $N = 100$ and $k_A = 6$, $m = 100 - 6 - (3 + 8 + 3)/2 = 87$, so $v = 87(2.90) + 1 + 24/2 = 241$. Then, $f^2 = (1 - .10)^{2.90} - 1 = .0370$, and $\lambda = .0370(24 + 24 + 1) = 9.8$, so the specifications are:

$$\mathbf{a} = .05 \qquad \mathbf{u} = 24 \qquad \mathbf{v} = 241 \qquad \lambda = 9.8.$$

The interpolated power value from Table 9.3.2 (for $\mathbf{a} = .05$) is a poor .34. We see here the debilitating effect of large $\mathbf{u}$ on power. Scanning the power values for the block $\mathbf{u} = 24$ reveals that it takes large $\lambda$ values to reach adequate power levels.

There are follow-up tests that will be of interest, for example, the relationship of unique aspects of the ability measures to the set of memory measures. The "unique" aspect of a variable in a set is that variable from which all the other variables in the set have been partialled. This partialling effects an orthogonalization of the variables, that is, whatever variance each shares with the others is removed, hence the term "unique." Here, where there are two ability measures, these would be ability 1•ability 2 and ability 2•ability 1. For ability 1•ability 2, for example, note that, in addition to the age/ed set, one other variable (ability 2) is being partialled from both sides, so set **A** contains $k_A = 4 + 1 = 5$ variables. Set **B** is the single variable, ability 1, so $k_X = k_B = 1$, and $k_Y = k_D$ remains 3. The **Y** set is the three memory measures from which are partialled the age/ed variables and ability 2 and the **X** set is ability 1 partialling the same variables. Assume that he posits a partial $R^2_{Y,X} = .15$ for each of these unique ability variables. What is the power of these tests?

$u = 3(1) = 3$, $m = 100 - 5 - (3 + 1 + 3)/2 = 91.5$, so $v = 91.5(1) + 1 - 3/2 = 91$. Since one of the sets (**X**) has only one variable, $s = 1$, so $f^2 = .15/(1 - .15) = .1765$, and $\lambda = .1765(3 + 91 + 1) = 16.8$. Summarizing,

$$\mathbf{a} = .01 \qquad \mathbf{u} = 3 \qquad \mathbf{v} = 91 \qquad \lambda = 16.8.$$

The interpolated power value from Table 9.3.1 is .81.

Two other types of follow-up tests would likely be pursued. One is the test of each of the three unique memory variables (e.g., memory 2 partialling memory 1 and memory 3) against the ability measures set, partialling in addition the age/ed variables as before. If the partial $R^2_{Y,X} = .12$ is posited, power at $\mathbf{a} = .01$ works out to .73, and at $\mathbf{a} = .05$ power is .89. The other test is between the unique aspect of a memory measure and the unique aspect of an ability score (e.g., memory 2 partialling memory 1 and memory 3 with

---

[3]I abandon the repetitive references to the standard equations for the ingredients of the power analysis, but continue to show the substitutions of the parameters.

ability 1 partialling ability 2), again also partialling the age/ed variables. (Note that this is a simple bivariate partial **r** with a total of 7 variables being partialled.) If the partial $R^2_{Y,X}$ is posited to be .10, power at .01 is .72 and at .05, .89. Readers may wish to see if they can arrive at these power values as an exercise.

Except for the poor power for testing the homogeneity of covariance assumption (i.e., the interaction), a chronic problem in both univariate and multivariate analysis of covariance, the planned tests show good to excellent power even at the **a** = .01 level. The psychologist will need to decide whether to increase his sample size to improve the power of the interaction test (see example 10.23), or to risk the assumption that the interaction effect is nonexistent or small and proceed with the research, as planned.

10.3.3.1   K-GROUP MANCOVA.   The multivariate analysis of covariance (MANCOVA), as has already been noted, is that special case of the multivariate APV wherein set **B** represents group membership in one or more nominal scales. From another perspective, it is a MANOVA to which there is added a set of covariates that is partialled from both the **D** and **B** sets. It has already been noted that covariates serve two important functions in data analysis: they reduce error variance (and thus increase power), and they "control" ("adjust for," "hold constant statistically") sources of variance that the analyst means to exclude from the analysis (Cohen & Cohen, 1982, Chapter 10).

From the perspective of SC, MANOVA calls upon the partial type of association, that is $R^2_{D \cdot A, B \cdot A}$, where **A** is the covariate set. For simple **K**-group (one-way) MANCOVA, Model 1 error is used (as it has been throughout to this point).

### Illustrative Example

**10.9**   Let us return to the experimental psychologist in example 10.5 who plans a learning experiment involving three experimental and one control group (with a total **N** = 50) and a **D** set made up of a time and an error score, with $R^2_{D,B}$ = .15. These specifications led to unsatisfactory power = .51 (at **a** = .05). Assume now that there is available a set of 2 verbal ability measures that relate to learning ability for this task. To the extent to which they do so there will be variance in the **D** set that is irrelevant to the issue of differences among the groups. If he treats these measures as a covariate set **A** and partials them from both **D** and **B**, his experiment is no longer about time and error scores, but rather about time and error scores from which ability variance has been removed. He can similarly conceptualize the groups as having had that ability variance removed; that is, the groups are "equated" for verbal ability: **B·A**. Whereas originally he estimated $R^2_{D,B}$ = .15, he has every reason to believe that with the variance in verbal ability removed, substantially more than .15 of the remaining variance in time and error scores can be accounted for. He may directly estimate a value for $R^2M_{D \cdot A, B \cdot A}$, or he may find it by positing population values for $R^2_{D,A}$ and $R^2_{D,A+B}$.[4] As given in Cohen (1982, p. 308, Equation 7),

$$(10.3.4) \qquad R^2_{D \cdot A, B \cdot A} = \frac{R^2_{D,A+B} - R^2_{D,A}}{1 - R^2_{D,A}}.$$

Thus, if he posits that $R^2_{D,A+B} = .50$ and $R^2_{D,A} = .35$, then $R^2_{D \cdot A, B \cdot A} = .23$. From (10.2.7), $L_p = 1 - .23 = .77$. Since $k_Y = 2$ and $k_X = 3$, $s = 2$ and $u = 2(3) = 6$ (all as before), but $f^2$ now equals .1396. Since the covariate set has 2 variables, $k_A = 2$, so $m = 50 - 2 - (2 + 3 + 3)/2 = 44$ and $v = 44 (2) + 1 - 6/2 = 86$. Finally, $\lambda = .1396 (6 + 86 + 1) = 13.0$. The new specifications are:

$$a = .05 \qquad u = 6 \qquad v = 86 \qquad \lambda = 13.0$$

Interpolating in Table 9.3.2, we find power = .74, far better than the .51 that was obtained in the absence of the covariate set. Note, however, that in increasing the proportion of variance some 50% (from .15 to .23), he is assuming a strong covariate set, that is, $R^2_{D,A} = .35$.

   Given that the dummy coding employed for treatments has the effect that each of the three variables in set **B**, when partialled by the other two, carries an experimental-control contrast, he can readily assess the power of these tests. Each of these is also of the partial type of association, but the covariate set now includes, in addition to the two ability measures, the other two dummy variables (Cohen & Cohen, 1983, Chapter 5). For example, $x_1 \cdot x_2 + x_3$ represents the experimental Group 1 vs. Control Group contrast. Combining these with the verbal ability covariates ($v_1$, $v_2$) results in the complete covariate set **A** for this contrast being $v_1 + v_2 + x_2 + x_3$ (so $k_A = 4$), and set **B** is made up of the single variable $x_1$ (so $k_X = k_B = 1$). $k_Y = k_D = 2$, as before. Since the smaller set has only one variable, $s = 1$. Assume that he posits $R^2_{D \cdot A, B \cdot A} = .15$. Since $s = 1$, $f^2 = .15/(1 - .15) = .1765$. The numerator df, $u = k_Y k_X = 2$, and given that $m = 50 - 4 - (2 + 1 + 3)/2 = 43$, the denominator df, $v = 43 (1) + 1 - 2 (1)/2 = 43$. Then, $\lambda = 1.765 (2 + 43 + 1) = 8.1$, and he has the specification summary:

$$a = .05 \qquad u = 2 \qquad v = 43 \qquad \lambda = 8.1$$

---

[4]The " + " sign between variables or sets signifies their combination. Thus, $x_1 \cdot x_2 + x_3$ is $x_1$ from which $x_2$ *and* $x_3$ are partialled.

Interpolating in Table 9.3.2 with (9.3.2), he finds power for the three individual tests of experimental-control contrasts to be .69. He may well consider increasing his sample size. (See example 10.24.)

10.3.3.2   BIPARTIAL ANALYSIS.   The logic of some investigations that relate two or more partialled sets requires that the partialling sets not be the same, thus $R^2_{Y,X}$ is $R^2_{D \cdot C, B \cdot A}$, where sets C and A are not (exactly) the same. This occurs for the obvious reason that what needs to be controlled in one set is not the same as what needs to be controlled in the other. For example, when working with a battery of cognitive ability scores B that are not age-standardized, the use of the partialled set B·A, where A is an age set, would be desirable, but whether the set to which it is to be related should also be partialled by A depends on the nature of the investigation and the hypothesis to be tested.

The reader may recall that $f^2$ for the bipartial is not $R^2$-complimentary (Section 10.2.3). It is best set by positing the population matrix and using the SC computer program to obtain the output from which $f^2$ is computed using Equation (10.2.5). Otherwise, the analyst has the option of using the conventional definitions of Section 10.2.2 or of directly positing $f^2$, guided by experience.

**Illustrative Example**

**10.10**   A medical research team mounts an experiment on the effect of nutritional supplementation during pregnancy on newborn somatic and behavioral characteristics with a plan to use a sample of 300 patients of a clinic in an urban ghetto. The women are to be randomly assigned to two treatment groups and a control groups (TRT, to be dummy coded; $k_{TRT} = 2$), and the babies assessed at birth for weight, length, and head circumference (SOM; $k_{SOM} = 3$) and also, within 48–96 hours after birth, for scores on four factors derived from a behavioral examination (BEH; $k_{BEH} = 4$). In order to adjust for (and reduce irrelevant variance in) differences among mothers in regard to such variables as prepregnant weight, parity, number of past low birthweight infants, etc., a set of maternal attribute variables will be employed as covariates (COV; $k_{COV} = 5$). In addition, the infant's sex is to be partialled from SOM and BEH to control for possible sex differences in those variables, and the infant's age in hours at the time of the behavioral examination is to be partialled from the BEH scores in order to control for the rapid changes in behavior that occur during that period.

In summary, the research factors to be studied are TRT·COV, SOM·COV + Sex, and BEH·COV + Sex + Age at Exam. The primary aim of the research is to test for treatment effects on the somatic and behavioral variables, but the team is also interested in the effect of the somatic set on the behavioral variables. Since none of the sets to be partialled are the same, the form of association here is of the bipartial type, that is, $D \cdot C$ with $B \cdot A$. All tests are to be performed using the $a = .01$ significance criterion.

For the treatment effects on the somatic variables, $D = SOM$, $C = COV + Sex$, $B = TRT$, and $A = COV$. Thus, $k_Y = k_D = 3$, $k_X = k_B = 2$, and for the partialling sets, $k_C = 6$ and $k_A = 5$. Therefore, $s = 2$, $u = 3$ (2) $= 6$, and given that $m = 300 - 6 - (3 + 2 + 3)/2 = 290$, $v = 290$ (2) $+ 1 - 6/2 = 578$. Either by positing the population correlation matrix or directly they set $f^2 = .04$. Therefore, $\lambda = .04 (6 + 578 + 1) = 23.4$. The specifications are thus:

$$a = .01 \qquad u = 6 \qquad v = 578 \qquad \lambda = 23.4,$$

and interpolating in Table 9.3.1, power is found to be .89.

On the assumption that this test will prove to be significant, they wish to determine the power of a follow-up test. If the two dummy variables of TRT are designated $t_1$ and $t_2$, then $t_1 \cdot t_2$ and $t_2 \cdot t_1$ carry, respectively, the Treatment 1 vs. Control and Treatment 2 vs. Control contrasts. The sets for the bipartial for the Treatment 1 contrast remain as before for $D$ and $C$, but $B$ is now $t_1$ and $A$ is now $t_2 + COV$. (For the Treatment 2 contrast, $t_1$ and $t_2$ are simply reversed.) Therefore, $k_Y$ remains 3, but $k_X = 1$; $k_C$ remains 6, but $k_A$ is now also 6. With only one variable in $B$, $s = 1$. For the df, $u = 3$ (1) $= 3$, and given that $m = 300 - 6 - (3 + 1 + 3)/2 = 290.5$, $v = 290.5 + 1 - 3/2 = 290$. The team posits $f^2 = .04$ for these two tests, so their $\lambda = .04 (3 + 290 + 1) = 11.8$. Their power specifications are:

$$a = .01 \qquad u = 3 \qquad v = 290 \qquad \lambda = 11.8,$$

and Table 9.3.1 gives power $= .63$ for $a = .01$. At $a = .05$, Table 9.3.2 gives power $= .83$.

Further follow-up tests may be employed to assess the two treatment vs. control contrasts on the individual SOM variables or on *unique* aspects of the SOM variables (designated $p_1$, $p_2$, $p_3$), e.g., $p_1 \cdot p_2 + p_3$. An example of one of the latter six tests is the treatment 1 vs. control contrast (adjusted by COV) of unique $p_1$ (adjusted by COV and Sex): the bipartial between $t_2 \cdot t_2 + COV$ and $p_1 \cdot p_2 + p_3 + COV + Sex$. Sets $B$ and $A$ remain as before, but set $D$ is now $p_1$, and set $C$ is now $p_2 + p_3 + COV + Sex$. Thus, $k_Y = k_D = 1$, $k_X = k_B = 1$, $k_C = 8$, and $k_A = 6$. Note that this is a bivariate relationship, so $s = u = 1$. $m = 300 - 8 - (1 + 1 + 3)/2 = 289.5$, so $v = 289.5$ (1) $+ 1 - 1/2 = 290$. They posit $f^2 = .03$, so $\lambda = .03 (1 + 290 + 1) = 8.8$. The specification summary is:

$$a = .01 \qquad u = 1 \qquad v = 290 \qquad \lambda = 8.8,$$

and Table 9.3.1 gives power $= .64$. Checking Table 9.3.2 for $a = .05$ gives power $= .84$.

For the treatment effects on the set of behavioral variables, set $\mathbf{B} = \text{TRT}$ and set $\mathbf{A} = \text{COV}$ as before (so $k_X = k_B = 2$ and $k_A = 5$), and set $\mathbf{D} = \text{BEH}$ and set $\mathbf{C} = \text{COV} + \text{Sex} + \text{Age}$, so $k_Y = k_D = 4$ and $k_C = 7$. $\mathbf{s}$ is again 2, $\mathbf{u} = 4\,(2) = 8$, $\mathbf{m} = 300 - 7 - (4 + 2 + 3)/2 = 288.5$, so $\mathbf{v} = 2\,(288.5) + 1 - 8/2 = 574$. $\mathbf{f}^2$ is posited as $.03$, so $\lambda = .03\,(8 + 574 + 1) = 17.5$. Summarizing,

$$a = .01 \qquad u = 8 \qquad v = 574 \qquad \lambda = 17.5,$$

and Table 9.3.1 gives power $= .70$. At $a = .05$, power $= .86$.

I omit detailing the power analysis of the treatment contrasts for the BEH set and the unique aspects of its variables because it is identical in form to that for the SOM set described above.

The research team will also assess the association between the two sets of outcome variables. $\text{SOM} \cdot \text{COV} + \text{Sex}$ with $\text{BEH} \cdot \text{COV} + \text{Sex} + \text{Age}$. Now $k_X = 3$, $k_Y = 4$, $k_A = 6$, and $k_C = 7$. From Table 10.2.1, $\mathbf{s} = 2.65$. For the $\mathbf{df}$, $\mathbf{u} = 4\,(3) = 12$, and $\mathbf{m} = 300 - 7 - (4 + 3 + 3)/2 = 288$, so $\mathbf{v} = 288\,(2.65) + 1 - 12/2 = 758$. They posit an $\mathbf{f}^2 = .05$, so $\lambda = .05\,(12 + 758 + 1) = 38.6$. Summarizing,

$$a = .01 \qquad u = 12 \qquad v = 758 \qquad \lambda = 38.6,$$

and Table 9.3.1 gives power $= .98$.

The pursuit of the setwise relationship between SOM and BEH down to unique aspects of each, e.g., of $p_2 \cdot p_2 + p_3$ with $b_1 \cdot b_2 + b_3 + b_4$, is left to the reader as an exercise. If $\mathbf{f}^2 = .03$, power at $a = .01$ works out to $.64$.

It is worth noting that when this study was actually done, the sample size was 650 (Cohen, 1982, pp. 326–329; Rush, Stein, & Susser, 1980). (See example 10.25.)

10.3.4  HIERARCHICAL ANALYSIS.  Research designs frequently employ more than one research factor operating on the dependent variable set. Each research factor is represented as a set of one or more variables, and the research factor becomes the unit of analysis. A familiar example of such designs is the balanced (orthogonal) factorial design of the analysis of variance (univariate or multivariate), but this is a rather special case (see Sections 10.3.2, 10.3.5, and 10.3.6). More generally, the research factors may be correlated with each other, with or without a compelling theory as to how this correlation comes about, and they may be quantitative or qualitative, or some of each. Depending on the nature of a given research factor $\mathbf{U}$, the investigator may be interested in its relationship to **Y** ignoring the other research factors or with one or more of them partialled out.

In hierarchical analysis, the research factors are ordered in a hierarchy at each stage of which the previously entered factors are partialled from the analysis. Thus, if the factors are ordered **U, V, W**, they are analyzed as the series of **X** sets: **U, V·U**, and **W·U + V**. It should be apparent that a hierarchical analysis is a series of APVs, in which each research factor is assessed in order and is then partialled from its successors in the hierarchy.

An important use of the hierarchical procedure occurs when an investigator posits an order of causal priority among research factors. The above ordering assumes that **U**'s effect on the dependent variables may be assessed ignoring **V** and **W**, because neither **V** nor **W** can cause (i.e., produce variation in) **U**. Generally, it is assumed that no later set can be a cause of an earlier set, although an earlier set need not be a cause of any later set. The effect of the partialling is to assure that variance in the dependent variables shared by research factors is systematically attributed to the set assumed to have causal priority.

Another application of hierarchical analysis occurs in exploratory studies where the investigator can assign, *a priori*, substantially different magnitudes of effects to the multiple research factors available for study, which are usually related to each other. Thus, the above ordering may reflect a study that is mostly about set **U**'s effects on set **Y**, with set **V** distinctly more weakly related and set **W** more weakly related still. This strategy tends to maximize power for the research factor of primary interest while highlighting unique effects of other research factors when they are present.

### Illustrative Examples

**10.11**   A psychiatric research team plans a records study of length of stay and level of functioning ($k_Y = 2$) using 400 ($= N$) randomly selected psychiatric admissions to eight hospitals in a state system. The three research factors to be studied are:

1. Set **U**, the patients' demographic characteristics (e.g., age, sex, socioeconomic status, ethnicity); $k_U = 9$.

2. Set **V**, scores on the nine scales of the Minnesota Multiphasic Personality Inventory (MMPI) given shortly after admission plus a missing data dichotomy; $k_V = 10$.

3. Set **W**, an effects-coded nominal (qualitative) scale that identifies from which of the eight hospitals the patient was admitted; $k_W = 7$.

The research factors are ordered in presumed causal priority. Thus, it is a safe bet that neither MMPI nor hospital can produce variation in demographic characteristics and that hospital cannot cause admission MMPI. Power analysis is to be applied first to **U**, then to **V·U**, and finally to **W·U + V**. The .01 significance criterion is to be used throughout.

The team posits that the research factor **U** accounts for .10 of the variance of the ($k_Y$ =) 2 dependent variables, so the whole association $R^2_{D,B}$ = .10. $k_X$ = 9 and **s** = 2. Since $L_W$ = 1 − $R^2_{D,B}$ = .90, $f^2$ = $.90^{-1/2}$ − 1 = .0541. **u** = 2 (9) = 18, **m** = 400 − (2 + 9 + 3)/2 = 393, so **v** = 393 (2) + 1 − 18/2 = 778. The noncentrality parameter, $\lambda$ = .0541 (18 + 778 + 1) = 43.1. The complete specifications are:

$$\mathbf{a} = .01 \qquad \mathbf{u} = 18 \qquad \mathbf{v} = 778 \qquad \lambda = 43.1$$

Reference to Table 9.3.1 reveals that the $\lambda$ value is beyond the table's limit and for **u** = 18, power exceeds .96.

Next in the hierarchy is the MMPI set, **V**. With set **U** partialled from both the dependent variable set and **V**, they posit that the proportion of variance accounted for is .05; this is the partial type of association, $R^2_{D \cdot A, B \cdot A}$, where **D** is the dependent variable set, **B** is the research factor **V**, and **A** is the research factor **U** that is to be partialled. $k_X$ = 10, $k_Y$ remains 2, and $k_A$ = 9. **s** = 2, and from (10.2.7), $L_P$ = 1 − $R^2_{D \cdot A, B \cdot A}$ = .95, so $f^2$ = $.95^{-1/2}$ − 1 = .0260. **u** = 2 (10) = 20, **m** = 400 − 9 − (2 + 10 + 3)/2 = 383.5, so **v** = 383.5 (2) + 1 + 20/2 = 758. Finally, $\lambda$ = .0260 (20 + 758 + 1) = 20.3. The specification summary is:

$$\mathbf{a} = .01 \qquad \mathbf{u} = 20 \qquad \mathbf{v} = 758 \qquad \lambda = 20.3,$$

and interpolation in Table 9.3.1 yields power = .55.

The last research factor in the hierarchy is hospital membership, **W**. The research team posits that it accounts for .075 of the variance in the set of two dependent variables, after both **U** and **V** have been partialled. Thus again the form of association is partial, but now set **A** is made up of research factors **U** and **V**. Since **s** remains 2, $f^2$ = $(1 − .075)^{-1/2}$ − 1 = .0398. $k_Y$ remains 2, $k_X$ = 7, and $k_A$ = 9 + 10 = 19. For the **df**, **u** = 2 (7) = 14, and given that **m** = 400 − 19 − (2 + 7 + 3)/2 = 375, **v** = 375 (2) + 1 − 14/2 = 744. $\lambda$ = .0398 (14 + 744 + 1) = 30.2, so the specification summary is:

$$\mathbf{a} = .01 \qquad \mathbf{u} = 14 \qquad \mathbf{v} = 744 \qquad \lambda = 30.2,$$

and Table 9.3.1 yields the interpolated power value of .89.

See example 10.26 for another perspective on this problem.

It is worth noting that the last analysis is in fact a "K-group MANCOVA" (see Section 10.3.3.1) on hospitals, with the covariate set comprised of research factors **U** and **V**. That is, it may be viewed as an assessment of hospital differences in the length of stay/level of functioning set, statistically controlling for the demographic characteristics and admission MMPI of the patients. If, instead of representing group membership, the **W** research factor were a set of seven quantitative variables, say symptom rating scale scores on admission, the last analysis would more generally have been an APV, but would have been carried out identically, and with identical results.

**10.12** A developmental psychologist is studying the persistence of personality traits using a data base for 120 (= **N**) subjects that contains ratings on three personality variables obtained at age 10. These three variables were rated by the subjects themselves (**U**), jointly by their parents (**V**), and by their teachers (**W**). The subjects rated themselves again for these variables when they were in their middle twenties, the latter constituting the dependent variable set. She anticipates that the three sets of ratings at age 10 are correlated with each other, but believes that the self ratings are much more strongly correlated with the young adult ratings than the other sets and particularly that the latter have less unique predictive ability. Her ordering for presumed potency is **U, V, W**, and she will use the **a** = .05 significance criterion.

She hypothesizes that the age 10 self-ratings (**U**) will account for .15 of the adult ratings variance. Since $k_Y = k_X = 3$, **s** = 2.43 (from Table 10.2.1). This is a whole association $R^2$–complimentary case, so $f^2 = (1 - .15)^{-1/2.43} - 1 = .0692$. She determines **u** = 3 (3) = 9 and **m** = 120 − (3 + 3 + 3)/2 = 115.5, so **v** = 115.5 (2.43) + 1 − 9/2 = 277. Thus, $\lambda$ = .0692 (9 + 277 + 1) = 19.9. Her specifications are:

$$\mathbf{a} = .05 \qquad \mathbf{u} = 9 \qquad \mathbf{v} = 277 \qquad \lambda = 19.9.$$

Interpolating with (9.3.2) in Table 9.3.2, she finds that the power for this test is .89.

Her next test will be of the parents' ratings, partialling the self-ratings. She posits .075 as the partial $R^2_{D \cdot A,B \cdot A}$, where **D** is the dependent variable set of adult self-ratings, **B** is the parent's ratings (**V**), and the set to be partialled, **A**, is the set of child's self-ratings (**U**); $k_A = 3$. This .075 represents the variance overlap of the parents' ratings and adult self-ratings when the child's self-ratings have been partialled from both, and is thus variance that is *uniquely* due to parents' ratings.

$k_Y = k_X = 3$, **s** = 2.43, and **u** = 9 (all as before). Since partial association is $R^2$-complimentary (10.2.7), $f^2 = (1 - .075)^{-1/2.43} - 1 = .0326$. **m** = 120 − 3 − (3 + 3 + 3)/2 = 112.5, so **v** = 112.5 (2.43) + 1 − 9/2 = 270, and $\lambda$ = .0326 (9 + 270 + 1) = 9.1, resulting in the specifications:

$$\mathbf{a} = .05 \qquad \mathbf{u} = 9 \qquad \mathbf{v} = 270 \qquad \lambda = 9.1.$$

The interpolated power value from Table 9.3.2 is .50. (See example 10.27 for determination of the **N** necessary for power = .75.)

Finally, the partial association for the teacher ratings, $R^2_{D \cdot A, B \cdot A}$, where **D** is (as throughout) the young adult self-ratings, **B** is the teacher ratings set (**W**), and **A** is the combined child self-ratings and parent ratings sets (**U** + **V**), is hypothesized to be .05. This represents unique (relative to child self-ratings and parent ratings) variance in adult self-ratings accounted for by teacher ratings

$k_Y = k_X = 3$, $s = 2.43$, and $u = 9$ (as throughout), but $k_A$ is now $3 + 3 = 6$. $f^2$ for the partial is $(1 - .05)^{-1/2.43} - 1 = .0213$. **m** now equals $120 - 6 - (3 + 3 + 3)/2 = 109.5$, so $v = 109.5 (2.43) + 1 - 9/2 = 263$. $\lambda = .0213 (9 + 263 + 1) = 5.8$, and the specification summary is:

$$a = .05 \qquad u = 9 \qquad v = 263 \qquad \lambda = 5.8,$$

and power is found from Table 9.3.2 to equal .32.

Thus, good power (.89) characterizes the analysis of the main research factor, but power for the tests of the unique relationships of the others is poor. For her to find the latter significant when the tests are performed would require either that the strength of association be greater than she supposes or that she be lucky (or both). It is important to note that if matters are pretty much as she suspects, then an ordering of the three sets in which the main factor was not first would produce less power for its test, exactly as would be the case if the research factor sets were instead single variables.

**10.13**   A political polling organization is planning a large-scale inquiry into political attitudes and preferences of the electorate using a probability sample of about 900 cases. Their data include the respondents' demographic characteristics and their ratings of three prospective presidential candidates of the same party. They plan a hierarchical analysis of the following four demographic characteristics, each to be treated as a research factor, in the order given: Age (1 variable), Sex (1 variable), Race (3 levels, hence 2 variables), and Education (2 variables, years of education and centered years of education squared).

It is decided that Model 2 error will be used, that is, at each level of the hierarchy, the error matrix will be the residual from prediction by all four research factors. The first series will use as the dependent variable set the 3 (= $k_Y$) candidate ratings, and, where the research factor is found to be significant, a second series of analyses will be performed on the *unique* candidate ratings, that is, each candidate's ratings from which the other two candidates' ratings have been partialled. This should have the effect of removing "halo" and result in a measure of candidate preference. The .01 significance criterion is to be used. Table 10.3.3 gives the relevant parameters for the analyses of the planned tests and provides the resulting power values as obtained from interpolating in Tables 9.3.1.

**Table 10.3.3**
Power Analysis Parameters and Results of Political Polling Study
(Example 10.13)

First Series: $k_Y = k_D = 3$

| X | $k_X$ | $k_C$ | $k_A$ | $k_G$ | s | u | v | $f^2$ | $\lambda$ | Power at $a = .01$ |
|---|---|---|---|---|---|---|---|---|---|---|
| Age | 1 | 0 | 0 | 5 | 1 | 3 | 891 | .02 | 17.9 | .86 |
| Sex·Age | 1 | 0 | 1 | 4 | 1 | 3 | 891 | .03 | 26.9 | .97 |
| Race·Age + Sex | 2 | 0 | 2 | 2 | 2 | 6 | 1782 | .01 | 17.9 | .76 |
| Ed·Age + Sex + Race | 2 | 0 | 4 | 0 | 2 | 6 | 1782 | .02 | 35.8 | .99 |

Second Series: $k_Y = k_D = 1$

| Age | 1 | 2 | 0 | 5 | 1 | 1 | 893 | .015 | 13.4 | .86 |
| Sex·Age | 1 | 2 | 1 | 4 | 1 | 1 | 893 | .015 | 13.4 | .86 |
| Race·Age + Sex | 2 | 2 | 2 | 2 | 1 | 2 | 893 | .01 | 9.0 | .55 |
| Ed·Age + Sex + Race | 2 | 2 | 4 | 0 | 1 | 2 | 893 | .015 | 13.4 | .77 |

Note that this design results in the use of four types of association: whole (for Age in the first series), X-semipartial (for the remainder of the first series), Y-semipartial (for Age in the second series), and bipartial (for the remainder of the second series). The type of association and error model is implied by where the zeros occur for $k_C$, $k_A$, and $k_G$ in Table 10.3.3.

As can be seen in the table, it is expected that the ES values for these research factors will be small, the directly posited $f^2$ values ranging from .01 to .03. These are for Model 2 error (except for Education, the last factor in the hierarchy, where $k_G = 0$ and $|E_2| = |E|$) and involve four different types of association.

Note that despite the small effect sizes posited and the .01 significance criterion, the power values are generally high (but see example 10.28). This is due to the large N in combination with the small set sizes that result in small u and s. The second series is, in fact, made up of hierarchical univariate MRC analyses, that is, they involve a single (albeit partialled) dependent variable.

10.3.5  FACTORIAL DESIGN MANOVA.  SC handles factorial design MANOVA by the use of Model 2 error. Consider a two-factor design for the factors (main effects) **U** and **V**, and the **U** × **V** interaction.

If **U** and **V** are orthogonal (balanced) experimentally manipulated conditions, then we will be interested in each unpartialled by (because they are independent of) the other. If nonorthogonal, to obtain "pure" main effects, we will need to assess the effects of **U·V** and **V·U**.

If either **U** or **V** (or both) are nonexperimental (e.g., diagnosis, college major) they must be entered hierarchically, ordered by assumed causal priority (see Section 10.3.4).

Thus, we may be interested in assessing the variance accounted for by any of the following sources: **U**, **U·V**, **V**, **V·U**, and the **U** × **V** interaction:

1. The proportion of variance **U** accounts for in the dependent variable set **D**, thus $R^2_{Y,X}$ is $R^2_{D,U}$, the whole type of association that we treated in the K-group MANOVA above.

2. The proportion of variance that **U·V** accounts for in set **D**, thus $R^2_{Y,X}$ is $R^2_{D,UV·V}$, an **X** semipartial type of association.

3. The same two types for **V** and **V·U**.

4. The proportion of variance accounted for by the **U** × **V** interaction, in which case $R^2_{Y,X}$ is $R^2_{D,UV·U+V}$, where **UV** is the usual product set (Cohen & Cohen, 1983, Chapter 8), and **U** + **V** is the combination of the two sets.

In the one-way MANOVA whole-association cases illustrated in the preceding examples we used Model 1 error. In those cases, the $|E|$ of Equation (10.2.1) for **L** is simply the complement of the $|H|$ matrix. Thus, scaled as correlation, to test for any source of variance (the hypothesis) **X**, $|H|$ is $R^2_{Y,X}$ and the $|E|$ for error Model 1 is

$$(10.3.5) \qquad |E_1| = 1 - R^2_{Y,X}.$$

In factorial designs, we wish to exclude from error, not only the variance due to the hypothesis **X**, but all the other research factors and interactions that together comprise the set **G**. Thus,

$$(10.3.6) \qquad |E_2| = 1 - R^2_{Y,X + G}$$

or, equivalently,

$$(10.3.7) \qquad |E_2| = 1 - R^2_{Y,Cells}.$$

$|E_2|$ is thus the within-cell or "pure" error variance that is standard in factorial designs.

For power analysis of any hypothesis in factorial designs (main effects or interactions), we specialize the error reduction ratio **g** of Equation (10.2.10) to

$$(10.3.8) \qquad g = (1 - R^2_{Y,Cells})/(1 - R^2_{Y,X}).$$

We then determine the Model 1 **L** as before, and from it the $f^2_1$. As noted in Section 2, to find the Model 2 $f^2$ we employ

$$(10.2.11) \qquad f^2_2 = f^2_1/g.$$

For example, in the two factor design, take **U** as the source of variance **X** whose $f^2_2$ is to be found. We posit $R^2_{D,U}$, take its complement as $L_W$ (10.2.6), and determine $f^2_1$ as $L^{-1/S} - 1$ (10.2.2). We then estimate $R^2_{D,Cells}$ as the proportion of between-cells variance, and its complement as $|\boldsymbol{E}_1|$. Since $|\boldsymbol{E}_1|$ is $1 - R^2_{D,U}$, we can find **g** from (10.3.8) and $f^2_2$ from (10.2.11).

When **X** is **U·V**, the operation proceeds similarly. Since this is an **X** semipartial type of association, find $L_{XS}$ from the posited $1 - R^2_{D·V,U·V}$ (10.2.9), then $f^2_1$ from (10.2.2). The within cell error $|\boldsymbol{E}_2|$ remains as before, but $|\boldsymbol{E}_1|$ is now $1 - R^2_{D,U·V}$, so the **g** ratio differs from before. Dividing $f^2_1$ by **g** produces $f^2_2$.

For the **UV** product set to be the **U** × **V** interaction, it must have partialled from it the **U** and **V** sets. Thus, the variance it accounts for is the **X** semipartial $R^2_{D,UV·U+V}$. In a two-factor design, the interaction is analyzed using Model 1 error, because there are no further sources of variance that can be used to reduce error.

The above generalizes to multifactor MANOVAs. The source of variance (**X**) of interest may be an unpartialled main effect or a main effect partialled by one or more other main effects. This will determine the type of association to employ for $R^2_{Y,X}$ and **L**, and $|\boldsymbol{E}_1|$ and $|\boldsymbol{E}_2|$ are defined by Equations (10.3.5) and (10.3.7), respectively, and **g** from Equation (10.3.8). The highest order interaction effect (if it is to be power-analyzed) includes all the main effects and all the other interactions in its definition, and it alone is therefore analyzed with Model 1 error.

### Illustrative Example

**10.14**   A psychiatric research team plans a cooperative research study in which patients in four mental hospitals are to be assigned randomly to two innovative treatment groups and one control group, and assessed following treatment. Hospitals (**H**) comprise a set of ($k_H$ = ) 3 effects-coded variables and treatments (**T**) a set of ($k_T$) = 2 dummy coded variables, the control group being the reference group. (See Cohen & Cohen, 1983, pp. 335–345 for the coding details and an MRC analysis of this design.) The dependent variable set **D** is made up of a mental status rating by an independent psychiatric rater and the patient's self rating of symptom status, thus $k_D$ = 2. Allowing for attrition, the research team plans a total **N** = 120, and they assume that, given the vagaries of clinical research, the cell sample sizes in this 3 × 4 design will not be equal or proportional, hence the design will be nonorthogonal. They intend that the **a** = .05 significance criterion will be used.

The research team is not much interested in hospital effects as such; they are included to serve as a statistical control variable in the assessment of treatments, and to assess the possibility that the treatment effects vary over (are conditional on) hospitals; that is, that there is an $H \times T$ interaction. Thus, for this research, a power analysis of the $H$ main effect need not be undertaken. However, in the interest of completeness, we will have them go through a power analysis of $H$.

They posit a value of $R^2_{Y,X} = R^2_{D,H} = .02$. For this test, $k_Y = k_D = 2$, $k_X = k_H = 3$ (the number of hospitals less 1), so $s = 2$ (Table 10.2.1). Since the type of association is whole, from (10.2.6) we find that $L_W = 1 - .02 = .98$, and from (10.2.2), $f^2 = .0102$. This is Model 1 $f^2$, and presumes $|E_1| = 1 - R^2_{D,H} = .98$. They anticipate that $R^2_{Y, \text{Cells}}$ (based on 11 df for the 12 cells of the design) $= .22$, so from (10.3.7), $|E_1| = .78$, and from (10.3.8), $g = .78/.98 = .7959$. Then from (10.2.11), the desired $f^2_2 = .0102/.7959 = .0128$. (Presumably, in a study in which $H$ was of serious interest, we would have a more robust ES for this main effect.) $u = 2 (3) = 6$, $m = 120 - 11 - (2 + 3 + 3)/2 = 105$, so $v = 107.5 (2) + 1 - (2) (2)/2 = 214$. Finally we find $\lambda = .0813 (4 + 214 + 1) = 2.8$. The specification summary is:

$$a = .05 \qquad u = 6 \qquad v = 208 \qquad \lambda = 2.8.$$

A glance at Table 9.3.2 at block $u = 6$ in the vicinity of $\lambda = 2$ shows that it is hardly worth the trouble to crank up the interpolation Equation (9.3.2) to determine power. Nevertheless, dutifully doing so, we find power $= .19$. (The research team reminds me that this test and its power is irrelevant to their research purpose. I, in turn, apologize for my pedagogic zeal.)

*Their* central interest is in the effect of treatments controlled for whatever hospital effects exist, that is, in $T \cdot H$. The team's collective judgment is that the population $R^2_{D,T \cdot H}$ (an $X$ semipartial) is somewhere in the vicinity of .12. For this test, $k_Y = 2$, $k_X = k_T = 2$, so $s = 2$. To find $f^2$, they need the $L_{XS}$ of (10.2.9), which calls for the partial $R^2_{D \cdot H, T \cdot H}$, which they posit to be .13. Note that this is assumed to be only slightly larger than the semipartial, because they do not expect a large $H$ effect on $D$. From (10.2.2), they find $f^2 = .0721$. This is the Model 1 $f^2$, and presumes $|E| = 1 - R^2_{D,T \cdot H} = .88$. Because, as noted above, they anticipate that $R^2_{Y,\text{Cells}} = .22$, from (10.3.7) $|E_2| = .78$, and from (10.3.1), $g = .78/.88 = .8864$. Then, from (10.2.11), the desired $f^2_2 = .0721/.8864 = .0813$.

$u = 2 (2) = 4$, $m = 120 - (3 + 6) - (2 + 2 + 3)/2 = 107.5$, so $v = 107.5 (2) + 1 - (2) (2)/2 = .0813 (4 + 214 + 1) = 17.8$. The specification summary is:

$$a = .05 \qquad u = 3 \qquad v = 214 \qquad \lambda = 17.8.$$

Entering Table 9.3.2 (for $a = .05$) and interpolating via (9.3.2) gives power $= .93$. That's splendid! They wonder what power would be at $a = .01$. From Table 9.3.1, for the same parameters, power is .82. Not bad at all.

The existence of an $\mathbf{H} \times \mathbf{T}$ interaction would indicate that the treatment effects vary across hospitals, a matter of considerable interest and concern, because it would mean that conclusions about treatment efficacy would require qualification. They posit that the proportion of the variance accounted for by the interaction, the $\mathbf{X}$ semipartial $R^2_{\mathbf{D},\mathbf{HT} \cdot \mathbf{H}+\mathbf{T}} = .08$, an amount they judge large enough to be important. As planned, what is the power of the interaction test?

To find $f^2$ requires the partial $R^2_{\mathbf{D} \cdot \mathbf{H}+\mathbf{T},\mathbf{HT} \cdot \mathbf{H}+\mathbf{T}}$, which they posit to be .09, and for $\mathbf{s} = 2$ gives .0483 for the $f^2$, which employs Model 1 error, $1 - R^2_{\mathbf{D},\mathbf{HT} \cdot \mathbf{H}+\mathbf{T}}$. (Since $\mathbf{H}$, $\mathbf{T}$, and their interaction exhaust the between cells variance, set $\mathbf{G}$ is empty, so it is Model 1 error we employ in testing the interaction in a two-factor design.) For the $\mathbf{df}$, $\mathbf{u} = k_Y k_X = k_D k_{HT} = 2 (6) = 12$, $\mathbf{m} = 120 - 5 - (2 + 6 + 3)/2 = 109.5$, so $\mathbf{v} = 109.5 (2) + 1 - (2) (6)/2 = 214$. Then, $\lambda = .0483 (12 + 214 + 1) = 11.0$, so the summary of the specifications for the interaction test is:

$$\mathbf{a} = .05 \qquad \mathbf{u} = 12 \qquad \mathbf{v} = 214 \qquad \lambda = 11.0.$$

Entering Table 9.3.2 and interpolating via (9.3.2) gives power $= .53$. That's rather poor.

Thus, although there is power to spare for the test of treatments, if the interaction accounts for as much as .09 of the variance, it is a fifty-fifty proposition that it will be detected.

If it is important to detect an interaction of that magnitude using this design, there is no avoiding increasing $\mathbf{N}$. Let's check out the effect of increasing $\mathbf{N}$ by 50% (to 180). Increasing $\mathbf{N}$ by 60 increases $\mathbf{v}$ by 2 (60) to 334. $\lambda$ is now .0483 (12 + 334 + 1) = 16.9, which yields power $= .77$, which may be found satisfactory by the research team. We return to this question after we have considered the rest of the power analysis. (Also, see example 10.29.)

A useful feature of SC (although not of MANOVA) is its ability to focus on unique aspects of a variable by partialling from it the other variables in its set, as we have already seen. The two dependent variables here, psychiatrist- and self-rating, $\mathbf{d_1}$ and $\mathbf{d_2}$, are likely to be correlated to some degree, yet the team is interested in that which is unique to each relative to the other. This is defined as each partialled by the other, $\mathbf{d_1} \cdot \mathbf{d_2}$ and $\mathbf{d_2} \cdot \mathbf{d_1}$. They are interested in a power analysis of the a proportion of variance accounted for by $\mathbf{T} \cdot \mathbf{H}$ in each of these unique dependent variables, which they posit to be .05. While this is a bipartial type of association, note that $k_Y = 1$, hence this can be treated (approximately) as a semipartial multiple $R^2$ with a partialled dependent variable, and from (9.2.2), $f^2_1 = .05/.95 = .0526$, which presumes $|\mathbf{E_1}| = .95$. Since $|\mathbf{E_2}| = 1 - R^2_{Y,\text{Cells}} = .78$, we find from (10.2.10) $\mathbf{g} = .78/.95 = .8211$, and from (10.2.11) $f^2_2 = .0526/.8211 = .0641$.

Since $k_Y = 1$ and $k_X = k_T = 2$, for the **df**, $u = 1(2) = 2$, $m = 120 - (3 + 6) - (1 + 2 + 3)/2 = 108$, so $v = 108(1) + 1 - 2/2 = 108$. From (10.3.1), $\lambda = .0641(2 + 108 + 1) = 7.1$. The specifications for these two tests of the unique components are:

$$a = .05 \qquad u = 2 \qquad v = 108 \qquad \lambda = 7.1$$

From the power Table 9.3.2, interpolating in $u = 2$ for $\lambda = 7.1$ and $v = 108$ with Equation (9.3.2), we find power $= .65$. One wishes it were higher.

Finally, because of the coding employed for **T**, the unique aspects of those two variables, $t_1 \cdot t_2 + H$ represent the contrast of each of the treatment groups with the control group, controlled for hospital differences. Each may be related to both the whole set **D** and the two unique dependent variables just considered.

Taking first the whole **D**, they posit $f^2_2$ directly as .08. Since $k_Y = 2$ and $k_X = 1$, $s = 1$. $u = 2(1) = 2$, $m = 120 - (4 + 6) - (2 + 1 + 3)/2 = 107$, so $v = 107(1) + 1 - 2(1)/2 = 107$. Now $\lambda = .08(2 + 107 + 1) = 8.8$. The summary for these tests:

$$a = .05 \qquad u = 2 \qquad v = 107 \qquad \lambda = 8.8.$$

Table 9.3.2 gives the interpolated power value of .76. At least some of the team members are likely to consider this not high enough, because the hypotheses of the effect of each treatment compared to the control are central to the investigation. There may also be some nervousness about the ES being overestimated (often, sadly, the case).

They then consider finally the effect of each treatment on the unique aspects of each outcome rating. They are interested in being able to detect an ES as large as $f^2_2 = .05$ for any of these four hypotheses. Note that we are now considering bipartials between two single variables, for example $t_1 \cdot t_2 + H$ with $d_2 \cdot d_1$, so $k_Y = k_X = 1$, $u = 1$, and $s = 1$. $m = 120 - (4 + 6) - (1 + 1 + 3)/2 = 107.5$, so $v = 107.5(1) + 1 - 1/2 = 108$. Thus, $\lambda = .05(1 + 108 + 1) = 5.5$. The summary specifications for each of these four tests is:

$$a = .05 \qquad u = 1 \qquad v = 108 \qquad \lambda = 5.5.$$

Interpolating in Table 9.3.2, we find power $= .64$. Although these hypotheses are presumably not central to the investigation, the research team is disappointed to find power here so low.

On the whole, for the specifications used, it seems that with the $N = 120$ that is planned, only the overall test of treatments would have good power (.93). The power of the test on each of the two treatment contrasts on the set of two dependent variables might seem barely adequate (.76), but that of treatments on unique aspects of the two ratings is rather poor (.65), and that of the treatment contrasts on unique ratings no better (.64). What is likely to be a more serious deficiency than the latter, however, is that the power to test the $\mathbf{H} \times \mathbf{T}$ interaction is so low (.53) that a serious inconsistency of effects across hospitals might well go undetected.

In the framework of this design and these parameters, it seems desirable to expend the necessary additional effort to increase the sample size. (See example 10.29 in Section 10.4 for determining the $\mathbf{N}$ necessary for power = .80.) However, an alternative design may result in greater power for these parameters. See example 10.15 for the factorial MANCOVA in the next section.

### 10.3.6 Factorial Design MANCOVA.

When, to a factorial design MANOVA we add a covariate set, we have a factorial design MANCOVA. Since a covariate set is involved, the basic type of association is partial, and because we will normally use within cells error to test main effects and interactions, we will employ Model 2 error.

**Illustrative Example**

**10.15** We return to our psychiatric research team of example 10.14. They were planning a cooperative research effort involving ($\mathbf{T}$) two treatments and a control ($\mathbf{k_T} = 2$), crossed with four ($\mathbf{H}$) hospitals ($\mathbf{k_H} = 3$), and utilizing psychiatrist rating and patient self-rating ($\mathbf{k_D} = 2$) as the dependent variable set. The total $\mathbf{N}$ was planned to be 120, and the tests were to be performed using an $\mathbf{a} = .05$ significance criterion. Planned as a MANOVA, while the power for the test on treatments ($\mathbf{T \cdot H}$) was high, power for other important tests in the design was poor, and a substantial increase in sample size seemed indicated.

Enter MANCOVA. The psychologist on the team suggested that their problem was that they had been planning for only post-treatment ratings. If they could organize the research so as to obtain pre-treatment ratings, they could study change rather than post-treatment status. Specifically, if the two pre-treatment ratings were used as a covariate set, they would in effect be studying *regressed* change, with a likely substantial increase in power. This tactic ("blocking," "having each subject serve as his or her own control") is a well established method for "improving precision," "increasing efficiency," or "reducing error" in experimental design. (See Section 11.4.)

Again, despite its irrelevance to the research but in the interest of completeness (and with apology), consider the power of the test on the hospital main effect, whose $\mathbf{R^2_{Y,X}} = \mathbf{R^2_{D,H}} = .02$. With the pre-treatment covariates partialled, they now posit $\mathbf{R^2_{Y,X}} = \mathbf{R^2_{D \cdot A, H \cdot A}} = .04$. From (10.2.7), $\mathbf{L} = 1$

$-.04 = .96$. For $s = 2$, from (10.2.2), the Model 1 $f^2 = .0206$. This presumes $|E_1| = 1 - R^2_{D,H+A}$, which, because of the strong relationship they expect between $D$ and $A$ (post and pre), they posit to be .45. But the Model 2 error that the analysis will employ will also remove from error the variance due to $T$ and the $H \times T$ interaction, $|E_2| = 1 - R^2_{D,H+T+HT+A}$, or $1 - R^2_{D,Cells+A}$, which they posit to be .25. (Note that in all, there are 13 independent variables in this $R^2$.) Thus, from (10.2.10), $g = .25/.45 = .5556$, and from (10.2.11), $f^2_2 = .0206/.5556 = .0371$. Note that although this ES remains quite small, it is nevertheless three times as large as in the original design (.0128). $u = 2 (3) = 6$ (as before), $m = 120 - (2 + 8) - (2 + 3 + 3)/2 = 106$, so $v = 106 (2) + 1 - 2 (3)/2 = 210$. Finally, from (10.3.1), we have $\lambda = .0371 (6 + 210 + 1) = 8.1$. The specifications are:

$$a = .05 \qquad u = 6 \qquad v = 210 \qquad \lambda = 8.1,$$

and interpolating in Table 9.3.2, we find power = .52. It is just as well that this test is not relevant to this research; nevertheless, it is noteworthy that the use of these covariates almost tripled the ES and strongly increased power. But note, too, that the covariate set was strongly related to the post-treatment measures, $D$; however, this is often the case when they are pre-treatment measures.

Turning to the test of major interest, that of $T \cdot H$, they hardly need to improve its power of .93 as found in the original design for which they posited $R^2_{D,T \cdot H} = .12$. Now it is the partial association they want, and in addition to the pair of pre-measures, $H$ will be partialled from both sides: Set $A$ in the expression $R^2_{D \cdot A, T \cdot A}$ contains five variables, the two pre-measures and the three variables that code $H$. They posit that $T$, adjusted for $H$ and pre-test measures will account for .25 of the variance in post-test measures, also adjusted for $H$ and pre-test measures. A less formal statement might be that $T$ is believed to account for .25 of the variance in (regressed) change, controlling for hospital effects.

$k_Y = 2$, and $k_X = k_T = 2$, so $s = 2$. From (10.2.7), they find $L = 1 - .25 = .75$, and from (10.2.2), the Model 1 $f^2 = .1547$. They expect that when $|E_2| = 1 - R^2_{D,Cells}$ is used, it will be about $(g =) .90$ as large, so from (10.2.11), $f^2_2 = .1547/.90 = .1719$. For the df, $u = 2 (2) = 4$, $m = 120 - (5 + 6) - (2 + 2 + 3)/2 = 105.5$, so $v = 105.5 (2) + 1 - 2 (2)/2 = 210$. Then, $\lambda = .1719 (4 + 210 + 1) = 37.0$. The specification summary is:

$$a = .05 \qquad u = 4 \qquad v = 210 \qquad \lambda = 37.0.$$

No interpolation is necessary in Table 9.3.2 — power is greater than .995. If $a = .01$ (Table 9.3.1) were specified, power would still be greater than .99!

It is for the test of the $H \times T$ interaction that the original design was underpowered — .53. They posited that the interaction accounted for $(R^2_{D,HT \cdot H + T} =)$ .09 of the variance in **D**. With the pretest measures to be employed as covariates, they need to posit the proportion of the variance in regressed change (i.e., in covariate-adjusted post-treatment ratings) for which the interaction accounts; they hypothesize that to be .16. The partial $R^2$ that they need in order to find $L_P$ from Equation (10.2.7) includes in its set of covariates, not only the two pre-experimental ratings, but also the combined **H** and **T** sets, the partialling of which from the **HT** product set defines the **H** × **T** interaction. Thus, the full covariate set **A** in $R^2_{D \cdot A, HT \cdot A}$ contains $(k_A =)$ 7 variables. They posit $R^2_{D \cdot A, HT \cdot A} = .18$. So $L = 1 - .18 = .82$, and, for $s = 2$, from (10.2.2) the Model 1 $f^2 = .1043$. (Recall that it is Model 1 error that is appropriate for this interaction test.)

As in the original design, $u = k_Y k_X = k_D k_{HT} = 2 (6) = 12$. **m** is now 120 $-7 - (2 + 6 + 3)/2 = 107.5$, so $v = 107.5 (2) + 1 - 2 (6)/2 = 210$. Thus, $\lambda = .1043 (12 + 210 + 1) = 23.3$. The specifications for this MANCOVA are:

$$a = .05 \qquad u = 12 \qquad v = 210 \qquad \lambda = 23.3.$$

Table 9.3.2 gives the interpolated power value of .90.

Compare this with the original design's .53 power with $N = 120$, or even the .77 power found for $N = 180$. It is true that these results depend on a strong covariate set, but such increases in power are not atypical when the measures used for pre and post have good psychometric properties.

Consider now the tests involving the two unique dependent variables, $d_1 \cdot d_2$ and $d_2 \cdot d_1$. With the two baseline ratings as covariates, they posit the effect of **T•H** on each of these as $f^2 = .14$. Thus, $k_Y = 1$, $k_X = k_T = 2$, and **s** $= 1$. For the **df**, $u = 1 (2) = 2$, $m = 120 - (5 + 6) - 1 + 2 + 3)/2 = 106$, so $v = 106 (1) + 1 - 1 (2)/2 = 106$. $\lambda = .14 (2 + 106 + 1) = 15.3$, so the specification summary is:

$$a = .05 \qquad u = 2 \qquad v = 106 \qquad \lambda = 15.3.$$

Interpolation in Table 9.3.2 gives power $= .94$. Compare this with the previous value in the MANOVA version of .65.

They now consider the tests of the contrasts of each of the treatment groups with the control group, controlled for hospital differences (as before), but now also controlled for the two pre-experimental rating covariates. For these two tests they posit $f^2_2 = .16$. As in the MANOVA version for these contrasts, $k_Y = 2$, and $k_X = 1$, so $s = 1$ and $u = 2$. $m = 120 - (6 + 6) - 2 (2 + 1 + 3)/2 = 105$, so $v = 105 (1) + 1 - 2 (1)/2 = 105$. From (10.3.1), $\lambda = .16 (2 + 105 + 1) = 17.3$, so

$$\mathbf{a} = .05 \qquad \mathbf{u} = 2 \qquad \mathbf{v} = 105 \qquad \lambda = 17.3.$$

Eyeball interpolation in Table 9.3.2 gives power $= .96$ for these two tests. Without the covariates, i.e., when the **X** set was post-ratings rather than regressed *change* in ratings, power was .76.

Finally, they assess the power of the four tests: each treatment contrast for each unique rating component, but now also employing the covariates. Because of the potent covariates, they now posit $\mathbf{f}^2_2 = .09$. The associations here are bipartials between two *single* variables, for example, $\mathbf{t_1 \cdot t_2 + H + A}$ with $\mathbf{d_2 \cdot d_1 + H}$. Thus, $\mathbf{k_Y} = \mathbf{k_X} = \mathbf{s} = \mathbf{u} = 1$ (as before); $\mathbf{m} = 120 - (6 + 6) - (1 + 1 + 3)/2 = 105.5$, so $\mathbf{v} = 105.5\,(1) + 1\,(1)/2 = 106$. $\lambda = .09\,(1 + 106 + 1) = 9.7$. The summary specification:

$$\mathbf{a} = .05 \qquad \mathbf{u} = 1 \qquad \mathbf{v} = 106 \qquad \lambda = 9.7.$$

Interpolating in Table 9.3.2 using (9.3.2) gives power $= .87$. Without the covariates, power for these four tests was .64.

The increase in power provided by the inclusion of the pre-experimental ratings as covariates on the tests involving unique components of **D** and **T·H** is sufficient to make the increase in **N** from 120 to 180 that was contemplated by the research team unnecessary. In fact, the use of a covariate set that greatly reduced error variance (without a material reduction of hypothesis variance) increased power more than the sample size increase with the MANOVA design.

With all that power, the research team contemplates the possibility of a budget reduction with its attendant reduction in **N**. What **N** would they need for power to be at least .80? See example 10.30.

## 10.4   DETERMINING SAMPLE SIZE

The determination of the **N** necessary to attain a desired level of power (given the other parameters) proceeds by inverting the procedures of the preceding section, where power was found as a function of **N**. As was the case there, we will employ the noncentrality parameter $\lambda$, a function of $\mathbf{f}^2$ (the effect size), and the numerator and denominator degrees of freedom, **u** and **v**, respectively, as shown in Equation (10.3.1).

Tables 9.4.1 and 9.4.2 of Chapter 9 give the $\lambda$ necessary for power values of .25, .50, .60, 2/3, .70(.05).95, and .99, for $\mathbf{u} = 1(1)15$, 18, 24, 30, 40, 48, 60, and 120, and $\mathbf{v} = 20$, 60, 120, and $\infty$. Interpolation for **u** and **v** is linear in their reciprocals (see below).

The procedure for determining **N** is as follows:

1. Enter Table 9.4.1 (for **a** = .01) or Table 9.4.2 (for **a** = .05) with the desired power, **u**, and a trial value of **v**, usually **v** = 120, and determine the value of $\lambda$.

2. Inverting Equation (10.3.1), a value of **v** is implied by this $\lambda$, $f^2$, and **u**:

(10.4.1)                               $$v = \frac{\lambda}{f^2} u - 1.$$

$f^2$ is set by means of the methods of Section 10.2.2.

3. To find the $\lambda$ for the implied **v**, one must interpolate in Tables 9.4.1–2. Interpolation between $\lambda$ values for a given **v** is linear in the reciprocals of the **v**'s. For the lower and upper tabled **v** values between which the implied **v** falls ($v_L$, $v_U$) and their respective $\lambda$ values ($\lambda_L$, $\lambda_U$), the interpolated value of $\lambda$ for **v** is given by Equation (9.4.2), restated here for convenience:

(10.4.2)                  $$\lambda = \lambda_L - \frac{1/v_L - 1/v}{1/v_L - 1/v_U}(\lambda_L - \lambda_U).$$

Note that when the trial **v** = 120 and the implied **v** > 120, which is frequently the case, $v_L$ = 120, $1/v_L$ = .00833, and $v_U$ = $\infty$, so $1/v_U$ = 0.

4. Substitute this $\lambda$ in Equation (10.4.1) to obtain the iterated value of **v**. Then, to find **N**, substitute in

(10.4.3)      $$N = \frac{1}{s}\left(v + \frac{u}{2} - 1\right) + \frac{k_Y + k_X + 3}{2} + \max(k_C, k_A + k_G),$$

whose terms are as defined in Equations (10.1.6–9).

The procedure is illustrated in the examples, which are organized by types of design, as in Section 10.3. The reader will find it useful to refer to Section 10.3 for a more detailed exposition of the particulars of the designs, and of the particulars and the rationale for setting the parameters for the examples, as needed.

10.4.1  WHOLE ASSOCIATION: QUANTITATIVE WITH QUANTITATIVE. In these problems, in $R^2_{Y,X}$, **Y** is a set **D** and **X** a set **B**, both made up of quantitative variables. For these problems, where neither partialled sets (**A** or **C**) nor Model 2 error and hence a set **G** (Section 10.1.2) are involved, the last term in Equation (10.4.3) equals zero.

**Illustrative Examples**

**10.16**  A market research company is planning an investigation of the relationship between personality traits and consumer attitudes, represented respectively by 6 and 4 measures. They estimate that the population $R^2_{Y,X}$ between these sets is .20. Using $a = .01$, for power $= .90$, what $N$ is required?

For $k_Y = 6$, $k_X = 4$, Table 10.2.1 gives $s = 3.49$. Since for whole association, $L$ is $R^2$–complementary, from (10.2.2), $f^2 = (1 - .80)^{-1/3.49} - 1 = .0660$. $u = 6(4) = 24$. Summarizing the ingredients for the determination of $N$,

$$
\begin{array}{ccc}
a = .01 & u = 24 & \text{power} = .90 \\
f^2 = .0660 & s = 3.49 & k_Y = 6 \qquad k_X = 4.
\end{array}
$$

First, Table 9.4.1 (for $a = .01$) gives for $u = 24$ at power $= .90$ for trial $v = 120$, $\lambda = 42.7$, and for $v = \infty$, $\lambda = 36.1$. To find the implied $v$, (10.4.1) gives $42.7/.0660 - 24 - 1 = 622$. Then, Equation (10.4.2) gives the interpolated $\lambda =$

$$
42.7 - \frac{.00833 - 1/622}{.00833 - 0}(42.7 - 36.1) = 37.4,
$$

which, when substituted back in Equation (10.4.1), gives the iterated value: $v = 37.4/.0660 - 24 - 1 = 542$. Substituting this value together with the other parameters in Equation (10.4.3), gives

$$
N = \frac{1}{3.49}\left(542 + \frac{24}{2} - 1\right) + \frac{4 + 6 + 3}{2} + 0 = 165.
$$

Thus, a sample of 165 cases will have a probability of rejecting the null hypothesis (at $a = .01$) in the relationship between the sets of personality and consumer attitude measures if the population $R^2_{Y,X} = .20$.

They will of course also be interested in various follow-up tests. One set of these is made up of the relationship between the set of personality measures and each of the unique consumer attitudes, the latter defined as an attitude score from which the other three attitude scores have been partialled. The form of association of $R^2_{Y,X}$ is $Y$-semipartial, $R^2_{D \cdot C,B}$, where $B$ is the personality set, $D$ is one of the attitude scores (say, $a_2$), and $C$ is a set made up of the other attitude scores ($a_1 + a_3 + a_4$). They posit $f^2 = .075$ (conventionally, between a "small" and "medium" ES), and wish to determine the $N$ for power $= .90$, at $a = .01$, as before. Now $k_Y = k_D = 1$, $k_X = k_B = 3$, and $k_C = 3$. With one dependent variable, what they have now is a multiple correlation with a partialled dependent variable, so $s = 1$, and $u = 3$. The specifications for these four tests are:

$$\mathbf{a} = .01 \qquad \mathbf{u} = 3 \qquad \text{power} = .90$$
$$\mathbf{f}^2 = .075 \qquad \mathbf{s} = 1 \qquad \mathbf{k_Y} = 1 \qquad \mathbf{k_X} = 3 \qquad \mathbf{k_C} = 3.$$

Table 9.4.1 gives for power $= .90$, $\mathbf{u} = 3$, for trial $\mathbf{v} = 120$, $\lambda = 20.1$, and at $\mathbf{v} = \infty$, $\lambda = 19.2$. From (10.4.1), the implied $\mathbf{v}$ is $20.1/.075 - 3 - 1 = 264$. Interpolating with (10.4.2) yields $\lambda = 19.6$, and substituting that value back into (10.4.1) gives an iterated $\mathbf{v} = 257$. When this value and the other parameters are substituted in (10.4.3), $\mathbf{N} = 264$.

Since this value is much larger than the 165 required for the test of the whole association, they check out the $\mathbf{N}$ for these tests when the desired power is dropped to .80. When the above procedure is repeated for the $\lambda$ values at power $= .80$ (16.1, 15.5), $\mathbf{N}$ works out to 214.

When the other hypotheses of interest to them are assessed for necessary $\mathbf{N}$ they will need to reconcile these demands as a function of their importance and the marginal cost of acquiring data (Cohen & Cohen, 1983, pp. 162, 164–165).

**10.17**   In example 10.2, a psychiatric epidemiologist was planning to study, in a sample of 100 delinquent adolescents, the relationship between $(\mathbf{k_Y} =)$ 8 measures of offense frequency and $(\mathbf{k_X} =)$ 6 ratings on dimensions of psychopathology. Her posited $\mathbf{R}^2_{Y,X}$ of .25, given that $\mathbf{s} = 4.92$, resulted in $\mathbf{f}^2 = .0602$. She found that power for the test at the intended $\mathbf{a} = .01$ was .51. Let's determine what sample size would be necessary for power to be .80 for these specifications:

$$\mathbf{a} = .01 \qquad \mathbf{u} = 48 \qquad \text{power} = .80$$
$$\mathbf{f}^2 = .0602 \qquad \mathbf{s} = 4.92 \qquad \mathbf{k_Y} = 8 \qquad \mathbf{k_X} = 6.$$

Table 9.4.1 gives, for $\mathbf{u} = 48$ and power $= .80$, for trial $\mathbf{v} = 120$, $\lambda = 51.2$, and for $\mathbf{v} = \infty$, $\lambda = 39.3$. From (10.4.1), the implied $\mathbf{v} = 801$, from (10.4.2), the interpolated $\lambda = 41.1$; substituting this in (10.4.1) gives the iterated $\mathbf{v} = 633$. Finally, (10.4.3) gives $\mathbf{N} = 142$.

We then checked power at the more lenient $\mathbf{a} = .05$ criterion, and found it to be .74. What $\mathbf{N}$ would be necessary for power $= .80$ using $\mathbf{a} = .05$? Except for the latter, the specifications are as above. Entering Table 9.4.2 (for $\mathbf{a} = .05$), we find for $\mathbf{u} = 48$ and power $= .80$, for trial $\mathbf{v} = 120$, $\lambda = 37.5$, and for $\mathbf{v} = \infty$, $\lambda = 29.7$. Again, (10.4.1) gives the implied $\mathbf{v} = 574$, which, when substituted in (10.4.2), gives the interpolated $\lambda = 31.3$. When this is substituted in (10.4.1), the iterated $\mathbf{v} = 471$, which finally from (10.4.3) gives $\mathbf{N} = 109$.

Thus, the epidemiologist would need to increase her sample by about 40% to attain .90 power, and by about 10% for .80 power, given the original parameters.

**10.18**   In example 10.3, our epidemiologist changed her plans. Retaining the planned **N** of 100, she planned to reduce $k_Y$ to 3 and $k_X$ to 2, in order to reduce **s** and thereby increase $f^2$ from .0660 to .1180, and also to reduce **u** from 48 to 6. Thus revised, she found power to be .88. She wondered what sample size would be needed to increase power to .90 for the revised specifications:

$$a = .01 \qquad u = 6 \qquad \text{power} = .90$$
$$f^2 = .1180 \qquad s = 2 \qquad k_Y = 3 \qquad k_X = 2.$$

From Table 9.4.1, for **u** = 6 at power = .90, for trial **v** = 120, $\lambda$ = 24.8, and for **V** = $\infty$, $\lambda$ = 23.2. From (10.4.1), the implied **v** = 203. Interpolating with (10.4.2), $\lambda$ = 24.1 which, when entered into (10.4.1) yields the iterated **v** = 198, which, entered into (10.4.3) with the other parameters, yields **N** = 104. a slight increase over the 100 she was provisionally planning.

However, the idea had occurred to her that the posited $R^2_{Y.X}$ = .20 may be overestimated, and she checked the power on the possibility that $R^2_{Y.X}$ = .175, leading to $f^2$ = .1010, which she found to be .80. Assuming this reduced ES, what **N** would she need to detect it? Except for this $f^2$ = .1010, the specifications remain as before, and going through the series of equations, the **v** implied by $f^2$ and **u** is 239, the interpolated $\lambda$ = 24.0, the iterated **v** = 231, and **N** = 120. Thus, the addition of 20 cases beyond her original plan will provide some insurance, in the event that the population $R^2_{Y.X}$ = .175, that power will be .90.

**10.19**   Let's review, from example 10.4, the clinical psychologist's planning of a study of the relationship between ($k_X$ =) 3 physiological anxiety measures and ($k_Y$=) 2 behavioral anxiety ratings in a sample of 38 cases, where an alternative-hypothetical population matrix yielded an $R^2_{Y.X}$ = .2653, which led, given that **s** = 2, to an $f^2$ = .1666. The test was to be performed at **a** = .05. These specifications resulted in power = .69. What **N** would be required for the conventional .80 power? The complete specifications are:

$$a = .05 \qquad u = 6 \qquad \text{power} = .80$$
$$f^2 = .1666 \qquad s = 2 \qquad k_Y = 2 \qquad k_X = 3.$$

In Table 9.4.2, we find that at **u** = 6 for power = .80, at trial **v** = 120, $\lambda$ = 14.3. Equation (10.4.1) gives the implied **v** as 79. With $\lambda$ = 15.0 at **v** = 60, (10.4.2) gives the interpolated $\lambda$ as 14.7, the iterated **v** from (10.4.1) is 81, and (10.4.3) gives the necessary **N** = 45. (Note that despite the fact that the trial **v** of 120 is much larger than the iterated **v** of 80, it is the case that either beginning with a trial **v** of 60, or reiterating the iterated value, or both, results in the same necessary $N = 45$. It is usually the case that following the proposed procedure with trial $v = 120$ will provide sufficient accuracy.) Thus, an increase of sample size from 38 to 45 will, for these specifications, increase power from .69 to .80.

In example 10.4, the clinical psychologist tried to improve power without increasing sample size by dropping one of the behavioral anxiety scales, which was relatively weakly related to the physiological set (see Table 10.3.2). This resulted in $R^2_{Y,X} = .2008$ (actually a multiple $R^2$, because now $k_Y = 1$), and, with $s = 1$, $f^2 = .2512$. He was disappointed to discover that for these revised specifications, power was .68, less than the .69 of his original plans. Clearly, there is no power advantage in dropping the anxiety scale. Nevertheless, out of curiosity perhaps, what sample size would be required for the revised plans to have power $= .80$? The specifications summary is:

$$a = .05 \quad u = 3 \quad \text{power} = .80$$
$$f^2 = .2512 \quad s = 1 \quad k_Y = 1 \quad k_X = 3.$$

For $u = 3$ and power $= .80$, Table 9.4.1 gives for trial $v = 120$, $\lambda = 11.1$ and Equation (10.4.1) gives the $v$ implied to be 40. For $v = 20$, $\lambda = 13.2$, and for $v = 60$, $\lambda = 11.5$, and (10.4.2) gives the interpolated $\lambda = 11.9$. Substituting this in (10.4.1) gives the iterated $v = 43$, and (10.4.3) gives the necessary $N$ for the revised specifications as 47.

10.4.2 WHOLE ASSOCIATION: CATEGORICAL WITH QUANTITATIVE; K GROUP MANOVA. The conditions here are as in the preceding section, except that set $X$ ($=$ set $B$) is a categorical variable (nominal scale); that is, one made up of $K$ mutually exclusive and exhaustive groups, and $k_X = K - 1$. These conditions are those of a simple (one-way) MANOVA or discriminant analysis. The $N$ that is solved for is the *total* $N$. The distribution of $N$ over the $K$ groups partly determines $R^2_{Y,X}$ (as in MRC, see Cohen & Cohen, 1983, pp. 190–193) and therefore $f^2$, so it must be taken into consideration when setting the latter.

**Illustrative Examples**

**10.20** The experimental psychologist of example 10.5 was planning a learning study involving samples of 20 control and 10 each of three experimental groups, total $N = 50$. The dependent variable set was made up of a time and an error score, $k_Y = 2$, and the independent variable set was made up of $k_X = K - 1 = 3$ dummy variables coding group membership. He estimated that $(R^2_{Y,X}=) .15$ of the variance was accounted for in the population, and planned a test at $a = .05$. Since $s = 2$, $f^2 = .0847$. These specifications led to the determination that power would be .51. How larger need $N$ be for power to be .80? The specifications are:

$$\mathbf{a} = .05 \qquad \mathbf{u} = 6 \qquad \text{power} = .80$$
$$\mathbf{f}^2 = .0847 \qquad \mathbf{s} = 2 \qquad \mathbf{k_Y} = 2 \qquad \mathbf{k_X} = 3.$$

In Table 9.4.2, at $\mathbf{u} = 6$ and power $= .80$, for trial $\mathbf{v} = 120$, $\lambda = 14.3$, and for $\mathbf{v} = \infty$, $\lambda = 13.6$. Applying (10.4.1), the implied $\mathbf{v} = 162$, and from (10.4.2) the interpolated $\lambda = 14.1$. Re-applying (10.4.1) to this value, the iterated $\mathbf{v} = 160$, and finally (10.4.3) gives the necessary $\mathbf{N} = 85$. Since $\mathbf{R}^2_{Y,X}$ (like all squared correlation coefficients) depends in part on the relative frequencies in the categorical variable, the total $\mathbf{N}$ here should be divided 34,17,17,17. (It is fortuitous, of course, that it can be exactly divided in the same proportions.)

Thus, the sample size would need to be increased by 70% to achieve the conventional power of .80.

In example 10.5, we investigated the consequence to power of dropping one of the two dependent variables while maintaining the $\mathbf{R}^2_{Y,X}$ (now a multiple $\mathbf{R}^2$) at .15. Since $\mathbf{s}$ is now 1, $\mathbf{f}^2$ more than doubles to .1765, and power worked out to .66, a clear improvement over the .51 when $\mathbf{k_Y} = 2$. We determine the $\mathbf{N}$ that would be required by the new specifications, which are:

$$\mathbf{a} = .05 \qquad \mathbf{u} = 3 \qquad \text{power} = .80$$
$$\mathbf{f}^2 = .1765 \qquad \mathbf{s} = 1 \qquad \mathbf{k_Y} = 1 \qquad \mathbf{k_X} = 3.$$

Table 9.4.2 gives for $\mathbf{u} = 3$ and power $= .80$ the necessary $\lambda$ values to substitute in Equations (10.4.1-3), and the necessary $\mathbf{N}$ is found to be 65 (which would be divided 26,13,13,13, again a fortuitously proportionately exact division).

**10.21**   The advertising researcher in example 10.6 planned a MANOVA in a multivariable study primarily as a device to control experimentwise Type I error. Her plan to study the ratings of users of four brands of detergents ($\mathbf{k_X} = \mathbf{K} - 1 = 3$) on 12 ($= \mathbf{k_Y}$) product characteristics, posited an overall $\mathbf{R}^2_{Y,X} = .15$, which results in $\mathbf{f}^2 = .0566$, and she determined that at $\mathbf{a} = .05$, power was .58. What $\mathbf{N}$ would be necessary for power to be .80 for these specifications, which are summarized as follows:

$$\mathbf{a} = .05 \qquad \mathbf{u} = 36 \qquad \text{power} = .80$$
$$\mathbf{f}^2 = .0566 \qquad \mathbf{s} = 2.95 \qquad \mathbf{k_Y} = 12 \qquad \mathbf{k_X} = 3?$$

There is no block of values in Table 9.4.2 for $\mathbf{u} = 36$, so to obtain the necessary $\lambda$ values, linear interpolation in the reciprocals of $\mathbf{u_L} = 30$ and $\mathbf{u_U} = 40$ is necessary. We can employ Equation (10.4.2) for this purpose, replacing $\mathbf{v}$ by $\mathbf{u}$:

(10.4.4)                    $$\lambda = \lambda_L - \frac{1/u_L - 1/u}{1/u_L - 1/u_U}(\lambda_L - \lambda_U).$$

In Table 9.4.2, for power = .80 and trial $v$ = 120: for $u$ = 30, $\lambda_L$ = 29.0 and for $u$ = 40, $\lambda_U$ = 33.8. Substituting in (10.4.2) gives for $u$ = 36 and $v$ = 120, $\lambda$ = 32.2. Similarly, applying (10.4.4) at $v = \infty$, where $\lambda_L$ = 24.5 and $\lambda_U$ = 27.6, gives for $u$ = 36 and $v = \infty$, $\lambda$ = 26.6. We can now find from (10.4.1) using the trial value of 120 for $v$, the implied $v$ = 32.2/.0566 − 36 − 1 = 532, from (10.4.2) the interpolated $\lambda$ = 27.9, from (10.4.1) the iterated $v$ = 455, and finally, from (10.4.3), $N$ = 169.

Then our advertising psychologist considered an alternative plan in which she would reduce her 12 ratings to $k_Y$ = 3 summary scores and posit the same $R^2_{Y,X}$ = .15. With the new $s$ = 2.43, $f^2$ = .0692, and for the original $N$ = 120, at $a$ = .05, power = .89. If she follows this plan and is prepared to have power = .80, she can do the study with fewer than 120 cases. How many fewer? The specifications are:

$$a = .05 \quad u = 9 \quad \text{power} = .80$$
$$f^2 = .0692 \quad s = 2.43 \quad k_Y = 3 \quad k_X = 3.$$

The values needed from Table 9.4.2 are, for $u$ = 9 and power = .80, at trial $v$ = 120, $\lambda$ = 16.7, and at $v = \infty$, $\lambda$ = 15.6. Going through the cycle of Equations (10.4.1–3), we find that $N$ = 98 cases will provide .80 power, a reduction of 22 (18%).

But she also found that the ANOVA test of each of the three individual summary scores, positing $R^2_{Y,X}$ = .05 (now a multiple $R^2$ or $\eta^2$ − see Cohen & Cohen, 1983, pp. 196–198),had power = .52 for $N$ = 120. Clearly,it would not do to reduce the sample size because of the power of the MANOVA. But now she asks, "What $N$ do I need for .80 power for these individual tests?" The specifications are now:

$$a = .05 \quad u = 3 \quad \text{power} = .80$$
$$f^2 = .0526 \quad s = 1 \quad k_Y = 1 \quad k_X = 3.$$

For $u$ = 3 and power = .80 in Table 9.4.2, at trial $v$ = 120, $\lambda$ = 11.1, and $v = \infty$, $\lambda$ = 10.9. Equations (10.4.1–3) yield $N$ = 209. Thus, rather than drop her $N$ of 120 because of the power of the MANOVA, she would need to increase it substantially in order to have adequate power for the ANOVA tests of the summary scores, which are, after all, the purpose of the investigation.

This fable offers some morals. Obviously, and most generally, the $N$ required for an investigation is the $N$ required by its most important hypotheses. It may be increased to accommodate less central hypotheses, but is decreased at the peril of the investigation. Less obviously, it will frequently be the case that the follow-up hypotheses, focusing on specific issues and therefore involving few (often one) hypothesis **df** $(= \mathbf{u})$, will have lower power and therefore require greater **N** than do the overall setwise relationships.

**10.4.2.1   2-GROUP MANOVA AND HOTELLING'S T².**   In Section 10.3.2.1, it was pointed out that Hotelling's $\mathbf{T}^2$ is the special case for $\mathbf{K} = 2$ of the one-way K-group MANOVA. Except for its provision of the Mahalanobis $\mathbf{D}^2$ as an ES measure, it offers nothing new for power analysis. See Section 10.3.2.1 for the relationship between $\mathbf{D}^2$ and $\mathbf{R}^2_{Y,X}$.

It was also pointed that the significance test and therefore the power analysis for a 2-group discriminant analysis is the same as for the 2-group MANOVA.

### Illustrative Example

**10.22**   The neuropsychologist in example 10.7 was planning a 2-group MANOVA comparing 50 Alzheimer patients and 40 normal controls on $(\mathbf{k_x}$ $=)$ 6 CAT scan measurements using the .05 significance level. His posited $\mathbf{R}^2_{Y,X} = .125$, which for $\mathbf{s} = 1$, led to $\mathbf{f}^2 = .1429$, and for these specifications, power was found to be .73. We compute the **N** necessary to bring power up to the conventional .80 level. The complete specifications are:

$$\mathbf{a} = .05 \qquad \mathbf{u} = 6 \qquad \text{power} = .80$$
$$\mathbf{f}^2 = .1429 \qquad \mathbf{s} = 1 \qquad \mathbf{k_Y} = 1 \qquad \mathbf{k_X} = 6.$$

Table 9.4.2 for $\mathbf{u} = 6$ at power $= .80$ gives for trial $\mathbf{v} = 120$, $\lambda = 14.3$, so Equation (10.4.1) gives the implied $\mathbf{v} = 14.3/.1429 - 6 - 1 = 93$. Table 9.4.2 gives, for $\mathbf{v} = 60$, $\lambda = 15.0$, and (10.4.2) then gives the interpolated $\lambda = 14.5$, which, when substituted in (10.4.2) gives the iterated $\mathbf{v} = 94$. Finally, (10.4.3) gives the necessary (total) $\mathbf{N} = 101$.

The power analysis of the tests of individual CAT scan measures could be analyzed as ordinary **t** tests, but he elected to test them in the SC framework. He posited $\mathbf{R}^2_{Y,X} = (\mathbf{r}^2_{pb} =) .05$, so $\mathbf{f}^2 = .0526$, and found that power for the planned **N** of 90 cases was .57. The specifications for the **N** necessary for power $= .80$ are:

$$\mathbf{a} = .05 \qquad \mathbf{u} = 1 \qquad \text{power} = .80$$
$$\mathbf{f}^2 = .0526 \qquad \mathbf{s} = 1 \qquad \mathbf{k_Y} = 1 \qquad \mathbf{k_X} = 1.$$

In Table 9.4.2 for $\mathbf{u} = 1$ and power $= .80$, at both $\mathbf{v} = 120$ and $\mathbf{v} = \infty$, $\lambda = 7.8$, and the implied $\mathbf{v}$ from (10.4.1) is 146. No interpolation for $\lambda$ nor therefore iteration of $\mathbf{v}$ is necessary, so, substituting in (10.4.3) results in $\mathbf{N} = 148$.

On further consideration, for reasons given in example 10.7, he also checked the necessary **N** for $f^2 = .0581$. With none of the other parameters changed, the procedure gives **N** = 126.

10.4.3   THE ANALYSIS OF PARTIAL VARIANCE AND THE ANALYSIS OF COVARIANCE.   In SC analysis of partial variance (APV), the form of association is partial — set **Y** is **D·A** and set **X** is **B·A**. For partial association, Wilks' **L** is $R^2$-complementary, which facilitates setting $f^2$ (see Section 10.2). In APV, the sets may contain variables of any kind. In the special case of the multivariate analysis of covariance (MANCOVA), set **B** is categorical and sets **D** and **A** are quantitative. (See Section 10.4.2 and Cohen & Cohen, 1983, Chapter 10, for details).

**Illustrative Example**

**10.23**   A study of the relationship between ability and memory described in example 10.8 was planned for **N** = 100. Although for **a** = .01 and the other parameters, power for the test of the overall relationship between three memory (**D**) and two ability (**B**) measures with age and education (**A**) partialled was .93, and was also satisfactory for the various follow-up tests contemplated (at least when **a** = .05), a problem was posed by the test of the ability by age/ed interaction, the existence of which would render invalid the assumption of regression homogeneity and therewith make the meaning of the ability-memory relationship ambiguous (see example 10.8 for the details of how this test is formulated).

It was found that, as planned, power of this test at **a** = .01 was .15. Matters were not much better if **a** was set at .05: power = .34. What **N** would be required for power = .80 for the interaction test? The specifications summary is:

$$a = .01 \qquad u = 24 \qquad \text{power} = .80$$
$$f^2 = .0370 \qquad s = 2.90 \qquad k_Y = 3 \qquad k_X = 8 \qquad k_A = 6.$$

Table 9.4.1, for **u** = 24 and power = .80, gives at trial **v** = 120, $\lambda$ = 35.6, and at **v** = $\infty$, $\lambda$ = 30.1. Equation (10.4.1) gives implied **v** = 937, (10.4.2) gives the interpolated $\lambda$ = 30.8, which, when substituted in (10.4.1), gives the iterated **v** = 808, and (10.4.3) gives **N** = 295. At **a** = .05, Table 9.4.2 gives $\lambda$ = 25.9 at **v** = 120 and $\lambda$ = 22.5 at **v** = $\infty$, and the result is **N** = 224.

These sample size far exceed his resources. It occurs to him that it may turn out that the relationships with age and education over his age range may turn out to be linear, in which case he can drop the squared terms from the age/ed set, leaving only two variables. This should help, because now the product set will have only ($k_X$ =) 4 (instead of 8) variables, and the interaction test will have $u = 12$ (instead of 24). Keeping the other parameters as before, the reader is invited to work out the sample size demand. The answer is that at $a = .01$, $N = 251$ (compared to 295), and at $a = .05$, $N = 190$. Thus, it helped, but not very much.

### 10.4.3.1 K-GROUP MANCOVA. This is the special case of the APV in which set **B** is a categorical variable (nominal scale) made up of **K** groups. As noted, Equation (10.4.3) gives the total **N**, and its distribution over the **K** groups relates to $R^2_{Y,X}$ and $f^2$. When not otherwise specified, equality is presumed.

### Illustrative Example

**10.24**   Our experimental psychologist of examples 10.5, 10.9, and 10.20 was planning a learning study involving 3 experimental groups of 10 cases each and one control group of 20 cases (total $N = 50$, $k_X = K - 1 = 3$) using time and error scores as dependent variables ($k_Y = 2$). In example 10.5, he found that for $R^2_{D.B} = .15$ ($f^2 = .0847$), power at $a = .05$ was .51. In example 10.20, he learned that for power $= .80$, his total **N** had to be 85. In example 10.9, he considered the effect of using a set of ($k_A =$) 2 verbal ability measures as covariates with the originally planned $N = 50$. The partial $R^2_{D.A,B-A}$ that was posited was .23, and $f^2 = .1396$. At $a = .05$, he found power $= .74$. What **N** would be needed to get power up to .80?

$$a = .05 \quad u = 6 \quad \text{power} = .80$$
$$f^2 = .1396 \quad s = 2 \quad k_Y = 2 \quad k_X = 3 \quad k_A = 2$$

The necessary values are found in Table 9.4.2 for $u = 6$ and power $= .80$: at trial $v = 120$, $\lambda = 14.3$, so Equation (10.4.1) gives the implied $v = 95$. The table gives for the lower $v = 60$, $\lambda = 15.0$, so (10.4.2) gives the interpolated $\lambda$ as 14.5. Iterating **v** and substituting in (10.4.3) gives $N = 55$, slightly more than originally planned, as expected.

But it was noted in example 10.9 that the follow-up tests of the contrasts of each experimental group with the control group resulted in power $= .69$, rather less than he would like. To increase this to .80, the specifications for **N** are (see example 10.9 for the rationale):

$$a = .05 \quad u = 2 \quad \text{power} = .80$$
$$f^2 = .1765 \quad s = 1 \quad k_Y = 2 \quad k_X = 1 \quad k_A = 4.$$

The values needed from Table 9.4.2 are, for $u = 2$ and power $= .80$, at trial $v = 120$, $\lambda = 9.7$, at $v = 20$, $\lambda = 11.1$, and at $v = 60$, $\lambda = 10.0$. Cycling through Equations 10.4.1–3, we find $N = 61$. (Using 60 as the trial $v$ gives the same result.)

It would seem that an $N$ of about 60, with 24 in the control group and 12 in each experimental group, would provide reasonably adequate power for these tests, and therefore power greater than .80 for the overall test. This presumes, of course, that neither the strength of the experimental effect nor that of the verbal ability covariates has been overestimated.

10.4.3.2  BIPARTIAL ANALYSIS.  In this form of analysis, the generic $R^2_{Y,X}$ is realized as $R^2_{D \cdot C, B \cdot A}$, the partialling sets differing for the dependent and independent variables. See Section 10.3.3.2 for the circumstances that require this design and the setting of $f^2$ for bipartial association.

### Illustrative Example

**10.25**  The bipartial analysis described in example 10.10, based on a sample of 300 pregnant women in an urban clinic, studied the effect of two nutritional supplementation treatments and a control on three somatic and four behavioral characteristics of their newborn infants. The treatments, and the somatic and behavioral characteristics were each controlled by partialling relevant sets of variables; see example 10.10 for the details.

With the planned $N = 300$, it was found that the major setwise bipartial associations had power greater than .80 at $a = .01$. However, follow-up *individual* treatment contrasts on the set of somatic variables and on the unique components of these individual behavior factors were found to have power respectively of .63 and .64. What $N$'s would be required for power = .80 at $a = .01$ for these tests?

Referring back to the details given in example 10.10, the two tests of treatment contrasts on the three somatic variables have the following specifications:

$$a = .01 \quad u = 3 \quad \text{power} = .80$$
$$f^2 = .04 \quad s = 1 \quad k_Y = 3 \quad k_X = 1 \quad k_C = 6 \quad k_A = 6.$$

From Table 9.4.1, we have at $u = 3$ and power = .80, $\lambda = 16.1$ for trial $v = 120$ and $\lambda = 15.5$ for $v = \infty$. Applying the procedure described in Section 3.4 using Equations (10.4.1–3), we find that the necessary $N = 398$.

The six tests comprised by the two treatment contrasts of the three unique somatic variables, described in detail in example 10.10, for $N = 300$ at $a = .01$ had power = .64. The specifications for the necessary $N$ for power = .80 for these tests are:

$$a = .01 \quad u = 1 \quad \text{power} = .80$$
$$f^2 = .03 \quad s = 1 \quad k_Y = 1 \quad k_X = 1 \quad k_C = 8 \quad k_A = 6.$$

Finding the relevant $\lambda$ values for $u = 1$ and power $= .80$ and applying Equations (10.4.1–3), we get $N = 400$.

10.4.4   HIERARCHICAL ANALYSIS.   When two or more research factors operate as independent variables, they may be ordered, with each factor partialled from those that succeed it in accounting for variance in the dependent variable set. The order may be one of presumed causal priority, defining a simple causal model. Another use of hierarchical analysis is in an effort to protect from power loss the major issues in an investigation while exploring secondary or tertiary issues. Section 10.3.4 provides details about the employment of these strategies.

**Illustrative Examples**

**10.26**   The psychiatric research team in example 10.11 was planning a records study of $N = 400$ state hospital psychiatric admissions. Using length of stay and level of functioning as a dependent variable set ($k_Y = 2$), they set up a hierarchy of the causal factors in the following order: **U**, demographic variables ($k_U = 9$), **V**, MMPI variables ($k_V = 10$), and **W**, a categorical variable coding which of eight hospitals the patient was in ($k_W = 7$). While power was quite high for the demographic variables and hospitals for the $f^2$'s posited and $a = .01$, for the MMPI set, power was only .55. What $N$ would be needed for this test to have power of .80? The specifications (see example 10.11 for the rationale) are:

$$a = .01 \quad u = 20 \quad \text{power} = .80$$
$$f^2 = .0260 \quad s = 2 \quad k_Y = 2 \quad k_X = 10 \quad k_A = 9.$$

Table 9.4.1 (for $a = .01$) gives from $u = 20$ for power $= .80$, at trial $v = 120$, $\lambda = 32.6$, and at $v = \infty$, $\lambda = 28.2$. Equation (10.4.1) gives the implied $v = 1233$, (10.4.2) gives the interpolated $\lambda$ for this $v$ as 28.6, which, when substituted in (10.4.1), gives an iterated $v = 1080$. When this is entered with the other parameters in (10.4.3), the necessary $N$ is found to be 561.

The planned $N$ of 400 falls far short of this $N$ demands. The investigators may not have the option of increasing the sample size. Since they have posited that the MMPI has a small ES, they may decide to forego trying to increase the power to detect it. If, when the investigation is undertaken (with $N = 400$), the MMPI effect is not significant, they should acknowledge the ambiguity of this result.

Alternatively, it is quite possible that a much smaller set of MMPI variables, selected either *a priori* or by factor- or cluster-analytic reduction, may be expected to account for all or nearly all of this multivariate relationship, and so may have greater power.

**10.27**   The longitudinal study by the developmental psychologist in example 10.12 had, for a sample of $N$ = 120 subjects, four sets of ratings on three personality variables: one set each by the subjects themselves, by their parents, and by their teachers, all at age 10, and a fourth set by the subjects made in their middle twenties. With the latter as the dependent variable set, the design was a hierarchical analysis with the three age 10 sets in the above order.

When power-analyzed in example 10.12, for the posited $f^2$'s at $a$ = .05, the test of the (whole) association of the age 10 self-ratings was found to have power = .89, but the tests of the partial associations of the parent and teacher ratings were respectively .50 and .32. Assuming that the data gathering has been completed, she does not have the option of increasing the sample size. However, she might wonder how large an $N$ she would have needed for these two tests to have power equal to (for the sake of variety) .75.

For the partial association of parents' ratings with the adult self-ratings, partialling the child self-ratings, she had posited $R^2_{Y,X}$ = .075, which, for $k_Y$ = $k_X$ = 3 and hence $s$ = 2.43, results in $f^2$ = .0692. The full specifications for determining this $N$ are:

$$a = .05 \quad u = 9 \quad \text{power} = .75$$
$$f^2 = .0692 \quad s = 2.43 \quad k_Y = 3 \quad k_X = 3 \quad k_A = 3.$$

Table 9.4.2 gives for $u$ = 9 and power = .75, at trial $v$ = 120, $\lambda$ = 15.1 and at $v$ = $\infty$, $\lambda$ = 14.2. Applying (10.4.1), the implied $v$ = 453 and (10.4.2) gives the interpolated $\lambda$ = 14.2. Applying (10.4.1) to this $\lambda$ yields the iterated $v$ = 433, and (10.4.3) finally gives the necessary $N$ = 187, some 50% more than she has available.

For the third set in the hierarchy, the teachers' ratings, the posited $R^2_{Y,X}$ with the adult self-ratings, partialling both the child self-ratings and the parents' ratings, was .05. With the same $k_Y$ = $k_X$ = 3, $s$ = 2.43, but now $k_A$ = 6, the specification summary is:

$$a = .05 \quad u = 9 \quad \text{power} = .75$$
$$f^2 = .0213 \quad s = 2.43 \quad k_Y = 3 \quad k_X = 3 = 3 \quad k_A = 6.$$

As before, the relevant $\lambda$'s are 15.1 for trial $v$ = 120 and 14.2 for $v$ = $\infty$. The cycle of Equations (9.4.1–3) gives the necessary $N$ = 285, more than twice the number available.

**10.28**   The study of attitudes toward presidential candidates planned by the political polling organization in example 10.13 had good power for most of the tests checked there. However, using Model 2 error with **N** = 900 and **a** = .01, the power of the test of the effect of Race partialling Age and Sex on unique candidate ratings was only .55 (see example 10.13 and Table 10.3.3 for the relevant parameters). What **N** would be needed for power = .80? The specification summary is:

$$\mathbf{a} = .01 \qquad \mathbf{u} = 2 \qquad \text{power} = .80$$
$$\mathbf{f}^2 = .01 \qquad \mathbf{s} = 1 \qquad \mathbf{k_Y} = 1 \qquad \mathbf{k_X} = 2 \qquad \mathbf{k_A} = 2 \qquad \mathbf{k_G} = 2.$$

Table 9.4.1 gives for **u** = 2 at power = .80, at trial **v** = 120, $\lambda$ = 14.3 and at **v** = $\infty$, $\lambda$ = 13.9. Equations (10.4.1–3) give **N** = 1397, some 50% more than planned.

Assuming their budget cannot support so large a sample, they may have to settle for less power, but surely, not .55! "What **N** do we need," the research director asks, "for two to one odds?", i.e., power = 2/3. The relevant $\lambda$ values from Table 9.4.1 are 11.2 and 10.9, and **N** works out to 1097. While pondering whether the costs of a 20% increase can be tolerated, the staff statistician points out that if the test meets the .05 significance criterion, the analyst will inevitably interpret it as real. Practically, then, the effective significance criterion is **a** = .05, not .01. What then is the **N** necessary for .80 power at **a** = .05?

The specifications are otherwise exactly as they were originally, but the relevant $\lambda$ values are obtained from Table 9.4.2. They are, for **v** = 120 and $\infty$, respectively 9.7 and 9.6. Putting them through the cycle of Equations (10.4.1–3), **N** = 965 is found. The research director okays **N** = 1000 for the study.

Note their forbearance in not tampering with the posited $\mathbf{f}^2$ = .01, the main source of their low power. In doing power analysis, the temptation is great to overstate the ES, a sure way to increase the computed power or reduce the computed necessary **N**. Obviously, however, doing so is self-deluding: an overstated ES simply results in overestimated power or underestimated **N**.

10.4.5   FACTORIAL DESIGN MANOVA.   In factorial design it is conventional to use the within cells variance for the error term for the main effects and interactions. This implies that, in general, Model 2 error will be employed in Wilks' **L** (10.2.1) and thus $\mathbf{f}^2$ (10.2.2). See Sections 10.2.3 and 10.3.5 for the details.

### Illustrative Example

**10.29**   Example 10.14 described a psychiatric research team planning a cooperative study involving two innovative treatments and a control treatment ($\mathbf{T}$, $k_T = 2$) replicated in four hospitals ($\mathbf{H}$, $k_H = 3$). The dependent variable set was made up of the patient's self-rating and a psychiatrist's rating on overall improvement. A total $\mathbf{N} = 120$ was planned, with $\mathbf{a} = .05$ as the significance criterion.

The research focus was, of course, on the treatment effects. The role of the $\mathbf{H}$ factor was primarily to allow for possible systematic hospital effects. The $\mathbf{H} \times \mathbf{T}$ interaction was also of interest, because, to the extent to which it operated, it would mean that the treatment effects were not the same in the four hospitals.

It was found in example 10.14 that while power for the test of $\mathbf{T} \cdot \mathbf{H}$ was quite high, power for the $\mathbf{H} \times \mathbf{T}$ interaction for the ES posited was only .53. Furthermore, the follow-up tests' power was not high, and one of them, the group of tests on the bipartials of the individual treatment effects on unique (mutually partialled) patient and psychiatrist improvement ratings was very poor, .54.

The effect of increasing $\mathbf{N}$ to 180 on the power of the $\mathbf{H} \times \mathbf{T}$ interaction was determined in example 10.14 to be .77. What $\mathbf{N}$ would be necessary for power $= .80$? The full specifications are:

$$\mathbf{a} = .05 \qquad \mathbf{u} = 12 \qquad \text{power} = .80$$
$$f^2 = .0483 \qquad \mathbf{s} = 2 \qquad k_Y = 2 \qquad k_X = 6 \qquad k_A = 5.$$

In Table 9.4.2, at $\mathbf{u} = 12$ and power $= .80$, at trial $\mathbf{v} = 120$, $\lambda = 18.8$ and at $\mathbf{v} = \infty$, $\lambda = 17.8$. Equation (9.4.1) gives implied $\mathbf{v} = 376$, Equation (9.4.2) gives the interpolated $\lambda = 18.1$, which, substituted in Equation (9.4.1), gives the iterated $\mathbf{v} = 362$. Finally, Equation (9.4.3) gives $\mathbf{N} = 194$, slightly more than the power $= .77$ for $\mathbf{N} = 180$, as would be expected.

As for the $\mathbf{N}$ necessary for power $= .80$ for the follow-up tests of the individual treatment effects on the unique outcome ratings, the specifications are:

$$\mathbf{a} = .05 \qquad \mathbf{u} = 1 \qquad \text{power} = .80$$
$$f^2 = .05 \qquad \mathbf{s} = 1 \qquad k_Y = 1 \qquad k_X = 1 \qquad k_A = 4 \qquad k_G = 6.$$

Table 9.4.2 at $\mathbf{u} = 1$ and power $= .80$ gives $\lambda = 7.8$ at both $\mathbf{v} = 120$ and $\mathbf{v} = \infty$, so no iteration of $\mathbf{v}$ is necessary. When the $\mathbf{v}$ implied in Equation (9.4.1) is substituted in Equation (9.4.3), the necessary $\mathbf{N}$ is found to be 166.

10.4.6 FACTORIAL DESIGN MANCOVA. The addition of a covariate set to a factorial design MANOVA results in a factorial design MANCOVA. The basic form of association is partial, and as in factorial design generally, within cell error, hence Model 2 error, is used.

### Illustrative Example

**10.30**   In the cooperative psychiatric study described in examples 10.14, 10.15, and 10.29, it was found that for the original MANOVA design, with the originally planned **N** = 120 and the ES's posited, power at **a** = .05 for several of the tests that would be performed was quite poor (example 10.14). In example 10.29 just above, it was found that for that design, a sample of 194 would be necessary for the interaction test to have power = .80. The research problem was reconsidered in example 10.15 as a MANCOVA, using two pre-test ratings paralleling the post-test ratings originally planned, resulting in what was in fact regressed change as the effective dependent variable set. The use of what was posited to be a powerful covariate set, that is, one that substantially reduced error variance, was to greatly increase the $f^2$'s and therefore the power of all the tests: the interaction test had power = .90, and the individual treatment contrasts on the unique ratings had power = .87.

So the research team has no problem about low power for even their weakest ES's with the planned **N** = 120. But it occurs to them that when the funding decision is made, it may be necessary for them to reduce their planned sample size. They then ask with regard to the interaction test, what **N** would be necessary for power to be at the conventional .80 level? The specifications for this test are:

$$\mathbf{a} = .05 \qquad \mathbf{u} = 12 \qquad \text{power} = .80$$
$$f^2 = .1043 \qquad \mathbf{s} = 2 \qquad \mathbf{k_Y} = 2 \qquad \mathbf{k_X} = 6 \qquad \mathbf{k_A} = 5.$$

The relevant $\lambda$ values from Table 9.4.2 (**u** = 12, power = .80) are 18.8 for **v** = 120 and 17.8 for **v** = $\infty$). Applying the standard procedure and Equations (10.4.1–3) gives **N** = 95.

The lowest power value in example 10.15 was .87, for the individual treatment contrasts on the unique outcome ratings. What **N** is required for power = .80 for these tests? The specification are:

$$\mathbf{a} = .05 \qquad \mathbf{u} = 1 \qquad \text{power} = .80$$
$$f^2 = .05 \qquad \mathbf{s} = 1 \qquad \mathbf{k_Y} = 1 \qquad \mathbf{k_X} = 1 \qquad \mathbf{k_A} = 4 \qquad \mathbf{k_G} = 6.$$

Table 9.4.2 gives $\lambda$ = 7.8 for both **v** = 120 and **v** = $\infty$ for the relevant **u** = 1, power = .80. **N** works out to 97.

Without the pressure of a cut in funding they would be ill-advised to reduce the planned **N** of 120. In power analysis it should always be kept in mind that power or necessary **N** is conditional on the posited ES, and that the latter may well be overstated.

# CHAPTER 11

# Some Issues in Power Analysis

## 11.1 INTRODUCTION

Because this book was written primarily as a handbook, some issues in power analysis were briefly touched upon here and there that deserve somewhat more detailed and integrated consideration. In this chapter I discuss what I believe to be the most important of these: effect size, the role of psychometric reliability and the efficacy of "qualifying" (differencing and partialling) variables.

## 11.2 EFFECT SIZE

Any reader who has penetrated this book to this point hardly needs convincing of the centrality of the concept of effect size (ES) to the determination of power or necessary sample size in research design.

Formally, ES is a crucial parameter in power analysis. While in routine data analysis the significance criterion is constrained by convention to be some low value (.05, sometimes .01), and desired power some high value (say, .80 or so), deciding the ES is a rather different matter. Rather less formally, to answer the question "What are my chances of finding it?", the researcher needs to have some idea of how big "it" is.

Not only is ES of central importance in power analysis, a moment's thought suggests that it is, after all, what science is all about. For sure, it's not about significance testing. A corollary of the long neglect of power analysis in behavioral science is a lack of a high degree of awareness of the magnitude of phenomena. I have elsewhere (1965) discussed the slippery slope of "If it's statistically significant, it's important, consequential, worth talking about, large, that is, *significant!*"

Contributing to the low consciousness of ES in large areas of behavioral science is the use of arbitrary measurement units. We rarely find ourselves dealing with dollars, years, centimeters, or bushels of manure (at least, not knowingly). Another source of our difficulty is that, until recently, the standard output of many of our procedures has been a tau statistic (Cohen, 1965), an **F**, **t**, or chi-square, together with the **P** values with (or without) their rewarding asterisks.

A partial solution to this problem is the use of "pure" (dimensionless, unit-free) measures of ES, what I called "rho" values in 1965. Prominent among these is the product moment correlation coefficient, **r**, of whatever variety (simple, partial, semipartial, bipartial in its bivariate, multiple, or multivariate form), and its square, interpreted as a proportion of variance (PV). This approaches being a common metric for ES. (But see Cooper, 1981, for the limitations of a common metric.) The various ES measures for the different tests given in the preceding chapters are (or can be) expressed as **r**'s or $r^2$'s, even relationships between nominal scales (see Cohen & Cohen, 1983, Appendix 4, on set correlation with contingency tables).

Add to this the proposed conventions for operational definitions of "small," "medium," and "large" ES, and a basis for coping with some of the troublesome problems of ES becomes available.

Note the careful qualification of the last statement. To begin with, these proposed conventions were set forth throughout with much diffidence, qualifications, and invitations not to employ them if possible. The values chosen had no more reliable a basis than my own intuition. They were offered as conventions because they were needed in a research climate characterized by a neglect of attention to issues of magnitude. The ES measures and conventions have been successful, widely adopted not only for power analysis, but more widely, for example, in ES surveys and in meta-analysis. But there are difficulties and much room for misunderstanding.

Consider **r** and $r^2$. The conventional .10, .30, .50, for "small," "medium," and "large" values for **r** look small. Smaller still are the .01, .09, .25 values for $r^2$. But squared or unsquared, these values may represent stronger degrees of association than they seem.

Item: Ozer (1985) makes a good case for the importance of the causal model in deciding whether $r^2$ or $r$ is the appropriate proportion of variance measure. He shows that in a causal model in which $x$ causes $y$, $r^2_{yx} = .25$ is a proper coefficient of determination and means that $x$ is accounting for a quarter of the variance in $y$. However, in a causal model in which some latent (unobserved) variable $Z$ causes both $x$ and $y$, the percentage of *shared* variance between $x$ and $y$ is not $r^2$, but $r$, not .25, but .50. Thus, sometimes at least, we should be thinking of the larger $r$ as a proportion of variance and not the usually much smaller $r^2$.

Item: Oakes (1982) tells us that our perception of the strength of association indicated by correlation coefficients is systematically and substantially overestimated. A sample of 30 academic psychologists, told to construct a correlation of .50 by supplying the paired values for a set of 12 ranks, gave results whose median $r$ was .76. Conversely, and quite consistently, a different sample of 30 psychologists, asked to estimate the correlation for a set of 12 paired rankings whose $r$ was actually .50, gave estimates whose median was .26. The discrepancies are of course more dramatic if expressed as $r^2$. Unless behavioral scientists in general are superior judges of these matters than British academic psychologists, our intuitions lead us to underestimate the $r$ that obtains for a given chunk of bivariate experience and overestimate the degree of association represented by a given value of $r$. I would expect that with the rapidly increasing ease of obtaining scatter plots, our intuitions should improve.

Item: Rosenthal and Rubin (1982) have made a valuable contribution to the understanding of ES with their binomial effect size display (BESD). They argue that "proportion of variance accounted for" invites a misleading impression that minimizes the ES relative to other ways of apprehending the size of an association, in particular, that of the BESD.

The layout in Table 11.1 illustrates their point. The $r$ (a fourfold point or $\phi$ coefficient) is .30, so $r^2 = .09$. I present this as a population BESD, in percent, with equal population sizes presumed (as is appropriate for the abstract treatment-control contrast). It is difficult to reconcile an increase in percent alive from 35 to 65 with "only 9% of the variance accounted for."

Rosenthal and Rubin show that the fact that the difference in propor-

TABLE 11.1
The Binomial Effect Size Display:
"Only" 9% of the Variance
is Accounted for

| Condition | Outcome % | | Total |
|-----------|-----------|------|-------|
|           | *Alive*   | *Dead* |     |
| Treatment | 65        | 35   | 100   |
| Control   | 35        | 65   | 100   |

tions (.65 − .35) equals the r is not a coincidence, but a necessity when the table is symmetrical (i.e., when the two values are equidistant from .50). This means, for example, that a difference in percent alive between .45 and .55, which most people would consider important (*alive*, mind you!), yields r = .10, and "only 1% of the variance accounted for," an amount that operationally defines a "small" effect in my scheme.

The difference in rates will approximate the r with departure from symmetry: for example, for proportions of .20 and .50, r = .314. Furthermore, Rosenthal and Rubin make a case for the use of the BESD as a "realistic representation of the size of treatment effect" when the outcome variable is continuous, provided that the groups are of equal size and variance. See their paper for the details.

I think there are two lessons to be learned from Rosenthal and Rubin. The first is the one they emphasize, namely, that in many circumstances (in particular, when at least one variable is binary), the amount of association, as intuited, is greater than $r^2$, the proportion of variance accounted for.

The second is subtly introduced by them in their choice of the content for their example. "Death" tends to concentrate the mind. But this in turn reinforces the principle that the size of an effect can only be appraised in the context of the substantive issues involved. An $r^2$ of .01 is indeed small in absolute terms, but when it represents a ten percentage point increase in survival, it may well be considered large. On the other hand, an entrance examination that accounts for 20% of the variance in freshman grade point average is no great shakes.

Final item: A dispute with a colleague about the role of chance in sport led Abelson (1985) to pose the question: "What percentage of the variance in athletic outcomes can be attributed to the skill of the players, as indexed by past performance?" He concretized the question in terms of batting skill of major league baseball players. In the course of the article, he describes the results of asking 61 knowledgeable (about both baseball and variance accounting) graduate students and faculty in the Department of Psychology at Yale to imagine a time at bat by an arbitrarily chosen major league baseball player, and to estimate the percentage of variance in getting/not getting a hit that is attributable to skill differential between hitters. Their median estimate was 25%.

Now, the issue is not trivial, at least not to the millions of fans of the game. "Everyone knows" that batting skill as represented by batting averages has substantial explanatory power. That's one reason why star players make such good money.

Applying a variance partitioning model to readily available batting statistics, Abelson found that the proportion of variance in the outcome of a given at bat accounted for by individual differences in skill (batting averages) was .00317! This is not a misprint — it is not .317, or even .0317. It is .00317, not quite one third of 1%.

Abelson's reaction to his finding (and mine, and no doubt yours) was one of incredulity. But neither he nor the editor and referees of Psychological Bulletin (nor I) could find any fault with his procedure. Abelson explains his counterintuitive discovery in terms of the cumulative effect within individual players and for the team as a whole. He gives as examples of potentially cumulative processes "educational interventions, the persuasive effects of advertising, and repeated decisions by ideologically similar policy makers." He writes

> . . . one should not necessarily be scornful of miniscule values for percentage variance explanation, provided there is statistical assurance that these values are significantly above zero, and that the degree of potential cumulation is substantial. On the other hand, in cases where the variables are by nature nonepisodic and therefore noncumulative (e.g., summary measures of personality traits), no improvement in variance explanation can be expected (1985, p. 133).

The next time you read that "only X% of the variance is accounted for," remember Abelson's Paradox.

To summarize: Effect size is indispensable in power analysis, as it is generally in science, and conventional operational definitions of ES have their use, but only as characterizations of absolute magnitude. However, the *meaning* of any given ES is, in the final analysis, a function of the context in which it is embedded. Thus, "only 50% of the variance" may be as valid a formulation in one context as "only 1% of the variance" is in another, and, conversely, "as much as 1% of the variance" is, in principle, no less valid a formulation than "as much as 50% of the variance."

## 11.3  RELIABILITY

It was pointed out in Section 3.2 that what might be a correlation of .25 between two variables assuming that each was measured without error, would turn out to be .10 if the variables were fallible, correlating only .63 with their respective true scores (i.e., if each variable's reliability coefficient was .40 = $.63^2$). The point I sought to make was that if we conceive our ES in terms of pure *constructs* rather than as fallible measures thereof, we will inevitably overestimate them.

Throughout the book, it has been assumed that it is the fallible *"observed"* scores, not the *"true"* scores of classical psychometric theory that provide the basis of population ES measurement. The well-known relationship between the two is a function of the measure's reliability, $r_{yy}$, defined as the ratio of true score variance to observed score variance, where the observed score variance is simply the sum of true score variance and error variance. Now, the effect of measurement error is to "attenuate" (reduce the absolute value of) population ES's from what they would be if there was no measurement error, i.e., if all the observed variance was true variance. Given the assumptions of the classical model (see any text in psychometric theory), the relationship between an ES on observes scores (ES), and the same ES on true scores (ES*) is a simple function of reliability. For example, given x and y as observed scores, and x* and y* as their true score counterparts,

(11.3.1) $$r_{xy} = r_{x^*y^*} \sqrt{r_{xx}} \sqrt{r_{yy}}.$$

Thus, the model has it that the r between the observed variables, that is, the *observed* r is the result of the attenuation of the correlation between true x and y by factors that are the square roots of their reliabilities. It follows from this simple equation that if either variable has perfect reliability, $\sqrt{1} = 1$ and it drops out of the equation.

Now, it is the latter situation that obtains for most of the ES measures in the preceding chapters. That is, they involve single quantitative dependent variables where the independent variable(s) are treated as "fixed" and error-free. Thus, if we let x in (11.3.1) represent one or more fixed independent variables (e.g., group membership, MRC regressors), we can write

(11.3.2) $$ES = ES^* \sqrt{r_{yy}},$$

which holds literally in many cases and figuratively (that is, conceptually) in the others. Specifically, we can write

(11.3.3) $$d = d^* \sqrt{r_{yy}},$$

(11.3.4) $$f = f^* \sqrt{r_{yy}},$$

and therefore,

(11.3.5) $$f^2 = f^{*2} r_{yy}.$$

This simple relationship was noted by (among others) Cleary & Linn (1969), who went on to show how increasing reliability by increasing test length and increasing N jointly affect power. (Using a simple model for the cost of testing, they provided some useful equations that give the N that maximizes power subject to the cost constraints.)

Given the simple relationship expressed in Equations (11.3.1–5), one can

1.2, that is, the **g** score would require 20% *larger* **n** than using **y** alone; 120 cases. The regression-adjusted **n**$_{y'}$ relative to **n**$_y$ requires only (11.4.12) $1 - .40^2 = .84$ as many, i.e., 84 cases.

3. See what happens if one is so benighted as to have a qualifying **x** whose **r** with **y** is zero, with a set of specifications that require 100 cases for just plain **y**: The **y** $-$ **x** difference would require 2 $(1 - 0)$ or twice as many cases to meet these specifications, while the regression-adjusted (actually *un*-adjusted) **n**$_{y'}$ requires $(1 - 0^2 = 1)$, i.e., the same number of cases as for un-qualified **y**. (Actually, the exact **n** demand would be trivially larger because of the loss of 1 **df** from the ANCOVA error term.)

As is evident from Equation (11.4.11), qualifying by differencing confers no advantage over ignoring **x** unless **r** is at least $+ .50$. Thus, an investigator would do well to assure that there is at least a substantial (and *positive*[2]) sample **r** within groups before qualifying by differencing. Because the **n** demand would be larger, it follows that for the original **n**, power would be smaller using difference scores.

On the other hand, provided that the demands of the model are met, the use of the regression adjustment of ANCOVA is always superior to differencing. The ratio $(1 + r)/2$ of Equation (11.4.13), for $-1 < r < +1$ (when **r** $= \pm 1$, there is, in fact, nothing to analyze), is always less than 1, and therefore necessarily more efficient than differencing (which we have seen is poorer than leaving **y** alone unless **r** is at least $+ .50$).

What if the qualifying variable **x** is not a literal pre-score that is measured in the same units as **y**? For differencing, and assuming the other model demands (including **m**$_{xA}$ = **m**$_{xB}$) are satisfied, the scores may be standardized, and one may proceed as before. The scaling of **x** constitutes no problem for regression adjustment, which requires only equality of the within group covariances.

In fact, for the regression adjustment of ANCOVA, one is not constrained to use a single variable (see Sections 9.3.2 and 9.4.3). A set of covariates **X** may be used simultaneously to qualify **y**, and the bivariate **r**$^2_{yx}$ in Equations (11.4.8) and (11.4.9) becomes the multiple **R**$^2_{y \cdot x}$, so that the relative **n** demand for a regression-adjusted **y** is linear in $1 - $ **R**$^2_{y \cdot x}$. Thus, if one can employ a set of covariates that account for 50% of the **y** variance, one needs only half the **n** than without it. And regression adjustment, or, more generally, partialling, is of course not limited to the single dependent variable case. It generalizes to multivariate analysis of covariance, or even further to set correlation (see Sections 10.3.3, and 10.3.6).

Moreover, although the demonstration of comparative power above was made for the two-group case in the interest of simplicity, the relative **n** for-

---

[2]Negative **r** is hardly worth discussing, but if it should occur, Equation (11.4.11) still works. For example, for **r** $= -.50$, it would take 2 $(1 - [-.50]) = 3$ times as many cases as for **y** alone.

mulas (11.4.11–13) hold for the **K**-group case of the analysis of variance/covariance, and beyond that for the multiple $R^2$ with nominal scales in all its generality (Chapter 9). (In principle, it even generalizes to the multivariate $R^2_{Y,X}$ of Chapter 10, but that statement requires some complicated qualifications.)

This demonstration is not intended to offer partialling as a panacea for all the occasions in data analysis where qualification is indicated. It makes model demands that frequently cannot be met; for example, no (or at least not much) measurement error in the independent variable(s) (fixed model), and homogeneity of regression (Cohen & Cohen, 1983, Chapter 10). Also, sometimes the desired qualification of **y** involves **x** in nonlinear operations, as in **y/x**, a problem which may or may not be successfully handled by logarithmic (or other nonlinear) transformations (Cohen & Cohen, 1983, Chapter 6).

But when it is appropriate, it is a powerful maneuver in data analysis.

# CHAPTER 12

# Computational Procedures

## 12.1 INTRODUCTION

Since this is a handbook intended for behavioral scientists, the computational procedures used to determine the power and sample size values of the tables were not given in the previous chapters so as not to interrupt the flow of the exposition of concepts and methods of application. Instead, this material is presented here for the interested reader. It may be used for computing power values or sample sizes in circumstances which are not covered by the tables provided.

All computed values were rounded to the *nearest* unit and are accurate within one or at most two units of the tabled value. Various computational checks were used, depending upon the function in question. For all tables, two additional checks were used: a monotonicity check throughout, and a check on consistency between power values and necessary sample size values where the latter fell within the range of the former and were independently determined. This check assures accuracy where it is most critical—when **n** is small.

Unless otherwise noted, where interpolation was necessary in tables which provided necessary computing values, linear interpolation was used because of the density of the argument relative to the needed accuracy.

## 12.2   t TEST FOR MEANS

12.2.1   POWER VALUES AND $d_c$. The approximation given by Dixon and Massey (1957, p. 253) was used for computing the power values in Tables 2.3.1–2.3.6. Expressing it in terms of $d$, solving for $z_{1-b}$, setting $n_1 = n_2 = n$ and $df = 2(n - 1)$, gives (using the present notation):

$$(12.2.1) \qquad z_{1-b} = \frac{d(n - 1)\sqrt{2n}}{2(n - 1) + 1.21(z_{1-a} - 1.06)} - z_{1-a}$$

where $z_{1-b}$ = the percentile of the unit normal curve which gives power,

$\qquad z_{1-a}$ = the percentile of the unit normal curve for the significance criterion—for one-tailed tests, $a = a_1$, and for two-tailed tests, $a = a_2/2$,

$\qquad d$ = the standardized mean difference [formula (2.2.1)], and

$\qquad n$ = the size of each sample.

This approximation was found to be quite accurate over the range of values of the tables when checked against available exact values. After all power values were computed, they were compared for the points made available by the computation of the $n$ tables (2.4.1), and the few inconsistencies reconciled with the latter, which is an exact procedure (see Section 12.2.2).

The $d_c$ values of the table, i.e., the sample $d$ value necessary for significance, were found from the following relationship:

$$(12.2.2) \qquad \delta = d\sqrt{\frac{n}{2}} = t_{1-a} + t_{1-b},$$

where $t_{1-a}$ and $t_{1-b}$ are percentile points for significance and power on the $t$ distribution for $df = 2(n - 1)$, and $\delta$ (delta) is the noncentrality parameter for noncentral $t$. As throughout, $a$ in the subscript is $a_1$ or $a_2/2$. Since the $d_c$ value occurs when power = .50, i.e., when $t_{1-b} = 0$, then

$$(12.2.3) \qquad d_c = t_{1-a}\sqrt{\frac{2}{n}}.$$

The necessary $t_{1-a}$ values were obtained from Owen (1962, Table 2.1).

12.2.2   SAMPLE SIZE VALUES. Owen (1965) provides tables for the noncentrality parameter of the $t$ test, $\delta$, as a function of degrees of freedom, $a$, and $b$. With equal sample sizes, each of $n$ cases,

$$(12.2.4) \qquad \delta = d\sqrt{\frac{n}{2}},$$

so that

(12.2.5) $$n = \frac{2\delta^2}{d^2}.$$

The **df** for trial in Owen's tables was estimated from the power tables, and $\delta$ was found and substituted in formula (12.2.5) together with the **d** value for the column being computed in order to find **n**. When $2(n-1)$ did not agree with the trial entry **df**, the table was reentered with new $\mathbf{df} = 2(n-1)$, until agreement was found.

Owen's (1965) tables serve for all the **a** values in the subtables of Table 2.4.1 except $\mathbf{a_1} = .10$, and for all the desired power values except .25, $\frac{2}{3}$, .75, and .85. The **n** entries for these cases were found by the following procedure; Formula (12.2.1) was rewritten as

(12.2.6) $$\frac{z_{1-a} + z_{1-b}}{d} = \frac{(n-1)\sqrt{2n}}{2(n-1) + 1.21(z_{1-a} - 1.06)}.$$

The left-hand side was found for a given table entry, and the integral value of **n** determined which made the right-hand side as nearly equal to it as possible.

## 12.3   THE SIGNIFICANCE OF A PRODUCT MOMENT r

12.3.1   POWER VALUES AND $r_c$. The **t** test for the significance of **r** is given by

(12.3.1) $$t = \frac{r\sqrt{df}}{\sqrt{1-r^2}}$$

where **r** = the sample **r** and $\mathbf{df} = n - 2$.

Solving formula (12.3.1) for **r** gives

(12.3.2) $$r = \sqrt{\frac{t^2}{t^2 + df}}.$$

Criterion values for **t** at the requisite values for **a** and $\mathbf{df} = n - 2$ were found from Owen (1962, Table 2.1) and applied in (12.3.2), yielding the $r_c$ necessary for significance at **a** for the given **df**.

To find the power values, two procedures were used. For $\mathbf{n} = 8$ (1) 25, 50, 100, 200, the tables provided by David (1938) were used. These tables give the frequency distribution of sample **r**'s for population $\mathbf{r} = .10$ (.10) .90 for the above **n**. The $r_c$ value for each row of the Tables 3.3.1–3.3.6 was located in the appropriate column in David's tables and the probability integral (**b**, the Type II error rate) found by linear interpolation.[1] The complement of this value is the value entered in the power tables of Chapter 3.

For **n** other than the above, power values were found by means of the arctanh **r** function, after several other approximations were checked and found inferior in their agreement with David. Graybill writes that the arctanh transformation " has the remarkable property of approximating the normal distribution even for fairly small **n** " (1961, p. 209). An even better approximation, recommended by Pearson and Hartley (1954, p. 29) was used, as well as their values for the transformation (Table 14):

$$(12.3.3) \qquad\qquad z' = \operatorname{arctanh} r + \frac{r}{2(n-1)}.$$

This transformation was applied to both the ES $= r_p$ (yielding $z_p{}'$) and $r_c$ (yielding $z_c{}'$). Then, for each necessary table value, the percentile value for the unit normal curve which gives power, $z_{1-b}$, was found from

$$(12.3.4) \qquad\qquad z_{1-b} = (z_p{}' - z_c{}')\sqrt{n-3}.$$

The resulting power values were found to agree with $\pm 1$ unit as tabled with those found from David (1938), as described above.

12.3.2 SAMPLE SIZE VALUES. Two procedures were used here. For **n** up to 40 (and where possible up to 60), the already computed power tables were used to find **n** for the given power value (i.e., inversely). Since most of these values were obtained via the David (1938) exact distribution tables, they were both more easily and more accurately determined than by transposition of (12.3.4) The other values were found by substituting $z_{1-a}/\sqrt{n-3}$ for $z_c{}'$ in formula (12.3.4), and solving for **n**:

$$(12.3.5) \qquad\qquad n = \left(\frac{z_{1-b} + z_{1-a}}{z_p{}'}\right)^2 + 3,$$

where $z_{1-b}$ and $z_{1-a}$ are, as before, the percentile values of the unit normal distribution for desired power and the **a** significance criterion (i.e., **a** in the subscript is $a_1$ or $a_2/2$).

## 12.4 Differences between Correlation Coefficients

12.4.1 POWER VALUES AND $q_c$. The significance test of the difference between **r**'s is accomplished via the Fisher **z** transformation, i.e., $z = \operatorname{arctanh} r$, and the ES is $q = z_1 - z_2$. Since the sample **q** is approximately normally

---

[1] Except for $n = 100$, $r_p = .40$, where an error in printing seems to have occurred in which all values are displaced upward by one interval. For these values the arctanh transformation procedure was used (see below).

distributed, power is given by

$$(12.4.1) \qquad x_{1-b} = q \sqrt{\frac{n-3}{2}} - x_{1-a},$$

where $x_{1-b}$ and $x_{1-a}$ are, respectively, the normal curve percentiles for power and significance criterion ($a$ in the subscript is $a_1$ or $a_2/2$). ($x$ is used in place of $z$ to denote the normal curve deviate in order to avoid confusion of the latter with the Fisher $r$ to $z$ transformation.) Owen (1962) was the source of both the $z$ transformation (Table 19.2) and normal curve values (Table 1.1).

For the $q_c$ values necessary for significance, which are those for which power is .50, and therefore $x_{.50} = 0$, we substitute $x_{1-b} = 0$ in formula (12.4.1) andsolve for $q_c$.

$$(12.4.2) \qquad q_c = x_{1-a} \sqrt{\frac{2}{n-3}}.$$

12.4.2   SAMPLE SIZE VALUES.   The $n$ values for Table 4.4.1 were found by solving formula (12.4.1) for $n$:

$$(12.4.3) \qquad n = 2 \left( \frac{x_{1-a} + x_{1-b}}{q} \right)^2 + 3,$$

where $n$ = the size of each sample yielding an $r$.

12.5   THE TEST THAT A PROPORTION IS .50 AND THE SIGN TEST

12.5.1   POWER VALUES AND v.   Except for a few values (see below), all the power values of Tables 5.3 were found from the Harvard tables of the cumulative binomial probability distribution (1955). For each value of $n$ of our standard set, the appropriate Harvard table for $P = .50$ was entered, and the value of $v$ (where $v > n - v$) was found which came nearest to the given $a$ value. Both $v$, the frequency needed for significance, and the " nearest " (exact) value of $a$ are given in Tables 5.3.1–5.3.6. Then, the distributions for each of our standard values of $P$ ($= .50 \pm g$) were entered with $v$ to determine the power for each $g$, i.e., the proportion of samples which equal or exceed $v$.

The Harvard tables are unusually comprehensive, giving distributions for 62 values of $P$ and 135 values of $n$, but it happens that none are given for $n = 250$, 350, and 450. For these values, power was found by means of the normal approximation:

$$(12.5.1) \qquad z_{1-b} = \frac{nP - v + .5}{\sqrt{nP(1 - P)}},$$

where the **v** necessary for significance at **a** ($=$**a**$_1$ or **a**$_2$/2) is

(12.5.2)                              $$v = \frac{n + z_{1-a}\sqrt{n+1}}{2},$$

rounding both **v** and power to the nearest value.

Formulas (12.5.1) and (12.5.2) can be used for nontabled values of **n**, **a**, and **g**. For **n** $> 50$, they agree closely with the exact value given by the Harvard tables.

12.5.2   SAMPLE SIZE VALUES.   As noted in Section 5.4, **n** values less than or equal to 50 given in Table 5.4.1 are for **a** no greater than and power no less than the value stated for the subtable (rather than nearest values). These **n** values are those obtained from the Harvard tables, which give **n** $= 1$ (1) 50. For **n** $> 50$, formula (12.5.2) was substituted in formula (12.5.1) and the latter solved for **n**, giving

(12.5.3)                     $$n = \left[\frac{2z_{1-a}\sqrt{P(1-P)} + z_{1-b}}{2P - 1}\right]^2,$$

rounding to the *nearest* value. Formula (12.5.3) may be used to determine values of **n** for values of power, **a**, or **g** not given in Table 5.4.1.

## 12.6   DIFFERENCES BETWEEN PROPORTIONS

12.6.1   POWER VALUES AND **h**$_c$. The significance test of the difference between proportions is accomplished through the use of the arcsin transformation, i.e., $\phi = 2$ arcsin $\sqrt{P}$, and the ES is **h** $= \phi_1 - \phi_2$. Since the sample **h** is approximately normally distributed, power is given by

(12.6.1)                          $$z_{1-b} = h\sqrt{\frac{n}{2}} - z_{1-a},$$

the **z** value being the normal curve percentiles for power and **a** level (**a** is **a**$_1$ or **a**$_2$/2).

Owen (1962, Table 9.9) was the source of the $\phi$ values for Table 6.2.1, and, as throughout, the normal curve values (his Table 1.1).

For **h**$_c$, the minimum sample difference in $\phi$'s necessary for significance, as before, set $z_{1-b}$ equal to zero in (12.6.1), and solve for **h**$_c$:

(12.6.2)                            $$h_c = z_{1-a}\sqrt{\frac{2}{n}}.$$

12.6.2 SAMPLE SIZE VALUES. The **n** values for Table 6.4.1 were found by solving formula (12.6.1) for **n**:

(12.6.3)
$$n = 2 \left( \frac{z_{1-a} + z_{1-b}}{h} \right)^2$$

where **n** = the sample size for each sample.

## 12.7 CHI-SQUARE TESTS FOR GOODNESS OF FIT AND CONTINGENCY TABLES

The preparation of the tables for this chapter was greatly facilitated by Haynam, Govindarajulu, and Leone's "Tables of the cumulative noncentral chi-square distribution" (1962). This definitive set of tables gives power as a function of the noncentrality parameter of noncentral chi square $\lambda$ (lambda), **a**, and **u** (Haynam et al., 1962, Table I). and $\lambda$ as a function of **a**, power, and **u** (Haynam et al., 1962, Table II). Many values of the arguments are presented, and it can readily be used to find power (Table I) and sample size (Table II) outside the limits of the tables provided in Chapter 7.

12.7.1 POWER VALUES. The relationship between $\lambda$, the noncentrality parameter, and **w**, the ES index, is simply

(12.7.1)
$$\lambda = w^2 N,$$

where **N** = the total sample size.

Table I of Haynam et al. (1962) was used for **a**, **u**, and $\lambda$ as found from (12.7.1), and power values were determined. Where interpolation for $\lambda$ was necessary, it was linear. It is recommended that when power value differences between adjacent **w** values of our Tables 7.3 are large (e.g., greater than .30), and intermediate values for **w** are needed, linear interpolation may give rise to errors in power ranging approximately up to between .05 and .10. When this degree of inaccuracy is excessive for the analyst's purpose, Table I of Haynam et al. (1962) may be readily used, with formula (12.7.1) providing the $\lambda$ value with which to find the exact power value. Milligan (1979) gives a short FORTRAN computer program for determining approximate power for any combination of the parameters.

12.7.2 SAMPLE SIZE VALUES. Table II of Haynam et al. (1962) was used for the **N** tables (Tables 7.4.1–7.4.15). The requisite **a**, **u**, and desired power were found and $\lambda$ was determined. Since transposing formula (12.7.1),

(12.7.2)
$$N = \frac{\lambda}{w^2},$$

the tabulated $\lambda$ was divided by the requisite $w^2$, and the resulting **N** found to the nearest integer. Due to the reciprocal relationship between **N** and $w^2$, formula (7.4.1) quite accurately gives **N** for nontabulated **w**, making unnecessary either interpolation for **w** in Tables 7.4, or reference to Haynam et al. (1962) for the **a**, **u**, and power entries provided by Tables 7.4.

## 12.8   THE ANALYSIS OF VARIANCE AND COVARIANCE

12.8.1   POWER AND $F_c$ VALUES. The criterion values needed for significance, $F_c$, were based on the (central) $F$ table provided by Owen (1962) in his Table 4.1. It contains as argument all the numerator $df (= u)$ needed for our Tables 8.3. For $v$ (denominator $df$), which for these tables is $(u + 1)$ $(n - 1)$, Owen gives as argument 1 (1), 30, 40, 48, 60, 80, 120, $\infty$. Interpolation between these values was linear in the reciprocal of the required values.

The basic procedure used for computing the tabled power values was Laubscher's square root normal approximation of noncentral $F$ (1960, Formula 6). In the present notation, this is

$$(12.8.1) \qquad z_{1-b} = \frac{\sqrt{2(u + \lambda) - \dfrac{u + 2\lambda}{u + \lambda}} - \sqrt{(2v - 1)\dfrac{uF_c}{v}}}{\sqrt{\dfrac{uF_c}{v} + \dfrac{u + 2\lambda}{u + \lambda}}}$$

where the noncentrality parameter is

$$(12.8.2) \qquad\qquad \lambda = f^2 n(u + 1),$$

and the denominator $df$ is

$$(12.8.3) \qquad\qquad v = (u + 1)(n - 1).$$

The unit normal percentile value for power, $z_{1-b}$, gave excellent agreement with exact value determinations given in the literature (e.g., Laubscher, 1960; Lehmer, 1944; Tang, 1938) and computed from tables supplied by the National Bureau of Standards (NBS tables, see Section 12.8.2) except when $n$ and $f$ are small. Therefore, Laubscher's cube root normal approximation of noncentral $F$ (1960, Formula 7) was also determined for all power values:

$$(12.8.4) \qquad z_{1-b} = \frac{1 - \dfrac{2(u + 2\lambda)}{9(u + \lambda)^2} - \left(1 - \dfrac{2}{9v}\right)\left(\dfrac{uF_c}{u + \lambda}\right)^{1/3}}{\left[\left(\dfrac{2}{9v}\right)\left(\dfrac{uF_c}{u + \lambda}\right)^{2/3} + \dfrac{2(u + 2\lambda)}{9(u + \lambda)^2}\right]^{1/2}}.$$

The cube root formula was used as a check and provided most of the power values for $n$, $f$ small except for smoothing and reconciliation at available points with the $n$ values computed from the NBS tables which are exact (see below).

12.8.2   SAMPLE SIZE VALUES. The sources used for computing the entries of the $n$ tables (8.4.1–8.4.9) give $\phi$ as a function of $a$, power, $u$, and $v$.

$$(12.8.5) \qquad\qquad \phi = \sqrt{\dfrac{\lambda}{u + 1}}$$

where $\lambda = $ the noncentrality parameter of the noncentral $F$ distribution.

The relationship between $\mathbf{f}$ and $\phi$ is simply

(12.8.6) $$\phi = \mathbf{f}\sqrt{\mathbf{n}},$$

so that

(12.8.7) $$\mathbf{n} = \left(\frac{\phi}{\mathbf{f}}\right)^2$$

The sources for the $\phi$ values were:

1. An unpublished tabular computer print-out furnished by the National Bureau of Standards, "Tables of Power Points of Analysis of Variance Tests" (NBS tables).[2] These tables provide $\phi$ for varying $\mathbf{u}$ and $\mathbf{v}$ at $\mathbf{a} = .01, .05, .10, .20$, and power $= .10, .50, .90, .95, .99$.

2. Lehmer (1944) provides $\phi$ values for varying $\mathbf{u}$ and $\mathbf{v}$ at $\mathbf{a} = .01, .05$, and power $= .70, .80$.

In both sources, the necessary $\mathbf{u}$ values are tabled, and interpolation for $\mathbf{v}$ was linear in the reciprocal.

## 12.9 MULTIPLE REGRESSION AND CORRELATION ANALYSIS[3]

12.9.1 POWER AS A FUNCTION OF $\lambda$, $\mathbf{u}$, $\mathbf{v}$, AND $\mathbf{a}$. The noncentrality parameter, $\lambda$, absorbs the information of the ES, $\mathbf{f}^2$, and the numerator ($\mathbf{u}$) and denominator ($\mathbf{v}$) degrees of freedom in Equation (9.3.1) : $\lambda = \mathbf{f}^2 (\mathbf{u} + \mathbf{v} + 1)$. Power is an increasing monotonic function of the distribution parameters $\lambda$, $\mathbf{v}$, and $\mathbf{a}$, and a decreasing monotonic function of $\mathbf{u}$. Because power does not vary greatly with $\mathbf{v}$ (beyond its absorption into $\lambda$), only four levels are provided, $\mathbf{v} = 20, 60, 120$, and $\infty$, with interpolation in the reciprocals as shown in Equation (9.3.2).

The relevant reference distribution is that of noncentral chi-square, whose parameters are $\lambda$, $\mathbf{u}$, $\mathbf{v}$, and $\mathbf{a}$. The power values in Tables 9.3.1 and 9.3.2 were derived from Tiku (1967), Laubscher (1960), and Haynam et al.. (1962).

---

[2] In a cover letter accompanying the NBS tables it is stated that partial checking of the computed values revealed no errors exceeding two units in the last (third) decimal place of the $\phi$ values. The maximum error in $\mathbf{n}$ when formula (10.8.7) is applied is .0011$\mathbf{n}$, i.e., slightly more than one-tenth of one percent and therefore quite negligible.

[3] In the Revised Edition (Cohen, 1977), the tables for power as a function of $\lambda$ and $\mathbf{u}$ (Tables 9.3.1–3) and those for $\lambda$ as a function of power and $\mathbf{u}$ (Tables 9.4.1–3) were approximate in that they were derived from the Haynam et al. (1962) tables for noncentral chi-square, and thus were based on infinite $\mathbf{v}$ (denominator $\mathbf{df}$). The present tables are also approximate but since they include the $\mathbf{u}$ parameter and have a denser argument for $\lambda$, they provide many more values and therefore are more accurate.

Tiku (1967) tables **b** (= 1 − power) as a function of the $\phi$ of Equation (12.8.5), which was readily converted to

$$(12.9.1) \qquad\qquad \lambda = \phi \sqrt{(u + 1)}.$$

Lagrangian 3-point interpolation was used for $\phi$. Tiku provides tables for **u** = 1(1)10, 12. Good agreement was found between the Tiku-derived power values and those of Chapter 8 (see Section 12.8.1).

For the remaining values of **u** except **u** = ∞, Laubscher's normalizing square root approximation to noncentral **F** (1960, Formula 6), given above as Equation (12.8.1), was used. An extensive Monte Carlo investigation of Laubscher's square root and cube root approximations showed them both to be quite accurate and led to the choice of the former (Cohen & Nee, 1987).

Finally, because the distribution of **F** when **v** = ∞ is the same as that of noncentral chi-square, the Haynam *et al.* (1962) tables were used for **v** = ∞.

12.9.2   $\lambda$ AS A FUNCTION OF POWER, **u**, **v**, AND **a**. The relationship of $\lambda$ to the other parameters of the noncentral **F** distribution is that it is an increasing monotonic function of power, **v** and **a**, and a decreasing monotonic function of **u**.

The $\lambda$ values for Tables 9.4.1 and 9.4.2 were found as follows: For each combination of **u**, **v**, and **a**, a low value of $\lambda$ was chosen, entered in the Laubscher square root formula (12.8.1), and the power determined. The value of $\lambda$ was incremented by .1 repeatedly to yield power over the range from .25 to .99, and the $\lambda$ values were determined that yielded power nearest to the tables' power argument (.25, .50, .60, . . . , .99).

# References

Abelson, R. P. A variance explanation paradox: When a little is a lot. *Psychological Bulletin,* 1985, **97,** 129–133.

Alexander, R. A., Carson, K. P., Alliger, G. M., & Barrett, G. V., Further consideration of the power to detect nonzero validity under range restriction. *Journal of Applied Psychology,* 1985, **70,** 451–460.

Anderson, R. B. *STAT POWER. An Apple computer program.* Cambridge, MA: Abt Associates, 1981.

Arkin, C. F. The t-test and clinical relevance. Is your $\beta$ error showing? *American Journal of Clinical Pathology,* 1981, **76,** 416–420.

Bangert-Drowns, R. L. Review of developments in meta-analytic method. *Psychological Bulletin,* 1986, **99,** 388–399.

Barcikowski, R. S. Optimum sample size and number of levels in a one-way random-effects analysis of variance. *Journal of Experimental Education,* 1973, **41,** 10–16.

Berelson, B., & Steiner, G. A. *Human behavior, an inventory of scientific findings.* New York: Harcourt, Brace & World, 1964.

Blalock, H. M., Jr. *Social statistics.* (2nd ed.) New York: McGraw-Hill, 1972.

Boneau, C. A. The effects of violations of assumptions underlying the t test. *Psychological Bulletin,* 1960, **57,** 49–64.

Boneau, C. A. A comparison of the power of the U and t test. *Psychological Review,* 1962, **69,** 246–256.

Bones, J. Statistical power analysis and geography. *Professional Geographer,* 1972, **24,** 229–232.

Borenstein, M., & Cohen, J. *Statistical power analysis: A computer program.* Hillsdale, NJ: Lawrence Erlbaum Associates, 1988.

Brewer, J. K. On the power of statistical tests in the American Educational Research Journal, *American Educational Research Journal,* 1972, **9,** 391–401.

Brewer, J. K., & Owen, P. W. A note on the power of statistical tests in the Journal of Educational Measurement. *Journal of Educational Measurement,* 1973, **10,** 71–74.

Budescu, D. V. The power of the F test in normal populations with heterogeneous variances. *Educational and Psychological Measurement,* 1982, **42,** 409–416.

Budescu, D. V., & Appelbaum, M. I. Variance stabilizing transformations and the power of the **F** test. *Journal of Educational Statistics*, 1981, **6**, 555–74.

Bureau of the Census, *1976 U.S. fact book*. New York: Grosset & Dunlap, 1975.

Campbell, J. D. *Manic-depressive disease*. Philadelphia: Lippincott, 1953.

Chase, L. J., & Baran, S. J. An assessment of quantitative research in mass communication. *Journalism Quarterly*, 1976, **53**, 308–311.

Chase, L. J., & Chase, R. B. A statistical power analysis of applied psychological research. *Journal of Applied Psychology*, 1976 **61**, 234–237.

Chase, L. J., & Tucker, R. K. A power-analytic examination of contemporary communication research. *Speech Monogrpahs*, 1975, **42**, 29–41.

Christensen, J. E., & Christensen, C. E. Statistical power analysis of health, physical education, and recreation research. *Research Quarterly*, 1977, **48**, 204–208.

Cleary, T. A. & Lynn, R. L. Error of measurement and the power of a statistical test. *British Journal of Mathematical and Statistical Psychology*, 1969, **22**, 49–55.

Cliff, N. *Analyzing multivariate data*. New York: Harcourt, Brace, Jovanovich, 1987.

Cohen, J. The statistical power of abnormal-social psychological research: A review. *Journal of Abnormal and Social Psychology*, 1962, **65**, 145–153.

Cohen, J. Some statistical issues in psychological research. In B. B. Wolman (Ed.), *Handbook of clinical psychology*. New York: McGraw-Hill, 1965. Pp. 95–121.

Cohen, J. Multiple regression as a general data-analytic system. *Psychological Bulletin*, 1968, **70**, 426–443.

Cohen, J. Approximate power and sample size determination for common one-sample and two-sample hypothesis tests. *Educational and Psychological Measurement*, 1970, **30**, 811–831.

Cohen, J. Statistical power analysis and research results. *American Educatioanl Research Journal*, 1973, **10**, 225–229.

Cohen, J. Set correlation as a general multivariate data-analytic method. *Multivariate Behavioral Research*, 1982 **17**, 301–341.

Cohen, J. *SETCOR: Set correlation analysis*. Evanston, IL: SYSTAT, 1989.

Cohen, J., & Cohen, P. *Applied multiple regression/correlation analysis for the behavioral sciences* (2nd ed.). Hillsdale, NJ: Lawrence Erlbaum Associates, 1983.

Cohen, J., & Nee, J. C. N. CORSET, a FORTRAN IV program for set correlation. *Educational and Psychological Measurement*, 1983, **43**,817–820.

Cohen, J., & Nee, J. C. N. Estimators for two measures of association for set correlation. *Educational and Psychological Measurement*, 1984, **44**, 907–917.

Cohen, J., & Nee, J. C. N. A comparison of two noncentral **F** approximations, with applications to power analysis in set correlation. *Multivariate Behavioral Research*, 1987, **22**, 483–490.

Cohen, J., & Struening, E. L. Opinions about mental illness: Mental hospital occupational profiles and profile clusters. *Psychological Reports*, 1963, **12**, 111–124.

Cohen, J., & Struening, E. L. Opinions about mental illness: Hospital social atmospheres and their relevance to effectiveness. *Journal of Consulting Psychology*, 1964, **28**, 291–298.

Cooper, H. M. On the significance of effects and the effects of significance. *Journal of Personality and Social Psychology*, 1981, **41**, 1013–1018.

Cooper, H. M., & Findley, M. Expected effect sizes: estimates for statistical power analysis in social psychology. *Personality and Social Psychology Bulletin*, 1982, **8**, 168–173.

Cox, D. R. *Planning of experiments*. New York: Wiley, 1958.

Cramer, E. M., & Nicewander, W.A. Some symmetric, invariant measures of multivariate association. *Psychometrika*, 1979, **44**, 43–54.

Crane, J. A. The power of social intervention experiments to discriminate differences between experimental and control groups. *Social Service Review*, 1976, **50**, 224–242.

Cronbach, L. J. *Essentials of psychological testing*. (2nd ed.) New York: McGraw-Hill, 1960.

Cureton, E. E. On correlation coefficients. *Psychometrika*, 1966, **31**, 605–607.

Dallal, G.E. *DESIGN*. Evanston, IL: SYSTAT, 1987.

Daly, J. A., & Hexamer, A. Statistical power in research in English education. *Research in the Teaching of English*, 1983, **17**, 157–164.

David, F. N. *Tables of the ordinates and probability integral of the distribution of the correlation coefficient in small samples*. Cambridge: University Press, 1938.

Davidson, P. O., & Costello, C. G. (Eds.) *N = 1: Experimental studies of single cases*. New York: Van Nostrand Reinhold, 1969.

Dixon, W. F., & Massey, F. J., Jr. *Introduction to statistical analysis*. (2nd ed.) New York: McGraw-Hill, 1957.

Edwards, A. L. *Experimental design in psychological research*. (4th ed.) New York: Holt, Rinehart, & Winston, 1972.

Fagley, N. S. Applied statistical power analysis and the interpretation of nonsignificant results by research consumers. *Journal of Counseling Psychology*, 1985, **32**, 391–396.

Fisher, R. A. *The design of experiments*. New York: Hafner, 1949.

Fiske, D. W., & Jones, L. V. Sequential analysis in psychological research. *Psychological Bulletin*, 1954, **51**, 264–275.

Flury, B. K., & Riedwyl, H. Standard distance in univariate and multivariate analysis. *The American Statistician*, 1986, **40**, 249–251.

Forsyth, R. A. A note on "Planning an experiment in the company of measurement error." *Applied Psychological Measurement*, 1978, **2**, 379–381.

Fowler, R. L. Testing for substantive significance is applied research by specifying nonzero effect null hypotheses. *Journal of Applied Psychology*, 1985, **70**, 215–218.

Freiman, J. A., Chalmers, T. C., Smith, H., & Kuebler, R. R. The importance of beta, the type II error and sample size in the design and interpretation of the randomized control trial: Survey of 71 "negative" trials. *New England Journal of Medicine*, 1978, **299**, 690–694.

Friedman, H. Magnitude of experimental effect and a table for its rapid estimation. *Psychological Bulletin*, 1968, **70**, 245–251.

Friedman, H. Simplified determinations of statistical power, magnitude of effect and research sample sizes. *Educational and Psychological Measurement*, 1982, **42**, 521–526.

Getzels, J. W., & Jackson, P. W. *Creativity and intelligence: Explorations with gifted students*. New York: Wiley, 1962.

Ghiselli, E. E. Dr. Ghiselli comments on Dr. Tupes note. *Personnel Psychology*, 1964, **17**, 61–63.

Glass, G. V., McGaw, B., & Smith, W. *Meta-analysis in social research*. Beverly Hills, CA: Sage, 1981.

Graybill, F. A. *An introduction to linear statistical models*. Vol. 1. New York: McGraw-Hill, 1961.

Guilford, J. P., & Fruchter, B. *Fundamental statistics in psychology and education*. (6th ed.) New York: McGraw-Hill, 1978.

Haase, R. F. Power analysis of research in counselor education. *Counselor Education and Supervision*, 1974, **14**, 124–132.

Haase, R. F. A Basic program to compute atypical values of alpha. *Educational and Psychological Measurement*, 1986, **66**, 629–632.

Haase, R. F., Waechter, D. M., & Solomon, G. S. How significant is a significant difference? Average effect size of research in counseling psychology. *Journal of Counseling Psychology*, 1982, **29**, 58–65.

Hall, J. C. The other side of statistical signficance: A review of type II errors in the Australian medical literature. *Australia and New Zealand Journal of Medicine*, 1982, **12**, 7–9.

Harrell, T. W., & Harrell, M. S. Army General Classification Test scores for civilian occupations. *Educational and Psychological Measurement*, 1945, **5**, 229–239.

Harvard University Computation Laboratory. *Tables of the cumulative binomial probability distribution.* Cambridge, Massachusetts: Harvard University Press, 1955.

Haynam, G. E., Govindarajulu, Z., & Leone, F. C. *Tables of the cumulative non-central chi-square distribution.* Cleveland: Case Institute of Technology Statistical Laboratory, 1962. (Case Statistical Laboratory, Publication No. 104.)

Hays, W. L. *Statistics.* (3rd ed.) New York. Holt, Rinehart, & Winston, 1981.

Hedges, L. V. Distribution theory for Glass's estimator of effect size and related estimators. *Journal of Educational Statistics*, 1981, **6**, 107–128.

Hedges, L. V., & Olkin, I. *Statistical methods for meta-analysis.* Orlando: Academic Press, 1985.

Hotelling, H. The generalization of Student's ratio. *Annals of Mathematical Statistics*, 1931, **2**, 360–378.

Hunter, J. E., Schmidt, F. L., & Jackson, G.B. *Meta-analysis: Cumulating research findings across studies.* Beverly Hills, CA: Sage, 1982.

Husén, T. *Psychological twin research.* Uppsala: Almquist & Wiksell, 1959.

Jensen, A. R. Review of the Maudsley Personality Inventory. In O. K. Buros (Ed.), *Sixth mental measurement yearbook.* Highland Park, NJ: Gryphon, 1965.

Jones, B. J., & Brewer, J. K. An analysis of the power of statistical tests reported in the Research Quarterly. *Research Quarterly*, 1972, **43**, 23–30.

Judd, C. M., & Kenny, D. A. *Estimating the effects of social interventions.* Cambridge, England: Cambridge University Press, 1981.

Katzell, R. A., & Dyer, F. J. Differential validity revived. *Journal of Applied Psychology*, 1977, **62**, 137–145.

Katzer, J., & Sodt, J. An analysis of the use of statistical testing in communication research. *Journal of Communication*, 1973, **23**, 251–265.

Koele, P. Calculating power in analysis of variance. *Psychological Bulletin*, 1982, **92**, 513–516.

Kraemer, H. C. Theory of estimation and testing of effect sizes: Use in power analysis. *Journal of Educational Statistics*, 1982, **8**, 93–101.

Kraemer, H. C. A strategy to teach the concept and application of power and statistical tests. *Journal of Educational Statistics*, 1985, **10**, 173–195.

Kroll, R. M., & Chase, L. J. Communication disorders: A power-analytic assessment of recent research. *Journal of Communication Disorders*, 1975, **8**, 237–247.

Laubscher, N. F. Normalizing the noncentral t and F distributions. *Annals of Mathematical Statistics*, 1960, **31**, 1105–1112.

Lehmer, E. Inverse tables of probabilities of error of the second kind. *Annals of Mathematical Statistics*, 1944, **15**, 388–398.

Levenson, R. L. Statistical power analysis: Implications for researchers, planners, and practitioners in gerontology. *Gerontologist*, 1980, **20**, 494–498.

Levin, J. R., & Subkoviak, M. J. Planning an experiment in the company of measurement error. *Applied Psychological Measurement*, 1977, **1**, 331–338.

MacKinnon, W. J. Compact table of twelve probability levels of the symmetric binomial cumulative distribution for sample sizes to 1,000. *Journal of the American Statistical Association*, 1959, **54**, 164–172.

MacKinnon, W. J. Concise table of three-place probabilities of the symmetric binomial cumulative distribution for sample sizes to 100. *Psychological Reports*, 1961, **10**, 291–300.

Mahalanobis, P. C. On the generalized distance in statistics. *Proceedings of the National Institute of Science, India*, 1936, **12**, 49–55.

Maxwell, S. E. Dependent variable reliability and determination of sample size. *Applied Psychological Measurement*, 1980, **4**, 253–260.

McNeil, K. A., Kelly, F. J., & McNeil, J. T. *Testing research hypotheses using multiple linear regression.* Carbondale, IL: Southern Illinois University Press, 1975.

Milligan, G. W. A computer program for calculating power of the chi-square test. *Educational and Psychological Measurement*, 1979, **39**, 681–684.

Milligan, G. W. Factors that affect Type I and Type II error rates in the analysis of multidimensional contingency tables using the loglinear model. *Psychological Bulletin*, 1980, **87**, 238–244.

National Bureau of Standards. *Tables of power points of analysis of variance tests,* 1963. Prepublication copy, not completely checked.

The New Information Please Almanac for 1966. New York: Simon & Schuster, 1965.

Neyman, J., & Pearson, E. S. On the use and interpretation of certain test critieria for purposes of statistical inference. *Biometrika*, 1928, **20A**, 175–240, 263–294.

Neyman, J., & Pearson, E. S. On the problem of the most efficient tests of statistical hypotheses. *Transactions of the Royal Society of London Series A*, 1933, **231**, 289–337.

Oakes, M. Intuiting strength of association from a correlation coefficent. *British Journal of Psychology*, 1982, **73**, 51–56.

Oakes, M. *Statistical inference: A commentary for the social and behavioral sciences.* New York: Wiley, 1986.

Olson, C. L. Comparative robustness of six tests in multivariate analysis of variance. *Journal of the American Statistical Association*, 1974, **69**, 894–908.

Olson, C. L. On choosing a test statistic in MANOVA. *Psychological Bulletin*, 1976, **83**, 579–586.

Orme, J. G., & Combs-Orme, T. D. Statistical power and type II errors in social work research. *Social Work Research & Abstracts*, 1986, **22**, 3–10.

Orme, J. G., & Tolman, R. M. The statistical power of a decade of social work education research. *Social Service Review*, 1986, **60**, 620–632.

Ottenbacher, K. Statistical power of research in occupational therapy. *Occupational Therapy Journal of Research*, 1982, **2**, 13–25.

Overall, J. E., & Dalal, S. N. Design of experiments to maximize power relative to cost. *Psychological Bulletin*, 1965, **64**, 339–350.

Overall, J. E., & Spiegel, D. K. Concerning least squares analysis of experimental data. *Psychological Bulletin*, 1969, **72**, 311–322.

Overall, J. E., Spiegel, D. K., & Cohen, J. Equivalence of orthogonal and nonorthogonal analysis of variance. *Psychological Bulletin*, 1975, **82**, 182–186.

Owen, D. B. *Handbook of statistical tables.* Reading, MA: Addison-Wesley, 1962.

Owen, D. B. The power of Student's **t**-test. *Journal of the American Statistical Association*, 1965, **60**, 320–333.

Ozer, D. J. Correlation and the coefficient of determination. *Psychological Bulletin*, 1985, **97**, 307–315.

Pearson, E. S., & Hartley, H. O. *Biometrika tables for statisticians.* Vol. I. Cambridge: University Press, 1964.

Pedhazur, E. J. *Multiple regression in behavioral research* (2nd ed.). New York: Holt, Rinehart & Winston, 1982.

Pennick, J. E., & Brewer, J. K. The power of statistical tests in science teaching research. *Journal of Research in Science Teaching, 9*, 377–381.

Peters, C. C., & VanVoorhis, W. R. *Statistical procedures and their mathematical bases.* New York: McGraw-Hill, 1940.

Peterson, R. A., Albaum, G., & Beltrami, R. F. A meta-analysis of effect sizes in consumer research. *Journal of Consumer Research*, 1985, **12**, 97–103.

Raju, N. S., Edwards, J. E., & LoVerde, M. A. Corrected formulas for computing sample sizes under indirect range restriction. *Journal of Applied Psychology*, 1985, **70**, 565–566.

Rao, C. R. *Linear statistical inference and its applications* (2nd ed.). New York: Wiley, 1975.

Reed, J. F., III, & Slaichart, W. Statistical proof in inconclusive 'negative' trials. *Archives of Internal Medicine*, 1981, **141**, 1307–1310.

Rosenthal, R., & Rubin, D. B. A simple, general purpose display of magnitude of experimental effect. *Journal of Educational Psychology*, 1982, **74**, 166–169.

Rossi, J. S., Rossi, S. R., & Cottrill, S. D. Statistical power of research in social and abnormal psychology. *Journal of Consulting and Clinical Psychology*, in press.

Rothpearl, A. B., Mohs, R. C., & Davis, K. L. Statistical power in biological psychiatry. *Psychiatry Research*, 1981, **5**, 257–266.

Rush, D., Stein, Z.A., & Susser, M. A randomized controlled trial of prenatal nutritional supplementation in New York City. *Pediatrics*, 1980, **65**, 683–697.

Sawyer, A. G., & Ball, A. D. Statistical power and effect size in marketing research. *Journal of Marketing Research*, 1981, **18**, 275–290.

Scheffé, H. *The analysis of variance*. New York: Wiley, 1959.

Schmidt, F. L., Hunter, J. E., & Urry, V. W. Statistical power in criterion-related validity studies. *Journal of Applied Psychology*, 1976, **61**, 473–485.

Sedlmeier, P., & Gigerenzer, G. Do studies of statistical power have an effect on the power of studies? *Psychological Bulletin*, in press.

Siegel, S. *Nonparametric statistics for the behavioral sciences*. New York: McGraw-Hill, 1956.

Stevens, J. P. *Applied multivariate statistics for the social sciences*. Hillsdale, NJ: Lawrence Erlbaum Associates, 1986.

Super, D. E. *Appraising vocational fitness*. New York: Harper & Row, 1949.

Tang, P. C. The power function of the analysis of variance tests with tables and illustrations of their use. *Statistical Research Memoirs*, 1938, **2**, 126–149.

Tiku, M. L. Tables of the power of the **F**-test. *Journal of the American Statistical Association*, 1967, **62**, 525–539.

Toft, C. A., & Shea, P. J. Detecting community-wide patterns: Estimating power strengthens statistical inference. *The American Naturalist*, 1983, **122**, 618–625.

Tversky, A., & Kahneman, D. Belief in the law of small numbers. *Psychological Bulletin*, 1971, **76**, 105–110.

Wald, A. *Sequential analysis*. New York: Wiley, 1947.

Walker, H., & Lev, J. *Statistical inference*. New York: Holt, Rinehart & Winston, 1953.

Ward, J.H., Jr., & Jennings, E. *Introduction to linear models*. Englewood Cliffs, NJ: Prentice-Hall, 1973.

Wechsler, D. *The measurement and appraisal of adult intelligence*. (4th ed.) Baltimore: Williams & Wilkins, 1958.

Welkowitz, J., Ewen, R. B., & Cohen, J. *Introductory statistics for the behavioral sciences*. (3rd ed.), New York: Academic Press, 1982.

Wilks, S. S. Certain generalizations in the analysis of variance. *Biometrika*, 1932, **24**, 471–494.

Winer, B. J. *Statistical principles in experimental design*. New York: McGraw-Hill, 1971.

Wooley, T.W. A comprehensive power-analytic investigation of research in medical education. *Journal of Medical Education*, 1983a, **58**, 710–715.

Wooley, T. W. Efficiency in public health research. The importance of *a priori* sample size estimation. *Proceedings of the 19th National Meeting of the Public Health Conference on Records and Statistics*. Washington: U. S. Department of Health and Human Services, 1983b.

Wooley, T. W., & Dawson, G. O. A follow-up power analysis of the tests used in Journal of Research in Science Teaching. *Journal of Research in Science Teaching*, 1983, **20**, 673–681.

Zimmerman, D. W., & Williams, R. H. Note on the reliability of experimental measures and the power of significance tests. *Psychological Bulletin*, 1986, **100**, 123–124.

# Index